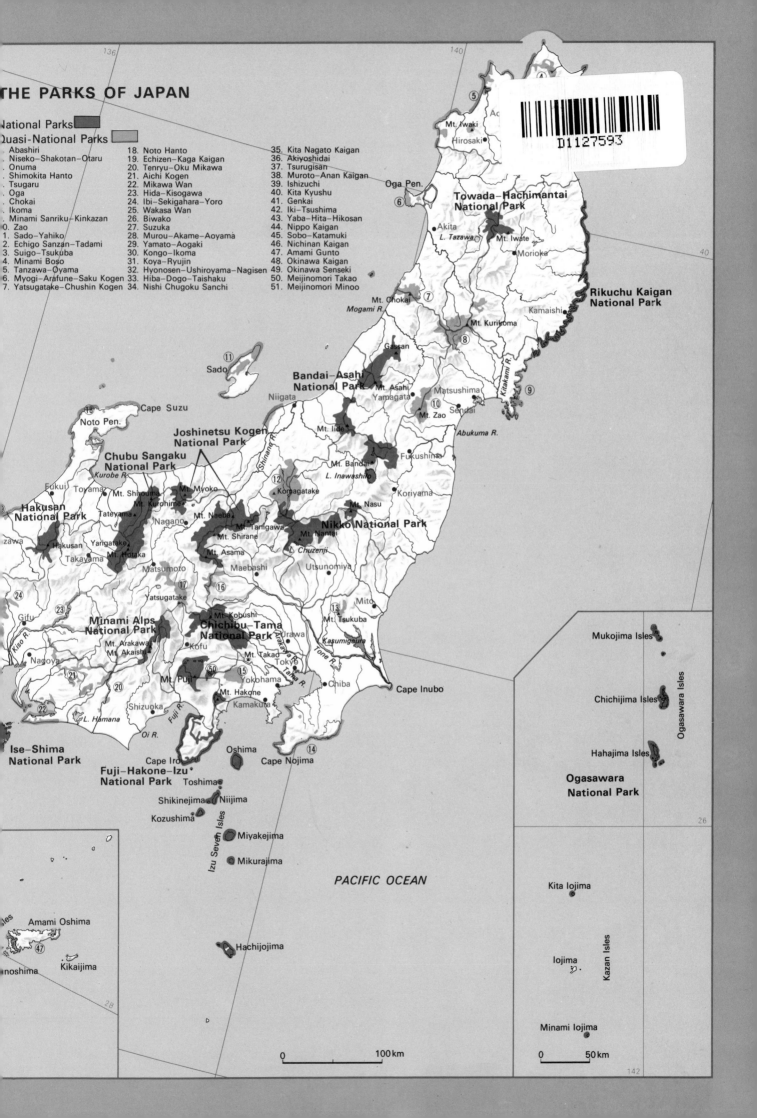

THE PARKS OF JAPAN

National Parks ▮
Quasi-National Parks ▮

1. Abashiri
2. Niseko–Shakotan–Otaru
3. Onuma
4. Shimokita Hanto
5. Tsugaru
6. Oga
7. Chokai
8. Ikoma
9. Minami Sanriku–Kinkazan
10. Zao
11. Sado–Yahiko
12. Echigo Sanzan–Tadami
13. Suigo–Tsukuba
14. Minami Boso
15. Tanzawa–Oyama
16. Myogi–Arafune–Saku Kogen
17. Yatsugatake–Chushin Kogen

18. Noto Hanto
19. Echizen–Kaga Kaigan
20. Tenryu–Oku Mikawa
21. Aichi Kogen
22. Mikawa Wan
23. Hida–Kisogawa
24. Ibi–Sekigahara–Yoro
25. Wakasa Wan
26. Biwako
27. Suzuka
28. Murou–Akame–Aoyama
29. Yamato–Aogaki
30. Kongo–Ikoma
31. Koya–Ryujin
32. Hyonosen–Ushiroyama–Nagisen
33. Hiba–Dogo–Taishaku
34. Nishi Chugoku Sanchi

35. Kita Nagato Kaigan
36. Akiyoshidai
37. Tsurugisan
38. Muroto–Anan Kaigan
39. Ishizuchi
40. Kita Kyushu
41. Genkai
42. Iki–Tsushima
43. Yaba–Hita–Hikosan
44. Nippo Kaigan
45. Sobo–Katamuki
46. Nichinan Kaigan
47. Amami Gunto
48. Okinawa Kaigan
49. Okinawa Senseki
50. Meijinomori Takao
51. Meijinomori Minoo

NATIONAL PARKS OF JAPAN

Mary Sutherland and Dorothy Britton

NATIONAL PA

RKS OF JAPAN

KODANSHA INTERNATIONAL LTD.
Tokyo, New York, San Francisco

PHOTO CREDITS: Camera Tokyo Service, 18, 22, 31, 40, 61, 71, 72, 78, 81, 88, 91, 92, 93, 94, 95; Dandi Photo, contents, 1, 26, 32, 42, 46, 47, 58, 62, 65, 69, 76, 90; Fine Photo Agency, contents, 2, 4, 10, 11, 13, 29, 34, 63, 75, 79, 82, 85, 87; Isogai Hiroshi (by courtesy of All Nippon Airway), 5, 15, 59, 77; Iwamiya Takeji, title page; Japan Travel Bureau, copyright page, 6, 8, 9, 12, 16, 23, 41, 43, 44, 50, 67, 74, 83, 89; Kaneko Hiroshi, 48; Kaneko Keizo, 20, 27, 28, 30; Midorikawa Yoichi, front jacket, 14, 68; Nakatani Yoshitaka, 3; Ohashi Haruzo, 24; Ojiro Akio, 39; Photo Library Tankei, copyright page, 21, 33, 52, 60, 64, 66, 70, 84; Sanei Photo Library, half title page, 17, 25, 36, 73, 80, 86; Shibazaki Koyo, 37, 53, 54; Shimizu Buko, 38; Shirahata Shiro, back jacket, 45, 51, 57; Uchiyama Akira, 7, 19, 35, 49, 56.

Maps by Kojima Michio. Line drawings on back endpapers by Katakura Kazuko.

Distributed in the United States by Kodansha International/USA Ltd. through Harper & Row, Publishers, Inc., 10 East 53rd Street, New York, New York 10022. In South America by Harper & Row, International Department. In Canada by Fitzhenry & Whiteside Ltd., 150 Lesmill Road, Don Mills, Ontario M3B 2T5. In Mexico & Central America by Harla S.A. de C.V., Apartado 30–546, Mexico 4, D.F. In the United Kingdom by Phaidon Press Ltd., Unit B, Ridgeway Trading Estate, Iver, Bucks SLO 9HW. In Europe by Boxerbooks, Inc., Limmatstrasse 111, 8031 Zurich. In Australia & New Zealand by Book Wise (Australia) Pty. Ltd., 104–8 Sussex Street, Sydney 2000. In Asia by Toppan Company (S) Pte. Ltd., No. 38 Liu Fang Road, Jurong Town, Singapore 2262.

Published by Kodansha International Ltd., 12–21, Otowa 2-chome, Bunkyo-ku, Tokyo 112 and Kodansha International/USA Ltd., 10 East 53rd Street, New York, New York 10022 and 44 Montgomery Street, San Francisco, California 94104. Photographs Copyright © 1980 by Kodansha International Ltd. Text Copyright in Japan 1980 by Kodansha International Ltd. All rights reserved. Printed in Japan.

LCC 75–30181
ISBN 0–87011–250–3
JBC 0072–785327–2361

CONTENTS

INTRODUCTION

Moreover he hath left you all his walks,
His private arbours, and new-planted orchards,
On this side Tiber; he hath left them you,
And to your heirs for ever; common pleasures
To walk abroad and recreate yourselves.

Shakespeare

In bequeathing park lands to the people of Rome two thousand years ago, Julius Caesar may well have realized that mankind needs nature's beauty for more than just health and recreation. People need nature, not only to recreate themselves, but also, themselves, to create.

"What has Fuji to do with our culture and civilization? We did not create it!" exclaimed a well-known Japanese statesman on seeing the immensely enlarged photograph of Mount Fuji which covered the whole of an important wall of the Japanese pavilion at a prestigious world fair. He was doubtless concerned lest the pavilion encourage the shallow "Fujiyama–cherry blossom–geisha" tourist view of his country.

But Fuji does indeed have a great deal to do with Japanese achievement. The natural environment of the land in which a people live inevitably molds and influences what they create. What kind of people would the Japanese have been, had they not been nurtured by the subtle symmetries of their sublime mountain and those clouds of delicate pink blossom in the spring? The art for which Japan is famous is the collective expression of a people probably more deeply sensitive to nature's infinite moods than the inhabitants of any other land.

Creative people the world over have been profoundly influenced by nature. The poet Wordsworth by his Lake District; philosopher and social reformer Rousseau by his beloved Lac de Bienne; art historian Bernard Berenson by a single tree in the Tuscan hills whose root-patterns crystallized for him his whole theory of aesthetics. Even an oil magnate: financial genius Calouste Gulbenkian said it was the structural beauty and harmony of nature that inspired his most successful company. Gulbenkian needed nature so much that he habitually conducted his business out of doors, sitting on camp chairs in beautiful parks.

The concept of a park—nature enclosed for man's delectation—goes way back to the kings of ancient Persia; it is from the name they used for their parks that our word "paradise" is derived. A medieval Latin word of Germanic origin, *parricus*, is the progenitor of the English word "park" and was first used in the early Middle Ages to describe spacious woodland reserved by royalty for the chase. The stag is still hunted by remnants of the French nobility at Rambouillet and Compiègne—well-kept forests of oak and beech outside Paris, which are now, of course, freely accessible to the public, although the hunt has right of way. In England's Windsor Great Park and Richmond Park, both near London, deer are no longer hunted, but they still inhabit the woods, adding to the enjoyment of the strolling populace.

It was the French who introduced into eleventh-century England stringent laws protecting forest parks, not for the people, but for the sport and pleasure of the king. Soon after William of Normandy conquered England in 1066, he enlarged existing royal hunting grounds to create the vast, hundred-thousand-acre New Forest. He did this by ruthlessly destroying villages, churches, and towns, making almost two thousand people homeless. Strict laws protected "every bush and tree within the Forest that doth bear fruit to feed the deer withal," and a man was to be blinded if he killed hart or hind.

In the sixteenth century King Henry VIII's love of hunting provided London with its eight thousand acres of parks and greenery—more than any other major capital city in the world. In the seventeenth century the monarchy opened up most of London's parks to the public; and members of the English public, two centuries later, themselves took the world's first significant step toward a coherent nature conservation movement, not to protect nature, but to claim some of it for the enjoyment of the common folk before too much park land became annexed to the country mansions of the rich and noble. In Britain in 1865, a Commons, Open Spaces and Footpaths Preservations Society was formed. It is important because it indirectly led to the establishment in the United States in 1872 of Yellowstone, the world's very first national park.

Japan, fresh out of her cocoon of isolation, was quick to follow suit, even if not on the scale of Yellowstone. A noted British expert on town and country planning has said that "what a nation does with its land is a good indication of its level of culture." In 1873, the fifth year of the Meiji "Rule of Enlightenment," Japan established as *ko-en* (literally "public parks") under government protection places traditionally visited in spring at cherry-blossom time or in autumn to enjoy the autumn colors. This is how Tokyo's Ueno Park came into being, although it was in fact established on temple land, already accessible to the people.

While Japan's move toward the establishment of

parks was timely in view of the industrialization soon to come, Japan had always been uniquely democratic in allowing the masses access to the countryside. No large tracts of woodland were reserved for royalty as in Europe. More than hunting, poetry and contemplation were the sport of kings in old Japan. Royal gardens were relatively small, and many, like Kyoto's Shugakuin, were cunningly devised to make vast natural vistas beyond *seem* to be part of the garden without actually fencing the countryside in. There was some hunting, to be sure, but it included the uniquely aesthetic *momiji-gari*, "hunting the autumn leaves." Like cherry-viewing in spring, these were picnics held in woodlands to enjoy the magnificent autumn colors behind temporary fences of elegant silken brocade. Common folk were free to visit the forests too. Japan can boast a people who are unique in their mass celebration of nature and whose veneration of trees and vegetarian way of life has meant that hillsides have not been denuded to create pasture as happened in Britain. What other people make to this day a holiday occasion out of the flowering of a tree?

Unique too, in old Japan, was the nature-protective role of religion. The essence of Shinto, the native animistic belief, is harmony with nature. Such was the people's awe and reverence for nature's holiness, they shrank from desecrating it. The gods were the keepers of the vast and beautiful park that was ancient Japan. Certain places—forests of huge cedars, specially imposing mountains and islands, places of great beauty—inspired such a sense of the presence of divinity that they were looked upon as shrines in themselves. Over the centuries the combination of Shinto belief in the spirits of mountains, rivers, stones, and all things, and Buddhist reverence for every form of life acted unconsciously to foster the creation of "nature reserves." Many areas subsequently designated as national parks have long been held in special religious regard.

Nevertheless, it was recreation rather than religion, and the burgeoning popularity of mountaineering as a sport that provided the impetus for large parks and Japan's modern park system. Paradoxically, it was an Englishman, Walter Weston, who started the craze of mountaineering at the turn of the century and who instilled in the minds of a people who climbed mountains because god was there the idea of climbing them simply because the mountains were there! (See Chubu Sangaku National Park.)

Japan passed a National Parks Law in 1931. This was twenty years after a petition was presented by concerned citizens requesting that the Grand Shrines and cedar forests at Nikko be placed under government care, and two years after the establishment of a National Parks Association of Japan, whose members included leading men of letters and business. Five years later, between 1934 and 1936, after much study and survey, twelve areas were designated national parks. The first three parks—the Inland Sea, Unzen, and Kirishima—were followed almost immediately by five more: Aso, Nikko, the Japan Alps, and Hokkaido's Akan and Daisetsuzan. Two years later, Towada, Fuji–Hakone, Yoshino–Kumano, and Daisen were added.

There was a clamor for more, better to exemplify the varied scenery of Japan's long string of islands, extending from icy northern regions to semitropical zones and displaying so much geological and seasonal variety. Once World War II was over, little time was lost in improving facilities in existing parks and creating new ones. Six more had been added by 1955. Many were enlarged. Now Japan has twenty-seven national parks, totaling about two million hectares (7,600 square miles)—5.4 percent of her total land area.

The more comprehensive 1957 Natural Parks Law replaced the 1931 legislation. The new system provides for three kinds of parks: national parks (*kokuritsu koen*), quasi-national parks (*kokutei koen*), and a large number of lesser local nature preserves called prefectural nature parks (*todofukenritsu shizen koen*). The 1972 Environment Preservation Law transferred administration of all parks from the Ministry of Health and Welfare to the Nature Conservation Bureau of the Environment Agency.

Japan's twenty-seven national parks fulfill strict requirements: outstanding scenic beauty and a distinctive physiography and geology peculiar to each locality as well as flora or fauna high in scientific value. Many include culturally significant features.

Forty-seven other beautiful areas of Japan which fall somewhat short of these criteria have been designated quasi-national parks, and their total area is about half that of the national parks. Criteria are subject to review, and some of today's national parks were first quasi-national parks then later upgraded. Thirty-nine out of both of these types of parks have tracts categorized as marine parks—an unusually high number, but one which vividly reflects Japan's island geography.

Tailoring the national park system to fit Japan's special needs was difficult. It was easy for America and Canada, young nations with vast virgin territories, to allocate thousands of hectares of uninhabited forest as government-owned park land. But, like Britain, Japan is small and densely populated, with a long history of private land ownership. Moreover, both countries need to use most of their land to survive.

In Japan, the government has had to create parks not necessarily where it owned land but where it recognized the need to preserve nature. In fact, the state owns only about half the land constituting national parks. The aim in creating parks by designation is to preserve natural beauty through mutual cooperation with landholders and to place controls on them (a number are industrial corporations) so that they do not destroy nature.

This system has given rise to some curious features, such as parks made up of widely scattered sections. An extreme example is the Inland Sea national park which consists of many parcels of land distributed among the ten prefectures bordering these beautiful island-studded waters. Even when tracts in one area form a cohesive unit they may still not be collectively large enough to warrant status as a separate park. The Fuji–Hakone–Izu National Park, easily accessible from Tokyo, comprises Mount Fuji and its environs combined with land at the tip of the Izu Peninsula more than a hundred kilometers away, with the Seven Isles of Izu thrown in, as it were, for good measure. Though widely separated, however, all share recreational popularity among Tokyoites, and together they form a convenient administrative unit.

The government's budget for the national parks is not large. Money paid out is twofold: direct subsidies to the prefectures, which are responsible for the day-to-day running of all parks with the assistance of about ninety national park rangers; and direct expenditure for the upkeep of state-owned land. In 1979, these amounts were 819 million and 1,059 million yen respectively (approximately four and five million dollars).

Land in the national parks is divided into three categories: normal park land, special areas, and special protection areas. Commercial enterprise and development is allowed on normal park land but planning is exercised to try and prevent the incursion of ugly urban sprawls. Sadly, however, there is often a conflict of interests between preserving the environment and catering to free-spending tourists. For instance, in Hokkaido's Shikotsu–Toya National Park a rare volcanic formation, Mount Showa Shinzan, while specially protected itself, is adjacent to normal park land marred by ramshackle souvenir stalls, parking lots, fast-food shops that can accommodate busloads at a time, and even an exhibition of bears. Land use and development in special areas is strictly controlled: trees may not be felled without permission, new structures built, or billboards erected, to name but a few of the restrictions. The special protection areas include sites of particular scientific or cultural value in heavily visited parks, as well as isolated tracts in remoter parks where nature can be left completely undisturbed and, in some cases, public access prohibited altogether. The ecosystem, a concept first formulated in 1935, is only beginning to be fully understood. The urgent need, worldwide, and especially in Japan, is to protect nature now not only *for* the people, but *from* the people. The delicate interrelationship between earth and plants and animal life is easily disturbed, resulting in the irrevocable destruction of nature. Sixty percent of all the land of the national parks belongs either to the special areas or the special protection areas.

The sheer volume of visitors to Japan's national parks is a problem of paramount importance. Is it a sign that the spirit of the poets who made arduous pilgrimages to their country's beauty spots centuries ago lives on in Japan today? Years before becoming internationally ubiquitous tourists, the Japanese assiduously visited famous places in their own land. They visit their national parks in droves. Over 316 million people "used" the national parks in 1977. That means every man, woman, and child in Japan passed through the national parks about three times in one year! Fuji–Hakone–Izu had the most with eighty million.

Access to many of Japan's parks has become too easy. More and more highways enable comfortable penetration of mountain fastnesses once only accessible on foot. One can even drive halfway up Mount Fuji. Exhaust fumes in the Japan Alps have forced the authorities to close some major park roads on summer weekends. Remoter parks such as Iriomote still remain "unspoiled," but the residents are in a quandary. They wish to preserve their semitropical paradise but they also want to increase visitors for the sake of the local economy.

Governments can make laws to try to curb pollution and the disfigurement and destruction of nature. They can impose fines on those who disregard the laws. But in the end it is the individual who must observe them. The hiker no less than the entrepreneur and the industrialist. Until people, as they "walk abroad and recreate themselves," learn enough discipline to leave behind nothing but their footprints, the last beautiful vistas left, even in national parks, may soon be only those in travel books such as this. Photographers have to take more and more pains to compose pictures not marred by the ugly man-made structures and discarded remnants of modern life that the sweeping eye of the observer cannot avoid. How indebted we are to these dedicated photographers who are putting nature's beauty on record before it is gone forever. Moreover, with their cameras—even better than we could with our own eyes—they are able to bring before us with startling vividness the marvelous scenic variety of these Islands of Japan, preserved for us in no small measure by these twenty-seven national parks pictured herein.

D.B. and M.S.

RISHIRI–REBUN–SAROBETSU
NATIONAL PARK

TWO ISLANDS AND A MARSH IN THE SUBARCTIC EXTREME NORTH
OF HOKKAIDO

1. The colorful day lily of north Hokkaido

2. Rishiri Island and Mount Rishiri from Momo-iwa on Rebun Island

SHIRETOKO NATIONAL PARK

A MOUNTAIN PENINSULA CALLED THE "END OF THE EARTH" BY THE AINU, BUTTRESSED BY SHEER CLIFFS AND BUFFETED BY KAMCHATKAN WINDS

3. An eagle glides past the cliffs of Shiretoko's northwest coast

4. One of the Shiretoko Five Lakes

5. These cliffs, on Shiretoko's northwest coast, look beguilingly welcoming in summer

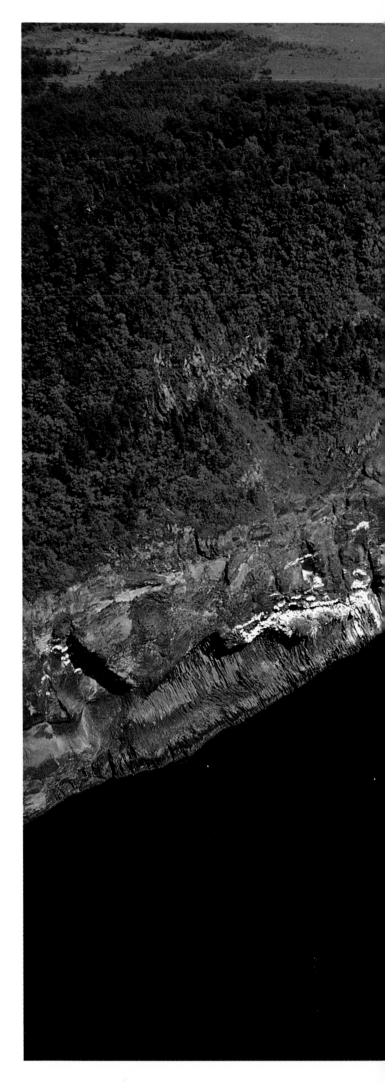

AKAN NATIONAL PARK

THREE OF THE WORLD'S LARGEST CRATER LAKES SURROUNDED BY
PRIMEVAL FORESTS

6. Lake Mashu, the deepest lake in the world after Lake Baikal in Siberia, under a mantle of mist

7. Japanese cranes on the frozen banks of the Akan River

8. Swans on Lake Kussharo

9. The clothing of the Ainu, many of whom live in the vicinity of Lake Akan, is noted for its striking patterns

DAISETSUZAN NATIONAL PARK

THE ROOF OF HOKKAIDO: THREE CLUSTERS OF MOUNTAINS SURROUND THE VAST SWEEP OF A PLATEAU

10. Mount Tokachi, with the vapors of the volcano providing a backdrop to the brilliance of the autumn leaves

11. A typical Hokkaido view of Mount Daisetsu

12. The Hagoromo Falls at Tenninkyo

SHIKOTSU–TOYA
NATIONAL PARK

JAPAN'S YOUNGEST VOLCANO CLINGS PARASITICALLY TO
THE BACK OF ITS EXTREMELY ACTIVE PARENT,
MOUNT USU

13. The lava dome of Showa Shinzan, Japan's youngest volcano

14. Mount Yotei, the Fuji of Hokkaido

15. Laka Toya and Nakanoshima, the "Island in the Middle" of the
lake—a common phenomenon in volcanic Japan

TOWADA–HACHIMANTAI NATIONAL PARK

MOUNTAINS, PLATEAUX, AND A LAKE IN JAPAN'S SNOW
COUNTRY, WITH ITS THATCHED ROOFS, FOLK ART, AND
FURIOUS FESTIVALS

16. Ice patterns of Lake Towada

17. Trees draped in snow on Mount Hakkoda

18. Oirase gorge in early summer, when the river is swollen with water
from snow melting on the surrounding peaks

RIKUCHU KAIGAN
NATIONAL PARK

WILDEST AND PERHAPS MOST BEAUTIFUL STRETCH OF
JAPAN'S COASTLINE——AND AMONG THE MOST
INACCESSIBLE

19. Black-tailed gulls

20. Wind-torn crags off Jodogahama (Paradise Beach)

21. Kitayamazaki in winter, when the cape bears a sprinkling of snow.

BANDAI–ASAHI NATIONAL PARK

22. Two products of volcanic activity: Mount Bandai and the marshlands of Nakasenuma

23, 24. Two shades of Goshikinuma (the Five-Color Marshes)

25. Mount Bandai: reflections of the mountain in paddy fields

RISHIRI-REBUN-SAROBETSU NATIONAL PARK

Sarobetsu Plain

Hokkaido, with its New England latitude and sub-arctic climate, is quite unlike the rest of Japan. The Japanese have a natural aversion to cold-weather living, and they mostly left the northern part of their archipelago to the aboriginal Ainu, whom they finally drove across the Tsugaru Straits into Hokkaido in the twelfth century after gradually pushing them further and further north. Hokkaido was not settled in earnest by the Japanese until the late nineteenth century, when dairy farming, the raising of cattle, sheep, and pigs, and the cultivation of crops and fruit such as apples and hops was begun on American lines. The wide open plains and gently rolling hills lend themselves to this kind of agriculture rather than to the rice cultivation suited to Japan's other islands with their abrupt hills and flat valleys. Crossing the straits from Honshu to Hokkaido is almost like going to a foreign land.

Two islands lying just west of Hokkaido's northern tip—towering Rishiri, 182 kilometers square, and gentle Rebun, half as big—combine with a nearby expanse of land on Hokkaido to form Rishiri–Rebun–Sarobetsu National Park. Besides being Japan's most northerly national park, the islands present an interesting reminder of a brush between the Czarist navy and Japan's Tokugawa shogunate almost two hundred years ago. Buried on Rishiri are some of the shogun's men who fell defending these offshore islands in 1807. The Russians attacked Japanese fishing settlements on Sakhalin and Kunashiri, and a hundred or so samurai sent from a fief near Kyoto successfully repulsed the aggressors.

Historical records first mention Hokkaido (or Yezo as it was called until this century) in connection with a foray made in the year 659 into what is now Russia's maritime provinces but was then most probably either uninhabited or Mongol-held land. The leader, Abe no Hirafu, made his base in Shiribeshi, not far from present-day Sapporo, capital of Hokkaido, but his expedition did little more than lead to further exploration and the establishment of island fishing posts.

In the following centuries, warriors fled across the the straits to Yezo from time to time during civil wars, eventually forming a fief called Matsumae with its castle seat at Hokkaido's southern tip. The colder regions still repelled all but the hard-pressed Ainu who had once regarded the whole of Japan as their home.

When population pressure finally drove the land-hungry Japanese to overcome their aversion to the cold and colonize Hokkaido with official sanction, their policy was to assimilate the Ainu, encouraging them to speak Japanese and adopt Japanese names. Ainu culture has been all but swallowed up, except as a tourist attraction. But an intriguing statistic claims the existence today of fifteen thousand full-blooded Ainu, almost two thousand more than the 1873 figure of 12,281. The distinctive proto-Caucasian element represented by the Ainu, whose blood must course through many Japanese veins, surely accounts for much that sets the Japanese apart from the peoples of the rest of Asia, making their land a sort of British Isles of the Orient.

A concerned Japanese linguist, proficient in both the Ainu and Eskimo tongues, whose efforts recently led to the promulgation of an Alaskan Native Language Act in the United States, is lobbying for similar measures in his own country to prevent the Ainu language from becoming totally extinct. Almost all that is left of it now are the Ainu words reflected in place names throughout Japan, especially in Hokkaido, hard to recognize since they are written and pronounced in Japanese fashion.

A remarkable British woman, Isabella Bird, who visited Hokkaido in 1878, living in Ainu homes, wrote what is still possibly the most readable and detailed account in English of Ainu beliefs, culture, and lifestyle in her book *Unbeaten Tracks in Japan*. She was enthusiastic both about the people and country:

"In Yezo the traveller is conscious of a freer atmosphere than he has breathed on the main island, and it is not only the air which circulates more freely. You can go off the roads and gallop for miles over breezy commons by the seashore, covered with red roses; you can swim rivers, and climb mountains. . . . There is a charm about the thinly peopled country, a fascination in the long moan of the Pacific between Tomakomai and Cape Erimo, in the glorious loneliness of the region round Volcano Bay and in the breeziness and freedom of Yezo life, which makes my memories of Yezo in some respects the most delightful which I have brought away from Japan."

Breezy Commons and Carpets of Flowers

Wildernesses such as Isabella Bird's "breezy commons by the seashore" are still to be found in Hokkaido aplenty, brilliant in summer with wild flowers of every hue from sunshine yellow to rose red, and varieties both familiar and strange. How she would have relished the marshlands of the Sarobetsu Plain, carpeted in June with orange and yellow day lilies and white-tufted cotton grass. In July the fields are a sea of white rhododendrons, lilies of the valley, black lilies, purple irises, and skunk cabbage—a kind of wild arum or calla lily. There are scattered woods of Japanese spruce, elm, mountain ash, and oak in this broad stretch of land, which undulates no more than from three to seven meters with the exception of a twenty-five-hectare eminence called Maruyama (Round Hill), which stands all of fourteen meters above sea level.

Sarobetsu derives from the Ainu *sar* (swamp) and *pet* (river), words which aptly describe this vast low-lying rectangle of marshy land five to eight kilometers wide and about twenty-seven kilometers long, crisscrossed by meandering streams. The land is rich, built up of layers of peat bog (decomposed moss, sedge grass,

and ditch weed) covered with fertile river silt. Its arable potential and 122 frostless days a year, thanks to favorable winds, combined to make a strong argument in favor of draining and reclaiming it as farmland. But in the end its one great drawback spared it so it could be added to the national park: the plain becomes waterlogged each spring when the snows melt, and the first good shower causes rivers and lakes to overflow.

Preserving Sarobetsu as a wild-flower reserve was the wiser choice. Swampy plains like this retard the rate at which fresh water runs off into the ocean, helping to recharge the supply of ground water. Moreover, as a coastal marsh, the plain, with its sand dunes lying alongside the Japan Sea, constitutes a self-repairing buffer against ravaging storm waves.

When the 8,129-hectare Sarobetsu Plain was added in 1974 to the islands of Rishiri and Rebun, already a quasi-national park, the whole area was upgraded to national park status. One of the best ways of seeing Sarobetsu is to leave the Soya main line train at Toyotomi and take a bus through the center of the plain to Wakkasakanai. An alternative is to take a bus from Wakkanai to Sakanoshita via Bakkai. Windswept Wakkanai, with its low scrub and gaily roofed houses, is Japan's most northerly town. From there, the Higashi Nihonkai ferry company runs two boats a day to both Rishiri and Rebun islands.

As the ferry from Wakkanai approaches the sister islands, the traveler can see what a complete contrast the two are. Rishiri is dominated by the upthrust figure of an extinct conical volcano, Mount Rishiri. From a distance, the deeply eroded black gullies on the mountainside and the irregularly shaped snow-covered summit suggest a bold work of art—a modern sculpture of chased metal inlaid with silver. Vigorous and strong, Rishiri gives the appearance of having wrenched itself free from the sea, while neighboring Rebun is flat and seems to ride gently upon the water. In fact, Rishiri is a volcanic island which came into existence only a matter of hundreds of thousands of years ago, while Rebun was created millions of years ago by the piling up of the earth's crust. Topographically and geologically, they are as different as can be.

The Smell of the North

Oshidomari on Rishiri Island, where my ferry docked, is a typical fishing port: a small fleet of masted fishing boats rock at anchor in the harbor; the weathered sides of the low warehouses are decorated with large black characters proclaiming the Fishermen's Cooperative, and nets are hung out like stage curtains to dry. Small, rusty cranes yank catches out of the holds. The smell of fish, salt water, and machine oil is all-pervasive. Still chilly, even in mid-

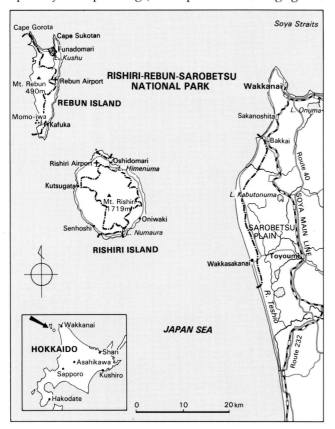

summer, the slanting rays of the sun bring the signboards and storefronts into sharp relief with the clarity of winter light. Beyond the harbor is a strip of beach where I saw children endeavoring to engage in a summer sport—swimming. But between dips they wrapped themselves up in heavy sweaters and even parkas, and, their limbs almost blue from the cold, they scurried up to a crackling bonfire.

I strolled up the main street toward the town hall, where I had an appointment to meet a park ranger. There, they told me the ranger had gone to Rebun to inspect park land and was returning on the next ferry. While I was waiting, I watched a friendly, talkative official inspect the fishermen's catch. For my benefit, he held up specimens as he worked, telling me what each one was—flounder, pieces of cod, herring (a local speciality), and crab. As he spoke, he hacked a piece off each and put all the pieces in a large pot. He tossed in a few fish heads for good measure, added water, and set the pot on the gas stove to simmer.

Before too long, the ranger arrived and we drove off on the single road that rings the island (perfect for cycling since traffic is light) to see some of the sights. A recent college graduate in forestry from Tokyo University, Ranger Matsumura had survived a highly competitive written examination to become a ranger and Rishiri was his first assignment. He was excited about having drawn "the frontier" as his first post and spoke enthusiastically about the park and the islands.

Our first stop was Himenuma (Maiden Lake), along whose shores is one of the three designated campsites on the island. Filled with carp and trout, the lake has enough fish to provide vacationers with breakfast, lunch, and dinner.

The terrain seemed to be an ideal habitat for the bears for which Hokkaido is famous. But the ranger explained that there were none on these two islands. "There's hardly ever a long enough calm on the rough channel between here and the mainland," he said; "so this is one short piece of water the bears just couldn't negotiate." The largest furred animals native to the islands are squirrels, field mice, and shrews. There are foxes and weasels, too, introduced at the turn of the century when it was thought that a trapping industry might be profitable. Probably the best known animal on the islands is the Sakhalin dog. Akin to Alaskan huskies, and known for their obedience and sturdiness, they have been used as sled dogs on Japanese polar expeditions. Rishiri and Rebun are also well known for the estuarine wading birds that flock there in summer.

The quickest way to find out about the islands is to visit the Rishiri Island Historical Society at Oniwaki (twenty minutes by bus from Oshidomari). It is housed in a one-story yellow clapboard building with sash

Mount Rishiri seen from Rebun Island

windows, chimneys, lightning rods, and gables. It was built to serve as Oniwaki's town hall in 1913 when Western-style architecture was popular in Japan. Only within the last decade has the building been converted to its present use.

The historical society has exhibitions on fishing, which has always been the mainstay of the economy of the island, as well as folk crafts and natural history. Archeological exhibits show that before the Ainu settled Rishiri, an aboriginal people of unknown extraction lived here. Then came the Ainu, to be followed about three hundred years ago by the first few Japanese. The Japanese settlers over the years came from all over the country and the folk craft on display reveals a variety of Japanese traditions, as well as objects of Ainu origin.

A small cemetery just outside Kutsugata (from where there is a ferry to Rebun) was the next stop on our island tour. There we saw the graves of the brave samurai from Kyoto who defended the islands in 1807. Their names have almost been obliterated by time and exposure. Local people believe that the spirits of these patriots who died so far from home still protect the island.

Rishiri's sister island, Rebun, with its gentle profile, is often called the "Isle of Flowers." More than three hundred varieties of alpine plants flourish here, including several types of crowfoot, poppies, and pinks. Though Rebun has only low, wind-swept hills, its northern latitude and climate provide a perfect habitat for mountain plants. Here, the creeping pines and delicate-looking alpine flowers are similar to those found at three thousand meters on Japan's main island, Honshu. Many plants found here are related to those of the Kurile Islands, as well as Sakhalin, Siberia, and Alaska, so Rebun is of great scientific interest to botanists. The best plant communities, collectively designated a Natural Monument, can be found around Momo-iwa (Peach Rock) on Rebun's southeast coast, from where there is a superb view of Mount Rishiri across the water.

M.S.

SHIRETOKO NATIONAL PARK

Rausu port

The Ainu called the mountainous, often mist-wrapped peninsula on the northeast of Hokkaido "Shiretoko." The name is apt, meaning "end of the earth," for the peninsula juts sixty-five kilometers into the cold, rough Sea of Okhotsk and looks chillingly inhospitable. Designated a national park in 1964, Shiretoko remains untamed and unspoiled—the wildest of all Japan's parks.

Two towns serve as gateways to the park: Rausu on the east, and Utoro on the northwest. I went first to Rausu because of the small ranger's station there. With its tile-roofed, weatherbeaten, one-story wooden buildings strung out in a line at the shore, Rausu is little more than a fishing village. Everyone knows everyone, and the place has some of the rugged charm of an Alaskan outpost.

The ranger's station in Rausu is a combination of office and home, not large, but warm and comfortable, up in the hills overlooking the town and its small harbor. While Ranger Hirano, an energetic man in his early thirties, was giving me some background information on the park, a friend strolled in to discuss the annual spring topic of snow damage, potholes, and road repairs. The ranger introduced his friend as Nakamura Kazuya and explained that he was a fisherman while at sea but found time while on land, especially in the long winter months, to work as a town official.

Warming my hands round the cup of tea that inevitably appeared, I listened eagerly to everything the two of them could tell me about the peninsula.

Only a couple of proper roads are open to visitors, running for twenty-five kilometers or so up either side of the peninsula from Rausu and Utoro respectively. Popular attractions on the narrow rocky coasts are the hot springs that gush out from the rocks to form shallow pools. They are best at low tide, since some disappear under the sea at high water, and they provide in particular a much-appreciated open-air bath for tourists in summer. One of these is quite near Kamu-iwakka waterfall on the northwestern coast.

Above all, what draws visitors to the park is Shiretoko's volcanic range and the magnificent cliffs that rim and buttress the peninsula. These are best seen from a boat. Tourist boats ply the waters surrounding Shiretoko from May to September, departing twice a day from Rausu to make the full four-hour trip to Utoro and vice versa. Boats from both ports also make a round trip to Cape Shiretoko, though passengers are not permitted to go ashore there. The fastest and most popular tour is the one-hour excursion from Utoro, which takes in the most spectacular cliff scenery. But I decided to take the longer boat trip from Rausu all the way round the peninsula. The ranger and his friend, quickly remembering all sorts of things they could do in Utoro, kindly offered to act as my guides.

Peninsula from the Sea

The early boat left at 5:30 A.M., just as a catch of flounder was being unloaded at the fishermen's cooperative. The sun soon warmed the damp air and the scent of resin from the thickly forested hills and mountains beyond came drifting out to sea where it mingled with the smell of the tide. A playful porpoise decided to befriend us and swam alongside all the way to the cape, occasionally leaping from the waves in shallow arcs.

After Rausu was well out of sight, Nakamura pointed to the shore, where strips of level ground at the water line afforded space for a few scattered huts. The huts, he told me, are used by fishermen from Rausu in the short summer season when the harvest of giant kelp, *konbu*, is on. *Konbu* is a sort of sea vegetable with thick, wide leaves—dark green in its natural state, but almost black and stiff as leather when it is dried and cut into sheets. It is an important ingredient in many Japanese recipes and is a basic element in soup stock.

I marveled at the vegetation. The hills were bright with angelica, Ezo dandelions, Hokkaido rhododendrons, tiger's tails, irises, and other flowering plants. To think that this rugged horn-shaped peninsula—surrounded by ice floes all winter—could burst into such bloom come spring! "A dwarf rose, of a deep crimson colour, with orange, medlar shaped hips, as large as crabs, and corollas three inches across, is one of

Oshinkoshin Falls near Utoro

the features of Yezo," wrote Isabella Bird in 1878.

Nakamura was looking forward to the coming season: "A few more months, and we'll be out there at the huts. We work all day, everybody together, gathering and drying—we dry it here, even though the sun isn't too hot, and the air isn't too dry—and at night everybody drinks by lantern light. At other times of the year, there's not a soul around that place."

As we neared the cape, Ranger Hirano, leaning against the rails at the stern, described his periodic treks deep into the interior of the peninsula, far past the point where there are any trails, treks that eventually bring him to the cape. Here at the foot of Mount Shiretoko, he has seen foxes, deer, hares, and the largest of Hokkaido's big brown bears. In a resigned tone, he added how occasionally he had to rescue overambitious hikers who went beyond the limited number of set trails and lost their way.

Nakamura broke in to direct my attention away from the cape and its unmanned lighthouse to the island of Kunashiri, which we could just make out to starboard. It is not part of the park, indeed, alas, no longer even part of Japan, but geographically it is a natural extension of Shiretoko. "The Russians seized it in 1945, two weeks after the end of the war. But we still consider it ours. We all know the waters there so well—good fishing, especially salmon: after all, we used to go there when we were young! But now every year some of us get caught."

Kunashiri is the second largest of the four Soviet-occupied islands off the coast of northeast Hokkaido. The others are Etorofu, Shikotan, and the Habomai group, only a stone's throw from the Nemuro Peninsula. All have indisputably been Japanese territory for centuries. Nakamura gave me his private views while a voice over the loudspeaker filled in the facts for the benefit of the other passengers: "The Japanese began trading with the Ainu and Gilyaks on these islands in the seventeenth century, and the Tokugawa government developed fishing on Kunashiri and Etorofu from the early 1800s. In an 1875 treaty with Japan, Czarist Russia recognized all the Kuriles as Japanese territory, but with the end of World War II came Soviet occupation. In the past three decades, over seven thousand Japanese fishermen, allegedly apprehended in restricted waters, have been taken by Russian patrol boats, detained on Shikotan, and eventually repatriated—an unwelcome addition to the natural dangers of fishing. Today the recovery of these northern territories is a major official objective."

Cliffs in Black and White

Finally, the cliffs of the northwest coast loomed into sight, rising to heights of two hundred meters and extending unbroken for ten-kilometer stretches, relenting only occasionally, as at the mouth of the Iwaobetsu River—a breeding ground for salmon and trout. These cliffs, with their black and white horizontal stripes, are a striking phenomenon: molten lava spread in sills through fossil-rich, sedimentary rock while the mass was still submerged; then volcanic activity beneath the ocean floor pushed the whole out of the sea, creating these massive cliffs.

Volcanic activity was not, however, the only force involved in the creation of these cliffs. The wind and sea have shaved them into fantastic shapes. The Ainu, as well as the Japanese, have given names to some: Penguin-no-hana (Penguin's Nose), Shishi-iwa (Lion Rock), Tako-iwa (Octupus Rock), Kannon-iwa (the Rock of Kannon, goddess of mercy). Here sea fowl—Temminck's cormorants, black-tailed gulls, and sooty guillemots—hover and screech, dive and settle in their nests. It is a sea-bird's paradise, and if one is lucky one

Mount Rausu seen from Utoro

may even catch a glimpse of the aerie of a rare white-tailed eagle. Narrow rivers, whose sources are in the mountains sixteen hundred meters up above, fall in cascades of white over the dark cliffs. In winter they freeze solid. Foliage tops the cliffs, and beyond them rises the Shiretoko range.

Three volcanic mountains, Shiretoko, Io, and Rausu, form a rugged backbone from the tip to the base of the peninsula. The Shiretoko mountains are part of the Chishima volcanic zone, which runs right down through the Kurile archipelago to the center of Hokkaido.

Of the Shiretoko group, only Mount Io (io is the Japanese for sulfur) is now active. History records that it erupts about every sixty years. When this unusual type of volcano erupts, out gushes almost pure liquid sulfur. As I watched the acrid smoke which constantly billows from the fumaroles at Io's summit, Nakamura explained that it was not until the middle of the seventeenth century that the mountain, and indeed the peninsula itself, were first mentioned in Japanese records. The most recent eruption took place in 1936 when something like seventeen thousand tons of sulfur were ejected in one night. He went on to tell me that for years a local family had had a mining concession in the area, but they eventually made a fortune overnight. Today the only visible trace of this enormous outpouring is the bright yellow of the seabed near the Kamuiwakka Falls. In the Ainu tongue, the name of the cascade means "Water of the Gods."

Visitors who want to see Mount Io's smoking vents and two great craters can hike up the path that runs from the Kamuiwakka Falls (where the paved road from Utoro ends) to the peak, a trek of about four hours. Ranger Hirano, who is an enthusiastic naturalist, told me about a plant unique to this mountain, the shiretoko sumire, a small white violet whose delicate blossoms defy the harsh environment and the strong sea winds.

At ten in the morning we finally docked at Utoro and bought breakfast on the pier from vendors selling delicious, fresh steamed crab. Then, bowing my thanks to my two guides, I caught a bus for the thirty-five-minute trip to the Shiretoko Five Lakes (Shiretoko Goko).

The volcanic plateau between Shiretoko's mountain spine and its cliffs cradles a great many lakes and marshes, but only the Shiretoko Five Lakes are easily accessible from the hotels, inns, and hostels of Utoro, popular for their hot-spring baths.

The lakes are like reservoirs, though none is very deep. They are natural hollows in the lava bed laid down around six hundred thousand years ago, a fact which also accounts for the marshy zone immediately surrounding the lakes. At the water's margin grow spatterdock and buckbean and other marsh plants, including skunk cabbage, whose Japanese name mizubasho (water plantain) is far pleasanter and more descriptive and whose funnellike white flowers, resembling stunted calla lilies, are among the first to blossom in spring.

Signposts along the route describe particular features of each lake, and some of them warn hikers and tourists not to leave the track: "The cliffs are only fifty meters away." Thick forests of birch, spruce, oak, and silver fir enfold the lakes and give a false impression of their altitude and distance from the sea.

M.S.

Drift ice from the Okhotsk Sea

AKAN NATIONAL PARK

Lake Akan

Akan National Park covers an area of 87,498 hectares and was established in 1934, making it one of the oldest national parks in Japan. Its exhilarating scenery is the product of prodigious volcanic activity. The park extends over the twin bowls of Akan and Kussharo. Each of these gigantic craters, or calderas, has a diameter of several tens of kilometers. Now carpeted with thick forest, they were created between a hundred and thirty thousand years ago (just yesterday by the geological calendar), when, after a series of violent eruptions, a group of volcanic cones collapsed. Subsequent volcanic activity within the large basins resulted in a number of new volcanoes, up to fifteen hundred meters in height. At the same time, lava flows created dams at various points, so that lakes were gradually formed.

Senpoku Pass overlooks the Akan caldera in the southwestern section of the park, while Bihoro Pass lies on the rim of the Kussharo caldera, to the northeast. These two vantage points, which are also the principal entryways to Akan National Park, command a view of a simple and pure landscape with thick subarctic forests, blue unpolluted lakes, and volcanoes—some dormant, some pluming white smoke.

Nature has been bountiful and generous in bestowing its beauty. The game and fish, the edible bulbs, berries and seeds of the underbrush attracted the Ainu to Akan and Kussharo long ago. They hunted and prospered in these mysterious woods of silver fir. Contributing to this primeval setting are the white-mottled foliage of the silvervine (a kind of catnip) and the large umbrellalike leaves of the *fuki* (bog rhubarb), under which, according to Ainu lore, live fairies adept at easing troubles of the heart. The edible stalks of the *fuki* are a common dish, and the flame red berries of the silvervine, aged with the right proportions of sugar and spirits, make a tangy homemade liqueur.

The road from Senpoku Pass leads to Akan Kohan Spa on the shore of Lake Akan. The spa provides an ideal base for exploring the southwestern section of the park: Lake Akan itself and Lakes Panke and Penke and the Akan volcanic cones—O-Akan, Me-Akan and Akan-Fuji. Accommodation ranges from youth hostels to expensive hotels, but all boast hot-spring baths. With its natural history exhibits, the Akan Visitors' Center in the middle of town can help the tourist decide what he or she will find most interesting.

Lake Akan is only a remnant of a vast expanse of water that once filled the whole of the Akan crater. Volcanic pressure squeezed the lake into its present shape, a small triangle with islands protruding. Its northwestern arm was severed from the main body of water and became the tiny "upper" lakes of Penke and Panke.

Plant without Leaves

Above all else, Lake Akan derives its fame from the fact that it is the home of a rare spherical water plant called *marimo*, or "ball moss," seen on sunny days floating close to the surface of the water. According to an Ainu legend, the plants are the tears of the maiden Setona who loved a hunter of unworthy tribal rank. The hunter, Manibe, was forced to flee the lakeside settlement forever after a struggle with Setona's betrothed, whom he killed. For years after—indeed, until her death—Setona would row herself far out on the lake to try to hear the strains of Manibe's flute, all the while weeping bitter tears into the water—every one of which is now a *marimo*.

In fact, the velvety green *marimo* (*Cladaphora sauteri*) are simply balls of thin, hairlike algae that have entwined and grown together. Different species of cladaphora are found in a number of alpine lakes in Switzerland and North America, but their distribution is very limited, and it is at Akan that this aquatic plant can best be studied.

Marimo lack true leaves, stems, roots, and vascular systems. They sometimes attach themselves to submerged rocks and timber in cold shallows or stream inlets and, if thickly clustered, look like an inviting bed of soft, rounded cushions. The rays of the sun attract them to the water's surface. The balls are formed by the rolling effect of currents, and their size is thus slowly increased millimeter by millimeter. *Marimo* range in diameter from three to twenty centimeters, though some unusually large specimens of forty centimeters have been discovered. The lifespan of the plant and the number of months or years they take to grow to a representative size is still unknown. At any rate, being locked into the winter ice at Akan appears not to affect them.

In 1949, the *marimo* were severely endangered when a sudden shift in the water level of the lake was precipitated by the use of its waters for the generation of electricity. Since *marimo* thrive in shallows, when the water level went down, many were exposed with the result that they withered and died. Following the lead of a group of schoolchildren, the villagers began to walk the shores, picking up the plants and pitching them back into the water. A campaign to protect the *marimo*, centering on a *marimo* festival, was initiated the same year. The festival, which takes place every year on October 10, when the autumn leaves are at their most colorful, has since become a major tourist attraction; the Ainu legends about the plant are enacted as part of the festival celebrations.

Visitors are no longer permitted to collect *marimo*, because in 1952 the plant was designated a Special Natural Treasure. The pleasure boat that tours Lake Akan stops at Churuimoshira, one of the four islands on the lake, where *marimo* can be observed growing in specially built tanks. Anglers at Lake Akan have to toss back *marimo* that get entangled in their lines, but they can keep the rainbow trout, lake salmon, and pond smelt they catch.

From the pleasure boat, one's gaze is attracted in summer by the purple azaleas thriving among the birches and in autumn by the red maples. Along the shore, there are a few rocky outcrops where the color of the water changes abruptly. These are places where hot springs pour into the lake.

Other evidence of the volcanic nature of Akan are a

Lake Kussharo

few small mud-ash basins. One called Bokke is close to the lake, a few minutes' walk from the visitors' center. The name Bokke imitates the sound of the gas bubbles, which, having risen sluggishly to the surface of the mud pot, pop open.

Around the lake rise the Akan volcanic cones. To the east is the dormant Mount O-Akan. This, the "Male Akan," is clothed in pines and has a stolid, dignified form. Across the lake is Mount Me-Akan, the "Female Akan," an active volcano with a smoking heart, which last erupted in 1955. A local explanation attributes the gash in the mountainside and the column of white smoke rising from the "distaff" peak to a wound sustained in a marital quarrel. Visitors invariably joke about the characterization of the larger, rumbling mountain as "female."

A subsidiary peak on the south side of Me-Akan is Mount Akan-Fuji, whose contours are said to be reminiscent of Mount Fuji itself. Any mountain bearing the slightest resemblance to Japan's best-known peak is liable to have the name Fuji tacked onto its own name. At least ten such "Fujis" spring to mind.

The northeastern part of the park can be approached via Bihoro Pass from the north, from Teshikaga Spa to the south, or along the Akan Transverse Road, which carries traffic across the park from west to east. On this scenic, winding road are two places worth a stop: Sogakudai (Two Mounts Lookout) from where O-Akan and Me-Akan can be seen in dramatic profile; and Sokodai (Two Lakes Lookout) from where there is a view of Lakes Penke and Panke in their primeval surroundings. The road goes on to Kawayu Spa to the east of Lake Kussharo. This spa also has a visitors' center and plenty of accommodation and is within easy access of the main sights of this part of the park.

Lake Kussharo with a perimeter of fifty-seven kilometers is the largest caldera lake in the world. Locals are proud of the color of the lake, a distinctive deep blue caused by the diffused reflection of sunlight on the abundant dissolved salts and minerals emanating from hot springs. Not to be outdone by stories of the monster of another famous lake, they spin tales of their own "Nessie" deep in Lake Kussharo, whom they call

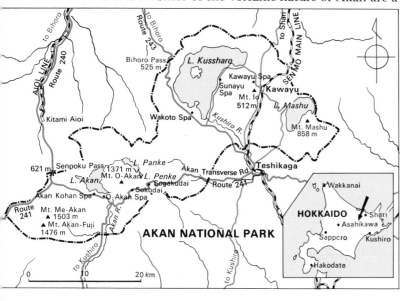

"Kutchie." In fact, because of the high mineral content of the water, the lake has few fish.

In the south is the miniature Wakoto Peninsula which just rises above the surface of the lake. Here, bubbling alkaline hot springs are used as open-air baths. Sunayu means "hot sand," and the beach on the northeast of the lake is just that. To warm one's hands by burying them or to walk barefoot there on a crisp evening produces a sensation unique for these latitudes. Camping is permitted at both these sites, and at Sunayu, people of Ainu descent give daily performances of native dances.

Savage Look Belied a Gentle People

Hokkaido has several Ainu *kotan*, or villages, where the Ainu dress and live as their forebears did—except that they do it for the benefit of tourists. Shiraoi is best known, but Akan National Park has a *kotan* at Akan Kohan Spa near Lake Akan in the west of the park. Yet the present-day Ainu who dress up to order and dance their slow, mournful dances that the tourists find rather boring mostly have short hair and are hardly distinguishable from Japanese. Few remember the ancient mother tongue, and only the very old can still sing the Ainu songs authentically, in wavery voices, playing the old instruments—one of which is a sort of wooden jew's-harp held in the mouth. To find out what this tribe were really like one must now go to sources like Isabella Bird and her late nineteenth-century account.

The Ainu were a gentle and courteous people, she tells us. "The savage look produced by masses of hair and beard, and the thick eyebrows, is mitigated by the softness in the creamy brown eyes, and is altogether obliterated by the exceeding sweetness of the smile." They were a handsome race, the women beautifully proportioned, the children pretty and attractive. The supposed ugliness of the women was simply due to "art and dirt" as she puts it. They seldom washed, out of a religious taboo against baring the body, and their good looks were marred by extensive tattooing. This custom was prohibited by the Japanese government about that time (1878), and Miss Bird relates how grieved they were, believing the gods would be angry, and repeating frequently: "It's part of our religion."

In winter, the Ainu wore hooded coats of animal skins and moccasins; in summer, simple loose garb woven from finely split bark—"a durable and beautiful fabric in various shades of natural buff." Isabella Bird continues: "Garments for holiday occasions are exceedingly handsome, being decorated with 'geometrical' patterns, in which the 'Greek fret' takes part, in coarse blue cotton, braided most dexterously with scarlet and white thread. Some take half a year to make." Else-where she says: "The 'jewels' of the women are large hoop earrings of silver or pewter, with attachments of a classical pattern, and silver neck ornaments." And she describes Ainu dwellings thus: "In their houses, as in their faces, the Ainos [sic] are more European than their conquerors, as they possess doorways, windows, central fireplaces, like those of the Highlanders of Scotland, and raised sleeping places."

Today, souvenir shops throughout Hokkaido sell not only miniatures of traditional Ainu garb and artifacts, but dozens of carved bears of all sizes. Many keep a bear cub tethered outside for local color. But the ancient Ainu venerated and "worshiped" the bear. They admired it for its strength, ferocity, and courage. No greater compliment could be paid a man than to say he was as strong as a bear, and a favorite young man would often be dubbed "the young bear."

The old bear cult entailed the capture of a small cub to be reared in the home of a chieftain, suckled by a highborn woman, and made the companion of a child until fully grown, when it would be caged and ceremoniously put to death with much feasting, propitiation, and invocation, and impassioned shouts of: "We kill you, O bear! Come back soon into an Ainu!"

In the northeastern corner of Akan National Park there is a remarkable crater lake—the world's deepest. The tiny isle curled like a sleeping bear cub on its gemlike aquamarine blue surface seems like a sort of celestial memorial to those hapless creatures caught in the web of a strange tradition. The Ainu call this strange isle Kamuitoo, "Island of the Gods." And indeed, Lake Mashu's thickly forested, sheer two-hundred-meter sides protect both lake and island from easy access by mere mortals.

M.S.

An Ainu with carved wooden bears

DAISETSUZAN NATIONAL PARK

Two of the Daisetsuzan peaks

Daisetsuzan National Park, known as the "roof of Hokkaido" and at the very center of this large island, enjoys several distinctions. Established in 1934, Daisetsuzan with its sweeping highlands and dramatic volcanic groups was not only one of Japan's first national parks, but together with Akan, established the same year, one of the first two parks in Hokkaido. Unlike the majority of Japan's national parks which are made up of scattered tracts of land, Daisetsuzan is a single vast tract. With an area of 231,000 hectares, it is, moreover, the largest park in Japan.

It has been easier here than with other parks to control development, and the greater part of the park is used to preserve nature, not to support the activities of man. This is due to the happy fact that ninety percent of Daisetsuzan National Park's land is owned directly by the national government.

Recreation areas at Daisetsuzan have been wisely confined to a generous band along the park's northwest and southeast perimeters, and nearby areas. Logging and reforestation, too, are kept to these same generally accessible areas and supervised by the government. The great Daisetsuzan forests in the interior of the park have been left untouched. The age and size of the park, and the fact that nearly all the land is owned outright by the state have contributed to making Daisetsuzan a great natural wilderness—despite the recreational and commercial facilities on its periphery.

At the very center of the park are the Ishikari Highlands, an area of undulating hills, few of which are more than fifteen hundred meters high, and vast forests.

The Ishikari Highlands were formed when a fault developed in the earth's crust during a period of volcanic activity, and the entire area was elevated as a monolithic block. The older volcanoes are nearby: the Daisetsuzan group to the north, the Tokachi group to the west (both with well-known ski resorts and good snow at least till May) and the Shikaribetsu group to the southeast (known for its hot springs). The park comprises these four distinctive areas: the central highlands surrounded by the three volcanic groups.

Wine from Chilled Latitudes

The name Tokachi is coming to be known now throughout Japan for its wine as well as for its skiing. The Tokachi mountains overlook a spacious plain whose inhabitants made a living from agriculture (including rice) and forestry. But in 1963, the small, century-old town of Ikeda, near Obihiro, began a wine making business that has grown by leaps and bounds.

A type of wild vine always grew on the plain and was once used to make a local liquor with an alcohol content nearly as high as brandy. When, in 1957, farmers were obliged to reduce rice production owing to a national surplus, Ikeda's mayor hit upon the idea of making wine. A subsidy of ¥55,000 was offered to every household planting four hectares of grapes. By 1964, Tokachi wine had been awarded an international bronze medal, followed by a silver the following year and a gold in 1968. The town now holds a Wine Festival in mid-February, following Sapporo's popular Snow Festival at the beginning of the month which attracts thousands from all over Japan to see the celebrated snow sculptures assembled on the wide main boulevard of Hokkaido's capital. Six hundred thousand visitors a year already flock to Ikeda whose "wine" theme is everywhere evident: the streets are paved with red-wine-colored asphalt, and lamps of white-wine-colored amber shed an alluring glow at night.

The mountains in Daisetsuzan National Park are not the loftiest in Japan by any means. Mount Asahi at 2,290 meters, for example, is not high in comparison to some of the mainland peaks, though it is the highest mountain in Hokkaido. But Hokkaido's northern latitude amply compensates for the modest height of its volcanoes creating an icy environment with more alpine plants and animals than almost anywhere else in the Japanese archipelago, and some arctic species as well.

The park takes its name from the Daisetsuzan group, which includes ten peaks all about 2,200 meters, among them Mount Daisetsu itself, Mount Asahi, and Kurodake (Black Mountain). Between these summits is

Tokachi Plain

a great plateau formed by a volcanic crater. The peaks in this group stretch for about forty-two kilometers from north to south and thirty kilometers east to west. While these mountains, like the nearby Tokachi group and the lesser Shikaribetsu mountains are not massive rocky peaks, they present a serene landscape characterized by wide, undulating plateaux with different kinds of vegetation as the altitude increases—needle-leaf and broad-leaf forests; creeping pines; and finally exposed rock with a few types of the hardiest kind of plantlife. When snow on these mountains finally begins to melt in late May and June, rocky outcrops form a colorful patchwork with stretches of alpine flowers, providing a scenic attraction which draws many hikers to the Daisetsuzan volcanic plateau.

Numerous Ainu legends mention Daisetsuzan, whose various summits were believed to contain the spirits of powerful gods. When the Ainu people faced such crises as contagious disease, forest fires, and poor hunting, they believed that the benevolent spirits of these mountain peaks would assume human form to help them—not something that I can vouch for personally since no such transmogrification occurred while I was there.

A Gorge Fit for Fairies

The highlight of my visit to Daisetsuzan National Park was the famous gorge called Sounkyo on the borders of the Daisetsuzan volcanic group. I boarded a bus in Asahikawa City bound for Sounkyo, and after about an hour I noticed walls of rock rising on either side of the road behind thick groves of evergreens and red pines. Further on, the walls became cliffs punctuated now and again by fine threadlike silvery waterfalls. And then all of a sudden the cliffs seemed to hem us in, and the valley became too narrow to accommodate a road as well as the river, so the road disappeared into tunnels hewn out of the face of the rock.

Slender columns of stone, jointed, and looking almost as if they had been fashioned by man gave me the feeling of being in the nave of a great natural cathedral. The spectacular basalt columns, characteristic of this gorge, are the result of quick contraction during the cooling of a lava mass millions of years ago. Some sections of the gorge have aptly whimsical names; two of the most famous are Obako and Kobako, "Big Box" and "Little Box." Looking up from the base of these confining two-hundred-meter cliffs to glimpse a sliver of blue sky indeed gives one the feeling of being "boxed in."

The Ainu call this place Pauchi Kotan, "settlement of the fairies," the high cliffs being the walls of the settlement. The fairies of Sounkyo were believed to have a unique skill: that of being able to weave such fine cloth that even the garments of the gods were inferior by comparison. A number of charming stories center on the magic cloth of the Sounkyo fairies.

The Japanese names for Sounkyo's waterfalls are of no less interest. The tallest are the Ryusei (Shooting Star) Falls and Ginga (Milky Way) Falls. Occasionally boulders and sturdy red pines or Sakhalin willows block the falling curtain of water and spread it out into the shape of a fan.

At the head of the gorge, just beyond the Obako and Kobako formations, much of the romance and mystery of the environs is dispelled by the newly constructed Daisetsuzan Dam and power station, which provide electricity for the Kamikawa district to

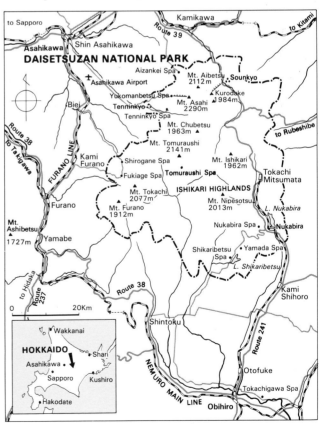

the north and irrigation water for the rice paddies there.

Ropeways and a Hike

To begin my ascent to the Daisetsuzan plateau, I returned to Sounkyo Spa, about halfway up the gorge. Sounkyo Spa is the terminus for the bus from Asahikawa City and is a village nestled at the foot of some of the lesser cliffs of the gorge. Small hotels and Japanese-style inns account for most of the buildings. All have hot-spring baths.

A modest museum at Sounkyo Spa has, in addition to displays on natural history, archeological exhibitions of stone implements used by the Okhotsk people, the first primitive inhabitants of the area who long predate the Ainu. Specimens of hornfels, green schist, pumice, cinnabar, and folds of mud stone are also on view, testifying to the volcanic nature of the mountains. Next to the museum is a small garden filled with some of the alpine plants for which Daisetsuzan is noted, among them flowering yellow rosebay and the pink hanging blossoms of the bleeding heart.

But I wanted to see the alpine vegetation in its natural habitat. I reached the Daisetsuzan plateau via the "ropeway," or cable car, that goes partway up the side of the 1,984-meter-high "Black Mountain," Kurodake.

Hiking from Kurodake to Mount Asahi and making

The Ginga Falls in Sounkyo

the descent to Yukomanbetsu is a day's walk, with plenty of time to study the alpine plants (many of which are so small that you really have to bend down to inspect them) and to enjoy the panoramic view of the Ishikari Highlands, stretched out below with their conifers and broad-leafed trees like a vast luxuriant carpet. The going is not very rough, and I met several groups of people on my way. Skirting the great crater of Mount Daisetsu, which has a diameter of two kilometers, I passed numerous small craters and tiny volcanic lakes and sputtering fissures.

I descended to Yukomanbetsu at the base of Mount Asahi by ropeway. Many mountains in Japan have these convenient cable cars to save hikers time and energy on their way up and down the mountain. I spent the night at a hostel in the tiny rustic spa of Yukomanbetsu. The hostel had a veranda facing Mount Asahi, and at sunset all the guests gathered there to watch the sun slide behind the noble profile of the mountain.

That evening I learned that Sounkyo is not the only gorge among the Daisetsuzan peaks. Tenninkyo (Angel Gorge), about as deep as Sounkyo, but with rock faces something less than sheer, is just south of Mount Asahi, only a short distance from Yukomanbetsu Spa.

Tenninkyo is noted for its Hagoromo (Feather Cloak) Falls, a 250-meter-high cascade which looks for all the world like that legendary garment, laid across the side of the verdant gorge in seven great diaphanous folds. The fourteenth-century Nō play *Hagoromo*, "The Feather Cloak," has been beautifully translated into English by Arthur Waley. He writes: "The story of the mortal who stole an angel's cloak and so prevented her return to heaven is very widely spread. It exists, with variations, in India, China, Japan, the Ryukyu Islands and Sweden." In the Nō play it is a fisherman who steals the robe, which the angel had hung on the branch of a pine tree. Without it, she is powerless to return to heaven:

> Like a bird without wings,
> I would rise, but robeless.
>
> . . . .
> This way, that way,
> Despair only.
>
> . . . .
> Strength failing.

Her pleading so touches his heart that he gives the cloak back to her after persuading her to perform him a heavenly dance. This waterfall, with its ethereal sparkle and gentle folds hidden amidst the verdure of the mountain gorge is indeed a vivid reminder of the ancient tale.

M.S.

SHIKOTSU–TOYA
NATIONAL PARK

Showa Shinzan

Shikotsu–Toya National Park is a veritable museum of volcanoes, with Showa Shinzan, one of the world's youngest—and strangest—volcanoes, as its prime attraction.

The story of Showa Shinzan goes back to late 1943, when tremors began north of Lake Toya, gently joggling the hundreds of snow-covered hectares as if they were a great white blanket. Soon, villagers in Sobetsu, the area most affected, found to their surprise during the next few weeks that the elevation of their homes and fields was gradually rising. The following spring, fields usually planted in wheat, flax, and beans had to be abandoned, a two-hundred-square-meter area having become a considerably high mound. Then a wierd bulge appeared in the middle of the mound and started to move slowly but perceptibly northward. The mysterious "walking mountain" continued to grow, and the fears of the villagers were confirmed when the earth exploded. Eruptions continued for months, forming seven craters, and stubborn farmers who had refused to leave their tilting homes finally decided to move to safety. In December, 1944, just a year after the first signs of volcanic activity, the climax came. A dome of hardened lava about 150 meters high thrust itself up from amidst the craters. The *shin-zan*, literally "new mountain," reached its maximum height of 405 meters above sea level in late 1945, and was officially named Showa Shinzan (Showa New Mountain). Showa is the name given to Emperor Hirohito's reign.

The sixty-five-year-old village postmaster, Mimatsu Masao, was one of the few local residents who did not look upon this rare natural phenomenon with superstition. Mimatsu kept a photographic record of Showa Shinzan's birth and as the volcano grew he became strongly identified with it. Something of a local hero, he calmly defied the lava flow and constant tremors and patrolled the base of the active volcano. As he became more and more interested in volcanology, he collected data which has proved invaluable in the study of volcanoes. To protect the area from exploitation, Mimatsu mortgaged his own property and persuaded the displaced farmers to sell him the twenty-four hectares now occupied by this smoking molehill. Mimatsu then got his privately owned mountain designated a Natural Monument in 1958, and when he died in 1972 he left if to the state, to be "held in trust for all Japanese people." Thus Showa Shinzan was duly incorporated into Shikotsu–Toya National Park (established in 1941).

Photographs hardly prepare one for the raw appearance of Showa Shinzan's brick-red lava dome, crowning its chunky yellow and brown contours, bare of vegetation. There is endless fascination in scrambling about on this "toy" volcano, still warm underfoot, to inspect miniature cones hissing steam and to finger the vermilion-colored lava outcrops. Though Showa Shinzan is by far the most popular attraction of this part of the park, it is a parasitic volcano, standing by the side of its 725-meter parent, Mount Usu, which is extremely active frequently showering the area with volcanic ash. Mount Usu is composed of three individual peaks—Big Usu, Little Usu and Yosomi (also known as Meiji Shinzan, having been formed in 1910 during Emperor Meiji's reign in exactly the same way as Showa Shinzan).

Next to these volcanoes lies Lake Toya, with islands that seem to drift on its limpid waters and a shoreline girdled by a thick belt of green. The Ainu called it Kimunto, literally "Lake of Hills," perhaps because the four major islands have profiles that suggest a range of hills. The largest is Nakanoshima (Middle Island), a

Lake Toya

perfect cone, thickly forested in green, riding the water of the lake with a grace that belies its size. Boats striped red and white ply the deep blue waters carrying visitors on an hour-long excursion from the popular hot-spring resort of Toyako Spa to Nakanoshima and its Forest Museum, an arboretum of Hokkaido trees—fir, maple, oak, elm, mountain ash, mountain birch, *katsura*, and cucumber trees.

Mount Yotei, rising in the distance on the far side of the lake from Showa Shinzan and Mount Usu, is also a part of the park. This extinct volcano is sometimes called Yezo-Fuji, a reference to its conical shape and Hokkaido's former name. Still another name for the same mountain is Shiribeshi, after the volcanic range dominating southwest Hokkaido. Mount Yotei rises to a height of 1,893 meters and great numbers of people (mainly from Sapporo) climb it during the summer climbing season. Its lower slopes are covered with dense primeval forests and its upper slopes are lava fields where more than 260 kinds of alpine plants flourish.

Top Hat on Sapporo's Doorstep

The mountainous terrain extending from Jozankei Spa in the north to Noboribetsu Spa in the southwest forms the largest part of this national park with Lake Shikotsu and the volcanoes that ring it at its center. Even though this stretch of park land falls within an area where sixty percent of Hokkaido's population lives (Sapporo is only an hour by bus), it is unspoiled,

Lake Toya seen from Mount Usu

unpolluted, and quiet. The uncommonly pretty lakeside resort of Shikotsu Kohan is a good base from which to explore the park. There are no hot springs at Shikotsu Kohan, but this log-cabin village blends perfectly with the environment to create a delightful atmosphere in which to go hiking, fishing, or simply relax.

The natural catastrophe that created Lake Shikotsu lives on in the oral tradition of the Ainu tribes who formerly settled this area. After a great, simultaneous eruption of Mounts Tarumae, Eniwa, and Fuppushi, the wide river valley that ran between these mountains sank and a great cavity, thirteen kilometers long and five kilometers wide, filled with water. This became Lake Shikotsu, the source of the Chitose River. According to the Ainu story, the eruptions resulted in great loss of human life and the destruction of many prosperous camps. The Ainu never returned to settle around the new lake, for they feared the spirits who seemed to be at battle there, where the waters sometimes boiled and jets of hot water pierced the quiet air with a sharp, violent hiss.

In cross section, Lake Shikotsu looks like an inverted top hat. The bed of the lake slopes gently down for about ten meters from the shore, then suddenly drops sheer to a depth of five hundred meters. The lake's extreme depth makes its water a memorable dark indigo blue. Aquatic life in the lake was not abundant before 1900—an indication of the lake's comparatively recent creation. Salmon trout from Lake Akan were successfully introduced just before the turn of the century, and since then small carp, bullhead, crayfish, and a type of red trout have also been stocked.

Of the three volcanoes surrounding Lake Shikotsu, Mount Tarumae is the least high at 1,024 meters, but its curious shape attracts the most attention. It looks like a half-finished pyramid and a constant plume of white smoke crowns its summit.

Tarumae was a cone-shaped volcano that "blew its

top" aeons ago. Then, in 1909, a one-hundred-meter-high loaflike lava crown formed on the leveled summit making it dome-shaped.

A bus runs from Shikotsu Kohan to a point halfway up Mount Tarumae where the forest ends abruptly. In summer, thick patches of white azaleas and clumps of pale purple *tarumaeso*, a kind of gentian unique to the mountain, surround the path that winds up to the summit. In contrast to the monochrome "moonscape" of volcanic rock and dust of the crater itself the view of the surrounding scenery presents an outstanding array of colors. Lake Shikotsu lies to the north, its deep blue set off by the backdrop of smoking Mount Eniwa and the dormant Mount Fuppushi. To the west is the Yufutsu Plain covered with forests toughened by wind and winter snows. And to the south is the rolling blue of the Pacific Ocean with the factory stacks of Tomakomai, Hokkaido's paper-making city, standing sentinel to one side.

The spectacular sight that rewards one after the two-hour hike up and over the crater lip is the smoking sulfur-rimmed crevice that runs through the lava dome. Guard rails prevent overeager tourists from getting too close to this giant dark slash that looks like a gateway with stairs down to the center of the earth. At times of activity, the crevice is measurably wider.

Infernal Valley with Heavenly Baths

The hot springs usually found in volcanic zones are valuable natural resources, and many of those within the boundaries of Shikotsu–Toya National Park have, of course, been developed into spas. Jozankei, on the upper reaches of the Toyohira River in the northern section of the park is convenient and popular. Famed for its rock-walled valleys, its lush vegetation in spring and summer, and sharp autumn colors, Jozankei has many hotels and Japanese-style inns. In winter, weekend skiers can relax their sore muscles in hot baths after a day on the slopes of Mounts Sapporo, Soranuma, and Izari.

The most famous of all, however, is Noboribetsu, which means in Ainu "Mountain River". There is no spa quite like it in the whole of Japan. Nestled in a narrow ravine, it has eleven different springs—sulfur, iron, alum, radium, salt, simple thermal, and variations thereof—that range in temperature from forty-five to ninety-five degrees centigrade. Twenty thousand gallons of water per minute pour out at times of maximum operation. Largest of all places to stay is the Daiichi Takimoto, a hostelry established in 1858 when a certain Takimoto Kinzo visited the area with his wife in search of a cure for her illness. They settled here and opened a small establishment, which grew and grew, until today it offers more than forty bathing pools (many quite large and some for mixed bathing) with ten different kinds of waters.

Just north of the cluster of wood and stucco buildings and bathhouses that comprise Noboribetsu Spa may be found the wellhead, called Jigokudani (Valley of Hell). A dried-out, cinder-crisp depression in the earth, just over a kilometer in diameter, Jigokudani is filled with smoking vents and cone-shaped sinters. A network of pipes of varying sizes crisscrosses the hissing bowl and draws off hot water. Visitors who want to descend partway into this "inferno" can make their way over railed catwalks. Jigokudani's parched appearance is heightened by the lush green that surrounds it. A deciduous virgin forest rises abruptly on the steep edges of the bowl. Another nearby wood is all maples and turns a blazing red in autumn.

A road winds through the village and on for four kilometers to Lake Kuttara, a perfectly circular crater lake renowned for its fishing. Here and there on the road to Kuttara are boiling mud swamps where tree saplings lie limp on the ground, like giant strands of spaghetti, asphyxiated by poisonous gases emitted from below the earth's surface.

In the 1970s, more than twelve million tourists visited Shikotsu–Toya National Park every year. Its great natural beauty and unusual volcanic scenery, together with its recreational facilities make it the most popular of the national parks in Hokkaido.

M.S.

Noboribetsu Spa

TOWADA–HACHIMANTAI NATIONAL PARK

Mount Hakkoda

The upper third of Japan's mainland is called the Tohoku and for people who think economic infrastructure is everything, the Tohoku might almost be considered a sort of Japanese hillbilly country. Indeed, if we apply the standards of demography and industrial development that we know from the great Tokyo-Osaka belt, this area, covering the six prefectures of Aomori, Iwate, Akita, Yamagata, Miyagi, and Fukushima, is poor and sparsely populated, with only one city, Sendai, with a population of over three hundred thousand. Here are sweeping plateaux, great caldera lakes, gushing hot springs and bubbling rills, grassy pastures and sleeping volcanoes on whose wide skirts grow forests of pine and beech.

In early medieval times, this wild country was beyond the established frontier. It was a place of banishment. As well as hearing their names in local Tohoku tales, we can read in the old chronicles of nobles and vassals who were exiled to the north even from as far away as Kyushu. We can also detect courtly origins in what are now common rustic songs.

As express trains whisk the modern traveler through the northern prefectures of Tohoku past ruins of castles on hillocks or clusters of thatched roofs, it is tempting to imagine under what dire conditions of exile and poverty the area's earliest inhabitants scraped a living.

Sugimoto Etsu, the author of that charming book *A Daughter of the Samurai*, writes of her childhood in the last years of Tokugawa rule in a place "which means 'Behind the Mountains,' . . . so shut off from the rest of Japan by the long [mountain] range that

during the early feudal days it was considered by the Government only a frozen outpost suitable as a place of exile for offenders too strong in position or influence to be treated as criminals. To this class belonged reformers. In those days Japan had little tolerance for reforms either in politics or religion, and an especially progressive thinker at court or a broad-minded monk was branded as equally obnoxious and sent to some desolate spot where his ambitions would be permanently crushed. [They] filled the graves of the little cemetery beyond the execution ground or lost themselves in some simple home among the peasants. Our literature holds many a pathetic tale of some rich and titled youth who, disguised as a pilgrim, wanders through the villages . . . searching for his lost father."

Rich in Fruit and Festivals

As the incessant wars of the early medieval period gave way to the peace of the Tokugawa shogunate, the northern part of the Tohoku came to be dominated by two important fiefs, Nanbu and Tsugaru. Commercial centers were not established in the area until the Meiji restoration and the advent of modern Japan. They are therefore only about a century old—boom towns built by pioneers and adventurers in the late nineteenth century when a concentrated government effort was directed at settling the northern mainland as well as using it as a jumping-off point for settling the large island of Hokkaido, even further north.

Life in the Tohoku has never been easy. The winter comes early and stays long. Paddies are small, dug out of a grudging soil that prefers to be covered with thick rough grass and beechy forests rather than rice. Fruit trees, however, do much better here. Most of Japan's best apples come from the Tohoku, and new local varieties such as the delicious *mutsu* (sold abroad as crispins) are constantly being developed. There are quinces, too, and walnuts. Trees are felled far up on high ridges and brought down by cables and on flatbed trucks; but not too long ago they were first sawed into lumber and then carried down on the back of plodding oxen or sure-footed packhorses.

Tohoku people speak in an unmistakable, heavily accented dialect, and this speech is often made fun of by city slickers who attribute the fact that they seem to speak with their mouths half-closed to the extreme cold of their native Tohoku winters. Nonetheless, people from northern Tohoku prefectures possess a directness and admirable vitality that must find its source in their forefathers' pioneering spirit.

The distinctiveness of Tohoku culture can be seen in annual local festivals, or *matsuri*, that preserve dances, costumes, and ceremonies long forgotten in other parts of Japan. It is the land, too, of blind women mediums who call up the spirits of the dead and of the other world, a vestige of Japan's most primitive beliefs.

Honshu's northernmost prefecture of Aomori was once the old Tsugaru domain. The people of Tsugaru are not only endowed with both musical and artistic talents, but have a real flair for show business. It is they who have commercialized the *minyo* (folk song) throughout Japan. Most of the leading *minyo* singers in Tokyo are from Aomori and carry on the Tsugaru tradition, famous for its brilliant *samisen* accompaniments in which the interludes are as long as the verses. Often heard and seen on radio and television, these virtuosos sometimes work themselves into such a frenzy of playing that their *samisen* seem about to explode.

During the long snowy winters, many of the inhabitants of Tsugaru engage in cottage industries, turning out all sorts of wicker-work and rice-straw objects, especially those doll-sized snow and rain capes brought home as souvenirs from a visit to the north country. Tsugaru lacquerwork also has a long tradition. This northern style, involving as many as forty coats of lacquer application, dates from the late seventeenth century. Under the patronage of the lord of Tsugaru, craftsmen of the castle town of Hirosaki were sent to Edo (Tokyo) to learn the art. Tsugaru-style lacquer evidently suits royal taste, for even today it is supplied to the Imperial Household.

The rival domains of Nanbu and Tsugaru were separated by a plateau and a string of mountains. Their buffer zone is today the Towada–Hachimantai National Park. While this corridor of mountains and greenery is surrounded by settlements that have long

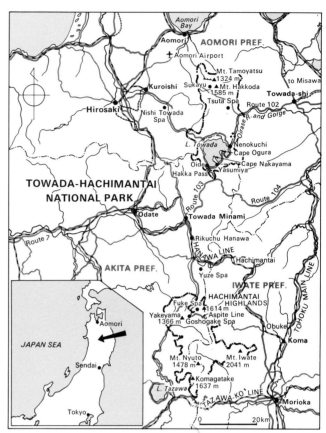

Lake Towada

and fascinating histories, the 83,000 hectares of the park itself are given over to nature and outdoor recreation.

The park consists of two separate areas. The northern sector centers on the great caldera lake, Towada, but also includes the rolling plateau of Hakkoda. The southern part of the park consists of another volcanic plateau: the highlands of Hachimantai. The Hachimantai highlands have several peaks and are generally more craggy than the northern Hakkoda plateau. Hachimantai's most prominent peak is Mount Iwate, sometimes called Tohoku's Fuji. The northern sector was designated a national park in 1936, making this one of the oldest parks in the country. The southern half was added in 1956.

A Lake with Volcanic Horns

Sixty-five kilometers due south from Aomori City on Mutsu Bay, and over the hump of the Hakkoda plateau, is the greatest attraction of the national park, Lake Towada. The lake is large, more than forty kilometers in circumference. Ferry-sized pleasure boats zigzag across the lake on nature-viewing outings. The dark inky hue of the lake's waters give an indication of its formidable depth, 330 meters.

Over a hundred thousand years ago (and even then, over the course of several tens of thousands of years), the lake was formed by the successive rise and fall of three volcanoes. The first was the greatest, and when

Oirase Gorge

the cone collapsed and lava ran off, the resulting crater became an almost perfectly round lake. Then, a second volcano arose, and when it collapsed, it left two ridges shaped like the horns of a water buffalo that project into the otherwise circular lake. At the very tip of one of these horns rose the third volcanic peak, Mount Ogura, with an elevation of around seven hundred meters. The summit of Mount Ogura is an excellent point from which to view the entire area. Another good spot is nearby Hakka Pass (640 meters) at the southwest end of the lake.

Most tourist amenities are clustered on the south shore, where the horns of land jut out into the lake. One interesting spot is the trout hatchery at Oide. The lake's salmon trout (*himemasu*) are particularly tasty. Anglers can fish their own, while gourmets and anglers alike can enjoy them on the menu of the local Japanese-style inns. Most inns and lodging houses here offer therapeutic hot-spring baths.

Lake Towada is at its most beautiful in late May dressed in fresh budding green or wearing the flaming colors of autumn in early October. The only river that has Lake Towada as its source is the Oirase, which flows eastward to the Pacific through a gorge that is one of the park's most popular spots. And so it should be, for with its leafy beeches and young pines growing on moss-covered, rocky islets in river shallows— backlit by bright sunlight—it presents a truly stunning sight. The bus from Yasumiya on the south shore of the lake toward Misawa takes you all the way through the gorge.

The Hakkoda area, north of the lake is best for camping and winter sports. From the heights of this undulating plateau, one can see both the Pacific on one side and the Japan Sea on the other. There is a wide variety of alpine plants to distract the lonely hiker and rustic hot springs to relieve the strain of a long day's

march. Dedicated skiers will find Hakkoda superb for spring skiing—even in late April, when enthusiasts ski down the slow, grainy slopes of Hakkoda dressed in T-shirt and shorts.

But beware! These mountains are not as mild as they appear. In January, 1902, Hakkoda was the scene of a great military tragedy. This was the era of Japan's modernization, and a modern army was being formed and trained, including men from all walks of life. Two hundred and ten soldiers of the Fifth Aomori Regiment were taking part in winter field maneuvers when a storm suddenly broke. The commanding officers felt that for the sake of "military honor" the practice march should continue; 199 of the men froze to death.

The Hachimantai section of the park, some fifty kilometers further south and easily accessible from Morioka, capital of Iwate Prefecture, lends itself to summer hiking and rustic vacations. This highland portion of the park straddles the prefectures of Akita and Iwate. Here there are boiling mud-pots, which some inns have put to use commercially as "beauty baths." From July to September, the area provides spectacular views of green mountainsides, and the cool temperature provides relief from city heat. In the past, the Hachimantai area attracted many artists, who appreciated not only the low tariffs, but also the peace and quiet. Doubtless they found inspiration in the handicrafts for which this area is famed. The noted sculptor Takamura Kotaro knew these mountains well, and the "father" of the folk art movement in Japan, Yanagi Soetsu, worked at a pottery not far east of Mount Iwate.

Because the topography is more complex here than further north, Hachimantai ski slopes provide challenging runs for the experienced skier. Nonetheless, the area has not been developed on a large scale for skiing and accommodation tends to be in Japanese-style inns or somewhat spartan lodging houses. At least most of them have hot-spring baths.

M.S.

Kogin embroidery, a famous Tsugaru craft

RIKUCHU KAIGAN
NATIONAL PARK

The Rikuchu Coast

Most of Japan is mountainous, but Iwate Prefecture, bulging out into the Pacific in the northeastern corner of Honshu, is almost entirely so. Rikuchu is the name of the old province whose boundaries coincided roughly with the modern Iwate Prefecture, and *kaigan* means coast, hence the name of this park. Stretching for 140 kilometers along the Pacific from Kitayamazaki (North Mountain Cape) halfway down Iwate's coastline as far as Kesennuma over the border in Miyagi Prefecture, this spectacular shoreline was designated a national park in 1955.

The Kitakami Highlands, which take up the larger part of the prefecture, fall steeply down to the coastline and their seaward spurs form grand and imposing headlands in the northern part of the coast, where the earth's crust has been thrust upward. The cliffs of Kitayamazaki, some nearly two hundred meters high are brilliant with rhododendrons in spring and early summer and reveal ancient Paleozoic chalk strata embedded with tiny fossils of the earliest forms of life. The coast presents a cavalcade of primeval wonders. Grottoed cliffs abound. And in Funakoshi Bay a strange island called Oshima has an awesome array of serried granite columns, a sort of geological "Parthenon," set upon a huge terrace of sedimentary rock patterned in rectangles like the immense room of a Japanese palace floored with a thousand *tatami* mats. This columnar outcrop is crowned by a dense growth of red pines, camphor trees, and a kind of camellia.

Funakoshi Bay is in the southern half of Iwate's coast, where the earth's crust sank, and water flooded the Kitakami range's seaward valleys and ravines, forming a succession of scenic inlets and fjordlike bays. This type of submerged coastline is known by the geological term ria (from the Spanish word *ria* meaning "estuary"), and its succession of long, narrow inlets of partially submerged, steep, thickly wooded river valleys creates a blue green, ragged seascape of beauty and variety. The ria coast begins near the town of Miyako, which boasts the loveliest spot of all: Jodogahama (Paradise Beach), with its sands of dazzling white trachyte quartz. Just offshore, its picturesqueness reflected in the aquamarine shallows, lies a row of jagged quartz peaks to which cling graceful dark green pines. A handsome forest of red pines graces the shoreline near Jodogahama, and all along the coast sea bird habitats abound. The Rikuchu coast is an ideal area to observe birds such as the black-tailed gull, the streaked sheerwater, Swinhoe's fork-tailed petrel, and the Madeiran fork-tailed petrel.

The proud ruggedness of Iwate's coast, punctuated by scenery of graceful beauty, reflects the character of its people. Often called the Tibet of Japan, Iwate is one of Honshu's most remote and inaccessible prefectures. The region is the poorest of the Tohoku prefectures but the warm and friendly people have always been proud and independent. In feudal days, they were quick to pick quarrels with their northern neighbors, the people of Tsugaru, now Aomori Prefecture, whose relative prosperity they resented. Though fine warriors, the people of Iwate lost most of their battles, impoverishing themselves even more.

Small quantities of various ores were found from time to time in Iwate's hills. Iwate, which was once also called Nanbu after the family whose domain it was, is still famous for its *Nanbu tetsu-bin*, teakettles and cauldrons made from a fine grade of iron. The teakettles, their sides often decorated with small raised nodules and whorls, are highly esteemed for use in the tea ceremony. *Sukiyaki* pans, similarly decorated, are also highly prized, and expensive. In the old days it seemed to these poor people that their remote mountains were full of gold.

> Tho' wild its hills and valleys be,
> Nanbu's rich and free!
> Look east, look west, and you behold
> Mountains chock-full of gold!

Thus sang the ox-herds who led their strings of yellow oxen down the mountain paths to the sea, the beasts laden with iron wares and the fine quality rice their single narrow fertile valley produced. But the seams of ore were few and far between, and the rice paddies were small, and the men who transported these few goods toiled hard and long. Singing was their consolation as they flung, full-throated, the tuneful melismas into the air to hear the echoing mountains fling them back again. This song is one of the loveliest of Japan's folk music. The elegant lilt of its melody betrays a culture alien to such a rugged region: the culture of tenth-century Heian-Period Kyoto. Many persons of standing were exiled to these remote mountains, or fled here. Noblemen from the capital banished to what for them must have seemed like the end of the earth. They even named their main port town Miyako, no doubt homesick for Kyoto, the real *miyako* (capital).

Delicate Flavor of Rugged Coastline

The Rikuchu Coast, bathed by both cold currents from the north and warm currents from the south is rich in tasty seafood of all sorts. That is one reason why so many sea birds are attracted here. And it may well have been the aristocratic exiles of yore, with their refined palates, who concocted the culinary delights which are now specialities of this area. The sea urchins gathered at Miyako and other places on the coast are particularly good, the edible portions are an egg-yolk yellow and are served freshly steamed in iridescent abalone shells. Oysters are another speciality. The species found here lack the usual tough, black, frilled mantles and their creamy flesh is rich and full-bodied, and tastes like *pâté de foie gras*.

The famous sculptor, Takamura Kotaro (1883–

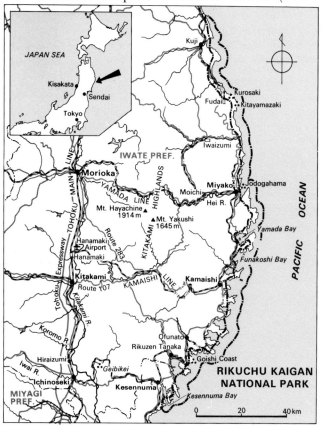

1956), who was the son of Takamura Koun, the leading sculptor of Meiji days, lived for a number of years during and after the war in one of Iwate's small mountain villages. In his celebrated essay "The Mountain People," he ascribes the fine musical feeling of these hill people to their devout Buddhism, and the way they used to gather monthly to chant sutras. There is something akin to Wales about Iwate with its old culture, and like the Welsh, the people are all good singers. They like to dance too. On the fifteenth day of the New Year, according to Takamura, the children of Ota village, where he lived, went from door to door, like our Christmas carolers, dancing and singing for rice cakes.

Horses, too, were an Iwate contribution to Japan's old economy, although Japanese race horses are now bred on the slopes of Mount Arao, across the border in Miyagi Prefecture. Like the ox-herds, the men who drove the rather rangy, early Japanese steeds to market sang their own songs—just as melodious and full of long cadenzas. Footsore and weary, as the lonely packhorse drivers led their strings of beasts over the difficult terrain, they too would keep up their spirits with music. The work was tedious, but fairly well paid for that time.

> Five *ryo* a day is the rate,
> But packhorse driving, how we hate!

Isabella Bird, the intrepid British woman who traveled the whole length of Japan in 1878 writes, as she neared the north of Honshu: "We met strings of packhorses the whole way, carrying salt-fish, which is taken throughout the interior."

The feudal lords of Nanbu were well known for their horses. They had their castle seat in the town of Morioka, where every June 15 a festival is still held called the *Chagu Chagu Umakko* (gee up, gee up, you little horse) festival when brightly costumed children ride through the town on gaily decorated horses.

The center of the ironware craft and other elegant folk crafts such as bambooware and straw artifacts, the city of Morioka also has a well-known university, Iwate University, specializing in education, engineering, agriculture and medicine. Iwate has produced more than one celebrated poet, a couple of noted statesmen, one of whom is Japan's fourteenth postwar prime minister, Suzuki Zenko, as well as the man who introduced modern science to Japan.

What Basho Missed

From Morioka it is just over two hours by express train to Miyako, a good place to begin one's visit to Rikuchu Kaigan National Park. The train follows the Hei River along a beautiful, scenic ravine with granite

Nanbu Tetsu-bin

boulders and jutting cliffs with basalt columns, and passes the foot of Mount Hayachine (1,914 meters) the highest peak in the Kitakami Highlands. The lovely white quartz "Paradise Beach," Jodogahama, is a twenty-minute bus ride from Miyako, and less by taxi. The graceful wind-shaped pines that cling to the precipitous rocks, admiring their own reflections in the crystal waters that lap the beach, are an unforgettable sight. The poet Basho likened the pines of Matsushima, a little further south, to beautiful women whom artifice had made even more beautiful still. What would he have written at Jodogahama? But on his seventeenth-century prose and poetry odyssey, *Narrow Road to a Far Province*, Basho did not go quite so far north; he went no further than Hiraizumi, a famous twelfth-century frontier stronghold. This area is the scene of one of the most celebrated incidents in Japanese history, the flight of Yoshitsune from his vengeful brother, Minamoto no Yoritomo, Japan's first ruling shogun. Basho alludes to these events in the following passage:

"We climbed up to the Takadachi, Yoshitsune's 'High Fort,' and saw below us the great Kitakami River, which flows from Nanbu Province. A tributary, the Koromo River, flows round Izumi Castle and joins the Kitakami here, below the fort. Yasuhira's stronghold stood beyond the Koromo Barrier Gate in a strategic position to guard the entrance to Nanbu Province and defend it against the Ainu tribesmen of the North. . . .

"But what a fleeting thing is military glory," he added. And then the poet wrote one of his most famous *haiku*:

> A mound of summer grass:
> Are warriors' heroic deeds
> Only dreams that pass?

Basho continues: "The road to Nanbu went on,

invitingly, even further north, but we reluctantly turned and retraced our steps to Iwate Village."

It is strange that Basho does not mention Genbikei. Only ten kilometers southwest from Hiraizumi, on the upper reaches of the limpid waters of the Iwai River, a tributary of the Kitakami, this gorge—sometimes called Itsukushi Gorge—was one of northeastern Japan's most famous beauty spots, celebrated for its rapids, pools, pine and cherry-clad rocks, and two-stage waterfall. Did Basho know how close he was to the southernmost end of our national park and the lovely beaches of Kesennuma? They were hardly accessible in those days, and he may not have known of their existence. Today it takes only a little over an hour by train from Ichinoseki (seven kilometers south of Hiraizumi) to Kesennuma via an even more spectacular gorge: Geibikei, thus named for its "Lion's Nose," a fantastic stalactite projecting from the middle of a cliff. This gorge was formed by the Satetsu River, another Kitakami tributary, flowing through steep walls of limestone.

The port of Kesennuma is renowned for its large limestone cave and is, like Miyako, a good base for sightseeing trips up and down the whole length of the park coastline especially by boat, providing the sea is calm enough. A stretch of marble cliffs almost a kilometer long adds to the scenic beauty of the southern end of the Rikuchu Coast.

It has been calculated that just over half of Japan's coastline has been commercially developed. But as long as stretches like that of Rikuchu Kaigan National Park are left largely unspoilt, we will always have proof of how beautiful was once the coastline of all the islands of the Japanese archipelago.

D.B.

Chagu Chagu Umakko

BANDAI–ASAHI NATIONAL PARK

Mount Bandai and Goshikinuma

In spring, Mount Bandai's lovely,
Fair as any blushing bride:
A gown of cherry blossoms;
On her brow white snow applied.

"Aizu Bandai-san" is one of Japan's most popular folk songs. It describes not only the beauties of the region's mountain landscapes but also tells how these mountains were once full of treasure—copper, the mainstay of the old economy. The song is best known for its catchy refrain recounting the cautionary tale about Ohara Shosuke. It was Shosuke's grandfather who made the fortune, probably in copper. In Yorkshire, the English have a saying: "From clogs to clogs in three generations." A similar adage in Japan is "The third generation hangs out the For Sale sign in beautiful calligraphy." Whatever the country, alas, how often is it that the man who has worked hard to amass enough wealth to secure the education and social standing of his children, and children's children, finds that his grandson is a mere dandy and wastrel!

Ohara Shosuke, pray tell
How did he squander his fortune away?
Morning sleeping, morning *sake*
Morning baths he loved too well
That's how he squandered his fortune, they say.
No wonder at all! No wonder at all!

At the foot of many-peaked Mount Bandai is the castle town of Aizu Wakamatsu, on whose outskirts lies Higashiyama Spa. Nestled among verdant hills,

inns cluster on both banks of a picturesque stream, the Yugawa (Hot Water River), offering the delights of bathing in very hot sulfated saline springs, especially good for rheumatism and neuralgia. One of the verses of the folk song invites the visitor to follow the insidious example of the young Shosuke.

If you like morning sleep,
Nice hot baths, and *sake* too,
Higashiyama's hostels
Are just the place for you!

Now called Fukushima, this prefecture was, in feudal times, known as Aizu Province, and its castle in Wakamatsu (renamed Aizu Wakamatsu in modern times) was the strongest fortress in northeastern Honshu. Fiercely loyal to the feudal cause—the lord of Aizu himself being a member of the ruling Tokugawa family—the Aizu men held out in 1868 until the castle was razed to the ground by the Emperor's forces. A modern reconstruction now dominates the city which is known today for its traditional lacquerware and its proximity to Lake Inawashiro, a popular boating and camping resort. Included in the national park, this lake is not only Japan's fourth largest, but it is also reputed to be the fourth clearest lake in the world. Celebrated for the view of Mount Bandai reflected in its crystalline waters, the lake is 514 meters above sea level, and was formed by volcanic action. Okinajima on its western shore is the birthplace of the renowned bacteriologist Dr. Noguchi Hideo (1876–1928) of yellow fever research fame.

Although, as the folk song says, the area surrounding Mount Bandai's peaks is lovely in springtime, when there is often enough snow left for skiing, October is the best time to visit the region. In autumn, the forests and woods in their gold and scarlet, the silvery miscanthus grass (*susuki*) of the heaths, and the dark green cypress groves contrast vividly with the sky blue waters of the hundred or so new marshy lakes and tarns formed as a result of the volcanic action. Most remarkable of all is Goshikinuma (the Five-Color Marshes), where the waters are tinted in strange, unnatural paint-box hues by the various volcanic rocks beneath.

Fatal Facelift

But Bandai is most famous for the complete change of scene it underwent to produce one of Japan's best virgin forests of broad-leafed trees. Bandai's topography is young: not yet a hundred years old. Beneath the lovely forests of larch and birch and the myriad lakes and ponds, eleven villages lie buried. Five hundred people lost their lives in 1888 when Mount Bandai erupted after lying dormant for a thousand years.

Noted by volcanologists the world over, the eruption gave a new name to their vocabulary, "Bandai-type." The explosion was horrendous, and blew off a third of the original mountain, darkening the sun and scattering ash and silica as far as Japan's Pacific coast. The volcano is dormant again, but remembrance of its cataclysmic origins lends special poignancy to the freshly abundant beauty of this place—all the more so while the memory of the graceful, lake-reflected profile of America's Mount St. Helens is still fresh, and how it was shattered in a catastrophic "twinkling of an eye" to become a mudscape littered with tree trunks. But in the words of the eighth-century Chinese poet Tu Fu: "Come spring, green grass will grow again" on the ruins, and, as with Mount Bandai, we shall become accustomed to the new outline.

Mount Bandai, one of Japan's three most important bird habitats, may be seen to good advantage from the new thirteen-kilometer Bandai-Azuma Lakeline toll road. Another new toll road, the eighteen-kilometer Bandai Goldline passes along the side of the mountain at mid-slope. It has opened up an easier ascent route than any of the previous three trails. The climb on foot past Hanitsu Shrine to Mount Bandai's Akahani peak takes three or four hours.

A breath-taking bird's-eye view of the whole of the Fukushima Prefecture section of the park may be had from the Bandai-Azuma Skyline road that curves over mountain ridges for nearly thirty kilometers at an average height of thirteen hundred meters as far as the Azuma volcanic zone, with its still active Mount Issaikyo and a cone-shaped "Little Fuji."

Rising 2,105 meters at the point where Yamagata, Fukushima, and Niigata prefectures meet, Mount Iide dominates a separate mountain area included in the

national park and noted for its beech forests and wildlife. Further north, straddling Niigata and Yamagata, is the Asahi section of the park. Like Mount Iide, the Asahi range, dominated by O-Asahi (Great Asahi; 1,870 meters), is a secluded habitat for black bears, the *kamoshika* (a kind of small mountain antelope), monkeys, weasels, squirrels, and flying squirrels, as well as some 110 varieties of alpine plants. The mountains are noted for their sculptured slopes of snow-eroded granite, their deep ravines and scenic gorges. On Asahi's lower slopes is a charming lake, Onuma (Great Marsh), adorned with floating "islets" of azalea and wisteria, drifting hither and yon with the wind.

Trinity of Holy Mountains

The Asahi range leads north to the celebrated Dewa Sanzan, the three holy mountains of Dewa, the old provincial name of the region. Gently sloping, conical Gassan (Moon Mountain) is, at an altitude of 1,980 meters, the highest of the three closely grouped peaks. A distant view of the Japan Sea across the lesser mountaintops can be had from its generous summit. A wealth of alpine flora grows there including Japanese primroses, wild poppies, and the rare *kuroyuri*, the Japanese black lily.

The cold Siberian winds blowing from the Japan Sea account for the deep snow that lies all year round, and makes skiing possible even in August. The famous seventeenth-century *haiku* poet Basho climbed Gassan

Azuma's "Little Fuji"

in the middle of summer and described the bitter cold: "We climbed for nineteen miles through cloud and mist and over ice and snow till it seemed as if we too shared the very path of the sun and moon! When we reached the summit, we were thoroughly chilled and could hardly breathe."

The second of the holy mountains, Yudono, is merely an outcrop on Gassan's southwest slope. Basho wrote that "what we saw on Yudono-yama, I am forbidden by the rules for mountain pilgrims to reveal." Like Masonic ritual, the ascetic disciplines practiced by the followers of Shugendo were strictly esoteric and it was forbidden to speak of them to the outside world. In Basho's time, a period of retreat in these holy mountains used to last seventy-five days and involved long fasts and many more flesh-mortifying endurance tests than are practiced today. These mountains were closed to ordinary people and one had to be ritually prepared to take part in such a retreat, as the devout poet and his companion undoubtedly were. Today's retreats are far shorter, although they still contain a host of difficult observances. Dr. Carmen Blacker of Cambridge University took part in such an exercise on Mount Haguro in 1963 and describes it in detail in her book *The Catalpa Bow*.

Haguro, a mere 419 meters, lies to Gassan's north and is the least high of the holy mountain trio. Centuries ago it was a center for *yamabushi*, the mountain hermits who gathered there for indoctrination in the rigorous practices of mind over

Gassan

matter that once endowed them with remarkable powers of healing and exorcism. The symbolic death and rebirth ritual still practiced there today is reminiscent of Jesus' words to Nicodemus: "Unless a man be born again, he cannot see the kingdom of God."

Basho wrote of Mount Haguro: "The temple . . . is of the Buddhist Tendai sect, whose doctrine . . . is as clear and radiant as the moon and . . . shines like a light.

"Cloisters stand row upon row, where mountain ascetics diligently practice these disciplines. The good emanating from this holy hill is most wonderful and awe-inspiring."

But now on Mount Haguro only a few of the buildings remain, as do but some of the magnificent old cryptomerias. Today's convenient but ubiquitous toll roads have eroded much of the former mystery and remoteness of the area.

Three of Basho's *haiku* sum up the erstwhile charm of the three holy mountains of Dewa:

> How many cloud shapes
> Capped the peak before the moon
> Rose on Moon Mountain?

> That I may not tell
> Of Yudono's wonders, tears
> On my coat sleeve fall.

> How cool the crescent moon,
> Faint above the leafy black
> Of Mount Haguro!

D.B.

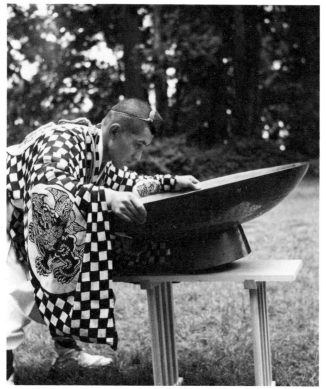

A *Yamabushi* on Mount Haguro

NIKKO NATIONAL PARK

DECORATION RUN RIOT AGAINST A NATURAL
BACKDROP OF UNPARALLELED SOBRIETY AND
SPLENDOR

26. Yomei Gate at the Tokugawa mausoleum, Nikko

27, 28. Water falls in sheets and cascades, left, at Yudaki near Lake Yunoko and in a ceaseless flow at Chuzenji's famed Kegon Falls atop Iroha Hill, right

29. Nikko day lilies on the Kirifuri Highlands

30. Thistles in the morning mist on moorland near Senjogahara

31. A forest of Japanese larch trees near Mount Nantai

32. The plain at Senjogahara in autumn

33. The Oze marshlands and their flora—the inelegantly named "skunk cabbage"

JOSHINETSU KOGEN
NATIONAL PARK

MAN'S ADAPTATION OF NATURE'S FACILITIES HAS
PRODUCED AN ALL-YEAR PLAYGROUND FOR TOKYOITES

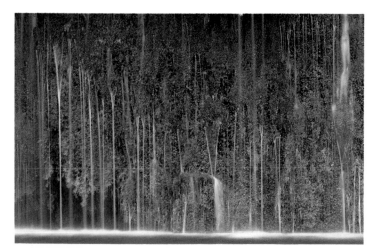

34. Karuizawa's Shiraito Falls

35. Macaque monkeys take a hot bath on the Shiga Highlands

36. Ichinokurasawa ravine in the rocky folds of Mount Tanigawa

37. Mount Asama and peach blossoms. Azaleas follow a few weeks later.

CHICHIBU–TAMA
NATIONAL PARK

ON TOKYO'S DOORSTEP, BUT IN PARTS SUGGESTING A
DELIGHTFULLY NEGLECTED GARDEN

38. Mitsumine Shrine

39. In the depths of Chichibu, Mount Mizugaki

40. The upper reaches of the Tama River, a world away from nearby
Tokyo

FUJI–HAKONE–IZU
NATIONAL PARK

JAPAN'S JEWEL, MOUNT FUJI; A BROOCH OF LAKES AND
MOUNTAINS; AND A NECKLACE OF ISLANDS

41. Odawara Castle, on the road to Hakone, surrounded by cherry blossoms. The castle was first built in the Kamakura Period (c. 13th century), but, as is the case with many Japanese castles, the present edifice is modern.

42. The west coast of the Izu Peninsula at Dogashima

43. Mount Fuji from Lake Kawaguchi

44. Mount Fuji reflected in paddy fields

45. There are times when Mount Fuji deigns to show itself only to its fellow peaks

OGASAWARA NATIONAL PARK

TOKYO'S ISLANDS STRUNG IN A FESTOON TOWARD THE
BECKONING WATERS OF THE TROPICS

46. The view across Futami Bay in the Chichijima group of islands

47. A Chichijima sunset transports one south to tropical climes

48. Wild goats on Yomejima (Daughter-in-law Island) in the Mukojima
group

CHUBU SANGAKU
NATIONAL PARK

PRECIPES, CRAGS, AND CREVICES TO TEST THE MOST
SEASONED ALPINIST

49. The *kamoshika* (Japanese antelope). Once numbers were diminish-
ing, but now overpopulation is the problem.

50. The Northern Alps reflected in Lake Taisho, Kamikochi

51. Yarigatake (Spear Mountain), known as Japan's Matterhorn, in the
center, with the north peak of Mount Hotaka on the right

52. The jagged, sulfur-yellow ridge of Mount Io is typical of the uncompromising ruggedness of the Northern Alps

53. The Shirouma range from Shirouma village. Ski slopes abound on these mountains.

54. This is the view of the Northern Alps from Hofukuji Pass that greeted the eye of William Weston, pioneer of mountain-climbing in Japan

MINAMI ALPS NATIONAL PARK

SOFTER, MORE SNOWY, BUT MIGHTIER THAN THE MORE
POPULAR NORTHERN ALPS

55. Alpine flora in the Southern Alps

56. A ptarmigan, or snow grouse

57. The summit of Mount Akaishi, deep within the Southern Alps and
difficult to reach.

ISE–SHIMA NATIONAL PARK

SHRINE TO THE SUN GODDESS AND PEARLS OF
PERFECT PROPORTIONS

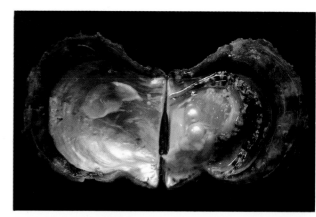

58. A pearl oyster with nacre and pearls. A pearl takes from two to five years to grow.

59. The pearl cultivation rafts of the Shima Peninsula are protected by the coastline
and warmed by the currents

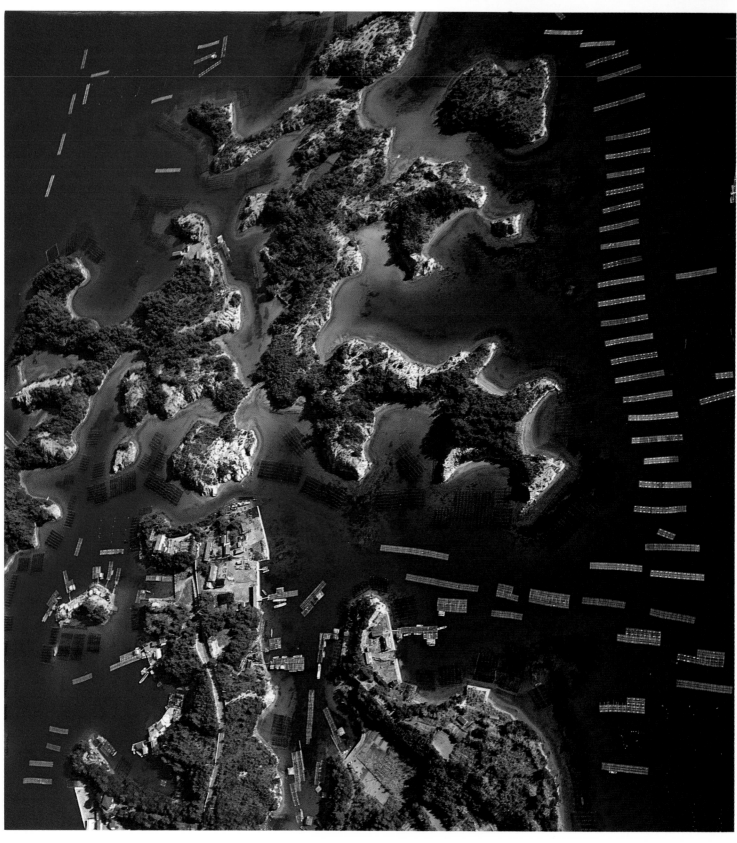

60. The Outer Shrine at Ise is rebuilt every twenty years, but the architectural style is never changed

61. Dawn is the best time to see Meoto-iwa (the Wedded Rocks) at Futami-ga-ura in Ise Bay

YOSHINO–KUMANO
NATIONAL PARK

MOUNTAINS AND FORESTS THAT SHELTERED TRAGIC HEROES OF
JAPANESE HISTORY

62. The Nachi Falls, a 130-meter cascade of sacred water

63. Hashikui-iwa (the Bridge Pier Rocks) near the tip of the Kii Peninsula at dawn

64. The cherry trees of Yoshino, from where Emperor Go-Daigo led his attempt to restore power to the throne

HAKUSAN NATIONAL PARK

ONE OF THE THREE MOUNTAINS THAT GUARDED MEDIEVAL
JAPAN'S GREAT HIGHWAYS

65. Black lilies growing on the slopes of Hakusan

66. One of the seven lakes of Hakusan. Scientists cannot decide how many of them are crater lakes.

NIKKO NATIONAL PARK

The "Sacred Bridge"

Readily accessible from Tokyo, Nikko is included on every foreign tourist's itinerary. But the Nikko he is led to see is a very limited, and in many ways misleading, view of one of Japan's four largest national parks, and one of the most varied and beautiful.

Nowadays, when life has become so hurried, and the tourist industry tries to cram as much as possible into the shortest time, two days at the very most are allotted to Nikko. After a box lunch on the train, tourists are piled into a coach at Nikko station and are taken straight to the gaudy shrines, whose exotic Oriental decorations jostle about in their minds with impressions of crowds of uniformed Japanese schoolchildren. An hour or so later, the tourists are screaming in terror as their coach awkwardly negotiates the hairpin bends of the one-way road hewn out of the steep mountainside leading to Lake Chuzenji. (Because of the steepness of the slope, one-way roads lead to and from Lake Chuzenji; altogether they have forty-eight hairpin bends, the number of symbols in Japan's *i-ro-ha* alphabet, so the roads are referred to as Irohazaka, Iroha Hill.) Our tourists pause briefly to peer down at the famous Kegon Falls, whose immense drop is better seen from below—but the trip to the bottom and back up again in the elevator takes too long. Then, all aboard for a quick cruise around the lake in a motor launch, while the tour guide points out the British, Belgian, Italian, and other embassy villas on its banks, barely visible through the lush foliage. On for the night to a ski lodge that might be anywhere in the world. Thus visitors to Japan, and most Japanese as well, "do" Nikko.

It was better in a bygone age. When I was taken there first as a child, the train journey took longer, and we arrived in time for tea at the delightful, rather Victorian Kanaya Hotel, next to the red Sacred Bridge over the Daiya River. My first impression of the nearby Tokugawa mausoleums was of the ancient cypresses shrouding the historical buildings with numinous mystery. As we watched the last rays of the setting sun filter through the dense branches and light up some of the carvings on the Yomei Gate, the deep boom of a temple bell reverberated through the forest and into my mind forever.

Japan's Buddhist temples and Shinto shrines are, most of them, set amid groves of beautiful trees that form an integral part of the sanctuary. To me, Japan's magnificent groves of cryptomerias are her cathedrals. These evergreen trees of the cypress family grow straight and tall. They reach up to heaven like spires, and amongst the great columns of their trunks there is the hallowed hush of the nave and transept of an immense cathedral. High overhead, their leafy branches meet like a cathedral's vaulted roof. And the manmade structures—the temples and shrines—seem to me more like the chapels one finds inside a European cathedral or abbey than buildings intended to stand alone. I am sure that the architects of Japan's ancient sanctuaries meant it to be that way and deliberately planned the buildings to harmonize with the trees in a manner that was oriented toward nature and formed an integrated whole. Each depends upon the other. Take the trees away, and most of Japan's temples and shrines would be unimposing.

Nikko's mountain group was explored and consecrated by the Buddhist monk Shodo, who is associated with the ascetic practices known as Shugendo. Shodo climbed to the summit of the principal peak in the year 767. Not only did this place have its cryptomeria "cathedral," but also a grand "cathedral close" of lakes, waterfalls, and rivers in the neighboring hills and mountains. It must have been Shodo who named the principal peak Mount Futaara, a transliteration of the Sanskrit term *Potalaka* (the Pure Land). The Chinese characters Shodo selected to write Futaara contain the meaning "two wildernesses," and while the characters are pronounced *futaara* in native Japanese, their other reading, derived from the Chinese, is *ni* and *ko*. Thus it was that over the centuries the peak and its surrounding area came to be called Niko rather than Futaara.

Illumination for the East

It is not known for sure who changed the Chinese characters that were read *niko* to different ones pronounced *nikko*, meaning "the sun's brilliance"; but the most likely candidate is the monk Tenkai, high priest to the first Tokugawa shogun, Ieyasu. Tenkai, a veritable Cardinal Wolsey, was known as the prime minister in black priest's robes. He was convinced that Nikko had the makings of a brilliant ecclesiastical center for the Kanto region surrounding Edo (Tokyo), the site of the shogun's castle. To this end, Tenkai founded a splendid Buddhist temple at Nikko called Rinnoji. He must have spoken frequently of Nikko's potential to his ruler, although the latter never visited it, and in choosing the Chinese characters meaning "sun's brilliance" to spell out its name, Tenkai would undoubtedly have been attempting to flatter the generalissimo, whose enlightened rule shone over the eastern provinces, and who was to be apotheosized and given the name Tosho, "Light of the East," upon his death.

Ironically the Sanskrit name Potalaka (*futaara*), which is a term from Buddhist theology and was bestowed on this sacred peak and its environs some time in the eighth century, is perpetuated in the Three Futaara Shrines, which since 1871 have been purely Shinto places of worship. The main shrine is 640 meters up, quite near the Tokugawa mausoleum; the intermediate shrine is 1,270 meters above sea level amid the cherry trees on Lake Chuzenji's shore; and the holiest of the shrines is at the summit of the mountain which has been known successively through history as Mount Futaara, Mount Kurokami, and today as Mount Nantai.

An extinct volcano, 2,484-meter-high Mount Nantai towers above Lake Chuzenji and is one of Japan's holiest mountains. Pilgrimages take place during the first week of August to the shrine at its summit. After purifying themselves by bathing in the icy lake, about ten thousand pilgrims each year start the steep four-hour ascent after the midnight bell, carrying lanterns, to greet the dawn upon the summit with its spectacular view of the eight eastern provinces of old, which Ieyasu promised to watch over forever in spirit.

Ieyasu died on April 17, 1616. He had asked that part of his remains be taken to Nikko after the first anniversary of his death and that a small shrine be built there in his memory. That November, the abbot Tenkai supervised the ground-breaking for a mausoleum at Nikko. Work progressed feverishly night and day through the icy winter months, and a fine complex of buildings was completed in time for the dedication ceremony on April 17, 1617. Yet, only sixteen years later, they were all replaced by new buildings—except the *torii* arch. (The original hall of worship was taken to Chorakuji, a temple in Ojima, Gunma Prefecture, where it may still be seen.)

It was Ieyasu's grandson, the third Tokugawa shogun, Iemitsu, who was responsible for rebuilding the mausoleum, on a far greater and more resplendent scale. Iemitsu felt that a posthumous boost to his grandfather's glory would do much to awe the people into continued subservience. He was evidently right. Over fifty years after the new mausoleum was built the poet Basho visited it and, much impressed, he wrote: "The august light of the Tokugawa rule illumines the whole firmament, and its beneficent rays reach into every corner of the land so that all the people may live in security and peace." The *haiku* he wrote there is a clever play on the meaning of the name Nikko.

> Holy, hallowed Shrine—
> Bright, as young green leaves in May,
> Like the sun, you shine!

The new mausoleum—the one we see today—took a year and a half to build. Japan's most celebrated artists and craftsmen came from Kyoto and Nara, spending months fabricating the marvels of intricate beauty that adorn every inch of the many buildings. Guilds of artisans vied with each other in craftsmanship; everything was done perfectly. Exotic woods were imported from China for the myriad painted carvings—betel palm, rosewood, ebony, sandalwood, persimmon, quince—and two and a half million small sheets of pure gold leaf were used. Yomei (Sunbright) Gate is so replete with detail that it is popularly known as the Sundown Gate, for the day is over before one has seen it all. This is the gate with the so-called Evil-averting Column, deliberately carved upside down to assure the gods that man was not trying to outdo nature. What was inadvertently placed upside down, however, was the shogunal crest on the bronze lantern presented by the Dutch in 1636, the year the mausoleum was completed. An understandable mistake for foreigners to commit, since the Tokugawa family crest's three hollyhock leaves are arranged concentrically inside a circle.

An Enlightened Ruler

"Age shall not weary them, nor the years condemn" the Tokugawa shrines, kept always "sunbright" and in good repair. But what of the man for whom all this splendor stands as an ever-fresh pean of praise? Ieyasu, first of the Tokugawa generalissimos, or shoguns, was a military and political genius. After unifying Japan, he ruled the country for thirteen years with keen wisdom, insight and humanity, ushering in the three hundred years of prosperity known as the Edo Period, in which the arts and crafts flourished and peace held sway. Though a dictator, and an effective one, Ieyasu was a benevolent autocrat. He was a man of culture and something of a philosopher, and played an instrumental part in promoting Confucianism in Japan.

Ieyasu's insight and humanity are evident in the singular grace and favor he showed toward Will Adams, the English navigator cast upon his shores. Against his own ministers' advice, the shogun spent hours in Adams's company, profiting from his knowledge in many ways, and showering honors—even a fiefdom—upon the Englishman. Ieyasu was indeed an enlightened ruler, eager to learn from the outside world and apply what he learnt for the good of his country.

At Nikko, the first shogun's ashes lie beyond the gold and vermilion, up 207 stone steps, high on the hill, where few tourists go. They are encased in a bronze pagoda-shaped tomb, deep amid the stately trees—on the very altar, as it were, of this beautiful cryptomeria cathedral. The British diplomat and raconteur A. B. Mitford (Lord Redesdale), who was stationed in Japan toward the end of the last century, writes: "There is no small amount of poetical feeling in this simple ending to so much magnificence: the sermon may have been preached by design, or it may have been by accident, but the lesson is there." It is not the only lesson. On the approach to the shrines, the feudal lords presented 118 bronze lanterns of handsome design. But one lord was poor and could ill afford such a contribution. Instead, he spent twenty years planting cryptomeria saplings along the road to Nikko for a distance of almost forty kilometers. Still intact along great stretches, the trees have proved the most splendid offering of all. The British traveler Isabella Bird visiting Nikko a century ago wrote: "There is a deep solemnity about this glorious avenue. Instinct alone would tell one that it leads to something which must be grand and beautiful like itself."

Grand and beautiful Nikko indeed is. Some say that the vivid gold and hectic red, the blues and greens and

Lake Chuzenji and the Kegon Falls (left)

ornate decorations of the shrines are too gaudy. That they are vulgar and in bad taste, far inferior to the sober refinement of the Katsura villa in Kyoto. But what about gaudy and flamboyant nature? In spring, when the magenta-colored azaleas burst forth; in autumn, when Nikko's hills are splashed with the flaming crimson and vermilion of the maples, the brilliant gold of the ginkgo trees, and the skies and lakes are a bright, cerulean blue: can you call nature vulgar and in bad taste?

The glory of Nikko is the arresting beauty of the famous mausoleum combined with the magnificent natural setting of this vast national park with all its seasonal variety. The mountains, the lakes, the waterfalls, the rivers, the hill-girt marshlands such as Oze with its fascinating flora, and the plateaux such as Senjogahara, the gorges, and above all, the trees—all profoundly complementing man's lovingly fabricated temples and shrines.

When you have seen all this, go to the tranquil ninth-century spa of Shionoyu, the "Hot Briny Waters." Here, near Shiobara at the northern edge of the national park, in outdoor baths hewn from the rocky side of a ravine above a gurgling stream, you can relax in health-giving waters right in the very bosom of nature. With autumn's crimson leaves and blue skies reflecting in your bath water, what better place in which to meditate upon man's relationship to nature—so well exemplified in Nikko?

D.B.

JOSHINETSU KOGEN NATIONAL PARK

Mount Shirane's crater lake

Among the summer resorts favored by Japanese and foreign residents alike are the birch-ringed uplands of Karuizawa and the rustic camping spots and cabin communities on Lake Nojiri. When the seasons change, ardent skiers appear on the panoramic, powdery slopes of the Shiga Highlands, Mount Naeba and Mount Myoko. The mention of any of these places conjures up images of craggy mountains and high, rolling plateaux, for they are all clustered on the volcanic heights of Honshu's mountain spine.

These favorite Japanese summer-and-winter vacation spots all fall within the boundaries of Joshinetsu Kogen National Park—an awkward name which is unlikely to ring a bell among even the most knowledgeable of travelers. Almost all the other national parks in the system are named after a distinguishing geographical feature: for example, Akan National Park after the great caldera lake. But Joshinetsu Kogen National Park takes its name, a Japanese-style acronym, from three old Japanese provinces—fiefdoms that lasted throughout the medieval period, until they were done away with in 1876—and the Japanese word for "highlands," *kogen*.

Jo is an alternate reading for the first character in Kozuke, present-day Gunma Prefecture. Shin is for timber-rich Shinano, today Nagano Prefecture, making up about two-thirds of the park. Etsu derives from the old province of Echigo, now Niigata Prefecture.

Covering 188,915 hectares but divided into two separate areas, Joshinetsu Kogen National Park ranks third in size, after Daisetsuzan and Bandai–Asahi

national parks. The larger part of the park is a roughly crescent-shaped block running from Mount Tanigawa past smoldering Mount Shirane and smoking Mount Asama down to Karuizawa. The other part is like a small star west of the crescent and includes Mount Togakushi, Mount Myoko, and Mount Kurohime, at the foot of which lies Lake Nojiri. The park covers a district where three volcanic zones converge (the Chokai, Nasu, and Fuji chains), a fact which accounts for its seventy volcanoes and one thousand hot springs.

Despite their shared volcanic nature, these mountains do not present an identical landscape. Variety abounds. The Tanigawa range (separated only from its Nikko cousins by a high valley) is largely aqueous rock, easily eroded. So, even though its highest peaks are no more than two thousand meters high, the deep ravines and sheer rock faces carved by wind and rain provide alpinists with a considerable challenge. Seen from a distance on a good day, the rock walls are crowded with climbers clinging on to their footholds like human flies.

In periods of extreme activity aeons ago, Mount Shirane, about fifty kilometers west of Mount Tanigawa as the crow flies, poured forth rivers of lava that remain as the sweeping Shiga Highlands. From the top of their ski runs, these snow-mantled Shiga slopes resemble an inviting, soft white quilt upon which the colorfully costumed skiers glint like sequins.

Mount Asama, at 2,542 meters, is Japan's tallest active volcano. Frequent eruptions have kept its upper slopes bare and arid, emphasizing its graceful lines and striking profile. But Asama's greatest interest lies at the foot of the mountain. A hike through the terrain at Asama's skirt is amply rewarding. Here grow peach trees and thick groves of azaleas with enormous blossoms and stands of larch and bright-barked birch that nest more species of birds than almost any other place in Japan. And for sharp contrast, the northeastern base of Asama presents the bleak and forlorn lavascape aptly called Onioshidashi, "The Devil's Discharge"—the result of a cataclysmic eruption in 1783.

The Myoko-Togakushi area has two distinct geographical features. Surrounding Mount Myoko are smooth rolling highlands of ejected lava, ideal for skiing. But the Togakushi peaks are craggy and boulder-strewn—a forbidding area that has been since ancient times a place of retreat for mountain ascetics.

Togakushi is also connected with Shinto myth. When the sun goddess, Amaterasu, retired to a cave in anger, thereby depriving the world of light, she blocked the cave with a large stone, and only after much coaxing and many blandishments did she emerge. The

Ski slopes on the Shiga Highlands

stone at the cave's entrance was supposedly hurled to earth as she stepped out and is one of Togakushi's crags. (See Ise–Shima National Park.) Four Shinto shrines form a small "pilgrim's circuit" of the rocky eminence. In pocketlike valleys here and there about the mountain are a scattering of *shukubo*, lodging houses run by priests that provided shelter in olden times for ascetics and pilgrims. Nowadays they are filled with a different kind of pilgrim—expert skiers who seek the physical challenge of the more hazardous slopes.

There is no "prime" season when it comes to the Joshinetsu highlands. This versatile park can be enjoyed year round. Just pick your sport—tennis, golf, hiking, rock climbing, cycling, skating, skiing—or, in a more sedentary vein, soaking in hot springs and simply admiring the views from the veranda of some old-style inn.

Many hot springs in the Joshinetsu area are very old, but were traditionally visited for their medicinal value, like Europe's spas. Summer sports and the escape to wind-cooled heights, the two notions on which the present hot-weather tourist industry rests have only been in vogue about a hundred years.

The Man Who Started It All

A British archdeacon and professor at the old Tokyo Imperial University, A. C. Shaw, "discovered" Karuizawa in 1886 and built a summer cottage there. Karuizawa was then just a tiny farming community, but it was on an ancient road from Edo (Tokyo) to the Japan Sea coast via Nagano, which was once often traveled by feudal lords with their retinues. Not far from Karuizawa the road passes the ruins of Komoro Castle, the subject of a celebrated modern poem by Shimazaki Toson (1872–1943), "On Traveling the Chikuma River." One of the stanzas reads:

Ah, what does the old castle tell?
What do the waves on the banks reply?
Think calmly of the world that has passed,
A hundred years are as yesterday.

A thousand meters above sea level, Karuizawa is a wide open plain, actually a type of volcanic bog. The archdeacon's summer spot is idyllically cool whilst Tokyo stews in humid heat. With an average temperature in summer of between twenty and twenty-one degrees centigrade, the air is so clean and pure that Karuizawa's residents jestingly call their resort a "roofless sanatorium."

Adept at finding cool "hill stations" like Simla and Darjeeling when cities became too hot for comfort, the British knew a good thing when they saw one. Following Shaw's example, many other foreigners—technical experts helping Japan in its turn-of-the-century push to industrialize—built rustic cabins in Karuizawa. Soon local high society caught onto the idea and some of Japan's most eminent families have had their second home here ever since, red-roofed summer villas surrounded by birch woods and ponds. Golf courses and tennis courts were built in sylvan settings. Building and development progressed at such a pace that now there are two Karuizawas, the original summer resort and a new town two kilometers away, near the second of the town's two train stations and the highway. The year-round residents number somewhere around fifteen thousand, but in summer the population is multiplied by ten. "Old" and "New" Karuizawa hold about 6,400 summer villas but this is not enough to meet current demand. Real estate developers have been busy zoning, developing, and selling off every plot of land they can lay their hands on within sight of Mount Asama and within easy striking distance of the golf links.

Its popularity and nearness to Tokyo make much of the park very crowded at times. Several of Japan's most famous hotels have branches here, principally in Karuizawa, and a not insignificant number of top Tokyo restaurants offer their high-priced dishes at these

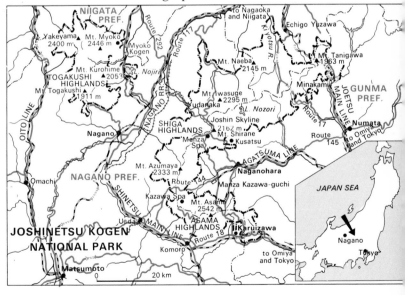

higher altitudes.

Karuizawa's social status was assured when it became known that one of its tennis courts had provided the setting for romance. It was here that no less a person than the crown prince, Emperor Hirohito's son, met, fell in love with, and courted his future spouse. This, ironically, played a large part in the transformation of Karuizawa from a rather exclusive summer resort to a haven for the *hoi polloi* from Tokyo's industrial satellite towns.

Old Karuizawa's main street is called the Ginza and specialty shops from the real Ginza in Tokyo, from Osaka, Kobe, and from Yokohama open summer branches here, following their clientele to the cool heights. At the top of the street, closed to traffic on weekends these days because the swell of strolling visitors is so great, stands a statue of A.C. Shaw, the man who started it all, solemnly presiding over the holiday fun.

Another Foreign Discovery

Lake Nojiri, a summer resort at the other end of the park, is a lava-dam lake in the shadow of Mount Kurohime. Like Karuizawa, it too was a foreign "discovery." The first vacationers here were mostly American missionaries, to whom this wooded lake country must have seemed like the vacation spots they knew as children in New England, upstate New York, and the Upper Michigan peninsula. Such "social action" groups as the YMCA and the YWCA, whose histories are related to early missionary activities, still maintain campsites and rugged cabins here. There is bathing and boating, fishing for salmon trout as well as carp. This lake is indented by so many little peninsulas, forty-eight in all, that the Japanese liken it to the *fuyo*, or hollyhock, leaf.

Most visitors to Nojiri come to enjoy the out-of-doors, but few Japanese fail to make a literary pilgrimage to nearby Kashiwabara, the home of Kobayashi Issa (1763–1827), whose fame as a writer of *haiku*

The Shiga Highlands

verse ranks second only to that of Basho. Issa's life was filled with family conflict, suffering, and poverty, and he spent many years wandering from place to place before returning to Nojiri in the last years of his life. He evolved a distinctive poetic style which Japanese greatly admire, and his works are filled with humor, satire, and compassion. Born in this winter wonderland, he made snow the theme of one of his most famous poems:

> Looks good enough to eat—
> snow falling
> fluffy, fluffy.

Issa may often have been hungry enough to want to eat the snow. Life was hard in the snow country in Issa's day, but snow has proved to be a source of "bread" to the poet's present-day descendants. The popularity of winter sports, particularly skiing, is a postwar development that has transformed the local people, once buckwheat farmers in summer and weavers of small bamboo goods in winter, into small-time entrepreneurs. Ski lifts now web the slopes of Mount Myoko and Mount Kurohime and many private homes have been opened to visitors as *minshuku*, holiday guest houses. Where formerly farmers thought only in terms of planting and harvesting, many are now part-timers and are happily and busily engaged in district innkeepers' associations "dreaming up" projects like village golf courses, tennis courts, and hiking trails, in addition to the expansion of wintertime amenities.

Each time I have visited Joshinetsu, I have noticed more and more sophistication in ways of helping visitors enjoy their holidays. This, of course, means greater inducement to spend your money. Slopes once trudged up, free, in boots, skis balanced over the shoulder, now have helicopters to take you to the best runs. Where once there were only rope tows (which meant staying wide awake lest you cross your ski-tips and tumble into the snowbank) there are now plastic-bubble gondolas as warm as the womb. Where once a mountaintop snack was just a welcome *onigiri*, the rice ball with a pickled plum heart, a leftover from the previous day's box-lunch on the train ride into the snow country, today there are little summit chalets that sell hamburgers and wine.

It is clear that much of Joshinetsu Kogen National Park is becoming a luxury year-round leisure center, with nature a controlled and accommodating backdrop. I am not one always to refuse a helicopter lift, but I feel sorry sometimes at not having to climb the mountain the hard way—so much is missed in the easy ascent.

M.S.

CHICHIBU–TAMA
NATIONAL PARK

Nakatsu Gorge near Lake Chichibu

Japan's most beautiful national parks are, on the whole, those which are furthest away from large cities. Their inaccessibility gives them an advantage, as it were. But Chichibu–Tama National Park lives on Tokyo's doorstep, a mere three-hour train ride away and has to retain its natural beauty despite the crowds. Surprisingly, it manages to do this with a considerable measure of success.

My own first impressions of the region as a whole were not overwhelmingly positive. Before I ever knew there was a national park in the mountains to the west of the capital, I used to spend a few days now and again in the countryside at a private farmhouse as a paying guest, not far by car from the town of Chichibu, the last stop for the Seibu-line trains that depart from Ikebukuro in Tokyo. Hospitable as my hosts were, their farm seemed to be in the spiritual shadow of the large cement factory and textile mills for which Chichibu is famed. It was not long before most of the farmers sold their lands, bordering a gently sloping attractive ravine, to developers, who constructed summer homes of the cheapest type. The tenants started throwing their garbage down the sides of the ravine into the small river, which had been the only delight of the area. There seemed little hope for the Chichibu district, the part that I had known being already permeated with rural decay. How could any place within striking distance of Tokyo and Yokohama be left unspoiled?

And then some friends told me about Tochimoto, a tiny village further up the valley in which Chichibu

stands, almost at the center of the national park. On a road that leads nowhere, it is situated beyond two of the park's most popular attractions: mountaintop Mitsumine Shrine and Lake Chichibu, a large man-made reservoir which supplies both electricity and water to Tokyo.

The park is comprised of the border lands of three prefectures as well as the Tokyo metropolitan district, and this reveals something about the terrain. It is "fringe land," neither prime nor arable. The fact that there are few roads on the map suggests impassability. Indeed, Chichibu–Tama's 120,000 hectares contain over twenty mountain peaks, and probably twice as many knife-sharp ravines. So, following Chichibu's "road to nowhere," my friends were certain they could find an "undiscovered" place like Tochimoto. Their descriptions were glowing. I was assured that visiting Tochimoto would be like stepping into old Japan, that it was a simple spot where modern conveniences were not yet considered essential. It was neat, it was clean, it was green and quiet, and the people gentle.

Checkpoint Hospitality

Tochimoto took a bit longer to get to than my old retreat, but not too much so. From the terminus of the Seibu line, a transfer and short ride on the local Chichibu line to Mitsumine-guchi, then a bus (or taxi when friends were there to split the fare) to my final destination.

The first time I went to Tochimoto, it was late at night when my friends and I arrived. Lake Chichibu, the moon reflected in its waters, was the last major landmark I knew, and still our taxi continued up and up on an ever-narrowing road through the dark forest. Every hairpin turn had a safety mirror, and our headlights jumped off them like darting fireflies on a summer night. We arrived in complete darkness, for it seemed the whole village was asleep. Soft night sounds—the breath of trees—issued from the steep wooded slopes immediately behind us. The only other sound was of rushing water, muffled as it rose from the depths of a ravine somewhere far below. Gingerly, my friends and I inched our way down a rocky incline (how far down I would only see in the morning light) to reach the house of the villager who was putting us up.

The whole Omura family—husband and wife and two small sons—had been waiting up and came out into their small yard to welcome us. Greetings all around and exclamations of surprise at city folk who only start traveling from Tokyo as the sun goes down.

The house easily passed muster. It was a generations-old two-story farmhouse with a gallery running the entire length of the front, overhung with deep eaves. Shuttered tight at night, the gallery was thrown open on fine days, as if to invite the surrounding vegetation into the house. There was an open hearth in the main sitting room (and the inevitable color television in a smaller sitting room off the kitchen); there were other large rooms with prettily decorated sliding doors and cupboards filled with neatly folded, downy *futon* for sleeping. Of course, it was drafty, as only a traditional Japanese house can be. Looking around at the solid beams and wooden jambs and thresholds between rooms glowing with a hand-rubbed luster, I wondered how the house would look in the bright, uncharitable light of morning.

But I was not disappointed. Next morning I saw that Tochimoto was all that had been promised—and more. It was a perfect example of that steep-sloped pine-scented rusticity which is as representative of Japan's countryside as are the vineyards and olive trees of the Mediterranean. Sitting at the side of the open gallery, I had an unobstructed view of the deep Kawamata valley. It was clear that spring had already come to the mountains on the opposite side of the valley. Leafy trees climbed its slopes in every shade of green, while the pines and cypresses were a much darker, almost bluish green. Among them, an occasional mountain cherry was in bloom. In the early light, I could not clearly make them out and took them at first for a delicate morning mist. I was reminded of Japan's beloved old song "Sakura, Sakura":

> Mist, or cloud, you might assume
> Till you smell their sweet perfume.

No houses at all stood on the mountain facing me and the march of trees was uninterrupted. The few fields that belonged to the house we were staying in and the others on the same side of the valley were small and they followed the steep contour of the land, with a minimum of banking and terracing. They were planted

Terraced rice fields near Chichibu

not in rice but in buckwheat (for *soba*), potatoes, squash, onions, and other robust foods. Neat fences of soft mountain stone divided the dry fields, and at the edge of the forest sections of the trunks of oak trees were stacked like log playhouses for growing *shiitake* mushrooms. Above the fields ran the road, and as I looked out that morning, I saw a group of village men with saws and rope setting off to cut timber. Their bantering voices floated across the thin mountain air.

I returned to Tochimoto many times. None of its regular man-made rhythms—pounding fresh steamed rice for *mochi* cakes, the relaxation of stolen hours fishing, picking ripe persimmons to hang and dry in the sun—defied the natural flow of things. Everything happened in proper order in its own time. In fact, the only "resident" of the village that I can remember as being out of kilter was an old rooster that in its last days crowed all through the night.

All Tochimoto villagers come from old stock. Four hundred years ago, the Tochimoto road was not much more than a path carved out of the mountainside, yet it provided one way of reaching the ancient imperial capital of Kyoto from areas north of Edo (Tokyo). But these mountains proved to be more treacherous to travelers than loftier, rockier chains. The harshness of the Chichibu heights is hidden by the healthy, rich-growing forests, but the mountains are steep-sided and crisscrossed with deep ravines. It didn't take much for travelers then (and hikers now) to lose their bearings. It was decided that a checkpoint should be set up somewhere behind Mount Mitsumine, whose shrine was a regional focus for pilgrims. So a site was selected, and a barrier gate or *sekisho* was built (and is still standing). The Omura family was appointed to manage the checkpoint—providing guides, meals, and beds; collecting tolls; and attending to other necessary duties. As the family grew, fields for simple crops were hacked out of the forest. The branch of the family with whom I lodged were descendents of the first barrier

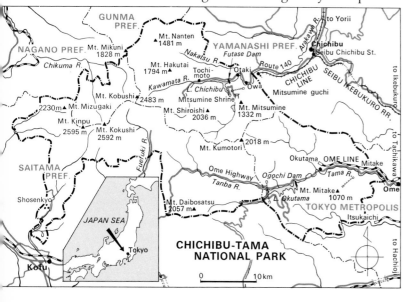

keepers, and so are the many other Omura families in the village. Perhaps the hospitality to travelers which Tochimoto villagers still unfailingly dispense is part of their shared heritage.

For me, every Tochimoto visit included a forty-five minute climb down the ravine to the Kawamata River—actually not much more than a generous stream—for the bucolic pleasures of fishing, swimming, and picnicking. I always found it hard to imagine this tranquil, leafy ravine was so close to the hub of bustling Japan. It had an enveloping, timeless feel to it, so that it came as no surprise to me when I discovered that the mountains and streams of this part of the country are among the very oldest in all Japan.

Water for the Millions

The Chichibu mountains which rise to heights of over two thousand meters are essentially gigantic rock piles formed as the earth's crust shifted and heaved. In a country of volcanoes, it is of some interest to find a mountain chain that is cold, and much older than all the "new" volcanic chains. Because the primary rock of these mountains is not volcanic but sedimentary, it is easily eroded and has crumbled into the rich topsoil that anchors forests firmly. Since the area experiences heavy rainfall, what were once gentle valleys have been bitten away into deep ravines. (The sedimentary limestone of Chichibu is the basis for the flourishing cement factories, the sort of industry that volcanoes cannot support!)

The mountains and the heavy rains make Chichibu not only a watershed, but also a major source of water for Tokyo and surrounding areas. Four large rivers, flowing in four different directions, have their sources in Chichibu. My Kawamata becomes the Arakawa, which in turn becomes the Sumida (although a second, larger outlet into the sea exists). There is also the Tanba (Red Wave) River, dammed at Okutama, which becomes the Tama River, the boundary between Tokyo and Kawasaki. The Fuefuki, one of whose tributaries flows through Shosenkyo, a gorge in Yamanashi Prefecture which is among the park's principal attractions, becomes the Fuji River in its lower reaches; and the Chikuma flows all the way north across Honshu to Niigata Prefecture where it empties into the Japan Sea as the Shinano, the longest river in all Japan. Dams made on the Arakawa (Lake Chichibu) and the Tama River (Lake Okutama) provide the water supply for many of the fifteen million people who live in the Tokyo-Yokohama area. In its own way, then, Chichibu–Tama National Park is also very much the hub of Japan—but how different from the country's nearby capital.

M.S.

FUJI–HAKONE–IZU NATIONAL PARK

Mount Fuji seen from Lake Yamanaka

Surely there is no mountain anywhere in the world as beautiful as Fuji. Its sublime profile must be familiar to millions who have never even visited Japan.

What is the secret of Mount Fuji's singular charm? Is it the setting? Fuji soars in solitary magnificence from a plain, dwarfing surrounding hills. People speak of its symmetry. But its beauty lies more in its imperfections. Fuji's slopes fall away in graceful sweeping curves of unequal length like the trailing hem of a Japanese bridal kimono. Its scalloped summit is exquisitely proportioned. And the erosion lines, artistically sculpted by wind, rain, and snow add elegance and poise.

Most probably, Fuji's great beauty can be attributed to its constantly changing aspect. In winter, cloaked from head to foot in snow. In summer, wearing but a filigreed snow tiara. Swathed in spring mists or boldly silhouetted against a vivid autumn sunset sky, Fuji is never twice the same. "Fuji bare and naked in a blaze of sunshine is beautiful," wrote an American anthropologist, Dr. Frederick Starr (1858–1933). "Fuji with its summit wrapped in cloud and mist is more beautiful; Fuji blotted out by the fog until but a hint or line is left is most beautiful." He climbed the mountain five times, and his words are carved on a monument to him at the foot of the Subashiri trail.

The seventeenth-century poet Basho found the mountain irresistible when it could not be seen at all:

> Rain obscures the scene—
> But Fuji still exerts a charm
> Even when unseen!

One never tires of Fuji's myriad moods and multitudinous settings. Hokusai, the woodblock artist, could easily have doubled his series of Thirty-Six Views and One Hundred Views without repeating himself.

There is a remarkable "presence" about this mountain. It is not surprising the Japanese should regard it as supernatural. To the aboriginal Ainu, Fuji personified fire, *fuchi*, from which word its name is thought to be derived. In Buddhist-infused modern Shinto, Fuji is the supreme symbol of ultimate purity and beauty, like the cherry blossom whose spirit, Konohana Sakuya Hime, the Goddess of Flowering Trees, is revered at Fuji's summit sanctuary, Sengen Shrine. There are 1,307 Sengen shrines throughout Japan, sacred to this deity. The main shrine, built in 1604, is at Fujinomiya at the foot of Fuji. Two million Japanese claim adherence to a centuries-old cult called Fuji-ko, the Society of Fuji. For them the mountain's grandeur mirrors the one divinely true absolute—the great unseen revealed in nature. "Mini-Fujis" abound, many in and about Tokyo. They were man-made in the Edo Period with lava from the mother mountain for those unable to ascend the real volcano. A round of several such Fujis is still performed today by Fuji-ko pilgrims every July, chanting the Fuji prayer that so resembles the old English litany "God be in my head and in my understanding."

Fuji is awesome. Even when most ingenuous, "bare and naked in a blaze of sunshine," she is not to be taken lightly. A British airline captain flew his plane-load of tourists close to her summit on just such a day. A reel of color film recovered from the wreck showed passengers had been recording the magnificent aerial view at the very moment one of Fuji's unique and sudden violent air currents hurled the aircraft to its destruction. On another apparently innocuous afternoon two seasoned Scandinavian alpinists, ignoring impassioned warnings, set off for a stroll up the "slope" they did not consider a real mountain. They were never seen alive again.

Dragon on Fuji's Summit

Fuji is officially open to the general public only during July and August, and the recommended period is limited to the four weeks between the middle of those months. Hundreds of thousands each year snake up the four "easy" trails five abreast and pack the overnight shelters like sardines. (There are three difficult trails, with no shelters, suitable only for experienced climbers.) Among the motley summer crowd of all ages are always a few Fuji-ko pilgrims, tinkling belled staff in hand, clad in traditional white garb, chanting: "Rokkon shojo; oyama wa seiten!" (Be pure, my six senses! Stay fair, O ye mountain!)

The year 1980 being a special Fuji year, half a million people reached the top. Legend says the volcano arose 2,340 years earlier, when the Year of the Monkey coincided with a year of wood. The zodiacal concurrence, called "Kanoesaru," happens only once every sixty years. A climb in Fuji's sexagenary birthyear counts as thirty-three climbs and bestows infinite blessings—and sixty years of health. Moreover, until 1870, when the ban was lifted, it was the only time women were permitted to climb the holy mountain, and they evidently took advantage of the privilege in droves. Edward de Fonblanque mentions the "enormous number" of women pilgrims in the Kanoesaru year 1860, the year of the first British ascent, led by Sir Rutherford Alcock. De Fonblanque was one of Alcock's party of eight. Judging by his words, Fuji's popularity is nothing new: "The annual pilgrimage," he wrote, "is . . . performed by thousands upon thousands."

Many climb through the summer night, reaching the summit in time to behold the dawn come up "like a dragon." Queuing to get one's staff branded with the final coveted red mark of the summit shrine (the other stations' marks are black) leaves little time to enjoy the breath-taking view before clouds begin to shroud the peak. On a clear morning you can see as far as the Japan Alps to the north and west, and southward to the distant Isles of Izu, afloat in the blue Pacific.

Fuji's summit offers two walks around the crater: an easy three-kilometer path and an hour's scramble over

the eight peaks, past the weather station (the world's highest constantly manned observatory) and past two holy, health-giving icy springs. The descent takes half as long as the arduous climb and weary legs have the help of two ash-slide "escalators."

One may now motor halfway up Fuji to the fifth station, where most begin the climb. There, at a height of about 2,500 meters, a fascinating midway circuit, the Ochudo, girdles the mountain. About nineteen kilometers long, it takes eight to ten hours to walk. With clouds above and trees below it roughly follows the timber line and is aptly called the "Border Twixt Heaven and Earth." It has its dangers, however, and much of it is closed. The path skirts the Hoei crater and crosses Osawa (Great Ravine), Mount Fuji's deep cleft on its seldom photographed west side, where the ominous rumble of sliding rocks is often heard.

Below this midway road are "enchanted" virgin forests filled with wierd lava caves and magnetic rocks that "bewitch" the compass so one must take great care not to lose one's way. Further down still are cherry groves and bright patches of wild azalea, where the hem of Fuji's splendid gown is a rich embroidery of five silvery lakes, and a waterfall, the Shiraito, whose "white threads" of subterranean Fuji water gush straight down out of a leafy cliff.

Dormant for two and three-quarter centuries, Fuji lulls many into forgetting she is a volcano. But people who live at her foot never forget. As the season draws to a close, bonfires are lit at all the trail stations and prayers are offered to the fire god. The last eruption, in 1707, formed the protruberance called Hoei Peak, a subsidiary crater, on the Gotenba trail. Will Fuji someday change its shape as Mount Bandai did in 1888, and America's Mount St. Helens in 1980? Fuji has kept her looks so far by confining her big eruptions to the main crater.

Japan's highest mountain, Fuji is 3,776 meters tall (or 12,385 feet, a figure which is more easily remembered as 12,365—a year's 12 months and 365 days). It is part of a long volcanic chain extending all the way from Yakeyama in Niigata Prefecture to Guam, far to the south in the Pacific. Fuji has erupted eighteen times in recorded history. The worst eruptions were in 800, 864, and in 1707, when fifteen centimeters of ash blanketed Edo (Tokyo). The only evidence of activity the mountain produces today are the hot vapors she occasionally spews from an eighty-degree-centigrade crevice outside her eastern rim.

Reeds and Riviera

Immediately southeast of Fuji lies a spacious composite volcano far, far older, worn down into rounded hills, completely extinct, but rich nevertheless in hot

Tea-picking in Shizuoka Prefecture

springs and sulfurous "Valleys of the Great and Lesser Boilings": Owakidani and Kowakidani. Approached from a steep valley filled with the sound of waterfalls and rivers, this area—embracing a grassy plateau and a placid caldera lake, Ashinoko (the Lake of Reeds), 723 meters above sea level—is Hakone, familiar to all tourists.

The ancient cedars beside Ashinoko have seen their share of history. Here, for 251 years until 1869, stood the famous Hakone Checkpoint of the Edo Period. Weary from the long hard climb, travelers between imperial Kyoto and military Edo had to pass this checkpoint, maintained by the Tokugawa shogun to monitor people's movements and make sure the feudal lords stayed loyal. The shogun kept Japan's 270-odd feudal lords busy maintaining an additional residence in Edo besides their provincial castles.

Directly south of Hakone is the balmy "Riviera" peninsula of Izu, shaped like a giant spearhead pointing southward into the Pacific. Aeons ago it was an island volcano. The bustling spa of Atami was its primeval crater, which tilted in the upheaval that joined the island to the mainland. The tilt formed Izu's game-rich mountain spine, and part of the crater sank on the east, causing a "Hot Sea," the meaning of Atami. Aquariums, cactus gardens, white sand beaches with old gnarled pines, and plum-blossom groves characterize Izu's spa-dotted east coast, while spots like Dogashima make its west side even more picturesque still.

The Izu Peninsula has long connections with Westerners in Japan. At Ito, between 1605 and 1610, Will Adams, the first Englishman to reach the shores of Japan, built for the shogun two European-style ships. And near the peninsula's southern tip is the old port of Shimoda where Townsend Harris, the first American envoy, spent fifteen months over a century ago in a temporarily secularized temple that is still standing. Shimoda's peaceful bay with its pine-clad islets has changed little, and mossy tombstones at Gyokusenji, Harris's temple, tell poignant tales of American sailors who fell ill, or fell from topgallant yards, and Russian Czarist sailors swept away by the tidal wave that followed a large earthquake in 1854. Commodore Perry's famous Black Ships, which brought Harris to

Shimoda in 1856, are commemorated in an annual festival held in May.

Almost an Octave of Islands

Southward from the Izu Peninsula the great Fuji volcanic chain thrusts out of the sea a succession of mountain peaks which include the Seven Isles of Izu, added in 1964 to the Fuji–Hakone National Park, originally designated in 1934. I saw them first at dusk from the deck of an ocean liner. A fantastic parade starkly silhouetted against the evening sky. After familiar Oshima (visible from my Hayama beach home) came tiny conical hat-shaped Toshima, separated from voluptuous-breasted Niijima by three rocks pointing like puritanical fingers up to heaven. The others followed on the horizon with their distinctive shapes, but one in particular, Shikine Island, appealed to the musician in me. It was flat, and lay on the horizon like a half-note rest on the top line of a watery musical staff. Beyond it was distant Miyake, with its active volcano, and next I saw steep little Mikura Island and, farthest out of all, semitropical Hachijo—playground for rich Tokyoites and easily reached by air. Oshima, too, is a popular resort, offering deep-sea fishing and golf and horseback rides across a desert of volcanic ash to its mid-island smoking crater.

But the islands between Oshima and Hachijo are more or less difficult of access. Gay in spring with red and white camellias and fragrant in summer with white spider lilies called hamayu (Crinum asiaticum) and gold-banded lilies (yamayuri), these islands' sparkling white beaches and jet black strands are visited only by the more adventurous fishers and campers via infrequent ferries named after flowers. Niijima and Shikine were once one (and still are administratively and in the count of the seven islands), but the sand dunes joining them were swept away by a tidal wave three hundred years ago. One hundred and twenty kilometers beyond the last Izu island, almost a third of the way to Japan's far Ogasawaras, lie a strange group of rocks which appear and disappear, known as the Myojin-sho (and on some maps as the Bayonnaise Rocks). A submarine eruption there in 1952 sank a research ship, killing thirty scientists and crew.

But Fuji's Goddess of Flowering Trees was smiling when I left Shimoda bound for intriguing Shikine, a few years back. Sitting on the deck of the Hydrangea in the crisp morning sunshine, I watched the mountains of Izu range themselves in rows like the hills in some ancient Japanese screen, and the lovely sugary summit of Mount Fuji slowly began to appear over the top of the farthest hills to wish me Godspeed.

D.B.

OGASAWARA NATIONAL PARK

Hybiscus on Chichijima

Everyone knows that Tokyo is the largest city in the world. But how many people are aware of the fact that it actually takes two days and a night by boat to reach the outer limits of the "city"? Like the Seven Isles of Izu, which extend in a chain from Tokyo Bay and are part of Fuji–Hakone–Izu National Park, the Ogasawara Islands, almost a thousand kilometers further out to sea, are administratively part of the metropolitan area.

The islands, which bear the name of the man who allegedly discovered them near the turn of the sixteenth century, Ogasawara Sadayori, were reincorporated into the Tokyo metropolitan government in 1968, when the territory was returned to Japan after an American occupation that began in 1945.

For such a remote and sparsely populated group of islands, the Ogasawaras have had a complex history. Although the first Japanese expeditions supposedly date back to the sixteenth century, the islands were left unsettled. Thus, this outer festoon of thirty islets, far from the mainland, came to be called the Munin (Uninhabited) Islands, from which the English name Bonin was corrupted. A couple of centuries later, the islands were vaguely claimed by both the British and the Americans. When whaling was in its heyday, there was a constant need for good deepwater harbors that could be used as mid-Pacific depots and ship chandleries. The first settlers, a small group of British, Americans, and Hawaiians, came in 1830 and built a wharf and raised the first structures at Port Lloyd (present-day Omura) on Chichijima, the largest island, although it measures no more than six kilometers by three. These Westerners stayed and became so prosperous on their little paradise that a generation later the Japanese began reasserting claims of sovereignty. By 1876, the Japanese managed to annex the islands. Immigration was encouraged. Not only were whaling and fishing attractive, but the hilly islands lent themselves to the cultivation of sugar cane, fruit, and exotic timbers such as sandalwood, ironwood, and rosewood. By the late 1930s, the Japanese population numbered around 7,700. When Japan embarked on its course of militarism, however, the islands were viewed in terms of their strategic location. The entire population, including those of Occidental descent, were removed to Tokyo, and the islands were garrisoned.

Today, the future of the Ogasawara Islands lies in tourism. On the same latitude as Okinawa, these islands have a similar subtropical climate, several good swimming beaches, and scenic wonders in abundance. With a view to maintaining a balance between the protection of virgin nature and the development of recreational and other facilities, over half the island area and several marine districts were designated a national park in 1972, one of the park system's newest.

Geological Relatives of Fuji

Nearly all the Ogasawara Islands have related names, making up a typical Japanese family. Chichi and Haha (Father and Mother) are the names both for the two major islands and for the family group which clusters around them. Others are Big Brother, Little Brother, Grandson, Big Sister and so on. To arrange for the marriage between Son-in-law Island and Daughter-in-law Island, there is even a Go-between Island. The archipelago is divided roughly into four groups: at the northern end of the chain is the Mukojima (Son-in-law Island) group. The next two groups further south cluster around and obtain their collective name from Chichijima and Hahajima respectively; while at the southernmost end of the Ogasawaras lie three widely separated islands collectively called the Kazan (Volcano) Islands. The entire chain was, in fact, pushed out of the sea by volcanic action and is geologically related to Mount Fuji, but these three display their volcanic nature more than the others. Here, bright yellow sulfur pits stand out in the midst of lush green foliage, and crevices emit plumes of acrid yellow smoke. Because of this, the islands are also known as the Io (Sulfur) Islands. In English, the central Sulfur Island has always been spelled not Iojima but Iwojima—a name immediately recognizable in modern history, for it was this very spit of volcanic rock, only three kilometers long, that was such a critical battleground in World War II.

Today, the only residents of Iojima are a few dozen men of the American Coast Guard and Japanese Maritime Self-Defense Forces who monitor an electronic navigational beam. There are no civilians. Visitors with permission from the military occasionally hitch a ride with the weekly flight bringing supplies. They trek up 169-meter-high Mount Suribachi, made famous by Joe Rosenthal's unforgettable photograph, to pay their respects at the two monuments, one Japanese and one American. The jungle has reclaimed the spaces once piled high with bodies. There is hardly a sound now where bombs once screamed through the air and burst. The sea is empty and wide—scarcely a ship in sight where once amphibian vessels clanked and chugged.

Iojima and Minami Iojima (South Sulfur Island) are not included in the national park, but Kita Iojima (North Sulfur Island) is. This tiny island with its wave-eroded cliffs rises straight up from the sea to a height of 804 meters on its north side, and forms an almost perfect cone.

Apart from the three Volcano Islands, the rest of the archipelago was formed by the piling up of volcanic materials such as basalt and andesite, when various volcanoes on the sea bed were young and active during the Tertiary Period. Aeons of battering by wind and waves has sculpted the craggy cliffs into fascinating shapes, such as Chihiro-iwa (Thousand Fathom Rock) on Chichijima, Oni-iwa (Devil's Rock) on Hahajima,

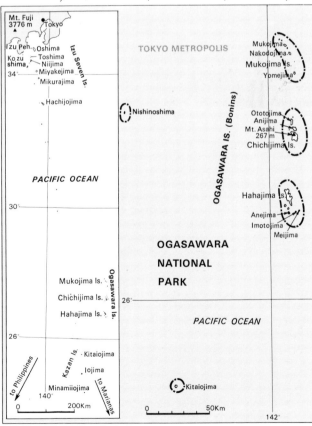

and Hari-no-iwa (Needle Rock) on Mukojima. Formations of coral limestone, too, are much in evidence. Just off Chichijima's southwest shore is a small island called Minamijima (South Island). Completely surrounded by a ring of tiny limestone reefs, the island is a small mountain of coral limestone shaped like a volcano with a sinkhole instead of a crater, into which rainwater disappears.

Beaches and Banyans

Those coastal sections of the park that are officially referred to as marine parks contain about forty varieties of coral, among which schools of iridescent tropical fish dart like spangles in the sunlit waters. The marine parks include the beautiful Anijima Channel, a narrow strip of deep cobalt blue between the steep, thickly wooded sides of Anijima (Big Brother Island) and Chichijima, where slim crescent-shaped beaches nestle in craggy cave-pitted coves. Chichijima, with its many deeply indented bays, abounds in scenic vistas, and the beach of Kominato is ideal for swimming. Another lovely beach is Miyukinohama on Hahajima. Lush subtropical vegetation covers most of the islands, including banyan trees and the rare *munin-yatsude*, with its eight-fingered leaves.

When the Ogasawaras were returned to Japan in 1968, Chichijima was the only island that was inhabited—with only 285 registered residents, mostly English-speaking descendants of the early settlers, hardly any of whom knew any Japanese, having lived under the American administration of the island for twenty-three years. The number had doubled by the ensuing year when the nostalgic evacuees had returned and Japanese from the mainland had arrived to begin the long task of rehabilitating the islands and providing tourist facilities. There is still a great deal of work to be done before the islands are ready to welcome tourists in earnest.

A ship leaves Tokyo Bay once a week and makes the thirty-eight-hour voyage to Chichijima's Futami Bay. Modest Japanese-style inns and guest houses exist on Chichijima and also on Hahajima—three hours from the larger island by thrice-weekly boat. Accommodation on the two islands combined, however, is far fewer than places on the ship from Tokyo. A growing number of people yearn to visit Japan's "new" island paradise, so it is essential to secure somewhere to stay before making the trip. All the more so since camping is not allowed.

The islands are best visited between April and August. During the rest of the year, rough seas make swimming dangerous. From late August to November, tropical typhoons sweep across the archipelago.

D.B. and M.S.

CHUBU SANGAKU NATIONAL PARK

The peaks of Tateyama

"The Japanese Alps are now without glaciers, and their scale is only about two thirds of the European Alps. But the ravines in the Japanese Alps are like paintings, rich with color. And the splendid calm of the dense woods covering the mountainsides exceeds any other scenery which I have ever seen while wandering in the European Alps."

Thus wrote the Reverend Walter Weston in his celebrated book *Mountaineering and Exploration in the Japanese Alps,* published in London in 1896. The name Japan Alps was first given to these mountains by another Englishman, William Gowland, in his 1888 *Japan Guide.* Many of the peaks were climbed for the first time by various Britons in those early days, but it was Weston, during his years as a missionary in Japan at the end of the last century, who popularized the name "Japan Alps" and pioneered here the sport of mountaineering—only forty years after its European beginnings.

When Weston came to Japan not long after the country had been opened to the West, her mountains were still considered the domain of spirits, and ordinary folk feared to venture very far into them. Only those mountains which had been climbed and consecrated by the early Japanese Buddhist saints such as Kukai and Shodo were considered "open" for pilgrimages by the devout. The imposing group of perpetually snow-covered peaks in the north of these Alps called Tateyama was consecrated in 703 and is one of the Three Sacred Mountains together with Hakusan and Fuji, which have both been designated national parks too.

Only fifty years before Weston scaled the slender pyramid of Yarigatake (Spear Mountain) with his knowledge of modern alpine techniques, a Buddhist monk, Banryu, reached the summit in 1826 and again in 1828 to formally consecrate it by placing there three Buddhist images. How he managed the difficult ascent in simple traditional white cotton pilgrim garb and straw sandals, assisted only by a wooden staff is mind-boggling. Although Yarigatake is ten meters lower than the tallest peak in this mountain group, it appears to tower above them all, and is certainly the most inviting.

Weston, an accomplished mountaineer who had climbed extensively in the Alps of Europe, dubbed soaring, pointed Yarigatake the Matterhorn of Japan. He scaled it successfully in 1892 after an earlier attempt was aborted by dense fog. The more Weston explored the peaks, cirques, valleys, ravines, and ridges of Japan's Alps, the greater was his enthusiasm for these mountains that combined, in such concentrated form, as rugged and challenging climbing as any alpinist could wish for with some of the most beautiful and varied alpine scenery in the world.

Broad glaciers had cut wide swaths through Europe's Alps, but the narrow V-shaped valleys of Honshu's mountains were carved by the abundant rain and melting snow that also fostered their lush verdure. And because Japan's mountains were only very slightly glaciated, her forests contain more varieties of plants, especially broad-leafed deciduous trees such as beech and oak, than Europe's alpine woods, where many types of flora were eliminated by the Ice Age.

The Japan Alps cross Honshu's center in three ranges. The northernmost Hida Range comprises this national park, known as Chubu Sangaku (Central Mountains) National Park but usually referred to as the Northern Japan Alps. Where the Hida Range abuts on the Japan Sea there was, in olden times, a fearsome, cliff-hanging route. The six kilometers where the Hokuriku main line train now winds along a rocky ledge in relative safety was described in 1689 by the poet Basho: "Today, we passed the most perilous places in all the North. The precarious path led us over boulders at the foot of a sheer cliff against which huge waves break."

Horses, Butterflies, and Melting Snow

The Northern Japan Alps consist of more than twenty mountains but six predominate, averaging three thousand meters in height. Northernmost is Mount Shirouma (White Horse). A sprawling mountain encompassing a two-kilometer-long snow valley and a large plateau carpeted in summer with alpine flowers, one imagines it to have been named after its white equine contours seen in winter. But its name has a more unusual derivation. By May the snow has melted enough to reveal a bare dark patch shaped like a horse when viewed from the villages below. When the snowless patch assumed its horse shape, farmers knew it was time to start preparing the rice paddies for sowing. So they called their alpine computer the Mountain of the Paddy Horse. And then somewhere along the way a geographical recorder must have mistakenly substituted the character shiro, "white," for the original shiro, "paddy field."

Melting snow gave its name to another peak. One of the Hida Range's smaller mountains is called Chogatake (Butterfly Mountain). But in this case it is the remaining snow itself that looks exactly like a giant butterfly or moth. Its "wings" never quite disappear, but when the "body" melts, the farmers in the valleys begin planting their rice.

Sacred Tateyama is the next major mountain in the Hida Range. Its several peaks include Oyama, with its eighth-century shrine, and Tsurugi (the Sword), whose eight sharp points are an alpinist's dream and gave rise to the saying "To climb 'the Sword'," which is a bit like our saying about crossing the Rubicon—a hazardous undertaking with no turning back. But some of Tateyama's sacred heights are now accessible by bus and cable car. Tateyama's ice-scoured peaks and ravines present rare traces of the Ice Age in Japan.

Further south is Matterhorn-like Yarigatake, followed closely by the immense five-peaked massif of Hotaka (Highcrest), two of whose peaks rise to 3,190 meters, making them the third highest in Japan after 3,776-meter-high Mount Fuji and the 3,192-meter Kita-dake (North Peak) of Mount Shirane in the Southern Alps. Then come Yakedake (Burnt Mountain) and Mount Norikura (Saddleback). Southernmost Norikura is the most accessible of the Northern Alps. Although over three thousand meters high, one may drive almost to the summit in one's own car or by bus. Fourteen and a half kilometers of fine highway, the Norikura Skyline, take you effortlessly up amid the snow-covered peaks and rich alpine flora.

The Northern Alps have their ration of extinct volcanic cones, but Yakedake, the "Burnt Mountain," is still excitingly active. It last erupted in 1962. Placid Lake Taisho at its foot was formed in the 1915 eruption, when lava choked up part of the Azusa River. The lake is named after the Taisho reign (1912–1925) in which it was born. The dead trees protruding from its water are a ghostly reminder of its fiery origin. Rubble and naked tree trunks on its slopes characterize this mountain, some of whose rocks are still hot to the touch and from whose yellow gashes sulfurous steam hisses forth. The 2,455-meter-high volcano makes an interesting and not too difficult hour and a half's climb.

The most difficult and dangerous climb is from Hotaka's Nishi (West) Peak to its Oku (Far) Peak. The trail follows the razor ridge of Hotaka's perilous ravine-creased rock wall known as Takidani (Valley of Waterfalls) and is barred by a menacing "gendarme" of perpendicular rock. Almost as arduous is the long trail north from Oku Hotaka traversing peak after peak to Yarigatake's pyramidal spearhead.

Where to Start and Which to Climb

There is something for everyone in the Japan Alps; and treks of varying difficulty and length, all well provided with huts and lodges, make it possible for even the novice hiker to enjoy the profusion of nature's delights scattered all over the area: the fields of delicately hued alpine flowers; the dense forests of both deciduous trees and conifers, melodious with bird song; the little lakes and tarns; the views near and far of strange mountain shapes and curious rock formations such as Mount Tsubakuro (Swallow) with its black and white birdlike outcrops and the zigzag ravines of Mount Sugoroku, named after an old board game resembling backgammon; the amphitheaterlike valleys, called cirques, whose "stages" are their summer ponds that reflect the drama of the surrounding peaks.

The Kurobe River bisects the Hida Range on its way north to the Japan Sea. In its upper reaches, the Kurobe

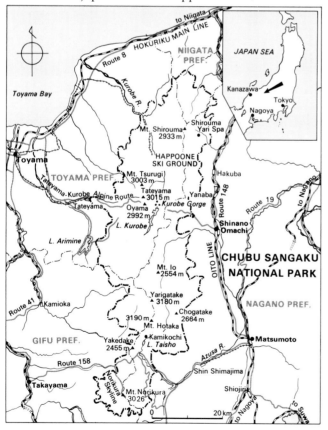

winds its way through forests between sacred Tateyama and Mount Shirouma, then through an eighty-kilometer-long gorge, one of Japan's most spectacular. It is easily reached by train, and is especially beautiful in autumn's blaze of gold and crimson. It terminates in the world's fifth largest arch-type dam, whose power station is discreetly hidden 150 meters underground so as not to mar the beauty of the gorge. The Kurobe area also boasts five spas. Nowhere in Japan is one very far from some delightful inn offering a natural hot-spring soak to relax body and mind. Not far east of the gorge is Shirouma Yari Spa, the highest in Japan at 2,100 meters above sea level.

The city of Omachi, thirty-five kilometers north of Matsumoto by train, is a convenient hour's journey by bus from the dam and is also one of the main bases for climbing the mountains of the Northern Japan Alps. It has an interesting mountaineering museum. But by far the most attractive base, to my mind, for an approach to the Alps—whether one is an expert climber, novice, or just plain nature lover—is the beautiful highland basin of Kamikochi, fifteen hundred meters above sea level, near the southern end of the Hida Range. Although crowded in summer, alas, it is a superb resort for all who love mountain scenery as well as being the ideal base for both hiking along the easier mountain trails and for setting out on more serious expeditions.

From Kappa Bridge, a suspension bridge spanning the sparkling waters of the Azusa (Catalpa) River, whose granite bed enhances the crystalline quality of the stream, a particularly fine view can be had of the towering escarpments of Hotaka. The Azusa River joins the Sai River and finally flows north into the Japan Sea in Niigata Prefecture as the great Shinano, the longest river in Japan. Tokyo's famed Imperial Hotel has its only branch hostelry at Kamikochi. A tasteful building with red-tiled roof, it blends nicely with the larch woods that line the peaceful river.

The Japanese are a grateful people, and Walter Weston, the father of mountaineering in Japan, is remembered in a memorial plaque on the banks of his beloved Azusa River about fifteen minutes' walk from Kappa (Water Sprite) Bridge. In the center of Weston Square, set into the rock face, is a relief of the genial-looking alpinist, and a commemoration is held there every year at the start of the climbing season. Most dedicated Japanese mountaineers try to attend so they can keep the spirit of their mentor informed of the great strides they have made in recent years: their many Himalayan triumphs, including the first woman on Everest. Weston's own exploits are far from forgotten. Climbers still talk of the remarkable manner in which he is said to have made his descent of Hotaka's formidable rock wall. Skillfully balancing himself with his alpenstock he slid down one of the steep snow-filled ravines at an astonishing speed.

The Weston Festival takes place on the first Sunday in June. But those who visit Kamikochi earlier are treated to the sight of the trees in their early green foliage and the blossoms of the wild pear above which the towering massif of Hotaka presides majestically, still thickly clad in winter snow. They can admire the *kesho-yanagi*, the fascinating "vanity willow," which put out shoots red as lipstick and then scatters powder-fine pollen as the spring wears on.

In Kamikochi, a morning's gentle stroll will take one to tiny Lake Tashiro with its myriad islets, made yellow as a topaz with algae in July, and then on to Lake Taisho with Yakedake reflected in its mirror surface. An afternoon's ramble in the opposite direction takes you to Hotaka Shrine on the banks of lovely Lake Myojin, where a monument commemorates Kamijo Kamonji, who—nature lover with an innate trail sense—accompanied Weston on his numerous climbs. A tiny hut reproduces the one in which Kamijo spent a solitary Thoreau-like existence at Kamikochi, the first person ever to live there. It is easy to see why Kamikochi, the Highlands of the Gods, came by its name in the days when it was considered a mysterious place and little visited.

Kamikochi can be reached in two hours by bus and train from Matsumoto. Matsumoto, a four-hour express-train ride from Tokyo, is a charming university town in the center of the great Matsumoto Basin, between the Sai River and Utsukushigahara. The spacious basin is a striking contrast to its distant ring of lofty mountains. The many-tiered tower of Matsumoto Castle, dating from 1504, dominates the city.

I first visited Matsumoto to interview violinist Suzuki Shinichi at his world-famous Talent Education Center. Whenever I think of Matsumoto, I remember the strains of Bach's Double Violin Concerto played with unbelievable beauty of phrasing, tone, and style by a host of children. Suzuki believes in the universality of musical talent. It is, he said, no different from the talent we all have at birth for mastering our various difficult mother tongues. Nothing is impossible for Suzuki. One little girl had been so crippled with polio she could not at first even hold the bow. "If a hundred tries are not enough, one must try a thousand times. One will inevitably succeed in the end." As he spoke, his eyes strayed to the mountains beyond, which were his daily inspiration. When I left, he gave me a *sumi* painting he had just completed of those far-off peaks of the Northern Japan Alps, with a few lines in graceful calligraphy: "Man is the child of his environment."

D.B.

MINAMI ALPS NATIONAL PARK

Mountain-climbing in the Southern Alps

Imagine Japan as a lady in kimono languidly reclining upon the blue Pacific. She wears a three-stranded *obi* around her ample waist, with Fuji as her jewelled *obi-dome*, or girdle brooch. From the Japan Sea, the Northern Alps' "strand"—the Hida Range—comes first only separated from the Central Alps, or Kiso Range, by the Kiso valley. Next to the Central Alps is the Ina valley followed by the girdle's third strand—the Southern Alps, or Akaishi Range. The Kofu Basin and Fuji River valley separate the Southern Alps from Mount Fuji, the jewel Japan wears on her girdle, sparkling over the Pacific in many-carat splendor.

Unlike the Northern Alps, the Southern Alps (*minami* means "south") have no volcanoes, even though not far away to their north, across the Suwa Basin, rises "Eight-Peak" Yatsugatake (a quasi-national park), whose much eroded volcanic cones are thought to have surpassed Fuji in magnitude aeons ago. The Southern Alps are tectonic mountains, some composed of granite and others of Paleozoic rock such as flintlike hornstone as well as sandstone and clay-slate. They lack the rugged escarpments and snowy ravines of their northern sisters. They are more gently contoured and more wooded, but these mountains yield nothing in stature and include Japan's highest peak next to Fuji, the 3,192 meter Kitadake (North Peak) of Mount Shirane.

Walter Weston, the British missionary who introduced the mountains he dubbed the Japan Alps to the world—and the sport of mountaineering to the Japanese—climbed extensively in the Southern Alps as well as in those of the north. At the annual Weston Festival at Kamikochi, the alpinists who come to honor the memory of the father of Japanese mountaineering always gather around a convivial bonfire that June night on the banks of the Azusa River. Seldom does the conversation fail to turn to Weston's exploits at the turn of the century and his celebrated tackling of a daunting pinnacle in the Southern Alps in 1903.

One of the three peaks of Hoozan (Phoenix Mountain) is called Jizo after the guardian bodhisattva of little children. It is so called because at its summit stands a huge perpendicular rock looking exactly like a giant statue of Jizo. A cleft near the top of the rock is still called Weston Crack. Having gained a foothold about thirty meters up the pinnacle, Weston weighted his rope with a heavy stone and threw it up into the crack, where it held fast. He then climbed up hand over hand and was soon at the summit of the Jizo peak. His feat is still cited as a classic example of rock climbing technique more than three-quarters of a century later.

Besides Jizo, the other two peaks on Phoenix Mountain are also named after Buddhist deities—Yakushi, after the physician of souls, and Kannon, after the goddess of mercy. The mountain is characterized by its clusters of stony outcrops of all sizes resembling hosts of Buddhist images.

A dramatic way to make one's first acquaintance with the Southern Alps is to take a night train on the

One of the Southern Alps' steep valleys

Chuo main line from Tokyo. It will bring you into the Kofu Basin just before dawn. Kofu is now thriving as Japan's wine country, its sunny plains having been found ideal for growing grapes. The train runs along the west side of the basin and enters a gorge formed by the upper reaches of the Fuji River, which flows from Kofu past Mount Fuji south into the Pacific. As the train winds along the banks of the Fuji River, the first red rays of dawn begin to streak across the dark sky and then, as if a curtain has been suddenly drawn open, on your left you see the peaks of Mount Kai Koma in startlingly bold rose-tinted relief, like a painted stage set. Soon the warm rays of the rising sun bathe the peaks in molten gold.

Many mountains in Japan are named *koma*, meaning "horse" or "colt." There is one in the neighboring Central Alps and one in Hakone. They are given the name because one or more dark horse-shaped patches appear on them as the snows of winter melt. In olden times the superstitious thought it meant the mountain was inhabited by equine gods. This Colt Mountain is called Kai Koma because it is in the old province of Kai. The one in the Kiso Range (the Central Alps) is called Kiso Koma.

Kai Koma is the northernmost of the Southern Alps, and is a granite peak 2,966 meters high. Just south comes 3,033-meter-high Mount Senjo followed by the three peaks of Hoozan, whose highest peak, Jizo, is 2,841 meters. After that comes Mount Shirane with its soaring 3,192-meter Kitadake, next to Fuji in height and the highest tectonic mountain in Japan. Shirane's other two peaks are 3,026-meter Mount Notori and 3,189-meter Ainodake, the "Peak-in-Between," Shiomi (Salt View), Arakawa (Wild River), Akaishi (Red Stone), and Hijiri (the Sage), all over three thousand meters, complete the Akaishi Range, which makes up the Southern Japan Alps.

Highbrow Mountains

Access to the Southern Alps is far easier now than it used to be. Nevertheless facilities for climbers and hikers, let alone motorists, are hardly developed at all compared with those in the Northern Alps. But therein lies the charm of these mountains. In summer the cirques of the Northern Alps are carpeted with orange nylon tents almost as densely as with wild flowers, and one must queue for the use of the chain and ladder leading to the summit of its "Matterhorn."

But here in the Southern Alps, nature still remains more or less unvisited. Huts and lodges for climbers have only recently been built and few of the trails have been "improved." Most bridges are of the giddily swinging variety. The mountains must still be climbed the hard way. Their appeal is for the serious moun-

Kitadake

taineer and the true nature lover. Both will be rewarded by the quietness and the purity of the nature they find here. Amid the virgin forests of beech, fir, Japanese hemlock, and spruce, and on the wooded hillsides and mountaintops, they are more apt to encounter the occasional mountain antelope and ptarmigan than hosts of other climbers.

How long the inaccessibility of the Southern Alps will be preserved is uncertain. Already the Chuo Expressway has reached Kofu. Now this once peaceful basin of farmland and vineyards can be reached by car from Tokyo in two hours. The local authorities are talking about villa development sites, ski grounds, and golf links. The pure air of the mountains is fast becoming polluted with exhaust fumes.

But the nationwide controversy aroused over the construction of the Super Norokawa Forestry Road was encouraging. Since the Northern Japan Alps have been made so accessible, obviously many hoped that the Southern Alps would be kept for those who really appreciate nature and are prepared to sacrifice comfort in order to escape for a while from the constraints of urban life.

Work on the forestry road was halted for five years while environmentalists studied its probable impact on nature in the park. Finally completed in November, 1979, it is now not quite so "super" as was originally intended. Unlike the nearby Yatsugatake Quasi-National Park's Venus Line, the Super Norokawa Forestry Road—hewn from sheer rock with a dizzying drop on one side—is not for the timid motorist. The Environment Agency ordered its 4.5-meter width cut by a meter for a short stretch, thereby making parking and passing impossible.

Two-Speed River

While access, already limited to forestry staff in winter, may be further restricted in the summer tourist

season as well, the Super Norokawa and its less ambitious sister, the Hayakawa Forestry Road, on the opposite bank, do now enable a few bus passengers and intrepid motorists to enjoy the delightful mountain scenery surrounding the Norokawa as it gurgles along its rocky bed between banks of lush verdure on its way to join the Fuji River. "Noro" is now written with characters meaning "meadow-way," but I am sure its original reading was *noro* meaning "slow," for soon, joined by another small stream, the name of the tributary changes to Hayakawa, or "Fast River," before it enters the Fuji River.

The tributary flows into the Fuji River near the charming spa of Shimobe. When I stayed there, my room at the inn was named "Seseragi," a lovely onomatopoeic word meaning "the murmuring of a stream." I remember how the pure mountain air was filled with the refreshingly soothing water music of the Fuji and its several tributaries, punctuated at intervals by the bush warbler's sweet signature tune.

The Hayakawa Forestry Road begins at Shimobe and winds along the west bank of the "Slow-Fast" tributary right up into the hills as far as Hirokawara (Wide Stream Vale) fifteen hundred meters above sea level, where there is a lodge and a campsite. Climbers make the steep eight-hour ascent of Shirane's Kitadake from here, right up to its summit, which is covered with a luxuriant growth of alpine plants.

From Hirokawara the more scenic Super Norokawa

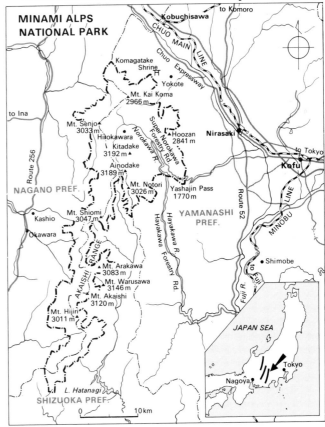

Forestry Road winds back down the east bank toward Kofu. Halfway along the Norokawa road, between Kannon Tunnel and Yashajin Tunnel, at an elevation of fourteen hundred meters, a splendid panorama presents itself of the three Shirane peaks across the deep ravine of the Norokawa. But the most celebrated viewpoint in the area is at Yashajin (She-Devil) Pass. An hour's climb from the bus stop at the opposite end of the long tunnel takes you to the pass itself, 1,770 meters high, with its magnificent bird's-eye view of most of the mountains in the Southern Alps. There is a lodge at the pass, and a campsite. It is particularly lovely here in April with spring at one's feet on the grassy slopes and the larches putting forth their young green shoots while winter lingers on the snowy alpine peaks beyond.

Branching off to Nirazaki before reaching Kofu, one will find an old motor road that takes one via Sawara Pond to the summit of 1,672-meter Mount Amari in fifty minutes. There at the summit azaleas and lilies-of-the-valley grow in profusion.

On the western side of the Southern Alps is the Ina valley through which flows the Tenryu (Heavenly Dragon) River. From the town of Iida, with its gorge of towering cliffs overhung with ancient pines through which one may "shoot the rapids," an old road runs to the foothills of the southernmost mountains of the Southern Alps; while a new road runs to the foothills of Kai Koma and Senjo, further north from the town of Ina. The valley is extremely fertile, particularly near the river, and produces rice of splendid quality. With the addition of crystalline water from the many small streams coursing down the alpine ravines, a deliciously mellow *sake* is made.

In its rice-producing heyday the prosperous Ina valley people fostered literature and the arts. They were such connoisseurs of theater that once there was no Kabuki actor worth his salt who had not appeared on an Iida stage. There was too an old saying that went "Do not marry your daughter to an Iida man unless she likes Kabuki."

The district was also once regarded as Japan's "treasure trove" because of the many private art collections there. But most were destroyed in World War II bombing raids. The only gold the people have there now are the flame-colored orbs of the ripe persimmons for which the valley is justly famous. It is said that the misty haze of moisture rising from the Tenryu River in the mornings and evenings gives a special sweetness to the local fruit. In late autumn all the farmhouses are festooned with the drying persimmons which appear in Tokyo stores as a winter delicacy.

D.B.

ISE–SHIMA NATIONAL PARK

Gokasho Bay

Through the towering wooden *torii* gateway, over the bridge, and into the magnificent forest of centuries-old camphor and cryptomeria they go. Pebbles crunch underfoot as visitors walk up the broad avenue under the great trees. Most stop at the banks of the Isuzu River to bend down and wash their hands and rinse their mouths in the crystal clear water flowing over chastened stones. In Shinto, cleanliness of both body and mind is essential. If this were any other shrine, these purification rituals would be performed at a basin in the forecourt, but using flowing water from a river is in keeping with the supremely natural setting of this shrine, the most ancient and most sacred of the eighty thousand Shinto shrines in Japan.

Here, Amaterasu Omikami, the sun goddess, from whom the imperial family traditionally claimed descent, is enshrined together with her relatives and attendant gods. Most of the buildings of the Grand Shrines of Ise are contained in two large compounds about six kilometers apart. The Naiku, or Inner Shrine, is dedicated to Amaterasu, while the Geku, or Outer Shrine, is dedicated to Toyouke, the goddess of agriculture and sericulture. Fourteen affiliated shrines are nearby and 109 smaller associated shrines are in the Ise area of the Shima Peninsula.

Amaterasu is the central figure in Japanese mythology. Her unruly brother Susano drove Amaterasu into a towering rage by running wildly through her heavenly rice paddies and ruining them; then he interrupted her violently as she taught her maids the art of weaving. The sun goddess retired to a cave in disgust and deprived heaven and earth of light. The other gods made a plan to coax her out. They hung a mirror and a jewel near its entrance, dancing and laughing uproariously. Curiosity got the better of Amaterasu and she peeped out of the cave, whereupon the gods drew her away and showed her their gifts—the mirror and jewel, which Amaterasu eventually gave to her grandson when he was sent to earth as a sign of her divine support. Together with a sacred sword, the mirror and curved jewel are the three objects recognized as Japan's imperial regalia.

In so far as Shinto is both the worship of nature and of ancestors, the veneration of Amaterasu at Ise has been particularly important: she was considered the divine progenitor of the imperial family and, by extension, of the entire Japanese people. Established around the fourth century and flourishing by the sixth, Amaterasu's shrine, the Naiku, is still closely associated with the imperial family. The sacred mirror preserved in the inner sanctuary is said to be the one the goddess gave her earthbound grandson as a symbol of herself.

Since medieval times it has been the custom for imperial princesses to assume the role of priestess. Even today, women of the imperial line, usually widows, assume this sacerdotal duty. At the rededication of the shrine in 1973 a daughter of Emperor Hirohito carried the sacred mirror to its newly built resting place.

All events of importance to the imperial family are duly reported here. When young Prince Hiro was accepted into the middle school of his choice, he came to Ise. Elected officials also come. Within a few days of being named to office, every new prime minister is photographed by newspapers paying his respects at Ise. The prime minister visits the shrine at New Year to pray for national welfare and prosperity.

Shinto was the state religion until 1945, and until that time, the Ise shrines were fully subsidized by the government. With the separation of church and state, however, Ise lost all its strictly nationalistic attributes, and some of its emotional appeal as well.

Twenty Years of Eternity

One of the most remarkable things about Ise is the fact that the wooden shrine buildings are razed and completely rebuilt every twenty years in accordance with ancient custom. While twenty years may not be long in the life of durable *hinoki* (Japanese cypress) wood, the shrines inevitably become soiled, and Shinto stresses spotless purity. "Behold, I make all things new," might well be a Shinto dictum. The first renewal was carried out in 690. Thereafter, regular rebuilding has continued at Ise except for certain times such as the Warring States Period (1467–1568), when civil war forced suspension for over a century. 1973 saw the

sixtieth renewal, rededication, and regeneration of Ise. This unique custom has preserved the original style of Japanese architecture unchanged through the ages, for the new buildings duplicate the old exactly.

The Inner Shrine's position, deep in a virgin forest of cryptomerias, heightens its mystery, but its architecture is the same as that of the Outer Shrine. At both the shrines, the central compounds are divided into eastern and western sectors (each measuring about 52 by 124 meters) for alternate use in each period of twenty years. The part "lying fallow" is spread with pure white gravel, and in the center a small shed protects the "heart pillar" in readiness for the next rebuilding.

The section of the compound in use is surrounded by a fence of plain unvarnished cryptomeria planks. The public is permitted only thus far, where a clear view of the shrine building—a small, narrow, gallery-encircled rectangle built high off the ground—is difficult. A maze of inner fences and white-curtained gateways keeps the sacred buildings from being viewed too closely by the profane visitor. But over the high fence-tops, one can catch an impressive glimpse of the unpainted, smooth, cypress-log crossbeams and ridgepoles, plain but for a few golden decorations that gleam in the sunshine as it filters through the trees. Visible too are the steep, thickly thatched roofs. All the elements are of the purest abstract beauty, making the buildings, archaic as they are, seem extremely modern in style.

The architecture at Ise is in the *shinmei*, or "divine," style, undeniably Japan's oldest. Thus, the shrines are an extremely valuable cultural property. Human rather than monumental proportions prevail; but nature's simplicity underlying the design lends a grandeur and dignity likened by the celebrated German architect Gropius to the intensity of the Greek Doric style. This

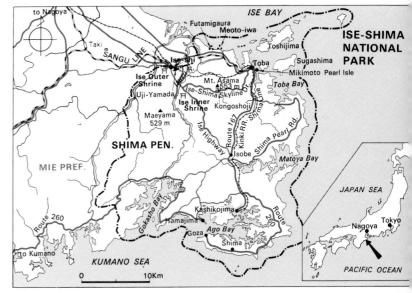

The Inner Shrine at Ise

native form of architecture developed long before the introduction of any influences from the Asian continent.

Building a new shrine takes just under nine years. It begins with a religious ceremony to the mountain god from whose domains many hundreds of trees with an average age of two centuries each will be cut. The timber comes from a national forest in the Kiso region in Nagano Prefecture, known for its fine wood. In the old days, logs were floated all the way to Ise. Dams have meant the partial adoption of overland transport, but local volunteers, singing and dressed in white, still haul the huge logs up the last leg of the journey, the Isuzu River, then into the shrine on wagons, in the ancient ceremony of *Okihiki*.

The carpentry work is carried out by about a hundred men, of whom only six are in the permanent employ of the shrine. The majority are local carpenters who set aside their usual work for a privileged period of two to four years. Blueprints exist for every structure, but it is the master carpenters who must remember and transmit to the junior carpenters their only sporadically exercised knowledge of how to put together the complex joints, using ancient, unfamiliar tools. Not a single nail is used. The most demanding and crucial part of the entire reconstruction is duplicating the inside of the main hall of the Inner Shrine where the sacred mirror is housed. This place is regarded as being so holy that direct observation of the existing structure is not permitted. The whole interior must be reconstructed from blueprints alone, aided only by the master carpenters' recollection of how they did it the previous time, so many years ago.

It is not only the buildings that are made anew every two decades. Over 2,500 articles, including elaborate vestments with thousand-year-old designs, fine swords, lacquerware, bows and arrows, and other fittings, are all replaced. In ancient days, the old works of art were burnt as a sacrifice, but today, "retired" objects are stored in treasuries in the shrine compounds to be displayed in rotation at the Ise Shrine Historical Museum. Lumber from the old main shrine buildings is used to repair shrine out-buildings.

Pearl Island

On the coast near Ise is Toba. With a mild climate prevailing all year round, Toba is a cultured pearl center and is also the gateway to the southern Shima Peninsula where much of the beautifully indented coastline is preserved in this national park.

At the turn of the century, Mikimoto Kokichi (1858–1955) chose a tiny, slim island just sixty meters long near Toba as a place to experiment with the cultivation of pearls. As long ago as the thirteenth century, the Chinese cultivated pearls in fresh-water mussels, but the gems they produced were imperfect, usually only hemispheres. But Mikimoto, through years of painstaking but inspired research, devised a way of growing perfectly rounded pearls. His success came in 1905, and today the world-famous company which Mikimoto founded is one of the largest, harvesting over twenty tons of pearls a year. Forty percent of Mikimoto pearls are grown in and around Ise Bay.

Mikimoto's Pearl Island in Toba was transformed from a working pearl farm into a tourist attraction in 1941. It draws about 1.3 million visitors annually, including crowned heads and presidents. An informative exhibit shows how pearls are grown.

Almost every shell-bearing mollusk, whether living in fresh water or salt, can produce "pearls" of sand grains coated with the same material as the mollusk's shell. Pearls produced by bivalve mollusks whose shells are lined with nacre, or mother-of-pearl, are the ones we value.

Pearls are formed when a foreign substance penetrates the oyster's mantle, where shell-secreting cells are located. These cells attach themselves to the invading material and generate layer upon layer of nacre until a gem-pearl results. Pearl cysts lodged in the oyster's mantle will develop into perfect spheres, but if they grow in another part of the body, they become irregular in shape and are known as "baroque" pearls.

Into a two- or three-year-old oyster, technicians insert a mother-of-pearl bead which acts as the nucleus of a pearl. These beads are punched out of the shells of a certain fresh-water mussel native to the Mississippi River. During the period when the nucleus is being coated with layers of nacre, the oysters are put into wire cages and suspended in warm, calm waters where they feed on plankton. It takes two to five years to grow a pearl. Large pearls are produced by starting with relatively larger nuclei since the maximum lute-shaped lake is reproduced in every detail. It has its "Seven Views" and a pine tree grown from a cutting taken from a celebrated Lake Biwa tree. Here the water is deep—deep enough to hold a dragon—and reflects, like a dark mirror, the loveliness of adjacent trees and the two-legged stone lantern at the water margin. And in contrast to this calm, in the distance there is the sound of a rushing torrent where the water tumbles down a hill and hurtles headlong to the climax of its symphony. But the noisy waterfall is not the end. There is a coda. A most unusual touch, and probably the earliest one of its kind in Japan: a fountain.

The poetic beauty of this garden, one of Japan's three most famous, was only part of its *raison d'être*. Its original purpose was practical. Lord Maeda's castle town needed water, so he had his engineers build an ingenious system of conduits and canals camouflaged as a beautiful garden. As for the fountain, it was mainly for the purpose of testing the water pressure.

All this water begins its long journey seaward high up in the cloud-enshrouded peaks of snowy Hakusan (White Mountain). A thousand years ago in the foothills of Hakusan, near a village called Tsurugi, a name which means "the place where the cranes come," the devout constructed a shrine where they could give thanks for the bountiful water and the trees and the rain and the sunshine—all the gifts of nature which are indispensable to man. They dedicated the shrine to Shirayama Hime, the Goddess of the White Mountain. Fire destroyed the main shrine in 1480, but the subordinate building, with its handsome roof, still stands deep in a venerable shade of ancient cryptomerias, above the tumultuous waters of the Tedori River. Tedori means "hand-clasping" and the river got its name from its swift currents, which made solitary fording of it unsafe.

When the Buddhists came to this region they chose as a site for their temple an eminence between two other rivers, set in a great wide valley surrounded by high hills, in what is now the city of Kanazawa. It was between the great mountain complex of Hakusan and the Japan Sea coast's wildly beautiful Noto Peninsula,

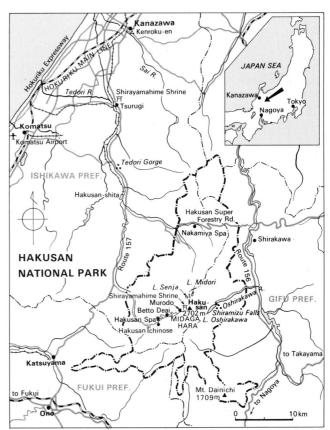

"Snow comes first to Hakusan"

shaped like a sea monster's head.

Perhaps it was the very prominence of its position that led to the temple's downfall, for, not content with a life of spiritual high-mindedness, the Buddhist monks gradually became more and more politically inclined and meddlesome until they held the whole of the surrounding countryside in sway. On its bluff between the two rivers, the temple was more like a formidable stronghold than a house of prayer.

This and similar ecclesiastical strongholds were subjugated by Oda Nobunaga in 1580 in an attempt to bring the whole nation under unified rule. He was soon succeeded by the great general Toyotomi Hideyoshi. But it was not until 1600 that a really stable feudal society was established by Tokugawa Ieyasu. By that time, the Maeda family was in possession of the bluff between the two rivers. On one side of the bluff they built an imposing castle with a deep moat, and where the Buddhist citadel had been, the third Lord Maeda laid out his beautiful water garden.

"We arrived in the great castle town of Kanazawa on the fifteenth day of the Seventh Moon," wrote the poet Basho in 1689. He and his companion had made the journey on foot down the Japan Sea coast after safely negotiating the perilous footpath at the base of the steep cliffs where the Hida Range of mountains abuts on the Japan Sea. (See Chubu Sangaku National Park.) They stayed in Kanazawa for several days, visiting famous places, and then went on to the nearby spa still celebrated for its health-giving hot springs, its lovely autumn foliage, and its proximity to the original Kutani-ware kilns. Basho writes: "On the road to Yamanaka Hot Springs, we could see White Mountain, which stayed behind us all the way."

Mountain Friend of Wildlife

Hakusan loomed benignly over travelers journeying along the Hokurikudo (North Land Road), who regarded the mountain as the dwelling place of gods who protected travelers. The even grander mountain complex of Tateyama shed its protective aura upon those who came and went on the upper portion of the same Hokurikudo, as did peerless Mount Fuji on the Pacific coast's well-known Tokaido (East Sea Road). The selection from ancient times of these mountains as the Three Sacred Mountains of Japan must partly have been due to the way their presence dominated the two main traffic routes.

Although Hakusan is not as lofty as the other two, it fills a large expanse of land with its arctic wildernesses whose snows the cold Siberian winds do little to melt, even in summer. In Japan, snow comes first to Hakusan, and stays there the longest. Hakusan is possibly the most unspoiled mountain in all the country. Few roads have penetrated the area. Climbing is the only way to see most of its varied alpine landscapes, although there are plenty of skiing facilities along certain parts of the mountain's ample skirt.

Hakusan, with its three main peaks, the highest of which is 2,702 meters, originated as a volcano with several craters, most of which are now filled with water. (Scientists disagree on the number of Hakusan's craters.) Midori-ga-ike (Green Pond) is the largest. But

Kanazawa Castle

Senja-ga-ike (Pond of the Thousand Serpents) is noted for its year-round ice and snow, and is the only sub-arctic lake in Honshu.

The mountain is rich in forests and colorful alpine flora. Creeping pines crown its summit, and its lower slopes are thick with virgin forests of white fir, beech, and Japanese oak. Japan's earliest botanists were active here, perhaps because of the mountain's relative nearness to the old capital city of Kyoto, and over thirty varieties of Japanese alpine plants are prefixed in the vernacular by the name Hakusan. Wild birds, too, are numerous. Among the many species found here are the lark, bush warbler, water ouzel, yellow wagtail, needle-tailed swift, ptarmigan, and the *inuwashi*, a rare Japanese eagle. Twenty-three kinds of animal inhabit the area, including monkeys, flying squirrels, and *kamoshika* (small mountain antelopes).

The private Hokuriku railway company's trains follow the Tedori River upstream past Tsurugi to Hakusan-shita. From there a bus makes a forty-minute journey further up the mountain to Ichinose. There are two trails to Hakusan's summit. A new twelve-kilometer route provides quite easy hiking, but the old, steep and difficult eleven-kilometer trail, taking six hours, is much more interesting. Both trails meet at Midagahara, 2,450 meters up, above which the scenery becomes more or less desolate. Not far from Midagahara, at Murodo, is a resthouse that is open in summer. Those who climb to the summit of Hakusan's highest point, Gozenmine (the Peak of the August Presence) may not only pay their respects at the shrine of Hakusan's deity, Shirayama Hime, but may also feast their eyes on the breath-taking view of at least seven well-known mountain peaks, including Matterhorn-like Yarigatake in the Japan Alps. The deep snow that blankets Hakusan's slopes for so much of the year makes climbing dangerous and impractical for more than about four weeks. The mountain is officially open only from mid-July to mid-August.

The countryside here is inhospitable, and the only people who once lived in Hakusan's valleys were foresters, cutting wood and making charcoal. Habitable land was scarce, and young couples could not set up separate dwellings. Here, as elsewhere in Japan's central mountains, many generations had to be housed together under one tall, steeply sloping roof containing at least three floors above the ground floor. A few of these picturesque old-style *gassho-zukuri* houses remain, particularly in Shirakawa, lending charm and character to the landscape. Some have been removed beam by beam to Tokyo to be reconstructed to become restaurants, like the popular "Furusato" that serves "old country" recipes, in keeping with its name.

D.B.

SETO NAIKAI NATIONAL PARK

THE ANCIENT HIGHWAY OF WATER THAT SERVED THE WESTERN HALF OF JAPAN

67. The shrine gateway at Miyajima can be reached on foot at low tide

68. The Shiwaku Islands, part of Kagawa Prefecture

69. The whirlpools of the Naruto Straits between Shikoku and Awaji Island are caused by the convergence of conflicting tides

70. Small ports like this one on Sanagi Island once provided a haven for the Inland Sea pirates

ASHIZURI–UWAKAI
NATIONAL PARK

DESTINATION FOR WHITE-CLAD PILGRIMS AND
JOURNEY'S END FOR DESPERATE LOVERS

71. A nocturnal view of Cape Ashizuri, magnet for many a typhoon

72. Usubae Beach near Cape Ashizuri

73. The "Dragon Skewers" of Tatsukushi

SANIN KAIGAN
NATIONAL PARK

SAND-DUNE ARABESQUE AND A GEOLOGICAL FANTASIA OF
A COASTLINE

74. Basalt columns at Genbu Cave—much of Japan is a geologist's dream

75. The Uradome Coast and its pine tree islets

76. The sand dunes of Tottori provide an illusion of Arabian desert in Japan

DAISEN–OKI NATIONAL PARK

LAND OF THE QUERULOUS THUNDER GOD AND LAGOONS
SHROUDED IN MIST

77. One face of a Jekyll-and-Hyde mountain, Daisen. The other face
rivals Fuji in its cone-shaped grace.

78. The Hiruzen Highlands near Daisen

SAIKAI NATIONAL PARK

AN "ABACUS-FULL" OF ISLANDS WHERE MISSIONARIES
FARED BETTER THAN MERCHANTS

79. A meadow of purple vetch on Fukue Island, largest island in the Goto
Chain

80. A few of the Ninety-Nine Islands, or Kujukushima, with Hirado
Island in the background

UNZEN–AMAKUSA
NATIONAL PARK

MOUNTAIN THAT RECALLS DAYS OF LEISURE AND ISLANDS
WITH MEMORIES OF MARTYRDOM

81. Sakitsu and its church on Shimojima, largest of the Amakusa Islands

82. Mount Unzen from behind azalea bushes in Niita Pass

83. Twin-peaked Mount Yufu and the thatched roof of a house in Yufu-in, a town in a balmy valley southwest of the mountain

84. Kusasenri (a Thousand Miles of Grass) between Mount Aso's Kishima and Eboshi peaks

85. Pastureland on the slopes of Mount Aso produces a landscape unusual for Japan

86. Mount Aso, the world's broadest volcano, has a circumference of 128 kilometers

KIRISHIMA–YAKU
NATIONAL PARK

FINGERS OF LAND CLUTCHING ONE ISLAND LET ANOTHER SLIP
OUT OF THEIR GRASP

87. The trunk of one of Yaku Island's thousand-year-old giant cedar trees

88. The volcano "island" of Sakurajima, which became a peninsula after a massive eruption in 1914

IRIOMOTE NATIONAL PARK

MANGROVE SWAMPS AND CORAL REEFS: WELCOME TO THE
TROPICAL "INVADERS" OF JAPAN

89. Orchids on Taketomi Island remind travelers they are as far south as
Taiwan

90. The traditional *sabani* boats of the Ryukyu Islands and fishing nets

91–94. Okinawa's submarine world of coral and the fish that are fortunate enough to inhabit it

95. The coral reef between Ishigaki and Iriomote islands extends twenty kilometers

SETO NAIKAI
NATIONAL PARK

The floating shrine on Miyajima

Seto Naikai, literally the "Sea within the Straits," as calm and protected as a vast salt-water lake, fills a basin between three of Japan's major islands—Honshu, Shikoku, and Kyushu. There are about seven hundred islands in this "Inland Sea," a quarter of which are uninhabited. Large islands like Awaji and Shodo are able to support fair-sized populations, while others are but spits of granite barely breaking the surface of the water. Many are volcanic in origin, but through the centuries erosion has softened their rugged contours to create a landscape of rounded island hills and white-sand beaches. A fault line far beneath caused the sea bed to rise and fall unevenly, creating deep crevices and countless outcrops.

The Inland Sea is only sixty-two kilometers at its widest point and between six and seven kilometers at its narrowest, so when making the 480-kilometer lengthwise journey from Osaka to Shimonoseki, at the western tip of Honshu, one is rarely out of sight of the mainland. When it does occasionally slip below the horizon, the numerous, inviting islands and constant nautical traffic assure one that civilization is never very far away.

The Inland Sea presents the traveler with a bewildering choice of passenger-carrying craft from small open boats with seats for only a few to large ferries with crowds sprawling on *tatami*-matted cabins. Whichever one chooses, it is a slow and sunny passage through an island-studded waterscape of great beauty. There are islands topped with red pines and bamboo, and others ringed with bands of silver beach. Some have neat fishing villages at the shore and mandarin orange groves or tidy terraced fields climbing up their hills. Traditional red *torii*—the arches that stand in front of all but the most perfunctory of shrines—can be spotted on even the smallest isles, some of which are barely more than outcrops covered with foliage. But modern Japan is also now very much a part of the Inland Sea and its scenery. What were quiet fishing towns less than thirty years ago have now become vast shipyards, petrochemical plants, and steel mills. Oil tankers, ore carriers, and other ocean-going vessels arrive and depart in procession, dwarfing the fishing boats which weave in and out of the shipping lanes.

The Inland Sea has in fact always been at the center of Japanese life, both cultural and commercial. In many ways, it was to west Japan what the great Tokaido (the road from Kyoto to Edo) was to the east of the country.

The *Record of Ancient Matters*, compiled in A.D. 711, the earliest Japanese chronicle, recounts (apocryphally, in point of fact) that the first emperor, Jinmu, moved through the Inland Sea from southern Kyushu and finally established himself in Yamato (near present-day Osaka) in 660 B.C., the traditional date of the unification of Japan. Many islands claim to have played host to Jinmu as he brought his rule eastward toward the center of the Japanese archipelago.

The Inland Sea was also the scene of the twelfth-century wars between the Minamoto and Taira clans, perhaps the most celebrated power struggle in Japanese history. The eclipse of the Taira was completed in 1185 at Dan-no-ura, near Shimonoseki at the westernmost extremity of the Inland Sea, with the mass suicide of the surviving Taira warriors and the drowning of the young Emperor Antoku.

Though the Taira lost, their bravery and courage still stir Japanese hearts, and many island communities take pride in having once harbored the Taira on their westerly progress toward their doom. Taira war fans are enshrined here and there (some more authentic than others, no doubt) and local lore and dances feature the heroes who passed by long ago.

Pirates' Shrine

In the fifteenth century, when the country was continually in a state of civil war, shipping and travel in these sheltered waters was made all the more dangerous by pirates and freebooters. Many islets and channels lent themselves to swooping raids: islands like Sanagi, one of the Shiwaku chain, whose wooded heights the buccaneers used as lookouts. At the imposing Oyamazumi Shrine on Omishima (an island in modern Ehime Prefecture) pirates prayed for success in their forays. In the sixteenth century, the merchants of

Osaka paid off the pirates to ensure the safe transport of cargoes. In the hills surrounding the harbor at Takehara on the northern, Honshu shore near Hiroshima, may be seen the tombs of the Murakami brothers, pirate-barons of the period. They are as imposing as the tombs of the most powerful of feudal lords.

For centuries, certain ports were known for their shipwrights; others as places to lay in supplies; still others for the elegance of their courtesans, who rivaled those of the capital with their gaily colored kimono and elaborately dressed hair.

The Inland Sea is also intimately connected with Japan's religious history. Many are the island temples said to have been founded by the great scholar-priest Kukai, who studied in China in the ninth century, introducing on his return home to Japan a new school of Buddhism. His journey back from China brought him through the Inland Sea where he first disseminated his new doctrine (see following chapter).

Seto Naikai National Park was originally designated in 1934 and then expanded in 1950 and 1956, and again in 1963. Today it comprises 63,000 hectares of widely scattered parcels of land. Some are included because of their scenic beauty and others for their historical associations—Kobe's green, refreshing Rokko Hills, for example, and parts of Awaji, the island famous for its puppets. Most spectacular is the Naruto Straits where Awaji and Shikoku almost brush up against each other. Its treacherous whirlpools that foam and swirl against the dark blue of the sea are a splendid sight, immortalized by the woodblock artist Hiroshige in his famous triptych. The Inland Sea's most celebrated panorama is traditionally observed from a hill called Washuzan across the water on the Honshu side from the city of Takamatsu in Shikoku. The outlook from Washuzan, which is near the picturesque old town of Kurashiki in Okayama Prefecture, encompasses all of the original section of the national park, considered the most beautiful portion of the Inland Sea—the part extending from Shodo Island in the east to Tomo near the city of Fukuyama to the west.

Even with its present additions, the park covers a tiny area in comparison with the Inland Sea's total extent of 96,000 square kilometers. The fact that the national park is not one single contiguous area poses monumental difficulties with regard to control of the environment. Pockets of land belonging to the park adjoin unprotected areas which continue to be used for commercial and industrial purposes. "Red tide" is a typical problem: chemical effluents make the sea phosphorous-rich and a type of algae flourishes, resulting in the deoxygenation of the sea water, threatening many forms of marine life.

Ankle-deep in Water

Undoubtedly the Inland Sea's best-known spot—more famous even than Washuzan—is Miyajima (Shrine Island) with its "floating" shrine and its huge red camphor-wood *torii* arch standing in the shallows and leading to the shrine buildings from the sea. This small island (also known as Itsukushima) makes an easy day trip from Hiroshima. At low tide, visitors can walk out to the *torii*, leaving tracks in the squelchy sand. But when the tide is in, the waters swirl beneath the long, roofed galleries and surround the outdoor stage intended for the traditional *bugaku* masked dances of the ancient court. In the evening, for a fee paid to the shrine office, all the large stone lanterns along the approach to the shrine, and the bronze lamps suspended along the open corridors, will be specially lit for you, bringing a romantic flicker to the lapping waters.

The island has been the site since ancient times of a shrine dedicated to three female deities, daughters of

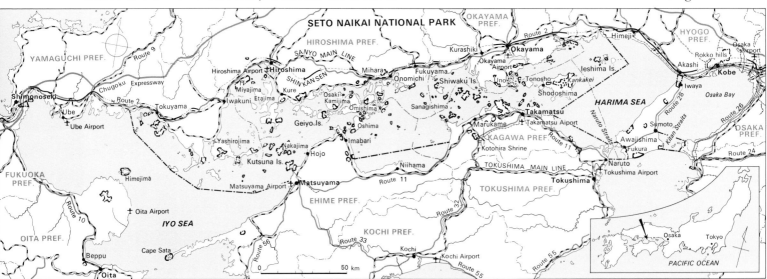

the thunder god, Susano. But the splendid architectural forms which have made the island (with the Amano-hashidate reef on the Japan Sea coast and the pine tree islands of Matsushima near Sendai in the north of the country) one of the three celebrated beauty spots of Japan are the result of the patronage of Taira no Kiyomori (1118–1181), who made Miyajima the Taira clan's tutelary shrine in the twelfth century.

Tradition has it that the island was considered so sacred that laymen were not allowed to set foot on it, so the Tairas conceived the idea of building out over the tidal flats so as to be able to approach the shrine by boat. The extraordinary natural beauty of Miyajima, shaped like a crouching dragon, does indeed give the visitor the impression that the island is imbued with a certain supernatural quality, and a once strictly enforced religious rule forbade the occurrence upon it of either human birth or death. Even today there are no cemeteries here; the dead are taken back to the mainland for burial and mourners undergo a purification ritual before returning to Miyajima.

Kiyomori did more than build the splendid "floating" shrine. He also brought here the best of the arts from Kyoto, the capital. Among the shrine's treasures are, for example, sensitively carved, lacquered wooden masks worn for *bugaku* dance, costumes used in No dramas, and exquisitely painted scrolls of religious texts. Sets of splendidly crafted medieval armor and other martial equipment are also to be seen, donated by Taira warriors after successful encounters with enemy troops.

While the shrine lies by the sea, a temple, the Gumonji, another of the island's attractions, stands atop Misen, which is, at 530 meters, the highest point on the island. The climb to the temple takes one through Momijidani (Maple Valley) Park, on the hillside behind the shrine, to a cable car station. Up most of the way by cable, and then it is only a short walk to the summit of Misen and its temple. The path, trodden smooth as terracotta, runs through a thick forest—the domain of darting monkeys.

From several points on this route, there are views of the shrine and the great *torii* looking like delicate toy models. In Hiroshima Bay, partially submerged oyster racks make geometric patterns in the blue water. But it is unlikely that any of the Taira ghosts would recognize the scene, for on the mainland of Honshu entire hillsides have been gouged into gigantic terraces for housing estates, while the cities of Hiroshima and Kure wear an uncompromisingly industrial, twentieth-century look. The large, strangely shaped island blocking the approach to both cities is Etajima, the site of the former Imperial Naval Academy and a large munitions depot during World War II and now a

Kankakei on Shodo Island

National Self-Defense Force Training School. Some islands, however, have managed to resist the incursions of the twentieth century's own type of freebooters, the developers, and have remained uninhabited, lying quietly and unassumingly in their bay. Further to the west and south are island hills and the gentle mountains of Shikoku, layer upon layer of them fading by imperceptible degrees into the haze of a Japanese summer sky.

Miyajima is the most popular part of the park for sightseeing. Shodo Island, the second largest island in the Inland Sea with an area of 172 square kilometers, has benefited from Miyajima's fame to the extent that it is not haunted by the large numbers of tour groups that can only fit in one island on their sightseeing gallop round this part of Japan. On Shodo Island, regularly scheduled buses run along the most scenic drives and provide access to most places of interest—from Kankakei, a gorge in the middle of the island, to the sugar-fine sands of Silver Beach in the north. Cars can be rented, and so too can bicycles, and that gives one the chance to see this charming island at a more leisurely and appropriate pace.

The quarry that supplied the granite for Osaka Castle is located on this island. Built between 1582 and 1586 by Toyotomi Hideyoshi, Osaka Castle was one of the greatest fortresses in the country. Some of the stones for the castle walls measured twelve meters by six. The castle was destroyed in 1615 only decades after it was completed, following the showdown between the Toyotomi and Tokugawa forces. The stone for Nihonbashi, the bridge at the heart of the city of Edo (Tokyo), is also said to have been quarried at this spot.

A peculiarity of Shodo is the mini-circuit of eighty-eight Shingon temples, based on Kukai's eighty-eight temples on the island of Shikoku. It takes only seven days to make the Shodo pilgrimage on foot, next to no time in comparison with the three weeks required for the Shikoku pilgrimage and therefore very popular.

M.S.

ASHIZURI–UWAKAI NATIONAL PARK

Cape Ashizuri

The wind that roils the sea and tumbles shells along the ocean floor and up onto beaches is the *kaiyose*, the "seashell-bringing" wind. It blows on the twentieth day of the Second Month of the lunar calendar, according to ancient lore. So, it must have been about the middle of April in 1687 that the poet Basho visited the lovely seaside resort on the outskirts of the town of Wakayama on the Kii Peninsula and wrote the following *haiku*:

> The seashell-bringing wind
> Has wrought its magic on the shore
> At Waka-no-ura

The Kii Peninsula points at the island of Shikoku like a chubby finger. From Tokyo, there are certainly faster ways of reaching Shikoku and its single national park, Ashizuri–Uwakai, than by ferry from a port on the Kii Peninsula. But I wanted to depart from Wakayama by sea for two reasons.

I wanted to begin the seashell-collecting journey I was making from the place where Basho penned one of my favorite poems. I also wanted to be able to have a look at rugged Shikoku from the sea, to see it as Ki no Tsurayuki did in the year 934. In his *Tosa Diary*, one of Japan's earliest literary masterpieces, this poet-governor describes his perilous month-long journey in a small boat round from his southern provincial capital, Tosa, to the imperial seat in Kyoto.

Until modern times, Shikoku (Four Fiefdoms) was one of the remoter parts of the country. The smallest of Japan's main islands, it is still the one least developed economically, and it retains much of its old faraway charm; this, in spite of the fact that each of its four provinces—now prefectures—can be reached today directly by air. I did not, however, take the ferry that goes from Wakayama all the way around Shikoku to its southernmost prefecture, Kochi, the nearest port of call to Ashizuri–Uwakai National Park. Instead I went straight across the Kii Channel from Wakayama to Tokushima, and from there, down to Kochi through the daunting range of mountains that made Tosa, the old name for Kochi, accessible only by sea until not so long ago.

A highway now runs along the Yoshino River's deep cleft through the island. The river's large boulders of red and green chlorite are seen best from a punt on the deep, still waters of Oboke Gorge *en route* from Tokushima to Kochi. Shikoku is famous for its handsome stones of varying hues and shapes, much sought-after for landscape gardens. They come from these river beds, and small chips carried downstream by spring torrents are polished by the thundering Pacific surf and cast up on Kochi's famed Katsura Beach. These are Kochi's "five-colored pebbles," well known among Japanese pebble collectors.

Tosa's Fighting Spirit

The city of Kochi, at the head of Tosa Bay, is dominated by a castle with many of its eighteenth-century buildings still standing in all their classic elegance. There, an unusual statue of a woman beside a horse caught my eye. Chiyo, wife of a poor samurai in the 1500s who could not afford a steed, bought her husband a handsome stallion with a precious inherited sum which she had kept hidden away in case of an emergency. Her selfless deed so captured the mind of Oda Nobunaga, the military ruler of the time, that he bestowed upon her husband the castle and fiefdom of Tosa. This man became the first of the Yamanouchi lords who were to rule the area for the following three centuries.

Tosa has been the ancestral home of some of Japan's greatest soldiers and statesmen. Yoshida Shigeru, post-war prime minister who formed five cabinets in all, was one of them. The fighting spirit is strong here. In Kochi, they show you the fighting dogs, whose contests are arranged in imitation of *sumo*. They show you the fighting cocks bred from a Siamese strain. And the few remaining freak cockerels—pure white or ebony black—bred in days of old to provide ten-meter-long tail feathers for the standards twirled aloft in feudal processions.

But I was more interested in the little stalls down on picturesque Katsura Beach near the city center, where fishwives were selling shells. The prized "Thatcheria," a pale pink pirouetting ballet dancer of a shell found only in Japanese waters, could be had for a few hundred yen.

"If you want more shells," one old woman said, "go where my husband brings them in." She directed me to a small port nearby. A five-minute drive by car and I had reached the place, a narrow wharf piled high with wooden boxes. Lifting the lid of one of the boxes, I was sent reeling by the smell of rotting shellfish. But what a gorgeous sight! The boxes were filled with the most beautiful shells.

After I had bought some from a fisherman, a small boy tugged at my sleeve. "Come and see my uncle. He will give you some for nothing!" Up a side street, in a shed, sat a young man next to an enormous box of shells out of which he was making cheap seaside souvenirs. "Help yourself," he said, smiling. The shells were weatherbeaten, but to my delight among them I spotted a rare Magnificent Wentletrap, and I was soon doing my best to try to persuade the man—to no avail—to accept payment for the shell.

Then on along the southward curving Pacific coast I sped in my hired car, stopping here and there at inviting beaches, always finding a treasured shell or two. Ashizuri–Uwakai National Park, one of Japan's newest, established in 1972, is a beautiful coastal stretch of granite cliffs, fantastic rocks, coral reefs and verdant islets, bathed by the warm Black Current.

The park begins at Cape Ashizuri, an eighteen-kilometer-long promontory. The Ashizuri Skyline road through the gentle rolling hills down the center of the promontory takes you to the famed lighthouse in less than half an hour. The hazardous cliff-clinging route around its circumference has barely enough room for a bus and a car to scrape past each other. Indeed, the sea road seems little wider than the original paths that must once have ringed the cape.

Possibly because of its remoteness, "lovers' leaps" abound on this precipitous cape. Groves of camellias, palms, and even banyan trees remind one how far south this corner of Shikoku extends into the Pacific, but to troubled and depressed souls Ashizuri evidently has the image of the last spot on earth. A warm-hearted proprietress of one of the many inns and hostels on the cape is known locally as a wise counselor, and she has often been called in by her neighboring hoteliers to talk with guests and travelers who seem grieved, troubled, or depressed.

Pilgrims Clad in White

Behind the Ashizuri lighthouse is a temple rebuilt three hundred years ago to replace an edifice eight hundred years older still. It was founded by Kukai, one of the most venerated Buddhist priests in all Japanese history. Kukai was born in the northeast of Shikoku in 773. A hundred years after his death in 835, he was "canonized" and given the title Kobo Daishi. It was he who devised the Japanese *hiragana* alphabet, and introduced the esoteric Shingon sect from China into Japan. He preached widely, sanctified mountains and built temples all over Japan, making arduous pilgrimages, living in caves, and performing miracles. He stressed a syncretic, tolerant, and aesthetic approach to religion, and taught that in the Supreme Buddha resided ultimate truth and that this was closest amid the beauties of nature.

Eighty-eight holy places on the island of Shikoku commemorate Kukai, and it has become a religious pilgrimage to visit them in a set order. From the city of Tokushima, the holy course circles the island clockwise, taking from forty days to two months to complete on foot, depending on age and fitness. I saw a group of pilgrims in a bus and several on foot, all clad in the traditional simple white cotton, staff in hand, and wearing wide sedge hats inscribed with some religious injunction.

Kongofukuji, Kukai's temple on Cape Ashizuri, is number thirty-eight of Shikoku's eighty-eight holy places. Here, on this scenic promontory, with the sound of the turbulent Pacific Ocean waves breaking far below, Kukai would have felt both the exhilaration and tranquility that nature inspires.

Looking northwest, over one hundred kilometers of

the Uwa coast—beautiful, varied, and deeply indented—beckons the traveler. Not far beyond the bustling fishing port of Tosa Shimizu stretches the Minokoshi shore, whose marine wonders are so many that some are bound to be "left unseen," the meaning of the name Minokoshi. A glass-bottomed boat and an undersea viewing shaft reveal the colorful fish and corals, while fantastic eroded sandstone rock formations beguile the eye above water all the way to Tatsukushi, "Dragon Skewers," named after the strange rock formations resembling bundles of giant petrified bamboo stems, a veritable outdoor museum of natural rock sculpture.

At Tatsukushi, I reached the object of my journey: the Shell Exhibition Hall, which houses the Kurohara Collection. Built near the rocky shore, its modern architecture blends well with nature and seems, in its abstract design, to reflect many of the fifty thousand exotic shells exhibited there. It must be the only museum in the world devoted exclusively to seashells. They are superbly and imaginatively exhibited. The low ceiling of the ground floor is of glass, covered with shells lit from below. Upstairs, one can lean over the balustrade and marvel at the shells' upperside convolutions lit by the sun through glass roof panels.

All sorts of objects connected with seashells are displayed, such as a complete lacquer-boxed set of the shell game of ancient Japan, played just like that old card game Pelmanism by matching the perfectly fitting halves of intricately painted clam shells.

At the entrance to the Hall of Shells is a polished granite slab incised with some curiously profound lines by the recently deceased literary scholar Mushanokoji Saneatsu:

My shell is the proof that once I lived:
Had I not lived, there would have been no shell.

The collection of shells was begun by a local artist

Katsura Beach near Kochi

fascinated by the architecture of mollusks in its infinite variety. Shikoku's southwest corner is called the "Typhoon Ginza," so many are the cyclones that pass this way. But shell collectors relish the good stirring up of the ocean bed, and Kurohara Kazuo was no exception. A pharmacist by profession, he is a fine artist in oils as well as an avid shell collector. He has discovered over thirty new varieties. Kurohara conducted me around his collection, showing me the rare cowrie bearing his name. He also told me which were the beaches where crayfish nets were hung to dry, and later, on the sand beneath them, I found many a treasure from deep under the sea.

Tearing myself away from Tatsukushi, I continued on through the national park following the road north along the coast of the Uwa Sea (Uwakai) and into the prefecture of Ehime. The character of the coast here changes to that of a typical "ria" formation of myriad narrow inlets and islands caused by the prehistoric submergence of mountain valleys. A thick green verdure covers the steep hills, and the deep, quiet fjordlike bays are lined with pearl-oyster rafts. I did not stop at the town of Uwajima, famed for its castle and archeological mounds, bull *sumo*, and October "Eight-Deer Dance," but drove on up to the celebrated viewpoint at Hokezu Pass.

Greenness is the impression that all Ehime gives as one looks down from the pass. The shades of green and other pastel tints are like the silken sleeves of the court ladies of old Kyoto—tree greens contrasted with sea blues and the soft orange color of the delicious mandarins that grow on sunny slopes. The landscape has a feminine beauty, appropriately enough as Ehime, the name of the prefecture, means "Maidens of Love." Perhaps this name derives from the ladies of pleasure who, centuries ago, are said to have plied their trade in boats on the calm waters of the Inland Sea off Ehime's northern coast, although in all likelihood the derivation of the prefecture's name is rather less whimsical than its meaning. The Japanese language is, in fact, full of false trails for the amateur etymologist.

The southward view from Hokezu Pass includes much of the park and is like a painting on an old Japanese screen. Hills and inlets and tiny islands. Island upon island blending into the misty blue Uwa Sea in the distance. As I feasted my eyes on this beautiful view, I thought of Kukai and then recollected those words engraved in granite at the Shell Museum. Like any other eager shell collector, I used to seek live specimens, heedlessly plundering tide pools on coral reefs. But I vowed that day to collect, henceforth, only the shells washed up on beaches or lying dead on the sand beneath the crayfish nets.

D.B.

SANIN KAIGAN NATIONAL PARK

Megane Domon (Eye-glasses Cave)

The poet Basho was vividly struck by the difference in mood between the Pacific Ocean coast and the Japan Sea coast. After a sojourn at the celebrated beauty spot of Matsushima, the "Pine Tree Isles," near Sendai on the Pacific coast, Basho trekked all the way across the spine of Honshu, the country's main island, to visit a lagoon on the Japan Sea coast, also celebrated for its pine-clad islets. In the clearing weather, he described his impressions of the latter:

"Though the lagoon called Kisakata was little more than two miles long and two miles wide, it reminded me of Matsushima. But in some ways, it was quite different. While Matsushima had a gay, laughing beauty, Kisakata's face was full of bitterness and rue. There was a feeling of the desolate loneliness and sorrow of a tormented soul.

> In Kisakata's rain,
> Mimosas droop, like fair Hsi-shih,
> Who languished with love's pain."

Although Basho was writing in the seventeenth century about a section of the Japan Sea coast eight hundred kilometers north of this national park, he might have been describing the Sanin Coast, with its sand dunes, lagoons, and secondary "Matsushimas."

Climatically and topographically, the two sides of Japan, the "front" and "back," differ dramatically. The benevolent, warm Black Current passes near the "front," which faces the bright waters of the Pacific Ocean where the sun shines for much of the year. The Pacific coast is protected from cold bleak winds

sweeping in from Siberia by the high mountains that form Honshu's spine. The winds blow and deep snows pile up, instead, on the unprotected "back" side of Japan, Ura Nihon. Winter there is long, gray, and snowy. Gun-metal seas pound the coast and the winds and waves form sand dunes and lagoons that are unknown on the Pacific side. The name Sanin itself means "in the shadows of the mountains," while the nearby Inland Sea coast of Honshu is known as Sanyo, "the sunny side of the mountains."

When the sun does shine on the silver gray waters of the Japan Sea's shores, the lagoons are veiled by soft mists which the sun seldom dispels. It is little wonder that Basho was reminded of the famed silk-clad Hsi-shih, that damsel of the ancient Chou Dynasty of China, sad in her unrequited love.

He might well have chosen the same image to describe tree-lined Koyama Lagoon on the Sanin Coast. Just outside the city of Tottori, the lagoon is sixteen kilometers in circumference and, like Basho's Kisakata Lagoon, contains many islands. But it is now completely enclosed and has in fact become a fresh-water lake rather than a true lagoon, although it was originally formed by silt from the Sendai River encircling a portion of the sea. The "lagoon" is characterized by a wide temperature range between its depths and shallows. The contour of its bed is ingeniously exploited by fishermen who make a living off the lagoon's abundance of eels, carp, and pond-smelt: the fish are "herded" into underwater fish traps made of heaps of stones in the shallows, out of which they can be readily scooped. A similar "lagoon" further west, Lake Togo, abounds in particularly delicious eels.

Koyama Lagoon and the city of Tottori are at the western end of Sanin Kaigan (Coast) National Park, quite near the celebrated sand dunes. With both the lagoon and the dunes within such easy reach and with the charm of the city itself to enjoy, Tottori is a good place from which to begin a trip through this park. In the late sixteenth century, Tottori was a castle town

The Sanin Coast

and was peopled by armorers, weavers, provisioners, grain merchants, and various tradesmen who catered to the garrison. Not long thereafter, the town became the seat of a rich fief, and so it remained until close to the end of the nineteenth century when Japan formed a modern government. Today it is the capital of Tottori Prefecture. Though Tottori has a political role and is a trading and market center, with lumber, rice, and fruit being bought and sold in large quantities, the city itself gives the feeling of a holiday resort. Within the city limits, as well as in the vicinity, there are many Japanese-style inns complete with natural hot springs, some gushing straight out of the sand, as at Hamasaka.

Stretching the Sands

The first day in Tottori normally includes a visit to the lagoon and dunes, with perhaps a stop at the Tottori Folk Art Museum, which has a fine exhibition of regional handicrafts, or at the old castle site or any one of the parklike grounds of old shrines and temples which dot the city. After an overnight stay to enjoy the hospitality of one of Tottori's old-style inns, you can drive eastward along the coast (or go by train) all the way to the town of Amino, at the other end of the park. It is only a distance of some eighty kilometers, so there is plenty of time to stop and enjoy the scenery along the way.

Sand dunes occur on many parts of the Japan Sea coast. They are the result of fine river sands washed out to sea being cast up against the shore by currents and high waves and being blown finally into great piles by strong Siberian winds. Tottori's dunes are caused by the Sendai (Thousand Generation) River, a name aptly suggesting the great antiquity of habitation in this coastal region, originally known as Inaba. Myths and legends persist here, connected with the ancient Izumo

tribe whose shrine lies further west on the same coast. According to one story, a certain crafty Inaba rabbit, washed out during a flood to the islet of Okinoshima, persuaded a host of fabulous turtlelike "crocodiles" (*wani*) to form him a bridge back to shore. Similar tales across the sea point to the possibility of a fourth-century invasion of southwest Japan by people from the Korean peninsula.

Sixteen kilometers long and about two kilometers wide, the Tottori dunes are Japan's largest. From the approach road, they sweep in two or three gentle, buff-colored hills and block a clear view of the sea. If you tramp over them, you will be in for a surprise. The last sandy hill suddenly descends sharply, forcing an awkward scramble down a hundred meters or so to a narrow shelf of a beach. This sharp descent to the lapping waves is quite unexpected after the seemingly endless "desert."

Indeed, because of the rippled patterns created on the dunes by high winds and even shimmering mirages in the distance on hot summer days, at times the Tottori dunes seem like footage out of *Lawrence of Arabia*, especially around sunset, when crowds are thin.

The dunes are one of the most popular sights on the entire Japan Sea coast, partly, no doubt, because of their decidedly un-Japanese and exotic quality. There are many tourist amenities, too, not only to attract visitors, but to ease the crush. An access road runs deep into the dunes so that tour buses can deposit tourists within easy distance of the last slope down to the sea. There is a place to rent skis for those who prefer to skim down the slopes. And, perhaps to sustain the Arabian image, there are a few horses for hire. Walking through deep sand is harder work than one imagines, so there are large cafeterias to serve revitalizing food and drink. For children there is a kiddyland, and for bored adults waiting for their tour buses, any number of arcade-type games.

So, alas, it is not entirely the remote, quiet, desert scene from *Lawrence*. It seems more like a Fellini dream sequence: carnival buildings on shifting sands, with dark-suited, tall gentlemen strolling aimlessly beneath the beating sun and fat ladies with gold teeth holding parasols sweating their way down to view the empty sea.

A Gallery of Sea Sculpture

Secondary versions of Matsushima, the "Pine Tree Isles," seem to proliferate all over Japan, just as "Mount Fujis" do. The Sanin Coast is no exception. The original Matsushima on Honshu's Pacific side has traditionally been considered one of Japan's three most outstanding beauty spots. The large bay is filled with

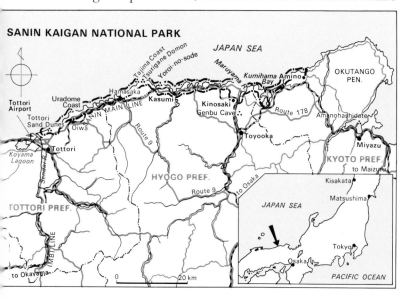

SANIN KAIGAN NATIONAL PARK

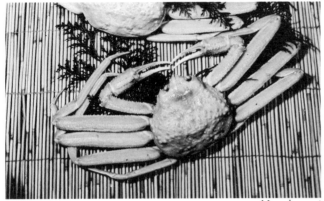

Matsuba-gani

more than 260 small islands, providing an endless variety of picturesque views and infinite inspiration for artists.

"There are countless islands," wrote Basho, "some tall, like fingers pointing to heaven; some lying prostrate on the waves; some grouped together in twos and threes; branching to the left or stretching to the right; some with babes upon their backs or clasped to their bosoms, like parents and grandparents. The pines are a deep, dark green. Their branches are bent by the salt sea winds into naturally graceful shapes, and they have a profound elegance."

As Basho's companion Sora gazed at the myriad islets far out in Matsushima Bay he wrote this *haiku*:

> To the Pine Tree Isles
>   You would need crane's wings to fly.
>   Little cuckoo bird!

But the Sanin Coast's pine-clad islets are not so far flung. They hug the coast, and are not even marked as dots on the average map, on which the Sanin Coast appears merely as a rather dull straight line, belying its great topographical interest and variety.

The islets are at Uradome (Coastal Riches), a little way east of the dunes—a mass of yellow beige rocks of all sizes that have been carved out of the cliff by the tempestuous winter seas. The large rocks are crowned with luxuriant pines whose roots cling precariously to crevices in the shaly rock. This "Matsushima" has a defiant beauty. Its verdant trees seem almost to dare the waves of the rough Japan Sea to try to dislodge them.

Scenic riches abound all along the Sanin Coast. The coastline near the port of Kasumi is designated an Outstanding Scenic Place. There stands Yoroi-no-sode, with its cliffs that resemble the sleeve-piece of a suit of ancient samurai armor, for which it is named. An assortment of strange rock formations includes Hachinosu-iwa (Beehive Rock), and Kujaku Domon (Peacock's Cave), which is lined with variegated basalt columns.

The Kasumi coast occupies the middle stretch of the Sanin park, and consists of volcanic rocks of various types that have undergone intense erosion by the sea over a long period of time. The strata are extremely complicated, and the whole area is a veritable geological museum and gallery of sea sculpture.

Sanin Kaigan National Park has several good coastal toll roads for motorists, but the best way to see the caves, arches, and varied rock formations of this enthralling coastline is by boat. Regular sightseeing craft ply out of Kasumi.

From November to March, the Kasumi fish market bustles with catches of *matsuba-gani*, pine-needle crab. A deep-sea member of the spider-crab family, *matsuba-gani* are a special delicacy of this region. The area is also famous for its delicious "Twentieth-Century" *nashi*, sent all over Japan from Tottori's orchards. The relatively dry rainy season and the fact that few typhoons strike here make it ideal for growing these crisp, juicy, applelike pears—a delightful fruit found only in Japan.

The national park ends at Amino on the Okutango Peninsula. Just on the other side of the peninsula, however, begins another park, the quasi-national Wakasa Bay park, which has a somewhat different topography—a ragged coastline with deeply indented bays and inlets. It includes the famed Amanohashidate, or "Heavenly Bridge." This narrow, pine-covered sand spit, over three kilometers long, enfolds a lagoon. Traditionally viewed upside down from between the legs, the Heavenly Bridge seems to be suspended in midair—truly a path for the gods. It is rendered this way by the great mid-nineteenth-century woodblock artist Hiroshige. Amanohashidate is the second of Japan's traditional three beauty spots, the first being Matsushima, and the third Miyajima, Shrine Island, a part of the Seto Naikai National Park.

D.B. and M.S.

Yoroi-no-sode

DAISEN–OKI NATIONAL PARK

The coast near the Great Shrine of Izumo

Daisen–Oki National Park takes its name from the mountain that dominates the area and the offshore islands you can see from its summit.

Daisen, "Great Mountain," (1,711 meters) is a veritable Janus: viewed from the west, the mountain has the appearance of a conical volcano and rivals Fuji in graceful symmetry, with deeply etched erosion lines artistically enhanced in winter by bold brush strokes of snow. Conical peaks throughout Japan are dubbed "Fujis" and provincial imitations abound, but Japan's peerless symbol really seems to have met its match here. That is, until you see another of Daisen's faces. Viewed from the north or south, it looks quite different. It is no longer Fuji, but a rugged escarpment that might have come straight out of the Japan Alps!

The Hiruzen pasturelands at Daisen's foot are ideal for gentle winter skiing and for summer camping. As for the four-hour climb to Daisen's summit, the reward is immediate—a breath-taking view across serried ranks of mist-bathed lesser peaks to the far-off Oki Islands in the Japan Sea.

The descent of Daisen is easy. In half the time it took to climb up and with less than half the effort, one reaches the remains of a great temple, Daisenji, founded in 718, which flourished in Japan's classical age. Fire has destroyed most of the hundred-odd buildings over the centuries, but Daisenji was once an important center of the Buddhist Tendai sect whose adherents came here to practice the rigorous Shugendo disciplines still followed on the three holy mountains of Dewa (see Bandai–Asahi National Park).

Daisen wears a dark green mantle of trees, the nationally protected *kyaraboku*—a dwarf creeping yew peculiar to Japan—and on its lower slopes are virgin forests of beech, oak, and maple, and groves of great red pines. To the west, another Fuji-like mountain, Mount Sanbe (1,126 meters), with its lovely alpine lake, joins Daisen in vigil over the Shimane Peninsula and its unusual topography.

The peninsula is unusual on two counts. While the word "peninsula" itself means "almost an island," most peninsulas are firmly joined to the mainland by their neck of *terra firma*—however narrow it may be—and most jut out more or less at right angles into the sea. The Shimane Peninsula, however, lies parallel to the mainland and is joined to it at either end by what are virtually sandbanks. The islandlike Shimane Peninsula is seventy kilometers wide and covered with hills. It is connected to the mainland at its western end by silt deposits laid down by the Hii and Kando rivers. The flat, silty expanse betwen the mouths of the two rivers is known as the Izumo Plain. At the eastern end of the peninsula, a sand spit, three kilometers wide and twenty long, created by the waves of the Japan Sea, would form an uninterrupted link with the peninsula were it not for a narrow channel at the town of Sakai Minato.

The central portion of this unusual peninsula, intent it would seem on becoming an island, bulges south, in effect dividing into two the waters that would make it an island. This is the site of Matsue, a city with a Venetian quality, built as it is between Lake Shinji on the west and the lagoon of Nakaumi on the east. Lake Shinji, fed by the Hii River, is a genuine fresh-water lake, while the lagoon is brackish, for the sea flows into it through the narrow channel at Sakai Minato on the north. The lagoon's name, Nakaumi, means "Inner Sea," and the great curved strip of land enclosing it, lined with pine forests, is appropriately called Yumigahama (Bow Beach), an excellent place for swimming.

Reminders of a Bygone Age

Matsue is a charming town. With its several canals and willow-lined embankments, it seems to be forever quietly admiring its own reflection in the shimmering waters all around. High on a hill among age-old pines, the dreaming battlements of a three-hundred-year-old castle look down on the town. It is one of the few castles in Japan still standing in its original state.

The people of Matsue preserve many of the niceties of a bygone age. The famed potter Kawai Kanjiro, born in Matsue, wrote: "A mannered leisure and a peculiarly Japanese grace of living distinguish the people of Matsue. They enhance the rocks in their gardens by keeping them moist, and they encourage

The Great Shrine of Izumo

moss to grow upon the stone lanterns. They polish the *sasa* leaves with oil, and wash the dust from the bamboo. They change the picture-scroll and flowers in the alcove every day. They are as much concerned with the color harmony between a food and its vessel as with its taste."

Lafcadio Hearn, the Irish-Greek author who found in Matsue his spiritual home, describes day-to-day life there in his *Glimpses of Unfamiliar Japan*.

Matsue was the seat of the lords of Izumo. The province is now called Shimane Prefecture, but the old name Izumo lives on in the name of Japan's oldest Shinto shrine, Izumo Taisha (the Great Shrine of Izumo). Approached through a magnificent avenue of ancient pine trees, the handsome shrine stands at the foot of pine-clad Yakumo (Eight Cloud) Hill at the western end of the Shimane Peninsula. Frequently rebuilt since its origin in the mists of time before these islands had been unified, the oldest building now dates back only to 1744, but the ancient type of architecture has been maintained.

The shrine commemorates Okuninushi no Mikoto, the Great God Ruler of the Land, and it was believed in olden times that during the Tenth Month of the lunar calendar all the Shinto gods congregated here. Because of their absence everywhere else, the Tenth Month was popularly known in the rest of Japan as the godless month, and many special taboos were observed during that period.

But the influence exerted by Okuninushi's father, the thunder god, Susano, is the one most tangible in Izumo today. Although Susano is better known for his capricious wildness than his occasional nobility, the tale told in Izumo about one of Susano's noble exploits is very similar to the Western myth of Saint George and the Dragon. Susano's dragon-slaying is recounted in the eighth-century *Record of Ancient Matters*.

The god came upon a couple who were mourning the seven of their eight daughters who had been devoured by an eight-headed dragon. The dragon was expected to come shortly for their remaining daughter,

the lovely maiden Inada. The god offered to attempt a rescue, asking for her hand in marriage should he succeed. He succeeded, of course, as gods do, and "eight clouds arose" as he and the maiden were joined in matrimony. Eight is a lucky number in Izumo, and Yakumo, "Eight Clouds," a lucky name. When he married a local girl and took Japanese nationality, Lafcadio Hearn adopted his wife's surname Koizumi and chose Yakumo for his Japanese given name.

Dragon-slaying Wine

The union of the god and the maiden continues to shed a blessing on Japanese couples marrying today. When I visited Izumo Taisha, a Shinto wedding was in progress there. But couples usually just pay their respects at Izumo and have their ceremonies at Yaegaki (Eightfold Fence) Shrine nearer Matsue. This shrine is supposed to be located on the very site of the palace where Susano and Inada lived as god and wife.

Yaegaki Shrine is solidly booked for weddings, and the wedding hall is decorated with a huge lifelike paper dragon with a single head resting on a *sake* barrel. For Susano overcame the eight-headed beast in the following manner: he had the girl's parents erect an eightfold fence and set a *sake* cask by each of the eight gates in the eight sections of the fence. When the dragon appeared, the lure proved effective; it drank its full and before too long began to feel drowsy. Finally it curled itself down onto the ground and fell asleep, enabling Susano to cut the fearsome creature to bits with his sword until the river ran red with its blood.

According to the myth, the dragon's tail concealed a miraculous sword. This clue has helped scholars unravel some of the symbols in Japanese myths. The rivers of Izumo *do* run red—with iron. The sands of the iron-rich Hii River once supported a thriving swordsmith's craft, recently revived. The boisterous

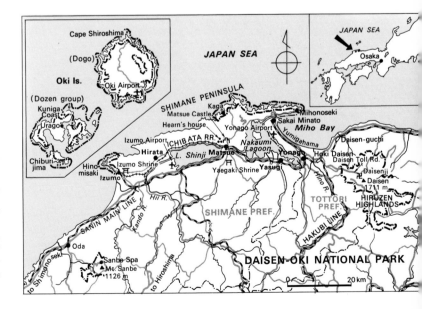

god Susano is now believed to represent the Izumo tribe, strong in prehistoric Japan but later conquered by Kyushu's Yamato tribe whose higher culture is symbolized by Susano's sister, Amaterasu, the goddess of light. It was the Yamato people who went on to establish the Japanese nation, and their sun goddess is enshrined at Ise. (See Ise–Shima National Park.)

Just beyond the Great Shrine of Izumo, the western extremity of the Shimane Peninsula around Hino-misaki (whose lighthouse is Japan's tallest) boasts a beautiful stretch of coast. The peninsula's eastern end is even lovelier. All the way from Kaga, with its sea-girt cave reminiscent of Capri, to the fishing port of Mihonoseki on the eastern tip is a succession of picturesque capes jutting out into the Japan Sea. Mihonoseki's seafarer shrine is Shinto's second oldest sanctuary after Izumo. The port is immortalized in the folk song "Seki no Gohon Matsu" (The Checkpoint's Five Pines—*seki* meaning "checkpoint" or "barrier"). Now only one of these trees remains. It is 350 years old, with a girth of four meters. In feudal times, the five pines were a vital navigational aid, and the villagers were aghast when the provincial lord proposed to fell the trees. The folk song is, in fact, a seventeenth-century environmental protest.

Nordic Touch to Islands

Mihonoseki was an important checkpoint because it was the port from which boats sailed to the "Islands Far Out to Sea." The distant Oki Islands were a convenient place of exile in premodern times for important political prisoners, including two emperors.

There is a daily ferry to the Oki Islands from

Cliffs on the Oki Islands

bustling Sakai Minato on the north end of the sand spit, across the lagoon channel from Mihonoseki. The trip to Oki takes a little over three hours. An air link has recently been added, closing the gap with the twentieth century that has kept these islands remote for so long. The Oki Islands are composed of a large major island called Dogo and a cluster of three smaller islands known as the Dozen group.

The island topography is spectacular, and the islanders have inherited a certain grace from the courtly inhabitants of long ago. There is here and there a Western note to the landscape. The grasslands atop cliffs where cattle graze seem almost Hebridean, while the valleys cradle rice paddies, old temples, and picturesque fishing villages. Then again, there seems to be something vaguely Norwegian about the fjords and forests of pine and cryptomeria. But the song of the *uguisu* reminds one that this is still Japan. In spring the woods and cherry groves are filled with the bush warbler's clear flute note building up in a joyous crescendo to its triplet flourish.

The forests of the large island, Dogo, are ideal for cultivating *shiitake* mushrooms (*Lentinus elodes*). Although to my mind not quite as tasty as the English field mushroom, which it resembles, the *shiitake*, grown commercially on special logs, makes up for this by its almost magical nutritional value. The ancient Chinese emperors, they say, considered it an elixir of youth and also an aphrodisiac. Did those exiled Japanese emperors—much influenced as they were by China—introduce *shiitake* to the Oki Islands? Today's scientists credit this delicious edible fungus with the power to reduce cholesterol levels in the blood quickly.

The greatest wonders of the Oki Islands are their coastal rock formations. The waves of the Japan Sea have chiseled and sculpted a riotous gamut of shapes from these multihued volcanic rocks. Visitors may hire boats from which to see the towering cliffs of whitish gray, splashed with red and yellow as from an impressionist's palette, with clumps of green shrubbery clinging miraculously to sheer precipices like lumps of paint. Through the blue of the sea, red rocks can be discerned at great depths. There are black and purple rocks too, as dark as the caverns visitors pass through before their boatman lights his burning torch.

There is also a miniature version of the Inland Sea (see Seto Naikai National Park). From the air, the forms of the islands in the Dozen group look like three giant swimmers, arms outstretched, treading water. The calm seas in their midst are busy with tiny craft as islanders go back and forth from isle to verdant isle. A halcyon scene, reminiscent perhaps of what the real Inland Sea used to be like long ago.

D.B.

SAIKAI NATIONAL PARK

Christian grave on Hirado Island

Had circumstances been more favorable when Europe sent its first missionaries and merchant adventurers to Japan in the mid and late sixteenth century, Hirado—the port where many of them landed—might have become, like Goa, Macao, Calcutta, Madras, Shanghai, or Hong Kong, a great Oriental trading center on which a rich empire was built. But in the case of Japan, suspicion and cautiousness conspired against both Christianity and trade taking deep root.

Hirado Island is one of the larger islands, now part of Nagasaki Prefecture, which ships from the south pass on their way to the industrial ports of northern Kyushu. Its port, also called Hirado, remains a small fishing town, not much larger today than when tall-masted galleons sailed past the sheltering headland to drop anchor—except that now the memory of those days has helped to inject the local economy with a bit of twentieth-century tourism. Especially in summer, visitors arrive in some numbers to admire the picturesque harbor and to see for themselves the relics of the brief, bygone days of Christianity and early European trade. For Hirado Island, most of which belongs to Saikai (West Sea) National Park, offers an unusual combination of natural beauty and exotic history—tatami-matted, wooden chapels, for instance, among rice paddies and bamboo groves.

Portuguese missionaries were the first to arrive, in 1542, and initially they experienced great success. Francis Xavier came to Japan in 1549, and stayed here for two years. Thousands were converted, including a number of influential feudal lords. The Dutch, on the other hand, had wordly, not spiritual, fortunes in mind when they set up a trading post, or "factory," in 1597, and so did the British.

Had the early Christian missionaries, both Jesuit and Franciscan, been content to sow the good seed and then quietly withdraw, or remain in small numbers concerning themselves with things purely spiritual rather than temporal, Japan's religious history might have been different. But the early Portuguese and Spanish priests inevitably found themselves dabbling in politics and supplying weapons to Christian clan lords.

The Christianization of Kyushu continued apace for fifty years, although the military rulers had already begun to have misgivings about the possible undermining effect of this foreign religious and cultural influence on the newly acquired unity of Japan. When the first Tokugawa shogun, Ieyasu (see Nikko National Park), was in power, he had his fears crystallized by an Englishman. Cast up on Japan's shores in 1600, ship's navigator Will Adams had fought under Drake against the Armada and held a wary view of the Spaniards. Forced to remain in Japan, Adams became an adviser and confidant to Ieyasu. In this period of religious and incipient national wars among the countries of Europe, it is no surprise to learn that Will Adams instilled in the shogun a distrust for Roman Catholic missionaries and indeed for all Spaniards. The expulsion of Portuguese and Spanish missionaries and traders from Japan ensued. Christianity was proscribed, and before long there were many Japanese martyrs, staunch in their new faith.

Traders were allowed to stay (this meant the Dutch), but in 1634 they were ordered to move to a tiny fan-shaped, artificial island of only thirteen thousand square meters known as Dejima in Nagasaki Bay. For the next two hundred years, Dejima was to be Japan's only window on the West. While most of the foreshore of Nagasaki Bay has now been reclaimed, the outlines of Dejima have been marked with brass studs. The narrow strip of water that separated the island from the town still remains in the form of a canal, and in 1958 a garden beside the canal and some of the original Dutch buildings were restored.

At the same time that Will Adams was inveighing against the Portuguese and Spanish and their tendency to colonize through religion, he was in contact with the East India Company about the trade opportunities that Japan offered. So a staff of six men was sent up from Bantam (present-day Indonesia) on the *Clove*, laden with five thousand pounds worth of goods with which to establish a "factory." The chief agent, or "factor," was Richard Cocks, then aged forty-seven, a native of Staffordshire. By the time the English arrived, the Portuguese and Spanish had already been edged out, with the exception of a few missionaries who dodged the authorities while trying to keep their undercover ministry alive. Cocks describes much of what he saw in his long letters and his diary. He mentions the solid Dutch settlement that was already standing in Hirado when the British arrived—a quay, a large well, and solid stonework walls like a bit of old Amsterdam amid the frame wood and paper-windowed houses of the natives.

Back to Batavia

Though both the Dutch and the English were originally allowed to set up their trading posts anywhere in Japan, the Dutch selected Hirado because it was close to the route of approach which foreign ships used and far from the Japanese seat of government. In trying to keep out of the immediate view of their host government, the Dutch had little idea about how peripheral Hirado was to the economic life of the country as a whole. The English followed the Dutch example, and by the time Will Adams found out his countrymen had established themselves in Hirado, it was too late to advise a move—they had been befriended by the local lord, the head of the Matsuura clan, for whom it was a financial boon to have traders in residence.

Bad luck was the lot of the English in Hirado. Ships were infrequent, not more than one a year. One vessel was even pirated by the Dutch and stripped of its cargo. Then, in 1617, the shogun restricted trading to established ports, which meant in effect that the entire country had to be serviced by a warehouse in backwater Hirado. Furthermore, the administrators of the East India Company ignored Cocks's pleas for more suitable trading goods—he wanted silk and guns—but his superiors kept supplying the Hirado factory an-

nually with woven cotton cloth, which samurai deigned just about good enough to use for spear covers. By 1623, the British were bankrupt. The factory was liquidated and Cocks was fetched back to Batavia (present-day Jakarta) to account for the failure. He died, mercifully, *en route* to London, where he would have been court-martialed. His letters and diary make clear that the poor affairs of the Hirado factory were not entirely his fault.

Most of the reminders of Hirado's intriguing history may be seen by walking from the town's northern headland southward along the crescent of the bay. In the north are the remains of the old Dutch settlement. A thick stone wall that today borders a village street was the limit of the settlement centuries ago. The foundations of the Dutch factor's residence are marked too. Quite near the port is a huge, double-troughed well, with one side used by ships taking on fresh water and the other by the Dutch residents. The stone quay is still intact, but most of it has been built over by ramshackle, wooden sheds used by fishermen.

Directly above the Dutch settlement is the Hirado Museum, which houses a collection of European memorabilia, including glassware, costumes, and the like. There are also letters to Hirado relatives from Japanese women who married foreign traders and had to live out their time in Indonesia and from the offspring of international romances who were exiled there after the Hirado factories were closed.

On the bluff of the northern headland, providing an excellent view of the bay, is Sakigata Park, with its cherries, azaleas, bamboos, and palms.

Nearer the bay, but also well situated on a bluff is the rambling Matsuura villa, with broad stone steps and a wood-and-wattle surrounding wall. This building dates from the early Meiji period, which makes it a little over a century old. The Matsuura family was in control when the European traders were here, however, and the exhibits that are now to be seen in the villa's main rooms are related to that period. Folding screens depict the Southern Barbarians: red-haired, long-nosed, tall and angular, wearing breeches and plumed hats. There are also maps and firearms and models of ships of the time. In a rustic annex in the garden, the tea ceremony is performed, while the garden itself offers a splendid and peaceful view of the port.

On a gentle slope at the very head of the bay is the Church of Saint Francis Xavier, with its tall spire giving the landscape a European touch. The church was built about a hundred years ago when freedom of religion was granted to the Japanese. With the reappearance of European missionaries in the 1870s, a group of crypto-Christians made themselves known. For over seven generations, they had kept their Chris-

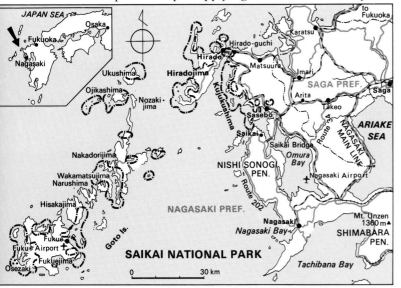

tian faith, practicing it in secret. For devotional objects, they used Buddhist and Shinto images with Christian symbolism cleverly worked into the design. Substituting tea for wine, they made the tea ceremony into a kind of Mass. Their prayers were a strange mixture of Latin, Portuguese, and local dialect. Some of the "ingrained" practices of the hidden Christians are still followed by the Roman Catholics who worship today at this church. (See Unzen–Amakusa National Park.)

There is one old and famous, but tiny bridge in Hirado that spans the narrow rivulet running through the middle of the town. It goes by two names: Saibashi (Good Luck Bridge) and Orandabashi (Dutch Bridge). Though built a century after the Dutch left Hirado, it was probably called Dutch Bridge because it is so sturdily made of stone just like the nearby Dutch settlement. In fact, the style of the bridge owes more to Chinese influence. Its double arch is reminiscent of Nagasaki's famed Meganebashi (Eye-glasses Bridge), built in 1634.

On the south side of Dutch Bridge, on the approach to the south side of the bay, are the remains of the English factory. A stone memorial, erected in 1928 by a member of the Matsuura family, is inscribed with the names of the Englishmen who came to Hirado. It includes Will Adams, John Saris (captain of the *Clove*), Richard Cocks, and the subordinate traders—among them one Tempest Peacock, who, from accounts in Cocks's diary, lived up to his name in every way and died a violent death in Indochina.

Just above the English memorial is Hirado Castle. The forebears of the Matsuuras built a rustic fortification here during the Kamakura Period (thirteenth century), when Hirado was one of the last native ports for envoys being sent to the Chinese court. The ferroconcrete building that stands today is in the style of a castle built in 1707.

A Proliferation of Islands

To see Hirado as its first Westerners did, take a ferry for the twenty-minute trip from Hirado-guchi on Kyushu. You can also drive to Hirado over the new 650-meter-long bridge built in 1977. Turn right, and after a few miles, the road will lead you into town the back way past the old Dutch Bridge. The most attractive way of approaching Hirado is by catching one of the eight sightseeing boats that leave Kashimae Pier in the old naval port city of Sasebo every day and wend their way for ninety minutes past island after island after island—far too many islands to count, but only an incorrigible pedant would quibble with the conventional total of ninety-nine, for these are the Kujukushima, the celebrated Niney-Nine Islands.

Despite Hirado Island's relatively small size and proximity to the large population centers of the north of Kyushu, it has remained by some miracle of oversight largely undeveloped. To be sure, Hirado and its immediate environs contain several sizable and architecturally undistinguished hotels. But the rest of the island boasts of little more than one beachside monstrosity and a couple of delightful little Japanese-style inns. Nearly all the roads are in an excellent state of repair and each little coastal village has its harbor. But the only modern buildings outside the town of Hirado are the hotel, a hospital, and several schools. The countryside is of a staggering beauty: in some places splashes of color, flowers around a hillside chapel, making it as bright and cheerful as the Mediterranean; but in other places deep, shady inlets under a somber sky imbuing it with a contemplative, moody grandeur—with the result that the traveler continually finds his emotional responses to the beauty of nature stimulated and provoked.

Five-Island Chain—Multiply by Thirty

Much further offshore, and a major component of this national park, is the Goto (Five-Island) Chain that in fact comprises 150 isles in all. (Island-counting seems not to have been the forte of the inhabitants of this park.) Until recently, it took a full four hours one way by boat from Nagasaki or Sasebo, but now a thirty-minute air service is available from Nagasaki airport.

During the eighteenth century, many crypto-Christians emigrated to these far-flung islands. The land was exceedingly poor, consisting of little more than eroded volcanoes and sea-carved cliffs, but the refugees were willing to put up with poverty for the protection afforded by remoteness.

The scenery of the islands is spectacular, especially the twenty-kilometer stretch of sheer cliffs, 160 meters high, at Osezaki on Fukue Island, largest of the islands, patterned with vivid, black and white stripes. The whole archipelago is geologically interesting, consisting of sedimentary rock mixed with a wide variety of igneous substances such as sandstone, shale, conglomerate, basalt, andesite, and granite.

Even today the population is mainly Christian, and villages are characterized by steepled churches and cemeteries with stone crosses—added to the scene, of course, within the last hundred years, now that belief in Jesus is no longer a crime. The people are more prosperous now, too. The islands are noted for their deep-sea fishing fleet, and they lend themselves, too, to the raising of cattle. Cows grazing on grasslands by the sea and wandering over the spacious yellow sands are a sight unfamiliar in most of Japan but common in the Goto Chain.

M.S.

UNZEN–AMAKUSA NATIONAL PARK

"Frost flowers" on Unzen

This most attractive national park has a special exotic quality given to it by its associations—both happy and tragic—with the Western world. Happy, because for many years before World War II it was the favorite holiday playground of European and American expatriates living and working in and around Shanghai, among them Pearl Buck.

Just as snow-capped Fuji greets air and sea visitors to Tokyo and Yokohama, it was another mountain, the graceful silhouette of Unzen, that told travelers from the South China Sea that they were nearing Japan. The old China hands found Unzen an ideal escape from the stifling heat of a Shanghai summer. It was they who first developed into a thriving resort these hills where cool, healthy mountain air, hot-spring baths, and superb views might be enjoyed less than an hour's drive up from a selection of delightful swimming beaches on the coast below.

The tragic connotations of the names Unzen and Amakusa lie in the memories they evoke of the persecution of Japan's Christians almost four hundred years ago. In 1612, Christian priests were banned from Japan, but missionaries continued to smuggle themselves in. Christian fervor among the peasant masses grew stronger and the shogun decided to clamp down altogether on the practice of the religion, making it a criminal offense. But a large number of the faithful continued to worship in secret, defying the most cruel persecution. Japan produced many Christian martyrs—some later canonized by Rome—and Unzen was the scene of much of their suffering.

Unzen, "Cloud Hermit" or "Cloud Mountain"—one can read both meanings into the name—is a relatively recently extinct volcano, a cluster of tholoid cones, whose once great activity molded the kidney-shaped Shimabara Peninsula. Unzen's volcanic core is highly evident in its many geysers and vents emitting steam and sulfurous gases. At what is today called Unzen Spa, 727 meters above sea level, multihued rivulets flow past mounds of whitish earth to a constantly boiling pond into which unfortunate Christians were often thrown during the seventeenth-century persecutions. A cross now marks the spot where the faithful were tried. Anyone suspected of being a Christian was obliged to trample upon the "sacred image"—a crude icon of Jesus Christ or the Virgin Mary. Refusal to do so meant the boiling pond.

Downhill, near the southern tip of the Shimabara Peninsula's coast, are the ruins of Hara Castle where 35,000 peasants, many of them Christians, died in 1637 in an abortive uprising known as the Shimabara Rebellion. Twenty-eight kilometers further along the coast are the ruins of Shimabara Castle, the headquarters of the government forces who put down the rebellion and massacred the 35,000. In its reconstructed castle building, historical relics of the early Japanese Christians and their hazardous underground activity are on display. Here one may see some of the *fumi-e* images on which they were forced to trample, worn thin by the pressure of thousands of feet. One can imagine the moral agony endured by many who outwardly went through the actions of denying their faith. Perhaps for the sake of relatives, perhaps simply out of fear.

Now only eggs are boiled in the pond—to provide guests at Unzen's inns with a breakfast novelty. The mountain resort is popular today with foreigners and Japanese alike. Near the infamous boiling pond, inns cluster, offering the delights of hot-spring baths. Unzen's fine golf course dates from the days of the old China hands. (It is beautifully landscaped, and I shall forever remember the one time I made a good drive down a lovely fairway only to have my ball swooped upon by an enormous black crow and carried off into the clouds!) Memorable too is the magnificent view from the top of Myoken, the second highest of Unzen's peaks. A ropeway takes one there in comfort, and the panorama is breath-taking, with its bird's-eye view of the intricate topography of the Shimabara Peninsula surrounded by the inland waters of the Ariake Sea to the north and Amakusa's skein of islands to the south.

Unzen is a resort for all seasons. In late spring and early summer the hillsides are ablaze with vivid azaleas, while the trees turn gold and crimson in the fall.

Winter has its "frost flowers" when branches sparkle and glisten with their celebrated silver thaw.

Buddhist Cloak for Christianity

Like several other archipelagos off the coast of Kyushu, the beautiful Amakusa Islands were tenacious strongholds of Christianity. Just how tenacious is shown by the fact that in 1905 not long after the ban on Christianity was lifted, five thousand Christians were found to be still practicing their faith in secret in a single village on one of the Amakusas. The stringent surveillance of the authorities of old reached everywhere, but the islands' sea moats must have been something of a safeguard. The anti-Christian law required everyone to register with their local Buddhist temple, and throughout Kyushu Christians endeavored to comply outwardly with the regulations while managing somehow to continue worshiping Jesus Christ and the Virgin Mary in secret. They displayed the proper Buddhist statuettes in their household shrines, but scratched crosses underneath or on the back in some inconspicuous place. Figurines of Kannon, the goddess of mercy, were ingeniously contrived to represent—to the initiated—the Holy Virgin. The goddess would be carved holding a child, or with a fish, an ancient Christian symbol. Many of these "Maria Kannon" and other cleverly camouflaged objects of secret worship can be seen today in collections like the one displayed at Hara Castle. On Shimojima (Lower Island), in the largest town of the Amakusas, Hondo, is a "Buddhist" temple called Myotokuji, where there is not only a celebrated Maria Kannon, but a statue of Jesus disguised as Jizo, the kindly Buddhist guardian of little children. Christian crosses have been subtly incorporated into decorative motifs carved into the temple's stone steps.

The descendants of those *kakure Kirishitan*, "hidden Christians," are devout Catholics today. At Hondo, a candlelight procession is made every November to a grotto built in 1958 to commemorate the centenary of the apparitions at Lourdes. Here and there in the Amakusas, in the middle of rice fields, or huddled among the simple gray-tiled dwellings of fisherfolk in villages such as Sakitsu on its small scenic fjord, one comes upon a Christian church built in the past century. It is fascinating to conjecture what Japan would have been like as a Christian nation, with steepled churches and spired cathedrals decorating the landscape instead of tree-shrouded Buddhist temples —all the more so, since a wave of temple destruction followed in the wake of the new faith as it began to take over in the sixteenth century. When the peasants rebelled against heavy taxation and merciless persecution in 1637, the people of Amakusa rose up also, and seized the castle at Tomioka. But they met their doom.

The tiny picturesque promontory of Tomioka, with its peaceful shore, is a popular beauty spot now. There is little left of its ill-fated castle. White sandy beaches and strikingly eroded cliffs characterize the lovely hilly isles of Amakusa (Heavenly Grasses). There are 120 islands in all, clustered around the two major islands, Kamijima and Shimojima (the latter being the biggest). Until quite recently the islands retained much of their old charm because of their remoteness. But in 1966 the spectacular Five Amakusa Bridges were completed, joining the archipelago to the mainland of Kyushu and carrying a highway, the Pearl Line, all the way to the bustling sardine, bonito, and yellowtail fishing port of Ushibuka at the southern tip of Shimojima. The bridges connect a series of small, pine-clad islets and one larger island between Misumi on the mainland twenty-five kilometers southeast of Kumamoto and Matsushima on Kamijima (Upper Island). The bridges are of four different types, and were featured on an attractive commemorative postage stamp. As a result of the bridges and the highway, the islands have become a popular tourist attraction. Subtropical flora flourish, and rare forms of marine life can be observed at Hondo's underwater observation shaft.

Unidentified Marine Pyrotechnics

The strangest local marine phenomenon is probably

the *shiranui*, or "mysterious fires," a curious form of marine luminescence that occurs mainly in the narrow inland waters of the Yatsushiro Sea, hemmed in between the Amakusa Islands and the Kyushu mainland. Kyushu-born writer Ryu Kankichi has this to say of this local *ignis fatuus*: "The phenomenon appears only in the seas off the Kyushu coasts and is seen twice each year. During the summer, the *shiranui* appear off the coast of the town of Yatsushiro, in Kumamoto Prefecture, with the Amakusa Islands in the distance. In winter, the fires are said to appear to the north, off the town of Omuta at a point overlooking the Ariake Sea. Their origin remains a mystery.

"What one can see is this: From a small hill called Yotsuyama, south of where Omuta merges with the town of Arao in Kumamoto Prefecture, one can look out in daylight across the bay to where the foothills of beautiful Mount Unzen trail like the train of a magnificent robe. By night, all that is visible are the lights of fishing vessels. But in mid-winter, at about one o'clock in the morning, the darkness on the horizon is broken by one or two 'fires.' These burning apparitions divide into more 'fires' which move right and left, joining and dividing in restless motion. After a while, a large blue-white flame appears on the left and moves across to the right at high speed, breaking up into many separate flames while in motion. As the spectacle continues, fires of various sizes and colours— red, white, and blue—appear and dance in various directions, alternately growing and shrinking in size.

"One observer who suspected that these 'fires' had their source in the lights of fishing vessels once pursued

The Five Amakusa Bridges

them in a power boat; but the elusive targets always kept ahead of him in a chase that had no end. Finally, the pursuer noted that while the 'fires' he was pursuing had gone out, other similar apparitions were by then burning far to the rear of his boat. Various theories prevail with regard to the origin of these fires, which blink, move, roll, and bounce in endless motion. One theory is that they are the result of flight by phosphorescent insects; another is that reflections from the lights of fishing vessels are the cause. It is also argued that they are a mirage of a kind to be found only in Ariake Bay, where the waters are affected by exceptionally strong tidal changes. Whatever the cause, these 'fires' are a weird phenomenon."

The wide tidal range of the Ariake Sea makes it ideal for farming laver, a delicious seaweed dried in thin sheets and used on *senbei*, the popular Japanese type of rice cracker. The wide tide gap is useful too in fishing. Traps are made of piles of rounded stones; fish swimming in at high tide are left high and dry when the water recedes.

Omuta is an industrial town surrounded by the Miike coalfields, Japan's largest. The blot it presents on the natural beauty of the area was already noted a century ago in one of Japan's best known folk songs. The lilting melody of the "Coal Miner's Dance" was popularized abroad by the American Army of Occupation:

> Lo! the moon is risen,
> The full moon is risen
> Over Miike Mine.
> But the chimneys are so high,
> The bright moon is smoky,
> Smoky all the time.

Not only is the eastern shore of the beautiful Ariake Sea now marred by chemical and industrial complexes like the one at Omuta, but on the Kyushu shore of the Yatsushiro Sea, which is even more beautiful, stand the noxious buildings of the nitrogen fixation industry of infamous Minamata, the city whose mercury effluent gave its name to a new, deforming ailment.

With these reminders of the damage, sometimes fatal, caused by rampant and untrammeled industrialization, we can indeed be thankful that much of the area's beauty has been saved by the national park. The mountain resort of Unzen, which covers most of the Shimabara Peninsula, was claimed for preservation as one of the first national parks in 1934. Twenty-two years later in 1956 the scenic coasts of the Amakusa Islands were added, preserving more of this beautiful part of the country so that not all of it would be overrun by "dark Satanic mills."

D.B.

ASO NATIONAL PARK

Mount Aso's crater

Right in the center of Kyushu, southernmost of Japan's four main islands, lies the great sprawling volcano called Aso. A monster of its kind, it is the biggest volcano in the world, although certainly not the highest. Aeons ago, it is believed to have risen to a far greater height than it does now, and its imposing presence dominated Kyushu. But over the millenia, it gradually eroded itself away in successive upheavals followed by violent explosions and subsequent depressions, till now it does not seem like a mountain at all but more like a giant molehill.

Aso's crater stretches for 16 kilometers from east to west and 32 kilometers from north to south, and is 128 kilometers in circumference. Although the volcano has actually been in action for about thirty million years, the present outer crater was probably formed only about 130,000 years ago. This main crater basin encompasses five smaller craters, of which one is still extremely active. It also includes two spacious green valleys where cattle graze. Over the ages, Aso has ejected a huge quantity of lava which flowed in every direction so that almost two-thirds of the whole of Kyushu is covered by lava ejected from Mount Aso at one time or another. The Gokase (Five Rapids) River that flows into the Pacific in Miyazaki Prefecture has cut, in its upper reaches, a spectacular gorge through one of Aso's lava flows. Known as Takachiho Gorge, it is in a quasi-national park adjacent to Aso National Park.

The gorge is celebrated for the curious shapes into which the mountain torrent has carved out the walls of solid andesite. One section resembles the pleats of a Japanese fan, or of a ceremonial *hakama* skirt. The gorge and its vicinity, centering around the village of Takachiho, are closely connected with the myths of Japan's origins, mimed in ancient sacred dances, the *Iwato kagura*, still performed there. The villagers seem to rejoice in a quiet pride, knowing their village was chosen by the gods. They show you what they claim is the very cave in which Amaterasu, the sun goddess, hid herself, throwing the whole world into darkness, until her companions coaxed her out again. The cave is well-nigh beyond reach, behind the piles of little stones left by the faithful in homage. (See Ise–Shima National Park.)

Almost adjacent to Aso National Park on the north is a second quasi-national park surrounding another gorge, the Yabakei—a region of outstanding beauty, particularly in autumn.

Aso has undergone many mutations in its long history. At one stage, the volcano actually sank and became a huge lake. It was out of this lake that the present crater with its five principal cones emerged in a succession of further eruptions. All the water eventually spilled away down fissures that had been opened up by the volcanic action. Twin rivers, still fed by subterranean springs, the Kurokawa (Black River) in the north and the Shirakawa (White River) in the south, are all that remain now of the lake.

The gently undulating, fertile pastureland created by Aso's thick deposits of volcanic ash over the ages was an invitation to farmers. There are now three towns inside the crater basin itself, supporting a population of about 70,000.

All around Mount Aso, too, the countryside is green and fertile. Driving with friends from America along

Kusasenri on the slopes of Mount Aso

the Trans-Kyushu Highway from the hot-spring resort of Beppu to the old castle town of Kumamoto, via Mount Aso, we were enchanted by the emerald green of central Kyushu's lush valleys. How we would like to live, we mused, in one of the prosperous-looking old farms, nestled among graceful bamboo groves on the hillsides, above fields of rice descending terrace-wise to crystalline streams. Each farm was a neat little compound with its handsome, white-walled storehouse decorated with black tiles interspersed with a ridged latticework of white plaster in diagonal crisscrosses. We made a detour to a place near Hita north of Mount Aso where the inhabitants of a remote little village make a characteristic type of earthenware baked with a glaze as green as their valleys.

Volcanic Battleground

But Aso's active crater is anything but green and fertile. There, for miles around, is nothing but desolation and signs of violent upheaval, nothing but sulfur yellow rocks and reddish earth, as if giant bulldozers had been at work pushing the earth's crust to prepare some gigantic building site. It is a forbidding area, relieved only by the bright attire of swarms of tourists, their gaily painted sightseeing buses, and the souvenir stalls, whose very tawdriness is an almost welcome sight in this treeless wasteland.

From Aso railway station, a road winds up a large mound of red earth and rock. Where the road ends, a

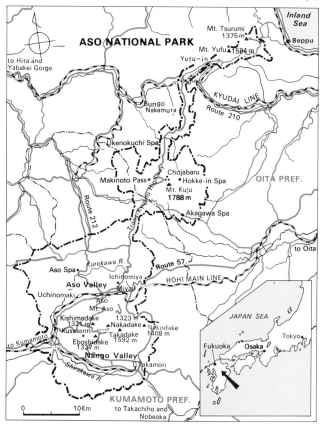

ropeway makes the four-minute crossing over a rock-strewn gully to the sides of the active crater, called Nakadake (Central Peak). Here one has the chilling feeling of being on a battleground. Concrete bunkers are provided, into which one can dive to take cover from sudden bombardments of molten rock. But tourists need not worry, as the volcanologists constantly keep a wary eye on the "enemy," and at the slightest sign that an eruption is imminent, tourists are kept a safe distance away behind cordons, disappointed of course at missing the close view of the crater they came so far to see. But all being well, one may advance to the very rim and look right down into the heart of the volcano. They say it is very spectacular at night.

There are seven fire holes, and the vents on the north side belch smoke and fire more or less continuously, accompanied by disconcerting rumbles. In the daytime the fire holes look no worse than belching chimney pots at the bottom of a yawning abyss. But the abyss itself is a commanding sight, rather like an oval, concentrated Grand Canyon. Its towering walls are vividly striped and zigzagged with alternate layers of volcanic ash, lava, and gravel.

Standing on the rim of Aso's active crater, you are fifteen hundred meters above sea level, but the rise has been so gradual you hardly have the feeling of being on the summit of the world's broadest volcano. To appreciate Mount Aso's enormous size and see the volcano in proper perspective, you must move further away—ideally, up to the top of Takadake, at 1,592 meters the tallest of Aso's five craters. From there you have a really good view of smoking Central Peak's elliptical form in its entirety.

But the pleasantest view of the volcano is to be had from the hot spring resort of Uchinomaki, on the outer ridge itself, also know as Aso Spa. Here, the whole dramatic panorama is unfolded before you in its immensity. One of Kyushu's most popular spas, Uchinomaki has many inns offering all the delights of the best Japanese *ryokan* together with soothing hot sulfur spring baths.

North of Mount Aso is another volcano just as old as Aso but now extinct. Mainland Kyushu's highest mountain at 1,788 meters, "Ninefold" Mount Kuju contrasts strikingly with its still wild and uncouth neighbor. Kuju is crowned with luxuriant alpine flora, and its skirt is densely forested. In early summer, the highlands near Hokke-in Spa are ablaze with the magenta azaleas (*Rhododendron kiusianum*) peculiar to Kyushu, while in winter, rime "blossoms" adorn the bare branches of the deciduous trees framing the snow-covered dome of Mount Kuju and giving an illusion of cherry trees in springtime. Mount Kuju and the other peaks in the range are typical tholoid volcanoes, whose eruptions have caused their crater rim to cave in, forming a sort of cupola, or dome, hence the name tholoid, which means "dome-shaped."

The Infernal Baths of Beppu

Another extinct volcano, Mount Yufu, at the park's northern extremity looks down on Beppu, north Kyushu's famous hot-spring resort. Between Kuju and Beppu stretch miles of rolling downs, a topography rare in Japan. The area is rich in scenic variety and has a goodly sprinkling of luxurious hot-spring inns.

Beppu, on the Inland Sea, at the northeastern extremity of Aso National Park, rivals Hokkaido's Noboribetsu in the abundance of its spas and the variety of its hot mineral springs—efficacious cures for an enormous number of diseases. (See Shikotsu–Toya National Park.) There are nine different chemical types in addition to the hot sand baths on the shore. Beppu comprises eight spas in all. The area is so rich in thermal activity that the prefectural government maintains an experimental station researching the possible agricultural uses of the waters, and Kyushu University has here an Institute of Balneotherapeutics for the study of the medical potential of hot-spring bathing.

In Beppu you feel that Mount Aso is not very far away. Its presence is like that of a mammoth subterranean dragon, whose fiery breath pushes up through the earth everywhere. Boiling ponds abound, each one a "hell" of some description or other. Many produce fiendish noises too, bubbles and infernal bangs, while some send clouds of devilish-hot mud shooting into the air. Ocean blue Umi-jigoku (Sea Hell) is said to be more than 120 meters deep. It is scalding hot, with a temperature of ninety-four degrees centigrade. Ninety-three-degree "Bloody Pond" is a gory vermilion and deeper still, and the source for four popular mud baths.

The people who flock to a Japanese spa such as Beppu do not come necessarily for its therapeutic benefits alone, like visitors to European watering places. Most of them come simply to enjoy the wonderfully relaxing hot baths in delightful conditions not found, to my knowledge, in any other land. In fact, the whole Japanese attitude to bathing is surely unique.

The Japanese are thought to have acquired their habit of soaking in very hot water for pleasure as well as for cleanliness nearly two thousand years ago. Wherever they came from (and this is still a subject of academic controversy), how the early migrants to these islands must have relished the natural hot water they found gushing from rocks throughout the land! No country is so blessed with thermal springs.

Even Japan's wild macaque monkeys (Beppu's Takasaki Hill is one of their habitats) have learnt to

Beppu's hot springs

warm themselves in natural hot-spring ponds. (The *Macaca fuscata* is a particularly intelligent species and the subject of some interesting studies by Japanese scientists.)

The ordinary Japanese bath today is obviously based on those original deep natural outdoor pools brimming over with piping hot-spring water, into which one could thoroughly immerse oneself while contemplating nature's beauty all around. A far cry from the bleakly utilitarian American shower and the full-length British tub, which looks so comfortable but whose vastness defies a satisfactory depth of hot water, leaving much of one's body prey to chilly draughts. Japanese ingenuity has extended even to the poor the luxury of a really hot bath daily. The simplest tub is deep enough for total immersion, feet drawn up; washing oneself outside, the same water does for the whole family; heating the water *in situ* leads to economies both in fuel and water, and plumbing is not essential. Simple basics to happy bathing not available elsewhere. Aesthetic touches are added whenever possible—a tub made of fragrant wood, a view into a garden, however tiny. And at a Japanese inn, whether it be a hot-spring resort or not, the baths are among the most important rooms of all, and all manner of aesthetic refinements are lavished upon them. One does not really know Japan until one has stayed at a Japanese inn and sampled the delights of an *ofuro*.

D.B.

KIRISHIMA–YAKU NATIONAL PARK

Mount Takachiho and Shinmoedake

One should begin a visit to this national park at Kirishima Shrine. Dedicated to the god Ninigi, grandson of the sun goddess, this peaceful Shinto shrine stands on the slopes of Mount Takachiho, deep in a grove of cryptomerias so old they might almost have known Japan's gods. For Takachiho with its twin craters and pointed peak is the very mountain upon which her gods are said to have descended.

According to the *Record of Ancient Matters*: "Then the Heavenly Grandson . . . Ninigi no Mikoto, left his heavenly throne . . . and descended to the earth along the heavenly bridge, pushing through the clouds and . . . came to rest on the peak of . . . Takachiho." The chronicle continues: "Then the Heavenly Grandson said 'This is indeed a wonderful place. The morning sun shines so brightly, and the setting sun glows . . . out unto Kasasa.' " Kasasa has been identified as the present Cape Sata. Japan's "in the beginning" goes back to the early ancestors of the present-day race, ancestors possibly from southern Asia, settling first in Kyushu, then joined by trans-Korean migrants—or invaders—moving eastward to found the Yamato state near Nara.

Crater-pocked, the Kirishima peaks present the sort of lunar landscape easy to associate with the descent of celestial ancestors from the heavens. But it is not all rocks and volcanic rubble: the slopes of the twenty-three craters are lush with verdure and many brim with water of varying hues. Ninigi no Mikoto's cedar-shadowed shrine on the banks of the sibilant Kirishima River is a perfect place to contemplate the kind of

beauty with which these islands of Japan are blessed. Look southward, and you can see in the far distance Kagoshima Bay, whose waters girdle an active volcano crowned with a halo of white smoke. And just north, waiting to be explored, Kirishima's volcanic landscape abounds in lakes, caldera lakes, streams, cascades, forests, and a fantasy of flora.

The highest of the dormant peaks, Karakuni (1,700 meters), affords a superb view across several of the crater lakes to Takachiho, which, like Shinmoedake, still has an active vent. The four principal crater lakes are each colored a different shade depending on the type of volcanic rock beneath. To the northwest lies the 1,200-meter-high Ebino Plateau, with more lakes and groves of Japanese oak and red pine. In May, the pale blossoms of the rare Japanese crab apple (*Malus spontanea Makino*) can be seen among the multitude of interesting plants and flowers for which the region is noted, and everywhere the slopes are vivid in spring and early summer with magenta splashes of wild Kirishima azalea (*Rhododendron kiusianum*).

Excellent highways crisscross the mountains, and a railway line conveniently circles the area, with an airport midway between the Kirishima mountains and the city of Kagoshima. Sprinkled all about the hills and streams are countless spas, where after a day of hiking or traveling by car one may relax luxuriously in beneficent hot-spring baths at some delightful inn. Near Maruo Spa is a waterfall as decorative as a scroll painting. And winter offers special attractions: skating on a crater lake, for example. Byakushi provides this novelty; and the trees in winter are adorned with a phenomenon the Japanese call "frost flowers."

Sakurajima: Volcano in the Back Garden

But the castle town of Kagoshima, south Kyushu's most important city, offers a wonder of an even more spectacular kind: a volcano in its own back garden, right in the middle of the bay. But no tame pet of a volcano this—I remember hearing rumblings the night I spent at a hot-spring inn nestled among the lava boulders at the very foot of the 1,118-meter-high triple-cratered mountain. Its first recorded eruption was in the year 708. There have been scores since then. In 1914, Sakurajima erupted with epoch-making force. Its magnitude would have made world headlines had it not coincided with the outbreak of World War I. Until 1914, the volcano had been completely surrounded by the waters of Kagoshima Bay. But on this occasion, part of the great lava flow choked up the channel on the opposite side from Kagoshima, joining the volcano to the mainland. The channel had been two hundred meters wide and seventy-two meters deep. Now the volcano is a peninsula. But it still retains the name

Sakurajima, meaning "Cherry Tree Island"—possibly because the volcano, in full eruption, resembles a giant cherry three in white-hot molten bloom.

The "island" volcano is a mere twenty-minute ferry ride from Kagoshima. A good road circles it, and a leisurely tour takes about two hours. One side consists mainly of grim, forbidding wildernesses of contorted lava. Signs in Japanese and English give details of the successive lava flows from one or other of the three craters that have gradually built the "island." Only one crater is active now. In one particularly inhospitable lava bed, I saw a tiny pine-tree sapling trying to gain a precarious foothold. Knowing the wind-sown baby pine would have little chance of survival I carefully uprooted it and now it is doing well in the garden of my home on the coast near Kamakura.

On the sheltered northern side of the lava "island," fruit trees flourish. Mandarins, summer oranges, kumquats, loquats. And the rich volcanic soil produces a giant strain of *daikon*, the elongated Japanese turnip. Specimens of this vegetable over a meter in girth and weighing forty-five kilograms are not uncommon! Kirishima *daikon*, pickled in *sake* lees or *miso* (fermented soybean paste) are a favorite local souvenir. At one picturesque little fishing hamlet at the volcano's foot, my eye was caught by clusters of huge, close-woven bamboo baskets. These, I was told, are used to store mackerel fry for bonito bait. They also had enormous wire-netted bamboo cages anchored offshore where they were rearing yellowtail. Their young, called *hamachi*, make a superb *sashimi*.

But I was not sorry to leave Sakurajima's rather disturbing volcanic eminence. I felt happier back in the city, viewing the volcano from Shiroyama (Castle Hill), a public park where once stood the stronghold of the Shimazu clan—one of the leading feudal families, who ruled their large fiefdom for almost seven hundred

years. It was known in olden times as the province of Satsuma, a name familiar to Westerners for its mandarin oranges and famous pottery. The Satsuma lords were innovative men: they were the first to adopt telegraphy, photography, modern glass-making, and cotton spinning. Firearms, too, reached Satsuma first. And so did Christianity. Xavier Park in Kagoshima commemorates the landing in 1549 of Saint Francis Xavier, one of the first Christian missionaries to arrive in Japan.

Looking south from Castle Hill one can see Mount Kaimon, a dormant volcano, standing like a lone sentinel at the tip of the Satsuma Peninsula guarding the narrow entrance to Kagoshima Bay. The people here call Kaimon the Satsuma Fuji, but its cone is, as it were, too perfect to be really attractive. Near it is the popular hot-spring resort of Ibusuki. The forty-five-kilometer trip south from Kagoshima down Kinko (Brocade Inlet) Bay, as Kagoshima Bay is often called, can be made in the same number of minutes, forty-five, by hovercraft.

Inns stand cheek by jowl all along Ibusuki beach. Some contain exotic "jungle baths"—indoor hot-spring pools where guests may relax in the beneficent waters while imagining themselves lost in a tropical rain forest. Most also offer the hot volcanic mud baths which have made Ibusuki famous. A little further south there are bays and inlets to explore, around the small promontory called Nagasakibana. Small pines like

Mount Kaimon

bonsai cling tenaciously to the rocky volcanic outcrops surrounding the promontory with the studied grace of a ballet dancer.

As one wends one's way back to the main highway from Nagasakibana, Mount Kaimon's almost artificially conical, pine-dark profile appears at every turn in a different place, as if it were participating in a game of geographical hide-and-seek. Back on the main road, a right-hand turning through thick pine woods takes one to a charming circular caldera lake noted for the unusual transparency of its waters. This is Lake Ikeda, the largest lake in Kyushu with a circumference of twenty-four kilometers.

Too Many Tips to Kyushu

I was intrigued by the curious insistence of the people here that Nagasakibana was the southernmost tip of Kyushu. The southernmost tip of the Satsuma Peninsula, yes. But surely, according to my map, Cape Sata at the end of the Osumi Peninsula on the other side of Kagoshima Bay extended at least another twenty kilometers south into the Pacific? But they were adamant. Later, crossing over from Yamakawa to the small town of Sata on the opposite cape, I began to understand why.

The ferry across the mouth of the bay runs infrequently and is obviously not geared to the tourist trade. Sata port is a dreary place, mostly used for loading pine logs and camphor wood. The good, scenic coastal road ends there, and most of the twenty-odd kilometers to the wild, rocky promontory—the true southernmost tip of Kyushu—is through rough, hilly country. The people of Sata seemed quite content to let the opportunists across the water boast about their being on the "southernmost tip" in their tourist brochures. But the ambitious are rewarded when they

Yaku Island's mountainous interior

explore the real south tip, with its exotic "jungles" of Chinese fan palm (*Livistonia chinensis*). Sata's best inn was bleak and draughty in the gale that arose when I was there. Unable to sleep for the rattling of ill-fitting shutters, I mused on the different use of certain words in different languages. In Britain, we are constantly talking about "fresh air" as something that needs letting in. In Japanese houses the problem is keeping it out.

The sea was too rough for the ferry on the following morning, so I drove back to Kagoshima along the high precipitous coast road on the Osumi Peninsula side of the bay, with a detour across to Uchi-no-ura on the Pacific coast where the air was redolent with the smell of camphor—the main industry being lumber, principally camphor wood. Back along the bay, the beaches were white with pumice—a reminder of their volcanic nature; for the bay itself was formed by the submergence of two calderas.

Ancient Arboreal Giants

This national park has one more wonder in store. On the map, Kagoshima Bay, with its two peninsulas, resembles the thumb and forefinger of a hand holding firmly a jewel, the volcano "isle" of Sakurajima. But a much larger jewel appears to have just slipped out of the grip of these fingers: the island of Yaku. Round as a large pearl, or a cannonball, it lies near long, flat Tanegashima, the island that gave its name to the matchlock musket in Japanese. For the first firearms to arrive in Japan were the property of three shipwrecked Portuguese who drifted ashore on this island in 1543.

Yaku Island, now also accessible by air, is a four-hour ferry trip from Kagoshima. This great mountainous cluster of peaks soars almost straight up from the warm Pacific to a height of 1,935 meters. Ninety percent of the island consists of mountains, remarkable for their primeval forests of *sugi*, or great cedars (*Cryptomeria japonica*), some of which grow to an immense height. The cedar is now a nationally protected tree in Japan. The cedars of Yaku (*Yaku-sugi*) are mostly over one thousand years old, and their wood has been prized for centuries for its fine-grained rings. Trees less than a thousand years old are not called *Yaku-sugi*, but simply "young cedars"! This small island, only a hundred kilometers in circumference, presents a dramatically wide climatic range. Skiing on its snowy hilltops may be followed thirty minutes later by sunbathing on its subtropical beaches, a fact the tourist industry is now busily promoting. But promoters still have one snag to combat—a local saying has it that on Yaku Island it rains thirty-five days in every month.

D.B.

IRIOMOTE NATIONAL PARK

A typical Okinawan tiled roof

Having lived in Tokyo where it sometimes seems as if all forms of life are about to be buried under a layer of concrete, I think of Iriomote as Japan's secret "tropical" paradise. One of the southernmost islands of the Ryukyu chain in Okinawa Prefecture, this island, with an area of 322 square kilometers, lies just one degree north of the Tropic of Cancer. Plunging down through the refreshing, clear waters surrounding Iriomote to explore its coral gardens was a wonderful change from diving down into the noise and clamor of Tokyo's subways.

I spent the first days snorkeling in the reef off Sonae, a tiny fishing hamlet. A random group of visitors, including myself, persuaded a local boatman to take us where the coral was most spectacular. The barrier reef which surrounds Iriomote has become hollow in many places, forming submarine canyons and caves—shimmering shapes and colors recall the underwater sea kingdom depicted in the Japanese fairy tale Urashima Taro. No aquarium exhibit can prepare one for the exhilaration of gliding through an enchanted marine garden of blue and gold.

Nestling among the fronds of seaweed were hosts of scallops and we pried open as many as we thought we could eat. One of my more experienced companions used a homemade spear, going after what looked to be the juiciest fish—not necessarily the most exotically colored. He persistently shook his head in answer to my gestures of encouragement, studiously refraining from stabbing at black scaleless stonefish or slow-moving blowfish emerging from behind staghorn and

fan coral like actors coming on stage. Despite their sluggish appearance, both these species are highly poisonous.

The local doctor, a sprightly gentleman in his sixties, treated my inevitable sunburn and a few patches of skin grazed by coral. He was the only doctor on this side of the island, looking after more than seven hundred people, and spoke as proudly of Iriomote, his "retirement" home, as he did of his native Kyoto where he had long practiced. To keep me out of the brilliant sunshine on the beach, he prescribed an easy one-day trek up the Urauchi River to the Mariyudo and Kanpira falls, the natural habitat of the Iriomote Wildcat.

Naturalists estimate there are about thirty to forty wildcats on Iromote, and with so few left they are on the point of extinction. This housecat-sized animal is nocturnal as well as being rare, with the result that it is scarcely seen even by islanders. The Iriomote Wildcat is of particular interest to zoologists. One of the most primitive of all the cat species, this animal is a "living fossil"; it has hardly changed its form for the last five to ten million years. The Iriomote Wildcat has been designated a Special Natural Living Monument, and visitors' general curiosity about it has made it the unofficial symbol of the island.

Journey into the Interior

As much for companionship and safety as for economy, the morning I chose for my trip up the Urauchi I waited in a thatched rustic shelter at the mouth of the river for tourists making a day trip from Ishigaki Island. Finally there were enough of us, twelve in all, to fill one boat and we took our places, weighing it down so much that the gunnels were only just above the surface of the water. Our boatman, his hand on the controls of the small chugging motor, headed the craft up river. We were entering a primitive, viridian world. The waters of this tidal river were a thick, dull bottle green, a total contrast to the clear blue of the ocean. The boatman warned us that young sharks liked to bask in the briny tidal flats.

The riverbanks were overgrown with dense mangroves; further inland were wild pineapple trees with small stunted fruit and stiff spiky leaves. Our little group must have looked like a band of explorers, complete with standard-bearers, although our standards were nothing more than long-poled butterfly nets held aloft, their white gauze waving softly like flags as we made for the interior.

After half an hour or so, the first part of our excursion ended abruptly at some rapids. The boatman anchored in midstream and we had to skip from boulder to boulder to reach firm ground. A forty-minute climb would bring us to the two waterfalls. Leaving the mangroves behind us, we walked single file along a narrow, spongy path through the jungle. The path itself was relatively clear, but foliage made a canopy overhead and vines crisscrossed like loose-hung skeins of thread. More than once I stumbled on stumps of large sappanwood trees, like giant webbed hands gripping the earth. Our boatman-cum-guide rapped lightly on one as we passed by, and the sound suggested that the wood was light and porous. Long, long ago, he said, islanders carved dugouts from these trees. They also made boats of Ryukyu pines, which we found growing in great numbers in the jungle.

The largest animals we saw were brilliantly plumed birds, land crabs, and a few small snakes, but none of the notorious, deadly *habu*, one of Japan's few poisonous snakes, found only in the Ryukyu and Amami islands. Once or twice I mistook white and pale-colored butterflies for tiny rays of light filtering through the dense green foliage. But the lepidopterists were quickly up and after them with their nets.

We emerged above the Mariyudo Falls, which drop in three stages some thirty meters into a dark deep pool, closely surrounded by thick groups of cycads and giant ferns. For the best part of the year, the river flows over only two-thirds of the width of its bed, so we were able to step off the bank onto the dry bed to view the falls. With some effort, I managed to scramble down from the top to a natural platform halfway

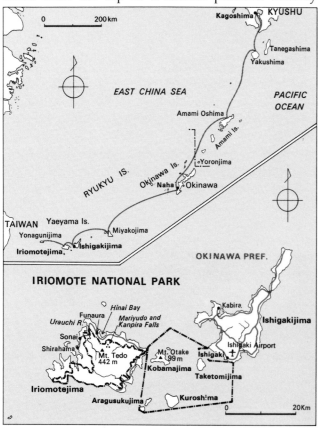

down the falls, and from there I worked my way behind the veil of the water which pours over a sizable ledge.

Kanpira, not far up the path from the Mariyudo Falls, is not a waterfall in the usual sense. Here, for most of the year, the river is hardly more than a stream, running over a gentle incline of about a hundred meters. But it is the riverbed that attracts one's attention. It is a bed of smooth undulating rock shot through with potholes that look like rows of tragic masks, open-mouthed and silent. How the power of water or wind had shaped these perfectly drilled shafts, I could not guess. Some were dry and shallow, while others appeared to be natural wells.

Weaving Beauty into Austerity

The island of Taketomi is also part of Iriomote National Park. This almost spherical island is more popular with tourists than primeval Iriomote not only because it is more accessible, but also because of its more manageable size. Its circumference is only twelve kilometers.

The absolute cleanliness and old-fashioned order of its one tiny village is an invitation to explore, and the apparent security of being well within sight of the so-called mainland of Ishigaki Island makes one feel that in a day's visit one can discover all there is in comfort. This is not the case, of course, but the initial impression of simplicity is one of Taketomi's lures.

I cycled around the village through streets lined with walls of coral rock, bleached white under the piercing sun, and past hedges of bougainvillea bright with mauve pink blossoms. Once or twice I passed women who had taken their weaving work to the streets. One was stringing freshly dyed thread onto pegs set in the coral-rock walls of the family compound, while another reeled thread, spread out on the dusty street in taut lines of several tens of yards.

Behind the coral-rock walls are traditional Okinawan wood-walled houses raised a meter or so off the ground and facing south to minimize the discomfort of the northern winter winds. The average house comprises two front rooms for living, eating and sleeping (into one of which the family shrine is installed), one back room, and a dirt-floor kitchen at ground level. If the roof is tiled (some are thatched), it will be in red, with strips of white cement joining the tiles, anchoring them firmly to withstand typhoon winds. There are also clay figures of lions on the roof to protect the house from evil spirits. I was told that formerly tiles were molded and baked at the site where a house was being built, and that the lions were slapped together with leftover clay. Because each was unique, there was a wide range of posture and fierceness of expression, but mass production of tiles has made this practice obsolete. Now the lions all have the same snarl.

It is difficult to get a good look at a traditional Okinawan house without an invitation to enter the compound because a screenlike barrier is built just inside the gap in the compound wall. This arrangement, which resembles the first stage of a maze, is not only for privacy, but also to keep out evil spirits which are believed to be able to travel only in straight lines.

The population of Taketomi is around three hundred. Most families work at subsistence farming, by hand or with water buffalo as beasts of burden. Many islanders are also involved in *minsa* weaving. The technique and style of *minsa* dates back to the seventeenth century, and the fabrics produced are of cotton, hemp, silk, and plantain. Just as their forebears did, the weavers today use natural dyes. One shade of blue, for example, comes from wild indigo; a striking clear yellow, from the bark of an indigenous tree called *fukugi*. Originally young girls wove small strips in the *minsa* style as amulets for their fiancés, most of whom were fishermen or sailors. It is said that the four-star and five-star patterns symbolize the spread of the tropical heavens, and a complicated single-line pattern called "centipede" holds the message, "Come back, come back to me, in this world and the next."

Today, *minsa* is woven out of a sense of duty to maintain the craft. The output is not great and emphasis is put on smaller items such as sashes, belts, and handbags, which visitors buy. The textiles are produced by a cooperative, with individuals working either at home or on looms at the Folk Art Museum in the village, depending on the step of production they are involved with.

The occupation of weaving on Taketomi did not always exist under such relaxed conditions. From the early seventeenth century to the late nineteenth century, the Ryukyu kingdom, though independent in name, had in fact bowed to the sovereignty of the powerful feudal lords of Satsuma in southern Kyushu and to the Chinese court. The tributary goods which the Okinawans had to pay their two overlords came in large part from the outer islands such as Taketomi, Iriomote, and Ishigaki, while the craft center at Shuri Castle in Naha, the capital, catered to the needs of the native Okinawan court. The suffering and privation the islanders endured to meet the intolerably heavy "taxes" is the source of many sad folk tales and songs of tragedy. One of the best known of such songs is Taketomi's famous "Asadoya Yunta," an old lilting ballad about a young man's ill-fated love for Kuyama, the beautiful daughter of the island's prominent Asadoya family. *Yunta* were "plaiting songs" sung while making mats and baskets of palm fronds and vines.

The Iriomote Wildcat

These days, tourism play an important part in Taketomi's economy. In addition to the charm of the village, there are some wide, spectacularly white, sandy beaches facing shallow, protected waters. Urban sun-worshippers on holiday come across from Ishigaki for the day and make believe they are castaways.

Like many of the southern Ryukyu Islands, Taketomi has its *hoshisuna* (star-sand) beach. This sand is to be found in pockets of exposed coral rock. If you separate a few grains from the rest, you will see that they are in fact miniature five-pointed stars. These are fossils of a tiny sea creature. Tourists have carried away just about all the star-sand there is on Taketomi, but for a modest price you can purchase a teaspoonful. For a bit of extra cash, local people on other islands where visitors are few prepare souvenir pouches of sand. The packet I bought contained the message "Star-sand brings good luck," and I asked whether this was a traditional belief. My question brought a wide smile and the reply that it probably had to do with public relations.

I marveled at life as I saw it both on Taketomi and Iriomote. The bare necessities are not easy to come by and there is a minimum of vanity. The people of these islands have responded to the land and the sea by accommodating themselves to nature rather than resisting it—straw hats and baskets are woven from screw pines; huge clay pots from local pits are for catching rain water or for boiling yams; and the roads and paths of crushed white coral have been taken from the sea. Their approach is not naive, but rather one that complements and reflects the power of the natural world which surrounds them. And although there is much that separates the Ryukyu Islands from the rest of the country, both in terms of culture and geography, this approach to life epitomizes the very best of traditional Japanese ideas of nature and man's position in the natural world.

M.S.

TRAVEL INFORMATION

*All times for trains, buses, and ferries are for expresses or special expresses and are approximate.

*Tokyo, Ueno, Shinjuku, Ikebukuro are all main line railway station in Tokyo.

*Private railways are denoted by the letters "RR."

*All flights from Tokyo leave from Haneda Airport.

NORTH JAPAN

Flights from Tokyo for Hokkaido:

1. Tokyo–Sapporo (Chitose); 1 hr 25 min; 25 flights a day.
   Chitose Airport–Sapporo City, 80 min by bus.
   (for Rishiri–Rebun–Sarobetsu, Daisetsuzan, Shikotsu-Toya parks)
2. Tokyo–Kushiro; 1 hr 45 min; 6 flights a day.
   Kushiro Airport–Kushiro City, 45 min by bus.
   (for Shiretoko, Akan parks)
3. Tokyo–Memanbetsu; 3 hr 15 min; 1 flight a day.
   Memanbetsu Airport–Abashiri City, 45 min by bus.
   (for Shiretoko, Akan parks)
4. Tokyo–Asahikawa; 2 hr 50 min; 3 flights a day.
   Asahikawa Airport–Asahikawa City, 30 min by bus.
   (for Rishiri–Rebun–Sarobetsu, Daisetsuzan parks)
5. Tokyo–Obihiro; 2 hr 40 min; 4 flights a day.
   Obihiro Airport–Obihiro City, 20 min by bus.
   (for Daisetsuzan park)
6. Tokyo–Hakodate; 1 hr 25 min; 6 flights a day.
   Hakodate Airport–Hakodate City, 20 min by bus.
   (for Shikotsu–Toya park)

Rishiri–Rebun–Sarobetsu National Park

RISHIRI—Washidomari: 3 hr by ship from Wakkanai port.
  —Rishiri Airport: 20 min by air, 1 flight a day from Wakkanai (1 hr from Sapporo by air, 1 flight a day; or JNR Soya Main Line, 8 hr from Sapporo).

REBUN—Funadomari: 3½ hr by ship from Wakkanai port.
  —Rebun Airport: 20 min by air, 1 flight a day from Wakkanai.

SAROBETSU—Wakkasakanai: 20 min by bus from Toyoumi (JNR Soya Main Line, 50 min from Wakkanai).

Shiretoko National Park

RAUSU—40 min by bus from Nemuroshibetsu (JNR Shibetsu Line, 2 hr 50 min from Kushiro).
  —4 hr by bus from Kushiro.

UTORO—1½ hr by bus from Shari (JNR Senmo Main Line, 2½ hr from Kushiro or 30 min from Abashiri).

SHIRETOKO FIVE LAKES—2 hr by bus from Shari.

Akan National Park

LAKE AKAN—2 hr by bus from Kushiro.
  —1½ hr by bus from Teshikaga (JNR Senmo Main Line, 1 hr 15 min from Kushiro).
  —40 min by bus from Kitami Aioi (JNR Aioi Line, 1 hr from Bihoro).

LAKE KUSSHARO—10 min by bus from Kawayu (JNR Senmo Main Line, 1 hr 45 min from Kushiro).
  —2 hr 45 min by bus from Bihoro (JNR Sekihoku Main Line, 3½ hr from Asahikawa).

LAKE MASHU—1 hr by bus from Teshikaga.

Daisetsuzan National Park

TENNINKYO—1 hr by bus from Asahikawa Airport.
  —1 hr 45 min by bus from Asahikawa (JNR Hakodate Main Line).
  —1 hr 50 min by bus from Sapporo.

SOUNKYO—2 hr by bus from Asahikawa.
  —1 hr by bus from Kamikawa (JNR Sekihoku Main Line, 1 hr from Asahikawa).

SHIKARIBETSU SPA—1 hr by bus from Nukabira (JNR Shihoro Line, 1 hr 45 min from Obihiro).

Shikotsu–Toya National Park

LAKE SHIKOTSU—45 min by bus from Chitose Airport (Sapporo).
  —1 hr 20 min by bus from Sapporo Station.
  —45 min by bus from Tomakomai (JNR Muroran Main Line, 1 hr from Sapporo).

JOZANKEI—1 hr by bus from Sapporo.

MT. YOTEI—15 min by bus from Kutchian (JNR Hakodate Main Line, 3½ hr from Hakodate).

LAKE TOYA—15 min by bus from Toya (JNR Muroran Main Line, 2 hr from Hakodate).
  —20 min by bus from Sobetsu (JNR Iburi Line, 15 min from Datemonbetsu).
  —2 hr 40 min by bus from Sapporo (via Jozankei).

NOBORIBETSU SPA—15 min by bus from Noboribetsu (JNR Muroran Main Line, 1½ hr from Sapporo).

Towada–Hachimantai National Park

LAKE TOWADA—Yasumiya: 3½ hr by bus (via Tsuta Spa) from Aomori (JNR Tohoku Main Line, 9 hr from Ueno).
  —1 hr 50 min by bus from Towada-shi (Towada Kanko RR, 25 min from Misawa).
  —1 hr 10 min from Towada Minami (JNR Hanawa Line, 2 hr from Morioka).

HACHIMANTAI—1½ hr by bus from Hachimantai Station (JNR Hanawa Line, 1 hr 45 min from Morioka) via Goshogake, Fuke spas.
  —1 hr by bus from Morioka.

Rikuchu Kaigan National Park

KUROSAKI—1½ hr by bus from Kuji (JNR Hachinohe Line, 1 hr 50 min from Hachinohe).

JODOGAHAMA—20 min by bus from Miyako (JNR Yamada Line, 2 hr from Morioka or 3 hr from Hanamaki).

KESENNUMA—JNR Ofunato Line, 1 hr from Ichinoseki (JNR Tohoku Main Line, 2 hr from Sendai) via Geibi Gorge.

Tokyo–Hanamaki by air; 1½ hr; 3 flights a day.
  Hanamaki Airport–Hanamaki City, 15 min by bus.
  Hanamaki Airport–Morioka City, 70 min by bus.

Bandai–Asahi National Park

MT. BANDAI—3½ hr by bus from Fukushima (JNR Tohoku Main Line, 3½ hr from Ueno).
  —1 hr 20 min by bus from Aizu Wakamatsu (JNR

Banetsu West Line, 1 hr from Koriyama, or 5 hr from Ueno).

—45 min by bus from Inawashiro (JNR Banetsu West Line, 40 min from Koriyama).

LAKE INAWASHIRO—20 min by bus from Aizu Wakamatsu.

—10 min by bus from Inawashiro.

MT. HAGURO—1 hr by bus from Tsuruoka (JNR Uetsu Main Line, 3 hr from Akita or 3 hr from Niigata).

MT. GASSAN—2 hr by bus from Tsuruoka.

MT. YUDONO—1 hr 40 min by bus from Tsuruoka.

CENTRAL JAPAN
Nikko National Park
NIKKO—Tobu RR, 1½ hr from Asakusa, Tokyo; or JNR Nikko Line, 2 hr 10 min from Ueno.

LAKE CHUZENJI—50 min by bus from Nikko.

SHIOBARA SPA—1½ hr by bus from Kinugawa Onsen (2 hr from Asakusa by Tobu RR).

—50 min by bus from Nishi Nasuno (JNR Tohoku Main Line, 2 hr 10 min from Ueno).

OZE MARSHLANDS—1 hr 50 min by bus from Numata (JNR Joetsu Line, 2½ hr from Ueno).

Joshinetsu Kogen National Park
MT. TANIGAWA—30 min by bus from Minakami (JNR Joetsu Line, 2 hr 10 min from Ueno).

KARUIZAWA—JNR Shinetsu Main Line, 2½ hr from Ueno.

MT. ASAMA—30 min by bus from Karuizawa.

—2½ hr by bus from Naganohara (JNR Agatsuma Line, 2 hr 50 min from Ueno).

SHIGA HIGHLANDS—40 min by bus from Yudanaka (Nagano RR, 45 min from Nagano).

—1½ hr by bus from Naganohara.

MYOKO HIGHLANDS—5 min by bus from Myoko Kogen (JNR Shinetsu Main Line, 4½ hr from Ueno).

LAKE NOJIRI—20 min by bus from Myoko Kogen.

MT. TOGAKUSHI—1 hr 10 min by bus from Nagano (JNR Shinetsu Main Line, 3 hr 20 min from Ueno).

Chichibu–Tama National Park
CHICHIBU—Seibu RR, 1 hr 20 min from Ikebukuro.

MITSUMINE-GUCHI—Chichibu RR, 20 min from Chichibu.

LAKE CHICHIBU—30 min by bus from Mitsumine-guchi.

LAKE OKUTAMA—20 min by bus from Okutama (JNR Ome Line, 1 hr from Tachikawa).

SHOSENKYO—30 min by bus from Kofu (JNR Chuo Main Line, 1 hr 50 min from Shinjuku).

Fuji–Hakone–Izu National Park
MT. FUJI (Fifth Station)—50 min by bus from Kawaguchi-ko (Fuji Kyuko RR, 1 hr from Otsuki; Shinjuku–Otsuki, JNR Chuo Main Line, 1 hr 15 min).

—50 min by bus from Gotenba (JNR Gotenba Line, 1 hr 50 min from Shinjuku; or 2 hr from Tokyo Station).

—2 hr by bus from Mishima (1 hr from Tokyo Station by JNR Shinkansen).

—3 hr by Chuo Express bus from Hamamatsucho (Tokyo) via Shinjuku (30 min), Lake Kawaguchi (2 hr 15 min), Lake Yamanaka (2 hr 30 min).

LAKE KAWAGUCHI—Fuji Kyuko RR, 1 hr from Otsuki.

—40 min by bus from Kofu (JNR Chuo Main Line, 1 hr 50 min from Shinjuku).

—1 hr 15 min by bus from Gotenba.

LAKE YAMANAKA—2 hr by bus from Odawara (40 min from Tokyo Station by JNR Shinkansen; or Odakyu RR, 1 hr 15 min from Shinjuku).

HAKONE YUMOTO—Odakyu RR, 1½ hr from Shinjuku.

—15 min by bus from Odawara.

ASHINOKO—40 min by bus from Odawara.

ITO—JNR Ito Line, 1 hr 50 min from Tokyo Station.

SHIMODA—Izu Kyuko RR, 2 hr 40 min from Tokyo Station.

SHUZENJI—Izu Hakone RR, 40 min from Mishima.

DOGASHIMA—2 hr 20 min by bus from Mishima.

—1 hr 45 min by bus from Shuzenji.

—1 hr by bus from Shimoda.

OSHIMA—7 hr by ship from Takeshiba pier, Tokyo.

—1 hr 40 min by ferry from Atami (60 min from Tokyo Station by JNR Shinkansen).

—1 hr 40 min by ferry from Ito.

Tokyo–Oshima by air; 40 min; 2 flights a day.

NIIJIMA—9 hr by ship from Takeshiba pier, Tokyo.

—2 hr 50 min by ship from Atami.

SHIKINEJIMA—10 hr by ship from Takeshiba pier, Tokyo.

MIYAKEJIMA—7 hr by ship from Takeshiba pier, Tokyo.

Tokyo–Miyakejima by air; 55 min; 2 flights a day.

HACHIJOJIMA—10 hr by ship from Takeshiba pier, Tokyo.

Tokyo–Hachijojima by air; 1 hr 5 min; 6 flights a day.

Ship departure dates depend on time of year.

Ogasawara National Park
CHICHIJIMA—Futami Bay: 30 hr by ship from Takeshiba pier, Tokyo.

Departure date depends on time of year.

Chubu Sangaku National Park
TATEYAMA AREA—1 hr by bus from Bijodaira (10 min by cable car from Tateyama: Toyama Chiho RR, 50 min from Toyama).

SHIROUMA, HAPPOONE AREA—45 min by bus from Shinano Omachi, Yanaba, Hakuba, or Hakuba Oike (JNR Oito Line, 5 hr–5½ hr from Shinjuku).

KAMIKOCHI—1½ hr by bus from Shinshimajima (Matsumoto RR, 35 min from Matsumoto).

—2½ hr by bus from Kiso Fukushima (JNR Chuo Main Line, 2 hr 10 min from Nagano).

NORIKURA AREA—1 hr 40 min by bus from Takayama (JNR Takayama Line, 3 hr from Nagoya).

Tokyo–Toyama by air; 1 hr 50 min; 4 flights a day.

Toyama Airport–Toyama City, 20 min by bus.

Minami Alps National Park
YASHAJIN PASS—1 hr 20 min by bus from Kofu (JNR Chuo Main Line, 1 hr 50 min from Shinjuku).

HIROKAWARA—2 hr from Kofu by bus.

—2 hr by bus from Minobu (JNR Minobu Line, 1 hr from Kofu).

KASHIO—40 min by bus from Ina Oshima (JNR Iida Line, 4 hr 50 min from Shinjuku).

Ise–Shima National Park

ISE OUTER SHRINE—7 min walk from Ise-shi (JNR Sangu Line, 1 hr 45 min from Nagoya).

ISE INNER SHRINE—20 min by bus from Ise-shi.

TOBA—JNR Sangu Line, 40 min from Taki (JNR Kise Main Line, 1½ hr from Nagoya).

KASHIKOJIMA—Kintetsu RR, 2 hr from Nagoya.

Yoshino–Kumano National Park

MT. YOSHINO—3 min by cable car from Yoshino (Kintetsu RR, 1 hr 40 min from Kyoto; or 1 hr 15 min from Abenobashi, Osaka).

ODAIGAHARA—2 hr 20 min by bus from Yamato Kamiichi (Kintetsu RR, 1 hr 10 min from Osaka).

DORO GORGE—Shiko: 30 min by bus from Shingu (JNR Kise Main Line, 3 hr 50 min from Nagoya).

NACHI FALLS—30 min by bus from Katsuura (JNR Kise Main Line, 3 hr 50 min from Nagoya).

HASHIKUI-IWA—5 min by bus from Kushimoto (JNR Kise Main Line, 1 hr from Shingu or 4 hr from Osaka).

SHIONOMISAKI—20 min by bus from Kushimoto.

Tokyo–Shirahama by air; 1 hr 45 min; 2 flights a day.
   Shirahama Airport–Shirahama, 20 min by bus.

Hakusan National Park

TEDORI GORGE—1 hr by bus from Kanazawa (Kenrokuen-shita).

BETTO DEAI—1½ hr by bus from Hakusan-shita (Hokuriku RR, 1 hr 20 min from Nomachi, Kanazawa).

HAKUSAN SPA—1 hr by bus from Hakusan-shita.

Tokyo–Komatsu by air; 1 hr 5 min; 4 flights a day.
   Komatsu Airport–Kanazawa City, 50 min by bus.

SOUTH JAPAN

Seto Naikai National Park

AWAJI ISLAND—Iwaya port: 25 min by ferry from Akashi (JNR Sanyo Main Line, 50 min from Osaka).

—Sumoto Port: 1 hr 40 min by ferry from Osaka port.

SHODO ISLAND—1 hr 15 min by ferry from Okayama port.
   —1½ hr by ferry from Uno (JNR Uno Line, 30 min from Okayama).
   —1 hr by ferry from Takamatsu.

MIYAJIMA—10 min by ferry from Miyajima-guchi (JNR Sanyo Main Line, 20 min from Hiroshima)

There are numerous ferries connecting mainland ports with islands.

Major ports are: Osaka, Kobe, Akashi, Okayama, Uno, Fukuyama, Onomichi, Mihara, Kure, Hiroshima, Tokuyama, Takamatsu, Marukame, Niihama, Imabari, Matsuyama.

Tokyo–Takamatsu by air; 2 hr 5 min; 4 flights a day.
   Takamatsu Airport–Takamatsu City, 30 min by bus.

Tokyo–Okayama by air; 2 hr; 2 flights a day.
   Okayama Airport–Okayama City, 35 min by bus.

Tokyo–Hiroshima by air; 2 hr 25 min; 6 flights a day.
   Hiroshima Airport–Hiroshima City, 30 min by bus.

Tokyo–Tokushima by air; 1 hr 55 min; 3 flights a day.
   Tokushima Airport–Tokushima City, 30 min by bus.

Tokyo–Matsuyama by air; 1 hr 20 min; 6 flights a day.
   Matsuyama Airport–Matsuyama City, 20 min by bus.

Ashizuri–Uwakai National Park

CAPE ASHIZURI—1½ hr by bus from Nakamura (JNR Nakamura Line, 2 hr 30 min from Kochi).

TATSUKUSHI—20 min by bus from Tosa Shimizu (1 hr by bus from Nakamura).
   —2 hr by bus from Sukumo (2 hr by bus from Uwajima).

UWAJIMA—JNR Yodo Line, 6 hr 40 min from Matsuyama.

Tokyo–Kochi by air; 2 hr 10 min; 3 flights a day.
   Kochi Airport–Kochi City, 30 min by bus.

Sanin Kaigan National Park

TOTTORI SAND DUNES—20 min by bus from Tottori (JNR Sanin Main Line, 4 hr from Kyoto).

URADOME COAST—10 min by bus from Iwami (JNR Sanin Main Line, 20 min from Tottori).

TAJIMA COAST, MEGANE DOMON, YOROI-NO-SODE—sightseeing boats leave from Kasumi.

GENBU CAVE—20 min by bus from Toyooka (JNR Sanin Main Line, 2½ hr from Kyoto).

Tokyo–Tottori by air; 2 hr; 2 flights a day.
   Tottori Airport–Tottori City, 25 min by bus.

Daisen–Oki National Park

MT. DAISEN—50 min by bus from Yonago (JNR Sanin Main Line, 5½ hr from Osaka).

HIRUZEN HIGHLANDS—1 hr by bus from Yonago.

MIHONOSEKI—1 hr 20 min by bus from Matsue (JNR Sanin Main Line, 6 hr from Osaka).

IZUMO TAISHA—25 min by bus from Izumo (JNR Sanin Main Line, 6 hr 50 min from Osaka).

HINOSAKI—30 min by bus from Taisha (Ichibata RR, 20 min from Izumo).

SANBE SPA—45 min by bus from Ota (JNR Sanin Main Line, 30 min from Izumo).

OKI ISLES—Saigo: 2 hr 50 min by ship from Sakai Minato (JNR Sakai Line, 45 min from Yonago).
   —Urago: 2½ hr by ship from Sakai Minato.

Yonago–Oki by air; 25 min; 1 flight a day.

Tokyo–Yonago by air; 2 hr 15 min; 3 flights a day.
   Yonago Airport–Yonago City, 30 min by bus.

Flights from Tokyo for Kyushu:
1. Tokyo–Fukuoka; 1½ hr; 18 flights a day.
   Fukuoka Airport–Fukuoka City, 30 min by bus.
   (for Saikai, Unzen–Amakusa parks)
2. Tokyo–Nagasaki (Omura); 1 hr 50 min; 5 flights a day.
   Omura Airport–Nagasaki City, 65 min by bus.
   (for Saikai, Unzen–Amakusa parks)
3. Tokyo–Kumamoto; 1 hr 45 min; 5 flights a day.
   Kumamoto Airport–Kumamoto City, 45 min by bus.
   (for Unzen–Amakusa, Aso parks)
4. Tokyo–Oita; 1 hr 45 min; 5 flights a day.
   Oita Airport–Oita City, 90 min by bus.
   Oita Airport–Beppu City, 60 min by bus.
   (for Aso park)
5. Tokyo–Kagoshima; 1 hr 40 min; 8 flights a day.

Kagoshima Airport–Kagoshima City, 60 min by bus. (for Kirishima–Yaku park)

Saikai National Park

HIRADO ISLAND—15 min by ferry from Hirado-guchi (JNR Omura Line, 2 hr 45 min from Nagasaki; or JNR Matsuura Line, 2½ hr from Hakata, Fukuoka).

—1 hr 20 min by bus from Sasebo (JNR Omura Line, 1 hr 40 min from Nagasaki).

—1 hr by ferry from Kashimae Sanbashi (30 min by bus from Sasebo) via Kujukushima.

GOTO CHAIN—Fukue: 12 hr by ship from Hakata; or 3½ hr by ship from Nagasaki.

Nagasaki–Fukue by air; 35 min; 3 flights a day.

Unzen–Amakusa National Park

UNZEN—2 hr 20 min by bus from Nagasaki (JNR Nagasaki Main Line, 3 hr from Hakata, Fukuoka).

—1 hr 20 min by bus from Isahaya (JNR Nagasaki Main Line, 30 min from Nagasaki).

—50 min by bus from Shimabara (Shimabara RR, 1 hr from Isahaya).

AMAKUSA—Hondo: 2 hr 20 min by bus from Kumamoto (JNR Kagoshima Main Line, 1 hr 40 min from Hakata, Fukuoka).

—Tomioka: 1 hr 10 min by bus from Hondo.

—Sakitsu: 1 hr 30 min by bus from Tomioka.

Aso National Park

MT. ASO—40 min by bus from Aso Station (JNR Hohi Main Line, 1 hr 20 min from Kumamoto).

YUFU-IN—JNR Kyudai Main Line, 1 hr from Oita.

—1 hr by bus from Beppu (JNR Nippo Main Line, 10 min from Oita).

MT. KUJU—1 hr by bus from Yufu-in.

Kirishima–Yaku National Park

SAKURAJIMA—15 min by ferry from Kagoshima Port (10 min by bus from Kagoshima).

MT. KAIMON—30 min by bus from Yamakawa (JNR Ibusuki Makurazaki Line, 1 hr from Nishi Kagoshima).

NAGASAKIBANA—20 min by bus from Yamakawa.

EBINO PLATEAU—2 hr by bus from Miyazaki (JNR Nippo Main Line, 2 hr 15 min from Kagoshima or 3 hr 15 min from Oita).

YAKU ISLAND—3½ hr by ship from Kagoshima Port.

Kagoshima–Yaku by air; 40 min; 2 flights a day.

Iriomote National Park

IRIOMOTE ISLAND—Ohara: 1 hr by ferry from Ishigaki (55 min by air from Naha, 8 flights a day).

—Funaura: 1 hr by ferry from Ishigaki.

—Shirahama: 2 hr 45 min by ferry from Ishigaki.

TAKETOMI—20 min by ferry from Ishigaki

Tokyo–Okinawa (Naha) by air; 2½ hr; 7 flights a day. Naha Airport–Naha City, 15 min by bus.

For further information, contact:
Japan Travel Bureau (JTB), tel. (03) 270–0372.
For details on travel to the Ogasawara Islands, contact:
Ogasawara Travel Center (Tokyo office), tel. (03) 452–3441.

Asahi Shimbun. *This is Japan*. Vols. 1–18. Tokyo: Asahi Shimbun Newspaper Publishing Co., 1954–1971.

Bird, Isabella L. *Unbeaten Tracks in Japan: An Account of Travels on Horseback in the Interior Including Visits to the Aborigines of Yezo and the Shrines of Nikko and Ise*. 1880. Reprint. Tokyo: Charles E. Tuttle Co., 1975.

Blacker, Carmen. *The Catalpa Bow: A Study of Shamanistic Practices in Japan*. London: George Allen and Unwin, 1975.

Britton, Dorothy. *A Haiku Journey: Basho's "Narrow Road to a Far Province."* Tokyo: Kodansha International, 1975 and (paperback) 1980.

———. *20 Folksongs of Japan*. Tokyo: Radio Japan, NHK; 1969.

Cocks, Richard. *Diary of Richard Cocks, Cape-Merchant in the English Factory in Japan*. Edited by N. Murakami. 2 vols. 1899. Reprint (3 vols.). Tokyo: Tokyo Daigaku Shiryo Hensanjo, 1978–.

Cooper, Michael. "The Second Englishman in Japan." *Transactions of the Asiatic Society of Japan*, in press.

Fujishima, Gaijiro, ed. *Nikko*. Tokyo: Kokusai Johosha, 1975.

Hearn, Lafcadio. *Glimpses of Unfamiliar Japan*. 1894. Reprint. Tokyo: Charles E. Tuttle Co., 1974.

Hisamatsu, Sen'ichi, ed. *Biographical Dictionary of Japanese Literature*. Tokyo: Kodansha International, 1976. (Translation of *haiku* by Issa.)

Japan National Tourist Organization. *All About Mount Fuji*. Tokyo: Japan Travel Bureau, 1963.

———. *The New Official Guide: Japan*. Tokyo: Japan Travel Bureau, 1975.

Keene, Donald. *Modern Japanese Literature*. Tokyo: Charles E. Tuttle Co., 1957. (Translation of poem by Shimazaki Toson.)

McQueen, Ian L. *Japan: A Guide for Travel and Understanding*. Melbourne: Lonely Planet Publications, forthcoming.

Mitford, A. B. (Lord Redesdale). *Tales of Old Japan*. 1871. Reprint. Tokyo: Charles E. Tuttle Co., 1966.

Miyawaka, Akira, ed. *Landscape of Japan*. 2 vols. Tokyo: Kokusai Johosha, 1975.

National Parks Association of Japan. *National Parks of Japan*. Tokyo: Tokyo News Service, 1957.

Oi, Michio. "The National Parks of Japan: A Brief Guide." In *These Splendored Isles: The Scenic Beauty of Japan*. Tokyo: John Weatherhill, 1970.

Sugimoto, Etsu Inagaki. *A Daughter of the Samurai*. 1926. Reprint. Tokyo: Charles E. Tuttle Co., 1966.

Waley, Arthur. *The No Plays of Japan*. London: George Allen and Unwin, 1921.

INDEX
Principal Place-names Only

PEARSON

Gary Johns • Alan M. Saks

Organizational Behaviour

Understanding and Managing Life at Work

Custom Edition for Concordia University

Taken from:
Organizational Behaviour: Understanding and Managing Life at Work,
Eighth Edition
by Gary Johns and Alan M. Saks

Cover Art: Courtesy of Digital Vision/Getty Images

Taken from:

Organizational Behaviour: Understanding and Managing Life at Work, Eighth Edition
by Gary Johns and Alan M. Saks
Copyright © 2011, 2008, 2005, 2001 by Pearson Canada, Inc.
Published by Prentice Hall
Toronto, Ontario

This special edition published in cooperation with Pearson Learning Solutions.

Pearson Learning Solutions, 501 Boylston Street, Suite 900, Boston, MA 02116
A Pearson Education Company
www.pearsoned.com

Printed in Canada

1 2 3 4 5 6 7 8 9 10 V092 16 15 14 13 12 11

000200010270742772

MHB

ISBN 10: 1-256-16905-6
ISBN 13: 978-1-256-16905-5

Brief Contents

Contents

PART ONE
An Introduction

LEARNING OBJECTIVES

After reading Chapter 1,
you should be able to:

1 Define *organizations*
and describe their basic
characteristics.

2 Explain the concept of
organizational behaviour
and describe the goals of
the field.

3 Define *management* and
describe what managers
do to accomplish goals.

4 Contrast the *classical
viewpoint* of management
with that which the *human
relations movement*
advocated.

5 Describe the *contemporary
contingency approach* to
management.

6 Explain what managers
do—their roles, activities,
agendas for action, and
thought processes.

7 Describe the societal and
global trends that are
shaping contemporary
management concerns.

Organizational Behaviour and Management

HOK in Canada Inc.

HOK in Canada Inc. is an international architectural planning and design firm that is a leader in pioneering sustainable building design practices. The company has 24 regional offices in North America, Asia, and Europe. In 2009, HOK in Canada was named as one of Canada's Top 100 Employers and one of Canada's greenest employers. Ever wonder what it's like to work at one of Canada's top employers?

For starters, the culture at HOK is very open, collaborative, and inclusive. According to Lui Mancinelli, senior vice-president and managing principal of HOK in Canada, employees are encouraged to speak their minds. "Our people are very vocal; they engage us in constantly improving what we do." They are also asked to provide input and feedback about the kinds of benefits they would like. The work environment is designed to stimulate creative thinking and innovation. The dress code is casual, and employees can listen to music while working. The company hosts social events throughout the year, such as an employee art show and parties to celebrate holidays. Employees are kept informed of organizational events through a company newsletter and the company's intranet site.

HOK conducts annual salary surveys and pays in the 75th percentile or over. Individual salaries are reviewed every six months. Bonuses are handed out twice a year and range from 5 percent to more than 50 percent of salary, depending on company profits. Spot bonuses are also provided for exceptional work or high performance.

Benefits at HOK in Canada include up to $4500 in tuition subsidies per year for studies related to an employee's position and up to $1500 for non-related courses. Family-friendly benefits include backup child care and elder care. Flexible work arrangements are also available, such as compressed and shortened workweeks, reduced summer hours, and telecommuting that allows employees to work at home on Fridays or a few days a week. Employees can also exercise at instructor-led Pilates classes and visit an onsite massage therapist.

HOK in Canada Inc. has been named one of Canada's Top 100 Employers and one of Canada's greenest employers.

Career development programs offer employees specialized training as well as subsidies for professional accreditations, in-house apprenticeships and training programs, skilled trades internships, online training programs, and a mentoring program.

What makes HOK in Canada one of Canada's greenest employers? HOK is committed to building sustainable communities and environments to reverse climate change and to ensure that employees work in a healthy environment. Its global policy is to design all projects to environmental standard or to a LEED (Leadership in Energy and Environmental Design) equivalent or higher. In Canada, the Toronto office has been awarded the LEED Gold certification, one of the first corporate interiors in Canada to receive the award, which recognizes structures that adhere to environmentally sustainable green building standards. It is a state-of-the-art green office space that includes sensor-operated lighting, energy-efficient windows, and green power from renewable energy sources. It was constructed using reused or recycled building materials. Environmental hazards have been removed, copiers and printers are located in enclosed spaces, and no harmful chemicals are used in cleaning or construction. Certain glues and contact cement have been banned from the office as well as the use of sugar packets and bleached coffee filters. Employees are encouraged to leave their cars at home with subsidies for public transit. In addition, bicycle parking and shower and change facilities are available to encourage employees to ride their bikes to work.

HOK in Canada supports a variety of local and international charitable initiatives, and employees receive paid time off to do volunteer work for their favourite charity. The company also donates its expertise to charitable causes such as the Hospital for Sick Children. A volunteer team of HOK in Canada landscape architects designed the hospital's new children's garden.

According to Lui Mancinelli, "Our real focus is on people, it's everything for us—quality, excellence—and supporting that is what it's all about for us." Is it any wonder that HOK in Canada is one of Canada's top employers?[1]

There are a variety of different organizations in which individuals work together to accomplish goals through group effort. Though the motivation of a television news station might differ from other organizations, all organizations strive for goal accomplishment and survival.

What we have here is an example of worklife and management—just what this book is about. The example also highlights many important aspects of organizational behaviour, such as organizational culture, communication, motivation, and learning. It raises some very interesting questions: Why do employees receive bonuses, and what effect does it have on their behaviour? Why does HOK in Canada provide employees many benefits, and what effect does this have on their attitudes and motivation? Why is HOK in Canada so concerned about the community and the environment? This book will help you uncover the answers to these kinds of questions.

In this chapter, we will define *organizations* and *organizational behaviour* and examine their relationship to management. We will explore historical and contemporary approaches to management and consider what managers do and how they think. The chapter concludes with some issues of concern to contemporary managers.

What Are Organizations?

Organizations. Social inventions for accomplishing common goals through group effort.

This book is about what happens in organizations. **Organizations** are social inventions for accomplishing common goals through group effort. HOK in Canada is obviously an organization, but so are the Toronto Blue Jays, the CBC, and a college sorority or fraternity.

Social Inventions

When we say that organizations are social inventions, we mean that their essential characteristic is the coordinated presence of *people,* not necessarily things. HOK in Canada owns a lot of things, such as equipment and offices. However, you are probably aware that, through advanced information technology and contracting out work, some contemporary organizations make and sell products, such as computers or clothes, without owning much of anything. Also, many service organizations, such as consulting firms, have little physical capital. Still, these organizations have people—people who present both opportunities and challenges. *The field of organizational behaviour is about understanding people and managing them to work effectively.*

Goal Accomplishment

Individuals are assembled into organizations for a reason. The organizations mentioned above have the very basic goals of providing architectural designs, winning baseball games, delivering news, and educating students. Non-profit organizations have goals such as saving souls, promoting the arts, helping the needy, or educating people. Virtually all organizations have survival as a goal. Despite this, consider the list of organizations that have failed to survive—Canadian Airlines, Eaton's, the Montreal Expos, and Jetsgo, just to name a few. *The field of organizational behaviour is concerned with how organizations can survive and adapt to change.* Certain behaviours are necessary for survival and adaptation. People have to

- be motivated to join and remain in the organization;
- carry out their basic work reliably, in terms of productivity, quality, and service;
- be willing to continuously learn and upgrade their knowledge and skills; and
- be flexible and innovative.[2]

The field of organizational behaviour is concerned with all these basic activities. Innovation and flexibility, which provide for adaptation to change, are especially important for contemporary organizations. Management guru Tom Peters has gone so far as to advise firms to "Get Innovative or Get Dead."[3]

Group Effort

The final component of our definition of organizations is that they are based on group effort. At its most general level, this means that organizations depend on interaction and coordination among people to accomplish their goals. Much of the intellectual and physical work done in organizations is quite literally performed by groups, whether they are permanent work teams or short-term project teams. Also, informal grouping occurs in all organizations because friendships develop and individuals form informal alliances to accomplish work. The quality of this informal contact in terms of communication and morale can have a strong impact on goal achievement. For all these reasons, *the field of organizational behaviour is concerned with how to get people to practise effective teamwork.*

Now that we have reviewed the basic characteristics of organizations, let's look more directly at the meaning and scope of organizational behaviour.

What Is Organizational Behaviour?

Organizational behaviour refers to the attitudes and behaviours of individuals and groups in organizations. The discipline of organizational behaviour systematically studies these attitudes and behaviours and provides insight about effectively managing and changing them. It also studies how organizations can be structured more effectively and how events in their external environments affect organizations. Those who study organizational behaviour are interested in attitudes—how satisfied people are with their jobs, how committed they feel to the goals of the organization, or how supportive they are of promoting women or minorities into management positions. Behaviours like cooperation, conflict, innovation, resignation, or ethical lapses are important areas of study in the field of organizational behaviour.

Using an organizational behaviour perspective, reconsider the HOK in Canada vignette that opened the chapter. The immediate question is: *What are the factors that make an organization a great place to work?* Although we will not answer this question directly, we can pose some subsidiary questions highlighting some of the topics that the field of organizational behaviour covers, which we will explore in later chapters.

Organizational behaviour. The attitudes and behaviours of individuals and groups in organizations.

- What is an organizational culture and what role does it play in an organization's success? The culture at HOK in Canada emphasizes collaboration, creativity, and social responsibility. How cultures are built and maintained is covered in Chapter 8.

- How do employees learn, and what is the role of training and career planning? At HOK in Canada, employees have access to a tuition reimbursement program and to training courses to help them advance in their careers. Learning is important for employee behaviour and performance. It is discussed in Chapter 2.

- How can organizations motivate employees, and how important is compensation? At HOK in Canada, employees receive above-average compensation and benefits as well as bonuses based on their performance and company profits. Chapter 5 describes different theories of motivation; the role of money as a motivator is discussed in Chapter 6.

- How should managers communicate to employees? Communication is the process of exchanging information, and effective organizational communication is essential for organizational competitiveness. At HOK in Canada, employees are asked to provide input and feedback, and they are kept informed through a company newsletter and intranet site. The company also conducts an employee satisfaction survey every 24 months.

These questions provide a good overview of some issues that those in the field of organizational behaviour study. Accurate answers to these questions would go a long way toward understanding why HOK in Canada is a successful organization and how other organizations can make changes to become more effective. Analysis followed by action is what organizational behaviour is all about.

Why Study Organizational Behaviour?

Why should you attempt to read and understand the material in *Organizational Behaviour*?

Organizational Behaviour Is Interesting

At its core, organizational behaviour is interesting because it is about people and human nature. Why does HOK in Canada focus so much on its employees, and what effect does this have on employee attitudes and behaviour? These questions are interesting because they help us understand why employees become committed to an organization and what motivates them to work hard.

Organizational Behaviour includes interesting examples of success as well as failure. Later in the text, we will study a company that receives thousands of job applications a week (WestJet); a company that successfully integrates generations in the workplace (L'Oreal); a company organized into families, villages, and tribes (Flight Centre); and a company that gives employees prizes for exercising and losing weight (DundeeWealth). All of these companies are extremely successful, and organizational behaviour helps explain why.

Organizational behaviour does not have to be exotic to be interesting. Anyone who has negotiated with a recalcitrant bureaucrat or had a really excellent boss has probably wondered what made them behave the way they did. Organizational behaviour provides the tools to find out why.

Organizational Behaviour Is Important

Looking through the lens of other disciplines, it would be possible to frame HOK in Canada's success in terms of architectural design or marketing. Notice, however, that underlying these perspectives, it is *still* about organizational behaviour. What happens in organizations often has a profound impact on people. It is clear that the impact of organizational behaviour does not stop at the walls of the organization. The consumers of an organization's products and services are also affected, such as the customers who rely on HOK in Canada for the design of their buildings. Thus, organizational behaviour is important to managers, employees, and consumers, and understanding it can make us more effective managers, employees, or consumers.

We sometimes fail to appreciate that there is tremendous variation in organizational behaviour. For example, skilled salespeople in insurance or real estate make many, many more sales than some of their peers. Similarly, for every Greenpeace or Sierra Club, there are dozens of failed organizations that were dedicated to saving the environment. The field of organizational behaviour is concerned with explaining these differences and using the explanations to improve organizational effectiveness and efficiency.

Organizational Behaviour Makes a Difference

Does organizational behaviour matter for an organization's competitiveness and performance? In his book *Competitive Advantage Through People*, Jeffrey Pfeffer argues that organizations can no longer achieve a competitive advantage through the traditional sources of success, such as technology, regulated markets, access to financial resources, and economies of scale.[4] Today, the main factor that differentiates organizations is their workforce or human capital, and the most successful organizations are those that effectively manage their employees. In other words, sustained competitive advantage and organizational effectiveness are increasingly related to the management of human capital and organizational behaviour. On the basis of a review of the popular and academic literature, Pfeffer identified 16 practices of companies that are effective through their management of people. Many of these practices, such as incentive pay, participation and empowerment, teams, job redesign, and training and skill development, are important topics in organizational behaviour and are discussed in this book. Pfeffer's research helps to point out that organizational behaviour is not just interesting and important but that it also makes a big difference for the effectiveness and competitiveness of organizations.

There is increasing evidence that management practices and organizational behaviour not only influence employee attitudes and behaviour, but also have an effect on an organization's effectiveness. In fact, companies like RBC Financial Group are at the forefront of a new wave of management practices that recognize that satisfied, high-performing employees are good for profits. A major overhaul of this company's human resources and management practices resulted in an improvement in both employee and customer satisfaction.[5]

This raises an interesting question: Are companies with good management who have implemented practices from organizational behaviour more successful? Are the best companies to work for also the most profitable? Some might argue that just because an organization is a great place to work does not necessarily mean that it is a great organization in terms of its competitiveness and performance. What do you think? To find out more, see the Research Focus: *Are the Best Companies to Work for the Best Companies?*

Now that you are familiar with organizational behaviour and the reasons for studying it, read You Be the Manager: *Organizational Change at Ornge* and answer the questions. At the end of the chapter, find out what Ornge did in The Manager's Notebook. This is not a test but rather an exercise to improve critical thinking, analytical skills, and management skills. Pause and reflect on these application features as you encounter them in each chapter.

RESEARCH FOCUS

Are the Best Companies to Work for the Best Companies?

In recent years, surveys of the best companies to work for have become very popular. While there is no doubt that being a great place to work is important, some have wondered whether the best places to work are also the best companies. For example, are the additional costs associated with being a great place to work (e.g., employee-friendly practices, outstanding pay and benefits) justified by higher firm performance? Do good employee relations and positive job attitudes contribute to the bottom line?

To find out, Ingrid Fulmer, Barry Gerhart, and Kimberly Scott conducted a study in which they compared 50 of the companies from Fortune magazine's 100 best list to a matched set of firms that have never been on the 100 best list but are comparable in terms of industry, size, and operating performance. Comparisons between the two samples indicated that the 100 best companies outperformed the matched group of companies on financial performance and stock returns. Financial performance as measured by return on assets (ROA) and market-to-book value of equity was generally better among the 100 best than among the matched group of organizations over a six-year period. Further, the six-year cumulative stock returns of the companies on the 100 best list outperformed a composite market index by 183 percentage points, or 95 percent!

To confirm this, they compared the sample from the 100 best companies to another sample of organizations from Hewitt Associates and The Gallup Organization on a measure of employee attitudes. The results indicated that the companies on the 100 best list did have more positive employee relations and attitudes compared to the other companies. Further, to assess the stability of job attitudes, the authors examined the relationship between the employee attitude measure over two years. The results indicated that the relationship was positive and significant and that there was little change from one year to the next. In other words, employee attitudes at the 100 best firms were highly positive and stable over time, providing some support for the belief that positive employee relations are a source of sustainable competitive advantage.

These findings provide the strongest evidence to date of a direct positive link between employee relations and attitudes and financial performance. They suggest that companies can create attractive workplaces without hurting the bottom line, and in many cases the 100 best exhibit superior performance.

Source: Based on Fulmer, I.S., Gerhart, B., & Scott, K.S. (2003). Are the 100 best better? An empirical investigation of the relationship between being a "great place to work" and firm performance. *Personnel Psychology, 56,* 965–993; Romero, E.J. (2004). Are the great places to work also great performers? *Academy of Management Executive, 18,* 150–152.

How Much Do You Know About Organizational Behaviour?

Although this is probably your first formal course in organizational behaviour, you already have a number of opinions about the subject. To illustrate this, consider whether the following statements are true or false. Please jot down a one-sentence rationale for your answer. There are no tricks involved!

1. Effective organizational leaders tend to possess identical personality traits.
2. Nearly all workers prefer stimulating, challenging jobs.
3. Managers have a very accurate idea about how much their peers and superiors are paid.
4. Workers have a very accurate idea about how often they are absent from work.
5. Pay is the best way to motivate most employees and improve job performance.

Now that you have your answers, do one more thing. Assume that the correct answer is opposite to the one you have given; that is, if your answer is "true" for a statement, assume that it is actually false, and vice versa. Now, give a one-sentence rationale why this opposite answer could also be correct.

YOU BE THE MANAGER

Organizational Change at Ornge

The Ontario Air Ambulance Service Company is a not-for-profit organization that began operations in January 2006. The transport medicine program began in 1977 with a single helicopter based in Toronto. Over the years, different regions throughout Ontario established bases with paramedics practising under regional base hospitals using either helicopters or airplanes.

In 2005, the Ontario Ministry of Health and Long-Term Care amalgamated the independent regions into one organization to coordinate all aspects of the aeromedical transport system. The organization has over 300 employees, including paramedics, pediatric transport nurses, transport medicine physicians, and a team of educators and researchers. While 200 of its employees work in Toronto, the rest are spread throughout the province. It is one of the largest programs of transport medicine in North America.

Dr. Christopher Mazza became president and CEO in 2006. He inherited not only the newly formed organization but also its employees, who were used to doing things a certain way. The ratio of service provided to service not provided was increasing, as were the cost overruns. According to Dr. Mazza, the organization was providing less help and its services were costing more. With a budget deficit projected to reach $165 million by 2011, he realized that "if we didn't change, the program was going to die."

The challenges for Dr. Mazza were considerable. Millions of Ontarians count on safe, efficient transport to ferry them from isolated parts of the province to hospitals for often life-saving medical care. "I had to come up with a mechanism that was going to allow me to do sustainable massive change, but [remain] respectful and human," Dr. Mazza said.

That meant first dealing with the fear of change by establishing a new workplace culture. In August 2006, the organization adopted a new name, Ornge (the

Millions of Ontarians count on safe, efficient transport to ferry them from isolated parts of the province to hospitals for often life-saving medical care.

colour of its aircraft), to better reflect the full scope of the services it provides. But what else should Dr. Mazza do to address employee fears of change and to change the organization? You be the manager.

QUESTIONS

1. What issues are particularly relevant from an organizational behaviour perspective? How is organizational behaviour relevant for the challenges facing Dr. Mazza?

2. What should Dr. Mazza do to change Ornge and why?

To find out what Dr. Mazza did to address organizational change at Ornge, see The Manager's Notebook.

Source: Based on Dwyer, A. (2009, March 23). Cultivating a corporate culture. *Globe and Mail*, B6; www.ornge.ca/AboutOrnge/Pages/Default.aspx.

Each of these statements concerns the behaviour of people in organizations. Furthermore, each statement has important implications for the functioning of organizations. If effective leaders possess identical personality traits, then organizations might sensibly hire leaders who have such traits. Similarly, if most employees prefer stimulating jobs, there are many jobs that could benefit from upgrading. In this book, we will investigate the extent to which statements such as these are true or false and why they are true or false.

The answers to this quiz may be surprising. Substantial research indicates that each of the statements in the quiz is essentially false. Of course, there are exceptions, but in general, researchers have found that the personalities of effective leaders vary a fair amount, many people prefer routine jobs, managers are not well informed about the pay of their peers and superiors, workers underestimate their own absenteeism, and pay is not always the most effective way to motivate workers and improve job performance. However, you should not jump to unwarranted conclusions based on the inaccuracy of these statements until we determine *why* they tend to be incorrect. There are good reasons for an organization to tie pay to job performance to motivate employees and to improve their performance. Also, we can predict who might prefer challenging jobs and who will be motivated by pay. We will discuss these issues in more detail in later chapters.

Experience indicates that people are amazingly good at giving sensible reasons why the same statement is either true or false. Thus, pay will always motivate workers because most people want to make more money and will work harder to get more pay. Conversely, workers will only work as hard as they have to, regardless of how much money they are paid. The ease with which people can generate such contradictory responses suggests that "common sense" develops through unsystematic and incomplete experiences with organizational behaviour.

However, because common sense and opinions about organizational behaviour do affect management practice, practice should be based on informed opinion and systematic study. To learn more about how to study organizational behaviour, see the Appendix. Now, let's consider the goals of organizational behaviour.

Goals of Organizational Behaviour

Like any discipline, the field of organizational behaviour has a number of commonly agreed-upon goals. Chief among these are effectively predicting, explaining, and managing behaviour that occurs in organizations. For example, in Chapter 6 we will discuss the factors that predict which pay plans are most effective in motivating employees. Then we will explain the reasons for this effectiveness and describe how managers can implement effective pay plans.

Predicting Organizational Behaviour

Predicting the behaviour of others is an essential requirement for everyday life, both inside and outside of organizations. Our lives are made considerably easier by our ability to anticipate when our friends will get angry, when our professors will respond favourably to a completed assignment, and when salespeople and politicians are telling us the truth about a new product or the state of the nation. In organizations, there is considerable interest in predicting when people will make ethical decisions, create innovative products, or engage in sexual harassment.

The very regularity of behaviour in organizations permits the prediction of its future occurrence. However, untutored predictions of organizational behaviour are not always as accurate. Through systematic study, the field of organizational behaviour provides a scientific foundation that helps improve predictions of organizational events. Of course, being able to predict organizational behaviour does not guarantee that we can explain the reason for the behaviour and develop an effective strategy to manage it. This brings us to the second goal of the field.

Explaining Organizational Behaviour

Another goal of organizational behaviour is to explain events in organizations—why do they occur? Prediction and explanation are not synonymous. Ancient societies were capable of predicting the regular setting of the sun but were unable to explain where it went or why it went there. In general, accurate prediction precedes explanation. Thus, the very regularity of the sun's disappearance gave some clues about why it was disappearing.

Organizational behaviour is especially interested in determining why people are more or less motivated, satisfied, or prone to resign. Explaining events is more complicated than predicting them. For one thing, a particular behaviour could have multiple causes. People may resign from their jobs because they are dissatisfied with their pay, because they are discriminated against, or because they have failed to respond appropriately to an organizational crisis. An organization that finds itself with a "turnover problem" is going to have to find out why this is happening before it can put an effective correction into place. This behaviour could have many different causes, each of which would require a specific solution. Furthermore, explanation is also complicated by the fact that the underlying causes of some event or behaviour can change over time. For example, the reasons people quit may vary greatly depending on the overall economy and whether there is high or low unemployment in the field in question. Throughout the book, we will consider material that should improve your grasp of organizational behaviour. The ability to understand behaviour is a necessary prerequisite for effectively managing it.

Managing Organizational Behaviour

Management is defined as the art of getting things accomplished in organizations. Managers acquire, allocate, and utilize physical and human resources to accomplish goals.[6] This definition does not include a prescription about how to get things accomplished. As we proceed through the text, you will learn that a variety of management styles might be effective depending on the situation at hand.

If behaviour can be predicted and explained, it can often be controlled or managed. That is, if we truly understand the reasons for high-quality service, ethical behaviour, or anything else, we can often take sensible action to manage it effectively. If prediction and explanation constitute analysis, then management constitutes action. Unfortunately, we see all too many cases in which managers act without analysis, looking for a quick fix to problems. The result is often disaster. The point is not to overanalyze a problem. Rather, it is to approach a problem with a systematic understanding of behavioural science.

Management. The art of getting things accomplished in organizations through others.

Early Prescriptions Concerning Management

For many years, experts interested in organizations were concerned with prescribing the "correct" way to manage an organization to achieve its goals. There were two basic phases to this prescription, which experts often call the classical view and the human relations view. A summary of these viewpoints will illustrate how the history of management thought and organizational behaviour has developed.

The Classical View and Bureaucracy

Most of the major advocates of the classical viewpoint were experienced managers or consultants who took the time to write down their thoughts on organizing. For the most part, this activity occurred in the early 1900s. The classical writers acquired their experience in military settings, mining operations, and factories that produced everything from cars to candy. Prominent names include Henri Fayol, General Motors executive James D. Mooney, and consultant Lyndall Urwick.[7] Although exceptions existed, the **classical viewpoint** tended to advocate a very high degree of specialization of labour and a very high degree of coordination. Each department was to tend to its own affairs, with centralized decision making from upper management providing coordination. To maintain control, the classical view suggested that managers have fairly few workers, except for lower-level jobs where machine pacing might substitute for close supervision.

Classical viewpoint. An early prescription on management that advocated high specialization of labour, intensive coordination, and centralized decision making.

Frederick Taylor (1856–1915), the father of **Scientific Management**, was also a contributor to the classical school, although he was mainly concerned with job design and the structure of work on the shop floor.[8] Rather than informal "rules of thumb" for job design, Taylor's Scientific Management advocated the use of careful research to determine the optimum degree of specialization and standardization. Also, he supported the development of written instructions that clearly defined work procedures, and he encouraged supervisors to standardize workers' movements and breaks for maximum efficiency. Taylor even extended Scientific Management to the supervisor's job, advocating "functional foremanship" whereby supervisors would specialize in particular functions. For example, one might become a specialist in training workers, while another might fulfill the role of a disciplinarian.

The practising managers and consultants had an academic ally in Max Weber (1864–1920), the distinguished German social theorist. Weber made the term "bureaucracy" famous by advocating it as a means of rationally managing complex organizations. During Weber's lifetime, managers were certainly in need of advice. In this time of industrial growth and development, most management was done by intuition, and nepotism and favouritism were rampant. According to Weber, a **bureaucracy** has the following qualities:

- A strict chain of command in which each member reports to only a single superior.
- Criteria for selection and promotion based on impersonal technical skills rather than nepotism or favouritism.
- A set of detailed rules, regulations, and procedures ensuring that the job gets done regardless of who the specific worker is.
- The use of strict specialization to match duties with technical competence.
- The centralization of power at the top of the organization.[9]

Weber saw bureaucracy as an "ideal type" or theoretical model that would standardize behaviour in organizations and provide workers with security and a sense of purpose. Jobs would be performed as intended rather than following the whims of the specific role occupant. In exchange for this conformity, workers would have a fair chance of being promoted and rising in the power structure. Rules, regulations, and a clear-cut chain of command that further clarified required behaviour provided the workers with a sense of security.

Even during this period, some observers, such as the "business philosopher" Mary Parker Follett (1868–1933), noted that the classical view of management seemed to take for granted an essential conflict of interest between managers and employees.[10] This sentiment found expression in the human relations movement.

The Human Relations Movement and a Critique of Bureaucracy

The human relations movement generally began with the famous **Hawthorne studies** of the 1920s and 1930s.[11] These studies, conducted at the Hawthorne plant of Western Electric near Chicago, began in the strict tradition of industrial engineering. They were concerned with the impact of fatigue, rest pauses, and lighting on productivity. However, during the course of the studies, the researchers (among others, Harvard University's Elton Mayo and Fritz Roethlisberger and Hawthorne's William J. Dickson) began to notice the effects of psychological and social processes on productivity and work adjustment. This impact suggested that there could be dysfunctional aspects to how work was organized. One obvious sign was resistance to management through strong informal group mechanisms, such as norms that limited productivity to less than what management wanted.

After World War II, a number of theorists and researchers, who were mostly academics, took up the theme begun at Hawthorne. Prominent names included Chris Argyris,

Alvin Gouldner, and Rensis Likert. The **human relations movement** called attention to certain dysfunctional aspects of classical management and bureaucracy and advocated more people-oriented styles of management that catered more to the social and psychological needs of employees. This critique of bureaucracy addressed several specific problems:

- Strict specialization is incompatible with human needs for growth and achievement.[12] This can lead to employee alienation from the organization and its clients.

- Strong centralization and reliance on formal authority often fail to take advantage of the creative ideas and knowledge of lower-level members, who are often closer to the customer.[13] As a result, the organization will fail to learn from its mistakes, which threatens innovation and adaptation. Resistance to change will occur as a matter of course.

- Strict, impersonal rules lead members to adopt the minimum acceptable level of performance that the rules specify.[14] If a rule states that employees must process at least eight claims a day, eight claims will become the norm, even though higher performance levels are possible.

- Strong specialization causes employees to lose sight of the overall goals of the organization.[15] Forms, procedures, and required signatures become ends in themselves, divorced from the true needs of customers, clients, and other departments in the organization. This is the "red-tape mentality" that we sometimes observe in bureaucracies.

Obviously, not all bureaucratic organizations have these problems. However, they were common enough that human relations advocates and others began to call for the adoption of more flexible systems of management and the design of more interesting jobs. They also advocated open communication, more employee participation in decision making, and less rigid, more decentralized forms of control.

Contemporary Management— The Contingency Approach

How has the apparent tension between the classical approach and the human relations approach been resolved? First, contemporary scholars and managers recognize the merits of both approaches. The classical advocates pointed out the critical role of control and coordination in getting organizations to achieve their goals. The human relationists pointed out the dangers of certain forms of control and coordination and addressed the need for flexibility and adaptability. Second, as we will study in later chapters, contemporary scholars have learned that management approaches need to be tailored to fit the situation. For example, we would generally manage a payroll department more bureaucratically than a research and development department. Getting out a payroll every week is a routine task with no margin for error. Research requires creativity that is fostered by a more flexible work environment.

Reconsider the four questions we posed earlier about the factors that make an organization a great place to work. Answering these questions is not an easy task, partly because human nature is so complex. This complexity means that an organizational behaviour text cannot be a "cookbook." In what follows, you will not find recipes to improve job satisfaction or service quality, with one cup of leadership style and two cups of group dynamics. We have not discovered a simple set of laws of organizational behaviour that you can memorize and then retrieve when necessary to solve any organizational problem. It is this "quick fix" mentality that produces simplistic and costly management fads and fashions.[16]

There is a growing body of research and management experience to help sort out the complexities of what happens in organizations. However, the general answer to many of the questions we will pose in the following chapters is "It depends." Which leadership style is most effective? This depends on the characteristics of the leader, those of the people being led, and what the leader is trying to achieve. Will an increase in pay lead to an increase in performance? This depends on who is getting the increase and the exact reason for the increase. These dependencies are called contingencies. The **contingency approach** to management recognizes that there is no one best way to manage; rather, an appropriate style depends on the demands of the situation. Thus, the effectiveness of a leadership style is contingent on the abilities of the followers, and the consequence of a pay increase is partly contingent on the need for money. Contingencies illustrate the complexity of organizational behaviour and show why we should study it systematically. Throughout the text we will discuss organizational behaviour with the contingency approach in mind.

Contingency approach. An approach to management that recognizes that there is no one best way to manage, and that an appropriate management style depends on the demands of the situation.

What Do Managers Do?

Organizational behaviour is not just for managers or aspiring managers. As we noted earlier, a good understanding of the field can be useful for consumers or anyone else who has to interact with organizations or get things done through them. Nevertheless, many readers of this text have an interest in management as a potential career. Managers can have a strong impact on what happens in and to organizations. They both influence and are influenced by organizational behaviour, and the net result can have important consequences for organizational effectiveness.

There is no shortage of texts and popular press books oriented toward what managers *should* do. However, the field of organizational behaviour is also concerned with what really happens in organizations. Let's look at several research studies that explore what managers *do* do. This provides a context for appreciating the usefulness of understanding organizational behaviour.

Managerial Roles

Canadian management theorist Henry Mintzberg conducted an in-depth study of the behaviour of several managers.[17] The study earned him a Ph.D. from the Massachusetts Institute of Technology (MIT) in 1968. In the Appendix, we discuss how he conducted the study and some of its more basic findings. Here, however, we are concerned with Mintzberg's discovery of a rather complex set of roles played by the managers: figurehead, leader, liaison person, monitor, disseminator, spokesperson, entrepreneur, disturbance handler, resource allocator, and negotiator. These roles are summarized in Exhibit 1.1.

Interpersonal Roles. Interpersonal roles are expected behaviours that have to do with establishing and maintaining interpersonal relations. In the *figurehead role*, managers serve as symbols of their organization rather than active decision makers.

EXHIBIT 1.1
Mintzberg's managerial roles.

Source: ODONNELL & KELLY, PORTALES: COMUNIDAD & CULTURA & WORKBK PKG, 1st Edition, © 2003. Reprinted by permission of Pearson Education, Inc. Upper Saddle River, NJ. Reprinted by permission.

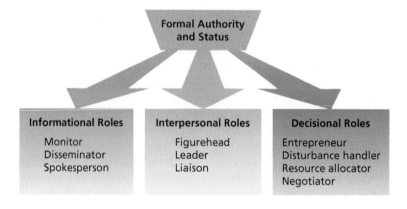

Examples of the figurehead role are making a speech to a trade group, entertaining clients, or signing legal documents. In the *leadership role*, managers select, mentor, reward, and discipline employees. In the *liaison role*, managers maintain horizontal contacts inside and outside the organization. This might include discussing a project with a colleague in another department or touching base with an embassy delegate of a country where the company hopes to do future business.

Informational Roles. These roles are concerned with the various ways managers receive and transmit information. In the *monitor role*, managers scan the internal and external environments of the firm to follow current performance and to keep themselves informed of new ideas and trends. For example, the head of research and development might attend a professional engineering conference. In the *disseminator role*, managers send information on both facts and preferences to others. For example, the R&D head might summarize what he or she learned at the conference in an email to employees. The *spokesperson role* concerns mainly sending messages into the organization's external environment—for example, drafting an annual report to stockholders or giving an interview to the press.

Decisional Roles. The final set of managerial roles Mintzberg discussed deals with decision making. In the *entrepreneur role*, managers turn problems and opportunities into plans for improved changes. This might include suggesting a new product or service that will please customers. In the *disturbance handler role*, managers deal with problems stemming from employee conflicts and address threats to resources and turf. In their *resource allocation role*, managers decide how to deploy time, money, personnel, and other critical resources. Finally, in their *negotiator role*, managers conduct major negotiations with other organizations or individuals.

Of course, the relative importance of these roles will vary with management level and organizational technology.[18] First-level supervisors do more disturbance handling and less figureheading. Still, Mintzberg's major contribution to organizational behaviour is to highlight the *complexity* of the roles managers are required to play and the variety of skills they must have to be effective, including leadership, communication, and negotiation. His work also illustrates the complex balancing act managers face when they must play different roles for different audiences. A good grasp of organizational behaviour is at the heart of acquiring these skills and performing this balancing act.

Managerial Activities

Fred Luthans, Richard Hodgetts, and Stuart Rosenkrantz studied the behaviour of a large number of managers in a variety of different kinds of organizations.[19] They determined that the managers engage in four basic types of activities:

- *Routine communication.* This includes the formal sending and receiving of information (as in meetings) and the handling of paperwork.
- *Traditional management.* Planning, decision making, and controlling are the primary types of traditional management.
- *Networking.* Networking consists of interacting with people outside of the organization and informal socializing and politicking with insiders.
- *Human resource management.* This includes motivating and reinforcing, disciplining and punishing, managing conflict, staffing, and training and developing employees.

Exhibit 1.2 summarizes these managerial activities and shows how a sample of 248 managers divided their time and effort, as determined by research observers (discipline and punishment were done in private and were not open to observation). Perhaps the most striking observation about this figure is how all these managerial activities involve dealing with people.

EXHIBIT 1.2

Summary of managerial activities.

Note: Figures do not total 100% due to rounding.

Source: Adapted from Luthans, F., Hodgetts, R.M., & Rosenkrantz, S.A. (1988). *Real managers.* Cambridge, MA: Ballinger. Reprinted by permission of Dr. F. Luthans on behalf of the authors.

One of Luthans and colleagues' most fascinating findings is how emphasis on these various activities correlated with managerial success. If we define success as moving up the ranks of the organization quickly, networking proved to be critical. The people who were promoted quickly tended to do more networking (politicking, socializing, and making contacts) and less human resource management than the averages in Exhibit 1.2. If we define success in terms of unit effectiveness and employee satisfaction and commitment, the more successful managers were those who devoted more time and effort to human resource management and less to networking than the averages in the exhibit. A good understanding of organizational behaviour should help you manage this trade-off more effectively, reconciling the realities of organizational politics with the demands of accomplishing things through others.

Managerial Agendas

John Kotter studied the behaviour patterns of a number of successful general managers.[20] Although he found some differences among them, he also found a strong pattern of similarities that he grouped into the categories of agenda setting, networking, and agenda implementation.

Agenda Setting. Kotter's managers, given their positions, all gradually developed agendas of what they wanted to accomplish for the organization. Many began these agendas even before they assumed their positions. These agendas were almost always informal and unwritten, and they were much more concerned with "people issues" and were less numerical than most formal strategic plans. The managers based their agendas on wide-ranging informal discussions with a wide variety of people.

Networking. Kotter's managers established a wide formal and informal network of key people both inside and outside of their organizations. Insiders included peers, employees, and bosses, but they also extended to these people's employees and bosses. Outsiders included customers, suppliers, competitors, government officials, and the press. This network provided managers with information and established cooperative relationships relevant to their agendas. Formal hiring, firing, and reassigning shaped the network, but so did informal liaisons in which managers created dependencies by doing favours for others.

Agenda Implementation. The managers used networks to implement the agendas. They would go *anywhere* in the network for help—up or down, in or out of the organization. In addition, they employed a wide range of influence tactics, from direct orders to subtle language and stories that conveyed their message indirectly.

John Kotter's research of successful business managers showed that exemplary managers practise agenda setting, networking, and agenda implementation. Michael Dell, of Dell Computers, is an example of such a manager.

The theme that runs through Kotter's findings is the high degree of informal interaction and concern with people issues that were necessary for the managers to achieve their agendas. To be sure, the managers used their formal organizational power, but they often found themselves dependent on people over whom they wielded no power. An understanding of organizational behaviour helps to recognize and manage these realities.

Managerial Minds

In contrast to exploring how managers act, which is the focus of the previous section, Herbert Simon and Daniel Isenberg have both explored how managers think.[21] Although they offer a wealth of observations, we will concentrate here on a specific issue that each examined in independent research—managerial intuition.

Some people think that organizational behaviour and its implications for management are just common sense. However, careful observers of successful managers have often noted that intuition seems to guide many of their actions. Isenberg's research suggests that experienced managers use intuition in several ways:

● to sense that a problem exists;

● to perform well-learned mental tasks rapidly (e.g., sizing up a written contract);

● to synthesize isolated pieces of information and data; and

● to double-check more formal or mechanical analyses ("Do these projections look correct?").

Does the use of intuition mean that managerial thinking is random, irrational, or undisciplined? Both Simon and Isenberg say no. In fact, both strongly dispute the idea that intuition is the opposite of rationality or that intuitive means unanalytical. Rather, good intuition is problem identification and problem solving based on a long history of systematic education and experience that enables the manager to locate problems within a network of previously acquired information. The theories, research, and management practices that we cover in *Organizational Behaviour* will contribute to your own information network and give you better managerial intuition about decisions that involve how to make an organization a great place to work and a financial success.

International managers must adapt to cross-cultural differences to successfully interact with potential clients and overseas affiliates.

International Managers

The research we discussed above describes how managers act and think in North America. Would managers in other global locations act and think the same way? Up to a point, the answer is probably yes. After all, we are dealing here with some very basic behaviours and thought processes. However, the style in which managers do what they do and the emphasis they give to various activities will vary greatly across cultures because of cross-cultural variations in values that affect both managers' and employees' expectations about interpersonal interaction. Thus, in Chapter 5 we study cross-cultural differences in motivation. In Chapter 9 we study cultural differences in leadership.

Geert Hofstede has done pioneering work on cross-cultural differences in values that we will study in Chapter 4. Hofstede provides some interesting observations about how these value differences promote contrasts in the general role that managers play across cultures.[22] He asserts that managers are cultural heroes and are even a distinct social class in North America, where individualism is treasured. In contrast, Germany tends to worship engineers and have fewer managerial types. In Japan, managers are required to pay obsessive attention to group solidarity rather than to star employees. In the Netherlands, managers are supposed to exhibit modesty and strive for consensus. In the family-run businesses of Taiwan and Singapore, "professional" management, North American style, is greatly downplayed. The contrasts that Hofstede raises are fascinating because the technical requirements for accomplishing goals are actually the same across cultures. It is only the *behavioural* requirements that differ. Thus, national culture is one of the most important contingency variables in organizational behaviour. The appropriateness of various leadership styles, motivation techniques, and communication methods depends on where one is in the world.

Some Contemporary Management Concerns

To conclude the chapter, we will briefly examine five issues with which organizations and managers are currently concerned. As with previous sections, our goal is to illustrate how the field of organizational behaviour can help you understand and manage these issues.

Diversity—Local and Global

The demographics of the North American population and workforce are changing and, as a result, both the labour force and customers are becoming increasingly culturally diverse. Contributing to this is the increased movement of women into paid employment, as well as immigration patterns. In Canada, visible minorities are the fastest growing segment of the population.[23] The annual report of Employment and Immigration Canada has projected that two-thirds of today's new entrants to the Canadian labour force will be women, visible minorities, aboriginal people, and persons with disabilities.[24] A report by Statistics Canada predicted that the number of visible minorities in Canada is expected to double by 2017 and will form more than half the population in greater Toronto and Vancouver, and immigrants will account for 22 percent of the population.[25] Native-born Caucasian North Americans frequently find themselves working with people whose ethnic backgrounds are very different from their own.

Diversity of age is also having an impact in organizations. In less than a decade, the workforce will be dominated by people over the age of 40. By the year 2015, 48 percent of Canada's working-age population will be between the ages of 45 and 64, compared to 29 percent in 1991.[26] With the elimination of mandatory retirement at age 65, along with the recent global recession in which many people saw their life savings diminish, a growing number of Canadians over 65 will remain in the workforce. A recent survey found that older Canadians are redefining the concept of retirement and that 75 percent of the participants who had not yet retired expected to continue working past the age of 65.[27] Perhaps you have observed people of various ages working in fast-food restaurants that were at one time staffed solely by young people. Both the re-entry of retired people into the workforce and the trend to remove vertical layers in organizations have contributed to much more intergenerational contact in the workplace than was common in the past. Organizations are beginning to adopt new programs in response to this demographic shift, such as flexible benefit plans, compressed workdays, and part-time jobs, to attract and retain older workers. For example, Orkin/PCO Services Corp. of Mississauga, a pest-control service, dealt with a shortage of pest-control specialists by introducing a more flexible part-time schedule with benefits to attract and retain employees who would otherwise have retired or left the industry.[28]

Diversity is also coming to the fore as many organizations realize that they have not treated certain segments of the population, such as women, homosexuals, and the disabled, fairly in many aspects of employment. Organizations have to be able to get the best from *everyone* to be truly competitive. Although legal pressures (such as the *Employment Equity Act*) have contributed to this awareness, general social pressure, especially from customers and clients, has also done so.

Finally, diversity issues are having an increasing impact as organizations "go global." Foreign sales by multinational corporations have exceeded $7 trillion and are growing 20 to 30 percent faster than their sales of exports.[29] Multinational expansion, strategic alliances, and joint ventures increasingly require employees and managers to come into contact with their counterparts from other cultures. Although many of these people have an interest in North American consumer goods and entertainment, it is naïve to assume that business values are rapidly converging on a North American model. As a result, North American organizations that operate in other countries need to understand how the workforce and customers in those countries are diverse and culturally different.

What does diversity have to do with organizational behaviour? The field has long been concerned with stereotypes, conflict, cooperation, and teamwork. These are just some of the factors that managers must manage effectively for organizations to benefit from the considerable opportunities that a diverse workforce affords.

Employee–Organization Relationships

Downsizing, restructuring, re-engineering, and outsourcing have had a profound effect on North American and European organizations in the past two decades. Companies such as General Motors, Ford, Levi Strauss, IBM, Air Canada, and Nortel each have laid off thousands of workers. These companies have eliminated high-paying manufacturing jobs, the once-secure middle-management jobs, and high-tech jobs. As well, there has been a major structural change in work arrangements. Full-time, full-year permanent jobs are being replaced by part-time work and temporary or contract work. It is expected that these work arrangements will become the future standard forms of work, and they will forever change the nature of employee–organization relationships.[30]

Surveys suggest that the consequences of these events are decreased trust, morale, and commitment, and shifting loyalties. Study after study shows worker have increasingly negative attitudes toward their jobs and organizations, suggesting that employee loyalty is a thing of the past. A survey by Towers Perrin management consultants found that one-third of employees are profoundly unhappy in their work and more than half of the employees sampled in both Canada and the United States have negative feelings about their jobs and are either actively or passively looking for other work. The key reasons for employees' unhappiness included boredom, overwork, concern about their future, and a lack of support and recognition from their bosses. The study also found that trust in senior management is declining, and only 17 percent of Canadian workers are highly engaged in their jobs and willing to put in extra effort.[31] In another study, the results indicated that employee morale and job satisfaction levels have fallen in the last decade. Employee satisfaction with bonuses, promotion policies, training programs, and co-workers is on the decline.[32]

Absenteeism in Canadian organizations is also on the rise. According to Statistics Canada, there has been an alarming and unprecedented increase in absenteeism rates since the mid-1990s. The increase in absenteeism has been found across all age groups and sectors and translates into millions of dollars in lost productivity. It has been estimated that the total cost of reported absenteeism in Canada is $15 billion annually. Although there is no one definitive cause, increasing stress levels and poorly designed jobs are major contributors. In fact, all types of employees are experiencing more workplace stress today than a decade ago, and the incidence of work-related illness is also on the rise.[33] A study of Canadian employees estimated that the direct cost of absenteeism due to high work–life conflict—a major stressor in the workplace—is approximately $3–5 billion per year, and when both direct and indirect costs are included in the calculation, work–life conflict costs Canadians approximately $6–10 billion per year.[34] Exhibit 1.3 presents some of the major findings from this study.

The field of organizational behaviour offers many potential solutions to these kinds of problems. For example, consider Radical Entertainment, a software company in Vancouver that has been ranked as one of Canada's best-managed private companies, where taking care of employees and creating a great place to work is a high priority. Employees have access to a fully equipped gym, flexible hours, enriched maternity leaves, and breakfast every morning. According to former company CEO Ian Wilkinson, "If creating a good place to work means that the people who work here will be inspired and that they will stay with us, then it's worth the cost."[35]

This book provides many other examples of organizations that have been able to build and maintain strong and positive employee–organization relationships.

A Focus on Quality, Speed, and Flexibility

Intense competition for customers, both locally and globally, has given rise to a strong emphasis on the quality of both products and services. Correctly identifying customer needs and satisfying them before, during, and after the sale (whether the consumer purchased a car or health care) are now seen as key competitive advantages. To obtain these advantages, many organizations have begun to pursue programs to achieve continuous improvement in the quality of their products or services.

Quality can be very generally defined as everything from speedy delivery to producing goods or services in an environmentally friendly manner. Quality tactics include

These findings are based on a sample of 31 571 Canadian employees who work for 100 medium to large organizations in the public, private, and nonprofit sections of the economy. The authors of the report concluded that the majority of Canada's largest employers cannot be considered to be best-practice employers.

What Workers Experience	Percentage of Employees
Employees reporting high levels of role overload	58%
Work responsibilities interfere with the ability to fulfill responsibilities at home	28%
Negative spillover from work to family	44%
Employees reporting high levels of stress	33%
Employees reporting high levels of burnout	32%
Employees reporting highly depressed mood	36%
Employees reporting high levels of job satisfaction	46%
Employees reporting high levels of organizational commitment	53%
Employees who think of leaving their current organization once a week or more	28%
Employees indicating high levels of absenteeism	46%
Employees reporting high levels of life satisfaction	41%

EXHIBIT 1.3

Work–Life Conflict in Canadian Organizations.

Source: Higgins, C., and Duxbury, L. (2003). *2001 National Work–Life Conflict Study* (Ottawa: Health Canada). Reproduced with permission of the authors.

extensive training, frequent measurement of quality indicators, meticulous attention to work processes, and an emphasis on preventing (rather than correcting) service or production errors. For example, automakers focus on solving problems that customers are most concerned about, such as wind noise, brake noise, fuel consumption, and ease of operating doors and hatches.[36]

Closely allied with quality is speed. LensCrafters makes glasses "in about an hour," and Domino's became famous for speedy pizza delivery. Local car dealers now do on-the-spot oil changes, whereas customers previously had to make an appointment days in advance. Perhaps even more important than this external manifestation of speed is the behind-the-scenes speed that has reduced the cycle time for getting new products to market. Firms such as Benetton and The Limited can move new fashions into stores in a couple of months instead of a couple of years, the former norm. Such speed can prove to be a real competitive advantage.

Finally, in addition to improving quality and speed, flexibility on the part of employees and organizations is also an important competitive advantage. Organizations today must operate in increasingly uncertain, turbulent, and chaotic environments that are being driven by the technological revolution and increasing globalization. For some organizations, the competition has become so fierce that it has been referred to as hyper-competition. Hypercompetitive environments are characterized by constant change and high levels of uncertainty. In order to survive in such an environment, organizations need to be flexible so that they can rapidly respond to changing conditions.

A good example of this is happening in the manufacturing sector, where organizations have begun to create jobs that are more mobile and flexible. At Lincoln Electric Co., the world's largest producer of arc welding equipment, workers receive continual cross-training, and they are moved wherever they are needed depending on the type and volume of orders the company receives. For example, salaried workers have been moved to hourly clerical jobs and are paid a different wage for each job assignment. Such job flexibility allows the company to operate with a lean workforce that has for decades contributed to productivity growth and profitability. Organizations require multiskilled workers as well as new organizational structures, cultures, and leaders to build an organization with strategic flexibility to survive and compete in the twenty-first century.[37]

What does the passion for quality, speed, and flexibility have to do with organizational behaviour? For one thing, all of these require a high degree of employee *involvement* and *commitment*. Often, this means that management must give employees the power to make on-the-spot decisions that were previously reserved for managers. In addition, quality, speed, and flexibility all require a high degree of *teamwork* between individuals and groups who might have some natural tendency to be uncooperative (such as the engineers and accountants involved in car design). The field of organizational behaviour is deeply concerned with such issues.

Talent Management

During the last decade, organizations have become increasingly concerned about talent management. **Talent management** refers to an organization's processes for attracting, developing, retaining, and utilizing people with the required skills to meet current and future business needs.[38] Consider this: A recent survey of senior executives from all over the world found that the two most important management challenges are

- recruitment of high-quality people across multiple territories, and
- improving the appeal of the company culture and work environment.[39]

The ability of organizations to attract and retain talent has always been important; however, today it has become especially critical for many organizations that are struggling to find the employees they need to compete and survive.

An increasing number of organizations are having trouble finding qualified people, a problem stemming in part from changing demographics that will result in a dramatic shortage of skilled workers over the next 10 years. The baby boomers will begin to retire in the next few years, which will create a large skills gap. It is predicted that there will be a 30 percent shortfall of workers between the ages of 25 and 44. This, combined with the increasing willingness of knowledge workers to relocate anywhere in the world and fewer Canadians entering the skilled trades, means that Canadian organizations will increasingly face severe shortages of labour. There are already shortages in scientific, technical, and high-tech industries and in senior management, communications, and marketing positions. A recent poll found that more than 60 percent of Canadian employers say that labour shortages are limiting their productivity and efficiency. Most of Canada's top CEOs believe that retaining employees has become their number-one priority, and attracting new employees is their fourth priority, just behind financial performance and profitability. Three-quarters of CEOs say they can't find enough competent employees.[40]

One industry where there is already a substantial labour shortage is the trucking industry, where the average turnover is 120 percent. However, for long-haul trucking company Coastal Pacific Xpress (CPX) of Surrey, British Columbia, the turnover rate is only 20 percent. The owners attribute this to the way the company treats its employees. The company provides a supportive environment that treats employees with respect. It pays for fitness memberships, offers flex-time, recognizes staff birthdays, and encourages colleagues to thank their co-workers with candy and thank-you notes. The company also has a profit-sharing program that has paid out more than $400 000 to employees in recent years (see Chapter 6).[41]

What does organizational behaviour have to do with talent management? Organizational behaviour provides the means for organizations to be designed and managed in ways that optimize talent attraction, development, retention, and performance.[42] For example, providing opportunities for learning and improving employees' job satisfaction and organizational commitment; designing jobs that are challenging, meaningful, and rewarding; providing recognition and monetary rewards for performance; managing a diverse workforce; offering flexible work arrangements; and providing effective leadership

Talent management. An organization's processes for attracting, developing, retaining, and utilizing people with the required skills to meet current and future business needs.

- Flexible work schedules (flex-time, telecommuting, job sharing, and compressed workweek)
- Stock options, profit sharing plans, and performance bonuses
- Extensive training and development programs
- Family assistance programs
- On-site fitness facilities, daycare, and wellness programs
- Career days and formal career plans
- Flexible or cafeteria-style benefit plans
- Monthly staff socials, family Christmas parties, and picnics
- Stress reduction programs
- Monthly all-employee meetings
- Formal workplace diversity programs to encourage women and minorities
- Employee recognition and reward programs

EXHIBIT 1.4
Management practices of the best companies to work for in Canada.

Sources: Brearton, S., & Daly, J. (2003, January). The 50 best companies to work for in Canada. *Report on Business Magazine, 19(2)*, 53–66; Hannon, G. (2002, January). The 50 best companies to work for. *Report on Business Magazine, 18(7)*, 41–52.

are just some of the factors that are important for the effective management of talent. These are, of course, some of the practices of the best companies to work for in Canada, and their annual rate of turnover is lower than the national average and half that of other companies.[43] To learn more about the management practices of the best companies to work for in Canada and their talent management strategies, see Exhibit 1.4.

A Focus on Corporate Social Responsibility

Organizations have become increasingly concerned about corporate social responsibility (CSR) and the need to be a good corporate citizen. **Corporate social responsibility** refers to an organization taking responsibility for the impact of its decisions and actions on its stakeholders. It has to do with an organization's overall impact on society at large and extends beyond the interests of shareholders to the interests and needs of employees and the community in which it operates. CSR involves a variety of issues that range from community involvement, environmental protection, safe products, ethical marketing, employee diversity, and local and global labour practices. Ultimately, CSR has to do with how an organization performs its core functions of producing goods and providing services and that it does so in a socially responsible way.[44] A good example of this is Unilever, a global company that produces a range of products from food to soap. Unilever's commitment to communities and the environment is integral to its business.[45]

What does a focus on social responsibility have to do with organizational behaviour? For starters, many CSR issues have to do with organizational behaviour such as an organization's treatment of employees; management practices such as managing diversity; work-family balance; and employment equity. Organizations that rank high on CSR are good employers because of the way they treat their employees and because of their management practices that promote employee well-being. As indicated earlier, these are the kinds of practices employed by the best companies to work for in Canada.

CSR also involves environmental, social, and governance (ESG) issues. Organizations' social and environmental actions are increasingly being scrutinized, and shareholders and consumers are holding firms to higher CSR standards on the environment, employment, and other social issues. Governance issues such as executive compensation have also begun to receive greater attention (see Chapter 6). CSR is so important that a number of research firms now rank and rate organizations on CSR.[46] In 2009, *Maclean's* published its inaugural list of the 50 Most Socially Responsible Corporations in Canada, corporations that are raising the standard of what it means to be a good corporate citizen.[47] These rankings, along with the belief that CSR has implications for an organization's reputation and financial performance, have led to an increasing number of organizations placing greater emphasis on CSR initiatives.

Corporate social responsibility (CSR). An organization taking responsibility for the impact of its decisions and actions on its stakeholders.

For example, many organizations make donations to charitable organizations and have implemented programs to help their communities. As indicated at the beginning of the chapter, HOK in Canada supports a variety of local and international charitable initiatives and donates its expertise to charitable causes, and employees receive paid time off to do volunteer work for their favourite charity. Cameo Corp. of Saskatoon, one of the world's largest producers of uranium, has a community investment program that focuses on improving the quality of life for people in the communities in which it operates. The company has contributed $3 million to the University of Saskatchewan to promote greater access for Aboriginal peoples, women, and northerners to studies in engineering and science. Unilever Canada has a community vitality fund and donates 1 percent of pre-tax profits to initiatives in children's health and water resources, which are both linked to its products. The company also encourages volunteerism and gives employees four afternoons off each year for community activities.[48]

A concern for the environment and green initiatives is also an example of CSR. Recall that HOK in Canada is one of Canada's greenest employers. Its global policy is to design all projects to environmental standard or to a LEED (Leadership in Energy and Environmental Design) equivalent or higher. The company's Toronto office features a state-of-the-art green interior that was constructed using reused or recycled building materials.

What does going green have to do with organizational behaviour? Green programs require changes in employees' attitudes and behaviours. For example, at Fairmont Hotels and Resorts, employees volunteer to be on green teams that meet monthly to brainstorm environmental initiatives. The company also recognizes and rewards employees for their efforts (see Chapter 2). The program has had a positive effect on employee engagement

APPLIED FOCUS

Green Management at the Delta Chelsea

In 2008, several hundred employees of the Delta Chelsea Hotel in Toronto took a tour at Turtle Island Recycling. The visit helped get employees more engaged in green initiatives by providing a big picture of what happens to the waste from the hotel and its impact on the environment.

"Those tours made a huge difference because our [recycling] results drastically improved after those visits," says Tracy Ford, public relations manager at the Delta Chelsea. "It's made such a difference in what our goals are with the hotel."

In 2008, 76 percent of all waste from the hotel was recycled, and by February 2009, that figure had risen to 81 percent. Much of that success is attributed to a green team made up of representatives from various departments—such as stewarding, catering, and housekeeping—that sets up a strategic plan and updates the hotel's environmental policy.

To spread the word, employee orientation includes a presentation on the hotel's green initiatives and policies, an internal newsletter dedicates a page to the environment, posters in elevators and message boards

on employee floors tout the cause, and a health and wellness day profiling the green team challenges employees to take a quiz for prizes.

The Delta Chelsea has also set a goal to be carbon-neutral. To help, the hotel recently launched a LivClean Eco-Stay Program, whereby guests can voluntarily pay $1 per stay to support emission-reduction projects. This will enable environmental initiatives within the hotel, facilitate assessment and reporting of its environmental impact, and assist in the development and expansion of the Hotel Association of Canada's Green Key Program, an "ECOmmodation" rating program. The hotel has been given a Green Key rating of four out of five.

The hotel's efforts have been recognized with an energy and environmental award from the Hotel Association of Canada. Going forward, the Delta plans to get a better understanding of the impact of its green initiatives on employee engagement by including questions on the green program in its annual employee survey.

Source: Based on Dobson, S. (2009, April 20). It pays to be green. *Canadian HR Reporter, 22(8)*, 15.

and motivation, and employees are proud to be working for an environmentally responsible organization.[49] For another example, see Applied Focus: *Green Management at the Delta Chelsea Hotel*.

In summary, CSR is becoming a major concern for organizations today, and some even issue CSR reports along with their annual reports. Hudson's Bay Company (Hbc) publishes a Corporate Social Responsibility Report every year that is available on its website. Such information is an indication of effective management practices and has been linked to improved financial performance. An organization's CSR also has implications for the recruitment and retention of employees as an increasing number of workers want to work for organizations that are environmentally friendly and rank high on CSR. For example, job candidates are attracted to Hbc because of its corporate social responsibility program. At Husky Injection Molding Systems Ltd. in Bolton, Ontario, job candidates and employees choose to work at the company because of its environmental responsibility program.[50] Organizational behaviour has much to offer organizations in their quest to become more socially responsible.

We hope this brief discussion of some of the issues that are of concern to organizations and managers has reinforced your awareness of using organizational behaviour to better understand and manage life at work. These concerns permeate today's workplace, and we will cover them in more detail throughout the book.

THE MANAGER'S NOTEBOOK

Organizational Change at Ornge

1. As described in the chapter, organizational behaviour refers to the attitudes and behaviours of individuals and groups in organizations, and the discipline of organizational behaviour provides insight about effectively managing and changing attitudes and behaviours. This is the crux of the challenge facing Dr. Mazza. He needs to change employees' attitudes and behaviours given that they are set on doing things the way they have in the past. As noted by Dr. Mazza, "If we didn't change, the program was going to die." In addition, now that the different regions are part of one organization, he needs to create a new organizational culture in which members from the different regions have the same beliefs, values, and expectations and are able to work together to accomplish the organization's goals. Thus, organizational behaviour is fundamental for the challenges that Ornge is facing.

2. In order to change employee attitudes and behaviours and create a new culture, Dr. Mazza brought in executives who could demonstrate three key components: innovation, collaboration, and compassion. He made it clear that hierarchical and judgmental behaviour and even gossip would not be tolerated. "I wanted to create an organization that took what I believe in as physician and put it into where we are working," he said. "And what I hoped

would happen, and is happening, is that I would create such an incredibly strong team that would have a family-like dynamic that they could take on anything." The organization also has a "safer-than-safe culture" to encourage employees "to be forthright about a mistake, rather than fearing the consequences and covering it up, so they can learn how to avoid it in the future," said Ornge's communications centre director Alan Stephen. The results of these initiatives are observable in both the level of workplace satisfaction and the bottom line. "Directors and managers are saying, 'We're seeing people coping better, the gossiping decreasing, and behaviour changing,'" Dr. Mazza said. And by questioning the old attitude of "we've always done it this way," Ornge has saved millions of dollars—it is now buying its own specially equipped helicopters and fixed-wing aircraft instead of leasing them. This is what the study of organizational behaviour is all about: understanding people and managing them to work effectively; understanding how organizations adapt to change and survive; and understanding how to get people to practice effective teamwork.

Source: Based on Dwyer, A. (2009, March 23). Cultivating a corporate culture. *Globe and Mail*, B6; www.ornge.ca/AboutOrnge/Pages/Default.aspx.

LEARNING OBJECTIVES CHECKLIST

1. *Organizations* are social inventions for accomplishing common goals through group effort. The basic characteristic of organizations is that they involve the coordinated efforts of people working together to accomplish common goals.

2. *Organizational behaviour* refers to the attitudes and behaviours of individuals and groups in an organizational context. The field of organizational behaviour systematically studies these attitudes and behaviours and provides advice about how organizations can manage them effectively. The goals of the field include the prediction, explanation, and management of organizational behaviour.

3. *Management* is the art of getting things accomplished in organizations through others. It consists of acquiring, allocating, and utilizing physical and human resources to accomplish goals.

4. The *classical view* of management advocated a high degree of employee specialization and a high degree of coordination of labour from the top of the organization. Taylor's Scientific Management and Weber's views on bureaucracy are in line with the classical position. The *human relations movement* pointed out

the "people problems" that the classical management style sometimes provoked and advocated more interesting job design, more employee participation in decisions, and less centralized control.

5. The *contemporary contingency* approach to management suggests that the most effective management styles and organizational designs are dependent on the demands of the situation.

6. Research on what managers do shows that they fulfill interpersonal, informational, and decisional roles. Important activities include routine communication, traditional management, networking, and human resource management. Managers pursue agendas through networking and use intuition to guide decision making. The demands on managers vary across cultures. A good grasp of organizational behaviour is essential for effective management.

7. A number of societal and global trends are shaping contemporary management concerns, including local and global diversity; changes in employee–organization relationships; the need to improve quality, speed, and flexibility; talent management; and a focus on corporate social responsibility.

DISCUSSION QUESTIONS

1. What are your goals in studying organizational behaviour? What practical advantages might this study have for you?

2. Consider absence from work as an example of organizational behaviour. What are some of the factors that might predict who is likely to be absent from work? How might you explain absence from work? What are some techniques that organizations use to manage absence?

3. Describe the assumptions about organizational behaviour that are reflected in television shows such as situation comedies and police dramas. How accurate are these portrayals? Do they influence our thinking about what occurs in organizations?

4. To demonstrate that you grasp the idea of contingencies in organizational behaviour, consider how closely managers should supervise the work of their employees. What are

some factors on which closeness of supervision might be contingent?

5. Management is the art of getting things accomplished in organizations through others. Given this definition, what are some factors that make management a difficult, or at least a challenging, occupation?

6. Use the contingency approach to describe a task or an organizational department where a more classical management style might be effective. Then do the same for a task or department where the human relations style would be effective.

7. What is corporate social responsibility (CSR) and what does it have to do with organizational behaviour? Explain how an understanding of organizational behaviour can help organizations become more socially responsible.

8. Why do studies of managerial behaviour reveal the importance of networking? What about the importance of human resource management? Explain the differences between these two behaviours and their importance for success.

9. What are some of the demands that increased workforce diversity and increased global operations make on managers? What are some of the opportunities that these trends offer to managers?

10. Describe how management practices and organizational behaviour can help organizations deal with the contemporary management concerns discussed in the chapter. In other words, what are some of the things that organizations can do to (a) manage local and global diversity, (b) improve employee–organization relationships, (c) improve quality, speed, and flexibility, (d) improve talent management, and (e) improve corporate social responsibility?

ON-THE-JOB CHALLENGE QUESTION

A recent report on the shortage of registered nurses (RNs) in Canada predicts that there could be a shortfall of 60 000 RNs by the year 2022. The shortage could have dire consequences for the provision of care, especially for the increasing number of seniors with chronic illnesses. Patients who are already experiencing long and frustrating wait times will suffer the brunt if nothing is done to ease burnout and declining morale among RNs. The average absentee rate for nurses is 14 days a year, which is about twice as high as for other professionals. According to Linda Silas, president of the Canadian Federation of Nurses Unions, the sheer stress of overwork, short-staffing, and lack of sometimes-basic equipment takes its toll. "It gets to a point where you have nurses so tired that when one of their colleagues calls in sick, they just say, 'Give me a warm body'—regardless if he or she has the education." Most nurses aren't looking for more money, Silas said. Average salaries range from a starting pay of $40 000 to $50 000 to a maximum salary of between $60 000 to $80 000 a year, depending on the province. However, the workforce is aging, and nurses are increasingly leaving the profession because of the physical and mental strain, the inflexibility of their work schedules, and the lack of time for education and research. About 8 000 nursing graduates start working each year. Research suggests that many show signs of burnout within the first 36 months on the job, and a large number of nurses leave the profession at a young age.

Explain how organizational behaviour can be used to predict, understand, and manage the nursing shortage in Canada. What do you think are some of the reasons for the nursing shortage and what are some solutions for averting the predicted shortfall? What should government and policy makers do to address the nursing shortage in Canada? How can organizational behaviour be used to curtail the nursing shortage?

Sources: Bailey, S. (2009, May 11). Canada headed for nursing crisis, report says. *Toronto Star* (online), www.thestar.com/printArticle/632605; Picard, A. (2009, May 12). Six steps urged to reverse RN shortfall. *Globe and Mail*, L1, L4; Tested solutions for eliminating Canada's registered nurse shortage. Canadian Nurses Association.www.cna-aiic.ca.

EXPERIENTIAL EXERCISE

Good Job, Bad Job

The purpose of this exercise is to help you get acquainted with some of your classmates by learning something about their experiences with work and organizations. To do this, we will focus on an important and traditional topic in organizational behaviour—what makes people satisfied or dissatisfied with their jobs (a topic that we will cover in detail in Chapter 4).

1. Students should break into learning groups of four to six people. Each group should choose a recording secretary.

2. In each group, members should take turns introducing themselves and then describing to the others either the best job or the worst job that they have ever had. Take particular care to explain why this particular job was either satisfying or dissatisfying. For example, did factors such as pay, co-workers, your boss, or the work itself affect your level of satisfaction? The recording secretary should make a list of the jobs group members held, noting which were "good" and which were "bad." (15 minutes)

3. Using the information from Step 2, each group should develop a profile of four or five characteristics that seem to contribute to dissatisfaction in a job and four or five characteristics that contribute to satisfaction. In other words, are there some common experiences among the group members? (10 minutes)

4. Each group should write its "good job" and "bad job" characteristics on the board. (3 minutes)

5. The class should reconvene, and each group's recording secretary should report on the specific jobs the group considered good or bad. The instructor will discuss the profiles on the board, noting similarities and differences. Other issues worth probing are behavioural consequences of job attitudes (e.g., quitting) and differences of opinion within the groups (e.g., one person's bad job may have seemed attractive to someone else). (15 minutes)

6. Why do you think that a good job for some people might be a bad job for others and vice versa? What are the implications of this for management and organizational behaviour?

EXPERIENTIAL EXERCISE

OB on TV

The purpose of this exercise is to explore the portrayal of organizational behaviour on television. Most experts on the function of TV as a communication medium agree on two points. First, although TV may present an inaccurate or distorted view of many specific events, the overall content of TV programming does accurately reflect the general values and concerns of society. Second, TV has the power to shape the attitudes and expectations of viewers. If this is so, we should pay some attention to the portrayal of work and organizational behaviour on TV.

Prepare this exercise before its assigned class:

1. Choose a prime-time TV show that interests you. (This means a show that airs between 8 p.m. and 10 p.m. in your viewing area. If your schedule prohibits this, choose another time.) The show in question could be a comedy, a drama, or a documentary, for example, *The Office* or *30 Rock*, *Grey's Anatomy*, or *the fifth estate*. Your instructor may give you more specific instructions about what to watch.

2. On a piece of paper, list the name of the program and its date and time of broadcast. Write the answers to the following questions during or immediately following the broadcast:

   a. What industry is the primary focus of the program? Use the following list to categorize your answer: agriculture; mining; construction; manufacturing; transportation; communication; wholesale trade; retail trade; finance; service; public administration. (Examples of service industries include hotel, health, law, education, newspaper, entertainment, and private investigation. Examples of public administration include justice, police work, and national security.)

   b. What industries or occupations are of secondary focus in the program?

   c. What exact job categories or occupational roles do the main characters in the program play? Use this list to categorize your answers: managerial; clerical; professional; sales; service; craftsperson; machine operator; labourer; law enforcement, military personnel; customer/patient/client; homemaker.

   d. Write several paragraphs describing how organizational life is portrayed in the program. For example, is it fun or boring? Does it involve conflict or cooperation? Are people treated fairly? Do they seem motivated? Is work life stressful?

   e. What aspects of the TV portrayal of organizational behaviour do you think were realistic? Which were unrealistic?

3. Be prepared to discuss your findings in class. Your instructor will have some research information about how organizational life has actually been portrayed on TV over the years.

Source: Inspired by the research of Leah Vande Berg and Nick Trujillo, as reported in Vande Berg, L., & Trujillo, N. (1989). *Organizational life on television.* Copyright © 1989. Ablex Publishing. Reproduced with permission of ABC-CLIO, LLC.

EXPERIENTIAL EXERCISE

OB in the News

Every day there are stories in the news about organizations, the workplace, careers, and jobs. Now that you are learning about organizational behaviour, you can begin to interpret and understand these stories in a more informed manner. So let's get started. Look for an article in your local newspaper that has something to do with work or organizations. Pay particular attention to articles in the business or careers section of the paper. Read the article as you normally would and then write a short summary of the article and what you have learned from it. Then read the article again, but this time answer the following questions:

1. What does the article tell you about organizational behaviour? Refer to the sections What Are Organizations? and What Is Organizational Behaviour? in this chapter to answer this question.

2. Use the events described in the article to explain why organizational behaviour is important and makes a difference.

3. How can the goals of organizational behaviour be used to better understand the events in the article or solve a problem or concern that is noted in the article? Be sure to relate each of the goals of

organizational behaviour to the article (i.e., predicting, explaining, and managing organizational behaviour).

4. Does the article address any of the contemporary management concerns described in the chapter? Try to interpret the article in terms of one or more of the contemporary management concerns.

5. Compare your first reading and interpretation of the article to your second reading and interpretation. What did you learn about the events in the article when interpreting it through your new organizational behaviour "lens"?

6. How can learning about organizational behaviour improve your understanding and interpretation of stories and events like the one described in your article.

CASE INCIDENT

My Mother's Visit

Last year, George was preparing for his mother's first visit to Canada. George had immigrated to Canada from Haiti six years ago. His dream was for his mother to come to Canada to meet his new family and live with them. He had been working hard and saving money for years to pay for his mother's airfare. Finally, everything was coming together. His mother's flight was booked and a big celebration was planned to mark her arrival. George had arranged to leave work at lunchtime to pick his mother up at the airport and take her to his house, where the guests would be waiting. He spent months planning the celebration and making the arrangements.

However, when the big day arrived, his boss handed him an assignment and told him he was not to leave until it was completed. When George described his plans, his boss cut him off and reminded him that the organization depends on employees to do whatever it takes to get the job done: "No excuses, George. You are

not to leave until the job is done!" George had to arrange for a taxi to pick up his mother, and her welcome celebration took place without him. George did not get home until late in the evening. The guests had left and his mother had gone to bed. George wondered why the assignment could not have waited until the next day, or why one of his co-workers couldn't have done it.

1. What does this incident tell you about management and organizational behaviour at George's organization?

2. How can organizational behaviour help to predict and explain the behaviour of George and his boss? What advice would you give to George and his boss in terms of managing organizational behaviour in the future?

3. What does this incident tell you about management and organizational behaviour in general?

CASE STUDY

Social Networking at Callsaurus Inc.

Callsaurus Inc. is an Ontario-based third-party inbound call-centre solutions provider with 800 employees in three locations. The call attendants, often college students or recent graduates, take in calls related to a variety of products from dozens of companies that have outsourced their toll-free customer service responsibilities to Callsaurus.

Productivity (e.g., number of calls answered per hour, percent of issues resolved with the first attendant)

is highly monitored. During slow times, when no calls are coming in, it is common for Callsaurus employees to surf the web—sometimes to get competitive information or to take online training, other times to catch up on personal business such as email and bill payments.

The company's current electronic communications policy allows for reasonable personal use of company equipment (phone, fax, email, and internet), as long as it does not interfere with customer service, productivity, or corporate security. However, employees are not able to download programs or applications unless they have permission from the director of IT, and certain websites, such as those relating to gaming, gambling, and pornography, are blocked by the company.

Recently, more and more employees have started accessing social networking sites such as YouTube, Facebook, and MySpace during office hours. The vice-president of operations, Dino Astrodon, is aware that several organizations, such as the City of Toronto, TD Canada Trust, and the Ontario government, have blocked access to these sites. To determine whether Callsaurus should do the same, he convened a meeting of the company's directors. Here is a sample of their comments:

Sales director: We must not block access to the internet. Our employees use it to research competitive offerings and also to go to technical sites to get more information. I'm thinking about launching a social networking strategy that would encourage our employees to access blogs, Facebook, and other sites, so that we can add to discussion forums, see what people are saying about our services, and respond accordingly.

Product support director: Maybe we should post stuff on YouTube to show how to use some of our products. That might cut down on our length of calls and make us more efficient.

HR director: There's a lot of information about us online right now. Social networking is about branding. If we are draconian in our policies, it will get out in the blogosphere and become impossible to attract the young, tech-savvy employees we need. Of course I want more productivity, but I don't want morale to suffer by imposing a no-internet policy.

Director of call-centre operations: Our productivity is suffering. We have employees who abuse the system. Some are addicted to Facebook and MySpace. They make personal calls, look for old classmates and, in one case, divulge company secrets online. We deal with these on a case-by-case basis, but it is time-consuming and frustrating. I think only managers and above should have access to social networking.

Corporate security director: Spending time on non-work-related sites is the same as stealing from the company. Whether it is pencils or time, stealing is stealing. Also, I don't want our company secrets out there for everyone to know. We don't even publicize our call-centre locations because we don't want disgruntled customers showing up at our doors!

Director of teleworking operations: With today's telecommunication technology, we have more and more people working from home and on flex-time, often using their personal computer for work purposes. Surely, we can't stop them from accessing 'inappropriate' sites . . . can we?

Director of IT: I'm concerned about bandwidth. Downloads and increased internet activity slow down our network. Also, it takes up our time to administer all the requests we get to download programs and add-ons. There's no way around it if we want to protect against a virus.

Director of finance: If we need to get more servers to accommodate all the increased internet activity, it's not coming out of my budget!

Astrodon left the meeting with more questions than answers. He knows Callsaurus needs to modify its internet policy, but he's not sure how to reflect the various directors' objectives (or even if he needs to consider everyone's comments in his decision). What should he do?

Source: Pekar, J. (2007, October/November). Saving face: Managing social networking sites in the workplace. *HR Professional, 24(5)*, 47–49. Reprinted with permission of *HR Professional* October/November 2007.

1. Refer to the case and describe how it sheds light on the meaning of organizations and organizational behaviour. Explain the relevance and importance of organizational behaviour for the issues described in the case.

2. Use examples from the case to explain the goals of organizational behaviour. In other words, what does the company need to predict, explain, and manage? How can the goals of organizational behaviour help the company decide what to do about employee use of the internet? Explain your answer.

3. Consider the relevance of each of the managerial roles and activities for Dino Astrodon. What roles and activities are most important for dealing with the incident described in the case? What does Dino Astrodon need to do and how should he proceed?

4. Consider the case in terms of the contemporary management concerns described in the chapter. In other words, to what extent are diversity, employee–organization relationships, quality, speed, and flexibility, talent management, and corporate social responsibility a concern and relevant?

5. Do you think the company should block employee access to the internet? How can organizational behaviour help you to understand the implications of blocking or not blocking employee access to the internet? How can organizational behaviour help Dino Astrodon decide what to do? What do you think he should do and why?

INTEGRATIVE CASE

Richard Ivey School of Business
The University of Western Ontario

Deloitte & Touche: Integrating Arthur Andersen

Written by Ken Mark and Gerard Seijts

Introduction

It was a rainy September morning. Terry Noble, the Toronto Group Managing Partner for Deloitte & Touche (Deloitte), stretched his back and contemplated the results of the most recent "Pulse Survey" that were just presented to him.

Noble co-chaired the national integration team that was faced with a huge challenge: to develop a company-wide plan to create support materials to aid the Deloitte people in integrating more than 1,000 Arthur Andersen (Andersen) people into their 5,600 person strong organization. Noble's team monitored the integration process through a monthly Pulse Survey, which would allow the team to benchmark unit to unit over time, and to take remedial action if, at specific stages, the integration goals were not attained.

The data that Noble just had seen did not come as a total surprise. In fact, he and the Deloitte senior management team were feeling a certain degree of backlash from a number of people in their own organization. Some Deloitte employees, it seemed, feared that Deloitte management, in its haste to consummate this new deal and welcome Andersen, was forgetting about its own employees. There was an attitude among some employees within Deloitte, the larger organization, that people coming from Andersen were "damaged goods" and that these people should be grateful that they had found a good home. Comments such as "Damn the torpedoes and let's get on with business," and "It's our way or the highway . . . after all, we acquired the Andersen business" began to surface. The cultural issues were showing up in day-to-day behavior. Noble mulled over how he might best address this issue. Should he address it at all? For example, he did not yet know whether the opinions voiced came from a few vocal employees, or if others in the Deloitte organization shared their sentiment. The integration issues were rather complicated because, at the outset, the integration message was interpreted by some as "a merger of two equals."

The Integration

On June 3, 2002, across Canada, approximately 1,000 Andersen people (700 professional staff, 200 support staff and 70 partners) would join Deloitte, effectively creating the country's largest professional services organization. The large majority of these people would be located in Toronto. Noble estimated that the value of Andersen annual billings brought to Deloitte was between Cdn$100 million and Cdn$180 million. If the integration were somehow mismanaged, annual billings would be around Cdn$90 million or even less. However, if the integration were successful, the number would be closer to the Cdn$180 million mark. The combined entity would employ 6,600 people in total, representing annual billings of approximately Cdn$1.1 billion.

A welcome breakfast involving 1,300 people was planned to kick off the integration at the Metro Toronto Convention Centre, followed by a series of introductory speeches. Colin Taylor, Deloitte's chief executive and managing partner stated:

> Now we're integrating the Andersen people and clients into Deloitte with the same energy, enthusiasm and speed that we brought to closing the transaction. We have a lot of work ahead of us and our goal is to make this transition absolutely seamless for our clients and as smooth as possible for our people.

At Deloitte, "Making a Difference Together" was the vision for the integrated organization that expressed the combined company's commitment to its clients and each other. It also expressed the belief that the integration with Andersen would strengthen existing capabilities. Deloitte included these words in a new logo created to highlight all integration communications. The logo symbolized Deloitte's conviction that, as the number one professional services firm in Canada, it will be even stronger and more successful in the marketplace (see Exhibit 1).

Deloitte & Touche

Deloitte in Canada was part of a worldwide group named Deloitte Touche Tohmatsu. Deloitte Touche Tohmatsu was a Swiss Verein, an association, and each of its national practices was a separate and independent legal entity.

In Canada, Deloitte had 2001 revenues of Cdn$895 million and 5,600 people (including 515 partners). Its main services were four-fold. Assurance and Advisory services provided attest services (financial audits of organizations, rendering an independent opinion). Financial Advisory services included investigative services directed at solving business crime and reorganization services to allow managers to regain control amid organizational crisis— essentially crisis management services. In addition, this group facilitated public offerings of stock or debt, mergers and acquisitions, and performed due diligence work for clients. Consulting-type services were offered to help clients develop and enhance their business strategies. Tax services supported personal and corporate filings as well as advised clients on how to achieve tax savings. Deloitte had offices in all major cities across Canada. The four services listed above were offered in each of these offices.

Andersen

Andersen Worldwide SC, a Swiss Societe Cooperative, was a co-ordinating entity for its autonomous member firms that had agreed to co-operate in the market with a common brand, philosophy, and technologies and practice methods. Thus, each Andersen Worldwide member firm, including Andersen in the United States and Andersen in Canada, had its own governance and capital structure. There were Andersen consultants serving clients in 390 locations around the world.

In 1960, Andersen established its Canadian practice with 26 people. Prior to 2002, it was considered the smallest of the five largest accounting firms in Canada with 1,300 people. At the time of the integration in 2002, Andersen had sized itself down to approximately 970 employees. The firm serviced clients across the country from seven offices located in Vancouver, Calgary, Winnipeg, Mississauga, Toronto, Ottawa and Montreal. It offered services that were very similar to those offered by Deloitte.

Noble was impressed with the Andersen organization in Canada, stating:

> *We knew that Andersen had the best litigation record of any professional services firm in Canada. We admired and envied Andersen. At Deloitte, we would often hold Andersen practices up as the industry benchmark, including their tools, skills, marketing, and knowledge management capabilities. Their link to a global network of consultants with expertise in a multitude of areas, and which could be accessed at any given time, was unparalleled.*

The Events that Led up to the Integration

In 1999, Enron had been the seventh largest U.S. company (based on reported revenues). For the last 10 years, it had evolved from a regional natural gas provider to, among other things, a trader of natural gas, electricity and other commodities, with retail operations in energy and other products. In 1998, Enron was number 73 on Fortune's annual list of "100 Best Companies to Work For."

Andersen U.S. provided Enron with Internal audit services as well as serving as Enron's external auditor. Although Andersen's international branches were legally separate from Andersen U.S., the Andersen name became a huge liability as a result of the Enron scandal. Andersen U.S. faced a felony charge of obstruction of justice, accused of trying to block a Securities and Exchange Commission (SEC) investigation into Enron's financial disclosures by destroying documents related to the accounting firm's audits.

In statements released to the media, Andersen stated that the action taken against its firm by the U.S. Department of Justice was "both factually and legally baseless." Nevertheless, the damage had been done and the company faced a crisis from which it would not recover.

Enron's collapse and allegations of illegal activity by Andersen created debate around auditor independence and scope of services. Criminal indictment of Andersen U.S. created a negative impact on the accounting profession. One of the questions that persisted in the public arena was whether an accounting firm could objectively perform an audit when it also made millions of dollars providing other services to the same client. Audit firms refuted that an audit could be enhanced by the extra knowledge the firm gained through its consulting arm.

The collapse of Enron and the court of public opinion effectively destroyed the Andersen brand in a few months. In accepting Andersen professionals, some Deloitte managers were concerned that the Enron fallout might carry over to the Deloitte brand.

The Integration Talks

Although it was thought that rival accounting firms — either KPMG or Ernst & Young — already had a deal to acquire Andersen, Deloitte's senior management team was pleasantly surprised when it found out that Andersen's U.S. tax practice had urged Andersen Canada to talk to Deloitte. In the United States, Andersen's tax practice had aligned with its Deloitte counterpart. In the first week of April 2002, Andersen Canada contacted Deloitte to begin integration talks.

On Friday, April 12, 2002, Deloitte completed a memorandum of agreement with Andersen Canada to integrate its practice with Deloitte. This transaction was subject to a due diligence review, partner approvals by both firms and regulatory approval. Because of its size, the transaction was subject to regulatory review by the Competition Bureau under Canada's Competition Act. Noble stated:

> *The run-up to the integration has been a disaster for Andersen. Despite their Canadian client base and staff remaining loyal, their phones were not ringing. Even when they were the frontrunner for new business, potential clients would almost always shy away from them. The day-to-day press surrounding Andersen was very negative.*

Andersen had been negotiating with KPMG and the media was speculating that a deal was imminent. Deloitte took a less public profile, avoiding speculation. Because both sides moved rapidly, the transaction was completed in six weeks. Closing the transaction quickly was critical because a lengthy process increased the risk that a major client and a significant number of talented professionals would be lost.

Alan Booth, director of National Human Resources with Deloitte, explained that the detailed negotiations on people and other critical integration issues proved very challenging due to various reasons, including:

1. Strict limitations on contact between Deloitte and Andersen to permit regulatory review;

2. Imminent systems loss at Andersen set to occur when it would withdraw from Andersen worldwide;

3. Numerous rumors that fed anxiety among people in both organizations; and

4. Co-ordination of messages to people from Deloitte and Andersen was greatly affected by the necessary contact limitations.

On Friday, May 31, 2002, at 5:00 p.m. Pacific Daylight Time, Andersen Canada "went dark." All its systems including phones, e-mail, and personal computers (PCs) were disconnected from the worldwide Andersen network. This signaled the beginning of the actual integration of the former Andersen people into the Deloitte organization.

The National Integration Team

A national integration team consisting of 12 individuals was formed to lead the integration. The team was co-chaired by Terry Noble, who had trained as a chartered accountant with Andersen in Canada, and Russ Robertson, Andersen's managing partner. Colin Taylor, Deloitte's chief executive, knew that both men had been classmates at the Western Business School undergraduate program at the University of Western Ontario, London, Canada, in the 1960s, and thus knew each other. Equal numbers of Deloitte and Andersen personnel were represented on the team. An effort was made to ensure that key people from both sides were involved, in order to guide the integration challenge. For example, heads of functions, integrating officers from the five Deloitte offices, and several "thought leaders" were part of the team.

The main goals of the integration team were to put together a company-wide plan for integration and to create support materials (e.g., "A Primer on Organizational Grieving") to aid the Deloitte people in integrating their new colleagues into their organization. Geographic and functional leaders were to execute the plan with support from national functions such as human resources (HR), information technology (IT) and finance. For example, HR was, to a large extent, responsible for communicating the Deloitte policies, as well as explaining administrative items, such as compensation, the incentive plan, pensions and benefits, and promotion policies. The IT department was responsible for issues such as a seamless transition of e-mail, telephone systems and computer applications. There were significant differences in the IT systems between the two companies. However, by the end of Monday, June 3, 2002, almost all new Deloitte people had their PCs reconfigured to the Deloitte systems, a new phone number, a connection to the network and new business cards to give to their clients.

The national integration team would monitor the integration process through an Internet-based Pulse Survey, which would allow the team to benchmark unit to unit over time, and to take immediate remedial action if in the various stages the integration goals were not attained. The Pulse Survey was conducted every month with a random sample of people from both organizations. For example, among other things, people were asked:

1. How they felt the integration was proceeding overall;
2. If they were kept informed about the personal impact integration would have on them;
3. Whether they perceived fair treatment;
4. Whether their ability to do their jobs was maintained or increased;
5. If they felt that client service levels were being maintained or improved; and
6. If they intended to remain with Deloitte one year into the future.

Participants in the survey were also given the opportunity to provide open comments on how they felt the integration was progressing, or any other message they wanted to communicate in confidence. All offices received detailed feedback on all of the questions that were incorporated in the survey. The questions that were part of the Pulse Survey are listed in Exhibit 2.

Once every two weeks, the managing partners of each of the five Deloitte offices would convene for a conference call to share updates and ideas, some of which resulted from the Pulse Survey. Best practices were identified, and integrating officers were encouraged to implement these practices across offices. Last, the integration team would present status updates to Deloitte's executive committee and board of directors.

Commenting on the Deloitte and Andersen integration, in November of 2002, Noble stated:

Integration is easier said than done. It takes at least three to five years. There is often a strong tendency on the part of those leading the change efforts to declare victory too soon. Early on we need to outline the present and future state of our organization. Cultures do not change that quickly. We do not want a situation where the integration unravels and turns into a bad business deal because we did not manage the process, people, systems, and business fundamentals in a proper fashion.

One thousand Andersen professionals are joining us and not one of them had chosen to be part of our organization. The integration is like an arranged marriage and we have to find common ground. The Andersen people probably have a fear that they will be taken over and their identity and sense of value will be lost. I'm sure that they are not prepared to let that happen.

There are workplace productivity issues that we will have to manage. At first, the Andersen people will be busy getting used to their new titles, new surroundings, and new colleagues. Many people will be concerned with "me" issues: my office, my promotion, my salary, my computer, my role and responsibilities, and so forth. While they have all that to sort through, our job is to figure out how to mitigate the productivity drop. A significant drop in our productivity could tie up the organization for years.

Of course, we want to be able to retain all of our clients—particularly those that are brought in by Andersen. We want our new clients to be proud of their association with Deloitte and confident in the ability of the combined entity to deliver quality and excellent service. Our combined client base needs to be convinced that Deloitte will not be affected by the aftershocks of the Andersen events in the U.S. We cannot afford to slip on our client service delivery. Otherwise there would not be enough work for our people.

Risks Identified by the Integration Team

As Noble saw it, the real challenge for the Deloitte and Andersen organizations was to move beyond the integrated HR and IT systems toward a unified, market-leading organization. The actual successes achieved in the marketplace would hold the combined entities together. For example, financial success served as glue and, as Noble observed, would all but ensure that partners felt they had shared in the success of the transaction. Essential to the long-term success of the integration, therefore, was that individuals would see (or feel in their pocket) that investing significant resources in the transaction, time and money, was indeed worth it. Noble believed that the Andersen people would be blamed if the combined organization missed the financial targets that it intended to achieve. Such scapegoating would detract from the integration efforts.

Noble identified the top three risk factors that threatened to derail the success of the integration: cultural misalignment and subsequent conflict, insufficient integration and lack of organizational synergies. Exhibits 3 and 4 describe the method and results of the cultural assessment that was conducted in July 2002 to determine the differences between the Deloitte and Andersen cultures.

The results of the assessment revealed how each organization viewed itself, the "other" organization and the challenges of the integration. The cultural gaps between members of the two organizations identified critical organizational issues that required special attention from the national integration team. It was quite clear that people from Deloitte and Andersen were different from an organizational culture point of view. Noble elaborated:

The Andersen organization is being told that they will join a new organization. They would not have volunteered to integrate with us if not for the crisis that occurred in the U.S. Will they be enthusiastic about the integration? Some of them may be. However, others may not completely understand why we do things in a certain way here at Deloitte. Addressing the differences between the two cultures was essential to successfully guiding the integration.

The great payoff will be, that if we do this right, and utilize the talent of Andersen employees, we will not only become the best professional services firm, but also the largest in the country.

Ultimately, "this is a talent play for us. We've got the best 1,000 people coming into our organization fully trained. We have to figure out how we can get their commitment to us and to serve our clients. We want the Andersen people to be proud of their new organization.

We will lose people, but we want to lose them for the right reasons. People may have goals or values that are different from the ones espoused at Deloitte. However, we don't want to lose people because of poor interpersonal treatment.

The September Meeting

The data from the Pulse Survey (the third since June of 2002) that Noble had received earlier in the morning confirmed, at least to some extent, what he had been hearing through the grapevine. The data suggested that a number of Deloitte employees feared that Deloitte management, in its haste to consummate the deal with Andersen and welcome the new employees, was forgetting about its own people. Some elements within the Deloitte organization did not understand the amount of attention given to the Andersen people, whom they viewed as "damaged goods." Comments indicating that it was time for all people involved in the integration to "get on with business and focus on the market" began to surface.

However, Noble was not certain of the number of individuals that shared such views. Were these the concerns of a few vocal people? Or did these individuals voice what many others in the Deloitte organization were thinking? Clearly, this was not the kind of feedback he was hoping for. The results from the Pulse Survey led Noble to contemplate how he and his colleagues from the integration team could best deal with the cultural differences in the short term. In his words:

There is the naive view that a new culture will be formed with relative ease. I doubt it. Cultures involve deep-seated beliefs. For example, at Andersen, there had always been a strong drive to focus on the clients' needs above everything else. In contrast, at Deloitte, while acknowledging the importance of commitment to quality and the client's needs, there was also a focus on employee issues.

A Frenchman and an Englishman will always retain their culture. But they can learn to work together to achieve a common goal. Or can they really?

It takes a lot of effort and patience to help new behaviors and practices grow deep roots.

In Noble's mind, this was a complex issue to manage. Furthermore, there were a number of situational constraints on actions that could be undertaken to address the issue. For example, Noble and his integration team had to contend with the fact that people were constantly on-site at the client's business. How then should managers work to resolve tensions that might arise between the two cultures? Moreover, taking the people from the two organizations to an off-site location to deal with the issue of cultural differences would certainly affect billable hours. Were we prepared to do that? On the other hand, addressing these and other issues in a timely and proper fashion could make the difference between being a good organization versus being great organization.

True integration would be hard to achieve without the knowledge, skill and, above all, the commitment of the Deloitte people. It was 10:29 a.m., and Noble got up to go to the meeting with the integration team.

QUESTIONS

1. Discuss the relevance of organizational behaviour for the issues that Deloitte & Touche are facing. How can organizational behaviour be used to help the integration team ensure that the integration is successful?

2. Explain how the goals of organizational behaviour can be used by the integration team to ensure that the integration is successful. Describe some of the things that the integration team might want to predict, explain, and manage.

3. Consider Terry Noble's role as co-chair of the national integration team in terms of Mintzberg's managerial roles. What roles does he exhibit and how effective is he in performing each role? What roles are most important and why?

4. To what extent are some of the contemporary management concerns described in Chapter 1 relevant for the integration team? What does the integration team need to be most concerned about and what should they do to be successful in managing the contemporary management concerns?

EXHIBIT 1
Deloitte's new logo for the integrated organization

Source: Company files.

EXHIBIT 2
Pulse survey questions

No.	Questions
1.	Overall, the integration is going well.
2.	The firm is committed to making the integration as smooth as possible for our people.
3.	I am being kept informed about how the integration will affect me.
4.	I am being treated fairly during the integration.
5.	My ability to do my job effectively has been maintained or improved as a result of the integration.
6.	I am confident dealing with client questions about the integration.
7.	Client service levels have been maintained or improved as a result of the integration.
8.	My clients are feeling positive about the integration.
9.	I intend to be with D&T one year from now.
	Overall score.

Methodology/Framework

Orientation

	Internal Integration	External Orientation	Red Tape	Bottom Line	Business Horizons/ Vision	Learning and Development
Measurement Dimensions	Teamwork Openness Management Support Communication Integrity Diversity Reward and Recognition Work Lifestyle Balance	Commitment to Quality Client Orientation External Competitiveness Market Orientation	Bureaucracy Action Orientation and Accountability Risk Propensity	Results Orientation	Goal Definition and Alignment Vision and Mission Organization Values	Learning and Development
Focus						

Findings from the focus groups, interviews, questionnaires, and documentation review were grouped based on 6 key cultural orientations, which are characterized by a series of measurement dimensions outlined above.

Making a Difference Together   15   DRAFT CONFIDENTIAL–NOT FOR DISTRIBUTION

EXHIBIT 3
Methodology used to test cultural alignment between Deloitte and Andersen

Source: Company files.

Overall Assessment

CULTURAL SYNERGIES		CULTURAL GAPS	
Dimension	**Degree of Alignment**	**Dimension**	**Degree of Alignment**
Commitment to Quality	◕	Bureaucracy	◔
Client Orientation	◕	Market Orientation	◔
Teamwork	◔	Diversity	◔
Communication	◔	Action Orientation and Accountability	◕
Openness	◔	Learning and Development	◕
Integrity	◔	Reward and Recognition	◕
External Competitiveness	◔	Organizational Values	◕
Results Orientation	◔	Work Lifestyle Balance	◕
Risk Propensity	◔	Management Support	◕
Vision and Mission	◔	Goal Definition and Alignment	◑

Legend: Degree of Cultural Alignment

⊕ ◔ ◑ ◕ ●

Ten areas were identified as having either a moderate or low degree of cultural alignment. The remaining ten areas revealed a relatively high degree of cultural alignment.

Making a Difference Together   19   DRAFT CONFIDENTIAL–NOT FOR DISTRIBUTION

EXHIBIT 4
Results of cultural assessment

Source: Company files.

PART TWO
Individual Behaviour

CHAPTERS

2	**3**	**4**	**5**	**6**
Personality and Learning	Perception, Attribution, and Diversity	Values, Attitudes, and Work Behaviour	Theories of Work Motivation	Motivation in Practice

Personality and Learning

DundeeWealth and PepsiCo

DundeeWealth is a Canadian-owned, independent wealth management company headquartered in Toronto, with more than 1100 employees in North America and Europe. The company recently launched a new program called "Health Is Wealth" that focuses on employees' wellness and fitness and includes regular competitions and prizes. According to the company's director of wellness, health, and safety, the aim of the program is to have healthier employees who are more productive and have less absenteeism.

The program includes everything from weight-loss competitions with prizes inspired by reality shows such as *The Biggest Loser* and *Taking It Off* to fitness breaks during sales meetings. To encourage employee participation, there are goals for weight loss and fitness with prizes such as $125 gift cards for sports gear, yoga gift baskets, and exercise equipment.

The company also offers employees fitness assessments and provides them with advice on how to set up a home training program. Healthy living is also encouraged when employees are away from home on business. For example, at a recent national sales meeting in Kelowna, British Columbia, employees were encouraged to spend less time at the buffet tables and more time in fitness classes and on scheduled walks. Employees received a ticket for a draw to win a $100 Lululemon gift certificate for each fitness activity they participated in. In the first year of the program, about 30 percent of employees participated. Early results indicate a reduction in sick days taken.

DundeeWealth is not alone in its efforts to change employee's lifestyle behaviour. More and more companies are focusing on fitness and wellness in an effort to lower health-care costs, increase productivity, reduce absenteeism, and attract and retain talent.

For example, PepsiCo, one of the world's largest food and beverage companies, has a program called HealthRoads that encourages employees to live healthier lifestyles through a combination of health assessments, fitness and nutrition programs, personalized coaching, and online tools and worksite initiatives. The program provides employees with financial

DundeeWealth recently launched a program called "Health Is Wealth" that focuses on employees' wellness and fitness and includes weight-loss competitions and prizes.

rewards for managing and improving their health. Employees can earn up to $250 a year in rewards and double that amount if their spouse or partner participates in the program. For example, they can earn up to $100 for taking a personal health assessment and for wellness coaching and $25 for healthy eating, weight management, exercise, and stress management. Employees who are smokers can avoid a $600 health benefit surcharge by participating in a smoking-cessation program and can earn up to $100 in rewards for successfully completing the program. To encourage a healthy pregnancy, the company offers expecting employees a $50 savings bond for their baby and a chance to participate in a $1500 raffle.

Sixty-eight percent of the company's 82 000 employees and spouses who are eligible for the program in the United States have registered for the program. Of those registered, 61 percent have taken a personal health assessment and 60 percent have reduced or eliminated at least one health risk. PepsiCo has so far reduced or eliminated more than 46 000 health risks. The company's annual rate of increase in health-care costs has dropped four percentage points since 2004.

In 2007, the HealthRoads program was launched in Asia, and PepsiCo UK has initiated a Fit for Life program to encourage healthier lifestyles and better work–life balance for its employees. A similar program called Vive Saludable (Live Healthy) has been implemented in Mexico.

In 2009, PepsiCo was one of 63 organizations recognized by the National Business Group on Health on its list of Best Employers for Healthy Lifestyles. PepsiCo was one of 17 large organizations to receive a Platinum Award, the highest level of recognition, for its HealthRoads program.[1]

Learning is a critical requirement for effective organizational behaviour, and as you probably know, for organizations to remain competitive in today's rapidly changing environment, employee learning must be continuous and life-long. As you can tell from the opening vignette, employees at DundeeWealth and PepsiCo are learning to live healthier lives. But how can organizations change employees' lifestyle behaviour? What learning principles and theories are involved? And are they effective? In this chapter we will focus on the learning process and see how learning in organizations takes place. While learning is necessary for the acquisition of knowledge, skills, and behaviours, studies in organizational behaviour have shown that behaviour is also a function of people's personalities. Therefore, we begin this chapter by considering personality and organizational behaviour, and then we will focus on learning.

What Is Personality?

The notion of personality permeates thought and discussion in our culture. We are bombarded with information about "personalities" in the print and broadcast media. We are sometimes promised exciting introductions to people with "nice" personalities. We occasionally meet people who seem to have "no personality." But exactly what *is* personality?

Personality is the relatively stable set of psychological characteristics that influences the way an individual interacts with his or her environment and how he or she feels, thinks, and behaves. An individual's personality summarizes his or her personal style of dealing with the world. You have certainly noticed differences in personal style among your parents, friends, professors, bosses, and employees. They are reflected in the distinctive way that they react to people, situations, and problems.

Where does personality come from? Personality consists of a number of dimensions and traits that are determined in a complex way by genetic predisposition and by one's long-term learning history. Although personality is relatively stable, it is certainly susceptible to change through adult learning experiences. And while we often use labels such as "high self-esteem" to describe people, we should always remember that people have a *variety* of personality characteristics. Excessive typing of people does not help us to appreciate their unique potential to contribute to an organization.

Personality. The relatively stable set of psychological characteristics that influences the way an individual interacts with his or her environment.

Personality and Organizational Behaviour

Personality has a rather long and rocky history in organizational behaviour. Initially, it was believed that personality was an important factor in many areas of organizational behaviour, including motivation, attitudes, performance, and leadership. In fact, after World War II, the use of personality tests for the selection of military personnel became widespread, and, in the 1950s and 1960s, it became popular in business organizations. This approach to organizational behaviour is known as the "dispositional approach" because it focuses on individual dispositions and personality. According to the dispositional approach, individuals possess stable traits or characteristics that influence their attitudes and behaviours. In other words, individuals are predisposed to behave in certain ways. However, decades of research produced mixed and inconsistent findings that failed to support the usefulness of personality as a predictor of organizational behaviour and job performance. As a result, there was a dramatic decrease in personality research and a decline in the use of personality tests for selection. Researchers began to shift their attention to factors in the work environment that might predict and explain organizational behaviour. This approach became known as the "situational approach." According to the situational approach, characteristics of the organizational setting, such as rewards and punishment, influence people's feelings, attitudes, and behaviour. For example, many studies have shown that job satisfaction and other work-related attitudes are largely determined by situational factors such as the characteristics of work tasks.[2]

Over the years, proponents of both approaches have argued about the importance of dispositions versus the situation in what is known as the "person–situation debate." Although researchers argued over which approach was the right one, it is now believed that both approaches are important for predicting and understanding organizational behaviour. This led to a third approach to organizational behaviour, known as the "interactionist approach," or "interactionism." According to the interactionist approach, organizational behaviour is a function of both dispositions and the situation. In other words, to predict and understand organizational behaviour, one must know something about an individual's personality and the setting in which he or she works. This approach is now the most widely accepted perspective within organizational behaviour.[3]

To give you an example of the interactionist perspective, consider the role of personality in different situations. To keep it simple, we will describe situations as being either "weak" or "strong." In weak situations it is not always clear how a person should behave, while in strong situations there are clear expectations for appropriate behaviour. As a result, personality has the most impact in weak situations. This is because in these situations (e.g., a newly formed volunteer community organization) there are loosely defined roles, few rules, and weak reward and punishment contingencies. However, in strong situations, which have more defined roles, rules, and contingencies (e.g., routine military operations), personality tends to have less impact.[4] Thus, as you can see, the extent to which personality influences people's attitudes and behaviour depends on the situation. Later in the text you will learn that the extent to which people perceive stressors as stressful and the way they react to stress is also influenced by their personality. This is another example of the interactionist approach to organizational behaviour.

One of the most important implications of the interactionist perspective is that some personality characteristics are useful in certain organizational situations. Thus, there is no one best personality, and managers need to appreciate the advantages of employee diversity. A key concept here is *fit*: putting the right person in the right job, group, or organization and exposing different employees to different management styles.

In recent years, there has been a resurgence of interest in personality research in organizational behaviour. One of the main problems with the early research on personality was the use of inadequate measures of personality characteristics. However, advances in measurement and trends in organizations have prompted renewed interest. For example, increased emphasis on service jobs with customer contact, concern about ethics and integrity, and contemporary interest in teamwork and cooperation all point to the potential contribution of personality.[5]

Another reason for the renewed interest in personality has been the development of a framework of personality characteristics known as the Five-Factor Model, or the "Big Five," which provides a framework for classifying personality characteristics into five general dimensions. This framework makes it much easier to understand and study the role of personality in organizational behaviour.[6]

In what follows, we first discuss the five general personality dimensions of the Five-Factor Model. Then we cover three well-known personality characteristics with special relevance to organizational behaviour. We then discuss recent developments in personality research. Later in the text, we will explore the impact of personality characteristics on job satisfaction, motivation, leadership, ethics, organizational politics, and stress.

The Five-Factor Model of Personality

People are unique, people are complex, and there are literally hundreds of adjectives that we can use to reflect this unique complexity. Yet, over the years, psychologists have discovered that there are about five basic but general dimensions that describe personality. These "Big Five" dimensions are known as the Five-Factor Model (FFM)

Extraversion	Emotional Stability	Agreeableness	Conscientiousness	Openness to Experience
Sociable, Talkative vs. Withdrawn, Shy	Stable, Confident vs. Depressed, Anxious	Tolerant, Cooperative vs. Cold, Rude	Dependable, Responsible vs. Careless, Impulsive	Curious, Original vs. Dull, Unimaginative

EXHIBIT 2.1
The Five-Factor Model of Personality.

of personality and are summarized in Exhibit 2.1 along with some illustrative traits.[7] The dimensions are:

- *Extraversion*—this is the extent to which a person is outgoing versus shy. Persons who score high on extraversion tend to be sociable, outgoing, energetic, joyful, and assertive. High extraverts enjoy social situations, while those low on this dimension (introverts) avoid them. Extraversion is especially important for jobs that require a lot of interpersonal interaction, such as sales and management, where being sociable, assertive, energetic, and ambitious is important for success.

- *Emotional stability/Neuroticism*—the degree to which a person has appropriate emotional control. People with high emotional stability (low neuroticism) are self-confident and have high self-esteem. Those with lower emotional stability (high neuroticism) tend toward self-doubt and depression. They tend to be anxious, hostile, impulsive, depressed, insecure, and more prone to stress. As a result, for almost any job the performance of persons with low emotional stability is likely to suffer. Persons who score high on emotional stability are likely to have more effective interactions with co-workers and customers because they tend to be more calm and secure.

- *Agreeableness*—the extent to which a person is friendly and approachable. More agreeable people are warm, considerate, altruistic, friendly, sympathetic, cooperative, and eager to help others. Less agreeable people tend to be cold and aloof. They tend to be more argumentative, inflexible, uncooperative, uncaring, intolerant, and disagreeable. Agreeableness is most likely to contribute to job performance in jobs that require interaction and involve helping, cooperating, and nurturing others, as well as in jobs that involve teamwork and cooperation.

- *Conscientiousness*—the degree to which a person is responsible and achievement-oriented. More conscientious people are dependable and positively motivated. They are orderly, self-disciplined, hard-working, and achievement-striving, while less conscientious people are irresponsible, lazy, and impulsive. Persons who are high on conscientiousness are likely to perform well on most jobs given their tendency towards hard work and achievement.

- *Openness to experience*—the extent to which a person thinks flexibly and is receptive to new ideas. More open people tend toward creativity and innovation. Less open people favour the status quo. People who are high on openness to experience are likely to do well in jobs that involve learning and creativity given that they tend to be intellectual, curious, and imaginative and have broad interests.

The "Big Five" dimensions are relatively independent. That is, you could be higher or lower in any combination of dimensions. Also, they tend to hold up well cross-culturally. Thus, people in different cultures use these same dimensions when describing the personalities of friends and acquaintances. There is also evidence that the "Big Five" traits have a genetic basis.[8]

Research Evidence. Research has linked the "Big Five" personality dimensions to organizational behaviour. First, there is evidence that each of the "Big Five" dimensions is related to job performance.[9] Generally, traits like those in the top half of Exhibit 2.1 lead to better job performance. Further, the "Big Five" dimensions that best predict job performance depend on the occupation. For example, high extraversion is important for managers and salespeople. However, high conscientiousness predicts performance in all jobs across occupations and is also the strongest predictor of all the "Big Five" dimensions of overall job performance.[10]

Second, research has also found that the "Big Five" are related to other work behaviours. For example, one study showed that conscientiousness is related to retention and attendance at work and is also an important antidote for counterproductive behaviours such as theft, absenteeism, and disciplinary problems.[11] Extraversion has also been found to be related to absenteeism; extraverts tend to be absent more often than introverts.[12]

The "Big Five" are also related to work motivation and job satisfaction. In a study that investigated the relationship between the "Big Five" and different indicators of work motivation, the "Big Five" were found to be significantly related to motivation. Among the five dimensions, neuroticism and conscientiousness were the strongest predictors of motivation, with the former being negatively related and the latter being positively related.[13] In another study, the "Big Five" were shown to be significantly related to job satisfaction. The strongest predictor was neuroticism (i.e., emotional stability) followed by conscientiousness, extraversion, and, to a lesser extent, agreeableness. Openness to experience was not related to job satisfaction. Higher neuroticism was associated with lower job satisfaction, while higher extraversion, conscientiousness, and agreeableness were associated with higher job satisfaction. Similar results have been found for life satisfaction. In addition, individuals with higher conscientiousness, extraversion, agreeableness, and emotional stability perform better on a team in terms of their performance of important team-relevant behaviours such as cooperation, concern, and courtesy to team members.[14]

The "Big Five" are also related to job search and career success. Extraversion, conscientiousness, openness to experience, and agreeableness have been found to relate positively to the intensity of a job seeker's job search, while neuroticism was negatively related. As well, conscientiousness was found to be positively related to the probability of obtaining employment.[15] In addition, high conscientiousness and extraversion and low neuroticism have been found to be associated with a higher income and occupational status. Perhaps most interesting is the fact that these personality traits were related to career success even when the influence of general mental ability had been taken into account. Furthermore, both childhood and adult measures of personality predicted career success during adulthood over a period of 50 years. These results suggest that the effects of personality on career success are relatively enduring.[16] But can personality predict an expatriate's effectiveness and success on a foreign work assignment? To learn more, see Global Focus: *Personality and Expatriate Effectiveness.*

As noted earlier, the "Big Five" personality dimensions are basic and general. However, years of research have also identified a number of more specific personality characteristics that influence organizational behaviour, including locus of control, self-monitoring, and self-esteem. Let's now consider each of these.

Locus of Control

Consider the following comparison. Laurie and Stan are both management trainees in large banks. However, they have rather different expectations regarding their futures. Laurie has just enrolled in an evening Master of Business Administration (MBA) program in a nearby university. Although some of her MBA courses are not immediately applicable to her job, Laurie feels that she must be prepared for greater responsibility as she moves up in the bank hierarchy. Laurie is convinced that she will achieve promotions because she studies hard, works hard, and does her job properly. She feels that an individual makes her own way in the world and that she can control her own destiny. She is certain that she can someday be the president of the bank if she really wants to be. Her personal motto is "I can do it."

Stan, on the other hand, sees no use in pursuing additional education beyond his bachelor's degree. According to him, such activities just do not pay off. People who get

GLOBAL FOCUS

Personality and Expatriate Effectiveness

Managing international assignments is both challenging and complex for organizations. The expatriate workforce is becoming more varied and global as multinational corporations rely more heavily on third-country nationals and less expensive intra-region transfers. The major international assignment challenge for organizations is selecting expatriates who will be effective.

However, when it comes to selecting candidates for expatriate assignments, many companies base their selection decisions on technical expertise and employee (or familial) willingness to go. Unfortunately, the result of this strategy is often poor expatriate adjustment, early returns, and inadequate job performance. With an estimated price tag of US$150 000 or more per person for adjustment failure in addition to an estimated US$80 000 for training, relocation, and compensation, organizations can ill afford to continue making expatriate selection decisions based on technical expertise and willingness to go.

But can personality predict expatriate adjustment and effectiveness? To find out, Margaret Shaffer, Hal Gregersen, David Harrison, J. Stewart Black, and Lori Ferzandi studied the "Big Five" as potential predictors of several dimensions of expatriate effectiveness. Expatriate effectiveness included three kinds of adjustment (work adjustment, interaction adjustment, and cultural adjustment): intentions to quit the assignment; and job performance.

The researchers collected data from a sample of expatriates and their spouses and colleagues from many nations living and working in Hong Kong, as well as Korean and Japanese expatriates on international assignments in numerous countries around the world. Because expatriates face highly uncertain and ambiguous situations, it represents a good example of a "weak situation," in which the norms for behaviour are unclear and individuals do not share a common understanding of what is expected of them.

The results indicated that emotional stability was positively related to an expatriate's work adjustment and negatively related to intentions to quit. Agreeableness was positively related to interaction adjustment, openness to experience was positively related to work adjustment and job performance, and extraversion was positively related to cultural adjustment. However, conscientiousness was not related to any indicator of expatriate effectiveness.

The results of this study demonstrate that the "Big Five" are important predictors of international assignment effectiveness. Each of the "Big Five" personality traits except conscientiousness was a significant predictor of at least one form of expatriate effectiveness. Expatriates who are emotionally stable, outgoing and agreeable, and high on openness to experience seem to function better than others on a foreign assignment.

Source: Based on Shaffer, M.A., Gregersen, H., Harrison, D.A., Black, J.S., & Ferzandi, L.A. (2006). You can take it with you: Individual differences and expatriate effectiveness. *Journal of Applied Psychology, 91*, 109–125.

promoted are just plain lucky or have special connections, and further academic preparation or hard work has nothing to do with it. Stan feels that it is impossible to predict his own future, but he knows that the world is pretty unfair.

Laurie and Stan differ on a personality dimension called **locus of control**. This variable refers to individuals' beliefs about the *location* of the factors that control their behaviour. At one end of the continuum are high internals (like Laurie), who believe that the opportunity to control their own behaviour resides within themselves. At the other end of the continuum are high externals (like Stan), who believe that external forces determine their behaviour. Not surprisingly, compared with internals, externals see the world as an unpredictable, chancy place in which luck, fate, or powerful people control their destinies.[17] (See Exhibit 2.2.)

Internals tend to see stronger links between the effort they put into their jobs and the performance level that they achieve. In addition, they perceive to a greater degree than externals that the organization will notice high performance and reward it.[18] Since internals believe that their work behaviour will influence the rewards they achieve, they are more likely to be aware of and to take advantage of information that will enable them to perform effectively.[19]

Locus of control. A set of beliefs about whether one's behaviour is controlled mainly by internal or external forces.

Research shows that locus of control influences organizational behaviour in a variety of occupational settings. Evidently, because they perceive themselves as being able to control what happens to them, people who are high on internal control are more satisfied with their jobs, earn more money, and achieve higher organizational positions.[20] In addition, they seem to perceive less stress, to cope with stress better, and to engage in more careful career planning.[21]

Self-Monitoring

We are sure that you have known people who tend to "wear their heart on their sleeves." These are people who act the way they feel and say what they think in spite of their social surroundings. We are also sure that you have known people who are a lot more sensitive to their social surroundings, a lot more likely to fit what they say and do to the nature of those surroundings regardless of how they think or feel. What we have here is a contrast in **self-monitoring**, which is the extent to which people observe and regulate how they appear and behave in social settings and relationships.[22] The people who "wear their heart on their sleeves" are low self-monitors. They are not so concerned with scoping out and fitting in with those around them. Their opposites are high self-monitors, who take great care to observe and control the images that they project. In this sense, high self-monitors behave somewhat like actors. In particular, high self-monitors tend to show concern for socially appropriate behaviour, to tune in to social and interpersonal cues, and to regulate their behaviour and self-presentation according to these cues.

How does self-monitoring affect organizational behaviour?[23] For one thing, high self-monitors tend to gravitate toward jobs that require, by their nature, a degree of role-playing and the exercise of their self-presentation skills. Sales, law, public relations, and politics are examples. In such jobs, the ability to adapt to one's clients and contacts is critical; so are communication skills and persuasive abilities, characteristics that high self-monitors frequently exhibit. High self-monitors perform particularly well in occupations that call for flexibility and adaptiveness in dealings with diverse constituencies. As well, a number of studies show that managers are inclined to be higher self-monitors than non-managers in the same organization. Self-monitoring is also significantly related to a number of work-related outcomes. High self-monitors tend to be more involved in their jobs, to perform at a higher level, and to be more likely to emerge as leaders. However, high self-monitors are also likely to experience more role stress and show less commitment to their organization.[24]

Promotion in the management ranks is often a function of subjective performance appraisals, and the ability to read and conform to the boss's expectations can be critical for advancement. Thus, the ability to regulate and adapt one's behaviour in social situations and to manage the impressions others form of them might be a career advantage for high self-monitors. In fact, in a study that tracked the careers of a sample of Master of Business Administration graduates, high self-monitors were more likely to change employers and locations and to receive more promotions than low self-monitors.[25]

Are high self-monitors always at an organizational advantage? Not likely. They are unlikely to feel comfortable in ambiguous social settings in which it is hard to determine exactly what behaviours are socially appropriate. Dealing with unfamiliar cultures (national or corporate) might provoke stress. Also, some roles require people to go against the grain or really stand up for what they truly believe in. Thus, high self-monitoring types would seem to be weak innovators and would have difficulty resisting social pressure.

Self-Esteem

How well do you like yourself? This is the essence of the personality characteristic called self-esteem. More formally, **self-esteem** is the degree to which a person has a positive self-evaluation. People with high self-esteem have favourable self-images. People with low self-esteem have unfavourable self-images. They also tend to be uncertain about the correctness of their opinions, attitudes, and behaviours. In general, people tend to be highly motivated to protect themselves from threats to their self-esteem.

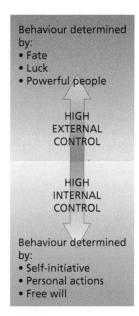

Behaviour determined by:
• Fate
• Luck
• Powerful people

HIGH EXTERNAL CONTROL

HIGH INTERNAL CONTROL

Behaviour determined by:
• Self-initiative
• Personal actions
• Free will

EXHIBIT 2.2
The internal/external locus of control continuum.

Self-monitoring. The extent to which people observe and regulate how they appear and behave in social settings and relationships.

Self-esteem. The degree to which a person has a positive self-evaluation.

One of the most interesting differences between people with high and low self-esteem has to do with the *plasticity* of their thoughts, attitudes, and behaviour, or what is known as "behavioural plasticity." According to **behavioural plasticity theory**, people with low self-esteem tend to be more susceptible to external and social influences than those who have high self-esteem—that is, they are more pliable. Thus, events and people in the organizational environment have more impact on the beliefs and actions of employees with low self-esteem. This occurs because, being unsure of their own views and behaviour, they are more likely to look to others for information and confirmation. In addition, people who have low self-esteem seek social approval from others, approval that they might gain from adopting others' views, and they do not react well to ambiguous and stressful situations. This is another example of interactionism, in that the effect of the work environment on people's beliefs and actions is partly a function of their self-esteem.[26]

Employees with low self-esteem also tend to react badly to negative feedback—it lowers their subsequent performance.[27] This means that managers should be especially cautious when using negative reinforcement and punishment, as discussed later in this chapter, with employees with low self-esteem. If external causes are thought to be responsible for a performance problem, this should be made very clear. Also, managers should direct criticism at the performance difficulty and not at the person. As we will explain shortly, modelling the correct behaviour should be especially effective with employees with low self-esteem, who are quite willing to imitate credible models and who also respond well to mentoring. Finally, organizations should try to avoid assigning those with low self-esteem to jobs (such as life insurance sales) that inherently provide a lot of negative feedback.

Organizations will generally benefit from a workforce with high self-esteem. Such people tend to make more fulfilling career decisions, they exhibit higher job satisfaction and job performance, and they are generally more resilient to the strains of everyday worklife.[28] What can organizations do to bolster self-esteem? Opportunity for participation in decision making, autonomy, and interesting work have been fairly consistently found to be positively related to self-esteem.[29] Also, organizations should avoid creating a culture with excessive and petty work rules that signal to employees that they are incompetent or untrustworthy.[30]

Recent Developments in Personality and Organizational Behaviour

In recent years, there have been a number of exciting developments in personality research in organizational behaviour. In this section, we briefly review five more recent personality variables that have been found to be important for organizational behaviour: positive and negative affectivity, proactive personality, general self-efficacy, and core self-evaluations.

Positive and Negative Affectivity. Have you ever known somebody who is always happy, cheerful, and in a good mood? Or perhaps you know someone who is always unhappy and in a bad mood. Chances are you have noticed these differences in people. Some people are happy most of the time, while others are almost always unhappy. These differences reflect two affective dispositions known as positive affectivity (PA) and negative affectivity (NA). Research has found that they are enduring personality characteristics and that there might be a genetic and biological basis to them.

People who are high on **positive affectivity** experience positive emotions and moods and view the world in a positive light, including themselves and other people. They tend to be cheerful, enthusiastic, lively, sociable, and energetic. People who are high on **negative affectivity** experience negative emotions and moods and view the world in a negative light. They have an overall negative view of themselves and the world around them, and they tend to be distressed, depressed, and unhappy.[31]

Behavioural plasticity theory. People with low self-esteem tend to be more susceptible to external and social influences than those who have high self-esteem.

Positive affectivity. Propensity to view the world, including oneself and other people, in a positive light.

Negative affectivity. Propensity to view the world, including oneself and other people, in a negative light.

Unlike the other personality traits discussed in this chapter, positive and negative affectivity are emotional dispositions that predict people's general emotional tendencies. Thus, they can influence people's emotions and mood states at work and influence job attitudes and work behaviour. Research on affective dispositions has found that people who are high on PA report higher job satisfaction and job performance, while those high on NA report lower job satisfaction and performance. Employees who have higher PA have also been found to be more creative at work. People who have high NA tend to experience more stressful work conditions and report higher levels of workplace stress and strain. NA has also been found to be associated with more counterproductive work behaviours (e.g., harassment, physical aggression), withdrawal behaviours (e.g., absenteeism, turnover), and occupational injury. Finally, there is some evidence that positive affect is a key factor that links happiness to success in life and at work.[32]

Proactive Personality.   How effective are you at taking initiative and changing your circumstances? Taking initiative to improve one's current circumstances or creating new ones is known as **proactive behaviour**. It involves challenging the status quo rather than passively adapting to present conditions. Some people are actually better at this than others because they have a stable disposition toward proactive behaviour, known as a "proactive personality." Individuals who have a **proactive personality** are relatively unconstrained by situational forces and act to change and influence their environment. Proactive personality is a stable personal disposition that reflects a tendency to take personal initiative across a range of activities and situations and to effect positive change in one's environment.[33]

> **Proactive behaviour.** Taking initiative to improve current circumstances or creating new ones.

> **Proactive personality.** A stable personal disposition that reflects a tendency to take personal initiative across a range of activities and situations and to effect positive change in one's environment.

Proactive individuals search for and identify opportunities, show initiative, take action, and persevere until they bring about meaningful change. People who do not have a proactive personality are more likely to be passive and to react and adapt to their environment. As a result, they tend to endure and to be shaped by the environment instead of trying to change it.[34] Proactive personality has been found to be related to a number of work outcomes, including job performance, tolerance for stress in demanding jobs, leadership effectiveness, participation in organizational initiatives, work team performance, and entrepreneurship. One study found that proactive personality is associated with higher performance evaluations because individuals with a proactive personality develop strong supportive networks and perform initiative-taking behaviours such as implementing solutions to organization or departmental problems or spearheading new programs. There is also evidence that persons with a proactive personality are more successful in searching for employment and career success. They are more likely to find a job, to receive higher salaries and more frequent promotions, and to have more satisfying careers.[35]

General Self-Efficacy.   General self-efficacy (GSE) is a general trait that refers to an individual's belief in his or her ability to perform successfully in a variety of challenging situations.[36] GSE is considered to be a *motivational* trait rather than an *affective* trait because it reflects an individual's belief that he or she can succeed at a variety of tasks rather than how an individual feels about him or herself. An individual's GSE is believed to develop over the life span as repeated successes and failures are experienced across a variety of tasks and situations. Thus, if you have experienced many successes in your life, you probably have high GSE, whereas somebody who has experienced many failures probably has low GSE. Individuals who are high on GSE are better able to adapt to novel, uncertain, and adverse situations. In addition, employees with higher GSE have higher job satisfaction and job performance.[37]

> **General self-efficacy.** A general trait that refers to an individual's belief in his or her ability to perform successfully in a variety of challenging situations.

Core Self-Evaluations.   Unlike the other personality characteristics described in this chapter, which are specific in themselves, **core self-evaluations** refers to a broad personality concept that consists of more specific traits. The idea behind the theory of core self-evaluations is that individuals hold evaluations about themselves and their

> **Core self-evaluations.** A broad personality concept that consists of more specific traits that reflect the evaluations people hold about themselves and their self-worth.

self-worth or worthiness, competence, and capability.[38] In a review of the personality literature, Timothy Judge, Edwin Locke, and Cathy Durham identified four traits that make up a person's core self-evaluation. The four traits have already been described in this chapter; they include self-esteem, general self-efficacy, locus of control, and neuroticism (emotional stability).

Research on core self-evaluations has found that these traits are among the best dispositional predictors of job satisfaction and job performance. People with more positive self-evaluations have higher job satisfaction and job performance. Furthermore, research has shown that core self-evaluations measured in childhood and in early adulthood are related to job satisfaction in middle adulthood. This suggests that core self-evaluations are related to job satisfaction over time. Core self-evaluations have also been found to be positively related to life and career satisfaction, and individuals with higher CSE perceive fewer stressors and experience less stress and conflict at work. One of the reasons for the relationship between core self-evaluations and job satisfaction is that individuals with a positive self-regard are more likely to perceive their jobs as interesting, significant, and autonomous than individuals with a negative self-regard. Persons with a positive self-regard experience their job as more intrinsically satisfying, and they are also more likely to have more complex jobs.[39]

What Is Learning?

So far in this chapter we have described how people's personalities can influence their work attitudes and behaviours. However, recall our earlier discussion that people's experiences and the work environment also have a strong effect on attitudes and behaviour. As you will learn in this section, the environment can change people's behaviour and even shape personalities and, as described at the start of the chapter, even people's lifestyle behaviours can be changed. To understand how this can happen, let's examine the concept of learning.

Learning occurs when practice or experience leads to a relatively permanent change in behaviour potential. The words *practice* or *experience* rule out viewing behavioural changes caused by factors like drug intake or biological maturation as learning. One does not learn to be relaxed after taking a tranquilizer, and a boy does not suddenly learn to be a bass singer at the age of 14. The practice or experience that prompts learning stems from an environment that gives feedback concerning the consequences of behaviour.

But what do employees learn in organizations? Learning in organizations can be understood in terms of taxonomies that indicate what employees learn, how they learn, and different types of learning experiences. The "what" aspect of learning can be described as learning content, of which there are four primary categories: practical skills, intrapersonal skills, interpersonal skills, and cultural awareness.[40]

Practical skills include job-specific skills, knowledge, and technical competence. Employees frequently learn new skills and technologies to continually improve performance and to keep organizations competitive. Constant improvement has become a major goal in many organizations today, and training can give an organization a competitive advantage.[41] *Intrapersonal skills* are skills such as problem solving, critical thinking, learning about alternative work processes, and risk taking. *Interpersonal skills* include interactive skills such as communicating, teamwork, and conflict resolution. Later in this book, we will discuss the ways in which teams are becoming the major building blocks of organizations, as well as the importance of effective communication for organizational success.

Finally, *cultural awareness* involves learning the social norms of organizations and understanding company goals, business operations, and company expectations and priorities. All employees need to learn the cultural norms and expectations of their organizations to function as effective organizational members. We discuss the learning of social norms and organizational culture in more detail in Chapter 8.

Now that we have considered the content of learning in organizations, let's turn to two theories that describe how people learn in organizations.

Learning. A relatively permanent change in behaviour potential that occurs due to practice or experience.

Operant Learning Theory

In the 1930s, psychologist B.F. Skinner investigated the behaviour of rats confined in a box containing a lever that delivered food pellets when pulled. Initially, the rats ignored the lever, but at some point they would accidentally pull it and a pellet would appear. Over time, the rats gradually acquired the lever-pulling response as a means of obtaining food. In other words, they *learned* to pull the lever. The kind of learning Skinner studied is called **operant learning** because the subject learns to operate on the environment to achieve certain consequences. The rats learned to operate the lever to achieve food. Notice that operantly learned behaviour is controlled by the consequences that follow it. These consequences usually depend on the behaviour, and this connection is what is learned. For example, salespeople learn effective sales techniques to achieve commissions and avoid criticism from their managers. The consequences of commissions and criticism depend on which sales behaviours salespeople exhibit.

Operant learning can be used to increase the probability of desired behaviours and to reduce or eliminate the probability of undesirable behaviours. Let's now consider how this is done.

Operant learning. Learning by which the subject learns to operate on the environment to achieve certain consequences.

Increasing the Probability of Behaviour

One of the most important consequences that influences behaviour is reinforcement. **Reinforcement** is the process by which stimuli strengthen behaviours. Thus, a *reinforcer* is a stimulus that follows some behaviour and increases or maintains the probability of that behaviour. The sales commissions and criticism mentioned earlier are reinforcers for salespeople. In each case, reinforcement serves to strengthen behaviours, such as proper sales techniques, that fulfill organizational goals. In general, organizations are interested in maintaining or increasing the probability of behaviours such as correct performance, prompt attendance, and accurate decision making. As described at the beginning of the chapter, DundeeWealth and PepsiCo are interested in maintaining and increasing the probability of various employee wellness behaviours, such as weight loss, exercise, and healthy eating. As we shall see, positive reinforcers work by their application to a situation, while negative reinforcers work by their removal from a situation.

Reinforcement. The process by which stimuli strengthen behaviours.

Positive Reinforcement

Positive reinforcement increases or maintains the probability of some behaviour by the *application* or *addition* of a stimulus to the situation in question. Such a stimulus is a positive reinforcer. In the basic Skinnerian learning situation described earlier, we can assume that reinforcement occurred because the probability of the lever operation increased over time. We can further assume that the food pellets were positive reinforcers because they were introduced after the lever was pulled.

Consider the experienced securities analyst who tends to read a particular set of financial newspapers regularly. If we had been able to observe the development of this reading habit, we might have found that it occurred as the result of a series of successful business decisions. That is, the analyst learns to scan those papers because his or her reading is positively reinforced by subsequent successful decisions. In this example, something is added to the situation (favourable decisions) that increases the probability of certain behaviour (selective reading). Also, the appearance of the reinforcer is dependent or contingent on the occurrence of that behaviour.

In general, positive reinforcers tend to be pleasant things, such as food, praise, money, or business success. However, the intrinsic character of stimuli does not determine whether they are positive reinforcers, and pleasant stimuli are not positive reinforcers when considered in the abstract. Whether or not something is a positive reinforcer depends only on whether it increases or maintains the occurrence of some behaviour by its application. Thus, it is improbable that the holiday turkey that employers give to all the employees of a manufacturing plant positively reinforces anything.

Positive reinforcement. The application or addition of a stimulus that increases or maintains the probability of some behaviour.

The only behaviour that the receipt of the turkey is contingent on is being employed by the company during the third week of December. It is unlikely that the turkey increases the probability that employees will remain for another year or work harder.

Negative Reinforcement

Negative reinforcement increases or maintains the probability of some behaviour by the *removal* of a stimulus from the situation in question. Also, negative reinforcement occurs when a response *prevents* some event or stimulus from occurring. In each case, the removed or prevented stimulus is a *negative reinforcer*. Negative reinforcers are usually aversive or unpleasant stimuli, and it stands to reason that we will learn to repeat behaviours that remove or prevent these stimuli.

Let's repeat this point, because it frequently confuses students of organizational behaviour: Negative reinforcers *increase* the probability of behaviour. Suppose we rig a cage with an electrified floor so that it provides a mild shock to its inhabitant. In addition, we install a lever that will turn off the electricity. On the first few trials, a rat put in the cage will become very upset when shocked. Sooner or later, however, it will accidentally operate the lever and turn off the current. Gradually, the rat will learn to operate the lever as soon as it feels the shock. The shock serves as a negative reinforcer for the lever pulling, increasing the probability of the behaviour by its removal.

Managers who continually nag their employees unless the employees work hard are attempting to use negative reinforcement. The only way employees can stop the aversive nagging is to work hard and be diligent. The nagging maintains the probability of productive responses by its removal. In this situation, employees often get pretty good at anticipating the onset of nagging by the look on their boss's face. This look serves as a signal that they can avoid the nagging altogether if they work harder.

Another example of negative reinforcement is PepsiCo's smoking cessation program, which was described at the beginning of the chapter. Recall that employees who do not participate in the program must pay a $600 benefits surcharge. However, if employees agree to participate in the program—the desired behaviour—then they do not have to pay the benefits surcharge. Thus, the benefits surcharge operates as a negative reinforcer to the extent that it increases the probability that employees will participate in the program. The only way that smokers can avoid the surcharge is to participate in the program. In other words, participating in the program removes the $600 surcharge, or negative reinforcer.

Negative reinforcers generally tend to be unpleasant things, such as shock, nagging, or threat of fines. Again, however, negative reinforcers are defined only by what they do and how they work, not by their unpleasantness. Above, we indicated that nagging could serve as a negative reinforcer to increase the probability of productive responses. However, nagging could also serve as a positive reinforcer to increase the probability of unproductive responses if an employee has a need for attention and nagging is the only attention the manager provides. In the first case, nagging is a negative reinforcer—it is terminated following productive responses. In the second case, nagging is a positive reinforcer—it is applied following unproductive responses. In both cases, the responses increase in probability.

Organizational Errors Involving Reinforcement

Experience indicates that managers sometimes make errors in trying to use reinforcement. The most common errors are confusing rewards with reinforcers, neglecting diversity in preferences for reinforcers, and neglecting important sources of reinforcement.

Confusing Rewards with Reinforcers. Organizations and individual managers frequently "reward" workers with things such as pay, promotions, fringe benefits, paid vacations, overtime work, and the opportunity to perform challenging tasks. Such rewards can fail to serve as reinforcers, however, because organizations do not make them contingent on specific behaviours that are of interest to the organization, such as attendance, innovation, or productivity. For example, many organizations assign overtime work on the basis of seniority, rather than performance or good attendance, even when the union contract does not require it. Although the opportunity to earn extra money might have strong potential as a reinforcer, it is seldom made contingent on some desired behaviour. Notice how the rewards for PepsiCo's HealthRewards program are contingent on specific behaviours, such as taking a personal health assessment.

Neglecting Diversity in Preferences for Reinforcers. Organizations often fail to appreciate individual differences in preferences for reinforcers. In this case, even if managers administer rewards after a desired behaviour, they may fail to have a reinforcing effect. Intuitively, it seems questionable to reinforce a workaholic's extra effort with time off from work, yet such a strategy is fairly common. A more appropriate reinforcer might be the assignment of some challenging task, such as work on a very demanding key project. Some labour contracts include clauses that dictate that supervisors assign overtime to the workers who have the greatest seniority. Not surprisingly, high-seniority workers are often the best paid and the least in need of the extra pay available through overtime. Even if it is administered so that the best-performing high-seniority workers get the overtime, such a strategy might not prove reinforcing—the usual time off might be preferred over extra money.

Managers should carefully explore the possible range of stimuli under their control (such as task assignment and time off from work) for their applicability as reinforcers for particular employees. Furthermore, organizations should attempt to administer their formal rewards (such as pay and promotions) to capitalize on their reinforcing effects for various individuals.

Neglecting Important Sources of Reinforcement. There are many reinforcers of organizational behaviour that are not especially obvious. While concentrating on potential reinforcers of a formal nature, such as pay or promotions, organizations and their managers often neglect those that are administered by co-workers or are intrinsic to the jobs being performed. Many managers cannot understand why a worker would persist in potentially dangerous horseplay despite threats of a pay penalty or dismissal. Frequently, such activity is positively reinforced by the attention provided by the joker's co-workers. In fact, on a particularly boring job, such threats might act as positive reinforcers for horseplay by relieving the boredom, especially if the threats are never carried out.

One very important source of reinforcement that managers often ignore is information that accompanies the successful performance of tasks. **Performance feedback** involves providing quantitative or qualitative information on past performance for the purpose of changing or maintaining performance in specific ways. This reinforcement is available for jobs that provide feedback concerning the adequacy of performance. For example, in some jobs, feedback contingent on performance is readily available. Doctors can observe the success of their treatment by observing the progress of their patients' health, and mechanics can take the cars they repair for a test drive. In other jobs, organizations must build some special feedback mechanism into the job. Performance feedback is most effective when it is (a) conveyed in a positive manner; (b) delivered immediately after the performance is observed (c) represented visually, such as in graph or chart form, and (d) specific to the behaviour that is being targeted for feedback.[42]

Another important source of reinforcement is social recognition. **Social recognition** involves informal acknowledgement, attention, praise, approval, or genuine appreciation for work well done from one individual or group to another. Research has shown that when social recognition is made contingent on employee behaviour it can be an effective means for performance improvement.[43] Thus, managers should understand that positive feedback and a "pat on the back" for a job well done is a positive reinforcer that is easy to administer and is likely to reinforce desirable behaviour.

Performance feedback. Providing quantitative or qualitative information on past performance for the purpose of changing or maintaining performance in specific ways.

Social recognition. Informal acknowledgement, attention, praise, approval, or genuine appreciation for work well done from one individual or group to another.

Reinforcement Strategies

What is the best way to administer reinforcers? Should we apply a reinforcer immediately after the behaviour of interest occurs, or should we wait for some period of time?

Should we reinforce every correct behaviour, or should we reinforce only a portion of correct responses?

To obtain the *fast acquisition* of some response, continuous and immediate reinforcement should be used—that is, the reinforcer should be applied every time the behaviour of interest occurs, and it should be applied without delay after each occurrence. Many conditions exist in which the fast acquisition of responses is desirable. These include correcting the behaviour of "problem" employees, training employees for emergency operations, and dealing with unsafe work behaviours. Consider the otherwise excellent performer who tends to be late for work. Under pressure to demote or fire this good worker, the boss might sensibly attempt to positively reinforce instances of prompt attendance with compliments and encouragement. To modify the employee's behaviour as quickly as possible, the supervisor might station herself near the office door each morning to supply these reinforcers regularly and immediately.

You might wonder when one would not want to use a continuous, immediate reinforcement strategy to mould organizational behaviour. Put simply, behaviour that individuals learn under such conditions tends not to persist when reinforced less frequently or stopped. Intuitively, this should not be surprising. For example, under normal conditions, operating the power switch on your stereo system is continuously and immediately reinforced by music. If the system develops a short circuit and fails to produce music, your switch-operating behaviour will cease very quickly. In the example in the preceding paragraph, the need for fast learning justified the use of continuous, immediate reinforcement. Under more typical circumstances, we would hope that prompt attendance could occur without such close attention.

Behaviour tends to be *persistent* when it is learned under conditions of partial and delayed reinforcement. That is, it will tend to persist under reduced or terminated reinforcement when not every instance of the behaviour is reinforced during learning or when some time period elapses between its enactment and reinforcement. In most cases, the supervisor who wishes to reinforce prompt attendance knows that he or she will not be able to stand by the shop door every morning to compliment the crew's timely entry. Given this constraint, the supervisor should compliment prompt attendance occasionally, perhaps later in the day. This should increase the persistence of promptness and reduce the employees' reliance on the boss's monitoring.

Let's recap. Continuous, immediate reinforcement facilitates fast learning, and delayed, partial reinforcement facilitates persistent learning (see Exhibit 2.3). Notice that it is impossible to maximize both speed and persistence with a single reinforcement strategy. Also, many responses in our everyday lives cannot be continuously and immediately reinforced, so in many cases it pays to sacrifice some speed in learning to prepare the learner for this fact of life. All this suggests that managers have to tailor reinforcement strategies to the needs of the situation. Often, managers must alter the strategies over time to achieve effective learning and maintenance of behaviour. For example, the manager training a new employee should probably use a reinforcement strategy that is fairly continuous and immediate (whatever the reinforcer). Looking over the employee's shoulder to obtain the fast acquisition of behaviour is appropriate. Gradually, however, the supervisor should probably reduce the frequency of reinforcement and perhaps build some delay into its presentation to reduce the employee's dependency on his or her attention.

EXHIBIT 2.3
Summary of reinforcement strategies and their effects.

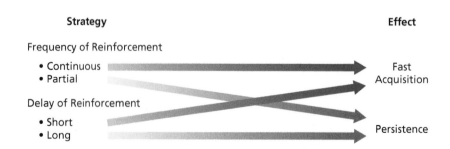

Reducing the Probability of Behaviour

Thus far in our discussion of learning, we have been interested in *increasing* the probability of various work behaviours, such as attendance or good performance. Both positive and negative reinforcement can accomplish this goal. However, in many cases, we encounter learned behaviours that we wish to *stop* from occurring. Such behaviours are detrimental to the operation of the organization and could be detrimental to the health or safety of an individual employee.

There are two strategies that can reduce the probability of learned behaviour: extinction and punishment.

Extinction

Extinction simply involves terminating the reinforcement that is maintaining some unwanted behaviour. If the behaviour is not reinforced, it will gradually dissipate or be extinguished.

Consider the case of a bright, young marketing expert who was headed for the "fast track" in his organization. Although his boss, the vice-president of marketing, was considering him for promotion, the young expert had developed a very disruptive habit—the tendency to play comedian during department meetings. The vice-president observed that this wisecracking was reinforced by the appreciative laughs of two other department members. He proceeded to enlist their aid to extinguish the joking. After the vice-president explained the problem to them, they agreed to ignore the disruptive one-liners and puns. At the same time, the vice-president took special pains to positively reinforce constructive comments by the young marketer. Very quickly, joking was extinguished, and the young man's future with the company improved.[44]

This example illustrates that extinction works best when coupled with the reinforcement of some desired substitute behaviour. Remember that behaviours that have been learned under delayed or partial reinforcement schedules are more difficult to extinguish than those learned under continuous, immediate reinforcement. Ironically, it would be harder to extinguish the joke-telling behaviour of a committee member who was only partially successful at getting a laugh than of one who was always successful at getting a laugh.

Extinction. The gradual dissipation of behaviour following the termination of reinforcement.

Punishment

Punishment involves following an unwanted behaviour with some unpleasant, aversive stimulus. In theory, when the actor learns that the behaviour leads to unwanted consequences, this should reduce the probability of the response. Notice the difference between punishment and negative reinforcement. In negative reinforcement a nasty stimulus is *removed* following some behaviour, increasing the probability of that behaviour. With punishment, a nasty stimulus is *applied* after some behaviour, *decreasing* the probability of that behaviour. If a boss criticizes her assistant after seeing her use the office phone for personal calls, we expect to see less of this activity in the future. Exhibit 2.4 compares punishment with reinforcement and extinction.

Punishment. The application of an aversive stimulus following some behaviour designed to decrease the probability of that behaviour.

Using Punishment Effectively

In theory, punishment should be useful in eliminating unwanted behaviour. After all, it seems unreasonable to repeat actions that cause us trouble. Unfortunately, punishment has some unique characteristics that often limit its effectiveness in stopping unwanted activity. First, while punishment provides a clear signal as to which activities are inappropriate, it does not by itself demonstrate which activities should *replace* the punished response. Reconsider the executive who chastises her assistant for making personal calls at the office. If the assistant makes personal calls only when she has caught up on her work, she might legitimately wonder what she is supposed to be doing during her

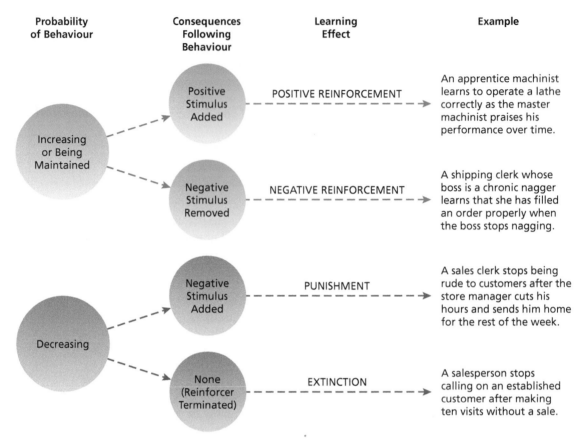

Probability of Behaviour	Consequences Following Behaviour	Learning Effect	Example
Increasing or Being Maintained	Positive Stimulus Added	POSITIVE REINFORCEMENT	An apprentice machinist learns to operate a lathe correctly as the master machinist praises his performance over time.
	Negative Stimulus Removed	NEGATIVE REINFORCEMENT	A shipping clerk whose boss is a chronic nagger learns that she has filled an order properly when the boss stops nagging.
Decreasing	Negative Stimulus Added	PUNISHMENT	A sales clerk stops being rude to customers after the store manager cuts his hours and sends him home for the rest of the week.
	None (Reinforcer Terminated)	EXTINCTION	A salesperson stops calling on an established customer after making ten visits without a sale.

EXHIBIT 2.4

Summary of learning effects.

occasional free time. If the boss fails to provide substitute activities, the message contained in the punishment may be lost.

Both positive and negative reinforcers specify which behaviours are appropriate. Punishment indicates only what is not appropriate. Since no reinforced substitute behaviour is provided, punishment only temporarily suppresses the unwanted response. When surveillance is removed, the response will tend to recur. Constant monitoring is very time consuming, and individuals become amazingly adept at learning when they can get away with the forbidden activity. The assistant will soon learn when she can make personal calls without detection. The moral here is clear: *Provide an acceptable alternative for the punished response.*

A second difficulty with punishment is that it has a tendency to provoke a strong emotional reaction on the part of the punished individual.[45] This is especially likely when the punishment is delivered in anger or perceived to be unfair. Managers who try overly hard to be patient with employees and then finally blow up risk overemotional reactions. So do those who tolerate unwanted behaviour on the part of their employees and then impulsively decide to make an example of one individual by punishing him or her. Managers should be sure that their own emotions are under control before punishing, and they should generally avoid punishment in front of observers.[46] Because of the emotional problems involved in the use of punishment, some organizations have downplayed its use in discipline systems. They give employees who have committed infractions *paid* time off to think about their problems.

In addition to providing correct alternative responses and limiting the emotions involved in punishment, there are several other principles that can increase the effectiveness of punishment.

- *Make sure the chosen punishment is truly aversive.* Organizations frequently "punish" chronically absent employees by making them take several days off work. Managers sometimes "punish" ineffective performers by requiring them to work overtime, which allows them to earn extra pay. In both cases, the presumed punishment may actually act as a positive reinforcer for the unwanted behaviour.

- *Punish immediately.* Managers frequently overlook early instances of rule violations or ineffective performance, hoping that things will "work out."[47] This only allows these behaviours to gain strength through repetition. If immediate punishment is difficult to apply, the manager should delay action until a more appropriate time and then reinstate the circumstances surrounding the problem behaviour. For example, the bank manager who observes her teller exhibiting inappropriate behaviour might ask this person to remain after work. She should then carry out punishment at the teller's window rather than in her office, perhaps demonstrating correct procedures and then role-playing a customer to allow the employee to practise them.

- *Do not reward unwanted behaviours before or after punishment.* Many supervisors join in horseplay with their employees until they feel it is time to get some work done. Then, unexpectedly, they do an about-face and punish those who are still "goofing around." Sometimes, managers feel guilty about punishing their employees for some rule infraction and then quickly attempt to make up with displays of good-natured sympathy or affection. For example, the boss who criticizes her assistant for personal calls might show up an hour later with a gift of flowers. Such actions present employees with extremely confusing signals about how they should behave, since the manager could be unwittingly reinforcing the very response that he or she wants to terminate.

- *Do not inadvertently punish desirable behaviour.* This happens commonly in organizations. The manager who does not use all his capital budget for a given fiscal year might have the department's budget for the next year reduced, punishing the prudence of his employees. Government employees who "blow the whistle" on wasteful or inefficient practices might find themselves demoted.[48] University professors who are considered excellent teachers might be assigned to onerous, time-consuming duty on a curriculum committee, cutting into their class preparation time.

In summary, punishment can be an effective means of stopping undesirable behaviour. However, managers must apply it very carefully and deliberately to achieve this effectiveness. In general, reinforcing correct behaviours and extinguishing unwanted responses are safer strategies for managers than the frequent use of punishment.

Social Cognitive Theory

It has perhaps occurred to you that learning and behaviour sometimes takes place in organizations without the conscious control of positive and negative reinforcers by managers. People often learn and behave through their own volition and self-influence. Thus, human behaviour is not simply due to environmental influences. Rather, people have the cognitive capacity to regulate and control their own thoughts, feelings, motivation, and actions. So, unlike operant learning theory, social cognitive theory emphasizes the role of *cognitive processes* in regulating people's behaviour. For example, people learn by observing the behaviour of others. Individuals can also regulate their behaviour by thinking about the consequences of their actions (forethought), setting performance goals, monitoring their performance and comparing it to their goals, and rewarding themselves for goal accomplishment. People also develop beliefs about their abilities through their interaction with the environment that influences their thoughts and behaviour.[49]

According to social cognitive theory, human behaviour can best be explained through a system of *triadic reciprocal causation,* in which personal factors and environmental factors work together and interact to influence people's behaviour. In addition, people's behaviour also influences personal factors and the environment. Thus, operant learning theory and social cognitive theory complement each other in explaining learning and organizational behaviour.[50]

According to Albert Bandura, social cognitive theory involves three components: observational learning, self-efficacy, and self-regulation.[51]

Observational Learning

Besides directly experiencing consequences, humans also learn by observing the behaviour of others. For instance, after experiencing just a couple of executive committee meetings, a newly promoted vice-president might look like an "old pro," bringing appropriate materials to the meeting, asking questions in an approved style, and so on. How can we account for such learning?

Observational learning is the process of observing and imitating the behaviour of others. With observational learning, learning occurs by observing or imagining the behaviour of others (models), rather than through direct personal experience.[52] Generally, observational learning involves examining the behaviour of others, seeing what consequences they experience, and thinking about what might happen if we act the same way. If we expect favourable consequences, we might imitate the behaviour. Thus, the new vice-president doubtless modelled his behaviour on that of the more experienced peers on the executive committee. But has reinforcement occurred here? It is *self-reinforcement* that occurs in the observational learning process. For one thing, it is reinforcing to acquire an understanding of others who are viewed positively. In addition, we are able to imagine that the reinforcers that the model experiences will come our way when we imitate his or her behaviour. Surely, this is why we imitate the behaviour of sports heroes and entertainers, a fact that advertisers capitalize on when they choose them to endorse products. In any event, observational learning is an important component of social cognitive theory.

What kinds of models are likely to provoke the greatest degree of imitation? In general, attractive, credible, competent, high-status people stand a good chance of being imitated. In addition, it is important that the model's behaviour provoke consequences that are seen as positive and successful by the observer. Finally, it helps if the model's behaviour is vivid and memorable—bores do not make good models.[53] In business schools, it is not unusual to find students who have developed philosophies or approaches that are modelled on credible, successful, high-profile business leaders. Popular examples include Microsoft's Bill Gates and former General Electric CEO Jack Welch, both of whom have been the object of extensive coverage in the business and popular press.

The extent of observational learning as a means of learning in organizations suggests that managers should pay more attention to the process. For one thing, managers who operate on a principle of "do as I say, not as I do" will find that what they do is more likely to be imitated, including undesirable behaviours such as expense account abuse. Also, in the absence of credible management models, workers might imitate dysfunctional peer behaviour if peers meet the criteria for strong models. For example, one study found that the antisocial behaviour of a work group was a significant predictor of an individual's antisocial workplace behaviour. Thus, individual's antisocial workplace behaviour can be shaped, in part, through the process of observation.[54] On a more positive note, well-designed performance appraisal and reward systems permit organizations to publicize the kind of organizational behaviour that should be learned and imitated.

Self-Efficacy

While observational learning may have helped the vice-president learn how to behave in an executive committee meeting, you may have wondered what made him so confident. Was he not full of self-doubt and worried that he would fail? This is known as self-efficacy. **Self-efficacy** refers to beliefs people have about their ability to successfully perform a specific task. At this point, it is important to note the difference between task-specific self-efficacy and some of the general personality traits discussed earlier in the chapter. In particular, unlike self-esteem and general self-efficacy, which are general personality traits, self-efficacy is a task-specific cognitive appraisal of one's ability to perform a specific task. Thus, it is not a generalized personality trait. Furthermore, people can have different self-efficacy beliefs for different tasks. For example, the vice-president might have strong self-efficacy for conducting an

Observational learning. The process of observing and imitating the behaviour of others.

Self-efficacy. Beliefs people have about their ability to successfully perform a specific task.

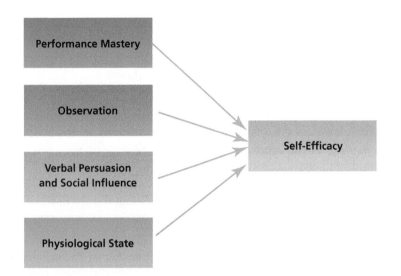

EXHIBIT 2.5
Determinants of
self-efficacy.

executive committee meeting, but low self-efficacy for doing well in a course on organizational behaviour![55]

Because self-efficacy is a cognitive belief rather than a stable personality trait, it can be changed and modified in response to different sources of information. As shown in Exhibit 2.5, self-efficacy is influenced by one's experiences and success performing the task in question (performance mastery), observation of others performing the task, verbal persuasion and social influence, and one's physiological or emotional state. Thus, the self-efficacy of the vice-president could have been strengthened by observing the behaviour of others during meetings, by encouragement from peers that he would do a great job, and perhaps by his own sense of comfort and relaxation rather than feelings of anxiety and stress while attending meetings. Finally, his mastery displayed during the meeting is also likely to further strengthen his self-efficacy beliefs.

Self-efficacy is a critical component of behaviour that can influence the activities people choose to perform, the amount of effort and persistence they devote to a task, affective and stress reactions, and job performance.[56] In the case of the vice-president, his strong sense of self-efficacy obviously contributed to his ability to perform like an "old pro" at the meeting.

Self-Regulation

In much of this chapter, we have been concerned with how organizations and individual managers can use learning principles to manage the behaviour of organizational members. However, according to social cognitive theory, employees can use learning principles to manage their *own* behaviour, making external control less necessary. This process is called **self-regulation**.[57]

How can self-regulation occur? You will recall that observational learning involved factors such as observation of models, imagination, imitation, and self-reinforcement. Individuals can use these and similar techniques in an intentional way to control their own behaviour. The basic process involves observing one's own behaviour (what is known as self-observation), comparing the behaviour with a standard, and rewarding oneself if the behaviour meets the standard (i.e., self-reinforcement). A key part of the process is people's pursuit of self-set goals that guide their behaviour. When there exists a discrepancy between one's goals and performance, individuals are motivated to modify their behaviour in the pursuit of goal attainment (a process known as *discrepancy reduction*). When individuals attain their goals, they are likely to set even higher and more challenging goals, a process known as *discrepancy production*. In this way, people continually engage in a process of setting goals in the pursuit of ever higher levels of performance. Thus, discrepancy reduction and discrepancy production lie at the heart of the self-regulatory process.[58]

Self-regulation. The use of learning principles to regulate one's own behaviour.

To illustrate some specific self-regulation techniques, consider the executive who finds that she is taking too much work home to do in the evenings and over weekends. While her peers seem to have most evenings and weekends free, her own family is ready to disown her due to lack of attention! What can she do?[59]

- *Collect self-observation data.* This involves collecting objective data about one's own behaviour. For example, the executive might keep a log of phone calls and other interruptions for a few days if she suspects that these contribute to her inefficiency.
- *Observe models.* The executive might examine the time-management skills of her peers to find someone successful to imitate.
- *Set goals.* The executive might set specific short-term goals to reduce telephone interruptions and unscheduled personal visits, enlisting the aid of her assistant, and using self-observation data to monitor her progress. Longer-term goals might involve four free nights a week and no more than four hours of work on weekends.
- *Rehearse.* The executive might anticipate that she will have to educate her co-workers about her reduced availability. So as not to offend them, she might practise explaining the reason for her revised accessibility.
- *Reinforce oneself.* The executive might promise herself a weekend at the beach with her family the first time she gets her take-home workload down to her target level.

Research has found that self-regulation can improve learning and result in a change in behaviour. For example, one study showed how a self-regulation program was used to improve work attendance among unionized maintenance employees. Those who had used over half their sick leave were invited by the human resources department to participate in an eight-week program with the following features:

- Discussion of general reasons for use of sick leave. High on the list were transportation problems, family difficulties, and problems with supervisors and co-workers.
- Self-assessment of personal reasons for absence and development of personal coping strategies.
- Goal setting to engage in behaviours that should improve attendance (short-term goals) and to improve attendance by a specific amount (long-term goal).
- Self-observation using charts and diaries. Employees recorded their own attendance, reasons for missing work, and steps they took to get to work.
- Identification of specific reinforcers and punishers to be self-administered for reaching or not reaching goals.

Compared with a group of employees who did not attend the program, the employees who were exposed to the program achieved a significant improvement in attendance, and they also felt more confident (i.e., higher self-efficacy) that they would be able to come to work when confronted with various obstacles to attendance.[60] In another study, training in self-regulation was found to significantly improve the sales performance of a sample of insurance salespeople.[61] Self-regulation programs have been successful in changing a variety of work behaviours and are an effective method of training and learning.[62]

Organizational Learning Practices

We began our discussion of learning by describing learning content, and then we focused on how people learn. In this final section, we review a number of organizational learning practices, including an application of operant learning called organizational behaviour modification, employee recognition programs, training programs, and career development.

Organizational Behaviour Modification

Organizational behaviour modification. The systematic use of learning principles to influence organizational behaviour.

Most reinforcement occurs naturally, rather than as the result of a conscious attempt to manage behaviour. **Organizational behaviour modification** (O.B. Mod) involves the

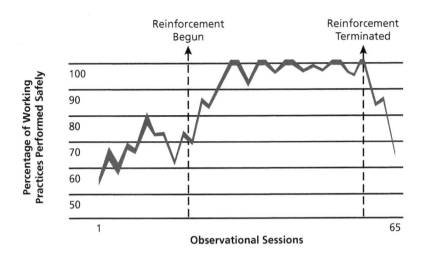

EXHIBIT 2.6
Percentage of safe working practices achieved with and without reinforcement.

Source: Adapted from Komaki, J., et al. (1978, August). A behavioral approach to occupational safety: Pinpointing and reinforcing safe performance in a food manufacturing plant. *Journal of Applied Psychology, 63*(4), 439. Copyright © 1978 by American Psychological Association. Adapted by permission.

systematic use of learning principles to influence organizational behaviour. For example, consider how one company used organizational behaviour modification through the reinforcement of safe working behaviour in a food-manufacturing plant. At first glance, accidents appeared to be chance events or wholly under the control of factors such as equipment failures. However, the researchers felt that accidents could be reduced if specific safe working practices could be identified and reinforced. These practices were identified with the help of past accident reports and advice from supervisors. Systematic observation of working behaviour indicated that employees followed safe practices only about 74 percent of the time. A brief slide show was prepared to illustrate safe versus unsafe job behaviours. Then, two reinforcers of safe practices were introduced into the workplace. The first consisted of a feedback chart that was conspicuously posted in the workplace to indicate the percentage of safe behaviours observers noted. This chart included the percentages achieved in observational sessions before the slide show, as well as those achieved every three days after the slide show. A second source of reinforcement was supervisors, who were encouraged to praise instances of safe performance that they observed. These interventions were successful in raising the percentage of safe working practices to around 97 percent almost immediately. When the reinforcers were terminated, the percentage of safe practices quickly returned to the level they were at before the reinforcement was introduced. (See Exhibit 2.6.)[63]

If you recall the programs at DundeeWealth and PepsiCo described at the beginning of the chapter, you will notice that they involve the use of O.B. Mod. to change employee's health behaviour. Notice that both companies use reinforcers (e.g., money and prizes) for health-related behaviours such as exercise, weight loss, and smoking cessation. As you can see, the key is to make the reinforcers contingent on specific behaviours.

In general, research supports the effectiveness of organizational behaviour modification programs. In addition to improvements in safety, O.B. Mod has also been found to have a positive effect on improving work attendance and task performance. The effects on task performance, however, tend to be stronger in manufacturing than in service organizations. As well, money, feedback, and social recognition have all been found to be effective forms of positive reinforcement. Although money has been found to have stronger effects on performance than social recognition and performance feedback, the use of all three together has the strongest effect on task performance. Research has also found that the effect of money on performance is greater when it is provided systematically through O.B. Mod compared to a routine pay-for-performance program.[64]

Employee Recognition Programs

Another example of an organizational learning practice that uses positive reinforcement is employee recognition programs. **Employee recognition programs** are formal

Employee recognition programs. Formal organizational programs that publicly recognize and reward employees for specific behaviours.

EXHIBIT 2.7 Types of recognition programs.

Source: Trends in Employee Recognition/WorldatWork. (2008, August 11). Service awards most popular. *Canadian HR Reporter*, *21*(14), 4.

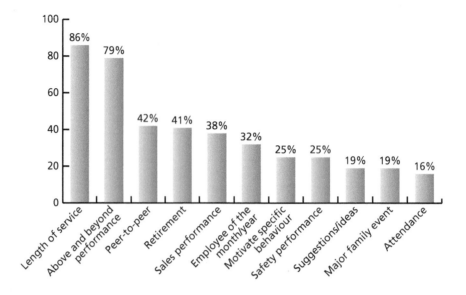

organizational programs that publicly recognize and reward employees for specific behaviours. Exhibit 2.7 shows some of the most popular types of employee recognition programs.

Many companies in Canada have some form of employee recognition program, and employees in the best companies to work for in Canada believe that they receive adequate recognition beyond compensation for their contributions and accomplishments. To be effective, however, a formal employee recognition program must specify (a) how a person will be recognized, (b) the type of behaviour being encouraged, (c) the manner of the public acknowledgment, and (d) a token or icon of the event for the recipient. A key part of an employee recognition program is public acknowledgment. Thus, a financial reward for good performance would not qualify as an employee recognition program if it was not accompanied by some form of public praise and recognition.[65]

An increasing number of organizations have begun to implement a new kind of recognition program called *peer recognition*. Before continuing, consider You Be the Manager.

YOU BE THE MANAGER

Peer Recognition at Ceridian Canada Ltd., Keller Williams Ottawa Realty, and IT/NET Ottawa Inc.

Peer recognition programs are showing up in organizations all across Canada as a growing number of employers see the value in encouraging employees to reward each other. It is a trend that goes along with a less hierarchical workplace where teamwork is valued over competition and employees are more likely to get ahead by patting each other on the back rather than by stabbing each other in the back. More companies are seeing the importance of recognizing their employees as a boost to morale, loyalty, retention, and recruiting.

Ceridian Canada Ltd. provides payroll and human resources management services to organizations across Canada. In addition to providing rewards for exceptional performance, the company has a unique peer recognition program. Employees can nominate co-workers for monthly prizes and quarterly cash awards and the chance to win the annual President's Club Award, which includes a paid vacation to a holiday destination.·

Ceridian recognizes 28 "star" employees each quarter and gives each a $100 gift certificate. At year end, 15 are selected to go on an overseas trip with spouses and senior executives. The destinations in previous years have included London, Paris, and Costa Rica, and the next trip will visit several African countries. "With prizes like these, the quest for recognition is 'quite competitive,'" says Jim Thomson, vice-president of human resources operations. He says that Ceridian's employees appreciate having an opportunity to praise each other. "We don't have to push this program at all," he says. "The employees like working with one another, and, when one of their co-workers does something above and beyond, they know they have a way of rewarding that."

Keller Williams Ottawa Realty is the largest single real estate office in Ottawa. The company has a peer-to-peer recognition program called Fill the Bucket. The program encourages employees to publicly acknowledge and thank each other for exceptional effort or work. All of the company's major meetings begin with at least one person's words of praise. According to team leader Sunny Daljit, the initiative helps reinforce positive, productive behaviour. But more importantly, he says, it fosters camaraderie, breaks down hierarchical barriers, and makes the company's meetings more productive because it frames them for success.

Keller Williams Ottawa Realty is one of many organizations that have implemented a peer recognition program.

IT/NET Ottawa Inc. provides consulting services in management and technology. The company has a peer-to-peer recognition program called My Thanks, in which employees are encouraged to acknowledge co-workers' exceptional work by sending them a cash-valued gift certificate. The value of the certificate is determined by who is awarding it and it can be done any time and as often as employees choose to recognize a co-worker. In 2007, the company spent approximately $4000 to $5000 on the program.

What do you think about peer recognition programs? Are they an effective way to reward employees and influence behaviour? You be the manager.

QUESTIONS

1. Based on operant learning theory, how can you make peer recognition programs effective?

2. How should peer recognition programs be designed to be most effective?

To find out how to make peer recognition programs effective, see The Manager's Notebook.

Sources: Anonymous. (2008, April 28). The power of peer recognition. A special report for the Great Place to Work® Institute Canada. *Globe and Mail,* GPTW5; Marron, K. (2006, February 15). High praise from colleagues counts. *Globe and Mail,* C1, C6. Reprinted with permission from Kevin Marron, freelance journalist, author, business writer; Ceridian Canada Ltd.: Canada's top 100 employers and Manitoba's top employers for 2009, www.eluta.ca/top-employer-ceridian-canada.

Employee recognition programs have been found to be related to a number of individual and organizational outcomes, including job satisfaction, performance and productivity, and lower turnover.[66] One study compared a public recognition program for improving work attendance with several other interventions. Employees with perfect attendance for an entire month had their names posted with a gold star for that month. At the end of each quarter, employees with no more than two absences received a personal card notifying and congratulating them. In addition, at the end of the year there was a plant-wide meeting to recognize good attendance, and small engraved mementos were awarded to employees who had perfect attendance during the entire year. The results indicated that employees had favourable perceptions of the program and that the program resulted in a decrease in absenteeism.[67] A survey of 26 000 employees in 31 organizations in the United States found that companies that invest the most in recognition programs have more than triple the profits of those that invest the least.[68]

A key factor in the implementation and success of employee recognition programs is to link them to organizational goals and make them relevant for employees throughout the organization. This is especially challenging for global organizations that have to consider regional and cultural differences. For an example of how one organization has implemented a strategic global recognition program, see Global Focus: *Strategic Global Recognition at Fairmont Hotels and Resorts.*

Training Programs

Training. Planned organizational activities that are designed to facilitate knowledge and skill acquisition to change behaviour and improve performance.

Training is one of the most common types of formal learning in organizations. **Training** refers to planned organizational activities that are designed to facilitate knowledge and skill acquisition to change behaviour and improve performance.[69] Employees learn a variety of skills by attending formal training programs. In addition to teaching employees technical skills required to perform their jobs, training programs also teach employees non-technical skills such as how to work in teams, how to provide excellent customer service, and ways to understand and appreciate cultural diversity.

Behaviour modelling training. One of the most widely used and effective methods of training, involving five steps based on the observational learning component of social cognitive theory.

Effective training programs include many of the principles of learning described earlier in the chapter, such as positive reinforcement, feedback, observational learning, strengthening employees' self-efficacy, and self-regulation. One of the most widely used and effective methods of training is **behaviour modelling training** (BMT), which is based on the observational learning component of social cognitive theory and involves the following steps:[70]

- Describe to trainees a set of well-defined behaviours (skills) to be learned.
- Provide a model or models displaying the effective use of those behaviours.
- Provide opportunities for trainees to practise using those behaviours.
- Provide feedback and social reinforcement to trainees following practice.
- Take steps to maximize the transfer of those behaviours to the job.

Many organizations have used behavioural modelling training to develop supervisory, communications, sales, and customer service skills. A recent review of behavioural modelling training research concluded that it has a positive effect on learning, skills, and job behaviour. The effects on behaviour were greatest when trainees were instructed to set goals and when rewards and sanctions were used in the trainees' work environment.[71] Training has been found to increase trainees' self-efficacy in addition to having a positive effect on learning and job behaviour.[72]

Career Development

While training can help employees learn to perform their current jobs more effectively, career development helps employees prepare for future roles and responsibilities.

GLOBAL FOCUS

Strategic Global Recognition at Fairmont Hotels and Resorts

Fairmont Hotels and Resorts is a global leader in the hospitality industry with a worldwide reputation for excellence. Headquartered in Toronto, the company has 30 000 employees in 60 countries.

In 2007, the company implemented a global strategic recognition program called Service Plus. According to Matthew Smith, executive director of learning and development, "We wanted to align our recognition program with Fairmont's mission statement and brand promise, and also to incorporate suggestions from the field. With the help of a task force and multiple colleague focus groups, we learned our hotels wanted more opportunities to recognize more individuals for memorable service moments. They also wanted to reward them in a more meaningful, personalized way."

To tie recognition to goals that enhance Fairmont's brand, the program features various award levels such as Memory Maker, for an outstanding show of thoughtfulness or creativity, and Star of the Month, for role models who embody company values, leadership, and years of service. Awards are presented to deserving employees in the lobby, dining area, hotel corridor, or anywhere an appreciated moment occurs.

Fairmont has also tied recognition to its chain-wide environmental program, which focuses on waste management, energy and water conservation, and the use of Earth-friendly products. Green Partnership is a comprehensive commitment to minimize the company's impact on the environment.

Each hotel has volunteer green teams that include employees from all departments that meet monthly to discuss and review ways to improve the operational performance in various departments. The environmental incentive program recognizes the green team that has performed the best, on a quarterly basis, and rewards two hotels that have had the best overall environmental performance each year. There is also an Enviro-Star award for the employee who embodies the principles of the Green Partnership "above and beyond."

Fairmont has won numerous awards and praise for its environmental initiatives and has been recognized as one of Canada's greenest and most Earth-friendly employers.

_____

Source: Based on Irvine, D. (2008, November 3). Bring back that lovin' feeling. *Canadian HR Reporter, 21*(19), 22; Dobson, S. (2007, March 26). Fairmont finds it's easy being green. *Canadian HR Reporter, 20*(6), 14; Yerema, R. (2009, April 23). The Green 30, *Maclean's* (online), www2.macleans.ca/2009/04/23/the-green-30/8/; www.fairmont.com.

Career development is an ongoing process in which individuals progress through a series of stages that consist of a unique set of issues, themes, and tasks. This usually involves a career planning and career management component. Career planning involves the assessment of an individual's interests, skills, and abilities in order to develop goals and career plans. Career management involves taking the necessary steps that are required to achieve an individual's goals and career plans. This often involves special assignments and activities that are designed to assist employees in their career development.[73]

Given the increasing emphasis on and importance of continuous and life-long learning, many organizations now have career development programs. For example, Dun & Bradstreet Canada, a business information services company, has a career development program for all of its employees. Employees have a file called a Leadership Action Plan that lists their strengths and career aspirations as well as a plan on how they will achieve their goals. The file is reviewed by a supervisor four times a year. In addition, an intranet site is available to help employees perform career assessments and access information about job opportunities within the company. The company believes that its career development program will provide it with a learning, knowledge, and skills advantage.[74] When TD Bank Financial Group surveyed its employees, it found that skills development and career development were the most important

Career development. An ongoing process in which individuals progress through a series of stages that consist of a unique set of issues, themes, and tasks.

factors for them. As a result, the company decided to invest more in employee career management and created a website to help employees with all aspects of managing their careers. The Career Advisor site is a comprehensive tool that enables employees to determine how best to develop themselves and overcome career challenges. Employees have access to a combination of interactive diagnostic instruments, personal reports, advice, tools, and action planning exercises.[75]

THE MANAGER'S NOTEBOOK

Peer Recognition at Ceridian Canada Ltd., Keller Williams Ottawa Realty, and IT/NET Ottawa Inc.

1. Peer recognition programs use rewards and praise as a way to recognize employees who have demonstrated outstanding performance. According to operant learning theory, to be most effective the rewards should be contingent on specific behaviours that are of interest to the organization, such as attendance, innovation, or productivity. This is especially important because employees are responsible for choosing co-workers for recognition, and such choices should not simply be based on who is most liked or who has the most friends in the company. The program also has to consider individual preferences for reinforcers. Rewards will not have a reinforcing effect if they are not desired by the employee. Therefore, it is important that a variety of rewards be available to suit individual preferences. Clearly, there are many rewards other than pay and promotions that can be effective reinforcers.

2. Peer recognition programs should be designed in the same manner as formal employee recognition programs. To be effective, they should specify (a) how a person will be recognized, (b) the type of behaviour being encouraged, (c) the manner of the public acknowledgment, and (d) a token or icon of the event for the recipient. Because the employee's peers are responsible for deciding who will be recognized, careful attention should be given to how this is done to ensure that the process is fair and that the expected behaviour has been demonstrated. The program also needs to be clear about what types of behaviours will be rewarded. Recognizing the wrong people and being inconsistent in how rewards are granted can create problems and undermine the program. Therefore, the program must have clear guidelines about what kind of behaviour will be recognized and how this will be done. At Ceridian, there are stringent criteria for nominations, and selections are made by committees composed of a mix of employees and managers. The company also holds employee focus groups to solicit feedback on its program and has acted on recommendations such as having more front-line staff and fewer senior executives on the selection committees.

LEARNING OBJECTIVES CHECKLIST

1. *Personality* is the relatively stable set of psychological characteristics that influences the way we interact with our environment. It has more impact on behaviour in weak situations than in strong situations.

2. According to the dispositional approach, stable individual characteristics influence people's attitudes and behaviours. The situational approach argues that characteristics in the work environment influence people's attitudes

and behaviour. The interactionist approach posits that organizational behaviour is a function of both dispositions and the situation.

3. The Five-Factor Model consists of five basic dimensions of personality: extraversion, emotional stability/neuroticism, agreeableness, conscientiousness, and openness to experience. Research has found that the "Big Five" are related to job performance, motivation, job satisfaction, and career outcomes.

4. People who have an *internal locus of control* are more satisfied with their jobs, earn more money, and achieve higher organizational positions. High *self-monitors* have good communication skills and persuasive abilities and are more likely to change employers and locations and to receive more promotions than individuals who are low self-monitors. People with high *self-esteem* tend to make more fulfilling career decisions, to exhibit higher job satisfaction and job performance, and to be generally more resilient to the strains of everyday worklife.

5. People who are high on *positive affectivity* experience positive emotions and moods and tend to view the world in a positive light, including themselves and other people. People who are high on *negative affectivity* experience negative emotions and moods and tend to view the world in a negative light. *Proactive personality* is a stable personal disposition that reflects a tendency to take personal initiative across a range of activities and situations and to effect positive change in one's environment. *General self-efficacy* (GSE) is a general trait that refers to an individual's belief in his or her ability to perform successfully in a variety of challenging situations. *Core self-evaluations* refer to a broad personality concept that consists of more specific traits.

6. *Learning* occurs when practice or experience leads to a relatively permanent change in behaviour potential. The content of learning in organizations consists of practical, intrapersonal and interpersonal skills, and cultural awareness.

7. *Operant learning* occurs as a function of the consequences of behaviour. If some behaviour is occurring regularly or increasing in probability, you can assume that it is being reinforced. If the reinforcer is added to the situation following the behaviour, it is a *positive reinforcer*.

If the reinforcer is removed from the situation following the behaviour, it is a *negative reinforcer*.

8. Behaviour is learned quickly when it is reinforced immediately and continuously. Behaviour tends to be persistent under reduced or terminated reinforcement when it is learned under conditions of delayed or partial reinforcement.

9. If some behaviour decreases in probability, you can assume that it is being either extinguished or punished. If the behaviour is followed by no observable consequence, it is being extinguished; that is, some reinforcer that was maintaining the behaviour has been terminated. If the behaviour is followed by the application of some unpleasant consequence, it is being punished.

10. According to social cognitive theory, people have the cognitive capacity to regulate and control their own thoughts, feelings, motivation, and actions. The main components of social cognitive theory are observational learning, self-efficacy, and self-regulation. Observational learning is the process of imitating others. Models are most likely to be imitated when they are high in status, attractive, competent, credible, successful, and vivid. *Self-efficacy* is the belief that one can successfully perform a specific task and is influenced by performance mastery, observation of others performing the task, verbal persuasion and social influence, and physiological arousal. *Self-regulation* occurs when people use learning principles to manage their own behaviour, thus reducing the need for external control. Aspects of self-regulation include collecting self-observation data, observing models, goal setting, rehearsing, and using self-reinforcement.

11. Organizational learning practices include organizational behaviour modification, employee recognition programs, training programs, and career development. *Organizational behaviour modification* is the systematic use of learning principles to influence organizational behaviour. Companies have successfully used it to improve employees' attendance, task performance, and workplace safety. *Employee recognition programs* are formal organizational programs that publicly recognize and reward employees for specific behaviours.

Training programs involve planned organizational activities that are designed to facilitate knowledge and skill acquisition to change behaviour and improve performance. *Career development* is an ongoing process in which individuals progress through a series of stages that consist of a unique set of issues, themes, and tasks. It involves a career planning and career management component.

DISCUSSION QUESTIONS

1. Consider the relevance of the dispositional, situational, and interactionist approaches to your own behaviour. Describe examples of your behaviour in a school or work situation that demonstrates each perspective of organizational behaviour.

2. Suppose that you are the manager of two employees, one who has an internal locus of control and another who has an external locus of control. Describe the leadership tactics that you would use with each employee. Contrast the management styles that you would employ for employees with high versus low self-esteem.

3. Consider some examples of behaviour that you repeat fairly regularly (such as studying or going to work every morning). What are the positive and negative reinforcers that maintain this behaviour?

4. We pointed out that managers frequently resort to punishing ineffective behaviour. What are some of the practical demands of the typical manager's job that lead to this state of affairs?

5. Discuss a situation that you have observed in which the use of punishment was ineffective in terminating some unwanted behaviour. Why was punishment ineffective in this case?

6. Describe a situation in which you think an employer could use organizational behaviour modification and an employee recognition program to improve or correct employee behaviour. Can you anticipate any dangers in using these approaches?

7. A supervisor in a textile factory observes that one of her employees is violating a safety rule that could result in severe injury. What combination of reinforcement, punishment, extinction, and social cognitive theory could she use to correct this behaviour?

8. Describe a job in which you think an employee recognition program might be an effective means for changing and improving employee behaviour. Explain how you would design the program and how you might use principles from operant learning theory and social cognitive theory.

9. Refer to Global Focus: *Personality and Expatriate Effectiveness* and consider the relationship between the "Big Five" personality characteristics and expatriate effectiveness. Why do you think that conscientiousness was the only trait not related to expatriate effectiveness, given that it has been found to be the best predictor of job performance among the "Big Five"? Why is openness to experience and agreeableness more important for expatriate effectiveness?

10. Compare and contrast operant learning theory and social cognitive theory. Describe how you would change an individual's behaviour according to each theory. What do you think is the best approach?

INTEGRATIVE DISCUSSION QUESTIONS

1. Refer to the material in Chapter 1 on Mintzberg's managerial roles and consider how personality might be a factor in how effectively a manager performs each role. Discuss the relationship among the "Big Five" personality dimensions, locus of control, self-monitoring, self-esteem, proactive personality, and general self-efficacy with each of the managerial roles.

2. Discuss how each of the organizational learning practices described in the chapter can be used by organizations to deal effectively with the contemporary management concerns discussed in Chapter 1 (i.e., diversity, both local and global; employee–organization relationships; quality, speed, and flexibility; talent management; and corporate social responsibility).

ON-THE-JOB CHALLENGE QUESTION

The recent downturn in the global economy has forced many organizations to rethink how they reward employees. As a result, many organizations have been thinking of how to replace financial rewards with less costly rewards and forms of recognition. For some companies, it has been necessary to cut employee rewards and recognition programs, especially when they have had to implement hiring freezes or slash the number of employees through layoffs. Other organizations have come up with creative and cost-effective ways to recognize employees. For example, Dimension Data Canada Inc. appointed a chief fun officer in its Toronto office who organizes monthly activities such as paintball, bowling, lunches, or hiring a massage therapist. At Montana's Cookhouse, employees can post praise of a co-worker's work in customer service, health and safety, and how they treat co-workers on the company's intranet site. The feedback is sent to the employee's manager, who then reads the feedback to staff.

What do you think organizations should do to reward and recognize employees during a recession? What do you think about the creative approaches that some companies have implemented? Are they effective ways to reward employees? What are the advantages and disadvantages of them? What advice would you give to organizations about rewarding and recognizing employees during a recession?

Source: Nixon, K. (2009, April 6). Recession-proof recognition. *Canadian HR Reporter, 22*(7), 14; Grant, T. (2009, March 21). Thanking staff without a fistful of dollars. *Globe and Mail,* B15.

EXPERIENTIAL EXERCISE

Proactive Personality Scale

Do you have a proactive personality? To find out, answer the 17 questions below as frankly and honestly as possible using the following response scale:

1–Disagree very much   5–Agree slightly

2–Disagree moderately   6–Agree moderately

3–Disagree slightly   7–Agree very much

4–Neither agree or disagree

_____ 1. I am constantly on the lookout for new ways to improve my life.

_____ 2. I feel driven to make a difference in my community, and maybe the world.

_____ 3. I tend to let others take the initiative to start new projects.

_____ 4. Wherever I have been, I have been a powerful force for constructive change.

_____ 5. I enjoy facing and overcoming obstacles to my ideas.

_____ 6. Nothing is more exciting than seeing my ideas turn into reality.

_____ 7. If I see something I don't like, I fix it.

_____ 8. No matter what the odds, if I believe in something I will make it happen.

_____ 9. I love being a champion for my ideas, even against others' opposition.

_____ 10. I excel at identifying opportunities.

_____ 11. I am always looking for better ways to do things.

_____ 12. If I believe in an idea, no obstacle will prevent me from making it happen.

_____ 13. I love to challenge the status quo.

_____ 14. When I have a problem, I tackle it head-on.

_____ 15. I am great at turning problems into opportunities.

_____ 16. I can spot a good opportunity long before others can.

_____ 17. If I see someone in trouble, I help out in any way I can.

Source: Bateman, T.S., & Crant, J.M. (1993). The proactive component of organizational behavior: A measure and correlates. *Journal of Organizational Behavior, 14,* 103–118. © 1993 John Wiley & Sons Limited. Reprinted with permission.

Scoring and Interpretation

You have just completed the Proactive Personality Scale developed by Thomas Bateman and J. Michael Crant. To score your scale, first subtract your response to question 3 from 8. For example, if you gave a response of 7 to question 3, give yourself a 1 (8 minus 7). Then add up your scores to all 17 items. Your total should be somewhere between 17 and 119. The higher you scored, the more proactive your personality is—you feel that you can change things in your environment.

The average score of 134 first-year MBA students with full-time work experience was 90.7. Thus, these people tended to see themselves as very proactive. In this research, people with a proactive personality tended to report more extracurricular and service activities and major personal achievements that involve constructive environmental change.

General Self-Efficacy

Want to learn about your general self-efficacy? Answer the 8 questions below as frankly and honestly as possible using the following response scale:

1–Strongly disagree   5-Strongly agree

2–Disagree   6–Agree moderately

3–Neither agree nor disagree

4–Agree

_____ 1. I will be able to achieve most of the goals that I have set for myself.

_____ 2. When facing difficult tasks, I am certain that I will accomplish them.

_____ 3. In general, I think that I can obtain outcomes that are important to me.

_____ 4. I believe I can succeed at most any endeavour to which I set my mind.

_____ 5. I will be able to successfully overcome many challenges.

_____ 6. I am confident that I can perform effectively on many different tasks.

_____ 7. Compared to other people, I can do most tasks very well.

_____ 8. Even when things are tough, I can perform quite well.

Source: Chen, G., Gully, S.M., & Eden, D. (2001). Validation of a new general self-efficacy scale. *Organizational Research Methods, 4, 62–83.*

Scoring and Interpretation

You have just completed the New General Self-Efficacy Scale developed by Gilad Chen, Stanley M. Gully, and Dov Eden. To obtain your general self-efficacy (GSE) score, add up your scores to all 8 items and divide by 8. Your total should be somewhere between 1 and 5. The higher your score, the greater your general self-efficacy.

GSE enables individuals to effectively adapt to novel and adverse environments and can help to explain motivation and performance in a variety of work contexts. The average score of 323 undergraduate students enrolled in several upper-level psychology courses was 3.87.

To facilitate class discussion and your understanding of proactive personality and GSE, form a small group with several other members of the class and consider the following questions:

1. Each group member should present their proactive personality and GSE score. Next, consider the extent to which each member has been involved in extracurricular and service activities and in personal accomplishments that involved environmental change and how they have adapted to novel and difficult situations. Have students with higher proactive personality scores been more involved in extracurricular and service activities? What about personal accomplishments and constructive change? Have students with higher GSE been more effective in adapting to novel and difficult situations? (Alternatively, members of the class may write their proactive personality and GSE scores, extracurricular and service activities, personal accomplishments, and experiences adapting to novel and difficult situations on a piece of paper and hand it in to the instructor. The instructor can then write the responses on the board for class discussion.)

2. When is a proactive personality and GSE most likely to be beneficial? When is it least likely to be beneficial?

3. Do you think organizations should hire people based on whether or not they have a proactive personality and on their GSE score? What are the implications of this?

4. Based on your proactive personality and GSE scores, what have you learned about yourself and your understanding of your behaviour in different situations?

5. How can knowledge of your proactive personality and GSE scores help you at school and at work? What can you do to become more proactive? What can you do to strengthen your GSE?

CASE INCIDENT

Courier Cats

To stay competitive, many organizations regularly upgrade their computer technology. This was the case for Courier Cats, a small but profitable courier firm. To improve the delivery and tracking of parcels, the company decided to invest in new software. It was expected that the new software would not only allow the company to expand its business but also improve the quality of service. Because the new software was much more complex and sophisticated than what the company had been using, employees had to attend a one-day training program to learn how to use the new system. However, six months after the system was implemented, many employees were still using the old system. Some employees refused to use the new software, while others did not think they would ever be able to learn how to use it.

1. Why do you think that the employees did not use the new software?

2. Can personality explain why some employees refused to use the new software? What personality characteristics are most relevant for explaining why some employees refused to use the new software while others had no trouble learning and using it?

3. What are some of the implications that stem from operant learning theory and social cognitive theory for increasing the probability that the employees will use the new software? What do you recommend for improving the use of the new software?

CASE STUDY

Howe 2 Ski Stores

The Howe 2 Ski Stores are a chain of three ski and windsurfing shops located in the suburbs of a large western coastal city. Maria Howe, a ski enthusiast and business major, opened the first store 10 years ago after her university graduation with financial backing from her family and several friends. From its inception, the Howe 2 store was intended to provide state-of-the-art equipment and clothing for skiers at all ski levels, from beginner to champion. It was to be staffed by employees who were themselves advanced skiers and could provide expert advice on the choice of clothing and equipment, and it was intended to have a quick response time that would permit the last-minute purchase of equipment and clothing to a ski trip.

Howe originally drew from a pool of skiing friends and fellow students to staff the stores and still prefers to hire part-time employees with skiing expertise who might leave in a year over more stable, full-time employees with less expertise and interest in the sport. Whether administrative staff, cashiers, clerks, or moulders (employees who fit bindings to skis), employees were encouraged to keep up to date on the latest skiing equipment and trends, attend ski vendor shows, try out demo equipment, and give feedback on the store's inventory in order to help provide the highest quality equipment and advice for the customer. Suggestion boxes were placed in the store, and Howe herself regularly collected, read, and acted upon the suggestions made by the clerks and customers. She developed special advertising campaigns to build an image for the nearby slopes in order to increase the market. As the business grew, Howe even added a line of rental equipment in order to lower the costs and encourage people to try the sport.

Although profits grew irregularly due to weather effects and the faddish nature of the sport, Howe's efforts paid off in the long term, and within four years business had grown sufficiently to permit the opening of a second Howe 2 Ski Store in another suburb about 16 kilometres from the location of the first store. In order to even out sales across the year, about six years ago Howe took a chance on the growing windsurfing market and the coastal location and added a line of equipment for this sport. This expanded market has enabled her to smooth out the number of sales occurring throughout the year.

Three years ago, Howe was able to open a third store, located within a 25-kilometre radius of the other two locations. Although managers have been hired to run each of the stores and the total number of employees has grown to 65, Howe's basic strategy has remained the same—high quality, state-of-the-art products, a knowledgeable staff, and quick response time. Profits from the stores have continued to grow, although at a slower rate. Competition from other ski stores has also increased noticeably within the last two years.

The threat of increased competition has been exacerbated by signs that employee productivity has begun to slide. Last year, there were eight occasions where expensive ski orders were not delivered in time for the customer's ski vacation. Although Howe used a variety of manoeuvres to retain the customers' patronage (e.g., paying for the customer to rent equipment of equivalent quality, arranging express delivery of the equipment to the customer as soon as it was received at the store, and lowering the price of the equipment), the costs of these late orders were high. She realized that word of mouth about these kinds of incidents could significantly damage the store's reputation. Furthermore, at least 15 percent of all ski orders were delivered more than two days late, even though customers did not miss a trip or vacation as a result.

In an attempt to respond to these difficulties, Howe instituted a merit performance system for the moulders (employees who fit the binding to skis). Although productivity seemed to increase for a while, waves of discontent popped up all over the stores. The moulders felt that their merit ratings were inaccurate because the store managers could not observe them working much of the time. Further, they argued that their performance levels would have been much higher had not other employees interrupted them with questions about appropriate bindings or failed to clearly identify the appropriate equipment on the sales orders. Other employees also complained because they were not given the opportunity for merit pay. The buyers, who visit ski shows, examine catalogues, and talk with sales representatives in order to decide on the inventory, argued that their work was essential for high sales figures and quality equipment. Sales clerks claimed that their in-depth familiarity with an extensive inventory and their sales skills were essential to increasing sales. They also noted their important role in negotiating a delivery date that the moulders could meet. Similar arguments were made by the people in the credit office who arranged for short-term financing if necessary and the cashiers who verified costs and checked credit card approvals. Even the stockers noted that the store would be in a bad way if they did not locate the correct equipment in a warehouse full of inventory and deliver it in a timely manner to the moulders.

Howe had to concede that the employees were correct on many of these points, so she suspended the merit plan at the end of the ski season and promised to re-evaluate its fairness. Even more convincing were several indications that productivity problems were not limited to moulder employees. Complaints about customer service increased 20 percent during the year. Several customers noted that they were allowed to stand, merchandise in hand, waiting for a clerk to help them, while clerks engaged in deep conversations among themselves. Although Howe mentioned this to employees in the stores when she visited and asked the store managers to discuss it in staff meetings, the complaints continued. A record number of "as is" skis were sold at the end of the season sale because they were damaged in the warehouse or the store or by the moulders. The closing inventory revealed that 20 percent of the rental equipment had been lost or seriously damaged without resulting charges to the renters because records were poorly maintained. Regular checks of the suggestion boxes in the store revealed fewer and fewer comments. Although less extreme, similar problems occurred in windsurfing season. Employees just didn't seem to notice these problems or, worse, didn't seem to care.

Howe was very bothered by all these factors and felt they could not be attributed to the growth of the business alone. She knew it would be impossible to maintain her competitive position with these events occurring.

Source: NKomo, S., Fottler, M., McAfee, R.B., & McQuarrie, F.A.E. (2007). Evaluating non-traditional incentive systems: Howe 2 Ski Stores. *Applications in human resource management: Cases, exercises, and skill builders.* First Canadian Edition. Scarborough, Ontario: Nelson. Original case contributed by M. Susan Taylor and J. Kline Harrison. Questions prepared by Alan M. Saks.

1. What are the main problems occurring in the Howe 2 Ski Stores? To what extent are the problems due to personality versus characteristics of the work environment?

2. What behaviours need to be maintained or increased and what behaviours should be reduced or eliminated?

3. What do you think of Maria Howe's attempt to respond to the difficulties in the stores? Use operant learning theory and social cognitive theory to explain the effects of her merit performance system. Why was it not more effective?

4. What do you think Maria Howe should do to respond to the difficulties in the stores? Refer to operant learning theory and social cognitive theory in answering this question.

5. What organizational learning practices might be effective for changing employee behaviours? Consider the potential of organizational behaviour modification, employee recognition programs, and training programs. Explain how you would implement each of these and their potential effectiveness.

6. What advice would you give Maria Howe on how to address the problems in her stores? Should she pay more attention to the personalities of the people she hires and/or should she make changes to the work environment? What employees and what behaviours should she focus on?

Perception, Attribution, and Diversity

Canada Post

Canada Post is responsible for collecting, transmitting, and delivering mail within Canada. The Crown corporation is one of the largest organizations in Canada. With 72 000 employees, Canada Post is committed to creating an inclusive and diverse workforce and works collaboratively with its stakeholders to promote workplace diversity.

For a long time, Canada Post was a very stable, homogenous workforce, according to Deborah Shelton, director of human rights and employment equity. "When Canada is becoming a more diverse culture and society, it's very important we have that same kind of balance in our workplace." In 2007, the company created a Corporate Employment Equity Plan for 2008–2010 to ensure that its workforce reflects the diversity of Canada's population. The plan includes hiring, training, retention, and promotion targets for the four designated groups under the Employment Equity Act: women, members of visible minorities, Aboriginal peoples, and persons with disabilities. It provides executives and managers with hiring and representation goals as well as action plans to achieve them.

Canada Post partners with Equitek Employment Equity Solutions to recruit job candidates who are hard to reach through traditional recruitment strategies. It also partners with local groups such as Local Agencies Serving Immigrants (LASI) to connect with new immigrants and attract a diverse workforce. Canada Post runs equity-awareness sessions for recruiters and has updated its recruitment policies and an external recruitment training manual to include sections on how to reach a more diverse labour market. It is also starting to use recruitment materials in languages such as Punjabi, Hindi, Spanish, and Arabic.

Canada Post already has a strong representation of female employees, including the role of president, senior vice-president of operations, and other senior, influential positions. Women now represent 48.9 percent of its employees. The numbers of visible minorities and persons with disabilities have also increased.

Targeted initiatives for Aboriginals include the Progressive Aboriginal Relations (PAR) program and the Canadian Union of Postal Workers

LEARNING OBJECTIVES

After reading Chapter 3, you should be able to:

1 Define *perception* and discuss some of the general factors that influence perception.

2 Explain *social identity theory* and *Bruner's model* of the perceptual process.

3 Describe the main biases in person perception.

4 Describe how people form *attributions* about the causes of behaviour.

5 Discuss various biases in attribution.

6 Discuss the concepts of *workforce diversity* and valuing diversity.

7 Discuss how racial, ethnic, gender, and age *stereotypes* affect organizational behaviour and what organizations can do to manage diversity.

8 Define *trust* perceptions and *perceived organizational* support and describe organizational support theory.

9 Discuss person perception and perceptual biases in human resources.

Canada Post is one of Canada's Top 100 Employers as well as one of Canada's Best Diversity Employers.

(CUPW) Aboriginal Hiring initiatives, which are helping to improve the representation rate, which is 1.9 percent, compared to the labour market availability of 2.5 percent. An Aboriginal relations advisor organizes sessions to raise awareness about Aboriginal workplace issues, which helps to educate employees about the concerns faced by the community on a day-to-day basis. The corporation also has an Aboriginal recruitment committee to help penetrate this market, and it received a PAR gold-level award in 2008 for its work in the Aboriginal community.

Canada Post also runs special events such as celebrations around Aboriginal Day or Black History Month, and it encourages people to self-identify. It also provides tools to help employees with disabilities, such as letter carriers who are hearing impaired who need to communicate with clients.

To track its success, Canada Post surveys employees on respect and fairness at work and investigates any complaints based on race or religion. They also conduct regular employment systems reviews to assess whether diversity and equity goals are being met. Annual briefings are provided for senior executives as well as national and regional managers on the corporation's employment equity representation and diversity goals.

In 2009, Canada Post was chosen as one of Canada's Top 100 Employers for the third year in a row as well as one of Canada's Best Diversity Employers, which recognizes employers across Canada that have exceptional workplace diversity and inclusiveness programs.[1]

Why has Canada Post made workplace equity and diversity a top priority? What effect do equity and diversity programs have on employee attitudes and behaviour? And why do organizations often harbour false assumptions and myths about women and visible minority employees? These are the kinds of questions that we will attempt to answer in this chapter. First, we will define perception and examine how various aspects of the perceiver, the object or person being perceived, and the situation influence perception. Following this, we will present a theory and model of the perceptual process, and we will consider some of the perceptual tendencies that we employ in forming impressions of people and attributing causes to their behaviour. We will then examine the role of perception in achieving a diverse workforce and how to manage diversity, perceptions of trust and perceived organizational support, and person perception in human resources. In general, you will learn that perception and attribution influence who gets into organizations, how they are treated as members, and how they interpret this treatment.

What Is Perception?

Perception is the process of interpreting the messages of our senses to provide order and meaning to the environment. Perception helps sort out and organize the complex and varied input received by our senses of sight, smell, touch, taste, and hearing. The key word in this definition is *interpreting*. People frequently base their actions on the interpretation of reality that their perceptual system provides, rather than on reality itself. If you perceive your pay to be very low, you might seek employment in another firm. The reality—that you are the best-paid person in your department—will not matter if you are unaware of the fact. However, to go a step further, you might be aware that you are the best-paid person and *still* perceive your pay as low in comparison with that of the CEO of your organization or your ostentatious next-door neighbour.

Some of the most important perceptions that influence organizational behaviour are the perceptions that organizational members have of each other. Because of this, we will concentrate on person perception in this chapter.

Perception. The process of interpreting the messages of our senses to provide order and meaning to the environment.

Components of Perception

Perception has three components—a perceiver, a target that is being perceived, and some situational context in which the perception is occurring. Each of these components influences the perceiver's impression or interpretation of the target (Exhibit 3.1).

"I'm only firing you to impress the people that I'm not firing."

EXHIBIT 3.1
Factors that influence
perception.

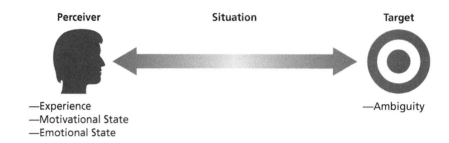

The Perceiver

—Experience
—Motivational State
—Emotional State

Situation

Target

—Ambiguity

The Perceiver

The perceiver's experience, needs, and emotions can affect his or her perceptions of a target.

One of the most important characteristics of the perceiver that influences his or her impressions of a target is experience. Past experiences lead the perceiver to develop expectations, and these expectations affect current perceptions. An interesting example of the influence of experience on perception is shown in Exhibit 3.2. It illustrates the perceptions of 268 managerial personnel in a Fortune 500 company concerning the influence of race and gender on promotion opportunities. As you can see, Caucasian men were much less likely to perceive race or gender barriers to promotion than were Caucasian women, non-Caucasian men, and non-Caucasian women.[2] Remember, these people were ostensibly viewing the same "objective" promotion system.

Frequently, our needs unconsciously influence our perceptions by causing us to perceive what we wish to perceive. Research has demonstrated that perceivers who have been deprived of food will tend to "see" more edible things in ambiguous pictures than will well-fed observers. Similarly, lonely university students might misperceive the most innocent actions of members of the opposite sex as indicating interest in them.

Emotions, such as anger, happiness, or fear, can influence our perceptions. We have all had the experience of misperceiving the innocent comment of a friend or acquaintance when we were angry. For example, a worker who is upset about not getting a promotion might perceive the consolation provided by a co-worker as gloating condescension. On the other hand, consider the worker who does get a promotion. She is so happy that she fails to notice how upset her co-worker is because he was not the one promoted.

In some cases, our perceptual system serves to defend us against unpleasant emotions. This phenomenon is known as **perceptual defence**. We have all experienced cases in which we "see what we want to see" or "hear what we want to hear." In many of these instances, our perceptual system is working to ensure that we do not see or hear things that are threatening.

Perceptual defence. The tendency for the perceptual system to defend the perceiver against unpleasant emotions.

The Target

Perception involves interpretation and the addition of meaning to the target, and ambiguous targets are especially susceptible to interpretation and addition. Perceivers have a need to resolve such ambiguities. You might be tempted to believe that providing more information about the target will improve perceptual accuracy.

EXHIBIT 3.2
Ratings of the perceived
importance of race and
gender for promotion
opportunity in executive
jobs.

Note: Table values are the percentages saying that race or gender was important or very important. N = number of cases.

Source: Reprinted with permission of the publisher from *Cultural diversity in organizations: Theory, research, & practice.* © 1993 by T. Cox Jr. Berrett-Koehler Publishers, Inc., San Francisco, CA. All rights reserved. www.bkconnection.com.

	Caucasian Men (N = 123)	Caucasian Women (N = 76)	Non-Caucasian Men (N = 52)	Non-Caucasian Women (N = 17)
Race	26	62	75	76
Gender	31	87	71	82

Unfortunately, this is not always the case. Writing clearer memos might not always get the message across. Similarly, assigning minority workers to a prejudiced manager will not always improve his or her perceptions of their true abilities. As we shall see shortly, the perceiver does not or cannot always use all the information provided by the target. In these cases, a reduction in ambiguity might not be accompanied by greater accuracy.

The Situation

Every instance of perception occurs in some situational context, and this context can affect what one perceives. The most important effect that the situation can have is to add information about the target. Imagine a casual critical comment about your performance from your boss the week before she is to decide whether or not you will be promoted. You will likely perceive this comment very differently from how you would if you were not up for promotion. Also, a worker might perceive a racial joke overheard on the job very differently before and after racial strife has occurred in the plant. In both of these examples, the perceiver and the target are the same, but the perception of the target changes with the situation.

Social Identity Theory

In the previous section, we described how characteristics of the perceiver, the target, and the situation influence the perceiver's interpretation of the target. In this section, we discuss social identity theory to help us understand how this happens. Let's begin with a simple question: "Who are you?" Chances are when you answer this question you say things like "student," "Canadian," "accountant," and so on. In other words, you respond in terms of various social categories to which you believe you belong. This is what social identity theory is all about.

According to **social identity theory**, people form perceptions of themselves based on their characteristics and memberships in social categories. As a result, our sense of self is composed of a personal identity and a social identity. Our *personal identity* is based on our unique personal characteristics, such as our interests, abilities, and traits. *Social identity* is based on our perception that we belong to various social groups, such as our gender, nationality, religion, occupation, and so on. Personal and social identities help us answer the question "Who am I?"

But why and how do we do this? As individuals, we categorize ourselves and others to make sense of and understand the social environment. The choice of specific categories depends on what is most salient and appropriate to the situation. For example, we might define people in a meeting according to their job title. Once a category is chosen, we tend to see members of that category as embodying the most typical attributes of that category, or what are called "prototypes." Similarly, once we locate ourselves in a social category we tend to perceive ourselves as embodying the prototypical characteristics of the category. In this way, we develop a sense of who and what we are, as well as our values, beliefs, and ways of thinking, acting, and feeling.[3]

In addition to forming self-perceptions based on our social memberships, we also form perceptions of others based on their memberships in social categories. This is because social identities are relational and comparative. In other words, we define members of a category relative to members of other categories. For example, the category of professor is meaningful in relation to the category of student. As the comparison category changes, so will certain aspects of the focal social identity. So when the authors of this text are in the classroom, they are perceived as professors by their students and as having whatever attributes the students attribute to professors. However, one of the authors of this text lives next door to a university student who perceives him not as a professor, but as a "baby boomer." Notice how her social categorization differs from those of the students in the classroom. As a result, her perception of the author will also

Social identity theory. A theory that states that people form perceptions of themselves based on their characteristics and memberships in social categories.

differ because the attributes and characteristics associated with the generation category of a "baby boomer" differ from those of the occupational category of "professor."

Social identity theory helps us understand how the components of the perceptual system operate in the formation of perceptions. We perceive people in terms of the attributes and characteristics that we associate with their social category relative to other categories. Thus, your perception of others is a function of how you categorize yourself (e.g., student) and your target (e.g., professor). If the situation changes, so might the categorization and the relation between the perceiver and the target. For example, in a hospital, medical students might be perceived as doctors by nurses and patients, but in the classroom they are likely to be perceived as medical students by their professors.[4]

Because people tend to perceive members of their own social categories in more positive and favourable ways than those who are different and belong to other categories, social identity theory is useful for understanding stereotyping and discrimination, topics we discuss later in this chapter. Now let's turn to a more detailed understanding of the perceptual process.

A Model of the Perceptual Process

In the previous section, we described how we form perceptions of ourselves and others based on social categories. But exactly how does the perceiver go about putting together the information contained in the target and the situation to form a picture of the target? Respected psychologist Jerome Bruner has developed a model of the perceptual process that can provide a useful framework for this discussion.[5] According to Bruner, when the perceiver encounters an unfamiliar target, the perceiver is very open to the informational cues contained in the target and the situation surrounding it. In this unfamiliar state, the perceiver really needs information on which to base perceptions of the target and will actively seek out cues to resolve this ambiguity. Gradually, the perceiver encounters some familiar cues (note the role of the perceiver's experience here) that enable her or him to make a crude categorization of the target, which follows from social identity theory. At this point, the cue search becomes less open and more selective. The perceiver begins to search out cues that confirm the categorization of the target. As this categorization becomes stronger, the perceiver actively ignores or even distorts cues that violate initial perceptions (see the left side of Exhibit 3.3). This does not mean that an early categorization cannot be changed. It does mean, however, that it will take a good many contradictory cues before one recategorizes the target, and that these cues will have to overcome the expectations that have been developed.

Let's clarify your understanding of Bruner's perceptual model with an example, shown on the right side of Exhibit 3.3. Imagine that a woman who works as an engineer for a large aircraft company is trying to size up a newly hired co-worker. Since he is an unfamiliar target, she will probably be especially open to any cues that might provide information about him. In the course of her cue search, she discovers that he has a master's degree in aeronautical engineering from Stanford University and that he graduated with top grades. These are familiar cues because she knows that Stanford is a top school in the field, and she has worked with many excellent Stanford graduates. She then proceeds to categorize her new co-worker as a "good man" with "great potential." With these perceptions, she takes a special interest in observing his performance, which is good for several months. This increases the strength of her initial categorization. Gradually, however, the engineer's performance deteriorates for some reason, and his work becomes less and less satisfactory. This is clear to everyone except the other engineer, who continues to see him as adequate and excuses his most obvious errors as stemming from external factors beyond his control.

Bruner's model demonstrates three important characteristics of the perceptual process. First, perception is *selective*. Perceivers do not use all the available cues, and

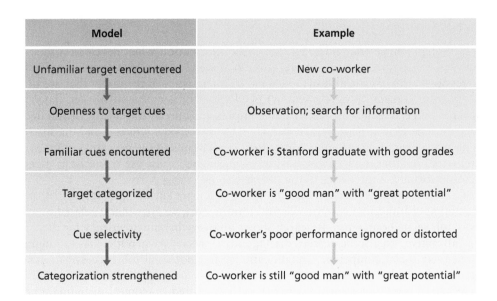

Model	Example
Unfamiliar target encountered	New co-worker
Openness to target cues	Observation; search for information
Familiar cues encountered	Co-worker is Stanford graduate with good grades
Target categorized	Co-worker is "good man" with "great potential"
Cue selectivity	Co-worker's poor performance ignored or distorted
Categorization strengthened	Co-worker is still "good man" with "great potential"

EXHIBIT 3.3
Bruner's model of the perceptual process and an example.

those they do use are thus given special emphasis. This means that our perception is efficient, and this efficiency can both aid and hinder our perceptual accuracy. Second, Bruner's model illustrates that our perceptual system works to paint a constant picture of the target. Perceptual *constancy* refers to the tendency for the target to be perceived in the same way over time or across situations. We have all had the experience of "getting off on the wrong foot" with a teacher or a boss and finding it difficult to change his or her constant perception of us. Third, the perceptual system also creates a consistent picture of the target. Perceptual *consistency* refers to the tendency to select, ignore, and distort cues in such a manner that they fit together to form a homogeneous picture of the target. We strive for consistency in our perception of people. We do not tend to see the same person as both good and bad or dependable and untrustworthy. Often, we distort cues that are discrepant with our general image of a person to make the cues consistent with this image. In the next section, we consider some specific perceptual biases that contribute to selectivity, constancy, and consistency in our perception of people.

Basic Biases in Person Perception

For accuracy's sake, it would be convenient if we could encounter others under laboratory conditions, in a vacuum or a test tube, as it were. Because the real world lacks such ideal conditions, the impressions that we form of others are susceptible to a number of perceptual biases.

Primacy and Recency Effects

Given the examples of person perception that we have discussed thus far, you might gather that we form our impressions of others fairly quickly. One reason for this fast impression formation is our tendency to rely on the cues that we encounter early in a relationship. This reliance on early cues or first impressions is known as the **primacy effect**. Primacy often has a lasting impact. Thus, the worker who can favourably impress his or her boss in the first few days on the job is in an advantageous position due to primacy. Similarly, the labour negotiator who comes across as "tough" on the first day of contract talks might find this image difficult to shake as the talks continue. Primacy is a form of selectivity, and its lasting effects illustrate the operation of constancy.

Sometimes, a **recency effect** occurs, in which people give undue weight to the cues they encountered most recently. In other words, last impressions count most. Landing a big contract today might be perceived as excusing a whole year's bad sales performance.

Primacy effect. The tendency for a perceiver to rely on early cues or first impressions.

Recency effect. The tendency for a perceiver to rely on recent cues or last impressions.

Reliance on Central Traits

Even though perceivers tend to rely on early information when developing their perceptions, these early cues do not receive equal weight. People tend to organize their perceptions around **central traits**, personal characteristics of the target that are of special interest to them. In developing her perceptions of her new co-worker, the experienced engineer seemed to organize her impressions around the trait of intellectual capacity. The centrality of traits depends on the perceiver's interests and the situation. Thus, not all engineers would organize their perceptions of the new worker around his intellectual abilities, and the established engineer might not use this trait as a central factor in forming impressions of the people she meets at a party.

Central traits often have a very powerful influence on our perceptions of others. Physical appearance is a common central trait in work settings that is related to a variety of job-related outcomes. Research shows an overwhelming tendency for those who are "attractive" to also be perceived as "good," especially when it comes to judgments about their social competence, qualifications, and potential job success.[6] In general, research shows that conventionally attractive people are more likely to fare better than unattractive people in terms of a variety of job-related outcomes, including employment potential, getting hired, being chosen as a business partner, given good performance evaluations, or being promoted.[7] Physical height, which is one of the most obvious aspects of appearance, has also been found to be related to job performance, promotions, and career success.[8] Taller and more attractive people are also more likely to be paid more. However, as discussed in Research Focus: *Weight-Based Bias in the Workplace*, individuals who are overweight tend to be evaluated negatively on a number of workplace outcomes. This bias is particularly relevant given that the rate of obesity among adults in North America has been increasing over the last 20 years.

Implicit Personality Theories

Each of us has a "theory" about which personality characteristics go together. These are called **implicit personality theories**. Perhaps you expect hardworking people to also be honest. Perhaps you feel that people of average intelligence tend to be most friendly. To the extent that such implicit theories are inaccurate, they provide a basis for misunderstanding.[9] The employee who assumes that her very formal boss is also insensitive might be reluctant to discuss a work-related problem with him that could be solved fairly easily.

Projection

In the absence of information to the contrary, and sometimes in spite of it, people often assume that others are like themselves. This tendency to attribute one's own thoughts and feelings to others is called **projection**. In some cases, projection is an efficient and sensible perceptual strategy. After all, people with similar backgrounds or interests often *do* think and feel similarly. Thus, it is not unreasonable for a capitalistic businessperson to assume that other businesspeople favour the free enterprise system and disapprove of government intervention in this system. However, projection can also lead to perceptual difficulties. The chairperson who feels that an issue has been resolved and perceives committee members to feel the same way might be very surprised when a vote is taken. The honest warehouse manager who perceives others as honest might find stock disappearing. In the case of threatening or undesirable characteristics, projection can serve as a form of perceptual defence. The dishonest worker might say, "Sure I steal from the company, but so does everyone else." Such perceptions can be used to justify the perceiver's thievery.

Stereotyping

One way to form a consistent impression of other people is simply to assume that they have certain characteristics by virtue of some category that they fall into as suggested

Central traits. Personal characteristics of a target person that are of particular interest to a perceiver.

Implicit personality theories. Personal theories that people have about which personality characteristics go together.

Projection. The tendency for perceivers to attribute their own thoughts and feelings to others.

RESEARCH FOCUS

Weight-Based Bias in the Workplace

Researchers have been investigating how body weight affects evaluative workplace outcomes such as hiring decisions and performance appraisals for nearly 30 years. Many studies have found evidence of a bias against overweight individuals in the workplace and have concluded that overweight individuals are systematically denigrated in comparison to their non-overweight co-workers. In fact, the evidence for discrimination against overweight individuals can be found at virtually every stage of the employment process, including hiring, placement, compensation, promotion, discipline, and termination.

Research on negative attitudes toward overweight people in the workplace has found that overweight individuals are perceived by their co-workers and supervisors as lacking self-discipline and self-control, being lazy and not trying as hard as others at work, possessing poor work habits, and having less conscientiousness, competency, skills, and ability than individuals of "average" weight. Overweight individuals are also viewed as being more likely to be absent from work and less likely to get along with and be accepted by their co-workers and subordinates.

In an effort to better understand the extent of the bias against overweight individuals in the workplace, Cort Rudolph and colleagues examined the results of previous research on body weight and workplace outcomes. Based on the results of 25 studies that have investigated weight-based bias in the workplace, the authors found that there is a significant negative relationship between body weight across all relevant evaluative workplace outcomes, including hiring decisions, promotion, and performance evaluation.

They also found that the negative effect of weight bias on hiring outcomes was significantly stronger than the effect on performance outcomes. Why might this be? The authors suggest that it is because the effects of bias are stronger when decision makers lack performance-relevant information about a target, such as when making hiring decisions. On the other hand, when decision makers have performance-relevant information about a target, such as when making performance evaluations or promotion decisions, the effects of bias are much lower. Without relevant information about a target, a decision maker is more likely to resort to body weight stereotypes and to make biased decisions.

Source: Reprinted from *Journal of Vocational Behaviour*, 74, Rudolph, C.W., Wells, C.L., Weller, M.D., and Baltes, B.B., A meta-analysis of empirical studies of weight-based bias in the workplace, 1–10, Copyright © 2009, with permission from Elsevier.

by social identity theory. This perceptual tendency is known as **stereotyping,** or the tendency to generalize about people in a social category and ignore variations among them. Categories on which people might base a stereotype include race, age, gender, ethnic background, social class, and occupation.[10] There are three specific aspects to stereotyping.[11]

Stereotyping. The tendency to generalize about people in a certain social category and ignore variations among them.

- We distinguish some category of people (college professors).
- We assume that the individuals in this category have certain traits (absent-minded, disorganized, ivory-tower mentality).
- We perceive that everyone in this category possesses these traits ("All my professors this year will be absent-minded, disorganized, and have an ivory-tower mentality").

People can evoke stereotypes with incredibly little information. In a "first impressions" study, the mere fact that a woman preferred to be addressed as "Ms." led to her being perceived as more masculine, more achievement-oriented, and less likeable than those who preferred the traditional titles "Miss" or "Mrs."[12]

Not all stereotypes are unfavourable. You probably hold favourable stereotypes of the social categories of which you are a member, such as student. However, these stereotypes are often less well developed and less rigid than others you hold. Stereotypes help us develop impressions of ambiguous targets, and we are usually pretty familiar with the people in our own groups. In addition, this contact helps us appreciate individual differences among group members, and such differences work against the development of stereotypes.

Language can be easily twisted to turn neutral or even favourable information into a basis for unfavourable stereotypes. For example, if British people do tend to be reserved, it is fairly easy to interpret this reserve as snobbishness. Similarly, if women who achieve executive positions have had to be assertive, it is easy to interpret this assertiveness as pushiness.

Knowing a person's occupation or field of study, we often make assumptions about his or her behaviour and personality. Accountants might be stereotyped as compulsive, precise, and one-dimensional, while engineers might be perceived as cold and calculating. Reflect on your own stereotypes of psychology or business students.

Not all stereotypes are inaccurate. You probably hold fairly correct stereotypes about the educational level of the typical university professor and the on-the-job demeanour of the typical telephone operator. These accurate stereotypes ease the task of developing perceptions of others. However, it is probably safe to say that most stereotypes are inaccurate, especially when we use them to develop perceptions of specific individuals. This follows from the fact that stereotypes are most likely to develop when we do not have good information about a particular group.

This raises an interesting question: If many stereotypes are inaccurate, why do they persist?[13] After all, reliance on inaccurate information to develop our perceptions would seem to be punishing in the long run. In reality, a couple of factors work to *reinforce* inaccurate stereotypes. For one thing, even incorrect stereotypes help us process information about others quickly and efficiently. Sometimes, it is easier for the perceiver to rely on an inaccurate stereotype than it is to discover the true nature of the target. The male manager who is required to recommend one of his 20 employees for a promotion might find it easier to automatically rule out promoting a woman than to carefully evaluate all his employees, regardless of gender. Second, inaccurate stereotypes are often reinforced by selective perception and the selective application of language that was discussed above. The Hispanic worker who stereotypes all non-Hispanic managers as unfair might be on the lookout for behaviours to confirm these stereotypes and fail to notice examples of fair and friendly treatment. If such treatment *is* noticed, it might be perceived as patronizing rather than helpful.

Attribution: Perceiving Causes and Motives

Attribution. The process by which causes or motives are assigned to explain people's behaviour.

Thus far, we have considered the components of perception, social identity theory, and Bruner's model of perception, and discussed some specific perceptual tendencies that operate as we form impressions of others. We will now consider a further aspect of impression formation—how we perceive people's motives. **Attribution** is the process by which we assign causes or motives to explain people's behaviour. The attribution process is important because many rewards and punishments in organizations are based on judgments about what really caused a target person to behave in a certain way.

Dispositional attributions. Explanations for behaviour based on an actor's personality or intellect.

In making attributions about behaviour, an important goal is to determine whether the behaviour is caused by dispositional or situational factors. **Dispositional attributions** suggest that some personality or intellectual characteristic unique to the person is responsible for the behaviour and that the behaviour thus reflects the "true person." If we explain a behaviour as a function of intelligence, greed, friendliness, or laziness, we are making dispositional attributions.

Situational attributions. Explanations for behaviour based on an actor's external situation or environment.

Situational attributions suggest that the external situation or environment in which the target person exists was responsible for the behaviour and that the person might have had little control over the behaviour. If we explain behaviour as a function of bad weather, good luck, proper tools, or poor advice, we are making situational attributions.

Obviously, it would be nice to be able to read minds to understand people's motives. Since we cannot do this, we are forced to rely on external cues and make inferences from these cues. Research indicates that as we gain experience with the behaviour of a target person, three implicit questions guide our decisions as to whether we should attribute the behaviour to dispositional or situational causes.[14]

- Does the person engage in the behaviour regularly and consistently? (Consistency cues)
- Do most people engage in the behaviour, or is it unique to this person? (Consensus cues)
- Does the person engage in the behaviour in many situations, or is it distinctive to one situation? (Distinctiveness cues)

Let's examine consistency, consensus, and distinctiveness cues in more detail.

Consistency Cues

Consistency cues reflect how consistently a person engages in a behaviour over time. For example, unless we see clear evidence of external constraints that force a behaviour to occur, we tend to perceive behaviour that a person performs regularly as indicative of his or her true motives. In other words, high consistency leads to dispositional attributions. Thus, one might assume that the professor who has generous office hours and is always there for consultation really cares about his or her students. Similarly, we are likely to make dispositional attributions about workers who are consistently good or poor performers, perhaps perceiving the former as "dedicated" and the latter as "lazy." When behaviour occurs inconsistently, we begin to consider situational attributions. For example, if a person's performance cycles between mediocre and excellent, we might look to variations in workload to explain the cycles.

Consistency cues.
Attribution cues that reflect how consistently a person engages in a behaviour over time.

Consensus Cues

Consensus cues reflect how a person's behaviour compares to that of others. In general, acts that deviate from social expectations provide us with more information about the actor's motives than conforming behaviours do. Thus, unusual, low-consensus behaviour leads to more dispositional attributions than typical, high-consensus behaviour. The person who acts differently from the majority is seen as revealing more of his or her true motives. The informational effects of low-consensus behaviour are magnified when the actor is expected to suffer negative consequences because of the deviance. Consider the job applicant who makes favourable statements about the role of big business in society while being interviewed for a job at General Electric. Such statements are so predictable in this situation that the interviewer can place little confidence in what they really indicate about the candidate's true feelings and motives. On the other hand, imagine an applicant who makes critical comments about big business in the same situation. Such comments are hardly expected and could clearly lead to rejection. In this case, the interviewer would be more confident about the applicant's true disposition regarding big business.

Consensus cues.
Attribution cues that reflect how a person's behaviour compares with that of others.

A corollary to this suggests that we place more emphasis on people's private actions than on their public actions when assessing their motives.[15] When our actions are not open to public scrutiny, we are more likely to act out our genuine motives and feelings. Thus, we place more emphasis on a co-worker's private statements about his boss than we do on his public relations with the boss.

Distinctiveness Cues

Distinctiveness cues reflect the extent to which a person engages in some behaviour across a variety of situations. When a behaviour occurs across a variety of situations, it lacks distinctiveness, and the observer is prone to provide a dispositional attribution

Distinctiveness cues.
Attribution cues that reflect the extent to which a person engages in some behaviour across a variety of situations.

about its cause. We reason that the behaviour reflects a person's true motives if it "stands up" in a variety of environments. Thus, the professor who has generous office hours, stays after class to talk to students, and attends student functions is seen as truly student-oriented. The worker whose performance was good in his first job as well as several subsequent jobs is perceived as having real ability. When a behaviour is highly distinctive, in that it occurs in only one situation, we are likely to assume that some aspect of the situation caused the behaviour. If the only student-oriented behaviour that we observe is generous office hours, we assume that they are dictated by department policy. If a worker performed well on only one job, back in 1995, we suspect that his uncle owned the company!

Attribution in Action

Frequently, observers of real life behaviour have information at hand about consistency, consensus, and distinctiveness. Let's take an example that shows how the observer puts such information together in forming attributions. At the same time, the example will serve to review the previous discussion. Imagine that Roshani, Mika, and Sam are employees who work in separate firms. Each is absent from work today, and a manager must develop an attribution about the cause to decide which action is warranted.

- *Roshani*—Roshani is absent a lot, her co-workers are seldom absent, and she was absent a lot in her previous job.
- *Mika*—Mika is absent a lot, her co-workers are also absent a lot, but she was almost never absent in her previous job.
- *Sam*—Sam is seldom absent, her co-workers are seldom absent, and she was seldom absent in her previous job.

Just what kind of attributions are managers likely to make regarding the absences of Roshani, Mika, and Sam? Roshani's absence is highly consistent, it is a low-consensus behaviour, and it is not distinctive, since she was absent in her previous job. As shown in Exhibit 3.4, this combination of cues is very likely to prompt a dispositional attribution, perhaps that Roshani is lazy or irresponsible. Mika is also absent consistently, but it is high-consensus behaviour in that her peers also exhibit absence. In addition, the behaviour is highly distinctive—she is absent only on this job. As indicated, this combination of cues will usually result in a situational attribution, perhaps that working conditions are terrible, or that the boss is nasty. Finally, Sam's absence is inconsistent. In addition, it is similar to that of co-workers and not distinctive, in that she was inconsistently absent on her previous job as well. As shown, this combination of cues suggests that some temporary, short-term situational factor is causing her absence. It is possible that a sick child occasionally requires her to stay home.

Biases in Attribution

As the preceding section indicates, observers often operate in a rational, logical manner in forming attributions about behaviour. The various cue combinations and the resulting attributions have a sensible appearance. This does not mean that such attributions are always correct but that they do represent good bets about why some behaviour occurred. Having made this observation, it would be naive to assume that attributions

EXHIBIT 3.4
Cue combinations and resulting attributions.

	Consistency	Consensus	Distinctiveness	Likely Attribution
Roshani	High	Low	Low	Disposition
Mika	High	High	High	Situation
Sam	Low	High	Low	Temporary Situation

are always free from bias or error. Earlier, we discussed a number of very basic perceptual biases, and it stands to reason that the complex task of attribution would also be open to bias. Let's consider three biases in attribution: the fundamental attribution error, actor–observer effect, and self-serving bias.[16]

Fundamental Attribution Error. Suppose you make a mistake in attributing a cause to someone else's behaviour. Would you be likely to err on the side of a dispositional cause or a situational cause? Substantial evidence indicates that when we make judgments about the behaviour of people other than ourselves, we tend to overemphasize dispositional explanations at the expense of situational explanations. This is called the **fundamental attribution error.**[17]

Why does the fundamental attribution error occur? For one thing, we often discount the strong effects that social roles can have on behaviour. We might see bankers as truly conservative people because we ignore the fact that their occupational role and their employer dictate that they act conservatively. Second, many people whom we observe are seen in rather constrained, constant situations (at work or at school) that reduce our appreciation of how their behaviour may vary in other situations. Thus, we fail to realize that the observed behaviour is distinctive to a particular situation. That conservative banker might actually be a weekend skydiver!

The fundamental attribution error can lead to problems for managers of poorly performing employees. It suggests that dispositional explanations for the poor performance will sometimes be made even when situational factors are the true cause. Laziness or low aptitude might be cited, while poor training or a bad sales territory is ignored. However, this is less likely when the manager has had actual experience in performing the employee's job and is thus aware of situational roadblocks to good performance.[18]

Actor–Observer Effect. It is not surprising that actors and observers often view the causes for the actor's behaviour very differently. This difference in attributional perspectives is called the **actor–observer effect.**[19] Specifically, while the observer might be busy committing the fundamental attribution error, the actor might be emphasizing the role of the situation in explaining his or her own behaviour. Thus, as actors, we are often particularly sensitive to those environmental events that led us to be late or absent. As observers of the same behaviour in others, we are more likely to invoke dispositional causes.

We see some of the most striking examples of this effect in cases of illegal behaviour, such as price fixing and the bribery of government officials. The perpetrators and those close to them often cite stiff competition or management pressure as causes of their ethical lapses. Observers see the perpetrators as immoral or unintelligent.[20]

Why are actors prone to attribute much of their own behaviour to situational causes? First, they might be more aware than observers of the constraints and advantages that the environment offered. At the same time, they are aware of their private thoughts, feelings, and intentions regarding the behaviour, all of which might be unknown to the observer. Thus, I might know that I sincerely wanted to get to the meeting on time, that I left home extra early, and that the accident that delayed me was truly unusual. My boss might be unaware of all of this information and figure that I am just unreliable.

Self-Serving Bias. It has probably already occurred to you that certain forms of attributions have the capacity to make us feel good or bad about ourselves. In fact, people have a tendency to take credit and responsibility for successful outcomes of their behaviour and to deny credit and responsibility for failures.[21] This tendency is called **self-serving bias,** and it is interesting because it suggests that people will explain the very same behaviour differently on the basis of events that happened *after* the behaviour occurred. If the vice-president of marketing champions a product that turns

Fundamental attribution error. The tendency to overemphasize dispositional explanations for behaviour at the expense of situational explanations.

Actor–observer effect. The propensity for actors and observers to view the causes of the actor's behaviour differently.

Self-serving bias. The tendency to take credit for successful outcomes and to deny responsibility for failures.

out to be a sales success, she might attribute this to her retailing savvy. If the very same marketing process leads to failure, she might attribute this to the poor performance of the marketing research firm that she used. Notice that the self-serving bias can overcome the tendency for actors to attribute their behaviour to situational factors. In this example, the vice-president invokes a dispositional explanation ("I'm an intelligent, competent person") when the behaviour is successful.

Self-serving bias can reflect intentional self-promotion or excuse making. However, again, it is possible that it reflects unique information on the part of the actor. Especially when behaviour has negative consequences, the actor might scan the environment and find situational causes for the failure.[22] To be sure, when a student does very well on an exam, he is very likely to make a dispositional attribution. However, upon receiving a failing grade, the same student is much more likely to find situational causes to explain his grade!

Person Perception and Workforce Diversity

The realities of workforce diversity have become an important factor for many organizations in recent years. **Workforce diversity** refers to differences among employees or potential recruits in characteristics such as gender, race, age, religion, cultural background, physical ability, or sexual orientation. The interest in diversity stems from at least two broad facts. First, the workforce is becoming more diverse. Second, there is growing recognition that many organizations have not successfully managed workforce diversity.

Workforce diversity.
Differences among recruits and employees in characteristics such as gender, race, age, religion, cultural background, physical ability, or sexual orientation.

The Changing Workplace

As we mentioned in Chapter 1, the composition of the labour force is changing.[23] Forty years ago, it was mainly Caucasian and male. Now, changing immigration patterns, the aging of baby boomers, and the increasing movement of women into paid employment make for a lot more variety. Immigrants to Canada from all parts of the world are making the Canadian population and labour force increasingly multicultural and multiethnic. According to Statistics Canada, the number of visible minorities in Canada is expected to double by 2017 and visible minorities will form more than half the population in greater Toronto and Vancouver. If current trends continue, one in every five persons in Canada will be non-white when Canada celebrates its 150th birthday in 2017.[24] And in less than a decade, 48 percent of Canada's working-age population will be between the ages of 45 and 64.[25]

The labour pool is changing, and at the same time many organizations are seeking to recruit more representatively from this pool so that they employ people who reflect their customer base—an effort to better mirror their markets. This is especially true in the growing service sector, where contact between organizational members and customers is very direct. As discussed in the chapter opening vignette, Canada Post has been very active in developing programs to hire, develop, and promote visible minorities, women, aboriginal people, and disabled persons, as have many other companies, including the YMCA in Toronto, Shell Canada Ltd., Federal Express Canada Ltd., the Royal Bank of Canada (RBC), and the RCMP, among others.[26]

The changing employment pool is not the only factor that has prompted interest in diversity issues. Globalization, mergers, and strategic alliances mean that many employees are required to interact with people from substantially different national or corporate cultures. Compounding all this is an increased emphasis on teamwork as a means of job design and quality enhancement.

Valuing Diversity

In the past, organizations were thought to be doing the right thing if they merely tolerated diversity—that is, if they engaged in fair hiring and employment practices with

1. Cost Argument	As organizations become more diverse, the cost of a poor job in integrating workers will increase. Those who handle this well will thus create cost advantages over those who don't.
2. Resource-Acquisition Argument	Companies develop reputations on favourability as prospective employers for women and ethnic minorities. Those with the best reputations for managing diversity will win the competition for the best personnel. As the labour pool shrinks and changes composition, this edge will become increasingly important.
3. Marketing Argument	For multinational organizations, the insight and cultural sensitivity that members with roots in other countries bring to the marketing effort should improve these efforts in important ways. The same rationale applies to marketing to subpopulations within domestic operations.
4. Creativity Argument	Diversity of perspectives and less emphasis on conformity to norms of the past (which characterize the modern approach to management of diversity) should improve the level of creativity.
5. Problem-Solving Argument	Heterogeneity in decision and problem solving groups potentially produces better decisions through a wider range of perspectives and more thorough critical analysis of issues.
6. System Flexibility Argument	An implication of the multicultural model for managing diversity is that the system will become less determinant, less standardized, and therefore more fluid. The increased fluidity should create greater flexibility to react to environmental changes (i.e., reactions should be faster and at less cost).

EXHIBIT 3.5

Competitive advantages to valuing and managing a diverse workforce.

Source: Cox, T.H., & Blake, S. (1991, August). Managing cultural diversity: Implications for organizational competitiveness. *Academy of Management Executive, 47,* 45–56.

respect to women and minorities. Firms were considered to be doing especially well if they assisted these people to "fit in" with the mainstream corporate culture by "fixing" what was different about them.[27] For example, women managers were sometimes given assertiveness training to enable them to be as hard-nosed and aggressive as their male counterparts!

Recently, some have argued that organizations should *value* diversity, not just tolerate it or try to blend everyone into a narrow mainstream. To be sure, a critical motive is the basic fairness of valuing diversity. However, there is increasing awareness that diversity and its proper management can yield strategic and competitive advantages. These advantages include the potential for improved problem solving and creativity when diverse perspectives are brought to bear on an organizational problem such as product or service quality. They also include improved recruiting and marketing when the firm's human resources profile matches that of the labour pool and customer base (see Exhibit 3.5). The results of a recent study indicate that more organizations are adopting diversity as part of their corporate strategy to improve their competitiveness in global markets. Another study found that organizations with more gender-diverse management teams have superior financial performance.[28]

However, if there is a single concept that serves as a barrier to valuing diversity, it is the stereotype. Let's now examine several workplace stereotypes and their consequences.

Stereotypes and Workforce Diversity

As described earlier, a stereotype is the tendency to generalize about people in a certain social category and ignore variations among them. Common workplace stereotypes are based on gender, age, race, and ethnicity. In the following section, we describe how stereotypes can have negative effects on how individuals are treated in organizations. It is also worth noting that in some situations in which a negative stereotype is salient, the perception that one might be judged on the basis of a stereotype can have a negative effect on one's behaviour and performance. This phenomenon, known as stereotype threat, occurs when members of a social group (e.g., visible minorities, women) feel they might be judged or treated according to a stereotype and that their behaviour or performance will confirm the stereotype. In other words, the existence of a stereotype threat can undermine a person's performance.

For example, when stereotyped group members take a test for educational admissions or employment, their performance might be lower if there are salient negative stereotype cues in the testing situation (e.g., women are not good at math, or ethnic minorities are inferior in intellectual abilities). Research has found evidence for stereotype threat effects for ethnicity/race stereotypes and gender-based stereotypes. The activation of a salient negative stereotype threat in a testing situation (e.g., asking test takers to report demographics prior to taking a test) has been found to result in lower cognitive ability and math test performance scores of minorities and women compared to non-threatening situations.[29] Let's now consider the nature of these stereotypes and their consequences in the workplace.

Racial and Ethnic Stereotypes. Racial and ethnic stereotypes are pervasive, persistent, frequently negative, and often self-contradictory. Most of us hold at least some stereotypical views of other races or cultures. Over the years, such stereotypes exhibit remarkable stability unless some major event, such as a war, intervenes to change them. Then, former allies can acquire negative attributes in short order.

Personal experience is unnecessary for such stereotype formation. In one study, people were asked to describe the traits of a number of ethnic groups, including several fictional ones. Although they had never met a Danerian, a Pirenian, or a Wallonian, this did not inhibit them from assigning traits, and those they assigned were usually unfavourable![30] Such stereotypes often contain contradictory elements. A common reaction is to describe a particular group as being too lazy, while at the same time criticizing it for taking one's job opportunities away.

There is a remarkable shortage of serious research into racial and ethnic matters in organizations.[31] However, what evidence there is shows that just getting in the door can be a problem. For example, whites have been found to advance further in the hiring process than blacks even when the applicants are the same age and physical size, have identical education and work experience, and share similar personalities.[32]

Even after visible minorities get in the door, career tracking based on racial or ethnic stereotypes is common. A study on the career satisfaction and advancement of visible minorities in Canada found that visible minorities perceive more barriers in their career advancement, including a lack of fairness in the process, and report less career satisfaction than white colleagues. In addition, 47 percent of visible minority managers and professionals reported feeling they were held to a higher standard of performance and 69 percent of visible minority respondents reported that in their career, "who you know" is more important than "what you know."[33] In the United States, almost one-quarter of workers from diverse backgrounds reported being discriminated against or treated unfairly at work. The most common example was not receiving credit for their work.[34]

Attributions can play an important role in determining how job performance is interpreted. For example, one study found that good performance on the part of African-American managers was seen to be due to help from others (a situational attribution), while good performance by Caucasian managers was seen to be due to their effort and abilities (a dispositional attribution).[35]

Racial and ethnic stereotypes are also important in the context of the increasing globalization of business. In one study, researchers asked American business students to describe Japanese and American managers along a number of dimensions. The students viewed Japanese managers as having more productive employees and being better overall managers. However, the students preferred to work for an American manager.[36] One can wonder how such students will respond to international assignments. Of course, all groups have stereotypes of each other. Japanese stereotypes of

Americans probably contribute to Americans not being promoted above a certain level in Japanese firms.

Finally, recent evidence suggests that organizations are simply reflections of the environments of which they are a part. Thus, if prejudice, negative stereotyping, ethnocentrism, and discrimination exist within the environment that an organization inhabits, it is very likely that these problems will surface within the organization itself.[37]

Gender Stereotypes. One of the most problematic stereotypes for organizations is the gender stereotype. Considering their numbers in the workforce, women are severely underrepresented in managerial and administrative jobs. Although women now occupy a significant and growing proportion of entry- and mid-level management positions, this is not the case for top-level positions, where they remain significantly under-represented. According to a study of 500 of Canada's top companies by Catalyst Canada, women hold only 14.4 percent of corporate officer positions, including presidents, executive vice-presidents, and chief operating officers. As a result, it's predicted that women's overall representation in corporate Canada will not reach 25 percent until 2025.[38]

There is evidence that gender stereotypes are partially responsible for discouraging women from business careers and blocking their ascent to managerial positions. This underrepresentation of women managers and administrators happens because stereotypes of women do not correspond especially well with stereotypes of businesspeople or managers.

What is the nature of gender stereotypes? A series of studies have had managers describe men in general, women in general, and typical "successful middle managers." These studies have determined that successful middle managers are perceived as having traits and attitudes that are similar to those generally ascribed to men. That is, successful managers are seen as more similar to men in qualities such as leadership ability, competitiveness, self-confidence, ambitiousness, and objectivity.[39] Thus, stereotypes of successful middle managers do not correspond to stereotypes of women. The trend over time in the results of these studies contains some bad news and some good news. The bad news is that *male* managers today hold the same dysfunctional stereotypes about women and management that they held in the early 1970s when researchers conducted the first of these studies. At that time, women managers held the same stereotypes as the men. The good news is that the recent research shows a shift by the women—they now see successful middle managers as possessing attitudes and characteristics that describe *both* men and women in general. However, although good managers are described today as possessing fewer masculine characteristics than in past decades, the most recent research indicates that both men and women of varying age, education, and work experience still describe a good manager as possessing predominantly masculine characteristics.[40]

Granting that gender stereotypes exist, do they lead to biased human resources decisions? The answer would appear to be yes. In a typical study, researchers asked male bank supervisors to make hypothetical decisions about workers who were described equivalently except for gender.[41] Women were discriminated against for promotion to a branch manager's position. They were also discriminated against when they requested to attend a professional development conference. In addition, female supervisors were less likely than their male counterparts to receive support for their request that a problem employee be fired. In one case, bias worked to *favour* women. The bank supervisors were more likely to approve a request for a leave of absence to care for one's children when it came from a female. This finding is similar to others that show that gender stereotypes tend to favour women when they are being considered for "women's" jobs (such as secretary) or for "women's" tasks (such as supervising other women), but not for traditional male jobs.[42] One recent study found that when women are successful in traditional male jobs, they are less liked. And being disliked had a negative effect on their evaluations and recommendations for rewards, including salary and special job opportunities.[43]

In general, research suggests that the above findings are fairly typical. Women suffer from a stereotype that is detrimental to their hiring, development, promotion, and salaries. Female managers are also more likely than male managers to have to make off-the-job sacrifices and compromises in family life to maintain their careers.[44] However, there is growing evidence that the detrimental effects of such stereotypes are reduced or removed when decision makers have good information about the qualifications and performance of particular women and an accurate picture of the job that they are applying for or seeking promotion into.[45] In particular, several studies reveal convincingly that women do not generally suffer from gender stereotypes in *performance evaluations* that their supervisors provide.[46] This is not altogether surprising. As we noted earlier, stereotypes help us process information in ambiguous situations. To the extent that we have good information on which to base our perceptions of people, reliance on stereotypes is less necessary. Day-to-day performance is often fairly easy to observe, and gender stereotypes do not intrude on evaluations.

On the other hand, hiring and promotion decisions might confront managers with ambiguous targets or situations and prompt them to resort to gender stereotypes in forming impressions. In fact, one recent study found that when participants read descriptions of mixed-sex pairs' team performance and were asked to evaluate the male and female members, females were rated as less competent, less influential in achieving a successful team outcome, and less likely to have taken on a leadership role unless there was specific information about the female member's excellent performance, or her contribution to the success of the team was irrefutable, or there was definitive information about the excellence of her past performance.[47] Thus, participants resorted to negative stereotype-based attributions in evaluating women's performance when there was ambiguity about the source of the team's success.

Fortunately, as shown in Exhibit 3.6, some Canadian organizations have been recognized as the best workplaces for women and have made efforts to ensure that women are represented in senior positions. For example, at Shell Canada Ltd. of Calgary there are more women than men on the list of potential senior managers.[48] Women have made the most significant progress moving into senior management and executive positions in the financial services industry. On the other hand, industries that tend to be stereotypically male, such as paper and forest products, steel production, motor vehicles and parts, oil and gas, and general manufacturing and construction, continue to have the lowest representation of women in senior positions.[49]

Organizations that remove perceptual barriers to the advancement of women have much to gain. A study of Fortune 500 companies found that companies with the highest representation of women in senior management positions have a 35 percent higher return on equity and a 34 percent greater return to shareholders than firms with the fewest women in senior positions.[50]

Age Stereotypes. Another kind of stereotype that presents problems for organizations is the age stereotype. Knowing that a person falls into a certain age range or belongs to a particular age generation, we have a tendency to make certain assumptions

EXHIBIT 3.6
Best Workplaces for
Women in Canada.

Source: © 2009 Great Place to
Work® Institute, Inc. All Rights
Reserved.

1 Environics
2 Keller Williams
3 Royal Lepage Performance
4 Ad Farm
5 Randstad Interim Inc.
6 Nintendo of Canada Ltd.
7 Quintiles Canada
8 Pottruff & Smith

about the person's physical, psychological, and intellectual capabilities. We will have more to say about generation differences and values in Chapter 4.

What is the nature of work-related age stereotypes? Older workers are seen as having less *capacity for performance*. They tend to be viewed as less productive, creative, logical, and capable of performing under pressure than younger workers. In addition, older workers are seen as having less *potential for development*. Compared with younger workers, they are considered more rigid and dogmatic and less adaptable to new corporate cultures. Not all stereotypes of older workers are negative, however. They tend to be perceived as more honest, dependable, and trustworthy (in short, more *stable*). In general, these stereotypes are held by both younger and older individuals.[51] It is worth noting that these stereotypes are essentially inaccurate. For example, age seldom limits the capacity for development until post-employment years.[52] Further, research has found that age and performance are unrelated, and some recent studies indicate a shift toward a more positive perception about older workers.[53]

However, the relevant question remains: Do age stereotypes affect human resources decisions? It would appear that such stereotypes can affect decisions regarding hiring, promotion, and skills development. In one study, researchers had university students make hypothetical recommendations regarding younger and older male workers. An older man was less likely to be hired for a finance job that required rapid, high-risk decisions. An older man was considered less promotable for a marketing position that required creative solutions to difficult problems. Finally, an older worker was less likely to be permitted to attend a conference on advanced production systems.[54] These decisions reflect the stereotypes of the older worker depicted above, and they are doubtless indicative of the tendency for older employees to be laid off during corporate restructuring.

Unfortunately, the reality for older workers is consistent with the research. According to the Ontario Human Rights Commission, discrimination on the basis of age is experienced by people as young as 40 to 45, who are often passed over for merit pay and promotions or pressured to take early retirement. In a blatant example of such discrimination, a job fair held in Toronto several years ago stated that the target audience was 18- to 54-year-olds. Many older workers were offended, and a complaint was

A public awareness campaign to combat age stereotypes and discrimination sponsored by Canada's Association for the Fifty-Plus and the Ontario Human Rights Commission featured this poster with the tag line: "Nobody has a shelf life."

made to the Ontario Human Rights Commission.[55] Again, however, we should recognize that age stereotypes may have less impact on human resources decisions when managers have good information about the capacities of the particular employee in question.

To combat age stereotypes and discrimination, Canada's Association for the 50 Plus (CARP) has worked with the Ontario Human Rights Commission on a public awareness campaign that included a poster featuring photographs of older people with the tag line, "Nobody has a shelf life. Stop age discrimination now."[56] Some organizations have implemented programs and practices to promote the hiring of older workers. To learn more, see Applied Focus: *Best Employers for 50-Plus Canadians*.

Managing Workforce Diversity

Given the prevalence of the stereotypes noted above, valuing diversity is not something that occurs automatically. Rather, diversity needs to be *managed* to have a positive impact on work behaviour and an organization. However, only 48 percent of visible minority mangers believe that their senior management demonstrates a commitment to diversity. So what does it mean to be committed to diversity? Before continuing, read You Be the Manager to find out what the Ottawa Police Service is doing about it.

What can organizations do to achieve and manage a diverse workforce? Clearly, they can do what Canada Post is doing with its Corporate Employment Equity Plan to

APPLIED FOCUS

Best Employers for 50-Plus Canadians

The Workplace Institute conducts research and provides consulting on mature workforce issues and best practices in Canada. It is also the founder and coordinator of the annual Best Employers Award for 50-Plus Canadians. The award recognizes and rewards organizations for innovative and effective programs or initiatives that lead the way to best practices for 50-plus workers while achieving organizational goals. Organizations are evaluated in the areas of career development, retention, recruitment, workplace culture/practices, benefits, management practices, health support, retirement/retiree practices, pension, and/or recognition.

In 2009, five companies from across Canada received a Best Employers Award for 50-Plus Canadians: Wal-mart Canada, Bethany Care Society, Catholic Children's Aid Society of Toronto, HSBC Bank Canada, and Seven Oaks General Hospital.

What are these companies doing that makes them best employers for 50-plus Canadians? In 2008, Wal-mart Canada introduced a program called Progressive Retirement Services to help the company retain and recruit more experienced workers through work–life flexibility options. Workers are encouraged to return as consultants, special project managers, or mentors.

Wal-mart has also implemented recognition programs and has a workplace culture that supports a diverse workforce of all ages.

Bethany Care Society, one of Western Canada's largest not-for-profit providers of health, housing, and support for seniors and persons with disabilities, has overhauled programs to focus more on the needs of current and potential 50-plus workers, who now make up more than one-third of its workforce. For example, it has a flexible matching benefits program that allows employees to invest employer contributions in retirement savings plans or cash them in. In addition, full benefits are offered to part-time employees, and most benefits are extended beyond age 65.

Seven Oaks General Hospital in Winnipeg, which is a leader among community health centres for its holistic approach to care, healing, and wellness, is developing a series of flexible retirement measures and incentives to keep potential retirees engaged and in the workforce.

Sources: Dobson, S. (2009, January 12). Age-free culture goal of top employers. *Canadian HR Reporter*, 22(1), 3; Creating an age-free workplace: Five companies awarded 2009 Best Employers Awards for 50-Plus Canadians. Workplace Institute. www.workplaceinstitute.org/bea-winners-2009.

YOU BE THE MANAGER

Wanted: Diversity at Ottawa Police Service

The Ottawa Police Service is facing the total turnover of its senior ranks. The majority of them will be retiring within the next 5 to 10 years. And as if that's not enough, most of those who will replace them have less than five years of experience. Set against this reality is the changing face of the city. One in five residents was born outside of Canada, and while this immigrant population isn't as sizable as it is in some other municipalities, it is still growing at twice the rate of the general population. With such a population shift, former police chief Vince Bevan has stated that "we would not be a legitimate police organization unless we had the capacity to communicate with and understand the diverse population that calls Ottawa home. . . . If we can't communicate with the victims, who is going to investigate crimes committed against them? And if we can't penetrate organized crime because we can't speak the language and don't understand the culture, who's going to halt its spread?"

Recruitment is also part of the problem. According to Staff Sergeant Syd Gravel, when police services talk of recruiting, what they usually mean is processing applications. "If the chief comes to me and says, 'We've got to hire 30 people,' I go and pull out 200 files from the filing cabinet from people who were naturally attracted to policing. And I go through the files and bring them down to 30 excellent candidates, and we would hire 30 people." The problem is that the names in that filing cabinet resemble less and less the names one encounters on Ottawa's streets.

Immigrant communities, however, have traditionally shown little interest in policing. Many immigrants come from nations where the police oppress rather than serve the public. Others arrive in Canada only to find themselves or their youth too often targeted by police using racial profiling. For these communities, a career with the police for their children just doesn't come up as an option to consider.

But the difficulties do not end with recruiting; the retention of women and visible minorities is also a problem. The results from focus groups that included officers and civilian staff who were women, visible minorities, gay, lesbian, bisexual, or transgender indicated that while white male officers didn't believe the organization had a retention problem, the female officers voiced discontent and a desire to leave the

Recruiting and retaining visible minority and female employees is a big problem for the Ottawa Police Service.

service. Civilian employees in the focus groups felt the same way, and while visible minority officers found the recruitment process to be fair and welcoming, once on board they felt that their peers viewed them as "employment equity hires." When a consultant looked at the retention rates of the 1200-strong force, he discovered that white men stayed roughly 29 years, women 15 years, and visible minorities 8 years.

What should the Ottawa Police Service do to create a more diverse workforce? You be the manager.

QUESTIONS

1. What should the Ottawa Police Service do to begin the process of creating a more diverse workforce?

2. What are some specific strategies that the Ottawa Police Service might employ to recruit and retain employees from diverse backgrounds?

To find out what the Ottawa Police Service is doing, consult The Manager's Notebook at the end of the chapter.

Source: Excerpted from Vu, U. (2005, April 25). Ottawa cops pursuing diversity. *Canadian HR Reporter*, 18(8), 1, 5; Crawford, T. (2006, April 1). A better mix. *Toronto Star*, L1, L2.

EXHIBIT 3.7

Common activities included in diversity programs.

Source: Jayne, M.E.A., & Dipboye, R.L. (2004, Winter). Leveraging diversity to improve business performance: Research findings and recommendations for organizations. *Human Resource Management*, 43(4), 409–424. © 2004 John Wiley & Sons, Inc. Used by permission.

Strategic Initiative	Sample Interventions
Recruiting	• Employee referral programs • Diverse recruiting teams • Internship programs and sponsored scholarships • Job posting and advertising initiatives targeting specific groups • Minority conference and job fair attendance • Recruiting efforts targeting universities and community colleges with diverse student bodies
Retention	• Corporate-sponsored employee resource or affinity groups • Employee benefits (e.g., adoption, domestic partner, eldercare, flexible health, and dependent spending accounts) • Work–life programs and incentives (e.g., on-site childcare, flexible work schedules, on-site lactation facilities)
Development	• Leadership development training programs • Mentoring programs
External Partnership	• Minority supplier programs • Community service outreach
Communication	• Award programs providing public recognition of managers and employees for diversity achievement • Newsletters, internal websites on diversity • Senior leadership addresses, town hall meetings, business updates
Training	• Awareness training on the organization's diversity initiative • Issue-based/prevention training (e.g., sexual harassment, men and women as colleagues) • Team-building and group-process training
Staffing and Infrastructure	• Dedicated diversity staff • Executive and local diversity councils

ensure that its workforce reflects the diversity of Canada's population. Some additional common examples are listed below.[57] For a more extensive list, see Exhibit 3.7.

- Select enough minority members to get them beyond token status. When this happens, the majority starts to look at individual accomplishments rather than group membership because they can see variation in the behaviours of the minority.
- Encourage teamwork that brings minority and majority members together.
- Ensure that those making career decisions about employees have accurate information about them rather than having to rely on hearsay and second-hand opinion.
- Train people to be aware of stereotypes.

A good example of a company that effectively manages workforce diversity is Boeing Canada Technology, Winnipeg Division, which has been recognized as one of Canada's Best Diversity Employers. The company actively promotes diversity, which helps to create a positive and respectful workplace and contributes to the overall success of the organization. In addition to employing 21 deaf people and providing them with BlackBerrys to communicate with co-workers and their supervisors, the company also employs the following diversity strategies:[58]

- Diversity days that feature a lunch from a particular culture accompanied by presentations that include dancers and singers to help employees learn about the diverse backgrounds of their co-workers.
- Diversity training that includes formal educational classes on respecting and honouring co-worker's origins, leanings, and affiliations.
- Language training for recent immigrants and others who want to improve their English, as well as training in American Sign Language (ASL).
- Monthly awareness campaigns that profile events in the calendar such as Ramadan.
- Aboriginal recruitment in partnership with the Centre for Aboriginal Human Resource Development in Winnipeg.
- Job shadowing in cooperation with Red River College's deaf students program in Winnipeg so that students can see and communicate with deaf employees at work.
- A volunteer employment equity and diversity team that meets biweekly to identify and discuss diversity initiatives and plan awareness programs.

Another organization that has been recognized as one of Canada's Best Diversity Employers is Corus Entertainment Inc., which manages nationwide employment equity committees that advise the company on diversity and equity issues and gather feedback from employees on future employment equity and diversity initiatives. The company also targets and develops women and visible minority candidates for managerial positions and has implemented a number of projects to increase the number of women in leadership positions throughout the company.[59]

Although diversity training programs are one of the most common approaches for managing diversity, there is little hard research on the success of these programs. However, there is some anecdotal evidence that these programs can actually cause disruption and bad feelings when all they do is get people to open up and voice their stereotypes and then send them back to work.[60] Awareness training should be accompanied by skills training that is relevant to the particular needs of the organization. This might include training in resolving intercultural conflict, team building, handling a charge of sexual harassment, or learning a second language.

Basic awareness and skills training are not the only components of managing diversity. Organizations must use a number of other tactics. In future chapters, we will consider the following:

- Attitude change programs that focus on diversity (Chapter 4).
- Recognizing diversity in employee needs and motives (Chapter 5).
- Using alternative working schedules to offer employees flexibility (Chapter 6).

In summary, many organizations today have implemented programs to manage diversity. For many organizations, diversity is believed to be a business imperative that can improve competitiveness and firm performance. Although some have questioned the benefits of diversity programs, it is generally believed that diversity can result in positive outcomes when organizations take certain actions in the management of diversity. According to Michele Jayne and Robert Dipboye, diversity programs will be most successful when the following actions are taken as part of a diversity initiative:[61]

- *Build senior management commitment and accountability.* Diversity programs involve change for the organization, and to be successful they require the visible, active, and ongoing involvement and commitment of senior management.

- *Conduct a thorough needs assessment.* To be effective, diversity programs need to be tailored to an organization's business, culture, and people. A thorough needs assessment of employees, jobs, and the organization will help to ensure that the right issues are identified and appropriate interventions are implemented.

- *Develop a well-defined strategy tied to business results.* The foundation for a successful diversity program is tying the diversity strategy to the business strategy and results. The diversity strategy should guide decision making and help employees understand and accept the business case for change and how diversity supports the business strategy.

- *Emphasize team building and group process training.* Team building and group process training can help ensure that the different skills and perspectives of a diverse group are used to improve task performance. These efforts encourage group members to share information and develop a deeper understanding of the resources available to the team.

- *Establish metrics and evaluate the effectiveness of diversity initiatives.* Diversity metrics should be established to track progress and evaluate the effectiveness of a diversity program.

Perceptions of Trust

Do you trust your boss and organization? This is a question that more and more people are asking themselves today, and research has found that employee trust toward management is on the decline.[62] One survey found that 47 percent of those who responded agreed that a lack of trust is a problem in their organization. In another survey, 40 percent indicated that they do not believe what management says.[63] A decline in trust can be a serious problem because trust perceptions influence organizational processes and outcomes, such as sales levels, net profits, and employee turnover.[64]

Trust has been defined as a willingness to be vulnerable and to take risks with respect to the actions of another party.[65] More specifically, "trust is a psychological state comprising the intention to accept vulnerability based upon positive expectations of the intentions or behaviour of another."[66] Trust perceptions toward management are based on three distinct perceptions: ability, benevolence, and integrity.[67] *Ability* refers to employee perceptions regarding management's competence and skills. *Benevolence* refers to the extent that employees perceive management as caring and concerned for their interests and willing to do good for them. *Integrity* refers to employee perceptions that management adheres to and behaves according to a set of values and principles that the employee finds acceptable. The combination of these three factors influences perceptions of trust.

How trusting would you be if you perceived your boss to be incompetent, unconcerned about your welfare, or driven by a set of values that you find unacceptable? Not surprisingly, higher perceptions of management ability, benevolence, and integrity are associated with greater perceptions of trust. Furthermore, perceptions of trust in management are positively related to job satisfaction, organizational commitment, job performance, and organizational citizenship behaviour, and negatively related to turnover intentions.[68]

Trust is also considered to be the most critical factor when judging best workplaces in Canada. According to the Great Place to Work Institute Canada, trust is the foundation for quality jobs and performance excellence. When the institute evaluates organizations for the best workplaces, they use a "Trust Index" to assess employees' perspective on what it is like to work in their organization. As shown in Exhibit 3.8, the trust model consists of five dimensions. To create a great workplace, managers need to build trust, which is achieved by practising credibility, respect, and fairness, and by encouraging pride and camaraderie among employees.[69]

Trust. A psychological state in which one has a willingness to be vulnerable and to take risks with respect to the actions of another party.

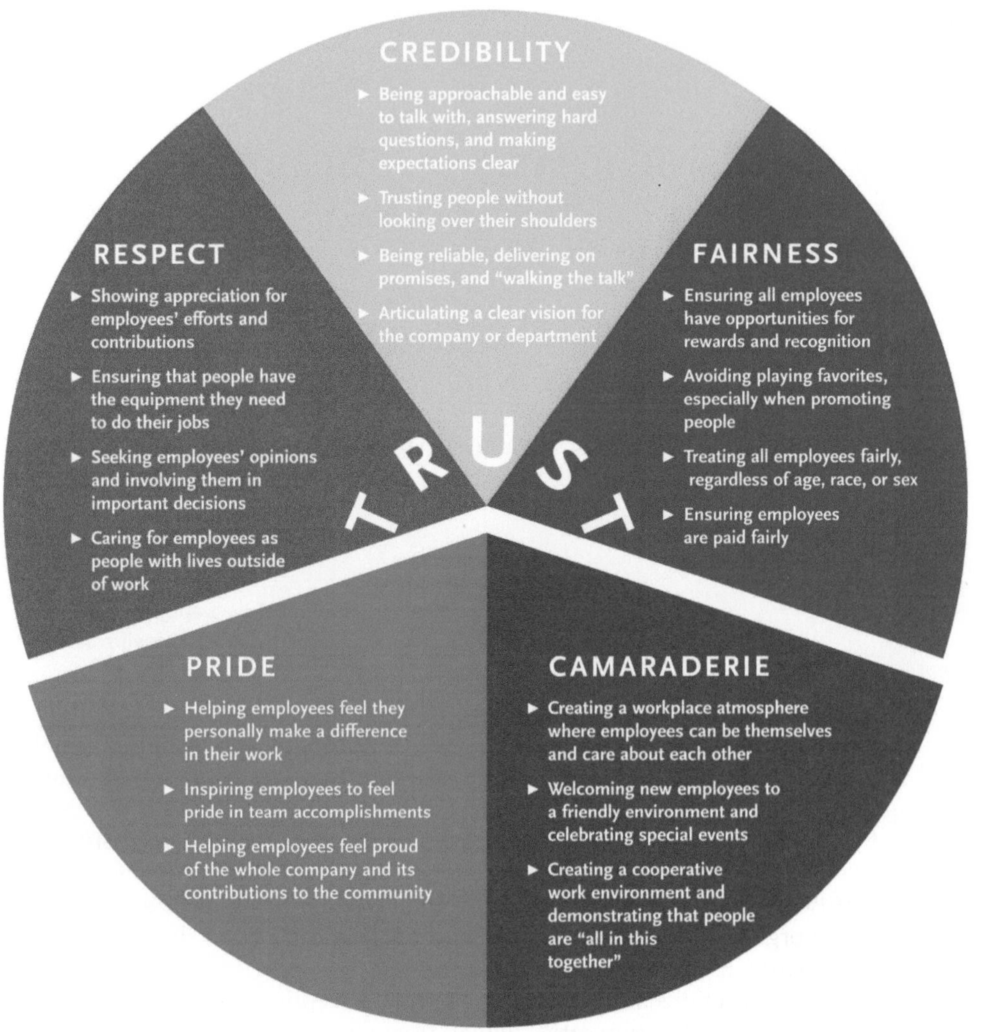

EXHIBIT 3.8
Trust Model.

Source: © 2005 Great Place to Work® Institute, Inc. All Rights Reserved.

Perceived Organizational Support

Whether or not you trust your boss and organization probably has a lot to do with how much they support you or, rather, your perceptions of support. **Perceived organizational support** (POS) refers to employees' general belief that their organization values their contribution and cares about their well-being. When employees have positive perceptions of organizational support, they believe that their organization will provide assistance when it is needed for them to perform their job effectively and to deal with stressful situations.[70]

According to **organizational support theory,** employees who have strong perceptions of organizational support feel an obligation to care about the organization's welfare and to help the organization achieve its objectives. They feel a greater sense of purpose and meaning and a strong sense of belonging to the organization. As a result, employees incorporate their membership and role within the organization into their social identity. In addition, when POS is strong, employees feel obligated to reciprocate the organization's care and support. As a result, POS has a number of positive consequences. Research has found that employees who have greater POS have higher job performance and are more satisfied with their jobs, more committed to the organization, and less likely to be absent from work and to quit. They are also more likely to have a positive mood at work and to be more involved in their job, and they are less likely to experience strain symptoms such as fatigue, burnout, anxiety, and headaches.[71]

Perceived organizational support. Employees' general belief that their organization values their contribution and cares about their well-being.

Organizational support theory. A theory that states that employees who have strong perceptions of organizational support feel an obligation to care about the organization's welfare and to help the organization achieve its objectives.

EXHIBIT 3.9
Predictors and
consequences of
perceived organizational
support.

Source: Based on Rhoades, L., &
Eisenberger, R. (2002). Perceived
organizational support: A review of
the literature. *Journal of Applied
Psychology, 87,* 698–714.

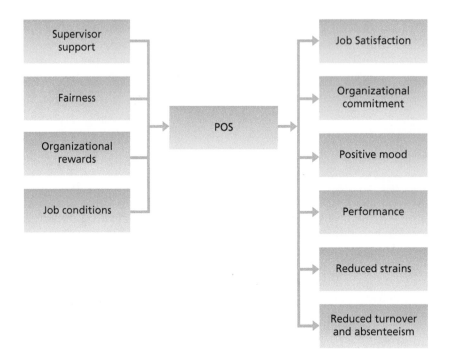

As shown in Exhibit 3.9, there are a number of factors that contribute to employees' POS. First, because supervisors function as representatives of their organizations through their actions and decisions, they represent the organization to employees. As a result, favourable treatment and support from supervisors, or *perceived supervisor support*, contributes strongly to POS. Interestingly, supervisors with more positive perceptions of POS are themselves perceived by employees as being more supportive. In addition, fair organizational procedures as well as favourable rewards and job conditions are also strongly related to POS.[72]

What can organizations do to improve employee perceptions of organizational support? One study found that supportive human resources practices that demonstrate an investment in employees and recognition of employee contributions are most likely to lead to the development of greater POS. Such practices signal to employees that the organization values and cares about them. Some examples of supportive human resources practices include participation in decision making, opportunities for growth and development, and a fair reward and recognition system.[73] Of course, equality and diversity programs such as those at Canada Post can also help to increase POS.

Person Perception in Human Resources

Perceptions play an important role in human resources and can influence who gets hired and how employees are evaluated once they are hired. Job applicants also form perceptions during the recruitment and selection process, and their perceptions influence their attraction to an organization and whether or not they decide to accept a job offer.

In this section, we consider the role of perceptions in three important areas of human resources: the employment interview, applicant perceptions of recruitment and selection, and the performance appraisal.

Perceptions in the Employment Interview

You have probably had the pleasure (or displeasure!) of sitting through one or more job interviews in your life. After all, the interview is one of the most common organizational selection devices, applied with equal opportunity to applicants for everything from the janitorial staff to the executive suite. With our futures on the line, we would like to think that the interview is a fair and accurate selection device, but is it? Research shows that the interview is a valid selection device, although it is far from perfectly accurate, especially when the interviewer conducts it in an unstructured, free-form format. The validity of the interview improves when interviewers conduct a more structured interview.[74]

What factors threaten the validity of the interview? To consider the most obvious problem first, applicants are usually motivated to present an especially favourable impression of themselves. As our discussion of the perception of people implies, it is difficult enough to gain a clear picture of another individual without having to cope with active deception! A couple of the perceptual tendencies that we already discussed in this chapter can also operate in the interview. For one thing, there is evidence that interviewers compare applicants to a stereotype of the ideal applicant.[75] In and of itself, this is not a bad thing. However, this ideal stereotype must be accurate, and this requires a clear understanding of the nature of the job in question and the kind of person who can do well in this job. This is a tall order, especially for the interviewer who is hiring applicants for a wide variety of jobs. Second, interviewers have a tendency to exhibit primacy reactions.[76] Minimally, this means that information the interviewer acquired early in the interview will have an undue impact on the final decision. However, it also means that information the interviewer obtained *before* the interview (for instance, by scanning the application form or resumé) can have an exaggerated influence on the interview outcome.

The interview is a difficult setting in which to form accurate impressions about a candidate. Interview validity increases when interviews are more structured.

A couple of perceptual tendencies that we have not discussed are also at work in interviews. First, interviewers have a tendency to give less importance to positive information about the applicant.[77] This tendency means that negative information has undue impact on the decision.[78] It might occur because interviewers get more feedback about unsuccessful hiring than successful hiring ("Why did you send me that idiot?"). It might also happen because positive information is not perceived as telling the interviewer much, since the candidate is motivated to put up a good front. In addition, **contrast effects** sometimes occur in the interview.[79] This means that the applicants who have been interviewed earlier affect the interviewer's perception of a current applicant, leading to an exaggeration of differences between applicants. For example, if the interviewer has seen two excellent candidates and then encounters an average candidate, she might rate this person lower than if he had been preceded by two average applicants (see Exhibit 3.10). This is an example of the impact of the situation on perception.

Contrast effects.
Previously interviewed job applicants affect an interviewer's perception of a current applicant, leading to an exaggeration of differences between applicants.

It is clear that the interview constitutes a fairly difficult setting in which to form accurate impressions about others. It is of short duration, a lot of information is generated, and the applicant is motivated to present a favourable image. Thus, interviewers often adopt "perceptual crutches" that hinder accurate perception.

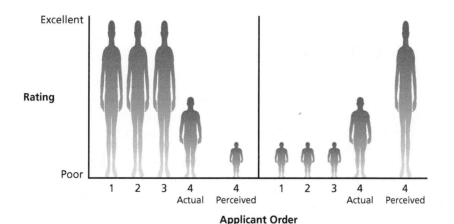

EXHIBIT 3.10
Two examples of contrast effects.

Earlier, we noted that the validity of the interview improves when it is structured. But what exactly is a structured interview? According to a study by Derek Chapman of the University of Calgary and David Zweig of the University of Toronto, interview structure involves four dimensions: *evaluation standardization* (the extent to which the interviewer uses standardized and numeric scoring procedures); *question sophistication* (the extent to which the interviewer uses job-related behavioural questions and situational questions); *question consistency* (the extent to which the interviewer asks the same questions in the same order of every candidate); and *rapport building* (the extent to which the interviewer does *not* ask personal questions that are unrelated to the job). They also found that interviews were more likely to be structured when the interviewer had formal interview training and focused on selection rather than recruitment during the interview.[80] Structured interviews probably reduce information overload and ensure that applicants can be more easily compared, since they have all responded to an identical sequence of questions.[81]

Perceptions of Recruitment and Selection

When you meet recruiters and complete employment tests, chances are you form perceptions of the organization. In fact, research indicates that how job applicants are treated during the recruitment and selection process influences their perceptions toward the organization and their likelihood of accepting a job offer. According to **signalling theory**, job applicants interpret their recruitment experiences as cues or signals about what it is like to work in an organization. For example, questions that are invasive and discriminatory might send a signal that the organization discriminates and does not value diversity; poor treatment during the hiring process might signal a lack of professionalism and respect of employees. These perceptions are important because they influence a job applicant's likelihood of remaining in the selection process and accepting a job offer.[82]

Applicants also form perceptions toward organizations based on the selection tests they are required to complete. This research has its basis in *organizational justice theory*, which is described in more detail in Chapter 4. Essentially, job applicants form more positive perceptions of the selection process when selection procedures are perceived to be fair. Furthermore, applicants who have more positive perceptions of selection fairness are more likely to view the organization favourably and to have stronger intentions to accept a job offer and recommend the organization to others. Among various selection procedures, employment interviews and work samples are perceived more favourably than cognitive ability tests, which are perceived more favourably than personality tests and honesty tests.[83]

Signalling theory. Job applicants interpret their recruitment experiences as cues or signals about what it is like to work in an organization.

Perceptions and the Performance Appraisal

Once a person is hired, however imperfectly, further perceptual tasks confront organization members. Specifically, the organization will want some index of the person's job performance for decisions regarding pay raises, promotions, transfers, and training needs.

Objective and Subjective Measures. It is possible to find objective measures of performance for certain aspects of some jobs. These are measures that do not involve a substantial degree of human judgment. The number of publications that a professor has in top journals is a good example. In general, though, as we move up the organizational hierarchy, it becomes more difficult to find objective indicators of performance. Thus, it is often hard to find quantifiable evidence of a manager's success or failure. When objective indicators of performance do exist, they are often contaminated by situational factors. For example, it might be very difficult to compare the dollar sales of a snowmobile salesperson whose territory covers British Columbia with one whose territory is Nova Scotia. Also, while dollar sales might be a good indicator of current sales performance, it says little about a person's capacity for promotion to district sales manager.

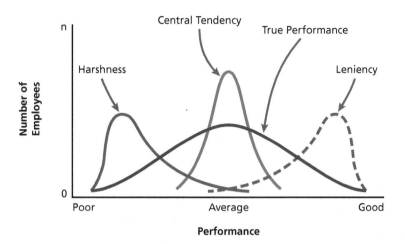

EXHIBIT 3.11
Leniency, harshness, and central tendency rater errors.

Because of the difficulties that objective performance indicators present, organizations must often rely on subjective measures of effectiveness, usually provided by managers. However, the manager is confronted by a number of perceptual roadblocks. He or she might not be in a position to observe many instances of effective and ineffective performance. This is especially likely when the employee's job activities cannot be monitored directly. For example, a police sergeant cannot ride around in six squad cars at the same time, and a telephone company supervisor cannot visit customers' homes or climb telephone poles with all of his or her installers. Such situations mean that the target (the employee's performance) is frequently ambiguous, and we have seen that the perceptual system resolves ambiguities in an efficient but often inaccurate manner. Even when performance is observable, employees often alter their behaviour so that they look good when their manager is around.

Rater Errors. Subjective performance appraisal is susceptible to some of the perceptual biases we discussed earlier—primacy, recency, and stereotypes. In addition, a number of other perceptual tendencies occur in performance evaluation. They are often called rater errors. One interrelated set of these tendencies includes leniency, harshness, and central tendency (Exhibit 3.11). **Leniency** refers to the tendency to perceive the performance of one's ratees as especially good, while **harshness** is the tendency to see their performance as especially ineffective. Lenient raters tend to give "good" ratings, and harsh raters tend to give "bad" ratings. Professors with reputations as easy graders or tough graders exemplify these types of raters. **Central tendency** involves assigning most ratees to a middle-range performance category—the extremes of the rating categories are not used. The professor who assigns 80 percent of her students Cs is committing this error.

Each of these three rating tendencies is probably partially a function of the rater's personal experiences. For example, the manager who has had an especially good group of employees might respond with special harshness when management transfers him to supervise a group of slightly less able workers. It is worth noting that not all instances of leniency, harshness, and central tendency necessarily represent perceptual errors. In some cases, raters intentionally commit these errors, even though they have accurate perceptions of workers' performance. For example, a manager might use leniency or central tendency in performance reviews so that his employees do not react negatively to his evaluation.

Another perceptual error that is frequently committed by performance raters is called the **halo effect**.[84] The halo effect occurs when the observer allows the rating of an individual on one trait or characteristic to colour the ratings on other traits or characteristics. For example, in a teacher evaluation system, a student might perceive his instructor as a nice person, and this might favourably influence his perception of the instructor's knowledge

Leniency. The tendency to perceive the job performance of ratees as especially good.

Harshness. The tendency to perceive the job performance of ratees as especially ineffective.

Central tendency. The tendency to assign most ratees to middle-range job performance categories.

Halo effect. The rating of an individual on one trait or characteristic tends to colour ratings on other traits or characteristics.

of the material and speed in returning exams and papers. Similarly, a manager might rate an employee as frequently late for work, and this might in turn lead her to devalue the employee's productivity and quality of work. As these examples illustrate, halo can work either for or against the ratee. In both cases, the rater fails to perceive differences *within* ratees. The halo effect tends to be organized around central traits that the rater considers important. The student feels that being nice is an especially important quality, while the manager places special emphasis on promptness. Ratings on these characteristics then affect the rater's perceptions of other characteristics.

Similar-to-me effect. A rater gives more favourable evaluations to people who are similar to the rater in terms of background or attitudes.

The **similar-to-me effect** is an additional rater error that may, in part, reflect perceptual bias. The rater tends to give more favourable evaluations to people who are similar to the rater in terms of background or attitudes. For example, the manager with an MBA degree who comes from an upper-middle-class family might perceive a similar employee as a good performer even though the person is only average. Similarly, a rater might overestimate the performance of an individual who holds similar religious and political views. Such reactions probably stem from a tendency to view our own performance, attitudes, and background as "good." We then tend to generalize this evaluation to others who are, to some degree, similar to us. Raters with diverse employees should be especially wary of this error.

Given all these problems, it should be clear that it is difficult to obtain good subjective evaluations of employee performance. Because of this, human resources specialists

EXHIBIT 3.12

Behaviourally anchored scale for rating customer service.

Source: Campbell, J.P., Dunnette, M.D., Lawler, E.E., III, & Weick, K.E., Jr. (1970). *Managerial behavior, performance, and effectiveness.* New York: McGraw-Hill. © The McGraw-Hill Companies, Inc. Used by permission.

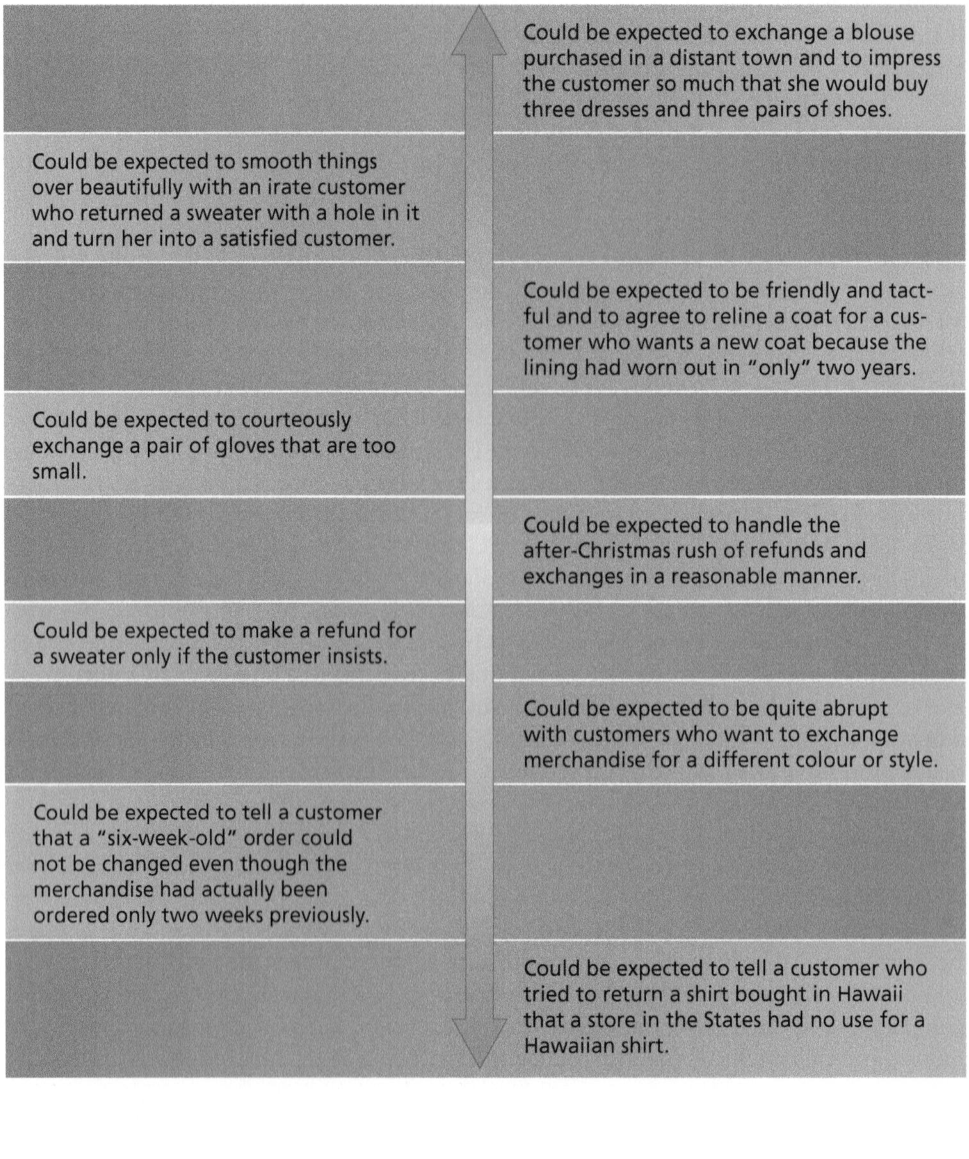

Could be expected to exchange a blouse purchased in a distant town and to impress the customer so much that she would buy three dresses and three pairs of shoes.

Could be expected to smooth things over beautifully with an irate customer who returned a sweater with a hole in it and turn her into a satisfied customer.

Could be expected to be friendly and tactful and to agree to reline a coat for a customer who wants a new coat because the lining had worn out in "only" two years.

Could be expected to courteously exchange a pair of gloves that are too small.

Could be expected to handle the after-Christmas rush of refunds and exchanges in a reasonable manner.

Could be expected to make a refund for a sweater only if the customer insists.

Could be expected to be quite abrupt with customers who want to exchange merchandise for a different colour or style.

Could be expected to tell a customer that a "six-week-old" order could not be changed even though the merchandise had actually been ordered only two weeks previously.

Could be expected to tell a customer who tried to return a shirt bought in Hawaii that a store in the States had no use for a Hawaiian shirt.

have explored various techniques for reducing perceptual errors and biases. There has been a tendency to attempt to reduce rater errors by using rating scales with more specific behavioural labels. The assumption here is that giving specific examples of effective and ineffective performance will facilitate the rater's perceptual processes and recall.

Exhibit 3.12 shows a behaviourally anchored rating scale that gives very specific behavioural examples (from top to bottom) of good, average, and poor customer service. It was developed for the J.C. Penney Company. With such an aid, the rater may be less susceptible to perceptual errors when completing the rating task, although the evidence for this is mixed.[85] Furthermore, there is also some evidence that a performance appraisal system that accurately measures employees' performance and ties it to rewards can increase employees' perceptions of trust toward management.[86]

THE MANAGER'S NOTEBOOK

Wanted: Diversity at Ottawa Police Service

1. In order to reach out to the diverse groups in Ottawa, the Ottawa Police Service needed to first find out how it is perceived as an employer. So they launched a process of consultation with community groups to find out what strategies they should put in place to help recruit a police service that reflects the community. The service's corporate planning section also put together focus groups of officers and civilian staff representing different groups. The recommendations of the community groups and the police staff were very similar. Telephone surveys of sworn officers and civilian employees on changes that management needed to make were also conducted. More than 90 recommendations emerged that were eventually distilled into 17 that formed the blueprint for the service's outreach recruitment program. A project team then took the recommendations to the Police Services Board and made a case for making the first recommendation—to be a diverse and bias-free organization—one of the 10 organizational values. The board approved, which means that henceforth, the chief is required by the Police Services Act to go to the board every three years and report on how the service is living up to that value.

2. In order to recruit and retain a more diverse workforce, the Ottawa Police Service developed programs to recruit from immigrant communities that have traditionally shown little interest in policing. For example, a volunteer recruiter initiative brings on board people from various communities to help the police recruit. After training, they go out with a pair of police employees, one uniformed and one civilian, to job fairs and career days to speak about policing as a career. Another program has the Ottawa police teaming up with the Ontario Provincial Police to go into an English-as-second-language class to teach young newcomers Criminal Code terminology and to talk about policing as a career. To help young candidates with entry requirements, the police service is setting up information sessions to prepare people for the aptitude tests, which are set by the province. Holding information sessions to explain to young immigrants what the tests are about or matching up mentors with young candidates to answer their questions one-on-one begins to put them on an equal footing to start the application process, says Staff Sergeant Syd Gravel. In another initiative, police and Somali youth play in a competitive basketball league in the hopes that Somali kids will see policing as a future occupation. To make the case that diversity means reaching out to all, not to some, the police service framed all the work in terms of being an employer of choice for all. According to former police chief Vince Bevan, "We wanted to make sure that we had a workplace where they would thrive, where they would be successful, and where they would be good ambassadors back to the community about what it was like to work for the Ottawa Police Service."

Sources: Excerpted from Vu, U. (2005, April 25). Ottawa cops pursuing diversity. *Canadian HR Reporter, 18*(8), 1, 5; Crawford, T. (2006, April 1). A better mix. *Toronto Star*, L1, L2.

LEARNING OBJECTIVES CHECKLIST

1. Perception involves interpreting the input from our senses to provide meaning to our environment. Any instance of perception involves a perceiver, a target, and a situational context. The experience, needs, and emotions of the perceiver affect perception, as does the ambiguity of the target.

2. According to social identity theory, people form perceptions of themselves and others based on their characteristics and memberships in social categories. Bruner's model of the perceptual process suggests that we are very receptive to cues provided by the target and the situation when we encounter an unfamiliar target. However, as we discover familiar cues, we quickly categorize the target and process other cues in a selective manner to maintain a consistent and constant picture of the target.

3. The main biases in person perception include primacy, recency, implicit personality theory, reliance on central traits, projection, and stereotyping. Stereotypes of gender, age, race, and ethnicity are especially problematic for organizations.

4. Attribution is the process of assigning causes or motives to people's behaviour. The observer is often interested in determining whether the behaviour is due to dispositional (internal) or situational (external) causes. Behaviour is likely to be attributed to the disposition of the actor when the behaviour (1) is performed consistently, (2) differs from that exhibited by other people, and (3) occurs in a variety of situations or environments. An opposite set of cues will prompt a situational attribution.

5. The tendency of observers to overemphasize dispositional attributions is known as the fundamental attribution error. In contrast, actors are more likely to explain their own behaviour in situational terms, and this actor–observer difference in attributions is known as the actor–observer effect. Our tendency to take credit for success and to deny responsibility for failure is known as the self-serving bias.

6. The changing nature of the workplace and increasing diversity have highlighted the importance of valuing and managing employee diversity, which can yield strategic and competitive advantages for the organization.

7. Racial, ethnic, gender, and age stereotypes can result in discriminatory human resources decisions and are a major barrier to valuing diversity. Organizations can use a number of tactics, including training, to manage diversity.

8. Perceptions of trust involve a willingness to be vulnerable and to take risks with respect to the actions of another party. Trust perceptions toward management are based on perceptions of ability, benevolence, and integrity. Perceived organizational support (POS) refers to perceptions about how much an organization values an individual's contribution and cares about one's well-being. According to organizational support theory, employees who have strong perceptions of organizational support feel an obligation to care about the organization's welfare and to help the organization achieve its objectives.

9. Judging the suitability of job applicants in an interview and appraising job performance are especially difficult perceptual tasks, in part because the target is motivated to convey a good impression. In addition, interviewers and performance raters exhibit a number of perceptual tendencies that are reflected in inaccurate judgments, including leniency, harshness, central tendency, and contrast, halo, and similar-to-me effects. Structured interviews can improve the accuracy of perceptions in the employment interview, and behaviourally anchored rating scales can improve performance appraisals. According to signalling theory, job applicants form perceptions about organizations on the basis of their recruitment and selection experiences, and their perceptions influence the likelihood that they will accept a job offer. Job applicants form more positive perceptions of the selection process when the selection procedures are perceived as being fair.

DISCUSSION QUESTIONS

1. Discuss how differences in the experiences of students and professors might affect their perceptions of students' written work and class comments.

2. Using implicit personality theory, explain how physical attractiveness influences job-related outcomes in employment interviews and performance appraisals.

3. Discuss the occupational stereotypes that you hold about computer programmers, the clergy, truck drivers, bartenders, and bankers. How do you think these stereotypes have developed? Has an occupational stereotype ever caused you to commit a socially embarrassing error when meeting someone for the first time?

4. Use Bruner's perceptual model (Exhibit 3.3) and social identity theory to explain why performance appraisals and interviewers' judgments are frequently inaccurate.

5. Discuss how perceptions of organizational support can influence employees' attitudes and behaviour. What can organizations do to develop positive perceptions of organizational support?

6. Suppose an employee does a particularly poor job on an assigned project. Discuss the attribution process that this person's manager will use to form judgments about this poor performance. Be sure to discuss how the manager will use consistency, consensus, and distinctiveness cues.

7. A study of small business failures found that owners generally cited factors such as economic depression or strong competition as causes. However, creditors of these failed businesses were much more likely to cite ineffective management. What attribution bias is indicated by these findings? Why do you think the difference in attribution occurs?

8. Discuss the factors that make it difficult for employment interviewers to form accurate perceptions of interviewees. Explain why a gender or racial stereotype might be more likely to affect a hiring decision than a performance appraisal decision. How can interviews and performance appraisals be designed to improve the accuracy of perceptions?

9. What are the implications of social identity theory for diversity in organizations? Describe some of the things that an organization can do to remove the barriers to workplace diversity. List some of the advantages gained by organizations that effectively manage a diverse workforce.

10. Explain stereotype threat effects and provide some examples of how they might occur in organizations and the consequences. What can organizations do to prevent stereotype threat effects?

INTEGRATIVE DISCUSSION QUESTIONS

1. Describe how the principles of operant learning theory and social cognitive theory can be used to manage workplace diversity and reduce the effects of workplace stereotypes. How can the organizational learning practices described in Chapter 2 be used for managing diversity?

2. Consider how the four basic types of managerial activities described in Chapter 1 (i.e., routine communication, traditional management, networking, and human resource management) can influence employees' perceptions of trust and perceived organizational support (POS). How should managers perform each of these activities to improve employees' perceptions of trust and POS?

ON-THE-JOB CHALLENGE QUESTION

Telecom giant Ericsson is the world's biggest supplier of mobile phone equipment and networks. Currently, the company employs 21 300 people in Sweden and about 50 500 in 140 other countries around the world. The company offered buyouts to up to 1000 of its employees in Sweden. It is a voluntary package, but it is only being offered to employees between the ages of 35 and 50. The company also announced plans to hire 900 new employees over the next three years, but only those who are under the age of 30. According to the company's global head of human resources, "The purpose of this program is to correct an age structure that is unbalanced. . . . We would like to make sure we employ more young people in order not to miss a generation in 10 years' time."

What do you think of Ericsson's voluntary buyout package and new hiring plans? Do perceptions have anything to do with their hiring plans? Is this something that Canadian organizations should consider? What are the implications?

Source: Acharya-Tom Yew, M. (2006, April 26). Is age 35 not judged as over the hill? *Toronto Star*, E1, E8. Reprinted with permission from Torstar Syndication Services.

EXPERIENTIAL EXERCISE

Beliefs about Older Workers

The items on the next page are an attempt to assess the attitudes people have about older workers. The statements cover many different opposing points of view; you may find yourself agreeing strongly with some of the statements, disagreeing just as strongly with others, and perhaps feeling uncertain about others.

Scoring and Interpretation

The scale you have just completed measures your attitudes toward older workers. To score your beliefs about older workers, subtract your responses to each of the following items from 6: 1, 2, 5, 6, 7, 8, 11, 13, 16, 17, 22, and 25. For example, if you put 2 for item 1, give yourself a 4 (6 minus 2). Then simply add up your resulting responses to all 27 items. Your score should fall somewhere between 27 and 135. Low scores indicate an overall negative belief about older workers, while high scores indicate positive beliefs. Thus, the higher your score, the more favourable your attitudes are toward older workers.

Research on older workers has generally found that a negative stereotype of older workers exists in organizations. The danger of this is that it can lead to negative attitudes and discriminatory behaviour toward older workers.

A study of 179 employees from three organizations obtained scores that ranged from 54 to 118. The average score was 90, which indicated somewhat positive beliefs about older workers. As reported in other studies, older workers had more positive beliefs about older workers than did younger workers. However, younger workers who had more interactions with older workers were found to have more positive beliefs about older workers.

To facilitate class discussion and your understanding of age stereotypes, form a small group with several other members of the class and consider the following questions. (Note that the instructor can also do this as a class exercise. Students should write their score, age, and interactions with older workers on a piece of paper and hand it in to the instructor, who can then determine the relationship between age, interactions with older workers, and beliefs about older workers.)

1. Students should first compare their scores to each other's and to the average score indicated above (90). Do group members have positive or negative beliefs about older workers? Do some group members have more positive or negative beliefs than others in the group?

2. Each member of the group should indicate his or her age. Determine the average age of the group and categorize those members above the average as being "older" and those below the average as being "younger." Then calculate the average score of the two age groups. Is there a difference in beliefs about older workers between older and younger group members?

3. Each group member should indicate how often they interact with older workers (daily, several times a week, once a week, or monthly). Based on group members' responses, create two categories that correspond to high and low interactions with older workers. Calculate the average score of these two groups. Is there a difference in beliefs about older workers between those who have more and those you have less interaction with older workers?

4. Why do some students have positive or negative beliefs about older workers? What are the implications of these beliefs at work and outside of work?

5. What can you do to develop more positive beliefs about older workers?

Source: Hassell, B.L., & Perrewe, P.L. (1995). An examination of beliefs about older workers: Do stereotypes still exist? *Journal of Organizational Behavior, 16,* 457–468.

Read each statement carefully. Using the numbers from 1 to 5 on the rating scale, mark your personal opinion about each statement in the blank space next to each statement. Remember, give your personal opinion according to how much you agree or disagree with each item. In all cases, older refers to people who are 50 years of age or older.

—1—	—2—	—3—	—4—	—5—
Strongly agree	Agree	Neither agree nor disagre	Disagree	Strongly disagree

____ 1. Older employees have fewer accidents on the job.

____ 2. Most companies are unfair to older employees.

____ 3. Older employees are harder to train for jobs.

____ 4. Older employees are absent more often than younger employees.

____ 5. Younger employees have more serious accidents than older workers.

____ 6. If two workers had similar skills, I'd pick the older worker to work with me.

____ 7. Occupational diseases are more likely to occur among younger employees.

____ 8. Older employees usually turn out work of higher quality.

____ 9. Older employees are grouchier on the job.

____ 10. Younger workers are more cooperative on the job.

____ 11. Older workers are more dependable.

____ 12. Most older workers cannot keep up with the speed of modern industry.

____ 13. Older employees are most loyal to the company.

____ 14. Older workers resist change and are too set in their ways.

____ 15. Younger workers are more interested than older workers in challenging jobs.

____ 16. Older workers can learn new skills as easily as other employees.

____ 17. Older employees are better employees.

____ 18. Older employees do not want jobs with increased responsibilities.

____ 19. Older workers are not interested in learning new skills.

____ 20. Older employees should "step aside" (take a less demanding job) to give younger employees advancement opportunities.

____ 21. The majority of older employees would quit work if they could afford it.

____ 22. Older workers are usually outgoing and friendly at work.

____ 23. Older workers prefer less challenging jobs than those they held when they were younger.

____ 24. It is a better investment to train younger workers rather than older workers.

____ 25. Older employees in our department work just as hard as anyone else.

____ 26. Given a choice, I would not work with an older worker on a daily basis.

____ 27. A person's performance declines significantly with age.

CASE INCIDENT

The New CEO

In March 2009, the Canadian National Institute for the Blind (CNIB) announced the appointment of John M. Rafferty as the organization's new president and CEO. CNIB is a nationwide charity that provides services and support to Canadians who are blind or visually impaired. Rafferty left a lucrative private-sector job to join CNIB. According to Al Jameson, chair of CNIB's national board of directors, Rafferty is an exceptional business leader whose skills and experience make him an excellent fit for CNIB. In fact, Rafferty has 13 years of national and international experience as a senior executive who has served in numerous leadership positions. However, Rafferty's appointment upset many people in the community and prompted criticism of CNIB. Some even referred to his hiring as despicable and a step backward.

Unlike all his predecessors and every top executive in the 91-year history of CNIB, Rafferty can see. He is CNIB's first "sighted" president and CEO. His hiring resulted in a complicated debate about identity and employment equity within Canada's diverse blind and visually impaired community. According to John Rae, vice-president of the Alliance for Equality of Blind Canadians (AEBC), the hiring of a sighted person as CEO is yet another example of CNIB "turning its back on the people it was set up to serve." By selecting Rafferty, CNIB has implied that blind Canadians qualified to lead a major organization do not exist. How can CNIB lobby corporations to hire the blind when it will not do so itself?

Sources: Dale, D. (2009, May 3). Debate stirs over hiring of sighted CNIB head: Board defends choice as critics ask how it can lobby firms to hire blind when it will not do so itself. *Toronto Star*, A1; Meet the President: John M. Rafferty. www.cnib.ca/en/about/who/president/default.aspx

1. Discuss the role of perceptions in people's reactions to the hiring of John Rafferty. Use Bruner's model of the perceptual process and social identity theory to explain people's perceptions and reactions.

2. Do you think CNIB should have hired John Rafferty as the organization's new president and CEO or should they have hired an individual who is blind or visually impaired? Explain your answer.

3. Does this incident have anything to do with equity and diversity? Explain your answer.

CASE STUDY

IVEY CTV Newsnet

Written by Professors Carol Tattersall and Christina A. Cavanagh

Richard Ivey School of Business
The University of Western Ontario

On January 15, 2000, Henry Kowalski, senior vice-president, news, had to move quickly to save the reputation of CTV (Canadian Television) Newsnet. Because of a technical error, a tape of its anchorperson, Avery Haines, making degrading remarks about various minorities, had been aired during a newscast. He had no doubt whatsoever about the integrity of Haines and that the apparent slurs were part of a private self-deprecating joke made, she believed, off-air. Still, none of these facts made his dilemma easier. It was up to him to address the situation, without delay.

CTV's Position in the Canadian Broadcasting Industry

CTV Inc. was one of Canada's pre-eminent communications companies, with conventional television operations across Canada. Its broadcasting signals reached 99 percent of English-speaking Canadians and offered a wide range of quality news, sports, information and entertainment programming. CTV Inc. had been in preliminary discussions with BCE (Bell Canada Enterprises), which announced a formal offer to purchase in March 2000.

During the previous four years, the company saw significant growth from its roots in family-run regional broadcasting, such as CFTO in Toronto. In February 1999, CTV Inc. was hoping to complete strategic negotiations that would expand the scale of its on-line operations. It was planning to launch an interactive site in the fall of 2000. At the CTV Inc. annual general meeting, Ivan Fecan, the chief executive officer, announced: "We expect to move into entertainment content production in a meaningful way, in fiscal 2000." While Fecan was clearly excited and optimistic about the direction the company was taking, he also, however, drew attention to the extra interest costs that would be incurred by acquisitions.

CTV's main competitor was Global Television, and at the beginning of the year, both companies were claiming to have won the 1999 fall ratings war, each interpreting differently the statistics compiled by Nielsen Research. Each of the competing broadcasters would have liked to be able to demonstrate definitively its edge in viewer numbers over the other, knowing the weight that advertisers would give to such ratings.

CTV's Goals and Corporate Philosophy

Fiscal 1999 was the first year of operation for the newly formed CTV Inc., although the brand known as CTV Network had been very well-known to Canadian audiences and advertisers for the past two decades. The consolidation of CTV and its owned affiliates, along with recent restructuring and innovations, had resulted in the creation of a truly integrated Canadian broadcasting and communications company.

Scope of operations included 25 television stations in Ontario, Saskatchewan, Alberta, British Columbia, Nova Scotia, and New Brunswick. Of these stations, 18 were affiliates of CTV, six were CBC affiliate television stations and one, CIVT, Vancouver, was an independent television station. CTV also owned ASN, a satellite-to-cable program undertaking and had ownership interests in four speciality cable television services: The Comedy Network; Outdoor Life Network; a headline news channel, CTV Newsnet; and CTV Sportsnet.

CTV Inc. had a 12 percent interest in History Television Inc. and held a licence for an additional speciality service, TalkTV, which was scheduled to launch in September 2000. CTV Inc. also had a controlling interest in Sports Specials/Pay-PerView for digital and DTH.

On March 5, 1999, CTV acquired a 68.46 percent interest in NetStar Communications Inc. The acquisition of NetStar was held in trust pending regulatory approvals. NetStar owned the Sports Network Inc. (TSN); Le Reseau des Sports (RDS) Inc.; Dome Productions Inc. (one of the largest mobile production facilities in Canada) and, through its 80 percent owned subsidiary, operated the Discovery Channel. NetStar also had a 24.95 percent interest in Viewer's Choice Canada Inc. CTV Inc. also had a 50 percent interest in Landscape Entertainment Corp., a production venture that would produce worldwide content for film, television and the Internet.

At fiscal year-end 1999, CTV Inc's. balance sheet showed total assets of $1.1 billion compared with $760 million at end of the previous year. Revenues for the first quarter of 2000 showed a slight decline over the same period the previous year, due mostly to softness in conventional television, which was down four percent compared with the previous year. Consequently, speciality channels such as CTV Newsnet and The Comedy Network were making significant revenue contributions and it was in this area that CTV Inc. would continue to focus.

Ivan Fecan further remarked that "CTV Inc. is still in the process of becoming the powerful, integrated broadcasting and communications organization it can and will be. We are leveraging the strengths of every part of the company to create a strong whole." He emphasized the company goal of helping clients to "extend their brands along the entire value chain, from the internet to local retail," and the need to maintain strong personal relationships and community roots across Canada.

CTV Inc. was clearly moving forward and enthusiastic about further expansion in the future, but it was also determined to continue to demonstrate that social commitment was still a priority. Fecan commended the involvement of individual employees in various fundraising and charitable activities. He also pointed to the contribution of CTV's programming, especially the Signature Series, which "had a significant impact on national awareness of injustice and sexual harassment of children," and stated the intention do many more projects like that.

The 24-hour news channel, CTV Newsnet, had always observed the company philosophy in its reporting, giving generous broadcast time to social issues, local, national and global. In January 2000, Canadian farmers were voicing their desperation about the crisis in Canadian agriculture, and the impossibility of family-owned farms remaining viable without increased government support. On January 16, a massive benefit concert was planned in Toronto solely to create awareness among urban dwellers on the problems faced by Canadian farmers.

One organizer, Liberal MP (Broadview-Greenwood) Dennis Mills, was quoted in *The Toronto Star* (January 13) as saying: "if we can get people to make legislators who live in cities—and 80 percent of Canada's parliamentarians do—more accountable in dealing with farming and agricultural issues, we'll have succeeded."

Canada's public station, CBC (Canadian Broadcasting Corporation), was planning to air a farm crisis program from 10:00 am Sunday, January 16 until 2:00 am Monday, January 17. On the morning of Saturday, January 15, CTV Newsnet, in keeping with its social awareness and community interest policies, was about to air the first of a series of its reports on the situation.

Henry Kowalski

Kowalski was a 25-year veteran of television news and had been with the CTV family since 1984. In the first six years of his career, he worked as head of assignment, specials producer, Toronto bureau chief and Vancouver bureau chief. In 1992, he was promoted to chief news editor, where he retooled the newscast and added several innovative features and segments.

His responsibilities included CTV's flagship *CTV News* with Lloyd Robertson and Sandie Rinaldo, all local newscasts on CTV's owned and operated stations across Canada, *Canada AM* and the highly acclaimed *W5*. Under his leadership, *CTV News* became Canada's most watched newscast, consistently ranking in the Nielsen top twenty.

In January 1997, Kowalski was promoted to senior vice-president and general manager, CTV News. He was responsible for guiding a team towards the successful launch of CTV Newsnet in October 1997 and for the remake of CFTO News, where he increased the audience and cemented it in first place in the competitive Toronto/Hamilton market.

CTV Newsnet's mandate was to become a significant force in Canadian journalism. In the highly competitive and over-serviced Canadian television market, Kowalski knew that a significant effort would be required to build a new service that would take a leadership position. He was no stranger to this type of challenge.

A New Anchor-Person

Early in December 1999, Kowalski signed 33-year-old Haines on a probationary contract to anchor the station's 24-hour cable news channel. Haines had been with the Toronto radio station CFRB for 11 years, having been hired straight from college by Bill Carroll, its news director.

Haines was eager to make the move from radio to television, and Kowalski was impressed with her qualifications: not only had she won several awards in newscasting, but she was well liked and respected by her peers and superiors and was already a popular radio personality with an enthusiastic following. He felt that she would be a good fit in the fast-paced and demanding milieu of television news and had the ability, ambition, and charisma that CTV Newsnet was looking to acquire. He had enjoyed the interview and found Haines relaxed, animated, composed, and personable. In all, he was very confident that Haines would quickly adapt and grow into this challenging position.

An Excellent Fit

Nearly two months had passed, and Kowalski was very pleased with Haine's progress. She had adjusted adeptly to the new medium, and her charisma translated well from voice to visual; she had impressive screen presence. Besides the implicit public approval, Haines seemed already to have gained the support and even affection of all her co-workers. She appeared inherently interested in everyone and everything and exuded a natural enthusiasm and charm.

It was not only personality, however, that distinguished the new employee but also her work ethic. Haines gave full commitment to her job; always willing to accept criticism and advice, to apply herself completely to every task, she was also creative and innovative where appropriate. Kowalski felt he had made a good decision and had acquired an employee who would be a great asset to CTV Newsnet.

Flubbed Lines

On Saturday, January 15, Haines was in the studio taping an introduction to a report on aid for Canadian farmers. For some reason, whether through lack of concentration, or simply because of a slip of the tongue, Haines stammered her way through the opening lines and completely garbled the message. Fortunately this was not a live broadcast, but as a relative newcomer in a very responsible position, Haines felt vulnerable and awkward.

Partly to cover her own embarrassment, but also to ease the tension for the other people in the studio, Haines started to make fun of her own ineptness. "I kind of like the stuttering thing," she laughed, "It's like equal opportunity, right? We've got a stuttering newscaster. We've got the black; we've got the Asian; we've got the woman. I could be a lesbian-folk-dancing-black-woman-stutterer." Someone joined in the banter, adding a few other possibilities, and Haines, responded in kind: "In a wheelchair . . . with a gimping rubber leg. Yeah, really. I'd have a successful career, let me tell you." Everyone in the studio knew the statements were very politically incorrect, but the repartee was harmless among those who understood its self-deprecating context and so typical of the gallows humour among journalists. No one was in the least offended, since Haines herself was a woman of African-Asian heritage. They knew she was poking fun at herself.

Meanwhile, everyone had relaxed, the technicians were ready to roll with a new tape, the original with the flubbed lines having been set aside. Haines went flawlessly through her farm-and-aid report, and the segment was ready to be aired later in the day.

A Technical Error

It had been a busy Saturday for the technical crew, but despite the re-take, everything was ready to go for the latest broadcast. The control room technician hit play and Haines, composed and pleasant, was on screen – stumbling through her intro to the farm-aid report. "Oh—! Oh—! Wrong tape! Wrong tape!" The cries went up in the studio control room. But things got worse. They realized that not only was the audience seeing Haines, CTV's Newsnet anchor, talking gibberish, they were watching and listening to the appallingly inappropriate exchange that had followed the flawed intro. The tape was rolling and the technical crews were so stunned that before they could react, the short tape had been played in its entirety.

Public Reaction

The phone lines at CTV's Agincourt studios were flashing instantly with messages from horrified and angry viewers, viewers who had come to trust the integrity and professionalism of CTV. Haines was doing another taped interview when her line-up editor rushed in to tell her about the awful error. Everyone scrambled, as they knew that Haine's comments would be aired by every competitive media source in the Greater Toronto area and could potentially spread beyond. It was essential to apologize on air as soon as possible. Haines was shaken and devastated, more for those she must have horribly offended than for her own sake. She was deeply disturbed that the public, would inevitably, and quite understandably, assume that her remarks represented her real views. She also knew that her position on CTV Newsnet was in jeopardy.

Henry Kowalski's Dilemma

Even before Haines's apologies were aired, Kowalski was in the CTV Newsnet studio, quickly trying to get a take on public reaction and to establish just how this major breach of process could have happened. Regardless of the details or of who was to blame, he was ultimately responsible for managing the brand created by CTV News and now he was faced with the unthinkable—damage control in the wake of a serious error.

Avery Haines had already demonstrated her talent and potential and clearly was a victim in the fiasco.

Nevertheless, Kowalski had to consider the effects of the incident not so much on individuals as on the growing reputation of CTV Newsnet and its ultimate backlash on the parent company, CTV Inc. They could lose major advertisers if the right actions weren't taken. Clearly, this was not going to be a good weekend.

Source: Professors Carol Tattersall and Christina A. Cavanagh prepared this case solely to provide material for class discussion. The authors do not intend to illustrate either effective or ineffective handling of a managerial situation. The authors may have disguised certain names and other identifying information to protect confidentiality.

1. What are people's perceptions of Avery Haines? Be sure to refer to the perceptions of Henry Kowalski, her co-workers, and CTV Newsnet viewers.

2. Why do viewers have different perceptions of Avery Haines than do her co-workers? Use Bruner's model of the perceptual process to explain people's perceptions of Avery Haines.

3. Use attribution theory to explain how co-workers and viewers responded to Haines's inappropriate comments. Why did her co-workers and the public react so differently?

4. Do you think the public's reaction to Haines's comments was reasonable? Discuss the possibility that the public response may be due to biases in person perception and attribution.

5. Haines was deeply disturbed that the public would assume that the bigotry inherent in her remarks represented her real views. Use the material in this chapter on perceptions and attributions to explain why the public believed that her remarks represented her real views. What does this case tell us about perceptions and attributions?

6. What do you think Avery Haines should do? What should Henry Kowalski do? Should Avery Haines be fired? Explain your answers.

After reading Chapter 4, you should be able to:

1 Define *values* and discuss the implications of cross-cultural variation in values for organizational behaviour.

2 Define *attitudes* and explain how people develop and change attitudes.

3 Explain the concept of *job satisfaction* and discuss some of its key contributors, including discrepancy, fairness, disposition, mood, and emotion.

4 Explain the relationship between job satisfaction and absenteeism, turnover, performance, organizational citizenship behaviour, and customer satisfaction.

5 Differentiate *affective, continuance,* and *normative commitment* and explain how organizations can foster *organizational commitment.*

Values, Attitudes, and Work Behaviour

L'Oréal Canada

Montreal's L'Oréal Canada is a subsidiary of the French L'Oréal Group, a prominent producer of cosmetics and personal care products. Their lines include L'Oréal Paris, Giorgio Armani, Ralph Lauren, Redken, Garnier, Biotherm, and Diesel, as well as those of the recently acquired Body Shop. Journalist Donna Nebenzahl describes three generations of L'Oréal employees.

It's not a new phenomenon, three generations in a single workplace, but the latest generation on the scene is causing a flurry of concern. That message came loud and clear to Marjolaine Rompré, director of learning development at L'Oréal Canada, a company that hires a large number of the Gen Y population, the most recent generation in the workplace.

By the late 1990s, the company realized that a work population that is one-third boomer (1947–1966), one-third Generation X (1967–1979), and one-third Generation Y (1980–1995) was going to have to figure out how to cope with the winds of change blown in by this younger generation. So it was up to Rompré, a young Boomer (born in 1961), to do something to alleviate the stress. Earlier generations, when they started at work, would go into meetings and observe and hardly speak, not wanting to ruffle feathers. Not so for the Gen Y population. "This new generation is so candid about participating and a lot freer," she said. "When we saw that, we realized we could be faced with an interesting problem. We called it Generation Shock."

So they decided to create a program for L'Oréal workers that would "valorize generational differences," which became the title, because they felt that Gen Y already received a lot of attention and the goal was to ensure that every group understood the other. In the end, she says, "the Ys told us they were so happy to learn why the baby boomers were so conservative and why Gen X didn't want to share information with them." They have brought in 500 employees so far, in an effort to reveal the values of each generation—and the common truth that each generation is more rebellious than the one before and always wants to change the world.

For instance, when they talk about security, the groups learn that for the post-war generation, the smallest, oldest group now known as traditionalists,

L'Oréal employees Jean Cardinal, Rosalie Nolin, and Dominic Savaria span the baby boom–Gen X–Gen Y gap.

security meant their savings. "They bought with cash and they had money in the bank," she said. For baby boomers, "their security was in the pension plan, because that was really created with their generation. You just had job security and pension plan." For the X generation, who came into a saturated market and had to fight for their jobs, security meant having a strong resumé. On the other hand, Rompré says, "for Gen Y, *security* is not a word in their vocabulary because they have such a safety net; their parents are there for them. They don't have the same outlook."

There's a certain self importance in this group, she says, mixed with extreme loyalty toward their colleagues, with whom many form lasting friendships. "There's a greater sense of community than among the Gen X. Baby boomers are about the team, while Gen X were very career-oriented, all about themselves." This, of course, is a response to Gen X's entrée into a very competitive and tight workplace, compared with Gen Y, who see work as a continuum from university. "For them, it's just another way of learning. They're really focused on their development," Rompré said. "They want to continue to grow and learn." At the same time, she points out, "they have an amazing sense of community and friendship. Families are smaller, with fewer siblings, so friends are important when growing up. Plus, mom and daddy are working." So when they get into the workplace, their colleagues become their friends and their social life takes place partly at work.

On the other hand, the previous generations were a lot more career and results focused. It was clear that when you started in a company, you would start at the bottom and work hard in order to earn your place. Not so for Gen Y. "This generation is the most schooled generation ever, and they want to have responsibility very early on," she said. They really want to be autonomous, yet they also want validation. They want to be independent, but like to work in teams. They want rapid success within the company, yet have a very strong desire to maintain work–life balance. They practise extensive freedom of speech and are very candid, but they lack political savvy.

They want to be everywhere at the same time, but have real difficulty managing priorities. They have great tolerance about religion, race and nationality, but are very quick to pass judgment on the competency of their bosses. "They won't respect you because you're their boss. They'll respect you because you're competent and approachable," Rompré said.

At L'Oréal, the course has been a huge success, generating so much buzz that the company had to add to the half-day sessions. Another sidenote within the company, where there are actually a number of Gen Ys who are now managing boomers and Gen Xs: Most of the Ys are children of baby boomers so there is an interesting relationship between the two groups. "The Xs had to fight much more, waiting for boomers to get out, but the baby boomers aren't threatened by Gen Y," she said. "In fact, they love to share and to show them the ropes."[1]

The L'Oréal Canada story illustrates how generational differences in values and work attitudes affect workplace behaviour. In this chapter we will discuss such values and attitudes. Our discussion of values will be particularly oriented toward cross-cultural variations in values and their implications for organizational behaviour. Our discussion of attitudes will explain attitude formation. Two critical attitudes are job satisfaction and organizational commitment. We will consider the causes and consequences of both.

What Are Values?

Values. A broad tendency to prefer certain states of affairs over others.

We might define **values** as "a broad tendency to prefer certain states of affairs over others."[2] The *preference* aspect of this definition means that values have to do with what we consider good and bad. Values are motivational, since they signal the attractive aspects of our environment that we seek and the unattractive aspects that we try to avoid or change. They also signal how we believe we *should* and *should not* behave.[3] The words *broad tendency* mean that values are very general and that they do not predict behaviour in specific situations very well. Knowing that a person generally embraces the values that support capitalism does not tell us much about how he or she will respond to a homeless person on the street this afternoon.

People tend to hold values structured around such factors as achievement, power, autonomy, conformity, tradition, and social welfare.[4] Not everyone holds the same values. Managers might value high productivity (an achievement value), while union officials might be more concerned with enlightened supervision and full employment (social values). We learn values through the reinforcement processes we discussed in Chapter 2. Most are socially reinforced by parents, teachers, and representatives of religions.

To solidify your understanding of values and their impact on organizational behaviour, let's examine some generational differences in values and see how work values differ across cultures.

Generational Differences in Values

Like L'Oréal Canada, many contemporary organizations are attempting to understand the implications of having four rather distinctive generations in the workplace at one time who are often required to work with one another. As shown in Exhibit 4.1, these generations comprise what are often called the Traditionalists, the baby

Generation	Percentage of Workforce	Assets in the Workplace	Leadership Style Preferences
Traditionalists Born 1922–1945	8%	Hard working, stable, loyal, thorough, detail-oriented, focused, emotional maturity	Fair, consistent, clear, direct, respectful
Baby Boomers Born 1946–1964	44%	Team perspective, delicated, experienced, knowledgeable, service-oriented	Treat as equals, warm and caring, mission-defined, democratic approach
Generation X Born 1965–1980	34%	Independent, adaptable, creative, techno-literate, willing to challenge the status quo	Direct, competent, genuine, informal, flexible, results-oriented, supportive of learning opportunities
Millennials Born 1981–2000	14% and increasing rapidly	Optimistic, able to multitask, tenacious, technologically savvy, driven to learn and grow, team-oriented, socially responsible	Motivational, collaborative, positive, educational, organized, achievement-oriented, able to coach

EXHIBIT 4.1

Four generations in today's workplace.

Source: Society for Human Resource Management (2009). The multigenerational workforce: Opportunity for competitive success. *SHRM Research Quarterly*, First Quarter, 1–9. Compiled from AARP (2007). *Leading a multigenerational workforce*. Washington, DC: AARP; Sabatini Fraone, J., Hartmann, D., & McNally, K. (2008). *The multigenerational workforce: Management implications and strategies for collaboration*. Boston: Boston College Center for Work & Family; Zemke, R., Raines, C., & Filipezak, B. (2000). *Generations at work*. New York: American Management Association.

boomers, Generation X, and the Millennials (or Generation Y). These generations are of course demarcated by being of different ages, but they are also distinguished by having grown up under rather different socialization experiences. For example, many traditionalists grew up in the shadow of two wars, baby boomers faced a vibrant economy (not to mention the sexual revolution and the advent of rock 'n' roll!), and Gen X and Y experienced more dual-career families and more divorce when growing up. It has been argued that these contrasting experiences, in turn, have led to notable value differences between the generations. For example, "latchkey kids" and those who know divorce might come to value the advice of authority figures less and the advice of friends more, compared to earlier generations. Such value differences might then underlie the differential workplace assets and preferences for leadership style highlighted in Exhibit 4.1.[10]

The popular press contains many stereotypes (Chapter 3) concerning the generations.[5] Thus, the Traditionalists are portrayed as being respectful of authority and having a high work ethic; boomers are viewed as optimistic workaholics; Gen X is seen as cynical, confident, and pragmatic; and Gen Y is said to be confident, social, demanding of feedback, and somewhat unfocused. In general, the latter two generations are seen as more accepting of diversity and striving for good work–life balance, and their comfort with technology is notable.

Are these stereotypes accurate? It has to be said that the study of inter-generational values and of related attitudes and behaviour is in its infancy. And it is inherently hard to tease out generational effects from those that simply reflect age or work experience. Most recent research points to more similarities than differences in values across generations.[6] However, there is some indication that Gen X and Y are more inclined to value status and rapid career growth than are boomers.[7] This may reflect valuing what one does not yet have, but it could also reflect the positive self-esteem movement to which later generations have been exposed. Indeed, there is evidence that the self-esteem of university students has increased over the years.[8] There is also evidence that Gen Ys especially value autonomy and that Xers, compared to boomers, are less loyal, more wanting of promotion, and more inclined toward work–life balance.[9] Research conducted by the Center for Creative Leadership concluded that all work generations share the same values but express them differently. For instance, most people value respect, but for older employees this means being deferred to, while for Gen X and Y this means being listened to.[10]

Any generational differences in work values or in the way values are expressed is important because there is much evidence that good "fit" between a person's values and those of the organization (person–organization fit) leads to positive work attitudes and behaviours, including reduced chances of quitting.[11] This means that organizations may have to tailor job designs, leadership styles, and benefits to the generational mix of their workforces.

Cultural Differences in Values

It is by now a cliché to observe that business has become global in its scope—Korean cars dot North American roads; your Dell helpdesk service provider resides in India; and entire lines of "Italian" cookware are made in China. All this activity obscures just how difficult it can be to forge business links across cultures. For example, research shows that anywhere from 16 to 40 percent of managers who receive foreign assignments terminate them early because they perform poorly or do not adjust to the culture.[12] Similarly, a lengthy history of failed business negotiations is attributable to a lack of understanding of cross-cultural differences. At the root of many of these problems is a lack of appreciation of basic differences in work-related values across cultures. On the other hand, consider the opportunities for organizations that are globally adept (and for graduating students who are cross-culturally sensitive!).

Work Centrality. Work itself is valued differently across cultures. One large-scale survey of over 8000 individuals in several nations found marked cross-national differences in the extent to which people perceived work as a central life interest.[13] Japan topped the list, with very high work centrality. Belgians and Americans exhibited average work centrality, and the British scored low. One question in the survey asked respondents whether they would continue working if they won a large amount of money in a lottery. Those with more central interest in work were more likely to report that they would continue working despite the new-found wealth.

The survey also found that people for whom work was a central life interest tended to work more hours. A reflection of this can be seen in Exhibit 4.2, which shows great variation in vacation time across cultures. This illustrates how cross-cultural differences in work centrality can lead to adjustment problems for foreign employees and managers. Imagine the unprepared British executive who is posted to Japan only to find that Japanese managers commonly work late and then socialize with co-workers or customers long into the night. In Japan, this is all part of the job, often to the chagrin of the lonely spouse. On the other hand, consider the Japanese executive posted to Britain who

Customer-friendly service is a high work priority in Japan. Tokyo Disneyland is considered the safest, cleanest, and most orderly Disney park in the world.

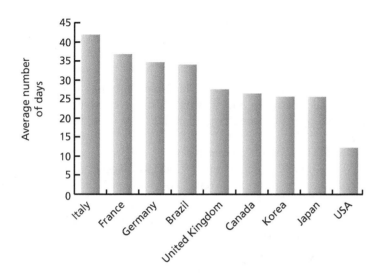

EXHIBIT 4.2
Vacation time across cultures.

Source: World Tourism Organization (WTO) as cited in Travel Industry Association of America (2002). World Tourism Overview. Retrieved July 18, 2003, from http://www.tia.org/ivis/worldtourism.asp#vacation. Reprinted by permission. © UNWTO, 9284403309.

finds out that an evening at the pub is *not* viewed as an extension of the day at the office and is therefore not a time to continue talking business.

Hofstede's Study. Dutch social scientist Geert Hofstede questioned over 116 000 IBM employees located in 40 countries about their work-related values.[14] (There were 20 different language versions of the questionnaire.) Virtually everyone in the corporation participated. When Hofstede analyzed the results, he discovered four basic dimensions along which work-related values differed across cultures: power distance, uncertainty avoidance, masculinity/femininity, and individualism/collectivism. Subsequent work with Canadian Michael Bond that catered more to Eastern cultures resulted in a fifth dimension, the long-term/short-term orientation.[15] More recently, the dimensions were verified and supplemented by the GLOBE project, headed by Professor Robert House.[16] You will learn more about this research, which involved more than 17 000 managers in 62 societies, when we cover leadership in Chapter 9.

- *Power distance.* **Power distance** refers to the extent to which society members accept an unequal distribution of power, including those who hold more power and those who hold less. In small power distance cultures, inequality is minimized, superiors are accessible, and power differences are downplayed. In large power distance societies, inequality is accepted as natural, superiors are inaccessible, and power differences are highlighted. Small power distance societies include Denmark, New Zealand, Israel, and Austria. Large power distance societies include the Philippines, Venezuela, and Mexico. Out of 40 societies, Canada and the United States rank 14 and 15, respectively, falling on the low power distance side of the average, which would be 20.

Power distance. The extent to which an unequal distribution of power is accepted by society members.

- *Uncertainty avoidance.* **Uncertainty avoidance** refers to the extent to which people are uncomfortable with uncertain and ambiguous situations. Strong uncertainty avoidance cultures stress rules and regulations, hard work, conformity, and security. Cultures with weak uncertainty avoidance are less concerned with rules, conformity, and security, and hard work is not seen as a virtue. However, risk taking is valued. Strong uncertainty avoidance cultures include Japan, Greece, and Portugal. Weak uncertainty avoidance cultures include Singapore, Denmark, and Sweden. On uncertainty avoidance, the United States and Canada are well below average (i.e., exhibiting weak uncertainty avoidance), ranking 9 and 10, respectively, out of 40.

Uncertainty avoidance. The extent to which people are uncomfortable with uncertain and ambiguous situations.

- *Masculinity/femininity.* More masculine cultures clearly differentiate gender roles, support the dominance of men, and stress economic performance. More feminine cultures accept fluid gender roles, stress sexual equality, and stress quality of life. In Hofstede's research, Japan is the most masculine society, followed by Austria, Mexico, and Venezuela. The Scandinavian countries are the most feminine. Canada ranks about mid-pack, and the United States is fairly masculine, falling about halfway between Canada and Japan. The GLOBE research identified two aspects to this dimension—how assertive people are and how much they value gender equality.

- *Individualism/collectivism.* More **individualistic** societies tend to stress independence, individual initiative, and privacy. More **collective** cultures favour interdependence and loyalty to one's family or clan. The United States, Australia, Great Britain, and Canada are among the most individualistic societies. Venezuela, Columbia, and Pakistan are among the most collective, with Japan falling about mid-pack. The GLOBE research uncovered two aspects to this dimension—how much the collective distribution of resources is stressed and how much one's group or organization elicits loyalty.

- *Long-term/short-term orientation.* Cultures with a long-term orientation tend to stress persistence, perseverance, thrift, and close attention to status differences. Cultures with a short-term orientation stress personal steadiness and stability, face-saving, and social niceties. China, Hong Kong, Taiwan, Japan, and South Korea tend to be characterized by a long-term orientation. The United States, Canada, Great Britain, Zimbabwe, and Nigeria characterized by a more short-term orientation. Hofstede and Bond argue that the long-term orientation, in part, explains prolific East Asian entrepreneurship.

Exhibit 4.3 compares the United States, Canada, Mexico, Japan, and West Africa on Hofstede's value dimensions. Note that the profiles for Canada and the United States are very similar, but they differ considerably from that of Mexico.

Hofstede has produced a number of interesting "cultural maps" that show how countries and regions cluster together on pairs of cultural dimensions. The map in Exhibit 4.4 shows the relationship between power distance and degree of individualism. As you can see, these two values tend to be related. Cultures that are more individualistic tend to downplay power differences, while those that are more collectivistic tend to accentuate power differences.

Implications of Cultural Variation

Exporting OB Theories. An important message from the cross-cultural study of values is that organizational behaviour theories, research, and practices from North America might not translate well to other societies, even the one located just south of Texas.[17] The basic questions (How should I lead? How should we make this decision?)

Individualism vs. collectivism. Individualistic societies stress independence, individual initiative, and privacy. Collective cultures favour interdependence and loyalty to family or clan.

EXHIBIT 4.3
Cross-cultural value comparisons.

Note: Time orientation data for Mexico unavailable.

Source: Graph by authors. Data from Hofstede, G. (2005). Cultures and organizations: Software of the mind. Copyright © 2005 Geert Hofstede. Reprinted with permission of the author.

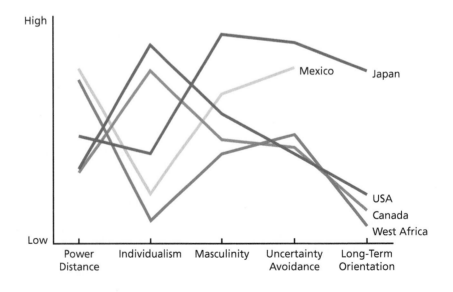

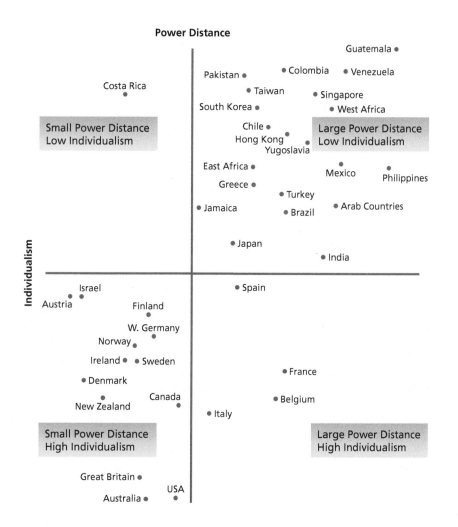

Power Distance

Small Power Distance
Low Individualism

Costa Rica

Pakistan •
• Colombia
Guatemala •
• Venezuela
• Taiwan
• Singapore
South Korea •
• West Africa

Chile •
Hong Kong •
Yugoslavia •

Large Power Distance
Low Individualism

East Africa •
Greece •
• Mexico
Philippines •

• Jamaica
• Turkey
• Brazil
• Arab Countries

• Japan
• India

Individualism

Israel •
Austria •
• Spain

Finland •

W. Germany •
Norway •
Ireland •   • Sweden
• Denmark

• France

New Zealand •   Canada •

Small Power Distance
High Individualism

• Belgium
• Italy

Large Power Distance
High Individualism

Great Britain •
USA •
Australia •

EXHIBIT 4.4

Power distance and individualism values for various countries and regions.

Source: Adapted from Hofstede, G. (1984) The cultural relativity of the quality of life concept. *Academy of Management Review*, 9, 389-398, p.391. This work is protected by copyright and it is being used with the permission of Access Copyright. Any alteration of its content or further copying in any form whatsoever is strictly prohibited unless otherwise permitted by law.

remain the same. It is just the *answers* that differ. For example, North American managers tend to encourage participation in work decisions by employees. This corresponds to the fairly low degree of power distance valued here. Trying to translate this leadership style to cultures that value high power distance might prove unwise. In these cultures, people might be more comfortable deferring to the boss's decision. Similarly, in individualistic North America, calling attention to one's accomplishments is expected and often rewarded in organizations. In more collective Asian or South American cultures, individual success might be devalued, and it might make sense to reward groups rather than individuals. Finally, in extremely masculine cultures, integrating women into management positions might require special sensitivity.

A good fit between company practices and the host culture is important. In general, the American culture is more similar to the French culture than the Japanese culture. However, the Walt Disney Company found that its specific human resources practices fit well with Japanese culture but not French culture (see Global Focus: *Disney in Japan vs. Disney in France*).

Importing OB Theories. Not all theories and practices that concern organizational behaviour are designed in North America or even in the West. The most obvious examples are "Japanese management" techniques, such as quality circles, total quality management, and just-in-time production. Although there are success stories of importing these techniques from Japan to North America, there are also examples of difficulties and failure. Many of the problems stem from basic value differences between Japan and North America. For example, the quest for continuous improvement and the heavy reliance on employee suggestions for improvement has had a mixed reaction.[18] In Japan,

GLOBAL FOCUS

Disney in Japan vs. Disney in France

Disney prides itself on friendly service and safe, clean, and orderly surroundings. And Disney feels that its employees, or "cast," must have what it calls a "wholesome American look" to be able to properly execute their smiling "roles" in the "happiest place on Earth." New employees are taught about these things at Disney University.

Providing this kind of service and atmosphere at Tokyo Disneyland was not difficult, because Disney's type of service orientation meshes easily with Japanese cultural norms. In fact, customer-friendly service is so important in Japanese corporate culture that new hires at Japanese companies have to take a 6- to 12-month training program just to learn customer service techniques. Among other things, they learn to adopt a special high-pitched voice as a mark of respect when talking to customers. The match between Disney's corporate norms and Japanese cultural norms is so good that of all the Disney theme parks worldwide, Tokyo Disneyland is the safest, cleanest, and most orderly.

At Disneyland Paris, on the other hand, Disney had trouble achieving its standards for customer service and park surroundings. Because French workplaces tend not to have dress codes, employees felt that Disney's dress code—which includes allowable lengths for dress, hair, and fingernails—limited their right to personal expression. Disneyland Paris also had problems getting its employees to smile the way they were taught at Disney University.

Inspections at Disneyland Paris have revealed all sorts of problems that make for a less than customer-friendly experience: messy grounds that lack the numerous sidewalk sweepers that are so prominent at other Disney parks, messy bathrooms with many broken stall doors, and unsmiling personnel. In one case, a food server got into an argument with a guest over the bill.

Unlike the custom in Japan and the United States, in France the customer isn't necessarily right. For example, waiters feel perfectly comfortable telling diners in their restaurant when they disapprove of their choice of dishes. Indeed, they take pride in doing so.

The mismatch between Disney's corporate norms and French cultural norms has resulted in a lot of negative press coverage. And in January 1995, Disneyland Paris was charged with having violated French labour laws for its attempt to impose the US dress code on its workers. Clearly, Disney's one-size-fits-all mentality needed to be adjusted to the differing cultural norms of France.

Source: Brannen, M.Y. (2004). When Mickey loses face: Recontextualization, semantic fit, and the semiotics of foreignness. *Academy of Management Review, 29*, 593–616.

---

cultural values have traditionally dictated a fairly high degree of employment security. Thus, working at a fast pace and providing suggestions for improvement will not put one out of a job. North American workers are uncertain about this.

Many of the Japanese-inspired means of organizing work are team-oriented. Since Japan has fairly collective cultural values, submerging one's own interests in those of the team is natural. Although employers have successfully used teams in North America, as you will see in Chapter 7, our more individualistic culture dictates that careful selection of team members is necessary.

Understanding cultural value differences can enable organizations to successfully import management practices by tailoring the practice to the home culture's concerns.

Appreciating Global Customers. An appreciation of cross-cultural differences in values is essential to understanding the needs and tastes of customers or clients around the world. Once relegated to the status of a marketing problem, it is now clear that such understanding fundamentally has to do with organizational behaviour. Errors occur with regularity. For instance, the initial French response to the Disneyland Paris theme park was less enthusiastic than Disney management had expected, probably due in part to Disney's failure to truly appreciate French tastes in food, lifestyle, and entertainment. South Korea's Samsung recalled a calendar featuring models displaying its products that was destined for overseas customers. Some North Americans were offended by Miss July's see-through blouse.

Appreciating the values of global customers is also important when the customers enter your own culture. Many firms have profited from an understanding of the increasing ethnic diversity in the United States, Canada, and Australia.

Developing Global Employees. Success in translating management practices to other cultures, importing practices developed elsewhere, and appreciating global customers are not things that happen by accident. Rather, companies need to select, train, and develop employees to have a much better appreciation of differences in cultural values and the implications of these differences for behaviour in organizations.

To get their designers to better appreciate the values of the North American market, Japanese and Korean car makers, including Nissan, Toyota, Hyundai, and Kia, have design studios in California. The top ranks of Detroit's automakers, once the protected realm of mid-westerners, are now liberally filled with Europeans or those with European or Asian experience. However, industry observers have noted that the recent financial woes of Detroit are due in part to poor global positioning. As we will see below, attitudes do not always get translated into behaviours.

As you proceed through the text, you will encounter further discussion about the impact of cultural values on organizational behaviour. Now, let's examine attitudes and see how they are related to values.

What Are Attitudes?

An **attitude** is a fairly stable evaluative tendency to respond consistently to some specific object, situation, person, or category of people. First, notice that attitudes involve *evaluations* directed toward *specific* targets. If I inquire about your attitude toward your boss, you will probably tell me something about how well you *like* him or her. This illustrates the evaluative aspect of attitudes. Attitudes are also much more specific than values, which dictate only broad preferences. For example, you could value working quite highly but still dislike your specific job.

Attitude. A fairly stable evaluative tendency to respond consistently to some specific object, situation, person, or category of people.

Our definition indicates that attitudes are *tendencies to respond* to the target of the attitude. Thus, attitudes often influence our behaviour toward some object, situation, person, or group.

Attitude ➤ Behaviour

Of course, not everyone who likes the boss goes around praising him or her in public for fear of being seen as too political. Similarly, people who dislike the boss do not always engage in public criticism for fear of retaliation. These examples indicate that attitudes are not always consistent with behaviour, and that attitudes provide useful information over and above the actions that we can observe. Behaviour is most likely to correspond to attitudes when people have direct experience with the target of the attitude and when the attitude is held confidently.[19]

Where do attitudes come from? Put simply, attitudes are a function of what we think and what we feel. That is, attitudes are the product of a related belief and value.[20] Given this point of view, we can now expand the attitude model presented above to include the thinking and feeling aspects of attitudes represented by beliefs and values.

BELIEF + VALUE ⇒ Attitude ➤ Behaviour

Thus, we can imagine the following sequence of ideas in the case of a person experiencing work–family conflict:

"My job is interfering with my family life." (Belief)

"I dislike anything that hurts my family." (Value)

"I dislike my job." (Attitude)

"I'll search for another job." (Behaviour)

This simple example shows how attitudes (in this case, job satisfaction) develop from basic beliefs and values, and how they affect organizational behaviour (in this case, turnover from the organization).

Organizations often attempt to change employee attitudes. Most attempts at attitude change are initiated by a communicator who tries to use persuasion of some form to modify the beliefs or values of an audience that supports a currently held attitude.[21] For example, management might hold a seminar to persuade managers to value workforce diversity, or it might develop a training program to change attitudes toward workplace safety. Persuasion that is designed to modify or emphasize values is usually emotionally oriented. A safety message that concentrates on a dead worker's weeping, destitute family exemplifies this approach. Persuasion that is slanted toward modifying certain beliefs is usually rationally oriented. A safety message that tries to convince workers that hard hats and safety glasses are not uncomfortable to wear reveals this angle. You have probably seen both these approaches used in AIDS awareness and anti-smoking campaigns.

The specific attitudes we are now going to cover, job satisfaction and organizational commitment, have a strong impact on people's positive contributions to their work.[22]

What Is Job Satisfaction?

Job satisfaction refers to a collection of attitudes that people have about their jobs. We can differentiate two aspects of satisfaction. The first of these is facet satisfaction, the tendency for an employee to be more or less satisfied with various facets of the job. The notion of facet satisfaction is obvious when we hear someone say, "I love my work but hate my boss" or "This place pays lousy, but the people I work with are great." Both these statements represent different attitudes toward separate facets of the speaker's job. The most relevant attitudes toward jobs are contained in a rather small group of facets: the work itself, compensation, career opportunities, recognition, benefits, working conditions, supervision, co-workers, and organizational policy.[23]

In addition to facet satisfaction, we can also conceive of overall satisfaction, an overall or summary indicator of a person's attitude toward his or her job that cuts across the various facets.[24] The statement "On the whole, I really like my job, although a couple of aspects could stand some improvement" is indicative of the nature of overall satisfaction. Overall satisfaction is an average or total of the attitudes individuals hold toward various facets of the job. Thus, two employees might express the same level of overall satisfaction for different reasons.

A popular measure of job satisfaction is the *Job Descriptive Index* (JDI).[25] This questionnaire is designed around five facets of satisfaction. Employees are asked to respond "yes," "no," or "?" (cannot decide) in describing whether a particular word or phrase is descriptive of particular facets of their jobs. Exhibit 4.5 shows some sample JDI

Job satisfaction. A collection of attitudes that workers have about their jobs.

EXHIBIT 4.5
Sample items from the Job Descriptive Index with "satisfied" responses.

Source: The Job Description Index, revised 1985, is copyrighted by Bowling Green State University. The complete forms, scoring key, instructions, and norms can be obtained from the Department of Psychology, Bowling Green State University, Bowling Green, Ohio, 43403. Reprinted with permission.

Work
- N Routine
- Y Creative
- N Tiresome
- Y Gives sense of accomplishment

People
- Y Stimulating
- Y Ambitious
- N Talk too much
- N Hard to meet

Promotions
- Y Good opportunity for advancement
- Y Promotion on ability
- N Dead-end job
- N Unfair promotion policy

Supervision
- Y Asks my advice
- Y Praises good work
- N Doesn't supervise enough
- Y Tells me where I stand

Pay
- Y Income adequate for normal expenses
- N Bad
- N Less than I deserve
- Y Highly paid

items under each facet, scored in the "satisfied" direction. A scoring system is available to provide an index of satisfaction for each facet. In addition, an overall measure of satisfaction can be calculated by adding the separate facet indexes.

Another carefully constructed measure of satisfaction, using a somewhat different set of facets, is the *Minnesota Satisfaction Questionnaire* (MSQ).[26] On this measure, respondents indicate how happy they are with various aspects of their job on a scale ranging from "very satisfied" to "very dissatisfied." Sample items from the short form of the MSQ include the following:

- The competence of my supervisor in making decisions
- The way my job provides for steady employment
- The chance to do things for other people
- My pay and the amount of work I do

Scoring the responses to these items provides an index of overall satisfaction as well as satisfaction on the facets on which the MSQ is based.

Firms such as Sears, Marriott, Scotiabank, The Keg, and Microsoft make extensive use of employee attitude surveys. For example, consider Applied Focus: *At RIM, Employee Satisfaction Supports a Culture of Innovation*.

What Determines Job Satisfaction?

When employees on a variety of jobs complete the JDI or the MSQ, we often find differences in the average scores across jobs. Of course, we could almost expect such differences. The various jobs might differ objectively in the facets that contribute to satisfaction. Thus, you would not be astonished to learn that a corporate vice-president was more satisfied with her job than a janitor in the same company. Of greater interest is the fact that we frequently find decided differences in job satisfaction expressed by individuals performing the same job in a given organization. For example, two nurses who work side by side might indicate radically different satisfaction in response to the MSQ item "The chance to do things for other people." How does this happen?

Discrepancy

You will recall that attitudes, such as job satisfaction, are the product of associated beliefs and values. These two factors cause differences in job satisfaction even when jobs are identical. First, people might differ in their beliefs about the job in question. That is, they might differ in their *perceptions* concerning the actual nature of the job. For example, one of the nurses might perceive that most of her working time is devoted to direct patient care, while the other might perceive that most of her time is spent on administrative functions. To the extent that they both value patient care, the former nurse should be more satisfied with this aspect of the job than the latter nurse. Second, even if individuals perceive their jobs as equivalent, they might differ in what they *want* from the jobs. Such desires are preferences that are dictated, in part, by the workers' value systems. Thus, if the two nurses perceive their opportunities to engage in direct patient care as high, the one who values this activity more will be more satisfied with the patient care aspect of work. The **discrepancy theory** of job satisfaction asserts that satisfaction is a function of the discrepancy between the job outcomes people want and the outcomes that they perceive they obtain.[27] For instance, there is strong evidence that satisfaction with one's pay is high when there is a small gap between the pay received and the perception of how much pay *should* be received.[28] At L'Oréal, for example, generational differences in values could have an impact on job satisfaction levels.

Discrepancy theory. A theory that job satisfaction stems from the discrepancy between the job outcomes wanted and the outcomes that are perceived to be obtained.

APPLIED FOCUS

At RIM, Employee Satisfaction Supports a Culture of Innovation

In the high-tech and creative domains, much of organizational success depends on attracting and retaining the very best talent and creating an atmosphere free from distractions and inconveniences so that the creative juices can flow. The stress of project deadlines is commonplace. Because of these factors, firms such as Google, Microsoft, and Research In Motion (RIM) go to extraordinary lengths to foster employee job satisfaction.

Nestled within Canada's Technology Triangle (Waterloo, Kitchener, Cambridge), RIM is one of the area's most well-known high-tech employers. It is best recognized as the creator of the BlackBerry wireless device and is seemingly unstoppable. In early 2009, RIM posted impressive annual results while the rest of the industry was struggling through the recession. So how does RIM do it?

RIM co-CEO and founder Mike Lazaridis attributes the company's success to its culture of innovation. "If you build the right culture and invest in the right facilities and you encourage and motivate and inspire both young and seasoned people and put them all in the right environment—then it really performs for you."

RIM is fanatical about attracting top university graduates who are crazy about wireless. Although RIM's reputation is strong, luring the brightest isn't an easy task. Waterloo is home to many other Canadian high-tech giants (e.g., OpenText) who are thirsty for local talent. RIM therefore promotes employee satisfaction right from the start by giving new employees a free BlackBerry on their very first day, not only to make them happy but also to ensure they intimately understand the company's core product.

At RIM's head office, creativity is encouraged through a campus-like environment. The 14 buildings boast employee lounges, full-service and self-service kitchens, a religious observance room, showering facilities, secure bike lock-ups, and, for those who want to stay late, escort to their cars. Along with standard financial and health benefits commonly found in high tech, RIM also supports employee well-being (e.g., onsite massages, flu shot clinics, discounted gym membership) and sponsors a number of local sports teams.

Employees are rewarded for innovation through the company's incentive programs, which focus on patent inventions, product ideas, and sales. Careers are managed through a number of mechanisms, including performance reviews, online career planning tools, feedback sessions, and training programs. RIM provides employee discounts for home computers and supports flexible working hours and telecommuting. Employees receive up to 100 percent tuition reimbursement for education related to their job and can take extended leave for personal reasons or to complete advanced degrees.

Employees are very much the centre of attention at RIM. In late 2008, at a time when most companies were cutting back on R&D, benefits, and employee recognition, RIM thanked everyone with a Tragically Hip and Van Halen concert at Toronto's Air Canada Centre.

Sources: Anonymous. (2008, April). BlackBerry: Innovation behind the icon. *Business Week* (online) (Lazaridis quote); Anonymous. (2009, April). How the BlackBerry duo plans to stay in motion. *Business Week* (online); Evans, B. (2005, June). Build your company's receptor capacity. *Information Week, (1042)*, 84; Yerema, R. (2009, January). Employer Review: Research In Motion Limited. Mediacorp Canada Inc. www.eluta.ca/top-employer-rim; www.rim.net.

Fairness

In addition to the discrepancy between the outcomes people receive and those they desire, another factor that determines job satisfaction is fairness. Issues of fairness affect both what people want from their jobs and how they react to the inevitable discrepancies of organizational life. As you will see, there are three basic kinds of fairness. Distributive fairness has to do with the outcomes we receive, procedural fairness concerns the process that led to those outcomes, and interactional fairness concerns how these matters were communicated to us.[29]

Distributive fairness. Fairness that occurs when people receive the outcomes they think they deserve from their jobs.

Distributive Fairness. Distributive fairness (often called distributive justice) occurs when people receive the outcomes they think they deserve from their jobs; that is, it involves the ultimate *distribution* of work rewards and resources. Above, we indicated that what people want from their jobs is a partial function of their value systems. In fact, however, there are practical limitations to this notion. You might value money and the luxurious lifestyle that it can buy very highly, but this does not suggest that you expect to receive a salary of $200 000 a year. In the case of many job facets, individuals want "what's fair." And how do we develop our conception of what is fair? **Equity theory** states that the inputs that people perceive themselves as investing in a job and the outcomes that the job provides are compared against the inputs and outcomes of some other relevant person or group.[30] Equity will be perceived when the following distribution ratios exist:

$$\frac{\text{My outcomes}}{\text{My inputs}} = \frac{\text{Other's outcomes}}{\text{Other's inputs}}$$

In these ratios, **inputs** consist of anything that individuals consider relevant to their exchange with the organization, anything that they give up, offer, or trade to their organization. These might include factors such as education, training, seniority, hard work, and high-quality work. **Outcomes** are those factors that the organization distributes to employees in return for their inputs. The most relevant outcomes are represented by the job facets we discussed earlier—pay, career opportunities, supervision, the nature of the work, and so on. The "other" in the ratio above might be a co-worker performing the same job, a number of co-workers, or even one's conception of all the individuals in one's occupation.[31] For example, the CEO of Microsoft probably compares his outcome/input ratio with those that he assumes exist for the CEOs of Google and Intel. You probably compare your outcome/input ratio in your organizational behaviour class with that of one or more fellow students.

Equity theory has important implications for job satisfaction. First, inequity itself is a dissatisfying state, especially when we are on the "short end of the stick." For example, suppose you see the hours spent studying as your main input to your organizational behaviour class and the final grade as an important outcome. Imagine that a friend in the class is your comparison person. Under these conditions, the following situations appear equitable and should not provoke dissatisfaction on your part:

You	Friend		You	Friend
You	**Friend**		**You**	**Friend**
C grade	A grade	or	A grade	C grade
50 hours	100 hours		60 hours	30 hours

In each of these cases, a fair relationship seems to exist between study time and grades distributed. Now consider the following relationships:

You	Friend		You	Friend
You	**Friend**		**You**	**Friend**
C grade	A grade	or	A grade	C grade
100 hours	50 hours		30 hours	60 hours

In each of these situations, an unfair connection appears to exist between study time and grades received, and you should perceive inequity. However, the situation on the left, in which you put in more work for a lower grade, should be most likely to prompt dissatisfaction. This is a "short end of the stick" situation. For example, the employee who frequently remains on the job after regular hours (input) and receives no special praise or extra pay (outcome) might perceive inequity and feel dissatisfied. Equity considerations also have an indirect effect on job satisfaction by influencing what people want from their jobs. If you study for 100 hours while the rest of the class averages 50 hours, you will expect a higher grade than the class average.

Consider a practical example of equity in action. During a business recession, the Canadian-based luxury hotel company Four Seasons did not lay off employees and thus threaten customer service like many of its competitors. Rather, executives accepted a pay freeze and workers were asked to vote on a temporary move to a four-day work week rather than five. The offer was accepted enthusiastically because it was seen as fair given extensive industry layoffs and the sacrifices made by company executives.[32]

Equity theory. A theory that job satisfaction stems from a comparison of the inputs one invests in a job and the outcomes one receives in comparison with the inputs and outcomes of another person or group.

Inputs. Anything that people give up, offer, or trade to their organization in exchange for outcomes.

Outcomes. Factors that an organization distributes to employees in exchange for their inputs.

In summary, the equitable distribution of work outcomes contributes to job satisfaction by providing for feelings of distributive fairness. However, let's remember our earlier discussion of cross-cultural differences in values. The equity concept suggests that outcomes should be tied to individual contributions or inputs. This corresponds well with the individualistic North American culture. In more collective cultures, *equality* of outcomes might produce more feelings of distributive fairness. In more feminine cultures, allocating outcomes according to *need* (rather than performance) might provide for distributive fairness.

Procedural Fairness. Procedural fairness (often called procedural justice) occurs when individuals see the process used to determine outcomes as reasonable; that is, rather than involving the actual distribution of resources or rewards, it is concerned with how these outcomes are decided and allocated. An example will illustrate the difference between distributive and procedural fairness. Out of the blue, Greg's boss tells him that she has completed his performance evaluation and that he will receive a healthy pay raise starting next month. Greg has been working very hard, and he is pleased with the pay raise (distributive fairness). However, he is vaguely unhappy about the fact that all this occurred without his participation. Where he used to work, the employee and the boss would complete independent performance evaluation forms and then sit down and discuss any differences. This provided good feedback for the employee. Greg wonders how his peers who got less generous raises are reacting to the boss's style.

Procedural fairness is particularly relevant to outcomes such as performance evaluations, pay raises, promotions, layoffs, and work assignments. In allocating such outcomes, the following factors contribute to perceptions of procedural fairness.[33] The allocator

- follows consistent procedures over time and across people;
- uses accurate information and appears unbiased;
- allows two-way communication during the allocation process; and
- welcomes appeals of the procedure or allocation.

Procedural fairness is especially likely to provoke dissatisfaction when people also see distributive fairness as being low.[34] One view notes that dissatisfaction will be "maximized when people believe that they *would* have obtained better outcomes if the decision maker had used other procedures that *should* have been implemented."[35] (Students who receive lower grades than their friends will recognize the wisdom of this observation!) Thus, Greg, mentioned above, will probably not react too badly to the lack of consultation while his peers who did not receive large raises might strongly resent the process that the boss used.

Interactional Fairness. Interactional fairness (often called interactional justice) occurs when people feel that they have received respectful and informative communication about some outcome.[36] In other words, it extends beyond the actual procedures used to the interpersonal treatment received when learning about the outcome. Respectful communication is sincere and polite and treats the individual with dignity; informative communication is candid, timely, and thorough. Interactional fairness is important because it is possible for absolutely fair outcomes or procedures to be perceived as unfair when they are inadequately or uncaringly explained.

Sometimes, lower-level managers have little control over procedures that are used to allocate resources. However, they almost always have the opportunity to explain these procedures in a thorough, truthful, and caring manner. Frequently, people who experience procedural unfairness are dissatisfied with the "system." On the other hand, people who experience interactional unfairness are more likely to be dissatisfied with the boss.

Both procedural and interactional fairness can to some extent offset the negative effects of distributive unfairness. In one interesting study, nurses who received a pay cut

---

Procedural fairness. Fairness that occurs when the process used to determine work outcomes is seen as reasonable.

Interactional fairness. Fairness that occurs when people feel they have received respectful and informative communication about an outcome.

due to hospital policy changes exhibited less insomnia when their supervisors were trained in the principles of interactional fairness compared to nurses with untrained supervisors.[37]

Disposition

Could your personality contribute to your feelings of job satisfaction? This is the essential question guiding research on the relationship between disposition and job satisfaction. Underlying the previous discussion is the obvious implication that job satisfaction can increase when the work environment changes to increase fairness and decrease the discrepancy between what an individual wants and what the job offers. Underlying the dispositional view of job satisfaction is the idea that some people are *predisposed* by virtue of their personalities to be more or less satisfied despite changes in discrepancy or fairness. This follows from the discussion in Chapter 2 on the dispositional approach and personality.

Some of the research that suggests that disposition contributes to job satisfaction is fascinating. Although each of these studies has some problems, as a group they point to a missing dispositional link;[38] for example,

- Identical twins raised apart from early childhood tend to have similar levels of job satisfaction.
- Job satisfaction tends to be fairly stable over time, even when changes in employer occur.
- Disposition measured early in adolescence is correlated with one's job satisfaction as a mature adult.

Taken together, these findings suggest that some personality characteristics originating in genetics or early learning contribute to adult job satisfaction.

Recent research on disposition and job satisfaction has centred around the "Big Five" personality traits (Chapter 2). People who are extraverted and conscientious tend to be more satisfied with their jobs, while those high in neuroticism are less satisfied.[39] Also, people who are high in self-esteem and internal locus of control are more satisfied.[40] Thus, in general, people who are more optimistic and proactive report higher job satisfaction. Mood and emotion may contribute to this connection, so we will now examine these topics.

Mood and Emotion

The picture we have painted so far of the determinants of job satisfaction has been mostly one of calculation and rationality: people calculate discrepancies, compare job inputs to outcomes, and so on. But what about the intense feelings that are sometimes seen in work settings—the joy of a closed business deal or the despair that leads to workplace homicides? Or what about that vague feeling of a lack of accomplishment that blunts the pleasure of a dream job? We are speaking here about the role of affect as a determinant of job satisfaction. Affect is simply a broad label for feelings. These feelings include **emotions**, which are intense, often short-lived, and caused by a particular event such as a bad performance appraisal. Common emotions include joy, pride, anger, fear, and sadness. Affect also refers to **moods**, which are less intense, longer-lived, and more diffuse feelings.

Emotions. Intense, often short-lived feelings caused by a particular event.

Moods. Less intense, longer-lived, and more diffuse feelings.

How do emotions and moods affect job satisfaction? Affective events theory, proposed by Howard Weiss and Russell Cropanzano, addresses this question.[41] Basically, the theory reminds us that jobs actually consist of a series of events and happenings that have the potential to provoke emotions or to influence moods, depending on how we appraise these events and happenings. Thus, seeing a co-worker being berated by a manager might provoke emotional disgust and lower one's job satisfaction, especially if it is a frequent occurrence. This illustrates that perceived unfairness, as discussed earlier, can affect job satisfaction via emotion. Also, a person's disposition can interact with job events to influence satisfaction. For instance, those who are neurotic and pessimistic may react to a minor series of job setbacks with a negative mood that depresses their job satisfaction.

An interesting way in which mood and emotion can influence job satisfaction is through **emotional contagion**. This is the tendency for moods and emotions to spread between people or throughout a group. Thus, people's moods and emotions tend to converge with interaction. Generally, teams experiencing more positive affect tend to be more cooperative, helpful, and successful, all of which are conditions that contribute to job satisfaction.[42] Emotional contagion can also occur in dealing with customers such that pleasant service encounters contribute to the service provider's satisfaction as well as to that of the customer.

Another interesting way in which mood and emotion can influence job satisfaction is through the need for **emotional regulation**. This is the requirement for people to conform to certain "display rules" in their job behaviour, in spite of their true mood or emotions. Often, this is referred to informally as "emotional labour." In one version, employees are expected to be perky and upbeat whether they feel that way or not, thus exaggerating positive emotions. In the other version, employees are supposed to remain calm and civil even when hassled or insulted, thus suppressing negative emotions. One study found that call centre employees averaged 10 incidents of customer aggression a day.[43] All jobs have their implicit display rules, such as not acting angry in front of the boss. However, service roles such as waiter, bank teller, and flight attendant are especially laden with display rules, some of which may be made explicit in training and via cues from managers.

What are the consequences of the requirement for emotional regulation? There is growing evidence that the frequent need to suppress negative emotions takes a toll on job satisfaction and increases stress.[44] Flight attendants can humour only so many drunk or angry air passengers before the experience wears thin! On the other hand, the jury is still out on the requirement to express positive emotions. Some research suggests that this display rule boosts job satisfaction.[45] If so, positive contagion from happy customers may be responsible. Of course, disposition may again enter the picture, as extraverts may be energized by requirements for positive display.

Do organizations pay a premium for emotional labour? The answer is sometimes. Theresa Glomb, John Kammeyer-Mueller, and Maria Rotundo studied the emotional labour and cognitive demands (thinking, decision making) required in various occupations (see Exhibit 4.6).[46] They found that those in occupations with high cognitive demands (the upper portion of the exhibit) tend to be paid more when the jobs are also high in emotional labour. Thus, lawyers tend to earn more than zoologists. On the other hand, occupations with low cognitive demands entail a wage penalty when emotional labour is higher. Thus, the "people jobs" in the lower right quadrant of the exhibit tend to be less well paid than the jobs in the lower left quadrant. As we will see shortly, pay is an important determinant of job satisfaction.

Consideration of mood and emotion helps explain a curious but commonplace phenomenon: how people with similar beliefs and values doing the same job for the same compensation can still exhibit very different satisfaction levels. This difference is probably a result of emotional events and subtle differences in mood that add up over time. We will revisit emotion when we study emotional intelligence (Chapter 5), decision making (Chapter 10), and stress (Chapter 12).

Exhibit 4.7 summarizes what research has to say about the determinants of job satisfaction. To recapitulate, satisfaction is a function of certain dispositional factors, the discrepancy between the job outcomes a person wants and the outcomes received, and mood and emotion. More specifically, people experience greater satisfaction when they meet or exceed the job outcomes they want, perceive the job outcomes they receive as equitable compared with those others receive, and believe that fair procedures determine job outcomes. The outcomes that people want from a job are a function of their personal value systems, moderated by equity considerations. The outcomes that people perceive themselves as receiving from the job represent their beliefs about the nature of that job.

Emotional contagion. Tendency for moods and emotions to spread between people or throughout a group.

Emotional regulation. Requirement for people to conform to certain "display rules" in their job behaviour in spite of their true mood or emotions.

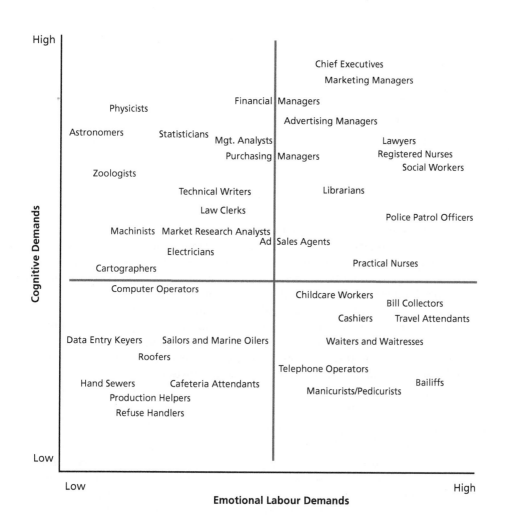

EXHIBIT 4.6
Occupations plotted by
emotional labour and
cognitive demands.

Source: Adapted from Glomb, T.M.,
Kammeyer-Mueller, J.D., & Rotundo,
M. (2004). Emotional labor demands
and compensating wage differentials.
Journal of Applied Psychology, 89,
700–714.

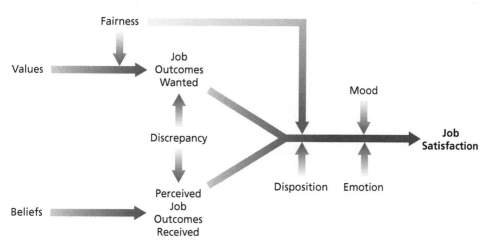

EXHIBIT 4.7
How discrepancy,
fairness, disposition,
mood, and emotion
affect job satisfaction.

Some Key Contributors to Job Satisfaction

From what we have said thus far, you might expect that job satisfaction is a highly personal experience. While this is essentially true, we can make some general statements about the facets that seem to contribute the most to feelings of job satisfaction for most North American workers. These include mentally challenging work, adequate compensation, career opportunities, and friendly or helpful colleagues.[47]

Mentally Challenging Work. This is work that tests employees' skills and abilities and allows them to set their own working pace. Employees usually perceive such work as personally involving and important. It also provides the worker with clear feedback regarding performance. Of course, some types of work can be too challenging, and this can result in feelings of failure and reduced satisfaction. In addition, some employees seem to prefer repetitive, unchallenging work that makes few demands on them.

Adequate Compensation. It should not surprise you that pay and satisfaction are positively related. However, not everyone is equally desirous of money, and some people are certainly willing to accept less responsibility or fewer working hours for lower pay. In most companies, one finds a group of employees who are especially anxious to earn extra money through overtime and another group that actively avoids overtime work.

Career Opportunities. The availability of career opportunities contributes to job satisfaction. Opportunity for promotion is an important contributor to job satisfaction because promotions contain a number of valued signals about a person's self-worth. Some of these signals may be material (such as an accompanying raise), while others are of a social nature (recognition within the organization and increased prestige in the community). Of course, there are cultural and individual differences in what people see as constituting a fair promotion system. Some employees might prefer a strict seniority system, while others might wish for a system based strictly on job performance. Many of today's flatter organizations no longer offer the promotion opportunities of the past. Well-run firms have offset this by designing lateral moves that provide for challenging work. Also, as discussed in Chapter 2, career development helps prepare employees to assume challenging assignments.

People. It should not surprise you that friendly, considerate, good-natured superiors and co-workers contribute to job satisfaction, especially via positive moods and emotions. There is, however, another aspect to interpersonal relationships on the job that contributes to job satisfaction. Specifically, we tend to be satisfied in the presence of people who help us attain job outcomes that we value. Such outcomes might include doing our work better or more easily, obtaining a raise or promotion, or even staying alive. For example, a company of soldiers in battle might be less concerned with how friendly their commanding officer is than with how competently he is able to act to keep them from being overrun by the enemy. Similarly, an aggressive young executive might like a considerate boss but prefer even more a boss who can clarify her work objectives and reward her for attaining them. The friendliness aspect of interpersonal relationships seems most important in lower-level jobs with clear duties and in various dead-end jobs. If pay is tied to performance or as jobs become more complex or promotion opportunities increase, the ability of others to help us do our work well contributes more to job satisfaction.

Context can certainly affect what contributes most to job satisfaction. Exhibit 4.8 shows the results of a survey conducted by the Society for Human Resource Management during the 2009 recession. As you can see, during this period, job security and benefits topped the list.

To see how Capital One enhances job satisfaction, check out You Be the Manager on page 130.

Consequences of Job Satisfaction

Dell, Sears, and L'Oréal Canada are firms that have maintained a competitive advantage by paying particular attention to employee satisfaction. Why is this so? Let's look at some consequences of job satisfaction.

Absence from Work

Absenteeism is an expensive behaviour in North America, costing billions of dollars each year. Such costs are attributable to "sick pay," lost productivity, and chronic

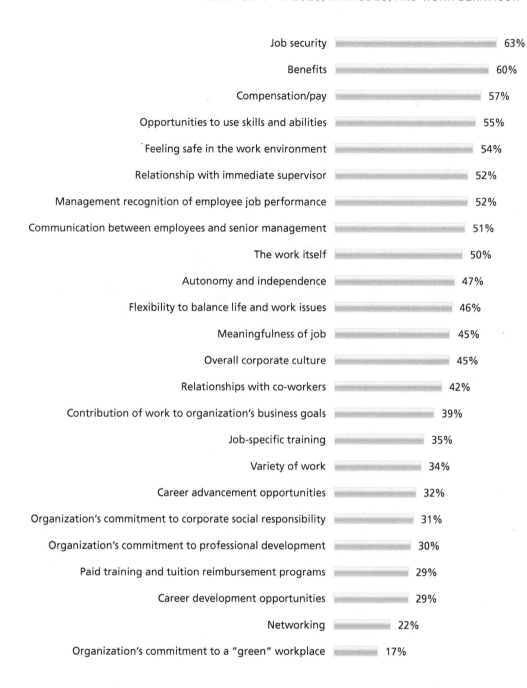

Job security	63%
Benefits	60%
Compensation/pay	57%
Opportunities to use skills and abilities	55%
Feeling safe in the work environment	54%
Relationship with immediate supervisor	52%
Management recognition of employee job performance	52%
Communication between employees and senior management	51%
The work itself	50%
Autonomy and independence	47%
Flexibility to balance life and work issues	46%
Meaningfulness of job	45%
Overall corporate culture	45%
Relationships with co-workers	42%
Contribution of work to organization's business goals	39%
Job-specific training	35%
Variety of work	34%
Career advancement opportunities	32%
Organization's commitment to corporate social responsibility	31%
Organization's commitment to professional development	30%
Paid training and tuition reimbursement programs	29%
Career development opportunities	29%
Networking	22%
Organization's commitment to a "green" workplace	17%

EXHIBIT 4.8
"Very important" aspects of employee job satisfaction.

Note: Percentages reflect respondents who answered "very important" on a scale where 1 = "very unimportant" and 4 = "very important."

Source: Society for Human Resource Management. (2009). *2009 Employee job satisfaction: Understanding the factors that make work gratifying.* Alexandria, VA: SHRM, p.6. © Society for Human Resource Management. Used by permission.

overstaffing to compensate for absentees. Many more days are lost to absenteeism than to strikes and other industrial disputes. Research shows that less-satisfied employees are more likely to be absent and that satisfaction with the content of the work is the best predictor of absenteeism.[48] However, the absence–satisfaction connection is not very strong. Several factors probably constrain the ability of many people to convert their like or dislike of work into corresponding attendance patterns:

● Some absence is simply unavoidable because of illness, weather conditions, or childcare problems. Thus, some very happy employees will occasionally be absent owing to circumstances beyond their control.

● Opportunities for off-the-job satisfaction on a missed day may vary. Thus, you might love your job but love skiing or sailing even more. In this case, you might skip work, while a dissatisfied person who has nothing better to do shows up.

YOU BE THE MANAGER

The Future of Work @ Capital One

The nature of the work to which people are drawn reflects the values that individuals espouse. Over the past century, work has moved from primarily blue collar, assembly-line jobs toward white collar, knowledge-based jobs. With the transition, employee values have also changed. Knowledge workers, who make up approximately one-third of the workforce in North America, seek a work environment that supports not only teamwork and collaboration but also privacy and flexibility. When the work environment cannot support these needs, employees can become dissatisfied because inability to concentrate and accomplish tasks can create frustration and anxiety, as can the challenges of trying to balance work life with personal life. When employees are not able to work when they want, how they want, and with whom they want, satisfaction can decline, resulting in absenteeism, turnover, and lower productivity.

At Capital One, one of the top 15 banks in the United States, caring for their knowledge workers has always been a top priority. Considered one of the best places to work by *Fortune* magazine, Capital One's key values include "Excellence" and "Do the Right Thing." Employees are encouraged to achieve corporate objectives by thinking independently and taking ownership of their ideas. The "test and learn" culture is played out through teamwork, collaboration, and innovative work practices. At the core of Capital One's culture is the importance of making data-driven decisions, which has positioned the IT function, and technology itself, in a strategic role.

To satisfy their knowledge workers, Capital One has invested in creating workspaces that support employee values. In the late 1990s, they embarked on a program with the aim of creating state-of-the-art facilities that encourage teamwork and collaboration. Drawing on theories of building and furniture utilization, Capital One implemented a standardized design of offices, cubicles, and conference rooms. But Capital One soon discovered a significant underutilization of office resources. They found that, on a daily basis, 40 percent of cubicles were left vacant, while another 30 percent were unoccupied for certain hours of the day. It appeared that employees were not using their workspace as originally intended. Capital One took this problem seriously. Even though the company had been recognized for its state-of-the-art facilities, changing workplace values were signalling that standard office designs were a thing of the past.

QUESTIONS

1. Although Capital One had implemented a state-of-the-art facility, employees did not appear to be taking advantage of the office resources in the way management intended. How could the work environment be affecting employees' job satisfaction?

2. How could the office space be redesigned to meet employees' needs? What role could technology play in the redesign of the office space?

To find out how Capital One increased job satisfaction by redesigning their office space, see The Manager's Notebook at the end of the chapter.

Source: Adapted from Khana, S., & New, J.R. (2008). Revolutionizing the workplace: A case study of the future of work program at Capital One. *Human Resource Management, 47*, 795–808.

- Some organizations have attendance control policies that can influence absence more than satisfaction does. In a company that doesn't pay workers for missed days (typical of many workplaces with hourly pay), absence may be more related to economic needs than to dissatisfaction. The unhappy worker who absolutely needs money will probably show up for work. By the same token, dissatisfied and satisfied workers might be equally responsive to threats of dismissal for absenteeism.

- In many jobs, it may be unclear to employees how much absenteeism is reasonable or sensible. With a lack of company guidelines, workers may look to the behaviour of their peers for a norm to guide their behaviour. This norm and its corresponding "absence culture" (see Chapter 7) might have a stronger effect than the individual employee's satisfaction with his or her job.[49]

The connection between job satisfaction and good attendance probably stems in part from the tendency for job satisfaction to facilitate mental health and satisfaction with life in general.[50] Content people will attend work with enthusiasm.

Turnover

Turnover refers to resignation from an organization, and it can be incredibly expensive. For example, it costs several thousand dollars to replace a nurse or a bank teller who resigns. As we move up the organizational hierarchy, or into technologically complex jobs, such costs escalate dramatically. For example, it costs millions of dollars to hire and train a single military fighter pilot. Estimates of turnover costs usually include the price of hiring, training, and developing to proficiency a replacement employee. Such figures probably underestimate the true costs of turnover, however, because they do not include intangible costs, such as work group disruption or the loss of employees who informally acquire special skills and knowledge over time on a job. All this would not be so bad if turnover were concentrated among poorer performers. Unfortunately, this is not always the case. In one study, 23 percent of scientists and engineers who left an organization were among the top 10 percent of performers.[51]

What is the relationship between job satisfaction and turnover? Research indicates a moderately strong connection, with less satisfied workers being more likely to quit.[52] However, the relationship between the attitude (job satisfaction) and the behaviour in question (turnover) is far from perfect. Exhibit 4.9 presents a model of turnover that can help explain this.[53] In the model, circles represent attitudes, ovals represent elements of the turnover process, and squares denote situational factors. The model shows that job satisfaction as well as commitment to the organization and various "shocks" (both discussed below) can contribute to intentions to leave. Research shows that such intentions

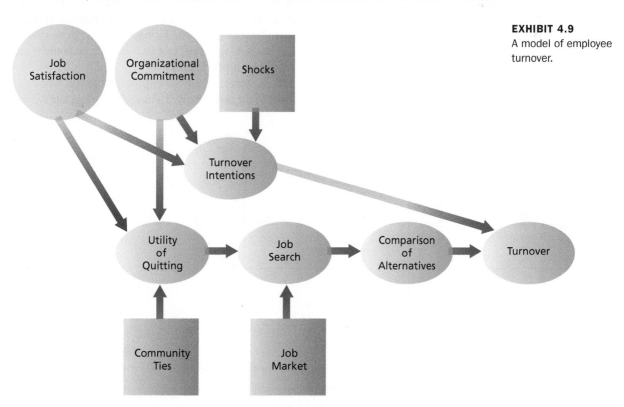

EXHIBIT 4.9
A model of employee turnover.

are very good predictors of turnover.[54] As shown, such intentions sometimes prompt turnover directly, even impulsively. On the other hand, reduced satisfaction or commitment can also stimulate a more deliberate evaluation of the utility of quitting and a careful job search and evaluation of job alternatives. The following are some reasons why satisfied people sometimes quit their jobs or dissatisfied people stay:

- Certain "shocks," such as a marital breakup, the birth of a child, or an unsolicited job offer in an attractive location, might stimulate turnover despite satisfaction with the current job.
- An employee's dissatisfaction with his or her specific job might be offset by a strong commitment to the overall values and mission of the organization.
- An employee might be so embedded in the community (due to involvement with churches, schools, or sports) that he or she is willing to endure a dissatisfying job rather than move.
- A weak job market might result in limited employment alternatives. Dissatisfaction is most likely to result in turnover when jobs are plentiful.[55]

Despite these exceptions, a decrease in job satisfaction often precedes turnover, and those who quit experience a boost in satisfaction on their new job. However, some of this boost might be due to a "honeymoon effect," in which the bad facets of the old job are gone, the good facets of the new job are apparent, and the bad facets of the new job are not yet known. Over time, as these bad facets are recognized, a "hangover effect" can occur, in which overall satisfaction with the new job decreases.[56] This pattern is shown in Exhibit 4.10, which traces job satisfaction at five points in time as a person moves between jobs A and B.

Performance

It seems sensible that job satisfaction contributes to less absenteeism and turnover, but does it also lead to improved job performance? After all, employees might be so "satisfied" that no work is accomplished! In fact, research has confirmed what folk wisdom and business magazines have advocated for many years—job satisfaction is associated with enhanced performance.[57] However, the connection between satisfaction and performance is complicated, because many factors influence motivation and performance besides job satisfaction (as we'll see in Chapter 5). Thus, research has led to some qualifications to the idea that "a happy worker is a productive worker."

All satisfaction facets are not equal in terms of stimulating performance. The most important facet has to do with the content of the work itself.[58] Thus, interesting, challenging

EXHIBIT 4.10

The honeymoon–hangover effect.

Source: Drawing by the authors, based on Boswell, W.R., Boudreau, J.W., & Tichy, J. (2005). The relationship between employee job change and job satisfaction: The honeymoon–hangover effect. *Journal of Applied Psychology, 90,* 882-892.

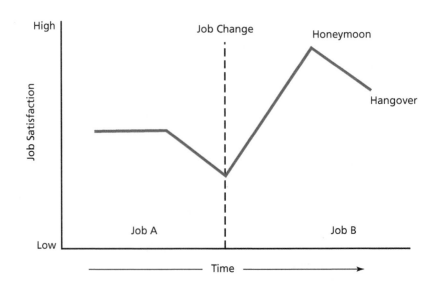

jobs are most likely to stimulate high performance (we will see how to design such jobs in Chapter 6). One consequence of this is the fact that the connection between job satisfaction and performance is stronger for complex, high-tech jobs in science, engineering, and computers and less strong for more routine labour jobs. In part, this is because people doing complex jobs have more control over their level of performance.

Another issue in the connection between job satisfaction and performance has to do with which of these is the cause and which the effect. Although job satisfaction contributes to performance, performance could also contribute to job satisfaction.[59] When good performance is *followed by rewards,* employees are more likely to be satisfied. However, many organizations do not reward good performance sufficiently. Thus, contemporary research indicates that satisfaction is more likely to affect performance, rather than the reverse.[60]

In addition to boosting formal job performance, satisfaction can also contribute to employees' informal, everyday behaviour and actions that help their organizations and their co-workers. Let's turn now to a discussion of this.

Organizational Citizenship Behaviour

Organizational citizenship behaviour (OCB) is voluntary, informal behaviour that contributes to organizational effectiveness.[61] In many cases, the formal performance evaluation system does not detect and reward it. Job satisfaction contributes greatly to the occurrence of OCB, more than it does to regular task performance, in fact.[62]

An example of OCB should clarify the concept. You are struggling to master a particularly difficult piece of software. A colleague at the next desk, busy on her own rush job, comes over and offers assistance. Irritated with the software, you are not even very grateful at first, but within 10 minutes you have solved the problem with her help. Notice the defining characteristics of this example of OCB:

- The behaviour is voluntary. It is not included in her job description.
- The behaviour is spontaneous. Someone did not order or suggest it.
- The behaviour contributes to organizational effectiveness. It extends beyond simply doing you a personal favour.
- The behaviour is unlikely to be explicitly picked up and rewarded by the performance evaluation system, especially since it is not part of the job description.

What are the various forms that OCB might take? As the software example indicates, one prominent form is *helping* behaviour, offering assistance to others. Another might be *conscientiousness* to the details of work, including getting in on the snowiest day of the year and not wasting organizational resources. A third form of OCB involves being a *good sport* when the inevitable frustrations of organizational life crop up—not everyone can have the best office or the best parking spot. A final form of OCB is *courtesy and cooperation.*[63] Examples might include warning the photocopy unit about a big job that is on the way or delaying one's own work to assist a colleague on a rush job.

Just how does job satisfaction contribute to OCB? Fairness seems to be the key. Although distributive fairness (especially in terms of pay) is important, procedural and interactional fairness from a supportive manager seem especially critical.[64] If the manager strays from the prescriptions for procedural fairness we gave earlier, OCB can suffer. If one feels unfairly treated, it might be difficult to lower formal performance for fear of dire consequences. It might be much easier to withdraw the less visible, informal activities that make up OCB. On the other hand, fair treatment and its resulting satisfaction might be reciprocated with OCB, a truly personalized input. OCB is also influenced by employees' mood at work. People in a pleasant, relaxed, optimistic mood are more likely to provide special assistance to others.[65]

Recent research has shown that OCB contributes to organizational productivity and efficiency and to reduced turnover.[66] Because of this, some firms do try to formally

Organizational citizenship behaviour. Voluntary, informal behaviour that contributes to organizational effectiveness.

When one worker voluntarily helps out another, it is an example of organizational citizenship, which positively affects organizational effectiveness.

recognize OCBs. Xilinx, the highly innovative leader in programmable logic components, fosters and publicizes nominations of people who go "above and beyond duty" to help peers, selecting some for special recognition and a token cash award.[67]

Customer Satisfaction and Profit

So far, we have established that job satisfaction can reduce employee absenteeism and turnover and increase employee performance and citizenship behaviour. But is it possible that employee satisfaction could actually affect *customer* satisfaction? That is, do happy employees translate into happy customers? And do happy employees actually contribute to the bottom line of the organization by increasing organizational profits? After all, we have warned that the translation of positive attitudes into positive employee behaviours is less than perfect and that such attitudes therefore might not affect the bottom line.

A growing body of evidence has established that employee job satisfaction is indeed translated into customer or client satisfaction and organizational profitability.[68] Thus, organizations with higher average levels of employee satisfaction are more effective. The same applies to units within larger organizations. Hence, local bank branches or insurance claims offices with more satisfied employees should tend to have more satisfied clients and generate more profits for the larger firm. Thus, it makes good sense to use employee satisfaction as one criterion in judging the effectiveness of local unit managers.

How does employee satisfaction translate into customer satisfaction? Reduced absenteeism and turnover contribute to the seamless delivery of service, as do the OCBs that stimulate good teamwork. Also, the mood mechanism, mentioned earlier, should not be discounted, as good mood among employees can be contagious for customers.

The Ford Motor Company and Sears have been particularly attentive to the links among employee satisfaction, customer satisfaction, and profit. In an 800-store study, Sears found a clear positive relationship between employee satisfaction and store profitability. In addition, improvements in employee satisfaction were mirrored in customer satisfaction, resulting in an estimated $200 million in added annual revenue.[69]

Let's turn now to another important work attitude—organizational commitment.

What Is Organizational Commitment?

Organizational commitment is an attitude that reflects the strength of the linkage between an employee and an organization. This linkage has implications for whether someone tends to remain in an organization. Researchers John Meyer and Natalie Allen have identified three very different types of organizational commitment:[70]

- **Affective commitment** is commitment based on a person's identification and involvement with an organization. People with high affective commitment stay with an organization because they *want* to.
- **Continuance commitment** is commitment based on the costs that would be incurred in leaving an organization. People with high continuance commitment stay with an organization because they *have* to.
- **Normative commitment** is commitment based on ideology or a feeling of obligation to an organization. People with high normative commitment stay with an organization because they think that they *should* do so.

Employees can be committed not only to their organization but also to various constituencies within and outside the organization. Thus, each type of commitment could also apply to one's work team, union, or profession.[71]

Organizational commitment. An attitude that reflects the strength of the linkage between an employee and an organization.

Affective commitment. Commitment based on identification and involvement with an organization.

Continuance commitment. Commitment based on the costs that would be incurred in leaving an organization.

Normative commitment. Commitment based on ideology or a feeling of obligation to an organization.

Key Contributors to Organizational Commitment

The causes of the three forms of commitment tend to differ. By far the best predictor of affective commitment is interesting, satisfying work of the type found in enriched jobs (see Chapter 6).[72] One mistake that organizations sometimes make is starting employees out in unchallenging jobs so they do not make any serious errors. This can have a negative impact on affective commitment. Role clarity and having one's expectations met after being hired also contribute to affective commitment.[73]

Continuance commitment occurs when people feel that leaving the organization will result in personal sacrifice, or they perceive that good alternative employment is lacking. Building up "side bets" in pension funds, obtaining rapid promotion, or being well integrated into the community where the firm is located can lock employees into organizations even though they would rather go elsewhere. Not surprisingly, continuance commitment increases with the time a person is employed by an organization.

Normative commitment ("I *should* stay here") can be fostered by benefits that build a sense of obligation to the organization. These might include tuition reimbursements or special training that enhances one's skills. Strong identification with an organization's product or service ("I should stay here because the Sierra Club is doing important work") can also foster normative commitment. Finally, certain socialization practices (see Chapter 8) that emphasize loyalty to the organization can stimulate normative commitment. For example, sports coaches often haze players who miss practice to stress the importance of loyalty to the team.

Consequences of Organizational Commitment

There is good evidence that all forms of commitment reduce turnover intentions and actual turnover.[74] Organizations plagued with turnover problems among key employees should look carefully at tactics that foster commitment. This is especially called for when turnover gets so bad that it threatens customer service. Many service organizations (e.g., restaurants and hotels), however, have traditionally accepted high turnover rates.

Organizations should take care, though, in their targeting of the kind of commitment to boost. Affective commitment is positively related to performance because it focuses attention on goals and thus enhances motivation (see Chapter 5).[75] However, continuance commitment is *negatively* related to performance, something you might have observed in dealing with burned-out bureaucrats.[76] An especially bad combination for both the employee and the organization is high continuance commitment coupled with low affective commitment—people locked into organizations that they detest. This happens very frequently during recessions.

Is there a downside to organizational commitment? Very high levels of commitment can cause conflicts between family life and work life. Also, very high levels of commitment have often been implicated in unethical and illegal behaviour, including a General Electric price-fixing conspiracy. Finally, high levels of commitment to a particular *form or style* of organization can cause a lack of innovation and lead to resistance when a change in the culture is necessary.[77]

Changes in the Workplace and Employee Commitment

Organizations are experiencing unprecedented change as a result of shifts in workforce demographics, technological innovations, and global competition.[78] In an era of lay-offs, downsizing, outsourcing, restructuring, and reengineering, there is evidence that employees are losing commitment to their organizations.[79] People often view their careers as a series of jobs with a variety of potential employers, or they even see themselves as freelancers rather than having a series of jobs in one organization.

John Meyer, Natalie Allen, and Laryssa Topolnytsky have studied commitment in a changing world of work, and they note that the impact of changes in the workplace on employee commitment can be seen in three main areas:[80]

- *Changes in the nature of employees' commitment to the organization.* Depending on the nature of workplace changes and how they are managed, employees' levels of affective, continuance, and normative commitment can increase or decrease. Thus, the commitment profiles of employees following a change will be different from what they were prior to the change, and maintaining high levels of affective commitment will be particularly challenging. Changes that are made in the organization's best interest but that are detrimental to employees' well-being are most likely to damage affective commitment.

- *Changes in the focus of employees' commitment.* Employees generally have multiple commitments. In particular, employee commitment can be directed to others within the organization, such as subunits or divisions, teams, the "new" organization, as well as entities outside the organization, such as one's occupation, career, or union. Therefore, changes in the workplace might alter the focus of employees' commitments both within and outside of the organization. As organizations increase in size following mergers and acquisitions, for example, employees are likely to shift their commitment to smaller organizational units, such as their particular division, branch, or team. As well, changes that threaten employees' future in the organization might result in a shift in commitment to entities outside the organization, such as one's profession, occupation, or personal career.

- *The multiplicity of employer–employee relationships within organizations.* As organizations attempt to cope and adapt to rapid change, they need to be flexible enough to shrink or expand their workforce. At the same time, they need a workforce that is flexible enough to get any job done. This creates a potential conflict as employees who do not have guaranteed job security may be unwilling to be as flexible as the organization would like or to have a strong affective commitment toward the organization. A potential solution to this problem is for organizations to have different relationships with employee groups. For example, an organization might have a group of core employees who perform the key operations required for organizational success. It would be important for this group of employees to have a high level of affective organizational commitment. Other employee groups would consist of those with contractual arrangements or individuals hired on a temporary basis who do not perform the core tasks and whose commitment to the organization is not as important. The idea of a multiplicity of employee–organization relationships enables organizations to have a flexible workforce and at the same time foster a high level of affective commitment among core employees.

In summary, changes in the workplace are having an impact on the nature of employee commitment and employee–employer relationships. It is therefore important that organizations understand how changes in the workplace can change the profile and focus of employees' commitment and the impact this can have on employee behaviour and organizational success.

THE MANAGER'S NOTEBOOK

Capital One

1. Capital One's original workspace design was based on a "one size fits all" approach. Using conventional theories of building and furniture utilization, they standardized the size of offices and cubicles and assigned office space based on hierarchy. Conference rooms were established as iconic representations of the corporate culture, taking up ample space in prime areas of the building. Although employees were provided with the tools to do their work, such as high-powered desktop computers and feature-rich phones, the design was based on the assumption that employees would either be in their cubicles working or in conference rooms for meetings. Capital One did not consider that their knowledge workers sought a diversity of workspace solutions that allowed them to work anywhere (within or outside the building), whenever and however they wanted. In lieu of working the way they were expected, they sought out workspaces that supported their need to collaborate, work independently, and work away from the office when required. Upon realizing the underutilization of resources, Capital One established a new program, called "The Future of Work." With the intent to increase job satisfaction, and ultimately business productivity, Capital One focused the program on the employee. They aimed to discover, with employees, what knowledge workers needed to be most productive and most happy. Capital One realized that, with the many generations of workers in their company and the diversity of cultures, employee needs varied considerably throughout the workday and the workweek. Their Future of Work program sought to provide a rich variety of work environments that allowed employees the flexibility they craved.

2. Capital One's Future of Work program was primarily concerned with the satisfaction of employees.

Although reducing facility costs and boosting productivity were also considered important, Capital One believed that things start with the employee. The Future of Work program therefore redirected the facility savings into technology programs in order to "untether" employees from their desks. Mobility tools such as laptops, mobile phones, BlackBerries, and voice-over-Internet Protocol (VOIP) telephony solutions were made available to ensure that employees could work from anywhere, whenever they chose, as long as WiFi or hard-wired internet connections were available. Workers were classified by the type of work they did and their mobility preferences. Each type of worker was then assigned a certain amount of office space and a set of mobility tools to support their work habits. For example, executives and directors were provided with both office space and BlackBerries or laptops, since they are often in the office during the day but also continue working when they leave. Teleworkers and mobile workers, on the other hand, were provided with plenty of mobility tools, but with shared rather than dedicated office space, in consideration of the fact that they were in the office less. In addition to the technology, the workspace itself was redesigned to include a variety of spaces, ranging from small enclaves to large project rooms, along with lounges and café-style settings, supported by power and data connections. Did all this work? Employees reported a 41 percent increase in overall workplace satisfaction, while facilities costs per employee dropped by almost half. Although overall productivity increases are difficult to measure, employees did report a greater facility in getting their work done, on their own and with their teams.

LEARNING OBJECTIVES CHECKLIST

1. *Values* are broad preferences for particular states of affairs. Values tend to differ across generations and across cultures. Critical cross-cultural dimensions of values include power distance, uncertainty avoidance, masculinity/femininity, individualism/collectivism, and time orientation. Differences in values across cultures set constraints on the export and import of organizational behaviour theories and management practices. They also have implications for satisfying global customers and developing globally aware employees.

2. *Attitudes* are a function of what we think about the world (our beliefs) and how we feel about the world (our values). Attitudes are important because they influence how we behave, although we have discussed several factors that reduce the correspondence between our attitudes and behaviours.

3. *Job satisfaction* is an especially important attitude for organizations. Satisfaction is a function of the discrepancy between what individuals want from their jobs and what they perceive that they obtain, taking into account fairness. Dispositional factors, moods, and emotions also influence job satisfaction. Factors such as challenging work, adequate compensation, career opportunities, and friendly, helpful co-workers contribute to job satisfaction.

4. Job satisfaction is important because it promotes several positive outcomes for organizations. Satisfied employees tend to be less likely to be absent or leave their jobs. While links between satisfaction and performance are not always strong, satisfaction with the work itself has been linked to better performance. Satisfaction linked to perceptions of fairness can also lead to citizenship behaviours on the part of employees. Satisfied workers may also enhance customer satisfaction.

5. *Organizational commitment* is an attitude that reflects the strength of the linkage between an employee and an organization. *Affective commitment* is based on a person's identification with an organization. *Continuance commitment* is based on the costs of leaving an organization. *Normative commitment* is based on ideology or feelings of obligation. Changes in the workplace can change the nature and focus of employee commitment as well as employer–employee relationships. To foster commitment, organizations need to be sensitive to the expectations of employees and consider the impact of policy decisions beyond economic issues.

DISCUSSION QUESTIONS

1. What are some of the conditions under which a person's attitudes might not predict his or her work behaviour?

2. What is the difference between procedural and interactional fairness? Give an example of each.

3. Explain how these people might have to regulate their emotions when doing their jobs: hair salon owner; bill collector; police officer; teacher. How will this regulation of emotion affect job satisfaction?

4. Using the model of the turnover process in Exhibit 4.9, explain why a very dissatisfied employee might not quit his or her job.

5. Explain why employees who are very satisfied with their jobs might not be better performers than those who are less satisfied.

6. Use equity theory to explain why a dentist who earns $100 000 a year might be more dissatisfied with her job than a factory worker who earns $40 000.

7. Mexico has a fairly high power distance culture, while the United States and Canada have lower power distance cultures. Discuss how effective management techniques might vary between Mexico and its neighbours to the north.

8. Describe some job aspects that might contribute to job satisfaction for a person in a more collective culture. Do the same for a person in a more individualistic culture.

9. Give an example of an employee who is experiencing distributive fairness but not procedural fairness. Give an example of an employee who is experiencing procedural fairness but not distributive fairness.

INTEGRATIVE DISCUSSION QUESTIONS

1. What role do perceptions play in the determination of job satisfaction? Refer to the components of perception in Chapter 3 and describe how perception plays a role in the determination of job satisfaction according to discrepancy theory, equity theory, and dispositions. How can perceptions be changed to increase job satisfaction?

2. Does personality influence values and job attitudes? Discuss how the "Big Five" personality dimensions, locus of control, self-monitoring, self-esteem, and positive and negative affectivity might influence occupational choice, job satisfaction, and organizational commitment (affective, continuance, and normative). If personality influences job satisfaction and organizational commitment, how can organizations foster high levels of these attitudes?

ON-THE-JOB CHALLENGE QUESTION

In 2006, Arthur Winston died at age 100. He had worked for 76 years for the Los Angeles Metropolitan Transportation Authority cleaning trains and buses. Although this is remarkable enough, it is even more remarkable that he missed only one day of work in his last 72 years, the day of his wife's funeral in 1988. At the time of his retirement on the eve of becoming 100, he headed a crew of 11 workers. Although he had aspired to become a mechanic when younger, the racial biases of the 1930s and 1940s prevented this career advancement. In 1996, Mr. Winston received a congressional citation from the US president as "Employee of the Century." Mr. Winston's incredible record was the object of extensive media coverage, both at home and abroad.

Use the material in the chapter to speculate on various reasons for Mr. Winston's awesome attendance record. What accounts for the great media interest in Mr. Winston?

Sources: (2006, April 14). MTA employee who retired at 100 has died in his sleep. http://cbs2.com/local/Arthur.Winston. MTA.2.515610.html; Marquez, M. (2006, March 22). Los Angeles man retires at 100. abcnews.go.com/US/WNT/ story?id=1756219.

EXPERIENTIAL EXERCISE

Attitudes toward Absenteeism from Work

In this exercise we will examine your attitudes toward absenteeism from work. Although you learned in the chapter that absence can stem from job dissatisfaction, the scenarios below show that a number of other factors can also come into play.

1. Working alone, please indicate the extent to which you think that the employee's absence in each of the following scenarios is legitimate or illegitimate by using one of the six answer categories that appear below. A legitimate absence might be considered acceptable, while an illegitimate absence might be considered unacceptable. This is a measure of your personal attitudes; there are no right or wrong answers. Add up your scores and divide by 7 to obtain an average. Lower scores represent less favourable attitudes toward absenteeism.

2. Working in groups of 3–5 people, discuss the ratings that each of you gave to each scenario. What are the major reasons that contributed to each of your ratings? Compare your average scores.

3. As a group, decide which scenario is *most* legitimate, and explain why. Then decide which scenario is *least* legitimate, and explain why. Compare with the norms provided below.

4. As managers, how would you react to the least legitimate situation? What would you do?

6	5	4	3	2	1
Extremely legitimate	Moderately legitimate	Slightly legitimate	Slightly illegitimate	Moderately illegitimate	Extremely illegitimate

1. Susan is a highly productive employee, but she is absent more often than her co-workers. She has decided to be absent from work to engage in some recreational activities because she believes that her absence would not affect her overall productivity. ___

2. John is an active member of his community social club. Occasionally, the club organizes community activities with the aim of improving the quality of community life. A few days before a planned community activity, much of the work has not been done and the club members are concerned that the activities will be unsuccessful. John has therefore decided to be absent from work to help the club organize its forthcoming activities. ___

3. Peter is a member of a project team that was charged with the responsibility of converting the company's information systems. The work entailed long hours, but the team was able to finish the project on time. Now that the project is completed, the long working hours have taken a toll and Peter feels quite stressed, so he has decided to stay away from work to recuperate. ___

4. Jane works in a low-paying job for which she is overqualified. She has been searching for a more suitable job through advertisements in the newspapers. She has been called for a job interview and has decided to call in sick to attend the interview. ___

5. Frank has a few months before his retirement and has lost the enthusiasm he used to have for his work. He believes he has contributed to making the company the success it is today. He recently joined a retired persons association where he feels his services are needed more. The association is organizing a safety awareness program for senior citizens, so he has decided to stay away from work to help. ___

6. Joan's co-workers normally use up all their sick leave. She is moving into a new house, and since she has not used up all her permitted sick leave, she has decided to call in sick so that she can finish packing for the move. ___

7. Anne does not feel challenged by her job and believes that she is not making any meaningful contribution to her organization. Her mother is going to the doctor for a routine medical checkup and because Anne believes the company will not miss her, she decided to stay away from work to accompany her mother. ___

Source: Scenarios developed by Helena M. Addae. Used with permission.

Scoring and Interpretation

As noted, lower scores represent less favourable attitudes toward absenteeism. Helena Addae, who developed the scenarios, administered them to over 1500 employees in nine countries. The average rating across the 7 scenarios was 3.09. Respectively, the average ratings for each scenario were: S1 = 2.39; S2 = 2.88; S3 = 3.96; S4 = 3.52; S5 = 3.12; S6 = 3.03; S7 = 2.70. Higher numbers indicate more legitimacy.

CASE INCIDENT

How Much Do You Get Paid?

Joan had been working as a reporter for a large television network for seven years. She was an experienced and hardworking reporter who had won many awards over the years for her outstanding work. The work was exciting and challenging, and at $75 000 a year plus benefits she felt well paid and satisfied. Then she found out that two recent graduates from one of the best schools of journalism in the United States had just been hired by her network at a starting salary of $80 000. Further, two other reporters who worked with Joan and had similar track records had just received job offers from American networks and were being offered $150 000 plus $10 000 for every award won for their reporting.

1. According to equity theory, how will these incidents influence Joan's job satisfaction and behaviour?

2. What should Joan do in response to her situation? What should her organization do?

CASE STUDY

The Well-Paid Receptionist

Harvey Finley did a quick double take when he caught a glimpse of the figure representing Ms. Brannen's salary on the year-end printout. A hurried call to payroll confirmed it. Yes, his receptionist had been paid $127 614.21 for her services last year. As he sat in stunned silence, he had the sudden realization that since his firm was doing so well this year, she would earn at least 10 to 15 percent more money during the current fiscal year. This was a shock, indeed.

Background

Harvey began his career as a service technician for a major manufacturer of copy machines. He received rather extensive technical training, but his duties were limited to performing routine, on-site maintenance and service for customers. After a year's experience as a service technician, he asked for and received a promotion to sales representative. In this capacity, he established many favourable contacts in the business community of Troupville and the surrounding towns. He began to think seriously about capitalizing on his success by opening his own business.

Then, seven years ago, he decided to take the plunge and start his own firm. He was tired of selling for someone else. When he mentioned his plan to his friends, they all expressed serious doubts; Troupville, a city of approximately 35 000 people located in the deep South, had just begun to recover from a severe recession. The painful memories of the layoffs, bankruptcies, and plummeting real estate values were too recent and vivid to be forgotten.

Undeterred by the skeptics, Harvey was optimistic that Troupville's slow recovery would soon become a boom. Even though his firm would certainly have to be started on a shoestring, Harvey thought his sales experience and technical competence would enable him to survive what was sure to be a difficult beginning. He was nervous but excited when he signed the lease on the first little building. A lifelong dream was either about to be realized or dashed forever. Troupville Business Systems was born.

While he had managed to borrow, rent, lease, or subcontract for almost everything that was absolutely necessary, he did need one employee immediately. Of course, he hoped the business would expand rapidly and that he would soon have a complete and competent staff. But until he could be sure that some revenue would be generated, he thought he could get by with one person who would be a combination receptionist/secretary and general assistant.

The typical salary for such a position in the area was about $30 000 per year; for Harvey, this was a major expense. Nevertheless, he placed what he thought was a well-worded ad in the "Help Wanted" section of the local newspaper. There were five applicants, four of whom just did not seem quite right for the position he envisioned. The fifth applicant, Ms. Cathy Brannen, was absolutely captivating.

Ms. Brannen was 27 years old with one child. Her resumé showed that she had graduated from a two-year office administration program at a state university. She had worked for only two employers following graduation, one for five years and the most recent for two years. Since returning to her hometown of Troupville two months ago, following her divorce, she had not been able to find suitable employment.

From the moment she sat down for the interview, Harvey and Ms. Brannen seemed to be on exactly the same wavelength. She was very articulate, obviously quite bright, and most importantly, very enthusiastic about assisting with the start-up of the new venture. She seemed to be exactly the sort of person Harvey had envisioned when he first began to think seriously about taking the plunge. He resisted the temptation to offer her the job on the spot, but ended the hour-long interview by telling her that he would check her references and contact her again very soon.

Telephone calls to her two former employers convinced Harvey that he had actually underestimated Ms. Brannen's suitability for the position. Each one said without equivocation that she was the best employee he had ever had in any position. Both former employers concluded the conversation by saying they would rehire her in a minute if she were still available. The only bit of disturbing information gleaned from these two calls was the fact that her annual salary had risen to $32 900 in her last job. Although Harvey thought that the cost of living was probably a bit higher in Houston, where she had last worked, he was not sure she would react favourably to the $30 000 offer he was planning to make. However, he was determined that, somehow, Cathy Brannen would be his first employee.

Ms. Brannen seemed quite pleased when Harvey telephoned her at home that same evening. She said she would be delighted to meet him at the office the next morning to discuss the position more fully.

Cathy Brannen was obviously very enthusiastic about the job as outlined in the meeting. She asked all the right questions, responded quickly and articulately to every query posed to her, and seemed ready to accept the position even before the offer was extended. When Harvey finally got around to mentioning the salary, there was a slight change in Cathy's eager expression. She stiffened. Since Harvey realized that salary might be a problem, he decided to offer Cathy an incentive of sorts in addition to the $30 000 annual salary. He told her that he realized his salary offer was lower than the amount she had earned on her last job. And he told her he understood that a definite disadvantage of working for a new firm was the complete absence of financial security. Although he was extremely reluctant to guarantee a larger salary because of his own uncertainty regarding the future, he offered her a sales override in the amount of two percent of sales. He explained that she would largely determine the success or failure of the firm. She needed to represent the firm in the finest possible manner to potential customers who telephoned and to those who walked in the front door. For this reason, the sales override seemed to be an appropriate addition to her straight salary. It would provide her with incentive to take an active interest in the firm.

Cathy accepted the offer immediately. Even though she was expecting a salary offer of $32 500, she hoped the sales override might make up the difference. "Who knows," she thought, "two percent of sales may amount to big money someday." It did not, however, seem very likely at the time.

Troupville Business Systems began as a very small distributor of copy machines. The original business plan was just to sell copy machines and provide routine, on-site service. More extensive on-site service and repairs requiring that a machine be removed from a customer's premises were to be provided by a regional distributor located in a major city approximately 100 miles from Troupville.

Troupville Business Systems did well from the start. Several important changes were made in the services the firm offered during the first year. Harvey soon found that there was a greater demand for the leasing of copy machines, particularly the large expensive models that he originally planned to sell. He also soon discovered that his customers wanted to be able to contract directly with his firm for all their service needs. Merely guaranteeing that he could get the machines serviced was not sufficient in the eyes of potential customers. In attempting to accommodate the market, he developed a complete service facility and began to offer leasing options on all models. These changes in the business all occurred during the first year. Growth during that year was steady, but not spectacular. While sales continued to grow steadily the second year, it was early in the third year that Harvey made what turned out to be his best decision. He entered the computer business.

Harvey had purchased a personal computer soon after Troupville Business Systems was founded. The machine and its capabilities fascinated him, although he knew virtually nothing about computers. He was soon a member of a local users club, was subscribing to all the magazines, and was taking evening computer courses at the local university—in short, he became a computer buff. Harvey recognized the business potential of the rapidly growing personal computer market, but he did not believe that his original business was sufficiently stable to introduce a new product line just yet.

During his third year of operations, he decided the time was right to enter the computer business. He added to his product line a number of personal computers popular with small businesses in the area. This key decision caused a virtual explosion in the growth of his firm. Several key positions were added, including that of a comptroller. By the fourth year of operations, computers produced by several other manufacturers had been added to Harvey's product line, and he had developed the capability of providing complete service for all products carried. His computer enterprise was not limited to business customers, because he quickly developed a significant walk-in retail trade. Rapid growth continued unabated.

During the first seven years of the company's existence, Cathy Brannen had proven truly indispensable. Her performance exceeded Harvey's highest expectations. Although her official position remained that of secretary/receptionist, she took it on herself to learn about each new product or service. During the early years, Harvey often thought that she did a better job than he did whenever a potential customer called in his absence. Even after he acquired a qualified sales staff, Harvey had no concerns when Cathy had to field questions from a potential customer because a regular salesperson was not available. The customer never realized that the professional young lady capably handling all inquiries was "only" the receptionist.

Cathy began performing fewer sales functions because of the increased number of professional salespersons, but her secretarial duties had expanded tremendously. She was still Harvey's secretary, and she continued to answer virtually every telephone call coming into the business. Since her office was in an open area, she still was the first to greet many visitors.

Cathy took a word-processing course at a local business school shortly after joining the firm. As she began working with Harvey's first personal computer, she, too, developed into a computer aficionado and became the best computer operator in the firm.

The Current Situation

Harvey was shaken by the realization that Cathy Brannen had been paid over $127 000 last year. As he wondered what, if anything, should be done about her earnings, he began to reflect on the previous seven years.

Success had come almost overnight. It seemed as though Troupville Business Systems could do nothing wrong. The workforce had grown at a rate of approximately 15 percent per year since the third year of operations. Seventeen people were now employed by the firm. While Harvey did acknowledge that some of this success was due to being in the right place at the right time, he also had reason to be proud of the choices he had made. Time had proven that all his major decisions had been correct. He also could not overestimate Cathy's contribution to the success of the firm. Yes, certainly, one of the most important days in the life of the firm was the day when Cathy responded to his ad in the newspaper.

Success had brought with it the ever-increasing demands on his time. He had never worked so hard, but the rewards were certainly forthcoming. First, there was the new Jaguar, then the new home on Country Club Drive, the vacation home on the coast, the European trips . . . Yes, success was wonderful.

During these years Cathy, too, had prospered. Harvey had not thought much about it, but he did remember making a joking comment the first day she drove her new Mercedes to work. He also remembered commenting on her mink coat at the company banquet last December. Cathy had been dazzling.

Now that Harvey realized what he was paying Cathy, he was greatly disturbed. She was making almost twice as much money as anyone else in the firm with the exception of himself. The best salesman had earned an amount in the low nineties last year. His top managers were paid salaries ranging from the high sixties to the mid-seventies. The average salary in the area for executive secretaries was now probably between $30 000 and $35 000 per year. A good receptionist could be hired for under $28 000, and yet Cathy had been paid $127 614.21 last year. The sales override had certainly enabled Cathy to share in the firm's success. Yes, indeed.

As Harvey thought more and more about the situation, he kept returning to the same conclusion. He felt something had to be done about her compensation. It was just too far out of line with other salaries in the firm. Although Harvey was drawing over $200 000 per year in salary and had built an equity in the business of more than $1 million, these facts did not seem relevant as he pondered what to do. It seemed likely that a number of other employees did know about Cathy's compensation level. Harvey wondered why no one ever mentioned it. Even the comptroller never mentioned Cathy's compensation. This did seem quite odd to Harvey, as the comptroller, Frank Bain, knew that Harvey did not even attempt to keep up with the financial details. He relied on Frank to bring important matters to his attention.

With no idea of how to approach this problem, Harvey decided to begin by making a list of alternatives. He got out a piece of paper and, as he stared at the blank lines, overheard Cathy's cheerful exchange with a customer in the next room.

Source: Case prepared by Roland B. Cousins, LaGrange College. Management cooperated in the field research for this case, which was written solely for the purpose of stimulating student discussion. All individuals and incidents are real, but names and data have been disguised at the request of the organization. Reprinted by permission from the Case Research Journal. Copyright 1992 by Roland B. Cousins and the North American Case Research Association. All rights reserved.

1. Use the ideas of distributive fairness and equity theory to explain why Harvey Finley thinks he pays Cathy Brannen too much.

2. Use the ideas of distributive fairness and equity theory to explain why Cathy Brannen might feel that her pay is fair.

3. What are the likely consequences for job satisfaction, organizational commitment, and behaviour if Ms. Brannen's pay level is known to other organizational members? Use equity theory to support your answer.

4. Suppose that you had been in Mr. Finley's position at the time that he hired Ms. Brannen. What would you have done differently to avoid the current situation while still attracting her to join the fledgling firm?

5. How might emotions be relevant to the events in the case?

6. What ethical or moral issues does this case raise?

7. What should Mr. Finley do now? Be sure to consider procedural and interactional fairness in framing your answer.

Theories of Work Motivation

Great Little Box Company

Great Little Box Company (GLBC) is a leading designer and manufacturer of custom and stock corrugated boxes and point-of-purchase displays. It began operations in 1982 in Burnaby, British Columbia, with just three employees. Today, the company has grown to more than 200 full- and part-time employees. It has locations in Kelowna, Victoria, and Everett, Washington, in addition to its head office in Richmond, which is a 76 200-square-metre facility on the banks of the Fraser River.

The company has had remarkable success since it began, with annual sales today of $30 million. Much of its success is attributed to the hard work and dedication of its employees, who receive ongoing skills training and career and personal development, as well as above-average compensation and benefits. To ensure that salaries are competitive, the company participates in salary surveys every 18 months and reviews individual salaries every 12 months.

Incentive compensation is linked to the company's overall business goals and to objectives that are part of employees' goals. At the beginning of each year, employees meet with their immediate supervisor to set individual performance goals. Performance reviews are held every quarter, and employees meet with their supervisor to review how well they met their goals and to establish goals for the next quarter.

Exceptional performance is recognized with special dinners, cash awards, and preferred parking spots. A suggestion program rewards employees for cost-savings ideas. Employees whose suggestions are implemented receive a share of the financial savings to the company. Employees can also receive a $10 reward any day of the week for catching a mistake, improving a work process, or providing better ideas for manufacturing in what is known as the $10'ers program. Incentives have also been established for each department and are paid out weekly, monthly, and quarterly.

Happy and motivated employees are the key to the success of the Great Little Box Company, which has been named The Best Company to Work for in BC.

GLBC also has a profit-sharing plan and encourages employees to save for their retirement through matching RSP contributions. Employees are kept up-to-date on the company's profits through monthly meetings that include frank discussions about all financial matters relating to the business. The company opens its books to employees and provides details on the company's financial status. The meetings ensure that employees know how the company is doing and what can be done to improve things. They are also a forum for employee input and for recognizing and rewarding employees for their efforts. Every month, 15 percent of the previous month's profits are shared equally among all employees regardless of an employee's position, seniority, and wage.

Employees also share the benefits of the company's success when it reaches its annual profitability goal. The annual profitability goal is known as the Big Outrageous Xtravaganza goal (or BOX goal), and when it is reached, the company treats all of its employees to an all-expenses-paid vacation to a sunny destination. Over the past 13 years, GLBC employees have enjoyed seven vacations to places such as Cabo San Lucas, Puerto Vallarta, and Las Vegas.

GLBC has consistently been recognized as one of Canada's 50 Best Managed Companies, and in 2009 it was chosen as one of Canada's Top 100 Employers and named The Best Company to Work for in BC. According to GLBC president and CEO Robert Meggy, "It is clear that happy and motivated employees are the key to success and longevity."[1]

Would you be motivated if you worked for Great Little Box Company? What kind of person would respond well to the company's motivational techniques? What underlying philosophy of motivation is GLBC using and what effect does it have on employees' motivation? These are some of the questions that this chapter will explore.

First, we will define motivation and distinguish it from performance. After that, we will describe several popular theories of work motivation and contrast them. Then we will explore whether these theories translate across cultures. Finally, we will present a model that links motivation, performance, and job satisfaction.

Why Study Motivation?

Why should you study motivation? Motivation is one of the most traditional topics in organizational behaviour, and it has interested managers, researchers, teachers, and sports coaches for years. However, a good case can be made that motivation has become even more important in contemporary organizations. Much of this is a result of the need for increased productivity to be globally competitive. It is also a result of the rapid changes that contemporary organizations are undergoing. Stable systems of rules, regulations, and procedures that once guided behaviour are being replaced by requirements for flexibility and attention to customers that necessitate higher levels of initiative. This initiative depends on motivation. According to GLBC president and CEO Robert Meggy, "Everything we do has to be by people who are well-motivated. I see it in the bottom line for us."[2]

What would a good motivation theory look like? In fact, as we shall see, there is no single all-purpose motivation theory. Rather, we will consider several theories that serve somewhat different purposes. In combination, though, a good set of theories should recognize human diversity and consider that the same conditions will not motivate everyone. Also, a good set of theories should be able to explain how it is that some people seem to be self-motivated, while others seem to require external motivation. Finally, a good set of theories should recognize the social aspect of human beings—people's motivation is often affected by how they see others being treated. Before getting to our theories, let's first define motivation more precisely.

What Is Motivation?

The term *motivation* is not easy to define. However, from an organization's perspective, when we speak of a person as being motivated, we usually mean that the person works "hard," "keeps at" his or her work, and directs his or her behaviour toward appropriate outcomes.

Basic Characteristics of Motivation

Motivation. The extent to which persistent effort is directed toward a goal.

We can formally define **motivation** as the extent to which persistent effort is directed toward a goal.[3]

Effort. The first aspect of motivation is the strength of the person's work-related behaviour, or the amount of *effort* the person exhibits on the job. Clearly, this involves different kinds of activities on different kinds of jobs. A loading dock worker might exhibit greater effort by carrying heavier crates, while a researcher might reveal greater effort by searching out an article in some obscure foreign technical journal. Both are exerting effort in a manner appropriate to their jobs.

Persistence. The second characteristic of motivation is the *persistence* that individuals exhibit in applying effort to their work tasks. The organization would not be likely to think of the loading dock worker who stacks the heaviest crates for two hours and then goofs off for six hours as especially highly motivated. Similarly, the researcher who makes an important discovery early in her career and then rests on her laurels for five years would not be considered especially highly motivated. In each case, workers have not been persistent in the application of their effort.

Direction. Effort and persistence refer mainly to the quantity of work an individual produces. Of equal importance is the quality of a person's work. Thus, the third characteristic of motivation is the *direction* of the person's work-related behaviour. In other words, do workers channel persistent effort in a direction that benefits the organization? Employers expect motivated stockbrokers to advise their clients of good investment opportunities and motivated software designers to design software, not play computer games. These correct decisions increase the probability that persistent effort is actually translated into accepted organizational outcomes. Thus, motivation means working smart as well as working hard.

Goals. Ultimately, all motivated behaviour has some goal or objective toward which it is directed. We have presented the preceding discussion from an organizational perspective—that is, we assume that motivated people act to enhance organizational objectives. In this case, employee goals might include high productivity, good attendance, or creative decisions. Of course, employees can also be motivated by goals that are contrary to the objectives of the organization, including absenteeism, sabotage, and embezzlement. In these cases, they are channelling their persistent efforts in directions that are dysfunctional for the organization.

Extrinsic and Intrinsic Motivation

Some hold the view that people are motivated by factors in the external environment (such as supervision or pay), while others believe that people can, in some sense, be self-motivated without the application of these external factors. You might have experienced this distinction. As a worker, you might recall tasks that you enthusiastically performed simply for the sake of doing them and others that you performed only to keep your job or placate your boss.

Experts in organizational behaviour distinguish between intrinsic and extrinsic motivation. At the outset, we should emphasize that there is only weak consensus concerning the exact definitions of these concepts and even weaker agreement about whether we should label specific motivators as intrinsic or extrinsic.[4] However, the following definitions and examples seem to capture the distinction fairly well.

Intrinsic motivation stems from the direct relationship between the worker and the task and is usually self-applied. Feelings of achievement, accomplishment, challenge, and competence derived from performing one's job are examples of intrinsic motivators, as is sheer interest in the job itself. Off the job, avid participation in sports and hobbies is often intrinsically motivated.

> **Intrinsic motivation.** Motivation that stems from the direct relationship between the worker and the task; it is usually self-applied.

Extrinsic motivation stems from the work environment external to the task and is usually applied by someone other than the person being motivated. Pay, fringe benefits, company policies, and various forms of supervision are examples of extrinsic motivators. At Great Little Box Company, profit sharing and cash awards for exceptional performance are examples of extrinsic motivators.

> **Extrinsic motivation.** Motivation that stems from the work environment external to the task; it is usually applied by others.

Obviously, employers cannot package all conceivable motivators as neatly as these definitions suggest. For example, a promotion or a compliment might be applied by the boss but might also be a clear signal of achievement and competence. Thus, some motivators have both extrinsic and intrinsic qualities.

Despite the fact that the distinction between intrinsic and extrinsic motivation is fuzzy, many theories of motivation implicitly make the distinction. For example, intrinsic and extrinsic factors are used in **self-determination theory** (SDT) to explain what motivates people and whether motivation is autonomous or controlled. When people

> **Self-determination theory.** A theory of motivation that considers whether people's motivation is autonomous or controlled.

are motivated by intrinsic factors, they are in control of their motivation, what is known as **autonomous motivation**. When people are motivated to obtain a desired consequence or extrinsic reward, their motivation is controlled externally, what is known as **controlled motivation**. However, it is worth noting that sometimes extrinsic factors can lead to autonomous motivation when an individual internalizes the values or attitudes associated with a behaviour and, as a result, no longer requires the extrinsic factor to motivate him or her to perform the behaviour. Thus, a key aspect of SDT is the extent to which one's motivation is autonomous versus controlled. This is an important distinction because autonomous motivation facilitates effective performance, especially on complex tasks.[5]

Autonomous motivation. When people are self-motivated by intrinsic factors.

Controlled motivation. When people are motivated to obtain a desired consequence or extrinsic reward.

The relationship between intrinsic and extrinsic motivators has been the subject of a great deal of debate.[6] Some research studies have reached the conclusion that the availability of extrinsic motivators can reduce the intrinsic motivation stemming from the task itself.[7] The notion is that when extrinsic rewards depend on performance, then the motivating potential of intrinsic rewards decreases. Proponents of this view have suggested that making extrinsic rewards contingent on performance makes individuals feel less competent and less in control of their own behaviour. That is, they come to believe that their performance is controlled by the environment and that they perform well only because of the money (this is what is meant by controlled motivation).[8] As a result, their intrinsic motivation suffers.

However, a review of research in this area reached the conclusion that the negative effect of extrinsic rewards on intrinsic motivation occurs only under very limited conditions, and they are easily avoidable.[9] As well, in organizational settings in which individuals see extrinsic rewards as symbols of success and as signals of what to do to achieve future rewards, they increase their task performance.[10] Thus, it is safe to assume that both kinds of rewards are important and compatible in enhancing work motivation. Let's now consider the relationship between motivation and performance.

Motivation and Performance

At this point, you may well be saying, "Wait a minute, I know many people who are 'highly motivated' but just don't seem to perform well. They work long and hard, but they just don't measure up." This is certainly a sensible observation, and it points to the important distinction between motivation and performance. **Performance** can be defined as the extent to which an organizational member contributes to achieving the objectives of the organization.

Performance. The extent to which an organizational member contributes to achieving the objectives of the organization.

Some of the factors that contribute to individual performance in organizations are shown in Exhibit 5.1.[11] While motivation clearly contributes to performance, the relationship is not one-to-one because a number of other factors also influence performance. For example, recall from Chapter 2 that personality traits such as the "Big Five" and core self-evaluations also predict job performance. You might also be wondering about the role of intelligence—doesn't it influence performance? The answer, of course, is yes—intelligence, or what is also known as mental ability, does predict performance. Two forms of intelligence that are particularly important for performance are general cognitive ability and emotional intelligence. Let's consider each before we discuss motivation.

EXHIBIT 5.1
Factors contributing to individual job performance.

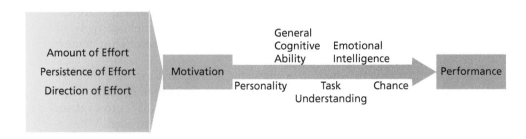

General Cognitive Ability. The term *cognitive ability* is often used to refer to what most people call intelligence or mental ability. Although there are many different types of specific cognitive abilities, in organizational behaviour we are often concerned with what is known as *general cognitive ability*. **General cognitive ability** is a term used to refer to a person's basic information processing capacities and cognitive resources. It reflects an individual's overall capacity and efficiency for processing information, and it includes a number of cognitive abilities, such as verbal, numerical, spatial, and reasoning abilities, that are required to perform mental tasks. Cognitive ability is usually measured by a number of specific aptitude tests that measure these abilities.[12]

Research has found that general cognitive ability predicts learning and training success as well as job performance in all kinds of jobs and occupations, including those that involve both manual and mental tasks. This should not come as a surprise because many cognitive skills are required to perform most kinds of jobs. General cognitive ability is an even better predictor of performance for more complex and higher-level jobs that require the use of more cognitive skills and involve more information processing.[13] Thus, both general cognitive ability and motivation are necessary for performance.

Given that cognitive ability is a strong predictor of performance, you might also wonder about the role of education in job performance. As you probably know, education is an important indicator of one's intelligence and it is important for obtaining employment. But how important is education for job performance? To find out, see Research Focus: *Does Education Predict Job Performance?*

General cognitive ability. A person's basic information processing capacities and cognitive resources.

RESEARCH FOCUS

Does Education Predict Job Performance?

Most organizations use education as an indicator of a job applicant's skill levels and ability and use education as a prerequisite in hiring decisions. There is substantial evidence that individuals' educational attainments are associated with positive career outcomes, including salary level, number of promotions, development opportunities, and job mobility. But does educational level predict job performance?

To find out, Thomas W.H. Ng and Daniel C. Feldman examined the results of 293 studies on education and job performance. They looked at three kinds of job performance. Core task performance refers to the basic required duties of a particular job. Citizenship performance refers to those extra behaviours engaged in by employees, over and above their core task requirements that actively promote and strengthen an organization's effectiveness (e.g., creativity). Counterproductive performance refers to voluntary behaviours that harm the well-being of the organization (e.g., theft, absenteeism). Education level refers to the academic credentials or degrees an individual has obtained.

The authors predicted that education would be positively related to core task performance and citizenship performance and negatively related to counterproductive performance as a result of the acquisition of task-relevant knowledge and work values that promote organizational effectiveness.

The results indicated that education was related to all three types of performance. More highly educated workers have higher core task performance, display greater creativity, and demonstrate more citizenship behaviours than less educated workers. Highly educated workers also engage in less counterproductive behaviours (i.e., workplace aggression, substance use, absenteeism). The authors also found that the relationships between education and performance were stronger for men than for women and stronger for Caucasian employees than for racial minorities. In addition, the relationship between education and core task performance was stronger for more complex jobs.

Overall, the results of this study confirm the long-held belief that education predicts job performance and provides some validity for the use of education level as a factor in the hiring process and for the benefits of an educated workforce.

Source: Excerpted from Ng, T.W.H. and Feldman, D.C. (2009). How broadly does education contribute to job performance? *Personnel Psychology*, 62, 89–134. Reprinted with permission of Wiley-Blackwell Publishing.

Emotional intelligence.
The ability to understand
and manage one's own
and other's feelings and
emotions.

Emotional Intelligence. Although the importance of general cognitive ability for job performance has been known for many years, researchers have only recently begun to study emotional intelligence. **Emotional intelligence** (EI) has to do with an individual's ability to understand and manage his or her own and others' feelings and emotions. It involves the ability to perceive and express emotion, assimilate emotion in thought, understand and reason about emotions, and manage emotions in oneself and others. Individuals high in EI are able to identify and understand the meanings of emotions and to manage and regulate their emotions as a basis for problem solving, reasoning, thinking, and action.[14]

Peter Salovey and John Mayer, who are credited with first coining the term *emotional intelligence,* have developed an EI model that consists of four interrelated sets of skills, or branches. The four skills represent sequential steps that form a hierarchy. The perception of emotion is at the bottom of the hierarchy, followed by (in ascending order) using emotions to facilitate thinking, understanding emotions, and the management and regulation of emotions. The four-branch model of EI is shown in Exhibit 5.2 and described below.[15]

1. *Perceiving emotions accurately in oneself and others:* This involves the ability to perceive emotions and to accurately identify one's own emotions and the emotions of others. An example of this is the ability to accurately identify emotions in people's faces and in non-verbal behaviour. People differ in the extent to which they can accurately identify emotions in others, particularly from facial expressions.[16] This step is the most basic level of EI and is necessary to be able to perform the other steps in the model.

2. *Using emotions to facilitate thinking:* This refers to the ability to use and assimilate emotions and emotional experiences to guide and facilitate one's thinking and reasoning. This means that one is able to use emotions in functional ways, such as making decisions and other cognitive processes (e.g., creativity, integrative thinking, inductive reasoning). This stage also involves being able to shift one's emotions and generate new emotions that can help one to see things in different ways and from different perspectives. This is an important skill because, as described in Chapter 10, emotions and moods affect what and how people think when making decisions.[17]

3. *Understanding emotions, emotional language, and the signals conveyed by emotions:* This stage involves being able to understand emotional information, the determinants and consequences of emotions, and how emotions evolve and change over time. At this stage, people understand how different situations and events generate emotions as well as how they and others are influenced by various emotions.[18] Individuals who are good at this know not to ask somebody who is in a bad mood for a favour, but rather to wait until the person is in a better mood or to just ask somebody else!

4. *Managing emotions so as to attain specific goals:* This involves the ability to manage one's own and others' feelings and emotions as well as emotional relationships. This is the highest level of EI because it requires one to have mastered the previous stages. At this stage, an individual is able to regulate, adjust, and change his or her own emotions as well as others' emotions to suit the situation. Examples of this include being able to stay calm when feeling angry or upset; being able to excite and enthuse others; or being able to lower another person's anger. To be effective at managing emotions, one must be able to perceive emotions, integrate and assimilate emotions, and be knowledgeable of and understand emotions.

Research on EI has found that it predicts performance in a number of areas, including job performance and academic performance.[19] One study found that college students' EI measured at the start of the academic year predicted their grade point averages at the end of the year. There is also some evidence that EI is most strongly related to job performance in jobs that require high levels of emotional labour, such as police officers and customer service representatives.[20] According to the results of one study, the importance of emotional intelligence for job performance depends on one's cognitive ability. Emotional intelligence was found to be most important for the job performance of employees with lower levels of cognitive ability and of less importance for the job performance of employees with high levels of cognitive ability.[21]

Managing emotions so as to attain specific goals

Understanding emotions, emotional language, and the signals conveyed by emotions

Using emotions to facilitate thinking

Perceiving emotions accurately in oneself and others

EXHIBIT 5.2
Four-branch model of emotional intelligence.

Source: Based on Mayer, J.D., Caruso, D.R., & Salovey, P. (2000). Emotional Intelligence meets traditional standards for an intelligence. *Intelligence, 27,* 267–298; Salovey, P., & Mayer, J.D. (1990). Emotional Intelligence. *Imagination, Cognition & Personality, 9,* 185–211. Used by permission of Baywood Publishing.

The Motivation–Performance Relationship

As shown in Exhibit 5.1, it is certainly possible for performance to be low even when a person is highly motivated. In addition to personality, general cognitive ability, and emotional intelligence, poor performance could also be due to a poor understanding of the task or luck and chance factors that can damage the performance of the most highly motivated individuals. Of course, an opposite effect is also possible. An individual with rather marginal motivation might have high general cognitive ability or emotional intelligence or might understand the task so well that some compensation occurs—what little effort the individual makes is expended very efficiently in terms of goal accomplishment. Also, a person with weak motivation might perform well because of some luck or chance factor that boosts performance. Thus, it is no wonder that workers sometimes complain that they receive lower performance ratings than colleagues who "don't work as hard."

In this chapter, we will concentrate on the motivational components of performance rather than on the other determinants in Exhibit 5.1. However, the message here should be clear: We cannot consider motivation in isolation. High motivation will not result in high performance if employees have low general cognitive ability and emotional intelligence, do not understand their jobs, or encounter unavoidable obstacles over which they have no control. Motivational interventions, such as linking pay to performance, simply *will not work* if employees are deficient in important skills and abilities.[22] Let's now turn to what motivates people and the process of motivation.

Need Theories of Work Motivation

The first three theories of motivation that we will consider are **need theories**. These theories attempt to specify the kinds of needs people have and the conditions under which they will be motivated to satisfy these needs in a way that contributes to performance. Needs are physiological and psychological wants or desires that individuals can satisfy by acquiring certain incentives or achieving particular goals. It is the behaviour stimulated by this acquisition process that reveals the motivational character of needs:

Need theories. Motivation theories that specify the kinds of needs people have and the conditions under which they will be motivated to satisfy these needs in a way that contributes to performance.

NEEDS ⟶ BEHAVIOUR ⟶ INCENTIVES AND GOALS

Notice that need theories are concerned with *what* motivates workers (needs and their associated incentives or goals). They can be contrasted with *process theories*, which are concerned with exactly *how* various factors motivate people. Need and process theories are complementary rather than contradictory. Thus, a need theory might contend that money can be an important motivator (what), and a process theory might explain the actual mechanics by which money motivates (how).[23] In this section, we will examine three prominent need theories of motivation.

Maslow's Hierarchy of Needs

Abraham Maslow was a psychologist who developed and refined a general theory of human motivation.[24] According to Maslow, humans have five sets of needs that are arranged in a hierarchy, beginning with the most basic and compelling needs (see the left side of Exhibit 5.3). These needs include:

1. *Physiological needs.* These include the needs that must be satisfied for the person to survive, such as food, water, oxygen, and shelter. Organizational factors that might satisfy these needs include the minimum pay necessary for survival and working conditions that promote existence.

2. *Safety needs.* These include needs for security, stability, freedom from anxiety, and a structured and ordered environment. Organizational conditions that might meet these needs include safe working conditions, fair and sensible rules and regulations, job security, a comfortable work environment, pension and insurance plans, and pay above the minimum needed for survival.

EXHIBIT 5.3
Relationship between
Maslow's and Alderfer's
need theories.

3. *Belongingness needs.* These include needs for social interaction, affection, love, companionship, and friendship. Organizational factors that might meet these needs include the opportunity to interact with others on the job, friendly and supportive supervision, opportunity for teamwork, and opportunity to develop new social relationships.

4. *Esteem needs.* These include needs for feelings of adequacy, competence, independence, strength, and confidence, and the appreciation and recognition of these characteristics by others. Organizational factors that might satisfy these needs include the opportunity to master tasks leading to feelings of achievement and responsibility. Also, awards, promotions, prestigious job titles, professional recognition, and the like might satisfy these needs when they are felt to be truly deserved.

5. *Self-actualization needs.* These needs are the most difficult to define. They involve the desire to develop one's true potential as an individual to the fullest extent and to express one's skills, talents, and emotions in a manner that is most personally fulfilling. Maslow suggests that self-actualizing people have clear perceptions of reality, accept themselves and others, and are independent, creative, and appreciative of the world around them. Organizational conditions that might provide self-actualization include absorbing jobs with the potential for creativity and growth as well as a relaxation of structure to permit self-development and personal progression.

Given the fact that individuals may harbour these needs, in what sense do they form the basis of a theory of motivation? That is, what exactly is the motivational premise of **Maslow's hierarchy of needs?** Put simply, the lowest-level unsatisfied need category has the greatest motivating potential. Thus, none of the needs is a "best" motivator; motivation depends on the person's position in the need hierarchy. According to Maslow, individuals are motivated to satisfy their physiological needs before they reveal an interest in safety needs, and safety must be satisfied before social needs become motivational, and so on. When a need is unsatisfied, it exerts a powerful effect on the individual's thinking and behaviour, and this is the sense in which needs are motivational. However, when needs at a particular level of the hierarchy are satisfied, the individual turns his or her attention to the next higher level. Notice the clear implication here that *a satisfied need is no longer an effective motivator.* Once one has adequate physiological resources and feels safe and secure, one does not seek more of the factors that met these needs but looks elsewhere for gratification. According to Maslow, the single exception to this rule involves self-actualization needs. He felt that these were "growth" needs that become stronger as they are gratified.

Maslow's hierarchy of needs. A five-level hierarchical need theory of motivation that specifies that the lowest-level unsatisfied need has the greatest motivating potential.

Alderfer's ERG Theory

Clayton Alderfer developed another need-based theory, called **ERG theory.**[25] It streamlines Maslow's need classifications and makes some different assumptions about the relationship between needs and motivation. The name ERG stems from Alderfer's

ERG theory. A three-level hierarchical need theory of motivation (existence, relatedness, growth) that allows for movement up and down the hierarchy.

compression of Maslow's five-category need system into three categories—existence, relatedness, and growth needs.

1. *Existence needs.* These are needs that are satisfied by some material substance or condition. As such, they correspond closely to Maslow's physiological needs and to those safety needs that are satisfied by material conditions rather than interpersonal relations. These include the need for food, shelter, pay, and safe working conditions.

2. *Relatedness needs.* These are needs that are satisfied by open communication and the exchange of thoughts and feelings with other organizational members. They correspond fairly closely to Maslow's belongingness needs and to those esteem needs that involve feedback from others. However, Alderfer stresses that relatedness needs are satisfied by open, accurate, honest interaction rather than by uncritical pleasantness.

3. *Growth needs.* These are needs that are fulfilled by strong personal involvement in the work setting. They involve the full utilization of one's skills and abilities and the creative development of new skills and abilities. Growth needs correspond to Maslow's need for self-actualization and the aspects of his esteem needs that concern achievement and responsibility.

As you can see in Exhibit 5.3, Alderfer's need classification system does not represent a radical departure from that of Maslow. In addition, Alderfer agrees with Maslow that, as lower-level needs are satisfied, the desire to have higher-level needs satisfied will increase. Thus, as existence needs are fulfilled, relatedness needs gain motivational power. Alderfer explains this by arguing that as more "concrete" needs are satisfied, energy can be directed toward satisfying less concrete needs. Finally, Alderfer agrees with Maslow that the least concrete needs—growth needs—become *more* compelling and *more* desired as they are fulfilled.

It is, of course, the differences between ERG theory and the need hierarchy that represent Alderfer's contribution to the understanding of motivation. First, unlike the need hierarchy, ERG theory does not assume that a lower-level need *must* be gratified before a less concrete need becomes operative. Thus, ERG theory does not propose a rigid hierarchy of needs. Some individuals, owing to background and experience, might seek relatedness or growth even though their existence needs are ungratified. Hence, ERG theory seems to account for a wide variety of individual differences in motive structure. Second, ERG theory assumes that if the higher-level needs are ungratified, individuals will increase their desire for the gratification of lower-level needs. Notice that this represents a *radical* departure from Maslow. According to Maslow, if esteem needs are strong but ungratified, a person will not revert to an interest in belongingness needs because these have necessarily already been gratified. (Remember, he argues that satisfied needs are not motivational.) According to Alderfer, however, the frustration of higher-order needs will lead workers to regress to a more concrete need category. For example, the software designer who is unable to establish rewarding social relationships with superiors or co-workers might increase his interest in fulfilling existence needs, perhaps by seeking a pay increase. Thus, according to Alderfer, an apparently satisfied need can act as a motivator by substituting for an unsatisfied need.

Given the preceding description of ERG theory, we can identify its two major motivational premises as follows:

1. The more lower-level needs are gratified, the more higher-level need satisfaction is desired.

2. The less higher-level needs are gratified, the more lower-level need satisfaction is desired.

McClelland's Theory of Needs

Psychologist David McClelland has spent several decades studying the human need structure and its implications for motivation. According to **McClelland's theory of needs,**

McClelland's theory of needs. A nonhierarchical need theory of motivation that outlines the conditions under which certain needs result in particular patterns of motivation.

needs reflect relatively stable personality characteristics that one acquires through early life experiences and exposure to selected aspects of one's society. Unlike Maslow and Alderfer, McClelland has not been interested in specifying a hierarchical relationship among needs. Rather, he has been more concerned with the specific behavioural consequences of needs. In other words, under what conditions are certain needs likely to result in particular patterns of motivation? The three needs that McClelland studied most have special relevance for organizational behaviour—needs for achievement, affiliation, and power.[26]

Individuals who are high in **need for achievement** (n Ach) have a strong desire to perform challenging tasks well. More specifically, they exhibit the following characteristics:

Need for achievement. A strong desire to perform challenging tasks well.

- *A preference for situations in which personal responsibility can be taken for outcomes.* Those high in n Ach do not prefer situations in which outcomes are determined by chance because success in such situations does not provide an experience of achievement.

- *A tendency to set moderately difficult goals that provide for calculated risks.* Success with easy goals will provide little sense of achievement, while extremely difficult goals might never be reached. The calculation of successful risks is stimulating to the high–n Ach person.

- *A desire for performance feedback.* Such feedback permits individuals with high n Ach to modify their goal attainment strategies to ensure success and signals them when success has been reached.[27]

People who are high in n Ach are concerned with bettering their own performance or that of others. They are often concerned with innovation and long-term goal involvement. However, these things are not done to please others or to damage the interests of others. Rather, they are done because they are *intrinsically* satisfying. Thus, n Ach would appear to be an example of a growth or self-actualization need.

Need for affiliation. A strong desire to establish and maintain friendly, compatible interpersonal relationships.

People who are high in **need for affiliation** (n Aff) have a strong desire to establish and maintain friendly, compatible interpersonal relationships. In other words, they like to like others, and they want others to like them! More specifically, they have an ability to learn social networking quickly and a tendency to communicate frequently with others, either face to face, by telephone, or in writing. Also, they prefer to avoid conflict and competition with others, and they sometimes exhibit strong conformity to the wishes of their friends. The n Aff motive is obviously an example of a belongingness or relatedness need.

Need for power. A strong desire to influence others, making a significant impact or impression.

People who are high in **need for power** (n Pow) strongly desire to have influence over others. In other words, they wish to make a significant impact or impression on them. People who are high in n Pow seek out social settings in which they can be influential. When in small groups, they act in a "high-profile," attention-getting manner. There is some tendency for those who are high in n Pow to advocate risky positions. Also, some people who are high in n Pow show a strong concern for personal prestige. The need for power is a complex need because power can be used in a variety of ways, some of which serve the power seeker and some of which serve other people or the organization. However, n Pow seems to correspond most closely to Maslow's self-esteem need.

McClelland predicts that people will be motivated to seek out and perform well in jobs that match their needs. Thus, people with high n Ach should be strongly motivated by sales jobs or entrepreneurial positions, such as running a small business. Such jobs offer the feedback, personal responsibility, and opportunity to set goals, as noted above. People who are high in n Aff will be motivated by jobs such as social work or customer relations because these jobs have as a primary task establishing good relations with others. Finally, high n Pow will result in high motivation in jobs that enable one to have a strong impact on others—jobs such as journalism and management. In fact, McClelland has found that the most effective managers have a low need for affiliation, a high need for power, and the ability to direct power toward organizational goals.[28] (We will study this further in Chapter 11.)

Research Support for Need Theories

Maslow's need hierarchy suggests two main hypotheses. First, specific needs should cluster into the five main need categories that Maslow proposes. Second, as the needs in a given category are satisfied, they should become less important, while the needs in the adjacent higher-need category should become more important. This second hypothesis captures the progressive, hierarchical aspect of the theory. In general, research support for both these hypotheses is weak or negative. This is probably a function of the rigidity of the theory, which suggests that most people experience the same needs in the same hierarchical order. However, there is fair support for a simpler, two-level need hierarchy comprising the needs toward the top and the bottom of Maslow's hierarchy.[29]

This latter finding provides some indirect encouragement for the compressed need hierarchy found in Alderfer's ERG theory. Several tests indicate fairly good support for many of the predictions generated by the theory, including expected changes in need strength. Particularly interesting is the confirmation that the frustration of relatedness needs increases the strength of existence needs.[30] The simplicity and flexibility of ERG theory seem to capture the human need structure better than the greater complexity and rigidity of Maslow's theory.

McClelland's need theory has generated a wealth of predictions about many aspects of human motivation. Recently, researchers have tested more and more of these predictions in organizational settings, and the results are generally supportive of the idea that particular needs are motivational when the work setting permits the satisfaction of these needs.[31]

Managerial Implications of Need Theories

The need theories have some important things to say about managerial attempts to motivate employees.

Appreciate Diversity. The lack of support for the fairly rigid need hierarchy suggests that managers must be adept at evaluating the needs of individual employees and offering incentives or goals that correspond to their needs. Unfounded stereotypes about the needs of the "typical" employee and naïve assumptions about the universality of need satisfaction are bound to reduce the effectiveness of chosen motivational strategies. The best salesperson might not make the best sales manager! The needs of a young recent college graduate probably differ from those of an older employee preparing for retirement. Thus, it is important to survey employees to find out what their needs are and then offer programs that meet their needs. For example, GLBC conducts an annual employee satisfaction survey to find out what employees want most and what they think of their salary.[32]

Appreciate Intrinsic Motivation. The need theories also serve the valuable function of alerting managers to the existence of higher-order needs (whatever specific label we apply to them). The recognition of these needs in many employees is important for two key reasons. One of the basic conditions for organizational survival is the expression of some creative and innovative behaviour on the part of members. Such behaviour seems most likely to occur during the pursuit of higher-order need fulfillment, and ignorance of this factor can cause the demotivation of the people who have the most to offer the organization. Second, observation and research evidence support Alderfer's idea that the frustration of higher-order needs prompts demands for greater satisfaction of lower-order needs. This can lead to a vicious motivational cycle—that is, because the factors that gratify lower-level needs are fairly easy to administer (e.g., pay and fringe benefits), management has grown to rely on them to motivate employees. In turn, some employees, deprived of higher-order need gratification, come to expect more and more of these extrinsic factors in exchange for their services. Thus, a cycle of deprivation, regression, and temporary gratification continues, at great cost to the organization.[33]

How can organizations benefit from the intrinsic motivation that is inherent in strong higher-order needs? First, such needs will fail to develop for most employees unless lower-level needs are reasonably well gratified.[34] Thus, very poor pay, job insecurity, and unsafe working conditions will preoccupy most workers at the expense of higher-order outcomes. Second, if basic needs are met, jobs can be "enriched" to be more stimulating and challenging and to provide feelings of responsibility and achievement (we will have more to say about this in Chapter 6). Finally, organizations could pay more attention to designing career paths that enable interested workers to progress through a series of jobs that continue to challenge their higher-order needs. Individual managers could also assign tasks to employees with this goal in mind.

Process Theories of Work Motivation

In contrast to need theories of motivation, which concentrate on *what* motivates people, **process theories** concentrate on *how* motivation occurs. In this section, we will examine three important process theories—expectancy theory, equity theory, and goal setting theory.

Expectancy Theory

The basic idea underlying **expectancy theory** is the belief that motivation is determined by the outcomes that people expect to occur as a result of their actions on the job. Psychologist Victor Vroom is usually credited with developing the first complete version of expectancy theory and applying it to the work setting.[35] The basic components of Vroom's theory are shown in Exhibit 5.4 and are described in more detail below.

- **Outcomes** are the consequences that may follow certain work behaviours. First-level outcomes are of particular interest to the organization; for example, high productivity versus average productivity, illustrated in Exhibit 5.4, or good attendance versus poor attendance. Expectancy theory is concerned with specifying how an employee might attempt to choose one first-level outcome instead of another. Second-level outcomes are consequences that follow the attainment of a particular first-level outcome. Contrasted with first-level outcomes, second-level outcomes are most personally relevant to the individual worker and might involve amount of pay, sense of accomplishment, acceptance by peers, fatigue, and so on.

- **Instrumentality** is the probability that a particular first-level outcome (such as high productivity) will be followed by a particular second-level outcome (such as pay) (this is also known as the *performance* $\longrightarrow$ *outcome* link). For example, a bank teller might figure that the odds are 50/50 (instrumentality =.5) that a good performance rating will result in a pay raise.

- **Valence** is the expected value of outcomes, the extent to which they are attractive or unattractive to the individual. Thus, good pay, peer acceptance, the chance of being fired, or any other second-level outcome might be more or less attractive to particular workers. According to Vroom, the valence of first-level outcomes is the sum of products of the associated second-level outcomes and their instrumentalities—that is,

$$\text{the valence of a particular} \atop \text{first-level outcome} = \sum \text{instrumentalities} \times \text{second-level valences}$$

In other words, the valence of a first-level outcome depends on the extent to which it leads to favourable second-level outcomes.

Process theories. Motivation theories that specify the details of how motivation occurs.

Expectancy theory. A process theory that states that motivation is determined by the outcomes that people expect to occur as a result of their actions on the job.

Outcomes. Consequences that follow work behaviour.

Instrumentality. The probability that a particular first-level outcome will be followed by a particular second-level outcome.

Valence. The expected value of work outcomes; the extent to which they are attractive or unattractive.

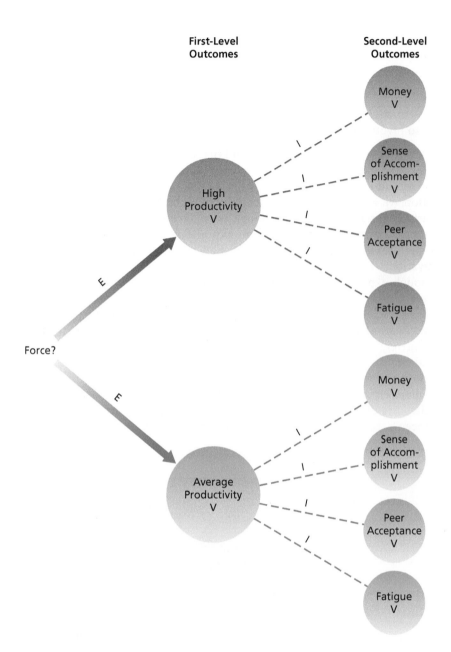

First-Level
Outcomes

Second-Level
Outcomes

EXHIBIT 5.4
A hypothetical expectancy
model (E = Expectancy,
I = Instrumentality,
V = Valence).

- **Expectancy** is the probability that the worker can actually achieve a particular first-level outcome (this is also known as the *effort* ⟶ *performance* link). For example, a machinist might be absolutely certain (expectancy = 1.0) that she can perform at an average level (producing 15 units a day), but less certain (expectancy = .6) that she can perform at a high level (producing 20 units a day).

- **Force** is the end product of the other components of the theory. It represents the relative degree of effort that will be directed toward various first-level outcomes.

According to Vroom, the force directed toward a first-level outcome is a product of the valence of that outcome and the expectancy that it can be achieved. Thus,

force = first-level valence × expectancy

We can expect an individual's effort to be directed toward the first-level outcome that has the largest force product. Notice that no matter how valent a particular first-level outcome might be, a person will not be motivated to achieve it if the expectancy of accomplishment approaches zero.

Expectancy. The
probability that a particular
first-level outcome can be
achieved.

Force. The effort directed
toward a first-level
outcome.

Believe it or not, the mechanics of expectancy theory can be distilled into a couple of simple sentences! In fact, these sentences nicely capture the premises of the theory:

- People will be motivated to perform in those work activities that they find attractive and that they feel they can accomplish.
- The attractiveness of various work activities depends on the extent to which they lead to favourable personal consequences.

It is extremely important to understand that expectancy theory is based on the perceptions of the individual worker. Thus, expectancies, valences, instrumentalities, and relevant second-level outcomes depend on the perceptual system of the person whose motivation we are analyzing. For example, two employees performing the same job might attach different valences to money, differ in their perceptions of the instrumentality of performance for obtaining high pay, and differ in their expectations of being able to perform at a high level. Therefore, they would likely exhibit different patterns of motivation.

Although expectancy theory does not concern itself directly with the distinction between extrinsic and intrinsic motivators, it can handle any form of second-level outcome that has relevance for the person in question. Thus, some people might find second-level outcomes of an intrinsic nature, such as feeling good about performing a task well, positively valent. Others might find extrinsic outcomes, such as high pay, positively valent.

To firm up your understanding of expectancy theory, consider Tony Angelas, a middle manager in a firm that operates a chain of retail stores (Exhibit 5.5). Second-level outcomes that are relevant to him include the opportunity to obtain a raise and the chance to receive a promotion. The promotion is more highly valent to Tony than

EXHIBIT 5.5
Expectancy model for Tony Angelas
(E = Expectancy,
I = Instrumentality,
V = Valence).

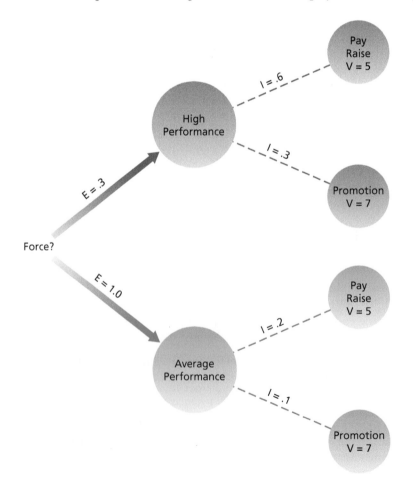

the raise (7 versus 5 on a scale of 10) because the promotion means more money *and* increased prestige. Tony figures that if he can perform at a very high level in the next few months, the odds are 6 in 10 that he will receive a raise. Thus, the instrumentality of high performance for obtaining a raise is .6. Promotions are harder to come by, and Tony figures the odds at .3 if he performs well. The instrumentality of average performance for achieving these favourable second-level outcomes is a good bit lower (.2 for the raise and only .1 for the promotion). Recall that the valence of a first-level outcome is the sum of the products of second-level outcomes and their instrumentalities. Thus, the valence of high performance for Tony is $(5 \times .6) + (7 \times .3) = 5.1$. Similarly, the valence of average performance is $(5 \times .2) + (7 \times .1) = 1.7$. We can conclude that high performance is more valent for Tony than average performance.

Does this mean that Tony will necessarily try to perform at a high level in the next few months? To determine this, we must take into account his expectancy that he can actually achieve the competing first-level outcomes. As shown in Exhibit 5.5, Tony is absolutely certain that he can perform at an average level (expectancy = 1.0) but much less certain (.3) that he can sustain high performance. Force is a product of these expectancies and the valence of their respective first-level outcomes. Thus, the force associated with high performance is $.3 \times 5.1 = 1.53$, while that associated with average performance is $1.0 \times 1.7 = 1.70$. As a result, although high performance is attractive to Tony, he will probably perform at an average level.

With all this complicated figuring, you might be thinking, "Look, would Tony really do all this calculation to decide his motivational strategy? Do people actually think this way?" The answer to these questions is probably no. Rather, the argument is that people *implicitly* take expectancy, valence, and instrumentality into account as they go about their daily business of being motivated. If you reflect for a moment on your behaviour at work or school, you will realize that you have certain expectancies about what you can accomplish, the chances that these accomplishments will lead to certain other outcomes, and the value of these outcomes for you.

Research Support for Expectancy Theory

Tests have provided moderately favourable support for expectancy theory.[36] In particular, there is especially good evidence that the valence of first-level outcomes depends on the extent to which they lead to favourable second-level consequences. We must recognize, however, that the sheer complexity of expectancy theory makes it difficult to test. We have already suggested that people are not used to *thinking* in expectancy terminology. Thus, some research studies show that individuals have a difficult time discriminating between instrumentalities and second-level valences. Despite this and other technical problems, experts in motivation generally accept expectancy theory.

Managerial Implications of Expectancy Theory

The motivational practices suggested by expectancy theory involve "juggling the numbers" that individuals attach to expectancies, instrumentalities, and valences.

Boost Expectancies. One of the most basic things managers can do is ensure that their employees *expect* to be able to achieve first-level outcomes that are of interest to the organization. No matter how positively valent high productivity or good attendance might be, the force equation suggests that workers will not pursue these goals if expectancy is low. Low expectancies can take many forms, but a few examples will suffice to make the point.

- Employees might feel that poor equipment, poor tools, or lazy co-workers impede their work progress.
- Employees might not understand what the organization considers to be good performance or see how they can achieve it.

- If performance is evaluated by a subjective supervisory rating, employees might see the process as capricious and arbitrary, not understanding how to obtain a good rating.

Although the specific solutions to these problems vary, expectancies can usually be enhanced by providing proper equipment and training, demonstrating correct work procedures, carefully explaining how performance is evaluated, and listening to employee performance problems. The point of all this is to clarify the path to beneficial first-level outcomes.

Clarify Reward Contingencies. Managers should also attempt to ensure that the paths between first- and second-level outcomes are clear. Employees should be convinced that first-level outcomes desired by the organization are clearly *instrumental* in obtaining positive second-level outcomes and avoiding negative outcomes. If a manager has a policy of recommending good performers for promotion, she should spell out this policy. Similarly, if managers desire regular attendance, they should clarify the consequences of good and poor attendance. To ensure that instrumentalities are strongly established, they should be clearly stated and then acted on by the manager. Managers should also attempt to provide stimulating, challenging tasks for workers who appear to be interested in such work. On such tasks, the instrumentality of good performance for feelings of achievement, accomplishment, and competence is almost necessarily high. The ready availability of intrinsic motivation reduces the need for the manager to constantly monitor and clarify instrumentalities.[37]

Appreciate Diverse Needs. Obviously, it might be difficult for managers to change the valences that employees attach to second-level outcomes. Individual preferences for high pay, promotion, interesting work, and so on are the product of a long history of development and are unlikely to change rapidly. However, managers would do well to analyze the diverse preferences of particular employees and attempt to design individualized "motivational packages" to meet their needs. Of course, all concerned must perceive such packages to be fair. Let's examine another process theory that is concerned specifically with the motivational consequences of fairness.

Equity Theory

Equity theory. A process theory that states that motivation stems from a comparison of the inputs one invests in a job and the outcomes one receives in comparison with the inputs and outcomes of another person or group.

In Chapter 4, we discussed the role of **equity theory** in explaining job satisfaction. To review, the theory asserts that workers compare the inputs that they invest in their jobs and the outcomes that they receive against the inputs and outcomes of some other relevant person or group. When these ratios are equal, the worker should feel that a fair and equitable exchange exists with the employing organization. Such fair exchange contributes to job satisfaction. When the ratios are unequal, workers perceive inequity, and they should experience job dissatisfaction, at least if the exchange puts the worker at a disadvantage vis-à-vis others.

But in what sense is equity theory a theory of motivation? Put simply, *individuals are motivated to maintain an equitable exchange relationship.* Inequity is unpleasant and tension-producing, and people will devote considerable energy to reducing inequity and achieving equity. What tactics can do this? Psychologist J. Stacey Adams has suggested the following possibilities:[38]

- Perceptually distort one's own inputs or outcomes.
- Perceptually distort the inputs or outcomes of the comparison person or group.
- Choose another comparison person or group.
- Alter one's inputs or alter one's outcomes.
- Leave the exchange relationship.

Notice that the first three tactics for reducing inequity are essentially psychological, while the last two involve overt behaviour.

To clarify the motivational implications of equity theory, consider Terry, a middle manager in a consumer products company. He has five years' work experience and an MBA degree and considers himself a good performer. His salary is $75 000 a year. Terry finds out that Maxine, a co-worker with whom he identifies closely, makes the same salary he does. However, she has only a Bachelor's degree and one year of experience, and he sees her performance as average rather than good. Thus, from Terry's perspective, the following outcome/input ratios exist:

$$\frac{\text{TERRY } \$75\,000}{\text{Good performance, MBA, 5 years}} \neq \frac{\text{MAXINE } \$75\,000}{\text{Average performance, Bachelor's, 1 year}}$$

In Terry's view, he is underpaid and should be experiencing inequity. What might he do to resolve this inequity? Psychologically, he might distort the outcomes that he is receiving, rationalizing that he is due for a certain promotion that will bring his pay into line with his inputs. Behaviourally, he might try to increase his outcomes (by seeking an immediate raise) or reduce his inputs. Input reduction could include a decrease in work effort or perhaps excessive absenteeism. Finally, Terry might resign from the organization to take what he perceives to be a more equitable job somewhere else.

Let's reverse the coin and assume that Maxine views the exchange relationship identically to Terry—same inputs, same outcomes. Notice that she too should be experiencing inequity, this time from relative overpayment. It does not take a genius to understand that Maxine would be unlikely to seek equity by marching into the boss's office and demanding a pay cut. However, she might well attempt to increase her inputs by working harder or enrolling in an MBA program. Alternatively, she might distort her view of Terry's performance to make it seem closer to her own. As this example implies, equity theory is somewhat vague about just when individuals will employ various inequity reduction strategies.

Gender and Equity. As an addendum to the previous example, it is extremely interesting to learn that both women and men have some tendency to choose same-sex comparison persons—that is, when judging the fairness of the outcomes that they receive, men tend to compare themselves with other men, and women tend to compare themselves with other women. This might provide a partial explanation for why women are paid less than men, even for the same job. If women restrict their equity comparisons to (lesser paid) women, they are less likely to be motivated to correct what we observers see as wage inequities.[39]

Research Support for Equity Theory

Most research on equity theory has been restricted to economic outcomes and has concentrated on the alteration of inputs and outcomes as a means of reducing inequity. In general, this research is very supportive of the theory when inequity occurs because of *underpayment*.[40] For example, when workers are underpaid on an hourly basis, they tend to lower their inputs by producing less work. This brings inputs in line with (low) outcomes. Also, when workers are underpaid on a piece-rate basis (e.g., paid $1 for each market research interview conducted), they tend to produce a high volume of low-quality work. This enables them to raise their outcomes to achieve equity. Finally, there is also evidence that underpayment inequity leads to resignation. Presumably, some underpaid workers thus seek equity in another organizational setting.

The theory's predictions regarding *overpayment* inequity have received less support.[41] The theory suggests that such inequity can be reduced behaviourally by increasing inputs or by reducing one's outcomes. The weak support for these strategies suggests either that people tolerate overpayment more than underpayment, or that they use perceptual distortion to reduce overpayment inequity.

Managerial Implications of Equity Theory

The most straightforward implication of equity theory is that perceived underpayment will have a variety of negative motivational consequences for the organization, including low productivity, low quality, theft, or turnover. On the other hand, attempting to solve organizational problems through overpayment (disguised bribery) might not have the intended motivational effect. The trick here is to strike an equitable balance.

But how can such a balance be struck? Managers must understand that feelings about equity stem from a *perceptual* social comparison process in which the worker "controls the equation"—that is, employees decide what are considered relevant inputs, outcomes, and comparison persons, and management must be sensitive to these decisions. For example, offering the outcome of more interesting work might not redress inequity if better pay is considered a more relevant outcome. Similarly, basing pay only on performance might not be perceived as equitable if employees consider seniority an important job input.

Understanding the role of comparison people is especially crucial.[42] Even if the best engineer in the design department earns $2000 more than anyone else in the department, she might still have feelings of inequity if she compares her salary with that of more prosperous colleagues in *other* companies. Awareness of the comparison people chosen by workers might suggest strategies for reducing felt inequity. Perhaps the company will have to pay even more to retain its star engineer.

Notice how equity is achieved at GLBC. Salary surveys are conducted every 18 months and individual salaries are reviewed every 12 months to make sure that salaries are competitive. In addition, all employees share equally in profit sharing. President and CEO Robert Meggy says, "I certainly believe in fair pay. You don't have to be the best paying but you have to be fair."[43]

Goal Setting Theory

As indicated in the chapter opening vignette, GLBC sets business goals and objectives for the organization as well as departments. In addition, employees meet with their immediate supervisor to set individual performance goals and to review how well they have met their goals.

One of the basic characteristics of all organizations is that they have goals. A **goal** is the object or aim of an action.[44] At the beginning of this chapter, individual performance was defined as the extent to which a member contributes to the attainment of these goals or objectives. Thus, if employees are to achieve acceptable performance, some method of translating organizational goals into individual goals must be implemented.

Goal. The object or aim of an action.

Unfortunately, there is ample reason to believe that personal performance goals are vague or nonexistent for many organizational members. Employees frequently report that their role in the organization is unclear, or that they do not really know what their boss expects of them. Even in cases in which performance goals would seem to be obvious because of the nature of the task (e.g., filling packing crates to the maximum to avoid excessive freight charges), employees might be ignorant of their current performance. This suggests that the implicit performance goals simply are not making an impression.

The notion of goal setting as a motivator has been around for a long time. However, theoretical developments and some very practical research have demonstrated when and how goal setting can be effective.[45]

What Kinds of Goals Are Motivational?

Goal setting theory. A process theory that states that goals are motivational when they are specific, challenging, and when organizational members are committed to them and feedback about progress toward goal attainment is provided.

According to **goal setting theory**, goals are most motivational when they are *specific* and *challenging* and when organizational members are *committed* to them. In addition, *feedback* about progress toward goal attainment should be provided.[46] The positive effects of goals are due to four mechanisms: they *direct* attention toward goal-relevant activities; they lead to greater *effort*; they increase and prolong *persistence*; and they lead

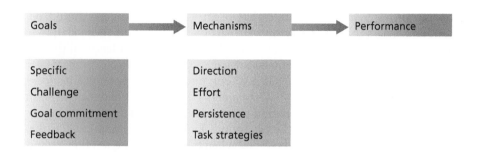

EXHIBIT 5.6
The mechanisms of goal setting.

Source: Locke, E.A., & Latham, G.P. (2002). Building a practically useful theory of goal setting and task motiv-ation. *American Psychologist, 57,* 705-717.

to the discovery and use of task-relevant *strategies* for goal attainment.[47] Exhibit 5.6 shows the characteristics of goals that are motivational and the mechanisms that explain the effects of goals on performance.

Goal Specificity. Specific goals are goals that specify an exact level of achievement for people to accomplish in a particular time frame. For example, "I will enroll in five courses next semester and achieve a *B* or better in each course" is a specific goal. Simi-larly, "I will increase my net sales by 20 percent in the coming business quarter" is a specific goal. On the other hand, "I will do my best" is not a specific goal, since level of achievement and time frame are both vague.

Goal Challenge. Obviously, specific goals that are especially easy to achieve will not motivate effective performance. However, goal challenge is a much more personal mat-ter than goal specificity, since it depends on the experience and basic skills of the organ-izational member. One thing is certain, however—when goals become so difficult that they are perceived as *impossible* to achieve, they will lose their potential to motivate. Thus, goal challenge is best when it is pegged to the competence of individual workers and increased as the particular task is mastered. One practical way to do this is to base initial goals on past performance. For example, an academic counsellor might encour-age a D student to set a goal of achieving Cs in the coming semester and encourage a C student to set a goal of achieving Bs. Similarly, a sales manager might ask a new sales-person to try to increase his sales by 5 percent in the next quarter and ask an experi-enced salesperson to try to increase her sales by 10 percent.

Goal Commitment. Individuals must be committed to specific, challenging goals if the goals are to have effective motivational properties. The effect of goals on perform-ance is strongest when individuals have high goal commitment. In a sense, goals really are not goals and cannot improve performance unless an individual accepts them and is committed to working toward them. This is especially important when goals are challenging and difficult to achieve. In a following section, we will discuss some factors that affect goal commitment.

Goal Feedback. Specific and challenging goals have the most beneficial effect when they are accompanied by ongoing feedback that enables the person to compare current performance with the goal. This is why a schedule of tasks to be completed often motiv-ates goal accomplishment. Progress against the schedule provides feedback. To be most effective, feedback should be accurate, specific, credible, and timely.

Enhancing Goal Commitment

It has probably not escaped you that the requirements for goal challenge and goal com-mitment seem potentially incompatible. After all, you might be quite amenable to accepting an easy goal but balk at accepting a tough one. Therefore, it is important to consider some of the factors that might affect commitment to challenging, specific goals, including participation, rewards, and management support.

Participation. It seems reasonable that organizational members should be more committed to goals that are set with their participation than to those simply handed down by their superior. Sensible as this sounds, the research evidence on the effects of participation is very mixed—sometimes participation in goal setting increases performance, and sometimes it does not.[48] If goal commitment is a potential *problem,* participation might prove beneficial.[49] When a climate of distrust between superiors and employees exists, or when participation provides information that assists in the establishment of fair, realistic goals, then it should facilitate performance. On the other hand, when employees trust their boss and when the boss has a good understanding of the capability of the employees, participation might be quite unnecessary for goal commitment.[50] Interestingly, research shows that participation can improve performance by increasing the *difficulty* of the goals that employees adopt.[51] This might occur because participation induces competition or a feeling of team spirit among members of the work unit, which leads them to exceed the goal expectations of the supervisor.

Rewards. Will the promise of extrinsic rewards (such as money) for goal accomplishment increase goal commitment? Probably, but there is plenty of evidence that goal setting has led to performance increases *without* the introduction of monetary incentives for goal accomplishment. One reason for this might be that many ambitious goals involve no more than doing the job as it was designed to be done in the first place. For example, encouraging employees to pack crates or load trucks to within 5 percent of their maximum capacity does not really involve a greater expenditure of effort or more work. It simply requires more attention to detail. Goal setting should, however, be compatible with any system to tie pay to performance that already exists for the job in question.

Supportiveness. There is considerable agreement about one factor that will *reduce* commitment to specific, challenging performance goals. When supervisors behave in a coercive manner to encourage goal accomplishment, they can badly damage employee goal commitment. For goal setting to work properly, supervisors must demonstrate a desire to assist employees in goal accomplishment and behave supportively if failure occurs, even adjusting the goal downward if it proves to be unrealistically high. Threat and punishment in response to failure will be extremely counterproductive.[52]

Goal Orientation and Types of Goals

Goal orientation. An individual's goal preferences in achievement situations.

A recent development in goal setting theory is research on people's preferences for different kinds of goals, or what is known as *goal orientation.* **Goal orientation** refers to an individual's goal preferences in achievement situations. It is a stable individual difference that affects performance. Some individuals have a preference for learning goals while others have a preference for performance-prove or performance-avoid goals. Individuals with a **learning goal orientation** are most concerned about learning something new and developing their competence in an activity by acquiring new skills and mastering new situations; they focus on acquiring new knowledge and skills and developing their competence. Individuals with a **performance-prove goal orientation** are most concerned about demonstrating their competence in performing a task by seeking favourable judgments about the outcome of their performance. Individuals with a **performance-avoid goal orientation** are most concerned about avoiding negative judgments about the outcome of their performance.[53]

Learning goal orientation. A preference to learn new things and develop competence in an activity by acquiring new skills and mastering new situations.

Performance-prove goal orientation. A preference to obtain favourable judgments about the outcome of one's performance.

Performance-avoid goal orientation. A preference to avoid negative judgments about the outcome of one's performance.

In the last several years, research has found that goal orientation is important for learning and performance. For example, a learning goal orientation has been found to be positively related to learning as well as academic, task, and job performance, while a performance-avoid orientation is negatively related to learning and lower task and job performance. A performance-prove orientation is not related to learning or performance outcomes. Thus, a learning goal orientation is most effective for learning and performance outcomes, while a performance-avoid goal orientation is detrimental for learning and performance.[54]

Although goal orientation is a stable individual difference, goals can be distinguished in terms of whether they are performance goals (e.g., achieve a specific performance outcome) or learning goals (e.g., discover strategies for solving a problem). In other words, it is possible to set a learning goal or a performance goal for an individual regardless of their goal orientation. As is described later, the effectiveness of a learning or performance goal depends on the nature of the task.

Goals can also be distinguished in terms of whether they are distal or proximal goals. A **distal goal** is a long-term or end-goal, such as achieving a certain level of sales performance. A **proximal goal** is a short-term or sub-goal that is instrumental for achieving a distal goal. Proximal goals involve breaking down a distal goal into smaller, more attainable sub-goals. Proximal goals provide clear markers of progress towards a distal goal because they result in more frequent feedback. As a result, individuals can evaluate their ongoing performance and identify appropriate strategies for the attainment of a distal goal. Distal goals are too far removed to provide markers of one's progress, making it difficult for individuals to know how they are doing and to adjust their strategies.[55]

Now that we have described different types of goals, you might be surprised to learn that goals do not always have to be conscious to be motivational. To learn more, see Research Focus: *Effects of Subconscious Goals on Performance.*

Distal goal. Long-term or end goals.

Proximal goal. Short-term or sub-goals.

Research Support for Goal Setting Theory

Goal setting theory is considered to be one of the most valid and practical theories of employee motivation. Several decades of research has demonstrated that specific, difficult goals lead to improved performance and productivity on a wide variety of tasks and occupations, including servicing drink machines, entering data, selling, teaching, and typing text. Studies reveal that the positive results of goal setting are not short lived—they persist over a long enough time to have practical value.[56] For example, in a now classic study conducted at Weyerhaeuser Company, a large forest products firm headquartered in Tacoma, Washington, truck drivers were assigned a specific, challenging performance goal of loading their trucks to 94 percent of legal weight capacity. Before setting this goal, management had simply asked the drivers to do their best to maximize their weight. Over the first several weeks, load capacity gradually increased to more than 90 percent and remained at this high level for seven years! In the first nine months alone, the company accountants conservatively estimated the savings at $250 000. These results were achieved without driver participation in setting the goal and without monetary incentives for goal accomplishment. Drivers evidently found the 94 percent goal motivating in and of itself; they frequently recorded their weights in informal competition with other drivers.[57]

In recent years, however, research has found that the effects of goal setting on performance depend on a number of factors. For example, when individuals lack the knowledge or skill to perform a novel or complex task, a specific and challenging performance goal can decrease rather than increase performance relative to a do-your-best goal. On the other hand, when a task is straightforward, a specific, high-performance goal results in higher performance than a do-your-best goal. Thus, a high-performance goal is most effective when individuals already have the ability to perform a task. However, when individuals are learning to perform a novel or complex task, setting a specific, high-learning goal that focuses on knowledge and skill acquisition will be more effective than a specific, high-performance goal or a do-your-best goal. This is because effective performance of complex tasks requires the acquisition of knowledge and skills, and a specific learning goal focuses one's attention on learning.[58]

Research has also found that proximal goals are especially important for novel and complex tasks and that distal goals can have a negative effect. However, when distal

RESEARCH FOCUS

Effects of Subconscious Goals on Performance

When we think of goals and goal setting, we naturally assume that it is a conscious process, and in fact goal setting theory is focused entirely on conscious motivation. But there is some evidence that subconscious goals can have the same effect on behaviour and performance as conscious goals. But how can people have subconscious goals? The answer is priming. Participants are exposed to stimuli such as a word or a picture of something relevant to the goal that one wants to prime them for. The stimulus triggers automatic goal activation that affects goal-directed cognition and behaviour without the person being aware of the process. Thus, subconscious goal motivation operates automatically, without intention, awareness, or conscious guidance.

A number of laboratory experiments have found that priming results in subconscious goals that influence behaviour and performance. But can priming result in subconscious goals in the workplace? To find out, Amanda Shantz and Gary Latham conducted an experiment in which they tested the effect of a primed goal alone and a specific, difficult consciously set goal on the performance of call centre employees who were fundraising for a university. Employees were randomly assigned to one of four conditions: a primed goal only, a conscious goal only, a primed goal and conscious goal, and a "do your best" goal condition.

At the start of their three-hour shift, the employees received an information packet that contained information about the university for whom they would be soliciting donations and recent awards to faculty and the university. In order to prime a subconscious goal, an achievement-related photograph of a woman winning a race was shown in the backdrop of the paper that the

information was printed on. The photograph was of Sonia O'Sullivan, an Irish athlete who won a silver medal in the 2000 Olympics. Participants in the conscious goal condition were given a specific high goal of $1200 to attain on their shift. The employees were told that management wanted to determine the usefulness of the information in the packet on their ability to raise money. They did not know that they were in an experiment.

To test the effects of the goal conditions, the employees in the four groups were compared on the amount of dollars they raised at the end of their shift. The results indicated that employees who were primed raised significantly more money than employees who were not primed and that employees who were assigned a conscious, difficult goal raised more money than employees were told to do their best. Thus, both the primed and conscious goals increased performance. However, employees in the conscious goal condition raised more money than employees in the primed-subconscious goal condition.

The results of this study suggest that organizations can motivate employees to achieve higher levels of performance by priming them with a subconscious achievement-related goal through the use of an image that depicts achievement. This study also shows that motivation is not always conscious and that subconscious goals can be activated through priming.

goals are accompanied with proximal goals they have a significant positive effect on the discovery and use of task-relevant strategies, self-efficacy, and performance.[59]

Finally, although we have focused on individual goal setting, the effect of group goal setting on group performance is similar to the effect of individual goal setting. Group goals result in superior group performance, especially when groups set specific goals and when the group members participate in setting the goals.[60]

Managerial Implications of Goal Setting Theory

The managerial implications of goal setting theory seem straightforward: Set specific and challenging goals and provide ongoing feedback so that individuals can compare their performance with the goal. While goals can be motivational in certain circumstances,

Drivers at Weyerhaeuser Company were assigned a specific, challenging performance goal of loading their trucks to 94 percent of legal weight capacity.

they obviously have some limitations. For example, as indicated earlier, the performance impact of specific, challenging goals is stronger for simpler jobs than for more complex jobs, such as scientific and engineering work. Thus, when a task is novel or complex and individuals need to acquire new knowledge and skills for good performance, setting a specific learning goal will be more effective than setting a high performance goal. Setting a high performance goal will be most effective when individuals already have the ability to perform a task effectively. In addition, proximal goals should be set in conjunction with distal goals when employees are learning a new task or performing a complex one.[61] In the next chapter, we will discuss a more elaborate application of goal setting theory, called *management by objectives*.

Now that you are familiar with motivation theories, try to use them to evaluate an actual motivation program. Please consult You Be the Manager: *Purolator's Early and Safe Return to Work Program*.

Do Motivation Theories Translate Across Cultures?

Are the motivation theories that we have described in this chapter culture-bound? That is, do they apply only to North America, where they were developed? The answer to this question is important for North American organizations that must understand motivational patterns in their international operations. It is also important to foreign managers, who are often exposed to North American theory and practice as part of their training and development.

It is safe to assume that most theories that revolve around human needs will come up against cultural limitations to their generality. For example, both Maslow and Alderfer suggest that people pass through a social stage (belongingness, relatedness) on their way to a higher-level personal growth or self-actualization stage. However, as we discussed in Chapter 4, it is well established that there are differences in the extent to which societies value a more collective or a more individualistic approach to life.[62] In individualistic societies (e.g., Canada, the United States, Great Britain, Australia), people tend to value individual initiative, privacy, and taking care of oneself. In more

YOU BE THE MANAGER

Purolator's Early and Safe Return to Work Program

Purolator's workers' compensation premiums were out of control. With 2130 claims filed in 2005, the company's bill for workers' compensation premiums came in around $13 million for the year. At Purolator, which employs 11 600 people across Canada, including 3000 couriers, 300 line haul truck drivers, and 500 call centre operators, 90 percent of the workers' compensation claims can be traced back to employees in two occupations: couriers and sorters.

Because their jobs require constant hauling, lifting, pushing, and pulling, soft tissue, orthopaedic and joint injuries make up the bulk of the claims. Psychological disability is also common, accounting for about one in five claims. Although the numbers are on par with the industry average, the costs were too high, particularly on the workers' compensation side. So Purolator decided to implement a program to improve claims management and disability accommodation.

Purolator developed a commitment to "early and safe return to work," fleshed out the models and processes to support that commitment, and hired a total of six occupational nurses and workers' compensation specialists to step into the roles of return-to-work coordinators. Their primary job is to coach managers and HR people on accommodating injured workers, and to liaise with physicians, unions, and workers' compensation boards.

One of the guiding principles in Purolator's return-to-work program is that it's not good enough just to put people back in an easy or light-duty job; they need to be put in jobs that are similar in the depot. That means that a courier might be put back into the job he had before he became a courier and that a worker on the dock who was loading trailers before he was injured might return to a job scanning freight or something similar.

However, making this happen and getting the numbers down also requires a change in managers' behaviour. How can Purolator motivate managers to change

**Employee absence because
of work-related injuries
was becoming a problem
at Purolator.**

their behaviour to help employees return to work and lower the number of days lost? You be the manager.

QUESTIONS

1. Use goal setting theory and expectancy theory to explain what Purolator can do to motivate managers to help employees return to work and lower the number of days lost to injuries.

2. How effective do you think a motivational program might be for lowering the days lost to injury? What is necessary to make it effective?

To find out what Purolator did and the results, see The Manager's Notebook at the end of the chapter.

Source: Excerpt from Vu, U. (2006, March 13). How Purolator dealt with skyrocketing costs. *Canadian HR Reporter*, 9, 10. Used with permission.

collective societies (e.g., Mexico, Singapore, Pakistan), more closely knit social bonds are observed, in which members of one's in-group (family, clan, organization) are expected to take care of each other in exchange for strong loyalty to the in-group.[63] This suggests that there might be no superiority to self-actualization as a motive in more collective cultures. In some cases, for example, appealing to employee loyalty might prove more motivational than the opportunity for self-expression because it

Cultures differ in how they define achievement. In collective societies where group solidarity is dominant, achievement may be more group-oriented than in individualistic societies.

relates to strong belongingness needs that stem from cultural values. Also, cultures differ in the extent to which they value achievement as it is defined in North America, and conceptions of achievement might be more group-oriented in collective cultures than in individualistic North America. Similarly, the whole concept of intrinsic motivation might be more relevant to wealthy societies than to developing societies.

With respect to equity theory, we noted earlier that people should be appropriately motivated when outcomes received "match" job inputs. Thus, higher producers are likely to expect superior outcomes compared with lower producers. This is only one way to allocate rewards, however, and it is one that is most likely to be endorsed in individualistic cultures. In collective cultures, there is a tendency to favour reward allocation based on equality rather than equity.[64] In other words, everyone should receive the same outcomes despite individual differences in productivity, and group solidarity is a dominant motive. Trying to motivate employees with a "fair" reward system might backfire if your definition of fairness is equity and theirs is equality.

Because of its flexibility, expectancy theory is very effective when applied cross-culturally. The theory allows for the possibility that there may be cross-cultural differences in the expectancy that effort will result in high performance. It also allows for the fact that work outcomes (such as social acceptance versus individual recognition) may have different valences across cultures.[65]

Finally, setting specific and challenging goals should also be motivational when applied cross-culturally, and, in fact, goal setting has been found to predict, influence, and explain behaviour in numerous countries around the world.[66] However, for goal setting to be effective, careful attention will be required to adjust the goal setting process in different cultures. For example, individual goals are not likely to be accepted or motivational in collectivist cultures, where group rather than individual goals should be used. Power distance is also likely to be important in the goal setting process. In cultures where power distance is large, it would be expected that goals be assigned by superiors. However, in some small power distance cultures in which power differences are downplayed, participative goal setting would be more appropriate. One limitation to the positive effect of goal setting might occur in those (mainly Far Eastern) cultures in which saving face is important. That is, a specific and challenging goal may not be very motivating if it suggests that failure could occur and if it results in a negative reaction. This would seem to be especially bad if it were in the context of the less-than-preferred individual goal setting. Failure in the achievement of a very specific goal could lead to loss of face. As well, in the so-called "being-oriented" cultures where people work only as much as needed to live and avoid continuous work, there tends to be some resistance to goal setting.[67]

International management expert Nancy Adler has shown how cultural blinders often lead to motivational errors.[68] A primary theme running through this discussion is that appreciating cultural diversity is critical in maximizing motivation.

Putting It All Together: Integrating Theories of Work Motivation

In this chapter, we have presented several theories of work motivation and attempted to distinguish between motivation and performance. In Chapter 4, we discussed the relationship between job performance and job satisfaction. At this point, it seems appropriate to review just how all these concepts fit together. Exhibit 5.7 presents a model that integrates these relationships.

Each of the theories helps us to understand the motivational process. First, in order for individuals to obtain rewards, they must achieve designated levels of performance. We know from earlier in this chapter that performance is a function of motivation as well as other factors, such as personality, general cognitive ability, emotional intelligence, understanding of the task, and chance. In terms of motivation, we are concerned with the amount, persistence, and direction of effort. Therefore, Boxes 1 through 5 in Exhibit 5.7 explain these relationships.

Perceptions of expectancy and instrumentality (expectancy theory) relate to all three components of motivation (*Box 1*). In other words, individuals direct their effort toward a particular first-level outcome (expectancy) and increase the amount and persistence of effort to the extent that they believe it will result in second-level outcomes (instrumentality). Goal setting theory (*Box 2*) indicates that specific and challenging goals that people are committed to, as well as feedback about progress toward goal attainment, will have a positive effect on amount, persistence, and direction of effort. Goal specificity should also strengthen both expectancy and instrumentality connections. The individual will have a clear picture of a first-level outcome to which her effort should be directed and greater certainty about the consequences of achieving this outcome.

Boxes 3 through 5 illustrate that motivation (*Box 3*) will be translated into good performance (*Box 5*) if the worker has the levels of general cognitive ability and emotional intelligence relevant to the job, and if the worker understands the task (*Box 4*). Chance can also help to translate motivation into good performance. If these conditions are not met, high motivation will not result in good performance.

Second, a particular level of performance (*Box 5*) will be followed by certain outcomes. To the extent that performance is followed by outcomes that fulfill individual needs (need theory) and are positively valent second-level outcomes (expectancy theory), they can be considered rewards for good performance (*Box 6*). In general, the connection

EXHIBIT 5.7
Integrative model of motivation theories.

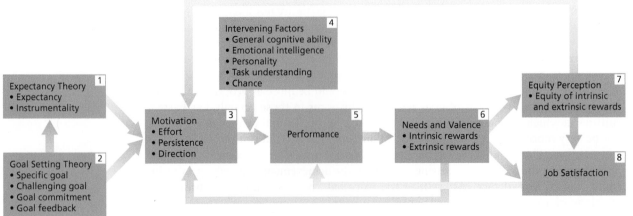

between performance and the occurrence of intrinsic rewards should be strong and reliable because such rewards are self-administered. For example, the nurse who assists several very sick patients back to health is almost certain to feel a sense of competence and achievement because such feelings stem directly from the job. On the other hand, the connection between performance and extrinsic rewards might be much less reliable because the occurrence of such rewards depends on the actions of management. Thus, the head nurse may or may not recommend attendance at a nursing conference (an extrinsic fringe benefit) for the nurse's good performance.

Third, to the extent that the rewards fulfill individual needs (need theory), then they will be motivational, as depicted by the path from rewards (*Box 6*) to motivation (*Box 3*). In addition, the rewards that individuals receive are also the outcomes of the equity theory equation and will be used by individuals to form perceptions of equity (*Box 7*). Perceptions of equity also influence motivation (*Box 3*) and job satisfaction (*Box 8*). You will recall that this relationship between job outcomes, equity, and job satisfaction was discussed in Chapter 4. According to equity theory, individuals in a state of equity have high job satisfaction. Individuals who are in a state of inequity experience job dissatisfaction. Also recall from Chapter 4 that good performance leads to job satisfaction if that performance is rewarded, and job satisfaction in turn leads to good performance.

In summary, each theory of motivation helps us to understand a different part of the motivational process. Understanding how the different theories of motivation can be integrated brings us to the topic of the next chapter—practical methods of motivation that apply the theories we have been studying in this chapter.

THE MANAGER'S NOTEBOOK

Purolator's Early and Safe Return to Work Program

1. Given that the focus of Purolator's program is to get employees back to work early and to lower the number of days lost to injury, it is possible to set clear targets. Thus, goal setting is particularly relevant in this situation and played a key part in the program. In rolling out the program, Purolator measured the lost time and severity of injuries at each of its 120 facilities across the country. Then they set targets (goals) for the company as a whole, for each division, each of the three depots, and each of the terminals. Another theory that is relevant is expectancy theory. Recall that according to expectancy theory, people will be motivated to perform work activities that they find attractive and that they feel they can accomplish. The attractiveness of various work activities depends on the extent to which they lead to favourable personal consequences. So the question for Purolator was how to get managers to be attracted to lowering the days lost to injuries. What they did was strengthen the instrumentality linkage—the probability that a first-level outcome (targets for lost days) will be followed by a particular second-level outcome. The second-

level outcome was the manager's pay. One of the most important things that Purolator did was to link performance to managers' compensation. About 10 percent of the managers' bonuses depends on meeting the targets for lost time and severity.

2. Managers were resistant to the program and saw accommodation as a potential drag on their productivity goals. But instead of softening productivity goals, Purolator held the line, believing that employees who were sitting at home doing nothing could instead be contributing to productivity goals. After showing managers a breakdown of the costs and demonstrating that for every dollar a claim costs the company in workers' compensation, another four dollars are spent on indirect costs, managers got the message. Now they work with HR on getting employees back to work and accommodated. The feedback from employees has been very positive. They feel that the company cares about them and they are more willing to come back and be engaged and work for the company. As for the number of days lost to injuries? In 2002 it was 9700, and in 2005 it was 6039.

LEARNING OBJECTIVES CHECKLIST

1. *Motivation* is the extent to which persistent effort is directed toward a goal. *Performance* is the extent to which an organizational member contributes to achieving the objectives of the organization.

2. *Intrinsic motivation* stems from the direct relationship between the worker and the task and is usually self-applied. *Extrinsic motivation* stems from the environment surrounding the task and is applied by others. *Self-determination theory* focuses on whether motivation is *autonomous* or *controlled*.

3. Performance is influenced by motivation as well as personality, general cognitive ability, emotional intelligence, task understanding, and chance factors. *General cognitive ability* refers to a person's basic information-processing capacities and cognitive resources. *Emotional intelligence* refers to the ability to manage one's own and other's feelings and emotions. Motivation will be translated into good performance if an individual has the general cognitive ability and emotional intelligence relevant to the job, and if he or she understands the task.

4. *Need theories* propose that motivation will occur when employee behaviour can be directed toward goals or incentives that satisfy personal wants or desires. The three need theories discussed are *Maslow's need hierarchy, Alderfer's ERG theory,* and *McClelland's theory of needs* for achievement, affiliation, and power. Maslow and Alderfer have concentrated on the hierarchical arrangement of needs and the distinction between intrinsic and extrinsic motivation. McClelland has focused on the conditions under which particular need patterns stimulate high motivation.

5. *Process theories* attempt to explain how motivation occurs rather than what specific factors are motivational. *Expectancy theory* argues that people will be motivated to engage in work activities that they find attractive and that they feel they can accomplish. The attractiveness of these activities depends on the extent to which they lead to favourable personal consequences.

6. *Equity theory* states that workers compare the inputs that they apply to their jobs and the outcomes that they get from their jobs with the inputs and outcomes of others. When these outcome/input ratios are unequal, inequity exists, and workers will be motivated to restore equity.

7. *Goal setting theory* states that goals are motivational when they are specific and challenging and when workers are committed to them and receive feedback about progress toward goal attainment. In some cases, companies can facilitate goal commitment through employee participation in goal setting and by financial incentives for goal attainment, but freedom from coercion and punishment seems to be the key factor in achieving goal commitment. *Goal orientation* refers to an individual's goal preferences in achievement situations. A *learning* goal orientation is a preference to learn new things and develop competence in an activity by acquiring new skills and mastering new situations. A *performance-prove goal orientation* is a preference to obtain favourable judgments about the outcome of one's performance, and a *performance-avoid goal orientation* is a preference to avoid negative judgments about the outcome of one's performance. A *distal goal* is a long-term or end goal, and a *proximal goal* is a short-term or sub-goal.

8. There are some cross-cultural limitations of the theories of motivation. For example, most theories that revolve around human needs will come up against cultural limitations to their generality as a result of differences in values across cultures. As for equity theory, trying to motivate employees with a "fair" reward system might backfire if the definition of fairness is other than equity (e.g., equality). Because of its flexibility, expectancy theory is very effective when applied cross-culturally and allows for the possibility that there may be cross-cultural differences in the expectancy that effort will result in high performance. It also allows for the fact that work outcomes (such as social acceptance versus individual recognition) may have different valences across cultures. Setting specific and challenging goals should also be motivational when applied cross-culturally. However, for goal setting to be effective, careful attention will be required to adjust the goal setting process in different cultures.

9. Performance is a function of motivation as well as other factors, such as personality, general cognitive ability, emotional intelligence, understanding of the task, and chance. Perceptions of expectancy and instrumentality influence motivation, as do specific and challenging goals that people are committed to and that are accompanied with feedback. Motivation will be translated into good performance if the worker has the levels of general cognitive ability and emotional intelligence relevant to the job and if the worker understands the task. Chance can also help to translate motivation into good performance. To the extent that performance leads to rewards that fulfill individual needs and are positively valent, they will be motivational. When the rewards are perceived as equitable, they will have a positive effect on motivation and job satisfaction. Furthermore, good performance leads to job satisfaction if that performance is rewarded, and job satisfaction in turn leads to good performance.

DISCUSSION QUESTIONS

1. Many millionaires continue to work long, hard hours, sometimes even beyond the usual age of retirement. Use the ideas developed in the chapter to speculate about the reasons for this motivational pattern. Is the acquisition of wealth still a motivator for these individuals?

2. Discuss a time when you were highly motivated to perform well (at work, at school, in a sports contest) but performed poorly in spite of your high motivation. How do you know that your motivation was really high? What factors interfered with good performance? What did you learn from this experience?

3. Use Maslow's hierarchy of needs and Alderfer's ERG theory to explain why assembly line workers and executive vice-presidents might be susceptible to different forms of motivation.

4. Colleen is high in need for achievement, Eugene is high in need for power, and Max is high in need for affiliation. They are thinking about starting a business partnership. To maximize the motivation of each, what business should they go into, and who should assume which roles or jobs?

5. Reconsider the case of Tony Angelas, which was used to illustrate expectancy theory. Imagine that you are Tony's boss and you think that he can be motivated to perform at a high level. Suppose you cannot modify second-level outcomes or their valences, but you can affect expectancies and instrumentalities. What would you do to motivate Tony? Prove that you have succeeded by recalculating the force equations to demonstrate that Tony will now perform at a high level.

6. Debate the following statements: *Of all the motivational theories we discussed in this chapter, goal setting theory is the simplest to implement. Goal setting is no more than doing what a good manager should be doing anyway.*

7. What are the implications of goal orientation for motivating a group of employees? When would it be best to set a learning goal versus a performance goal? When it would be best to set a proximal versus a distal goal? Describe a situation in which it would be best to set a learning goal and a situation in which it would be best to set a performance goal. Describe a situation when it would be best to set a proximal goal and a situation in which it would be best to set a distal goal.

8. Critique the following assertion: *People are basically the same. Thus, the motivation theories discussed in the chapter apply equally around the globe.*

9. Describe self-determination theory and provide an example of when your motivation was controlled and autonomous. What factors contributed to your autonomous and controlled motivation?

10. What is the relationship between cognitive ability and emotional intelligence with job performance? When would emotional intelligence be most important for a person's job performance? When is cognitive ability especially important for job performance?

INTEGRATIVE DISCUSSION QUESTIONS

1. Refer to the cross-cultural dimensions of values described in Chapter 4 (i.e., work centrality, power distance, uncertainty avoidance, masculinity/femininity, individualism/collectivism, and long-term/short-term orientation) and discuss the implications of each value for exporting the work motivation theories discussed in this chapter across cultures. Based on your analysis, how useful are the theories described in this chapter for understanding and managing motivation across cultures? What are the implications?

2. Consider the basic characteristics of motivation in relation to operant learning theory and social cognitive theory. What are the implications of operant learning theory and social cognitive theory for motivation, and how do they compare to the theories of work motivation described in this chapter?

ON-THE-JOB CHALLENGE QUESTION

Employee theft is a major problem for organizations in Canada and the United States. According to one study, employee theft costs Canadian organizations more than $120 billion a year and is the cause of 30 percent of business failures. The study also found that 79 percent of employees admit to stealing or considering it. Another study found that as many as one out of every 28 employees was apprehended for theft in 2007 in the United States. Although employee theft has usually involved things like inflated expense accounts, cooking the books, stealing merchandise, or pocketing money from cash sales, organizations are increasingly finding themselves the victims of time theft.

Time theft occurs when employees steal their employer's time by engaging in unauthorized personal activities during working hours, such as visiting social networking sites and chat lines or spending time out of the office fulfilling one's personal agenda (e.g., playing golf) rather than meeting with clients or making sales calls. Time theft also occurs when employees take longer breaks for coffee or meals, make personal phone calls at work, send or receive email not related to work, and surf the web for personal reasons.

Why are employees motivated to steal from their organization? Use the theories of motivation discussed in the chapter to answer this question. What can organizations do to prevent employee theft? Consider the implications of each theory of motivation for preventing employee theft.

Sources: Sherr, I. (2009, July 11). U.S. retailers struggle with theft by employees; Outpaces shoplifting, fraud. Tech solutions yield surprises. *Gazette* (Montreal), C6; Levitt, H. (2009, May 20). Employers must beware of the time wasters: Ways to make staff accountable for time away from the office. *Edmonton Journal*, F4; Levitt, H. (2008, August 20). Hands off the cookie jar or pay the price. *Ottawa Citizen*, F3; Buckingham, R. (2008, April 1). Time theft growing in the workplace. *Telegraph-Journal* (Saint John), B1.

EXPERIENTIAL EXERCISE

What Is Your Goal Orientation?

The following scale is a measure of goal orientation. Answer each of the statements as accurately and honestly as possible using the following response scale:

1–Strongly disagree   5–Slightly agree
2–Moderately disagree   6–Moderately agree
3–Slightly disagree   7–Strongly agree
4–Neither disagree nor agree

____ 1. It's important for me to impress others by doing a good job.

____ 2. If I don't succeed at a difficult task, I plan to try harder the next time.

____ 3. I worry that I won't always be able to meet the standards set by others.

____ 4. I avoid tasks that I may not be able to complete.

____ 5. It's better to stick with what works than risk failing at a task.

____ 6. The opportunity to extend my range of abilities is important to me.

_____ 7. I avoid circumstances where my performance will be compared to that of others.

_____ 8. I like to meet others' expectations of me.

_____ 9. The opportunity to learn new things is important to me.

_____ 10. I'm not interested in impressing others with my performance.

_____ 11. I am always challenging myself to learn new concepts.

_____ 12. I get upset when other people do better than I do.

_____ 13. Most of the time, I stay away from tasks that I know I won't be able to complete.

_____ 14. I don't care what others think of my performance.

_____ 15. I don't enjoy taking on tasks if I am unsure whether I will complete them successfully.

_____ 16. The opportunity to do challenging work is important to me.

_____ 17. Typically, I like to be sure that I can successfully perform a task before I attempt it.

_____ 18. I value what others think of my performance.

_____ 19. I prefer to work on tasks that force me to learn new things.

_____ 20. In learning situations, I tend to set fairly challenging goals for myself.

_____ 21. I don't like having my performance compared negatively to that of others.

Scoring and Interpretation

To obtain your score, first subtract your response to questions 10 and 14 from 8. For example, if you gave a response of 1 to question 10, give yourself a 7 (8 minus 1). To obtain your score on each goal orientation, add your scores as follows:

> Learning goal orientation: Add items 2, 6, 9, 11, 16, 19, and 20.
>
> Performance-prove goal orientation: Add items 1, 5, 8, 12, 18, and 10.
>
> Performance-avoid goal orientation: Add items 3, 4, 7, 13, 15, 17, and 21.

Your total for each of the three goal orientations should be somewhere between 7 and 49. The higher your score, the higher your goal orientation. To facilitate class discussion and your understanding of goal orientation, form a small group with several other members of the class and consider the following questions:

1. Each group member should present their goal orientation scores. Rank your three scores from highest to lowest. What is your primary goal orientation? What is the primary goal orientation of most members of your group?

2. Given your primary goal orientation, how might it affect your academic performance? How might it affect your performance at work?

3. Given your primary goal orientation, what type of goal should you set for yourself in the future? When should you set a learning goal versus a performance goal?

4. How can knowledge of your primary goal orientation help you in your future studies and grades? How can it help you at work?

5. Based on the results of this exercise, what have you learned about yourself? What kind of goals should you focus on at school and at work?

Source: Zweig, D., and Webster, J. (2004). Validation of a multidimensional measure of goal orientation. *Canadian Journal of Behavioural Science*, 36:3, 232–243. Copyright 2004, Canadian Psychological Assocation. Used with permission.

CASE INCIDENT

Mayfield Department Stores

As competition in the retail market began to heat up, it became necessary to find ways to motivate the sales staff of Mayfield Department Stores to increase sales. Therefore, a motivational program was developed with the help of a consulting firm. Each month, employees in the department with the highest sales would have a chance to win a trip to Mexico. At the end of the year, the names of all employees in those departments that had the highest sales for at least one month would have their name entered into a draw and three names would be chosen to win a one-week trip to Mexico paid for by Mayfield.

1. According to need theories of motivation and goal setting theory, will this program be motivational? Explain your answer.

2. Discuss the motivational potential of the program according to expectancy theory and equity theory. Will the program motivate the sales staff and improve sales?

3. How would you change the program to make it more effective for motivating employees? Use expectancy theory and goal setting theory to explain how to improve the program.

CASE STUDY

DATATRONIC

DATATRONIC is a company started by George Pandry and Rolin Martin, two friends who had just graduated with degrees in business administration and saw an opportunity to start their own business. With an increasing number of organizations conducting employee attitude surveys, they saw a need for data input and analyses as well as for the design of web-based surveys. With a loan from their parents, they rented space, purchased 20 used computers, and set up shop. They hired some students they knew at the university and began advertising their services. Employees were paid minimum wage and usually worked three-hour shifts in the mornings and afternoons several days a week.

The assignment of projects to employees was fairly straightforward. Whenever a new project was accepted by DATATRONIC, Rolin would review the job and then set a deadline for completion based on the nature of the project and the customer's needs. While some employees only worked on web-based surveys, all employees were able to input data and conduct some basic data analyses. If a project required more advanced data analysis, it was assigned to one of a handful of employees who were able to do it. It was George's responsibility to check on the progress of projects and make sure they were completed by the deadline. Once a project was completed, Rolin would review it and check for mistakes and errors. If a project was found to have errors, Rolin would send it back to the employee who worked on it, with instructions on what needed to be corrected and the new deadline. If the corrections were minor, then the employee would be asked to do them immediately and put aside what he or she was currently working on. If the corrections were more substantial, then the employee's current project would be given to another employee so that the employee could work on the project that required corrections.

Within a relatively short period of time, DATATRONIC was having trouble keeping up with demand. In fact, business was so good they had to hire more employees and purchase more computers. After about six months, however, they began to notice some problems. An increasing number of projects were not being completed on time, and customers were beginning to complain. In some cases, George and Rolin had to give big discounts to customers who threatened to take their business elsewhere.

In order to try to deal with the increasing missed deadlines, George decided to keep a close eye on employees during their shifts. He soon came to the conclusion that many of them were friends and spent too much time chatting and socializing while they were supposed to be working.

After discussing the problem with Rolin, it was decided that the best thing to do was to keep a closer eye on employees while they worked. So the next day, George began watching employees and even standing over them while they worked. Whenever some of the employees began to talk with each other, George rushed over to remind them that they were there to work and not to talk. Some of the employees were surprised at this sudden change and didn't understand what the problem was. George told them that too many projects were not being completed on time and that talking would no longer be tolerated while employees are working. "You get paid for working here, not socializing and talking to your friends," George was often heard saying. "Stop talking and get back to work."

By the end of the month, however, things still had not improved. While the employees were no longer talking to each other when George was watching over them, many projects were still not being completed on time. George and Rolin decided that they should focus on those employees who were the main source of the problem. After reviewing the records of all employees, they made a list showing the number of projects each employee had completed on time as well as the number that were late. They then posted the list on a large board at the front of the office room. Employees were told that from now on, George and Rolin would be keeping track of how many employees' projects were completed on time and that they would fire people who were late completing more than one project a month.

This did not sit well with the employees. Many of them complained that it was unfair to blame them for being late because some projects were much more demanding than others and the deadlines were often unreasonable. However, George and Rolin insisted that the deadlines were based on the size and difficultly of the projects.

Many of the students relied on the extra money they made from DATATRONIC to pay for their books, supplies, and the occasional dinner or night out, so being fired was a concern to them. Within a few weeks, almost all projects were being completed on time. George and Rolin concluded that their latest strategy was working, and the list of employees at the front of the room was showing a marked increase in projects completed on time for all employees.

However, by the end of the month a new problem became apparent. Many of the completed data files were full of mistakes, the data analysis was often incomplete and incorrect, and the web-based surveys were often missing questions and contained all sorts of errors. As a result, almost 50 percent (15 jobs per month) of all jobs had to be completely redone. This turned out to be a rather costly problem. Each job took between 10 and 50 hours and cost DATATRONIC hundreds of dollars to fix. This also meant that projects were not being completed on time because they had to be redone and checked after the deadline. More and more customers began to complain and to demand a reduction in the cost of their projects.

To make matters worse, some of the best employees decided to quit. Over a period of three months, DATA-TRONIC lost an average of three employees a month. Every time an employee quit, they had to replace him or her, and the cost of replacement was beginning to be a problem. The cost of advertising, interviewing, and hiring a new employee was estimated to be about $5000.

While employees were at one time bringing their friends to DATATRONIC, this was no longer enough to fill all the jobs. As a result, it became increasingly difficult to find and hire new workers. In desperation, George and Rolin decided to increase the pay to new hires to above minimum wage. This, however, did not sit well with current employees, some of whom had been with DATATRONIC since it first began. Some of DATATRONIC's experienced employees threatened to quit if they did not receive a pay increase. George and Rolin did not see how they could increase the pay of all their current employees. However, they realized that something had to be done—and fast.

They came up with a three-pronged approach. First, they decided to give those employees who were threatening to quit a pay increase equal to what new hires were receiving. Second, they decided to offer a $100 bonus at the end of every month to the employee who performed best on completion time and quality. The employee with the most projects completed with the fewest errors would receive the bonus. And third, they decided that employees who turned in projects with substantial errors would be required to correct them on their own time, without pay.

When the employees heard about these changes they became less cooperative with each other and less willing to offer help and assistance. Before the announcement, although employees engaged in less socializing during working hours, they maintained a friendly and collegial atmosphere, with workers frequently asking each other for help and providing assistance to new hires. However, with the new bonus program and the possibility of having to correct errors without pay, this was no longer the case. Employees not only stopped talking to each other, they also stopped helping each other. This was especially hard on the new hires, who often needed help and advice from the more experienced employees.

At the end of the first month under the new bonus program, George and Rolin called a meeting and told the employees that Mika Salomn had completed three projects and had made only one error. She happily accepted her bonus cheque for $100 and was congratulated for her excellent performance. Some of the other employees clapped and congratulated her, but others seemed less enthused. Nonetheless, the number of mistakes and projects that had to be returned to workers for corrections began to decline.

George and Rolin felt that they had finally found the solution to solving the problems at DATATRONIC. However, by the end of the week, three other employees began demanding a pay increase and several others complained that they should have received the bonus because their performance was just as good as Mika's. To make matters worse, three new hires and two of DATATRONIC's most experienced employees decided to quit.

George and Rolin couldn't understand how something so good had become so bad. They wondered whether they should give all employees a pay increase equal to the new hires. Or maybe they need to do something about the bonus program. They were at a loss as to what to do next and wondered if maybe it was time to start a new business.

1. What factors do you think contribute to the performance of the employees at DATATRONIC? Refer to Exhibit 5.1 to explain your answer.

2. Consider the needs of the employees at DATATRONIC. What is most likely to motivate them? How important are intrinsic and extrinsic motivators? Is their motivation autonomous or controlled?

3. Discuss the motivational strategies being used at DATATRONIC. What are employees motivated to do? How do the theories of motivation help us understand employees' motivation and performance and the effectiveness of motivational strategies?

4. Using the theories of motivation, what advice would you give George and Rolin on how to motivate employees at DATATRONIC? Be sure to refer to the need theories and the process theories of motivation.

5. What would you do to motivate DATATRONIC employees? Be specific in terms of how to motivate them using the motivation theories to complete projects on time without errors and to stay at DATATRONIC.

Motivation in Practice

WestJet Airlines

On February 29, 1996, with 220 employees and three aircraft, Calgary-based WestJet Airlines began operations, charging only $118 for a return fare to Vancouver while the major airlines were charging up to $600. In its first 10 months of operation, the debt-free airline brought in $37.2 million in revenues while operating only three aircraft between Calgary, Vancouver, Kelowna, Winnipeg, and Edmonton. By 1998, revenues had grown to $125.8 million, more western Canadian cities were added, the number of employees had doubled, and earnings grew from $870 000 to $6.5 million. WestJet was making money while its big competitors continued to record huge losses. In fact, the company has consistently ranked as one of the most profitable airlines in North America. And since its initial public offering of 2.5 million common shares in 1999, its share price has increased more than 240 percent. Company revenues grew by 27 percent between 2005 and 2006, and full-year revenue rose nearly 20 percent in 2008 to a record $2.5 billion and a profit of $178.1 million.

In addition to its discount fares and low-cost operation, WestJet is known for how it motivates its employees. The company aligns employees' interests with the interests of the company through a number of programs that make everyone at WestJet an owner. For example, WestJet has a generous profit-sharing plan that is designed to encourage everyone to maximize profits. Employees share in profits that are equivalent to the company's profit margin, up to 20 percent. So if the airline's profit margin is 10 percent, then 10 percent of the net income is spread among employees (prorated to salary). Profit Sharing Day is held twice a year, at which time cheques are handed out to employees. The company has handed out more than $8 million on such days, with an average cheque amount of $9000. WestJet has paid out more than $130 million in proft sharing to its employees since 1996.

WestJet also has an employee stock ownership plan. Employees are encouraged to buy shares in the company, and for every $1 a worker invests, the company matches it. Employees can also choose to receive

WestJet uses a number of motivational practices that align the interests of employees with those of the organization, including profit sharing, employee stock ownership plans, and alternative working schedules.

up to 20 percent of their salary in shares, which the company also matches 100 percent. More than 80 percent of the airline's employees are shareholders, and many of the original employees who invested in the company before it went public now have generous portfolios. In fact, some of WestJet's flight attendants have more than $400 000 in stock, and some of its pilots are millionaires.

WestJet employees also have a great deal of freedom and autonomy in how they perform their jobs. A pillar of the company's culture is that employees in direct contact with customers not only have a stake in the success of the company through profit sharing but also are openly encouraged to contribute ideas about how the airline is run. In addition, employees are given the freedom to make judgment calls when dealing directly with customers without having to check in with a supervisor. For example, call centre representatives have the authority to waive fees and override fares in certain circumstances. WestJet also offers employees alternative working schedules, including flexible scheduling, telecommuting, and shortened work weeks.

WestJet has become the most successful low-cost carrier in Canadian history and is one of Canada's top 100 employers and one of the most respected companies in Canada. In 2008, for the fourth consecutive year, WestJet was ranked as having one of the most admired corporate cultures in Canada and was chosen as one of Alberta's Top Employers for 2009. Perhaps it's not surprising that the company receives an average of 1200 to 1500 resumés every week![1]

Notice the motivational strategies that WestJet employs: a profit-sharing plan, an employee stock ownership plan, jobs that are designed to provide employees with freedom and autonomy, and alternative working schedules. In this chapter, we will discuss four motivational techniques: money, job design, Management by Objectives, and alternative working schedules. In each case, we will consider the practical problems that are involved in implementing these techniques. The chapter will conclude with a discussion of the factors that an organization needs to consider when choosing a motivational strategy.

Money as a Motivator

The money that employees receive in exchange for organizational membership is in reality a package made up of pay and various fringe benefits that have dollar values, such as insurance plans, sick leave, and vacation time. Here, we will be concerned with the motivational characteristics of pay itself.

So just how effective is pay as a motivator? How important is pay for you? Chances are you don't think pay is as important as it really is for you. In fact, employees and managers seriously underestimate the importance of pay as a motivator.[2] Yet the motivation theories described in Chapter 5 suggest that pay is, in fact, a very important motivator.

According to Maslow and Alderfer, pay should prove especially motivational to people who have strong lower-level needs. For these people, pay can be exchanged for food, shelter, and other necessities of life. However, suppose you receive a healthy pay raise. Doubtless, this raise will enable you to purchase food and shelter, but it might also give you prestige among friends and family, signal your competence as a worker, and demonstrate that your boss cares about you. Thus, using need hierarchy terminology, pay can also function to satisfy social, self-esteem, and self-actualization needs. If pay has this capacity to fulfill a variety of needs, then it should have especially good potential as a motivator. How can this potential be realized? Expectancy theory provides the clearest answer to this question. According to expectancy theory, if pay can satisfy a variety of needs, it should be highly valent, and it should be a good motivator to the extent that *it is clearly tied to performance*.

Research on pay and financial incentives is consistent with the predictions of need theory and expectancy theory. Financial incentives and pay-for-performance plans have been found to increase performance and lower turnover. Research not only supports the motivational effects of pay but also suggests that pay may well be the most important and effective motivator of performance. In general, the ability to earn money for outstanding performance is a competitive advantage for attracting, motivating, and retaining employees.[3] Let's now find out how to link pay to performance on production jobs.

Linking Pay to Performance on Production Jobs

The prototype of all schemes to link pay to performance on production jobs is piece-rate. In its pure form, **piece-rate** is set up so that individual workers are paid a certain sum of money for each unit of production they complete. For example, sewing machine operators might be paid two dollars for each dress stitched, or punch press operators might be paid a few cents for each piece of metal fabricated. More common than pure piece-rate is a system whereby workers are paid a basic hourly wage and paid a piece-rate differential on top of this hourly wage. For example, a forge operator might be paid 8 dollars an hour plus 30 cents for each unit he produces. In some cases, of course, it is very difficult to measure the productivity of an individual worker because of the nature of the production process. Under these circumstances, group incentives are sometimes employed. For example, workers in a steel mill might be paid an hourly wage and a monthly bonus for each ton of steel produced over some minimum quota. These various schemes to link pay to performance on production jobs are called **wage incentive plans**.

Piece-rate. A pay system in which individual workers are paid a certain sum of money for each unit of production completed.

Wage incentive plans. Various systems that link pay to performance on production jobs.

"Because of my ridiculously low pay per course,
I will only be able to give partial answers, vague suggestions,
and half-truths. Okay--let's get started . . . . "

Compared with straight hourly pay, the introduction of wage incentives usually leads to substantial increases in productivity.[4] One review reports a median productivity improvement of 30 percent following the installation of piece-rate pay, an increase not matched by goal setting or job enrichment.[5] Also, a study of 400 manufacturing companies found that those with wage incentive plans achieved 43 to 64 percent greater productivity than those without such plans.[6]

One of the best examples of the successful use of a wage incentive plan is the Lincoln Electric Company. Lincoln Electric is the world's largest producer of arc welding equipment, and it also makes electric motors. The company offers what some say are the best-paid factory jobs in the world. The company uses an intricate piece-rate pay plan that rewards workers for what they produce. The firm has turned a handsome profit every quarter for more than 50 years and has not laid off anyone for more than 40 years. Employee turnover is extremely low, and Lincoln workers are estimated to be roughly twice as productive as other manufacturing workers.[7] Other companies that use wage incentive plans include Steelcase, the Michigan manufacturer of office furniture, and Nucor, a steel producer. However, not as many organizations use wage incentives as we might expect. What accounts for this relatively low utilization of a motivational system that has proven results?[8]

Potential Problems with Wage Incentives

Despite their theoretical and practical attractiveness, wage incentives have some potential problems when they are not managed with care.

Wage incentive programs that link pay to performance on production jobs have been shown to improve employee productivity.

Lowered Quality. It is sometimes argued that wage incentives can increase productivity at the expense of quality. While this may be true in some cases, it does not require particular ingenuity to devise a system to monitor and maintain quality in manufacturing. However, the quality issue can be a problem when employers use incentives to motivate faster "people processing," such as conducting consumer interviews on the street or in stores. Here, quality control is more difficult.

Differential Opportunity. A threat to the establishment of wage incentives exists when workers have different opportunities to produce at a high level. If the supply of raw materials or the quality of production equipment varies from workplace to workplace, some workers will be at an unfair disadvantage under an incentive system. In expectancy theory terminology, workers will differ in the expectancy that they can produce at a high level.

Reduced Cooperation. Wage incentives that reward individual productivity might decrease cooperation among workers. For example, to maintain a high wage rate, machinists might hoard raw materials or refuse to engage in peripheral tasks, such as keeping the shop clean or unloading supplies.

Consider what happened when Solar Press, an Illinois printing and packaging company, installed a team wage incentive. It wasn't long before both managers and employees began to spot problems. Because of the pressure to produce, teams did not perform regular maintenance on the equipment, so machines broke down more often than before. When people found better or faster ways to do things, some hoarded them from fellow employees for fear of reducing the amount of their own payments. Others grumbled that work assignments were not fairly distributed, that some jobs demanded more work than others. They did, but the system did not take this into account.[9]

Incompatible Job Design. In some cases, the way jobs are designed can make it very difficult to implement wage incentives. On an assembly line, it is almost impossible to identify and reward individual contributions to productivity. As pointed out above, wage incentive systems can be designed to reward team productivity in such a circumstance. However, as the size of the team *increases*, the relationship between any individual's productivity and his or her pay *decreases*. For example, the impact of your productivity in a team of two is much greater than the impact of your productivity in a team of ten. As team size increases, the linkage between your performance and your pay is erased, removing the intended incentive effect.

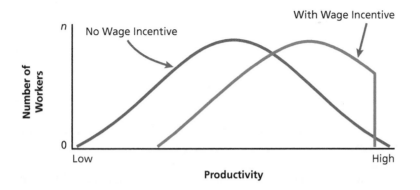

EXHIBIT 6.1
Hypothetical productivity
distributions, with and
without wage incentives,
when incentives promote
restriction.

Restriction of Productivity. A chief psychological impediment to the use of wage incentives is the tendency for workers to restrict productivity. This restriction is illustrated graphically in Exhibit 6.1. Under normal circumstances, without wage incentives, we can often expect productivity to be distributed in a "bell-shaped" manner—a few workers are especially low producers, a few are especially high producers, and most produce in the middle range. When wage incentives are introduced, however, workers sometimes come to an informal agreement about what constitutes a fair day's work and artificially limit their output accordingly. In many cases, this **restriction of productivity** can decrease the expected benefits of the incentive system, as in Exhibit 6.1.

Why does restriction often occur under wage incentive systems? Sometimes it happens because workers feel that increased productivity due to the incentive will lead to reductions in the workforce. More frequently, however, employees fear that if they produce at an especially high level, an employer will reduce the rate of payment to cut labour costs. In the early days of industrialization, when unions were non-existent or weak, this often happened. Engineers studied workers under normal circumstances, and management would set a payment rate for each unit of productivity. When management introduced the incentive system, workers employed legitimate shortcuts that they had learned on the job to produce at a higher rate than expected. In response to this, management simply changed the rate to require more output for a given amount of pay! Stories of such rate-cutting are often passed down from one generation of workers to another in support of restricting output under incentive systems. As you might expect, restriction seems less likely when a climate of trust and a history of good relations exist between employees and management.

> **Restriction of productivity.** The artificial limitation of work output that can occur under wage incentive plans.

Linking Pay to Performance on White-Collar Jobs

Compared to production jobs, white-collar jobs (including clerical, professional, and managerial) frequently offer fewer objective performance criteria to which pay can be tied. To be sure, company presidents are often paid annual bonuses that are tied to the profitability of the firm, and salespeople are frequently paid commissions on sales. However, trustworthy objective indicators of individual performance for the majority of white-collar jobs are often difficult to find. Thus, performance in many such jobs is evaluated by the subjective judgment of the performer's manager.

Attempts to link pay to performance on white-collar jobs are often called **merit pay plans.** Just as straight piece-rate is the prototype for most wage incentive plans, there is also a prototype for most merit pay plans: Periodically (usually yearly), managers are required to evaluate the performance of employees on some form of rating scale or by means of a written description of performance. Using these evaluations, the managers then recommend that some amount of merit pay be awarded to individuals over and above their basic salaries. This pay is usually incorporated into the subsequent year's salary cheques. Since the indicators of good performance on some white-collar jobs (especially managerial jobs) can be unclear or highly subjective, merit pay can provide an especially tangible signal that the organization considers an employee's performance "on track." Individuals who see a strong link between rewards and performance tend to

> **Merit pay plans.** Systems that attempt to link pay to performance on white-collar jobs.

perform better.[10] In addition, white-collar workers (especially managers) particularly support the notion that performance should be an important determinant of pay.[11]

Merit pay plans are employed with a much greater frequency than wage incentive plans and have become one of the most common forms of motivation in Canadian organizations.[12] In a tight labour market, merit pay is often used by organizations to attract and retain employees and as an alternative to wage increases.[13]

However, despite the fact that merit pay can stimulate effective performance, that substantial support exists for the idea of merit pay, and that most organizations claim to provide merit pay, it appears that many of these systems now in use are *ineffective*. In fact, a recent survey found that 83 percent of organizations with a pay-for-performance system said it was only somewhat successful or not working at all.[14] Many individuals who work under such plans do not perceive a link between their job performance and their pay. There is also evidence that pay is, in fact, *not* related to performance under some merit plans.[15] Adding more evidence of ineffectiveness are studies that track pay increases over time. For example, one study of managers showed that pay increases in a given year were often uncorrelated with pay increases in adjacent years.[16] From what we know about the consistency of human performance, such a result seems unlikely if organizations are truly tying pay to performance. In most organizations, seniority, the number of employees, and job level account for more variation in pay than performance does. Perhaps it is not surprising then that there has been an increasing number of disputes over unpaid or underpaid bonuses that are winding up in the courts.[17]

Potential Problems with Merit Pay Plans

As with wage incentive plans, merit pay plans have several potential problems if employers do not manage them carefully. Before continuing, read You Be the Manager: *Merit Pay at Toronto City Hall*.

Low Discrimination. One reason that many merit pay plans fail to achieve their intended effect is that managers might be unable or unwilling to discriminate between good performers and poor performers. In Chapter 3, we pointed out that subjective evaluations of performance can be difficult to make and are often distorted by a number of perceptual errors. In the absence of performance rating systems designed to control these problems, managers might feel that the only fair response is to rate most employees as equal performers. Effective rating systems are rarely employed. Surveys show consistent dissatisfaction with both giving and receiving performance evaluations.[18] Even when managers feel capable of clearly discriminating between good and poor performers, they might be reluctant to do so. If the performance evaluation system does not assist the manager in giving feedback about his or her decisions to employees, the equalization strategy might be employed to prevent conflicts with them or among them. If there are true performance differences among employees, equalization over-rewards poorer performers and under-rewards better performers.[19]

Small Increases. A second threat to the effectiveness of merit pay plans exists when merit increases are simply too small to be effective motivators. In this case, even if rewards are carefully tied to performance and managers do a good job of discriminating between more and less effective performers, the intended motivational effects of pay increases may not be realized. Ironically, some firms all but abandon merit when inflation soars or when they encounter economic difficulties. Just when high motivation is needed, the motivational impact of merit pay is removed. Sometimes a reasonable amount of merit pay is provided, but its motivational impact is reduced because it is spread out over a year or because the organization fails to communicate how much of a raise is for merit and how much is for cost of living.

To overcome this visibility problem, some firms have replaced conventional merit pay with a **lump sum bonus** that is paid out all at one time and not built into base pay.

Lump sum bonus. Merit pay that is awarded in a single payment and not built into base pay.

YOU BE THE MANAGER

Merit Pay at Toronto City Hall

Non-unionized employees at Toronto City Hall receive merit pay as part of their compensation package. The system pays a bonus of up to 3 percent to managers who meet agreed performance goals, on top of cost-of-living increases of up to 3.25 percent.

However, the city's merit pay system for non-unionized staff became an issue in 2009, when politicians led by Councillor Peter Milczyn urged the budget committee to cut the $8.5 million set aside for it.

The city's merit pay system has long been controversial. Critics have argued that a major flaw in the program is that most non-union city hall staff are eligible for it and most get it. In all, some 3000 employees are eligible, and city finance officials say about 90 percent of them get the maximum merit pay, which amounts to 3 percent of their salaries, while another 5 percent receive a 1 percent increase on top of the cost of living increases and raises for moving up the salary scale. The cost of all these hikes is $133 million, of which about $8.5 million is pure bonus.

Councillor Peter Milczyn has stated that the performance merit pay system is exorbitant. "It does not achieve the goals of truly rewarding those who perform exceptionally." He has argued that "unless you're doing something extraordinary for the city, you're already being paid a good wage with excellent benefits and a fabulous pension and job security. Why should we give you a bonus as well?" He is calling for the mayor to suspend the bonus system until meaningful reforms are introduced.

Toronto Mayor David Miller said he is reviewing the system of performance bonuses given to senior civil servants and considering using the savings to top up Toronto's depleted welfare services. A review of the management compensation program, particularly performance pay, is being conducted.

What do you think about the City of Toronto's merit pay system? What do you think the mayor should do? You be the manager.

Most non-union city hall employees receive the maximum amount of merit pay.

QUESTIONS

1. What do you think is wrong with the city's merit pay system? What should David Miller do about it?

2. If you were to change the city's merit pay system, what would you do to make it more effective?

To find out what David Miller wants to do, see The Manager's Notebook at the end of the chapter.

Sources: Vincent, D. (2009, February 20). Merit pay on mayor's chopping block: City's generous system long been controversial. *Toronto Star*, A3; Hanes, A. (2009, February 20). Miller reviews bonus system of senior staff: Acknowledges criticism of cash beyond salaries. *National Post*, A8; Vincent, D., Moloney, P., & Spears, J. (2009, April 8). Councillors freeze pay for others: City politicians under fire for eliminating staffers' cost-of-living while keeping their own. *Toronto Star*, GT2; Levy, S. (2008, December 23). Merit pay blues at City Hall. *Toronto Sun* (online), www.torontosun.com; Lewington, J. (2008, July 12). City wants tighter merit purse strings. *Globe and Mail*, A9; Lewington, J. (2009, March 24). Miller wants to freeze non-union salaries. *Globe and Mail*, A11.

Such bonuses have become a common method to motivate and retain employees at all levels of an organization. They get people's attention! However, with the recent financial crises along with government loans to struggling companies, executive compensation and bonuses have become a very contentious issue. In the United States, executive compensation is believed to be one of the reasons why many companies engaged in the kind of risky and unethical behaviour that helped trigger the financial crisis and a global recession. To find out more, see Ethical Focus: *Excessive Executive Bonuses*.

ETHICAL FOCUS

Excessive Executive Bonuses

Bonuses have long been recognized as part of executive compensation, with some executives receiving bonuses in the hundreds of thousands of dollars. But with the downturn in the global economy and the bailout of large corporations in both Canada and the United States, excessive bonuses have led to public outrage and raised concerns about fairness, equity, and ethics. As a result, executive bonuses have begun to receive increasing scrutiny.

The outrage over executive bonuses was particularly evident when it was discovered that the insurance company AIG Inc. paid out US$165 million in retention bonuses to its employees at the same time that it was accepting $5 billion in bailout funds from the US government. To make matters worse, some of the bonuses were paid to the traders and executives whose risky financial behaviour had caused AIG's near collapse. AIG's CEO Edward Liddy told a congressional hearing in Washington that he was concerned about the safety of AIG employees and has requested that employees voluntarily return at least half of their bonuses.

The outrage over executive bonuses has resulted in a number of actions by government and shareholders, who are demanding greater links between pay and performance. In the United States, a new compensation czar will set the salaries and bonuses of some of the top financiers and industrialists. Strict new pay rules for the largest recipients of government loans will prevent executives from receiving bonuses that exceed one-third of their annual salary, and bonuses will be deferred until after government loans have been repaid.

The United States is also considering "say-on-pay" legislation that will give shareholders more say on executive pay as shareholders have begun to demand a voice in determining executive pay policies. In Canada, Sun Life Financial Inc. is one of a handful of Canadian companies that have agreed to give shareholders an advisory vote on executive compensation. At BCE Inc., shareholders demanded that the board cut pay and bonuses for executives and directors and requested a "say-on-pay" vote on executive compensation.

It is generally believed that these actions will result in executive compensation practices that more tightly tie pay to performance, with a focus on the overall performance of the organization.

Sources: Kuhnhenn, J., & Raum, T. (2009, March 19). AIG chief wants half of bonuses back. *Toronto Star*, B1, B5; McFarland, J. (2009, March 12). Sun Life gives shareholders say on pay. *Globe and Mail*, B10; McFarland, J., & Avery S. (2009, April 2). How much is too much? *Globe and Mail*, B1, B4; McKenna, B. (2009, June 11). U.S. moves to curb executive pay. *Globe and Mail*, B1, B4; Dimma, W. (2009, June 22). Outrage abounds, but will it change anything? *Globe and Mail*, B2; (2009, February 22). City's merit pay has no merit. www.torontosun.com.

When merit pay makes up a substantial portion of the compensation package, management has to take extreme care to ensure that it ties the merit pay to performance criteria that truly benefit the organization. Otherwise, employees could be motivated to earn their yearly bonus at the expense of long-term organizational goals.

Pay Secrecy. A final threat to the effectiveness of merit pay plans is the extreme secrecy that surrounds salaries in most organizations. It has long been a principle of human resource management that salaries are confidential information, and management frequently implores employees who receive merit increases not to discuss these increases with their co-workers. Notice the implication of such secrecy for merit pay plans: Even if merit pay is administered fairly, is contingent on performance, and is generous, employees might remain ignorant of these facts because they have no way of comparing their own merit treatment with that of others. As a consequence, such secrecy might severely damage the motivational impact of a well-designed merit plan. Rather incredibly, many organizations fail to inform employees about the average raise received by those doing similar work.

Given this extreme secrecy, you might expect that employees would profess profound ignorance about the salaries of other organizational members. In fact, this is not true—in the absence of better information, employees are inclined to "invent" salaries for other members. Unfortunately, this invention seems to reduce both satisfaction and

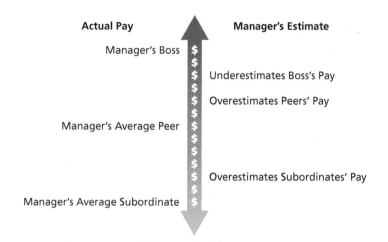

Actual Pay

Manager's Boss

Manager's Average Peer

Manager's Average Subordinate

Manager's Estimate

Underestimates Boss's Pay

Overestimates Peers' Pay

Overestimates Subordinates' Pay

EXHIBIT 6.2
A manager's estimates of pay earned by boss, peers, and subordinates.

motivation. Specifically, several studies have shown that managers have a tendency to overestimate the pay of their employees and their peers and to underestimate the pay of their superiors (see Exhibit 6.2).[20] In general, these tendencies will reduce satisfaction with pay, damage perceptions of the linkage between performance and rewards, and reduce the valence of promotion to a higher level of management.

An interesting experiment examined the effects of pay disclosure on the performance and satisfaction of pharmaceutical salespeople who operated under a merit pay system. At the time of a regularly scheduled district sales meeting, each of the 14 managers in the experimental group presented to his or her employees the new open salary administration program. The sales staff were given the individual low, overall average, and individual high merit raise amounts for the previous year. The raises ranged from no raise to $75 a month, with a company average of $43. Raises were classified according to district, region, and company increases in pay. Likewise, salary levels (low, average, and high) were given for sales staff on the basis of their years with the company (1 to 5; 5 to 10; 10 to 20; and more than 20 years). Specific individual names and base salaries were not disclosed to the sales staff. However, this information could be obtained from the supervisor. Each person's performance evaluation was also made available by the district manager for review by his or her other sales staff.[21]

After the pay disclosure was implemented, the sales staff in the experimental group revealed significant increases in performance and satisfaction with pay. However, since performance consisted of supervisory ratings, it is possible that supervisors felt pressured to give better ratings under the open pay system, in which their actions were open to scrutiny. This, of course, raises an important point. If performance evaluation systems are inadequate and poorly implemented, a more open pay policy will simply expose the inadequacy of the merit system and lead managers to evaluate performance in a manner that reduces conflict. Unfortunately, this might be why most organizations maintain relative secrecy concerning pay. One exception was the now defunct NeXT Computers, founded by Steve Jobs, which had a completely open salary system. Although many public and civil service jobs have open pay systems, most make little pretence of paying for performance.

Using Pay to Motivate Teamwork

Some of the dysfunctional aspects of wage incentives and merit pay stem from their highly individual orientations. People sometimes end up pursuing their own agendas (and pay) at the expense of the goals of their work group, department, or organization. As a result, some firms have either replaced or supplemented individual incentive pay with plans designed to foster more cooperation and teamwork.[22] Notice that each of the plans we discuss below has a somewhat different motivational focus. Organizations have to choose pay plans that support their strategic needs.

Profit Sharing. Profit sharing is one of the most commonly used group-oriented incentive systems and, as described at the beginning of the chapter, is a key component of WestJet's motivational system. In years in which the firm makes a profit, some of this is returned to employees in the form of a bonus, sometimes in cash and sometimes in a deferred retirement fund. Such money is surely welcome, and it may reinforce some identification with the organization. For example, at Apex Public Relations in Toronto, the company allocates 15 percent of its profit to all of its employees every year. Larsen & Shaw Ltd., a hinge-making company in Walkerton, Ontario, has a profit-sharing plan for its 100 employees. The company shares 11 percent of its pre-tax profits every December and June. The amount an employee receives is based on his or her years of service, base pay, and performance, which is evaluated twice a year.[23]

However, it is unlikely that profit sharing, as normally practised, is highly motivational. Its greatest problem is that too many factors beyond the control of the workforce (such as the general economy) can affect profits no matter how well people perform their jobs. Also, in a large firm, it is difficult to see the impact of one's own actions on profits.

Profit sharing seems to work best in smaller firms that regularly turn a handsome profit, like WestJet. The company is small and has consistently been profitable. For another example of a small company with a successful profit-sharing plan, see Applied Focus: *Profit Sharing at Coastal Pacific Xpress.*

Employee Stock Ownership Plans (ESOPs). In recent years, **employee stock ownership plans (ESOPs)** have also become a popular group-oriented incentive. These plans allow employees to own a set amount of the company's shares. Employees are often allowed to purchase shares at a fixed price, and some organizations, like WestJet, match employee contributions. ESOPs provide employees with a stake in a company's future earnings and success and help to create a sense of ownership. They also serve a number of other purposes, including attracting and retaining talent; motivating employee performance; focusing employee attention on organizational performance; creating a culture of ownership; educating employees about the business; and conserving cash by substituting options for cash.[24]

In Canada, many of the best companies to work for, including WestJet, offer stock options to a majority of their employees. For example, at the Royal Bank of Canada, 85 percent of employees are enrolled in a share ownership plan that matches 50 cents for every dollar an employee invests, up to 6 percent of his or her salary. At PCL Constructors in Edmonton, only employees are permitted to own company stocks. The company has realized a profit every year since 1977, when it became 100 percent employee owned.[25] Husky Injection Molding Systems Ltd. has a share-purchasing plan in which approximately 25 percent of the company's shares are held by employees. Employees at Husky can earn company shares by doing things that help the environment and community. At Hudson's Bay Company, employees receive $1 worth of company shares for every $6 they invest, an immediate return of 17 percent.[26]

Employee stock options are believed to increase employees' loyalty and motivation because they align employees' goals and interests with those of the organization and create a sense of legal and psychological ownership. There is some evidence that ESOPs can improve employee retention and profitability.[27] A study conducted by the Toronto Stock Exchange found that companies with employee stock ownership plans outperformed those that do not on a number of performance indicators, including profit growth, net profit margin, productivity, return on average total equity, and return on capital.[28]

However, like profit sharing, ESOPs work best in small organizations that regularly turn a profit. In larger organizations it is more difficult for employees to see the connection between their efforts and company profits because many factors can influence the value of a company's stock besides employee effort and performance. In addition, ESOPs lose their motivational potential in a weak economy when a company's share price goes down.

APPLIED FOCUS

Profit Sharing at Coastal Pacific Xpress

Coastal Pacific Xpress (CPX) is one of British Columbia's biggest trucking companies. The Surrey-based company began in 1986 with one truck and trailer and now has more than 300 trucks and 900 trailers, making it one of the fastest-growing temperature-controlled truckload carriers in British Columbia. The company operates throughout North America and serves major markets in Canada and the United States. It focuses on temperature-controlled and just-in-time overnight deliveries. Over the past five years, the company has grown by 500 percent.

This might not seem like such a big deal if it weren't for the fact that there is an alarming shortage of long-haul truck drivers in Canada and the United States. According to Statistics Canada, 18 percent of Canadian truck drivers are 55 or older (compared with 13 percent of the general workforce), making it one of the oldest workforces in the country. According to the Canadian Trucking Human Resources Council, the industry currently employs more than 500 000 people and needs to attract 30 000 to 45 000 new drivers annually. However, in recent years it has hired only between 5700 and 18 100.

Part of the problem is the relatively low pay, long hours, and extended periods on the road that keep young job seekers away from an occupation that is perceived as unattractive. But this doesn't seem to be a problem at CPX, whose guiding principle is employees come first, customers come second, and profits third.

What does it mean to put employees first? The owners say they set out to build a company that treats truck drivers with respect. According to co-owner Jim Mickey, "Our intention has always been to create a shared success, shared reward-type environment, one where the president isn't necessarily more valuable than a truck driver."

In August 2005, they put their money where their mouths are. They handed out bonus cheques totalling more than $400 000 to more than 400 employees. The owners intend to give out bonuses every year that the company makes a profit. "My goal is to do $1 million next year. I would love to have a BBQ and pass out double what we did this year," says Mickey. In August 2006, the company paid out more than $400 000 in profits to 475 employees and drivers in recognition of their role in helping the company generate revenue of $100 million for the fiscal year that ended May 31, 2006—a 41 percent ($71 million) increase over 2005!

The company's approach seems to be working. In an industry with an average turnover of 120 percent, CPX is doing far better, with only 20 percent turnover in 2006, down from 22 percent in 2005—one of the lowest in the industry. In 2008, CPX was ranked as one of B.C.'s Top Employers for the third consecutive year and recognized as one of the 50 Best Workplaces in Canada for the second consecutive year.

Sources: Klie, S. (2005, September 26). "Employees first" at CPX. *Canadian HR Reporter, 1*, 3; Galt, V. (2006, February 24). Better shifts, better training, better pay. *Globe and Mail*, C1; Hood, S.B. (2006, April 10–23). Truck stop: A shortage of long-haul drivers threatens to impede commerce. *Canadian Business, 79(8)*, 24; Anonymous. (2006, August 10). Breaking the rules: Hundreds of CPX o-o's see big raises from profit sharing program. *Today's Trucking* (online), www.todaystrucking.com/news.cfm?intDocID=16557&CFID=; www.cpx.ca.

Gainsharing. Gainsharing plans are group incentive plans that are based on improved productivity or performance over which the workforce has some control.[29] Such plans often include reductions in the cost of labour, material, or supplies. When measured costs decrease, the company pays a monthly bonus according to a predetermined formula that shares this "gain" between employees and the firm. For example, a plan installed by Canadian pulp and paper producer Fraser Papers rewards employees for low scrap and low steam usage during production. The plan sidesteps the cost of steam generation and the international price for paper, things over which the workforce lacks control.[30]

Gainsharing plans have usually been installed using committees that include extensive workforce participation. This builds trust and commitment to the formulas that are used to convert gains into bonuses. Also, most plans include all members of the work unit, including production people, managers, and support staff.

Gainsharing. A group pay incentive plan based on productivity or performance improvements over which the workforce has some control.

The most common gainsharing plan is the Scanlon Plan, developed by union leader Joe Scanlon in the 1930s.[31] The plan stresses participatory management and joint problem solving between employees and managers, but it also stresses using the pay system to reward employees for this cooperative behaviour. Thus, pay is used to align company and employee goals. The Scanlon Plan has been used successfully by many small, family-owned manufacturing firms. Also, in recent years, many large corporations (such as General Electric, Motorola, Carrier, and Dana) have installed Scanlon-like plans in some manufacturing plants.[32] The turnaround of the motorcycle producer Harley-Davidson is, in part, attributed to the institution of gainsharing.

In a study in a unionized auto parts manufacturing plant, a Scanlon gainsharing program was negotiated as part of a joint union–management effort to respond to economic downturns and competitive challenges in the auto industry. Management and the union were extensively involved in the development and implementation of the plan, which consisted of a formal employee suggestion program and a formula for determining the amount of total cost savings that was to be divided equally among plant employees. The plan had a positive effect on the number of suggestions provided by employees, and the cumulative number of suggestions implemented was associated with lower production costs.[33] In general, productivity improvements following the introduction of Scanlon-type plans support the motivational impact of this group wage incentive.[34] However, perception that the plan is fair is critical.[35]

Skill-Based Pay. The idea behind **skill-based pay** (also called pay for knowledge) is to motivate employees to learn a wide variety of work tasks, irrespective of the job that they might be doing at any given time. The more skills that are acquired, the higher the person's pay.[36] Companies use skill-based pay to encourage employee flexibility in task assignments and to give them a broader picture of the work process. It is especially useful on self-managed teams (Chapter 7), in which employees divide up the work as they see fit. It is also useful in flexible manufacturing, in which rapid changes in job demands can occur. Quebec's Bell Helicopter Textron plant uses skill-based pay for its aircraft assemblers to enhance their flexibility.

Training costs can be high with a skill-based pay system. Also, when the system is in place, it has to be used. Sometimes, managers want to keep employees on a task they are good at rather than letting them acquire new skills. However, skill-based programs can have positive consequences. A study on the effects of a skill-based pay system in a large organization that manufactures vehicle safety systems reported an increase in productivity, lower labour costs per part, and a reduction in scrap following implementation of a skill-based pay program.[37]

Skill-based pay. A system in which people are paid according to the number of job skills they have acquired.

At Quebec's Bell Helicopter Textron plant, skill-based pay encourages flexibility in the aircraft assemblers' work assignments and provides them with an overall picture of the work process.

PAY PLAN	DESCRIPTION	ADVANTAGES	DISADVANTAGES
Profit sharing	Employees receive a cash bonus based on organization profits	• Employees have a sense of ownership. • Aligns employee goals with organization goals. • Only pays when the organization makes a profit.	• Many factors beyond the control of employees can affect profits. • It is difficult for employees to see the impact of their actions on organization profits.
Employee stock ownership	Employees can own a set amount of the organization's shares.	• Creates a sense of legal and psychological ownership for employees. • Aligns employees' goals and interests with those of the organization.	• Many factors can influence the value of an organization's shares, regardless of employees' effort and performance. • It is difficult for employees to see the connection between their efforts and the value of their organization's stocks. • They lose their motivational potential in a weak economy when the value of an organization's stocks decline.
Gainsharing	When measured costs decrease, employees receive a bonus based on a predetermined formula.	• Aligns organization and employee goals. • Encourages teamwork and cooperative behaviour.	• Bonuses might be paid even when the organization does not make a profit. • Employees might neglect objectives that are not included in the formula.
Skill-based pay	Employees are paid according to the number of job skills they acquire.	• Encourages employees to learn new skills. • Greater flexibility in task assignments. • Provides employees with a broader picture of the work process.	• Increases the cost of training. • Labour costs can increase as employees acquire more skills.

EXHIBIT 6.3
Teamwork pay plans.

Exhibit 6.3 compares the various pay plans that organizations use to motivate teamwork. Research has found that group-based financial incentives can have a positive effect on the collective efforts of employees and business-unit outcomes.[38]

Job Design as a Motivator

If the use of money as a motivator is primarily an attempt to capitalize on extrinsic motivation, current approaches to using job design as a motivator represent an attempt to capitalize on intrinsic motivation. In essence, the goal of job design is to identify the characteristics that make some tasks more motivating than others and to capture these characteristics in the design of jobs. Although it is often believed that money is the primary work motivator, many workers are actually motivated more by stimulating, challenging, and meaningful work.[39] But how do you design jobs to make them more motivating? Let's begin with a review of traditional views of job design.

Traditional Views of Job Design

From the beginning of the Industrial Revolution until the 1960s, the prevailing philosophy regarding the design of most non-managerial jobs was job simplification. The historical roots of job simplification are found in social, economic, and technological forces that existed even before the Industrial Revolution. This preindustrial period was characterized by increasing urbanization and the growth of a free market economy, which prompted a demand for manufactured goods. Thus, a division of labour within society occurred, and specialized industrial concerns using newly developed machinery emerged to meet this demand. With complex machinery and an uneducated, untrained workforce, these organizations recognized that *specialization* was the key to efficient productivity. If the production of an object could be broken down into very basic, simple steps, even an uneducated and minimally trained worker could contribute his or her share by mastering one of these steps.

The zenith of job simplification occurred in the early 1900s, when industrial engineer Frederick Winslow Taylor presented the industrial community with his principles of Scientific Management.[40] From Chapter 1, you will recall that Taylor advocated extreme division of labour and specialization, even extending to the specialization of supervisors in roles such as trainer, disciplinarian, and so on. Also, he advocated careful standardization and regulation of work activities and rest pauses. Intuitively, jobs designed according to the principles of scientific management do not seem intrinsically motivating. The motivational strategies that management used during this period consisted of close supervision and the use of piece-rate pay. But it would do a disservice to history to conclude that job simplification was unwelcomed by workers, who were mostly non-unionized, uneducated, and fighting to fulfill their basic needs. Such simplification helped them to achieve a reasonable standard of living. However, with a better-educated workforce whose basic needs are fairly well met, behavioural scientists have begun to question the impact of job simplification on performance, customer satisfaction, and the quality of working life.

Job Scope and Motivation

Job scope can be defined as the breadth and depth of a job.[41] **Breadth** refers to the number of different activities performed on the job, while **depth** refers to the degree of discretion or control the worker has over how these tasks are performed. "Broad" jobs require workers to *do* a number of different tasks, while "deep" jobs emphasize freedom in *planning* how to do the work.

As shown in Exhibit 6.4, jobs that have great breadth and depth are called high-scope jobs. A professor's job is a good example of a high-scope job. It is broad because it involves the performance of a number of different tasks, such as teaching, grading, doing research, writing, and participating in committees. It is also deep because there is considerable discretion in how academics perform these tasks. In general, professors have a fair amount of freedom to choose a particular teaching style, grading format, and research area. Similarly, management jobs are high-scope jobs. Managers perform a wide variety of activities (supervision, training, performance evaluation, report writing) and have some discretion over how they accomplish these activities.

Job scope. The breadth and depth of a job.

Breadth. The number of different activities performed on a job.

Depth. The degree of discretion or control a worker has over how work tasks are performed.

EXHIBIT 6.4
Job scope as a function of job depth and job breadth.

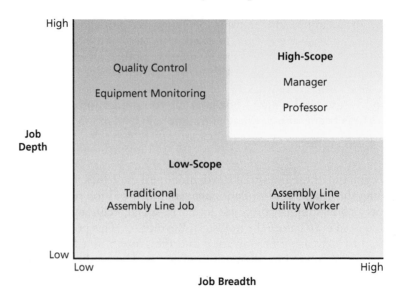

The classic example of a low-scope job is the traditional assembly line job. This job is both "shallow" and "narrow" in the sense that a single task (such as bolting on car wheels) is performed repetitively and ritually, with no discretion as to method. Traditional views of job design were attempts to construct low-scope jobs in which workers specialized in a single task.

Occasionally, we encounter jobs that have high breadth but little depth, or vice versa. For motivational purposes, we can also consider these jobs to be relatively low in scope. For example, a utility worker on an assembly line fills in for absent workers on various parts of the line. While this job involves the performance of a number of tasks, it involves little discretion as to when or how the worker performs the tasks. On the other hand, some jobs involve a fair amount of discretion over a single, narrowly defined task. For example, quality control inspectors perform a single, repetitive task, but they might be required to exercise a fair degree of judgment in performing this task. Similarly, workers who monitor the performance of equipment (such as in a nuclear power plant) might perform a single task but again be required to exercise considerable discretion when a problem arises.

The motivational theories we discussed in the previous chapter suggest that high-scope jobs (*both* broad and deep) should provide more intrinsic motivation than low-scope jobs. Maslow's need hierarchy and ERG theory both seem to indicate that people can fulfill higher-order needs by the opportunity to perform high-scope jobs. Expectancy theory suggests that high-scope jobs can provide intrinsic motivation if the outcomes derived from such jobs are attractive.

One way to increase the scope of a job is to assign employees *stretch assignments*, something that many organizations have begun to do. Stretch assignments offer employees challenging opportunities to broaden their skills by working on a variety of tasks with new responsibilities. Oakville, Ontario–based Javelin Technologies Inc., which develops design and engineering software for the manufacturing industry, uses stretch assignments as a way to keep employees interested and challenged in their positions.[42]

Another approach for increasing the scope of an individual's job is **job rotation**, which involves rotating employees to different tasks and jobs in an organization. This often involves working in different functional areas and departments. Job rotation is used by many companies, such as Bell Canada, Telus Corp., and Pitney Bowes, and it has been increasing in popularity. Each year, Pitney Bowes Canada assigns five or six new recruits two years in job rotation. In addition to providing employees with a variety of

Job rotation. Rotating employees to different tasks and jobs in an organization.

In his classic film *Modern Times*, Charlie Chaplin performed a typical low-scope job working on an assembly line.

challenging assignments, job rotation is also effective for developing new skills and expertise that can prepare employees for future roles.[43] In the next section, we discuss a model of how to design high-scope jobs.

The Job Characteristics Model

The concept of job scope provides an easy-to-understand introduction to why some jobs seem more intrinsically motivating than others. However, we can find a more rigorous delineation of the motivational properties of jobs in the Job Characteristics Model that J. Richard Hackman and Greg Oldham developed (Exhibit 6.5).[44] As you can observe, the Job Characteristics Model proposes that there are several "core" job characteristics that have a certain psychological impact on workers. In turn, the psychological states induced by the nature of the job lead to certain outcomes that are relevant to the worker and the organization. Finally, several other factors (moderators) influence the extent to which these relationships hold true.

Core Job Characteristics. The Job Characteristics Model shows that there are five core job characteristics that have particularly strong potential to affect worker motivation: skill variety, task identity, task significance, autonomy, and job feedback. In general, higher levels of these characteristics should lead to the favourable outcomes shown in Exhibit 6.5. Notice that **skill variety**, the opportunity to do a variety of job activities using various skills and talents, corresponds fairly closely to the notion of job breadth we discussed earlier. **Autonomy**, the freedom to schedule one's own work activities and decide work procedures, corresponds to job depth. However, Hackman and Oldham recognized that one could have a high degree of control over a variety of skills that were perceived as meaningless or fragmented. Thus, the concepts of task significance and task identity were introduced. **Task significance** is the impact that a job has on others. **Task identity** is the extent to which a job involves doing a complete piece of work, from beginning to end. In addition, they recognized that

Skill variety. The opportunity to do a variety of job activities using various skills and talents.

Autonomy. The freedom to schedule one's own work activities and decide work procedures.

Task significance. The impact that a job has on other people.

Task identity. The extent to which a job involves doing a complete piece of work, from beginning to end.

EXHIBIT 6.5
The Job Characteristics Model.

Source: J. Richard Hackman & Greg R. Oldham, Work Redesign (Prentice Hall Organizational Development Series), 1st Ed. © 1980. Reproduced by Pearson Education, Inc., Upper Saddle River, NJ. Electronically reproduced by permission of Pearson Education, Inc., Upper Saddle River, NJ.

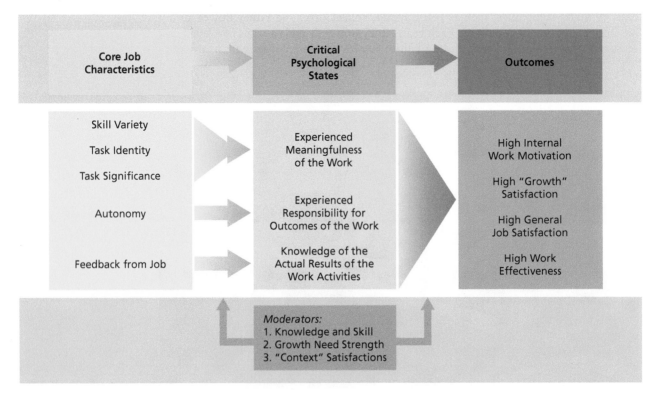

1. Skill variety
   High variety: The owner-operator of a garage who does electrical repair, rebuilds engines, does body work, and interacts with customers.
   Low variety: A body shop worker who sprays paint eight hours a day.

2. Task identity
   High identity: A cabinet maker who designs a piece of furniture, selects the wood, builds the object, and finishes it to perfection.
   Low identity: A worker in a furniture factory who operates a lathe solely to make table legs.

3. Task significance
   High significance: Nursing the sick in a hospital intensive care unit.
   Low significance: Sweeping hospital floors.

4. Autonomy
   High autonomy: A telephone installer who schedules his or her own work for the day, makes visits without supervision, and decides on the most effective techniques for a particular installation.
   Low autonomy: A telephone operator who must handle calls as they come according to a routine, highly specified procedure.

5. Job feedback
   High feedback: An electronics factory worker who assembles a radio and then tests it to determine if it operates properly.
   Low feedback: An electronics factory worker who assembles a radio and then routes it to a quality control inspector who tests it for proper operation and makes needed adjustments.

EXHIBIT 6.6
Core job characteristics examples.

feedback, information about one's performance effectiveness, is also essential for high intrinsic motivation. People are not motivated for long if they do not know how well they are doing. High and low levels of each of the core job characteristics are described in Exhibit 6.6.

Hackman and Oldham developed a questionnaire called the Job Diagnostic Survey (JDS) to measure the core characteristics of jobs. The JDS requires job holders to report the amount of the various core characteristics contained in their jobs. From these reports, we can construct profiles to compare the motivational properties of various jobs. For example, consider the JDS profiles for lower-level managers in a utility company (collected by one of the authors of this text) and those for keypunchers in another firm (reported by Hackman and Oldham). While the managers perform a full range of managerial duties, the keypunchers perform a highly regulated job—anonymous work from various departments is assigned to them by a supervisor, and their output is verified for accuracy by others. Not surprisingly, the JDS profiles reveal that the managerial jobs are consistently higher on the core characteristics than are the keypunching jobs.

According to Hackman and Oldham, an overall measure of the motivating potential of a job can be calculated by the following formula:

$$\text{Motivating potential score} = \frac{\text{Skill variety} + \text{Task identity} + \text{Task significance}}{3} \times \text{Autonomy} \times \text{Job feedback}$$

Since the JDS measures the job characteristics on seven-point scales, a motivating potential score could theoretically range from 1 to 343. For example, the motivating potential score for the keypunchers' jobs is 20, while that for the managers' jobs is 159. Thus, the managers are more likely than the keypunchers to be motivated by the job itself. The average motivating potential score for 6930 employees on 876 jobs has been calculated at 128.[45]

Feedback. Information about the effectiveness of one's work performance.

Critical Psychological States. Why are jobs that are higher on the core characteristics more intrinsically motivating? What is their psychological impact? Hackman and Oldham argue that work will be intrinsically motivating when it is perceived as meaningful, when the worker feels responsible for the outcomes of the work, and when the worker has knowledge about his or her work progress. As shown in Exhibit 6.5, the Job Characteristics Model proposes that the core job characteristics affect meaningfulness, responsibility, and knowledge of results in a systematic manner. When an individual uses a variety of skills to do a "whole" job that is perceived as significant to others, he or she perceives the work as meaningful. When a person has autonomy to organize and perform the job as he or she sees fit, the person feels personally responsible for the outcome of the work. Finally, when the job provides feedback about performance, the worker will have knowledge of the results of this opportunity to exercise responsibility.

Outcomes. The presence of the critical psychological states leads to a number of outcomes that are relevant to both the individual and the organization. Chief among these is high intrinsic motivation. When the worker is truly in control of a challenging job that provides good feedback about performance, the key prerequisites for intrinsic motivation are present. The relationship between the work and the worker is emphasized, and the worker is able to draw motivation from the job itself. This will result in high-quality productivity. By the same token, workers will report satisfaction with higher-order needs (growth needs) and general satisfaction with the job itself. This should lead to reduced absenteeism and turnover.

Moderators. Hackman and Oldham recognize that jobs that are high in motivating potential do not always lead to favourable outcomes. Thus, as shown in Exhibit 6.5, they propose certain moderator or contingency variables (Chapter 1) that intervene between job characteristics and outcomes. One of these is the job-relevant knowledge and skill of the worker. Put simply, workers with weak knowledge and skills should not respond favourably to jobs that are high in motivating potential, since such jobs will prove too demanding. Another proposed moderator is **growth need strength**, which refers to the extent to which people desire to achieve higher-order need satisfaction by performing their jobs. Hackman and Oldham argue that those with high growth needs should be most responsive to challenging work. Finally, they argue that workers who are dissatisfied with the context factors surrounding the job (such as pay, supervision, and company policy) will be less responsive to challenging work than those who are reasonably satisfied with context factors.

Growth need strength. The extent to which people desire to achieve higher-order need satisfaction by performing their jobs.

Research Evidence. In tests of the Job Characteristics Model, researchers usually require workers to describe their jobs by means of the JDS and then measure their reactions to these jobs. Although there is some discrepancy regarding the relative importance of the various core characteristics, these tests have generally been very supportive of the basic prediction of the model—workers tend to respond more favourably to jobs that are higher in motivating potential.[46]

A recent review of research on the Job Characteristics Model found that all five core job characteristics were positively related to the outcomes in the model (i.e., job satisfaction, growth satisfaction, internal work motivation) as well as other outcomes, including supervisor satisfaction, co-worker satisfaction, compensation satisfaction, promotion satisfaction, organizational commitment, and job involvement. In addition, some of the core job characteristics (e.g., autonomy and feedback from the job) were also related to behavioural (e.g, absenteeism, performance) and well-being (e.g., anxiety, stress) outcomes. With respect to the critical psychological states, there was strong support for the role of experienced meaningfulness of the work but less support for experienced responsibility and no support for the role of knowledge of results. These results suggest that experienced meaningfulness is the most critical psychological state.[47] Where the model seems to falter is in its predictions about growth needs and context satisfaction. Evidence that these factors influence reactions to job design is weak or contradictory.[48]

Job Enrichment

Job enrichment is the design of jobs to enhance intrinsic motivation, the quality of working life, and job involvement. **Job involvement** refers to a cognitive state of psychological identification with one's job and the importance of work to one's total self-image. Employees who have challenging and enriched jobs tend to have higher levels of job involvement. In fact, all of the core job characteristics have been found to be positively related to job involvement. Employees who are more involved in their job have higher job satisfaction and organizational commitment and are less likely to consider leaving their organization.[49]

WestJet is a good example of the benefits of job enrichment. As indicated in the chapter opening vignette, WestJet employees have a high degree of latitude in how they perform their jobs, without interference from supervisors. They also have the freedom to make decisions about what they do and how they do it. This helps to explain the high degree of job involvement and positive job attitudes among WestJet employees as well as the company's low rate of turnover.

In general, job enrichment involves increasing the motivating potential of jobs via the arrangement of their core characteristics. There are no hard and fast rules for the enrichment of jobs. Specific enrichment procedures depend on a careful diagnosis of the work to be accomplished, the available technology, and the organizational context in which enrichment is to take place. However, many job enrichment schemes combine tasks, establish client relationships, reduce supervision, form teams, or make feedback more direct.[50]

- *Combining tasks.* This involves assigning tasks that might be performed by different workers to a single individual. For example, in a furniture factory a lathe operator, an assembler, a sander, and a stainer might become four "chair makers"; each worker would then do all four tasks. Such a strategy should increase the variety of skills employed and might contribute to task identity as each worker approaches doing a unified job from start to finish.

- *Establishing external client relationships.* This involves putting employees in touch with people outside the organization who depend on their products or services. An example of this might be to give line workers letters from customers who have problems with service or a product.[51] Such a strategy might involve the use of new (interpersonal) skills, increase the identity and significance of the job, and increase feedback about one's performance.

- *Establishing internal client relationships.* This involves putting employees in touch with people who depend on their products or services within the organization. For example, billers and expediters in a manufacturing firm might be assigned permanently to certain salespeople, rather than working on any salesperson's order as it comes in. The advantages are similar to those mentioned for establishing external client relationships.

- *Reducing supervision or reliance on others.* The goal here is to increase autonomy and control over one's own work. For example, management might permit clerical employees to check their own work for errors instead of having someone else do it. Similarly, firms might allow workers to order needed supplies or contract for outside services up to some dollar amount without obtaining permission. As indicated earlier, the lack of interference from supervisors at WestJet is a good example of this job enrichment technique.

- *Forming work teams.* Management can use this format as an alternative to a sequence of "small" jobs that individual workers perform when a product or service is too large or complex for one person to complete alone. For example, social workers who have particular skills might operate as a true team to assist a particular client, rather than passing the client from person to person. Similarly, stable teams can form to construct an entire product, such as a car or boat, in lieu of an

Job enrichment. The design of jobs to enhance intrinsic motivation, quality of working life, and job involvement.

Job involvement. A cognitive state of psychological identification with one's job and the importance of work to one's total self-image.

assembly line approach. Such approaches should lead to the formal and informal development of a variety of skills and increase the identity of the job.

- *Making feedback more direct.* This technique is usually used in conjunction with other job design aspects that permit workers to be identified with their "own" product or service. For example, an electronics firm might have assemblers "sign" their output on a tag that includes an address and toll-free phone number. If a customer encounters problems, he or she contacts the assembler directly. In Sweden, workers who build trucks by team assembly are responsible for service and warranty work on "their" trucks that are sold locally.

Potential Problems with Job Enrichment

Despite the theoretical attractiveness of job enrichment as a motivational strategy, and despite the fact that many organizations have experimented with such programs, enrichment can encounter a number of challenging problems.

Poor Diagnosis. Problems with job enrichment can occur when it is instituted without a careful diagnosis of the needs of the organization and the particular jobs in question. Some enrichment attempts might be half-hearted tactical exercises that really do not increase the motivating potential of the job adequately. An especially likely error here is increasing job breadth by giving employees more tasks to perform at the same level while leaving the other crucial core characteristics unchanged—a practice known as **job enlargement**. Thus, workers are simply given *more* boring, fragmented, routine tasks to do, such as bolting intake manifolds and water pumps onto engines. On the other side of the coin, in their zeal to use enrichment as a cure-all, organizations might attempt to enrich jobs that are already perceived as too rich by their incumbents (some refer to this as *job engorgement!*).[52] This has happened in some "downsized" firms in which the remaining employees have been assigned too many extra responsibilities. Rather than increasing motivation, this can lead to role overload and work stress.

Job enlargement. Increasing job breadth by giving employees more tasks at the same level to perform but leaving other core characteristics unchanged.

Lack of Desire or Skill. Put simply, some workers do not *desire* enriched jobs. Almost by definition, enrichment places greater demands on workers, and some might not relish this extra responsibility. Even when people have no basic objections to enrichment in theory, they might lack the skills and competence necessary to perform enriched jobs effectively. Thus, for some poorly educated or trained workforces, enrichment might entail substantial training costs. In addition, it might be difficult to train some workers in certain skills required by enriched jobs, such as social skills.

Demand for Rewards. Occasionally, workers who experience job enrichment ask that greater extrinsic rewards, such as pay, accompany their redesigned jobs. Most frequently, this desire is probably prompted by the fact that such jobs require the development of new skills and entail greater responsibility. Sometimes such requests are motivated by the wish to share in the financial benefits of a successful enrichment exercise. In one documented case, workers with radically enriched jobs in a General Foods dog food plant in Topeka, Kansas, sought a financial bonus based on the system's success.[53] Equity in action!

Union Resistance. Traditionally, North American unions have not been enthusiastic about job enrichment. In part, this is due to a historical focus on negotiating with management about easily quantified extrinsic motivators, such as money, rather than the soft stuff of job design. Also, unions have tended to equate the narrow division of labour with preserving jobs for their members. Faced with global competition, the need for flexibility, and the need for employee initiative to foster quality, companies and unions have begun to dismantle restrictive contract provisions regarding job design.

Fewer job classifications mean more opportunities for flexibility by combining tasks and using team approaches.

Supervisory Resistance. Even when enrichment schemes are carefully implemented to truly enhance the motivating potential of deserving jobs, they might fail because of their unanticipated impact on other jobs or other parts of the organizational system. A key problem here concerns the supervisors of the workers whose jobs have been enriched. By definition, enrichment increases the autonomy of employees. Unfortunately, such a change might "disenrich" the boss's job, a consequence that will hardly facilitate the smooth implementation of the job redesign. Some organizations have responded to this problem by effectively doing away with direct supervision of workers performing enriched jobs. Others use the supervisor as a trainer and developer of individuals in enriched jobs. Enrichment can increase the need for this supervisory function.

Recent Developments in Job Design: Work Design

Although the Job Characteristics Model and job enrichment have received the most attention and are considered to be the most dominant theoretical models of job design, they have been criticized for being too narrow in that they focus on a limited number of motivational job characteristics. In recent years, more comprehensive models of job design have been developed that go beyond the core job characteristics and include other important aspects of work design, such as social and contextual characteristics.

Based on a review of the literature, Frederick Morgeson and Stephen Humphrey developed a work design model (they use the term "*work* design" as opposed to "*job* design" because it acknowledges both the job and the broader work environment) that consists of a wider variety of work design characteristics. **Work design characteristics** refer to the attributes of the task, job, and social and organizational environment and consist of three categories: motivational characteristics, social characteristics, and work context characteristics. The motivational characteristics category includes *task characteristics,* which are similar to the core job characteristics of the Job Characteristics Model (autonomy, task variety, task significance, task identity, and feedback from the job), as well as *knowledge characteristics* that refer to the kinds of knowledge, skill, and ability demands required to perform a job. Note that they make a distinction between task variety and skill variety in that task variety involves the degree to which a job requires employees to perform a wide range of tasks on the job, while skill variety reflects the extent to which a job requires an individual to use a variety of different skills to perform a job.

Social characteristics have to do with the interpersonal and social aspects of work and include social support, interdependence, interaction outside of the organization, and feedback from others. *Work context characteristics* refer to the context within which work is performed and consist of ergonomics, physical demands, work conditions, and equipment use. See Exhibit 6.7 for more detail on the work design characteristics.

Morgeson and Humphrey developed a scale called the Work Design Questionnaire (WDQ) to measure the work design characteristics, and it is currently the most comprehensive measure of work design available. The scale can be used for research purposes and as a diagnostic tool to assess the motivational properties of jobs prior to work redesign.

Although much less research has been conducted on the knowledge, social, and work context characteristics than the task characteristics, research has found that they are also related to work attitudes and behaviours. In fact, the social characteristics are even more strongly related to some outcomes (i.e., turnover intentions, organizational commitment) than the motivational characteristics. Thus, knowledge, social, and work context characteristics represent an important addition to the study of work design. Overall, the results of a recent review of work design research indicate that work design characteristics have a large and significant effect on employee attitudes and behaviours.[54]

Work design characteristics. Attributes of the task, job, and social and organizational environment.

EXHIBIT 6.7
Work Design
Characteristics.

Source: Morgeson, F.P., & Humphrey,
S.E. (2006). The work design questionnaire (WDQ): Developing and
validating a comprehensive measure
for assessing job design and the
nature of work, *Journal of Applied
Psychology, 91*, 1321–1339;
Humphrey, S.E. Nahrgang, J.D., &
Morgeson, F.P. (2007). Integrating
motivational, social, and contextual
work design features: A meta-analytic
summary and theoretical extension of
the work design literature. *Journal of
Applied Psychology, 92*, 1332–1356.
Copyright © 2006, 2007 by the
American Psychological Association.
Reproduced with permission.

Task Characteristics. How the work itself is accomplished and the range and nature of tasks associated with a particular job.
  a. *Autonomy*. The extent to which a job allows freedom, independence, and discretion to schedule work, make decisions, and choose the methods used to perform tasks.
  b. *Task variety*. The degree to which a job requires employees to perform a wide range of tasks on the job.
  c. *Task significance*. The degree to which a job infuences the lives of others, whether inside or outside the organization.
  d. *Task identity*. The degree to which a job involves a whole piece of work, the results of which can be easily identified.
  e. *Feedback from job*. The degree to which the job provides direct and clear information about the effectiveness of task performance.

Knowledge Characteristics. The kinds of knowledge, skill, and ability demands that are placed on an individual as a function of what is done on the job.
  a. *Job complexity*. The extent to which the tasks on a job are complex and difficult to perform.
  b. *Information processing*. The degree to which a job requires attending to and processing data or other information.
  c. *Problem solving*. The degree to which a job requires unique ideas or solutions and reflects the more active cognitive processing requirements of a job.
  d. *Skill variety*. The extent to which a job requires an individual to use a variety of different skills to complete the work.
  e. *Specialization*. The extent to which a job involves performing specialized tasks or possessing specialized knowledge and skill.

Social Characteristics. The interpersonal and social aspects of work.
  a. *Social support*. The degree to which a job provides opportunities for advice and assistance from others.
  b. *Interdependence*. The degree to which the job depends on others and others depend on it to complete the work.
  c. *Interaction outside the organization*. The extent to which the job requires employees to interact and communicate with individuals external to the organization.
  d. *Feedback from others*. The extent to which others (e.g., coworkers and supervisors) in the organization provide information about performance.

Contextual Characteristics. The context within which work is performed including the physical and environmental contexts.
  a. *Ergonomics*. The degree to which a job allows correct or appropriate posture and movement.
  b. *Physical demands*. The amount of physical activity or effort required on the job.
  c. *Work conditions*. The environment within which a job is performed (e.g., the presence of health hazards, noise, temperature, and cleanliness of the working environment).
  d. *Equipment use*. The variety and complexity of the technology and equipment used in a job.

Management by Objectives

**Management by
Objectives (MBO).** An
elaborate, systematic,
ongoing program designed
to facilitate goal establishment, goal accomplish-
ment, and employee
development.

In Chapter 5, we discussed goal setting theory, which states that a specific, challenging goal can be established to solve a particular performance problem. **Management by Objectives (MBO)** is an elaborate, systematic, ongoing management program designed to facilitate goal establishment, goal accomplishment, and employee development.[55] The concept was developed by management theorist Peter Drucker. The objectives in MBO are simply another label for goals. In a well-designed MBO program, objectives for the organization as a whole are developed by top management and diffused down through the organization through the MBO process. In this manner, organizational objectives are translated into specific behavioural objectives for individual members. Our primary focus here is with the nature of the interaction between managers and individual workers in an MBO program.

Although there are many variations on the MBO theme, most manager–employee interactions share the following similarities:

1. The manager meets with individual workers to develop and agree on employee objectives for the coming months. These objectives usually involve both current job performance and personal development that may prepare the worker to perform other tasks or seek promotion. The objectives are made as specific as possible and quantified, if feasible, to assist in subsequent evaluation of accomplishment. Time frames for accomplishment are specified, and the objectives may be given priority according to their agreed importance. The methods to achieve the objectives may or may not be topics of discussion. Objectives, time frames, and priorities are put in writing.

2. There are periodic meetings to monitor employee progress in achieving objectives. During these meetings, people can modify objectives if new needs or problems are encountered.

3. An appraisal meeting is held to evaluate the extent to which the agreed upon objectives have been achieved. Special emphasis is placed on diagnosing the reasons for success or failure so that the meeting serves as a learning experience for both parties.

4. The MBO cycle is repeated.

Over the years, a wide variety of organizations have implemented MBO programs. At Hewlett-Packard, MBO, and metrics to measure progress, was the cornerstone of the company's management philosophy for nearly six decades.[56] At Toronto-based pharmaceutical firm Janssen-Ortho Inc., each employee's goals are tied to a list of corporate objectives. Employees can earn a yearly bonus of up to 20 percent if they and the company meet their goals.[57]

Research Evidence. Overall, the research evidence shows that MBO programs result in clear productivity gains.[58] However, a number of factors are associated with the failure of MBO programs. For one thing, MBO is an elaborate, difficult, time-consuming process, and its implementation must have the full commitment of top management. One careful review showed a 56 percent average gain in productivity for programs with high top management commitment, and a 6 percent gain for those with low commitment.[59] If such commitment is absent, managers at lower levels simply go through the motions of practising MBO. At the very least, this reaction will lead to the haphazard specification of objectives and thus subvert the very core of MBO—goal setting. A frequent symptom of this degeneration is the complaint that MBO is "just a bunch of paperwork."[60] Indeed, at this stage, it is!

Even with the best of intentions, setting specific, quantifiable objectives can be a difficult process. This might lead to an overemphasis on measurable objectives at the expense of more qualitative objectives. For example, it might be much easier to agree on production goals than on goals that involve employee development, although both might be equally important. Also, excessive short-term orientation can be a problem with MBO. Finally, even if reasonable objectives are established, MBO can still be subverted if the performance review becomes an exercise in browbeating or punishing employees for failure to achieve objectives.[61]

Alternative Working Schedules as Motivators for a Diverse Workforce

Most Canadians work a five-day week of approximately 40 hours—the "nine-to-five grind." However, many organizations, like WestJet, have modified these traditional working schedules. The purpose of these modifications is not to motivate people to work harder and thus produce direct performance benefits. Rather, the purpose is to meet diverse workforce needs and promote job satisfaction. In turn, this should facilitate recruiting the best personnel and reduce costly absenteeism and turnover. For example, realizing that the traditional banking approach of rigid schedules and inattention to employee's personal preferences was driving staff away and compromising customer service, the Royal Bank of Canada made some major changes to its human resources policies. As a result, the bank now offers its employees flexible work hours, compressed workweeks, job sharing, telecommuting, and other innovative work arrangements. These changes appear to be paying off. Employees are happier, more customers are giving the bank their business, and the bank has been ranked as the most respected company in Canada.[62]

Flex-Time

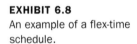

Flex-time. An alternative work schedule in which arrival and departure times are flexible.

One alternative to traditional working schedules is **flex-time**, which was first introduced on a large scale in Europe. In its most simple and common form, management requires employees to report for work on each working day and work a given number of hours. However, the times at which they arrive and leave are flexible, as long as they are present during certain core times. For example, companies might permit employees to begin their day anytime after 7 a.m. and work until 6 p.m., as long as they put in eight hours and are present during the core times of 9:15 a.m. until noon and 2:00 p.m. until 4:15 p.m. (Exhibit 6.8). Other systems permit employees to tally hours on a weekly or monthly basis, although they are still usually required to be present during the core time of each working day.[63]

Flex-time is obviously well suited to meeting the needs of a diverse workforce since it allows employees to tailor arrival and departure times to their own transportation and childcare situations. It should reduce absenteeism, since employees can handle personal matters during conventional business hours.[64] Also, flexible working hours signal a degree of prestige and trust that is usually reserved for executives and professionals.

When jobs are highly interdependent, such as on an assembly line, flex-time becomes an unlikely strategy. To cite an even more extreme example, we simply cannot have members of a hospital operating room team showing up for work whenever it suits them! In addition, flex-time might lead to problems in achieving adequate supervisory

EXHIBIT 6.8
An example of a flex-time schedule.

Source: Adapted from Ronen, S. (1981). *Flexible working hours: An innovation in the quality of work life.* New York: McGraw-Hill, p. 42. Reprinted by permission of the author.

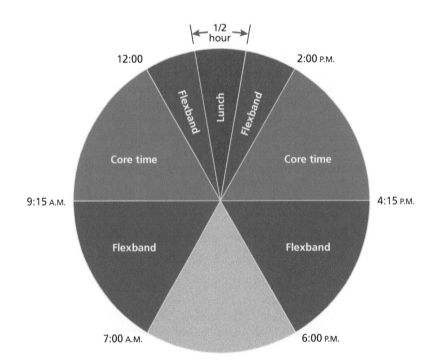

"... AM I INTERESTED IN AN ALTERNATIVE WORK ARRANGEMENT?,... YES,... I'D LIKE TO TELECOMMUTE FROM A COMPUTER EQUIPPED HOT TUB ON FLEX TIME..."

coverage. For these reasons, not surprisingly, flex-time is most frequently implemented in office environments. For instance, in a bank, the core hours might be when the bank is open to the public.

Although flex-time has generally been limited to white-collar personnel, it has been applied in a variety of organizations, including insurance companies (ING Insurance), financial institutions (RBC), and government offices (many Canadian and American civil service positions). According to one survey, 66 percent of organizations offered flexible work schedules.[65]

Research Evidence. We can draw a number of conclusions from the research on flex-time.[66] First, employees who work under flex-time almost always prefer the system to fixed hours. In addition, work attitudes generally become more positive, and employers report minimal abuse of the arrangement. When measured, absenteeism and tardiness have often shown decreases following the introduction of flex-time, and first-line supervisors and managers are usually positively inclined toward the system. Interestingly, slight productivity gains are often reported under flex-time, probably due to better use of scarce resources or equipment rather than to increased motivation. A review of research on flex-time concluded that it has a positive effect on productivity, job satisfaction, and satisfaction with work schedule, and that it lowers employee absenteeism.[67]

Compressed Workweek

A second alternative to traditional working schedules is the **compressed workweek**. This system compresses the hours worked each week into fewer days. The most common compressed workweek is the 4–40 system, in which employees work four 10-hour days each week rather than the traditional five 8-hour days. Thus, the organization or department might operate Monday through Thursday or Tuesday through Friday, although rotation schemes that keep the organization open five days a week are also employed.[68]

Like flex-time, the shorter workweek might be expected to reduce absenteeism because employees can pursue personal business or family matters in what had been working time. In addition, the 4–40 schedule reduces commuting costs and time by 20 percent and provides an extra day a week for leisure or family pursuits. Although the longer

Compressed workweek. An alternative work schedule in which employees work fewer than the normal five days a week but still put in a normal number of hours per week.

workday could pose a problem for single parents, a working couple with staggered off-days could actually provide their own childcare on two of five "working" days.

Technical roadblocks to the implementation of the 4–40 workweek include the possibility of reduced customer service and the negative effects of fatigue that can accompany longer working days. The latter problem is likely to be especially acute when the work is strenuous.

Research Evidence. Although research on the effects of the four-day week is less extensive than that for flex-time, a couple of conclusions do stand out.[69] First, people who have experienced the four-day system seem to *like* it. Sometimes this liking is accompanied by increased job satisfaction, but the effect might be short-lived.[70] In many cases, the impact of the compressed workweek might be better for family life than for worklife. Second, workers have often reported an increase in fatigue following the introduction of the compressed week. This might be responsible for the uneven impact of the system on absenteeism, sometimes decreasing it and sometimes not. Potential gains in attendance might be nullified as workers take an occasional day off to recuperate from fatigue.[71] Finally, the more sophisticated research studies do not report lasting changes in productivity due to the shortened workweek.[72] According to a review of research on the compressed workweek, there is a positive effect on job satisfaction and satisfaction with work schedule, but no effect on absenteeism or productivity.[73]

Job and Work Sharing

Job sharing occurs when two part-time employees divide the work (and perhaps the benefits) of a full-time job.[74] The two can share all aspects of the job equally, or some kind of complementary arrangement can occur in which one party does some tasks and the co-holder does other tasks.

Job sharing is obviously attractive to people who want to spend more time with small children or sick elders than a conventional five-day-a-week routine permits. By the same token, it can enable organizations to attract or retain highly capable employees who might otherwise decide against full-time employment.

Work sharing involves reducing the number of hours employees work to avoid layoffs when there is a reduction in normal business activity. The Government of Canada has a work-sharing program that is designed to help employers and workers avoid temporary layoffs. For example, NORDX/CDT, a Montreal-based firm that makes cables used in fibre-optic networks, introduced a work sharing program to cut costs while keeping workers employed. The program reduces the workweek by one to three days for some employees over a short-term period; 272 employees work one day less per week. Employees receive employment-insurance benefits for the days they are not working, up to 55 percent of their salary.

Many companies all across Canada implemented work sharing programs to save jobs and avoid layoffs during the recent recession. For example, Rogers Communications gave full-time staff the opportunity to reduce their workweek and accept a 20 percent pay cut in order to avoid layoffs to 20 percent of its staff. Buhler Industries Inc. of Winnipeg implemented a three-day workweek for its 200 employees instead of letting 90 workers go or shutting down its tractor-manufacturing plant for four months. In British Columbia, Photon Control Inc. saved 10 jobs by implementing a four-day workweek when its revenues declined, saving the company about $17 000 a month without having to downsize. Work sharing not only cuts costs, saves jobs, and avoids layoffs, but it allows organizations to retain highly skilled workers so they can quickly rebound when the economy and business improves.[75]

Research Evidence. There is virtually no hard research on job and work sharing. However, anecdotal reports suggest that the job sharers must make a concerted effort to communicate well with each other and with superiors, co-workers, and clients. Such

Job sharing. An alternative work schedule in which two part-time employees divide the work of a full-time job.

Work sharing. Reducing the number of hours employees work to avoid layoffs when there is a reduction in normal business activity.

communication is greatly facilitated by contemporary computer technology and voice mail. However, job sharing can result in coordination problems if communication is not adequate. Also, problems with performance appraisal can occur when two individuals share one job.

Telecommuting

In recent years, an increasing number of organizations have begun to offer employees telecommuting, or what is sometimes called telework. By **telecommuting**, employees are able to work at home but stay in touch with their offices through the use of communications technology, such as a computer network, voice mail, and electronic messages.[76] Like the other types of alternative working arrangements, telecommuting provides workers with greater flexibility in their work schedules.

Many companies first began implementing telecommuting in response to employee requests for more flexible work arrangements.[77] With the growth in communication technologies, however, other factors have also influenced the spread of telecommuting. For example, telecommuting is changing the way that organizations' recruit and hire people. When telecommuting is an option, companies can hire the best person for a job, regardless of where they live in the world, through *distant staffing*.[78] Distant staffing enables employees to work for a company without ever having to come into the office or even be in the same country!

Telecommuting has grown considerably over the last few years, and demand is expected to continue to grow in the coming years. It is estimated that approximately 11 million North Americans are telecommuting and that 51 percent of North American companies offer some form of telecommuting, including one in four Fortune 1000 companies. In Canada, it has been estimated that more than 1.5 million Canadians are telecommuting.[79]

An interesting trend in telecommuting that has started to appear in the United States and Canada is telework centres that provide workers all of the amenities of a home office in a location close to their home. Related to this is the emergence of *distributed work programs*, which involve a combination of remote work arrangements that allow employees to work at their business office, a satellite office, and a home office. At Bell Canada, all employees are eligible to participate in the company's distributed work

Telecommuting. A system by which employees are able to work at home but stay in touch with their offices through the use of communications technology, such as a computer network, voice mail, and electronic messages.

program. Employees can choose to work from home all of the time, or they can work a few days a week at one of Bell's satellite offices. More than 2000 of its 42 000 workers in Canada telecommute, either from home or from one of 13 satellite offices.[80]

Research Evidence. Telecommuting has often been touted as having benefits to organizations and individuals. For example, organizations stand to benefit from lower costs as a result of a reduction in turnover and need for office space and equipment, and they can attract employees who see it as a desirable benefit. For individuals, it has been suggested that telecommuting can improve work–life balance and increase productivity.[81] But does telecommuting deliver on these benefits? A recent review of research on telecommuting found that telecommuting has small but positive effects on perceived autonomy and lower work–family conflict. It also has a positive effect on job satisfaction and job performance and results in lower stress and turnover intentions. Telecommuting was found to have no detrimental effect on the quality of workplace relationships or one's career prospects. In addition, a greater frequency of telecommuting (more than 2.5 days a week) was associated with a greater reduction in work–family conflict and stress. The authors found that the positive effects of telecommuting were mostly due to an increase in perceived autonomy. In other words, one of the reasons that telecommuting has positive effects on attitudes and behaviours is because it increases employees' perceptions of autonomy.[82]

Negative aspects of telecommuting can result from damage to informal communication. These include decreased visibility when promotions are considered, problems in handling rush projects, and workload spillover for non-telecommuters. And more frequent telecommuting has a negative effect on relationships with co-workers.[83] Other potential problems include distractions in the home environment, feelings of isolation, and overwork. In addition, telecommuting may not be appropriate in organizations where customers are frequently at the office or where co-workers need to constantly collaborate on rush projects. Nor is telecommuting appropriate for all employees.[84]

Despite the benefits and the growing popularity of telecommuting, many companies are hesitant to implement telecommuting programs because of concerns about trust and control and worries that employees will not be as productive. Many managers are uncomfortable with the prospect of not being able to keep an eye on their employees while they work.[85] Therefore, it is important that there is a strong perception of trust between employees and management before an organization implements a telecommuting program and that the program is preceded by careful planning and accompanied by clear guidelines to govern the arrangement.

Motivation Practices in Perspective

As we have illustrated in this chapter, organizations have a lot of options when it comes to motivating their employees. Confused about what they should do? The concepts of *fit* and *balance* can help resolve this confusion. First, the motivational systems chosen should have a good fit with the strategic goals of the organization. Ultimately, employee attraction and retention and the speed, quality, and volume of output involve some tradeoffs, and an organization will not be able to achieve all of these outcomes with one motivational strategy. Second, balance among the components of a motivational system is critical. Job design and work schedules must allow employees to achieve the goals that are set, and the incentive system needs to be directed toward this achievement.

As we indicated in Chapter 1, there are no simple formulas to improve employee attitudes and performance, nor is there a set of laws of organizational behaviour that can be used to solve organizational problems. Like all of organizational behaviour, when it comes to employee motivation, there is no "cookbook" to follow. Thus, while many of the best companies to work for in Canada use the motivational practices described in this chapter, this does not mean that these practices will always be effective or that other organizations should follow suit. Clearly, the motivational practices used by the best companies are effective because they *fit* in to and are part of a larger organizational culture and system of management practices. For example, the motivational practices of WestJet described at the beginning of the chapter are part of an organizational culture that fosters a family atmosphere, employee ownership, and an objective to maximize profits.

The choice of motivational practices requires a thorough diagnosis of the organization as well as a consideration of employee needs. The most effective approach will depend on a combination of factors, including employee needs (e.g., money, challenging work), the nature of the job (e.g., individual, group work), characteristics of the organization (e.g., strategy, culture), and the outcome that an organization wants to achieve (e.g., diversity, learning). Ultimately, motivational systems that make use of a variety of motivators—such as performance-based pay and job enrichment—used in conjunction with one another are likely to be most effective.[86]

THE MANAGER'S NOTEBOOK

Merit Pay at Toronto City Hall

1. There are a number of problems with the merit pay program at Toronto City Hall. For starters, almost everybody eligible for merit not only receives it but also gets the maximum permitted. This of course suggests that merit pay is not tied to performance. A related issue is that there are probably some limitations of the performance review process that are failing to discriminate levels of performance. Managers are either unable or unwilling to discriminate between good performers and poor performers. As a result, most employees are rated as equal performers. Thus, the system over-rewards poor performers and under-rewards the best performers. All this suggests that the merit pay system is not having the intended motivational effects and, like most merit pay systems, is ineffective. According to Toronto Mayor David Miller, if he has his way, merit pay for senior staff will get the axe. "We're looking at not having that kind of performance pay, just the standard," Miller said. "I would anticipate that we will be changing the pay structure of senior civil servants this year; whether that's in time for the budget or not, I can't make a commitment to," he told reporters. "But it will have an impact on the way people are paid, particularly the performance bonus." However, the city's last attempt to cap merit pay resulted in a lawsuit. In 2004, the city tried to reduce the merit pay bonus from 3 percent to 1 percent but lost the case in arbitration.

2. In order for the City of Toronto's merit pay program to be effective, it must be tied to performance. There must be a rigorous performance evaluation system in place that allows and requires managers to discriminate between good and poor performers. The system must clearly indicate the criteria for merit pay, and it should be given only to those employees who meet or exceed the criteria. As stated by Councillor Doug Holyday, who is a member of the employee and labour relations committee, the system should be revamped for everyone, not just senior management, and merit pay should go only to exceptional employees. Giving it to everybody makes a mockery of the concept, according to Holyday. Councillor Peter Milczyn said that merit pay should be awarded only for "extraordinary achievement," such as a project that saves the city money. In February 2008, Mayor Miller's blue ribbon panel suggested that the merit pay system be reformed; it should not be "automatic," and increases should be in line with the general labour market. In April 2009, councillors on the city's executive committee agreed to eliminate cost-of-living and merit increases for non-union city staff. A possible revamp of the merit pay system for non-union employees would not take effect until 2011.

LEARNING OBJECTIVES CHECKLIST

1. Money should be most effective as a motivator when it is made contingent on performance. Schemes to link pay to performance on production jobs are called *wage incentive plans. Piece-rate*, in which workers are paid a certain amount of money for each item produced, is the prototype of all wage incentive plans. In general, wage incentives increase productivity, but their introduction can be accompanied by a number of problems, one of which is the restriction of production.

2. Attempts to link pay to performance on white-collar jobs are called *merit pay plans*. Evidence suggests that many merit pay plans are less effective than they could be because merit pay is inadequate, performance ratings are mistrusted, or extreme secrecy about pay levels prevails.

3. Compensation plans to enhance teamwork include *profit sharing, employee stock ownership, gainsharing,* and *skill-based pay*. Each of these plans has a different motivational focus, so organizations must choose a plan that supports their strategic needs.

4. Recent views advocate increasing the scope (breadth and depth) of jobs to capitalize on their inherent motivational properties, as opposed to the job simplification of the past. The *Job Characteristics Model*, developed by Hackman and Oldham, suggests that jobs have five core characteristics that affect their motivating potential: *skill variety, task identity, task significance, autonomy,* and *feedback*. When jobs are high in these characteristics, favourable motivational and attitudinal consequences should result.

5. Job enrichment involves designing jobs to enhance intrinsic motivation, job involvement, and the quality of working life. Some specific enrichment techniques include combining tasks, establishing client relationships, reducing supervision and reliance on others, forming work teams, and making feedback more direct.

6. In recent years, more comprehensive models of job design have been developed that go beyond the core job characteristics and include other important work design characteristics. *Work design characteristics* refer to the attributes of the task, job, and social and organizational environment.

7. *Management by Objectives (MBO)* is an elaborate goal-setting and evaluation process that organizations typically use for management jobs. Objectives for the organization as a whole are developed by top management and diffused down through the organization and translated into specific behavioural objectives for individual members.

8. Some organizations have adopted alternative working schedules, such as *flex-time, compressed workweeks, job and work sharing,* or *telecommuting*, with expectations of motivational benefits. These schemes have the potential to reduce absenteeism and turnover and to enhance the quality of working life for a diverse workforce.

9. Organizations need to conduct a diagnostic evaluation to determine the motivational practice that will be most effective. This requires a consideration of employee needs, the nature of the job, organizational characteristics, and the outcome that is of most concern to the organization.

DISCUSSION QUESTIONS

1. Describe some jobs for which you think it would be difficult to link pay to performance. What is it about these jobs that provokes this difficulty?

2. Why do you think employees and managers seriously underestimate the importance of pay as a motivator? What are the implications of this for organizations' use of pay to motivate employees? What are the consequences?

3. Imagine two insurance companies that have merit pay plans for salaried, white-collar personnel. In one organization, the plan truly rewards good performers, while in the other it does not. Both companies decide to make

salaries completely public. What will be the consequences of such a change for each company? (Be specific, using concepts such as expectancy, instrumentality, job satisfaction, and turnover.)

4. You are, of course, familiar with the annual lists of the world's 10 worst-dressed people or 10 worst movies. Here's a new one: A job enrichment consultant has developed a list of the 10 worst jobs, which includes a highway toll collector, roofer, bank guard, garbage collector, and elevator operator. Use the five core job characteristics to describe each of these jobs. Could you enrich any of these jobs? How? Which should be completely automated? Can you add some jobs to the list?

5. What are the essential distinctions between gainsharing, profit sharing, and employee stock ownership? How effective is each pay plan, and what are the advantages and disadvantages?

6. Some observers have argued that the jobs of the prime minister of Canada and the president of the United States are "too big" for one person to perform adequately. This probably means that the jobs are perceived as having too much scope or being too enriched. Use the Job Characteristics Model to explore the accuracy of this observation.

7. Imagine an office setting in which a change to a four-day workweek, flex-time, or telecommuting would appear to be equally feasible to introduce. What would be the pros and cons of each system? How would factors such as the nature of the business, the age of the workforce, and the average commuting distance affect the choice of systems?

8. How is the concept of workforce diversity related to the motivational techniques discussed in the chapter?

9. Although an increasing number of organizations are offering their employees the opportunity to telecommute, many employees who have tried it don't like it and prefer to be in the workplace. Why do you think some employees do not want to telecommute and some have even returned to the workplace after trying it? What can organizations do to ensure that employees' telecommuting experiences are successful?

10. Refer to the work design characteristics in Exhibit 6.7. What work design characteristics are most important for you and why? If you were to redesign the job you currently hold or a job you have previously held, what work design characteristics would you change?

INTEGRATIVE DISCUSSION QUESTIONS

1. Merit pay plans often require that managers conduct performance evaluations of their employees to determine the amount of merit pay to be awarded. Discuss some of the perceptual problems and biases described in Chapter 3 that could create problems for a merit pay plan. What can be done to improve performance evaluations and the success of merit pay plans?

2. Using each of the motivation theories described in Chapter 5, explain how job design and job enrichment can be motivational.

According to each theory, when is job design and job enrichment most likely to be effective for motivating workers?

3. In Chapter 2, employee recognition programs were discussed as an organizational learning practice. Using the material presented in this chapter, describe the potential for employee recognition programs as a motivational practice. What aspects of employee recognition programs might be especially important for a motivational program?

ON-THE-JOB CHALLENGE QUESTION

In the summer of 2009, civic workers in Toronto walked off the job, leaving Toronto residents without garbage collection, city-run daycare, swimming pools, and a wide range of other services after a legal strike was called by the city's 24 000 unionized workers. The workers accused the city of dragging its feet, while the city cited budget pressure. One of the most contentious issues was a sick leave plan that allows city employees to bank up to 18 sick days a year and, after at least 10 years of service, cash them out at half their value on retirement. The maximum paid out to those with at least 25 years of service is six months. The union was determined to protect the 18 sick days a year, while the city was asking for concessions on sick days and was looking to replace the benefit with a "short-term disability plan." The city claimed that it cannot afford the retirement pay-out given the economic situation. The union claimed that the city was using the recession as an excuse to rip their agreement to pieces.

Comment on the motivational effects of the sick days plan. What does it motivate employees to do? What does it not motivate them to do? If you were to change the sick days plan, how would you change it and why? Do you think sick plans that allow employees to cash banked sick days are an effective way to motivate employees?

Sources: Contenta, S. (2009, July 5). Right to banked sick days a waning trend in Ontario; Striking workers face "tough" battle in effort to keep benefit that's been mostly faded out in last 20 years. *Toronto Star*, A8; Wente, M. (2009, July 16). Someone will have to pay for a two-tier job system, and it's not the tooth fairy. *Globe and Mail*, A17; Lewington, J. (2009, June 22). Garbage strike is here after talks break down. *Globe and Mail*, A1; Blaze Carlson, K. (2009, June 22). Unions, City hit breaking point: Toronto strike appears imminent despite assurances of "good progress." *National Post*, A1.

EXPERIENTIAL EXERCISE

Task Characteristics Scale

How would you describe your job? The questions below are from the Work Design Questionnaire (WDQ). They provide you the opportunity to evaluate the task characteristics of the job you currently hold or one you have held in the past. For each question, indicate the extent to which you agree or disagree. Alternatively, you can use this scale to assess your task characteristics preferences by replacing the beginning of each question with "I would like a job that allows me to . . ."

Use the following response scale when answering each question.

1–Strongly disagree   4–Agree

2–Disagree   5–Strongly agree

3–Neither disagree nor agree

____ 1. The job allows me to make my own decisions about how to schedule my work.

____ 2. The job allows me to decide on the order in which things are done on the job.

____ 3. The job allows me to plan how I do my work.

____ 4. The job gives me a chance to use my personal initiative or judgment in carrying out the work.

____ 5. The job allows me to make a lot of decisions on my own.

____ 6. The job provides me with significant autonomy in making decisions.

____ 7. The job allows me to make decisions about what methods I use to complete my work.

____ 8. The job gives me considerable opportunity for independence and freedom in how I do the work.

____ 9. The job allows me to decide on my own how to go about doing my work.

____ 10. The job involves a great deal of task variety.

____ 11. The job involves doing a number of different things.

____ 12. The job requires the performance of a wide range of tasks.

____ 13. The job involves performing a variety of tasks.

____ 14. The results of my work are likely to significantly affect the lives of other people.

____ 15. The job itself is very significant and important in the broader scheme of things.

____ 16. The job has a large impact on people outside the organization.

____ 17. The work performed on the job has a significant impact on people outside the organization.

____ 18. The job involves completing a piece of work that has an obvious beginning and end.

____ 19. The job is arranged so that I can do an entire piece of work from beginning to end.

____ 20. The job provides me the chance to completely finish the pieces of work I begin.

____ 21. The job allows me to complete work I start.

____ 22. The work activities themselves provide direct and clear information about the effectiveness (e.g., quality and quantity) of my job performance.

____ 23. The job itself provides feedback on my performance.

____ 24. The job itself provides me with information about my performance.

Scoring and Interpretation

You have just completed the task characteristics scales of the Work Design Questionnaire (WDQ). A study of a sample of 540 individuals who had at least 10 years of full-time work experience resulted in the following mean scores for each task characteristic (scores range from 1 to 5; note that there are three different scales for autonomy: work scheduling autonomy, decision-making autonomy, and work methods autonomy):

Work scheduling autonomy:	3.93
Decision-making autonomy:	4.12
Work methods autonomy:	3.99
Task variety:	4.13
Task significance:	3.95
Task identity:	3.61
Feedback from the job:	3.91

To obtain your score on each task characteristic, calculate your scores as shown below. Note that your scores can range from 1 to 5, with higher scores indicating a great amount of the task characteristic in your job (or in the case of preferences, a greater preference for the task characteristic).

Work scheduling autonomy: Add items 1, 2, and 3 and divide by three.

Decision-making autonomy: Add items 4, 5, and 6 and divide by three.

Work methods autonomy: Add items 7, 8, and 9 and divide by three.

(Note that you can obtain an overall score of autonomy by adding your score for questions 1 to 9 and dividing by nine).

Task variety: Add items 10, 11, 12, and 13 and divide by four.

Task significance: Add items 14, 15, 16, and 17 and divide by four.

Task identity: Add items 18, 19, 20, and 21 and divide by four.

Feedback from job: Add items 22, 23, and 24 and divide by three.

Source: Morgeson, F.P., & Humphrey, S.E. (2006). The work design questionnaire (WDQ): Developing and validating a comprehensive measure for assessing job design and the nature of work. *Journal of Applied Psychology, 91*, 1321–1339. Copyright © 2006 by the American Psychological Association. Reproduced with permission.

To facilitate class discussion and your understanding of the task characteristics and job design, form a small group with several other members of the class and consider the following questions:

1. Each group member should present his or her score on each task characteristic. What task characteristics do group members score high and low on? Is there any consistency among group members in terms of the highest and lowest task characteristics? (Note: If you answered the question in terms of task characteristics preferences, discuss your highest and lowest preferences).

2. Each group member should describe his or her job and provide specific examples of what contributes to their task characteristics scores. What is it about the job that contributes to a high or low score on each task characteristic? (Note: If you answered the question in terms of task characteristics preferences, discuss your ideal job based on your task characteristics scores. Be specific in terms of how you would like your job to be designed).

3. Consider your job attitudes (e.g., job satisfaction, organizational commitment) and behaviours (e.g., job performance, absenteeism) in terms of your task characteristics scores. To what extent do the task characteristics contribute to your job attitudes and behaviours? (Note: If you answered the question in terms of task characteristics preferences, describe how the task characteristics might influence your job attitudes and behaviours. What task characteristics do you think would be most important for you and why?).

4. If you could redesign your job, what task characteristics would you focus on? What exactly would you do to redesign your job? Be specific in terms of how your job would change. What effect do you think these changes would have on your job attitudes and behaviours? (Note: If you answered the question in terms of task characteristics preferences, discuss how knowledge of your task characteristics scores can assist you in your job search, questions you will ask interviewers, and your job choice decision. How will knowledge of your task characteristics preferences assist in you in the future?)

CASE INCIDENT

The Junior Accountant

After graduating from business school, Sabrita received a job offer from a large accounting firm to work as a junior accountant. She was ranked in the top 10 of her class and could not have been happier. During the first six months, however, Sabrita began to reconsider her decision to join a large firm. This is how she described her job: Every day her supervisor brought several files for her to audit. He told her exactly in what order to do them and how to plan her day and work. At the end of the day, the supervisor would return to pick up the completed files. The supervisor collected the files from several other junior accountants and put them all together and completed the audit himself. The supervisor would then meet the client to review and discuss the audit. Sabrita did not ever meet the clients, and her supervisor never talked about his meeting with them or the final report. Sabrita felt very discouraged and wanted to quit. She was even beginning to reconsider her choice of accounting as a career.

1. Describe the job characteristics and critical psychological states of Sabrita's job. According to the Job Characteristics Model, how motivated is Sabrita and what is she likely to do?

2. Evaluate Sabrita's job on each of the work design characteristics described in Exhibit 6.7. What work design characteristics are particularly low? Based on your evaluation, what factors do you think are contributing to Sabrita's attitudes and intention to quit?

3. How would you redesign Sabrita's job to increase its motivating potential? Be sure to describe changes you would make to the work design characteristics as well as job enrichment schemes that you might use to redesign her job.

CASE STUDY

Chang Koh Metal Ptd. Ltd. in China

Chang Koh Metal Ptd. Ltd. was founded in Singapore in 1982 by Teo Kai San, a first generation Straits-born Chinese. The company's operations were in the production of metal-stamping precision parts. In 1993, the company expanded its operations by establishing a plant in Putian, China, the area of China from which Teo Kai San's parents had emigrated. The founder's son, Andrew Teo, was appointed as general manager. Andrew was 29 years old and had an engineering degree from the National University of Singapore. Prior to joining his father's company, Andrew had worked for an American multinational company in Singapore and had progressed to the rank of line manager, a position with substantial authority and responsibility. Andrew joined his father's company because he felt that his success in the multinational was a sign of his skills, indicating that he deserved a senior position in his father's company on the basis of merit rather than family connections. He also felt that the systems and practices he had learned at the mutinational would enable him to bring more updated management practices to Chang Koh Metal.

Since Andrew's father believed it was important to have in a position of authority a person who was knowledgeable about the local area, he appointed a relative from Putian, Jian Wei, as the plant manager to assist Andrew in the plant's operations. A primary reason for choosing China as the site for a plant was the belief that Singaporean Chinese should find it easy to work with the Chinese in China. After all, the two groups shared a common cultural heritage. The other advantages were the readily available supply of labour—Singapore was experiencing full employment, and the company found it difficult to recruit qualified production workers—and the lower operating costs. After a year in China, however, Andrew was not sure the plan to venture there had been wise. Although the labour costs were much lower than in Singapore, productivity was disappointing, and a number of management and labour problems had arisen, which he felt were frustrating his efforts to control the plant efficiently.

Staffing Procedure

Andrew had learned from his previous work experience that it was important to hire the right people with the appropriate qualifications and place them in the positions to which they were best suited in order to ensure smooth operations. But his efforts were hindered by Jian Wei's peculiar hiring practices. To fill open positions, Jian Wei would contact city officials and friends and relatives and ask them for recommendations on whom to hire. Most of the time the people hired did not have the skills needed to perform the tasks for which they were hired. Andrew vigorously protested against Jian Wei's practices and instituted formalized procedures to follow in recruitment and selection that called for systematic advertising of positions, evaluation of candidates, and hiring based on qualifications. Jian Wei became upset because he argued that his practices were necessary as a way to keep the channels of communication and mutual exchange open with important officials because the company might need their help in future business dealings. This disagreement created tension between the two men.

Productivity and Quality Issues

The plant in China employed about 150 workers. Andrew adopted the same salary system as he had seen used by his former employer and paid these workers a fixed salary based on the number of hours worked. However, their productivity rates were very low, and the workers demonstrated very little commitment to meeting the company's goals. After three months, Andrew scrapped the salary system and instead instituted a piece-rate system in which the workers were paid a minimum base salary supplemented by an incremental rate for each unit produced above a certain number. In other words, if the workers produced at or below the minimum production standard for the day, they received the minimum wage. If they produced above that rate, they received additional money for each extra piece produced.

For the following two months, Andrew was proud of his innovative management because the results were impressive. Company productivity targets were met, the workers were exerting themselves energetically, and they were even willing to work overtime at the same rate as the usual work day in order to make extra money. However, within a short period of time, he began to receive several complaints from customers about the low quality of the goods they were receiving from the company. Parts that should have been rejected were instead shipped to customers.

In response, Andrew had the quality control and manufacturing specifications printed on large posters and posted around the plant for all to see. He set up a quality control department and implemented 100 percent quality checks. However, all these efforts failed to stop poor-quality products from reaching the customers. As he investigated, he discovered that those in the quality control department were inspecting the parts but were passing almost everything that they inspected. He held a training session for the quality control inspectors, pointed out defective parts to them, and had them demonstrate to him that they could distinguish poor quality from good quality. Since it was clear that they could do so, he sent them back to the production floor, convinced that they would now begin to perform as a true quality control unit. Yet within a short period of time it became apparent that the unit was not doing the job any better than it had before the training session.

Andrew expressed his frustration to Jian Wei and demanded that he take action to improve the situation. Jian Wei protested that the quality control members' actions were completely understandable—they knew that rejected parts would not be added to the total that would count toward the incentive rate compensation and would therefore reduce the wages production workers would receive. They would not take money out of the pockets of the production workers. Andrew felt that the quality control workers should be shown that failure to act would take money out of their own pockets, so he suggested that a system of demerit points be set up for the quality control employees that would lead to deductions from their wages. However, Jian Wei strongly disagreed with the idea, arguing that it was unfair to penalize these employees for doing what they believed was right. Finally, a compromise was reached in which more supervisors were hired for the quality control department to provide closer supervision of the workers. In addition, Andrew arranged to have all final products shipped to Singapore for final inspection before they were sent out to customers.

Rules and Regulations

About 15 technicians were responsible for the maintenance of machinery. At any one time, one machine would be set aside for maintenance work. Ninety percent of the time, a machine that was designated as "in maintenance" actually sat unused. To Andrew's dismay, he found that the technicians regularly used the "in maintenance" machine to do moonlighting work to make extra income. To Andrew, this practice was a clear violation of company rules and regulations, a fact that warranted dismissal of the supervisor of the technicians, who had not only condoned the activity but had actually participated in it. Jian Wei supported the employees. He argued that the machine would have been left idle anyway, so what was the harm? All activities were conducted outside normal working hours, and the technicians' jobs were not being neglected. No additional costs were incurred by the factory, except in the operation of the machine. Jian Wei thought that, as boss, Andrew needed to show much more understanding and sensitivity to the issue than he had. It was unfair to single out one person for punishment, especially when the company had not suffered any losses. In addition, Jian Wei was dismayed to hear Andrew talk about dismissing an employee. He said that such practice just was not done in China—no true Chinese person would think about removing a person's "iron rice bowl." Reluctantly, Andrew agreed to Jian Wei's recommendation to resolve the issue by transferring the technicians' supervisor to another department.

Problems like these made Andrew very doubtful that the operation in China could ever be turned into a profitable venture. His father had been willing to grant Andrew some time to get the plant up and running before he expected results, but now he was starting to ask questions about why the plant was still losing money and why no trend in the direction of profitability was evident in the financial performance figures. He had recently asked Andrew to come up with a concrete plan to turn the situation around. Andrew was wondering what he could do.

Source: Begley, T. (1998). Chang Koh Metal Ptd. Ltd. In China. In G. Oddou and M. Mendenhall (Eds.), Cases in International Organizational Behaviour. Reprinted by permission of John Wiley & Sons, Inc. Questions prepared by Alan Saks.

1. Comment on the fixed salary system that Andrew adopted from his former employer. Why was this system not effective for motivating the plant workers?

2. Do you think that scrapping the fixed salary system and replacing it with the piece-rate system was a good idea? What are some of the strengths and weaknesses of the piece-rate system?

3. Why was Andrew unsuccessful in his efforts to improve product quality? Do you think that a system of demerit points and wage deductions for the quality control workers would have been effective?

Would having more supervisors in the quality control department and shipping products to Singapore for final inspection solve the problem? What do you think would be an effective way to improve product quality?

4. Were cross-cultural differences a factor in the effectiveness of the salary systems? How effective do you think each system would have been if the plant were located in North America?

5. Discuss the potential effects of implementing an MBO program in the plant. Do you think it

would improve productivity and solve some of the problems?

6. Are there any conditions under which the piece-rate system might have been more effective?

7. What are some alternative ways to use pay to motivate the workers at the plant? Are there alternatives to the piece-rate system? How effective are they likely to be? What does this case say about using money as a motivator?

8. What should Andrew do now? What would you do?

INTEGRATIVE CASE

Deloitte & Touche: Integrating Arthur Andersen

At the end of Chapter 1 you were introduced to the Deloitte & Touche: Integrating Arthur Andersen Integrative Case. The case questions focused on issues pertaining to the relevance and goals of organizational behaviour, managerial roles, and contemporary management concerns. Now that you have completed Part 2 of the text and the chapters on Individual Behaviour, you can return to the Integrative Case and focus on issues related to learning, perceptions, fairness and job attitudes, motivation, and pay plans by answering the following questions.

QUESTIONS

1. How important is learning for the successful integration of the two firms? What do employees need to learn and what organizational learning practices should be used? Be sure to consider the use and application of each of the organizational learning practices described in Chapter 2.

2. Consider the perceptions held by employees of both firms. To what extent are person perception biases affecting these perceptions? What are the implications of these perceptions for the integration of the two firms and what does the integration team need to do?

3. Use social identity theory to explain the perceptions that employees at each firm have of themselves and those at the other firm. According to social identity theory, what does the integration team need to understand and what should they do?

4. Consider the role of trust and perceived organizational support (POS) in the case. How important

are they for the successful integration of the two firms and to what extent do employees at each firm have positive perceptions of trust and organizational support? What should the integration team and management do to create positive perceptions of trust and organizational support?

5. Discuss in detail how issues of fairness are relevant to this case. Do you expect that distributive, procedural, or interactional fairness is most important here? Please be sure to consider both the current Deloitte personnel and the incoming Andersen personnel.

6. Speculate about how mood and emotion might have figured in the case events. Was there a need for emotional regulation?

7. Consider the job satisfaction and organizational commitment of the Andersen employees. What should the integration team focus on if they want the Andersen employees to be satisfied with their new jobs, committed to their new organization, and willing to stay rather than quit? What about the Deloitte & Touche employees?

8. Discuss the relevance of motivation in the case. How important is motivation and describe what employees need to be motivated to do and how to motivate them to do it? Explain how each of the theories of motivation can be used to motivate employees.

9. Do you think the integration team should consider using money to motivate employees? What kind of pay plan would you recommend and why? What other motivational practices would you recommend for the successful integration of the two firms? Explain your answer.

myOBlab

Visit MyOBLab at **www.pearsoned.ca/myoblab** for access to online tutorials, interactive exercises, videos, and much more.

CHAPTERS

7	**8**	**9**	**10**	**11**	**12**
Groups and Teamwork	Social Influence, Socialization, and Culture	Leadership	Decision Making	Power, Politics, and Ethics	Conflict and Stress

CHAPTER 7

LEARNING OBJECTIVES

After reading Chapter 7, you should be able to:

1 Define *groups* and distinguish between *formal* and *informal* groups.

2 Discuss group development.

3 Explain how group size and member diversity influence what occurs in groups.

4 Review how *norms*, *roles*, and *status* affect social interaction.

5 Discuss the causes and consequences of *group cohesiveness*.

6 Explain the dynamics of *social loafing*.

7 Discuss how to design and support *self-managed teams*.

8 Explain the logic behind *cross-functional teams* and describe how they can operate effectively.

9 Understand *virtual teams* and what makes them effective.

Groups and Teamwork

Ralston Foods

Headquartered in St. Louis, Missouri, Ralcorp has more than 3000 employees and is the largest store-brand manufacturer in the United States. It includes four separate food categories: Ralston ready-to-eat and hot cereals; Bremner crackers and cookies; Nutcracker/Flavor House Brands jar and can snack nuts and candy; and Carriage House mayonnaise, salad dressings, jams, jellies, and peanut butter.

The Ralston Foods' Sparks, Nevada, plant, located on the outskirts of Reno, is a small segment of Ralcorp's $1.2-billion organization. The plant opened as a pet-food producer in 1972, but was shut down in 1990. At that time, Daniel Kibbe was brought in to retrofit the facility into a cereal plant. Kibbe viewed this major change as a way to create a new culture at the Sparks plant: a culture focused on groups and teams.

Many millions of dollars were spent redesigning and retrofitting the plant over an 18-month period, from mid-1990 to 1991. In July 1991, Kibbe and his management team met with 58 laid-off employees from the pet-food operation and explained the new participative culture to them. At first they were pretty skeptical. Their response was, "We've heard that before; you'll never let us do those things." But Kibbe stayed the course. Initially, they started delegating a lot of little things that were empowering in nature, such as allowing the workers to renegotiate the vending service contract at the plant that had previously been a source of dissatisfaction. That kind of empowerment spread throughout the plant as they moved into the start-up process. Group members were involved in all aspects—hiring, equipment checkout, developing work rules, skill-based pay, schedules, and training.

The Sparks culture is based on the recognition that traditional systems have failed to tap the true potential of group members. The system is based on an environment of credibility, trust, and openness. The work group orientation drives the organization. There are operating work groups, support work groups, and a leadership work group composed of the entire management staff, including operating and staff managers, group leaders, and the plant manager. In most cases, work groups, which range in size from 8 to 50 members, are broken down into smaller teams

Ralston Foods has been able to use self-directed work groups to its advantage in its Sparks, Nevada, cereal plant.

ranging from 3 to 10 members. The six operating work groups function in all areas of the plant, including three in operations, which comprises the mill, processing, and packing areas, plus three more in the maintenance, storeroom, and warehouse areas. Two of these groups are totally self-directed; four are semi-autonomous.

In addition to work groups, there are cross-functional committees that meet regularly. Most committee members are volunteers, and group members represent their work group. Some are only formed for short-term needs, such as business response, specific continuous improvement projects, and culture day (an off-site day in which all group members participate in team-building activities and training). There are also ongoing committees responsible for the following areas or issues: continuous improvement, food safety, community activities, employee activities, hiring task force, policy, safety, and PEO (Plant Emergency Organization).

The two self-directed work groups in the plant are the warehouse and mill groups. Neither of these groups has had a group leader for five or six years. The self-directed groups consistently have a better, more dependable performance than those with group leaders. They also tend to be tougher on disciplinary problems than work groups with leaders. The work groups with leaders have gotten good at referring to the group leader for decisions they are reluctant to make—such as dealing with a poor performer. Self-directed groups do meet with a group manager once a week, but other than that, the groups have to deal with all the issues themselves. They just elevate themselves to the level needed.

Through a mix of trust, performance measurement and rewards, training and development, and leadership, Kibbe has succeeded in transforming the culture at Ralston's Sparks plant and has demonstrated the power of teamwork.[1]

This vignette shows how critical groups or teams are in determining organizational success. In this chapter, we will define the term *group* and discuss the nature of formal groups and informal groups in organizations. After this, we will present the details of group development. Then, we will consider how groups differ from one another structurally and explore the consequences of these differences. We will also cover the problem of social loafing. Finally, we will examine how to design effective work teams.

What Is a Group?

We use the word "group" rather casually in everyday discourse—for example, special-interest group or ethnic group. However, for behavioural scientists, a **group** consists of two or more people interacting interdependently to achieve a common goal.

Interaction is the most basic aspect of a group—it suggests who is in the group and who is not. The interaction of group members need not be face to face, and it need not be verbal. For example, employees who telecommute can be part of their work group at the office even though they live kilometres away and communicate via email. Interdependence simply means that group members rely to some degree on each other to accomplish goals. All groups have one or more goals that their members seek to achieve. These goals can range from having fun to marketing a new product to achieving world peace.

Group memberships are very important for two reasons. First, groups exert a tremendous influence on us. They are the social mechanisms by which we acquire many beliefs, values, attitudes, and behaviours. Group membership is also important because groups provide a context in which *we* are able to exert influence on *others*.

Formal work groups are groups that organizations establish to facilitate the achievement of organizational goals. They are intentionally designed to channel individual effort in an appropriate direction. The most common formal group consists of a manager and the employees who report to that manager. In a manufacturing company, one such group might consist of a production manager and the six shift supervisors who report to him or her. In turn, the shift supervisors head work groups composed of themselves and their respective subordinates. Thus, the hierarchy of most organizations is a series of formal, interlocked work groups. As the Ralston Foods case shows, all this direct supervision is not always necessary. Nevertheless, Ralston's self-managed teams are still formal work groups.

Other types of formal work groups include task forces and committees. *Task forces* are temporary groups that meet to achieve particular goals or to solve particular problems, such as suggesting productivity improvements. *Committees* are usually permanent groups that handle recurrent assignments outside the usual work group structures. For example, a firm might have a standing committee on work–family balance. Although their terminology varies a bit, Ralston Foods makes extensive use of committees and task forces.

In addition to formal groups sanctioned by management to achieve organizational goals, informal grouping occurs in all organizations. **Informal groups** are groups that emerge naturally in response to the common interests of organizational members. They are seldom sanctioned by the organization, and their membership often cuts across formal groups. Informal groups can either help or hurt an organization, depending on their norms for behaviour. We will consider this in detail later.

Group Development

Even relatively simple groups are actually complex social devices that require a fair amount of negotiation and trial and error before individual members begin to function as a true group. While employees often know each other before new teams are formed, simple familiarity does not replace the necessity for team development.

Group. Two or more people interacting interdependently to achieve a common goal.

Formal work groups. Groups that are established by organizations to facilitate the achievement of organizational goals.

Informal groups. Groups that emerge naturally in response to the common interests of organizational members.

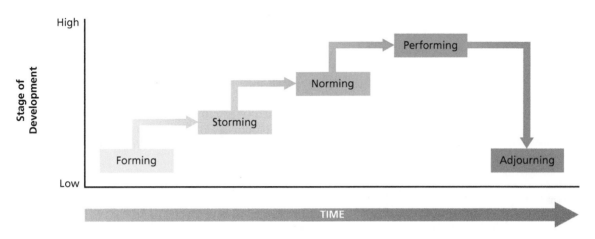

EXHIBIT 7.1
Stages of group development.

Typical Stages of Group Development

Leaders and trainers have observed that many groups develop through a series of stages over time.[2] Each stage presents the members with a series of challenges they must master to achieve the next stage. These stages (forming, storming, norming, performing, and adjourning) are presented in Exhibit 7.1.

Forming. At this early stage, group members try to orient themselves by "testing the waters." What are we doing here? What are the others like? What is our purpose? The situation is often ambiguous, and members are aware of their dependency on each other.

Storming. At this second stage, conflict often emerges. Confrontation and criticism occur as members determine whether they will go along with the way the group is developing. Sorting out roles and responsibilities is often at issue here. Problems are more likely to happen earlier, rather than later, in group development.

Norming. At this stage, members resolve the issues that provoked the storming, and they develop social consensus. Compromise is often necessary. Interdependence is recognized, norms are agreed to, and the group becomes more cohesive (we will study these processes later). Information and opinions flow freely.

Performing. With its social structure sorted out, the group devotes its energies toward task accomplishment. Achievement, creativity, and mutual assistance are prominent themes of this stage.

Adjourning. Some groups, such as task forces and design project teams, have a definite life span and disperse after achieving their goals. Also, some groups disperse when corporate layoffs and downsizing occur. At this adjourning stage, rites and rituals that affirm the group's previous successful development are common (such as ceremonies and parties). Members often exhibit emotional support for each other.[3]

The stages model is a good tool for monitoring and troubleshooting how groups are developing. However, not all groups go through these stages of development. The process applies mainly to new groups that have never met before. Well-acquainted task forces and committees can short-circuit these stages when they have a new problem to work out.[4] Also, some organizational settings are so structured that storming and norming are unnecessary for even strangers to coalesce into a team. For example, most commercial airline cockpit crews perform effectively even though they can be made up of virtual strangers who meet just before takeoff.[5]

Punctuated Equilibrium

When groups have a specific deadline by which to complete some problem-solving task, we can often observe a very different development sequence from that described above. Connie Gersick, whose research uncovered this sequence, describes it as a **punctuated equilibrium model** of group development.[6] *Equilibrium* means stability, and the research revealed apparent stretches of group stability punctuated by a critical first meeting, a midpoint change in group activity, and a rush to task completion. In addition to many real-world work groups, Gersick studied student groups doing class projects, so see if this sequence of events sounds familiar to you.

> **Punctuated equilibrium model.** A model of group development that describes how groups with deadlines are affected by their first meetings and crucial midpoint transitions.

Phase 1. Phase 1 begins with the first meeting and continues until the midpoint in the group's existence. The very first meeting is critical in setting the agenda for what will happen in the remainder of this phase. Assumptions, approaches, and precedents that members develop in the first meeting end up dominating the first half of the group's life. Although it gathers information and holds meetings, the group makes little visible progress toward the goal.

Midpoint Transition. The midpoint transition occurs at almost exactly the halfway point in time toward the group's deadline. For instance, if the group has a two-month deadline, the transition will occur at about one month. The transition marks a change in the group's approach, and how the group manages the change is critical for the group to show progress. The need to move forward is apparent, and the group may seek outside advice. This transition may consolidate previously acquired information or even mark a completely new approach, but it crystallizes the group's activities for Phase 2 just like the first meeting did for Phase 1.

Phase 2. For better or for worse, decisions and approaches adopted at the midpoint get played out in Phase 2. It concludes with a final meeting that reveals a burst of activity and a concern for how outsiders will evaluate the product.

Exhibit 7.2 shows how the punctuated equilibrium model works for groups that successfully or unsuccessfully manage the midpoint transition.

What advice does the punctuated equilibrium model offer for managing product development teams, advertising groups, or class project groups?[7]

- Prepare carefully for the first meeting. What is decided here will strongly determine what happens in the rest of Phase 1. If you are the coach or adviser of the group, stress *motivation and excitement* about the project.

- As long as people are working, do not look for radical progress during Phase 1.

EXHIBIT 7.2
The punctuated equilibrium model of group development for two groups.

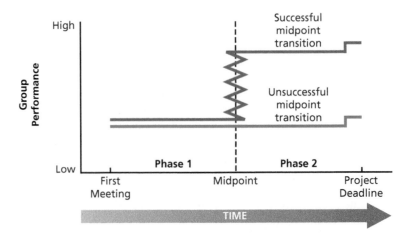

- Manage the midpoint transition carefully. Evaluate the strengths and weaknesses of the ideas that people generated in Phase 1. Clarify any questions with whoever is commissioning your work. Recognize that a fundamental change in approach must occur here for progress to occur. Essential issues are not likely to "work themselves out" during Phase 2. At this point, a group coach should focus on the *strategy* to be used in Phase 2.
- Be sure that adequate resources are available to actually execute the Phase 2 plan.
- Resist deadline changes. These could damage the midpoint transition.

As noted, the concept of punctuated equilibrium applies to groups with deadlines. Such groups might also exhibit some of the stages of development noted earlier, with a new cycle of storming and norming following the midpoint transition.

Group Structure and Its Consequences

Group structure refers to the characteristics of the stable social organization of a group—the way a group is "put together." The most basic structural characteristics along which groups vary are size and member diversity. Other structural characteristics are the expectations that members have about each other's behaviour (norms), agreements about "who does what" in the group (roles), the rewards and prestige allocated to various group members (status), and how attractive the group is to its members (cohesiveness).

Group Size

Of one thing we can be certain—the smallest possible group consists of two people, such as a manager and a particular employee. It is possible to engage in much theoretical nitpicking about just what constitutes an upper limit on group size. However, given the definition of group that we presented earlier, it would seem that congressional or parliamentary size (300 to 400 members) is somewhere close to this limit. In practice, most work groups, including task forces and committees, usually have between 3 and 20 members.

Size and Satisfaction. The more the merrier? In theory, yes. In fact, however, members of larger groups rather consistently report less satisfaction with group membership than those who find themselves in smaller groups.[8] What accounts for this apparent contradiction?

For one thing, as opportunities for friendship increase, the chance to work on and develop these opportunities might decrease owing to the sheer time and energy required. In addition, in incorporating more members with different viewpoints, larger groups might prompt conflict and dissension, which work against member satisfaction. As group size increases, the time available for verbal participation by each member decreases. Also, many people are inhibited about participating in larger groups.[9] Finally, in larger groups, individual members identify less easily with the success and accomplishments of the group. For example, a particular member of a 4-person cancer research team should be able to identify his or her personal contributions to a research breakthrough more easily than a member of a 20-person team can.

Size and Performance. Satisfaction aside, do large groups perform tasks better than small groups? This question has great relevance to practical organizational decisions: How many people should a bank assign to evaluate loan applications? How many carpenters should a construction company assign to build a garage? If a school system decides to implement team teaching, how big should the teams be? The answers to these and similar questions depend on the exact task that the group needs to accomplish and on how we define good performance.[10]

Additive tasks. Tasks in which group performance is dependent on the sum of the performance of individual group members.

Disjunctive tasks. Tasks in which group performance is dependent on the performance of the best group member.

Process losses. Group performance difficulties stemming from the problems of motivating and coordinating larger groups.

Some tasks are **additive tasks.** This means that we can predict potential performance by adding the performances of individual group members together. Building a house is an additive task, and we can estimate potential speed of construction by adding the efforts of individual carpenters. Thus, for additive tasks, the potential performance of the group increases with group size.

Some tasks are **disjunctive tasks.** This means that the potential performance of the group depends on the performance of its *best member.* For example, suppose that a research team is looking for a single error in a complicated computer program. In this case, the performance of the team might hinge on its containing at least one bright, attentive, logical-minded individual. Obviously, the potential performance of groups doing disjunctive tasks also increases with group size because the probability that the group includes a superior performer is greater.

We use the term "potential performance" consistently in the preceding two paragraphs for the following reason: As groups performing tasks get bigger, they tend to suffer from process losses.[11] **Process losses** are performance difficulties that stem from the problems of motivating and coordinating larger groups. Even with good intentions, problems of communication and decision making increase with size—imagine 50 carpenters trying to build a house. Thus, actual performance = potential performance – process losses.

These points are summarized in Exhibit 7.3. As you can see in part (a), both potential performance and process losses increase with group size for additive and disjunctive tasks. The net effect is shown in part (b), which demonstrates that actual performance increases with size up to a point and then falls off. Part (c) shows that the *average* performance of group members decreases as size gets bigger. Thus, up to a point, larger groups might perform better as groups, but their individual members tend to be less efficient.

EXHIBIT 7.3

Relationships among group size, productivity, and process losses.

Source: From Steiner, I.D. (1972). *Group process and productivity.* New York: Academic Press, p. 96. Copyright © 1972.

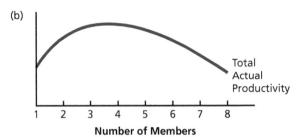

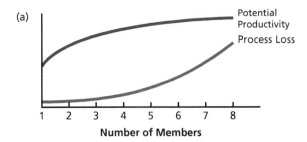

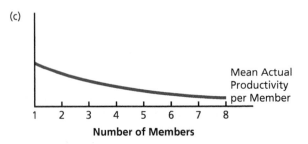

We should note one other kind of task. **Conjunctive tasks** are those in which the performance of the group is limited by its *poorest performer*. For example, an assembly-line operation is limited by its weakest link. Also, if team teaching is the technique used to train employees how to perform a complicated, sequential job, one poor teacher in the sequence will severely damage the effectiveness of the team. Both the potential and actual performance of conjunctive tasks would decrease as group size increases because the probability of including a weak link in the group goes up.

In summary, for additive and disjunctive tasks, larger groups might perform better up to a point but at increasing costs to the efficiency of individual members. By any standard, performance on purely conjunctive tasks should decrease as group size increases.

Conjunctive tasks. Tasks in which group performance is limited by the performance of the poorest group member.

Diversity of Group Membership

Imagine an eight-member product development task force composed exclusively of 30-something white males of Western European heritage. Then imagine another task force with 50 percent men and 50 percent women from eight different ethnic or racial backgrounds and an age range from 25 to 55. The first group is obviously homogeneous in its membership, while the latter is heterogeneous or diverse. Which task force do you think would develop more quickly as a group? Which would be most creative?

Group diversity has a strong impact on interaction patterns—more diverse groups have a more difficult time communicating effectively and becoming cohesive (we will study cohesiveness in more detail shortly).[12] This means that diverse groups might tend to take longer to do their forming, storming, and norming.[13] Once they do develop, more and less diverse groups are equally cohesive and productive.[14] However, diverse groups sometimes perform better when the task requires cognitive, creativity-demanding tasks and problem solving rather than more routine work because members consider a broader array of ideas.[15] In general, any negative effects of "surface diversity" in age, gender, or race seem to wear off over time. However, "deep diversity" in attitudes toward work or how to accomplish a goal can badly damage cohesiveness.[16]

All this speaks well for the concepts of valuing and managing diversity, which we discussed in Chapter 3. When management values and manages diversity, it offsets some of the initial process loss costs of diversity and capitalizes on its benefits for group performance.

Group Norms

Social **norms** are collective expectations that members of social units have regarding the behaviour of each other. As such, they are codes of conduct that specify what individuals ought and ought not to do and standards against which we evaluate the appropriateness of behaviour.

Norms. Collective expectations that members of social units have regarding the behaviour of each other.

' Much normative influence is unconscious, and we are often aware of such influence only in special circumstances, such as when we see children struggling to master adult norms or international visitors sparring with the norms of our culture. We also become conscious of norms when we encounter ones that seem to conflict with each other ("Get ahead" but "Don't step on others") or when we enter new social situations. For instance, the first day on a new job, workers frequently search for cues about what is considered proper office etiquette: Should I call the boss "mister"? Can I personalize my workspace?

Norm Development. *Why* do norms develop? The most important function that norms serve is to provide regularity and predictability to behaviour. This consistency provides important psychological security and permits us to carry out our daily business with minimal disruption.

What do norms develop *about?* Norms develop to regulate behaviours that are considered at least marginally important to their supporters. For example, managers are more likely to adopt norms regarding the performance and attendance of employees than norms concerning how employees personalize and decorate their offices. In general, less deviation is accepted from norms that concern more important behaviours.

How do norms develop? As we discussed in Chapter 4, individuals develop attitudes as a function of a related belief and value. In many cases, their attitudes affect their behaviour. When the members of a group *share* related beliefs and values, we can expect them to share consequent attitudes. These shared attitudes then form the basis for norms.[17] Notice that it really does not make sense to talk about "my personal norm." Norms are *collectively* held expectations, depending on two or more people for their existence.

Why do individuals tend to comply with norms? Much compliance occurs simply because the norm corresponds to privately held attitudes. In addition, even when norms support trivial social niceties (such as when to shake hands or when to look serious), they often save time and prevent social confusion. Most interesting, however, is the case in which individuals comply with norms that *go against* their privately held attitudes and opinions. For example, couples without religious convictions frequently get married in religious services, and people who hate neckties often wear them to work. In short, groups have an extraordinary range of rewards and punishments available to induce conformity to norms. In the next chapter, we will examine this process in detail.

Some Typical Norms. There are some classes of norms that seem to crop up in most organizations and affect the behaviour of members. They include the following:

- *Dress norms.* Social norms frequently dictate the kind of clothing people wear to work.[18] Military and quasi-military organizations tend to invoke formal norms that support polished buttons and razor-sharp creases. Even in organizations that have adopted casual dress policies, employees often express considerable concern about what they wear at work. Such is the power of social norms.

- *Reward allocation norms.* There are at least four norms that might dictate how rewards, such as pay, promotions, and informal favours, could be allocated in organizations:

  a. Equity—reward according to inputs, such as effort, performance, or seniority.

  b. Equality—reward everyone equally.

  c. Reciprocity—reward people the way they reward you.

  d. Social responsibility—reward those who truly need the reward.[19]

  Officially, of course, most Western organizations tend to stress allocation according to some combination of equity and equality norms—give employees what they deserve, and no favouritism.

- *Performance norms.* The performance of organizational members might be as much a function of social expectations as it is of inherent ability, personal motivation, or technology.[20] Work groups provide their members with potent cues about what an appropriate level of performance is. New group members are alert for these cues: Is it all right to take a break now? Under what circumstances can I be absent from work without being punished? (See Research Focus: *Absence Cultures— Norms in Action.*) The official organizational norms that managers send to employees usually favour high performance. However, work groups often establish their own informal performance norms, such as those that restrict productivity under a piece-rate pay system. The self-directed warehouse and mill groups at Ralston Foods, which are tougher disciplinarians than groups with conventional leaders, are clear exceptions.

RESEARCH FOCUS

Absence Cultures—Norms in Action

On first thought, you might assume that absenteeism from work is a very individualized behaviour, a product of random sickness or of personal job dissatisfaction. Although these factors contribute to absenteeism, there is growing evidence that group norms also have a strong impact on how much work people miss.

We can see cross-national differences in absenteeism. Traditionally, absence has been rather high in Scandinavia, lower in the United States and Canada, and lower yet in Japan and Switzerland. Clearly, these differences are not due to sickness but rather to differences in cultural values about the legitimacy of taking time off work. These differences get reflected in work group norms.

Within the same country and company, we can still see group differences in absenteeism. A company that Gary Johns studied had four plants that made the same products and had identical human resources policies. Despite this, one plant had a 12 percent absence rate while another had an absence rate of 5 percent. Within one plant, some departments had virtually no absence while others approached a rate of 25 percent!

Moving to the small group level, Johns also studied small customer service groups in a utility company. Despite the fact that all employees were doing the same work in the same firm, there were again striking cross-group differences in absenteeism, ranging from 1 to 13 percent.

These normative differences in absenteeism across groups are called absence cultures. How do they develop? People tend to adjust their own absence behaviour to what they see as typical of their group. Then, other factors come into play. In the utility company study, the groups that monitored each other's behaviour more closely had lower absence. A Canadian study found that air traffic controllers traded off calling in sick so that their colleagues could replace them at double overtime. A UK study found that industrial workers actually posted "absence schedules" so that they could take time off without things getting out of hand! All these are examples of norms in action.

The norms underlying absence cultures can dictate presence as well as absence. Recent studies show that "presenteeism," coming to work when feeling unwell, is prevalent in many human services occupations.

Source: Some of the research bearing on absence cultures is described in Johns, G. (2008). Absenteeism and presenteeism: Not at work or not working well. In J. Barling & C.L. Cooper (Eds.), *Sage Handbook of Organizational Behavior* (Vol. 1). London: Sage.

Roles

Roles are positions in a group that have a set of expected behaviours attached to them. Thus, roles represent "packages" of norms that apply to particular group members. As we implied in the previous section, many norms apply to all group members to be sure that they engage in *similar* behaviours (such as restricting productivity or dressing a certain way). However, the development of roles is indicative of the fact that group members might also be required to act *differently* from one another. For example, in a committee meeting, not every member is required to function as a secretary or a chairperson, and these become specific roles that are fulfilled by particular people.

In organizations, we find two basic kinds of roles. Designated or *assigned roles* are formally prescribed by an organization as a means of dividing labour and responsibility to facilitate task achievement. In general, assigned roles indicate "who does what" and "who can tell others what to do." In a software firm, labels that we might apply to formal roles include president, software engineer, analyst, programmer, and sales manager. In addition to assigned roles, we invariably see the development of *emergent roles*. These are roles that develop naturally to meet the social–emotional needs of group members or to assist in formal job accomplishment. The class clown and the office gossip fulfill emergent social–emotional roles, while an "old pro" might emerge to assist new group members learn their jobs. Other emergent roles might be assumed by informal leaders or by scapegoats who are the targets of group hostility.

Roles. Positions in a group that have a set of expected behaviours attached to them.

EXHIBIT 7.4
A model of the role
assumption process.

Source: Adapted from Katz, D. et al.
(1966, 1978). *The Social Psychology
of Organizations*, 2nd edition, p.196.
© 1966, 1978 John Wiley & Sons
Inc. New York. Reprinted by permission of John Wiley & Sons, Inc.

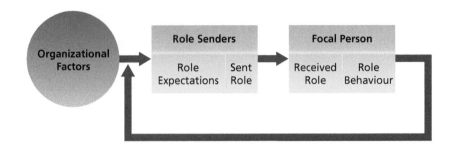

Role Ambiguity. Role ambiguity exists when the goals of one's job or the methods of performing it are unclear. Ambiguity might be characterized by confusion about how performance is evaluated, how good performance can be achieved, or what the limits of one's authority and responsibility are.

Exhibit 7.4 shows a model of the process that is involved in assuming an organizational role. As you can see, certain organizational factors lead role senders (such as managers) to develop role expectations and "send" roles to focal people (such as employees). The focal person "receives" the role and then tries to engage in behaviour to fulfill the role. This model reveals a variety of elements that can lead to ambiguity.

Role ambiguity. Lack of clarity of job goals or methods.

- *Organizational factors.* Some roles seem inherently ambiguous because of their function in the organization. For example, middle management roles might fail to provide the "big picture" that upper management roles do. Also middle management roles do not require the attention to supervision necessary in lower management roles.
- *The role sender.* Role senders might have unclear expectations of a focal person. Even when the sender has specific role expectations, they might be ineffectively sent to the focal person. A weak orientation session, vague performance reviews, or inconsistent feedback and discipline may send ambiguous role messages to employees.
- *The focal person.* Even role expectations that are clearly developed and sent might not be fully digested by the focal person. This is especially true when he or she is new to the role. Ambiguity tends to decrease as length of time in the job role increases.[21]

What are the practical consequences of role ambiguity? The most frequent outcomes appear to be job stress, dissatisfaction, reduced organizational commitment, lowered performance, and intentions to quit.[22] Managers can do much to reduce unnecessary role ambiguity by providing clear performance expectations and performance feedback, especially for new employees and for those in more intrinsically ambiguous jobs.

Role Conflict. Role conflict exists when an individual is faced with incompatible role expectations. Conflict can be distinguished from ambiguity in that role expectations might be crystal clear but incompatible in the sense they are mutually exclusive, cannot be fulfilled simultaneously, or do not suit the role occupant.

Role conflict. A condition of being faced with incompatible role expectations.

- **Intrasender role conflict** occurs when a single role sender provides incompatible role expectations to the role occupant. For example, a manager might tell an employee to take it easy and not work so hard, while delivering yet another batch of reports that require immediate attention. This form of role conflict seems especially likely to also provoke ambiguity.

Intrasender role conflict. A single role sender provides incompatible role expectations to a role occupant.

- If two or more role senders differ in their expectations for a role occupant, **intersender role conflict** can develop. Employees who straddle the boundary between the organization and its clients or customers are especially likely to encounter this form of conflict. Intersender conflict can also stem exclusively from within the organization. The classic example here is the first-level manager, who serves as the interface between "management" and "the workers." From above, the manager might be pressured to get the work out and keep the troops in line. From below, he or she might be encouraged to behave in a considerate and friendly manner.

Intersender role conflict. Two or more role senders provide a role occupant with incompatible expectations.

- Organizational members necessarily play several roles at one time, especially if we include roles external to the organization. Often, the expectations inherent in these several roles are incompatible, and **interrole conflict** results.[23] One person, for example, might fulfill the roles of a functional expert in marketing, head of the market research group, subordinate to the vice-president of marketing, and member of a product development task force. This is obviously a busy person, and competing demands for her time are a frequent symptom of interrole conflict.

- Even when role demands are clear and otherwise congruent, they might be incompatible with the personality or skills of the role occupant—thus, **person–role conflict** results.[24] Many examples of "whistle-blowing" are signals of person–role conflict. The organization has demanded some role behaviour that the occupant considers unethical.

As with role ambiguity, the most consistent consequences of role conflict are job dissatisfaction, stress reactions, lowered organizational commitment, and turnover intentions.[25] Managers can help prevent employee role conflict by avoiding self-contradictory messages, conferring with other role senders, being sensitive to multiple role demands, and fitting the right person to the right role.

Status

Status is the rank, social position, or prestige accorded to group members. Put another way, it represents the group's *evaluation* of a member. Just *what* is evaluated depends on the status system in question. However, when a status system works smoothly, the group will exhibit clear norms about who should be accorded higher or lower status.

Formal Status Systems. All organizations have both formal and informal status systems. Since formal systems are most obvious to observers, let's begin there. The formal status system represents management's attempt to publicly identify those people who have higher status than others. It is so obvious because this identification is implemented by the application of *status symbols* that are tangible indicators of status. Status symbols might include titles, particular working relationships, pay packages, work schedules, and the physical working environment. Just what are the criteria for achieving formal organizational status? One criterion is often seniority in one's work group. Employees who have been with the group longer might acquire the privilege of choosing day shift work or a more favourable office location. Even more important than seniority, however, is one's assigned role in the organization—one's job. Because they perform different jobs, secretaries, labourers, managers, and executives acquire different statuses. Organizations often go to great pains to tie status symbols to assigned roles.

Why do organizations go to all this trouble to differentiate status? For one thing, status and the symbols connected to it serve as powerful magnets to induce members to aspire to higher organizational positions (recall Maslow's need for self-esteem). Second, status differentiation reinforces the authority hierarchy in work groups and in the organization as a whole, since people *pay attention* to high-status individuals.

Informal Status Systems. In addition to formal status systems, one can detect informal status systems in organizations. Such systems are not well advertised, and they might lack the conspicuous symbols and systematic support that people usually accord the formal system. Nevertheless, they can operate just as effectively. Sometimes, job performance is a basis for the acquisition of informal status. The "power hitters" on a baseball team or the "cool heads" in a hospital emergency unit might be highly evaluated by co-workers for their ability to assist in task accomplishment. Some managers who perform well early in their careers are identified as "fast trackers" and given special job assignments that correspond to their elevated status. Just as frequently, though, informal status is linked to factors other than job performance, such as gender or race. For example, the man who takes a day off work to care for a sick child may be praised as a model father. The woman who does the same may be questioned about her work commitment.

Interrole conflict. Several roles held by a role occupant involve incompatible expectations.

Person–role conflict. Role demands call for behaviour that is incompatible with the personality or skills of a role occupant.

Status. The rank, social position, or prestige accorded to group members.

Consequences of Status Differences. Status differences have a paradoxical effect on communication patterns. Most people like to communicate with others at their own status or higher rather than with people who are below them.[26] The result should be a tendency for communication to move up the status hierarchy. However, if status differences are large, people can be inhibited from communicating upward. These opposing effects mean that much communication gets stalled.

Status also affects the amount of various group members' communication and their influence in group affairs. As you might guess, higher-status members do more talking and have more influence.[27] Some of the most convincing evidence comes from studies of jury deliberations, in which jurors with higher social status (such as managers and professionals) participate more and have more effect on the verdict.[28] Unfortunately, there is no guarantee that the highest-status person is the most knowledgeable about the problem at hand!

Reducing Status Barriers. Although status differences can be powerful motivators, their tendency to inhibit the free flow of communication has led many organizations to downplay status differentiation by doing away with questionable status symbols. The goal is to foster a culture of teamwork and cooperation across the ranks. The high-tech culture of Silicon Valley has always been pretty egalitarian and lacking in conspicuous status symbols, but even old-line industries are getting on the bandwagon, doing away with reserved parking and fancy offices for executives.

Some organizations employ phoney or misguided attempts to bridge the status barrier. Some examples of "casual Friday" policies (which permit the wearing of casual clothes on Fridays) only underline status differences the rest of the week if no other cultural changes are made.

Many observers note that email has levelled status barriers.[29] High-speed transmission, direct access, and the opportunity to avoid live confrontation often encourage lower-status parties to communicate directly with organizational VIPs. This has even been seen in the rank-conscious military.

Group Cohesiveness

Group cohesiveness. The degree to which a group is especially attractive to its members.

Group cohesiveness is a critical property of groups. Cohesive groups are those that are especially attractive to their members. Because of this attractiveness, members are especially desirous of staying in the group and tend to describe the group in favourable terms.[30]

The arch-stereotype of a cohesive group is the major league baseball team that begins September looking like a good bet to win its division and make it to the World Series. On the field we see well-oiled, precision teamwork. In the clubhouse, all is sweetness and joviality, and interviewed players tell the world how fine it is to be playing with "a great bunch of guys."

Cohesiveness is a relative, rather than absolute, property of groups. While some groups are more cohesive than others, there is no objective line between cohesive and non-cohesive groups. Thus, we will use the adjective *cohesive* to refer to groups that are more attractive than average for their members.

Factors Influencing Cohesiveness

What makes some groups more cohesive than others? Important factors include threat, competition, success, member diversity, group size, and toughness of initiation.

Threat and Competition. External threat to the survival of the group increases cohesiveness in a wide variety of situations.[31] As an example, consider the wrangling, uncoordinated corporate board of directors that quickly forms a united front in the

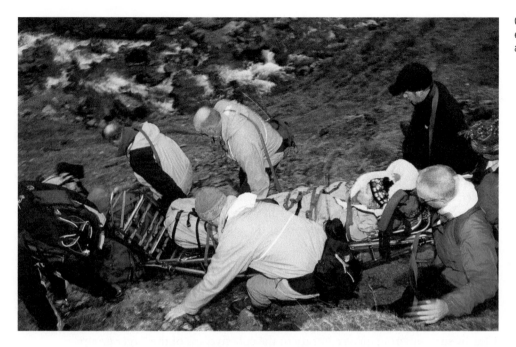

Cohesive groups lead to effective goal accomplishment.

face of a takeover bid. Honest competition with another group can also promote cohesiveness.[32] This is the case with the World Series contenders.

Why do groups often become more cohesive in response to threat or competition? They probably feel a need to improve communication and coordination so that they can better cope with the situation at hand. Members now perceive the group as more attractive because it is seen as capable of doing what has to be done to ward off threat or to win. There are, of course, limits to this. Under *extreme* threat or very *unbalanced* competition, increased cohesiveness will serve little purpose. For example, the partners in a firm faced with certain financial disaster would be unlikely to exhibit cohesiveness because it would do nothing to combat the severe threat.

Success. It should come as no surprise that a group becomes more attractive to its members when it has successfully accomplished some important goal, such as defending itself against threat or winning a prize.[33] By the same token, cohesiveness will decrease after failure, although there may be "misery loves company" exceptions. The situation for competition is shown graphically in Exhibit 7.5. Fit-Rite Jeans owns two small clothing stores (A and B) in a large city. To boost sales, it holds a contest between

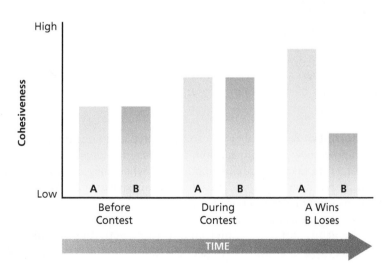

EXHIBIT 7.5
Competition, success, and cohesiveness.

the two stores, offering $150 worth of merchandise to each employee of the store that achieves the highest sales during the next business quarter. Before the competition begins, the staff of each store is equally cohesive. As we suggested above, when competition begins, both groups become more cohesive. The members become more cooperative with each other, and in each store there is much talk about "us" versus "them." At the end of the quarter, store A wins the prize and becomes yet more cohesive. The group is especially attractive to its members because it has succeeded in the attainment of a desired goal. On the other hand, cohesiveness plummets in the losing store B—the group has become less attractive to its members.

Member Diversity. Earlier, we pointed out that groups that are diverse in terms of gender, age, and race can have a harder time becoming cohesive than more homogeneous groups. However, if the group is in agreement about how to accomplish some particular task, its success in performing the task will often outweigh surface dissimilarity in determining cohesiveness.[34]

Size. Other things being equal, bigger groups should have a more difficult time becoming and staying cohesive. In general, such groups should have a more difficult time agreeing on goals and more problems communicating and coordinating efforts to achieve those goals. Earlier, we pointed out that large groups frequently divide into subgroups. Clearly, such subgrouping is contrary to the cohesiveness of the larger group.

Toughness of Initiation. Despite its rigorous admissions policies, the Harvard Business School does not lack applicants. Similarly, exclusive yacht and golf clubs might have waiting lists for membership extending several years into the future. All this suggests that groups that are tough to get into should be more attractive than those that are easy to join.[35] This is well known in the armed forces, where rigorous physical training and stressful "survival schools" precede entry into elite units such as the Special Forces or the Rangers.

Consequences of Cohesiveness

From the previous section, it should be clear that managers or group members might be able to influence the level of cohesiveness of work groups by using competition or threat, varying group size or composition, or manipulating membership requirements. The question remains, however, as to whether *more* or *less* cohesiveness is a desirable group property. This, of course, depends on the consequences of group cohesiveness and who is doing the judging.

More Participation in Group Activities. Because members wish to remain in the group, voluntary turnover from cohesive groups should be low. Also, members like being with each other; therefore, absence should be lower than in less cohesive groups. In addition, participation should be reflected in a high degree of communication within the group as members strive to cooperate with and assist each other. This communication might well be of a more friendly and supportive nature, depending on the key goals of the group.[36]

More Conformity. Because they are so attractive and coordinated, cohesive groups are well equipped to supply information, rewards, and punishment to individual members. These factors take on special significance when they are administered by those who hold a special interest for us. Thus, highly cohesive groups are in a superb position to induce conformity to group norms.

Members of cohesive groups are especially motivated to engage in activities that will *keep* the group cohesive. Chief among these activities is applying pressure to deviants to get them to comply with group norms. Cohesive groups react to deviants by increasing the amount of communication directed at these individuals.[37] Such communication contains information to help the deviant "see the light," as well as veiled threats about what might happen if he or she does not. Over time, if such communication is ineffective in inducing conformity, it tends to decrease. This is a signal that the group has isolated the deviant member to maintain cohesiveness among the majority.

More Success. Above, we pointed out that successful goal accomplishment contributes to group cohesiveness. However, it is also true that cohesiveness contributes to group success—in general, cohesive groups are good at achieving their goals. Research has found that group cohesiveness is related to performance.[38] Thus, there is a reciprocal relationship between success and cohesiveness.

Why are cohesive groups effective at goal accomplishment? Probably because of the other consequences of cohesiveness we discussed above. A high degree of participation and communication, coupled with active conformity to group norms and commitment, should ensure a high degree of agreement about the goals the group is pursuing and the methods it is using to achieve those goals. Thus, coordinated effort pays dividends to the group.

Since cohesiveness contributes to goal accomplishment, should managers attempt to increase the cohesiveness of work groups by juggling the factors that influence cohesiveness? To answer this question, we must emphasize that cohesive groups are especially effective at accomplishing *their own* goals. If these goals happen to correspond with those of the organization, increased cohesiveness should have substantial benefits for group performance. If not, organizational effectiveness might be threatened. In fact, one study of paper-machine work crews found that group cohesiveness was related to the productivity of the crews that accepted the goals of the organization. Cohesiveness did not improve productivity in work crews that did not accept the goals of the organization.[39] One large-scale study of industrial work groups reached the following conclusions:

- In highly cohesive groups, the productivity of individual group members tends to be fairly similar to that of other members. In less cohesive groups there is more variation in productivity.

- Highly cohesive groups tend to be *more* or *less* productive than less cohesive groups, depending on a number of variables.[40]

These two facts are shown graphically in Exhibit 7.6. The lower variability of productivity in more cohesive groups stems from the power of such groups to induce conformity. To the extent that work groups have productivity norms, more cohesive groups should be better able to enforce them. Furthermore, if cohesive groups accept

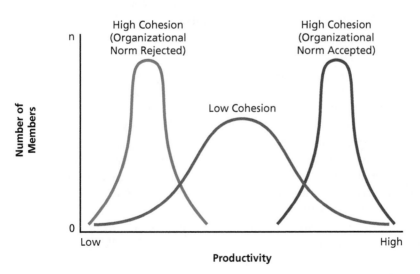

EXHIBIT 7.6
Hypothetical productivity curves for groups varying in cohesiveness.

organizational norms regarding productivity, they should be highly productive. If cohesive groups reject such norms, they are especially effective in limiting productivity.

One other factor that influences the impact of cohesiveness on productivity is the extent to which the task really requires interdependence and cooperation among group members (e.g., a football team versus a golf team). Cohesiveness is more likely to pay off when the task requires more interdependence.[41]

In summary, cohesive groups tend to be successful in accomplishing what they wish to accomplish. In a good labour relations climate, group cohesiveness on interdependent tasks should contribute to high productivity. If the climate is marked by tension and disagreement, cohesive groups may pursue goals that result in low productivity.

Social Loafing

Have you ever participated in a group project at work or school in which you did not contribute as much as you could have because other people were there to take up the slack? Or have you ever reduced your effort in a group project because you felt that others were not pulling their weight? If so, you have been guilty of social loafing. **Social loafing** is the tendency that people have to withhold physical or intellectual effort when they are performing a group task.[42] The implication is that they would work harder if they were alone rather than part of the group. Earlier we said that process losses in groups could be due to coordination problems or to motivation problems. Social loafing is a motivation problem.

People working in groups often feel trapped in a social dilemma, in that something that might benefit them individually—slacking off in the group—will result in poor group performance if everybody behaves the same way. Social loafers resolve the dilemma in a way that hurts organizational goal accomplishment. Notice that the tendency for social loafing is probably more pronounced in individualistic North America than in more collective and group-oriented cultures.

As the questions above suggest, social loafing has two different forms. In the *free rider effect*, people lower their effort to get a free ride at the expense of their fellow group members. In the *sucker effect*, people lower their effort because of the feeling that others are free riding, that is, they are trying to restore equity in the group. You can probably imagine a scenario in which the free riders start slacking off and then the suckers follow suit. Group performance suffers badly.

What are some ways to counteract social loafing?[43]

- *Make individual performance more visible.* Where appropriate, the simplest way to do this is to keep the group small in size. Then, individual contributions are less likely to be hidden. Posting performance levels and making presentations of one's accomplishments can also facilitate visibility.

- *Make sure that the work is interesting.* If the work is involving, intrinsic motivation should counteract social loafing.

- *Increase feelings of indispensability.* Group members might slack off because they feel that their inputs are unnecessary for group success. This can be counteracted by using training and the status system to provide group members with unique inputs (e.g., having one person master computer graphics programs).

- *Increase performance feedback.* Some social loafing happens because groups or individual members simply are not aware of their performance. Increased feedback, as appropriate, from the boss, peers, and customers (internal or external) should encourage self-correction. Group members might require assertiveness training to provide each other with authentic feedback.

- *Reward group performance.* Members are more likely to monitor and maximize their own performance (and attend to that of their colleagues) when the group receives rewards for effectiveness.

Social loafing. The tendency to withhold physical or intellectual effort when performing a group task.

What Is a Team?

We began this chapter with a simple question: "What is a group?" Now you may be asking yourself, "What is a team?" Some have suggested that a team is something more than a group. They suggest that a group becomes a team when there exists a strong sense of shared commitment and when a synergy develops such that the group's efforts are greater than the sum of its parts.[44] While such differences might be evident in some instances, our definition of a group is sufficient to describe most teams that can be found in organizations. The term "team" is generally used to describe "groups" in organizational settings. Therefore, for our purposes in this chapter, we use the terms interchangeably. Teams have become a major building block of organizations and are now quite common in North America.[45] The reasons for this vary, but in many cases it is an attempt to improve efficiency, quality, customer satisfaction, innovation, or the speed of production. Research has shown improvements in organizational performance in terms of both efficiency and quality as a result of team-based work arrangements.[46]

You will recall that in Chapter 2 we defined self-efficacy as beliefs individuals have about their ability to successfully perform a task. When it comes to teams, collective efficacy is also important to ensure high performance.[47] **Collective efficacy** consists of *shared* beliefs that a team can successfully perform a given task. Notice that self-efficacy doesn't necessarily translate into collective efficacy—five skilled musicians do not necessarily result in a good band. In the following sections we cover the factors that contribute to collective efficacy in a team.

Collective efficacy. Shared beliefs that a team can successfully perform a given task.

Designing Effective Work Teams

The double-edged nature of group cohesiveness suggests that a delicate balance of factors dictates whether a work group is effective or ineffective. In turn, this suggests that organizations should pay considerable attention to how work groups are designed and managed.

A good model for thinking about the design of effective work groups is to consider a successful sports team. In most cases, such teams are small groups made up of highly skilled individuals who are able to meld these skills into a cohesive effort. The task they are performing is intrinsically motivating and provides very direct feedback. If there are status differences on the team, the basis for these differences is contribution to the team, not some extraneous factor. The team shows an obsessive concern with obtaining the right personnel, relying on tryouts or player drafts, and the team is coached, not supervised. With this informal model in mind, let's examine the concept of group effectiveness more closely.

J. Richard Hackman of Harvard University (co-developer of the Job Characteristics Model, Chapter 6) has written extensively about work group effectiveness.[48] According to Hackman, a work group is effective when (1) its physical or intellectual output is acceptable to management and to the other parts of the organization that use this output, (2) group members' needs are satisfied rather than frustrated by the group, and (3) the group experience enables members to *continue* to work together.

What leads to group effectiveness? In colloquial language, "sweat, smarts, and style." Put more formally, as Hackman notes, group effectiveness occurs when high effort is directed toward the group's task, when great knowledge and skill are directed toward the task, and when the group adopts sensible strategies for accomplishing its goals. And just how does an organization achieve this? As with Ralston Foods, there is growing awareness in many organizations that the answer is self-managed work teams.

Self-Managed Work Teams

Self-managed work teams (SMWTs) generally provide their members with the opportunity to do challenging work under reduced supervision. Other labels that we often apply to such groups are autonomous, semi-autonomous, and self-directed. The general idea,

Self-managed work teams (SMWTs). Work groups that have the opportunity to do challenging work under reduced supervision.

which is more important than the label, is that the groups regulate much of their own members' behaviour. Much interest in such teams was spurred by the success of teams in Japanese industry.

Critical to the success of self-managed teams are the nature of the task, the composition of the group, and the various support mechanisms in place.[49] Notice that many of the suggestions that follow should improve coordination, discourage social loafing, and foster collective efficacy.

Tasks for Self-Managed Teams. Experts agree that tasks assigned to self-managed work teams should be complex and challenging, requiring high interdependence among team members for accomplishment. In general, these tasks should have the qualities of enriched jobs, which we described in Chapter 6. Thus, teams should see the task as significant, they should perform the task from beginning to end, and they should use a variety of skills. The point here is that self-managed teams have to have something useful to self-manage, and it is fairly complex tasks that capitalize on the diverse knowledge and skills of a group. Taking a number of olive stuffers on a food-processing assembly line, putting them in distinctive jumpsuits, calling them the Olive Squad, and telling them to self-manage will be unlikely to yield dividends in terms of effort expended or brainpower employed. The basic task will still be boring, a prime recipe for social loafing!

Outside the complexity requirement, the actual range of tasks for which organizations have used self-managed teams is wide, spanning both blue- and white-collar jobs. In the white-collar domain, complex service and design jobs seem especially conducive to self-management. In the blue-collar domain, General Mills and Chaparral Steel of Midlothian, Texas, make extensive use of self-managed work groups. In general, these groups are responsible for dividing labour among various subtasks as they see fit and making a variety of decisions about matters that impinge on the group. When a work site is formed from scratch and lacks an existing culture, the range of these activities can be very broad. Consider the self-managed teams formed in a new UK confectionery plant.

> *Production employees worked in groups of 8 to 12 people, all of whom were expected to carry out each of eight types of jobs involved in the production process. Group members were collectively responsible for allocating jobs among themselves, reaching production targets and meeting quality and hygiene standards, solving local production problems, recording production data for information systems, organizing breaks, ordering and collecting raw materials and delivering finished goods to stores, calling for engineering support, and training new recruits. They also participated in selecting new employees. Within each group, individuals had considerable control over the amount of variety they experienced by rotating their tasks, and each production group was responsible for one product line. Group members interacted informally throughout the working day but made the most important decisions—for example, regarding job allocation—at formal weekly group meetings where performance was also discussed.[50]*

If a theme runs through this discussion of tasks for self-managed teams, it is the breakdown of traditional, conventional, specialized *roles* in the group. Group members adopt roles that will make the group effective, not ones that are simply related to a narrow specialty.

Composition of Self-Managed Teams. How should organizations assemble self-managed teams to ensure effectiveness? "Stable, small, and smart" might be a fast answer.[51]

- *Stability*. Self-managed teams require considerable interaction and high cohesiveness among their members. This, in turn, requires understanding and trust. To achieve this, group membership must be fairly stable. Rotating members into and out of the group will cause it to fail to develop a true group identity.[52]

- *Size*. In keeping with the demands of the task, self-managed teams should be as small as is feasible. The goal here is to keep coordination problems and social loafing to a minimum. These negative factors can be a problem for all groups, but they can be especially difficult for self-managed groups. This is because reduced supervision means that there is no boss to coordinate the group's activities and search out social loafers who do not do their share of the work.

- *Expertise*. It goes without saying that group members should have a high level of expertise about the task at hand. Everybody does not have to know everything, but the group as a *whole* should be very knowledgeable about the task. Again, reduced supervision discourages "running to the boss" when problems arise, but the group must have the resources to successfully solve these problems. One set of skills that all members should probably possess to some degree is *social skills*. Understanding how to talk things out, communicate effectively, and resolve conflict is especially important for self-managed groups.

- *Diversity*. Put simply, a team should have members who are similar enough to work well together and diverse enough to bring a variety of perspectives and skills to the task at hand. A product planning group consisting exclusively of new, male MBAs might work well together but lack the different perspectives that are necessary for creativity. Concerning diversity, check out Global Focus: *Diversity on Multicultural Self-Managed Work Teams.*

GLOBAL FOCUS

Diversity on Multicultural Self-Managed Work Teams

Over the last several decades, companies have turned to self-managed work teams (SMWTs) to accomplish important tasks and solve organizational problems. For managers and researchers alike, the issue of how to assemble a strong team has been of great interest. The advent of the global economy has added a new question concerning successful team composition: How can managers build an effective team made up of individuals from different cultures? Furthermore, since various cultures can be represented in a single country, this question not only concerns multinational teams, but also within-nation teams made up of individuals with different cultural values.

Researchers Bradley Kirkman and Debra Shapiro undertook a study to assess how cultural diversity affects SMWT performance. Instead of simply using nationality as a measure of culture, Kirkman and Shapiro measured cultural values directly to capture within-country differences. They believed that diversity in cultural values would be more important for team performance than how high a team scored on a particular value. They also believed that diversity on various cultural values would affect performance differently in different countries, depending on their dominant cultural orientation. To test these beliefs, Kirkman and Shapiro studied 15 SMWTs in an American chemical firm and 19 SMWTs in an electronic component manufacturer in the Philippines, and assessed how cultural value diversity affected team performance.

What did they find? Cultural diversity measured directly had a greater impact on team performance than simple demographic (e.g., age, gender) diversity. They also found that diversity in cultural values within teams affected performance more than whether a team had an overall high or low score on a particular value. Finally, they found a different pattern of results concerning diversity and performance for the American teams versus the teams from the Philippines. For example, diversity on collectivism, power distance, and determinism had negligible or positive effects on performance on the Philippine teams, but negative effects on the US teams. Overall, the lessons for managers are that (a) cultural diversity on SMWTs is not automatically good or bad, (b) managers need to carefully consider cultural diversity issues when assembling a team, and (c) managers need to understand that diversity effects can vary across countries.

Source: Based on Kirkman, B.L., & Shapiro, D.L. (2005). The impact of cultural value diversity on multicultural team performance. *Advances in International Management (Managing Multinational Teams: Global Perspectives)*, 18, 33–67.

One way of maintaining appropriate group composition might be to let the group choose its own members, as occurred at the confectionery plant we described above. A potential problem with this is that the group might use some irrelevant criterion (such as race or gender) to unfairly exclude others. Thus, human resources department oversight is necessary, as are very clear selection criteria (in terms of behaviours, skills, and credentials). The selection stage is critical, since some studies (including the one conducted in the confectionary plant) have shown elevated turnover in self-managed teams.[53] "Fit" is important, and it is well worth expending the extra effort to find the right people. At Britain's Pret A Manger sandwich and coffee shops, job seekers work in a shop for a day and then the staff votes on whether they can join the team.[54]

The theme running through this discussion of team composition favours *high cohesiveness* and the development of group *norms* that stress group effectiveness.

Supporting Self-Managed Teams. A number of support factors can assist self-managed teams in becoming and staying effective. Reports of problems with teams can usually be traced back to inadequate support.

- *Training.* In almost every conceivable instance, members of self-managed teams will require extensive training. The kind of training depends on the exact job design and on the needs of the workforce. However, some common areas include:
  - *Technical training.* This might include math, computer use, or any tasks that a supervisor formerly handled. Cross-training in the specialties of other teammates is common.
  - *Social skills.* Assertiveness, problem solving, and routine dispute resolution are skills that help the team operate smoothly.
  - *Language skills.* This can be important for ethnically diverse teams. Good communication is critical on self-managed teams.
  - *Business training.* Some firms provide training in the basic elements of finance, accounting, and production so that employees can better grasp how their team's work fits into the larger picture.
- *Rewards.* The general rule here is to try to tie rewards to team accomplishment rather than to individual accomplishment while still providing team members with some individual performance feedback. Microsoft's European product support group went from individual rewards to team-based rewards when it found that the former discouraged engineers from taking on difficult cases.[55] Gain sharing, profit sharing, and skill-based pay (Chapter 6) all seem to be compatible reward systems for a team environment. Skill-based pay, used at Ralston Foods, is especially attractive because it rewards the acquisition of multiple skills that can support the team. To provide individual performance feedback, some firms have experimented with peer (e.g., team member) performance appraisals. Many have also done away with status symbols that are unrelated to group effectiveness (such as reserved parking and dining areas).
- *Management.* Self-management will not receive the best support when managers feel threatened and see it as reducing their own power or promotion opportunities. Some schooled in the traditional role of manager may simply not adapt. Those who do can serve important functions by mediating relations *between* teams and by dealing with union concerns, since unions are often worried about the cross-functional job sharing in self-management. One study found that the most effective managers in a self-management environment encouraged groups to observe, evaluate, and reinforce their own task behaviour.[56] This suggests that coaching teams to be independent enhances their effectiveness.[57]

Michael Campion and his colleagues have studied team characteristics and group effectiveness in teams of professional and non-professional workers.[58] Their results

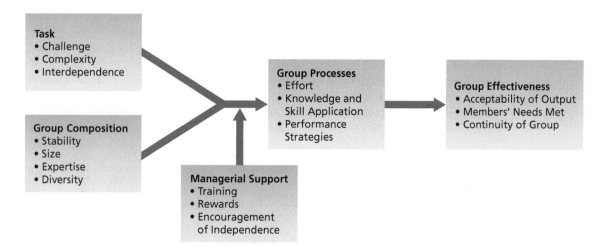

EXHIBIT 7.7
Factors influencing work group effectiveness.

Source: Based in part on Hackman, J.R. (1987). "The Design of Work Teams" in J.W. Lorsch, ed., *Handbook of Organizational Behaviour*. Englewood Cliffs, NJ: Pearson Education. Used by permission of J.W. Lorsch.

provide strong support for many of the relationships shown in Exhibit 7.7. For example, they found that task characteristics were related to most measures of group effectiveness, including productivity, team member satisfaction, and manager and employee judgments of group effectiveness. Group composition characteristics were related to only a few of the effectiveness measures. In particular, teams perceived as too large for their tasks were rated as less effective than teams perceived as an appropriate size or too small. Managerial support was related to many of the measures of effectiveness and was found to be one of the best predictors of group performance in another recent study.[59] Campion and colleagues found that group processes were the best predictors of group effectiveness, which is consistent with Exhibit 7.7. Overall, research has shown improvements in team productivity, quality, customer satisfaction, and safety following the implementation of self-managed work teams.[60]

Cross-Functional Teams

Let's look at another kind of team that contemporary organizations are using with increasing frequency. **Cross-functional teams** bring people with different functional specialties together to better invent, design, or deliver a product or service.

A cross-functional team might be self-managed and permanent if it is doing a recurrent task that is not too complex. If the task is complex and unique (such as designing a car), cross-functional teams require formal leadership, and their lives will generally be limited to the life of the specific project. In both cases, the "cross-functional" label means that such diverse specialties are necessary that cross-training is not feasible. People have to be experts in their own area but able to cooperate with others.

Cross-functional teams, which have been used in service industries such as banking and hospitals, are probably best known for their successes in product development.[61] Thus, Rubbermaid uses teams to invent and design a remarkable variety of innovative household products. Similarly, Thermos used a team to invent a very successful ecologically friendly electric barbecue grill. It sped to the market in record time.

The general goals of using cross-functional teams include some combination of innovation, speed, and quality that comes from early coordination among the various specialties. We can see their value by looking at the traditional way auto manufacturers designed cars in North America.[62] First, stylists determined what the car would look like and then passed their design on to engineering, which developed mechanical specifications and blueprints. In turn, manufacturing considered how to construct what the stylists and engineers designed. Somewhere down the line, marketing and accounting got their say. This process invariably leads to problems. One link in the chain might

Cross-functional teams. Work groups that bring people with different functional specialties together to better invent, design, or deliver a product or service.

have a difficult time understanding what the previous link meant. Worse, one department might resist the ideas of another simply because they "were not invented here." The result of all this is slow, expensive development and early quality problems. In contrast, the cross-functional approach gets all the specialties working together from day one. A complex project, such as a car design, might have over 30 cross-functional teams working at the same time. Applied Focus: *A Diverse Team Creates the New Camaro* describes a small part of the cross-functional teamwork that produced the new Chevy, which is built in Oshawa, Ontario.

APPLIED FOCUS

A Diverse Team Creates the New Camaro

The handful of designers who gave birth to the all new Camaro were a diverse group. That theme continued as it was developed all around the globe. When Design Director Tom Peters got a hush-hush assignment from Ed Welburn, VP of Global Design, to come up with a new Camaro to be shown at an upcoming auto show, he was beyond excited. The chance to redefine an American icon is every car designer's dream. Trying to keep his project top secret, he assembled a small team of his most talented young designers. They were SangYup Lee and Steve Kim from Korea and Vlad Kapitonov from Russia. Tom wanted a diverse group who didn't grow up with the Camaro in their backyard— who would bring a fresh perspective to the design. He asked his team to design "the meanest street-fighting dog they've ever seen" and to look at modern aircraft for influence. He did this right before a holiday break.

SangYup took that directive literally, feverishly sketching at the airport on his way to visit family in Korea. Vlad and Steve sketched over break too, and when everybody regrouped at the design lair known as Studio X, Tom knew he had picked the right guys. Sketches were chosen—SangYup's for the front, and Vlad's for the rear. Designer Micah Jones nailed the interior, fusing high design with high technology. Using these sketches as a guide, the car was fast-tracked to a full-size clay and then fitted with an engine and drivetrain so that it could swagger onto the world's stage at the 2006 North American International Auto Show. And that's where the story really began. Tom and his team now had to build a production car that would lose none of the jaw-dropping style of the concept—a job that would require a flawless blend of engineering and technology.

The team crisscrossed the world in this effort, beginning in Australia. There, the engineering group at Holden were chosen because of their rear-wheel-drive

Three GM designers who worked on the Camaro: Micah Jones, Rebecca Waldmeir, and SangYup Lee.

prowess. Working closely with Tom's team, they created a platform that delivered the pure power any car bearing the name Camaro would need. The Camaro took plenty of other side trips on its journey from concept to production car. It was cold-weather tested in Sweden. Warm-weather tested in Death Valley. And the mighty SS was track tested at Nürburgring, where it clocked a world-class 8:19.

The result of all this combined passion is nothing short of spectacular. You might see a beautifully modern American car when you look at the new Camaro. But Tom Peters sees a car drawn by a Korean, engineered in Australia, tested in Germany, and built in North America. Because he knows firsthand that the only way to build a world-class car is to have the best people in the world build it!

Sources: Excerpted from Chevrolet advertising copy. (2009, May). *Road & Track*, 30. General Motors Corp. Used with permission, GM Media Archives.

The speed factor can be dramatic. Manufacturers have reduced the development of a new car model by several years. Boeing used a cross-functional team to reduce certain design analyses from two weeks to only a few minutes.

Principles for Effectiveness. Research has discovered a number of factors that contribute to the effectiveness of cross-functional teams. We will illustrate several of these factors with examples from a past redesign of the Ford Mustang.[63]

- *Composition.* All relevant specialties are necessary, and effective teams are sure not to overlook anyone. Auto companies put labour representatives on car design teams to warn of assembly problems. On the Mustang project, outside suppliers were represented.

- *Superordinate goals.* **Superordinate goals** are attractive outcomes that can only be achieved by collaboration. They override detailed functional objectives that might be in conflict (e.g., finance versus design). On the Mustang project, the superordinate goal was to keep the legendary name alive in the face of corporate cost cutting.

- *Physical proximity.* Team members have to be located (sometimes relocated) close to each other to facilitate informal contact. Mustang used a former furniture warehouse in Allen Park, Michigan, to house its teams.

- *Autonomy.* Cross-functional teams need some autonomy from the larger organization, and functional specialists need some authority to commit their function to project decisions. This prevents meddling or "micromanaging" by upper level or functional managers.

- *Rules and procedures.* Although petty rules and procedures are to be avoided, some basic decision procedures must be laid down to prevent anarchy. On the Mustang project, it was agreed that a single manufacturing person would have a veto over radical body changes.

- *Leadership.* Because of the potential for conflict, cross-functional team leaders need especially strong people skills in addition to task expertise. The "tough engineer" who headed the Mustang project succeeded in developing his people skills for that task.

One of the goals of several of these principles is to ensure that team members share mental models. **Shared mental models** mean that team members share identical information about how they should interact and what their task is. Shared mental models contribute greatly to effective team performance, at least when the shared knowledge is an accurate reflection of reality.[64] Although shared mental models are important for all teams, they are a particular challenge to instill in cross-functional teams due to the divergent backgrounds of the team members. Consider this product development team:

> *The team is given the mandate to make a "tough truck." The designer, thinking in terms of styling, conceptualizes "tough" as "powerful looking." The designer then sketches a vehicle with a large grille and large tires, creating a very powerful stance. When seeing this mock-up, an engineer, thinking in terms of functionality and conceptualizing tough as implying durability, is unhappy with the design because it compromises the vehicle's power. Maintaining hauling capacity with large tires implies the need for greater torque output from the engine, adding expense and difficulty to the engineer's part of the problem. When the engineer suggests 16- rather than 20-inch wheels, the designer balks, claiming it makes the vehicle look cartoonish rather than tough.[65]*

Clearly, the designer and the engineer don't share mental models of what "tough" means, and this problem can be greatly magnified with the participation of other functions and disciplines. It can also be magnified in virtual teams, a subject we will now turn to.

Superordinate goals. Attractive outcomes that can only be achieved by collaboration.

Shared mental models. Team members share identical information about how they should interact and what their task is.

Virtual Teams

Virtual teams. Work groups that use technology to communicate and collaborate across time, space, and organizational boundaries.

With the increasing trends toward globalization and the rapid development of high-tech communication tools, a new type of team has emerged that will surely be critical to organizations' success for years to come: virtual teams. **Virtual teams** are work groups that use technology to communicate and collaborate across space, time, and organizational boundaries.[66] Along with their reliance on computer and electronic technology, the primary feature of these teams is the lack of face-to-face contact between team members due to geographic dispersion. This geographic separation often entails linkages across countries and cultures. Furthermore, virtual teams are often cross-functional in nature. Technologies used by virtual teams can be either asynchronous (email, fax, voice mail), allowing team members to reflect before responding, or synchronous (chat, groupware), allowing team members to communicate dynamically in real time. Although not so long ago they were only a dream, virtual teams are now spreading across the business landscape and are used by numerous companies, such as CAE, Sabre Inc., IBM, and Texas Instruments.

Advantages of Virtual Teams. Why are these teams becoming so popular? Because managers are quickly learning that linking minds through technology has some definite advantages:

- *Around-the-clock work.* Globally, using a virtual team can create a 24-hour team that never sleeps. In these "follow the sun" teams, a team member can begin a process in London and pass it on to another team member in New York for more input. From New York, the work can be forwarded to a colleague in San Francisco who, after more work, can send it along to Hong Kong for completion.[67] In today's non-stop economy, the benefits of such continuous workflows are huge.

- *Reduced travel time and cost.* Virtual teaming reduces travel costs associated with face-to-face meetings. In the past, important meetings, key negotiation sessions, and critical junctures in projects required team members to board planes and travel long distances. In the virtual environment, expensive and time-consuming travel can be mostly eliminated. Virtual teams can therefore lead to significant savings of time, money, and security concerns over air travel also make virtual teams an attractive alternative.

- *Larger talent pool.* Virtual teams allow companies to expand their potential labour markets and to go after the best people, even if these people have no interest in relocating. The nature of virtual teams can also give employees added flexibility, allowing for a better work–life balance, which is an effective recruiting feature.[68]

Challenges of Virtual Teams. While the advantages highlighted above are appealing, many commentators have pointed out that virtual teams can also involve some disadvantages.[69] The lesson seems to be that managers must recognize that these teams present unique challenges and should not be treated as regular teams that just happen to use technology.

- *Trust.* Several commentators have noted that trust is difficult to develop between virtual team members. People typically establish trust through physical contact and socialization, which are simply not available to virtual team members. For more on this challenge, see You Be the Manager.

- *Miscommunication.* The loss of face-to-face communication presents certain risks for virtual teams. Humans use many non-verbal cues to communicate meaning and feeling in a message. Using technology, the richness of face-to-face communication is lost and miscommunication can result (see Chapter 10). These risks can be

YOU BE THE MANAGER

Creating Trust in Virtual Teams at Orange

Multinational companies have a dual challenge of globalizing operations for purposes of efficiencies and localizing delivery of products and services to support national differences. At Orange, this challenge became all the more obvious when it expanded operations in the late 1990s to become a large, pan-European company. Orange is the mobile operator of France Telecom, providing services to 57 million customers across 17 countries. With presence in Europe, the Middle East, and Africa, Orange realized that to protect and strengthen the Orange brand, product development previously performed within host countries needed to become a global initiative. Although it is tempting to centralize a team that has a global mandate, Orange pursued virtual team collaboration, which allows firms to increase diversity in their teams and potentially achieve greater productivity and creativity. At Orange, virtual teams were becoming a way of life, as with many high-tech, global corporations, but there were clearly challenges, rooted in the fact that there were less interpersonal similarities (e.g., common backgrounds and experience) among team members.

Within the product development organization at Orange, virtual teams were usually led by a product manager. Members of the team not only had primary responsibilities to the virtual team but also did work for local teams and various functions. As with other virtual teams, those at Orange were required to work across time zones, cultures, and reporting lines. Virtuality meant that team members were unable to interact informally, in face-to-face meetings. Communicating through electronic media (e.g., email, phone, video conferencing) greatly reduced the ability to interact through non-verbal cues. The lack of informal communication was considered to be a large barrier in team productivity. As one team leader expressed, "Work really only starts after that first face-to-face meeting."

Cultural distance also affected the virtual teams at Orange. In one virtual team, conference calls between the UK and Paris offices became particularly strained. The British employees, in an effort to enhance meeting productivity, used humour to encourage participation, but this approach backfired. Without the benefit of seeing facial expressions, paired with the difficulty of

At Orange, the creation and leadership of virtual teams is based on the fundamental need to create trust quickly and embed this trust throughout the life of the team.

relating to the jokes themselves, Parisian employees felt increasingly isolated from their British counterparts and, as with other virtual teams at Orange, had low trust in their colleagues' ability to perform.

Because virtual teams at Orange were vital to the company's overall global strategy, management was keen to find ways to enhance team performance, productivity, and innovation. It was clear that work had to be done to overcome the trust barrier that existed between many of the virtual team members.

QUESTIONS

1. Why is trust important in virtual teams, and what influences the degree of trust among team members?

2. How can trust be developed and maintained in virtual teams?

To find out how Orange increased trust between virtual team members, see The Manager's Notebook at the end of this chapter.

Source: Adapted from Lawley, D. (2006, May/June). Creating trust in virtual teams at Orange. *Knowledge Management Review*, 12–17.

particularly high on global virtual teams, as attempts at humour or the use of unfamiliar terms can lead to messages being misconstrued. Some organizations, such as Chevron, encourage global team members to avoid humour or metaphors when communicating online.[70]

- *Isolation.* People have needs for companionship. In self-contained offices, co-workers can meet for lunch, share stories, talk about their kids, and socialize outside of work. Unfortunately, these more casual interactions are not usually possible for virtual teams, a lack that can lead to team members having feelings of isolation and detachment.

- *High costs.* Savings in areas such as travel must be weighed against the costs of cutting-edge technology. Initial set-up costs can be substantial. Budgets must also be devoted to maintenance since, in the virtual environment, the firm's technology must run flawlessly, 24 hours a day, 7 days a week.

- *Management issues.* For managers, virtual teams can create new challenges in terms of dealing with subordinates who are no longer in view. How can you assess individual performance, monitor diligence, and ensure fairness in treatment when your team is dispersed around the globe?

Bradley Kirkman and colleagues studied 65 virtual teams at Sabre Inc., a leader in web-based travel reservations, and found that many of these challenges could be managed and, in some cases, turned into opportunities.[71] They found that trust, although developed differently than in face-to-face teams, was still possible through team member responsiveness, consistency, and reliability. Training and once-a-year team-building exercises in which members actually meet also build trust and clarify communication standards at Sabre. Furthermore, Kirkman and colleagues found that virtual communication reduced instances of stereotyping, discrimination, personality conflicts, and the formation of cliques, which often create problems in conventional work environments. Finally, in terms of performance assessments, the view at Sabre is that technology actually leads to more objective, transparent, and unbiased information being available to both employees and managers.

Lessons Concerning Virtual Teams. Overall, a number of lessons are beginning to emerge about what managers must do or keep watch for when developing virtual teams.[72]

- *Recruitment.* Choose team members carefully in terms of attitude and personality so that they are excited about these types of teams and can handle the independence and isolation that often define them. Find people with good interpersonal skills, not just technical expertise.

- *Training.* Invest in training for both technical and interpersonal skills. At Sabre, cooperation and interpersonal skills were rated much higher in importance than technical skills by virtual team members.

- *Personalization.* Encourage team members to get to know each other, either by encouraging informal communication using technology or by arranging face-to-face meetings whenever possible. Reduce feelings of isolation by setting aside time for chit-chat, acknowledging birthdays, and so on.

- *Goals and ground rules.* On the management side, virtual team leaders should define goals clearly, set rules for communication standards and responses, and provide feedback to keep team members informed of progress and the big picture.

The key appears to be recognizing the ways in which these teams are different than those based in a single office environment but not falling into the trap of focusing solely on technology. Many of the general recommendations that apply to any work team also apply to virtual teams. These teams are made up of individuals who have the same feelings and needs as workers in more traditional environments. Virtual teams must be real teams, if not by location, then in mind and spirit.

A Word of Caution: Teams as a Panacea

Teams can be a powerful resource for organizations, and this chapter has identified some of the important lessons leading to team success. However, switching from a traditional structure to a team-based configuration is not a cure-all for an organization's problems, even though some managers fall prey to the "romance of teams."[73] It is likely that the research to date on teams has focused almost exclusively on viable, ongoing teams, with little attention being paid to failed or unsuccessful teams. Also, the emergence of many teams has been the result not of employee demand but of managers' desire for greater organizational returns. Some observers therefore suggest that the team approach puts unwanted pressure and responsibilities on workers. Others have noted that many organizations have rushed to deploy teams with little planning, often resulting in confusion and contradictory signals to employees. Good planning and continuing support are necessary for the effective use of teams.[74]

THE MANAGER'S NOTEBOOK

Creating Trust in Virtual Teams at Orange

1. Trust is an important ingredient in all teams, regardless of the proximity of members. Trust is considered to enhance overall team performance because it reduces the need for formal checks and balances and increases team members' ability to work through interpersonal challenges. When trust is low, teams require a higher degree of control and leadership, which reduces overall productivity and increases costs. In virtual teams, trust is harder to achieve due to the perceived distances (e.g., geographical and cultural) between team members. To overcome this challenge, members of virtual teams need to be aligned in their thoughts and actions about the work they have been assigned. In virtual teams, trust is built upon the perceived ability of team members, benevolence between team members, positive feelings about each other, and the overall integrity of the group. At Orange, experience confirmed that three principles are necessary for building trust in teams: small team size, strong leadership, and a common working framework. At first, Orange attempted to run large, lengthy, cross-functional initiatives through the use of virtual teams. But the company found that the number of relationships and the complexity of the work created significant trust barriers. Over time, Orange moved to smaller virtual teams (under 10 members) to achieve more focused mandates over a shorter period. In addition, Orange recognized that more effective leaders were those who could recognize cultural differences and bridge those differences between members through the use of a common framework. For example, one way to ensure "equality" in a team is to have everyone join a conference call by phone, regardless of the fact that some members are located in the same place and could talk face-to-face.

2. At Orange, experience indicated that leaders of virtual teams are better off focusing on outputs rather than on team processes. Since it is impossible to know what each team member is doing at any particular time, measuring outputs allows each team member to work when and how he or she chooses, respecting local customs and norms. Orange and their consultants also realized that the start-up of a team is a crucial period when leaders need to develop clear team objectives. To encourage a culture of trust within the team, leaders must therefore be good communicators and coaches, naturally trustworthy of others, and independent workers. From the start, the leader must demonstrate trust in team members and encourage trust among team members by identifying their track records and nature of expertise. This effort must be complemented by seeking trust from stakeholders of the project, which, in turn, will generate further trust within the team. At Orange, the creation and leadership of virtual teams is now based on the fundamental need to create trust quickly and to embed this trust throughout the life of the team. Trust has become a planned activity to be achieved through the building of knowledge (understanding objectives and the contribution of others) and team formation.

LEARNING OBJECTIVES CHECKLIST

1. A *group* consists of two or more people interacting interdependently to achieve a common goal. *Formal work groups* are groups that organizations establish to facilitate the achievement of organizational goals. *Informal groups* are groups that emerge naturally in response to the common interests of organizational members.

2. Some groups go through a series of developmental stages: forming, storming, norming, performing, and adjourning. However, the *punctuated equilibrium* model stresses a first meeting, a period of little apparent progress, a critical midpoint transition, and a phase of goal-directed activity.

3. As groups get bigger, they provide less opportunity for member satisfaction. When tasks are *additive* (performance depends on the addition of individual effort) or *disjunctive* (performance depends on that of the best member), larger groups should perform better than smaller groups if the group can avoid *process losses* due to poor communication and motivation. When tasks are *conjunctive* (performance is limited by the weakest member), performance decreases as the group gets bigger, because the chance of adding a weak member increases. Diverse groups will generally develop at a slower pace and be less cohesive than homogeneous groups. While the effects of surface-level demographic diversity can wear off over time, deep diversity differences regarding attitudes are more difficult to overcome.

4. *Norms* are expectations that group members have about each other's behaviour. They provide consistency to behaviour and develop as a function of shared attitudes. In organizations, both formal and informal norms often develop to control dress, reward allocation, and performance. *Roles* are positions in a group that have a set of expected behaviours associated with them. *Role ambiguity* refers to a lack of clarity of job goals or methods. *Role conflict* exists when an individual is faced with incompatible role expectations, and it can take four forms: *intrasender, intersender, interrole*, and *person–role*. Both ambiguity and conflict have been shown to provoke job dissatisfaction, stress, and lowered commitment. *Status* is the rank or prestige that a group accords its members. Formal status systems use status symbols to reinforce the authority hierarchy and reward progression. Informal status systems also operate in organizations. Although status differences are motivational, they also lead to communication barriers.

5. *Cohesive groups* are especially attractive to their members. Threat, competition, success, and small size contribute to cohesiveness, as does a tough initiation into the group. The consequences of cohesiveness include increased participation in group affairs, improved communication, and increased conformity. Cohesive groups are especially effective in accomplishing their own goals, which may or may not be those of the organization.

6. *Social loafing* occurs when people withhold effort when performing a group task. This is less likely when individual performance is visible, the task is interesting, there is good performance feedback, and the organization rewards group achievement.

7. Members of *self-managed work teams* do challenging work under reduced supervision. For greatest effectiveness, such teams should be stable, small, well trained, and moderately diverse in membership. Group-oriented rewards are most appropriate.

   Teams perform best when they have high *collective efficacy*, a shared belief that they can perform a given task. Sharing identical information (*shared mental models*) contributes to such efficacy.

8. *Cross-functional teams* bring people with different functional specialties together to better invent, design, or deliver a product or service. They should have diverse membership, a *superordinate* goal, some basic decision rules, and reasonable autonomy. Members should work in the same physical location, and team leaders require people skills as well as task skills.

9. *Virtual teams* use technology to communicate and collaborate across time, space, and organizational boundaries. These teams offer many advantages, such as reduced travel costs, greater potential talent, and continuous workflows, but pose dangers in terms of miscommunication, trust, and feelings of isolation.

DISCUSSION QUESTIONS

1. Describe the kind of skills that you would look for in members of self-managed teams. Explain your choices. Do the same for virtual teams.

2. Debate: *Effective teamwork is more difficult for individualistic Americans, Canadians, and Australians than for more collectivist Japanese.*

3. When would an organization create self-managed teams? When would it use cross-functional teams? When would it employ virtual teams?

4. Suppose that a group of United Nations representatives from various countries forms to draft a resolution regarding world hunger. Is this an additive, disjunctive, or conjunctive task? What kinds of process losses would such a group be likely to suffer? Can you offer a prediction about the size of this group and its performance?

5. Explain how a cross-functional team could contribute to product or service quality. Explain how a cross-functional team could contribute to speeding up product design.

6. Mark Allen, a representative for an international engineering company, is a very religious person who is active in his church. Mark's direct superior has instructed him to use "any legal means" to sell a large construction project to a foreign government. The vice-president of international operations had informed Mark that he could offer a generous "kickback" to government officials to clinch the deal, although such practices are illegal. Discuss the three kinds of role conflict that Mark is experiencing.

7. Some organizations have made concerted efforts to do away with many of the status symbols associated with differences in organizational rank. All employees park in the same lot, eat in the same dining room, and have similar offices and privileges. Discuss the pros and cons of such a strategy. How might such a change affect organizational communications?

8. You are an executive in a consumer products corporation. The president assigns you to form a task force to develop new marketing strategies for the organization. You are permitted to choose its members. What things would you do to make this group as cohesive as possible? What are the dangers of group cohesiveness for the group itself and for the organization of which the group is a part?

INTEGRATIVE DISCUSSION QUESTIONS

1. What role do perceptions play in group development? Refer to the perceptual process and biases in Chapter 3 and discuss the implications for each stage of group development. What are the implications for improving the development of groups?

2. How can groups be motivated? Consider the implications of each of the work motivation theories described in Chapter 5. What do the theories tell us about how to motivate groups?

ON-THE-JOB CHALLENGE QUESTION

ISE Communications was one of the pioneers in using self-managed work teams. The teams were put in place to improve manufacturing flexibility and customer service, both factors being crucial in the highly competitive circuit board industry. Its conversion from an assembly line style of circuit board manufacturing to teams who identified with "their own" products and customers was deemed a great success by industry observers. One interesting result was that the teams were extremely obsessed with monitoring the promptness and attendance of their members, more so than managers had been before the conversion to teams. They even posted attendance charts and created punishments for slack team members.

Use your understanding of both group dynamics and teams to explain why the employees became so concerned about attendance when they were organized into teams. What had changed?

Source: Barker, J.R. (1993). Tightening the iron cage: Concertive control in self-managing teams. *Administrative Science Quarterly, 38*, 408–437.

EXPERIENTIAL EXERCISE

NASA

The purpose of this exercise is to compare individual and group problem solving and to explore the group dynamics that occur in a problem-solving session. It can also be used in conjunction with Chapter 10. The instructor will begin by forming groups of four to seven members.

The situation described in this problem is based on actual cases in which men and women lived or died, depending on the survival decisions they made. Your "life" or "death" will depend on how well your group can share its present knowledge of a relatively unfamiliar problem, so that the group can make decisions that will lead to your survival.

The Problem

You are a member of a space crew originally scheduled to rendezvous with a mother ship on the lighted surface of the moon. Due to mechanical difficulties, however, your ship was forced to land at a spot some 200 miles from the rendezvous point. During landing, much of the equipment aboard was damaged, and, because survival depends on reaching the mother ship, the most critical items available must be chosen for the 200-mile trip. On the next page are listed the fifteen items left intact and undamaged after the landing. Your task is to rank them in terms of their importance to your crew in reaching the rendezvous point. In the first column (step 1) place the number 1 by the first most important, and so on, through number 15, the least important. You have fifteen minutes to complete this phase of the exercise.

After the individual rankings are complete, participants should be formed into groups having from four to seven members. Each group should then rank the fifteen items as a team. This group ranking should be a general consensus after a discussion of the issues, not just the average of each individual ranking. While it is unlikely that everyone will agree exactly on the group ranking, an effort should be made to reach at least a decision that everyone can live with. It is important to treat differences of opinion as a means of gathering more information and clarifying issues and as an incentive to force the group to seek better alternatives. The group ranking should be listed in the second column (step 2).

The third phase of the exercise consists of the instructor providing the expert's rankings, which should be entered in the third column (step 3). Each participant should compute the difference between the individual ranking (step 1) and the expert's ranking (step 3), and between the group ranking (step 2) and the expert's ranking (step 3). Then add the two "difference" columns—the smaller the score, the closer the ranking is to the view of the experts.

Source: From Ritchie, *Organization and People*, 3rd edition. © 1984 South-Western, a part of Cenage Learning, Inc. Reproduced by permission. www.cengage.com/permissions.

Discussion

The instructor will summarize the results on the board for each group, including (a) the average individual accuracy score, (b) the group accuracy score, (c) the gain or loss between the average individual score and the group score, and (d) the lowest individual score (i.e., the best score) in each group.

The following questions will help guide the discussion:

1. As a group task, is the NASA exercise an additive, disjunctive, or conjunctive task?

2. What would be the impact of group size on performance in this task?

3. Did any norms develop in your group that guided how information was exchanged or how the decision was reached?

4. Did any special roles emerge in your group? These could include a leader, a secretary, an "expert," a critic, or a humorist. How did these roles contribute to or hinder group performance?

5. Consider the factors that contribute to effective self-managed teams. How do they pertain to a group's performance on this exercise?

6. How would group diversity help or hinder performance on the exercise?

NASA tally sheet

Items	Step 1 Your individual ranking	Step 2 The team's ranking	Step 3 Survival expert's ranking	Step 4 Difference between Step 1 & 3	Step 5 Difference between Step 2 & 3
Box of matches					
Food concentrate					
50 feet of nylon rope					
Parachute silk					
Portable heating unit					
Two .45 calibre pistols					
One case dehydrated milk					
Two 100-lb. tanks of oxygen					
Stellar map (of the moon's constellation)					
Life raft					
Magnetic compass					
5 gallons of water					
Signal flares					
First aid kit containing injection needles					
Solar-powered FM receiver-transmitter					
Total					
(The lower the score the better)				Your score	Team score

CASE INCIDENT

The Group Assignment

Janet, a student, never liked working on group assignments; however, this time she thought it would be different because she knew most of the people in her group. But it was not long before things started going badly. After the first meeting, the group could not agree when to meet again. When they finally did meet, nobody had done anything, and the assignment was due in two weeks. The group then agreed to meet again the next day to figure out what to do. However, two of the group members did not show up. The following week Janet tried in vain to arrange for another meeting, but the other group members said they were too busy and that it would be best to divide the assignment up and have each member work on a section. The night before the assignment was due the group members met to give Janet their work. Finally, Janet thought, we are making progress. However, when she got home and read what the other members had written she was shocked at how bad it was. Janet spent the rest of the night and early morning doing the whole assignment herself. Once the course ended, Janet never spoke to any of the group members again.

1. Refer to the typical stages of group development and explain the development of Janet's group.

2. To what extent was group cohesiveness a problem in Janet's work group? What might have made the group more cohesive?

CASE STUDY

The Creativity Development Committee

Tom was the manager of three research and development laboratories for a large chemical and materials corporation. He supervised general operations, budgeting, personnel, and proposal development for the labs. Each lab had several projects, and each project team was headed by a project director, who was usually a scientist or an engineer. Tom had been project director for 10 years in another of the corporation's labs and had been promoted to lab manager 4 years ago. Although he had to transfer across the country to take this job, he felt he had earned the respect of his subordinates. He had been regarded as an outsider at first, but he worked hard to be accepted, and the lab's productivity had gone up over the last two years. Tom's major worry was keeping track of everything. His busy schedule kept him from close supervision over projects.

As in most labs, each project generally went its own way. As long as it produced results, a project enjoyed a high degree of autonomy. Morale was usually high among research staff. They knew they were on the leading edge of the corporation's success and they enjoyed it. The visibility and importance of innovative research were shown by the fact that project directors were regularly promoted upward.

It was in this milieu that Tom decided that productivity might be further increased if research creativity were heightened. Research teams often met to discuss ideas and to decide on future directions. In these meetings ideas were often improved upon, but they could also be killed or cut off. Tom had studied research on decision making, which indicated that groups often suppress good ideas without a hearing; the research suggested ways of preventing this suppression and enhancing group creativity. Tom hoped to harness these findings by developing standard procedures through which idea development would be enhanced rather than hindered in these meetings. Tom asked four project directors if they were willing to work with him to review the research and meet regularly over the summer to help formulate appropriate procedures. The four agreed to take on the task and the group began its work enthusiastically.

During the first six weeks of the summer the group met weekly to discuss relevant articles and books and to hear consultants. The group was able to narrow down a set of about 15 procedures and programs to 4 prime possibilities. Eventually, 2 programs emerged as possibilities. However, as the list was narrowed from 4 to 2, there was a clear split in how the group felt.

One procedure was strongly favoured by three of the project directors. The fourth project director liked the procedure better than the other option but was less vocal in showing her support for it. In general, the project directors felt the procedure they favoured was far more consistent with what project teams were currently doing and with the problems faced by the corporation. They believed the second program, which involved a lot of writing and the use of special voting procedures, was too abstract for working research scientists to accept. It would be difficult, they said, to use this procedure because everyone would have to fill out forms and explain ideas in writing before a meeting could be held. Because of already heavy workloads, their people would not go along with the program. Researchers would ridicule the program and be prejudiced against future attempts to stimulate creativity.

Tom argued that the second program was more comprehensive, had a broader conception of problems, and would help develop more creative ideas than the first, which was a fairly conservative "brainstorming" process. Although discussion focused on the substantive nature of each program and its reaction to the objective of creativity, the project directors knew that the program Tom favoured was one he had been trained in at his former lab. Tom was a good friend of the consultant who had developed it. The project directors talked outside meetings about this friendship and questioned whether it was shaping Tom's attitudes. The climate of the group, which had initially been positive and enthusiastic, grew tense as issues connected to the power relations between the manager and project directors surfaced.

Although the project directors knew Tom could choose the program he wanted, how the final choice would be made was never clarified at the beginning of the summer. The time that the project directors spent reading and evaluating the programs created an implicit expectation that they would have an equal say in the final choice. At the same time, the project directors had all worked at the lab for at least four years and had experienced first-hand the relative power of managers and project directors. They heard horror stories of project directors who had got on the manager's "wrong side" and been denied promotion or fired. When push came to shove, they expected the manager to have greater power and to be willing to use it.

At its final meeting the group discussed the two programs for quite some time, but there seemed to be little movement. Somewhat hesitantly, Tom turned to each project director individually and asked, "How upset would you be if I choose the program I prefer?" One project director said he was uncomfortable answering. Two indicated that they felt they would have difficulty using the creativity program as it was currently designed. The fourth said that she thought she could live with it. After these answers were given, Tom told the project directors he would leave a memo in their mailboxes informing them of the final decision.

Two weeks after this discussion, the project directors were told that the second program, the one the manager preferred, would be ordered. The memo also said that the other program would be used, on an experimental basis, by one of the 18 projects. The decision caused considerable resentment. The project directors felt "used." They saw little reason in having spent too much time discussing programs if Tom was just going to choose the program he wanted, regardless of their preferences. When the program began in the fall, one of the project directors told his team that the program would be recommended rather than required, and he explained that it might have to be adapted extensively to fit the unit's style. He made this decision without telling the manager. While the move was in clear violation of Tom's authority, he knew Tom could not visit the teams often and was therefore unlikely to find out about it. Another project director instituted the program but commented afterward that he felt he had not integrated it into his unit well. He questioned how much effort he had actually invested in making the program "work."

The incident had a significant impact on the way Tom was seen by the project directors. Several commented that they had lost their respect for Tom, that they saw Tom as someone who was willing to manipulate people for his own purposes. This opinion filtered to other project directors and scientists through the "grapevine" and caused Tom considerable difficulties in a labour grievance during the following year. In this dispute several researchers banded together and defied the manager because they believed he would eventually back down. In addition, the project director who made the program optional for these workers served as a model for similar defiance by others. Once the directors saw that "optional" use of the program would be go unpunished, they felt free to do it themselves, and Tom's control was further reduced. Tom eventually transferred to another division of the corporation.

Source: Folger, et al. WORKING THROUGH CONFLICT, Case 4.3, "The Creativity Development Committee," pp. 107–109, © 1997. Reproduced by permission of Pearson Education, Inc.

1. Discuss how the stages of group development and the punctuated equilibrium model apply to the Creativity Development Committee. Did the group progress through any of the stages of these models? Did the group fail to resolve any issues implied by these models?

2. Is the choice of the best creativity development program an additive, disjunctive, or conjunctive task? Explain your reasoning. Discuss the implications of the task type for what happened on the committee.

3. Did role ambiguity surface in the case? If so, how so?

4. Did role conflict surface in the case? If so, which type or types occurred?

5. How did status issues emerge in the committee?

6. Did the committee share a mental model about its goals and procedures?

CHAPTER 8

Social Influence, Socialization, and Culture

Google Canada

Google was co-founded by Larry Page and Sergey Brin in 1998 while they were students at Stanford University. Today, Google is one of the world's largest internet search engines and the most popular website. Google's world headquarters building, known as the Googleplex, is located in Mountain View, California.

Google has more than 20 000 employees in offices around the world, and its employees speak dozens of languages. However, it has managed to maintain a small-company feel thanks to a culture that includes collaboration, a flat structure with very little hierarchy, kitchens that serve healthy food and encourage employees to eat together and socialize, and perks such as in-house massages. The company even has a chief culture officer to ensure that it maintains its core values and culture. To encourage a sense of ownership, Google employees receive stock grants or options.

In 2008, Google Canada opened its first official Canadian headquarters in downtown Toronto. Given the company's commitment to being environmentally responsible, it is no surprise that the Toronto headquarters was built with the environment in mind. For example, they kept the existing concrete floor rather than using new floor material. The cafeteria floor is made of recycled Canadian bicycle tires from landfills. And rather than using new chairs in the lobby waiting area, the company purchased stadium seats from the old Montreal Forum. Many of the green ideas came from employees and involved using existing materials of the building or reusing or recycling other materials.

As part of the company's green initiative, employees are encouraged to use public transportation or their own green solution to get to work; those that do so receive a monthly subsidy that is added to their pay. A bike room with showers is provided to encourage a healthy lifestyle. The cafeteria offers free breakfasts, lunch, and snacks and a dietary expert is responsible for the selection of food along with a menu that details how healthy each item is.

Eric Morris, a senior account executive in the Toronto office, describes the work environment as more than an office where people work. "It's not

just a bunch of cubicles, work spaces, desks and meeting rooms, but also a social environment where co-workers can collaborate in a less formal but more impactful environment." The informal work environment of the Toronto office, which consists of low barriers between work stations, was created to facilitate socializing and collaboration. Google offices also have game rooms to bring employees together from different areas of the company. Rock Band video game stations and yoga balls encourage relaxed breaks.

The Google culture also encourages innovation through its "20 percent time" program, which enables employees to work together or separately on something other than their job for one day out of five. This allows employees to work on new ideas and collaborate with each other. Gmail and Google Outreach came out of the 20 percent time program.

Another important part of the Google culture is transparency. The company holds weekly TGIF meetings, where company executives and founders Sergey Brin and Larry Page, along with CEO Eric Schmidt, address employees and answer any questions they have about Google. The Google culture of open communication also influences the hiring process, which involves several rounds of interviews in which employees and managers participate. As a result, employees have some input into the direction of the company and who they will be working with.

Google has won many awards for its work environment. *Fortune* magazine ranked Google as one of America's most admired companies and the best place to work in the United States. Google Canada was ranked as the best place to work in Canada in 2009.[1]

This description of Google Canada raises a number of interesting questions. What exactly is an organizational culture and what effect does it have on employees? What does it mean to have a strong culture and how are cultures built and maintained? These are the kinds of questions that we will probe in this chapter.

First, we will examine the general issue of social influence in organizations—how members have an impact on each other's behaviour and attitudes. Social norms hold an organization together, and conformity to such norms is a product of social influence. Thus, the next section discusses conformity. Following this, we consider the elaborate process of organizational socialization, the learning of attitudes, knowledge, and behaviours that are necessary to function in an organization. Socialization both contributes to and results from the organizational culture, the final topic that we will explore.

Social Influence in Organizations

In the previous chapter, we pointed out that groups exert influence over the attitudes and behaviour of their individual members. As a result of social influence, people often feel or act differently from how they would as independent operators. What accounts for such influence? In short, in many social settings, and especially in groups, people are highly *dependent* on others. This dependence sets the stage for influence to occur.

Information Dependence and Effect Dependence

We are frequently dependent on others for information about the adequacy and appropriateness of our behaviour, thoughts, and feelings. How satisfying is this job of mine? How nice is our boss? How much work should I take home to do over the weekend? Should we protest the bad design at the meeting? Objective, concrete answers to such questions might be hard to come by. Thus, we must often rely on information that others provide.[2] In turn, this **information dependence** gives others the opportunity to influence our thoughts, feelings, and actions via the signals they send to us.[3]

Information dependence. Reliance on others for information about how to think, feel, and act.

Individuals are often motivated to compare their own thoughts, feelings, and actions with those of others as a means of acquiring information about their adequacy. The effects of social information can be very strong, often exerting as much or more influence over others as objective reality.[4]

As if group members were not busy enough tuning in to information provided by the group, they must also be sensitive to the rewards and punishments the group has at its disposal. Thus, individuals are dependent on the *effects* of their behaviour as determined by the rewards and punishments provided by others. **Effect dependence** actually involves two complementary processes. First, the group frequently has a vested interest in how individual members think and act because such matters can affect the goal attainment of the group. Second, the member frequently desires the approval of the group. In combination, these circumstances promote effect dependence.

Effect dependence. Reliance on others due to their capacity to provide rewards and punishment.

In organizations, plenty of effects are available to keep individual members "under the influence." Managers typically have a fair array of rewards and punishments available, including promotions, raises, and the assignment of more or less favourable tasks. At the informal level, the variety of such effects available to co-workers is staggering. They might reward cooperative behaviour with praise, friendship, and a helping hand on the job. Lack of cooperation might result in nagging, harassment, name calling, or social isolation.

Social Influence in Action

One of the most obvious consequences of information and effect dependence is the tendency for group members to conform to the social norms that have been established by the group. In the last chapter, we discussed the development and function of such norms, but we have postponed until now the discussion of why norms are supported. Put simply, much of the information and many of the effects on which group members are dependent are oriented toward enforcing group norms.

Motives for Social Conformity

The fact that Roman Catholic priests conform to the norms of the church hierarchy seems rather different from the case in which convicts conform to norms that prison officials establish. Clearly, the motives for conformity differ in these two cases. What is needed, then, is some system to classify different motives for conformity.[5]

Compliance. Compliance is the simplest, most direct motive for conformity to group norms. It occurs because a member wishes to acquire rewards from the group and avoid punishment. As such, it primarily involves effect dependence. Although the complying individual adjusts his or her behaviour to the norm, he or she does not really subscribe to the beliefs, values, and attitudes that underlie the norm. Most convicts conform to formal prison norms out of compliance. Similarly, very young children behave themselves only because of external forces.

> **Compliance.**
> Conformity to a social norm prompted by the desire to acquire rewards or avoid punishment.

Identification. Some individuals conform because they find other supporters of the norm attractive. In this case, the individual identifies with these supporters and sees him or herself as similar to them. Although there are elements of effect dependence here, information dependence is especially important—if someone is basically similar to you, then you will be motivated to rely on that person for information about how to think and act. **Identification** as a motive for conformity is often revealed by an imitation process in which established members serve as models for the behaviour of others. For example, a newly promoted executive might attempt to dress and talk like her successful, admired boss. Similarly, as children get older, they might be motivated to behave themselves because such behaviour corresponds to that of an admired parent with whom they are beginning to identify.

> **Identification.**
> Conformity to a social norm prompted by perceptions that those who promote the norm are attractive or similar to oneself.

Internalization. Some conformity to norms occurs because individuals have truly and wholly accepted the beliefs, values, and attitudes that underlie the norm. As such, **internalization** of the norm has happened, and conformity occurs because it is seen as *right,* not because it achieves rewards, avoids punishment, or pleases others. That is, conformity is due to internal, rather than external, forces. In general, we expect that most religious leaders conform to the norms of their religion for this reason. Similarly, the career army officer might come to support the strict discipline of the military because it seems right and proper, not simply because colleagues support such discipline. In certain organizational settings, some of these motives for conformity are more likely than others.

> **Internalization.**
> Conformity to a social norm prompted by true acceptance of the beliefs, values, and attitudes that underlie the norm.

The Subtle Power of Compliance

In many of the examples given in the previous section, especially those dealing with effect dependence, it is obvious that the doubting group member is motivated to conform only in the compliance mode—that is, he or she really does not support the belief, value, and attitude structure underlying the norm but conforms simply to avoid trouble or obtain rewards. Of course, this happens all the time. Individuals without religious beliefs or values might agree to be married in a church service to please others. Similarly, a store cashier might verify a credit card purchase by a familiar customer even though he feels that the whole process is a waste of time. These examples of compliance seem trivial enough, but a little compliance can go a long way.

A compliant individual is necessarily *doing* something that is contrary to the way he or she *thinks* or *feels.* Such a situation is highly dissonant and arouses a certain tension in the individual. One way to reduce this dissonance is to cease conformity. This is especially likely if the required behaviour is at great variance with one's values or moral standards. However, this might require the person to adopt an isolated or scapegoat role, which are equally unpleasant prospects. The other method of reducing dissonance is to gradually accept the beliefs, values, and attitudes that support the norm in question. This is more likely when the required behaviour is not so discrepant with one's current value system.

Consider Mark, an idealistic graduate of a college social work program who acquires a job with a social services agency. Mark loves helping people but hates the bureaucratic red tape and reams of paperwork that are necessary to accomplish this goal. However, to acquire the approval of his boss and co-workers and to avoid trouble, he follows the rules to the letter of the law. This is pure compliance. Over time, however, Mark begins to *identify* with his boss and more experienced co-workers because they are in the enviable position of controlling those very rewards and punishments that are so important to him. Obviously, if he is to *be* one of them, he must begin to think and feel like them. Finally, Mark is promoted to a supervisory position, partly because he is so cooperative. Breaking in a new social worker, Mark is heard to say, "Our rules and forms are very important. You don't understand now, but you will." The metamorphosis is complete—Mark has *internalized* the beliefs and values that support the bureaucratic norms of his agency.

Although this story is slightly dramatized, the point that it makes is accurate—simple compliance can set the stage for more complete identification and involvement with organizational norms and roles. The process through which this occurs in organizations is known as *organizational socialization*, the focus of the next section.

Organizational Socialization

The story of Mark, the social worker, in the previous section describes how one individual was socialized into a particular organization. **Socialization** is the process by which people learn the attitudes, knowledge, and behaviours that are necessary to function in a group or organization. It is a learning process in which new members must acquire knowledge, change their attitudes, and perform new behaviours. Socialization is also the primary means by which organizations communicate the organization's culture and values to new members.[6]

Exhibit 8.1 depicts the socialization process. In particular, it shows how different socialization methods (e.g., employee orientation programs) influence a number of immediate or proximal socialization outcomes, such as learning, which lead to more

Socialization. The process by which people learn the attitudes, knowledge, and behaviours that are necessary to function in a group or organization.

EXHIBIT 8.1
The socialization process.

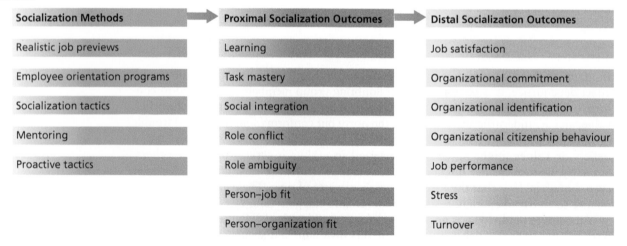

Socialization Methods	Proximal Socialization Outcomes	Distal Socialization Outcomes
Realistic job previews	Learning	Job satisfaction
Employee orientation programs	Task mastery	Organizational commitment
Socialization tactics	Social integration	Organizational identification
Mentoring	Role conflict	Organizational citizenship behaviour
Proactive tactics	Role ambiguity	Job performance
	Person–job fit	Stress
	Person–organization fit	Turnover

distal or longer-term outcomes such as attitudes (e.g., job satisfaction) and behaviours (e.g., turnover).

Learning during socialization has often been described in terms of content areas or domains of learning, such as the task, role, group, and organization domain. New-comers need to acquire the knowledge and skills necessary to perform their job duties and *tasks*; they need to learn the appropriate behaviours and expectations of their *role*; they need to learn the norms and values of their *work group*; and they need to learn about the *organization*, such as its history, traditions, language, politics, mission, and culture. As newcomers learn about each of these areas, they should begin to master their tasks and integrate with others in their work group and the organization. This should also help to reduce their role ambiguity and role conflict. In Chapter 7, we described how different factors can lead to role ambiguity and role conflict. One of the goals of socialization is to provide new hires with information and knowledge about their role to avoid problems of role conflict and role ambiguity.

An important objective of organizational socialization is for newcomers to achieve a good fit. There are generally two kinds of fit that are important for socialization. First, newcomers must acquire the knowledge and skills necessary to perform their work tasks and roles. This is known as person–job fit, or P–J fit. **Person–job fit** refers to the match between an employee's knowledge, skills, and abilities and the require-ments of a job. Second, newcomers must also learn the values and beliefs that are important to the group and organization. This is known as **person–organization fit,** or P–O fit, and refers to the match between an employee's personal values and the values of an organization.[7] Research has found that both P–J and P–O fit are strongly influ-enced by the socialization process and are related to job attitudes and behaviours.[8]

One of the primary goals of organizational socialization is to ensure that new employees learn and understand the key beliefs, values, and assumptions of an organiz-ation's culture and for individuals to define themselves in terms of the organization and what it is perceived to represent. This is known **as organizational identification,** and as shown in Exhibit 8.1, it is also a distal outcome of socialization. Organizational identi-fication reflects an individual's learning and acceptance of an organization's culture.[9]

In summary, socialization is important because it has a direct effect on proximal socialization outcomes (e.g., learning, P–J fit, and P–O fit), which lead to more positive distal outcomes (e.g., organizational identification). As we shall see, some of this process might occur before organization membership formally begins, while some of it occurs once the new member enters the organization. Furthermore, socialization is an ongoing process by virtue of continuous interaction with others in the workplace. However, socialization is most potent during certain periods of membership transition, such as when one is promoted or assigned to a new work group, and especially when one joins a new organization.[10]

Person–job fit. The match between an employee's knowledge, skills, and abili-ties and the requirements of a job.

Person–organization fit. The match between an employee's personal values and the values of an organization.

Organizational identification. The extent to which an individual defines him- or herself in terms of the organization and what it is perceived to represent.

Stages of Socialization

Since organizational socialization is an ongoing process, it is useful to divide this process into three stages.[11] One of these stages occurs before entry, another immedi-ately follows entry, and the last occurs after one has been a member for some period of time. In a sense, the first two stages represent hurdles for achieving passage into the third stage (see Exhibit 8.2).

Anticipatory Socialization. A considerable amount of socialization occurs even before a person becomes a member of a particular organization. This process is called anticipatory socialization. Some anticipatory socialization includes a formal process of skill and attitude acquisition, such as that which might occur by attending college or university. Other anticipatory socialization might be informal, such as that acquired through a series of summer jobs or even by watching the portrayal of organizational life in television shows and movies. Some organizations begin to socialize job candidates

EXHIBIT 8.2

Stages of organizational
socialization.

Source: Based on Feldman, D.C.
(1976). A contingency theory of
socialization. *Administrative Science
Quarterly, 21,* 433–452; Feldman,
D.C. (1981). The multiple socialization of organization members.
*Academy of Management Review,
6,* 309–318.

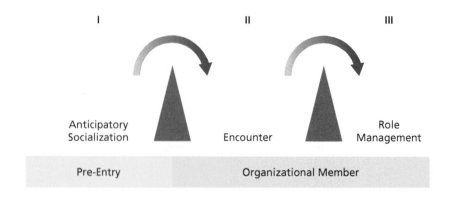

even before they are hired at recruitment events, where organizational representatives discuss the organization with potential hires. As we shall see shortly, organizations vary in the extent to which they encourage anticipatory socialization in advance of entry. As well, not all anticipatory socialization is accurate and useful for the new member.

Encounter. In the encounter stage, the new recruit, armed with some expectations about organizational life, encounters the day-to-day reality of this life. Formal aspects of this stage might include orientation programs and rotation through various parts of the organization. Informal aspects include getting to know and understand the style and personality of one's boss and co-workers. At this stage, the organization and its experienced members are looking for an acceptable degree of conformity to organizational norms and the gradual acquisition of appropriate role behaviour. Recruits, on the other hand, are interested in having their personal needs and expectations fulfilled. If successful, the recruit will have complied with critical organizational norms and should begin to identify with experienced organizational members.

Role Management. Having survived the encounter stage and acquired basic role behaviours, the new member's attention shifts to fine tuning and actively managing his or her role in the organization. Following some conformity to group norms, the new recruit might now be in a position to modify the role to better serve the organization. This might require forming connections outside the immediate work group. The organizational member must also confront balancing the now-familiar organizational role with non-work roles and family demands. Each of these experiences provides additional socialization to the role occupant, who might begin to internalize the norms and values that are prominent in the organization.

Now that we have seen a basic sketch of how socialization proceeds, let's look in greater detail at some of the key issues in the process.

Unrealistic Expectations and the Psychological Contract

People seldom join organizations without expectations about what membership will be like and what they expect to receive in return for their efforts. In fact, it is just such expectations that lead them to choose one career, job, or organization over another. Management majors have some expectations about what they will be doing when they become management trainees at IBM. Similarly, even 18-year-old army recruits have notions about what military life will be like. Unfortunately, these expectations are often unrealistic, and obligations between new members and organizations are often breached.

Unrealistic Expectations. Research indicates that people entering organizations hold many expectations that are inaccurate and often unrealistically high. As a result, once they enter an organization they experience a reality shock and their expectations are not met.[12] In one study of telephone operators, for example, researchers obtained people's expectations about the nature of the job *before* they started work. They also looked at these employees' perceptions of the actual job shortly *after* they started work. The results indicated that many perceptions were less favourable than expectations. A similar result occurred for students entering an MBA program. The extent to which newcomers' expectations are met (or unmet) has important implications for their work adjustment. Research has found that newcomers who have higher met expectations have higher job satisfaction, organizational commitment, job performance, and job survival and lower intentions to leave.[13]

Why do new members often have unrealistic expectations about the organizations they join?[14] To some extent, occupational stereotypes, such as those we discussed in Chapter 3, could be responsible. The media often communicate such stereotypes. For example, a person entering nursing training might have gained some expectations about hospital life from watching the television show *Grey's Anatomy*. Those of us who teach might also be guilty of communicating stereotypes. After four years of study, the new management trainee at IBM might be dismayed to find that the emphasis is on *trainee* rather than *management*! Finally, unrealistic expectations may also stem from overzealous recruiters who paint rosy pictures to attract job candidates to the organization. Taken together, these factors demonstrate the need for socialization.

Psychological Contract. When people join organizations, they have beliefs and expectations about what they will receive from the organization in return for what they give the organization. Such beliefs form what is known as the psychological contract. A **psychological contract** refers to beliefs held by employees regarding the reciprocal obligations and promises between them and their organization.[15] For example, an employee might expect to receive bonuses and promotions in return for hard work and loyalty.

Unfortunately, psychological contract breach appears to be a common occurrence. Perceptions of **psychological contract breach** occur when an employee perceives that his or her organization has failed to fulfill one or more of its promises or obligations in the psychological contract. One study found that 55 percent of recent MBA graduates reported that some aspect of their psychological contract had been broken by their employer.[16] This often results in feelings of anger and betrayal and can have a negative effect on employees' work attitudes and behaviour. A review of research on the impact of psychological contract breach found that breach is related to affective reactions (higher feelings of contract violation and mistrust toward management), work attitudes (lower job satisfaction and organizational commitment, and higher turnover intentions), and work behaviours (lower organizational citizenship behaviour and job performance). The results of this study indicate that psychological contract breach can have a negative effect on employee job attitudes and behaviours because it results in negative emotions that stem from feelings of violation and mistrust toward management.[17]

Why does psychological contract breach occur? As is the case with unrealistic expectations, recruiters are often tempted to promise more than their organization can provide to attract the best job applicants. In addition, newcomers often lack sufficient information to form accurate perceptions concerning their psychological contract. As a result, there will be some incongruence or differences in understanding between an employee and the organization about promised obligations. In addition, organizational changes, such as downsizing and restructuring, can cause organizations to knowingly break promises made to an employee that they are either unable or unwilling to keep.[18]

It is therefore important that newcomers develop accurate perceptions in the formation of a psychological contract. Many of the terms of the psychological contract are established during anticipatory socialization. Therefore, organizations need to ensure that truthful and accurate information about promises and obligations is communicated to new members before and after they join an organization. Incongruence

Psychological contract. Beliefs held by employees regarding the reciprocal obligations and promises between them and their organization.

Psychological contract breach. Employee perceptions that his or her organization has failed to fulfill one or more its promises or obligations of the psychological contract.

and psychological contract breach are less likely in organizations where socialization is intense.[19] This further demonstrates the importance of and need for organizational socialization.

Methods of Organizational Socialization

Organizations differ in the extent to which they socialize their new hires. This is in part owing to the fact that some organizations make use of other organizations to help socialize their members. For example, hospitals do not develop experienced cardiologists from scratch. Rather, they depend on medical schools to socialize potential doctors in the basic role requirements of being a physician. Similarly, business firms rely on business schools to send them recruits who think and act in a business-like manner. In this way, a fair degree of anticipatory socialization may exist before a person joins an organization. On the other hand, organizations such as police forces, the military, and religious institutions are less likely to rely on external socialization. Police academies, boot camps, and seminaries are set up as extensions of these organizations to aid in socialization.

Organizations that handle their own socialization are especially interested in maintaining the continuity and stability of job behaviours over a period of time. Conversely, those that rely on external agencies to perform anticipatory socialization are oriented toward maintaining the potential for creative, innovative behaviour on the part of members—there is less "inbreeding." Of course, reliance on external agents might present problems. The engineer who is socialized in university courses to respect design elegance might find it difficult to accept cost restrictions when he or she is employed by an engineering firm. For this reason, organizations that rely heavily on external socialization always supplement it with formal training and orientation or informal, on-the-job training.

The point is that organizations differ in terms of *who* does the socializing, *how* it is done, and *how much* is done. Most organizations, however, make use of a number of methods of socialization, including realistic job previews, employee orientation programs, socialization tactics, and mentoring.

Realistic Job Previews

We noted earlier that new organizational members often harbour unrealistic, inflated expectations about what their jobs will be like. When the job actually begins and it fails to live up to these expectations, individuals experience "reality shock," and job dissatisfaction results. As a consequence, costly turnover is most likely to occur among newer employees who are unable to survive the discrepancy between expectations and reality. For the organization, this sequence of events represents a failure of socialization.

Obviously, organizations cannot control all sources of unrealistic job expectations, such as those provided by television shows and glorified occupational stereotypes. However, they *can* control those generated during the recruitment process by providing job applicants with realistic job previews. **Realistic job previews** provide a balanced, realistic picture of the positive and negative aspects of the job to applicants.[20] Thus, they provide "corrective action" to expectations at the anticipatory socialization stage. Exhibit 8.3 compares the realistic job preview process with the traditional preview process that often sets expectations too high by ignoring the negative aspects of the job.

How do organizations design and conduct realistic job previews? Generally, they obtain the views of experienced employees and human resources staff about the positive and negative aspects of the job. Then, they incorporate these views into booklets or video presentations for applicants.[21] A video might involve interviews with job incumbents discussing the pros and cons of their jobs. Some companies have managers

Realistic job previews. The provision of a balanced, realistic picture of the positive and negative aspects of a job to applicants.

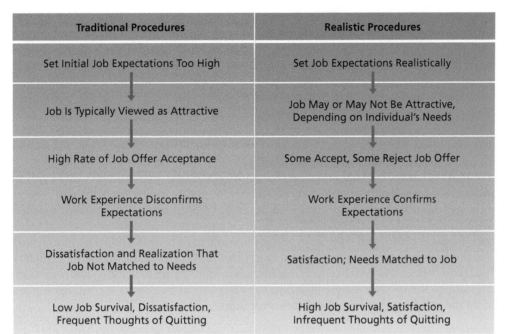

Traditional Procedures	Realistic Procedures
Set Initial Job Expectations Too High	Set Job Expectations Realistically
Job Is Typically Viewed as Attractive	Job May or May Not Be Attractive, Depending on Individual's Needs
High Rate of Job Offer Acceptance	Some Accept, Some Reject Job Offer
Work Experience Disconfirms Expectations	Work Experience Confirms Expectations
Dissatisfaction and Realization That Job Not Matched to Needs	Satisfaction; Needs Matched to Job
Low Job Survival, Dissatisfaction, Frequent Thoughts of Quitting	High Job Survival, Satisfaction, Infrequent Thoughts of Quitting

EXHIBIT 8.3

Traditional and realistic job previews compared.

Source: Wanous, J.P. (1975 July-August). Tell it like it is at realistic job previews. *Personnel*, 50–60 © 1975 American Management Association, New York. All rights reserved.

and employees communicate realistic information to job candidates in person. For example, Scotiabank has managers from various business lines explain the day-to-day job realities to prospective job candidates. Steel maker Dofasco Inc. of Hamilton, Ontario, has a team of employees, which includes members from the senior ranks to the most recently hired, join student ambassadors at campus recruitment events, where they are available for one-on-one conversations with job candidates.[22] Realistic previews have been designed for jobs as diverse as telephone operators, life insurance salespeople, US Marine Corps recruits, and supermarket workers.

Sometimes realistic previews use simulations to permit applicants to actually sample the work. For example, in an effort to recruit more women, the Ontario Provincial Police (OPP) have staged recruiting camps in which the women experience typical OPP policing activities, including shooting a handgun, completing 6 a.m. fitness drills, and responding to mock crimes.[23]

Research Evidence. Evidence shows that realistic job previews are effective in reducing inflated expectations and turnover and improving job performance.[24] What is less clear is exactly why turnover reduction occurs. Reduced expectations and increased job satisfaction are part of the answer. It also appears that realistic previews cause those not cut out for the job or who have low P–J and P–O fit perceptions to withdraw from the application process, a process known as *self-selection*.[25] As a result, applicants who perceive a good P–J and P–O fit are more likely to remain in the hiring process and to accept a job offer. Although the turnover reductions generated by realistic previews are small, they can result in substantial financial savings for organizations.[26] Providing realistic job previews can also help prevent perceptions of psychological contract breach.[27]

Employee Orientation Programs

Once newcomers enter an organization, socialization during the encounter stage usually begins with an orientation program. **Employee orientation programs** are designed to introduce new employees to their job, the people they will be working with, and the

Employee orientation programs. Programs designed to introduce new employees to their job, the people they will be working with, and the organization.

organization. The main content of most orientation programs consists of health and safety issues, terms and conditions of employment, and information about the organization, such as its history and traditions. Another purpose of employee orientation programs is to begin conveying and forming the psychological contract and to teach newcomers how to cope with stressful work situations.[28] A new type of orientation program that is designed to help newcomers cope with stress is called Realistic Orientation Program for Entry Stress (ROPES). Like a realistic job preview, ROPES provides newcomers with realistic information; however, it also teaches newcomers how to use cognitive and behavioural coping techniques to manage workplace stressors. For an example of how ROPES has been used, see Global Focus: *ROPES and Cultural Socialization*.

Most orientation programs take place during the first week of entry and last one day to one week. Some organizations realize the importance of orientation and invest a considerable amount of time and resources in it. At Starbucks, new employees receive 24 hours of training in their first 80 hours of employment. CEO Howard Schultz greets new hires via video, and they learn about the company's history and its obsession with quality and customer service. According to Schultz, "For people joining the company, we try to define what Starbucks stands for, what we're trying to achieve, and why that's relevant to them." Not surprisingly, the turnover rate at Starbucks is considerably less than the average rate in the specialty-coffee industry.[29]

GLOBAL FOCUS

ROPES and Cultural Socialization

As business becomes increasingly global, more workers are relocating to different countries. This means that socialization needs to focus on preparing new hires and current employees not only for the organization where they will be working (organizational socialization) but also for the culture (cultural socialization). But how do you socialize people for different countries and prepare them for the enormous amount of stress they will experience working and living in a different culture?

The answer is a new kind of orientation program called ROPES, which stands for Realistic Orientation Program for Entry Stress. ROPES provides realistic information about tasks and the environment and also teaches cognitive and behavioural coping techniques to manage stressors and lower stress. But how effective is ROPES for cultural socialization?

To find out, Jinyan Fan and John P. Wanous conducted a study among new Asian international graduate students at a large university in the United States in which they compared ROPES to a more traditional orientation program. Based on interviews with international students, ROPES was designed to teach international students how to cope with three major stressors: (1) the fast pace of the academic quarter system (the university has three quarters versus the more common two semester system), (2) language difficulties, and (3) social interaction difficulties.

The 72 participants were randomly assigned to receive ROPES or a more traditional orientation session that focused mostly on students' immediate concerns, such as how to keep legal status in the United States, how to ensure personal safety, how to connect a home phone, and so forth.

To test the effectiveness of ROPES, participants completed questionnaires to measure their expectations, anxiety, stress, and adjustment. The results indicated that the ROPES participants reported lower expectations at the end of the orientation program, lower stress and higher academic and interaction adjustment six and nine months after the program, and higher retention two years later. Further, the positive effects of ROPES became stronger over time. The results also indicated that the better academic and interaction adjustment of the ROPES participants was partly due to a reduction in stress. In other words, ROPES was more effective for cultural socialization than the traditional orientation program because it lowered stress.

Source: Based on Fan, J., & Wanous, J.P. (2008). Organizational and cultural entry: A new type of orientation program for multiple boundary crossings. *Journal of Applied Psychology 93*, 1390–1400. Copyright © 2008 by the American Psychological Association. Reproduced with permission.

INSTITUTIONALIZED TACTICS		INDIVIDUALIZED TACTICS
Collective Formal	CONTEXT TACTICS	Individual Informal
Sequential Fixed	CONTENT TACTICS	Random Variable
Serial Investiture	SOCIAL TACTICS	Disjunctive Divestiture

EXHIBIT 8.4
Socialization tactics.

Research Evidence. Orientation programs are an important method of socialization because they can have an immediate effect on learning and a lasting effect on the job attitudes and behaviours of new hires. One study found that newly hired employees who attended an orientation program were more socialized in terms of their knowledge and understanding of the organization's goals and values, history, and involvement with people, and also reported higher organizational commitment compared to employees who did not attend the orientation program.[30] A study conducted at Corning Inc. concluded that employees who completed a full orientation program were 69 percent more likely to remain with the company after three years. Other companies have also seen substantial decreases in their rate of turnover as a result of employee orientation programs.[31]

Socialization Tactics

Although realistic job previews and orientation programs play an important role in the socialization of new employees, the socialization process does not end at the conclusion of an orientation program. So what happens to new hires once the orientation program has ended?

John Van Maanen and Edgar Schein developed a theory of socialization that helps us understand and explain the socialization process. They suggested that there are six **socialization tactics** that organizations can use to structure the early work experiences of new hires and individuals who are in transition from one role to another. Each of the six tactics consists of a bipolar continuum; they are described below.[32] Exhibit 8.4 depicts the six socialization tactics.

Socialization tactics.
The manner in which organizations structure the early work experiences of newcomers and individuals who are in transition from one role to another.

Collective versus Individual Tactics. When using the collective tactic, a number of new members are socialized as a group, going through the same experiences and facing the same challenges. Army boot camps, fraternity pledge classes, and training classes for salespeople and flight attendants are common examples. In contrast, the individual tactic consists of socialization experiences that are tailor-made for each new member. Simple on-the-job training and apprenticeship to develop skilled craftspeople constitute individual socialization.

Formal versus Informal Tactics. Formal tactics involve segregating newcomers from regular organizational members and providing them with formal learning experiences during the period of socialization. Informal tactics, however, do not distinguish a newcomer from more experienced members and rely more on informal and on-the-job learning.

Sequential versus Random Tactics. Sequential versus random tactics have to do with whether there is a clear sequence of steps or stages during the socialization process. With a sequential tactic, there is a fixed sequence of steps leading to the assumption of the role, whereas with the random tactic, there is an ambiguous or changing sequence.

Fixed versus Variable Tactics. If socialization is fixed, there is a time table for the newcomer's assumption of the role. If the tactic is variable, then there is no time frame to indicate when the socialization process ends and the newcomer assumes his or her new role.

Serial versus Disjunctive Tactics. The serial tactic refers to a process in which newcomers are socialized by experienced members of the organization. The disjunctive tactic refers to a socialization process where role models and experienced organization members do not groom new members or "show them the ropes."

Investiture versus Divestiture Tactics. Divestiture tactics refer to what is also known as debasement and hazing. This occurs when organizations put new members through a series of experiences that are designed to humble them and strip away some of their initial self-confidence. Debasement is a way of testing the commitment of new members and correcting for faulty anticipatory socialization. Having been humbled and stripped of preconceptions, members are then ready to learn the norms of the organization. An extreme example is the rough treatment and shaved heads of US Marine Corps recruits. Sometimes organizations prefer not to use debasement or hazing as part of the socialization of newcomers. Rather, they employ the investiture socialization tactic, which affirms the incoming identity and attributes of new hires rather than denying them and stripping them away. Organizations that carefully select new members for certain attributes and characteristics would be more likely to use this tactic.

Institutionalized versus Individualized Socialization. The six socialization tactics can be grouped into two separate patterns of socialization. *Institutionalized socialization* consists of collective, formal, sequential, fixed, serial, and investiture tactics. *Individualized socialization* consists of individual, informal, random, variable, disjunctive, and divestiture tactics. The main difference between these two dimensions is that institutionalized socialization reflects a more formalized and structured program of socialization that reduces uncertainty and encourages new hires to accept organizational norms and maintain the status quo. On the other hand, individualized socialization reflects a relative absence of structure that creates ambiguity and encourages new hires

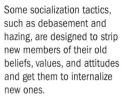

Some socialization tactics, such as debasement and hazing, are designed to strip new members of their old beliefs, values, and attitudes and get them to internalize new ones.

to question the status quo and develop their own approach to their role. In addition, the tactics have also been distinguished in terms of the *context* in which information is presented to new hires, the *content* provided to new hires, and the *social* aspects of socialization.[33] As shown in Exhibit 8.4, the collective–individual and formal–informal tactics represent the context of socialization; the sequential–random and fixed–variable represent the content of socialization; and the serial–disjunctive and investiture–divestiture represent the social aspects of socialization.

Why would an organization choose institutionalized over individualized socialization? Institutionalized socialization tactics are effective in promoting organizational loyalty, esprit de corps, and uniformity of behaviour among those being socialized. This last characteristic is often very important. No matter where they are in the world, soldiers know whom to salute and how to do it. Similarly, air passengers need not expect any surprises from cabin crew, thanks to the flight attendants' institutionalized socialization.

When socialization is individualized, new members are more likely to take on the particular characteristics and style of those who are socializing them. Thus, two newly hired real estate agents who receive on-the-job training from their bosses might soon think and act more like their bosses than like each other. As you can see, uniformity is less likely under individualized socialization.

Institutionalized socialization is always followed up by some individualized socialization as the member joins his or her regular work unit. For example, rookie police officers are routinely partnered with more experienced officers. At this point, they will begin to develop some individuality in the style with which they perform their jobs.

Research Evidence. Research on socialization tactics supports the basic predictions regarding the effects of institutionalized and individualized socialization on newcomers' roles, attitudes, and behaviour. Institutionalized socialization tactics have been found to be related to proximal outcomes, such as lower role ambiguity and conflict and more positive perceptions of P–J and P–O fit, as well as distal outcomes, such as more positive job satisfaction and organizational commitment and lower stress and turnover. In addition, the institutionalized socialization tactics result in a more custodial role orientation, in which new hires accept the status quo and the requirements of their tasks and roles. On the other hand, the individualized socialization tactics result in a more innovative role orientation, in which new recruits might change or modify the way they perform their tasks and roles. It is also worth noting that among the different socialization tactics, the social tactics (serial–disjunctive and investiture–divestiture) have been found to be the most strongly related to socialization outcomes. This is consistent with research that has found that organizations that are more successful at socializing newcomers help them to establish a broad network of relationships with co-workers.[34]

Mentoring

It should be apparent from our discussion of socialization tactics that supervisors and peers play an important role in the socialization process. While effective relationships between supervisors and their employees do influence the socialization and career success of individuals within an organization, one particularly important relationship is between a newcomer or apprentice and a mentor.

A **mentor** is an experienced or more senior person in the organization who gives a junior person special attention, such as giving advice and creating opportunities to assist him or her during the early stages of his or her career. While someone other than the junior person's boss can serve as a mentor, often the supervisor is in a unique position to provide mentoring. For mentors to be effective, they must perform two types of mentor functions: career and psychosocial functions.

Mentor. An experienced or more senior person in the organization who gives a junior person special attention, such as giving advice and creating opportunities to assist him or her during the early stages of his or her career.

Career Functions of Mentoring. A mentor provides many career-enhancing benefits to an apprentice.[35] These benefits are made possible by the senior person's experience, status, knowledge of how the organization works, and influence with powerful people in the organization. The career functions of mentoring include:

- *Sponsorship.* The mentor might nominate the apprentice for advantageous transfers and promotions.
- *Exposure and visibility.* The mentor might provide opportunities to work with key people and see other parts of the organization.
- *Coaching and feedback.* The mentor might suggest work strategies and identify strengths and weaknesses in the apprentice's performance.
- *Developmental assignments.* The mentor can provide challenging work assignments that will help develop key skills and knowledge that are crucial to career progress.

Psychosocial Functions of Mentoring. Besides helping directly with career progress, mentors can provide certain psychosocial functions that are helpful in developing the apprentice's self-confidence, sense of identity, and ability to cope with emotional traumas that can damage a person's effectiveness. These include:

- *Role modelling.* This provides a set of attitudes, values, and behaviours for the junior person to imitate.
- *Provide acceptance and confirmation.* This provides encouragement and support and helps the apprentice gain self-confidence.
- *Counselling.* This provides an opportunity to discuss personal concerns and anxieties concerning career prospects, work–family conflicts, and so on.

Formal Mentoring Programs. Mentoring relationships have often been of an informal nature, such that the individuals involved chose to enter into a mentoring relationship with each other without the direct involvement of their organization. But can organizations formally assign mentors to apprentices and achieve the career outcomes normally associated with more spontaneous, informal mentor–apprentice relationships? The answer appears to be yes because formal mentoring programs have become increasingly popular in recent years.[36] For example, Telvent Canada Ltd., a Calgary-based company that develops information management systems, started a formal mentoring program a number of years ago. Although it was originally offered to new hires to help get them up to speed, it is now available to all of the company's employees. Bell Canada launched a company-wide online mentor program several years ago called Mentor Match, which is open to all of its employees. The program is available on the company's intranet, and employees must apply to be either a mentor or a protege.[37]

Women and Mentors. One factor that inhibits women's career development compared with that of their male counterparts is the difficulty women have historically faced in establishing an apprentice–mentor relationship with a senior person in the organization.[38] The lack of mentors and role models is a major barrier for the career advancement of many women.[39] The problem goes well beyond the traditional gender stereotyping we discussed in Chapter 3. It stems from the fact that senior people, who are in the best position to be mentors, are frequently men. A young woman attempting to establish a productive relationship with a senior male associate faces complexities that the male apprentice does not. Part of the problem is the lack of experience many male mentor candidates have in dealing with a woman in roles other than daughter,

Many research efforts have documented the importance of having a mentor when starting one's career and how it can influence career success.

wife, or mother. Often, a woman's concerns are going to be different from those her male mentor experienced at that stage in his career. As a result, the strategies that he models might have limited relevance to the female apprentice. Perhaps the greatest difficulty is associated with fears that their relationship will be perceived as involving intimacy. Concerns about appearances and what others will say can make both people uncomfortable and get in the way of a productive relationship.

Because of these concerns, the prospective female apprentice faces more constraints than her male counterpart. Research has confirmed that cross-gender mentor–apprentice dyads are less likely to get involved in informal after-work social activities. These activities can help apprentices establish relationships with other influential people in a relaxed setting. Research also confirms that apprentices in a cross-gender dyad are less likely to see their mentor as a role model and, therefore, are less likely to realize the developmental benefits of an effective model.[40]

How critical is mentoring to a woman's career? The research evidence suggests that mentoring is even more critical to women's career success than it is to men's. Women who make it to executive positions invariably had a mentor along the way. This is true for on-half to two-thirds of male executives.[41] Recent studies also indicate that a majority of women (61 percent) have had a mentor, and almost all (99 percent) say that their mentor has had an impact on the advancement of their career.[42]

Thus, for women with these career aspirations, finding a mentor appears to be a difficult but crucial task. The good news is that an increasing number of organizations are developing mentoring and networking programs. For example, Deloitte has a program called Developing Leaders, in which experienced partners mentor and coach male and female partners who demonstrate leadership potential. Mentors are carefully chosen, and their skills and experience are matched to the new partner's goals and aspirations. In addition, women at Deloitte have developed networking and mentoring opportunities for themselves through a program called Women's Business Development Groups. The group organizes networking events and meets with other women's business groups and organizes an annual Spring Breakfast during which prominent women are invited to speak.[43] These kinds of networking opportunities are extremely important because research has found that exclusion from informal networks is one of the major roadblocks to the advancement of women.[44]

Race, Ethnicity, and Mentoring. Limited racial and ethnic diversity at higher levels of organizations constrain the mentoring opportunities available to younger minority group employees. Research shows that mentors tend to select apprentices who are similar to them in terms of race and nationality as well as gender.[45] While there are exceptions, research confirms that minority apprentices in cross-ethnic group mentoring relationships tend to report less assistance than those with same-race mentors.[46]

Cross-race mentoring relationships seem to focus on instrumental or career functions of mentoring (e.g., sponsorship, coaching, and feedback) and provide less psychosocial support functions (e.g., role modelling, counselling) than is generally seen in same-race dyads.[47] Although the increasing diversity of organizations makes this tendency less problematic, it suggests that minority group members should put extra efforts into developing a supportive network of peers who can provide emotional support and role modelling as well as the career functions. It also means that organizations must do more to provide mentoring opportunities for minority employees, just as some have done for women. One organization that is doing this is IBM, where an Asian Task Force identifies and develops talented Asian employees across North America who might benefit from mentoring.[48]

Research Evidence. Many research efforts have documented the importance of having a mentor when starting one's career and how it can influence career success.[49] A review of this research found that mentored individuals had higher objective career outcomes, such as compensation and number of promotions, and higher subjective outcomes, including greater satisfaction with one's job and career and greater career commitment. They were also more likely to believe that they will advance in their career. However, mentoring tends to be more strongly related to the subjective than to the objective career outcomes. Furthermore, in comparisons of the effects of the two mentoring functions, the psychosocial function was found to be more strongly related to satisfaction with the mentoring relationship, while the career function was more strongly related to compensation and advancement. Both functions were found to be just as important in generating positive attitudes toward one's job and career.[50]

Research on formal mentoring programs has found that they are just as beneficial as informal relationships and are certainly more beneficial than not having mentors at all. In addition, formal mentoring programs have been found to be most effective when the mentor and protégé have input into the matching process and when they receive training prior to the mentoring relationship, especially training that is perceived to be of a high quality.[51]

Proactive Socialization

You may recall from Chapter 2 that individuals learn by observing and imitating the behaviour of others. You also learned how people with a proactive personality have a tendency to behave proactively and to effect positive change in their environment. Thus, it should not surprise you that newcomers can be proactive in their socialization and in the management of their careers through the use of proactive behaviours. In fact, observation has been found to be one of the most common ways by which newcomers learn on the job, and newcomer self-regulation behaviour has been found to be related to lower anxiety and stress and to a more successful socialization.[52]

Proactive socialization refers to the process in which newcomers play an active role in their socialization through the use of a number of proactive behaviours. Exhibit 8.5 describes the major types of proactive socialization behaviours. One of the most important proactive behaviours that newcomers can employ during their socialization is to request feedback about their performance and to seek information about their work tasks and roles as well as about their group and organization. Recall that

Proactive socialization. The process through which newcomers play an active role in their own socialization through the use of a number of proactive socialization behaviours.

General socializing. Participating in social office events and attending social gatherings (e.g., parties, outings, clubs, lunches).

Boss relationship building. Initiating social interactions to get to know and form a relationship with one's boss.

Networking. Socializing with and getting to know members of the organization from various departments and functions.

Feedback-seeking. Requesting information about how one is performing one's tasks and role.

Information-seeking. Requesting information about one's job, role, group and organization.

Observation. Observing and modelling the behaviour of appropriate others.

Behavioural self-management. Managing one's socialization through self-observation, self-goal setting, self-reward, and rehearsal.

Relationship building. Initiating social interactions and building relationships with others in one's area or department.

Job change negotiation. Attempts to change one's job duties or the manner and means by which one performs one's job in order to increase the fit between oneself and the job.

Involvement in work-related activities. Participating in "extra-curricular" work-related activities that are work-related but not part of one's job.

Career-enhancing strategies. Engaging in behaviours to improve one's career opportunities, such as working on varied tasks and job assignments and seeking additional job responsibilities.

Informal mentor relationships. Forming relationships with experienced organization members who act as informal mentors.

EXHIBIT 8.5
Proactive socialization behaviours.

Sources: Ashford, S.J., & Black, J.S. (1996). Proactivity during organizational entry: The role of desire for control. *Journal of Applied Psychology, 81*, 199–214; Feij, J.A., Whitely, W.T., Peiro, J.M., & Taris, T.W. (1995). The development of career-enhancing strategies and content innovation: A longitudinal study of new workers. *Journal of Vocational Behavior, 46*, 231–256; Griffin, A.E.C., Colella, A., & Goparaju, S. (2000). Newcomer and organizational socialization tactics: An interactionist perspective. *Human Resource Management Review, 10*, 453–474.

organizational socialization is about learning the attitudes, knowledge, and behaviours that are necessary to function as an effective member of a group and organization. One way for new employees to learn is to seek information from others in the organization.[53]

Newcomers can acquire information by requesting it, by asking questions, and by observing the behaviour of others. In addition, there are different sources that can be used to acquire information, such as supervisors, co-workers, mentors, and written documents. However, research has found that newcomers rely primarily on observation, followed by interpersonal sources (i.e., supervisors and co-workers). Furthermore, they tend to seek out task-related information the most, especially during the early period of socialization, followed by role, group, and organization information.

In addition to feedback and information seeking, newcomers can also be proactive by socializing, networking, and building relationships with co-workers and members of the organization, negotiating job changes to improve P–J fit, engaging in career enhancing strategies to improve one's career opportunities, getting involved in different work-related activities to acquire new knowledge and skills, and finding a mentor.[54] As indicated earlier, having a mentor is extremely important for one's socialization and career development.

Research Evidence. Research has found that feedback and information seeking is related to greater knowledge of different content areas as well as to higher job satisfaction, organizational commitment, and job performance, and lower levels of stress, intentions to quit, and turnover. Supervisors are the information source most strongly related to positive socialization outcomes. In addition, newcomers who are more proactive in their use of the different proactive behaviours have been found to report more learning and positive socialization outcomes.[55]

Organizational Culture

The last several pages have been concerned with socialization into an organization. To a large degree, the course of that socialization both depends on and shapes the culture of the organization. As indicated in the chapter-opening vignette, the culture of Google Canada is unique and helps to create a work environment that is a great place to work. But what exactly is an organizational culture? Let's examine culture, a concept that has gained the attention of both researchers and practising managers.

What Is Organizational Culture?

At the outset, we can say that organizational culture is not the easiest concept to define. Informally, culture might be thought of as an organization's style, atmosphere, or personality. This style, atmosphere, or personality is most obvious when we contrast what it must be like to work in various organizations, such as Suncor Energy Inc., the Royal Bank of Canada, WestJet, or Google Canada. Even from their mention in the popular press, we can imagine that these organizations provide very different work environments. Thus, culture provides uniqueness and social identity to organizations.

Organizational culture.
The shared beliefs, values, and assumptions that exist in an organization.

More formally, **organizational culture** consists of the shared beliefs, values, and assumptions that exist in an organization.[56] In turn, these shared beliefs, values, and assumptions determine the norms that develop and the patterns of behaviour that emerge from these norms. The term "shared" does not necessarily mean that members are in close agreement on these matters, although they may well be. Rather, it means that they have had uniform exposure to them and have some minimum common understanding of them. Several other characteristics of culture are important.

- Culture represents a true "way of life" for organizational members, who often take its influence for granted. Frequently, an organization's culture becomes obvious only when it is contrasted with that of other organizations or when it undergoes changes.

- Because culture involves basic assumptions, values, and beliefs, it tends to be fairly stable over time. In addition, once a culture is well established, it can persist despite turnover among organizational members, providing social continuity.

- The content of a culture can involve matters that are internal to the organization or external. Internally, a culture might support innovation, risk taking, or secrecy of information. Externally, a culture might support "putting the customer first" or behaving unethically toward competitors.

- Culture can have a strong impact on both organizational performance and member satisfaction.

Culture is truly a social variable, reflecting yet another aspect of the kind of social influence that we have been discussing in this chapter. Thus, culture is not simply an automatic consequence of an organization's technology, products, or size. For example, there is some tendency for organizations to become more bureaucratic as they get larger. However, the culture of a particular large organization might support an informal, non-bureaucratic atmosphere as is the case at Google, which has maintained a small-company, informal work environment.

Subcultures. Smaller cultures that develop within a larger organizational culture that are based on differences in training, occupation, or departmental goals.

Can an organization have several cultures? The answer is yes. Often, unique **subcultures** develop that reflect departmental differences or differences in occupation or training.[57] A researcher who studied Silicon Valley computer companies found that technical and professional employees were divided into "hardware types" and "software types." In turn, hardware types subdivided into engineers and technicians, and software types subdivided into software engineers and computer scientists. Each group had its own values, beliefs, and assumptions about how to design computer systems.[58] Effective organizations will develop an overarching culture that manages such divisions. For instance, a widely shared norm might exist that in effect says, "We fight like hell until a final design is chosen, and then we all pull together."

The "Strong Culture" Concept

Some cultures have more impact on the behaviour of organizational members than others. In **a strong culture**, the beliefs, values, and assumptions that make up the culture are both intense and pervasive across the organization.[59] In other words, they are strongly supported by the majority of members, even cutting across any subcultures that might exist. Thus, the strong culture provides great consensus concerning "what the organization is about" or what it stands for. In weak cultures, on the other hand, beliefs, values, and assumptions are less strongly ingrained or less widely shared across the organization. Weak cultures are thus fragmented and have less impact on organizational members. All organizations have a culture, although it may be hard to detect the details of weak cultures.

To firm up your understanding of strong cultures, let's consider thumbnail sketches of some organizations that are generally agreed to have strong cultures.

Strong culture. An organizational culture with intense and pervasive beliefs, values, and assumptions.

- *Hilti (Canada) Corp.* For 10 years, the construction-equipment manufacturer in Mississauga, Ontario, developed a can-do attitude using "Gung Ho!" as its mantra and a culture that emphasizes the importance of worthwhile work, being in control of achieving your goals, and celebrating others' successes. The company takes its culture so seriously that "Gung Ho!" was transformed into a new program called Culture Journey to ensure that all employees know what Hilti stands for and expects. Most of the company's employees have gone through the mandatory two-day Culture Journey, which reintroduces them to the company's culture. In addition, all new recruits now get two days of "culture training" before they begin four weeks of product and sales training, and that's after four weeks of pre-training! Hilti has been ranked as one of the best workplaces in Canada.[60]

- *Boston Pizza.* Based in Richmond, British Columbia, Boston Pizza is the number-one casual dining chain in Canada, with more than 325 restaurants across the country. It has a culture of teamwork and fun that emphasizes fit over skills when hiring. The company hires people who fit the culture, or what they call the Boston Pizza fit. A three-pillar success strategy involves a commitment to franchisee profitability, building the brand, and continually improving the guest experience. Incentive programs reward franchisees and their staff for delivering above-standard quality. Boston Pizza has been recognized as having one of Canada's most admired corporate cultures.[61]

- *WestJet Airlines.* WestJet is known for its relaxed, fun, and youthful culture and for fostering a family atmosphere and a desire to maximize profits that has inspired extremely high employee motivation and commitment. WestJet has consistently been ranked as having one of the 10 most admired corporate cultures in Canada and even has a culture department to ensure that employees remain happy and engaged. Interestingly, the airline and its culture are modelled after the successful Dallas-based airline Southwest Airlines.[62] To find out about some of the other companies with the most admired corporate cultures in Canada, see Exhibit 8.6.

Three points are worth emphasizing about strong cultures. First, an organization need not be big to have a strong culture. If its members agree strongly about certain beliefs, values, and assumptions, a small business, school, or social service agency can have a strong culture. Second, strong cultures do not necessarily result in blind conformity. For example, a strong culture at 3M supports and rewards *non*-conformity in the form of innovation and creativity. Finally, Hilti, Boston Pizza, and

EXHIBIT 8.6

Canada's 10 most admired corporate cultures of 2008.

Source: Excerpt from "Canada's 10 Most Admired Corporate Cultures of 2008." Waterstone Human Capital Ltd. Toronto, Ontario.

Organization
Boston Pizza International Inc.
Four Seasons Hotels and Resorts
Intuit Canada
McDonald's Restaurants of Canada Ltd.
Purolator Courier Ltd.
RBC
Shoppers Drug Mart
Tim Hortons
WestJet
Yellow Pages Group

WestJet are obviously successful organizations. Thus, there is a strong belief that strong cultures are associated with greater success and effectiveness.

Assets of Strong Cultures

Organizations with strong cultures have several potential advantages over those lacking a strong culture. See Applied Focus: *Culture and Customer Service at Print Audit* to learn about the advantages of a strong customer service–oriented culture.

Coordination. In effective organizations, the right hand (e.g., finance) knows what the left hand (e.g., production) is doing. The overarching values and assumptions of strong cultures can facilitate such communication. In turn, different parts of the organization can learn from each other and can coordinate their efforts. This is especially important in decentralized, team-oriented organizations. Notice that coordination and collaboration are facilitated at Google Canada by providing places for employees to communicate and socialize with each other, its "20 percent time" program, and weekly TGIF meetings.

Conflict Resolution. You might be tempted to think that a strong culture would produce strong conflicts within an organization—that is, you might expect the intensity associated with strongly held assumptions and values to lead to friction among organizational members. There may be some truth to this. Nevertheless, sharing core values can be a powerful mechanism that helps to ultimately resolve conflicts—a light in a storm, as it were. For example, in a firm with a core value of excellent customer service, it is still possible for managers to differ about how to handle a particular customer problem. However, the core value will often suggest an appropriate dispute resolution mechanism—"Let's have the person who is closest to the customer make the final decision."

Financial Success. Does a strong culture pay off in terms of dollars and cents—that is, do the assets we discussed above get translated into bottom-line financial success? The answer seems to be yes, as long as the liabilities discussed below can be avoided.

One study of insurance companies found that firms whose managers responded more consistently to a culture survey (thus indicating agreement about the firm's culture) had greater asset and premium growth than those indicating disagreement.[63] Another study had members of six international accounting firms complete an organizational culture values survey. Because all firms were in the same business, there is some similarity to their value profiles (e.g., attention to detail is valued over innovation). However, close inspection shows that the six firms actually differ a good deal in their value profiles. Two of the firms tended to emphasize the work task values of detail and stability and to deemphasize a team orientation and respect for people. Comparatively, three other firms tended to emphasize these interpersonal relationship values. The author determined that the two firms that emphasized work task values had much higher employee turnover rates compared to the three firms that emphasized interpersonal relationship values, a fact that was estimated to cost them between $6 and $9 million a year.[64]

There is growing consensus that strong cultures contribute to financial success and other indicators of organizational effectiveness *when the culture supports the mission, strategy, and goals of the organization.*[65] A good example is WestJet Airlines. A key aspect of WestJet's corporate culture is a universal desire to maximize profits. The company has not only become one of the most profitable airlines in North America, but it is also the most successful low-cost carrier in Canadian history. According to former company CEO Clive Beddoe, WestJet's corporate culture is the primary reason for its extraordinary performance. "The entire environment is conducive to bringing out the best in people," he says. "It's the culture that creates the passion to succeed."[66]

Perhaps it's no wonder, then, that executives across Canada have consistently ranked WestJet as having one of the most admired corporate cultures in Canada. Most of the executive respondents also believe that there is a direct correlation between culture and an organization's health and financial performance and that corporate

APPLIED FOCUS

Culture and Customer Service at Print Audit

Print Audit is a fast-growing print management software company based in Calgary, Alberta. It develops print tracking and auditing software that enables organizations to analyze, reduce, and recover their printing volumes and costs. According to President and Chief Executive Officer John MacInnes, the company enables its 5000 customers around the world to lower the cost and environmental impact of printing and photocopying.

In addition to its environmental achievements, Print Audit has also been winning awards for its customer service and technical support. In 2004, the company received the National Quality Institute's (NQI) Canada Award of Excellence for Quality, and in 2005 and 2008, it received the Gold Customer Service Award for Small Business. The NQI bases its award in part on a company's culture, and it was impressed with Print Audit's vision statement: "To have fun, build great products and 'wow' the customer."

Key to Print Audit's success is its high-quality customer service and close relationships with its customers. Unlike other companies, which emphasize how fast you get somebody off the phone, Print Audit is concerned with whether they solved an issue to the caller's 100 percent satisfaction. They even call customers back to make sure they are satisfied. Callers are greeted by a live person and not an automated message, and the company contacts customers 15 and 45 days after they purchase any product or service to ensure they are fully satisfied.

What makes Print Audit's approach different? The company's five corporate values: family first, fun, growth, integrity, and respect. "Nowhere in our values does it say, 'Get them off the phone,'" says MacInnes. "It comes down to respect. These people have paid us money that they've worked hard for and it is our job to make sure they are satisfied with what they've bought from us." Employees are encouraged to send thank-you cards as well as flowers and gifts to customers. The company's annual flower bill is $10 000.

According to MacInnes, "The biggest hurdle is making sure that the people working here share the same values." So when hiring, Print Audit conducts multiple interviews, including one that thoroughly assesses a job candidate's fit with its service-oriented culture. This is one reason why the company has a retention rate close to 100 percent. In fact, only two people have left Print Audit during its nine years in business.

In the last eight years, Print Audit has achieved an average of 362 percent annual growth. As for the awards the company has won, MacInnes says, "The most meaningful awards we receive are the ones which recognize the values and priorities that we hold most dear."

Sources: Dunsdon, N. (2008, October 14). The customer is all right. *Globe and Mail*, E6; Anonymous (2008, September 9). Print Audit wins National Customer Service Award, Targeted News Service; Atchison, C. (2009, May). Masters of one (Guaranteeing 'wow' service every time. *Profit, 28(2)*, 18; www.printaudit.com.

culture has a tangible impact on their long-term success and an organization's ability to recruit, manage, and retain the best people. In fact, the 10 Canadian organizations listed in Exhibit 8.6 had a three-year average revenue growth that was 37 percent higher than that of the S&P/TSX 60, and a three-year average asset growth that was 147 percent higher than the S&P/TSX 60.[67]

Liabilities of Strong Cultures

On the other side of the coin, strong cultures can be a liability under some circumstances.

Resistance to Change. The mission, strategy, or specific goals of an organization can change in response to external pressures, and a strong culture that was appropriate for past success might not support the new order. That is, the strong consensus about common values and appropriate behaviour that makes for a strong culture can prove to be very resistant to change. This means that a strong culture can damage a firm's ability to innovate.

An excellent example is the case of IBM. A strong culture dedicated to selling and providing excellent service for mainframe computers contributed to the firm's remarkable success. However, this strong culture also bred strong complacency that damaged the company's ability to compete effectively with smaller, more innovative firms. IBM's strong mainframe culture limited its competitiveness in desktop computing, software development, and systems compatibility.

Another good example is the sales culture of software giant Oracle Corporation, which has been described as hyperaggressive and tough as nails—the toughest ever seen in the industry. Oracle salespeople have been accused of using brute-force tactics, heavy-handed sales pitches, and even routinely running roughshod over customers. Although the culture was once the envy of the industry and the major reason Oracle became the world's second-largest software company, the industry has changed, and now the culture has been described as its own worst enemy. CEO Larry Ellison set out to change the company's aggressive sales culture, and one of the first things he did was eliminate a long-established incentive system that encouraged furious sales pushes, over-promising, and steep discounts.[68]

Culture Clash. Strong cultures can mix as badly as oil and water when a merger or acquisition pushes two of them together under the same corporate banner.[69] Both General Electric and Xerox, large organizations with strong cultures of their own, had less-than-perfect experiences when they acquired small high-tech Silicon Valley companies with unique cultures. In both cases, the typical scenario concerns a freewheeling smaller unit confronting a more bureaucratic larger unit.

The merger of Hewlett-Packard and Compaq also raised concerns about a culture clash given the different work habits, attitudes, and strategies of the two companies. For example, Hewlett-Packard is known for careful, methodical decision making while Compaq has a reputation for moving fast and correcting mistakes later. Hewlett-Packard is engineering-oriented and Compaq is sales-oriented. The merger involved a vicious battle inside Hewlett-Packard that was described as a corporate civil war. Now that the companies have merged, employees who were once rivals have to work together and learn new systems. They have to resolve culture clashes and overcome the fact that more often than not, high-tech mergers fail. This, however, is nothing new to Compaq. The company experienced a culture clash when it merged with Digital Equipment Corp. in 1998. Many of the promised benefits did not materialize, product decisions were not made quickly or were changed, and confused customers took their business elsewhere.[70]

Pathology. Some strong cultures can threaten organizational effectiveness simply because the cultures are, in some sense, pathological.[71] Such cultures may be based on beliefs, values, and assumptions that support infighting, secrecy, and paranoia, pursuits that hardly leave time for doing business. The collapse of Enron has been blamed in part on a culture that valued lies and deception rather than honesty and truth, and the collapse of WorldCom has been attributed to a culture of secrecy and blind obedience in which executives were encouraged to hide information from directors and auditors and told to simply follow orders. The use of unethical and fraudulent accounting practices was part and parcel of both cultures. Similarly, when Garth Drabinsky and Myron Gottlieb, co-founders of the theatre company Livent Inc., were sentenced for fraud and forgery, Superior Court Justice Mary Lou Benotto stated that the two men presided over a corporation whose culture was one of dishonesty and what she called a "cheating culture."[72]

Another example of a pathological culture is NASA's culture of risk taking. Although the cause of the fatal crash of the *Columbia* space shuttle in February 2003 was a chunk of foam about the size of a briefcase, the root cause was NASA's culture that downplayed space-flight risks and suppressed dissent. A report by the Columbia Accident Investigation Board concluded that "NASA's organizational culture had as much to do with this accident as foam did." The report indicated that the culture of NASA has sacrificed safety in the pursuit of budget efficiency and tight schedules. One of the board's recommendations was that the "self-deceptive" and "overconfident" culture be changed.[73]

Contributors to the Culture

How are cultures built, maintained, and changed? In this section, we consider two key factors that contribute to the foundation and continuation of organizational cultures. Before continuing, please consult You Be the Manager:*Changing the Culture at Yellow Pages Group*.

CEO Frank Stronach of Magna International is a classic example of a founder whose values have shaped the organization's culture.

The Founder's Role. It is certainly possible for cultures to emerge over time without the guidance of a key individual. However, it is remarkable how many cultures, especially strong cultures, reflect the values of an organization's founder.[74] The imprint of Walt Disney on the Disney Company, Sam Walton on Wal-Mart, Ray Kroc on McDonald's, Thomas Watson on IBM, Frank Stronach on Magna International, Mary Kay Ash on Mary Kay Cosmetics, and Bill Gates on Microsoft is obvious. As we shall see shortly, such an imprint is often kept alive through a series of stories about the founder passed on to successive generations of new employees. This provides continuing reinforcement of the firm's core values.

In a similar vein, most experts agree that top management strongly shapes the organization's culture. The culture will usually begin to emulate what top management "pays attention to." For example, the culture of IBM today is much different than it was under the leadership of Thomas Watson, who created a culture that reflected his own personality. Louis Gerstner, Jr., who took over as CEO in 1993 until his retirement in 2002, made diversity a top priority. As a result, the culture of IBM became a more people-friendly one in which individuals are valued for their unique traits, skills, and contributions—a sharp contrast to the culture of conformity under the leadership of Thomas Watson. Today, IBM is regarded as a leader in workplace diversity.[75]

Sometimes the culture begun by the founder can cause conflict when top management wishes to see an organization change direction. At Apple Computer, Steven Jobs nurtured a culture based on new technology and new products—innovation was everything. When top management perceived this strategy to be damaging profits, it introduced a series of controls and changes that led to Jobs's resignation as board chair.[76] At Oracle, many people who are familiar with the company believed that to change the culture they must also change the CEO.

Socialization. The precise nature of the socialization process is a key to the culture that emerges in an organization because socialization is one of the primary means by which individuals can learn the culture's beliefs, values, and assumptions. Weak or fragmented cultures often feature haphazard selection and a nearly random series of job assignments that fail to present the new hire with a coherent set of experiences. On the other hand, Richard Pascale of Stanford University notes that organizations with strong cultures go to great pains to expose employees to a careful, step-by-step socialization process (Exhibit 8.7).[77]

- *Step 1—Selecting Employees.* New employees are carefully selected to obtain those who will be able to adapt to the existing culture, and realistic job previews are provided to allow candidates to deselect themselves (i.e., self-selection). As an example, Pascale cites Procter & Gamble's series of individual interviews, group interviews, and tests for brand management positions. Another good example is the interview process conducted by Google, in which employees participate in the selection of new hires who fit the Google culture.

- *Step 2—Debasement and Hazing.* Debasement and hazing provoke humility in new hires so that they are open to the norms of the organization.

- *Step 3—Training "in the Trenches."* Training begins "in the trenches" so that employees begin to master one of the core areas of the organization. For example, even experienced MBAs will start at the bottom of the professional ladder to ensure that they understand how *this* organization works. At Lincoln Electric, an extremely successful producer of industrial products, new MBAs literally spend

YOU BE THE MANAGER

Changing the Culture at Yellow Pages Group

With over 2000 employees, Montreal-based Yellow Pages Group (YPG) is Canada's largest telephone directories publisher and has been an industry leader since it published its first directory in 1908. YPG is the official publisher for Bell's directories in Canada and for TELUS directories. YPG now publishes more than 330 directories with a total circulation of 28 million copies reaching over 90 percent of Canadians. It also owns some of Canada's leading internet directories, such as YellowPages.ca, and seven local online guides, generating an average of five million unique visitors each month.

Today, YPG's market performance is impressive, with 12-month increases of 113 percent in revenues, 580 percent in profits, and 310 percent in earnings per share. However, achieving this success has required a considerable change in the company's culture. In the 1980s, the introduction of the colour red into advertisements in the profitable yet lethargic telephone business was considered "innovative." In recent years, the business has changed drastically in response to new competitive pressures like the internet that require content-rich product offerings, brand leadership, and innovative thinking. It also requires a customer-focused and result-oriented corporate culture, according to YPG president and CEO Marc P. Tellier.

However, YPG's culture was less than dynamic. According to Tellier, there was a "sense of entitlement" in the business and little accountability for results. The culture needed to change. "We like to characterize this business as a 100-year-old start-up," says Tellier. The cultural shift started with internal marketing of three new YPG guiding principles after Kohlberg Kravis Roberts & Co. and Ontario Teachers' Merchant Bank acquired control of YPG from BCE Inc. in 2002. First, says Tellier, there had to be open, honest, and timely communication. "We put a lot of emphasis on the three words because if it's not open, it's not honest," he says. "And importantly, if it's not timely, what's the point?" Second, the organization would promote the

Rejuvenating a 100-year-old "start-up."

"sense of excellence." Third, there would only be fact-based decision making. "There are no sacred cows," says Tellier. "Everything should be questioned."

But what should the new culture be like? What values are required to respond to new competitive pressures? And what will it take to change employee behaviours and accept the new culture? You be the manager.

QUESTIONS

1. What kind of culture should the company build and what values should be emphasized?

2. What should the company do to build the culture and change employee behaviours?

To find out about YPG's new culture and how it was changed, see The Manager's Notebook at the end of the chapter.

Source: Excerpt from 2005 Canadian corporate culture study. Waterstone Human Capital Ltd. Toronto, Ontario. Used by permission.

eight weeks on the welding line so that they truly come to understand and appreciate Lincoln's unique shop floor culture.

- *Step 4—Reward and Promotion.* The reward and promotion system is carefully used to reinforce those employees who perform well in areas that support the goals of the organization.

- *Step 5—Exposure to Core Culture.* Again and again, the culture's core beliefs, values, and assumptions are asserted to provide guidance for member behaviour.

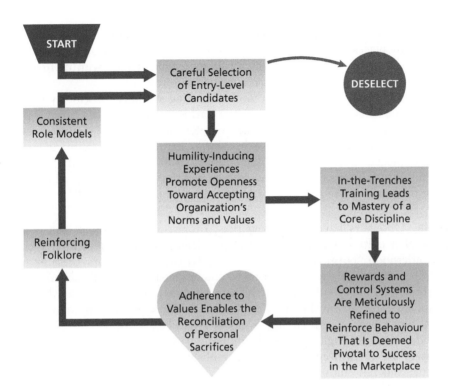

EXHIBIT 8.7
Socialization steps in strong cultures.

Source: Copyright © 1985, by The Regents of the University of California. Reprinted from the *California Management Review*, Vol. 27, No. 2. by permission of The Regents.

This is done to emphasize that the personal sacrifices required by the socialization process have a true purpose.

- *Step 6—Organizational Folklore.* Members are exposed to folklore about the organization, stories that reinforce the nature of the culture. We examine this in more detail below.
- *Step 7—Role Models.* Identifying people as "fast-trackers" provides new members with role models whose actions and views are consistent with the culture. These role models serve as tangible examples for new members to imitate.

Pascale is careful to note that it is the *consistency* among these steps and their mutually reinforcing properties that make for a strong culture. For example, it is remarkable how many of these tactics the Disney company uses. Selection is rigorous, and grooming standards serve as mild debasement. Everyone begins at the bottom of the hierarchy. Pay is low, but promotion is tied to performance. Folklore stresses core values ("Walt's in the park"). And better performers serve as role models at Disney University or in paired training.

At Four Seasons Hotels and Resorts, where the company wants new employees to buy in to the team philosophy and a "service mindset," all new hires—from hotel managers to dishwashers—go through four interviews during the selection process; once hired, they enter a three-month socialization program.[78]

Diagnosing a Culture

Earlier, we noted that culture represents a "way of life" for organizational members. Even when the culture is strong, this way of life might be difficult for uninitiated outsiders to read and understand. One way to grasp a culture is to examine the symbols, rituals, and stories that characterize the organization's way of life. For insiders, these symbols, rituals, and stories are mechanisms that teach and reinforce the culture.

Symbols. At the innovative Chaparral Steel Company in Texas, employees have to walk through the human resources department to get to their lockers. Although this facilitates communication, it also serves as a powerful symbol of the importance that the company places on its human resources. For years, IBM's "respect for the individual" held strong symbolic value, which was somewhat shaken with its first-ever lay-offs. Such symbolism is a strong indicator of corporate culture.[79]

Some executives are particularly skilled at using symbols consciously to reinforce cultural values. Retired chairman and CEO Carl Reichardt of Wells Fargo was known as a fanatic cost cutter. According to one story, Reichardt received managers requesting capital budget increases while sitting in a tatty chair. As managers made their cases, Reichardt picked at the chair's exposed stuffing, sending a strong symbolic message of fiscal austerity. This was in case they had missed the message conveyed by having to pay for their own coffee and their own office Christmas decorations![80]

Rituals. Observers have noted how rites, rituals, and ceremonies can convey the essence of a culture.[81] For example, at Tandem, a California computer company, Friday afternoon "popcorn parties" are a regular ritual. (For years, these parties were called "beer busts." We will leave it up to you to decide whether this change of names is symbolic of a major cultural shift!) The parties reinforce a "work hard, play hard" atmosphere and reaffirm the idea that weekly conflicts can be forgotten. The Disney picnics, beach parties, and employee nights are indicative of a peer-oriented, youth-oriented culture. At Flight Centre, the monthly parties called "buzz nights," at which employees are recognized for their accomplishments, are indicative of a youthful, energetic, and fun culture. At Mary Kay Cosmetics, elaborate "seminars" with the flavour of a Hollywood premiere combined with a revival meeting are used to make the sales force feel good about themselves and the company. Pink Cadillacs and other extravagant sales awards reinforce the cultural imperative that any Mary Kay woman can be successful. Rituals need not be so exotic to send a cultural message. In some companies, the annual performance review is an act of feedback and development. In others, it might be viewed as an exercise in punishment and debasement.

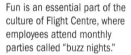

Fun is an essential part of the culture of Flight Centre, where employees attend monthly parties called "buzz nights."

Stories. As we noted earlier, the folklore of organizations—stories about past organizational events—is a common aspect of culture. These stories, told repeatedly to successive generations of new employees, are evidently meant to communicate "how things work," whether they are true, false, or a bit of both. Anyone who has spent much time in a particular organization is familiar with such stories, and they often appear to reflect the uniqueness of organizational cultures. However, research indicates that a few common themes underlie many organizational stories.

- Is the big boss human?
- Can the little person rise to the top?
- Will I get fired?
- Will the organization help me when I have to move?
- How will the boss react to mistakes?
- How will the organization deal with obstacles?[82]

Issues of equality, security, and control underlie the stories that pursue these themes. Also, such stories often have a "good" version, in which things turn out well, and a "bad" version, in which things go sour. For example, there is a story that Ray Kroc, McDonald's founder, cancelled a franchise after finding a single fly in the restaurant.[83] This is an example of a sour ending to a "How will the boss react to mistakes?" story. Whether the story is true, its retelling is indicative of one of the core values of the McDonald's culture—a fanatical dedication to clean premises.

THE MANAGER'S NOTEBOOK

Changing the Culture at Yellow Pages Group

The Yellow Pages Group is an excellent example of how an organization can change its culture and the actions involved in the process. In the last four years, the company was ranked as having one of the 10 most admired corporate cultures in Canada, and it has also been recognized as one of Canada's Top 100 Employers and one of the 10 Best Companies to Work For.

1. Management's objectives included building a performance-driven culture that focused on results, with more employee accountability and respect in the workplace. Six values, or "ground rules," were promoted to encourage behavioural changes: customer focus, compete to win, teamwork, passion, respect, and open communication.

2. One of the first things the company did was demonstrate that the organization's own people were important contributors. Internal talent was promoted to highly visible positions, while others were recruited from the outside for some key roles. According to Tellier, efforts were made to ensure they had the "right people in the right seat on the right bus." In addition, small things like printing the ground rules on the back of employees' security access cards had a big impact. And because the company did not have a common message or language in the marketplace, they developed the YPG Value Equation, which became a kind of internal script that highlights the organization's strengths and superior market position. "You have to create a framework in terms of how you get there and how you live it day-in and day-out with a set of values that people can relate to," says Tellier. Management also played an important role. In its efforts to question internal processes, the company ended up redesigning all reporting methods to encourage greater individual accountability. Senior management also demonstrated teamwork, such as spending one day a week making calls with the advertising force. Most importantly, "we were conscious about not making cultural change an objective in and of itself. While corporate culture is what we're trying to drive," says Tellier, "culture is a by-product of other behaviours. Our focus was on accomplishments that we were incredibly proud of, such as our heritage, brand, and products. We then made people accountable for their actions and started expecting more of ourselves."

LEARNING OBJECTIVES CHECKLIST

1. There are two basic forms of social dependence. *Information dependence* means that we rely on others for information about how we should think, feel, and act. *Effect dependence* means that we rely on rewards and punishments provided by others. Both contribute to conformity to norms.

2. There are several motives for conformity to social norms. One is *compliance*, in which conformity occurs mainly to achieve rewards and avoid punishment. It is mostly indicative of effect dependence. Another motive for conformity is *identification* with other group members. Here, the person sees himself or herself as similar to other organizational members and relies on them for information. Finally, conformity may be motivated by the *internalization* of norms, and the person is no longer conforming simply because of social dependence.

3. *Socialization* is the process by which people learn the attitudes, knowledge, and behaviours that are necessary to function in a group or organization. It is a process that affects proximal socialization outcomes (e.g., learning about one's tasks, roles, group, and organization) as well as distal socialization outcomes (e.g., job satisfaction, turnover). Organizational members learn norm and role requirements through three stages of socialization: anticipatory, encounter, and role management.

4. People entering organizations tend to have expectations that are inaccurate and unrealistically high that can cause them to experience a reality shock when they enter an organization. The *psychological contract* refers to beliefs held by employees regarding the reciprocal obligations and promises between them and their organization. *Psychological contract breach* is common and can have a negative effect on employees' work attitudes and behaviours. Socialization programs can help new hires form realistic expectations and accurate perceptions of the psychological contract.

5. *Realistic job previews* can help new members cope with initial unrealistic expectations. *Employee orientation programs* introduce new employees to their job, the people they will be working with, and the organization. *Socialization tactics* refer to the manner in which organizations structure the early work experiences of newcomers and individuals who are in transition from one role to another. Institutionalized socialization reflects a formalized and structured program of socialization, while individualized socialization reflects a relative absence of structure. *Mentors* can assist new members during socialization and influence their career success by performing career and psychosocial functions. New members can play an active role in their socialization through the use of *proactive socialization behaviours*, such as feedback and information seeking.

6. *Organizational culture* consists of the shared beliefs, values, and assumptions that exist in an organization. *Subcultures* can develop that reflect departmental or occupational differences. In *strong cultures*, beliefs, values, and assumptions are intense, pervasive, and supported by consensus. An organization's founder and its socialization practices can strongly shape a culture.

7. The assets of a strong culture include good coordination, appropriate conflict resolution, and financial success. Liabilities of a strong culture include inherent pathology, resistance to change, and culture clash when mergers or acquisitions occur.

8. Symbols, rituals, and stories are often useful for diagnosing a culture.

DISCUSSION QUESTIONS

1. Compare and contrast information dependence with effect dependence. Under which conditions should people be especially information-dependent? Under which conditions should people be especially effect-dependent?

2. Describe an instance of social conformity that you have observed in an organizational setting. Did compliance, identification, or internalization motivate this incident? Were the results beneficial for the organization? Were they beneficial to the individual involved?

3. Consider how you were socialized into the college or university where you are taking your organizational behaviour course. Did you have

some unrealistic expectations? Where did your expectations come from? What outside experiences prepared you for college or university? Did you experience institutionalized or individualized socialization? What proactive socialization behaviours did you employ to facilitate your socialization?

4. What are the pros and cons of providing realistic job previews for a job that is objectively pretty bad? What about for a job that is pretty good?

5 Imagine that you are starting a new business in the retail trade. You are strongly oriented toward providing excellent customer service. What could you do to nurture a strong organizational culture that would support such a mission?

6. Discuss the advantages and disadvantages of developing a strong organizational culture

and some socialization practices that you would recommend for building a strong organizational culture.

7. Describe how you would design a new-employee orientation program. Be sure to indicate the content of your program and what knowledge and information employees will acquire from attending the program. What are some of the outcomes that you would expect from your orientation program?

8. What is the difference between a traditional orientation program and a Realistic Orientation Program for Entry Stress (ROPES)? What is the difference between a realistic job preview (RJP) and ROPES? Why and when would you use each of these (traditional orientation program, ROPES, and RJP)?

INTEGRATIVE DISCUSSION QUESTIONS

1. What are the implications of social cognitive theory for social influence and socialization? Discuss the practical implications of each component of social cognitive theory (i.e., observational learning, self-efficacy, and self-regulation) for the socialization of new organization members. Describe how you would design an orientation program for new employees based on social cognitive theory. Consider the implications of social cognitive theory for mentoring. What does social cognitive theory say about why mentoring is important and how to make it effective?

2. Refer to the work-related values that differ across cultures in Chapter 4 (i.e., work centrality, power distance, uncertainty avoidance, masculinity/femininity, individualism/collectivism, long-term/short-term orientation) and consider how the culture of an organization in Canada might lead to conflicts in a country with different work-related values. Give some examples of the kind of organizational culture that might conflict with the various work-related values in other countries. What are the implications of this for Canadian companies that wish to expand abroad?

ON-THE-JOB CHALLENGE QUESTION

CN Rail is the largest freight railway in Canada, with 22 696 employees. It operates the largest rail network in Canada and the only transcontinental network in North America—in eight provinces in Canada and 16 states in the United States. In 1995, CN went public after decades of government ownership. The company underwent a transformation that involved acquiring the Illinois Central Railroad in 1998. As a result, it is now considered to be "North America's Railroad."

In 2007, Canada's Transport minister ordered a review of the railway after a five-year period in which there was a steep increase in collisions and derailments. One of the conclusions of the resulting report was the following: "CN's strict adherence to a rules-based approach, focused largely on disciplinary actions when mistakes are made, has

instilled a 'culture of fear and discipline' and is counter to an effective safety management system. CN needs to acknowledge this openly and take concrete steps to improve."

CN's goal is to be the best transportation company in North America. Does it need to change the culture to obtain its goal?

Explain how the culture at CN Rail can contribute to collisions and derailments. How can safety be influenced by an organization's culture? How important is it for CN to change its culture? What do they need to do to change the culture and improve safety?

Sources: Vu, U. (2008, July 14). Culture of fear rules safety at CN. *Canadian HR Reporter, 21(13)*, 1, 20; Johnson, J., Dakens, L., Edwards, P., & Morse, N. (2008). *Switchpoints.* Hoboken, NJ: John Wiley & Sons, Inc.; www. cn.ca.

EXPERIENTIAL EXERCISE

Socialization Preferences and Experience

The purpose of this exercise is for you to learn about how you would like to be socialized when you join an organization and how you have been socialized in a current or previous organization. By comparing your preferences to your most recent socialization experience, you can better understand how socialization can influence your job attitudes and behaviour.

Part 1: Your Socialization Preferences

Indicate your preference for each of the socialization tactics listed below using the following response scale:

1 = Dislike very much

2 = Dislike

3 = Neither like nor dislike

4 = Like

5 = Like very much

To what extent would you like or dislike:

_____ 1. To be extensively involved with other new hires in common, job-related training activities.

_____ 2. To go through a set of training experiences that are specifically designed to give newcomers a thorough knowledge of job-related skills.

_____ 3. The organization to change your values and beliefs.

_____ 4. To see a clear pattern in the way one role leads to another or one job assignment leads to another.

_____ 5. To have experienced organizational members see advising or training newcomers as one of their main job responsibilities.

_____ 6. To be able to predict your future career path in the organization by observing other people's experiences.

_____ 7. To have other newcomers be instrumental in helping you to understand your job requirements.

_____ 8. To be physically apart from regular organizational members during your training.

_____ 9. To have to "pay your dues" before you are fully accepted.

_____ 10. For each stage of the training process to expand and build upon the job knowledge gained during the preceding stages of the process.

_____ 11. To gain a clear understanding of your role in the organization by observing your senior colleagues.

_____ 12. To have good knowledge of the time it will take you to go through the various stages of the training process in the organization.

_____ 13. For the organization to put all newcomers through the same set of learning experiences.

_____ 14. To avoid performing any of your normal job responsibilities until you are thoroughly familiar with departmental procedures and work methods.

_____ 15. To be transformed or changed into a different kind of person.

_____ 16. For the movement from role to role and function to function, to build up experience and a track record, to be very apparent in the organization.

_____ 17. To receive little guidance from experienced organizational members about how you should perform your job.

_____ 18. To have your progress through the organization follow a fixed timetable of events.

_____ 19. For most of your training to be carried out apart from other newcomers.

_____ 20. For much of your job knowledge to be acquired informally on a trial and error basis.

_____ 21. To be accepted by the organization for who you are as a person.

_____ 22. For the organization to put newcomers through an identifiable sequence of learning experiences.

_____ 23. To have a lot of access to people who have previously performed your role in the organization.

_____ 24. To have a clear idea of when to expect a new job assignment or training exercise in the organization.

_____ 25. To experience a sense of "being in the same boat" among newcomers in the organization.

_____ 26. To be very aware that you are seen as "learning the ropes" in the organization.

_____ 27. To feel that experienced organizational members hold you at a distance until you conform to their expectations.

_____ 28. To have the steps in the career ladder clearly specified in the organization.

_____ 29. To generally be left alone to discover what your role should be in the organization.

_____ 30. For most of your knowledge of what may happen to you in the future to come informally, through the grapevine, rather than through regular organizational channels.

Part 2: Your Socialization Experience

Answer each of the questions above again but this time in terms how you were socialized in your current organization if you are employed or the most recent organization where you were last employed. For each statement, use the following scale to indicate how accurately it describes your socialization experiences when you joined the organization:

1 = Strongly disagree

2 = Disagree

3 = Neither agree nor disagree

4 = Agree

5 = Strong agree

Scoring and Interpretation

This scale measures the six socialization tactics. To calculate your scores on each tactic, you first must subtract your response to questions 3, 9, 15, 17, 19, 20, 27, 29, 39 from 6. For example, if you gave a response of 5 to question 3, give yourself a 1 (6 minus 5). Then calculate your score for each socialization tactic by adding up your answers as follows:

Collective versus individual tactic: Add your answers to questions 1, 7, 13, 19, and 25.

Formal versus informal tactic: Add your answers to questions 2, 8, 14, 20, and 26.

Investiture versus divestiture tactic: Add your answers to questions 3, 9, 15, 21, and 27.

Sequential versus random tactic: Add your answers to questions 4, 10, 16, 22, and 28.

Serial versus disjunctive tactic: Add your answers to questions 5, 11, 17, 23, and 29.

Fixed versus variable tactic: Add your answers to questions 6, 12, 18, 24, and 30.

For each scale your total score should be somewhere between 5 and 25. Higher scores reflect the institutionalized end of the scale (collective, formal, investiture, sequential, serial, and fixed). You can calculate a total score for all tactics by adding your responses to all 30 questions. Your total scale should fall between 30 and 150. Higher scores reflect a preference for institutionalized socialization. To calculate your

socialization experience scores, follow the same procedures but this time use your answers from Part 2.

To compare your socialization preferences to your socialization experience, calculate a socialization preference difference score by subtracting your socialization experience score from your socialization preference score for each tactic. For example, if your collective–individual socialization preference score was 25 and your socialization experience score was 10, the difference would be 15. A small difference indicates greater congruence between your socialization preference and experience. Large differences indicate a discrepancy between how you prefer to be socialized and the way you were socialized.

To facilitate class discussion and your understanding of socialization tactics, form a small group with several other members of the class and consider the following questions:

1. Each group member should present their preference score of each socialization tactic. What is the average of the group for each tactic? For each of the six tactics, do most group members prefer the institutionalized or individualized end of continuum? Each group member should explain their preference for each tactic.

2. Each group member should present their experience score of each socialization tactic. What is the average of the group for each tactic? For each of the six tactics, did most group members experience institutionalized or individualized socialization? Each group member should explain how they were socialized and what effect it had on them.

3. Each group member should present their socialization preference–experience difference score for each tactic. What are largest and smallest differences and for which tactics? Do some members have larger differences than others? Compare and contrast the experiences of those who have large to those who have smaller difference scores. Be sure to consider the effect your socialization on your learning, job attitudes, and behaviour.

4. How can an understanding of your socialization preferences assist in your future jobs? How can organizations improve their socialization process by understanding the socialization preferences of new hires?

5. What are the implications for organizations that do not consider the socialization preferences of new hires?

Source: Based on Jones, G.R. (1986). Socialization tactics, self-efficacy, and newcomers' adjustments to organizations. *Academy of Management Journal, 29*, 262–279; Ashforth, B.E., Sluss, D.M., & Saks, A.M. (2007). Socialization tactics, proactive behavior, and newcomer learning: Integrating socialization models. *Journal of Vocational Behavior, 70*, 447–462.

CASE INCIDENT

The Reality Shock

Soon after starting his new job, Jason began to wonder about the challenging work he was supposed to be doing, the great co-workers he had been told about, and the ability to attend training and development programs. None of these things seemed to be happening as promised and as he had expected. To make matters worse, he had spent most of the first month working on his own and reading about the organization's mission, history, policies, and so on. Jason began to wonder whether he had chosen the right job and organization. He was feeling very dissatisfied and seriously thinking about quitting.

1. Explain how Jason's anticipatory socialization might be contributing to his disappointment and job attitudes. How might this situation have been prevented?

2. Explain how unrealistic expectations and the psychological contract can help us understand Jason's situation.

3. Comment on the use of socialization tactics in Jason's socialization. What tactics do you think were used and what effect did they have on Jason?

4. Given Jason's current situation, is there anything the organization can do to prevent him from quitting? What should Jason do? Is there anything the organization should do so other new hires don't have the same experience as Jason?

CASE STUDY

Changing the Culture at Home Depot

Part 1

Home Depot is one of the business success stories of the past quarter-century. Founded in 1978 in Atlanta by Bernard Marcus and Arthur Blank, the company grew to more than 1100 big-box stores by the end of 2000; it reached the $40 million revenue mark faster than any retailer in history. The company's success stemmed from several distinctive characteristics, including the warehouse feel of its orange stores, complete with low lighting, cluttered aisles, and sparse signage; a "stack it high, watch it fly" philosophy that reflected a primary focus on sales growth; and extraordinary store manager autonomy, aimed at spurring innovation and allowing managers to act quickly when they sensed a change in local market conditions. Today, Home Depot is the second-largest retailer in the United States after Wal-Mart.

Home Depot's culture, set primarily by the charismatic Bernard Marcus (known among employees as Bernie), was itself a major factor in the company's success. It was marked by an entrepreneurial high-spiritedness and a willingness to take risks; a passionate commitment to customers, colleagues, the company, and the community; excellent customer service and respect for all people; and an aversion to anything that felt bureaucratic or hierarchical. The company's philosophy of customer service—"whatever it takes"—emphasizes the importance of cultivating a relationship with customers. The company structure was viewed as an inverted pyramid, with stores and customers at the top and senior management at the bottom.

Long-time Home Depot executives recall the disdain with which store managers used to view directives from headquarters. Because everyone believed that managers should spend their time on the sales floor with customers, company paperwork often ended up buried under piles on someone's desk, tossed in a wastebasket, or even marked with a company-supplied "B.S." stamp and sent back to the head office. Such behaviour was seen as a sign of the company's unflinching focus on the customer. "The idea was to challenge senior managers to think about whether what they were sending out to the stores was worth store managers' time," says Tom Taylor, the company's former executive vice-president for merchandising and marketing who started at Home Depot in 1983 as a parking lot attendant.

There was a downside to this state of affairs, though. Along with arguably low-value corporate paperwork, an important store safety directive might disappear among the unread memos. And while their sense of entitled autonomy might have freed store managers to respond to local market conditions, it paradoxically made the company as a whole less flexible. A regional buyer might agree to give a supplier of, say, garden furniture, prime display space in dozens of stores in exchange for a price discount of 10 percent—only to have individual store managers ignore the agreement because they thought it was a bad idea. And as the chain mushroomed in size, the lack of strong career development programs was leading Home Depot to run short of the talented store managers on whom its business model depended.

All in all, the cultural characteristics that had served the retailer well when it had 200 stores started to undermine it when Lowe's began to move into Home Depot's big metropolitan markets from its small-town base in the mid-1990s. Individual autonomy and a focus on sales at any cost eroded profitability, particularly as stores weren't able to benefit from economies of scale that an organization the size of Home Depot should have enjoyed.

When Robert Nardelli arrived at Home Depot in December 2000, the deck seemed stacked against the new CEO. He had no retailing experience and, in fact, had spent an entire career in industrial, not consumer, businesses. His previous job was running General Electric's power systems division, whose multimillion-dollar generating plants for industry and governments were a far cry from $10 light switches for do-it-yourselfers. Nardelli was also taking over what seemed to be a wildly successful company with a 20-year record of growth that had outpaced even Wal-Mart—but with latent financial and operational problems that threatened its continued growth, and even its future, if they weren't quickly addressed.

Nardelli's arrival at Home Depot came as a shock. No one had expected that Bernie Marcus (then chairman) and Arthur Blank (then CEO) would be leaving anytime soon. Most employees simply couldn't picture the company without these father figures. And if there was going to be change at the top of the organization, in which promotions had nearly always come from within, no one wanted, as Nardelli himself acknowledges, an outsider who would "GE-ize their company and culture."

To top it off, Nardelli's exacting and tough-minded approach, which he learned at General Electric, set him on a collision course with the freewheeling yet famously close-knit culture fostered by his predecessors, Marcus and Blank. It was this culture that Nardelli had to reshape if he hoped to bring some big-company muscle to the entrepreneurial organization (which, with revenue of $46 billion in 2000, was sometimes referred to as a "$40 billion start-up") and put the retailer's growth on a secure foundation.

Nardelli laid out a three-part strategy: enhance the core by improving the profitability of current and future stores in existing markets; extend the business by offering related services such as tool rental and home installation of Home Depot products; and expand the market, both geographically and by serving new kinds of customers, such as big construction contractors.

To meet his strategy goals, Nardelli had to build an organization that understood the opportunity in, and the importance of, taking advantage of its growing scale. Some functions, such as purchasing (or merchandising), needed to be centralized to leverage the buying power that a giant company could wield. Previously autonomous functional, regional, and store operations needed to collaborate—merchandising needed to work more closely with store operations, for instance, to avoid conflicts like the one over the placement of garden furniture. This would be aided by making detailed performance data transparent to all the relevant parties simultaneously so that people could base decisions on shared information. The merits of the current store environment needed to be re-evaluated; its lack of signage and haphazard layout made increasingly less sense

for time-pressed shoppers. And a new emphasis needed to be placed on employee training, not only to bolster the managerial ranks but also to transform orange-aproned sales associates from cheerful greeters into knowledgeable advisers who could help customers solve their home improvement problems. As Nardelli likes to say, "What so effectively got Home Depot from zero to $50 billion in sales wasn't going to get it to the next $50 billion." The new strategy would require a careful renovation of Home Depot's strong culture.

Shortly after arriving, Nardelli hired an old colleague from GE, Dennis Donovan, as his head of human resources. By placing a trusted associate in a position known for its conspicuous lack of influence in most executive suites—and by making him one of Home Depot's highest-paid executives—Nardelli signalled that changing the culture would be central to getting the company where it needed to go.

Before reading Part 2 of the case, answer the following questions:

1. Does Home Depot need to change its culture? What are the consequences it faces if it does or does not change the culture?

2. Describe Home Depot's culture and the role it has played in the company's success. How should the culture change? What norms and patterns of behaviour need to be developed? How should the new culture differ from the old culture?

3. Do you agree with the board's decision to hire an outsider as the new CEO, especially someone who has worked in a company in a different industry and with a very different culture? What are the advantages and disadvantages of this?

4. What are some of the risks and obstacles that Nardelli faces in trying to change the culture of Home Depot? What should he do to manage them?

5. How should Nardelli change the culture of Home Depot? What does he have to do, and how should he proceed?

Part 2

On January 3, 2007, Home Depot announced that the company and Nardelli had "mutually agreed" that Nardelli would resign. Dennis Donovan tendered his resignation on February 1, 2007.

Although Nardelli's departure was related to his compensation and the board's desire to reduce his 2006 pay package, there is much more to this story. Much of it has to do with what he tried to do to the Home Depot culture. According to one writer, "His failure was rooted in his decision to take a hammer to the people-oriented culture that was the essence of the Home Depot experience." The old Home Depot was staffed with experts who were always ready and willing to help customers. It was this personal touch that Nardelli changed.

He got rid of many employees and replaced full-timers with part-time staff to cut costs. As a result, Home Depot went from having great customer service to being a place where it was hard to find help. His centralization of purchasing made the company more efficient, but it eroded the entrepreneurial culture. Store managers were measured on an array of metrics such as the average hourly labour rate, none of which were related to customer service. Stores became dirty and employees surly and scarce. Some claim that what Nardelli did was ruin the Home Depot culture.

People now question whether Nardelli was the right person for the job given his background at GE, where front-line staff are not as important. By all accounts, Nardelli seems to have GE-ized the Home Depot service culture. It has been reported that upon hearing the news of Nardelli's departure, store workers were celebrating. This is not likely to have caused Nardelli much concern, as he negotiated a $210 million retirement package upon his departure. Never mind that company earnings fell 3.1 percent in the third quarter of 2006, to $1.5 billion.

Following Nardelli's resignation in January 2007, Frank Blake became chairman and CEO of Home Depot. Blake joined Home Depot in 2002 as executive vice-president, Business Development and Corporate Operations. Tim Crow replaced Dennis Donovan as vice-president of Human Resources following Donovan's resignation. Crow has also been with Home Depot since 2002, first as vice-president of Organization, Talent, and Performance Systems and then as senior vice-president. One of his most critical tasks will be to revive the Home Depot culture of strong customer service. This will not be easy. Over the last several years the company that was once famous for its helpful employees has become the subject of blog rants about bad experiences with disengaged and hard-to-find employees. Home Depot fell eight points in seven years on the University of Michigan's American Customer Satisfaction index, the largest drop for any retailer in the index.

Crow says he is focused on three priorities: creating a sense of ownership among Home Depot's 330 000 associates, making sure they have the product knowledge that customers want, and aligning rewards and recognition programs to boost morale. He has introduced a new Success Sharing program that gives everyone in a store a cash bonus if they achieve their sales plans. Homer Badges are given to associates who are recognized for "living Home Depot values." Associates who earn three badges get a cash bonus. The Aprons on the Floor program invites employees to develop ways to spend more time working with customers. The company held a luncheon for the first winners of the program, and each team member received a badge and a $100 gift card.

6. What do you think about the changes that Nardelli made to Home Depot? Why wasn't he more successful? What else should he have done? What should he have not done?

7. What do you think of Tim Crow's three priorities and some of the new programs he has introduced? What effect will they have on employees and the culture?

8. Compare and contrast Nardelli's initiatives to the new priorities and programs being implemented by Tim Crow. How are they different and what are the implications of them for employees and the culture?

9. What should the new chairman and CEO Frank Blake and the new human resources vice-president Tim Crow do? Should they focus on culture? How should they proceed?

10. What does this case say about the role of founders and leadership for organizational culture? What does it say about the effect of culture on employees and organizations? What does it say about building, maintaining, and changing an organization's culture?

Sources: Excerpt from Charan, R. (2006). Home Depot's blueprint for culture change. *Harvard Business Review, 84(4),* 60–70; Hollon, J. (2007, January 15). Other sources include Nardelli's tear-down job. *Workforce Management, 86(1),* 34; Ruiz, G. (2007, February 12). Home Depot's new HR leader faces tall order. *Workforce Management, 86(3),* 4; Reingold, J. (2008, September 29). Home Depot's total rehab. *Fortune,* 159; Marquez, J. (2008, July 14). Home remodel. *Workforce Management, 87(12),* 1, 24, 26, & 28; www.homedepot.com.

Leadership

LEARNING OBJECTIVES

After reading Chapter 9, you should be able to:

1 Define *leadership* and discuss the role of formal and *strategic leadership*.

2 Explain and critically evaluate the *trait* approach to leadership.

3 Explain the concepts of *consideration, initiating structure,* and *leader reward* and *punishment behaviour* and their consequences.

4 Describe and evaluate *Fiedler's Contingency Theory, Cognitive Resource Theory,* and *House's Path-Goal Theory.*

5 Explain how and when to use *participative leadership* using the Vroom and Jago model.

6 Describe and evaluate *Leader–Member Exchange Theory.*

7 Discuss the merits of *transactional* and *transformational leadership.*

8 Define and discuss *ethical* and *authentic* leadership.

9 Explain the role that culture plays in leadership effectiveness and describe *global leadership.*

10 Describe gender differences in leadership and explain why women are underrepresented in leadership roles in organizations.

Michael McCain of Maple Leaf Foods

Michael McCain comes from a family that has a long history in the Canadian food business. His father, Wallace, along with his brothers, founded McCain Foods Ltd., the world's largest producer of French fries. Michael McCain had always been regarded by his family as leadership material. After graduating from the University of Western Ontario, where he earned an honours degree in business administration, he joined McCain Foods, where he held positions in sales, sales management, marketing management, and information systems management. In 1986, he became president of McCain Citrus Inc., and in 1990, he was appointed president and CEO of McCain Foods USA Inc.

In 1995, McCain joined Maple Leaf Foods as president and chief operating officer. At the time, Canada's largest meat company was demoralized and antiquated. He became instrumental in bringing modern management practices to the company and upgrading the company's approach to talent management after he was promoted to president and CEO in 1999. He implemented a new corporate strategy in the face of a high Canadian dollar and rising farm commodity costs to move Maple Leaf Foods away from a commodity pork processor to a value-added branded producer of bread and meats. During the restructuring process he was praised internally and externally for his ability to engage the entire company and for acting decisively as the CEO when the time was right. He is credited for leading the transformation of Maple Leaf Foods into a major food processor and exporter.

However, on August 23, 2008, Maple Leaf Foods found itself facing the most serious crisis in its history. Packaged meat from its Toronto plant was being blamed for a listeriosis outbreak that caused persons who had consumed it to become sick and, in some cases, die. The listeriosis outbreak was the biggest food safety crisis in Canada's history and prompted the country's largest-ever meat recall. In a televised statement, Michael McCain announced that he had closed the plant and ordered a recall of its products. He apologized and expressed sympathy for the victims. During a press conference, he told reporters, "Going through the crisis, there are two advisers I've paid no attention to. The first are the lawyers, and the second are the accountants. It's not about money or legal liability—this is about our being accountable for providing consumers with safe food." He continued, "It's about public health and our

Michael McCain is credited for leading the transformation of Maple Leaf Foods into a major food processor and exporter. During the listeriosis outbreak in 2008 he was praised for his transparency and focus on consumers' health over the bottom line.

consumers and people, that's where we're spending our time and attention. . . . The buck stops here." McCain became the human face of a company that cared about its customers. McCain was praised for his transparency and his focus on consumers' health over the bottom line.

Although McCain's actions appeared expertly crafted to crisis management experts, he refused to call what he had done "crisis management." It was simply doing what was right, and doing what was right came directly from the company's ingrained values. "This is not about some contrived strategy," McCain said. "It's just about a tragic situation and an organization's desire to make it right. . . . The core principle here was to first do what's in the interest of public health, and second to be open and transparent in taking accountability. For the team, this was almost not a decision—it was obvious. It's just what we are."

After the outbreak, McCain announced a program of continuous improvement in food safety that includes establishing a food safety advisory council made up of experts from around the world, and the creation of a new executive position of chief food safety officer. The company also said it will work with government and other companies to enhance food safety across the entire industry. In addition, Maple Leaf Foods has agreed to pay as much as $27 million to settle lawsuits stemming from the listeriosis outbreak that was responsible for the deaths of 22 people. The Canadian Press named Michael McCain the 2008 CEO of the year.[1]

Michael McCain is a case study in leadership. But what exactly is leadership, and what makes a leader successful? Would Michael McCain be successful in another organization and in other leadership situations? These are the kinds of issues that this chapter tackles.

First, we will define leadership and find out if we can identify special leadership traits. After this, we will examine the consequences of various leadership behaviours and examine theories contending that effective leadership depends on the nature of the work situation. Following this are discussions of participation, leader–member exchange theory, transactional and transformational leadership, ethical and authentic leadership, and culture and global leadership. We conclude the chapter with a discussion of gender differences in leadership.

What Is Leadership?

Several years ago, an article in *Report on Business Magazine* highlighted the perceived importance of leadership in business and public affairs. The cover story, "The Toughest SOBs in Business," profiles Canada's toughest bosses and suggests that effective leaders have a rare combination of vision, skills, expertise, and toughness. In another cover story on the 25 most powerful executives in Canada, it is suggested that powerful leaders have influence and the ability to get their way with governments, the public, partners, and peers. Perhaps it's not surprising that organizations in North America spend billions of dollars each year to make their leaders more effective.[2] But what exactly is leadership?

Leadership occurs when particular individuals exert influence on the goal achievement of others in an organizational context. Effective leadership exerts influence in a way that achieves organizational goals by enhancing the productivity, innovation, satisfaction, and commitment of the workforce.

Leadership. The influence that particular individuals exert on the goal achievement of others in an organizational context.

As demonstrated in the chapter-opening vignette, leadership has a strong effect on an organization's strategy, success, and very survival. Just consider Michael McCain's role in developing and implementing a new corporate strategy and in the company's response to the listeriosis outbreak. His actions demonstrate the importance of what is known as strategic leadership.

Strategic leadership refers to a leader's "ability to anticipate, envision, maintain flexibility, think strategically, and work with others to initiate changes that will create a viable future for the organization." Strategic leaders can provide an organization with a sustainable competitive advantage by helping their organizations compete in turbulent and unpredictable environments and by exploiting growth opportunities. Strategic leaders are open and honest in their interactions with the organization's stakeholders, and they focus on the future.[3]

Strategic leadership. Leadership that involves the ability to anticipate, envision, maintain flexibility, think strategically, and work with others to initiate changes that will create a viable future for the organization.

In theory, *any* organizational member can exert influence on other members, thus engaging in leadership. In practice, though, some members are in a better position to be leaders than others. Individuals with titles such as *manager, executive, supervisor,* and *department head* occupy formal or assigned leadership roles. As part of these roles they are *expected* to influence others, and they are given specific authority to direct employees. Of course, the presence of a formal leadership role is no guarantee that there is leadership. Some managers and supervisors fail to exert any influence on others. These people will usually be judged to be ineffective leaders. Thus, leadership involves going beyond formal role requirements to influence others.

Individuals might also emerge to occupy informal leadership roles. Since informal leaders do not have formal authority, they must rely on being well liked or being perceived as highly skilled to exert influence. In this chapter we will concentrate on formal leadership.

Michael McCain is an excellent example of formal leadership. Some might even say he is a born leader. But are leaders born or made? Before continuing, see You Be the Manager: *Leadership Development at Business Development Bank of Canada (BDC).*

YOU BE THE MANAGER

Leadership Development at Business Development Bank of Canada (BDC)

Many organizations report a gap between their current leadership talent and future leadership needs. In order to address leadership gaps, companies such as Business Development Bank of Canada (BDC) identify employees who have the potential to move into leadership roles.

BDC is a Crown corporation based in Montreal that provides financing and consulting services for small and medium-sized businesses. It focuses primarily on the technology and export sectors of the economy and provides entrepreneurs with financing and a range of business consulting services. It serves its clients through a network of 92 branches across Canada.

To ensure it has future leaders, BDC selects employees for promotion based on their skills and achievements. However, very often the employees selected do not have experience leading/managing and inspiring others and may face various challenges when they are promoted into management positions.

At one point, BDC realized that a significant number of employees who were promoted were having difficulties achieving the expected results and required training and coaching. Other companies have had similar problems with high-potential employees who are not prepared for leadership roles. One study found that 27 percent of 109 employees who were rated as having high potential for senior management were rated as high risks for failure once they were promoted.

In order to address this problem, BDC implemented a leadership transition program to better prepare and develop employees with leadership potential. But how do you prepare employees to be leaders? You be the manager.

Business Development Bank of Canada (BDC) has implemented a program to evaluate and develop employees with leadership potential.

QUESTIONS

1. What kinds of experiences should the leadership transition program provide employees with leadership potential?

2. How effective will the program be in increasing the success of new leaders? Can you "make" effective leaders?

To find out more about BDC's leadership transition program, see The Manager's Notebook at the end of the chapter.

Sources: Immen, W. (2007, November 23). Primed to sail, not to fail. *Globe and Mail*, C1; Carlson, D. (2007, March 3). Potential managers play high-stakes game. *Vancouver Sun*, D4; Klie, S. (2008, October 20). Holistic approach to developing leaders best. *Canadian HR Reporter, 21(18)*, 14; Yerema, R., & Caballero, R. (2009, January 12). Employer Review: Business Development Bank of Canada/BDC, www.eluta.ca/top-employer-bdc; www.bdc.ca.

Are Leaders Born? The Search for Leadership Traits

Given Michael McCain's family history, you might be tempted to conclude that he is a born leader. But then again, with his business education and experience you might just as easily conclude that he was, in fact, groomed and trained to become a leader. Throughout history, social observers have been fascinated by obvious examples of successful interpersonal influence, whether the consequences of this influence were good, bad, or mixed. Individuals such as Henry Ford, Martin Luther King, Jr., Barbara Jordan, Ralph Nader, and Jack Welch have been analyzed and reanalyzed to discover what made them leaders and what set them apart from less successful leaders. The

" Some men are born great, some achieve greatness, and some are allowed to work for great men like me. "

implicit assumption here is that those who become leaders and do a good job of it possess a special set of traits that distinguish them from the masses of followers. While philosophers and the popular media have advocated such a position for centuries, trait theories of leadership did not receive serious scientific attention until the 1900s.

Research on Leadership Traits

During World War I the US military recognized that it had a leadership problem. Never before had the country mounted such a massive war effort, and able officers were in short supply. Thus, the search for leadership traits that might be useful in identifying potential officers began. Following the war, and continuing through World War II, this interest expanded to include searching for leadership traits in populations as diverse as school children and business executives. Some studies tried to differentiate traits of leaders and followers, while others were a search for traits that predicted leader effectiveness or distinguished lower-level leaders from higher-level leaders.[4]

Just what is a trait, anyway? **Traits** are personal characteristics of the individual, including physical characteristics, intellectual ability, and personality. Research has shown that many, many traits are not associated with whether people become leaders or how effective they are. However, sometimes we think that people are more likely to be a leader or that they are a more effective leader simply because they possess certain characteristics that we believe are associated with leadership. As described in Research Focus: *Leader Categorization Theory and Racial Bias*, this can result in racial bias and discrimination.

Research also shows that some traits are associated with leadership. Exhibit 9.1 provides a list of these traits.[5] As you might expect, leaders (or more successful leaders) tend to be higher than average on these dimensions, although the connections are not very strong. Notice that the list portrays a high-energy person who really wants to have an impact on others but at the same time is smart and stable enough not to abuse his or her power. Interestingly, this is a very accurate summary description of Michael McCain.

Traits. Individual characteristics such as physical attributes, intellectual ability, and personality.

Intelligence
Energy
Self-confidence
Dominance
Motivation to lead
Emotional stability
Honesty and integrity
Need for achievement

EXHIBIT 9.1
Traits associated with leadership effectiveness.

In recent years, there has been a renewed interest in the study of leadership traits, and a number of studies have shown that certain traits are more closely linked to leadership emergence and effectiveness. For example, one study found that three of the "Big Five" dimensions of personality (agreeableness, extraversion, and openness to experience) are related to leadership behaviours. A review of research on intelligence and leadership found that although there is a significant relationship between intelligence and leadership, it is considerably lower than previously thought.[6] Many prominent firms use personality tests and assessment centres to measure leadership traits when making hiring and promotion decisions. However, there are some aspects to the trait approach that limit its ultimate usefulness.

Limitations of the Trait Approach

Even though some traits appear to be related to leadership, there are several reasons why the trait approach is not the best means of understanding and improving leadership.

In many cases, it is difficult to determine whether traits make the leader or whether the opportunity for leadership produces the traits. For example, do dominant individuals tend to become leaders, or do employees become more dominant *after* they successfully occupy leadership roles? This distinction is important. If the former is true, we

RESEARCH FOCUS

Leader Categorization Theory and Racial Bias

Are you more likely to think that somebody is a leader just because of their race? According to research by Ashleigh Rosette, Geoffrey Leonardelli, and Katherine Phillips, there is a good chance that you are more likely to view somebody who is white as a leader than somebody who is a racial minority. The authors based their predictions on a theory called leadership categorization theory. According to leadership categorization theory, people are more likely to view somebody as a leader and to evaluate them as a more effective leader when they possess prototypical characteristics of leadership.

A leadership prototype is a standard example or typical leader category that individuals develop over time based on a set of beliefs about the behaviours and characteristics of leaders. Persons who possess the characteristics that are consistent with an observer's leadership prototype are more likely to be viewed as leaders and to be evaluated more favourably. The authors of the study predicted that this might explain racial bias in who occupies top leadership positions. That is, race, and specifically being white, might be a central characteristic of the business leader prototype.

To find out, the authors conducted four studies in which student participants read a newspaper article about a fictitious company and then answered questions about the race of the leader and the effectiveness of the leader described in the article. As predicted by leader categorization theory, leaders, but not employees, were more often assumed to be white by white and non-white participants regardless of whether the organization portrayed in the article was in the financial services or social services industry and regardless of the percentage of white individuals in the organization and in leadership positions. White and non-white participants also evaluated white leaders as more effective and as having more leadership potential than non-white leaders when the leader was credited with their organization's success. This is the very situation where racial bias can undermine non-white leaders' career potential.

These results demonstrate that being white is a characteristic of the business leader prototype. In other words, whites are perceived to be prototypical business leaders and receive more favourable evaluations compared to non-white leaders. Thus, race can result in biased evaluations of leadership through the process of leader categorization, and this has implications for the likelihood that an individual will be promoted to leadership positions and a leader's likelihood of career advancement.

Source: Based on Rosette, A.S., Leonardelli, G.J., & Phillips, K.W. (2008). The White standard: Racial bias in leader categorization. *Journal of Applied Psychology, 93*, 758–777. Used with permission. Copyright © 2008 by the American Psychological Association. Adapted with permission.

might wish to seek out dominant people and appoint them to leadership roles. If the latter is true, this strategy will not work.

Even if we know that dominance, intelligence, or tallness is associated with effective leadership, we have few clues about what dominant or intelligent or tall people *do* to influence others successfully. As a result, we have little information about how to train and develop leaders and no way to diagnose failures of leadership.

The most crucial problem of the trait approach to leadership is its failure to take into account the *situation* in which leadership occurs. Intuitively, it seems reasonable that top executives and first-level supervisors might require different traits to be successful. Similarly, physical prowess might be useful in directing a logging crew but irrelevant to managing a team of scientists.

In summary, although there are some traits that are associated with leadership success, traits alone are not sufficient for successful leadership. Traits are only a precondition for certain actions that a leader must take to be successful. In other words, possessing the appropriate traits for leadership makes it possible—and even more likely—that certain actions will be taken and will be successful.[7] Let's now consider what "actions" or behaviours are important for leadership.

The Behaviour of Leaders

The trait approach is mainly concerned with what leaders *bring* to a group setting. The limitations of this approach gradually promoted an interest in what leaders *do* in group settings. Of particular interest were the behaviours of certain group members that caused them to *become* leaders and the behaviour of assigned or appointed leaders. What are the crucial behaviours such leaders engage in, and how do these behaviours influence employee performance and satisfaction? In other words, is there a particular *leadership style* that is more effective than other possible styles?

The most involved, systematic study of leadership to date was begun at Ohio State University in the 1940s. The Ohio State researchers began by having employees describe their superiors along a number of behavioural dimensions. Statistical analyses of these descriptions revealed that they boiled down to two basic kinds of behaviour—consideration and initiating structure.

Co-operators president and CEO Kathy Bardswick is a good example of a leader who exhibits leader consideration behaviour.

Consideration and Initiating Structure

Consideration is the extent to which a leader is approachable and shows personal concern and respect for employees. The considerate leader is seen as friendly and egalitarian, expresses appreciation and support, and is protective of group welfare. Co-operators president and CEO Kathy Bardswick is a good example of someone who exhibits leader consideration behaviour. After she became CEO in 2001, she participated in 90 town hall meetings across the country to learn about employee concerns and answer their questions. Upon learning that employees were stressed and feeling the heat of public outrage at the high cost of auto insurance, she introduced a number of initiatives to assist employees, including a wellness program, recognition programs, and flexible work hours. In 2004, for the first time, the Co-operators were named one of the 50 Best Employers in Canada.[8]

Consideration. The extent to which a leader is approachable and shows personal concern and respect for employees.

Initiating structure is the degree to which a leader concentrates on group goal attainment. The structuring leader clearly defines and organizes his or her role and the roles of followers, stresses standard procedures, schedules the work to be done, and assigns employees to particular tasks.

Initiating structure. The degree to which a leader concentrates on group goal attainment.

It is important to note that consideration and initiating structure are not incompatible; a leader could be high, low, or average on one or both dimensions.

The Consequences of Consideration and Structure

The association between leader consideration, leader initiating structure, and employee responses has been the subject of hundreds of research studies. In general, this research shows that consideration and initiating structure both contribute positively to employees' motivation, job satisfaction, and leader effectiveness. However, consideration tends to be more strongly related to follower satisfaction (leader satisfaction and job satisfaction), motivation, and leader effectiveness, while initiating structure is slightly more strongly related to leader job performance and group performance.[9] In addition, there is some evidence that the relative importance of consideration and initiating structure varies according to the nature of the leadership situation. To verify this, consider the following:

- When employees are under a high degree of pressure due to deadlines, unclear tasks, or external threat, initiating structure increases satisfaction and performance. (Soldiers stranded behind enemy lines should perform better under directive leadership.)

- When the task itself is intrinsically satisfying, the need for high consideration and high structure is generally reduced. (The teacher who really enjoys teaching should be able to function with less social–emotional support and less direction from the principal.)

- When the goals and methods of performing the job are very clear and certain, consideration should promote employee satisfaction, while structure might promote dissatisfaction. (The job of refuse collection is clear in goals and methods. Here, employees should appreciate social support but view excessive structure as redundant and unnecessary.)

- When employees lack knowledge as to how to perform a job, or the job itself has vague goals or methods, consideration becomes less important, while initiating structure takes on additional importance. (The new astronaut recruit should appreciate direction in learning a complex, unfamiliar job.)[10]

As you can see, the effects of consideration and initiating structure often depend on characteristics of the task, the employee, and the setting in which work is performed.

Leader Reward and Punishment Behaviours

Assigned leaders can do other things besides initiate structure and be considerate. Two additional leader behaviours that have been the focus of research are leader reward behaviour and leader punishment behaviour. **Leader reward behaviour** provides employees with compliments, tangible benefits, and deserved special treatment. When such rewards are made *contingent on performance*, employees should perform at a high level and experience job satisfaction. Under such leadership, employees have a clear picture of what is expected of them, and they understand that positive outcomes will occur if they achieve these expectations. **Leader punishment behaviour** involves the use of reprimands or unfavourable task assignments and the active withholding of raises, promotions, and other rewards. You will recall from Chapter 2 that punishment is extremely difficult to use effectively and, when it is perceived as random and not contingent on employee behaviour, employees react negatively, with great dissatisfaction.

How effective is leader reward and punishment behaviour? A recent study examined research on leader reward and punishment behaviour and found these behaviours to be very effective. Contingent leader reward behaviour was found to be positively related to employees' perceptions (e.g., trust in supervisor), attitudes (e.g., job satisfaction and organizational commitment), and behaviour (e.g., effort, performance, organizational citizenship behaviour). And while contingent leader punishment behaviour was related to more favourable employee perceptions, attitudes, and behaviour, *noncontingent* punishment behaviour was related to unfavourable outcomes. The authors noted that the relationships were much stronger when rewards and punishment were made contingent on employee behaviour, leading them to conclude that the manner in which leaders administer rewards and punishment is a critical determinant of their

Leader reward behaviour. The leader's use of compliments, tangible benefits, and deserved special treatment.

Leader punishment behaviour. The leader's use of reprimands or unfavourable task assignments and the active withholding of rewards.

effectiveness. In other words, as described in Chapter 2, the key to effective reward and punishment is that it be administered contingent on employee behaviour and performance. The study also suggested that the reason leader reward and punishment behaviour is related to employee attitudes and behaviours is because it leads to more positive perceptions of justice and lower role ambiguity.[11]

Situational Theories of Leadership

We have referred to the potential impact of the situation on leadership effectiveness several times. Specifically, *situation* refers to the *setting* in which influence attempts occur. The basic premise of situational theories of leadership is that the effectiveness of a leadership style is contingent on the setting. The setting includes the characteristics of the employees, the nature of the task they are performing, and characteristics of the organization.

A good example of the importance of the situation for the effectiveness of a leader comes from WestJet Airlines. A number of years ago, the airline hired Steve Smith to take over as CEO. At the time, Smith was running Air Canada's regional airline in Ontario. WestJet liked his amiable, energetic personality. However, once he was on the job it became apparent that Smith's top-down leadership style and lack of openness with employees did not fit with WestJet's more open, bottom-up, collaborative style of leadership. WestJet's employee association resented his approach and Smith eventually resigned. This is a good example of how the effectiveness of a leader's style is contingent on the situation.[12]

The situational leadership theories described below are among the best known and most studied. They consider situational variables that seem especially likely to influence leadership effectiveness.

Fiedler's Contingency Theory and Cognitive Resource Theory

Fred Fiedler of the University of Washington has spent over three decades developing and refining a situational theory of leadership called **Contingency Theory**.[13] This name stems from the notion that the association between *leadership orientation* and *group effectiveness* is contingent on (depends on) the extent to which the *situation is*

Contingency Theory. Fred Fiedler's theory that states that the association between leadership orientation and group effectiveness is contingent on how favourable the situation is for exerting influence.

Situational theories of leadership explain how leadership style must be tailored to the demands of the task and the qualities of employees.

favourable for the exertion of influence. In other words, some situations are more favourable for leadership than others, and these situations require different orientations on the part of the leader.

Leadership orientation is measured by having leaders describe their **Least Preferred Co-Worker** (LPC). This person may be a current or past co-worker. In either case, it is someone with whom the leader has had a difficult time getting the job done. The leader who describes the LPC relatively favourably (a high LPC score) can be considered *relationship* oriented—that is, despite the fact that the LPC is or was difficult to work with, the leader can still find positive qualities in him or her. On the other hand, the leader who describes the LPC unfavourably (a low LPC score) can be considered *task* oriented. This person allows the low-task competence of the LPC to colour his or her views of the personal qualities of the LPC ("If he's no good at the job, then he's not good, period").

Fiedler has argued that the LPC score reveals a personality trait that reflects the leader's motivational structure. High LPC leaders are motivated to maintain interpersonal relations, while low LPC leaders are motivated to accomplish the task. Despite the apparent similarity, the LPC score is *not* a measure of consideration or initiating structure. These are observed *behaviours,* while the LPC score is evidently an *attitude* of the leader toward work relationships.

Situational Favourableness. Situational favourableness is the "contingency" part of Contingency Theory—that is, it specifies when a particular LPC orientation should contribute most to group effectiveness. Factors that affect situational favourableness, in order of importance, are the following:

- *Leader–member relations.* When the relationship between the leader and the group members is good, the leader is in a favourable situation to exert influence. A poor relationship should damage the leader's influence and even lead to insubordination or sabotage.

- *Task structure.* When the task at hand is highly structured, the leader should be able to exert considerable influence on the group. Clear goals, clear procedures to achieve these goals, and straightforward performance measures enable the leader to set performance standards and hold employees responsible.

- *Position power.* Position power is the formal authority granted to the leader by the organization to tell others what to do. The more position power the leader holds, the more favourable is the leadership situation.

According to Fiedler, the situation is most favourable for leadership when leader–member relations are good, the task is structured, and the leader has strong position power—for example, a well-liked army sergeant who is in charge of servicing jeeps in the base motor pool. The situation is least favourable when leader–member relations are poor, the task is unstructured, and the leader has weak position power—for instance, the disliked chairperson of a voluntary homeowner's association who is trying to get agreement on a list of community improvement projects.

As shown in Exhibit 9.2, we can arrange the possible combinations of situational factors into eight octants that form a continuum of favourability. The model indicates that a task orientation (low LPC) is most effective when the leadership situation is very favourable (octants I, II, and III) *or* when it is very unfavourable (octant VIII). On the other hand, a relationship orientation (high LPC) is most effective in conditions of medium favourability (octants IV, V, VI, and VII). Why is this so? In essence, Fiedler argues that leaders can "get away" with a task orientation when the situation is favourable—employees are "ready" to be influenced. Conversely, when the situation is very unfavourable for leadership, task orientation is necessary to get anything accomplished. In conditions of medium favourability, the boss is faced with some combination of an unclear task or a poor relationship with employees. Here, a relationship orientation will help to make the best of a situation that is stress-provoking but not impossibly bad.

Least Preferred Co-Worker. A current or past co-worker with whom a leader has had a difficult time accomplishing a task.

Favourableness	High ←							→ Low
Leader-Member Relations	Good				Poor			
Task Structure	Structured		Unstructured		Structured		Unstructured	
Position Power	Strong	Weak	Strong	Weak	Strong	Weak	Strong	Weak
	I	II	III	IV	V	VI	VII	VIII
Most Effective Leader Orientation	Task				Relationship			Task

EXHIBIT 9.2
Predictions of leader effectiveness from Fiedler's Contingency Theory of leadership.

Research Evidence. The conclusions about leadership effectiveness in Exhibit 9.2 are derived from many studies that Fiedler summarizes.[14] However, Contingency Theory has been the subject of as much debate as any theory in organizational behaviour.[15] Fiedler's explanation for the superior performance of high LPC leaders in the middle octants is not especially convincing, and the exact meaning of the LPC score is one of the great mysteries of organizational behaviour. It does not seem to be correlated with other personality measures or predictive of specific leader behaviour. It now appears that a major source of the many inconsistent findings regarding Contingency Theory is the small sample sizes that researchers used in many of the studies. Advances in correcting for this problem statistically have led recent reviewers to conclude that there is reasonable support for the theory.[16] However, Fiedler's prescription for task leadership in octant II (good relations, structured task, weak position power) seems contradicted by the evidence, suggesting that his theory needs some refinement.

Cognitive Resource Theory. In recent years, Fiedler has revised contingency theory and developed a new leadership theory called **Cognitive Resource Theory (CRT)**. The focus of CRT is the conditions in which a leader's cognitive resources (intelligence, expertise, and experience) contribute to effective leadership. The essence of CRT is that the importance of intelligence for leadership effectiveness depends on the following conditions: the directiveness of the leader, group support for the leader, and the stressfulness of the situation. Leader intelligence is predicted to be most important when the leader is directive, the group supports the leader, and the situation is low-stress, because the leader is able to think clearly and use his or her intelligence. In high-stress situations a leader's cognitive resources are impaired, so there his or her work experience will be most important.[17]

Research on CRT has found some support for the prediction that experience predicts performance in high-stress situations, while intelligence predicts performance in low-stress situations.[18] These results help us understand Michael McCain's effective handling of the listereosis outbreak, which was undoubtedly a very stressful situation in which his years of leadership experience came in handy. Leader intelligence has also been found to be more strongly related to group performance when the leader is directive and has the support of the group.[19] Thus, CRT indicates that traits are important for leadership effectiveness in certain situations.

House's Path-Goal Theory

Robert House, building on the work of Martin Evans, has proposed a situational theory of leadership called Path-Goal Theory.[20] Unlike Fiedler's Contingency Theory, which relies on the somewhat ambiguous LPC trait, **Path-Goal Theory** is concerned with the situations under which various leader *behaviours* are most effective.

The Theory. Why did House choose the name Path-Goal for his theory? According to House, the most important activities of leaders are those that clarify the paths to various

Cognitive Resource Theory. A leadership theory that focuses on the conditions in which a leader's cognitive resources (intelligence, expertise, and experience) contribute to effective leadership.

Path-Goal Theory. Robert House's theory concerned with the situations under which various leader behaviours (directive, supportive, participative, achievement-oriented) are most effective.

goals of interest to employees. Such goals might include a promotion, a sense of accomplishment, or a pleasant work climate. In turn, the opportunity to achieve such goals should promote job satisfaction, leader acceptance, and high effort. Thus, *the effective leader forms a connection between employee goals and organizational goals.*

House argues that to provide *job satisfaction* and *leader acceptance,* leader behaviour must be perceived as immediately satisfying or as leading to future satisfaction. Leader behaviour that employees see as unnecessary or unhelpful will be resented. House contends that to promote employee *effort,* leaders must make rewards dependent on performance and ensure that employees have a clear picture of how they can achieve these rewards. To do this, the leader might have to provide support through direction, guidance, and coaching. For example, the bank teller who wishes to be promoted to supervisor should exhibit superior effort when his boss promises a recommendation contingent on good work and explains carefully how the teller can do better on his current job.

Leader Behaviour. Path-Goal Theory is concerned with the following four specific kinds of leader behaviour:

- *Directive behaviour.* Directive leaders schedule work, maintain performance standards, and let employees know what is expected of them. This behaviour is essentially identical to initiating structure.

- *Supportive behaviour.* Supportive leaders are friendly, approachable, and concerned with pleasant interpersonal relationships. This behaviour is essentially identical to consideration.

- *Participative behaviour.* Participative leaders consult with employees about work-related matters and consider their opinions.

- *Achievement-oriented behaviour.* Achievement-oriented leaders encourage employees to exert high effort and strive for a high level of goal accomplishment. They express confidence that employees can reach these goals.

According to Path-Goal Theory, the effectiveness of each set of behaviours depends on the situation that the leader encounters.

Situational Factors. Path-Goal Theory has concerned itself with two primary classes of situational factors—employee characteristics and environmental factors. Exhibit 9.3 illustrates the role of these situational factors in the theory. Put simply, the impact of leader behaviour on employee satisfaction, effort, and acceptance of the leader depends on the nature of the employees and the work environment. Let's consider these two situational factors in turn, along with some of the theory's predictions.

According to the theory, different types of employees need or prefer different forms of leadership. For example,

- Employees who are high need achievers (Chapter 5) should work well under achievement-oriented leadership.

- Employees who prefer being told what to do should respond best to a directive leadership style.

- When employees feel that they have rather low task abilities, they should appreciate directive leadership and coaching behaviour. When they feel quite capable of performing the task, they will view such behaviours as unnecessary and irritating.

EXHIBIT 9.3
The Path-Goal Theory of leadership.

Source: From *Journal of Contemporary Business, 3(4),* 89. Reprinted by permission.

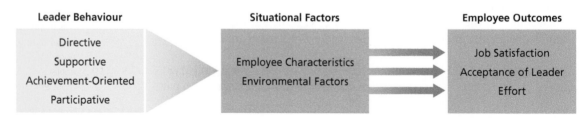

Leader Behaviour	Situational Factors	Employee Outcomes
Directive Supportive Achievement-Oriented Participative	Employee Characteristics Environmental Factors	Job Satisfaction Acceptance of Leader Effort

As you can observe from these examples, leaders might have to tailor their behaviour to the needs, abilities, and personalities of individual employees.

Also, according to the theory, the effectiveness of leadership behaviour depends on the particular work environment. For example,

- When tasks are clear and routine, employees should perceive directive leadership as a redundant and unnecessary imposition. This should reduce satisfaction and acceptance of the leader. Similarly, participative leadership would not seem to be useful when tasks are clear, since there is little in which to participate. Obviously, such tasks are most common at lower organizational levels.

- When tasks are challenging but ambiguous, employees should appreciate both directive and participative leadership. Such styles should clarify the path to good performance and demonstrate that the leader is concerned with helping employees to do a good job. Obviously, such tasks are most common at higher organizational levels.

- Frustrating, dissatisfying jobs should increase employee appreciation of supportive behaviour. To some degree, such support should compensate for a disliked job, although it should probably do little to increase effort.

As you can see from these examples of environmental factors, effective leadership should *take advantage of* the motivating and satisfying aspects of jobs while *offsetting or compensating for* those job aspects that demotivate or dissatisfy.

Research Evidence. In general, there is some research support for most of the situational propositions discussed above. In particular, there is substantial evidence that supportive or considerate leader behaviour is most beneficial in supervising routine, frustrating, or dissatisfying jobs and some evidence that directive or structuring leader behaviour is most effective on ambiguous, less-structured jobs.[21] The theory appears to work better in predicting employees' job satisfaction and acceptance of the leader than in predicting job performance.[22]

Participative Leadership: Involving Employees in Decisions

In the discussion of Path-Goal Theory, we raised the issue of participative leadership. Because this is such an important topic, we will devote further attention to participation.

What Is Participation?

At a very general level, **participative leadership** means involving employees in making work-related decisions. The term "involving" is intentionally broad. Participation is not a fixed or absolute property but a relative concept. This is illustrated in Exhibit 9.4. Here, we see that leaders can vary in the extent to which they involve employees in decision making. Minimally, participation involves obtaining employee opinions before making a decision. Maximally, it allows employees to make their own decisions within agreed-on limits. As the "area of freedom" on the part of employees increases, the leader is behaving in a more participative manner. There is, however, an upper limit to the area of employee freedom available under participation. Participative leadership should not be confused with the *abdication* of leadership, which is almost always ineffective.

Participation can involve individual employees or the entire group of employees that reports to the leader. For example, participation on an individual basis might work best when setting performance goals for particular employees, planning employee development, or dealing with problem employees. On the other hand, the leader might involve the entire work group in decision making when determining vacation schedules, arranging for telephone coverage during lunch hour, or deciding how to allocate scarce resources such as travel money or secretarial help. As these

Participative leadership. Involving employees in making work-related decisions.

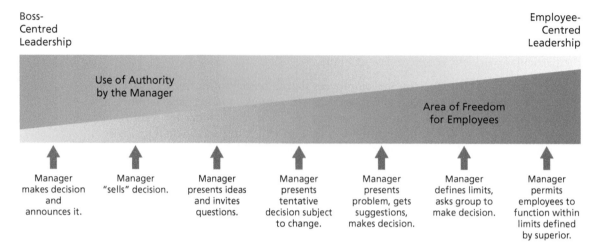

Boss-Centred Leadership

Employee-Centred Leadership

Use of Authority by the Manager

Area of Freedom for Employees

| Manager makes decision and announces it. | Manager "sells" decision. | Manager presents ideas and invites questions. | Manager presents tentative decision subject to change. | Manager presents problem, gets suggestions, makes decision. | Manager defines limits, asks group to make decision. | Manager permits employees to function within limits defined by superior. |

EXHIBIT 9.4

Employee participation in decision making can vary.

Source: printed by permission of the *Harvard Business Review*. An exhibit from "How to Choose a Leadership Pattern" by Robert Tannenbaum and Warren H. Schmidt (1958, March/April). Copyright © 1958 by the President and Fellows of Harvard College; all rights reserved.

examples suggest, the choice of an individual or group participation strategy should be tailored to specific situations.

Potential Advantages of Participative Leadership

During the restructuring process at Maple Leaf Foods, Michael McCain fostered teamwork and collaboration and was praised internally and externally for his ability to engage the entire company. Just why might participation be a useful leadership technique? What are its potential advantages?

Motivation. Participation can increase the motivation of employees.[23] In some cases, participation permits them to contribute to the establishment of work goals and to decide how they can accomplish these goals. It might also occur to you that participation can increase intrinsic motivation by enriching employees' jobs. In Chapter 6, you learned that enriched jobs include high task variety and increased employee autonomy. Participation adds some variety to the job and promotes autonomy by increasing the "area of freedom" (see Exhibit 9.4).

Quality. Participation can enhance quality in at least two ways. First, an old saying argues that "two heads are better than one." While this is not always true, there do seem to be many cases in which "two heads" (participation) lead to higher-quality decisions than the leader could make alone.[24] In particular, this is most likely when employees have special knowledge to contribute to the decision. In many research and engineering departments, it is common for the professional employees to have technical knowledge that is superior to that of their boss. This occurs either because the boss is not a professional or because the boss's knowledge has become outdated. Under these conditions, employee participation in technical matters should enhance the quality of decisions.

Participation can also enhance quality because high levels of participation often empower employees to take direct action to solve problems without checking every detail with the boss. Empowerment gives employees the authority, opportunity, and motivation to take initiative and solve problems.

Acceptance. Even when participation does not promote motivation or increase the quality of decisions, it can increase the employees' acceptance of decisions. This is especially likely when issues of *fairness* are involved.[25] For example, consider the problems of scheduling vacations or telephone coverage during lunch hours. Here, the leader could probably make high-quality decisions without involving employees. However, the decisions might be totally unacceptable to the employees because they perceive them as unfair. Involving employees in decision making could result in solutions of equal quality that do not provoke dissatisfaction. Public commitment and ego involvement probably contribute to the acceptance of such decisions.

Potential Problems of Participative Leadership

You have no doubt learned that every issue in organizational behaviour has two sides. Consider the potential difficulties of participation.

Time and Energy. Participation is not a state of mind. It involves specific behaviours on the part of the leader (soliciting ideas, calling meetings), and these behaviours use time and energy. When a quick decision is needed, participation is not an appropriate leadership strategy. The hospital emergency room is not the place to implement participation on a continuous basis!

Loss of Power. Some leaders feel that a participative style will reduce their power and influence. Sometimes, they respond by asking employees to make trivial decisions of the "what colour shall we paint the lounge" type. Clearly, the consequences of such decisions (for motivation, quality, and acceptance) are near-zero. A lack of trust in employees and a fear that they will make mistakes is often the hallmark of an insecure manager. On the other hand, the contemporary call for flatter hierarchies and increased teamwork make such sharing of power inevitable.

Lack of Receptivity or Knowledge. Employees might not be receptive to participation. When the leader is distrusted, or when a poor labour climate exists, they might resent "having to do management's work." Even when receptive, employees might lack the knowledge to contribute effectively to decisions. Usually, this occurs because they are unaware of *external constraints* on their decisions.

Vroom and Jago's Situational Model of Participation

How can leaders capitalize on the potential advantages of participation while avoiding its pitfalls? Victor Vroom and Arthur Jago have developed a model that attempts to specify in a practical manner when leaders should use participation and to what extent they should use it. (The model was originally developed by Vroom and Philip Yetton).[26]

Vroom and Jago begin with the recognition that there are various degrees of participation that a leader can exhibit. For issues involving the entire work group, the following range of behaviours is plausible (A stands for autocratic, C for consultative, and G for group; I indicates an individual, and II indicates that a group is involved):

AI. You solve the problem or make the decision yourself, using information available to you at the time.

AII. You obtain the necessary information from your employees, then decide the solution to the problem yourself. You may or may not tell your employees what the problem is in getting the information from them. The role played by your employees in making the decision is clearly one of providing the necessary information to you, rather than generating or evaluating alternative solutions.

CI. You share the problem with the relevant employees individually, getting their ideas and suggestions without bringing them together as a group. Then you make the decision, which may or may not reflect your employees' influence.

CII. You share the problem with your employees as a group, obtaining their collective ideas and suggestions. Then you make the decision, which may or may not reflect your employees' influence.

GII. You share the problem with your employees as a group. Together you generate and evaluate alternatives and attempt to reach agreement (consensus) on a solution. Your role is much like that of chairperson. You do not try to influence the group to adopt "your" solution, and you are willing to accept and implement any solution that has the support of the entire group.[27]

Which of these strategies is most effective? According to Vroom and Jago, this depends on the situation or problem at hand. In general, the leader's goal should be to make high-quality decisions to which employees will be adequately committed without undue delay. To do this, he or she must consider the questions in Exhibit 9.5. The quality requirement (QR) for a problem might be low if it is very unlikely that a technically bad decision could be made or if all feasible alternatives are equal in quality. Otherwise, QR is probably high. The commitment requirement (CR) is likely to be high if employees are very concerned about which alternative is chosen or if they will have to actually implement the decision. The problem is structured (ST) when the leader understands the current situation, the desired situation, and how to get from one to the other. Unfamiliarity, uncertainty, or novelty in any of these matters reduces problem structure. The other questions in Exhibit 9.5 are fairly self-explanatory. Notice, however, that all are oriented toward preserving either decision quality or commitment to the decision.

By tracing a problem through the decision tree, the leader encounters the prescribed degree of participation for that problem. In every case, the tree shows the fastest

EXHIBIT 9.5

The Vroom and Jago decision tree for participative leadership.

QR	Quality Requirement:	How important is the technical quality of this decision?
CR	Commitment Requirement:	How important is subordinate commitment to the decision?
LI	Leader's Information:	Do you have sufficient information to make a high-quality decision?
ST	Problem Structure:	Is the problem well structured?
CP	Commitment Probability:	If you were to make the decision by yourself, is it reasonably certain that your subordinate(s) would be commited to the decision?
GC	Goal Congruence:	Do subordinates share the organizational goals to be attained in solving the problem?
CO	Subordinate Conflict:	Is conflict among subordinates over preferred solutions likely?
SI	Subordinate Information:	Do subordinates have sufficient information to make a high-quality decision?

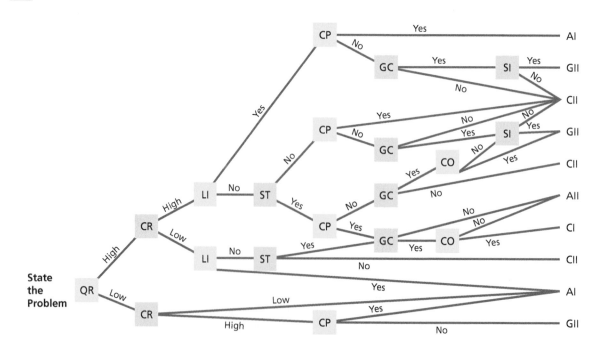

approach possible (i.e., the most autocratic) that still maintains decision quality and commitment. In many cases, if the leader is willing to sacrifice some speed, a more participative approach could stimulate employee development (as long as quality or commitment is not threatened).

Research Evidence. The original decision model developed by Vroom and Yetton, on which the Vroom and Jago model is based, has substantial research support.[28] Following the model's prescriptions is more likely to lead to successful managerial decisions than unsuccessful decisions. The model has been used frequently in management development seminars.

But does participative leadership result in beneficial outcomes? There is substantial evidence that employees who have the opportunity to participate in work-related decisions report more job satisfaction than those who do not. Thus, most workers seem to *prefer* a participative work environment. However, the positive effects of participation on productivity are open to some debate. For participation to be translated into higher productivity, it would appear that certain facilitating conditions must exist. Specifically, participation should work best when employees feel favourably toward it, when they are intelligent and knowledgeable about the issue at hand, and when the task is complex enough to make participation useful.[29] In general, these conditions are incorporated into the Vroom and Jago model. Like any other leadership strategy, the usefulness of participation depends on the constraints of the situation.

Leader–Member Exchange Theory (LMX)

An important component of leadership is the nature of the relationship that develops between leaders and employees. One theory of leadership that explains leader–employee relationships is **Leader–Member Exchange** or **LMX Theory**. Unlike other theories of leadership that focus on leader traits and behaviours, the LMX theory focuses on the dyadic relationship between a leader and an employee. In other words, it is a relationship-based approach to leadership.

The basic idea is that over time and through the course of their interactions, different types of relationships develop between leaders and employees. As a result, each relationship that a leader develops with an employee will be different and unique. In terms of LMX theory, these relationships will differ in terms of the *quality* of the relationship. Effective leadership processes result when leaders and employees develop and maintain high-quality social exchange relationships.[30]

Leader–Member Exchange (LMX) Theory. A theory of leadership that focuses on the quality of the relationship that develops between a leader and an employee.

Research Evidence. Research on LMX theory has shown that the relationships between leaders and employees do in fact differ in terms of the quality of the relationship. High-quality relationships, or high LMX, involve a high degree of mutual influence and obligation as well as trust, loyalty, and respect between a leader and an employee. High LMX leaders provide employees with challenging tasks and opportunities, greater latitude and discretion, task-related resources, and recognition. In high-quality relationships, employees perform tasks beyond their job descriptions. At the other extreme are low-quality relationships, or low LMX. Low LMX is characterized by low trust, respect, obligation, and mutual support. In low-quality relationships, the leader provides less attention and latitude to employees, and employees do only what their job descriptions and formal role requirements demand.[31]

Research has found that the quality of LMX is related to a number of employee outcomes, including higher overall satisfaction, satisfaction with supervision, organizational commitment, organizational citizenship behaviour, role clarity, job performance, and lower role conflict and turnover intentions. In general, research on LMX theory has found that higher-quality LMX relationships result in a number of positive outcomes for leaders, employees, work units, and organizations.[32]

Transactional and Transformational Leadership

Thus far in the chapter, we have been studying various aspects of what we can call transactional leadership. **Transactional leadership** is leadership that is based on a fairly straightforward exchange relationship between the leader and the followers—employees perform well, and the leader rewards them; the leader uses a participatory style, and the employees come up with good ideas. For the most part, transactional leadership behaviour involves *contingent reward behaviour,* as discussed earlier in the chapter, and management by exception. Similar to path-goal theory, the leader clarifies expectations and establishes the rewards for meeting them. **Management by exception** is the degree to which leaders take corrective action on the basis of results of leader–follower transactions. Thus, they monitor follower behaviour, anticipate problems, and take corrective actions before the behaviour creates serious problems.[33] Although it might be difficult to do well, such leadership is routine, in the sense that it is directed mainly toward bringing employee behaviour in line with organizational goals.

However, you might have some more dramatic examples of leadership in mind, examples in which leaders have had a more profound effect on followers by giving them a new vision that instilled true commitment to a project, a department, or an organization. Such leadership is called **transformational leadership** because the leader decisively changes the beliefs and attitudes of followers to correspond to this new vision and motivates them to achieve performance beyond expectations.[34]

Popular examples of transformational leadership are easy to find—consider Herb Kelleher's founding of Southwest Airlines, former Disney CEO Michael Eisner's role in improving Disney's performance, Steven Jobs's vision in bringing the Apple Macintosh to fruition, or former Hewlett-Packard CEO Carly Fiorina's orchestration of the merger with Compaq Computer and her transformation of Hewlett-Packard's structure and culture. Each of these leaders went beyond a mere institutional figurehead role and even beyond a transactional leadership role to truly transform employees' thinking about the nature of their businesses. However, these prominent examples should not obscure the fact that transformational leadership can occur in less visible settings. For example, a new coach might revitalize a sorry peewee soccer team, or an energetic new director might turn around a moribund community association using the same types of skills.

But what *are* the skills of these exceptional transformational leaders who encourage considerable effort and dedication on the part of followers? Bernard Bass of the State University of New York at Binghamton has conducted extensive research on transformational leaders.[35] Bass notes that transformational leaders are usually good at the transactional aspects of clarifying paths to goals and rewarding good performance. But he also notes other qualities that set transformational leaders apart from their transactional colleagues. In particular, there are four key dimensions of transformational leader behaviour: intellectual stimulation, individualized consideration, inspirational motivation, and charisma.[36]

Intellectual Stimulation

Intellectual stimulation contributes, in part, to the "new vision" aspect of transformational leadership. People are stimulated to think about problems, issues, and strategies in new ways. The leader challenges assumptions, takes risks, and solicits followers' ideas. Often, creativity and novelty are at work here. For example, Steve Jobs was convinced that the Apple Macintosh had to be extremely user friendly. As you might imagine, many of the technical types who wanted to sign on to the Mac project needed to be convinced of the importance of this quality, and Jobs was just the person to do it, raising their consciousness about what it felt like to be a new computer user.

Individualized Consideration

Individualized consideration involves treating employees as distinct individuals, indicating concern for their needs and personal development, and serving as a mentor or coach when appropriate. The emphasis is a one-on-one attempt to meet the concerns and needs of the individual in question in the context of the overall goal or mission. Bass implies that individualized consideration is particularly striking when military leaders exhibit it because the military culture generally stresses impersonality and "equal" treatment. General "Stormin'" Norman Schwarzkopf, commander of American troops during the Gulf War, was noted for this.

Inspirational Motivation

Inspirational motivation involves the communication of visions that are appealing and inspiring to followers. Leaders with inspirational motivation have a strong vision for the future based on values and ideals. They stimulate enthusiasm, challenge followers with high standards, communicate optimism about future goal attainment, and provide meaning for the task at hand. They inspire followers using symbolic actions and persuasion.[37]

Charisma

Charisma (also known as *idealized influence*) is the fourth and by far the most important aspect of transformational leadership. In fact, many authors simply talk about charismatic leadership, although a good case can be made that a person could have charisma without being a leader. **Charisma** is a term stemming from a Greek word meaning *favoured* or *gifted*.

Charisma. The ability to command strong loyalty and devotion from followers and thus have the potential for strong influence among them.

Charismatic individuals have been portrayed throughout history as having personal qualities that give them the potential to have extraordinary influence over others. They tend to command strong loyalty and devotion, and this, in turn, inspires enthusiastic dedication and effort directed toward the leader's chosen mission. In terms of the concepts we developed in Chapter 8, followers come to trust and *identify* with charismatic leaders and to *internalize* the values and goals they hold. Charisma provides the *emotional* aspect of transformational leadership.

It appears that the emergence of charisma is a complex function of traits, behaviours, and being in the right place at the right time.[38] Prominent traits include self-confidence, dominance, and a strong conviction in one's beliefs. Charismatic leaders often act to create an impression of personal success and accomplishment. They hold high expectations for follower performance while at the same time expressing confidence in followers' capabilities. This enhances the self-esteem of the followers. The goals set by charismatic leaders often have a moral or ideological flavour to them. In addition, charismatic leaders often emerge to articulate the feelings of followers in times of stress or discord. If these feelings go against an existing power structure, the leader might be perceived as especially courageous.

Charisma has been studied most intensively among political leaders and the leaders of social movements. Winston Churchill, Martin Luther King, Jr., Nelson Mandela, Pierre Elliott Trudeau, and Gandhi appear charismatic. Among American presidents, one study concludes that Jefferson, Jackson, Lincoln, Kennedy, and Reagan were charismatic, while Coolidge, Harding, and Buchanan were not.[39] Among business leaders, Frank Stronach, Richard Branson, Jack Welch, and the late Mary Kay Ash of Mary Kay Cosmetics are often cited as charismatic.

Although charisma is considered to be an important aspect of transformational leadership, it has also been treated as a distinct theory of leadership in its own right and often studied independent of the other dimensions of transformational leadership. Charismatic leadership has been found to be strongly related to follower satisfaction

Richard Branson of Virgin
Group is a charismatic leader
who commands strong loyalty
and devotion from his
employees.

and leadership effectiveness.[40] Several studies have investigated the charisma of CEOs and its relationship to organizational performance. The results of these studies, however, are mixed. Although CEOs who are perceived to be more charismatic tend to be perceived as more effective, only one study has found charismatic leadership to be directly related to firm performance. Two studies found a relationship, but only when the environment was perceived to be uncertain. However, several studies have found that CEO transformational leadership is positively related to organizational performance.[41]

In passing, we must also mention that charisma has a dark side, a side that is revealed when charismatic leaders abuse their strong influence over others for purely personal reasons.[42] Such people often exploit the needs of followers to pursue a reckless goal or mission. Adolf Hitler and cult leader David Koresh personify extreme examples of charismatic abuse. We will explore the abuse of power further in Chapter 11.

Research Evidence. In the last two decades, there have been more published studies on transformational leadership than all other popular theories of leadership. A review of all these studies found transformational leadership to be strongly related to follower motivation and satisfaction (satisfaction with leader and job satisfaction), leader performance, leader effectiveness, individual, group, and organizational performance. Interestingly, contingent reward leadership behaviour was also strongly related to all of these outcomes, and management by exception was moderately related to follower motivation, satisfaction with the leader, leader job performance, and leader effectiveness. Comparisons between transformational leadership and contingent reward behaviours indicated that transformational leadership was more strongly related to follower satisfaction with the leader and leader effectiveness, while contingent reward was more strongly related to follower job satisfaction and leader job performance. However, transformational leadership is especially effective during times of change and for obtaining employees' commitment to a change.[43]

Why are transformational leaders so effective? According to recent studies, transformational leaders are instrumental in developing high-quality LMX relationships, identification with one's work unit, self-efficacy, and for enhancing employees' perceptions of the five core job characteristics of the job characteristics model (see Chapter 6).[44] Overall, research indicates that the best leaders are both transformational and transactional.

Ethical and Authentic Leadership

The leadership theories described in this chapter so far focus on how leaders can improve the performance and effectiveness of individuals and groups. This should not be surprising, as most organizations and their shareholders want competent leaders who can make the company profitable. However, given the profound impact that leaders have on the lives of so many people inside and outside of an organization, ethics is also is a fundamental component of effective leadership. It is now generally understood that ethical leadership is a critical component of leadership effectiveness and long-term business success.

Ethical leadership involves the demonstration of normatively appropriate conduct (e.g., openness and honesty) through personal actions and interpersonal relationships, and the promotion of such conduct to followers through two-way communication, reinforcement, and decision making. Ethical leaders model what is deemed to be normatively appropriate behaviour, such as honesty, trustworthiness, fairness, and care. They make ethics salient in the workplace and draw attention to it by engaging in explicit ethics-related communications and by setting ethical standards. They reward

Ethical leadership. The demonstration of normatively appropriate conduct through personal actions and interpersonal relationships, and the promotion of such conduct to followers through two-way communication, reinforcement, and decision making.

Suncor Energy Inc. CEO Rick George exhibits ethical leadership by supporting environmentally friendly programs and policies.

ethical conduct and discipline those who don't follow ethical standards (notice the use of contingent leader reward and punishment behaviour). Ethical leaders also consider the ethical consequences of their decisions and make principled and fair decisions that can be observed and emulated by others. Ethical leaders care about people and the broader society and seek to do the right thing personally and professionally.[45]

For example, consider Michael McCain's decision to take personal responsibility for the listeriosis outbreak. Other leaders might have avoided accountability and been more concerned about profits and lawsuits. McCain's primary concern to protect consumers and ignore lawyers and accountants is an example of ethical leadership. Some leaders, such as Suncor Energy Inc. CEO Rick George, display ethical leadership by supporting environmentally friendly programs and policies.[46]

What should leaders do to develop an ethical culture and workplace? According to Terry Thomas, John Schermerhorn, and John Dienhart, leaders must have a strong commitment to ethics and be willing to do even the small, every-day things that help to raise awareness, and reinforce the importance, of ethics, including:[47]

- *Communicate a clear and consistent positive ethics message from the top.* Commitment to ethics must be stated often and clearly; ethics messages must be supported by positive examples of senior executives making tough choices that are driven by company values.

- *Create and embrace opportunities for everyone in the organization to communicate positive ethics, values, and practices.* Employees must experience a "voice" in the ethics culture and be encouraged to express concerns and preferences; they must have easy and secure access to mechanisms for doing so, including advice lines and tip lines for reporting violations; all questions and concerns must be followed to closure; all systematic sources of recurring problems must be traced and rectified.

- *Ensure consequences for ethical and unethical conduct.* Ethical performance should be recognized and rewarded, visibly and regularly; unethical behaviour should be met with sanctions up to and including termination, with no exclusions for senior executives.

Boeing's CEO Jim McNerney is a good example of an ethical leader who has taken these kinds of initiatives in an effort to build an ethical culture. For example, he has linked pay and bonuses to how well executives embrace "Boeing values," such as promoting integrity and avoiding abusive behaviour. He has also established financial incentives for managers based not solely on a rising stock price but on improved performance.[48]

Research Evidence. Ethical leadership is a new and emerging area of leadership, and therefore very little research has been conducted so far. However, ethical leadership has been found to be positively associated with employee perceptions of honesty, fairness, and effectiveness and with less counterproductive behaviour. Employees of ethical leaders have been found to be more satisfied with their supervisor, more willing to devote extra effort to one's job, and more willing to report problems to management. In another study, the extent to which ethics was an important part of an organization's culture was influenced by the ethics and moral development of the leader. In other words, the ethical behaviour of leaders had a significant influence on the ethical culture of the organization. Finally, although ethical leadership is important at all levels of an organization, the ethical leadership of immediate supervisors is likely to have the greatest effect on employees.[49]

Authentic Leadership

Do leaders always act in a manner that is consistent with their true personal values and beliefs? As it turns out, some leaders are more authentic than others when it comes to what they say and what they do. Just consider what Michael McCain said and did in response to the listeriosis outbreak. He apologized and expressed sympathy for the victims and accepted full responsibility and accountability for the outbreak. He said that he was doing what was right, and doing what was right came directly from the company's ingrained values. According to McCain, "The core principle here was to first do what's in the interest of public health, and second to be open and transparent in taking accountability. For the team, this was almost not a decision—it was obvious. It's just what we are."[50] McCain's words and actions are an excellent example of what is known as authentic leadership.

Authentic leadership is a positive form of leadership that involves being true to oneself. Authentic leaders know and act upon their true values, beliefs, and strengths, and they help others do the same. Their conduct and behaviour is guided by their internal values. In other words, there is a consistency between their values, beliefs, and actions. As a result, authentic leaders earn the respect and trust of their followers.

Although authentic leadership includes an ethical component, it involves more than just being ethical. Authentic leadership consists of four related but distinct dimensions:[51]

- *Self-awareness*. An understanding of one's strengths and weaknesses and an awareness of one's impact on others. Authentic leaders gain insight into themselves through interactions with others.

- *Relational transparency*. The presenting of one's true or authentic self to others and the sharing of information and expressions of one's true thoughts and feelings.

- *Balanced processing*. The objective analysis of relevant information before making a decision and consideration of views that challenge one's own position.

- *Internalized moral perspective*. The internal moral standards and values that guide one's behaviour and decision making. Authentic leaders exhibit behaviour that is consistent with their internal values and standards.

Research Evidence. Although research on authentic leadership is just beginning to emerge, there is evidence that the followers of authentic leaders report higher organizational citizenship behaviour, organizational commitment, job satisfaction, and satisfaction with their supervisor, and that they have higher job performance. Authentic leadership promotes trust and respect towards organizational leaders.

There is also evidence that the components of authentic leadership generalize across cultures.[52] Let's now turn to a more detailed consideration of culture and leadership.

Authentic leadership. A positive form of leadership that involves being true to oneself. Authentic leaders know and act upon their true values, beliefs, and strengths, and they help others do the same.

Culture and Global Leadership

Are the various leadership styles equally effective across cultures? This is a question that researchers have been asking for decades. Fortunately, we have learned a great deal about this over the last 10 years, thanks to the most extensive and ambitious study ever undertaken on global leadership. The Global Leadership and Organizational Behaviour (GLOBE) research project involved 170 researchers who worked together for 10 years collecting and analyzing data on cultural values and practices and leadership attributes from over 17 000 managers in 62 societal cultures. The results provide a rich and detailed account of cultural attributes and global leadership dimensions around the world.[53]

The project team first identified nine cultural dimensions that distinguish one society from another and have important managerial implications. Some of these dimensions are similar to Hofstede's, which were described in Chapter 4, but many of them were developed by GLOBE. Exhibit 9.6 lists and defines the nine cultural dimensions. Using these nine dimensions, GLOBE identified 10 culture clusters from the 62 culture samples. The culture clusters differ with respect to how they score on the nine culture dimensions.

Second, GLOBE wanted to know whether the same attributes that lead to successful leadership in one country lead to success in other countries. What they found was

EXHIBIT 9.6

Cultural Dimensions from the GLOBE Project

Source: Javidan, M., Dorfman, P.W., de Luque, M.S., & House, R.J. In the eye of the beholder: Cross-cultural lessons in leadership from Project GLOBE. *Academy of Management Perspectives, 20,* Table 4, p. 75.

The GLOBE conceptualized and developed measures of nine cultural dimensions. These are aspects of a country's culture that distinguish one society from another and have important managerial implications. The nine cultural dimensions are as follows:

Performance Orientation: The degree to which a collective encourages and rewards (and should encourage and reward) its members for improvement and excellence in their performance.

Assertiveness: The degree to which individuals are (and should be) assertive, confrontational, and aggressive in their interactions with others.

Future Orientation: The extent to which individuals prepare (and should prepare) for the future, for example, by delaying gratification, planning ahead, and investing in the future.

Humane Orientation: The degree to which a collective encourages and rewards (and should encourage and reward) individuals for their fairness, altruism, generosity, caring, and kindness to others.

Institutional Collectivism: The degree to which the institutional practices of organizations and society encourage and reward (and should encourage and reward) collective distribution of resources and collective action.

In-Group Collectivism: The degree to which individuals express (and should express) pride, loyalty, and cohesiveness in their families or organizations.

Gender Egalitarianism: The degree to which a collective minimizes (and should minimize) gender inequality.

Power Distance: The degree to which members of a collective expect (and should expect) power to be distributed evenly.

Uncertainty Avoidance: The extent to which a society, organization, or group relies (and should rely) on social norms, rules, and procedures to lessen the unpredictability of future events.

Implicit leadership theory. A theory that states that individuals hold a set of beliefs about the kinds of attributes, personality characteristics, skills, and behaviours that contribute to or impede outstanding leadership.

that citizens in each nation have implicit assumptions regarding requisite leadership qualities, something known as implicit leadership theory. According to **implicit leadership theory**, individuals hold a set of beliefs about the kinds of attributes, personality characteristics, skills, and behaviours that contribute to or impede outstanding leadership. These belief systems are assumed to affect the extent to which an individual accepts and responds to others as leaders. GLOBE found that these belief systems are shared among individuals in common cultures, something they call *culturally endorsed implicit leadership theory (CLT)*. Further, they identified 21 primary and 6 global leadership dimensions that are contributors to or inhibitors of outstanding leadership. The six global leadership dimensions are as follows:[54]

- *Charismatic/Value-Based.* A broadly defined leadership dimension that reflects the ability to inspire, to motivate, and to expect high performance outcomes from others on the basis of firmly held core beliefs.

- *Team-Oriented.* Emphasizes effective team building and implementation of a common purpose or goal among team members.

- *Participative.* The degree to which managers involve others in making and implementing decisions.

- *Humane-Oriented.* Reflects supportive and considerate leadership, but also includes compassion and generosity.

- *Autonomous.* Refers to independent and individualistic leadership.

- *Self-Protective.* Focuses on ensuring the safety and security of the individual.

Third, GLOBE created leadership profiles for each national culture and cluster of cultures based on their scores on the six global leadership dimensions. They then compared the ten culture clusters on the leadership profiles and found that cultures and clusters differ significantly on all six of the global leadership dimensions. For example, compared to other culture clusters, Canada and the United States score high on the charismatic/value-based, participative, and humane-oriented dimensions, low on the self-protective dimension, and medium on the team-oriented and the autonomous dimensions.

Finally, to determine what is considered important for leadership effectiveness across cultures, GLOBE examined a large number of leader attributes. They found that while the cultures do differ on many aspects of leadership effectiveness, they also have many similarities. In fact, they found many attributes, such as being honest, decisive, motivational, and dynamic, to be universally desirable; these are believed to facilitate outstanding leadership in all GLOBE countries. They also found leadership attributes such as loners, irritable, egocentric, and ruthless to be deemed ineffective in all GLOBE countries. And as you might expect, they also found that some attributes are *culturally contingent*. In other words, some attributes are effective in some cultures but are either ineffective or even dysfunctional in others. Exhibit 9.7 provides some examples of universally desirable, universally undesirable, and culturally contingent leadership attributes.[55]

The results of the GLOBE project are important because they show that while there are similarities across cultures in terms of what are considered to be desirable and undesirable leadership attributes, there are also important differences. This means that managers need to understand the similarities and differences in what makes someone an effective leader across cultures if they are to be effective global leaders.

Global Leadership

For multinational organizations, global leadership is a critical success factor. But what is global leadership? **Global leadership** involves having leadership capabilities to function effectively in different cultures and being able to cross language, social, economic, and political borders.[56] The essence of global leadership is the ability to influence people who are not like the leader and come from different cultural backgrounds.

Global leadership. A set of leadership capabilities required to function effectively in different cultures and the ability to cross language, social, economic, and political borders.

EXHIBIT 9.7
Cultural Views of Leadership Effectiveness from the GLOBE Project.

Source: Javidan, M., Dorfman, P.W., de Luque, M.S., & House, R.J. In the eye of the beholder: Cross-cultural lessons in leadership from Project GLOBE. *Academy of Management Perspectives, 20,* 69–70.

The following is a partial list of leadership attributes that are universal facilitators, universal inhibitors, or culturally contingent.

Universal Facilitators of Leadership Effectiveness

- Demonstrating trustworthiness, a sense of justice, and honesty
- Having foresight and planning ahead
- Encouraging, motivating, and building confidence; being positive and dynamic
- Being communicative, informed, a coordinator, and team integrator (team builder)

Universal Impediments to Leadership Effectiveness

- Being a loner and asocial
- Being irritable and uncooperative
- Imposing your views on others

Culturally Contingent Endorsement of Leader Attributes

- Being individualistic
- Being constantly conscious of status
- Taking risks

Bonnie Brooks, the Bay's first female CEO, is an example of a global business leader. Her international experience includes 11 years in Hong Kong.

This means that to succeed, global leaders need to have a global mindset, tolerate high levels of ambiguity, and exhibit cultural adaptability and flexibility.[57]

A good example of a global leader is Bonnie Brooks, who became the Bay's first female CEO in August 2008. She has 35 years of international retail experience, including 11 years in Hong Kong, where she was president of Lane Crawford Joyce Group, a conglomerate that runs more than 500 stores in nine Asian countries. Brooks is credited with transforming Lane Crawford into a luxury retailer. As the Bay's new CEO she is responsible for revitalizing Canada's oldest department store.[58]

What makes Bonnie Brooks a global leader? According to Hal Gregersen, Allen Morrison, and Stewart Black, global leaders have the following four characteristics:[59]

- *Unbridled inquisitiveness.* Global leaders must be able to function effectively in different cultures in which they are required to cross language, social, economic, and political borders. A key characteristic of global leaders is that they relish the opportunity to see and experience new things.

- *Personal character.* Personal character consists of two components: an emotional connection to people from different cultures and uncompromising integrity. The ability to connect with others involves a sincere interest and concern for them and a willingness to listen to and understand others' viewpoints. Global leaders also demonstrate an uncompromising integrity by maintaining high ethical standards and loyalty to their organization's values. This demonstration of integrity results in a high level of trust throughout the organization.

- *Duality.* For global leaders, duality means that they must be able to manage uncertainty and balance global and local tensions. Global leaders are able to balance the tensions and dualities of global integration and local demands.

- *Savvy.* Because of the greater challenges and opportunities of global business, global leaders need to have business and organizational savvy. Global business savvy means that global leaders understand the conditions they face in different countries and are able to recognize new market opportunities for their organization's goods and services. Organizational savvy means that global leaders are well informed of their organization's capabilities and international ventures. As for the Bay, Bonnie Brooks is believed to be one of the few executives with the savvy to lead a turnaround.

Earlier in this chapter, we discussed research on leadership traits. By now you may be wondering if global leaders are born or made. The answer appears to be both; that is, global leaders are born and then made. Individuals with the potential to become global leaders have experience working or living in different cultures, they speak more than one language, and have an aptitude for global business.

However, becoming an effective global leader requires extensive training that consists of travel to foreign countries, teamwork with members of diverse backgrounds, and formal training programs that provide instruction on topics such as international and global strategy, business and ethics, cross-cultural communication, and multicultural team leadership. The most powerful strategy for developing global leaders is work experience, transfers, and international assignments. Transfers and international assignments enable leaders to develop many of the characteristics that global leaders require to be successful. Long-term international assignments are considered to be especially effective.[60] Many companies, such as GE, Citigroup, Shell, Siemens, and Nokia, use international assignments to develop global leaders.[61]

In summary, developing global leaders is becoming increasingly important for organizations around the world. To be successful in the global economy, it is critical for an organization to identify and develop leaders who have the capability to become global leaders. For many organizations, however, this will not be easy, as many report that they do not have enough global leaders now or for the future, and they do not have a system in place for developing them.[62]

However, there is some evidence that certain countries produce more global leaders than others. Karl Moore and Henry Mintzberg of McGill University found that those countries that are considered to be the most global in terms of their involvement in world trade and investment, such as Canada, the Netherlands, Switzerland, Belgium, Ireland, Sweden, Denmark, Singapore, Australia, and Finland, tend to have more than their share of good global leaders given their size. Why is this? They are all middle-economy countries that are dependent on foreign trade. As a result, they must be able to understand and empathize with persons in other cultures. For Canadians, this comes naturally. According to Moore and Mintzberg, it is a strength of Canadians that they learn from the cradle to take into account other perspectives, a key requirement of global managers working for global companies. Living in a multicultural environment like Canada is excellent preparation for being a global manager. As a result, Canadian companies like Bombardier are way ahead of most organizations in big countries like the United States when it comes to global leadership.[63]

Gender and Leadership

Do men and women adopt different leadership styles? A number of popular books have argued that women leaders tend to be more intuitive, less hierarchically oriented, and more collaborative than their male counterparts. Is this true? Notice that two opposing logics could be at work here. On the one hand, different socialization experiences could lead men and women to learn different ways of exerting influence on others. On the other hand, men and women should be equally capable of gravitating toward the style that is most appropriate in a given setting. This would result in no general difference in style.

However, a number of reviews have found that there are some differences in leadership style between men and women in organizational settings. For example, researchers Alice Eagly and Blair Johnson concluded that women have a tendency to be more participative or democratic than men, and as a result, they are changing the business world.[64] How is this so? One theory holds that women have better social skills, which enable them to successfully manage the give-and-take that participation requires. Another theory holds that women avoid more autocratic styles because they violate gender stereotypes and lead to negative reactions. This might explain why a study on gender and leadership found that women are perceived by themselves and their co-workers as performing significantly better as managers than do men.[65]

In a review of the leadership styles of men and women based on 45 studies, women leaders were found to be more transformational than men leaders, and they also engaged in more of the contingent reward behaviours associated with transactional leadership. Men leaders engaged in more of the other components of transactional leadership, such as management by exception and **laissez-faire leadership**, which is the avoidance or absence of leadership. What is most interesting about these findings is that those aspects of leadership style in which women exceed men are all positively related to leadership effectiveness, while those leadership aspects in which men exceed women have weak, negative, or null relations to leadership effectiveness. The authors concluded that these findings attest to the ability of women to be highly effective leaders in contemporary organizations.[66]

Laissez-faire leadership. A style of leadership that involves the avoidance or absence of leadership.

While the evidence clearly indicates that women can be highly effective leaders, the reality is that women hold very few top leadership positions in Canadian organizations. An exception is Annette Verschuren, who is president of Home Depot Canada and oversees Home Depot operations in China. When she was featured in a cover story in *Report on Business* magazine in 2007, the magazine made note of the fact that she was the only woman to appear on the magazine's cover in the past year—a sad reflection of the fact that so few women occupy the top echelons of Canada's largest organizations.[67]

The most recent census of women corporate officers and top earners of the FP500 indicates that women hold only 16.9 percent of corporate officer roles. This is particularly low when you consider that women make up 47.1 percent of the total workforce and 37.2 percent of management positions. Further, only 37 women occupy top executive offices (vice-presidents, chief operating officers, chief financial officers) of Canada's 100 largest publicly traded companies. Women also hold a minority of senior leadership positions in the United States and Europe.[68] How can we explain this obvious gender bias in leadership?

For decades the explanation has been the **glass ceiling** metaphor—the invisible barrier that prevents women from advancing to senior leadership positions in organizations. However, Alice Eagly and Linda Carli have recently suggested that a more accurate metaphor is a *labyrinth*, because of the many twists, turns, detours, and dead ends that women encounter along their way up the organizational hierarchy. In other words, the lack of women leaders is the sum of all of the barriers women face rather than one particular barrier (i.e., the glass ceiling) at the top of the organization.[69]

So what are the barriers that women encounter in organizations? According to Eagly and Carli, they include:[70]

- *Vestiges of prejudice.* Men continue to receive higher wages and faster promotions than women with equal qualifications at all organizational levels.

- *Resistance to women's leadership.* Men are perceived as having *agentic* traits, which convey assertion and control and are generally associated with effective leadership. Women are perceived as having *communal* traits, which convey a concern for the compassionate treatment of others. A recent study found that perceivers associate agentic leadership traits with male leaders to a greater extent than with female leaders. In other words, males are perceived as having traits that are associated with leadership. Exhibit 9.8 shows some common agentic and communal leadership traits.

- *Issues of leadership style.* Women leaders often struggle to find an appropriate leadership style that reconciles the communal traits associated with females and the agentic traits associated with leaders. This results in a double bind. When women exhibit an agentic style they are criticized for lacking communal traits, and when

Glass ceiling. An invisible barrier that prevents women from advancing to senior leadership positions in organizations.

Annette Verschuren is president of Home Depot Canada and one of the few women to hold a senior leadership position in a Canadian organization.

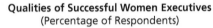

Agentic Traits

Dedicated: Worked late all week in order to finish the project.

Charismatic: When speaking, motivates employees.

Intelligent: Displays extraordinary talent and competence in every project.

Determined: Does not give up on a project when complications arise.

Aggressive: Fights to get the work group necessary resources.

Competitive: Emphasizes that the team needs to be number one.

Communal Traits

Caring: Always shows concern for the well being of the team.

Sensitive: Is responsive to the feelings of employees at work.

Honest: Always makes sure that credit is not taken for employee's good ideas.

Understanding: Listens when subordinates are having a personal conflict.

Compassionate: Extends employees deadlines when they have important family commitments.

Sympathetic: Expresses concern with subordinates that are going through difficult times.

EXHIBIT 9.8

Agentic and Communal Leadership Traits

Source: Reprinted from *Organizational Behavior and Human Decision Processes 101*, Scott, K. A., & Brown, D. J., Female first, leader second? Gender bias in the encoding of leadership behavior, 230–242. Copyright © 2006 Elsevier Inc. All Rights Reserved. Reprinted with permission from Elsevier.

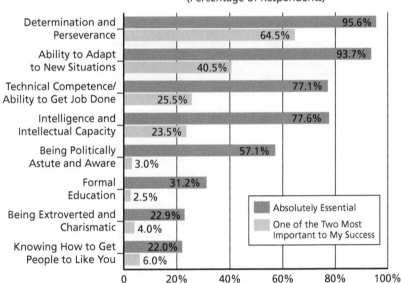

EXHIBIT 9.9

Qualities of successful women executives.

Source: *Women in Management*, Richard Ivey School of Business, The University of Western Ontario.

they exhibit a communal style they are criticized for not being agentic enough to be a leader. However, as shown in Exhibit 9.9, many of the qualities of successful women executives are in fact agentic.

- *Demands of family life.* Women remain more responsible for domestic work and child rearing and as a result they have fewer years of work experience and fewer hours of employment. This slows their career progress and results in lower pay.

- *Underinvestment in social capital.* Women have less time for socializing with colleagues and developing social networks and often have difficulty breaking in to social networks because these are predominantly male. As a result, women have less social capital.

Given the many obstacles that women face, what can organizations do to increase the number of women in senior leadership positions? As shown in Exhibit 9.10, a combination of programs and interventions is required. For an example of how an organization has succeeded in the advancement of women, see Applied Focus: *The Advancement of Women Initiative at Scotiabank.*

EXHIBIT 9.10

The Advancement of
Women in Organizations

Source: Reprinted by permission of
the *Harvard Business Review*. Exhibit
from "Women and the Labyrinth of
Leadership" by A.H. Eagly and L.L.
Carli, 101 (2007). Copyright ©
2007 by the Harvard Business
School Publishing Corporation;
all rights reserved.

According to Alice Eagly and Linda Carli, legislation that requires organizations to eliminate inequitable practices is not effective for the advancement of women when inequality in an organization is embedded in the organization's culture and structure. If organizations want to remove the barriers that prevent women from advancing to leadership roles, they should do the following:

- Increase people's awareness of the psychological drivers of prejudice toward female leaders, and work to dispel those perceptions.
- Change the long-hours norm.
- Reduce the subjectivity of performance evaluation.
- Use open-recruitment tools, such as advertising and employment agencies, rather than relying on informal social networks and referrals to fill positions.
- Ensure a critical mass of women in executive positions—not just one or two women—to head off the problems that come with tokenism.
- Avoid having a sole female member of any team.
- Help shore up social capital.
- Prepare women for line management with appropriately demanding assignments.
- Establish family-friendly human resources practices.
- Allow employees who have significant parental responsibility more time to prove themselves worthy of promotion.
- Welcome women back.
- Encourage male participation in family-friendly benefits.

APPLIED FOCUS

The Advancement of Women Initiative at Scotiabank

In 1993, Scotiabank established a task force on the advancement of women in an effort to recruit, develop, and advance more women into senior leadership positions. However, the program did not set targets for fear of a negative backlash within the bank, and there were no measures of progress. As a result, 10 years later women still held less than 20 percent of senior management positions.

In 2003, the bank re-launched the Advancement of Women Initiative with some important changes. For example, ScotiaWomen's Connection provides an online resources guide with information and tools to support networking and mentoring. Quarterly networking sessions are held for women at all levels of the organization that feature speakers, professional development, and career information sessions.

In addition, the bank now measures women's progress toward targets in senior-level positions on an ongoing basis. Managers and all executive vice-presidents are accountable for the advancement of women. It is part of their performance review, which, in turn, is tied to compensation.

Today, women comprise 70 percent of Scotiabank's total Canadian workforce and just over 50 percent of its management staff. The number of women at all senior levels in the bank has nearly doubled between 2003 and 2006. Scotiabank has increased the percentage of women at the senior management level from 18.9 percent in 2003 to 31.0 percent in 2006. In the most senior roles, the percentage of women has increased from 26.7 percent in 2003 to 36.8 percent in 2006. In 2007, three of Scotiabank's female vice-presidents were on the 100 most powerful Canadian women list, and three other of its leaders were listed on the 100 most powerful Canadian women alumnae.

The Advancement of Women Initiative was expanded in 2007 and can now be found in many countries where the bank operates. It is considered to be a model of how to develop and promote female leaders.

In 2007, Scotiabank received the prestigious Catalyst Award for its Advancement of Women Initiative, and in 2009, it was chosen as one of Canada's 35 best diversity employers.

Sources: Klie, S. (2009, April 6). Women make small gains. *Canadian HR Reporter*, 22(7), 2, 3; Galt, V. (2007, April 5). How to hammer the glass ceiling. Globe and Mail, B1; Diversity is strength, Advancement of women. www.scotiabank.com; Scotiabank—Unlocking potential, delivering results: The Advancement of Women (AoW) Initiative. 2007 Catalyst Award Winner; www.catalyst.org.

THE MANAGER'S NOTEBOOK

Leadership Development at Business Development Bank of Canada (BDC)

BDC has been recognized for its leadership practices. In 2007, it was the first and only Canadian organization listed on Fortune's list of Top Companies for Leaders. BDC has also been recognized for its excellence in Leadership Development and was selected as one of Canada's Top 100 Employers for 2007, 2008, and 2009.

1. The leadership transition program includes classroom learning, job shadowing, and coaching, and high potentials are given projects that stretch their experiences. Participants also attend an Executive Assessment Centre, where they participate in a simulation in which they role-play a manager. The simulation involves juggling a variety of tasks, making vital business decisions, and staying in character while role-playing a day-in-the life of a specifically titled executive. Performances are recorded on video and reviewed. BDC is one of an increasing number of organizations using the assessment centre to identify potential leaders and prepare them to move up the corporate ladder. According to BDC's senior director of learning strategies, "Basically, we're preparing people who'd be put into first level of managerial roles within 18 to 24 months."

2. The program has improved the transition to leadership and increased the number of newly promoted managers that meet expectations. High-potential employees are now better prepared for leadership roles, and their transition is more successful. Further, those who realize that management is not for them drop out of the program before moving into a leadership role. Thus, employees who have the potential to become leaders need to be developed to become effective leaders.

LEARNING OBJECTIVES CHECKLIST

1. *Leadership* occurs when an individual exerts influence on others' goal achievement in an organizational context. Individuals with titles such as manager, executive, supervisor, and department head occupy formal or assigned leadership roles. As part of these roles, they are expected to influence others, and they are given specific authority to direct employees. Individuals may also emerge to occupy informal leadership roles. Since informal leaders do not have formal authority, they must rely on being well liked or being perceived as highly skilled to exert influence. *Strategic leadership* involves the ability to anticipate, envision, maintain flexibility, think strategically, and work with others to initiate changes that will create a viable future for the organization.

2. Early studies of leadership were concerned with identifying physical, psychological, and intellectual *traits* that might predict leader effectiveness. While some traits appear to be related to leadership capacity, there are no traits that guarantee leadership across various situations.

3. Studies of the behaviour of leaders have concentrated on *initiating structure* and *consideration* as well as *leader reward* and *punishment behaviours*. Both consideration and initiating structure contribute positively to employees' motivation, job satisfaction, and leader effectiveness. Consideration tends to be more strongly related to follower satisfaction, motivation, and leader effectiveness, while initiating structure is slightly more

strongly related to leader job performance and group performance. Leader contingent reward and punishment behaviour is positively related to employees' perceptions, attitudes, and behaviour.

4. *Fiedler's Contingency Theory* is a situational theory of leadership that suggests that different leadership orientations are necessary depending on the favourableness of the situation for the leader. Favourableness depends on the structure of the task, the position power of the leader, and the relationship between the leader and the group. Fiedler argues that *task-oriented* leaders perform best in situations that are either very favourable or very unfavourable. *Relationship-oriented* leaders are said to perform best in situations of medium favourability. *Cognitive Resource Theory* (CRT) is a refinement of contingency theory that focuses on the conditions in which a leader's cognitive resources contribute to effective leadership. *House's Path-Goal Theory* is a situational theory of leadership that suggests that leaders will be most effective when they are able to clarify the paths to various subordinate goals that are also of interest to the organization. According to House, the effectiveness of directive, supportive, participative, and achievement-oriented behaviour depends on the nature of the subordinates and the characteristics of the work environment.

5. *Participative* leader behaviour involves employees in work decisions. Participation can increase employee motivation and lead to higher-quality and more acceptable decisions. The *Vroom and Jago model* specifies how much participation is best for various kinds of decisions. Participation works best when employees are desirous of participation, when they are intelligent and knowledgeable, and when the task is reasonably complex.

6. *Leader–Member Exchange Theory* is concerned with the quality of the relationship that develops between a leader and an employee. High-quality relationships, or high LMX, involve a high degree of mutual influence and obligation as well as trust, loyalty, and respect between a leader and an employee. Higher-quality LMX relationships

result in positive outcomes for leaders, employees, work units, and organizations.

7. *Transactional* leadership is leadership that is based on a straightforward exchange relationship between the leader and the followers and involves *contingent reward behaviour* and *management by exception*. *Transformational leaders* modify the beliefs and attitudes of followers to correspond to a new vision. They provide intellectual stimulation, individualized consideration, and inspirational motivation. They also have *charisma*, the ability to command extraordinary loyalty, dedication, and effort from followers.

8. *Ethical leadership* involves the demonstration of normatively appropriate conduct through personal actions and interpersonal relationships and the promotion of such conduct to followers through two-way communication, reinforcement, and decision making. *Authentic leadership* is a positive form of leadership that involves being true to oneself. Authentic leaders know and act upon their true values, beliefs, and strengths and they help others do the same.

9. The GLOBE project found that there are many leadership attributes that are universally desirable or universally undesirable in all cultures, as well as some attributes that are culturally contingent, that is, they will be effective in some cultures but ineffective or dysfunctional in others. *Global leaders* can function effectively in different cultures and are characterized by their inquisitiveness, personal character, global business and organizational savvy, and their ability to manage the dualities of global integration and local demands.

10. There are some differences in leadership style between men and women in organizational settings. Women leaders tend to be more transformational than men leaders, and they also engage in more contingent reward behaviours. Men leaders engage in more management by exception and laissez-faire leadership. Women remain underrepresented in senior leadership positions as a result of many barriers and obstacles that have been described as a labyrinth of leadership.

DISCUSSION QUESTIONS

1. Are leaders born or made? Consider each perspective (leaders born versus made) and the implications of each for organizations. What does each perspective suggest that organizations should do to ensure that they have effective leaders?

2. Contrast the relative merits of consideration and initiating structure as well as leader reward and punishment behaviour in the following leadership situations: running the daily operations of a bank branch; commanding an army unit under enemy fire; supervising a group of college students who are performing a hot, dirty, boring summer job. Use House's Path-Goal Theory to support your arguments.

3. What is the main premise behind Cognitive Resource Theory (CRT) and how does it extend Fiedler's Contingency Theory? What does CRT say about research on leadership traits? What does it tell us about the role of traits for leadership effectiveness?

4. Describe a situation that would be ideal for having employees participate in a work-related decision. Discuss the employees, the problem, and the setting. Describe a situation in which participative decision making would be an especially unwise leadership strategy. Why is this so?

5. What are transformational leaders skilled at doing that gives them extraordinary influence over others? Why do you think women are more likely to be transformational leaders than men? Describe a leadership situation in which a transformational leader would probably not be the right person for the job.

6. What are the main findings from the GLOBE project and what are the implications for leadership across cultures? If a leader from Canada takes on an assignment in another culture, will he or she be successful? What is most likely to improve the chances of success?

7. Identify a leader who you think is a global leader and describe the characteristics and behaviours that make that person a global leader. Do you think that global leaders are born or made? What advice would you give an organization that needs more global leaders?

8. Leadership traits are considered to be important for leadership because they can lead to certain actions that are required for effective leadership. Review each of the traits in Exhibit 9.1 and discuss how they might be related to different leadership styles and behaviours (e.g., consideration, initiating structure, directive, supportive, participative, achievement oriented, transformational, LMX, ethical, authentic, and global).

9. What does it mean to be an ethical leader, and how can ethical or unethical leadership impact an organization? What about an authentic leader?

10. Describe Leadership Categorization Theory and how it explains racial and gender bias in leadership. What can organizations do to remove the barriers that restrict the movement of non-whites and women into leadership positions?

INTEGRATIVE DISCUSSION QUESTIONS

1. Consider the relationship between leadership and organizational culture. Using the approaches to leadership discussed in this chapter (e.g., leadership traits, behaviours, situational theories, participative leadership, LMX theory, transformational leadership, ethical and authentic leadership), describe how a leader can influence the culture of an organization. Based on your analysis, do you think that leaders have a strong influence on an organization's culture?

2. What effect does leadership have on employee motivation? Using each of the theories of motivation described in Chapter 5, discuss the implications for leadership. In other words, according to each theory, what should a leader do to motivate employees?

3. Refer to the material in Chapter 3 on perceptions and gender stereotypes and compare and contrast it with the material presented in this chapter on women and leadership. What does the material in Chapter 3 tell us about women and leadership? Why do you think women are more likely to be transformational leaders than men? Can women be more effective leaders than men? What have you learned about perceptions, stereotypes, and reality?

4. Refer to the material in Chapter 2 on learning and discuss the implications of learning theories for ethical leadership. In other words, what should ethical leaders do to create an ethical workplace? Similarly, refer to the material in Chapter 8 on culture and explain what a leader might do to create an ethical organizational culture.

ON-THE-JOB CHALLENGE QUESTION

The Bay is Canada's oldest department store, with 94 stores across the country. However, like other department stores in North America, store productivity has been slipping for years, and the Bay has been losing market share to speciality chains and global discounters. In August 2008, Bonnie Brooks was appointed president and CEO of the Bay. She is the Bay's first female CEO, and her mandate is to lead the Bay's ambitious revival strategy. She has more than 30 years of experience in the retail fashion industry. Before returning to Canada, Brooks was president of Lane Crawford Joyce Group, a conglomerate that runs more than 500 stores in nine Asian countries. Brooks is credited with transforming Lane Crawford into a luxury retailer. So why did she decide to return to Canada to run the much smaller Bay? According to Brooks, "The role to transform the Bay from its existing format to world class was too compelling to pass up. Building exceptional retail destinations is not only my profession, it's my passion." It is believed that the Bay must make dramatic changes if it is to survive. The vision is to make it the dominant Canadian department store by improving the quality of its brands, its stores, and its service.

However, the Bay has been subject to numerous failed makeovers over the past decade. While there are many skeptics, according to industry experts Brooks is one of the few executives with the savvy to change the Bay. They say she will bring a sense of fashion, style, and glamour to the job.

Refer to the theories and approaches to leadership discussed in the chapter and describe the kind of leader that Bonnie Brooks should be and the type of leadership that is required to transform the Bay. What do the various theories suggest she needs to do to be an effective leader at the Bay? What advice would you give her?

Sources: Flavelle, D. (2008, August 6). The Bay's new boss: Fashion expert Bonnie Brooks says she'll bring her passion for "building exceptional retail destinations" to Canada's oldest department store. *Toronto Star*, B3; Kingston, A. (2009, March 16). Bonnie of the Bay. *Maclean's, 122(9)*, 34–36; Strauss, M. (2009, April 23). The pragmatic fashionista. *Globe and Mail*, B1, B7.

EXPERIENTIAL EXERCISE

Ethical Leadership Scale (ELS)

How ethical is your leader? To find out, answer the 10 questions below as frankly and honestly as possible about your current supervisor if you are employed or the most recent supervisor you had in your last job. Use the following response scale:

1–Strongly disagree

2–Disagree

3–Neither agree or disagree

4–Agree

5–Strongly agree

My supervisor . . .

_____ 1. Listens to what employees have to say.

_____ 2. Disciplines employees who violate ethical standards.

_____ 3. Conducts his/her personal life in an ethical manner.

_____ 4. Has the best interests of employees in mind.

_____ 5. Makes fair and balanced decisions.

_____ 6. Can be trusted.

_____ 7. Discusses business ethics or values with employees.

_____ 8. Sets an example of how to do things the right way in terms of ethics.

_____ 9. Defines success not just by results but also by the way that they are obtained.

_____ 10. When making decisions, asks, "What is the right thing to do?"

Scoring and Interpretation

You have just completed the Ethical Leadership Scale (ELS) developed by Michael E. Brown, Linda K. Trevino, and David A. Harrison. To obtain your score, add up your responses to the 10 questions and divide by 10. Your total should be somewhere between 1 and 5. Higher scores indicate a more ethical leader. The average score of 87 MBA students in a large public university in the United States was 3.37. In a sample of 123 undergraduate seniors in business, the average ELS score was 3.46.

Source: Reprinted from *Organizational Behavior and Human Decision Processes 97*, Brown, M.E., Trevino, L.K. & Harrison, D.A. (2005). Ethical leadership: A social learning perspective for construct development and testing, 117–134. Copyright © 2005 Elsevier Inc. All Rights Reserved. Reprinted with permission from Elsevier.

To facilitate class discussion and your understanding of ethical leadership, form a small group with several members of the class and consider the following questions:

1. Each group member should present their ELS score. What is the range of scores (highest and lowest) and the average score in your group? Overall, how ethical are group members' supervisors?

2. Each group member should provide examples of what makes their supervisor an ethical or unethical leader. Be specific in describing supervisor behaviours that are ethical or unethical. Based on group members' answers, what are some of the main differences between ethical and unethical leaders?

3. Each group member should consider the impact that their supervisor has had on them, their co-workers, and the organization. Be specific in describing the effects that their ethical or unethical behaviour has had on people's attitudes and behaviours as well as on the organization (e.g., sales or productivity).

4. What does your supervisor need to do differently to be a more ethical leader?

5. If you are now or have been in a leadership position in the past, how ethical have you been? Take the ELS again but this time thinking about yourself in a current or previous leadership role. How ethical are you (or were you)? What do you have to do to become a more ethical leader?

EXPERIENTIAL EXERCISE

Leadership Jazz

The purpose of this exercise is to learn about the effect of leadership on individual and group creativity. For this exercise, students will work in small groups (no more than five people). The instructor will assign a leader to each group and will also decide what kind of leader he or she will be. Each group will be required to create musical instruments using only the resources they have with them, which they will use to play a tune/song in front of the class. The class will evaluate each group's performance.

Procedure

Students should form small groups with no more than five people. The instructor will then assign a leader in each group and instruct that person on what kind of leader to be (e.g., transactional, transformational, considerate, task-oriented, participative, etc.). This will enable comparisons across groups. Alternatively, the instructor can let the leaders of each group choose their leadership style. Whatever the case, the leader should not reveal to the group his/her leadership style until after the exercise. The leader of each group is responsible for his or her group's performance in creating musical instruments and for their performance of a tune or song. Once the groups have been formed and the leaders assigned, the exercise should proceed as follows:

Step 1: Each group will have 10–15 minutes to create musical instruments using any materials they have with them. They must not leave the room or their workspace to search for materials. Groups should try to create as many musical instruments as they can, creating a variety of instruments that can be used in a band or orchestra. Thus, the goal is both quantitative (number of instruments) and qualitative (variety of instruments).

Step 2: Each group will have 10–15 minutes to decide on several tunes/songs to play and to rehearse them in preparation for their performance in front of the class. The group should decide on what tune to play for the class and focus on the quality of their performance. Each group should have a backup tune/song in case another group plays the same one they have chosen. This will help to ensure that each group plays a different tune/song. Keep in mind that the quality of the performance is important.

Step 3: Each group will perform a tune/song (two to three minutes maximum) in front of the class that no other group has performed (each group should be prepared to perform more than one song in case their first choice is played by another group).

Step 4: The class will rate the performance of each group using the following criteria:

- quantity of instruments used
- variety of instruments used
- recognizability of tune/song
- uniqueness of tune/song
- quality of performance

After all the groups have performed their tune/song, the class votes for the best group for each of the criteria listed above and for the overall best group.

Discussion

The discussion should focus on how the group members responded to the leader and the effect of the leader on the group's creativity and performance. To facilitate class discussion, consider the following questions:

1. How did group members respond to their leader and what effect did the leader have on individual group member's behaviour, creativity, and performance?

2. What effect did the leader have on the creativity and performance of each group? Group members should comment on what their leader did that was helpful and encouraged creativity and what their leader did that was not helpful and did not encourage creativity. What else could the leader have done to improve the group's creativity and performance? How important is leadership for individual and group creativity? What can leaders do to encourage creativity?

3. What style of leadership was most effective? At this point, the leaders can disclose their leadership style. What type of leader was associated with the group that received the highest score on the performance criteria? What type of leader was associated with the group that received the lowest score on the performance criteria? What type of leadership was most effective for overall group creativity and performance?

4. Consider the role of situational theories of leadership. Does the task of creating and playing musical instruments require a certain style of leadership? Did some members of each group respond better to their leader than others?

5. If you were to do this task over again, what type of leader would you prefer and why? What type of leader would be most effective? Discuss the theories of leadership to support your answers.

Source: Lengnick-Hall, M.L., & Lengnick-Hall, C.A. (1999). Leadership jazz: An exercise in creativity. *Journal of Management Education, 23,* 65–70. Copyright © 1999, OBTS Teaching Society for Management Educators. Reprinted by Permission of SAGE Publications.

CASE INCIDENT

Fran-Tech

A mid-level manager at Fran-Tech, a Seattle software company, received a CD-ROM set containing the source code for a competitor's software product. The competitor is the market leader in the software niche in which both companies compete; it is crushing Fran-Tech in the marketplace. An anonymous note accompanying the package stated that the package was sent by a disgruntled employee of the competitor and urged the recipient to use the data "as you see fit." The manager receiving the data was considered to be a "star" performer by her boss and her peers.

1. What do you think the manager is likely to do in this situation? What should she do and why?

2. Explain the relevance of ethical leadership in this situation. What will an ethical leader do and why? What will an unethical leader do?

3. Consider how the manager's response to this situation can impact the ethical behaviour of her employees in the organization. What are some of the potential implications of her actions for employees and the organization?

Source: Thomas, T., Schermerhorn, J.R., Jr., & Dienhart, J.W. (2004). Strategic leadership of ethical behavior in business. *Academy of Management Executive, 18,* 56–66.

CASE STUDY

Computer Services Team at AVIONICS

John Johnson, a top executive at AVIONICS who is partially responsible for information systems, is contemplating a government contract directive that calls for an integration of the computer information systems into a "service centre" concept. He is also aware that management has issued a directive to cut costs, and that he has not been inspired by the service centre manager's performance for some time. He wondered if the service contract idea is an opportunity to address all three issues at once.

John is known for his ability to empower people. He is dedicated to continual process improvement techniques, and he has put together a number of process improvement teams, focusing on concurrent engineering and total quality management (TQM). He prides himself on his ability to help teams improve quality and process. People respect John's abilities, and he has moved up rapidly in the organization. His excellent interpersonal skills have made him well-liked and influential at AVIONICS.

In John's readings of total quality management and process improvement, he has been impressed with the concept of a "leaderless team" or "autonomous work group." He wonders if the service centre concept could be an opportunity to experiment with the idea. After some thought, he decides to lay off the computer information systems supervisor and create a leaderless team. He changed the name from "computer information systems" to "computer service centre," and let team members know that their purpose was to integrate their systems to provide quality service to the customers.

As John expected, the laid-off supervisor, Glen Smith, was not happy and immediately filed a grievance, requesting reinstatement. He was allowed to stay as a member of the team until a decision could be made about his status. Even with the grievance, John felt satisfied that he had solved some of his problems. Glen wouldn't be a problem now that he was just a member.

John decided to start the team off right with a two-day, intensive training session. At the training session, he told the team members he was empowering them to change their own destiny. "You have the opportunity to control your own work," John enthusiastically told them. "No one is a leader—you are all responsible. That means if you have a problem, don't come running to me—you are in charge!"

Using large sheets of newsprint, the group listed their goals and expectations. They decided they wanted to achieve a collective identity. John instructed them on breakthrough analysis and told them about leaderless teams. Team members were impressed by John's knowledge of the subject. William Ashby, a Macintosh specialist, listened with interest. He really liked what

John was saying about total quality management. He had read a few books on the subject and, listening to John, he felt inspired about really doing it.

The First Meeting

Shortly after the off-site training session, team members gathered for their first meeting. Eight people sat at a large rectangular table. William, the Macintosh specialist, looked around the room. He had more or less worked with several of these people in the past; at least they had shared the same large office space. There was Alyne, the VAX systems administrator, and her assistant, Frank. William recognized Russ, the IBM PC specialist and his counterpart. Glen, their former supervisor, was there, trying to blend in. Three other people he didn't know very well were also present: Rachel, the database support specialist, Harold, from business operations, and the assistant business manager, Carol.

A few people chatted with each other. Carol appeared engrossed in a memo. Glen sat with his arms folded, leaning back in his chair. William wondered who was going to get the meeting started. People were looking uncomfortable, waiting and wondering what would happen next. "Maybe I should say something," William thought to himself. He cleared his throat.

"Well, here we all are," he said. William hesitated, to see if anyone else wanted to take the lead. Everyone except Carol, who still seemed engrossed in her memo, stared at him. "I guess we should get started," William announced, hoping someone would offer a suggestion. He waited again. Again, everyone stared at him.

"Well, I for one was really excited about what John had to say at our off-site training." William looked around the room; a few people's heads nodded. "So I guess we should get started," William repeated, feeling a bit foolish.

Glen, the former supervisor, sat watching the group. "Oh, brother!" he thought. "This is going to be a problem, a real problem." He watched William struggle to lead the group.

William continued: "John suggested that we elect a leader from among ourselves to act as a volunteer leader of sorts. Does anyone have any suggestions?"

"Yeah, let's hurry this up," said Russ, the IBM PC specialist. "I've got 10 people who need to be hard-wired breathing down my neck." Russ continued, "I nominate you, William. You seem interested, and I really don't care who our leader is."

Some of the people looked at Russ with embarrassment. They had lots of work to do, too, but wouldn't have put it so bluntly. "He sure is a pain," thought Alyne. She turned to William and smiled. "Yes, I think

William would be good. Would you be interested, William?" she asked.

"Well, I guess I would. I've never played on a formal team before, and I don't know what to do, but I'm willing to give it a shot." William felt the blood rising up to his ears. "I guess, unless there are any objections, I'll volunteer to be leader." Since no one said anything, William became the leader.

The group spent the next 20 minutes trying to figure out what it was supposed to be doing. They weren't sure what a TQM team was, or what it meant to integrate their various jobs to "create a service team." Most of the people sat and listened while William, Alyne, and Rachel talked. Russ stated again that he really needed to get back to work. The group decided to continue the discussion during the next meeting, a week away.

The Volunteer Leader Prepares

William told his wife that night about his election as leader of the group. "I'm not sure what to do. Maybe I'll check out the bookstore, and see if I can find some books on the subject." William drove to the bookstore and searched through the business section. He found several books on TQM that looked promising, plus one called How to Make Prize Winning Teams, which he thought was a real find. That night, William began reading the book. He was inspired by what he read, and he thought it was "doable" for his team.

The next week, the team gathered once more around the rectangular table. Russ, the IBM specialist, was absent because of "pressing business," but everyone else was present. William started things off by telling them about the books. He suggested that everyone should get a copy and read it.

"I think we need to begin figuring out how to improve our work," William told them. He proceeded to tell them about how they should look at each of their areas, and look for ways to improve it. William looked down at the notes he had taken from the book. He wanted to make sure he told them all exactly how it should be done; he didn't want to get it wrong.

Alyne interrupted him. She didn't like the way William seemed to be telling them what to do. "I think before we go charging down that street, we need to decide how we are going to decide things. I, for one, don't want people telling me what to do about my area." A few people nodded. "I think everyone should have a vote in these changes."

"Yes, I agree," said Frank, her assistant. "Majority rules; no one should have more say-so than anyone else."

"Fine," said William, but he couldn't help feeling that something had just gone wrong. The team agreed to vote on all matters. People started fidgeting in their seats, so William suggested that they end the meeting. "Everyone should try to buy the books and read them before our next meeting," he said.

During the next few months, William tried in vain to get the group to read the books. He thought if they would read them, they'd understand what he'd been talking about.

He felt pretty disheartened as he spoke to his wife that night. "Everyone wants to just go along," he told her. "We've got all these individuals on the team, and they only seem to care about their own turf. I thought we were starting to make progress last week when a few people started talking about the common complaint their customers had about reaching them, but then it became a discussion about why their customers didn't understand. I've learned you can't dictate to them. I have to win them over, but I don't know how. I'm going for a drive to think this out."

As William drove toward the beach, he thought about his job. He wasn't having much fun. Every meeting was the same thing. Members had to vote on every little thing that was brought up. If someone in the group didn't want to do it, that person just didn't vote. Or the person would go along with everyone else and vote but not follow through. He saw no evidence that anyone wanted to make it work. He wished he could go to his supervisor, John, but John had maintained a strict hands-off approach with the team since the in-service training. He felt that John had cut them loose, to sink or swim. They were definitely sinking.

"Maybe there is too much diversity on this team," he thought. "I need training on how to bring a diverse group together." He decided to see if he could get some training to help him out of the hole he'd crawled into.

William Voted Out

When William approached the human resources department about the training, he was told that his group did not have the budget for that kind of training. William angrily left the office, feeling very discouraged.

Over the next two months, it became painfully obvious that the group wasn't working. Some team members argued constantly, and some avoided conflict at all cost. Carol, the assistant business manager, requested a stress leave. She felt she couldn't take the problems and responsibility any longer. No one could agree on the team's goals, or how they were going to integrate their "service team." They felt frustrated with John, their manager, and thought he was unpredictable. John had a reputation for being a supportive and creative manager, yet with this team he was distant. They wondered why he didn't act like the manager others said he was.

Finally, at one meeting six months after the team began, Alyne, the VAX specialist, spoke up, "Look, William, this isn't working. We need a new leader." Everyone else agreed and, after some discussion, they voted in Glen, their former supervisor, as their "volunteer" leader. Glen, who had recently won his grievance against the layoff, was ready for the assignment.

William felt hurt. "That's it, I give up," he thought. "From now on, I'm looking out for my own group. I've been neglecting the Mac users, but no more."

About the time that Glen became "volunteer" leader, John was transferred to another assignment, and

Barbara, the director of business management, became the group's manager. She told team members they needed to get better at serving their customers.

Glen, who had more leadership skills than William, recognized that the team was at a crisis point. He decided to try to build trust among the team members by working on continuous process improvement (CPI). He thought they might be able to pull it off if they just had enough time.

After four months, Barbara, the team manager, pulled the plug and ordered the team to go back to the structure it had nearly a year ago. A few people, and particularly Glen, were disappointed. "I was just beginning to feel like we were going to make it. The other team members were right—the company doesn't support teams. They just give a lot of lip service, but there is no management commitment."

Source: Harvey, Carol; Allard, M. June, *Understanding and Managing Diversity*, 4th ed. ©N/A. Reproduced by Pearson Education, Inc., Upper Saddle River, NJ. Questions prepared by Alan Saks.

1. Discuss John's and William's leadership behaviour in terms of consideration, initiating structure, reward, and punishment. What behaviours did they exhibit and which behaviours do you think they should have exhibited? Explain your answer.

2. Use House's Path-Goal Theory to analyze the leadership situation facing the computer services team. What leadership behaviour does the theory suggest? What leadership behaviour did John and William exhibit and what effect did it have on members of the team?

3. Use Fiedler's Contingency Theory and Cognitive Resource Theory (CRT) to analyze the leadership situation. What leadership style does the theory suggest? What leadership style did John and William exhibit and what do the theories say about their effectiveness as leaders?

4. Discuss the merits of LMX theory and transactional and transformational leadership for the computer services team. What do these theories tell us about how John and William could have been more effective leaders?

5. Based on your reading of the case and your answers to the previous questions, what should John and William have done differently to be more effective leaders?

6. What do the events in the case tell us about the effects of leadership on individuals, teams, and organizations? Was the computer services team a big mistake or could things have turned out differently? Explain your answer.

PEARSON
myOBlab

Visit MyOBLab at **www.pearsoned.ca/myoblab** for access to online tutorials, interactive exercises, videos, and much more.

Decision Making

LEARNING OBJECTIVES

After reading Chapter 10, you should be able to:

1 Define *decision making* and differentiate well-structured and ill-structured problems.

2 Compare and contrast perfectly *rational decision making* with decision making *under bounded rationality*.

3 Discuss the impact of *framing* and *cognitive biases* on the decision process.

4 Explain the process of *escalation of commitment* to an apparently failing course of action.

5 Consider how emotions and mood affect decision making.

6 Summarize the pros and cons of using groups to make decisions, with attention to the *groupthink* phenomenon and risk assessment.

7 Discuss techniques for improving organizational decision making.

The 2008–2009 Economic Meltdown

In March 2009, the Dow Jones Industrial Average dipped below 7000, closing at about half of its peak value achieved in October 2007. At the same time, Stephan Schwarzman, CEO of Blackstone Group LP, a private equity company, said that 45 percent of the world's wealth had been destroyed by the global credit crisis. Around the world, both developed and developing countries declared that they had entered a recession, with some analysts suggesting that a depression was looming. The cost of a barrel of oil had dropped to $50, approximately one-third of its all-time high, reached in July 2008. Although Canada was relatively better positioned than other countries, it too suffered from the economic meltdown. The Bank of Canada rate was pushed down to an all-time low of 0.75 percent, while the national unemployment rate neared 8 percent. Governments at all levels projected large deficits, while bailout packages became prominent on the political agenda.

As the *Washington Post* reported in October 2008, the financial crisis was created through a complicated web of policy decisions that could be traced as far back as a decade. Opinions varied about which specific policies and decisions were most responsible, but one thing that most observers agreed on was that a contributing factor was the overabundance of subprime mortgages granted in the United States. These are mortgages that are issued using lower than normal credits standards to people with risky credit profiles (e.g., weak credit history, late or missed payments).

The trouble actually began with a series of decisions made much earlier. A 1992 study by the Boston Federal Reserve Board suggested that discrimination by lenders was preventing some Americans from achieving home ownership. The study spurred a rash of political activity that led to a movement which suggested that home ownership should be a right, not a privilege. President Clinton, followed by President Bush, pressured the Federal National Mortgage Association and the Federal Home Loan Mortgage Corporation (respectively known as Fannie Mae and Freddie Mac) to ease the credit requirements on mortgages to broaden the accessibility of home-ownership. Through weak regulation (which some called "self-regulation"), banks were encouraged to provide mortgages to subprime borrowers on financially inflated real estate. In turn, Fannie Mae and Freddie Mac would buy up the loans so that the banks could lend even more. In the meantime, Fannie Mae and Freddie Mac packaged the mortgage loans and sold them to Wall Street investors in the form of derivatives, financial instruments used to manage the risk associated with an underlying security (in this case, the

The 2008–2009 economic meltdown revealed flawed decision making.

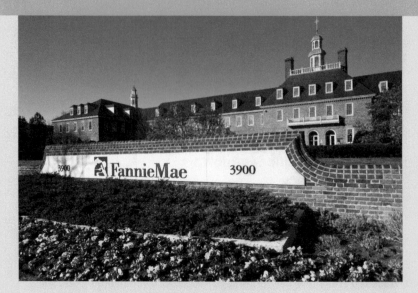

mortgages themselves). The Wall Street investors, in turn, protected their investments by selling "credit-default swaps," in which the buyer of the swap pays the seller (through a series of payments) and is potentially rewarded financially should the credit instrument go into default. Finally, the Federal Reserve Board did its part by holding interest rates low.

This house of cards, created by a series of risky decisions, was founded upon assumptions that the economy would stay strong, real estate prices would continue to rise, and the subprime borrowers would somehow find a way to pay their mortgages, even though they had no money. In other words, the subprime mortgage market, and the derivatives that supported it, would thrive in a strong economy because escalating house prices would be a source of wealth for new buyers.

In the face of the belief that the right of home ownership was playing a central role in the US economy, publications such as *The Economist* frequently pointed out the fragility of the economic situation. Notable analysts, such as Brooksley E. Born, head of the Commodity Futures Trading Commission, argued as far back as 1998 that the obscure and ever-growing derivative market carried significant economic risks. But the arguments of Born and others fell on deaf ears. By 2003, home ownership was contributing more than 20 percent to the US gross domestic product and was considered to be responsible for the healthy US economy. The home ownership program and the associated derivatives market were so successful that by mid-2008 the derivatives market reached a whopping US$530 trillion. Who would have thought that only a few months later, the US government would have to concoct bailout packages in the order of hundreds of billions of dollars to buy back mortgage bonds issued by Fannie Mae and Freddie Mac?

In hindsight, it seems that the global financial crisis and, more specifically, the collapse of the subprime mortgage market could have been avoided. However, closer analysis suggests that the meltdown resulted from a series of decisions, all of which were founded upon a set of principles that were created and backed by the American people, through the office of the presidency. Starting with framing home ownership as a right rather than a privilege, politicians, bankers, investors, homeowners, and shareholders all supported the subprime market, voting with their money or their homes.[1]

In the case of the economic meltdown, how could so many people misjudge the risks and make such a series of apparently bad decisions? We will find out in this chapter. First, we will define decision making and present a model of a rational decision-making process. As we work through this model, we will be especially concerned with the practical limitations of rationality. After this, we will investigate the use of groups to make decisions. Finally, the chapter closes with a description of some techniques to improve decision making.

What Is Decision Making?

Consider the following questions that might arise in a variety of organizational settings:

- How much inventory should our store carry?
- Where should we locate the proposed community mental health centre?
- Should I remain at this job or accept another?
- How many classes of Philosophy 200 should our department offer next semester?
- Should our diplomats attend the summit conference?

Common sense tells us that someone is going to have to do some decision making to answer such questions. **Decision making** is the process of developing a commitment to some course of action.[2] Three things are noteworthy about this definition. First, decision making involves making a *choice* among several action alternatives—the store can carry more or less inventory, and the mental health centre can be located at the north or south end of town. Second, decision making is a *process* that involves more than simply the final choice among alternatives—if you decide to accept the offer of a new job, we want to know *how* this decision was reached. Finally, the "commitment" mentioned in the definition usually involves some commitment of *resources,* such as time, money, or personnel—if the store carries a large inventory, it will tie up cash.

In addition to conceiving of decision making as the commitment of resources, we can describe it as a process of problem solving.[3] A **problem** exists when a gap is perceived between some existing state and some desired state. For example, the chairperson of the Philosophy department might observe that there is a projected increase in university enrolment for the upcoming year and that his course schedule is not completed (existing state). In addition, he might wish to adequately service the new students with Philosophy 200 classes and at the same time satisfy his dean with a timely, sensible schedule (desired state). In this case, the decision-making process involves the perception of the existing state, the conception of the desired state, and the steps that the chairperson takes to move from one state to the other.

> **Decision making.** The process of developing a commitment to some course of action.

> **Problem.** A perceived gap between an existing state and a desired state.

Well-Structured Problems

For a **well-structured** problem, the existing state is clear, the desired state is clear, and how to get from one state to the other is fairly obvious. Intuitively, these problems are simple, and their solutions arouse little controversy. This is because such problems are repetitive and familiar.

- Assistant bank manager—which of these 10 car loan applications should I approve?
- Welfare officer—how much assistance should this client receive?
- Courier—which delivery route should I use?

Because decision making takes time and is prone to error, organizations (and individuals) attempt to program the decision making for well-structured problems. A **pro-**

> **Well-structured problem.** A problem for which the existing state is clear, the desired state is clear, and how to get from one state to the other is fairly obvious.

Program. A standardized way of solving a problem.

gram is simply a standardized way of solving a problem. As such, programs short-circuit the decision-making process by enabling the decision maker to go directly from problem identification to solution.

Programs usually go under labels such as *rules, routines, standard operating procedures,* or *rules of thumb.* Some programs come from experience and exist only "in the head." Other programs are more formal. At UPS, drivers' routes are programmed to avoid left-hand turns so that they don't idle waiting for oncoming traffic to clear. In one year, this saved three million gallons of fuel and reduced emissions by 32 000 metric tons.[4] You are probably aware that routine loan applications are "scored" by banks according to a fixed formula that takes into account income, debt, previous credit, and so on. Unfortunately, in the subprime mortgage fiasco, problematic credit scores were simply ignored.

Many of the problems encountered in organizations are well structured, and programmed decision making provides a useful means of solving these problems. However, programs are only as good as the decision-making process that led to the adoption of the program in the first place. In computer terminology, "garbage in" will result in "garbage out." For example, Nebraska enacted a "safe haven" law by which unwanted infants could be left at hospitals rather than abandoned. However, the law used the word "child," which resulted in a number of unruly teenagers (some from other states) being deposited at Nebraska hospitals![5]

These difficulties of programmed decision making are seen in the ineffective hiring procedures that some firms use. To solve the recurrent problem of choosing employees for lower-level jobs, almost all companies use application forms. These forms are part of a decision program. However, some firms have persisted in asking for information (such as age or marital status) that violates equal employment and human rights legislation or is not job-related. Costly lawsuits have resulted.

Ill-Structured Problems

Ill-structured problem. A problem for which the existing and desired states are unclear and the method of getting to the desired state is unknown.

The extreme example of an **ill-structured problem** is one in which the existing and desired states are unclear and the method of getting to the desired state (even if clarified) is unknown. For example, a vice-president of marketing might have a vague feeling that the sales of a particular product are too low. However, she might lack precise information about the product's market share (existing state) and the market share of its most successful competitor (ideal state). In addition, she might be unaware of exactly how to increase the sales of this particular product.

Ill-structured problems are generally unique; that is, they are unusual and have not been encountered before. In addition, they tend to be complex and involve a high degree of uncertainty. As a result, they frequently arouse controversy and conflict among the people who are interested in the decision. For example, consider the following:

- Should we vaccinate the population against a new flu strain when the vaccination may have some bad side effects?
- Should we implement a risky attempt to rescue political hostages?
- In which part of the country should we build a new plant?

It should be obvious that ill-structured problems such as these cannot be solved with programmed decisions. Rather, the decision makers must resort to non-programmed decision making. This simply means that they are likely to try to gather more information and be more self-consciously analytical in their approach. Ill-structured problems can entail high risk and stimulate strong political considerations. This was apparent in the political blame game that followed the 2008–2009 economic meltdown. We will concentrate on such ill-structured problems in this chapter.

The Compleat Decision Maker—A Rational Decision-Making Model

Exhibit 10.1 presents a model of the decision process that a rational decision maker might use. When a problem is identified, a search for information is begun. This information clarifies the nature of the problem and suggests alternative solutions. These are carefully evaluated, and the best is chosen for implementation. The implemented solution is then monitored over time to ensure its immediate and continued effectiveness. If difficulties occur at any point in the process, repetition or recycling may be affected.

It might occur to you that we have not yet determined exactly what a "rational" decision maker is. Before we discuss the specific steps of the model in detail, let's contrast two forms of rationality.

Perfect versus Bounded Rationality

The prototype for **perfect rationality** is the familiar Economic Person (formerly Economic Man), whom we meet in the first chapter of most introductory textbooks in economics. Economic Person is the perfect, cool, calculating decision maker. More specifically, he or she

- can gather information about problems and solutions without cost and is thus completely informed;
- is perfectly logical—if solution A is preferred over solution B, and B is preferred over C, then A is necessarily preferable to C; and
- has only one criterion for decision making—economic gain.

Perfect rationality. A decision strategy that is completely informed, perfectly logical, and oriented toward economic gain.

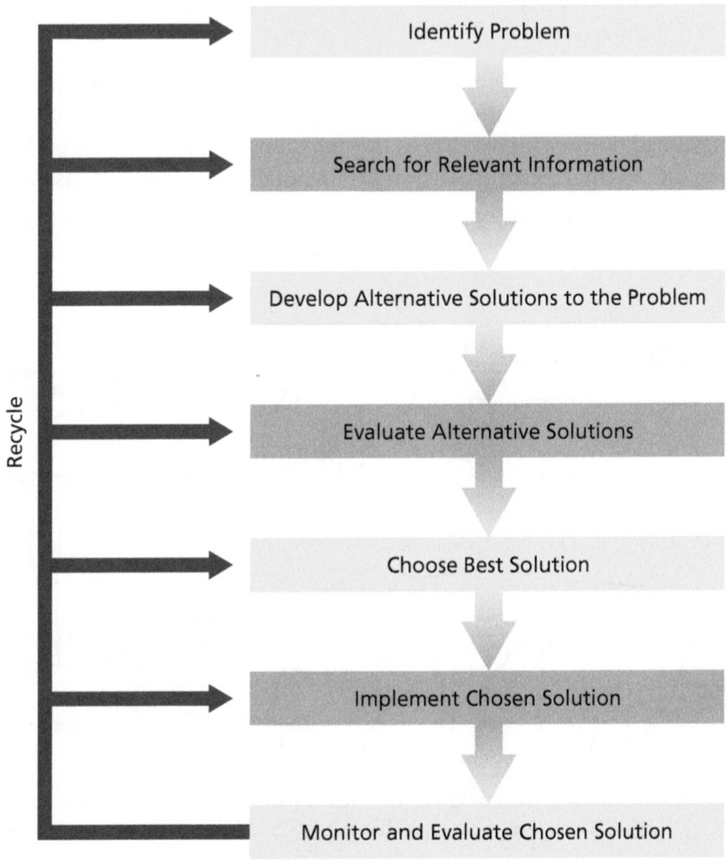

EXHIBIT 10.1
The rational decision-making process.

Identify Problem

Search for Relevant Information

Develop Alternative Solutions to the Problem

Evaluate Alternative Solutions

Choose Best Solution

Implement Chosen Solution

Monitor and Evaluate Chosen Solution

Recycle

While Economic Person is useful for theoretical purposes, the perfectly rational characteristics embodied in Economic Person do not exist in real decision makers. Nobel Prize winner Herbert Simon recognized this and suggested that managers use **bounded rationality** rather than perfect rationality.[6] That is, while they try to act rationally, they are limited in their capacity to acquire and process information. In addition, time constraints and political considerations (such as the need to please others in the organization) act as bounds to rationality.

Framing and cognitive biases both illustrate the operation of bounded rationality, as does the impact of emotions and mood on decisions. **Framing** refers to the (sometimes subtle) aspects of the presentation of information about a problem that are assumed by decision makers.[7] A frame could include assumptions about the boundaries of a problem, the possible outcomes of a decision, or the reference points used to decide if a decision is successful.[8] As we shall see, how problems and decision alternatives are framed can have a powerful impact on resulting decisions.

Cognitive biases are tendencies to acquire and process information in a particular way that is prone to error. These biases constitute assumptions and shortcuts that can improve decision-making efficiency, but they frequently lead to serious errors in judgment. We will see how they work in the following pages.

After we work through the rational decision-making model, we will consider how emotions and mood affect decisions.

Problem Identification and Framing

You will recall that a problem exists when a gap occurs between existing and desired conditions. Such gaps might be signalled by dissatisfied customers or vigilant employees. Similarly, the press might contain articles about legislation or ads for competing products that signal difficulties for the organization. The perfectly rational decision maker, infinitely sensitive and completely informed, should be a great problem identifier. Bounded rationality, however, can lead to the following difficulties in problem identification:[9]

- *Perceptual defence.* In Chapter 3, we pointed out that the perceptual system may act to defend the perceiver against unpleasant perceptions. For example, the fact that people assumed no-down-payment subprime loans despite poor credit histories could have been due to their perceptual systems' incapacity to dwell on disaster scenarios.

- *Problem defined in terms of functional specialty.* Selective perception can cause decision makers to view a problem as being in the domain of their own specialty

Bounded rationality. A decision strategy that relies on limited information and that reflects time constraints and political considerations.

Framing. Aspects of the presentation of information about a problem that are assumed by decision makers.

Cognitive biases. Tendencies to acquire and process information in an error-prone way.

"IT'S BEGINNING TO SHOW SOME HUMAN CHARACTERISTICS— FAULTY REASONING, FORGETFULNESS AND REPETITION."

Source: *Current Contents*, July 17, 1989.

even when some other perspective might be warranted. For example, employees with a marketing background might fixate on a marketing solution to poor sales even though the problem resides in bad design.

- *Problem defined in terms of solution.* This form of jumping to conclusions effectively short-circuits the rational decision-making process. When Coca-Cola changed its time-honoured formula to produce a "new" Coke, it appears that it prematurely defined its market share problem in terms of a particular solution—we need to change our existing product. In a more recent example, it is now clear that subprime loans were not an appropriate solution for discrimination in the mortgage market.

- *Problem diagnosed in terms of symptoms.* "What we have here is a morale problem." While this might be true, a concentration on surface symptoms will provide the decision maker with few clues about an adequate solution. The real problem here involves the cause of the morale problem. Low morale due to poor pay suggests different solutions than does low morale due to boring work.

When a problem is identified, it is necessarily framed in some way. Consider how different it is to frame a $10 000 expenditure as a cost (something to be avoided) versus an investment (something to be pursued). Or, consider how different it is to frame a new product introduction as a military campaign against competitors versus a crusade to help customers. In each case, the facts of the matter might be the same, but the different decision frames might lead to very different decisions. In the subprime mortgage debacle, framing home ownership as a right rather than a privilege had unforeseen negative decision consequences.

Rational decision makers should try to be very self-conscious about how they have framed problems ("We have assumed that this is a product innovation problem."). Also, they should try out alternative frames ("Let's imagine that we don't need a new product here."). Finally, decision makers should avoid overarching, universal frames (corporate culture gone wild). While it is a good idea to "put customers first," we do not want to frame every problem as a customer service problem.[10]

Information Search

As you can see in Exhibit 10.1, once a problem is identified, a search for information is instigated. This information search may clarify the nature or extent of the problem and begin to suggest alternative solutions. Again, our perfectly rational Economic Person is in good shape at this second stage of the decision-making process. He or she has free and instantaneous access to all information necessary to clarify the problem and develop alternative solutions. Bounded rationality, however, presents a different picture. The information search might be slow and costly.

Too Little Information. Sometimes, decision makers do not acquire enough information to make a good decision. Several cognitive biases contribute to this. For one thing, people tend to be mentally lazy and use whatever information is most readily available to them. Often, this resides in the memory, and we tend to remember *vivid, recent* events.[11] Although such events might prove irrelevant in the context of the current problem, we curtail our information search and rely on familiar experience. The manager who remembers that "the last time we went to an outside supplier for parts, we got burned" may be ignoring the wisdom of contracting out a current order.

Another cognitive bias that contributes to an incomplete information search is the well-documented tendency for people to be overconfident in their decision making.[12] This difficulty is exacerbated by **confirmation bias**, the tendency to seek out information that conforms to one's own definition of or solution to a problem. According to one expert, this ceremonial information search leads to "decision-based evidence making" rather than evidence-based decision making![13]

Confirmation bias. The tendency to seek out information that conforms to one's own definition of or solution to a problem.

Critics of the US invasion of Iraq cited both overconfidence and confirmation bias. Similarly, in the fatal 1986 *Challenger* space launch, only a limited range of data about the impact of temperature on mechanical failure was examined, leading to a disastrous cold weather launch choice. Another sort of inadequate information was apparent during the 2008–2009 economic meltdown. Many of the derivative financial products were so mathematically complicated that executives simply didn't understand how risky they were.

Too Much Information. While the bounds of rationality often force us to make decisions with incomplete or imperfect information, *too much* information can also damage the quality of decisions. **Information overload** is the reception of more information than is necessary to make effective decisions. As you might guess, information overload can lead to errors, omissions, delays, and cutting corners.[14] In addition, decision makers facing overload often attempt to use all the information at hand, then get confused and permit low-quality information or irrelevant information to influence their decisions.[15] Perhaps you have experienced this when writing a term paper—trying to incorporate too many references and too many viewpoints into a short paper can lead to a confusing, low-quality end product. More is not necessarily better.

However, decision makers seem to *think* that more is better. Why is this so? For one thing, even if decisions do not improve with additional information, confidence in the decisions will increase.[16] Second, decision makers may fear being "kept in the dark"

Information overload.
The reception of more information than is necessary to make effective decisions.

Information overload can lead to errors, omissions, delays, and stress.

and associate the possession of information with power. One research review concludes that managers

- gather much information that has little decision relevance;
- use information that they collected and gathered after a decision to justify that decision;
- request information that they do not use;
- request more information, regardless of what is already available; and
- complain that there is not enough information to make a decision even though they ignore available information.[17]

Finally, information search often involves seeking advice from various parties, including trade associations, government agencies, and consultants. Research reveals that people have a cognitive bias to value advice for which they have paid over free advice of equal quality. No wonder there are so many consulting firms![18]

Alternative Development, Evaluation, and Choice

Perfectly informed or not, the decision maker can now list alternative solutions to the problem, examine the solutions, and choose the best one. For the perfectly rational, totally informed, ideal decision maker, this is easy. He or she conceives of all alternatives, knows the ultimate value of each alternative, and knows the probability that each alternative will work. In this case, the decision maker can exhibit **maximization**—that is, he or she can choose the alternative with the greatest expected value. Consider a simple example:

Maximization. The choice of the decision alternative with the greatest expected value.

	Ultimate Value	Probability	Expected Value
Alternative 1	$100 000 Profit	.4	$40 000 Profit
Alternative 2	$ 60 000 Profit	.8	$48 000 Profit

Here, the expected value of each alternative is calculated by multiplying its ultimate value by its probability. In this case, the perfectly rational decision maker would choose to implement the second alternative.

Unfortunately, things do not go so smoothly for the decision maker working under bounded rationality. He may not know all alternative solutions, and he may be ignorant of the ultimate values and probabilities of success of those solutions that he knows. Again, cognitive biases come into play. In particular, people are especially weak intuitive statisticians, and they frequently violate standard statistical principles. For example,[19]

- People avoid incorporating known existing data about the likelihood of events ("base rates") into their decisions. For instance, firms continue to launch novelty food products (e.g., foods squeezed from tubes or foods developed by celebrities) even though they have a very high failure rate in the market.
- Large samples warrant more confidence than small samples. Despite this, data from a couple of (vivid) focus groups might be given more weight than data from a large (but anonymous) national survey.
- Decision makers often overestimate the odds of complex chains of events occurring— the scenario sounds sensible despite being less likely with every added link in the chain. During the 2008–2009 economic meltdown, it was implicitly assumed that the economy would remain healthy *and* real estate prices would continue to rise *and* people would find a way to pay their escalating mortgages.
- People are poor at revising estimates of probabilities and values as they acquire additional information. A good example is the **anchoring effect**, which illustrates that

Anchoring effect. The inadequate adjustment of subsequent estimates from an initial estimate that serves as an anchor.

decision makers do not adjust their estimates enough from some initial estimate that serves as an anchor. For example, in one study, real estate agents allowed the *asking price* of a house to unduly influence their *professional evaluation* of the house.[20]

It is possible to reduce some of these basic cognitive biases by making people more accountable for their decisions. This might include requiring reasoned reports, formal presentations of how the decision was reached, and so on. However, it is critical that this accountability be in place *before* a decision is reached. After-the-fact accountability often increases the probability of biases, as people try to protect their identity as good decision makers.[21] It is now clear that deregulation of the banking industry reduced accountability and contributed to the 2008–2009 economic meltdown.

The perfectly rational decision maker can evaluate alternative solutions against a single criterion—economic gain. The decision maker who is bounded by reality might have to factor in other criteria as well, such as the political acceptability of the solution to other organizational members—will the boss like it? Since these additional criteria have their own values and probabilities, the decision-making task increases in complexity. Decision expert Paul Nutt found that the search for alternatives is often very limited in strategic decision making and that firms invest very little money in exploring alternatives.[22]

The bottom line here is that the decision maker working under bounded rationality frequently "satisfices" rather than maximizes.[23] **Satisficing** means that the decision maker establishes an adequate level of acceptability for a solution and then screens solutions until he or she finds one that exceeds this level. When this occurs, evaluation of alternatives ceases, and the solution is chosen for implementation. For instance, the human resources manager who feels that absenteeism has become too high might choose a somewhat arbitrary acceptable level (e.g., the rate one year earlier), then accept the first solution that seems likely to achieve this level. Few organizations seek to *maximize* attendance.

Satisficing. Establishing an adequate level of acceptability for a solution to a problem and then screening solutions until one that exceeds this level is found.

Risky Business

Choosing between decision alternatives often involves an element of risk, and the research evidence on how people handle such risks is fascinating. Consider this scenario that decision researcher Max Bazerman developed. Which alternative would you choose?

> *Robert Davis, head of the legal staff of a Fortune 500 company, has delayed making one of the most critical recommendations in the organization's history. The company is faced with a class action suit from a hostile group of consumers. While the organization believes that it is innocent, it realizes that a court may not have the same perspective. The organization is expected to lose $50 million if the suit is lost in court. Davis predicts a 50 percent chance of losing the case. The organization has the option of settling out of court by paying $25 million to the "injured" parties. Davis's senior staff has been collecting information and organizing the case for over six months. It is time for action. What should Davis recommend?*

Alternative A   Settle out of court and accept a sure *loss* of $25 million,

or

Alternative B   Go to court expecting a 50 percent probability of a $50 million loss.[24]

Notice that these two solutions are functionally equivalent in terms of dollars and cents (50 percent of $50 million = $25 million). Nonetheless, you probably tended to choose alternative B—about 80 percent of students do. Notice also that alternative B is the riskier of the two alternatives in that it exposes the firm to a *potential* for greater loss.

Now, consider two further descriptions of the alternatives. Which solution would you choose?

Alternative C   Settle out of court and *save* $25 million that could be lost in court,

or

Alternative D   Go to court expecting a 50 percent probability of *saving* $50 million.

Again, these two solutions are functionally equivalent in monetary terms (and equivalent to options A and B). Yet, you probably chose solution C—80 percent of students do. Notice that this is the *less* risky alternative, in that the firm is not exposed to a potential $50 million loss.

This is a graphic example of the power of framing. Alternatives A and B frame the problem as a choice between losses, while C and D frame it as a choice between gains or savings. Research by Daniel Kahneman and Amos Tversky shows that when people view a problem as a choice between losses, they tend to make risky decisions, rolling the dice in the face of a sure loss. When people frame the alternatives as a choice between gains they tend to make conservative decisions, protecting the sure win.[25] It is very important to be aware of what reference point you are using when you frame decision alternatives. It is not necessarily wrong to frame a problem as a choice between losses, but this can contribute to a foolish level of risk taking.

We should emphasize that learning history can modify these general preferences for or against risk.[26] For example, suppose that a firm has become very successful by virtue of a series of risky decisions and is now faced with sitting on a handsome market share or investing in a product that could boost its share even higher. This win-win scenario would normally provoke conservatism, but the firm's historical success may tempt managers to choose the risky course of action and invest in the new product.

Solution Implementation

When a decision is made to choose a particular solution to a problem, the solution must be implemented. The perfectly rational decision maker will have factored any possible implementation problems in to his or her choice of solutions. Of course, the bounded decision maker will attempt to do the same when estimating probabilities of success. However, in organizations, decision makers are often dependent on others to implement their decisions, and it might be difficult to anticipate their ability or motivation to do so.

A good example of implementation problems occurs when products such as cars are designed, engineered, and produced in a lengthy series of stages. For example, engineering might have to implement decisions made by designers, and production planning might have to implement decisions made by engineering. As we noted in Chapter 7, this sequential process frequently leads to confusion, conflict, and delay unless cross-functional teams are used during the decision-making process. When they work well, such teams are sensitive to implementation problems.

Solution Evaluation

When the time comes to evaluate the implemented solution, the decision maker is effectively examining the possibility that a new problem has occurred: Does the (new) existing state match the desired state? Has the decision been effective? For all the reasons we stated previously, the perfectly rational decision maker should be able to evaluate the effectiveness of the decision with calm, objective detachment. Again, however, the bounded decision maker might encounter problems at this stage of the process.

Justification. As we said earlier, people tend to be overconfident about the adequacy of their decisions. Thus, substantial dissonance can be aroused when a decision turns out to be faulty. One way to prevent such dissonance is to avoid careful tests of the adequacy of the decision. As a result, many organizations are notoriously lax when it comes to evaluating the effectiveness of expensive training programs or advertising campaigns. If the bad news cannot be avoided, the erring decision maker may devote his or her energy to trying to justify the faulty decision.

The justification of faulty decisions is best seen in the irrational treatment of sunk costs. **Sunk costs** are permanent losses of resources incurred as the result of a decision.[27] The key word here is "permanent." Since these resources have been lost (sunk) due to a past decision, they should not enter into future decisions. Psychologist Barry Staw has studied how, despite this, people often "throw good resources after bad," acting as if they can recoup sunk costs. This process is **escalation of commitment** to an apparently failing course of action, in which the escalation involves devoting more and more resources to actions implied by the decision.[28] For example, suppose an executive authorizes the purchase of several new machines to improve plant productivity. The machines turn out to be very unreliable, and they are frequently out of commission for repairs. Perfect rationality suggests admitting to a mistake here. However, the executive might authorize an order for more machines from the same manufacturer to "prove" that he was right all along, hoping to recoup sunk costs with improved productivity from an even greater number of machines. Dissonance reduction is not the only reason that escalation of commitment to a faulty decision may occur. A social norm that favours *consistent* behaviour by managers may also be at work.[29] Changing one's mind and reversing previous decisions might be perceived as a sign of weakness, a fate to be avoided at all costs.

Escalation of commitment sometimes happens even when the current decision maker is not responsible for previous sunk costs. For example, politicians might continue an expensive, unnecessary public works project that was begun by a previous political administration. Here, dissonance reduction and the appearance of consistency are irrelevant, suggesting some other causes of escalation. For one thing, decision makers might be motivated to not appear wasteful.[30] ("Even though the airport construction is way over budget and flight traffic doesn't justify a new airport, let's finish the thing. Otherwise, the taxpayers will think we've squandered their money.") Also, escalation of commitment might be due to the way in which decision makers frame the problem once some resources have been sunk. Rather than seeing the savings involved in reversing the decision, they may frame the problem as a decision between a sure loss of x dollars (which have been sunk) and an uncertain loss of $x + y$ dollars (maybe the additional investment will succeed). As we noted earlier, when problems are framed this way, people tend to avoid the certain loss and go with the riskier choice, which in this case is escalation.[31] In addition to these situational causes, personality, moods, and emotions can affect escalation. For instance, people high on neuroticism and negative affectivity (Chapter 2) are *less* likely to escalate since they try to avoid stressful predicaments.[32]

Escalation can occur in both competitive and non-competitive situations. A non-competitive example can be seen in the overvaluation of stocks by Wall Street analysts in advance of a market crash. Competitive, auction-like situations seem especially likely to prompt escalation because they often involve time pressure, rivalry, interested audiences, and the desire to be the first mover. These factors contribute to emotional arousal (see below) and stimulate escalation.[33] The Vietnam and Iraq wars have been cited as prime examples of competitive escalation.

Are there any ways to prevent the tendency to escalate commitment to a failing course of action? Logic and research suggest the following:[34]

- Encourage continuous experimentation with reframing the problem to avoid the decision trap of feeling that more resources *have* to be invested. Shift the frame to saving rather than spending.

- Set specific goals for the project in advance that must be met if more resources are to be invested. This prevents escalation when early results are "unclear."

Sunk costs. Permanent losses of resources incurred as the result of a decision.

Escalation of commitment. The tendency to invest additional resources in an apparently failing course of action.

- Place more emphasis when evaluating managers on *how* they made decisions and less on decision outcomes. This kind of accountability is the sensible way to teach managers not to fear failure.

- Separate initial and subsequent decision making so that individuals who make the initial decision to embark on a course of action are assisted or replaced by others who decide if a course of action should be continued. Banks often do this when trying to decide what to do about problem loans.

It may be tempting to think that using groups to make decisions will reduce the tendency toward escalation. However, groups are *more* prone than individuals to escalate commitment.[35]

For a particularly dark example of non-competitive escalation, see Ethical Focus: *Rogue Traders Get Trapped in Escalation.* It illustrates how more and more resources are dedicated to trying to turn around a flawed investment strategy.

Hindsight. The careful evaluation of decisions is also inhibited by faulty hindsight. Hindsight refers to the tendency to review the decision-making process that was used to find out what was done right (in the case of success) or wrong (in the case of failure). While hindsight can prove useful, it often reflects a cognitive bias.

> **Hindsight.** The tendency to review the decision-making process to find what was done right or wrong.

ETHICAL FOCUS

Rogue Traders Get Trapped in Escalation

Backed by the wealth of large investment companies, traders deal in financial instruments on their employers' behalf. Over the years, a number of traders have gone "rogue," losing tons of money and repeatedly covering up the fact, trying to recoup their losses and refusing to accept sunk costs. One of the most notorious rogue traders is Jérôme Kerviel, who was charged in 2008 for losing 5 billion Euros trading on behalf of France's Société Générale. Kerviel was accused of fraudulent activity because he knowingly broke company policies in an effort to create an exorbitant amount of wealth. Not all rogue traders, however, appear to be motivated by personal gain. Take, for example, John Rusnak, who lost US$691 million at Allfirst Bank. Unlike some rogue traders, Rusnak was considered to be an introverted family man. According to court documents, he received a modest salary of $108 000 and a bonus of $78 000 in 2001. When Rusnak was arrested in 2002, he appeared to be less of an intentional fraud and more of a cover-up artist, a term used by consultant Hugo Pound for traders who make risky, high-return investments in an effort to recoup earlier losses. Apparently Rusnak's trouble began in 1997, when he lost a large amount of money in a questionable trading strategy. Instead of admitting failure to the bank, because he had positioned himself as a savvy trader, Rusnak sold fictitious options, which generated fictitious returns. He then invested heavily in real options, hoping to recover his losses. Over a four-year period, Rusnak repeatedly threw good company money after his bad investments, digging himself deeper and deeper into a hole. Rusnak's behaviour, as with other cover-up artists, is a clear example of escalation of commitment. In this case, Rusnak couldn't accept his original losses and write them off as sunk costs. Although he likely knew that the facade would one day come undone, he continued along the destructive path in order to please his employer and save face. As explained by Nick Leeson, another infamous cover-up artist, "For the trader, it feels like being carried away by a hot-air balloon; if you don't jump off immediately, you can't jump off at all." In 2009, John Rusnak was released on parole before the end of his seven-and-a-half-year jail term. Although he legally owes $691 million, it's not clear how much he will actually be able to pay back.

Sources: Anonymous. (2009, January 29). Rogue trader Rusnak released from prison. *Toronto Star*, B2; DiBiagio, T.M. (2002). *Indictment of United States of America versus John M. Rusnack*. The United States District Court for the District of Maryland, www.usdoj.gov/; Leith, W. (2002, October 26). How to lose a billion. *Guardian* (online), www.guardian.co.uk (quote); Lichfield, J. (2009, January 23). Jérôme Kerviel: Secrets of the rogue trader. *The Independent* (online), www.independent.co.uk; McNee, A. (2002). Allied Irish Banks Case Study. *eRisk*, www.erisk.com; Pignal, S. (2009, January 24). They Bet the Bank. *Financial Times*, 24; Barry Staw, personal communication (2009, July 31).

The classic example of hindsight involves the armchair quarterback who "knew" that a chancy intercepted pass in the first quarter was unnecessary because the team won the game anyway! The armchair critic is exhibiting the knew-it-all-along effect. This is the tendency to assume, after the fact, that we knew all along what the outcome of a decision would be. In effect, our faulty memory adjusts the probabilities that we estimated before making the decision to correspond to what actually happened.[36] This can prove quite dangerous. The money manager who consciously makes a very risky investment that turns out to be successful might revise her memory to assume that the decision was a sure thing. The next time, the now-confident investor might not be so lucky! Such dynamics may have played a role in the derivative and credit-default swap arena in 2008–2009.

Another form of faulty hindsight is the tendency to take personal responsibility for successful decision outcomes while denying responsibility for unsuccessful outcomes.[37] Thus, when things work out well, it is because *we* made a careful, logical decision. When things go poorly, some unexpected *external* factor messed up our sensible decision!

How Emotion and Mood Affect Decision Making

Thus far, we have discussed decision making from a mainly cognitive perspective, focusing on the rational decision-making model and illustrating the limits to rationality. However, our coverage of decision justification and hindsight suggests a considerable emotional component to many organizational decisions—people don't like to be wrong, and they often become emotionally attached to the failing course of action that signals escalation of commitment.

At the outset, it should be emphasized that emotionless decision making would be poor decision making, and the rational model is not meant to suggest otherwise. Some of the most graphic evidence for this comes from unfortunate cases in which people suffer brain injuries that blunt their emotions while leaving their intellectual functions intact. Such individuals often proceed to make a series of poor life decisions because they are unable to properly evaluate the impact of these decisions on themselves and others; they have no feeling.[38] One can imagine the negative consequences if NASA's manned spacecraft were designed by emotionless rather than caring engineers. In fact,

Decision makers in a good mood can overestimate the likelihood of good events and use shortcut decision strategies.

during the 2005 *Discovery* mission, it was suggested that some of the caution-focused decisions, such as the delay in landing and decision to set down in California, were made by mission control personnel still suffering emotional effects of the 2003 *Columbia* tragedy. Strong emotions frequently figure in the decision-making process that corrects ethical errors (Chapter 11), and so-called whistle-blowers often report that they were motivated by emotion to protest decision errors. Strong (positive) emotion has also been implicated in creative decision making and the proper use of intuition to solve problems. Such intuition (Chapter 1) can lead to the successful short-circuiting of the steps in the rational model when speed is of the essence.

Despite these examples of how emotion can help decision making, there are many cases in which strong emotions are a hindrance. The folk saying "blinded by emotion" has some truth to it, as people experiencing strong emotions are often self-focused and distracted from the actual demands of the problem at hand. Most of our information about the impact of emotions on decisions is anecdotal, because people are often reluctant to participate in field research about emotional issues and because it is not ethical to invoke strong emotions in lab research. One clever field study did document how excessive pride led highly paid CEOs to pay too much for firms they were acquiring.[39] Other business-press evidence implicates angry CEOs losing their heads in competitive bidding for acquisitions (escalation of commitment). A common theme over the years has been how excessive emotional conflict between business partners or family business members provokes questionable business decisions.

In contrast to the case for strong emotions, there is much research on the impact of mood on decision making. You will recall from Chapter 4 that moods are relatively mild, unfocused states of positive or negative feeling. The research on mood and decision making reveals some very interesting paradoxes. For one thing, mood is a pretty low-key state, and you might be inclined to think it would not have much impact on decisions. In fact, there is plenty of evidence that mood affects *what* and *how* people think when making decisions. Also, you might imagine that the impact of mood would be restricted to mundane, structured decision problems. In fact, mood has its greatest impact on uncertain, ambiguous decisions of the type that are especially crucial for organizations. Here is what the research reveals:[40]

- People in a positive mood tend to remember positive information. Those in a negative mood remember negative information.

- People in a positive mood tend to evaluate objects, people, and events more positively. Those in a negative mood provide more negative evaluations.

- People in a good mood tend to overestimate the likelihood that good events will occur and underestimate the occurrence of bad events. People in a bad mood do the opposite.

- People in a good mood adopt simplified, shortcut decision-making strategies, more likely violating the rational model. People in a negative mood are prone to approach decisions in a more deliberate, systematic, detailed way.

- Positive mood promotes more creative, intuitive decision making.

As you can see, it makes perfect sense to hope for your job interview to be conducted by a person in a good mood or to try to create a good mood on the part of your clients! Notice that the impact of mood on decision making is not necessarily dysfunctional. If the excesses of optimism can be controlled, those in a good mood can make creative decisions. If the excesses of pessimism can be controlled, those in a negative mood can actually process information more carefully and effectively. In a very interesting simulation of foreign currency trading, it was found that traders in a good mood performed more poorly (by losing money) than those in bad or neutral moods. Those in a bad mood performed better, but were rather conservative. Traders in a neutral mood did best, tolerating risk but not being overconfident.[41] Thus, the investment practitioners' advice to remain calm during turbulent markets has some validity.

One suspects that some of the subprime house buyers knew they couldn't really afford a house but were lured by the positive vibes of their real estate agents.

A fine example of how mood and emotion can lead to faulty decision making can be seen in the "dot.com meltdown" that began in the late 1990s. In this era, hundreds of firms were formed to exploit the potential wealth of e-commerce. An economic boom, ready capital, advancing technology, and the model of a few overnight "internet millionaires" created a positive mood that led to overly intuitive decisions, false creativity, and exaggerated optimism. Mood is contagious, and many start-up firms, fearing to be left behind, were founded with vague goals and vaguer business plans. Many consisted of little more than a website, and "hits" were confused with cash flow. The ensuing crash left the firms founded on careful business decision–making principles to enjoy the spoils of the technology revolution. It was exactly this kind of giddy emotion, fuelled by big bonuses, that led Wall Street executives to ignore the coming subprime mortgage meltdown.

Before continuing, check out You Be the Manager: *Preventing Surgical Decision Errors at Toronto General Hospital.*

Rational Decision Making—A Summary

The rational decision-making model in Exhibit 10.1 provides a good guide for how many decisions *should* be made but offers only a partially accurate view of how they *are* made. For complex, unfamiliar decisions, such as choosing an occupation, the rational model provides a pretty good picture of how people actually make decisions.[42] Also, organizational decision makers often follow the rational model when they agree about the goals they are pursuing.[43] On the other hand, there is plenty of case study evidence of short-circuiting the rational model in organizational decisions, in part because of the biases we discussed above.[44] A study of 356 decisions in medium to large organizations in the United States and Canada found that half the decisions made in organizations fail. These failures were found to be primarily due to the use of poor tactics on the part of managers who impose solutions, limit the search for alternatives, and use power to implement their plans.[45] However, true experts in a field will often short-circuit the rational model, using their intuitive knowledge base stored in memory to skip steps logically.[46] Exhibit 10.2 summarizes the operation of perfect and bounded

EXHIBIT 10.2
Perfectly rational decision making contrasted with bounded rationality.

Stage	Perfect Rationality	Bounded Rationality
Problem Identification	Easy, accurate perception of gaps that constitute problems	Perceptual defence; jump to solutions; attention to symptoms rather than problems; mood affects memory
Information Search	Free; fast; right amount obtained	Slow; costly; reliance on flawed memory; obtain too little or too much
Development of Alternative Solutions	Can conceive of all	Not all known
Evaluation of Alternative Solutions	Ultimate value of each known; probability of each known; only criterion is economic gain	Potential ignorance of or miscalculation of values and probabilities; criteria include political factors; affected by mood
Solution Choice	Maximizes	Satisfices
Solution Implementation	Considered in evaluation of alternatives	May be difficult owing to reliance on others
Solution Evaluation	Objective, according to previous steps	May involve justification, escalation to recover sunk costs, faulty hindsight

YOU BE THE MANAGER

Preventing Surgical Decision Errors at Toronto General Hospital

Every year, between 9000 and 23 000 people die in Canadian hospitals due to surgical errors. Although many preventable deaths occur during an operation, some of them also stem from pre-op or post-op errors. Surgical operations are done by some of the most highly trained professionals, yet still mistakes are made in this emotion-laden environment.

Toronto General Hospital and its two sister hospitals, Toronto Western and Princess Margaret, form the University Health Network (UHN). These hospitals, like all other hospitals in the country, sometimes fall victim to human error. Considering that the complication rate in higher-income area hospitals is approximately 10.3 percent, more than 2000 of the UHN's 23 000 annual surgical patients may suffer from preventable complications.

"[Surgery] is one of the areas where we have tremendous skills and resources," says Dr. Ross Baker, a health policy professor at the University of Toronto. "And then we go in and somebody forgets to do something they should do as a matter of course, and the outcome is an infection or complication of some sort."

For years, medical researchers have sought ways to reduce errors that occur in the operating room, not only to save lives but also to save money. Prevention requires an understanding of possible negative events and their associated causes. Once the scenarios have been identified, a set of procedures can be created to help prevent them from occurring. Also at issue is establishing means to manage any negative events that do occur to avoid adverse complications. Both approaches come with challenges. First, it may be difficult to predict potential problems because hospital staff and procedures are constantly changing. Second, errors may not always be identified in real time.

One might wonder why a highly professional team of doctors and nurses would fail to identify or respond to a potentially deadly error, especially when they have the collective technical knowledge to identify such errors. The problem, it seems, is not so much related to knowledge; rather, it often stems from the complex professional relationships that exist between doctors and nurses, and between the surgical leader and the rest of the team. Like a pilot in command of a plane, the lead surgeon carries significant responsibility and authority. Team members often feel threatened about speaking up, even if they believe that a problem

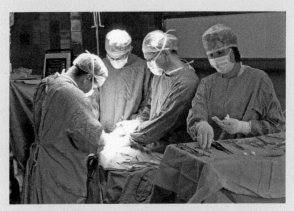

In surgical teams, members often find it difficult to speak up, even if they believe that a problem exists.

exists. Eliminating preventable complications, therefore, requires both systemic and behavioural changes.

Dr. Bryce Taylor, UHN's surgeon in chief, takes the problem very seriously: "With approximately 234 million surgeries performed each year worldwide, we owe it to our patients to look at every opportunity to prevent complications during and after surgery."

QUESTIONS

1. Is there a programmed decision-making process that would support the prevention and correction of surgical errors?

2. What role may emotions play in the decision behaviour of operating room personnel?

To find out what happened at Toronto General, see The Manager's Notebook at the end of the chapter.

Sources: Blackwell, T. (2009, January 15). Checklists cut surgical mistakes by a third. *National Post*, A1, A5 (Baker quote); Blatt, R., Christianson, M.K., & Sutcliffe, K.M. (2006). A sensemaking lens on reliability. *Journal of Organizational Behavior, 27*, 491–515; Haynes, A.B., Weiser, T.G., Berry, W.R., Lipsitz, S.R., Breizat, A-H.S., Dellinger, et al. (2009). A surgical safety checklist to reduce morbidity and mortality in a global population. *New England Journal of Medicine, 360*, 491–499; Nembhardi, I.M., & Edmondson, A.C. (2006). Making it safe: The effects of leader inclusiveness and professional status on psychological safety and improvement efforts in health care teams. *Journal of Organizational Behavior, 27*, 941–966; Priest, L. (2009, January 15). Simple checklist saves lives in the operating room, study finds. *Globe and Mail*, A4; Anonymous (2009, January 14). *Results show surgical safety checklist drops deaths and complications by more than one third*, University Health Network, www.uhn.com (Taylor quote).

EXHIBIT 10.3
Summary of cognitive
biases in decision
making.

- Decision makers tend to be overconfident about the decisions that they make.
- Decision makers tend to seek out information that confirms their own problem definitions and solutions. (Confirmation bias)
- Decision makers tend to remember and incorporate vivid, recent events into their decisions.
- Decision makers fail to incorporate known existing data about the likelihood of events into their decisions.
- Decision makers ignore sample sizes when evaluating samples of information.
- Decision makers overestimate the odds of complex chains of events occurring.
- Decision makers do not adjust estimates enough from some initial estimate that serves as an anchor as they acquire more information. (Anchoring effect)
- Decision makers have difficulty ignoring sunk costs when making subsequent decisions.
- Decision makers overestimate their ability to have predicted events after-the-fact, take responsibility for successful decision outcomes, and deny responsibility for unsuccessful outcomes. (Hindsight)

rationality at each stage of the decision process. Exhibit 10.3 summarizes the various cognitive biases that we have covered.

Group Decision Making

Many, many organizational decisions are made by groups rather than individuals, especially when problems are ill structured. In this section, we consider the advantages and problems of group decision making.

Why Use Groups?

There are a number of reasons for employing groups to make organizational decisions.

Decision Quality. Experts often argue that groups or teams can make higher-quality decisions than individuals. This argument is based on the following three assumptions:

- Groups are *more vigilant* than individuals are—more people are scanning the environment.
- Groups can *generate more ideas* than individuals can.
- Groups can *evaluate ideas better* than individuals can.

At the problem identification and information search stages, vigilance is especially advantageous. For example, a member of the board of directors might notice a short article in an obscure business publication that has great relevance for the firm. In searching for information to clarify the problem suggested in the article, other members of the board might possess unique information that proves useful.

When it comes to developing alternative solutions, more people should literally have more ideas, if only because someone remembers something that others have forgotten. In addition, members with different backgrounds and experiences may bring different perspectives to the problem. This is why undergraduate students, graduate students, faculty, and administrators are often included on university task forces to improve the library or course evaluation system.

When it comes to evaluating solutions and choosing the best one, groups have the advantage of checks and balances—that is, an extreme position or incorrect notion held by one member should be offset by the pooled judgments of the rest of the group.

These characteristics suggest that groups *should* make higher-quality decisions than individuals can. Shortly, we will find out whether they actually do.

Decision Acceptance and Commitment. As we pointed out in our discussion of participative leadership in Chapter 9, groups are often used to make decisions on the premise that a decision made in this way will be more acceptable to those involved. Again, there are several assumptions underlying this premise:

- People wish to be involved in decisions that will affect them.
- People will better understand a decision in which they participated.
- People will be more committed to a decision in which they invested personal time and energy.

The acceptability of group decisions is especially useful in dealing with a problem described earlier—getting the decision implemented. If decision makers truly understand the decision and feel committed to it, they should be willing to follow through and see that it is carried out.

Diffusion of Responsibility. High quality and acceptance are sensible reasons for using groups to make decisions. A less admirable reason to employ groups is to allow for **diffusion of responsibility** across the members in case the decision turns out poorly. In this case, each member of the group will share part of the burden of the negative consequences, and no one person will be singled out for punishment. Of course, when this happens, individual group members often "abandon ship" and exhibit biased hindsight—"I knew all along that the bid was too high to be accepted, but they made me go along with them."

Diffusion of responsibility. The ability of group members to share the burden of the negative consequences of a poor decision.

Do Groups Actually Make Higher-Quality Decisions Than Individuals?

Is the frequent use of groups to make decisions warranted by evidence? The answer is yes. One review concludes that "groups usually produce more and better solutions to problems than do individuals working alone."[47] Another concludes that group performance is superior to that of the average individual in the group.[48] More specifically, groups should perform better than individuals when

- the group members differ in relevant skills and abilities, as long as they do not differ so much that conflict occurs;
- some division of labour can occur;
- memory for facts is an important issue; and
- individual judgments can be combined by weighting them to reflect the expertise of the various members.[49]

To consolidate your understanding of these conditions, consider a situation that should favour group decision making: A small construction company wishes to bid on a contract to build an apartment complex. The president, the controller, a construction boss, and an engineer work together to formulate the bid. Since they have diverse backgrounds and skills, they divide the task initially. The president reviews recent bids on similar projects in the community; the controller gets estimates on materials costs; the engineer and construction boss review the blueprints. During this process, each racks his or her brain to recall lessons learned from making previous bids. Finally, they put their information together, and each member voices an opinion about what the bid should be. The president decides to average these opinions to arrive at the actual bid, since each person is equally expert in his or her own area.

Equal weighting of opinions and averaging is inappropriate when some group members have more expertise concerning a particular problem, and it is critical for decision success that such expertise is recognized by the group. However, if several group members share the same view about a problem, this shared view can prevail in spite of the knowledge held by a single expert.[50]

Disadvantages of Group Decision Making

Although groups have the ability to develop high-quality, acceptable decisions, there are a number of potential disadvantages to group decision making.

Time. Groups seldom work quickly or efficiently compared with individuals. This is because of the process losses (Chapter 7) involved in discussion, debate, and coordination. The time problem increases with group size. When the speed of arriving at a solution to a problem is a prime factor, organizations should avoid using groups.

Conflict. Many times, participants in group decisions have their own personal axes to grind or their own resources to protect. When this occurs, decision quality may take a back seat to political wrangling and infighting. In the example about the construction company we presented earlier, the construction boss might see it to his advantage to overestimate the size of the crew required to build the apartments. On the other hand, the controller might make it her personal crusade to pare labour costs. A simple compromise between these two extreme points of view might not result in the highest-quality or most creative decision. In general, groups will make better decisions when their members feel psychologically safe.

Domination. The advantages of group decision making will seldom be realized if meetings are dominated by a single individual or a small coalition. Even if a dominant person has good information, this style is not likely to lead to group acceptance and commitment. If the dominant person is particularly misinformed, the group decision is very likely to be ineffective.

Groupthink. Have you ever been involved in a group decision that you knew was a "loser" but that you felt unable to protest? Perhaps you thought you were the only one who had doubts about the chosen course of action. Perhaps you tried to speak up, but others criticized you for not being on the team. Maybe you found yourself searching for information to confirm that the decision was correct and ignoring evidence that the decision was bad. What was happening? Were you suffering from some strange form of possession? Mind control?

In Chapter 8, we discussed the process of conformity, which can have a strong influence on the decisions that groups make. The most extreme influence is seen when **groupthink** occurs. This happens when group pressures lead to reduced mental efficiency, poor testing of reality, and lax moral judgment.[51] In effect, unanimous acceptance of decisions is stressed over quality of decisions.

Psychologist Irving Janis, who developed the groupthink concept, felt that high group cohesiveness was at its root. It now appears that other factors are more important.[52] These include strong identification with the group, concern for their approval, and the isolation of the group from other sources of information. However, the promotion of a particular decision by the group leader appears to be the strongest cause.[53] Janis provides a detailed list of groupthink symptoms:

- *Illusion of invulnerability.* Members are overconfident and willing to assume great risks. They ignore obvious danger signals.

Groupthink. The capacity for group pressure to damage the mental efficiency, reality testing, and moral judgment of decision-making groups.

- *Rationalization.* Problems and counterarguments that members cannot ignore are "rationalized away." That is, seemingly logical but improbable excuses are given.

- *Illusion of morality.* The decisions the group adopts are not only perceived as sensible, they are also perceived as *morally* correct.

- *Stereotypes of outsiders.* The group constructs unfavourable stereotypes of those outside the group who are the targets of their decisions.

- *Pressure for conformity.* Members pressure each other to fall in line and conform with the group's views.

- *Self-censorship.* Members convince themselves to avoid voicing opinions contrary to the group.

- *Illusion of unanimity.* Members perceive that unanimous support exists for their chosen course of action.

- *Mindguards.* Some group members may adopt the role of "protecting" the group from information that goes against its decisions.[54]

For an example of some of these symptoms, see Research Focus: *"Pluralistic Ignorance" on Corporate Boards.*

Obviously, victims of groupthink are operating in an atmosphere of unreality that should lead to low-quality decisions. We can see this in the decision-making process concerning NASA's Hubble Space Telescope in the 1990s, where an aberration in the telescope's primary mirror was the source of the astronomical repair costs.[55] To begin with, a dominant leader in charge of the internal mirror tests appears to have isolated the mirror project team from outside sources of information. Symptoms of groupthink followed: At least three sets of danger signals that the mirror was flawed were ignored or explained away (illusion of invulnerability and rationalization); an outside firm,

RESEARCH FOCUS

"Pluralistic Ignorance" on Corporate Boards

Corporate boards of directors are appointed to oversee the strategy and performance of organizations. Many such boards are made up of highly qualified and experienced executives. Nonetheless, there are countless examples of boards seemingly ignoring prominent signals that the companies they govern are in serious trouble. What accounts for this apparent contradiction between board member expertise and failed oversight? Could group dynamics have something to do with it?

Researchers James Westphal and Michael Bednar studied the contribution of "pluralistic ignorance" to the failure of corporate boards to call for strategic change in the face of poor firm performance. Pluralistic ignorance occurs when most group members feel concern about certain policies or practices but at the same time feel that the other group members support the policies and practices. It is thought that this ignorance stems from the self-censorship and illusion of

unanimity aspects of groupthink—people are reticent to voice what they think are minority opinions.

Using questionnaires completed by outside directors of low-performing firms, Westphal and Bednar found that they underestimated the degree of concern felt by other board members. The stronger this tendency, the less likely board members were to voice their concerns and the more likely their firms were to persist in ineffective strategies. In direct contradiction to the idea that cohesiveness contributes to groupthink, boards with stronger friendship ties and those that were more homogeneous in terms of business background and gender were less likely to exhibit pluralistic ignorance.

Source: Westphal, J.D., & Bednar, M.K. (2005). Pluralistic ignorance in corporate boards and firms' strategic persistence in response to low firm performance. *Administrative Science Quarterly, 50,* 262–298.

Kodak, was dismissed as too incompetent to test the mirror (stereotype of outsiders); the consultant who suggested that Kodak test the mirror received bitter criticism but still felt he did not protest enough in the end (mindguarding and self-censorship); the defence of the isolated working methods was viewed as more "theological" than technical (illusion of morality).

What can prevent groupthink? Leaders must be careful to avoid exerting undue pressure for a particular decision outcome and concentrate on good decision processes. Also, leaders should establish norms that encourage and even reward responsible dissent, and outside experts should be brought in from time to time to challenge the group's views.[56] Some of the decision-making techniques we discuss later in the chapter should help prevent the tendency as well.

How Do Groups Handle Risk?

Almost by definition, problems that are suitable for group decision making involve some degree of risk and uncertainty. This raises a very important question: Do groups make decisions that are more or less risky than those of individuals? Or will the degree of risk assumed by the group simply equal the average risk preferred by its individual members? Consider the following scenario:

> *An accident has just occurred at a nuclear power plant. Several corrections exist, ranging from expensive and safe to low-cost but risky. On the way to an emergency meeting, each nuclear engineer formulates an opinion about what should be done. But what will the group decide?*

Conventional wisdom provides few clear predictions about what the group of engineers will decide to do. It is sometimes argued that groups will make riskier decisions than individuals because there is security in numbers—that is, diffusion of responsibility for a bad decision encourages the group to take greater chances. On the other hand, it is often argued that groups are cautious, with the members checking and balancing each other so much that a conservative outcome is sure to occur. Just contrast the committee-laden civil service with the swashbuckling style of independent operators such as Ted Turner and Donald Trump!

Given this contradiction of common sense, the history of research into group decision making and risk is instructive. A Massachusetts Institute of Technology student, J.A.F. Stoner, reported in a master's thesis that he had discovered clear evidence of a **risky shift** in decision making.[57] Participants in the research reviewed hypothetical cases involving risk, such as those involving career choices or investment decisions. As individuals, they recommended a course of action. Then they were formed into groups, and the groups discussed each case and came to a joint decision. In general, the groups tended to advise riskier courses of action than the average risk initially advocated by their members. This is the risky shift. As studies were conducted by others to explore the reasons for its causes, things got more complicated. For some groups and some decisions, **conservative shifts** were observed. In other words, groups came to decisions that were *less* risky than those of the individual members before interaction.

It is now clear that both risky and conservative shifts are possible, and that they occur in a wide variety of real settings, including investment and purchasing decisions. But what determines which kind of shift occurs? A key factor appears to be the initial positions of the group members before they discuss the problem. This is illustrated in Exhibit 10.4. As you can see, when group members are somewhat conservative before interaction (the Xs), they tend to exhibit a conservative shift when they discuss the problem. When group members are somewhat risky initially (the •s), they exhibit a risky shift after discussion. In other words, *group discussion seems to polarize or exaggerate*

Risky shift. The tendency for groups to make riskier decisions than the average risk initially advocated by their individual members.

Conservative shift. The tendency for groups to make less risky decisions than the average risk initially advocated by their individual members.

Position of Group Members Before Discussion:

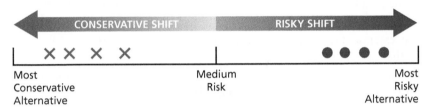

Position of Group Members After Discussion:

EXHIBIT 10.4
The dynamics of risky and conservative shifts for two groups.

the initial position of the group.[58] Returning to the nuclear accident, if the engineers initially prefer a somewhat conservative solution, they should adopt an even more conservative strategy during the meeting.

Why do risky and conservative shifts occur when groups make decisions? Evidence indicates two main factors:[59]

- Group discussion generates ideas and arguments that individual members have not considered before. This information naturally favours the members' initial tendency toward risk or toward conservatism. Since discussion provides "more" and "better" reasons for the initial tendency, the tendency ends up being exaggerated.

- Group members try to present themselves as basically similar to other members but "even better." Thus, they try to one-up others in discussion by adopting a slightly more extreme version of the group's initial stance.

A somewhat worrisome research finding is that groups that communicate via computer are inclined to polarize even more than face-to-face groups.[60]

In summary, managers should be aware of the tendency for group interaction to polarize initial risk levels. If this polarization results from the sensible exchange of information, it might actually improve the group's decision. However, if it results from one-upmanship, it might lead to low-quality decisions.

Improving Decision Making in Organizations

Managers can improve the success of their decisions by using various tactics, such as making the need for action clear at the outset, setting objectives, carrying out an unrestricted search for solutions, and getting key people to participate.[61] It stands to reason that organizational decision making can improve if decision makers receive encouragement to follow more closely the rational decision-making model shown in Exhibit 10.1. This should help to preclude the various biases and errors that we have alluded to throughout the chapter. Each of the following techniques has this goal.

Training Discussion Leaders

When organizations use group decision making, an appointed leader often convenes the group and guides the discussion. The actions of this leader can "make or break" the decision. On the one hand, if the leader behaves autocratically, trying to "sell" a preconceived decision, the advantages of using a group are obliterated, and decision acceptance can suffer. If the leader fails to exert *any* influence, however, the group might develop a low-quality solution that does not meet the needs of the organization. The use of role-playing training to develop these leadership skills has increased the quality and acceptance of group decisions. The following are examples of the skills that people learn in discussion leader training:[62]

- State the problem in a non-defensive, objective manner. Do not suggest solutions or preferences.
- Supply essential facts and clarify any constraints on solutions (e.g., "We can't spend more than $25 000.").
- Draw out all group members. Prevent domination by one person, and protect members from being attacked or severely criticized.
- Wait out pauses. Do not make suggestions or ask leading questions.
- Ask stimulating questions that move the discussion forward.
- Summarize and clarify at several points to mark progress.

Stimulating and Managing Controversy

Full-blown conflict among organizational members is hardly conducive to good decision making. Individuals will withhold information, and personal or group goals will take precedence over developing a decision that solves organizational problems. On the other hand, a complete lack of controversy can be equally damaging, since alternative points of view that may be very relevant to the issue at hand will never surface. Such a lack of controversy is partially responsible for the groupthink effect, and it also contributes to many cases of escalation of commitment.

Research shows a variety of ways to stimulate controversy in decision-making groups: incorporating members with diverse ideas and backgrounds, forming subgroups to "tear the problem apart," and establishing norms that favour the open sharing of information.[63] However, these tactics must be managed carefully to ensure that open conflict does not result.

Devil's advocate. A person appointed to identify and challenge the weaknesses of a proposed plan or strategy.

One interesting method of controversy stimulation is the appointment of a **devil's advocate** to challenge existing plans and strategies. The advocate's role is to challenge the weaknesses of the plan or strategy and state why it should not be adopted. For example, a bank might be considering offering an innovative kind of account. Details to be decided include interest rate, required minimum balance, and so on. A committee might be assigned to develop a position paper. Before a decision is made, someone would be assigned to read the paper and "tear it apart," noting potential weaknesses. Thus, a decision is made in full recognition of the pros and cons of the plan. The controversy promoted by the devil's advocate improves decision quality.[64] However, to be effective, the advocate must present his or her views in an objective, unemotional manner.

Traditional and Electronic Brainstorming

Brainstorming. An attempt to increase the number of creative solution alternatives to problems by focusing on idea generation rather than evaluation.

Brainstorming is the brainchild of a Madison Avenue advertising executive.[65] Its major purpose is to increase the number of creative solution alternatives to problems. Thus, **brainstorming** focuses on the *generation* of ideas rather than the *evaluation* of ideas. If a group generates a large number of ideas, the chance of obtaining a truly creative solution is increased.

Brainstorming was originally conceived as a group technique. It was assumed that, in generating ideas, group members could feed off each other's suggestions and be stimulated to offer more creative solutions. To ensure this, the group is encouraged to operate in a freewheeling, off-the-wall manner. No ideas should be considered too extreme or unusual to be voiced. In addition, no criticism of ideas should be offered, since this can inhibit useful lines of thinking. For instance, an advertising agency might convene a group to generate names for a new toothpaste or soft drink. Similarly, a government agency might convene a group to generate possible solutions for welfare fraud.

Traditional brainstorming has not fulfilled its full creative promise. Research has shown conclusively that individuals working alone tend to generate more ideas than those in groups.[66] In other words, four people working independently (and encouraged to be creative and non-evaluative) will usually generate more ideas than the same people working as a team. Why is this? Likely explanations include inhibition, domination of the group by an ineffective member, or the sheer physical limitations of people trying to talk simultaneously.

However, brainstorming can provide advantages that extend beyond the mere number of ideas generated. Researchers Robert Sutton and Andrew Hargadon studied IDEO, the incredibly successful product and services design firm based in Palo Alto, California. One of the most innovative companies in the world. IDEO makes extensive use of brainstorming. They found that the procedure results in a number of important creative and business advantages. In terms of the organizational culture, they found that it helps organizational memory and supports a culture of wisdom— that is, ideas from one session can be used on subsequent, unrelated projects, and participants learn to appreciate the good ideas of others. At the individual level, the sessions motivate and stimulate the engineers and allow them to show off their good ideas to their colleagues. Finally, IDEO uses the brainstorming sessions to impress their clients, who really get to see how the design process unfolds. Thus, brainstorming shapes the organizational culture, helps retain good talent, and contributes to client confidence.[67]

An alternative to traditional brainstorming is electronic brainstorming. **Electronic brainstorming** uses computer-mediated communication to accomplish the same goal as traditional brainstorming: the generation of novel ideas without evaluation. As we noted, face-to-face interaction actually reduces individual brainstorming performance. But what happens if people brainstorm as an electronic group?

Once over the size of two members, electronic brainstorming groups perform better than face-to-face groups in terms of both quantity and quality of ideas.[68] Also, as electronic groups get larger, they tend to produce more ideas, but the ideas-per-person measure remains stable. In contrast, as face-to-face groups get bigger, fewer and fewer ideas per person are generated (remember social loafing from Chapter 7). What accounts for the success of electronic brainstorming? Reduced inhibition about participating and the ability for people to enter ideas simultaneously without waiting for others seem to be the main reasons. Notice that these factors become especially critical as the group gets bigger. Some organizations have done electronic brainstorming with groups of up to 30 members.

Electronic brainstorming. The use of computer-mediated technology to improve traditional brainstorming practices.

Nominal Group Technique

The fact that nominal (in name only) brainstorming groups generate more ideas than interacting brainstorming groups gave rise to the **nominal group technique** (NGT) of decision making. Unlike brainstorming, NGT is concerned with both the generation of ideas and the evaluation of these ideas.

Nominal group technique. A structured group decision-making technique in which ideas are generated without group interaction and then systematically evaluated by the group.

Imagine a meeting room in which 7 to 10 individuals are sitting around a table in full view of each other; however, at the beginning of the meeting they do not speak to each other. Instead, each individual is writing ideas on a pad of paper in front of him or her. At the end of 5 to 10 minutes, a structured sharing of ideas takes place. Each individual, in round-robin fashion, presents one idea from his or her private list. A recorder writes that idea on a flip chart in full view of other members. There is still no discussion at this point of the meeting—only the recording of privately narrated ideas. Round-robin listing continues until all members indicate they have no further ideas to share. Discussion follows during the next phase of the meeting; however, it is structured so that each idea receives attention before independent voting. This is accomplished by asking for clarification, or stating support or non-support of each idea listed on the flip chart. Independent voting then takes place. Each member privately, in writing, selects priorities by rank-ordering (or rating). The group decision is the mathematically pooled outcome of the individual votes.[69]

As you can see, NGT carefully separates the generation of ideas from their evaluation. Ideas are generated nominally (without interaction) to prevent inhibition and conformity. Evaluation permits interaction and discussion, but it occurs in a fairly structured manner to be sure that each idea gets adequate attention. NGT's chief disadvantage would seem to be the time and resources required to assemble the group for face-to-face interaction. The Delphi technique was developed, in part, to overcome this problem.

The Delphi Technique

Delphi technique. A method of pooling a large number of expert judgments by using a series of increasingly refined questionnaires.

The **Delphi technique** of decision making was developed at the Rand Corporation to forecast changes in technology. Its name derives from the future-telling ability of the famous Greek Delphic Oracle.[70] Unlike NGT, the Delphi process relies solely on a nominal group—participants do not engage in face-to-face interaction. Thus, it is possible to poll a large number of experts without assembling them in the same place at the same time. We should emphasize that these experts do not actually make a final decision; rather, they provide information for organizational decision makers.

The heart of Delphi is a series of questionnaires sent to respondents. Minimally, there are two waves of questionnaires, but more is not unusual. The first questionnaire is usually general in nature and permits free responses to the problem. For example, suppose the CEO of a large corporation wishes to evaluate and improve the firm's customer service. A random sample of employees who have worked closely with customers would receive an initial questionnaire asking them to list the strengths and weaknesses of the existing approach to customers. The staff would collate the responses and develop a second questionnaire that might share these responses and ask for suggested improvements. A final questionnaire might then be sent asking respondents to rate or rank each improvement. The staff would then merge the ratings or rankings mathematically and present them to the president for consideration.

A chief disadvantage of Delphi is the rather lengthy time frame involved in the questionnaire phases, although email and other web-based solutions can speed up sending and receiving. In addition, its effectiveness depends on the writing skills of the respondents and their interest in the problem, since they must work on their own rather than as part of an actual group. Despite these problems, Delphi is an efficient method of pooling a large number of expert judgments while avoiding the problems of conformity and domination that can occur in interacting groups.

THE MANAGER'S NOTEBOOK

Preventing Surgical Decision Errors at Toronto General Hospital

1. To help cut surgical errors, medical researchers drew upon the experience of airline pilots, who use a safety checklist before takeoff. In 2008, the World Health Organization issued a set of guidelines for safe surgery. Harvard professor Dr. Atul Gawande and a team of physicians from eight city hospitals worldwide (including Toronto General) transformed the WHO guidelines into a 19-item Surgical Safety Checklist. Such checklists are especially effective for preventing procedural errors. The checklist is applied at three critical stages of the surgical process: before anaesthesia, before skin incision, and before the patient leaves the operating room. As part of their research, Dr. Gawande and his team, including UHN Chief Surgeon Dr. Bryce Taylor, tested the checklist in each of the eight hospitals, with impressive results. Although there was a greater decrease in preventable deaths in lower-income versus higher-income hospitals, all eight institutions experienced significant drops in complication rates. Dr. Taylor was so impressed with the results that the checklist is now being used by all three UHN hospitals under his watch. Should the checklist be fully implemented across Canada, it is possible that more than 60 000 complications could be avoided each year. Dr. Gawande's own experience convinced him that the checklist should be used worldwide; he argues that its use could prevent millions of complications and deaths each year and save billions of dollars in health-care costs.

2. Studies have indicated that nurses do not always speak up in the operating room out of fear of reprisal. Although both nurses and doctors ultimately serve the needs of the patient, their respective training serves different purposes. Physicians have in-depth knowledge on surgical procedures, positioning them as leaders in the operating room. Consequently, because nurses are on the lower end of the status hierarchy, they may refrain from challenging physicians out of fear of being punished. The traditional operating room structure, in which the lead surgeon is considered to be the ultimate boss, may also intimidate residents and anaesthesiologists. So when problems do arise, they may be overlooked by a submissive surgical team. The essential problem is one in which the emotions of discomfort or outright fear lead to decisions being made with inadequate information. Thus, the person on the team who is most knowledgeable about a problem may not offer decision input. Toronto General Hospital understood that changing the surgical team culture from one of command-and-control to one of collaborative learning could encourage effective group decision making through the elimination of fear. The introduction of the Surgical Safety Checklist encouraged all team members to speak up either prior to, during, or after the operation. The researchers from Toronto General Hospital were so convinced that the procedures borrowed from aviation could save lives that they even invited a senior Air Canada training pilot to talk with the surgical teams.

LEARNING OBJECTIVES CHECKLIST

1. *Decision making* is the process of developing a commitment to some course of action. Alternatively, it is a problem-solving process. A problem exists when a gap is perceived between some existing state and some desired state. Some problems are well structured. This means that existing and desired states are clear, as is the means of getting from one state to the other. Well-structured problems are often solved with programs which simply standardize solutions. Programmed decision making is effective as long as the program is developed rationally and as long as conditions do not change. Ill-structured problems

contain some combination of an unclear existing state, an unclear desired state, or unclear methods of getting from one state to the other. They tend to be unique and non-recurrent, and they require non-programmed decision making, in which the rational model comes into play.

2. *Rational decision making* includes (1) problem identification, (2) information search, (3) development of alternative solutions, (4) evaluation of alternatives, (5) choice of the best alternative, (6) implementation, and (7) ongoing evaluation of the implemented alternative. The imaginary, perfectly rational decision maker has free and easy access to all relevant information, can process it accurately, and has a single ultimate goal—economic maximization. Real decision makers must suffer from *bounded rationality*. They do not have free and easy access to information, and the human mind has limited information processing capacity and is susceptible to a variety of cognitive biases. In addition, time constraints and political considerations can outweigh anticipated economic gain. As a result, bounded decision makers usually *satisfice* (choose a solution that is "good enough") rather than maximize.

3. *Framing* refers to the aspects of the presentation of information about a problem that are assumed by decision makers. A frame could include assumptions about the boundaries of a problem, the possible outcomes of a decision, or the reference points used to decide if a decision is successful. Problems that are framed as an investment versus a cost, or as a potential gain versus a potential loss, can affect decision-making processes. *Cognitive biases* are tendencies to acquire and process information in a particular way that is prone to error. These biases constitute assumptions and shortcuts that can improve decision-making efficiency, but they frequently lead to serious errors in

judgment. Examples include overemphasizing recent information, overconfidence based on past success, perceptual defence, and faulty hindsight.

4. *Escalation of commitment* is the tendency to invest additional resources in an apparently failing course of action. This tendency emerges from people's desires to justify past decisions and attempts to recoup sunk costs incurred as the result of a past decision.

5. Although emotions can enhance the decision-making process in relation to correcting ethical errors or when dealing with creative problems, they can also distract and unsettle decision makers and lead to poor choices. Research has shown that mood can also have an important impact on the decision-making process, especially for uncertain or ambiguous problems. Mood can affect information recall, evaluation, creativity, time reference, and projected outcomes.

6. Groups can often make higher-quality decisions than individuals because of their vigilance and their potential capacity to generate and evaluate more ideas. Also, group members might accept more readily a decision that they have been involved in making. Given the appropriate problem, groups will frequently make higher-quality decisions than individuals. However, using groups takes a lot of time and may provoke conflict. In addition, groups may fall prey to *groupthink,* in which social pressures to conform to a particular decision outweigh rationality. Groups may also make decisions that are more risky or conservative than those of individuals.

7. Attempts to improve organizational decision making have involved training discussion leaders, stimulating controversy, *brainstorming, the nominal group technique,* and the *Delphi technique.*

DISCUSSION QUESTIONS

1. The director of an urban hospital feels that there is a turnover problem among the hospital's nurses. About 25 percent of the staff resigns each year, leading to high replacement costs and disruption of services. Use the decision model in Exhibit 10.1 to explore how the director might proceed to solve this problem. Discuss probable bounds to the rationality of the director's decision.

2. Describe a decision-making episode (in school, work, or your personal life) in which you experienced information overload. How did you respond to this overload? Did it affect the quality of your decision?

3. Many universities must register thousands of students for courses each semester. Is this a well-structured problem or an ill-structured

problem? Does it require programmed decisions or non-programmed decisions? Elaborate.

4. An auditing team fails to detect a case of embezzlement that has gone on for several months at a bank. How might the team members use hindsight to justify their faulty decisions?

5. A very cohesive planning group for a major oil company is about to develop a long-range strategic plan. The head of the unit is aware of the groupthink problem and wishes to prevent it. What steps should she take?

6. Discuss the implications of diffusion of responsibility, risky shift, and conservative shift for the members of a parole board. Also, consider the role of emotion and mood.

7. Discuss how the concepts of groupthink and escalation of commitment might be related to some cases of unethical decision making (and its cover-up) in business.

8. What are the similarities and differences of the nominal group technique and the Delphi technique? What are the comparative advantages and disadvantages?

INTEGRATIVE DISCUSSION QUESTIONS

1. Consider the role of communication in decision making. Explain how barriers to effective manager–employee communication can affect decision making in organizations. How can personal and organizational approaches for improving communication improve decision making?

2. Does group structure influence group decision making? Explain how each of the following structural characteristics might influence group decision quality, acceptance and commitment, and diffusion of responsibility: group size, diversity, norms, roles, status, and cohesiveness.

ON-THE-JOB CHALLENGE QUESTION

Although automotive journalists love BMW's award-winning cars, they complained for years about BMW's complicated iDrive electronic interface. The menu-driven interface, which uses a knob on the centre console and a display screen, controls several hundred functions related to climate control, sound system, and navigation. In 2006, *Car and Driver* magazine used the words "maddening," "exasperating," and "curse" in referring to iDrive. Most automotive journalists intensely disliked the feature, even though BMW felt that it reinforced their image as a technology leader and represented the wave of the future in automotive electronics. Finally, for the 2009

model, BMW made significant changes that prompted *Road & Track* to claim that iDrive was now as easy to use as an iPhone.

BMW was obviously aware of the repeated criticism of iDrive. What factors might have accounted for their decision not to do away with or significantly simplify the system for such a long time? What might have accounted for their change with the 2009 model?

Sources: Swann, T. (2006, November). Four upscale sedans to ward off old-guy blues. *Car and Driver,* 88–97; Mitani, S. (2009, February). BMW 750 Li: Softer, but better in almost every way. *Road & Track,* 28.

EXPERIENTIAL EXERCISE

The New Truck Dilemma

Preparation for Role-Playing

The instructor will:

1. Read the general instructions to the class as a whole.

2. Place data regarding name, length of service, and make and age of truck on the chalkboard for ready reference by all.

3. Divide the class into groups of six. Any remaining members should be asked to join one of the groups and serve as observers.

4. Assign roles to each group by handing out slips with the names Chris Marshall, Terry, Sal, Jan, Sam, and Charlie. Ask each person to read his or her own role only. Instructions should not be consulted once role-playing has begun.

5. Ask the Chris Marshalls to stand up when they have completed reading their instructions.

6. When all Chris Marshalls are standing, ask that each crew member display conspicuously the slip of paper with his or her role name so that Chris can tell who is who.

The Role-Playing Process

1. The instructor will start the role-playing with a statement such as the following: "Chris Marshall has asked the crew to wait in the office. Apparently Chris wants to discuss something with the crew. When Chris sits down that will mean he or she has returned. What you say to each other is entirely up to you. Are you ready? All Chris Marshalls please sit down."

2. Role-playing proceeds for 25 to 30 minutes. Most groups reach agreement during this interval.

Collection of Results

1. Each supervisor in turn reports his or her crew's solution. The instructor summarizes these on the chalkboard by listing the initials of each repair person and indicating with arrows which truck goes to whom.

2. A tabulation should be made of the number of people getting a different truck, the crew members considering the solution unfair, and the supervisor's evaluation of the solution.

Discussion of Results

1. A comparison of solutions will reveal differences in the number of people getting a different truck, who gets the new one, the number dissatisfied, and so on. Discuss why the same facts yield different outcomes.

2. The quality of the solution can be measured by the trucks retained. Highest quality would require the poorest truck to be discarded. Evaluate the quality of the solutions achieved.

3. Acceptance is indicated by the low number of dissatisfied repair people. Evaluate solutions achieved on this dimension.

4. List problems that are similar to the new truck problem. See how widely the group will generalize.

General Instructions

This is a role-playing exercise. Do not read the roles given below until assigned to do so by your instructor!

Assume that you are a repair person for a large utility company. Each day you drive to various locations in the city to do repair work. Each repair person drives a small truck, and you take pride in keeping it looking good. You have a possessive feeling about your truck and like to keep it in good running order. Naturally, you would like to have a new truck too, because a new truck gives you a feeling of pride.

Here are some facts about the trucks and the crew that reports to Chris Marshall, the supervisor of repairs:

Terry—17 years with the company, has a 2-year-old Ford

Sal—11 years with the company, has a 5-year-old Dodge

Jan—10 years with the company, has a 4-year-old Ford

Sam—5 years with the company, has a 3-year-old Ford

Charlie—3 years with the company, has a 5-year-old Chevrolet

Most of you do all your driving in the city, but Jan and Sam cover the jobs in the suburbs.

You will be one of the people mentioned above and will be given some further individual instructions. In acting your part in role-playing, accept the facts as well as assume the attitude supplied in your specific role. From this point on, let your feelings develop in accordance with the events that transpire in the role-playing process. When facts or events arise that are not covered by the roles, make up things that are consistent with the way it might be in a real-life situation.

When the role-playing begins, assume that Chris Marshall called the crew into the repair office.

Role for Chris Marshall, Supervisor. You are the supervisor of a repair crew, each of whom drives a small service truck to and from various jobs. Every so often you get a new truck to exchange for an old one, and you have the problem of deciding which one of your crew gets the new truck. Often there are hard feelings because each person seems to feel entitled to the new truck, so you have a tough time being fair. As a matter of fact, it usually turns out that whatever you decide, most of the crew consider it wrong. You now have to face the issue again because a new truck has just been allocated to you for assignment. The new truck is a Chevrolet.

To handle this problem, you have decided to put the decision up to the crew themselves. You will tell them about the new truck and will put the problem in terms of what would be the fairest way to assign the truck. Do not take a position yourself because you want to do what the crew thinks is most fair. However, be sure that the group reaches a decision.

Role for Terry. When a new Chevrolet truck becomes available, you think you should get it because you have most seniority and do not like your present truck. Your own car is a Chevrolet, and you prefer a Chevrolet truck such as you drove before you got the Ford.

Role for Sal. You feel you deserve a new truck. Your present truck is old, and since the more senior crew member has a fairly new truck, you should get the next one. You have taken excellent care of your present Dodge and have kept it looking like new. People deserve to be rewarded if they treat a company truck like their own.

Role for Jan. You have to do more driving than most of the other crew because you work in the suburbs. You have a fairly old truck and feel you should have a new one because you do so much driving.

Role for Sam. The heater in your present truck is inadequate. Since Charlie backed into the door of your truck, it has never been repaired to fit right. The door lets in too much cold air, and you attribute your frequent colds to this. You want a warm truck since you have a good deal of driving to do. As long as it has good tires, brakes, and is comfortable, you do not care about its make.

Role for Charlie. You have the poorest truck in the crew. It is five years old, and before you got it, it had been in a bad wreck. It has never been good, and you have put up with it for three years. It is about time you got a good truck to drive, and you feel the next one should be yours. You have a good accident record. The only accident you had was when you sprung the door of Sam's truck when he opened it as you backed out of the garage. You hope the new truck is a Ford, since you prefer to drive one.

Source: Adapted from Maier, N.R.F., & Verser, G.C. (1982). *Psychology in industrial organizations* (5th ed.). Copyright 1982 Wadsworth, a part of Cengage Learning, Inc. Adapted by permission, www.cengage.com/permissions.

CASE INCIDENT

The Restaurant Review

After emigrating from New Orleans to his adopted city of Vancouver, Christophe Touché had worked as head chef at a neighbourhood pub for five years while saving money and planning to open his own restaurant. At the pub, he perfected several Cajun specialties that would form the core of the menu of his new restaurant, Cajun Sensation. After his restaurant had been open for two months, Christophe was delighted to receive a phone call from the local newspaper food critic who had dined anonymously at the restaurant the previous evening and was calling to verify some of the ingredients and techniques he used in his cooking. Two days later, delight turned to dismay as Christophe read the restaurant review. Although the critic praised the inventiveness of some dishes, others were described as "heavy handed." The staff was described as "charming but amateurish." And the wine list was described as "well chosen but overpriced." The review concluded, "In sum, this very new restaurant has both problems and promise." It was local custom to post restaurant reviews prominently at the restaurant entrance to capture walk-by trade. At a staff meeting, opinions varied about what to do. One member suggested posting the review, as it noted that the new establishment had been open only two months. Another suggested posting only favourable excerpts from the review. A third offered to write an angry letter to the paper's editor. Christophe wasn't sure what to do.

1. What are some of the factors that might lead Christophe to make a poor decision about the review?

2. What would you do in this situation, and why?

CASE STUDY

Standard Media Plan

It was a late Saturday afternoon in mid-December, and Bob Smith, a research analyst for L&H Marketing Research, was working furiously to complete the media plan portion of the Standard Grooming Products report. Standard was considering introducing a men's hairspray and needed demographic characteristics and media habits of male hairspray users, as well as attitudinal information about such product attributes as oiliness, stickiness, masculinity and fragrance.

The findings were to be presented Monday afternoon, and a long series of problems and delays had forced Bob to come in on Saturday to finish the report. Complicating matters, Bob felt that his boss, Barry Michaels, expected the statistical analysis to be consistent with L&H's initial recommendations to Standard. Bob, Barry and Marjorie Glass, from Standard's advertising agency, were to meet Monday morning to finalize L&H's presentation to Standard.

Back in September, Bob had recommended surveying 250 users of men's hairspray from each of 15 metropolitan areas. Charles Chastain from Standard's marketing department had argued that conclusions about local usage in each city would not be accurate unless each city's sample size was proportional to its population. That is, the sample sizes for larger cities should be larger than for smaller cities. Furthermore, Charles feared that males in metropolitan areas differed from rural males on usage or other important characteristics. Bob finally convinced Charles that sample sizes proportional to population would mean only 5 to 10 interviews in some smaller cities—too few to draw statistically valid conclusions. Furthermore, expanding the survey to include rural users would have required committing more money to the project—money Standard didn't want to spend. Since Standard was a new account with big potential, a long-term relationship with them would be valuable. (Business at L&H had been slow this past year.) Feeling "under the gun," Bob met with Barry and Charles, who agreed to reduce the sample to 200 men in each of only 11 metropolitan areas.

In October, a Des Moines, Iowa, pretest revealed that the questionnaire's length was driving the cost per completed interview to about $18. Total expenses would be well over budget if that cost held for the 15 metro areas. If the survey costs exceeded $65,000 (counting the pilot study), precious little money would be left for the focus groups, advertising, and packaging pretesting in L&H's contract with Standard (see Table 10.1).

In early November, a new problem arose. After surveying eight metro areas, Bob discovered that his assistant, with whom he had a good long-term relationship, had accidentally deleted all questions on media habits from the questionnaire given to L&H's vendor for the phone interviews. When telling Barry and Charles of the missing questions problem, Bob omitted indicating the source of the problem. Barry and Charles became visibly angry at the vendor, but after much discussion, they decided there was too little time to hire a new vendor and resample the eight areas. Therefore, they agreed to reinsert the media questions for the remaining three cities and just finish the survey.

Bob's task now was to make the most of the data he had. Because responses from each of the three cities were reasonably similar, and each city came from a different region (East, West and Midwest), Bob felt confident that the three-city data were representative. Therefore, he decided to base the media plan on the large differences between his results and the national averages for adult men—making sports magazines and newspapers the primary vehicles for Standard's advertising (see Table 10.2).

Bob's confidence in the media plan based on sports magazines and newspapers was bolstered by a phone conversation with Marjorie Glass. Until a short time ago, her agency had handled the advertising for American Toiletries, so she had valuable information about this competitor's possible responses to Standard's new product. Marjorie liked Bob's recommendations, had no misgivings about using information about a former client, and agreed to support the media plan in Monday's meeting. Indeed, Bob thought, Marjorie had been a big help.

The Standard project had put a great deal of stress on Bob, who hated spending weekends away from his

TABLE 10.1
Proposed Budget

Type of Expense	Amount (US$)
Phone survey	58 000
Focus group study	8 000
Advertising pretesting	25 000
Package pretesting	14 000
Miscellaneous expenses	5 000
Proposal total expenses	110 000

TABLE 10.2
Comparison of Media Habits, Three-City Sample of Male Hairspray Users versus U.S. Adult Males

Male Media-Use	Male Hairspray Users in Three Cities	National Male Hairspray Users
Magazines, % of users (at least one subscription)		
News	28	19
Entertainment	4	3
Sports	39	20
Other	9	6
Newspaper subscription, % of users (at least one daily)	35	14
Favourite radio format, % of users		
Pop/rock	51	48
Country	26	37
EZ listening	7	6
News/talk	5	4
Other	11	5
Hours watching television per week, per user		
Total	17.5	23.5
Dramas	6.3	8.4
Comedies	7.8	7.3
News	1.1	3.9
Other	2.3	3.9

family—especially near Christmas! If the presentation went well and more business was forthcoming, Bob suspected he would be spending even more weekends here. But if the presentation went poorly or the data collection errors became an issue, then Standard might look elsewhere for market research, thus jeopardizing Bob's future with L&H. Either way, he felt apprehensive. He wondered how he should present his results and how much information he should share with the client. Should he reveal to Standard any or all of the problems L&H experienced in conducting the project? Or should he simply present his results and recommendation as credible bases to proceed with Standard's media plan and not mention technical issues? The question really was about the level of understanding that his client would want about the basis of the recommendations. He also thought that his boss, Barry Michaels, would be much more concerned about how well the proposals fit with L&H's initial recommendations and would certainly be upset if he lost the account. The choices weren't easy. Bob wished he could turn to somebody outside the organization to share his dilemma and seek a fresh, independent perspective.

1. Given the formal definition of the word problem presented in the chapter, what is the problem faced by Bob Smith? Is the problem well structured or ill structured?

2. What are some of the bounds or limits on rationality that affect attempts to solve the problem Bob faces? What would a satisficing solution be?

3. Is Bob suffering from too little information or too much? Defend your answer.

4. How has Bob framed his problem? What would be an alternative frame?

5. Does the case contain any elements of groupthink or escalation of commitment? Please explain.

6. Discuss how confirmation bias and the anchoring effect (Exhibit 10.4) pertain to Bob's concern about Barry Michaels's interest that the marketing proposal fit the initial recommendation to the client.

7. Are there ethical issues in this case?

8. What should Bob do?

Source: Excerpted from Boland, R.J., Jr., Singh, J., Salipante, P., Aram, J.D., Fay, S.Y., & Kanawattanachai, P. (2001). Knowledge representations and knowledge transfer. *Academy of Management Journal, 44,* 393–417, Appendix B.

LEARNING OBJECTIVES

After reading Chapter 11,
you should be able to:

1 Define *power* and review
the bases of individual
power.

2 Explain how people obtain
power in organizations.

3 Discuss the concept of
empowerment.

4 Review various *influence
tactics*.

5 Provide a profile of power
seekers.

6 Explain *strategic contingencies* and discuss how
subunits obtain power.

7 Define *organizational politics*
and discuss its various
forms.

8 Define *ethics* and review
the ethical dilemmas that
managers face.

9 Define *sexual harassment*
and discuss what organizations can do to prevent it
and how they should
respond to allegations.

Power, Politics, and Ethics

Enron

When energy-trading giant Enron filed for bankruptcy in December 2001, it was the seventh-largest corporation in the United States. A firm that had been the darling of the investment community and had been called America's most innovative company by *Fortune* was gone with no apparent warning. What caused Enron's downfall? The house of cards collapsed when it was revealed that the firm had used shady accounting practices to hide more than a billion dollars of debt and losses in outside firms that it had created. Transferring poor financial results to these partnership firms made it appear that Enron was in excellent financial health and allowed its stock price to soar. As such, executives got rich and investors were defrauded. In the end, rank-and-file employees, the vast majority of whom knew nothing about these partnership firms, suffered the most through the loss of their jobs and, in many cases, the loss of their life savings.

The fall of Enron also ensnared its external auditors, Arthur Andersen, the fifth-largest accounting firm in the United States until it was destroyed by the Enron mess. Many questioned how Andersen could have approved these financial practices for years. Although the accounting firm stated it had been duped by Enron, it was revealed that it shredded thousands of documents relating to Enron between September and December 2001. Andersen was indicted on obstruction of justice charges in March 2002 and was found guilty that June.

As investigations into the unethical and illegal activities unfolded, it became clear that power, politics, and corporate cultures fuelled by greed were an important part of the story. Enron had been a traditional energy company in the 1980s, with standard assets such as oil pipelines. In the 1990s, Jeff Skilling was chosen by CEO Kenneth Lay to steer the company in a new direction. As Lay faded into the background, Skilling transformed Enron's business and culture, and the company sold off hard assets and entered the complicated business of energy trading. Enron went from a traditional energy company to the biggest e-commerce company in the United States. For several years, the wheeling and dealing paid off, and Enron executives became rich beyond their wildest dreams. Underlying the apparent success, however, was a corporate culture based on cutthroat competition, paranoia, and the relentless pursuit of profit. Skilling created an in-your-face culture in which positive results and growth were all that

1400 Smith Street

Enron illustrates how the abuse of power and politics contributes to unethical corporate behaviour.

mattered. Those who preached fundamentals or suggested more traditional business approaches were labelled dinosaurs and were marginalized. Skilling also used political tactics and power to outmanoeuvre potential internal rivals. By December 2000, Skilling had surrounded himself with a team of yes-people, had wiped out all internal opponents, and collected his ultimate prize: promotion to the position of CEO, replacing Ken Lay, who stayed on as board chair. In Skilling's Enron, his right-hand man was CFO Andrew Fastow, another young shark who rose quickly and was not afraid to use bully tactics. Fastow set up and partially owned many of the partnership firms in which Enron hid its losses. It has been reported that Fastow made more than $30 million from these partnerships and enriched family and friends along the way. By the second half of 2002, it became clear that Enron's fortune and success were mere illusions. Barely six months into his term as CEO, Skilling resigned, citing personal reasons. In November 2002, Fastow was charged in criminal court with fraud, money laundering, and conspiracy. More indictments followed in May 2003, including one for Fastow's wife. Fastow was convicted and sentenced to 10 years in prison. Jeff Skilling and Ken Lay were indicted on fraud and insider trading charges and were convicted in 2006. Skilling was sentenced to 24 years in prison, a sentence currently under review. Lay died of a heart attack only weeks after his conviction. Among the most shocking revelations was that Enron executives cashed out $1.1 billion of stock from 1999 to 2001, before any trouble was disclosed to the public, and that Ken Lay continued to encourage employees to buy stock even after executive whistle-blower Sherron Watkins had warned him of the fraudulent practices.

In the case of Andersen, many point to the $1 million per week for auditing and the $27 million in consulting revenue that the accounting firm received from Enron as the reason they did not stop the questionable practices. Information also surfaced about the culture of greed within the accounting firm, in which income apparently overruled the obligation to be impartial and vigilant.

In all, two once-respected firms were destroyed, public confidence in corporations and entities designed to stop fraud was shaken, and millions of people were adversely affected by these scandals. Not the most promising start for business in the 21st century.[1]

This vignette illustrates the main themes of this chapter—power, politics, and ethics. First, we will define power and discuss the bases of individual power. Then we will examine how people get and use power and who seeks it. After this, we will explore how organizational subunits, such as particular departments, obtain power, define organizational politics, and explore the relationship of politics to power. Finally, we will look at ethics in organizations and sexual harassment.

At one time, power and politics were not considered polite topics for coverage in organizational behaviour textbooks. At best, they were seen as irrational and at worst, as evil. Now, though, organizational scholars recognize what managers have known all along—that power and politics are *natural* expressions of life in organizations. They often develop as a rational response to a complex set of needs and goals, and their expression can be beneficial. However, they can also put a strain on ethical standards, as was the case at Enron and Anderson.

What Is Power?

Power. The capacity to influence others who are in a state of dependence.

Power is the capacity to influence others who are in a state of dependence. First, notice that power is the *capacity* to influence the behaviour of others. Power is not always perceived or exercised.[2] For example, most professors hold a great degree of potential power over students in terms of grades, assignment load, and the ability to embarrass students in class. Under normal circumstances, professors use only a small amount of this power.

Second, the fact that the target of power is dependent on the powerholder does not imply that a poor relationship exists between the two. For instance, your best friend has power to influence your behaviour and attitudes because you are dependent on him or her for friendly reactions and social support. Presumably, you can exert reciprocal influence for similar reasons.

Third, power can flow in any direction in an organization. Often, members at higher organizational levels have more power than those at lower levels. However, in specific cases, reversals can occur. For example, the janitor who finds the president in a compromising position with a secretary might find himself in a powerful position if the president wishes to maintain his reputation in the organization!

Finally, power is a broad concept that applies to both individuals and groups. On the one hand, an individual marketing manager might exert considerable influence over the staff who report to her. On the other, the marketing department at XYZ Foods might be the most powerful department in the company, able to get its way more often than other departments. But from where do the marketing manager and the marketing department obtain their power? We explore this issue in the following sections. First, we consider individual bases of power. Then we examine how organizational subunits, such as the marketing department, obtain power.

The Bases of Individual Power

If you wanted to marshal some power to influence others in your organization, where would you get it? As psychologists John French and Bertram Raven explained, power can be found in the *position* that you occupy in the organization or the *resources* that you are able to command.[3] The first base of power—legitimate power—is dependent on one's position or job. The other bases (reward, coercive, referent, and expert power) involve the control of important resources. If other organizational members do not respect your position or value the resources you command, they will not be dependent on you, and you will lack the power to influence them.

Legitimate Power

Legitimate power derives from a person's position or job in the organization. It constitutes the organization's judgment about who is formally permitted to influence whom, and it is often called authority. As we move up the organization's hierarchy, we find that members possess more and more legitimate power. In theory, organizational equals (e.g., all vice-presidents) have equal legitimate power. Of course, some people are more likely than others to *invoke* their legitimate power—"Look, *I'm* the boss around here."

Organizations differ greatly in the extent to which they emphasize and reinforce legitimate power. At one extreme is the military, which has many levels of command, differentiating uniforms, and rituals (e.g., salutes), all designed to emphasize legitimate power. On the other hand, the academic hierarchy of universities tends to downplay differences in the legitimate power of lecturers, professors, chairpeople, and deans.

When legitimate power works, it often does so because people have been socialized to accept its influence. Experiences with parents, teachers, and law enforcement officials cause members to enter organizations with a degree of readiness to submit to (and exercise) legitimate power. In fact, employees consistently cite legitimate power as a major reason for following their boss's directives, even across various cultures.[4] This is one reason why juries failed to believe that Skilling and Lay were "out of the loop" in the Enron fiasco.

Legitimate power. Power derived from a person's position or job in an organization.

Reward Power

Reward power means that the powerholder can exert influence by providing positive outcomes and preventing negative outcomes. In general, it corresponds to the concept of positive reinforcement discussed in Chapter 2. Reward power often backs up legitimate power. That is, managers are given the chance to recommend raises, do performance evaluations, and assign preferred tasks to employees. Of course, *any* organizational member can attempt to exert influence over others with praise, compliments, and flattery, which also constitute rewards.

At Enron, those who bought into Jeff Skilling's vision for the company were well rewarded. Many became rich beyond their wildest dreams. Lavish parties, exclusive clubs, and special privileges for managers and their families were available for those who went along with the change of direction. Around Houston, the company's home base, Porsche became known as Enron's company car.

Reward power. Power derived from the ability to provide positive outcomes and prevent negative outcomes.

Coercive Power

Coercive power is available when the powerholder can exert influence using punishment and threat. Like reward power, it is often a support for legitimate power. Managers might be permitted to dock pay, assign unfavourable tasks, or block promotions. Despite a strong civil service system, even US government agencies provide their executives with plenty of coercive power. At Enron, while employees who followed Jeff Skilling's cultural shift were rewarded, the consequences for those who did not were

Coercive power. Power derived from the use of punishment and threat.

very unpleasant. Executives who clashed with Skilling were shipped off to other departments, sometimes overseas, and all managers faced regular performance reviews that could be particularly brutal. In fact, after every review, the bottom 15 percent would be fired immediately.

Of course, coercive power is not perfectly correlated with legitimate power. Lower-level organizational members can also apply their share of coercion. For example, consider work-to-rule campaigns that slow productivity by strictly adhering to organizational procedures. Cohesive work groups are especially skilful at enforcing such campaigns.

In Chapter 2, we pointed out that the use of punishment to control behaviour is very problematic because of emotional side effects. Thus, it is not surprising that when managers use coercive power, it is generally ineffective and can provoke considerable employee resistance.[5]

Referent Power

Referent power. Power derived from being well liked by others.

Referent power exists when the powerholder is *well liked* by others. It is not surprising that people we like readily influence us. We are prone to consider their points of view, ignore their failures, seek their approval, and use them as role models. In fact, it is often highly dissonant to hold a point of view that is discrepant from that held by someone we like.[6]

Referent power is especially potent for two reasons. First, it stems from *identification* with the powerholder. Thus, it represents a truer or deeper base of power than reward or coercion, which may stimulate mere compliance to achieve rewards or avoid punishment. In this sense, charismatic leaders (Chapter 9) have referent power. Second, *anyone* in the organization may be well liked, irrespective of his or her other bases of power. Thus, referent power is available to everyone from the janitor to the president.

Friendly interpersonal relations often permit influence to extend across the organization, outside the usual channels of legitimate authority, reward, and coercion. For example, a production manager who becomes friendly with the design engineer through participation in a task force might later use this contact to ask for a favour in solving a production problem.

Expert Power

Expert power. Power derived from having special information or expertise that is valued by an organization.

A person has **expert power** when he or she has special information or expertise that the organization values. In any circumstance, we tend to be influenced by experts or by those who perform their jobs well. However, the more crucial and unusual this expertise, the greater is the expert power available. Thus, expert power corresponds to difficulty of replacement. Consider the business school that has one highly published professor who is an internationally known scholar and past federal cabinet minister. Such a person would obviously be difficult to replace and should have much greater expert power than an unpublished lecturer.

One of the most fascinating aspects of expert power occurs when lower-level organizational members accrue it. Many secretaries have acquired expert power through long experience in dealing with clients, keeping records, or sparring with the bureaucracy. Frequently, they have been around longer than those they serve. In this case, it is not unusual for bosses to create special titles and develop new job classifications to reward their expertise and prevent their resignation.

Expert power is a valuable asset for managers. Of all the bases of power, expertise is most consistently associated with employee effectiveness.[7] Also, research shows that employees perceive women managers as more likely than male managers to be high in expert power.[8] Women often lack easy access to more organizationally based forms of power, and expertise is free for self-development. Thus, being "better" than their male counterparts is one strategy that women managers have used to gain influence.

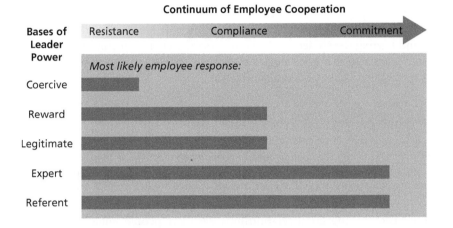

EXHIBIT 11.1
Employee responses
to bases of power.

Source: Steers, R.M., & Black, J.S.
(1994). *Organizational behavior*,
4th ed. © 1991. Reproduced by
permission of Pearson Education,
Inc., Upper Saddle River, NJ.

Exhibit 11.1 summarizes likely employee responses to various bases of managerial power. As you can see, coercion is likely to produce resistance and lack of cooperation. Legitimate power and reward power are likely to produce compliance with the boss's wishes. Referent and expert power are most likely to generate true commitment and enthusiasm for the manager's agenda.

How Do People Obtain Power?

Now that we have discussed the individual bases of power, we can turn to the issue of how people *get* power—that is, how do organizational members obtain promotions to positions of legitimate power, demonstrate their expertise, and get others to like them? And how do they acquire the ability to provide others with rewards and punishment? Rosabeth Moss Kanter, an organizational sociologist, has provided some succinct answers: Do the right things, and cultivate the right people.[9]

Doing the Right Things

According to Kanter, some activities are "righter" than others for obtaining power. She argues that activities lead to power when they are extraordinary, highly visible, and especially relevant to the solution of organizational problems.

Extraordinary Activities. Excellent performance of a routine job might not be enough to obtain power. What one needs is excellent performance in *unusual* or *non-routine* activities. In the large company that Kanter studied, these activities included occupying new positions, managing substantial changes, and taking great risks. For example, consider the manager who establishes and directs a new customer service program. This is a risky, major change that involves the occupancy of a new position. If successful, the manager should acquire substantial power.

Visible Activities. Extraordinary activities will fail to generate power if no one knows about them. People who have an interest in power are especially good at identifying visible activities and publicizing them. The successful marketing executive whose philosophy is profiled in *Fortune* will reap the benefits of power. Similarly, the innovative surgeon whose techniques are reported in the *New England Journal of Medicine* will enhance his influence in the hospital.

Relevant Activities. Extraordinary, visible work may fail to generate power if no one cares. If nobody sees the work as relevant to the solution of important organizational problems, it will not add to one's influence. The English professor who wins two Pulitzer Prizes will probably not accrue much power if his small college is financially strapped and hurting for students. He would not be seen as contributing to the solution of pressing organizational problems. In another college, these extraordinary, visible activities might generate considerable influence.

Cultivating the Right People

An old saying advises, "It's not what you know, it's *who* you know." In reference to power in organizations, there is probably more than a grain of truth to the latter part of this statement. Kanter explains that developing informal relationships with the right people can prove a useful means of acquiring power.

Outsiders. Establishing good relationships with key people outside one's organization can lead to increased power within the organization. Sometimes this power is merely a reflection of the status of the outsider, but, all the same, it may add to one's internal influence. The assistant director of a hospital who is friendly with the president of the American Medical Association might find herself holding power by association. Cultivating outsiders may also contribute to more tangible sources of power. Organizational members who are on the boards of directors of other companies might acquire critical information about business conditions that they can use in their own firms. Enron cultivated strong political ties in Washington through large contributions to political parties. Although they were abandoned by political friends once the problems were revealed, many suggest that their contacts allowed them to operate with little oversight and to gain many favours over the years.

Subordinates. At first blush, it might seem unlikely that power can be enhanced by cultivating relationships with subordinates. However, as Kanter notes, an individual can gain influence if she is closely identified with certain up-and-coming subordinates—"I taught her everything she knows." In academics, some professors are better known for the brilliant Ph.D. students they have supervised than for their own published work. Of course, there is also the possibility that an outstanding subordinate will one day become one's boss! Having cultivated the relationship earlier, one might then be rewarded with special influence.

Cultivating subordinate interests can also provide power when a manager can demonstrate that he or she is backed by a cohesive team. The research director who can oppose a policy change by honestly insisting that "My people won't stand for this" knows that there is strength in numbers.

At Enron, a team of key subordinates helped Jeff Skilling advance his vision for the firm and build his internal empire. As a result, these subordinates were given a very long leash and a great deal of power for themselves. In the end, these powerful subordinates were allowed to operate with little oversight, which eventually led to the ethical lapses.

Peers. Cultivating good relationships with peers is mainly a means of ensuring that nothing gets in the way of one's *future* acquisition of power. As one moves up through the ranks, favours can be asked of former associates, and fears of being "stabbed in the back" for a past misdeed are precluded. Organizations often reward good "team players" with promotions on the assumption that they have demonstrated good interpersonal skills. On the other side of the coin, people often avoid contact with peers whose reputation is seen as questionable.

Superiors. Liaisons with key superiors probably represent the best way of obtaining power through cultivating others. As we discussed in Chapter 8, such superiors are often called *mentors* or *sponsors* because of the special interest they show in a promising subordinate. Mentors can provide power in several ways. Obviously, it is useful to be identified as a protégé of someone higher in the organization. More concretely, mentors can provide special information and useful introductions to other "right people."

Empowerment—Putting Power Where It Is Needed

Early organizational scholars treated power as something of a fixed quantity: An organization had so much, the people on the top had a lot, and lower-level employees had a little. Our earlier analysis of the more informal sources of power (such as being liked and being an expert) hints at the weakness of this idea. Thus, contemporary views of power treat it less as a fixed-sum phenomenon. This is best seen in the concept of **empowerment**, which means giving people the authority, opportunity, and motivation to take initiative to solve organizational problems.[10]

In practice, having the authority to solve an organizational problem means having legitimate power. This might be included in a job description, or a boss might delegate it to a subordinate.

Having opportunity usually means freedom from bureaucratic barriers and other system problems that block initiative. In a service encounter, if you have ever heard "Sorry, the computer won't let me do that" or "That's not my job," you have been the victim of limited opportunity. Opportunity also includes any relevant training and information about the impact of one's actions on other parts of the organization.

The motivation part of the empowerment equation suggests hiring people who will be intrinsically motivated by power and opportunity and aligning extrinsic rewards with successful performance. Also, leaders who express confidence in subordinates' abilities (especially transformational leaders, Chapter 9) can contribute to empowerment.[11] A good example occurred when a nay-saying union shop steward, doubting General Electric's commitment to changing its corporate culture, explained a recurrent problem with a supplier's component. His manager, sensing he was correct, chartered a plane, and the subordinate left that same night to visit the supplier and solve the problem.[12] It goes without saying that managers have to be tolerant of occasional mistakes from empowered employees.

People who are empowered have a strong sense of self-efficacy (Chapter 2), the feeling that they are capable of doing their jobs well and "making things happen." Empowering lower-level employees can be critical in service organizations, where providing customers with a good initial encounter or correcting any problems that develop can be essential for repeat business. The Nordstrom chain of stores is one firm that is known for empowering sales personnel to make on-the-spot adjustments or search out merchandise at other stores. Customers have even had enthusiastic store personnel change flat tires. This dedication to customer service enables Nordstrom to spend only a fraction of the industry average on advertising.

Under its Power to Please program, staff at Canada's Delta Hotels have the authority to handle special guest requests without seeking manager approval, deal with customer complaints on the spot, and have input on how they fulfill their tasks. For example, staff can handle requests for extra towels or more coffee directly, housekeepers have input on the type of cleaning products the hotel uses, and a front desk staffer can take it upon him- or herself to send up a platter from room service following a guest complaint.[13]

There is growing evidence that empowerment fosters job satisfaction and high performance.[14] However, empowerment does not mean providing employees with a maximum amount of unfettered power. Rather, used properly, empowerment puts power where it is *needed* to make the organization effective. This depends on organizational strategy and customer expectations. The average Taco Bell customer does not expect highly empowered counter personnel who offer to make adjustments to the posted menu—a friendly, fast, efficient encounter will do. On the other hand, the unempowered

Empowerment. Giving people the authority, opportunity, and motivation to take initiative and solve organizational problems.

Delta Hotels focuses on empowerment.

waiter in a fancy restaurant who is fearful of accommodating reasonable adjustments and substitutions can really irritate customers. Speaking generally, service encounters predicated on high volume and low cost need careful engineering. Those predicated on customized, personalized service need more empowered personnel.[15] For an instructive exception, see Applied Focus: *Tim Hortons Franchise Lacks Empowerment*.

You might wonder whether organizational members could have *too much* power. Exhibit 11.2 nicely illustrates the answer. People are empowered, and should exhibit effective performance, when they have sufficient power to carry out their jobs. Above, we mainly contrasted empowerment with situations in which people had inadequate power for effective performance. However, as the exhibit shows, excessive power can lead to abuse and ineffective performance. One is reminded of the recurrent and inappropriate use of government aircraft by political bigwigs as an example. As we will see in the following sections, the fact that people can have too much power does not always inhibit them from seeking it anyway!

EXHIBIT 11.2
Relationship between power and performance.

Source: Whetten, David A.; Cameron, Kim S. *Developing Management Skills*, 3rd ed. © 1995. Reproduced by permission of Pearson Education, Inc., Upper Saddle River, NJ.

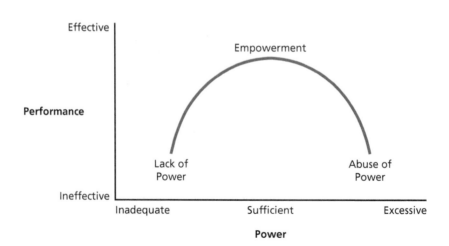

APPLIED FOCUS

Tim Hortons Franchise Lacks Empowerment

Tim Hortons Inc. has squelched what could have become a PR disaster over the Timbit Affair. At the same time, the company has been served a stinging lesson on how following franchise rules too zealously can stifle the ability of front-line workers to keep the customer satisfied. The coffee and doughnut chain, one of the most valued brands in the country, rehired a London, Ont. employee just hours after she was fired for giving away one 16-cent timbit to the restless child of a regular customer.

"When the dust settles, Tim Hortons did absolutely the right thing, which is to reconsider and say, 'if we had to do it over again, we wouldn't do it quite this way,'" said Hugh Christie, a lawyer who heads the labour and employment national group at Gowlings.

Media outlets jumped on the tale of the 27-year-old single mother of four, shunted aside by a Canadian corporate icon. Head office didn't take long to respond. Rather than go on the offensive, Tims ate humble pie. Hours after her firing, Nicole Lilliman was reinstated. But she doesn't want to go back to the same store. Ms. Lilliman will now work at a nearby location, said spokeswoman Rachel Douglas. She will be paid for the missed days. "When something comes out of London and gets this amount of press coverage, it's a learning [experience] for the entire chain," Ms. Douglas said. "The lesson is appropriate ways to treat your staff. Using proper processes . . . and making sure everyone's aware." She stressed that the whole sorry saga was a "mistake that shouldn't have happened," and that franchises set their own policies on freebies.

Events unfolded Monday, when a long-time customer came in with a fussy toddler. Ms. Lilliman, who's worked at the store for three years, spontaneously gave the child a doughnut hole to quiet her. She thought nothing of it, according to the London Free Press, until Wednesday, when she was hauled into the office and told she'd been caught on video giving away free food. The experience "was hell," she told the newspaper. "When I told my daughter I lost my job she started crying. She's only six, and she doesn't know. She said 'we won't have any food any more.'"

The fate of her manager is still being decided. It certainly hit a nerve with the public. *Globe* readers posted more than 800 comments on the story yesterday, making it one of the most-talked about stories in the history of globeandmail.com.

The Timbit Affair offers insights into how much discretion individual employees should have, and how front-line workers are the real faces of the corporate brand. "The best customer service happens when people on the front lines have decision-making power and it's assumed that they can problem-solve on the spot," said Kadi Kaljuste, senior vice-president at consultant firm Hill & Knowlton, who praised Ms. Lilliman for using common sense. Giving employees leeway to figure out solutions isn't a new idea. U.S. fashion retailer Nordstrom Inc. and airline WestJet Airlines Ltd. have both won plaudits for their customer service—and handing that trust to employees is partly why, Ms. Kaljuste says. It's an important reminder of how "the brand values cascade right down to the front line," said Paul Cubbon, marketing instructor at UBC's Sauder School of Business.

So what are policies like at Tims competitors? Dunkin Donuts lets stores set policies on giveaways. Starbucks lets customers try food and drinks.

Influence Tactics—Putting Power to Work

As we discussed earlier, power is the potential to influence others. But exactly how does power result in influence? Research has shown that various **influence tactics** convert power into actual influence. These are specific behaviours that powerholders use to affect others.[16] These tactics include the following:

- Assertiveness—ordering, nagging, setting deadlines, and verbally confrontng;
- Ingratiation—using flattery and acting friendly, polite, or humble;

Influence tactics. Tactics that are used to convert power into actual influence over others.

- Rationality—using logic, reason, planning, and compromise;
- Exchange—doing favours or offering to trade favours;
- Upward appeal—making formal or informal appeals to organizational superiors for intervention; and
- Coalition formation—seeking united support from other organizational members.

What determines which influence tactics you might use? For one thing, your bases of power.[17] Other things being equal, someone with coercive power might gravitate toward assertiveness, someone with referent power might gravitate toward ingratiation, and someone with expert power might try rationality. Of course, rationality or its appearance is a highly prized quality in organizations, and its use is viewed positively by others. Thus, surveys show that people report trying to use rationality very frequently.

As you can guess, the use of influence tactics is also dependent on just whom you are trying to influence—subordinates, peers, or superiors. Subordinates are more likely to be the recipients of assertiveness than peers or superiors. Despite the general popularity of rationality, it is most likely to be directed toward superiors. Exchange, ingratiation, and upward appeal are favoured tactics for influencing both peers and subordinates.[18]

Which influence tactics are most effective? Some of the most interesting research has concerned upward influence attempts directed toward superiors. It shows that, at least for men, using rationality as an influence tactic was associated with receiving better performance evaluations, earning more money, and experiencing less work stress. A particularly ineffective influence style is a "shotgun" style that is high on all tactics with particular emphasis on assertiveness and exchange. In this series of studies, women who used ingratiation as an influence tactic received the highest performance evaluations (from male managers).[19] Another study showed that top managers who used ingratiation with their CEOs were inclined to receive appointments to corporate boards with whom the CEO was connected.[20] Thus, flattery and opinion conformity work even at the very top of organizations!

Who Wants Power?

Who wants power? At first glance, the answer would seem to be everybody. After all, it is both convenient and rewarding to be able to exert influence over others. Power whisks celebrities to the front of movie lines, gets rock stars the best restaurant tables, and enables executives to shape organizations in their own image. Actually, there are considerable individual differences in the extent to which individuals pursue and enjoy power. On television talk shows, we occasionally see celebrities recount considerable embarrassment over the unwarranted power that public recognition brings.

Earlier we indicated that some people consider power a manifestation of evil. This is due, in no small part, to the historic image of power seekers that some psychologists and political scientists have portrayed. This is that power seekers are neurotics who are covering up feelings of inferiority, striving to compensate for childhood deprivation, or substituting power for lack of affection.[21]

There can be little doubt that these characteristics do apply to some power seekers. Underlying this negative image of power seeking is the idea that some power seekers feel weak and resort primarily to coercive power to cover up, compensate for, or substitute for this weakness. Power is sought for its own sake and is used irresponsibly to hurt others. Adolf Hitler comes to mind as an extreme example.

But can one use power responsibly to influence others? Psychologist David McClelland says yes. In Chapter 5, we discussed McClelland's research on need for power (n Pow). You will recall that n Pow is the need to have strong influence over others. This need is a reliable personality characteristic—some people have more n Pow than others.[22] Also, just as many women have high n Pow as men.[23] People who are high in n Pow in its "pure" form conform to the negative stereotype depicted above—they are rude, sexually

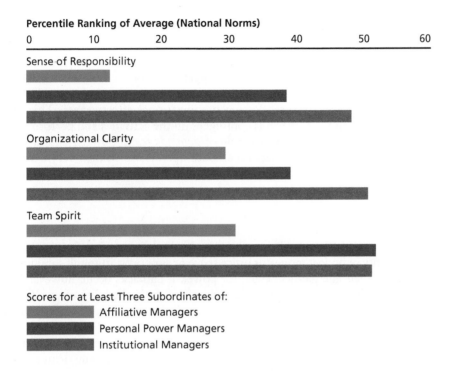

EXHIBIT 11.3
Responses of subordinates of managers with different motive profiles.

Source: McClelland, D.C., & Burnham, D.H. (1976, March/April). Power is the great motivator. *Harvard Business Review*. Copyright © 1976 by the President and Fellows of Harvard College; all rights reserved.

exploitative, abuse alcohol, and show a great concern with status symbols. However, when *n* Pow is responsible and controlled, these negative properties are not observed. Specifically, McClelland argues that the most effective managers

- have high *n* Pow;
- use their power to achieve organizational goals;
- adopt a participative or "coaching" leadership style; and
- are relatively unconcerned with how much others like them.

McClelland calls such managers *institutional managers* because they use their power for the good of the institution rather than for self-aggrandizement. They refrain from coercive leadership but do not play favourites, since they are not worried about being well liked. His research reveals that institutional managers are more effective than *personal power managers,* who use their power for personal gain, and *affiliative managers,* who are more concerned with being liked than with exercising power. Exhibit 11.3 shows that institutional managers are generally superior in giving subordinates a sense of responsibility, clarifying organizational priorities, and instilling team spirit.[24] We can conclude that the need for power can be a useful asset, as long as it is not a neurotic expression of perceived weakness.

Finally, what happens when people want power but cannot get it because they are locked in a low-level job or faced with excessive rules and regulations? People react to such powerlessness by trying to gain control, but if they cannot succeed, they feel helpless and become alienated from their work.[25] This is something that empowerment is designed to prevent.

Controlling Strategic Contingencies— How Subunits Obtain Power

Thus far, we have been concerned with the bases of *individual* power and how individual organizational members obtain influence. In this section, we shift our concern to **subunit power.** Most straightforwardly, the term "subunit" applies to organizational

Subunit power. The degree of power held by various organizational subunits, such as departments.

departments. In some cases, subunits could also refer to particular jobs, such as those held by software engineers or environmental lawyers.

How do organizational subunits acquire power—that is, how do they achieve influence that enables them to grow in size, get a bigger share of the budget, obtain better facilities, and have greater impact on decisions? In short, they control **strategic contingencies**, which are critical factors affecting organizational effectiveness. This means that the work *other* subunits perform is contingent on the activities and performance of a key subunit. Again, we see the critical role of *dependence* in power relationships. If some subunits are dependent on others for smooth operations (or their very existence), they are susceptible to influence. We turn now to the conditions under which subunits can control strategic contingencies.

Strategic contingencies.
Critical factors affecting organizational effectiveness that are controlled by a key subunit.

Scarcity

Differences in subunit power are likely to be magnified when resources become scarce.[26] When there is plenty of budget money or office space or support staff for all subunits, they will seldom waste their energies jockeying for power. If cutbacks occur, however, differences in power will become apparent. For example, well-funded quality-of-worklife programs or organizational development efforts might disappear when economic setbacks occur because the subunits that control them are not essential to the firm's existence.

Subunits tend to acquire power when they are able to *secure* scarce resources that are important to the organization as a whole. One study of a large American state university found that the power of academic departments was associated with their ability to obtain funds through consulting contracts and research grants. This mastery over economic resources was more crucial to their power than was the number of undergraduates taught by the department.[27]

Uncertainty

Organizations detest the unknown. Unanticipated events wreak havoc with financial commitments, long-range plans, and tomorrow's operations. The basic sources of uncertainty exist mainly in the organization's environment—government policies might change, sources of supply and demand might dry up, or the economy might take an unanticipated turn. It stands to reason that the subunits that are most capable of coping with uncertainty will tend to acquire power.[28] In a sense, these subunits are able to protect the others from serious problems. By the same token, uncertainty promotes confusion, which permits *changes* in power priorities as the organizational environment changes. Those functions that can provide the organization with greater control over what it finds problematic and can create more certainty will acquire more power.[29]

Changes in the sources of uncertainty frequently lead to shifts in subunit power. Thus, HR departments gained power when government legislation regarding employment opportunity was first passed, and departments concerned with environmental impact have gained power with the current interest in "green" organizations. Units dealing with business ethics or environmental concerns gain or lose power in response to the latest scandal or the newest piece of legislation involving clean air or water.

Centrality

Other things being equal, subunits whose activities are most central to the work flow of the organization should acquire more power than those whose activities are more peripheral.[30] A subunit's activities can be central in at least three senses. First, it may influence the work of most other subunits. The finance or accounting department is a good example here—its authority to approve expenses and make payments affects every other department in the firm.

Centrality also exists when a subunit has an especially crucial impact on the quantity or quality of the organization's key product or service. This is one reason for the former low power of human resources departments—their activities were then seen as fairly remote from the primary goals of the organization.

Finally, a subunit's activities are more central when their impact is more immediate. As an example, consider a large city government with a fire department, a police department, and a public works department. The impact of a lapse in fire or police services will be felt more immediately than a lapse in street repairs. This gives the former departments more potential for power acquisition.

Substitutability

A subunit will have relatively little power if others inside or outside the organization can perform its activities. If the subunit's staff is non-substitutable, however, it can acquire substantial power.[31] One crucial factor here is the labour market for the specialty performed by the subunit. A change in the labour market can result in a change in the subunit's influence. For example, the market for scientists and engineers is notoriously cyclical. When jobs are plentiful, these professionals command high salaries and high influence in organizations. When jobs are scarce, this power wanes. In the 1990s, there was a shortage of engineers and scientists, with a consequent increase in their bargaining power. Precisely in line with the strategic contingencies idea, this shortage provided real opportunities for properly trained women and members of minorities to move into positions of power from which they were excluded when there were plenty of white male engineers and scientists to go around.[32]

If the labour market is constant, subunits whose staff is highly trained in technical areas tend to be less substitutable than those that involve minimal technical expertise. For example, in a telecommunications company, managers can fill in for striking telephone operators, but not for highly trained IT personnel.

Finally, if work can be contracted out, the power of the subunit that usually performs these activities is reduced. Typical examples include temporary office help, off-premises data entry, and contracted maintenance, laboratory, and security services. The subunits that control these activities often lack power because the threat of "going outside" can counter their influence attempts.

Organizational Politics—Using and Abusing Power

In the previous pages, we have avoided using the terms "politics" or "political" in describing the acquisition and use of power. This is because not all uses of power constitute politics.

The Basics of Organizational Politics

Organizational politics is the pursuit of self-interest within an organization, whether or not this self-interest corresponds to organizational goals.[33] Frequently, politics involves using means of influence that the organization does not sanction or pursuing ends or goals that it does not sanction.[34]

We should make several preliminary points about organizational politics. First, political activity is self-conscious and intentional. This separates politics from ignorance or lack of experience with approved means and ends. Second, we can conceive of politics as either individual activity or subunit activity. Either a person or a whole department could act politically. Finally, it is possible for political activity to have beneficial outcomes for the organization, even though these outcomes are achieved by questionable tactics.

We can explore organizational politics using the means/ends matrix in Exhibit 11.4. It is the association between influence means and influence ends that determines whether activities are political and whether these activities benefit the organization.

Organizational politics. The pursuit of self-interest in an organization, whether or not this self-interest corresponds to organizational goals.

EXHIBIT 11.4

The dimensions of
organizational politics.

Source: From Mayes, B.T., & Allen,
R.T. (1977). Toward a definition of
organizational politics, *Academy of
Management Review, 2*, 672-678,
p. 675. Reprinted by permission.

	Influence Ends	
Influence Means	Organizationally Sanctioned	Not Sanctioned by Organization
Organizationally Sanctioned	Nonpolitical Job Behaviour **I**	**II** Organizationally Dysfunctional Political Behaviour
Not Sanctioned by Organization	Political Behaviour Potentially Functional to the Organization **III**	**IV** Organizationally Dysfunctional Political Behaviour

- *I. Sanctioned means/sanctioned ends.* Here, power is used routinely to pursue agreed-on goals. Familiar, accepted means of influence are employed to achieve sanctioned outcomes. For example, a manager agrees to recommend a raise for an employee if she increases her net sales by 30 percent in the next six months. There is nothing political about this.

- *II. Sanctioned means/not-sanctioned ends.* In this case, acceptable means of influence are abused to pursue goals that the organization does not approve of. For instance, a head nurse agrees to assign a subordinate nurse to a more favourable job if the nurse agrees not to report the superior for stealing medical supplies. While job assignment is often a sanctioned means of influence, covering up theft is not a sanctioned end. This is dysfunctional political behaviour.

- *III. Not-sanctioned means/sanctioned ends.* Here, ends that are useful for the organization are pursued through questionable means. For example, although officials of the Salt Lake City Olympic Committee were pursuing a sanctioned end—the 2002 Winter Olympics—the use of bribery and vote-buying as a means of influence was not sanctioned by the committee.

- *IV. Not-sanctioned means/not-sanctioned ends.* This quadrant may exemplify the most flagrant abuse of power, since disapproved tactics are used to pursue disapproved outcomes. For example, to increase his personal power, the head of an already overstaffed legal department wishes to increase its size. He intends to hire several of his friends in the process. To do this, he falsifies workload documents and promises special service to the accounting department in exchange for the support of its manager.

We have all seen cases in which politics have been played out publicly to "teach someone a lesson." More frequently, though, politicians conceal their activities with a "cover story" or "smoke screen" to make them appear legitimate.[35] Such a tactic will increase the odds of success and avoid punishment from superiors. A common strategy is to cover non-sanctioned means and ends with a cloak of rationality.

Do political activities occur under particular conditions or in particular locations in organizations? Research suggests the following:[36]

- Managers report that most political manoeuvring occurs at middle and upper management levels rather than at lower levels.

- Some subunits are more prone to politicking than others. Clear goals and routine tasks (e.g., production) might provoke less political activity than vague goals and complex tasks (e.g., research and development).

- Some issues are more likely than others to stimulate political activity. Budget allocation, reorganization, and personnel changes are likely to be the subjects of politicking. Setting performance standards and purchasing equipment are not.

- In general, scarce resources, uncertainty, and important issues provoke political behaviour.

Highly political climates result in lowered job satisfaction, lowered feelings of organizational support, and increased turnover intentions.[37] When it comes to performance, evidence indicates that politics take a toll on older workers but not on younger workers, perhaps due to stress factors.[38]

At Enron, the upper management echelons were steeped in organizational politics. Jeff Skilling's strongest rival at the firm was Rebecca Mark, another hotshot brought in by Ken Lay, who became known as one of America's most powerful women in business. Skilling used political tactics to outmanoeuvre and undercut Mark at every turn. In the end, he received the ultimate reward when he was named as Lay's replacement.

The Facets of Political Skill

It is one thing to engage in organizational politics, but it is another thing to do it skillfully, because pursuing self-interest can encounter resistance. Gerald Ferris and colleagues define **political skill** as "the ability to understand others at work and to use that knowledge to influence others to act in ways that enhance one's personal or organizational objectives."[39] Notice that this definition includes two aspects—comprehending others and translating this comprehension into influence. Research by Ferris and colleagues indicates that there are four facets to political skill:

- *Social astuteness.* Good politicians are careful observers who are tuned in to others' needs and motives. They can "read" people and thus possess emotional intelligence, as discussed in Chapter 5. They are active self-monitors (Chapter 2) who know how to present themselves to others.

- *Interpersonal influence.* The politically skilled have a convincing and persuasive interpersonal style but employ it flexibly to meet the needs of the situation. They put others at ease.

- *Apparent sincerity.* Influence attempts will be seen as manipulative unless they are accompanied by sincerity. A good politician comes across as genuine and exhibits high integrity.

- *Networking ability.* **Networking** involves establishing good relations with key organizational members or outsiders to accomplish one's goals. Networks provide a channel for favours to be asked for and given. An effective network enhances one's organizational reputation, thus aiding influence attempts.

Political skill, as measured by these four facets, is positively related to rated job performance. Also, more skilled politicians are less inclined to feel stressed in response to role conflict, evidently due to better coping.[40] If you would like to assess your own political skill, complete the Experiential Exercise *Political Skill Inventory* at the end of the chapter.

Because networking is such a critical aspect of power acquisition and political success, let's examine it in more detail. In essence, networking involves developing informal social contacts to enlist the cooperation of others when their support is necessary. Upper-level managers often establish very large political networks both inside and outside the organization (Exhibit 11.5). Lower-level organizational members might have a more restricted network, but the principle remains the same. One study of general managers found that they used face-to-face encounters and informal small talk to bolster their political networks. They also did favours for others and stressed the obligations of others to them. Personnel were hired, fired, and transferred to bolster a workable network, and the managers forged connections among network members to create a climate conducive to goal accomplishment.[41]

Monica Forret and Thomas Dougherty determined that there are several aspects to networking:[42]

- Maintaining contacts—giving out business cards, sending gifts and thank you notes
- Socializing—playing golf, participating in company sports leagues, having drinks after work

Political skill. The ability to understand others at work and to use that knowledge to influence others to act in ways that enhance one's personal or organizational objectives.

Networking. Establishing good relations with key organizational members and outsiders to accomplish one's goals.

EXHIBIT 11.5
A typical upper-level manager's external network.

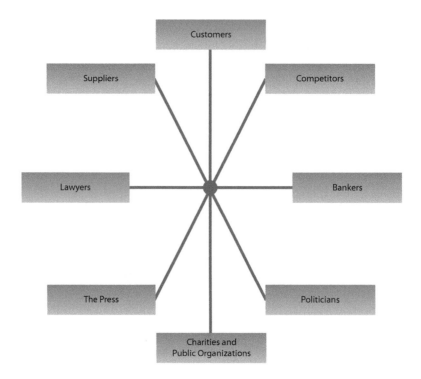

- Engaging in professional activities—giving a workshop, accepting a speaking engagement, teaching, publishing, appearing in the media
- Participating in community activities—being active in civic groups, clubs, and church events
- Increasing internal visibility—accepting high-profile work projects, sitting on important committees and task forces

The authors found that those high in self-esteem and extraversion (Chapter 2) were more likely to engage in networking behaviours. They also found that engaging in professional activities and increasing internal visibility were most associated with career success (i.e., compensation, promotions, perceived success).[43] However, this

Networking is an effective way to develop informal social contacts.

applied only to men, despite the fact that men and women engaged in networking equally, except for socializing, where men perhaps had the edge. Forret and Dougherty make the important point that networking has increased in importance as people become more self-reliant and less reliant on organizations to plot their career futures.

Being central in a large network provides power because you have access to considerable resources, such as knowledge. This is especially true if the network is diverse (the people you know don't know each other) and consists of those who themselves hold power.[44] One study in a leading bank revealed that those who were promoted most quickly to senior vice-president had very different networks from regular vice-presidents. Their networks bridged the bank, cutting across different divisions and regions and including people of diverse tenure and functional expertise. In turn, these networks were used to make up for the limitations of formal organizational structure.[45]

Machiavellianism—The Harder Side of Politics

Have you ever known people who had the following characteristics?

- Act very much in their own self-interest, even at the expense of others.
- Cool and calculating, especially when others get emotional.
- High self-esteem and self-confidence.
- Form alliances with powerful people to achieve their goals.

These are some of the characteristics of individuals who are high on a personality dimension known as Machiavellianism. **Machiavellianism** is a set of cynical beliefs about human nature, morality, and the permissibility of using various tactics to achieve one's ends. The term derives from the 16th-century writings of the Italian civil servant Niccolo Machiavelli, who was concerned with how people achieve social influence and the ability to manipulate others. Machiavellianism is a stable personality trait (Chapter 2).

Compared with "low Machs," "high Machs" are more likely to advocate the use of lying and deceit to achieve desired goals and to argue that morality can be compromised to fit the situation in question. In addition, high Machs assume that many people are excessively gullible and do not know what is best for themselves. Thus, in interpersonal situations, the high Mach acts in an exceedingly practical manner, assuming that the ends justify the means. Not surprisingly, high Machs tend to be convincing liars and good at "psyching out" competitors by creating diversions. Furthermore, they are quite willing to form coalitions with others to outmanoeuvre or defeat people who get in their way.[46] In summary, high Machs are likely to be enthusiastic organizational politicians.

Do high Machs feel guilty about the social tactics they utilize? The answer would appear to be no. Since they are cool and calculating rather than emotional, high Machs seem to be able to insulate themselves from the negative social consequences of their tactics. You might wonder how successful high Machs are at manipulating others and why others would tolerate such manipulation. After all, the characteristics we detail above are hardly likely to win a popularity contest, and you might assume that targets of a high Mach's tactics would vigorously resist manipulation by such a person. Again, the high Mach's rationality seems to provide an answer. Put simply, it appears that high Machs are able to accurately identify situations in which their favoured tactics will work. Such situations have the following characteristics:

- The high Mach can deal face to face with those he or she is trying to influence.
- The interaction occurs under fairly emotional circumstances.
- The situation is fairly unstructured, with few guidelines for appropriate forms of interaction.[47]

In combination, these characteristics reveal a situation in which the high Mach can use his or her tactics because emotion distracts others. High Machs, by remaining calm and rational, can create a social structure that facilitates their personal goals at the expense of

Machiavellianism. A set of cynical beliefs about human nature, morality, and the permissibility of using various tactics to achieve one's ends.

others. Thus, high Machs are especially skilled at getting their way when power vacuums or novel situations confront a group, department, or organization. For example, imagine a small family business whose president dies suddenly without any plans for succession. In this power vacuum, a high Mach vice-president would have an excellent chance of manipulating the choice of a new president. The situation is novel, emotion provoking, and unstructured, since no guidelines for succession exist. In addition, the decision-making body would be small enough for face-to-face influence and coalition formation.

Defensiveness—Reactive Politics

So far, our discussion of politics has focused mainly on the proactive pursuit of self-interest. Another form of political behaviour, however, is more reactive in that it concerns the defence or protection of self-interest. The goal here is to reduce threats to one's own power by avoiding actions that do not suit one's own political agenda or avoiding blame for events that might threaten one's political capital. Blake Ashforth and Ray Lee describe some tactics for doing both.[48]

Astute organizational politicians are aware that sometimes the best action to take is no action at all. A number of defensive behaviours can accomplish this mission:

- *Stalling.* Moving slowly when someone asks for your cooperation is the most obvious way of avoiding taking action without actually saying no. With time, the demand for cooperation may disappear. The civil service bureaucracy is infamous for stalling on demands from acting governments.

- *Overconforming.* Sticking to the strict letter of your job description or to organizational regulations is a common way to avoid action. Of course, the overconformer may be happy to circumvent his job description or organizational regulations when it suits his political agenda.

- *Buck passing.* Having someone else take action is an effective way to avoid doing it yourself. Buck passing is especially dysfunctional politics when the politician is best equipped to do the job but worries that it might not turn out successfully ("Let's let the design department get stuck with this turkey.").

Another set of defensive behaviours is oriented around the motto "If you can't avoid action, avoid blame for its consequences." These behaviours include:

- *Buffing.* Buffing is the tactic of carefully documenting information showing that an appropriate course of action was followed. Getting "sign offs," authorizations, and so on are examples. Buffing can be sensible behaviour, but it takes on political overtones when doing the documenting becomes more important than making a good decision. It is clearly dysfunctional politics if it takes the form of fabricating documentation.

- *Scapegoating.* Blaming others when things go wrong is classic political behaviour. Scapegoating works best when you have some power behind you. One study found that when organizations performed poorly, more-powerful CEOs stayed in office and the scapegoated managers below them were replaced. Less powerful CEOs were dismissed.[49]

The point of discussing these defensive political tactics is not to teach you how to do them. Rather, it is to ensure that you recognize them as political behaviour. Many of the tactics are quite mundane. However, viewing them in context again illustrates the sometimes subtle ways that individuals pursue political self-interest in organizations. Politics, like power, is natural in all organizations. Whether or not politics is functional for the organization depends on the ends that are pursued and the influence means that are used.

Ethics in Organizations

In 2008, Linda Keen, the president of the Canadian Nuclear Safety Commission, was dismissed from her post by the Conservative government, citing her "lack of leadership." The commission headed by Keen had ordered a shutdown of the 50-year-old

Chalk River nuclear reactor because of safety concerns. The reactor, which generates 40 percent to 60 percent of the world's vital medical isotopes used in nuclear medicine, was restarted following an emergency measure in the House of Commons. Prime Minster Stephen Harper had called Keen a partisan because she was appointed by the Liberal government. In the following months, heavy water leaks occurred, which eventually forced the shutdown of the reactor.[50] What are the ethics of this story?

For our purposes, **ethics** can be defined as systematic thinking about the moral consequences of decisions. Moral consequences can be framed in terms of the potential for harm to any stakeholders in the decision. **Stakeholders** are simply people inside or outside the organization who have the potential to be affected by the decision. This could range from the decision makers themselves to "innocent bystanders."[51] Ethics is a major branch of philosophy, and we will not attempt to describe the various schools of ethical thought. Instead, we will focus on the kinds of ethical issues that organizational decision makers face and some of the factors that stimulate unethical decisions.

Over the years, researchers have conducted a number of surveys to determine managers' views about the ethics of decision making in business.[52] Some striking similarities across studies provide an interesting picture of the popular psychology of business ethics. First, far from being shy about the subject, a large majority agree that unethical practices occur in business. Furthermore, a substantial proportion (between 40 percent and 90 percent according to the particular study) report that they have been pressured to compromise their own ethical standards when making organizational decisions. Finally, in line with the concept of self-serving attributions, managers invariably tend to see themselves as having higher ethical standards than their peers and sometimes their superiors.[53] The unpleasant picture emerging here is one in which unethical behaviour tempts managers, who sometimes succumb but feel that they still do better than others on moral grounds. This situation is not helped by the fact that top managers tend to see their organizations as being more ethical than do those lower in the hierarchy.[54] This is not a recipe for ethical vigilance.

In case you think that students are purer than organizational decision makers, think again. Research is fairly consistent in showing that business students have looser ethical standards than practising managers, at least when responding to written descriptions of ethical issues.[55] Among business students, undergraduates have been found to be more ethical than MBA students.[56] In fact, in a large survey, 56 percent of MBA students admitted to cheating during the past year, compared with 47 percent of non-business grad students.[57] Research results are mixed in terms of whether women are more morally aware than men, but on the whole it appears that women act more ethically.[58]

Ethics. Systematic thinking about the moral consequences of decisions.

Stakeholders. People inside or outside of an organization who have the potential to be affected by organizational decisions.

The Nature of Ethical Dilemmas

What are the kinds of ethical dilemmas that most frequently face organizational decision makers? Exhibit 11.6 shows the results of a Conference Board study of corporate codes of business ethics. The figures indicate the extent to which various issues are covered for the firms' own employees, its suppliers, and its joint venture partners. As can be seen, contractual and legally mandated issues find the most consensus (e.g., bribery, conflict of interest, proprietary information). The important but more subjective matters at the bottom of the list are less likely to be addressed.

Ethical issues are often occupationally specific. As an example, let's consider the ethical dilemmas faced by the various subspecialties of marketing.[59] Among market researchers, telling research participants the true sponsor of the research has been an ongoing topic of debate. Among purchasing managers, where to draw the line in accepting favours (e.g., sports tickets) from vendors poses ethical problems. Among product managers, issues of planned obsolescence, unnecessary packaging, and differential pricing (e.g., charging more in the inner city) raise ethical concerns. When it comes to salespeople, how far to go in enticing customers and how to be fair in expense

EXHIBIT 11.6
Issues covered
in corporate codes
of ethics.

Source: *Global corporate ethics
practices: A developing consensus*
(Report Number: R-1243-99-RR),
Ronald E. Berenbeim, The Conference
Board, Inc. www.conference-board.org.

	Employees	Suppliers/ Vendors	Joint Venture Partners
Bribery/improper payments	92%	45%	27%
Conflict of interest	92	37	26
Security of proprietary information	92	30	25
Receiving gifts	90	46	25
Discrimination/equal opportunity	86	25	22
Giving gifts	84	48	26
Environment	78	27	24
Sexual harassment	78	22	17
Antitrust	76	27	23
Workplace safety	71	20	18
Political activities	71	11	13
Community relations	62	8	13
Confidentiality of personal information	52	11	11
Human rights	50	14	17
Employee privacy	48	8	10
Whistle-blowing	46	10	10
Substance abuse	42	12	12
Nepotism	28	5	8
Child labour	15	8	7

account use have been prominent ethical themes. Finally, in advertising, the range of ethical issues can (and does) fill books. Consider, for example, the decision to use sexual allure to sell a product.

In contrast to these occupationally specific ethical dilemmas, what are the common themes that run through ethical issues that managers face? An in-depth interview study of an occupationally diverse group of managers discovered seven themes that defined their moral standards for decision making.[60] Here are those themes and some typical examples of associated ethical behaviour:

- *Honest communication.* Evaluate subordinates candidly; advertise and label honestly; do not slant proposals to senior management.

- *Fair treatment.* Pay equitably; respect the sealed bid process; do not give preference to suppliers with political connections; do not use lower-level people as scapegoats.

- *Special consideration.* The "fair treatment" standard can be modified for special cases, such as helping out a long-time employee, giving preference to hiring the disabled, or giving business to a loyal but troubled supplier.

- *Fair competition.* Avoid bribes and kickbacks to obtain business; do not fix prices with competitors.

- *Responsibility to organization.* Act for the good of the organization as a whole, not for self-interest; avoid waste and inefficiency.

- *Corporate social responsibility.* Do not pollute; think about the community impact of plant closures; show concern for employee health and safety.

- *Respect for law.* Legally avoid taxes, do not evade them; do not bribe government inspectors; follow the letter and spirit of labour laws.

Before continuing, have a look at the You Be the Manager feature.

YOU BE THE MANAGER

Plagiarism at Raytheon

What would you do if you found out that the CEO of a big company had passed off someone else's work as his own? This was the question faced by Carl Durrenberger, an engineer and market developer at Hewlett-Packard in San Diego. When he was cleaning out his desk he found a copy of *The Unwritten Laws of Engineering*, written by California engineering professor W.J. King and published by the American Society of Mechanical Engineers in 1944. It had been a present from his boss several years ago, and he read a couple of the rules, amused at the outdated language.

Imagine Durrenberger's surprise when he read some of the rules again just a few days later in a news article originally published in *USA Today* about the highly successful CEO of the Raytheon Company, a defence contractor based near Boston with annual sales of US$22 billion. The article referred to another publication, *Swanson's Unwritten Rules of Management*, by Raytheon's CEO, William Swanson. According to Swanson, his book was a compilation of management tips he had come up with over the years. A few years ago, because the maxims had become very popular with corporate executives, Raytheon published the rules in a booklet.

Durrenberger grabbed his copy of King's book and noted the following similarities between Swanson's rules and King's book.

Swanson: "Don't get excited in engineering emergencies: Keep your feet on the ground."
King: "Do not get excited in engineering emergencies—keep your feet on the ground."
Swanson: "Cultivate the habit of making quick, clean-cut decisions."
King: "Cultivate the habit of making brisk, clean-cut decisions."

Durrenberger initially gave Swanson the benefit of the doubt, thinking that perhaps the writer of the USA Today article had forgotten to credit King. He emailed the writer to point out the omission. He then did a bit of research on the internet and discovered that the problem lay with Swanson: He had been passing the rules off as his own for years. When Durrenberger hadn't heard back from USA Today, he decided to publish his email to the newspaper on his blog. He titled the entry "Bill Swanson of Raytheon is a Plagiarist." A New York Times reporter read it, and soon the story became nationwide news.

At first, Swanson and Raytheon claimed that the lack of attribution of King's book was an oversight on

A question of plagiarism lands Raytheon's CEO in an embarrassing situation.

the part of Swanson's staff. But when it appeared that this explanation would not satisfy the public, Swanson finally accepted personal responsibility for the omission. During Raytheon's annual meeting, he apologized to the company's board, its shareholders, its employees, and "to those whose material I wish I had treated with greater care."

QUESTIONS

1. What is the nature of Swanson's breach of ethics? Suggest some possible causes that could explain Swanson's plagiarism.

2. Prior to the scandal, Swanson was regarded as a very successful CEO and had received a large raise based on Raytheon's strong financial performance. Who are the stakeholders affected by Swanson's actions? Do you believe that Swanson should be fired for his indiscretion? How does it compare to student plagiarism?

To find out how Raytheon's board reacted, see The Manager's Notebook at the end of the chapter.

Sources: Excerpted with editing from Darce, K. (2006, May 13). How, why a blogger calls CEO a plagiarist. *San Diego Union-Tribune*, H1; Marquez, J. (2006, May 22). Sanctions on Raytheon CEO deemed fitting. *Workforce Management, 85*, 8 (Treviño and Sonnenfeld quotes—Manager's Notebook); Cullen, L.T. (2006, May 15). Rule No. 1: Don't copy. *Time, 167,* 41 (Wicks quote—Manager's Notebook); Weisman, R. (2006, March 16). Raytheon chief's pay jumps 25.5 percent to over $7M. *Boston Globe*, A1.

Causes of Unethical Behaviour

What are the causes of unethical behaviour? Knowing the answer to this question is important so that you can anticipate the circumstances that warrant special vigilance.

Knowing the causes of unethical behaviour can aid in its prevention. Because the topic is sensitive, you should appreciate that this is not the easiest area to research. The major evidence comes from surveys of executive opinion, case studies of prominent ethical failures, business game simulations, and responses to written scenarios involving ethical dilemmas.

Gain. Although the point might seem mundane, it is critical to recognize the role of temptation in unethical activity. The anticipation of healthy reinforcement for following an unethical course of action, especially if no punishment is expected, should promote unethical decisions.[61] Consider Dennis Levine, the Drexel Burnham Lambert investment banker who was convicted of insider trading in one of Wall Street's biggest scandals.

> *It was just so easy. In seven years I built $39,750 into $11.5 million, and all it took was a 20-second phone call to my offshore bank a couple of times a month—maybe 200 calls total. My account was growing at 125% a year, compounded. Believe me, I felt a rush when I would check the price of one of my stocks on the office Quotron and learn I'd just made several hundred thousand dollars. I was confident that the elaborate veils of secrecy I had created—plus overseas bank-privacy laws—would protect me.*[62]

A slightly more subtle example of the role of gain can be seen in compensation systems designed around very high bonuses. Such systems have often been implicated in ethically questionable behaviour, as ethics are sacrificed to boost income.

Role Conflict. Many ethical dilemmas are actually forms of role conflict (Chapter 7) that get resolved in an unethical way. For example, consider the ethical theme of corporate social responsibility we listed above. Here, an executive's role as custodian of the environment (do not pollute) might be at odds with his or her role as a community employer (do not close the plant that pollutes).

A very common form of role conflict that provokes unethical behaviour occurs when our "bureaucratic" role as an organizational employee is at odds with our role as the member of a profession.[63] For example, engineers who in their professional role opposed the fatal launch of the space shuttle *Challenger* due to cold weather were pressured to put on their bureaucratic "manager's hats" and agree to the launch. Both the insurance and brokerage businesses have been rocked by similar ethics problems. Agents and brokers report being pressured as employees to push products that are not in the best interests of their clients. Frequently, reward systems (i.e., the commission structure) heighten the conflict, which then becomes a conflict of interest between self and client.

Competition. Stiff competition for scarce resources can stimulate unethical behaviour. This has been observed in both business game simulations and industry studies of illegal acts, in which trade offences, such as price fixing and monopoly violations, have been shown to increase with industry decline.[64] For example, observers cite a crowded and mature market as one factor prompting price fixing violations in the folding-carton packaging industry.[65] We should note one exception to the "competition stresses ethics" thesis. In cases in which essentially *no* competition exists, there is also a strong temptation to make unethical decisions. This is because the opportunity to make large gains is not offset by market checks and balances. Prominent examples have occurred in the defence industry, in which monopoly contracts to produce military hardware have been accompanied by some remarkable examples of overcharging taxpayers.

Personality. Are there certain types of personalities that are more prone to unethical decisions? In fact, the cynical and those with external locus of control (Chapter 2) are less tuned in to ethical matters.[66] Also, people with strong economic values (Chapter 4) are more likely to behave unethically than those with weaker economic values.[67] Finally, people with a high need for personal power (especially Machiavellians) may be prone to make unethical decisions, using this power to further self-interest rather than for the good of the organization as a whole.

More broadly, there are marked individual differences in the degree of sophistication that people use in thinking about moral issues.[68] Some people are morally disengaged, rejecting responsibility for their actions and using euphemistic labelling to obscure moral issues.[69] For example, a broken political promise might be described as a "non-core promise" to deflect censure. Other people are morally attentive, spotting moral issues and thinking about moral matters.[70] Research shows that less disengagement and more attentiveness is associated with more ethical behaviour.

Remember that we have a tendency to exaggerate the role of dispositional factors, such as personality, in explaining the behaviour of others (Chapter 3). Thus, when we see unethical behaviour, we should look at situational factors, such as competition and the organization's culture, as well as the personality of the actor.

Organizational and Industry Culture. Bart Victor and John Cullen found that there were considerable differences in ethical values across the organizations they studied.[71] These differences involved factors such as consideration for employees, respect for the law, and respect for organizational rules. In addition, there were differences across groups within these organizations. This suggests that aspects of an organization's culture (and its subcultures) can influence ethics.[72] This corresponds to the repeated finding in executive surveys that the conduct of peers and superiors is viewed as strongly influencing ethical behaviour, for good or for bad. The presence of role models helps to shape the culture (Chapter 8). If these models are actually rewarded for unethical behaviour, rather than punished, the development of an unethical culture is likely. In fact, firms convicted of illegal acts often tend to be repeat offenders.[73] Remember, no one thing creates a "culture of corruption" in organizations. Rather, it is often a combination of factors, such as evaluating managers solely "by the numbers," denying responsibility, denying injury to others, and teaching (low power) newcomers corrupt practices that lead to unethical corporate cultures.[74]

It has become clear that the illegal activities at Enron and Andersen cannot simply be attributed to a few bad apples. Report after report has underlined the culture of greed at these firms, which encouraged cutthroat politics, intimidation, and an almost exclusive focus on positive financial results. Since managers at these firms were excessively rewarded for such behaviours over the years, is it any wonder that things spun out of control?

Observers of the folding-carton price-fixing scandal we mentioned above noted how top managers frequently seemed out of touch with the difficulty of selling boxes in a mature, crowded market. They put in place goal setting and reward systems (e.g., commission forming 60 percent of income), systems that are much more appropriate for products on a growth cycle, that almost guaranteed unethical decisions.[75] In fact, research shows that upper-level managers generally tend to be naïve about the extent of ethical lapses in those below them. This can easily contribute to a success-at-any-cost culture.[76]

Finally, a consideration of culture suggests the conditions under which corporate codes of ethics might actually have an impact on decision making. If such codes are specific, tied to the actual business being done, and correspond to the reward system, they should bolster an ethical culture. If vague codes that do not correspond to other cultural elements exist, the negative symbolism might actually damage the ethical culture.

Whistle-blowing

In spite of the catalogue of causes of unethical behaviour discussed above, individuals occasionally step forward and "blow the whistle" on unethical actions. For instance, former tobacco executive Dr. Jeffrey Wigand (portrayed in the movie *The Insider*) leaked evidence to *60 Minutes* that consumers had been misled about the addictiveness of nicotine for many years. Similarly, Spc. Joseph Darby leaked photos showing abuse of prisoners at Iraq's Abu Ghraib prison.

Whistle-blowing. Disclosure of illegitimate practices by a current or former organizational member to some person or organization that may be able to take action to correct these practices.

Whistle-blowing occurs when a current or former organizational member discloses illegitimate practices to some person or organization that may be able to take action to correct these practices.[77] Thus, the whistle may be blown either inside or outside of the offending organization, depending on the circumstances. The courage of insiders to call attention to organizational misdoing is especially important in large contemporary organizations, because their very complexity often allows for such misdoing to be disguised from outsiders. Also, given pervasive conflicts of interest, there is no guarantee that external watchdogs (Arthur Andersen in the case of Enron) will do the job.[78] Most organizations seem to rely on vague open door policies rather than having specific channels and procedures for whistle-blowers to follow (see Exhibit 11.6). This is not the best way to encourage principled dissent.

Not everyone at Enron stood idly by while fraud unfolded around them. Sherron Watkins, a vice-president with a master's degree in accounting, courageously spoke out against the fraudulent accounting practices and notified Ken Lay. Watkins's testimony at the hearings into the scandal also provided crucial information as to the breadth and depth of the problems at Enron. At telecommunications giant WorldCom, Cynthia Cooper, an internal auditor, discovered fraudulent bookkeeping entries. Cooper discussed her findings with the company's controller and with the CFO, but was told not to worry about it and to stop her review. Instead, she immediately went over her boss's head and called the board chair's audit committee. Two weeks later, WorldCom disclosed its misstatements, leading to the largest bankruptcy in American history. In the end, both women were singled out for their courage to speak up under conditions of intense pressure to remain silent. For their actions, Sherron Watkins and Cynthia Cooper, along with whistle-blower Coleen Rowley of the FBI, were named *Time*'s Persons of the Year.[79]

Sexual Harassment—When Power and Ethics Collide

As indicated in Exhibit 11.6, 78 percent of the codes of ethics examined by the Conference Board mentioned sexual harassment. In recent years, a number of high-profile sexual harassment cases have made news headlines and brought increased attention to this problem. In addition to numerous cases reported in the American and Canadian military, many organizations, including Mitsubishi, Astra, Sears, and Del Laboratories, have found themselves involved in costly litigation cases.[80] The failure of these organizations to effectively respond to charges of sexual harassment has cost them millions of dollars in settlements as well as lower productivity, increased absenteeism, and turnover. As well, the effects on employees can include decreased job satisfaction and organizational commitment as well as reduced psychological and physical well-being.[81]

The following is a fairly comprehensive definition of sexual harassment:

The EEOC [Equal Employment Opportunity Commission] regulatory guidelines state that unwelcome sexual advances, requests for sexual favours, and other verbal or physical conduct of a sexual nature constitute sexual harassment when submission to requests for sexual favours is made explicitly or implicitly a term or condition of employment; submission to or rejection of such requests is used as a basis for employment decisions; or such conduct unreasonably interferes with work performance or creates an intimidating, hostile, or offensive work environment. On the basis of these guidelines, current legal frameworks generally support two causes of action that claimants may state: coercion of sexual cooperation by threat of job-related consequences (quid pro quo harassment) and unwanted and offensive sex-related verbal or physical conduct, even absent any job-related threat (hostile work environment).[82]

Sexual harassment is a form of unethical behaviour that stems, in part, from the abuse of power and the perpetuation of a gender power imbalance. Managers who use their position, reward, or coercive power to request sexual favours or demonstrate verbal or physical conduct of a sexual nature as a condition of employment or as a basis for employment decisions toward those in less powerful positions are abusing their power and acting in an unethical manner. While the most severe forms of sexual harassment are committed by supervisors, the most frequent perpetrators are actually co-workers. Although co-workers do not necessarily have the same formal power bases as supervisors, power differences often exist among co-workers and can also play a role in co-worker sexual harassment. Whether the harasser is a supervisor or a co-worker, he or she is likely to be more powerful than the person being harassed,[83] and the most vulnerable victims are those who cannot afford to lose their jobs.[84] Clients and customers can also engage in harassment, as seen in Research Focus: *Who Gets Sexually Harassed?*

Sexual harassment is also prevalent in hostile work environments that perpetuate the societal power imbalance between men and women. For example, the higher incidences of sexual harassment reported in the military are believed to be partly a function of the rigid hierarchy and power differentials in the organizational structure.[85] Incidents of harassment and organizational inaction to complaints of harassment are also more likely in male-dominated industries and organizations in which men attempt to maintain their dominance relative to women.[86]

RESEARCH FOCUS

Who Gets Sexually Harassed?

Research shows that women are more likely than men to be sexually harassed. But what are the reasons that some women are harassed and others are not? Noting that most research on the topic has dealt with harassers from inside organizations (mostly peers and bosses), Hilary Gettman and Michele Gelfand chose to study sexual harassment stemming from clients and customers. Many service jobs are performed by women, who are required to spend virtually their entire workday with customers. Other jobs (e.g., sales rep) require the development of strong client relationships. In a web-based survey of professional women, 86 percent reported having experienced sexist hostility, 40 percent reported unwanted sexual attention, and 8 percent reported sexual coercion. They found that harassment increased when the proportion of men in the client base increased and when the clients were perceived as holding at lot of power

(e.g., were very important to company business). They also found that minority women were more likely to be harassed. Harassment in turn led to job dissatisfaction, health complaints, psychological distress, and turnover intentions.

Jennifer Berdahl found that harassment was more likely to be experienced by women who exhibited traditionally masculine personality traits (such as independence, assertiveness, and dominance). In other words, the motive was punishment for gender role "deviance" rather than sexual desire. In general, women in male-dominated organizations were more likely to be harassed, and those with masculine personality traits received the most harassment.

Source: Gettman, H.J., & Gelfand, M.J. (2007). When the customer shouldn't be king: Antecedents and consequences of sexual harassment by clients and customers. *Journal of Applied Psychology, 92*, 757–770; Berdahl, J.L. (2007). The sexual harassment of uppity women. *Journal of Applied Psychology, 92*, 425–437.

Unfortunately, many organizations are slow to react to complaints of sexual harassment. This phenomenon has been labelled the "deaf ear syndrome," which refers to the "inaction or complacency of organizations in the face of charges of sexual harassment."[87] A review found three main reasons why organizations fail to respond: inadequate organizational policies and procedures for managing harassment complaints; defensive managerial reactions; and organizational features that contribute to inertial tendencies (e.g., international companies in the United States have problems managing sexual harassment).[88]

Organizations can effectively deal with allegations of sexual harassment and increase their responsiveness by taking a number of important measures. Ellen Peirce, Carol Smolinski, and Benson Rosen offer the following recommendations:

- *Examine the characteristics of deaf ear organizations.* Managers should examine their own organizations to determine if they have any of the characteristics that would make them susceptible to the deaf ear syndrome.

- *Foster management support and education.* Sexual harassment training programs are necessary to educate managers on how to respond to complaints in a sensitive and respectful manner.

- *Stay vigilant.* Managers must monitor the work environment and remove displays of a sexual nature and factors that can contribute to a hostile work environment.

- *Take immediate action.* Failure to act is likely to result in negative consequences for the organization and the victims of sexual harassment. Organizations considered to be the best places for women to work are known for their swift action and severe handling of harassers.

- *Create a state-of-the-art policy.* Sexual harassment policies and procedures need to clearly define what constitutes harassment and the sanctions that will be brought to bear on those found guilty of it.

- *Establish clear reporting procedures.* User-friendly policies need to be designed so that there are clear procedures for filing complaints and mechanisms in place for the impartial investigation of complaints. The privacy of those involved must also be protected.[89]

In general, organizations that are responsive to complaints of sexual harassment have top management commitment, provide comprehensive education programs, continuously monitor the work environment, respond to complaints in a thorough and timely manner, and have clear policies and reporting procedures.[90] An example is DuPont, which has developed a sexual harassment awareness program called A Matter of Respect. It includes interactive training programs, peer-level facilitators who are trained to meet with victims or potential victims, and a 24-hour hotline. As the company has become more international, so has its training on sexual harassment, which is now provided in Japan, China, Mexico, and Puerto Rico.[91]

Employing Ethical Guidelines

A few simple guidelines, regularly used, should help in the ethical screening of decisions. The point is not to paralyze your decision making but to get you to think seriously about the moral implications of your decisions before you make them.[92]

- Identify the stakeholders that will be affected by any decision.
- Identify the costs and benefits of various decision alternatives to these stakeholders.
- Consider the relevant moral expectations that surround a particular decision. These might stem from professional norms, laws, organizational ethics codes, and principles such as honest communication and fair treatment.

- Be familiar with the common ethical dilemmas that decision makers face in your specific organizational role or profession.
- Discuss ethical matters with decision stakeholders and others. Do not think ethics without talking about ethics.
- Convert your ethical judgments into appropriate action.

What this advice does is enable you to recognize ethical issues, make ethical judgments, and then convert these judgments into behaviour.[93]

Training and education in ethics have become very popular in North American organizations. Evidence indicates that formal education in ethics does have a positive impact on ethical attitudes.[94]

THE MANAGER'S NOTEBOOK

Plagiarism at Raytheon

1. Swanson's ethical breach can be framed in several ways. First, plagiarism represents dishonest communication. Second, plagiarism is a form of unfair treatment of an original author who is not getting credit for his or her own ideas. Third, Swanson's actions can be viewed as a breach of his responsibility toward Raytheon, which suffered negative publicity due to the story. Finally, plagiarism can be viewed as a lack of respect for copyright laws. How could such an ethical lapse be explained? While Swanson's mistake could possibly be an innocent oversight, there are several possible ethics-related explanations that could provide insight. First, while Swanson's maxims did not necessarily result in personal financial gain, they certainly earned him considerable fame. His book of "rules" was available for free download on the Raytheon website, and it is estimated that more than 300 000 are in circulation. In addition to gaining distribution and initial positive news coverage of his "rules," Swanson was also a sought-after speaker. Second, personality could be an explanation for this type of breach by a CEO. Need for power, personal values, and moral reasoning can all influence a CEO's decisions and actions in such situations. Finally, there are also cultural factors that could explain how a CEO could be led to plagiarize. Many larger-than-life businesspeople, such as Jack Welch and Donald Trump, are known by the general public more for their business writings than their particular accomplishments. In this era of the CEO-superstar, the allure of publishing for the masses must be extremely appealing.

2. On the one hand, Swanson's indiscretion seems to be something of a victimless crime. No money changed hands, no individual was harmed in any way, and the original author was long deceased. Still, the slip seems particularly troubling because it came from the head of one of the country's most powerful corporations, one that is responsible for manufacturing high-security defence products for the military. In this era of heightened military security, questions about Swanson's integrity and honesty could damage the credibility of the company. "If I were a board member or a shareholder, it would raise questions in my mind about how honest, transparent and responsible a CEO is being in other dealings," said Andy Wicks, co-director of the University of Virginia's Olsson Center for Applied Ethics. As such, the primary stakeholder in this ethical breach appears to be Swanson's firm, Raytheon. At the May 2006 annual shareholders' meeting, Raytheon's board announced that Swanson's raise was cancelled and that his eligible stock grants were being reduced by 20 percent. The salary cut represented a reduction of approximately $1 million. According to Linda Treviño, director of the Shoemaker Program in Business Ethics at Pennsylvania State University, the board's response was appropriate: "What he did was a mistake, and that was wrong, but he didn't profit from it and it wasn't intentional." Others believe he got off easy. "If any of Raytheon's military customers did this when they were in school, they would have been thrown out," said Jeff Sonnenfeld, senior associate dean at the Yale School of Management.

LEARNING OBJECTIVES CHECKLIST

1. *Power* is the capacity to influence others who are in a state of dependence. People have power by virtue of their position in the organization (legitimate power) or by virtue of the resources that they command (reward, coercion, friendship, or expertise).

2. People can obtain power by doing the right things and cultivating the right people. Activities that lead to power acquisition need to be extraordinary, visible, and relevant to the needs of the organization. People to cultivate include outsiders, subordinates, peers, and superiors.

3. *Empowerment* means giving people the authority, opportunity, and motivation to solve organizational problems. Power is thus located where it is needed to give employees the feeling that they are capable of doing their jobs well.

4. *Influence tactics* are interpersonal strategies that convert power into influence. They include assertiveness, ingratiation, rationality, exchange, upward appeal, and coalition formation. Rationality (logic, reason, planning, compromise) is generally the most efficient tactic.

5. Effective managers often have a high need for power. While individuals with high *n* Pow can, in some circumstances, behave in an abusive or dominating fashion, they can also use their power responsibly. Managers with high *n* Pow are effective when they use this power to achieve organizational goals.

6. Organizational subunits obtain power by controlling *strategic contingencies*. This means that they are able to affect events that are critical to other subunits. Thus, departments that can obtain resources for the organization will acquire power. Similarly, subunits gain power when they are able to reduce uncertainty, when their function is central to the workflow, and when other subunits or outside contractors cannot perform their tasks.

7. *Organizational politics* occur when influence means that are not sanctioned by the organization are used or when non-sanctioned ends are pursued. The pursuit of non-sanctioned ends is always dysfunctional, but the organization may benefit when non-sanctioned means are used to achieve approved goals. Several political tactics were discussed: *Networking* is establishing good relations with key people to accomplish goals. It contributes to political skill along with political astuteness, interpersonal influence, and apparent sincerity. *Machiavellianism* is a set of cynical beliefs about human nature, morality, and the permissibility of using various means to achieve one's ends. Situational morality, lying, and "psyching out" others are common tactics. *Defensiveness* means avoiding taking actions that do not suit one's political agenda and avoiding blame for negative events.

8. *Ethics* is systematic thinking about the moral consequences of decisions. Of particular interest is the impact on stakeholders, people who have the potential to be affected by a decision. Ethical dilemmas that managers face involve honest communication, fair treatment, special consideration, fair competition, responsibility to the organization, social responsibility, and respect for law. Causes of unethical behaviour include the potential for gain, role conflict, the extremes of business competition (great or none), organizational and industry culture, and certain personality characteristics.

9. *Sexual harassment* is a form of unethical behaviour that stems from the abuse of power and the perpetuation of a gender imbalance in the workplace. Steps that can be taken to prevent and deal with harassment include training and education, clear and formal policies, vigilance, detection of the "deaf ear" syndrome, and rapid response.

DISCUSSION QUESTIONS

1. Contrast the bases of power available to an army sergeant with those available to the president of a voluntary community association. How would these differences in power bases affect their influence tactics?

2. Are the bases of individual power easily substitutable for each other? Are they equally effective? For example, can coercive power substitute for expert power?

3. Suppose that you are an entrepreneur who has started a new chain of consumer electronics stores. Your competitive edge is to offer excellent customer service. What would you do to empower your employees to help achieve this goal?

4. Imagine that you are on a committee at work or in a group working on a project at school that includes a "high Mach" member. What could you do to neutralize the high Mach's attempts to manipulate the group?

5. Discuss the conditions under which the following subunits of an organization might gain or lose power: legal department; research and development unit; public relations department. Use the concepts of scarcity, uncertainty, centrality, and substitutability in your answers.

6. Differentiate between power and politics. Give an example of the use of power that is not political.

7. Is it unethical to occasionally surf the internet at work? Is it unethical to download pornography? Defend your answers.

8. Is sexual harassment more likely to be a problem in some occupations and types of organizations? Describe those occupations and organizational cultures where sexual harassment is most likely to be a problem. What can be done to prevent sexual harassment in these occupations and organizations?

INTEGRATIVE DISCUSSION QUESTIONS

1. Consider the role of politics and ethics in decision making. How can organizational politics be a source of effective or ineffective decision making in organizations? In what way can the causes of unethical behaviour influence decision making?

2. How can an organization create an ethical workplace where ethical behaviour is the norm? Refer to the organizational learning practices in Chapter 2, attitude change in Chapter 4, ethical leadership in Chapter 9, and the contributors to organizational culture in Chapter 8 to answer this question.

ON-THE-JOB CHALLENGE QUESTION

In the fall of 2006, Patricia Dunn was removed as the chair of the board of Hewlett-Packard, one of the world's premier technology companies. Dunn, whose position earned US$300 000 a year, had been frustrated and angered by leaks to the media of sensitive boardroom discussions that might affect HP's stock price. To deal with the problem, she authorized a private investigation firm to seek out the identity of those responsible for the leaks. HP directors, employees, and journalists were the target of the investigation. Among other things, investigators posed as these people ("pretexting") to obtain their confidential telephone records and set up an email sting to fool a reporter. Dunn claimed she was assured that all actions taken were legal and proper,

but the invasion of privacy did not sit well with a congressional committee investigating the matter. Two directors and a high-level legal advisor also resigned in the turmoil surrounding the events.

How were power and politics implicated in the events at HP? What are the ethics of using private investigators to probe leaks to the press? Was Dunn a victim in this affair?

Sources: Associated Press. (2006, September 28). Patricia Dunn: Others knew about HP probe. www.MSNBC.com; Robertson, J. (2006, September 26). Patricia Dunn resigns as HP chairwoman, Mark Hurd takes over as chairman. www.canada.com, Canadian Press; Robertson, J. (2006; September 12). HP chairwoman Dunn to step down. www.globeandmail.com, Associated Press.

EXPERIENTIAL EXERCISE

Political Skill Inventory

Early in the chapter we discussed political skill. This exercise will allow you to assess your political skill set.

Instructions: Using the following 7-point scale, please place the number on the blank before each item that best describes how much you agree with each statement about yourself.

1 = strongly disagree   5 = slightly agree

2 = disagree   6 = agree

3 = slightly disagree   7 = strongly agree

4 = neutral

1. _____ I spend a lot of time and effort at work networking with others.

2. _____ I am able to make most people feel comfortable and at ease around me.

3. _____ I am able to communicate easily and effectively with others.

4. _____ It is easy for me to develop good rapport with most people.

5. _____ I understand people very well.

6. _____ I am good at building relationships with influential people at work.

7. _____ I am particularly good at sensing the motivations and hidden agendas of others.

8. _____ When communicating with others, I try to be genuine in what I say and do.

9. _____ I have developed a large network of colleagues and associates at work whom I can call on for support when I really need to get things done.

10. _____ At work, I know a lot of important people and am well connected.

11. _____ I spend a lot of time at work developing connections with others.

12. _____ I am good at getting people to like me.

13. _____ It is important that people believe I am sincere in what I say and do.

14. _____ I try to show a genuine interest in other people.

15. _____ I am good at using my connections and network to make things happen at work.

16. _____ I have good intuition or savvy about how to present myself to others.

17. _____ I always seem to instinctively know the right things to say or do to influence others.

18. _____ I pay close attention to people's facial expressions.

Scoring and Interpretation

To compute your overall political skill, add up your scores and divide the total by 18. Scores below 2.3 indicate low political skill and scores over 4.6 signal high political skill. You can also compute your scores for the various dimensions of political skill. To determine your social astuteness, sum answers 5, 7, 16, 17, and 18 and divide by 5. To determine your interpersonal influence, sum answers 2, 3, 4, and 12 and divide by 4. To assess your networking ability, sum answers 1, 6, 9, 10, 11, and 15 and divide by 6. Finally, to compute your apparent sincerity, sum answers 8, 13, and 14 and divide by 3. It is also useful to see how others rate your political skill. Have someone who knows you well use the scale to rate you and compare his or her rating with yours.

Source: Ferris, G.R., Treadway, D.C., Kolodinsky, R.W., Hochwarter, W.A., Kacmar, C.J., Douglas, C., & Frink, D.D. (2005). Development and validation of the Political Skill Inventory. *Journal of Management, 31,* 126–152.

CASE INCIDENT

Doubling Up

The business school at Canadian Anonymous University prided itself on its international programs, which spanned Eastern Europe, North Africa, and South America. Many of the faculty enjoyed teaching in these programs, as it offered them a chance for free travel and the opportunity to sometimes avoid the harsh extremes of the Canadian climate. In addition, the teaching was well paid, offering a more reliable source of additional income than consulting. The university's auditor recently determined that several faculty members had been teaching in the international programs at the same time that they were scheduled to be teaching undergraduate classes at CAU. This was possibly due to the loose connection between the international programs office and the academic departments. After some investigation, it was determined that these faculty members had been subcontracting their CAU teaching to graduate students (at rather low rates) to enable themselves to teach internationally. One faculty member defended the practice as "gaining global exposure." Another claimed that developing countries "deserved experienced professors." A third claimed to be underpaid without the international teaching.

1. What kind of organizational politics are at work here?

2. What influence tactics might the profs have used to get the grad students to fill in for them?

3. Discuss the ethics of the professors "doubling up" on their teaching.

CASE STUDY

WestJet Spies on Air Canada

Stephen Smith is the type of boss who keeps his door open. As president of Zip, a short-lived Air Canada subsidiary, he was known as easygoing and approachable, regularly walking around the Calgary office to check in with people. He also happens to be the former CEO of WestJet Airlines, Air Canada's archrival. All of which may be why he was the one to receive a phone call last December from a man identifying himself only as a WestJet employee. "I'm all for tough competition," said the voice on the phone, "but I have to draw the line at dishonest conduct."

Then the caller dropped a bomb: WestJet was dipping into private Air Canada files online and passing the information around the executive suite. The tipster reported that he had seen a multicoloured page filled with Air Canada's flight load data—industry jargon for the number of passengers flying on a specific flight—on a senior executive's computer. Smith suddenly feared WestJet brass might have access to a private site used by Air Canada employees to book their own travel, from which the snoopers could gauge which routes make money and which don't—invaluable information in a business built on tight margins. If he was right, *this* could explain why WestJet seemed to be making all the right strategic decisions of late, such as flipping its Montreal–Vancouver flight from evening to morning.

Smith wasn't alone in his office when the call came. A colleague, Michael Rodyniuk, was also there, according to an affidavit Smith filed later. Unbeknownst to the WestJet snitch, Smith's phone displayed his name and number. As Smith was jotting notes from the conversation, he pulled out an extra sheet of paper and says he indicated to Rodyniuk to write down the information.

That phone call, which couldn't have lasted more than five minutes, eventually triggered a massive civil lawsuit over corporate espionage, one that provides a rare glimpse of the dirty tricks rivals resort to in the name of competition. Although none of the parties would go on the record for this story, affidavits, transcripts and background interviews reveal just how ruthless the airline business has become in this country, where Air Canada is battling a posse of up-and-comers, most notably the feisty WestJet, as it emerges from bankruptcy protection. Even in its early stages the case has uncovered fresh incriminating material, but it will be months, possibly years, before the various players

get their days in court. It may never get that far—many observers expect an out-of-court settlement. Still, the critical battle is playing out in the court of public opinion, where the two airlines' public personas so far seem reversed: Air Canada, long thought to be a corporate bully, appears to be the victim, while WestJet, for years the darling of investors and the flying public, has been cast as the bad guy.

In its statement of claim, which accuses WestJet of "high-handed and malicious" conduct, Air Canada says the company surreptitiously tapped into its employee website and set up a "screen scraper," a program designed to automatically lift data off one site and dump it into another. WestJet boosted its own profits using that information, says Air Canada, claiming a whopping $220 million in damages. In reply, WestJet dismissed the suit as an attempt to embarrass a rival and in a countersuit accuses the national carrier of stealing its confidential information. It says Air Canada sent investigators to pilfer one of its executive's garbage—and has pictures to prove it.

What pushes this story into the realm of the absurd is that neither airline denies the accusations—what's disputed is whether doing so was wrong. WestJet admits a senior executive, Mark Hill, entered Air Canada's website; Clive Beddoe, the company's CEO, even apologized to shareholders for Hill's actions while discussing WestJet's tumbling profits this summer. For its part, Air Canada readily admits it took the garbage—in fact, it uses the reconstituted pages as evidence for its case. But almost in mirror fashion, they both scoff at the recriminations. WestJet says its so-called crime coughed up data that was neither confidential nor important. Air Canada's investigators deny they trespassed on private property. If there weren't jobs and investors' money at stake, and possibly even the fragile health of the national airline industry, these suits and countersuits could be likened to a spat between siblings that's getting out of control.

And now Jetsgo Corporation, the young Montreal-based discounter, has entered the fray. Among the documents Air Canada had pasted back together, it discovered a summary of Jetsgo load factors. Last week, Jetsgo CEO Michel Leblanc asked Air Canada for a copy of that document. All of which poses an intriguing question: Just how widespread was WestJet's espionage?

While the audacity of the tactics may be shocking, there is nothing new in companies spying on each other, says Norman Inkster, who led the RCMP from 1987 to 1994 and now runs a private investigation firm. But in the old days it usually meant breaking into rivals' offices. Today, it's about hacking into websites and electronic files—tactics that Inkster says can be difficult to detect and hugely damaging. If Smith hadn't been tipped off, chances are Air Canada would never have discovered WestJet's scheme.

As much as five months before the mole's disturbing call, Rodyniuk, the executive who Smith says was in his office that day, had mentioned that a WestJet co-founder, Mark Hill, seemed to have oddly accurate data on Air Canada's flight loads. Rodyniuk, Zip's director of marketing and sales, had known Hill for more than a decade. The two regularly bantered back and forth by e-mail. Occasionally Hill, known as a genius for industry numbers, would taunt Rodyniuk about Air Canada's woes. "Winnipeg–London at 27 percent isn't doing much for your bottom line," he wrote on January 15, 2004. "I'd be willing to bet my next profit-share cheque that YWG-YXU [the airports' call letters] has the lowest load factor of any domestic route operated by AC today. C'mon. Fess up."

Hill's name also came up in Smith's conversation with the informant, who said Hill was the source of the sensitive data. Smith immediately made two calls: one to Air Canada's CEO Robert Milton, and the other to security. An investigation was launched.

First stop: the employee website. A standard airline perk allows employees to travel almost for free on flights with open seats. Workers receive a personal code so they can check which flights are available. Air Canada's manager of online services, Gerald Gunn, found that someone—or something—had used a single access code to enter the site an astounding 243 630 times between May 15, 2003, and March 19, 2004, for an average of 786 hits a day. In one extraordinary day, the site was tapped 4973 times.

It didn't take long to determine the code used over and over belonged to Jeffrey Lafond, a former Canadian Airlines employee who had accepted a buyout as Canadian was being taken over by Air Canada. Part of his package included two Air Canada tickets a year for five years.

Last winter, as Air Canada secretly tried to piece together what WestJet knew and how, Rodyniuk continued his e-mail relationship with Hill. In February, he broached a new subject: He wondered if WestJet might have a job for him.

Here the storyline gets contentious. Air Canada claims Rodyniuk and Hill met for dinner on March 18. The following morning, Air Canada's employee website was entered using Lafond's code for the last time. On March 24, Rodyniuk quit his job at Zip. The next day, he showed up at WestJet as director of revenue. Air Canada believes Rodyniuk tipped Hill off to its investigation.

In his affidavit, Rodyniuk disputes Smith's account of the tipster phone call. He says he only learned about the call when Smith asked for help checking out a former Canadian Airlines employee. Rodyniuk admits he wrote down the name and number on the slip of paper, but that information didn't come from Smith's phone display; it came from directory assistance.

Meanwhile, as Gunn was combing through Air Canada's website looking for signs of infiltration, the company's law firm, Lerners, decided to engage in some espionage of its own. It hired a private detective agency, IPSA International, to do some sleuthing of a grittier nature than WestJet's high-tech screen scraping. Hill often worked from his home in Victoria's exclusive Oak Bay suburb. IPSA's job was to get Hill's trash: It might reveal how WestJet was using the data it took from Air Canada's site. Tipped off by a neighbour who'd seen a suspicious white truck, Hill caught the IPSA workers last April. "Do you work for Air Canada?" he shouted at them, snapping photos of the men and their truck as they loaded his trash and recycling bins into their pickup. The pictures were printed in newspapers, and the incident gave Hill and WestJet something to be indignant about. The garbage was on private property, says Hill, whose countersuit accuses the private dicks and Air Canada of trespassing.

Hill's recycling material included shredded papers. After sorting the trash, the IPSA men sent the strips to a company in Houston that specializes in reconstituting shredded papers. They turned out to be reports comparing Air Canada's and WestJet's flight loads, according to Air Canada affidavits.

The day after Hill snapped the photos, and two weeks after Rodyniuk jumped to WestJet, Air Canada filed a lawsuit against WestJet, Mark Hill, and Jeffrey Lafond. And that's when things got interesting.

Some of the best drama in the case—and some of Air Canada's best evidence—came in pre-trial cross-examinations, which took place in a vast glass-walled conference room at the company's law firm. Earl Cherniak, Air Canada's lawyer, is like a sharpshooter—quiet, precise, and dangerous. In late June, he questioned Lafond. The session was well attended: at least eight lawyers, a couple of airline executives, and Hill, who was to be examined immediately after. Lafond admitted providing his employee and personal ID numbers for Air Canada's website to Hill, but said he didn't think the load factor information was relevant. The transcript of the 2½ hour cross-examination reads like a school principal grilling a cheating student. Had Lafond asked Hill how the information would be used? Did he know it would be used 243 000 times? Did he know it was used on an automated basis? No, no, and no, Lafond answered.

"Mr. Hill never told you that?"

"No."

"So you had no idea, when you were giving Mr. Hill this access that he would use it in that way?"

"That's correct."

"Yes. But if you had known that, you wouldn't have given it to him, would you?"

"Again, I don't think the load factor information is very relevant," said Lafond. (He nonetheless asked Hill for—and got, on the same day he handed over the codes—an indemnity saying WestJet would take care of him for "any reason.")

At the beginning of Lafond's grilling, Hill kept busy doing a crossword puzzle. By the time it was his turn in the hot seat, however, Hill was no longer nonchalant. At one point during questioning, he was shaking, says one person who was in the room. Hill told Cherniak that when he first got Lafond's access code he spent 90 minutes each evening going into the Air Canada website and analyzing its data. Later, he asked a West-Jet computer expert to create a program that would retrieve the data automatically. But, said Hill over and over, the load factor information was available from other sources. Airlines hire people to stand at airport gates and count passengers as they board or exit flights, he pointed out. And, over and over, Cherniak told Hill that he was volunteering information for which he hadn't been asked. (Hill resigned from WestJet this summer, saying it was in his and WestJet's best interests they part company.)

In its defence, WestJet doesn't deny accessing Air Canada's website, but it points the finger at Hill as the one who did the dirty work. Besides, says WestJet, its rival's troubles aren't the result of Hill's actions, and the flight load information Hill obtained was of little value.

Much of the case will ultimately revolve around this point. As one lawyer put it, if you are hit by a car running a red light, the case against the driver will be much tougher if you were left brain-damaged than if you're lightly bruised. The next step in this case may well determine whether Air Canada was bruised or bashed by its rival's actions. In July, WestJet was ordered to turn over its executives' hard drives for an independent review, which should help answer some outstanding questions. Who at WestJet knew? Who used the data? And how useful was it? Claude Proulx, an airline analyst, noted in a July report that WestJet's load factors "deteriorated significantly" after it stopped scraping Air Canada's data. Meanwhile, Air Canada's traffic figures have improved substantially.

In the end, both airlines may be harshly judged. With few controls on its employee website, Air Canada left itself wide open to snoops. WestJet's Hill took advantage of his competition's lax security. But most importantly, both—whether as a tactic to divert attention from falling profits or a ploy to appear less of a bully—have blown things way out of proportion.

1. Did WestJet employees engage in unethical behaviour in this series of events? Did Air Canada employees? Defend your answers.

2. Who are the relevant stakeholders in this situation?

3. Does Air Canada's apparently weak security in this matter reduce any blame to be apportioned to WestJet?

4. Do arguments that the load data was useless or that it was available from other sources reduce the seriousness of the online snooping?

5. Who gained and lost power in this case?

6. On May 29, 2006, a settlement was announced. WestJet agreed to pay Air Canada $5 million in costs and to donate $10 million to children's charities in the name of the two airlines. It also apologized and described its conduct as unethical. Is this a fair outcome? Does it change your views about your answers to the previous questions?

After reading Chapter 12, you should be able to:

1 Define *interpersonal conflict* and review its causes in organizations.

2 Explain the *types of conflict* and the process by which conflict occurs.

3 Discuss the various *modes of managing conflict.*

4 Review a range of *negotiation techniques.*

5 Discuss the merits of *stimulating conflict.*

6 Distinguish among *stressors*, *stress*, and *stress reactions.*

7 Discuss the role that personality plays in stress.

8 Review the sources of stress encountered by various organizational role occupants.

9 Describe *behavioural, psychological,* and *physiological reactions* to stress and discuss techniques for managing stress.

Conflict and Stress

The Toronto Hair War: Glo versus Gliss

A dispute between two of Yorkville's ritziest hair salons has degenerated into a sniping war involving seized garbage, surprise searches, and a $6.4 million lawsuit. The fight centres on Glo Salon & Spa, a high-end beauty purveyor on [Toronto's] Avenue Road that caters to some of the city's wealthiest women. A Glo cut and colour starts at about $200 and goes up quickly from there.

"(Hairstyling) is a dirty little business," laughed Luis Pacheco, co-owner of nearby Hair on the Avenue, who is watching this scrap from the sidelines. "It's like a cesspool."

Three years ago, hairstylist Perry Neglia and a partner sold Glo to Mary Louise Abrahamse, who was new to the salon business. As part of the $450,000 sale, Neglia agreed to continue working at Glo for a year and not to open a competing business for three years. It's not clear who did what to whom over the next three years, but it's plain that relations between Abrahamse and some of her new staff became strained. On April 1, the day after his non-compete clause expired, Neglia opened a rival salon 100 metres up the street, calling it Gliss. Over the next several weeks, a steady stream of Glo hairstylists and colour technicians followed Neglia the short walk up Avenue Road. More importantly, "a high percentage" of their clients came with them, according to Neglia. He and his new staffers contacted long-time customers to let them know about the switch. "It would be rude not to tell them," Neglia said in an interview. "It would look like we didn't want to take them. They'd feel jilted."

"She thinks she bought the clients," Jarmil Kulik, Neglia's new partner and a former Glo stylist, said of Abrahamse. "And nobody does that," said Neglia. As a result, Glo was left with a denuded staff without well-developed client rosters, according to Abrahamse's lawsuit. One of her lawyers, Bob Klotz, said in an interview that his client's business has been "destroyed." Abrahamse declined comment.

For several weeks, things settled to a low boil. But while Neglia and his staff were building their new business, Abrahamse was working behind the scenes to unsettle them. She hired private investigators to go through Gliss's trash. They sent dummy clients into Gliss to look around. The object of the search was to determine what, if anything, Gliss staff had removed from Glo. Key to that investigation were the so-called

Former Glo staff, now at Gliss, embroiled in a $6.4 million suit.

"colour cards" that are used to chart the chemical formula for colouring hair. The cards often contain a client's contact info. Abrahamse's legal team asserts that the cards are her property. Neglia counters that cards were the property of individual staffers when he owned Glo, and that the rule was not changed after he sold the business. He claims that his staff copied the information on the cards and left the originals at Glo. "That way (the customers) have a choice about which salon they want to go to," said Neglia in an interview. The practice of taking cards and luring away clients often causes ugly breakups in the hairstyling business but is so pervasive that most salon owners grudgingly accept it. "Clients have free will, too. There's no ownership," said Hair on the Avenue owner Pacheco. "Is it fair to take [the cards]? I would say so."

The investigators found enough to persuade a judge to issue an Anton Piller order, an extraordinary legal device that allows a private search without notice so that evidence cannot be destroyed. On the morning of June 4, a team of lawyers and forensic technicians, including a videographer, arrived to search Gliss. "It was like something out of *Law & Order*," said stylist Stephen Jackson, one of those who left Glo to join Neglia. At the same time, another half-dozen people turned up at Neglia's home. Both groups brought police officers to act as peacekeepers. Staffers at Gliss were told to hand over cellphones, the contents of which were then copied. A total of six computers at the business and at Neglia's home were confiscated and cloned. About a thousand colour cards and binders with client information were also taken and have yet to be returned. All of that property is now being held by an independent auditor. Neglia, Kulik, Jackson and five other former Glo staff members then learned they were being sued for a total of $6.4 million. "It's mind-boggling," said Brian Menzies, a colourist and co-defendant.

The fight has caused a flutter around Yorkville, where dozens of high-end salons have clustered in the years since Vidal Sassoon opened his landmark shop in the late '60s. "I think everyone thinks Mary Louise is out of her mind, that she's crazy," said Marianne Marshall, the city's top beauty trade headhunter. She said both Abrahamse and Neglia are her clients. It's also raising questions among hair professionals and their clients about who owns what in the prim world of beauty salons. "What is she (Abrahamse) suing for?" said Marlene Hore, an advertising exec who moved up the street to Gliss to continue getting her hair done by Jackson. "Don't I have a right to go wherever I want to have my hair cut?"

On Monday, Justice Colin Campbell thought better of the Anton Piller order. He intends to set it aside, dealing a blow to Abrahamse's suit. However, Klotz said that his client intends to continue. "Sure, Mary Louise is mad," said headhunter Marshall. "But suing Perry (Neglia) is not going to accomplish anything. This way, everyone gets dragged through the mud. And, in the end, I don't think she's going to win."[1]

In this chapter, we will define *interpersonal conflict*, discuss its causes, and examine various ways of handling conflict, including negotiation. Then we will explore *work stress*, noting its causes and the consequences that it can have for both individuals and organizations. Various strategies for managing stress will be considered.

What Is Conflict?

Interpersonal conflict

The process that occurs when one person, group, or organizational subunit frustrates the goal attainment of another.

Interpersonal conflict is a process that occurs when one person, group, or organizational subunit frustrates the goal attainment of another. Thus, the curator of a museum might be in conflict with the director over the purchase of a particular work of art. Likewise, the entire curatorial staff might be in conflict with the financial staff over cutbacks in acquisition funds.

In its classic form, conflict often involves antagonistic attitudes and behaviours, as seen in the drama concerning the Toronto hair salons. As for attitudes, the conflicting parties might develop a dislike for each other, see each other as unreasonable, and develop negative stereotypes of their opposites ("Those scientists should get out of the laboratory once in a while"). Antagonistic behaviours might include name calling, sabotage, or even physical aggression. In some organizations, the conflict process is managed in a collaborative way that keeps antagonism at a minimum. In others, conflict is hidden or suppressed and not nearly so obvious (e.g., some gender conflict).[2]

Causes of Organizational Conflict

It is possible to isolate a number of factors that contribute to organizational conflict.[3]

Group Identification and Intergroup Bias

An especially fascinating line of research has shown how identification with a particular group or class of people can set the stage for organizational conflict. In this work, researchers have typically assigned people to groups randomly or on the basis of some trivial characteristic, such as eye colour. Even without interaction or cohesion, people have a tendency to develop a more positive view of their own "in-group" and a less positive view of the "out-group," of which they are not a member.[4] The ease with which this unwarranted intergroup bias develops is disturbing.

Why does intergroup bias occur? Self-esteem is probably a critical factor. Identifying with the successes of one's own group and disassociating oneself from out-group failures boosts self-esteem and provides comforting feelings of social solidarity. Research by one of your authors, for example, found that people felt that their work group's attendance record was superior to that of their occupation in general (and, by extension, other work groups).[5] Attributing positive behaviour to your own work group should contribute to your self-esteem.

In organizations, there are a number of groups or classes with which people might identify. These might be based on personal characteristics (e.g., race or gender), job function (e.g., sales or production), or job level (e.g., manager or non-manager). Furthermore, far from being random or trivial, differences between groups might be accentuated by real differences in power, opportunity, clients serviced, and so on. For instance, the merger between Air Canada and Canadian Airlines made firm identities very salient for employees, and these identities persisted even after the companies merged into a single entity. The best prognosis is that people who identify with some groups will tend to be leery of out-group members. The likelihood of conflict increases as the factors we cover below enter into the relationship between groups.

The increased emphasis on teams in organizations generally places a high premium on getting employees to identify strongly with their team. The prevalence of intergroup bias suggests that organizations will have to pay special attention to managing relationships *between* these teams.

Interdependence

When individuals or subunits are mutually dependent on each other to accomplish *their own* goals, the potential for conflict exists. For example, the sales staff is dependent on the production department for the timely delivery of high-quality products. This is the only way sales can maintain the goodwill of its customers. On the other hand, production depends on the sales staff to provide routine orders with adequate lead times. Custom-tailored emergency orders will wreak havoc with production schedules and make the production department look bad. In contrast, the sales staff and the office maintenance staff are not highly interdependent. Salespeople are on the road a lot and should not make great demands on maintenance. Conversely, a dirty office probably will not lose a sale.

Interdependence can set the stage for conflict for two reasons. First, it necessitates interaction between the parties so that they can coordinate their interests. Conflict will not develop if the parties can "go it alone." Second, as we noted in the previous chapter, interdependence implies that each party has some *power* over the other. It is relatively easy for one side or the other to abuse its power and create antagonism.

Interdependence does not *always* lead to conflict. In fact, it often provides a good basis for collaboration through mutual assistance. Whether interdependence prompts conflict depends on the presence of other conditions, which we will now consider.

Differences in Power, Status, and Culture

Conflict can erupt when parties differ significantly in power, status, or culture.

Power. If dependence is not mutual but one-way, the potential for conflict increases. If party A needs the collaboration of party B to accomplish its goals but B does not need A's assistance, antagonism may develop. B has power over A, and A has nothing with which to bargain. A good example is the quality control system in many factories. Production workers might be highly dependent on inspectors to approve their work, but this dependence is not reciprocated. The inspectors might have a separate boss, their own office, and their own circle of friends (other inspectors). In this case, production workers might begin to treat inspectors with hostility, one of the symptoms of conflict.

Status. Status differences provide little impetus for conflict when people of lower status are dependent on those of higher status. This is the way organizations often work, and most members are socialized to expect it. However, because of the design of the work, there are occasions when employees who technically have lower status find themselves giving orders to, or controlling the tasks of, higher-status people. The restaurant business provides a good example. In many restaurants, lower-status servers give orders and initiate queries to higher-status chefs. The latter might come to resent this reversal of usual lines of influence.[6] In some organizations, junior staff are more adept with information technology than senior staff. Some executives are defensive about this reversal of roles.

Culture. When two or more very different cultures develop in an organization, the clash in beliefs and values can result in overt conflict. Hospital administrators who develop a strong culture centred on efficiency and cost-effectiveness might find themselves in conflict with physicians who share a strong culture based on providing excellent patient care at any cost. A telling case of cultural conflict occurred when Apple Computer expanded and hired professionals away from several companies with their own strong cultures.

> During the first couple of years Apple recruited heavily from Hewlett-Packard, National Semiconductor, and Intel, and the habits and differences in style among these companies were reflected in Cupertino. There was a general friction between the rough and tough ways of the semiconductor men (there were few women) and the people who made computers, calculators, and instruments at Hewlett-Packard. . . . Some of the Hewlett-Packard men began to see themselves as civilizing influences and were horrified at the uncouth rough-and-tumble practices of the brutes from the semiconductor industry. . . . Many of the men from National Semiconductor and other stern backgrounds harboured a similar contempt for the Hewlett-Packard recruits. They came to look on them as prissy fusspots.[7]

Ambiguity

Ambiguous goals, jurisdictions, or performance criteria can lead to conflict. Under such ambiguity, the formal and informal rules that govern interaction break down. In addition, it might be difficult to accurately assign praise for good outcomes or blame for bad outcomes when it is hard to see who was responsible for what. For example, if sales drop following the introduction of a "new and improved" product, the design group might blame the marketing department for a poor advertising campaign. In response, the marketers might claim that the "improved" product is actually inferior to the old product.

Ambiguous performance criteria are a frequent cause of conflict between managers and employees. The basic scientist who is charged by a chemical company to "discover new knowledge" might react negatively when her boss informs her that her work is inadequate. This rather open-ended assignment is susceptible to a variety of interpretations. Conflict is not uncommon in the film and entertainment industry, in part because a great deal of ambiguity surrounds just what is needed to produce a hit movie or show. In the up-market atmosphere of Yorkville's hair salons, there is apparent ambiguity about who "owns" client information such as "colour cards."

Scarce Resources

In the previous chapter, we pointed out that differences in power are magnified when resources become scarce. This does not occur without a battle, however, and conflict often surfaces in the process of power jockeying. Limited budget money, secretarial support, or lab space can contribute to conflict. Scarcity has a way of turning latent or disguised conflict into overt conflict. Two scientists who do not get along very well may be able to put up a peaceful front until a reduction in lab space provokes each to protect his or her domain. In the chapter-opening vignette, the battle between Glo and Gliss was most decidedly provoked by scarce resources—wealthy customers willing to pay $200 for a haircut and colour.

Types of Conflict

Is all conflict the same? The answer is no. It is useful to distinguish among relationship, task, and process conflict.[8] **Relationship conflict** concerns interpersonal tensions among individuals that have to do with their relationship per se, not the task at hand. So-called "personality clashes" are examples of relationship conflicts. **Task conflict** concerns disagreements about the nature of the work to be done. Differences of opinion about goals or technical matters are examples of task conflict. Finally, **process conflict** involves disagreements about how work should be organized and accomplished. Disagreements about responsibility, authority, resource allocation, and who should do what all constitute process conflict.

In the context of work groups and teams, task, relationship, and process conflict tend to be detrimental to member satisfaction and team performance. In essence, such conflict prevents the development of cohesiveness (Chapter 7). Occasionally, some degree of task conflict might actually be beneficial for team performance, especially when the task is non-routine and requires a variety of perspectives to be considered and when it does not degenerate into relationship conflict.[9] Thus, not all conflict is detrimental, and we shall return to some potential benefits of conflict later in the chapter.

Relationship conflict. Interpersonal tensions among individuals that have to do with their relationship per se, not the task at hand.

Task conflict. Disagreements about the nature of the work to be done.

Process conflict. Disagreements about how work should be organized and accomplished.

Conflict Dynamics

A number of events occur when one or more of the causes of conflict we noted above take effect. We will assume here that the conflict in question occurs between groups, such as organizational departments. However, much of this is also relevant to conflict within teams or between individuals. Specifically, when conflict begins, we often see the following events transpire:

- "Winning" the conflict becomes more important than developing a good solution to the problem at hand.
- The parties begin to conceal information from each other or to pass on distorted information.
- Each side becomes more cohesive. Deviants who speak of conciliation are punished, and strict conformity is expected.
- Contact with the opposite party is discouraged except under formalized, restricted conditions.
- While the opposite party is negatively stereotyped, the image of one's own position is boosted.
- On each side, more aggressive people who are skilled at engaging in conflict may emerge as leaders.[10]

You can certainly see the difficulty here. What begins as a problem of identity, interdependence, ambiguity, or scarcity quickly escalates to the point that the conflict process *itself* becomes an additional problem. The elements of this process then work against the achievement of a peaceful solution. The conflict continues to cycle "on its own steam," as illustrated in the "Hair War" vignette.

Modes of Managing Conflict

How do you tend to react to conflict situations? Are you aggressive? Do you tend to hide your head in the sand? As conflict expert Kenneth Thomas notes, there are several basic reactions that can be thought of as styles, strategies, or intentions for dealing with conflict. As shown in Exhibit 12.1, these approaches to managing conflict are a function of both how *assertive* you are in trying to satisfy your own or your group's concerns and how *cooperative* you are in trying to satisfy those of the other party or group.[11] It should be emphasized that none of the five styles for dealing with conflict in Exhibit 12.1 is inherently superior. As we will see, each style might have its place given the situation in which the conflict episode occurs. To diagnose how you manage conflict, try the Experiential Exercise at the end of the chapter.

Avoiding

Avoiding. A conflict management style characterized by low assertiveness of one's interests and low cooperation with the other party.

The **avoiding** style is characterized by low assertiveness of one's own interests and low cooperation with the other party. This is the "hiding the head in the sand" response. Although avoidance can provide some short-term stress reduction from the rigours of conflict, it does not really change the situation. Thus, its effectiveness is often limited.

Of course, avoidance does have its place. If the issue is trivial, information is lacking, people need to cool down, or the opponent is very powerful and very hostile, avoidance might be a sensible response.

Accommodating

Accommodating. A conflict management style in which one cooperates with the other party while not asserting one's own interests.

Cooperating with the other party's wishes while not asserting one's own interests is the hallmark of **accommodating**. If people see accommodation as a sign of weakness, it does not bode well for future interactions. However, it can be an effective reaction when you are wrong, the issue is more important to the other party, or you want to build good will.

Competing

Competing. A conflict management style that maximizes assertiveness and minimizes cooperation.

A **competing** style tends to maximize assertiveness for your own position and minimize cooperative responses. In competing, you tend to frame the conflict in strict win-lose terms. Full priority is given to your own goals, facts, or procedures. Bill Gates, the billionaire czar of Microsoft, tends to pursue the competing style:

> *Gates is famously confrontational. If he strongly disagrees with what you're saying, he is in the habit of blurting out, "That's the stupidest . . . thing I've ever heard!" People tell stories of Gates spraying saliva into the face of some hapless*

EXHIBIT 12.1

Approaches to managing organizational conflict.

Source: Thomas, K.W. (1992). "Conflict and Negotiations in Organizations" in M.D. Dunnette & L.M. Hough (Eds.) *Handbook of Industrial and Organizational Psychology* (2nd Ed., Vol. 3). Palo Alto, CA: Consulting Psychologists Press. Used by permission of the publisher.

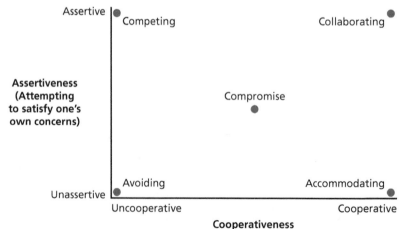

employee as he yells, "This stuff isn't hard! I could do this stuff in a weekend!"
What you're supposed to do in a situation like this, as in encounters with griz-
zly bears, is stand your ground: if you flee, the bear will think you're game and
will pursue you, and you can't outrun a bear.[12]

The competing style holds promise when you have a lot of power, you are sure of your facts, the situation is truly win-lose, or you will not have to interact with the other party in the future. This style is illustrated in the chapter-opening vignette.

Compromise

Compromise combines intermediate levels of assertiveness and cooperation. Thus, it is itself a compromise between pure competition and pure accommodation. In a sense, you attempt to satisfice (Chapter 10) rather than maximize your outcomes and hope that the same occurs for the other party. In the law, a plea bargain is an example of a compromise between the defending lawyer and the prosecutor.

Compromise places a premium on determining rules of exchange between the two parties. As such, it always contains the seeds for procedural conflict in addition to whatever else is being negotiated. Also, compromise does not always result in the most creative response to conflict. Compromise is not so useful for resolving conflicts that stem from power asymmetry, because the weaker party may have little to offer the stronger party. However, it is a sensible reaction to conflict stemming from scarce resources. Also, it is a good fallback position if other strategies fail.

Compromise. A conflict management style that combines intermediate levels of assertiveness and cooperation.

Collaborating

In the **collaborating** mode, both assertiveness and cooperation are maximized in the hope that an integrative agreement occurs that fully satisfies the interests of both parties. Emphasis is put on a win–win resolution, in which there is no assumption that someone must lose something. Rather, it is assumed that the solution to the conflict can leave both parties in a better condition. Ideally, collaboration occurs as a problem-solving exercise (Chapter 10). It probably works best when the conflict is not intense and when each party has information that is useful to the other. Although effective collaboration can take time and practice to develop, it frequently enhances productivity and achievement.[13]

Collaborating. A conflict management style that maximizes both assertiveness and cooperation.

Some of the most remarkable examples of collaboration in contemporary organizations are those between companies and their suppliers. Traditionally, adversarial competition in which buyers try to squeeze the very lowest price out of suppliers, who are frequently played off against each other, has dominated these relationships. This obviously does not provide much incentive for the perpetually insecure suppliers to invest in improvements dedicated toward a particular buyer. Gradually, things have changed, and now it is common for organizations to supply extensive engineering support and technical advice to their suppliers.

Collaboration also helps to manage conflict inside organizations. Our discussion of cross-functional teams in Chapter 7 is a good example. Also, research shows that collaboration between organizational departments is particularly important for providing good customer service.[14]

Managing Conflict with Negotiation

The stereotype we have of negotiation is that it is a formal process of bargaining between labour and management or buyer and seller. However, job applicants negotiate for starting salaries, employees negotiate for better job assignments, and people with sick kids negotiate to leave work early. To encompass all these situations, we might define **negotiation** as "a decision-making process among interdependent parties who do not share identical preferences."[15] Negotiation constitutes conflict management, in that it is an attempt to either prevent conflict or resolve existing conflict.

Negotiation. A decision-making process among interdependent parties who do not share identical preferences.

Collaboration can provide unions and management with win–win solutions.

Negotiation is an attempt to reach a satisfactory exchange among or between the parties. Sometimes, negotiation is very explicit, as in the case of the labour negotiation or the buyer–seller interaction. However, negotiation can also proceed in a very implicit or tacit way.[16] For instance, when an employee is trying to get a more interesting job assignment or to take off from work early, the terms of the exchange are not likely to be spelled out very clearly. Still, this is negotiation.

It has become common to distinguish between distributive and integrative negotiation tactics.[17] **Distributive negotiation** assumes a zero-sum, win-lose situation in which a fixed pie is divided up between the parties. If you re-examine Exhibit 12.1, you can imagine that distributive negotiation occurs on the axis between competition and accommodation. In theory, the parties will more or less tend toward some compromise. On the other hand, **integrative negotiation** assumes that mutual problem solving can result in a win–win situation in which the pie is actually enlarged before distribution. Integrative negotiation occurs on the axis between avoiding and collaborating, ideally tending toward the latter.

Distributive and integrative negotiations can take place simultaneously. We will discuss them separately for pedagogical purposes.

Distributive negotiation. Win-lose negotiation in which a fixed amount of assets is divided between parties.

Integrative negotiation. Win–win negotiation that assumes that mutual problem solving can enlarge the assets to be divided between parties.

Distributive Negotiation Tactics

Distributive negotiation is essentially single-issue negotiation. Many potential conflict situations fit this scenario. For example, suppose you find a used car that you really like. Now, things boil down to price. You want to buy the car for the minimum reasonable price, while the seller wants to get the maximum reasonable price.

The essence of the problem is shown in Exhibit 12.2. Party is a consulting firm who would like to win a contract to do an attitude survey in Other's firm. Party would like to make $90 000 for the job (Party's target) but would settle for $70 000, a figure that provides for minimal acceptable profit (Party's resistance point). Other thinks that the survey could be done for as little as $60 000 (Other's target) but would be willing to spend up to $80 000 for a good job (Other's resistance point). Theoretically, an offer in the settlement range between $70 000 and $80 000 should clinch the deal, if the negotiators can get into this range. Notice that every dollar that Party earns is a dollar's worth of cost for Other. How will they reach a settlement?[18]

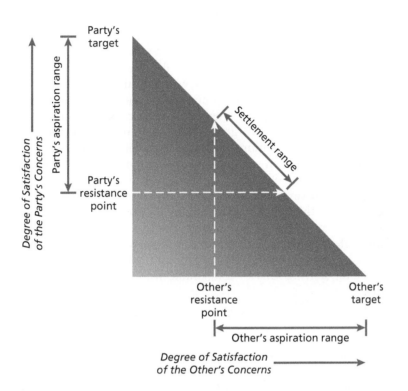

EXHIBIT 12.2

A model of distributive negotiation.

Source: Thomas, K.W. (1992). "Conflict and Negotiations in Organizations" in M.D. Dunnette & L.M. Hough (Eds.) *Handbook of Industrial and Organizational Psychology* (2nd Ed., Vol. 3). Palo Alto, CA: Consulting Psychologists Press. Used by permission of the publisher.

Threats and Promises. *Threat* consists of implying that you will punish the other party if he or she does not concede to your position. For example, the Other firm might imply that it will terminate its other business with the consulting company if Party does not lower its price on the attitude survey job. *Promises* are pledges that concessions will lead to rewards in the future. For example, Other might promise future consulting contracts if Party agrees to do the survey at a lower price. Of course, the difference between a threat and a promise can be subtle, as when the promise implies a threat should no concession be made.

Threat has some merit as a bargaining tactic if one party has power over the other that corresponds to the nature of the threat, especially if no future negotiations are expected or if the threat can be posed in a civil and subtle way.[19] If power is more balanced and the threat is crude, a counterthreat could scuttle the negotiations, despite the fact that both parties could be satisfied in the settlement range. Promises have merit when your side lacks power and anticipates future negotiations with the other side. Both threat and promises work best when they send interpretable signals to the other side about your true position, what really matters to you. Careful timing is critical.

Firmness versus Concessions. How about intransigence—sticking to your target position, offering few concessions, and waiting for the other party to give in? Research shows that such a tactic is likely to be reciprocated by the other party, thus increasing the chances of a deadlock.[20] On the other hand, a series of small concessions early in the negotiation will often be matched. Good negotiators often use face-saving techniques to explain concessions. For example, the consulting firm might claim that it could reduce the cost of the survey by making it web-based rather than based on paper questionnaires.

Persuasion. Verbal persuasion or debate is common in negotiations. Often, it takes a two-pronged attack. One prong asserts the technical merits of the party's position. For example, the consulting firm might justify its target price by saying "We have the most qualified staff. We do the most reliable surveys." The other prong asserts the fairness of the target position. Here, the negotiator might make a speech about the expenses the company would incur in doing the survey.

Verbal persuasion is an attempt to change the attitudes of the other party toward your target position. Persuaders are most effective when they are perceived as expert, likable, and unbiased. The obvious problem in distributive negotiations is bias—each party knows the other is self-interested. One way to deal with this is to introduce some unbiased parties. For example, the consulting firm might produce testimony from satisfied survey clients. Also, disputants often bring third parties into negotiations on the assumption that they will process argumentation in an unbiased manner.

Salary negotiation is a traditional example of distributive bargaining. A review of studies on gender differences in negotiation outcomes found that although men negotiated significantly better outcomes than women, the overall difference between men and women was small. However, even small differences in salary and wage negotiations would be perpetuated through subsequent salary increases based on percentage of pay. Furthermore, differences in negotiation outcomes could also be a factor in creating a "glass ceiling" effect to the extent that women are less effective in negotiating opportunities and positions of power and status. Thus, training programs that enable women to negotiate better starting salaries comparable with men can have short- and long-term benefits.[21]

Integrative Negotiation Tactics

As we noted earlier, integrative negotiation rejects a fixed-pie assumption and strives for collaborative problem solving that advances the interests of both parties. At the outset, it is useful but sobering to realize that people have a decided bias for fixed-pie thinking. A good example is seen in the North American manufacturing sector, where such thinking by both unions and management badly damaged the global competitiveness of manufacturing firms.[22]

Why the bias for fixed-pie thinking? First, integrative negotiation requires a degree of creativity. Most people are not especially creative, and the stress of typical negotiation does not provide the best climate for creativity in any event. This means that many of the role models that negotiators have (e.g., following labour negotiations on TV) are more likely to use distributive than integrative tactics. To complicate matters, if you are negotiating for constituents, they are also more likely to be exposed to distributive tactics and likely to pressure you to use them. Nevertheless, attempts at integrative negotiation can be well worth the effort.[23]

Copious Information Exchange. Most of the information exchanged in distributive bargaining is concerned with attacking the other party's position and trying to persuade them of the correctness of yours. Otherwise, mum's the word. A freer flow of information is critical to finding an integrative settlement. The problem, of course, is that we all tend to be a bit paranoid about information being used against us in bargaining situations. This means that trust must be built slowly. One way to proceed is to give away some non-critical information to the other party to get the ball rolling. As we noted earlier, much negotiation behaviour tends to be reciprocated. Also, ask the other party a lot of questions, and *listen* to their responses. This is at odds with the tell-and-sell approach used in most distributive negotiations. If all goes well, both parties will begin to reveal their true interests, not just their current positions.

Framing Differences as Opportunities. Parties in a negotiation often differ in their preferences, for everything from the timing of a deal to the degree of risk that each party wants to assume. Traditionally, such differences are framed as barriers to negotiations. However, such differences can often serve as a basis for integrative agreements because, again, they contain information that can telegraph each party's real interests. For instance, imagine that two co-workers are negotiating for the finishing date of a project that they have to complete by a certain deadline. Due to competing demands, one wants to finish it early, and the other wants to just make the deadline. In the course of the discussion, they realize that they can divide the labour such that one begins the project while the other finishes it, satisfying both parties fully (notice that this is not a compromise).

Cutting Costs. If you can somehow cut the costs that the other party associates with an agreement, the chance of an integrative settlement increases. For example, suppose that you are negotiating with your boss for a new, more interesting job assignment, but she does not like the idea because she relies on your excellent skills on your current assignment. By asking good questions (see above), you find out that she is ultimately worried about the job being done properly, not about your leaving it. You take the opportunity to inform her that you have groomed a subordinate to do your current job. This reduces the costs of her letting you assume the new assignment.

Integrative solutions are especially attractive when they reduce costs for *all* parties in a dispute. For example, firms in the computer and acoustics industries have joined together to support basic research on technology of interest to all firms. This reduces costly competition to perfect a technology that all parties need anyway.

Increasing Resources. Increasing available resources is a very literal way of getting around the fixed-pie syndrome. This is not as unlikely as it sounds when you realize that two parties, working together, might have access to twice as many resources as one party. One of your authors once saw two academic departments squabbling to get the approval to recruit one new faculty member for whom there was a budget line. Seeing this as a fixed pie leads to one department winning all or to the impossible compromise of half a recruit for each department. The chairs of the two departments used their *combined* political clout to get the dean to promise that they could also have exclusive access to one budget line the following year. The chairs then flipped a coin to see who would recruit immediately and who would wait a year. This minor compromise on time was less critical than the firm guarantee of a budget line.

Introducing Superordinate Goals. As discussed in Chapter 7, superordinate goals are attractive outcomes that can be achieved only by collaboration.[24] Neither party can attain the goal on its own. Superordinate goals probably represent the best example of creativity in integrative negotiation because they change the entire landscape of the negotiation episode. Many observers have noted how the terrorist attacks on September 11, 2001, created a superordinate goal that prompted collaboration among nations that otherwise might have been mired in conflict over more trivial matters.

Superordinate goals. Attractive outcomes that can be achieved only by collaboration.

Third Party Involvement

Sometimes, third parties come into play to intervene between negotiating parties.[25] Often, this happens when the parties reach an impasse. For example, a manager might have to step in to a conflict between two employees or even between two departments. In other cases, third party involvement exists right from the start of the negotiation. For example, real estate agents serve as an interface between home sellers and buyers.

Mediation. The process of mediation occurs when a neutral third party helps to facilitate a negotiated agreement. Formal mediation has a long history in labour disputes, international relations, and marital counselling. However, by definition, almost any manager might occasionally be required to play an informal mediating role.

What do mediators do?[26] First, almost anything that aids the *process* or *atmosphere* of negotiation can be helpful. Of course, this depends on the exact situation at hand. If there is tension, the mediator might serve as a lightning rod for anger or try to introduce humour. The mediator might try to help the parties clarify their underlying interests, both to themselves and to each other. Occasionally, imposing a deadline or helping the parties deal with their own constituents might be useful. Introducing a problem-solving orientation to move toward more integrative bargaining might also be appropriate.

The mediator might also intervene in the *content* of the negotiation, highlighting points of agreement, pointing out new options, or encouraging concessions.

Research shows that mediation has a fairly successful track record in dispute resolution. However, mediators cannot turn water into wine, and the process seems to work best when the conflict is not too intense and the parties are resolved to use negotiation to deal with their conflict. If the mediator is not seen as neutral or if there is dissension in the ranks of each negotiating party, mediation does not work so well.[27]

Arbitration.   The process of arbitration occurs when a third party is given the authority to dictate the terms of settlement of a conflict (there is also non-binding arbitration, which we will not consider here). Although disputing parties sometimes agree to arbitration, it can also be mandated formally by law or informally by upper management or parents. The key point is that negotiation has broken down, and the arbitrator has to make a final distributive allocation. This is not the way to integrative solutions.

In *conventional arbitration*, the arbitrator can choose any outcome, such as splitting the difference between the two parties. In *final offer arbitration*, each party makes a final offer, and the arbitrator chooses one of them. This latter invention was devised to motivate the two parties to make sensible offers that have a chance of being upheld. Also, fear of the all-or-nothing aspect of final arbitration seems to motivate more negotiated agreement.[28]

One of the most commonly arbitrated disputes between employers and employees is dismissal for excessive absenteeism. One study found that the arbitrators sided with the company in over half of such cases, especially when the company could show evidence of a fair and consistently applied absentee policy.[29]

Is All Conflict Bad?

In everyday life, there has traditionally been an emphasis on the negative, dysfunctional aspects of conflict. This is not difficult to understand. Discord between parents and children, severe labour strife, and international disputes are unpleasant experiences. To some degree, this emphasis on the negative aspects of conflict is also characteristic of thinking in organizational behaviour. However, there is growing awareness of some potential *benefits* of organizational conflict.[30] In fact, we suggested this in our previous distinction among task, process, and relationship conflict.

The argument that conflict can be functional rests mainly on the idea that it promotes necessary organizational change:

$$\text{CONFLICT} \longrightarrow \text{CHANGE} \longrightarrow \text{ADAPTATION} \longrightarrow \text{SURVIVAL}^{31}$$

In other words, for organizations to survive, they must adapt to their environments. This requires changes in strategy that may be stimulated through conflict. For example, consider the museum that relies heavily on government funding and consistently mounts exhibits that are appreciated only by "true connoisseurs" of art. Under a severe funding cutback, the museum can survive only if it begins to mount exhibits with more popular appeal. Such a change might occur only after much conflict within the board of directors.

Just how does conflict promote change? For one thing, it might bring into consideration new ideas that would not be offered without conflict. In trying to "one up" the opponent, one of the parties might develop a unique idea that the other cannot fail to appreciate. In a related way, conflict might promote change because each party begins to monitor the other's performance more carefully. This search for weaknesses means that it is more difficult to hide errors and problems from the rest of the organization. Such errors and problems (e.g., a failure to make deliveries on time) might be a signal that changes are necessary. Finally, conflict may promote useful change by signalling that a redistribution of power is necessary. Consider the human resources department that must battle with managers to get diversity programs implemented. This conflict might be a clue that some change is due in power priorities.

All this suggests that there are times when managers might use a strategy of **conflict stimulation** to cause change. But how does a manager know when some conflict might be a good thing? One signal is the existence of a "friendly rut," in which peaceful relationships take precedence over organizational goals. Another signal is seen when parties that should be interacting closely have chosen to withdraw from each other to avoid overt conflict. A third signal occurs when conflict is suppressed or downplayed by denying differences, ignoring controversy, and exaggerating points of agreement.[32]

The causes of conflict, discussed earlier, such as scarcity and ambiguity, can be manipulated by managers to achieve change.[33] For example, when he was appointed vice-chairman of product development at General Motors, Robert Lutz sent out a memo entitled "Strongly-Held Beliefs." In it, the product czar said that GM undervalued exciting design, and he panned corporate sacred cows such as the extensive use of consumer focus groups and product planning committees. Lutz stimulated conflict by signalling a shift of resources from marketing to design.[34]

Conflict in organizations, warranted or not, often causes considerable stress. Let's now turn to this topic.

> **Conflict stimulation.** A strategy of increasing conflict to motivate change.

A Model of Stress in Organizations

During the last decade, stress has become a serious concern for individuals and organizations. In fact, the headline of a news article referred to excessive stress as "the plague," and a popular business magazine named a special issue "The Limit," in recognition of workers being pushed to the limit like never before at all levels in the workplace.[35] A recent US National Institute for Occupational Safety and Health survey found that 40 percent of workers found their jobs extremely or very stressful, and the US Bureau of Labor Statistics determined that stress is a leading cause of worker disability.[36] In fact, in an American Psychological Association survey, work was reported to be a potent source of stress, edging out health and relationships.[37] Stress has been estimated to cost US businesses $300 billion annually and Canadian businesses $16 billion.[38]

These dramatic figures should not obscure the fact that stress can be part of the everyday routine of organizations. The model of a stress episode in Exhibit 12.3 can guide our introduction to this topic.[39]

Stressors

Stressors are environmental events or conditions that have the potential to induce stress. There are some conditions that would prove stressful for just about everyone. These include such things as extreme heat, extreme cold, isolation, or hostile people. More interesting is the fact that the individual personality often determines the extent to which a potential stressor becomes a real stressor and actually induces stress.

> **Stressors.** Environmental events or conditions that have the potential to induce stress.

> **EXHIBIT 12.3**
> Model of a stress episode.

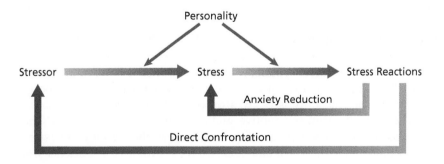

Stress

Stress. A psychological reaction to the demands inherent in a stressor that has the potential to make a person feel tense or anxious.

Stress is a psychological reaction to the demands inherent in a stressor that has the potential to make a person feel tense or anxious because the person does not feel capable of coping with these demands.[40] Stress is not intrinsically bad. All people require a certain level of stimulation from their environment, and moderate levels of stress can serve this function. In fact, one would wonder about the perceptual accuracy of a person who *never* experienced tension. On the other hand, stress does become a problem when it leads to especially high levels of anxiety and tension. Obviously, the Hair War described in the chapter-opening vignette has provoked much stress.

Stress Reactions

Stress reactions. The behavioural, psychological, and physiological consequences of stress.

Stress reactions are the behavioural, psychological, and physiological consequences of stress. Some of these reactions are essentially passive responses over which the individual has little direct control, such as elevated blood pressure or a reduced immune function. Other reactions are active attempts to *cope* with some previous aspect of the stress episode. Exhibit 12.3 indicates that stress reactions that involve coping attempts might be directed toward dealing directly with the stressor or simply reducing the anxiety generated by stress. In general, the former strategy has more potential for effectiveness than the latter because the chances of the stress episode being *terminated* are increased.[41]

Often, reactions that are useful for the individual in dealing with a stress episode may be very costly to the organization. The individual who is conveniently absent from work on the day of a difficult inventory check might prevent personal stress but leave the organization short handed (provoking stress in others). Thus, organizations should be concerned about the stress that individual employees experience.

Throughout the book, we have been careful to note cross-cultural differences in OB. However, the stress model presented here appears to generalize across cultures. That is, similar factors provoke stress and lead to similar stress reactions around the globe.[42]

Personality and Stress

Personality (Chapter 2) can have an important influence on the stress experience. As shown in Exhibit 12.3, it can affect both the extent to which potential stressors are perceived as stressful and the types of stress reactions that occur. Let's look at three key personality traits.

Locus of control. A set of beliefs about whether one's behaviour is controlled mainly by internal or external forces.

Locus of Control. You will recall from Chapter 2 that **locus of control** concerns people's beliefs about the factors that control their behaviour. Internals believe that they control their own behaviour, while externals believe that their behaviour is controlled by luck, fate, or powerful people. Compared with internals, externals are more likely to feel anxious in the face of potential stressors.[43] Most people like to feel in control of what happens to them, and externals feel less in control. Internals are more likely to confront stressors directly because they assume that this response will make a difference. Externals, on the other hand, are anxious but do not feel that they are masters of their own fate. Thus, they are more prone to simple anxiety-reduction strategies that only work in the short run.

Type A behaviour pattern. A personality pattern that includes aggressiveness, ambitiousness, competitiveness, hostility, impatience, and a sense of time urgency.

Type A Behaviour Pattern. Interest in the **Type A behaviour pattern** began when physicians noticed that many sufferers of coronary heart disease, especially those who developed the disease relatively young, exhibited a distinctive pattern of behaviours and emotions.[44] Individuals who exhibit the Type A behaviour pattern tend to be aggressive and ambitious. Their hostility is easily aroused, and they feel a great sense of time urgency. They are impatient, competitive, and preoccupied with their work. The Type A individual can be contrasted with the Type B, who does not exhibit these extreme characteristics. Compared with Type B individuals, Type A people report heavier workloads, longer work hours, and more conflicting work demands.[45] We will see later that such factors turn out to be potent stressors. Thus, either Type A people encounter more stressful situations than Type B people do, or they perceive themselves as doing so. In turn, Type A individuals are likely to exhibit adverse physiological reactions in response to stress. These include elevated blood pressure, elevated heart rate, and modified blood chemistry. Frustrating, difficult, or competitive events are especially likely to prompt these adverse reactions. Type A individuals seem to have a strong need to control their work environment. This is doubtless a full-time task that stimulates their feelings of time urgency and leads them to overextend themselves physically.[46]

Research has made it increasingly clear that the major component of Type A behaviour that contributes to adverse physiological reactions is hostility and repressed anger. This may also be accompanied by exaggerated cynicism and distrust of others. When these factors are prominent in a Type A individual's personality, stress is most likely to take its toll.[47]

Negative Affectivity. Negative affectivity is the propensity to view the world, including oneself and other people, in a negative light. It is a stable personality trait that is a major component of the "Big Five" personality dimension neuroticism (Chapter 2). People high in negative affectivity tend to be pessimistic and downbeat. As a consequence, they tend to report more stressors in the work environment and to feel more subjective stress. They are particularly likely to feel stressed in response to the demands of a heavy workload.[48]

Several factors might be responsible for the susceptibility to stress of those who are high in negative affectivity. These include (a) a predisposition to *perceive* stressors in the workplace, (b) hypersensitivity to existing stressors, (c) a tendency to gravitate to stressful jobs, (d) a tendency to *provoke* stress through their negativity, or (e) the use of passive, indirect coping styles that avoid the real sources of stress.[49]

> **Negative affectivity.** Propensity to view the world, including oneself and other people, in a negative light.

Stressors in Organizational Life

A study found that among a sample of employed Canadians, the most common source of stress is *workplace* stressors.[50] In this section, we will examine potential stressors in detail. Some stressors can affect almost everyone in any organization, while others are likely to affect people who perform particular roles.

Executive and Managerial Stressors

Executives and managers make key organizational decisions and direct the work of others. In these capacities, they experience some special forms of stress.

Role Overload. Role overload occurs when one must perform too many tasks in too short a time period, and it is a common stressor for managers, especially in today's downsized organizations.[51] The open-ended nature of the managerial job is partly responsible for this heavy and protracted workload.[52] Management is an ongoing *process*, and there are few signposts to signify that a task is complete and that rest and relaxation are permitted. Especially when coupled with frequent moves or excessive travel, a heavy workload often provokes conflict between the manager's role as an organizational member and his or her role as a spouse or parent. Thus, role overload may provoke stress, at the same time preventing the manager from enjoying the pleasures of life that can reduce stress.

> **Role overload.** The requirement for too many tasks to be performed in too short a time period.

Heavy Responsibility. Not only is the workload of the executive heavy, but it can have extremely important consequences for the organization and its members. A vice-president of labour relations might be in charge of a negotiation strategy that could result in either labour peace or a protracted and bitter strike. To complicate matters,

"You've been working awfully hard lately.
If you need a little fresh air and sunshine,
you can go to www.fresh-air-and-sunshine.com"

the personal consequences of an incorrect decision can be staggering. For example, the courts have fined and even jailed executives who have engaged in illegal activities on behalf of their organizations. Finally, executives are responsible for people as well as things, and this influence over the future of others has the potential to induce stress. The executive who must terminate the operation of an unprofitable division, putting many out of work, or the manager who must lay off an employee, putting one out of work, may experience guilt and tension.[53]

Operative-Level Stressors

Operatives are individuals who occupy non-professional and non-managerial positions in organizations. In a manufacturing organization, operatives perform the work on the shop floor and range from skilled craftspeople to unskilled labourers. As is the case with other organizational roles, the occupants of operative positions are sometimes exposed to a special set of stressors.

Poor Physical Working Conditions. Operative-level employees are more likely than managers and professionals to be exposed to physically unpleasant and even dangerous working conditions. Although social sensibility and union activity have improved working conditions over the years, many employees must still face excessive heat, cold, noise, pollution, and the chance of accidents.

Poor Job Design. Although bad job design can provoke stress at any organizational level (executive role overload is an example), the designs of lower-level blue- and white-collar jobs are particular culprits. It might seem paradoxical that jobs that are too simple or not challenging enough can act as stressors. However, monotony and boredom can prove extremely frustrating to people who feel capable of handling more complex tasks. Thus, research has found that job scope can be a stressor at levels that are either too low or too high.[54]

Boundary Role Stressors, Burnout, and Emotional Labour

Boundary roles. Positions in which organizational members are required to interact with members of other organizations or with the public.

Boundary roles are positions in which organizational members are required to interact with members of other organizations or with the public. For example, a vice-president of public relations is responsible for representing his or her company to the public. At other levels, receptionists, sale reps, and installers often interact with customers or suppliers.

Occupants of boundary role positions are especially likely to experience stress as they straddle the imaginary boundary between the organization and its environment. This is yet another form of role conflict in which one's role as an organizational member might be incompatible with the demands made by the public or other organizations. A classic case of boundary role stress involves sales reps. In extreme cases, customers desire fast delivery of a custom-tailored product, such as a new software application. The sales rep might be tempted to "offer the moon" but at the same time is aware that such an order could place a severe strain on his or her organization's software development team. Thus, the sales rep is faced with the dilemma of doing his or her primary job (selling), while protecting another function (software development) from unreasonable demands that could result in a broken delivery contract.

A particular form of stress (and accompanying stress reactions) experienced by some boundary role occupants is burnout. **Burnout,** as Christina Maslach, Michael Leiter, and Wilmar Schaufeli define it, is a syndrome made up of emotional exhaustion, cynicism, and low self-efficacy (Chapter 2).[55] Burnout was originally studied among those working in some capacity with people. Frequently, these people are organizational clients who require special attention or who are experiencing severe problems. Thus, teachers, nurses, paramedics, social workers, and police are especially likely candidates for burnout. However, it has now been established that burnout can occur even among non-boundary spanners.

Burnout follows a process that begins with emotional exhaustion (left side of Exhibit 12.4). The person feels fatigued in the morning, drained by the work, and frustrated by the day's events. One way to deal with this extreme exhaustion is to become cynical and distance oneself from one's clients, the "cause" of the exhaustion. In the extreme, this might involve depersonalizing them, treating them like objects, and lacking concern for what happens to them. The clients might also be seen as blaming the employee for their problems. Finally, the burned-out individual develops feelings of low self-efficacy and low personal accomplishment—"I can't deal with these people, I'm not helping them, I don't understand them." In fact, because of the exhaustion and depersonalization, there might be more than a grain of truth to these feelings. Although the exact details of this progression are open to some question, these three symptoms paint a reliable picture of burnout.[56]

Burnout seems to be most common among people who entered their jobs with especially high ideals. Their expectations of being able to "change the world" are badly frustrated when they encounter the reality shock of troubled clients (who are often perceived as unappreciative) and the inability of the organization to help them. Teachers get fed up with being disciplinarians, nurses get upset when patients die, and police officers get depressed when they must constantly deal with the "losers" of society. For an illustration, see Ethical Focus: *Workplace Violence Prompts Stress among Health and Social Service Providers.*

Burnout. A syndrome of emotional exhaustion, cynicism, and reduced self-efficacy.

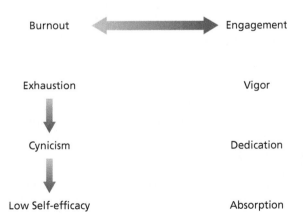

EXHIBIT 12.4
The burnout–engagement continuum.

ETHICAL FOCUS

Workplace Violence Prompts Stress among Health and Social Service Providers

Health care and social assistance workers are much more likely to file compensation claims over violence in the workplace than employees in other Canadian sectors, a CBC News investigation suggests. In some provinces, the rate of violence-related claims is 12 times higher than for all other industries, according to databases from provincial workplace safety insurance boards that the CBC gained access to after three years of negotiation. Some of the databases are more detailed than others, and incidents are recorded in different ways, so numbers can't be compared across the board. However, the databases show the following:

- Nova Scotia health care and social assistance workers reported 3.59 violent incidents per 1000 workers between 1994 and 2004, among the highest rates in the country for workers in those sectors.
- Ontario health care and social assistance workers reported 5333 violent incidents between the years 1997 and 2004, out of 12 383 reported by all workers. That's an average of 1.21 incidents per 1000 workers, compared to 0.17 incidents per 1000 workers in other industries.
- Quebec's health and social assistance sector recorded 1.43 incidents per 1000 workers between 1994 and 2004.
- Annually, Ontario health care and social assistance workers lost 24.5 days per 1000 workers due to violence, compared to four lost days per 1000 workers in all other incidents.

Not even police officers are exposed to more violence at work than nurses, the numbers for at least two provinces indicate. In Nova Scotia, 358 registered nurses filed claims stemming from violence between 1994 and 2004, compared to 96 police officers who did so in the same time period. During the same decade in British Columbia, 769 practical nurses or nurse's aides filed claims based on violent incidents, compared to 335 police officers. Health care workers say the trend to de-institutionalize people with mental illnesses, bringing them into emergency rooms, is one reason for the increase in violence. And with an aging population, more people with dementia are in long-term care facilities. In addition, some nurses report they're so busy working in an overburdened system that they don't have time to defuse little crises before they escalate into full-fledged attacks.

A union representing 14 000 health care and social service workers in BC says they are being punched, grabbed, pushed, and threatened verbally by their patients and clients. In rare cases, some are even killed. "If you were working in a grocery store, you wouldn't tolerate someone ramming a grocery cart into you because the stock wasn't on the shelf," said Cindy Stewart, who speaks for the Health Sciences Association of British Columbia. "You wouldn't tolerate one of your customers punching you, or slapping you, grabbing you, or spitting on you, or verbally abusing you. That wouldn't be tolerated in those kinds of work environments—and yet it is a daily occurrence in the health sector."

Source: Excerpted from CBC News (2006). Health, social service workers top targets of violence. Retrieved April 24, 2006, from www.cbc.ca/story/canada/national/2006/04/24/workplace-violence060424.html. Used by permission.

What are the consequences of burnout? Some individuals bravely pursue a new occupation, often experiencing guilt about not having been able to cope in the old one. Others stay in the same occupation but seek a new job. For instance, the burned-out nurse may go into nursing education to avoid contact with sick patients. Some people pursue administrative careers in their profession, attempting to "climb above" the source of their difficulties. These people often set cynical examples for idealistic subordinates. Finally, some people stay in their jobs and become part of the legion of "deadwood," collecting their paycheques but doing little to contribute to the mission of the organization. Many "good bureaucrats" choose this route.[57]

Much boundary role stress stems from the frequent need for such employees to engage in "emotional labour." You will recall from Chapter 4 that emotional labour involves regulating oneself to suppress negative emotions or to exaggerate positive ones. Thus, police officers are not supposed to express anger at unsafe motorists or drunks, and salon employees are supposed to act friendly and sympathetic to boorish clients. Such suppression and acting takes a toll on cognitive and emotional resources over time.

The Job Demands–Resources Model and Work Engagement

It is obvious that organizations should strive to avoid causing burnout and the extreme detachment from the job that it causes. In fact, organizations should strive to foster exactly the *opposite* of burnout—extreme engagement and enthusiasm for the job. In recent years the subject of engagement has captured the attention of both researchers and managers. In part, this is due to rather low self-reported levels of engagement. Surveys indicate that only 17 percent of Canadians are highly engaged in their work, 66 percent are moderately engaged, and 17 percent are disengaged.[58]

Work engagement can be defined as "a positive work-related state of mind that is characterized by vigor, dedication, and absorption."[59] (See the right side of Exhibit 12.4.) Vigor involves high levels of energy and mental resilience at work; dedication means being strongly involved in your work and experiencing a sense of significance, enthusiasm, and challenge; absorption refers to being fully concentrated on and engrossed in your work. In particular, the first two dimensions—vigor and dedication—position engagement as the opposite of burnout.

What determines whether employees tend toward engagement versus burnout? According to the **job demands–resources model** the work environment can be described in terms of demands and resources.[60] Job demands are physical, psychological, social, or organizational features of a job that require sustained physical or psychological effort that in turn can result in physiological or psychological costs. Common demands include work overload, time pressure, role ambiguity, and role conflict. Job resources refer to features of a job that are functional in that they help achieve work goals, reduce job demands, and stimulate personal growth, learning, and development. Job resources can come from the organization (e.g., pay, career opportunities, job security), interpersonal and social relations (e.g., supervisor and co-worker support, team climate), the organization of work (e.g., role clarity, participation in decision making), and the task itself (e.g., task significance, autonomy, performance feedback). A central assumption of the model is that high job resources foster work engagement, while high job demands exhaust employees physically and mentally and lead to burnout. Indeed, research has found that job demands are related to burnout, disengagement, and health problems, while job resources lead to work engagement, organizational citizenship behaviour, and organizational commitment. Also, it shows that resources can buffer the negative impact of job demands on well-being.[61]

Exhibit 12.5 shows the results of a survey of 11 000 UK workers in 26 occupations. The occupations are ranked in terms of several outcomes of stress. The low-ranked jobs are "worse," and those in italics are worse than average. These are the jobs that make high demands while supplying limited resources. Later in the chapter we will suggest some ways to reduce stress or improve the ability to cope that involve reducing demands and/or increasing resources.

Some General Stressors

To conclude our discussion of stressors that people encounter in organizational life, we will consider some that are probably experienced equally by occupants of all roles.

Interpersonal Conflict. From our earlier discussion of interpersonal conflict, you may correctly guess that it can be a potent stressor, especially for those with strong avoidance tendencies. The entire range of conflict, from personality clashes to intergroup strife, is

Work engagement. A positive work-related state of mind that is characterized by vigor, dedication, and absorption.

Job demands–resources model. A model that specifies how job demands cause burnout and job resources cause engagement.

EXHIBIT 12.5
Occupations ranked on physical health, psychological well-being, and job satisfaction.

Note: The most stressful jobs have the lowest ranks. Jobs worse than average are indicated in italics.

Source: Johnson S. (2009). Organizational screening: The ASSET model. In S. Cartwright & C.L. Cooper (Eds.), *The Oxford handbook of organizational well-being*. Oxford: Oxford University Press, p. 145.

Rank	Physical health	Psychological well–being	Job satisfaction
1	*Ambulance*	*Social services providing care*	*Prison officer*
2	*Teachers*	*Teachers*	*Ambulance*
3	*Social services providing care*	*Fire brigade*	*Police*
4	*Customer services–call center*	*Ambulace*	*Customer services–call center*
5	*Bar staff*	*Vets*	*Social services providing care*
6	*Prison officer*	*Lecturers*	*Teachers*
7	*Mgmt (private sector)*	*Clerical and admin*	*Nursing*
8	*Clerical and admin*	*Mgmt (private sector)*	*Medical/dental*
9	*Police*	*Prison Officer*	*Allied health professionals*
10	*Teaching assistant*	*Research–academic*	Bar staff
11	*Head teachers*	*Police*	Mgmt (private sector)
12	*Secretarial/business support*	*Customer services–call center*	Fire brigade
13	*Research–academic*	*Director (public sector)*	Vets
14	*Lecturers*	*Allied health professionals*	Clerical and admin
15	*Senior police*	*Bar staff*	Mgmt (public sector)
16	*Nursing*	*Nursing*	Lecturers
17	*Mgmt (public sector)*	*Medical/dental*	Head teachers
18	*Allied health professionals*	*Senior police*	Teaching assistant
19	*Medical/dental*	*Secretaria/business support*	Secretarial/business support
20	Accountant	*Head teachers*	Director (public sector)
21	Fire brigade	*Mgmt (public sector)*	Research–academic
22	Vets	*Accountant*	Senior police
23	Director (public sector)	*Teaching assistant*	School lunchtime supervisors
24	Analyst	Analyst	Accountant
25	School lunchtime supervisors	School lunchtime supervisors	Analyst
26	Director/MD (private sector)	Director/MD (private sector)	Director/MD (private sector)

especially likely to cause stress when it leads to real or perceived attacks on our self-esteem or integrity. Although conflict can lead to stress in many settings outside of work, we often have the option of terminating the relationship, of "choosing our friends," as it were. This option is often not available at work.

A particular manifestation of interpersonal conflict that has received increased attention in recent years is workplace bullying. **Bullying** can be defined as repeated negative behaviour directed toward one or more individuals of lower power or status that creates a hostile work environment.[62] Research has clearly demonstrated that it is a potent source of stress and negative well-being.[63]

A number of factors distinguish bullying as a stress-inducing form of conflict.[64] Although bullying can involve physical aggression, it is most commonly a more subtle form of psychological aggression and intimidation. This can take many forms, such as incessant teasing, demeaning criticism, social isolation, or sabotaging others' tools and equipment. An essential feature of bullying is its persistence, and a single harsh incident would not constitute such behaviour. Rather, it is the *repeated* teasing, criticism, or undermining that signals bullying. Another key feature of the bullying process is some degree of power or status imbalance between the bully and the victim. Thus, managers have often been identified as bullies by subordinates. However, power imbalance can be subtle, and in some settings even work peers might lack power due to

Bullying. Repeated negative behaviour directed toward one or more individuals of lower power or status that creates a hostile work environment.

their gender, race, physical stature, low job security, or educational credentials. Also, there is power in numbers, in that subordinates might team up to harass their boss. This is an example of a phenomenon closely associated to bullying called *mobbing*. Mobbing occurs when a number of individuals, usually direct co-workers, "gang up" on a particular employee.[65] Mobbing can be especially intimidating and stressful because it restricts the availability of social support that might be present when there is only a single bully.

The essential point is that victims of bullying and mobbing experience stress because they feel powerless to deal with the perpetrator(s). Most observers note that a combination of factors work together to stimulate this dysfunctional behaviour.

Norway, Sweden, France, and the provinces of Quebec and Saskatchewan have enacted laws that pertain to bullying in the workplace.[66] Various organizations have also done their part. The US Department of Veterans Affairs and IBM both have active anti-bullying programs. IBM fired several factory workers who mobbed their new supervisor to drive home its seriousness about its policy.[67]

Before continuing, consider You Be the Manager: *Bullying at Veterans Affairs.*

Work–Family Conflict. Work–family conflict occurs when either work duties interfere with family life or family life interferes with work responsibilities.[68] A study found that it is costing Canadian companies $6 billion to $10 billion a year in absenteeism, and the Canadian health care system $425 million in increased visits to the doctor.[69]

Two facts of life in contemporary society have increased the stress stemming from the interrole conflict between being a member of one's family and the member of an organization. First, the increase in the number of households in which both parents work and the increase in the number of single-parent families has led to a number of stressors centred around childcare. Finding adequate daycare and disputes between partners about sharing childcare responsibilities can prove to be serious stressors. Second, increased life spans have meant that many people in the prime of their careers find themselves providing support for elderly parents, some of whom may be seriously ill. This inherently stressful eldercare situation is often compounded by feelings of guilt about the need to tend to matters at work.

Women are particularly victimized by stress due to work–family conflict, although it is a rapidly growing problem for men as well. Much anecdotal evidence suggests that women who take time off work to deal with pressing family matters are more likely than men to be labelled disloyal or undedicated to their work. Also, many managers seem to be insensitive to the demands that these basic demographic shifts are making on their employees, again compounding the potential for stress.[70]

Occupations that require a high degree of teamwork or responsibilities for others tend to provoke the most work–family conflict (e.g., police detectives, firefighters, family doctors). At the other extreme, tellers, insurance adjusters, and taxi drivers report much lower levels.[71]

Job Insecurity and Change. Secure employment is an important goal for almost everyone, and stress may be encountered when it is threatened. During the last decade, organizations have undergone substantial changes that have left many workers unemployed and threatened the security of those who have been fortunate enough to remain in their jobs. The trend toward mergers and acquisitions, along with re-engineering, restructuring, and downsizing, has led to increasingly high levels of stress among employees who either have lost their jobs or must live with the threat of more layoffs, the loss of friends and co-workers, and an increased workload.[72] The fear of job loss has become a way of life for employees at all organizational levels.[73]

At the operative level, unionization has provided a degree of employment security for some, but the vagaries of the economy and the threat of technology and other organizational changes hang heavily over many workers. Among professionals, the very

YOU BE THE MANAGER

Bullying at Veterans Affairs

Jobs in the social service sector regularly entail emotional labour, with workers confronted on a daily basis with high demands from clients concerning social, emotional, and medical problems. While such client–service provider interactions can be emotionally draining, such a work environment can also be a breeding ground for workplace aggression and bullying.

With this in mind, the United States Department of Veterans Affairs (VA), in collaboration with university researchers, launched the Workplace Stress and Aggression Project. The VA provides patient care and federal benefits to veterans and their dependents through central offices, benefits offices, and medical facilities. In the post-September 11 era, the VA had seen an increase in activity with the conflicts in Afghanistan and Iraq. The goal of the project was to assess the prevalence of workplace aggression and bullying within the VA, to understand their impact on employee satisfaction, VA performance, and veteran satisfaction, and to develop intervention strategies.

The research team used archival data, questionnaires, interviews, and discussion groups. Results of the initial surveys clearly indicated that workplace aggression and bullying were issues within the VA. Overall, 36 percent of employees surveyed reported being bullied at work. Bullying was defined as persistent patterns of aggression that workers experienced at least once a week. Of the 36 percent, 29 percent indicated they experienced aggression in the workplace one to five times a week, while 7 percent reported experiencing six or more aggression episodes a week. Another 58 percent of employees reported that they experienced workplace aggression, albeit not on a weekly basis, while only 6 percent of employees indicated that they suffered no workplace aggression. Aggression could be physical or verbal, active (e.g., in a confrontation) or passive (e.g., through exclusion), or direct (e.g., personally targeted) or indirect (e.g., defacing property or spreading rumours). Most incidents were of the verbal, passive, and indirect variety.

Employees indicated that 44 percent of the aggression they experienced emanated from co-workers, 35 percent came from supervisors, and 12 percent came from veterans. In terms of impact on personal well-being, they suffered more stress and lower job satisfaction when a supervisor was the source of the aggression than when co-workers or clients were the

High levels of bullying at various Veterans Affairs facilities worried executives.

source. The research team also found that bullying was linked to lower employee and organizational performance and increases in stress, absenteeism, lateness, turnover, and worker compensation claims. With this data in hand, the project team's focus turned to understanding why aggression occurred and what could be done to reduce it.

QUESTIONS

1. What do you think some of the primary causes of workplace aggression and bullying within the VA might be? Do you think the causes would be different across the various VA facilities?

2. Suggest an intervention strategy to reduce the incidence of aggression and bullying in the VA workplace. Who should be involved?

To find out how the VA responded, see The Manager's Notebook at the end of the chapter.

Sources: Scaringi, J., et al. (Undated). *The VA workplace stress and aggression project—final report*; Neuman, J.H., and Keashly, L. (2005, August). Reducing aggression and bullying: An intervention project in the U.S. Department of Veterans Affairs. In J. Raver (Chair), *Workplace bullying: International perspectives on moving from research to practice.* Symposium presented at the annual meeting of the Academy of Management, Honolulu, HI; Neuman, J.H. (2004). Injustice, stress, and aggression in organizations. In R.W. Griffin and A.M. O'Leary-Kelly (Eds.), *The dark side of organizational behavior.* San Francisco, CA: Jossey-Bass.

specialization that enables them to obtain satisfactory jobs becomes a millstone whenever social or economic forces change. For example, aerospace scientists and engineers have long been prey to the boom-and-bust nature of their industry. When layoffs occur, these people are often perceived as overqualified or too specialized to easily obtain jobs in related industries. Finally, the executive suite does not escape job insecurity. Recent pressures for corporate performance have made cost-cutting a top priority, and one of the surest ways to cut costs in the short run is to reduce executive positions and thus reduce the total management payroll. Many corporations have greatly thinned their executive ranks in recent years.

Role Ambiguity. We have already noted how role conflict—having to deal with incompatible role expectations—can provoke stress. There is also substantial evidence that role ambiguity can provoke stress.[74] From Chapter 7, you will recall that role ambiguity exists when the goals of one's job or the methods of performing the job are unclear. Such a lack of direction can prove stressful, especially for people who are low in their tolerance for such ambiguity. For example, the president of a firm might be instructed by the board of directors to increase profits and cut costs. While this goal seems clear enough, the means by which it can be achieved might be unclear. This ambiguity can be devastating, especially when the organization is doing poorly and no strategy seems to improve things.

Sexual Harassment. In Chapter 11, we discussed sexual harassment in terms of the abuse of power and a form of unethical behaviour. Sexual harassment is a major workplace stressor, with serious consequences for employees and organizations that are similar to or more negative than those of other types of job stressors.[75] Sexual harassment in the workplace is now considered to be widespread in both the public and private sectors, and most harassment victims are subjected to ongoing harassment and stress.[76] The negative effects of sexual harassment include decreased morale, job satisfaction, organizational commitment, and job performance, and increased absenteeism, turnover, and job loss. Sexual harassment has also been found to have serious effects on the psychological and physical well-being of harassment victims.[77] Victims of sexual harassment experience depression, frustration, nervousness, fatigue, nausea, hypertension, and symptoms of posttraumatic stress disorder.[78] Organizations in which sexual harassment is most likely to be a problem are those that have a climate that is tolerant of sexual harassment and where women are working in traditionally male-dominated jobs and in a male-dominated workplace.[79]

Exhibit 12.6 summarizes the sources of stress at various points in the organization.

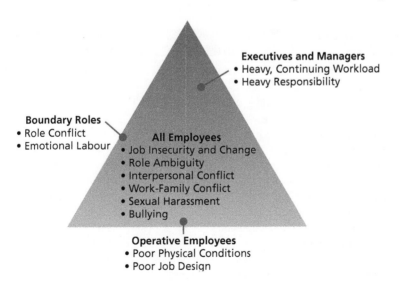

Executives and Managers
- Heavy, Continuing Workload
- Heavy Responsibility

Boundary Roles
- Role Conflict
- Emotional Labour

All Employees
- Job Insecurity and Change
- Role Ambiguity
- Interpersonal Conflict
- Work-Family Conflict
- Sexual Harassment
- Bullying

Operative Employees
- Poor Physical Conditions
- Poor Job Design

EXHIBIT 12.6
Sources of stress at various points in the organization.

Reactions to Organizational Stress

In this section, we examine the reactions that people who experience organizational stress might exhibit. These reactions can be divided into behavioural, psychological, and physiological responses. In general, reactions that result in an addition to one's resources can be seen as good coping with stress. Reactions that increase demands constitute bad coping. Exhibit 12.7 shows how a sample of more than 31 000 Canadian employees reported coping with stress.

Behavioural Reactions to Stress

Behavioural reactions to stress are overt activities that the stressed individual uses in an attempt to cope with the stress. They include problem solving, seeking social support, modified performance, withdrawal, and the use of addictive substances.

Problem Solving. In general, problem solving is directed toward terminating the stressor or reducing its potency, not toward simply making the person feel better in the short run. Problem solving is reality-oriented, and while it is not always effective in combating the stressor, it reveals flexibility and realistic use of feedback. Most examples of a problem-solving response to stress are undramatic because problem solving is generally the routine, sensible, obvious approach that an objective observer might suggest. Consider the following examples of problem solving.

- *Delegation.* A busy executive reduces her stress-provoking workload by delegating some of her many tasks to a capable assistant.
- *Time management.* A manager who finds the day too short writes a daily schedule, requires his subordinates to make formal appointments to see him, and instructs his secretary to screen phone calls more selectively.
- *Talking it out.* An engineer who is experiencing stress because of poor communication with her non-engineer superior resolves to sit down with the boss and hammer out an agreement concerning the priorities on a project.
- *Asking for help.* A salesperson who is anxious about his company's ability to fill a difficult order asks the production manager to provide a realistic estimate of the probable delivery date.
- *Searching for alternatives.* A machine operator who finds her monotonous job stress-provoking applies for a transfer to a more interesting position for which the pay is identical.

EXHIBIT 12.7
How Canadian employees cope with stress.

Source: Higgins, C., Duxbury, L., and Lyons, S. (2006). *Reducing work-life conflict: What works? What doesn't?* Ottawa: Health Canada, p. 131. Reproduced with the permission of the Minister of Public Works and Government Services Canada, 2009.

Coping Strategies	% of Sample Who Use		
	Rarely	Weekly	Daily
Prioritize	9%	21%	69%
Schedule, organize and plan my time more carefully	22%	32%	47%
Talked with family or friends	26%	29%	45%
Just work harder (I try to do it all)	31%	26%	43%
Find some other activity to take my mind off it	36%	32%	32%
Talked with colleagues at work	40%	27%	32%
Delegate work to others	49%	24%	27%
Sought help from family or friends	51%	25%	23%
Just try and forget about it	60%	20%	19%
Sought help from colleagues at work	65%	19%	16%
Have an alcoholic drink	65%	23%	12%
Use prescription, over-the-counter or other drugs	86%	4%	11%
Reduce the quality of the things I do	72%	18%	10%

Seeking Social Support. Speaking generally, social support simply refers to having close ties with other people. In turn, these close ties can affect stress by bolstering self-esteem, providing useful information, offering comfort and humour, or even providing material resources (such as a loan). Research evidence shows that the benefits of social support are double-barrelled. First, people with stronger social networks exhibit better psychological and physical well-being. Second, when people encounter stressful events, those with good social networks are likely to cope more positively. Thus, the social network acts as a buffer against stress.[80]

Off the job, individuals might find social support in a spouse, family, or friends. On the job, social support might be available from one's superior or co-workers. Research evidence suggests that the buffering aspects of social support are most potent when they are directly connected to the source of stress. This means that co-workers and superiors may be the best sources of support for dealing with work-related stress. But most managers need better training to recognize employee stress symptoms, clarify role requirements, and so on. Unfortunately, some organizational cultures, especially those that are very competitive, do not encourage members to seek support in a direct fashion. In this kind of setting, relationships that people develop in professional associations can sometimes serve as an informed source of social support.

Performance Changes. Stress or stressors frequently cause reduced job performance.[81] However, this statement needs to be qualified slightly. Some stressors are "hindrance" stressors in that they directly damage goal attainment. These include things like role ambiguity and interpersonal conflict. Such stressors damage performance. On the other hand, some stressors are challenging. These include factors such as heavy workload and responsibility. Such stressors can damage performance, but they sometimes stimulate it via added motivation.[82]

Withdrawal. Withdrawal from the stressor is one of the most basic reactions to stress. In organizations, this withdrawal takes the form of absence and turnover. Compared with problem-solving reactions to stress, absenteeism fails to attack the stressor directly. Rather, the absent individual is simply attempting short-term reduction of the anxiety prompted by the stressor. When the person returns to the job, the stress is still there. From this point of view, absence is a dysfunctional reaction to stress for both the individual and the organization. The same can be said about turnover if a person resigns from a stressful job on the spur of the moment merely to escape stress. However, a good case can be made for a well-planned resignation in which the intent is to assume another job that should be less stressful. This is actually a problem-solving reaction that should benefit both the individual and the organization in the long run. Absence, turnover, and turnover intentions have often been linked with stress and its causes.[83] For an ironic counterexample, see Research Focus: *Presenteeism in the Workplace.*

Use of Addictive Substances. Smoking, drinking, and drug use represent the least satisfactory behavioural responses to stress for both the individual and the organization. These activities fail to terminate stress episodes, and they leave employees less physically and mentally prepared to perform their jobs. We have all heard of hard-drinking newspaper reporters and advertising executives, and it is tempting to infer that the stress of their boundary role positions is responsible for their drinking. Indeed, cigarette and alcohol use are associated with work-related stress.[84]

Psychological Reactions to Stress

Psychological reactions to stress primarily involve emotions and thought processes rather than overt behaviour, although these reactions are frequently revealed in the individual's speech and actions. The most common psychological reaction to stress is the use of defence mechanisms.[85]

Defence mechanisms are psychological attempts to reduce the anxiety associated with stress. Notice that, by definition, defence mechanisms concentrate on *anxiety*

Defence mechanisms. Psychological attempts to reduce the anxiety associated with stress.

RESEARCH FOCUS

Presenteeism in the Workplace

Presenteeism refers to going to work when one is ill. Although both managers and work researchers have been interested in absenteeism for years, it is only recently that presenteeism has become a subject of concerted interest. Some of this interest is stimulated by the finding that the aggregate productivity loss that occurs due to working while ill is much greater than that attributed to absence. Presentees are at work, but they are often not working at full capacity. What would cause people to go to work even though they are suffering from asthma, allergies, migraines, or respiratory problems? Many factors appear to be stress-related. This is ironic because it means that some stressors can cause both absenteeism and presenteeism.

High job demands and time pressure have been associated with presenteeism; people feel under pressure to get work done and sense the work piling up if they are absent. This is especially likely if there is a lack of backup, an increasing possibility in today's down sized organizations. Job insecurity may also prompt people to go to work when they are ill. Thus, non-permanent employees exhibit less absenteeism than their permanent counterparts, and this might signal presenteeism on their part. Strict policies against absence and team-oriented work designs have also been implicated in presenteeism. In team settings, people might feel they are letting the team down if they book off sick.

Depression, which is frequently associated with stress, is one of the most common health problems connected to presenteeism. This may be because people do not view it as a legitimate reason to be absent or fear disclosing it as reason for their absence.

Source: Johns, G. (2010). Presenteeism in the workplace: A review and research agenda. *Journal of Organizational Behavior*, in press.

reduction rather than on actually confronting or dealing with the stressor. Some common defence mechanisms include the following:

- *Rationalization* is attributing socially acceptable reasons or motives to one's actions so that they will appear reasonable and sensible, at least to oneself. For example, a male nurse who becomes very angry and abusive when learning that he will not be promoted to supervisor might justify his anger by claiming that the female head nurse discriminates against men.

- *Projection* is attributing one's own undesirable ideas and motives to others so that they seem less negative. For example, a sales executive who is undergoing conflict about offering a bribe to an official of a foreign government might reason that the official is corrupt.

- *Displacement* is directing feelings of anger at a "safe" target rather than expressing them where they may be punished. For example, a construction worker who is severely criticized by the boss for sloppy workmanship might take out his frustrations in an evening hockey league.

- *Reaction formation* is expressing oneself in a manner that is directly opposite to the way one truly feels, rather than risking negative reactions to one's true position. For example, a low-status member of a committee might vote with the majority on a crucial issue rather than stating his true position and opening himself up to attack.

- *Compensation* is applying one's skills in a particular area to make up for failure in another area. For example, a professor who is unable to get his or her research published might resolve to become a superb teacher.

Is the use of defence mechanisms a good or bad reaction to stress? Used occasionally to temporarily reduce anxiety, they appear to be a useful reaction. For example, the construction worker who displaces aggression in an evening hockey league rather than attacking a frustrating boss might calm down, return to work the next day, and "talk it out" with the boss. Thus, the occasional use of defence mechanisms as short-term anxiety reducers probably benefits both the individual and the organization. In fact, people with "weak defences" can be incapacitated by anxiety and resort to dysfunctional withdrawal or addiction.

When the use of defence mechanisms becomes a chronic reaction to stress, however, the picture changes radically. The problem stems from the very character of defence mechanisms—they simply do not change the objective character of the stressor, and the basic conflict or frustration remains in operation. After some short-term relief from anxiety, the basic problem remains unresolved. In fact, the stress might *increase* with the knowledge that the defence has been essentially ineffective.

Physiological Reactions to Stress

Can work-related stress kill you? This is clearly an important question for organizations, and it is even more important for individuals who experience excessive stress at work. Many studies of physiological reactions to stress have concentrated on the cardiovascular system, specifically on the various risk factors that might prompt heart attacks. For example, work stress is associated with electrocardiogram irregularities and elevated levels of blood pressure, cholesterol, and pulse.[86] Stress has also been associated with the onset of diseases such as respiratory and bacterial infections due to its ill effects on the immune system.[87] The accumulation of stress into burnout has been particularly implicated in cardiovascular problems.[88]

Organizational Strategies for Managing Stress

This chapter would be incomplete without a discussion of personal and organizational strategies to manage stress. In general, these strategies either reduce demands on employees or enhance their resources.

Job Redesign

Organizations can redesign jobs to reduce their stressful characteristics. In theory, it is possible to redesign jobs anywhere in the organization to this end. Thus, an overloaded executive might be given an assistant to reduce the number of tasks he or she must perform. In practice, most formal job redesign efforts have involved enriching operative-level jobs to make them more stimulating and challenging.

Especially for service jobs, there is growing evidence that providing more autonomy in how service is delivered can alleviate stress and burnout.[89] Call centre workers, fast-food employees, some salespeople, and some hospitality workers are highly "scripted" by employers, with the idea that uniformity will be appreciated by customers. This idea is debatable, but what is not debatable is that this lack of personal control goes against the research-supported prescriptions of job enrichment (Chapter 6) and empowerment (Chapter 11), and the job demands–resources model of stress (this chapter). Boundary role service jobs require a high degree of emotional regulation in any event, and some degree of autonomy allows employees to cope with emotional labour by adjusting their responses to the needs of the moment in line with their own personalities. Guidelines about desired service outcomes can replace rigid scripts, especially for routine (non-emergency) encounters. Also, excessive electronic monitoring should be avoided in call centres.[90]

Police officers must deal with a unique type of on-the-job stress: workplace violence. There has been an upswing in psychological counselling for officers experiencing stress reactions.

A special word should be said about the stressful job designs that often emerge from heavy-handed downsizings, restructurings, and mergers. Common symptoms of such jobs are extreme role overload, increased responsibility without corresponding authority to act, and the assignment of tasks for which no training is provided. Executives overseeing such change efforts should obtain professional assistance to ensure proper job designs.

"Family-Friendly" Human Resource Policies

To reduce stress associated with dual careers, childcare, and eldercare, many organizations are beginning to institute "family-friendly" human resource policies.[91] These policies generally include some combination of formalized social support, material support, and increased flexibility to adapt to employee needs. The website connectmoms.com is dedicated to hooking up working mothers with such family-friendly employers.

In the domain of social support, some firms distribute newsletters, such as *Work & Family Life,* that deal with work–family issues. Others have developed company support groups for employees dealing with eldercare problems. Some companies have contracted specialized consultants to provide seminars on eldercare issues.

A welcome form of material support consists of corporate daycare centres. Flexibility (which provides more *control* over family issues) is also important, and includes flex-time, telecommuting, and job sharing (Chapter 6), as well as family leave policies that allow time off for caring for infants, sick children, and aged dependents. Although many firms boast of having such flexible policies, a common problem is encouraging managers to *use* them in an era of downsizing and lean staffing.

According to connectmoms.com, firms that are noted for their family-friendly human resource policies include BC Hydro, Kraft Canada, RBC, and WestJet. In general, research shows that perceptions of flexibility, a reasonable workload, supportive supervision, and a supportive culture are associated with less work–family conflict and higher job satisfaction and organizational commitment.[92]

Stress Management Programs

Some organizations have experimented with programs designed to help employees "manage" work-related stress. Such programs are also available from independent off-work sources. Some of these programs help physically and mentally healthy employees prevent problems due to stress. Others are therapeutic in nature, aimed at individuals who are already experiencing stress problems. Although the exact content of the programs varies, most involve one or more of the following techniques: meditation,

Companies are striving to be much more "family friendly" than in the past. Some organizations offer daycare for children of employees.

training in muscle-relaxation exercises, biofeedback training to control physiological processes, training in time management, and training to think more positively and realistically about sources of job stress.[93] Evidence suggests that these applications are useful in reducing physiological arousal, sleep disturbances, and self-reported tension and anxiety.[94]

Work–Life Balance, Fitness, and Wellness Programs

Many people have argued that a balanced lifestyle that includes a variety of leisure activities combined with a healthy diet and physical exercise can reduce stress and counteract some of the adverse physiological effects of stress. For some organizations, work–life balance programs and quality-of-life benefits have become a strategic retention tool. Employees are increasingly demanding work–life balance benefits, and employers are realizing that by providing them they can increase commitment and reduce turnover.

At Husky Injection Molding Systems, the cafeteria serves only healthy food. The company's head office in Bolton, Ontario, has a naturopath, a chiropractor, a medical doctor, a nurse, and a massage therapist on staff, and employees are encouraged to use the company's large fitness centre.[95] The DundeeWealth investment firm features weight-loss contests, fitness classes, and consultation on home training programs.[96]

Studies show that fitness training is associated with improved mood, a better self-concept, reduced absenteeism, enhanced job satisfaction, and reports of better performance.[97] Work–life programs are also believed to result in lower health care costs. Some of these improvements probably stem from stress reduction.

THE MANAGER'S NOTEBOOK

Bullying at Veterans Affairs

1. Many of the well-known sources of conflict in the workplace can lead to aggression and bullying. Power and status differences between individuals, rivalries between groups, uncertainty and competition, and a noxious organizational culture can all facilitate bullying and aggression. The VA project team found many of these conditions at the various sites. However, they generally found a distinctive pattern of causes of bullying at each facility. At some sites, a lack of cooperation, respect, and fairness were drivers of aggression and bullying. At other sites, diversity management was the primary issue. Sites that had recently made significant new hires often had clashes between newcomers and old-timers. Sites with poor leadership and a lack of goal alignment were also problems. The results were often communication breakdowns, misinformation, and the growth of rumours. Overall, the project team identified issues in the work climate, although they varied in content from site to site, as the key factor in workplace aggression and bullying.

2. The VA project team realized that, unlike many organizational development prescriptions advocating the establishment of best practices to resolve problems, interventions to quell workplace aggression and bullying would need to be customized at each site to deal with each specific work climate. However, the general process they developed to do this was common to all. In the 11 sites that participated in the more comprehensive version of the project, the research team created action teams of organizational members to guide the project and develop needed interventions. The exercise of bringing people together to learn and discuss issues surrounding bullying and aggression in itself transformed the work climate in a positive way. Interventions often focused on some form of what are known as High Involvement Work Systems, involving information sharing and empowerment. In a follow-up two years after the original data gathering exercise, the research team found that, compared with the 15 sites that did not participate in the intervention, the 11 focal sites reported fewer incidents of aggressive behaviour and fewer injury stress–related behaviours. Work attitudes and performance indicators also improved at the 11 intervention sites compared with the 15 other sites.

LEARNING OBJECTIVES CHECKLIST

1. *Interpersonal conflict* is a process that occurs when one person, group, or organizational unit frustrates the goal attainment of another. Such conflict can revolve around facts, procedures, or the goals themselves. Causes of conflict include intergroup bias, high interdependence, ambiguous jurisdictions, and scarce resources. Differences in power, status, and culture are also a factor.

2. *Types of conflict* include *relationship, task,* and *process* conflict. Conflict dynamics include the need to win the dispute, withholding information, increased cohesiveness, negative stereotyping of the other party, reduced contact, and emergence of aggressive leaders.

3. Modes of managing conflict include *avoiding, accommodating, competing, compromise,* and *collaborating.*

4. *Negotiation* is a decision-making process among parties that do not have the same preferences. *Distributive negotiation* attempts to divide up a fixed amount of outcomes. Frequent tactics include threats, promises, firmness, concession making, and persuasion. *Integrative negotiation* attempts to enlarge the amount of outcomes available via collaboration or problem solving. Tactics include exchanging copious information, framing differences as opportunities, cutting costs, increasing resources, and introducing *superordinate goals.*

5. When managers perceive that employees are in a rut or avoiding disagreements at the cost of not dealing with important issues, they may want to *stimulate* conflict to reinvigorate the workplace. Although conflict is often considered a negative occurrence, conflict can also be necessary for and beneficial to organizational change initiatives. In the context of change, conflict can generate new ideas, lead to more careful monitoring of the actions of others, and lead to a redistribution of power within the organization.

6. *Stressors* are environmental conditions that have the potential to induce stress. *Stress* is a psychological reaction that can prompt tension or anxiety because an individual feels incapable of coping with the demands made by a stressor. *Stress reactions* are the behavioural, psychological, and physiological consequences of stress.

7. Personality characteristics can cause some individuals to perceive more stressors than others, experience more stress, and react more negatively to this stress. In particular, people with *external locus of control*, high *negative affectivity*, and *Type A behaviour pattern* are prone to such reactions.

8. At the managerial or executive level, common stressors include *role overload* and high responsibility. At the *operative level*, poor physical working conditions and underutilization of potential owing to poor job design are common stressors. *Boundary role occupants* often experience stress in the form of conflict between demands from inside the employing organization and demands from outside. Emotional labour may also provoke stress. *Burnout* may occur when a job produces emotional exhaustion, cynicism, and low self-efficacy. Job insecurity and change, role ambiguity, sexual harassment, interpersonal conflict, and work–family conflicts have the potential to induce stress in all organizational members.

   Work engagement is a positive state of mind about work involving dedication, absorption, and vigour. The *job demands–resources model* explains how demands lead to burnout and resources lead to engagement.

9. *Behavioural reactions* to stress include problem solving, modified performance, withdrawal, and the use of addictive substances. *Problem solving* is the most effective reaction because it confronts the stressor directly and thus has the potential to terminate the stress episode. The most common psychological reaction to stress is the use of *defence mechanisms* to temporarily reduce anxiety. The majority of studies on physiological reactions to stress implicate cardiovascular risk factors. Strategies that can reduce organizational stress include job redesign, family-friendly human resource policies, stress management programs, and work–life balance programs.

DISCUSSION QUESTIONS

1. The manager of a fast-food restaurant sees that conflict among the staff is damaging service. How might she implement a superordinate goal to reduce this conflict?

2. A company hires two finance majors right out of college. Being in a new and unfamiliar environment, they begin their relationship cooperatively. However, over time, they develop a case of deep interpersonal conflict. What factors could account for this?

3. What are some of the factors that make it a real challenge for conflicting parties to develop a collaborative relationship and engage in integrative negotiation?

4. Two social workers just out of college join the same county welfare agency. Both find their case loads very heavy and their roles very ambiguous. One exhibits negative stress reactions, including absence and elevated alcohol use. The other seems to cope very well. Use the stress episode model to explain why this might occur.

5. Imagine that a person who greatly dislikes bureaucracy assumes her first job as an investigator in a very bureaucratic government tax office. Describe the stressors that she might encounter in this situation. Give an example of a problem-solving reaction to this stress. Give an example of a defensive reaction to it.

6. What factors might explain why bullying persists? How do workplace bullies get away with it?

7. Compare and contrast the stressors that might be experienced by an assembly line worker and the president of a company.

8. Discuss the advantages and disadvantages of hiring employees with Type A personality characteristics.

INTEGRATIVE DISCUSSION QUESTIONS

1. Does personality influence the way individuals manage conflict? Consider the relationship among each of the following personality characteristics and the five approaches to managing conflict described in this chapter: the "Big Five" dimensions of personality, locus of control, self-monitoring, self-esteem, need for power, and Machiavellianism.

2. Can leadership be a source of stress in organizations? Refer to the leadership theories described in Chapter 9 (e.g., leadership traits, behaviours, situational theories, participative leadership, strategic leadership, and LMX theory) and explain how leadership can be a source of stress. According to each theory, what can leaders do to reduce stress and help employees cope with it?

ON-THE-JOB CHALLENGE QUESTION

A Harris/Decima poll commissioned by Expedia.ca determined that almost 25 percent of Canadians fail to use all the vacation days they are entitled to during the year. The unused days ranged from 1.39 in the province of Quebec to 2.81 in Alberta. Although these numbers seem small, they project nationally to 34 million unused days a year. Despite this, 42 percent of those polled reported being tired, stressed, and in need of a vacation.

What do you think explains the reluctance of so many people to forego deserved vacation time? If you were or are a manager, how would you react to staff who don't use all their vacation days? What are the long-term implications of this behaviour?

Source: Covert, K. (2009, July 9). Vacation phobia spreads. *National Post*, FP11.

EXPERIENTIAL EXERCISE

Strategies for Managing Conflict

Indicate how often you use each of the following by writing the appropriate number in the blank. Choose a number from a scale of 1 to 5, with 1 being "rarely," 3 being "sometimes," and 5 being "always." After you have completed the survey, use the scoring key to tabulate your results.

_____ 1. I argue my position tenaciously.

_____ 2. I put the needs of others above my own.

_____ 3. I arrive at a compromise both parties can accept.

_____ 4. I don't get involved in conflicts.

_____ 5. I investigate issues thoroughly and jointly.

_____ 6. I find fault in other persons' positions.

_____ 7. I foster harmony.

_____ 8. I negotiate to get a portion of what I propose.

_____ 9. I avoid open discussions of controversial subjects.

_____ 10. I openly share information with others in resolving disagreements.

_____ 11. I enjoy winning an argument.

_____ 12. I go along with the suggestions of others.

_____ 13. I look for a middle ground to resolve disagreements.

_____ 14. I keep my true feelings to myself to avoid hard feelings.

_____ 15. I encourage the open sharing of concerns and issues.

_____ 16. I am reluctant to admit I am wrong.

_____ 17. I try to help others avoid "losing face" in a disagreement.

_____ 18. I stress the advantages of "give and take."

_____ 19. I encourage others to take the lead in resolving controversy.

_____ 20. I state my position as only one point of view.

Scoring Key
Managing Strategy

Total your responses to these questions

Competing 1, 6, 11, 16_____

Accommodating 2, 7, 12, 17_____

Compromising 3, 8, 13, 18_____

Avoiding 4, 9, 14, 19_____

Collaborating 5, 10, 15, 20_____

Primary conflict management strategy (highest score): _____

Secondary conflict management strategy (next-highest score): _____

Source: Whetten, D.A., & Cameron, K.S. _Developing management skills_ (7th ed.) © 2008. Reproduced by Pearson Education, Inc., Upper Saddle River, NJ. Electronically reproduced by permission of Pearson Education, Inc., Upper Saddle River, NJ.

CASE INCIDENT

Air Canada and Canadian Airlines

When Air Canada and Canadian Airlines merged in 2000, one of the most difficult challenges was handling the integration of employees who had once been bitter rivals. In the months leading up to the merger, Canadian Airline employees began sporting "Better dead than red!" buttons in reference to their rival's corporate colour, while the head of Air Canada's pilots' union outraged Canadian Airlines pilots when he suggested that the successful Air Canada would be contaminated by a virus from the "sick" Canadian Airlines if the two airlines merged. Once the companies merged, a particular sore point became the question of seniority. Although Air Canada was the "winner" in the merger and the failing Canadian was the "loser," Canadian employees tended to have more overall seniority than their Air Canada peers. Conflict ensued, with Canadian employees expecting to be at the top of the seniority roster and Air Canada employees claiming that the Canadian people should feel lucky to have jobs at all. Years after the merger, tension still ran high between the employees of the two former rivals.

Sources: Brent, P. (1999, December 6). Air Canada's challenge: Soothe bitter feelings of intense combatants. _National Post_, C4; Naumetz, T. (1999, September 30). Air Canada pilot fears "virus" from merger: Employees voice concerns for job security. _Ottawa Citizen_, C1; Nicol, J., & Clark, A. (2000, May 22). Unfriendly skies. _Maclean's_, 34–37; Viera, P. (2003, June 27). Labour board upholds seniority ruling covering airline pilots. _National Post_, FP5.

1. What were the roots of the conflict between Air Canada employees and their colleagues who were previously part of Canadian Airlines?

2. How could this conflict have been better managed?

3. On the seniority issue, what negotiation tactics would you have recommended?

CASE STUDY

The Last Straw

Jerry Lambert has been employed by the University of Upper Ontario for 26 years. He first came to the university in the mid-1970s as a master's student in information technology and became a teaching assistant to Professor Jane Burnett. Eager to learn and thrilled with the teaching aspects of this job, Jerry convinced Professor Burnett to let him do some in-class work. The professor finally agreed, and was impressed with Jerry's natural teaching ability and dedication. At the end of the school year, the professor went on sabbatical and suggested to her department that Jerry take over her class for the time that she would be away. Because of the shortage of information technology professors at the time, and in light of Professor Burnett's glowing recommendation, Jerry was hired as an instructor.

In the meantime, Jerry had taken a summer job as a junior programmer in the university's computing services department. By the end of the summer, he had been offered a full-time job with this department. Since Jerry was thinking of marrying, he promptly decided to take the job, as well as the part-time teaching position. He also decided not to pursue his Ph.D. degree for the time being. Jerry soon earned a reputation as an excellent communicator, valiant worker, and dedicated instructor. Since information systems were relatively new at the time, most instructors and workers in this area were young. Jerry was young, had a friendly, outgoing personality, and was a quick learner. He fit in well and quickly built up a group of friends and associates within his department and elsewhere.

Over the years, Jerry obtained a number of promotions and more part-time teaching contracts. The teaching contracts were given on a one-semester basis. Therefore, Jerry had no guarantee of having any of them renewed. However, he had always had one or two classes per semester, so the situation seemed relatively stable. In the early 1980s, Jerry decided that he should pursue his Ph.D. degree and returned to school part-time. At the same time, he started to do some consulting work on his own. This very full schedule stimulated him but left very little time for his personal life. Within a short time, he and his wife were divorced.

Jerry continued with his work, obtaining two more promotions. He was unable to continue his studies, however, because of lack of time. Finally, he became manager of training services for the university's information systems department. Jerry was very happy with this position, which gave him the opportunity to combine his interests. Three years after he had obtained this position, Jerry felt comfortable. He had a nice job, a cottage in the country, and had just bought a house in an affluent section of town. Although there was a large mortgage on the house, Jerry felt comfortable with it since his income allowed him to meet the payments. Jerry had recently remarried, and his wife was expecting a baby.

Three months ago, the university president announced that there would be massive cutbacks in management and support staff at the university. Within a month, Jerry heard rumours that his section was being targeted for downsizing. Jerry tried repeatedly to get confirmation or disconfirmation of these rumours from his boss, Patricia Jones. However, Patricia remained vague and evasive. At one point, Mario, a fellow manager, told Jerry in confidence that Patricia had asked other managers' opinion about Jerry's department and that some of these managers had said that they felt that Jerry's job and department were "non-essential." "I am not supposed to tell you this," Mario said, "but if I was in your shoes I'd like to know if my job was in danger." Jerry thanked him and kept the information confidential; however, he couldn't help feeling that his other colleagues, Mario excepted, were "stabbing him in the back." "They are all looking out for themselves without any thought as to what makes sense," he fumed. "What a bunch of self-centred turkeys!"

To make matters worse, a month later, Jerry stepped into the parking lot to find that his car had been stolen. Later on, he discovered that his insurance did not cover the full cost of replacing the car. His wife took this news badly and started feeling ill. Her doctor ordered complete bed rest for the next three months, until the baby was due. She told Jerry that she was tired of hearing about his speculations concerning doom and gloom at work. To avoid irritating his wife, Jerry started keeping his work-related problems to himself. Last week, Jerry was told that some of his teaching contracts might not be renewed because the university planned to save money by assigning a larger teaching load to full-time professors. Concerned with the unstable situation of both his full-time job and his contract work at the university, Jerry pursued additional teaching assignments with the local community college. He is now teaching five nights a week and feeling exhausted since the workload amounts to having two full-time jobs. To make matters worse, constant worry is keeping him awake at night. In addition, he has been suffering from recurring colds and has been having frequent headaches.

This morning, his secretary walked into his office in tears, saying that Jerry's boss, Patricia, had just told her that she was being laid off. This was a shock for Jerry, who had not been forewarned about this by Patricia. Obviously, having his secretary laid off while being kept completely in the dark did not bode well for Jerry's department. Although he tried to sympathize with his secretary's plight, Jerry could not help but feel terribly angry at the way the situation was being handled. He tried to reach his boss but was told that Patricia was in a meeting. By the end of the day, Jerry still hadn't heard from Patricia. Feeling a knot in his stomach that would not go away, Jerry rushed from his office to his evening class, carrying a pile of assignments to return to his students. On the way out the door, a colleague bumped into him, sending the assignments flying. Upset, Jerry lashed out at his colleague, calling him an idiot.

Source: Case prepared by Nicole Bérubé. Used with permission.

1. Jerry is clearly experiencing stress. What stress reactions does he exhibit? What are the stressors that prompted this reaction?

2. Is Jerry experiencing burnout? If so, what factors might be responsible? Feel free to speculate, given the nature of his job and family situation.

3. Is interpersonal conflict an issue in the case? What are its causes?

4. Evaluate Patricia's management style. How should Jerry deal with her?

5. How could the University of Upper Ontario do a better job of dealing with the issues raised in the case?

INTEGRATIVE CASE

Deloitte & Touche: Integrating Arthur Andersen

At the end of Part Two of the text, on Individual Behaviour, you answered a number of questions about the Deloitte & Touche Integrative Case that dealt with issues related to learning, perceptions, fairness and job attitudes, motivation, and pay plans. Now that you have completed Part Three of the text and the chapters on Social Behaviour and Organizational Processes, you can return to the Integrative Case and enhance your understanding of some of the main issues associated with social behaviour and organizational processes by answering the following questions that deal with groups, socialization and culture, leadership, communication, conflict, and stress.

QUESTIONS

1. Given that employees from the two firms will be working together in groups, what are the implications for group development and group cohesiveness? What advice would you give the integration team for designing effective work teams?

2. Is organizational socialization relevant for the integration of Arthur Andersen employees? What would you tell the integration team about organizational socialization and how it can be helpful for the integration process?

3. What methods of organizational socialization can be used to integrate the Arthur Andersen employees? Be sure to explain how you would use each of the methods described in Chapter 8 and indicate what you think would be most effective for the successful integration of Arthur Andersen employees.

4. Review the results of the cultural assessment of the two firms and then compare and contrast their cultures. How are they similar and different and what are the implications for the successful integration of the two firms?

5. What should the integration team do about the cultural differences between the two firms? Should they integrate the Arthur Andersen employees into the existing Deloitte & Touche culture or should they create a new culture? What do you think the integration team should do and how should they proceed?

6. How important is leadership for the successful integration of the two firms? Consider the implications of the different leadership theories described in Chapter 9 (situational theories, leader-member exchange theory, transformational and transactional leadership, ethical and authentic leadership, and strategic leadership) for the successful integration of the two firms. What type of leadership do you think is most important and likely to be effective and why?

7. Identify some challenges or barriers to effective communication in the case. How did Deloitte try to counteract these barriers?

8. Although there is no evidence of open conflict in the case, there is plenty of potential for it. What are some factors that might cause conflict between the Deloitte and Andersen contingents?

9. Consider the potential for stress among the employees of both firms. What stressors are employees most likely to experience and why? What can the integration team do to minimize these stressors and help employees cope with stress?

Research in Organizational Behaviour

Research is a way of finding out about the world through objective and systematic information gathering. The key words here are *objective* and *systematic*, and it is these characteristics that separate the outcomes of the careful study of organizational behaviour from opinion and common sense.

Understanding how researchers conduct their research is important to the study of organizational behaviour for several reasons. First of all, you should be aware of how the information presented in this book was collected. This should increase your confidence in the advantages of systematic study over common sense. Second, you will likely encounter reports, in management periodicals and the popular press, of interventions to improve organizational behaviour, such as job redesign or employee development programs. A critical perspective is necessary to differentiate those interventions that are carefully designed and evaluated from useless or even damaging ones. Those backed by good research deserve the greatest confidence. Occasionally, a manager may have to evaluate a research proposal or consultant's intervention to be carried out in his or her own organization. A brief introduction to research methodology should enable you to ask some intelligent questions about such plans. Third, knowledge and understanding of organizational behaviour research is necessary for managers to make better decisions through evidence-based management. Your knowledge of organizational behaviour research can enable you to practice evidence-based management.

Evidence-based management involves translating principles based on the best scientific evidence into organizational practices. By using evidence-based management, managers can make decisions based on the best available scientific evidence from social science and organizational research, rather than personal preference and unsystematic experience. Evidence-based management derives principles from research evidence and translates them into practices that solve organizational problems. The use of evidence-based management is more likely to result in the attainment of organizational goals, including those affecting employees, stockholders, and the public in general.[1]

Trained behavioural scientists who have backgrounds in management, applied psychology, or applied sociology carry out research in organizational behaviour. While this introduction will not make you a trained behavioural scientist, it should provide an appreciation of the work that goes into generating accurate knowledge about organizational behaviour.

LEARNING OBJECTIVES

After reading the Appendix, you should be able to:

1 Explain what *a hypothesis* is and define the meaning of a *variable*.

2 Distinguish between *independent* and *dependent* variables and *moderating* and *mediating variables*.

3 Differentiate *reliability* from *validity* and *convergent validity* from *discriminant validity*.

4 Understand *observational research* and distinguish between *participant* and *direct observation*.

5 Describe *correlational research* and explain why causation cannot be inferred from correlation.

6 Explain *experimental research* and the meaning of *internal validity* and discuss threats to internal validity.

7 Discuss the relative advantages and disadvantages of different research techniques.

8 Describe *random sampling* and *external validity* and the role they play in the research process.

9 Explain the *Hawthorne effect* and how it can occur.

10 Discuss the basic ethical concerns to which researchers must attend.

The Basics of Organizational Behaviour Research

All research in organizational behaviour begins with a question about work or organizations. Sometimes this question might stem from a formal theory in the field. For example, a motivation theory called equity theory (see Chapter 5) is concerned with peoples' reactions to fairness or lack of it. Equity theory suggests the following research question: What do people do when they perceive their pay to be too low in comparison to other people's pay? Other times, a research question might stem from an immediate organizational problem. For example, a human resources manager might ask herself: How can we reduce absenteeism among our customer service personnel?

Often, research questions are expressed as hypotheses. A **hypothesis** is a formal statement of the expected relationship between two variables. **Variables** are simply measures that can take on two or more values. Temperature is a variable, but so are pay, fairness, and absenteeism. A formal hypothesis stemming from equity theory might be this: The less fair people perceive their pay to be, the more likely they will be to resign their jobs. Here, a variable that can take on many values, perceived fairness, is linked to a variable made up of two values, staying or leaving. The human resources manager might develop this hypothesis: The introduction of a small attendance bonus will reduce absenteeism. Here, a variable with two values, bonus versus no bonus, is related to one that can take on many values, days of absenteeism.

Types of Variables

In most research, we are concerned with two kinds of variables: the independent variable and the dependent variable. The **independent variable** is a predictor or cause of variation in a dependent variable. The **dependent variable** is a variable that will vary as a result of changes in the independent variable. So in the first example, pay fairness perceptions is the independent variable and resigning is the dependent variable. In the second example, the attendance bonus is the independent variable and absenteeism is the dependent variable. In both cases, scores on the dependent variable are expected to vary as a function of scores on the independent variable.

Two other kinds of variables that we are sometimes interested in are mediating variables and moderating variables. A **moderating variable** is a variable that affects the nature of the relationship between an independent and a dependent variable such that the relationship depends on the level of the moderating variable. Moderating variables are like contingency variables in that they indicate when an independent variable is most likely to be related to a dependent variable. In the example above about the attendance bonus, a moderating variable might be pay satisfaction. If the bonus only reduces the absenteeism of employees who are *not* satisfied with their pay and has no effect on the absenteeism of employees who *are* satisfied with their pay, then we would conclude that pay satisfaction moderates the effect of the bonus on absenteeism.

Sometimes we want to know why an independent variable predicts or causes a dependent variable. In such cases, we are interested in a mediating variable. A **mediating variable** is a variable that intervenes or explains the relationship between an independent and a dependent variable. To return to the attendance bonus example, we might want to know why the bonus reduces absenteeism. One possibility might be that the bonus increases people's *motivation* to come to work. Thus, motivation intervenes or mediates the relationship between the attendance bonus and absenteeism.

Measurement of Variables

Good researchers carefully measure the variables they choose. For one thing, a measure should exhibit high reliability. **Reliability** is an index of the consistency of a research subject's responses. For example, if we ask someone several questions about how fair

---

Evidence-based management. Translating principles based on the best scientific evidence into organizational practices.

Hypothesis. A formal statement of the expected relationship between two variables.

Variables. Measures that can take on two or more values.

Independent variable. The variable that predicts or is the cause of variation in a dependent variable.

Dependent variable. The variable that is expected to vary as a result of changes to the independent variable.

Moderating variable. A variable that affects the nature of the relationship between an independent and a dependent variable such that the relationship depends on the level of the moderating variable.

Mediating variable. A variable that intervenes or explains the relationship between an independent and a dependent variable.

Reliability. An index of the consistency of a research subject's responses.

his or her pay is, the person should respond roughly the same way to each question. Similarly, the person should respond roughly the same way to the same questions next week or next month if there has been no change in pay.

Measures should also exhibit high validity. **Validity** is an index of the extent to which a measure truly reflects what it is supposed to measure. For instance, a good measure of perceived pay fairness should not be influenced by employees' feelings of fairness about other workplace factors, such as supervision. Also, a researcher would expect people who are objectively underpaid to report high pay unfairness and for them to report increased fairness if their pay were increased. Researchers are often able to choose measures with a known history of reliability and validity.

Good measures should also be strongly related to other measures of the same variable and should not be related to measures of different variables. For example, a measure of job satisfaction should be highly correlated to other measures of job satisfaction. This is known as **convergent validity**, and it exists when there is a strong relationship between different measures of the same variable. In addition, good measures should not be related to measures of different variables. For example, a measure of job satisfaction should not be strongly related to measures of job performance. This is known as **discriminant validity**, and it exists when there is a weak relationship between measures of different variables. Good measures should have both convergent and discriminant validity. Thus, a measure of job satisfaction should be more strongly related to other measures of job satisfaction than to measures of job performance.

There are three basic kinds of research techniques: observation, correlation, and experimentation. As you will see, each begins with a research question or questions. Correlation and experimentation are most likely to test specific hypotheses and devote explicit attention to measurement quality.

> **Validity.** An index of the extent to which a measure truly reflects what it is supposed to measure.

> **Convergent validity.** When there is a strong relationship between different measures of the same variable.

> **Discriminant validity.** When there is a weak relationship between measures of different variables.

Observational Techniques

Observational research techniques are the most straightforward ways of finding out about behaviour in organizations and thus come closest to the ways in which we develop common-sense views about such behaviour. In this case, *observation* means just what it implies—the researcher proceeds to examine the natural activities of people in an organizational setting by listening to what they say and watching what they do. The difference between our everyday observations and the formal observations of the trained behavioural scientist is expressed by those key words *systematic* and *objective*.

First, the researcher approaches the organizational setting with extensive training concerning the nature of human behaviour and a particular set of questions that the observation is designed to answer. These factors provide a systematic framework for the business of observing. Second, the behavioural scientist attempts to keep a careful ongoing record of the events that he or she observes, either as they occur or as soon as possible afterwards. Thus, excessive reliance on memory, which may lead to inaccuracies, is unnecessary. Finally, the behavioural scientist is well informed of the dangers of influencing the behaviour of those whom he or she is observing and is trained to draw reasonable conclusions from his or her observations. These factors help ensure objectivity.

The outcomes of observational research are summarized in a narrative form, sometimes called a *case study*. This narrative specifies the nature of the organization, people, and events studied, the particular role of and techniques used by the observer, the research questions, and the events observed.

> **Observational research.** Research that examines the natural activities of people in an organizational setting by listening to what they say and watching what they do.

Participant Observation

One obvious way for a researcher to find out about organizational behaviour is to actively participate in this behaviour. In **participant observation** the researcher becomes a functioning member of the organizational unit he or she is studying to conduct the research. At this point you may wonder, "Wait a minute. What about objectivity?

> **Participant observation.** Observational research in which the researcher becomes a functioning member of the organizational unit being studied.

What about influencing the behaviour of those being studied?" These are clearly legitimate questions, and they might be answered in the following way: In adopting participant observation, the researcher is making a conscious bet that the advantages of participation outweigh these problems. It is doubtless true in some cases that "there is no substitute for experience." For example, researcher Robert Sutton wanted to find out how employees cope with jobs that require them to express negative emotions.[2] To do this, he trained and then worked as a bill collector. This is obviously a more personal experience than simply interviewing bill collectors.

Another advantage to participant observation is its potential for secrecy—the subjects need not know that they are being observed. This potential for secrecy does raise some ethical issues, however. Sociologist Tom Lupton served as an industrial worker in two plants in England to study the factors that influenced productivity.[3] Although he could have acted in secrecy, he was required to inform management and union officials of his presence to secure records and documents, and he thus felt it unfair not to inform his workmates of his purpose. It should be stressed that his goals were academic and that he was *not* working for the managements of the companies involved. Sometimes, however, secrecy seems necessary to accomplish a research goal, as the following study of "illegal" industrial behaviour shows.

Joseph Bensman and Israel Gerver investigated an important organizational problem: What happens when the activities that appear to be required to get a job done conflict with official organizational policy?[4] Examples of such conflicts include the punch press operator who must remove the safety guard from his machine to meet productivity standards, the executive who must deliver corporate money to a political slush fund, or the police officer who cannot find time to complete an eight-page report to justify having drawn her revolver on a night patrol.

The behaviour of interest to Bensman and Gerver was the unauthorized use of taps by aircraft plant workers. A tap is a hard steel hand tool used to cut threads into metal. The possession of this device by aircraft assemblers was strictly forbidden because the workers could use it to correct sloppy or difficult work like the misalignment of bolt holes in two pieces of aircraft skin or stripped lock nuts; both of these problems could lead to potential structural weaknesses or maintenance problems.

Possession of a tap was a strict violation of company policy, and a worker could be fired on the spot for it. On the other hand, since supervisors were under extreme pressure to maintain a high quota of completed work, the occasional use of a tap to correct a problem could save hours of disassembly and realignment time. How was this conflict resolved? The answer was provided by one of the authors, who served as a participant observer while functioning as an assembler. Put simply, the supervisors and inspectors worked together to encourage the cautious and appropriate use of taps. New workers were gradually introduced to the mysteries of tapping by experienced workers, and the supervisors provided refinement of skills and signals as to when a tap might be used. Taps were not to be used in front of inspectors or to correct chronic sloppy work. If "caught," tappers were expected to act truly penitent in response to a chewing out by the supervisors, even if the supervisors themselves had suggested the use of the tap. In short, a *social ritual* was developed to teach and control the use of the tap to facilitate getting the work out without endangering the continued presence of the crucial tool. Clearly, this is the kind of information about organizational behaviour that would be extremely difficult to obtain except by participant observation.

Direct Observation

Direct observation.
Observational research in which the researcher observes organizational behaviour without taking part in the studied activity.

In **direct observation** the researcher observes organizational behaviour without participation in the activity being observed. There are a number of reasons why one might choose direct observation over participant observation. First, there are many situations in which the introduction of a new person into an existing work setting would severely disrupt and change the nature of the activities in that setting. These are cases in which the "influence" criticism of participant observation is especially true. Second, there are many job tasks that a trained behavioural scientist could not be expected to learn for research purposes. For example, it seems unreasonable to expect a researcher to spend years acquiring the skills of a pilot or banker to be able to investigate what happens in the cockpit of an airliner or in a boardroom. Finally, participant observation places rather severe limitations on the observers' opportunity to record information. Existence of these conditions suggests the use of direct observation. In theory, the researcher could carry out such observation covertly, but there are few studies of organizational behaviour in which the presence of the direct observer was not known and explained to those being observed.

Henry Mintzberg's study of the work performed by chief executives of two manufacturing companies, a hospital, a school system, and a consulting firm provides an excellent example of the use of direct observation.[5] At first glance, this might appear to be an inane thing to investigate. After all, everybody knows that managers plan, organize, lead, and control, or some similar combination of words. In fact, Mintzberg argues that we actually know very little about the routine, everyday behaviour managers use to achieve these vague goals. Furthermore, if we ask managers what they do (in an interview or questionnaire), they usually respond with a variation of the plan-organize-lead-control theme.

Mintzberg spent a week with each of his five executives, watching them at their desks, attending meetings with them, listening to their phone calls, and inspecting their mail. He kept detailed records of these activities and gradually developed a classification scheme to make sense of them. What Mintzberg found counters the common-sense view that some hold of managers—sitting behind a large desk, reflecting on their organization's performance, and affixing their signatures to impressive documents all day. In fact, Mintzberg found that his managers actually performed a terrific amount of work and had little time for reflection. On an average day, they examined 36 pieces of mail, engaged in five telephone conversations, attended eight meetings, and made one tour of their facilities. Work-related reading encroached on home lives. These activities were varied, unpatterned, and of short duration. Half the activities lasted less than nine minutes, and 90 percent less than one hour. Furthermore, these activities tended to be directed toward current, specific issues rather than past, general issues. Finally, the managers revealed a clear preference for verbal communications, by either telephone or unscheduled face-to-face meetings; in fact, two-thirds of their contacts were of this nature. In contrast, they generated an average of only one piece of mail a day.

In summary, both participant and direct observation capture the depth, breadth, richness, spontaneity, and realism of organizational behaviour. However, they also share some weaknesses. One of these weaknesses is a lack of control over the environment in which the study is being conducted. Thus, Mintzberg could not ensure that unusual events would not affect the executives' behaviour. Also, the small number of observers and situations in the typical observational study is problematic. With only one observer, there is a strong potential for selective perceptions and interpretations of observed events. Since only a few situations are analyzed, the extent to which the observed behaviours can be generalized to other settings is limited. (Do most executives behave like the five that Mintzberg studied?) It is probably safe to say that observational techniques are best used to make an initial examination of some organizational event on which little information is available and to generate ideas for further investigation with more refined techniques.

Correlational Techniques

Correlational research attempts to measure variables precisely and examine relationships among these variables without introducing change into the research setting. Correlational research sacrifices some of the breadth and richness of the observational techniques for more precision of measurement and greater control. It necessarily involves

Correlational research.
Research that attempts to measure variables precisely and examine relationships among these variables without introducing change into the research setting.

some abstraction of the real event that is the focus of observation to accomplish this precision and control. More specifically, correlational approaches differ from observational approaches in terms of the nature of the data researchers collect and the issues they investigate.

The data of observational studies are most frequently observer notes. We hope that these data exhibit reliability and validity. Unfortunately, because observations are generally the products of a single individual viewing a unique event, we have very little basis on which to judge their reliability and validity.

The data of correlational studies involve surveys and interviews as well as existing data. **Surveys** involve the use of questionnaires to gather data from participants, who answer questions on the relevant variables. The **interview** is a technique in which the researcher asks respondents a series of questions to gather data on the variables of interest. Interview data can be quantitative and similar to that obtained from a survey, or it can be more qualitative and descriptive. The type of data obtained will depend on the purpose of the interview and the nature of the questions asked. **Existing data** come from organizational records and include productivity, absence, and demographic information (e.g., age, gender). Variables often measured by surveys and interviews include:

- employees' perceptions of how their managers behave on the job,
- the extent to which employees are satisfied with their jobs, and
- employees' reports about how much autonomy they have on their jobs.

It is possible to determine in advance of doing research the extent to which such measures are reliable and valid. Thus, when constructing a questionnaire to measure job satisfaction, the researcher can check its reliability by repeatedly administering it to a group of workers over a period of time. If individual responses remain fairly stable, there is evidence of reliability. Evidence of the validity of a questionnaire might come from its ability to predict which employees would quit the organization for work elsewhere. It seems reasonable that dissatisfied employees would be more likely to quit, and such an effect is partial evidence of the validity of a satisfaction measure.

In addition to differing in the nature of the data collected, correlational studies differ from observational studies in terms of the kinds of events they investigate. Although the questions investigated by observational research appear fairly specific (What maintains an "illegal" behaviour such as tapping? What do executives do?), virtually any event relevant to the question is fair game for observation. Thus, such studies are extremely broad-based. Correlational research sacrifices this broadness to investigate the relationship (correlation) between specific, well-defined variables. The relationship between the variables of interest is usually stated as a hypothesis of the relationship between an independent and a dependent variable. Using the variables mentioned above, we can construct three sample hypotheses and describe how they would be tested.

- Employees who are satisfied with their jobs will tend to be more productive than those who are less satisfied. To test this, a researcher might administer a reliable, valid questionnaire concerning satisfaction and obtain production data from company records.
- Employees who perceive their supervisor as friendly and considerate will be more satisfied with their jobs than those who do not. To test this, a researcher might use reliable, valid questionnaires or interview measures of both variables.
- Older employees will be absent less than younger employees. To test this, a researcher might obtain data concerning the age of employees and their absenteeism from organizational records.

In each case, the researcher is interested in a very specific set of variables, and he or she devotes effort to measuring them precisely.

A good example of a correlational study is that of Belle Rose Ragins and John Cotton, who studied employees' willingness to serve as mentors to newer organizational

Surveys. The use of questionnaires to gather data from participants, who answer questions on the relevant variables.

Interview. A technique in which the researcher asks respondents a series of questions to gather data on the variables of interest.

Existing data. Data that is obtained from organizational records, such as productivity, absence, and demographic information.

members.[6] Mentorship was defined as helping a junior person with career support and upward mobility. The major focus of the study was the relationship between gender (the independent variable) and willingness to mentor (the dependent variable). The authors reviewed literature that hypothesized that women may face more barriers to becoming mentors than men because they are in a minority in many employment settings. The authors were also interested in the relationships between age, organizational rank, length of employment, and prior mentorship experience and willingness to mentor.

These variables were measured with questionnaires completed by more than 500 employees in three research and development organizations. The researchers found that men and women were equally willing to serve as mentors, although the women perceived more barriers (e.g., lack of qualifications and time) to being a mentor. They also found that higher rank and prior experience as a mentor or a protégé were associated with greater willingness to mentor. Notice that a study such as this could also incorporate existing data from records. For example, we might hypothesize that those with better performance evaluations would be more confident about serving as mentors.

Correlation and Causation

A final important point should be made about correlational studies. Consider a hypothesis that friendly, considerate supervisors will have more productive employees than unfriendly, inconsiderate supervisors. In this case, a researcher might have some employees describe the friendliness of their supervisors on a reliable, valid questionnaire designed to measure this variable and obtain employees' productivity levels from company records. The results of this hypothetical study are plotted in Exhibit A.1, where each dot represents an employee's response to the questionnaire in conjunction with his or her productivity. In general, it would appear that the hypothesis is confirmed—that is, employees who describe their supervisor as friendly tend to be more productive than those who describe him or her as unfriendly. As a result of this study, should an organization attempt to select friendly supervisors or even train existing supervisors to be more friendly to obtain higher productivity? The answer is no. The training and selection proposal assumes that friendly supervisors *cause* their employees to be productive, and this may not be the case. Put simply, supervisors might be friendly *if* their employees are productive. This is a possible interpretation of the data, and it does not suggest that selection or training to make supervisors friendly will achieve higher productivity. This line of argument should not be unfamiliar to you. Heavy smokers and cigarette company lobbyists like to claim that smoking is related to the incidence of lung cancer because cancer proneness prompts smoking, rather than vice versa. The point here is that *correlation does not imply causation*. How can we find out which factors cause certain organizational behaviours? The answer is to perform an experiment.

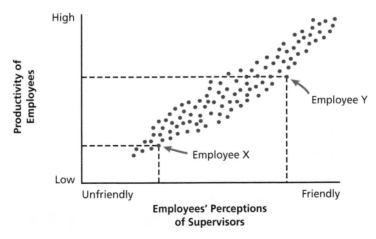

EXHIBIT A.1

Hypothetical data from a correlational study of the relationship between supervisory friendliness and employee productivity.

Experimental Techniques

If observational research involves observing nature, and correlational research involves measuring nature, **experimental research** involves manipulating nature. In an experiment, a variable is manipulated or changed under controlled conditions, and the consequence of this manipulation for some other variable is measured. If all other conditions are truly controlled, and a change in the second variable follows the change that was introduced in the first variable, we can infer that the first change has caused the second change.

In experimental language, the variable that the researcher manipulates or changes is the independent variable. The variable that the independent variable is expected to affect is the dependent variable. Consider the following hypothesis: The introduction of recorded music into the work setting will lead to increased productivity. In this hypothesis, the independent variable is music, which is expected to affect productivity, the dependent variable. Consider another hypothesis: Stimulating, challenging jobs will increase the satisfaction of the workforce. Here, the design of the job is the independent variable and satisfaction is the dependent variable.

Let's return to our hypothesis that friendly, considerate supervisors will tend to have more productive employees. If we wish to determine whether friendly supervision contributes to employee productivity, the style of supervision becomes the independent variable, and productivity becomes the dependent variable. This means that the researcher must manipulate or change the friendliness of some supervisors and observe what happens to the productivity of their employees. In practice, this would probably be accomplished by exposing the bosses to some form of human relations training designed to teach them to be more considerate and personable toward their workers.

Exhibit A.2 shows the results of this hypothetical experiment. The line on the graph represents the average productivity of a number of employees whose supervisors have received our training. We see that this productivity increased and remained higher following the introduction of the training. Does this mean that friendliness indeed increases productivity and that we should proceed to train all of our supervisors in this manner? The answer is again *no*. We cannot be sure that *something else* did not occur at the time of the training to influence productivity, such as a change in equipment or job insecurity prompted by rumoured layoffs. To control this possibility, we need a control group of supervisors who are not exposed to the training, and we need productivity data for their employees. A **control group** is a group of research subjects who have not been exposed to the experimental treatment, in this case not exposed to the training. Ideally, these supervisors should be as similar as possible in experience and background to those who receive the training, and their employees should be performing at the same level. The results of our improved experiment are shown in Exhibit A.3. Here, we see that the productivity of the employees whose supervisors were trained increases following training, while that of the control supervisors remains constant. We can, thus, infer that the human relations training affected employee productivity.

Experimental research. Research that changes or manipulates a variable under controlled conditions and examines the consequences of this manipulation for some other variable.

Control group. A group of research subjects who have not been exposed to the experimental treatment.

EXHIBIT A.2
Hypothetical data from an experiment concerning human relations training.

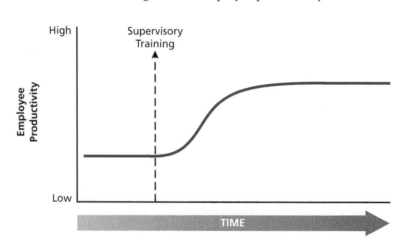

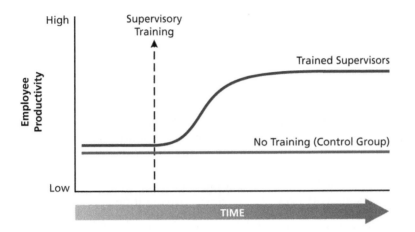

EXHIBIT A.3
Hypothetical data from an improved experiment concerning human relations training.

The extent to which a researcher can be confident that changes in a dependent variable are due to the independent variable is known as **internal validity**. Note that this is different from the validity of a measure, which was discussed earlier. Internal validity has to do with the validity of an experimental design. To return to the example above, if a control group was not included in the design, then the internal validity would be low because other factors might explain the improvement in productivity. What are some of these other factors? Perhaps something happened at the same time that the supervisors were trained, such as a pay increase or bonus, or perhaps new equipment or technology was implemented. Factors that are alternative explanations for the results of an experiment are called *threats to internal validity* (see Exhibit A.4). Without a control group, there are many threats to internal validity that might be responsible for a change in productivity. However, with a control group, one can have much more confidence that the improvement was due to the training program. Thus, internal validity increases the confidence that one has in concluding that the training program was the cause of the improvement in productivity and not something else.

John Ivancevich and Herbert Lyon conducted an interesting experiment that examined the effects of a shortened workweek on the employees of a company that manufactures food-packaging equipment.[7] The independent variable was the length of the

Internal validity. The extent to which a researcher has confidence that changes in a dependent variable are due to the independent variable.

EXHIBIT A.4
Threats to Internal Validity

Selection of participants. When participants selected for the experimental group differ from those in the control group in some way that influences the results of an experiment.

Testing. The process of completing a survey and answering questions at the start of an experiment might sensitize participants to the study and influence how they respond to the same questions after the experiment.

Instrumentation. If different measures are used at different times during the course of an experiment, then any changes in participants' scores might be due to differences in the measures used.

Statistical regression. This is the tendency of scores on a measure to shift over time toward the mean score. Participants who perform poorly on a test before an experiment might have higher scores after an experiment simply due to regression toward the mean.

History. Events or factors that occur during the course of an experiment and can explain changes in the dependent variable.

Maturation. Natural changes in participants that are due to the passage of time (e.g., job experience) and can result in changes in the dependent variable.

Mortality. When certain types of participants drop out of an experiment before it has ended and those who remain and complete the dependent measures differ in some way from those who dropped out.

workweek (4 days, 40 hours versus 5 days, 40 hours). Two of the company's divisions were converted to a 4–40 week from a 5–40 week. A third division, remaining on the 5–40 schedule, served as a control group. Workers in the control division were similar to those in the other divisions in terms of age, seniority, education, and salary. The dependent variables (measured one month before the conversion and several times after) included the workers' responses to a questionnaire concerning job satisfaction and stress, absence data from company records, and performance appraisals conducted by supervisors. After 12 months, several aspects of satisfaction and performance showed a marked improvement for the 4–40 workers when compared with the 5–40 workers. However, at 25 months this edge existed for only one aspect of satisfaction— satisfaction with personal worth. The authors concluded that benefits that had been proposed for the 4–40 workweek were of short-term duration.

A Continuum of Research Techniques

You might reasonably wonder which of the research techniques just discussed is most effective. As shown in Exhibit A.5, these methods can be placed on a continuum ranging from rich, broad-based, and loosely controlled (observation) to specific, precise, and rigorous (experimentation). The method that researchers use to investigate organizational behaviour is dictated by the nature of the problem that interests them. In the writing of this section of the chapter, special pains were taken to choose examples of problems that were well suited to the research techniques employed to investigate them. Bensman and Gerver were interested in variables that were not well defined. The variables were thus not easy to isolate and measure precisely, and observation was the appropriate technique. Furthermore, "tapping" was a controversial issue, and the researchers would have had to develop considerable trust to investigate it with questionnaires or formal interviews. Similarly, Mintzberg insists that questionnaires and interviews have failed to tell us what executives actually do. Ragins and Cotton, who studied mentoring, were interested in specific variables that were relatively easily measured. On the other hand, they were not in a position to manipulate the causes of intention to mentor. Ivancevich and Lyon were also interested in a specific set of variables, and they conducted their research on the short workweek in a situation where it was both possible and ethical to manipulate the workweek. In all these cases, the research technique the researchers chose was substantially better than dependence on common sense or opinion.

Combining Research Techniques

Robert Sutton and Anat Rafaeli tested what might seem to be an obvious hypothesis— that friendly, pleasant behaviour on the part of sales clerks would be positively associated with store sales.[8] As obvious as this might seem, it would be a good idea to confirm it before spending thousands of dollars on human relations training for clerks. The study combined correlational and observational methods. In the quantitative correlational part of the study, teams of researchers entered a large North American chain's 576 convenience stores and, posing as shoppers, evaluated the friendliness of the sales clerks on rating scales. They also recorded other factors, such as the length of the line at the register. Existing data from company records provided the total annual

EXHIBIT A.5
Continuum of research techniques.

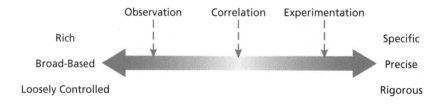

sales each store recorded. When the researchers analyzed the data, the results were surprising—the "unfriendly" stores tended to chalk up higher sales!

To understand this unexpected result, the authors resorted to qualitative, observational research techniques. Specifically, each author spent extensive time in many of the convenience stores directly observing transactions between customers and clerks. In addition, each spent time as a participant-observer, actually doing the sales clerk's job. This observation resolved the mystery. The researchers found that when the stores were busy, the sales clerks tended to stop the small talk, concentrate on their work, and process customers as quickly as possible. This behaviour corresponded to customers' expectations for fast service in a convenience store. When business was slow, clerks tended to be friendly and engage in small talk to relieve boredom. Since the busier stores generated higher sales, it is not surprising that their clerks were less friendly. In fact, further analysis of the correlational data showed that clerks were less friendly when the lines were longer.

This study illustrates how two research techniques can complement each other. It also shows that correlation does not imply causation. Although sales were negatively correlated with friendliness, volume of sales affected the expression of friendliness, not the other way around. Of course, these results would probably not generalize to sales settings in which customers expect more personal attention.

Issues and Concerns in Organizational Behaviour Research

As in every field of study, particular issues confront researchers in organizational behaviour. Three of these issues include sampling, Hawthorne effects, and ethical concerns.

Sampling

Researchers are usually interested in generalizing the results of their research beyond their study. The extent to which the results of a study generalize to other samples and settings is known as **external validity**. External validity will be greater when the results of a study are based on large, random samples. Large samples ensure that the results they obtain are truly representative of the individuals, groups, or organizations being studied and not merely the product of an extreme case or two.

Random sampling means that the research participants have been randomly chosen from the population of interest. Random samples ensure that all relevant individuals, groups, or organizations have an equal probability of being studied and give confidence in the generalizability of the findings. As was noted earlier, observational studies usually involve small samples, and they are seldom randomized. Thus, generalizing from such studies is a problem. However, a well-designed observational study that answers important questions is surely superior to a large-sample, randomized correlational study that enables one to generalize about a trivial hypothesis.

In experimental research, randomization means randomly assigning subjects to experimental and control conditions. To illustrate the importance of this, we can reconsider the hypothetical study on human relations training. Suppose that instead of randomly assigning supervisors to the experimental and control groups, managers nominate supervisors for training. Suppose further that to "reward" them for their long service, more-experienced supervisors are nominated for the training. This results in an experimental group containing more-experienced supervisors and a control group containing less-experienced supervisors. If supervisory experience promotes employee productivity, we might erroneously conclude that it was the *human relations training* that led to any improved results and that our hypothesis is confirmed. Poor sampling due to a lack of randomization has biased the results in favour of our hypothesis. To achieve randomization, it would be a good idea to ascertain that the employees of the experimental and

External validity. The extent to which the results of a study generalize to other samples and settings.

Random sampling. The research participants are randomly chosen from the population of interest.

control supervisors were equally productive *before* the training began. Random sampling is another way to lower the threats to internal validity. In this example, the threat to internal validity was due to the fact that the supervisors in the experimental condition had more experience than those in the control group (as shown in Exhibit A.4, this threat to internal validity is called *selection of participants*), and this might explain the results of the experiment. Thus, it is important that when conducting an experiment the participants are randomly assigned to the experimental and control groups. This helps to ensure that the participants in both conditions do not differ on important variables such as experience and increases internal validity.

Hawthorne Effect

The Hawthorne effect was discovered as a result of a series of studies conducted at the Hawthorne plant of the Western Electric Company near Chicago many years ago. As explained in Chapter 1, these studies examined the effects of independent variables, such as rest pauses, lighting intensity, and pay incentives, on the productivity of assemblers of electrical components.[9]

In a couple of these loosely controlled experiments, unusual results occurred. In the illumination study, both experimental and control workers improved their productivity. In another study, productivity increased and remained high despite the introduction and withdrawal of factors such as rest pauses, shortened workdays, and so on. These results gave rise to the term **Hawthorne effect**, which might be defined as a favourable response of subjects in an organizational experiment to a factor other than the independent variable that is formally being manipulated. Researchers have concluded that this "other factor" is psychological in nature, although it is not well understood.[10] Likely candidates include subjects' reactions to special attention, including feelings of prestige, heightened morale, and so on. The point is that researchers might misinterpret the true reason for any observed change in behaviour because research subjects can have unmeasured feelings about their role in the research.

To return to the human relations training experiment, a Hawthorne effect might occur if the experimental subjects are grateful to management for selecting them for this special training and resolve to work harder back on the job. The supervisors might put in longer hours thinking up ways to improve productivity that have nothing to do with the training they received. However, the researcher could easily conclude that the human relations training improved productivity.

It is very difficult to prevent Hawthorne effects. However, it is possible, if expensive, to see whether they have occurred. To do so, investigators establish a second experimental group that receives special treatment and attention but is not exposed to the key independent variable. In the human relations experiment, this could involve training that is not expected to increase productivity. If the productivity of the supervisors' employees in both experimental groups increases equally, the Hawthorne effect is probably present. If productivity increases only in the human relations training condition, it is unlikely to be due to the Hawthorne effect.

Ethics

Researchers in organizational behaviour, no matter who employs them, have an ethical obligation to do rigorous research and to report that research accurately.[11] In all cases, the psychological and physical well-being of the research subjects is of prime importance. In general, ethical researchers avoid unnecessary deception, inform participants about the general purpose of their research, and protect the anonymity of research subjects. For example, in a correlational study involving the use of questionnaires, investigators should explain the general reason for the research and afford potential subjects the opportunity to decline participation. If names or company identification numbers are required to match responses with data in employee files (e.g., absenteeism or subsequent turnover),

Hawthorne effect. A favourable response by subjects in an organizational experiment that is the result of a factor other than the independent variable that is formally being manipulated.

investigators must guarantee that they will not make individual responses public. In some observation studies and experiments, subjects may be unaware that their behaviour is under formal study. In these cases, researchers have special obligations to prevent negative consequences for subjects. Ethical research has a practical side as well as a moral side. Good cooperation from research subjects is necessary to do good research. Such cooperation is easier to obtain when people are confident that ethical procedures are the rule, not the exception.

LEARNING OBJECTIVES CHECKLIST

1. All research in organizational behaviour begins with a basic question about work or organizations. Frequently, researchers express the question as a *hypothesis*, a formal statement of the expected relationship between two variables. *Variables* are simply measures that can take on two or more values.

2. In most research, we are concerned with two kinds of variables. The *independent variable* is a predictor or cause of variation in a dependent variable. The *dependent variable* is a variable that will vary as a result of changes in the independent variable. Two other kinds of variables that we are sometimes interested in are mediating variables and moderating variables. A *moderating variable* is a variable that affects the nature of the relationship between an independent and dependent variable such that the relationship depends on the level of the moderating variable. A *mediating variable* is a variable that intervenes or explains the relationship between an independent and dependent variable.

3. Careful measurement of variables is important in research. *Reliability* is an index of the consistency of a research subject's responses. *Validity* is an index of the extent to which a measure truly reflects what it is supposed to measure. *Convergent validity* exists when there is a strong relationship between different measures of the same variable. *Discriminant* validity exists when there is a weak relationship between measures of different variables.

4. In *observational research*, one or a few observers assess one or a few instances of organizational behaviour in its natural setting. In *participant observation*, the observer actually takes part in the activity being observed. In *direct observation*, the assessment occurs without the active participation of the researcher.

5. Compared with observation, *correlational research* techniques attempt to measure the variables in question more precisely by using questionnaires, interviews, and existing data. No change is introduced into the research setting. One problem with correlational research is its inability to imply causation. Researchers use experiments to overcome this problem.

6. In *experimental research*, the investigator actually changes or manipulates some factor in the organizational setting and measures the effect that this manipulation has on behaviour. In experimental language, the variable that the researcher manipulates or changes is the independent variable and the variable that the independent variable is expected to affect is the dependent variable. Causation can be inferred from a carefully designed experiment that has high internal validity. *Internal validity* refers to the confidence that the researcher has in concluding that changes in the dependent variable are due to the independent variable. Threats to internal validity are alternative explanations for the results of an experiment. The use of a control group and random assignment to experimental and control conditions increases internal validity and lowers threats to internal validity.

7. The method that researchers use to investigate organizational behaviour is dictated by the nature of the problem under investigation. When variables are not well defined and not easy to isolate and measure precisely, *observation* is an appropriate technique. Some of the weaknesses of observational research include a lack of control over the environment in which the study is being conducted and the small number of observers and situations in the typical observational study. Observational techniques are best used to make an initial examination of some organizational event on which little information is available and to

generate ideas for further investigation with more refined techniques. When the researcher is interested in specific variables that are well defined and relatively easy to measure but cannot be manipulated, *correlational research* is an appropriate technique. Correlational research provides more precision and greater control than observational techniques; however, it cannot be used to study causation. When the researcher is interested in causation and the effect of an independent variable on a dependent variable and it is both possible and ethical to manipulate the independent variable, *experimental research* is an appropriate technique. Experimental research provides the greatest amount of rigour but sacrifices the breadth and richness of less rigorous techniques like observational research.

8. *External validity* refers to the extent to which the results of a study generalize to other samples and settings. External validity will be greater when the results of a study are based on large, random samples. A *random sample* means that the research participants have been randomly chosen from the population of interest. This ensures that all relevant individuals, groups, or organizations have an equal probability of being studied and give confidence in the generalizability of the findings.

9. The *Hawthorne effect* refers to a favourable response of subjects in an organizational experiment to a factor other than the independent variable that is formally being manipulated. Researchers have concluded that this "other factor" is psychological in nature, although it is not well understood. Likely candidates include subjects' reactions to special attention, including feelings of prestige, heightened morale, and so on. The point is that researchers might misinterpret the true reason for any observed change in behaviour because research subjects can have unmeasured feelings about their role in the research.

10. Researchers in organizational behaviour have an ethical obligation to do rigorous research and to report that research accurately. In all cases, the psychological and physical well-being of the research subjects is of prime importance. In general, ethical researchers avoid unnecessary deception, inform participants about the general purpose of their research, and protect the anonymity of research subjects.

References

Chapter 1

1. Dobson, S. (2008). Building a sustainable culture. *Canadian HR Reporter, 21(18)*, 18, 21; Yerema, R. (2009, March 27). Employer Review: HOK Canada, Inc.: Chosen as one of Canada's top 100 employers and Greater Toronto's top employers for 2009. www.eluta.ca/top-employer-hok-canada; Yerema, R. (2009, April 16). Employer Review: HOK Canada, Inc.: Chosen as one of Canada's greenest employers for 2009. www.eluta.ca/green-at-hok-canada; Chai, C.C. (2008, October 18). LEED-ing by example: Design firm's award-winning and environmentally friendly office makes other firms green with envy. *Toronto Star,* R4; (2008, October 18). Building a sustainable culture in Canada. Ideas work news archive; www.hokcanada.com.
2. Katz, D. (1964). The motivational basis of organizational behavior. *Behavioral Science, 9,* 131–146.
3. Peters, T. (1990, Fall). Get innovative or get dead. *California Management Review,* 9–26.
4. Pfeffer, J. (1994). *Competitive advantage through people: Unleashing the power of the work force.* Harvard Business School Press: Boston.
5. Chisholm, P. (2000, May 29). What the boss needs to know. *Maclean's, 113(22),* 18–22.
6. Wren, D. (1987). *The evolution of management thought* (3rd ed.). New York: Wiley.
7. For a summary of their work and relevant references, see Wren, 1987.
8. Taylor, F.W. (1967). *The principles of scientific management.* New York: Norton.
9. Weber, M. (1974). *The theory of social and economic organization* (A.M. Henderson & T. Parsons, Trans.). New York: Free Press.
10. See Wren, 1987.
11. Roethlisberger, F.J., & Dickson, W.J. (1939). *Management and the worker.* Cambridge, MA: Harvard University Press; Wrege, C.D., & Greenwood, R.G. (1986). The Hawthorne studies. In D.A. Wren & J.A. Pearce II (Eds.) (1986), *Papers dedicated to the development of modern management.* Academy of Management.

12. Argyris, C. (1957). *Personality and organization.* New York: Harper.
13. Likert, R. (1961). *New patterns of management.* New York: McGraw-Hill.
14. Gouldner, A.W. (1954). *Patterns of industrial bureaucracy.* New York: Free Press.
15. Selznick, P. (1949). *TVA and the grass roots: A study in the sociology of formal organizations.* Berkeley: University of California Press.
16. Abrahamson, E. (1991). Managerial fads and fashions: The diffusion and rejection of innovations. *Academy of Management Review, 16,* 586–612; Johns, G. (1993). Constraints on the adoption of psychology-based personnel practices: Lessons from organizational innovation. *Personnel Psychology, 46,* 569–592.
17. Mintzberg, H. (1973). *The nature of managerial work.* New York: Harper & Row. See also Mintzberg, H. (1994, Fall). Rounding out the manager's job. *Sloan Management Review,* 11–26.
18. See Gibbs, B. (1994). The effects of environment and technology on managerial roles. *Journal of Management, 20,* 581–604; Kraut, A.I., Pedigo, P.R., McKenna, D.D., & Dunnette, M.D. (1989, November). The role of the manager: What's really important in different management jobs. *Academy of Management Executive,* 286–293.
19. Luthans, F., Hodgetts, R.M., & Rosenkrantz, S.A. (1988). *Real managers.* Cambridge, MA: Ballinger.
20. Kotter, J.P. (1982). *The general managers.* New York: Free Press.
21. Simon, H.A. (1987, February). Making management decisions: The role of intuition and emotion. *Academy of Management Executive,* 57–64; Isenberg, D.J. (1984, November–December). How senior managers think. *Harvard Business Review,* 80–90. See also Sims, H.P., Jr., & Gioia, D.A. (Eds.) (1986). *The thinking organization: Dynamics of organizational social cognition.* San Francisco: Jossey-Bass.
22. Hofstede, G. (1993, February). Cultural constraints in management theories. *Academy of Management Executive,* 81–94.
23. Crawford, M. (1993, May). The new office etiquette. *Canadian Business,* 22–31.

24. Kanungo, R.N. (1998). Leadership in organizations: Looking ahead to the 21st century. *Canadian Psychology, 39(1–2),* 71–82.
25. Mahoney, J. (2005, March 23). Visible majority by 2017. *Globe and Mail,* A1, A7.
26. Mingail, H. (2004, September 29). Wise ways for retraining older workers. *Globe and Mail,* C8.
27. Galt, V. (2006, March 15). 65 means freedom to start a whole new career. *Globe and Mail,* C1, C2.
28. Galt, V. (2005, September 20). Few firms adopt plans to retain aging staff. *Globe and Mail,* B7.
29. Javidan, M., Dorfman, P.W., de Luque, M.S., & House, R.J. (2006). In the eye of the beholder: Cross cultural lessons in leadership from Project GLOBE. *Academy of Management Perspectives, 20,* 67–90.
30. Armstrong-Stassen, M. (1998). Alternative work arrangements: Meeting the challenges. *Canadian Psychology, 39,* 108–123; Meyer, J.P., Allen, N.J., & Topolnytsky, L. (1998). Commitment in a changing world of work. *Canadian Psychology, 39,* 83–93.
31. Galt, V. (2003, January 28). One-third of employees loathe their jobs, consultants find. *Globe and Mail,* B1, B6; Galt, V. (2005, November 15). Fewer workers willing to put in 110%. *Globe and Mail,* B1, B6; Carniol, N. (2005, November 15). Fewer workers willing to give 100 per cent. *Toronto Star,* D1, D11.
32. (2002, August 26). Workers' morale sliding. *Globe and Mail,* B11 (Reuters News Agency).
33. Attersley, J. (2005, November 7). Absence makes the bottom line wander. *Canadian HR Reporter,* R2; Chisholm, 2000, May 29; Galt, V. (2003, June 4). Workers rack up increased sick time. *Globe and Mail,* C1, C3.
34. Duxbury, L., & Higgins, C. (2003). *Work–life conflict in Canada in the new millennium: A status report.* Ottawa: Health Canada.
35. Chisholm, P. (2001, March 5). Redesigning work. *Maclean's, 114(10),* 34–38.
36. Shirouzu, N., & White, J.B. (2002, April 1). Car makers focus on quality.

Globe and Mail, p. B8 (reprinted from the *Wall Street Journal*).

37. Ansberry, C. (2002, March 27). Jobs morph to suit rapidly changing times. *Globe and Mail*, C2; Hitt, M.A., Keats, B.W., & DeMarie, S.M. (1998). Navigating in the new competitive landscape: Building strategic flexibility and competitive advantage in the 21st century. *Academy of Management Executive, 12*, 22–42.

38. Lockwood, N.R. (2006). Talent management: Driver for organizational success. *2006 SHRM Research Quarterly*. Alexandria, VA: Society for Human Resource Management.

39. Lawler, E.E. (2008). *Talent: Making people your competitive advantage*. San Francisco, CA: John Wiley & Sons.

40. McLaren, C. (2002, February 8). Ways to win top talent. *Globe and Mail*, C1.

41. Klie, S. (2005, September 26). "Employees first" at CPX. *Canadian HR Reporter*, 1, 3; (2006, August 10). Breaking the rules: Hundreds of CPX o-o's see big raises from profit sharing program. *Today's Trucking* (online), www.todaystrucking.com/news.cfm?intDocID=16557&CFID.

42. Lawler (2008).

43. McKay, S. (2001, February). The 35 best companies to work for in Canada. *Report on Business Magazine*, 53–62; Toda, B.H. (2000, February). The rewards: Being a good employer draws talent and unlocks success. *Report on Business Magazine*, 33.

44. Bansal, P., Maurer, C., & Slawinski, N. (2008, January/February). Beyond good intentions: Strategies for managing your CSR performance. *Ivey Business Journal, 72(1)*, 1–8.

45. Unilever. Our values. www.unilever.ca/ourvalues/default.asp.

46. Bansal, P., Maurer, C., & Slawinski, N. (2008, January/February).

47. Birenbaum, R., Lang, H., Linley, D., MacMahon, Mann, B., Sabour, A., Sosa, I., Stein, G., & White, A. (2009, June 22). 50 most socially responsible corporations. *Maclean's, 122(23)*, 42–49.

48. McLaren, D. (2008, December 10). Doing their part—with goals in mind. *Globe and Mail*, B7.

49. Johne, M. (2007, October 10). Show us the green, workers say. *Globe and Mail*, C1, C6.

50. Johne, M. (2007, October 10).

Chapter 2

1. Immen, W., & Brown-Bowers, A. (2008, April 16). Employers get the fitness bug. *Globe and Mail*, C1;

www.dundeewealth.com; Pallarito, K. (2008, November). The Pepsi challenge: Sustaining employee participation in wellness. *Workforce Management (Crain's Benefits Outlook 2009)*, 12;(2009, June 24). PepsiCo recognized by National Business Group on Health as a leading employer promoting healthy lifestyles for its employees. News Release. www.pepsico.com; PepsiCo employee wellness program. www.pepsico.com.

2. George, J.M. (1992). The role of personality in organizational life: Issues and evidence. *Journal of Management, 18*, 185–213; Mount, M.K., & Barrick, M.R. (1995). The big five personality dimensions: Implications for research and practice in human resources management. In K.M. Rowland & G. Ferris (Eds.), *Research in personnel and human resources management*(Vol. 13, 153–200). Greenwich, CT: JAI Press.

3. George, 1992; Weiss, H.M., & Adler, S. (1984). Personality and organizational behavior. In B.M. Staw & L.L. Cummings (Eds.), *Research in organizational behavior* (Vol. 6, 1–50). Greenwich, CT: JAI Press.

4. Adler, S., & Weiss, H.M. (1988). Recent developments in the study of personality and organizational behavior. In C.L. Cooper & I. Robertson (Eds.), *International review of industrial and organizational psychology*. New York: Wiley.

5. Moses, S. (1991, November). Personality tests come back in I/O. *APA Monitor*, 9.

6. Mount & Barrick, 1995.

7. Digman, J.M. (1990). Personality structure: Emergence of the five-factor model. *Annual Review of Psychology, 41*, 417–440; Hogan, R.T. (1991). Personality and personality measurement. In M.D. Dunette & L.M. Hough (Eds.), *Handbook of industrial and organizational psychology* (2nd ed., Vol. 2). Palo Alto, CA: Consulting Psychologists Press; Barrick, M.R., & Mount, M.K. (1991). The big five personality dimensions and job performance: A meta-analysis. *Personnel Psychology, 44*, 1–26; Barrick, M.R., Mount, M.K., & Judge, T.A. (2001). Personality and performance at the beginning of the new millennium: What do we know and where do we go next? *International Journal of Selection and Assessment, 9*, 9–30; Barrick, M.R., Mount, M.K., & Gupta, R. (2003). Meta-analysis of the relationship between the five-factor model of personality and Holland's occupational types. *Personnel*

Psychology, 56, 45–74; Ng, T.W.H., Eby, L.T., Sorensen, K.L., & Feldman, D.C. (2005). Predictors of objective and subjective career success: A meta-analysis. *Personnel Psychology, 58*, 367–408.

8. Judge, T.A., Higgins, C.A., Thorensen, C.J., & Barrick, M.R. (1999). The Big Five personality traits, general mental ability, and career success across the life span. *Personnel Psychology, 52*, 621–652.

9. Hough, L.M., Eaton, N. K., Dunnette, M.D., Kamp, J.D., & McCloy, R.A. (1990). Criterion-related validities of personality constructs and the effect of response distortion on those validities. *Journal of Applied Psychology, 75*, 581–595; Tett, R.P., Jackson, D.N., & Rothstein, M. (1991). Personality measures as predictors of job performance: A meta-analytic review. *Personnel Psychology, 44*, 703–742.

10. Barrick & Mount, 1991; Ones, D.S., Dilchert, S., Viswesvaran, C., & Judge, T.A. (2007). In support of personality assessment in organizational settings. *Personnel Psychology, 60*, 995–1027; Barrick, M.R., Mount, M.K., & Judge, T.A. (2001).

11. Ones, D.S., Viswesvaran, C., & Schmidt, F.L. (1993). Comprehensive meta-analysis of integrity test validities: Findings and implications for personnel selection and theories of job performance. Journal of Applied Psychology, 78, 679–703.

12. Judge, Higgins, Thorensen, & Barrick, 1999.

13. Judge, T.A., & Ilies, R. (2002). Relationship of personality to performance motivation: A meta-analytic review. *Journal of Applied Psychology, 87*, 797–807.

14. Judge, T.A., Heller, D., & Mount, M.K. (2002). Five-factor model of personality and job satisfaction: A meta-analysis. *Journal of Applied Psychology, 87*, 530–541; Morgeson, F.P., Reider, M.H., & Campion, M.A. (2005). Selecting individuals in team settings: The importance of social skills, personality characteristics, and team work knowledge. *Personnel Psychology, 58*, 583–611.

15. Kanfer, R., Wanberg, C.R., & Kantrowitz, T.M. (2001). Job search and employment: A personality-motivational analysis and meta-analytic review. *Journal of Applied Psychology, 86*, 837–855.

16. Judge, Higgins, Thorensen, & Barrick, 1999.

17. Rotter, J.B. (1966). Generalized expectancies for internal versus external controls of reinforcement.

Psychological Monographs, 80 (Whole no. 609).

18. Szilagyi, A.D., & Sims, H.P., Jr. (1975). Locus of control and expectancies across multiple organizational levels. *Journal of Applied Psychology, 60,* 638–640.

19. Szilagyi, A.D., Sims, H.P., Jr., & Keller, R.T. (1976). Role dynamics, locus of control, and employee attitudes and behavior. *Academy of Management Journal, 19,* 259–276.

20. Andrisani, P.J., & Nestel, G. (1976). Internal-external control as contributor to and outcome of work experience. *Journal of Applied Psychology, 61,* 156–165.

21. For evidence on stress and locus of control, see Anderson, C.R. (1977). Locus of control, coping behaviors, and performance in a stress setting: A longitudinal study. *Journal of Applied Psychology, 62,* 446–451. For evidence on career planning, see Thornton, G.C., III. (1978). Differential effects of career planning on internals and externals. *Personnel Psychology, 31,* 471–476.

22. Snyder, M. (1987). *Public appearances/private realities: The psychology of self-monitoring.* New York: W.H. Freeman; Gangestad, S.W., & Snyder, M. (2000). Self-monitoring: Appraisal and reappraisal. Psychological Bulletin, 126(4), 530–555.

23. Snyder, 1987; Gangestad & Snyder, 2000.

24. Day, D.V., Schleicher, D.J., Unckless, A.L., & Hiller, N.J. (2002). Self-monitoring personality at work: A meta-analytic investigation of construct validity. *Journal of Applied Psychology, 87,* 390–401.

25. Kilduff, M., & Day, D.V. (1994). Do chameleons get ahead? The effects of self-monitoring and managerial careers. *Academy of Management Journal, 37(4),* 1047–1060.

26. Brockner, J. (1988). *Self-esteem at work: Research, theory, and practice.* Lexington, MA: Lexington.

27. Brockner, 1988.

28. Brockner, 1988.

29. Pierce, J.L., Gardner, D.G., Cummings, L.L., & Dunham, R.B. (1989). Organization-based self-esteem: Construct definition, measurement, and validation. Academy of Management Journal, 32, 622–648; Tharanou, P. (1979). Employee self-esteem: A review of the literature. Journal of Vocational Behavior, 15, 1–29.

30. Pierce, J.L., Gardner, D.G., Dunham, R.B., & Cummings, L.L. (1993). Moderation by organization-based self-esteem of role condition–employee response relationships. *Academy of Management Journal, 36,* 271–288.

31. George, J.M. (1996). Trait and state affect. In K.R. Murphy (Ed.), *Individual differences and behavior in organizations.* San Francisco, CA: Jossey-Bass.

32. George, 1996; Thoresen, C.J., Kaplan, S.A., Barsky, A.P., Warren, C.R., & de Chermont, K. (2003). The affective underpinnings of job perceptions and attitudes: A meta-analytic review and integration. *Psychological Bulletin, 129,* 914–945; Lyubomirsky, S., King, L., & Diener, E. (2005). The benefits of frequent positive affect: Does happiness lead to success? *Psychological Bulletin, 131,* 803–855; Kaplan, S., Bradley, J.C., Luchman, J.N., & Haynes, D. (2009). On the role of positive and negative affectivity in job performance: A meta-analytic investigation. *Journal of Applied Psychology, 94,* 162–176.

33. Crant, M.J. (2000). Proactive behaviour in organizations. Journal of Management, 26, 435–462; Seibert, S.E., Kraimer, M.L., & Crant, J.M. (2001). What do proactive people do? A longitudinal model linking proactive personality and career success. *Personnel Psychology, 54,* 845–874.

34. Bateman, T.S., & Crant, J.M. (1993). The proactive component of organizational behavior: A measure and correlates. *Journal of Organizational Behavior, 14,* 103–118.

35. Seibert, Kraimer, & Crant, 2001; Thompson, J.A. (2005). Proactive personality and job performance: A social capital perspective. *Journal of Applied Psychology, 90,* 1011–1017; Brown, D.J., Cober, R.T., Kane, K., Levy, P.E., & Shalhoop, J. (2006). Proactive personality and the successful job search: A field investigation with college graduates. Journal of Applied Psychology, 91, 717–726.

36. Chen, G., Gully, S.M., & Eden, D. (2001). Validation of a new general self-efficacy scale. *Organizational Research Methods, 4,* 62–83.

37. Chen, Gully, & Eden, 2001.

38. Judge, T.A., Erez, A., Bono, J.E., & Thoresen, C.J. (2003). The core self-evaluation scale: Development of a measure. *Personnel Psychology, 56,* 303–331.

39. Judge, T.A., & Bono, J.E. (2001). Relationship of core self-evaluations traits—self-esteem, generalized self-efficacy, locus of control, and emotional stability—with job satisfaction and job performance: A meta-analysis. *Journal of Applied Psychology, 86,* 80–92; Judge, T.A., Bono, J.E., & Locke, E.A. (2000). Personality and job satisfaction: The mediating role of job characteristics. *Journal of Applied Psychology, 85,* 237–249; Judge, Erez, Bono, & Thoresen, 2003; Judge, T.A., Locke, E.A., & Durham, C.C. (1997). The dispositional causes of job satisfaction: A core evaluations approach. In B.M. Staw & L.L. Cummings (Eds.), *Research in organizational behavior* (Vol. 19, 151–188). Greenwich, CT: JAI Press; Judge, T.A., Bono, J.E., Erez, A., & Locke, E.A. (2005). Core self-evaluations and job and life satisfaction: The role of self-concordance and goal attainment. *Journal of Applied Psychology, 90,* 257–268; Kammeyer-Mueller, J.D., Judge, T.A., & Scott, B.A. (2009). The role of core self-evaluations in the coping process. *Journal of Applied Psychology, 94,* 177–195; Judge, T.A. (2009). Core self-evaluations and work success. *Current Directions in Psychological Science, 18,* 58–62; Johnson, R.E., Rosen, C.C., & Levy, P.E. (2008). Getting to the core of core self-evaluation: A review and recommendations. *Journal of Organizational Behavior, 29,* 391–413.

40. Day, N. (1998, June). Informal learning gets results. *Workforce,* 31–35.

41. Pfeffer, J. (1994). *Competitive advantage through people: Unleashing the power of the work force.* Boston, MA: Harvard Business School Press.

42. Peterson, S.J., & Luthans, F. (2006). The impact of financial and nonfinancial incentives on business-unit outcomes over time. *Journal of Applied Psychology, 91,* 156–165.

43. Peterson & Luthans, 2006.

44. Luthans, F., & Kreitner, R. (1975). *Organizational behavior modification.* Glenview, IL: Scott, Foresman.

45. However, more research is necessary to establish the extent of this in organizations. See Arvey, R.D., & Ivancevich, J.M. (1980). Punishment in organizations: A review, propositions, and research suggestions. *Academy of Management Review, 5,* 123–132.

46. Punishment in front of others can be effective under restricted conditions. See Trevino, L.K. (1992). The social effects of punishment in organizations: A justice perspective. *Academy of Management Review, 17,* 647–676.

47. Orsgan, D.W., & Hamner, W.C. (1982). *Organizational behavior: An applied psychological approach* (Revised ed.). Plano, TX: Business Publications.

48. See Parmerlee, M.A., Near, J.P., & Jensen, T.C. (1982). Correlates of

whistle-blowers' perceptions of organizational retaliation. *Administrative Science Quarterly, 27,* 17–34.

49. Bandura, A. (1991). Social cognitive theory of self-regulation. *Organizational Behavior and Human Decision Processes, 50,* 248–287.

50. Bandura, A. (1989). Human agency in social cognitive theory. *American Psychologists, 44,* 1175–1184. For a presentation of operant learning theory, see Honig, W.K., & Staddon, J.E.R. (Eds.). (1977). *Handbook of operant behavior.* Englewood Cliffs, NJ: Prentice-Hall. For a presentation of social learning theory, see Bandura, A. (1986). *Social foundations of thought and action.* Englewood Cliffs, NJ: Prentice-Hall.

51. Bandura, 1986.

52. Luthans, F., & Kreitner, R. (1985). *Organizational behavior modification and beyond: An operant and social learning approach.* Glenview, IL: Scott, Foresman; Manz, C.C., & Sims, H.P., Jr. (1981). Vicarious learning: The influence of modeling on organizational behavior. *Academy of Management Review, 6,* 105–113.

53. Bandura, 1986; Goldstein, A.P., & Sorcher, M. (1974). *Changing supervisor behavior.* New York: Pergamon.

54. Robinson, S.L., & O'Leary-Kelly, A.M. (1998). Monkey see, monkey do: The influence of work groups on the antisocial behavior of employees. *Academy of Management Journal, 41,* 658–672; Goulet, L.R. (1997). Modelling aggression in the workplace: The role of role models. *Academy of Management Executive, 11,* 84–85.

55. Bandura, A. (1997). *Self-efficacy: The exercise of control.* New York, NY: W.H. Freeman.

56. Bandura, 1997; Stajkovic, A.D., & Luthans, F. (1998). Self-efficacy and work-related performance: A meta-analysis. *Psychological Bulletin, 124,* 240–261.

57. Bandura, 1991; Manz, C.C., & Sims, H.P., Jr. (1980). Self-management as a substitute for leadership: A social learning theory perspective. *Academy of Management Review, 5,* 361–367; Hackman, J.R. (1986). The psychology of self-management in organizations. In M.S. Pollack & R. Perloff (Eds.), Psychology and work. Washington, DC: American Psychological Association.

58. Bandura, 1986, 1989, 1991; Kanfer, F.H. (1980). Self-management methods. In F.H. Kanfer & A.P. Goldstein (Eds.), *Helping people change: A textbook of methods* (2nd ed.). New York: Pergamon.

59. Luthans & Kreitner, 1985; Manz & Sims, 1980.

60. Frayne, C., & Latham, G. (1987). Application of social learning theory to employee self-management of attendance. *Journal of Applied Psychology, 72,* 387–392.

61. Frayne, C.A., & Geringer, J.M. (2000). Self-management training for improving job performance: A field experiment involving salespeople. *Journal of Applied Psychology, 85,* 361–372.

62. Gist, M.E., Stevens, C.K., & Bavetta, A.G. (1991). Effects of self-efficacy and post-training intervention on the acquisition and maintenance of complex interpersonal skills. *Personnel Psychology, 44,* 837–861; Stevens, C.K., Bavetta, A.G., & Gist, M.E. (1993). Gender differences in the acquisition of salary negotiation skills: The role of goals, self-efficacy, and perceived control. *Journal of Applied Psychology, 78,* 723–735.

63. Komaki, J., Barwick, K.D., & Scott, L.R. (1978). A behavioral approach to occupational safety: Pinpointing and reinforcing safe performance in a food manufacturing plant. *Journal of Applied Psychology, 63,* 434–445. For a similar study, see Haynes, R.S., Pine, R.C., & Fitch, H.G. (1982). Reducing accident rates with organizational behavior modification. *Academy of Management Journal, 25,* 407–416.

64. Stajkovic, A.D., & Lutans, F. (1997). A meta-analysis of the effects of organizational behavior modification on task performance, 1975–95. *Academy of Management Journal, 40,* 1122–1149; Stajkovic, A.D., & Luthans, F. (2003). Behavioral management and task performance in organizations: Conceptual background, meta-analysis, and test of alternative models. *Personnel Psychology, 56,* 155–194; Stajkovic, A.D., & Luthans, F. (2001). Differential effects of incentive motivators on work performance. *Academy of Management Journal, 44,* 580–590.

65. Markham, S.E., Scott, K.D., & McKee, G.H. (2002). Recognizing good attendance: A longitudinal, quasi-experimental field study. *Personnel Psychology, 55,* 639–660.

66. Markham, Scott, & McKee, 2002; Well-structured employee reward/recognition programs yield positive results. (1999, November). *HRFocus, 1,* 14, 15.

67. Markham, Scott, & McKee, 2002.

68. Klie, S. (2006, August 14). Recognition equals profits. *Canadian HR Reporter, 19(14),* 18.

69. Saks, A.M., & Haccoun, R.R. (2010). *Managing performance through training and development* (5th ed.). Toronto: Nelson.

70. Taylor, P.J., Russ-Eft, D.F., & Chan, D.W.L. (2005). A meta-analytic review of behavior modeling training. *Journal of Applied Psychology, 90,* 692–709.

71. Taylor, Russ-Eft, & Chan, 2005.

72. Saks, A.M. (1997). Transfer of training and self-efficacy: What is the dilemma? Applied Psychology: An International Review, 46, 365–370.

73. DeSimone, R.L., Werner, J.M., & Harris, D.M. (2002). *Human resource development.* Orlando, FL: Harcourt College.

74. Harding, K. (2003, February 5). Firms offer a hand up the ladder. *Globe and Mail,* C3.

75. Brown, D. (2005, June 20). TD gives employees tool to chart career paths. *Canadian HR Reporter, 18(12),* 11, 13.

Chapter 3

1. Dobson, S. (2009, March 9). Employers rewarded for diversity. *Canadian HR Reporter, 22(5),* 5, 6; Campbell, J. (2009, February 25). Canada Post delivers on diversity. *Ottawa Citizen,* D6; Sankey, D. (2009, February 21). StatsCan, Canada Post lead by example in diversity hiring. *CanWest News;* Sankey, D. (2009, February 25). Federal agencies lead by example. *Ottawa Citizen,* D8; About Us. Canada Post. www.canadapost.ca; Acting responsibly social responsibility report. www.canadapost.ca.

2. Cox, T., Jr. (1993). *Cultural diversity in organizations: Theory, research, & practice.* San Francisco: Berrett-Koehler.

3. Ashforth, B.E. (2001). *Role transitions in organizational life: An identity-based persepctive.* Mahwah, NJ: Lawrence Erlbaum Associates, Inc.; Ashforth, B.E., & Mael, F. (1989). Social identity theory and the organization. *Academy of Management Review, 14,* 20–39.

4. Ashforth, 2001; Ashforth & Mael, 1989.

5. Bruner, J.S. (1957). On perceptual readiness. *Psychological Review, 64,* 123–152.

6. Eagly, A.H., Ashmore, R.D., Makhijani, M.G., & Longo, L.C. (1991). What is beautiful is good, but . . . : A meta-analytic review of research on the physical attractiveness stereotype. *Psychological Bulletin, 110,* 109–128; Hosoda, M., Stone-Romero, E.F., & Coats, G. (2003). The effects of

physical attractiveness on job-related outcomes: A meta-analysis of experimental studies. *Personnel Psychology, 56,* 431–462.

7. Stone, E.F., Stone, D.L., & Dipboye, R.L. (1992). Stigmas in organizations: Race, handicaps, and physical unattractiveness. In K. Kelley (Ed.), *Issues, theory and research in industrial/ organizational psychology.* New York: Elsevier; Hosoda, Stone-Romero, & Coats, 2003.

8. Judge, T.A., & Cable, D.M. (2004). The effect of physical height on workplace success and income: Preliminary test of a theoretical model. *Journal of Applied Psychology, 89,*428–441.

9. See Krzystofiak, F., Cardy, R., & Newman, J.E. (1988). Implicit personality and performance appraisal: The influence of trait inferences on evaluations of behavior. *Journal of Applied Psychology, 73,* 515–521.

10. Fiske, S.T. (1993). Social cognition and social perception. *Annual Review of Psychology, 44,* 155–194.

11. Secord, P.F., Backman, C.W., & Slavitt, D.R. (1976). *Understanding social life: An introduction to social psychology.* New York: McGraw-Hill. For elaboration, see Wilder, D.A. (1986). Social categorization: Implications for creation and reduction of intergroup bias. *Advances in Experimental Social Psychology, 19,* 291–349.

12. Dion, K.L., & Schuller, R.A. (1991). The Ms. stereotype: Its generality and its relation to managerial and marital status stereotypes. *Canadian Journal of Behavioural Science, 23,* 25–40.

13. For a more complete treatment see Falkenberg, L. (1990). Improving the accuracy of stereotypes within the workplace. *Journal of Management, 16,* 107–118.

14. Kelley, H.H. (1972). Attribution in social interaction. In E.E. Jones, E.E., Kanhouse, D.E., Kelley, H.H., Nisbett, R.E., Valins, S., & Weiner, B. (Eds.), *Attribution: Perceiving the causes of behavior.* Morristown, NJ: General Learning Press. For an integrative attribution model, see Medcof, J.W. (1990). PEAT: An integrative model of attribution processes. *Advances in Experimental Social Psychology, 23,* 111–209.

15. Baron, R.A., Byrne, D., & Griffitt, W. (1974). *Social psychology: Understanding human interaction.* Boston: Allyn and Bacon.

16. This discussion of attribution biases draws upon Fiske, S.T., & Taylor, S.E. (1984). *Social cognition.* Reading, MA: Addison-Wesley.

17. Jones, E.E. (1979). The rocky road from acts to dispositions. *American Psychologist, 34,* 107–117; Ross, L. (1977). The intuitive psychologist and his shortcomings: Distortions in the attribution process. *Advances in Experimental Social Psychology, 10,* 173–220.

18. Mitchell, T.R., & Kalb, L.S. (1982). Effects of job experience on supervisor attributions for a subordinate's poor performance. *Journal of Applied Psychology, 67,* 181–188.

19. Watson, D. (1982). The actor and the observer: How are their perceptions of causality divergent? *Psychological Bulletin, 92,* 682–700.

20. Sonnenfeld, J. (1981). Executive apologies for price fixing: Role biased perceptions of causality. *Academy of Management Journal, 24,* 192–198; Waters, J.A. (1978, Spring). Catch 20.5. Corporate morality as an organizational phenomenon. *Organizational Dynamics,* 2–19.

21. Greenwald, A.G. (1980). The totalitarian ego: Fabrication and revision of personal history. *American Psychologist, 35,* 603–618; Tetlock, P.E. (1985). Accountability: The neglected social context of judgment and choice. *Research in Organizational Behavior, 7,* 297–332.

22. Pyszczynski, T., & Greenberg, J. (1987). Toward an integration of cognitive and motivational perspectives on social inference: A biased hypothesis-testing model. *Advances in Experimental Social Psychology, 20,* 197–340.

23. This section relies on Jackson, S.E., & Alvarez, E.B. (1992). Working through diversity as a strategic imperative. In S.E. Jackson (Ed.), *Diversity in the workplace: Human resources initiatives.* New York: Guilford Press; Mahoney, J. (2005, March 23). Visible majority by 2017. *Globe and Mail,* A1, A7.

24. Mahoney, 2005, March 23.

25. Mingail, H. (2004, September 29). Wise ways for retraining older workers. *Globe and Mail,*C8.

26. Crawford, 2006, April 1; Galt, V. (2005, March 2). Diversity efforts paying off: Shell CFO. *Globe and Mail,*B1, B20; Vu, U. (2004, November 8). FedEx holds managers accountable for diversity. *Canadian HR Reporter,* 17(19),3; Shaw, A. (2006, May 22). Hiring immigrants makes good business sense. Canadian HR Reporter, 19(10),21; Keung, N. (2006, March 18). Wanted: Minorities. *Toronto Star,*B1, B3.

27. Cox, 1993; Cox, T., Jr. (1991, May). The multicultural organization. *Academy of Management Executive, 5,* 34–47.

28. Crone, G. (1999, February 18). Companies embracing workplace diversity. *Financial Post,*C11; Galt, V. (2004, January 27). Firms excel with women in senior ranks: Study. *Globe and Mail,* B5.

29. Nguyen, H.-H.D., & Ryan, A.M. (2008). Does stereotype threat affect test performance of minorities and women? A meta-analysis of experimental evidence. *Journal of Applied Psychology, 93,*1314–1334.

30. Hartley, E.L. (1946). *Problems in prejudice.* New York: King's Crown Press.

31. Alderfer, C.P., & Thomas, D.A. (1988). The significance of race and ethnicity for organizational behavior. In C.L. Cooper & I. Robertson (Eds.), *International review of industrial and organizational psychology.* New York: Wiley; Cox, T., Jr., & Nkomo, S.M. (1990). Invisible men and women: A status report on race as a variable in organization behavior research. *Journal of Organizational Behavior, 11,* 419–431.

32. Sharpe, R. (1993, September 14). Losing ground. *Wall Street Journal,* A1, 12, 13.

33. Immen, W. (2007, June 29). Minorities still see barriers in way to the top. *Globe and Mail,* C1.

34. (2007, June 29). Discrimination reported as a continuing issue in U.S. *Globe and Mail,*C1.

35. Greenhaus, J.H., & Parasuraman, S. (1993). Job performance attributions and career advancement prospects: An examination of gender and race effects. *Organizational Behavior and Human Decision Processes, 55,* 273–297.

36. Powell, G.N. (1992). The good manager: Business students' stereotypes of Japanese managers versus stereotypes of American managers. *Group & Organizational Management, 17,* 44–56.

37. Brief, A.P., Umphress, E.E., Dietz, J., Burrows, J.W., Butz, R.M., Scholten, L. (2005). Community matters: Realistic group conflict theory and the impact of diversity. *Academy of Management Journal, 48,* 830–844.

38. Galt, V. (2005, May 4). Glass ceiling still tough to crack. *Globe and Mail,* C1, C2; Flavelle, D. (2005, April 28). Women advance up ranks slowly. *Toronto Star,*D1, D12; Perry, A. (2009, March 6). Women climbing corporate ranks: Study. *Toronto Star,* B3

39. Brenner, O.C., Tomkiewicz, J., & Schein, V.E. (1989). The relationship between sex role stereotypes and requisite management characteristics revisited. *Academy of Management Journal, 32,* 662–669; Heilman, M.E., Block, C.J., Martell, R.F., & Simon, M.C. (1989). Has anything changed? Current characterizations of men, women, and managers. *Journal of Applied Psychology, 74,* 935–942; Schein, V.E. (1975). Relationships between sex role stereotypes and requisite management characteristics among female managers. *Journal of Applied Psychology, 60,* 340–344.

40. Brenner et al., 1989; Powell, G.N., Butterfield, D.A., & Parent, J.D. (2002). Gender and managerial stereotypes: Have the times changed? *Journal of Management, 28*(2), 177–193.

41. Rosen, B., & Jerdee, T.H. (1974). Influence of sex role stereotypes on personnel decisions. *Journal of Applied Psychology, 59,* 9–14.

42. Cohen, S.L., & Bunker, K.A. (1975). Subtle effects of sex role stereotypes on recruiters' hiring decisions. *Journal of Applied Psychology, 60,* 566–572. See also Rose, G.L., & Andiappan, P. (1978). Sex effects on managerial hiring decisions. *Academy of Management Journal, 21,* 104–112.

43. Heilman, M.E., Wallen, A.S., Fuchs, D., & Tamkins, M.M. (2004). Penalties for success: Reactions to women who succeed at male gender-typed tasks. *Journal of Applied Psychology, 89,* 416–427.

44. Parasuraman, S., & Greenhaus, J.H. (1993). Personal portrait: The life-style of the woman manager. In E.A. Fagenson (Ed.), *Women in management: Trends, issues, and challenges in managerial diversity.* Newbury Park, CA: Sage; Cleveland, J.N., Vescio, T.K., & Barnes-Farrell, J.L. (2005). Gender discrimination in organizations. In R.L. Dipboye & A. Colella (Eds.), *Discrimination at work: The psychological and organizational bases.* Mahwah, NJ: Lawrence Erlbaum Associates.

45. Tosi, H.L., & Einbender, S.W. (1985). The effects of the type and amount of information in sex discrimination research: A meta-analysis. *Academy of Management Journal, 28,* 712–723.

46. For a review, see Latham, G.P., Skarlicki, D., Irvine, D., & Siegel, J.P. (1993). The increasing importance of performance appraisals to employee effectiveness in organizational settings in North America. In C.L. Cooper & I. Robertson (Eds.), *International review of industrial and organizational psychology.* New York: Wiley. For a representative study, see Pulakos, E.D., White, L.A., Oppler, S.A., & Borman, W.C. (1989). Examination of race and sex effects on performance ratings. *Journal of Applied Psychology, 74,* 770–780; Cleveland, Vescio, & Barnes-Farrell, 2005.

47. Heilman, M.E., & Haynes, M.C. (2005). No credit where credit is due: Attributional rationalization of women's success in male-female teams. *Journal of Applied Psychology, 90,* 905–916.

48. Galt, 2005, March 2.

49. Galt, 2005, May 4.

50. Won, S. (2004, November 8). Women climbing the ranks at banks. *Globe and Mail,* C1, C2.

51. Rosen, B., & Jerdee, T.H. (1976). The nature of job-related age stereotypes. *Journal of Applied Psychology, 61,* 180–183. See also Gibson, K.J., Zerbe, W.J., & Franken, R.E. (1992). Job search strategies for older job hunters: Addressing employers' perceptions. *Canadian Journal of Counselling, 26,* 166–176.

52. Gibson et al., 1992.

53. Cole, T. (2000, June). Revenge of the fortysomethings. *Report on Business Magazine,* 34–40; McEvoy, G.M., & Cascio, W.F. (1989). Cumulative evidence of the relationship between employee age and job performance. *Journal of Applied Psychology, 74,* 11–17. For a broader review on age, see Rhodes, S.R. (1983). Age related differences in work attitudes and behavior. *Psychological Bulletin, 93,* 328–367.

54. Rosen, B., & Jerdee, T.H. (1976). The influence of age stereotypes on managerial decisions. *Journal of Applied Psychology, 61,* 428–432. Also see Dietrick, E.J., & Dobbins, G.J. (1991). The influence of subordinate age on managerial actions: An attributional analysis. *Journal of Organizational Behavior, 12,* 367–377.

55. Galt, V. (2002, October 16). What am I, chopped liver? *Globe and Mail,* C1, C6.

56. Galt, 2002, October 16.

57. Falkenberg, 1990; Fiske et al., 1991.

58. Shaw, A. (2008, May 5). Boeing puts diversity to work—silently. *Canadian HR Reporter, 21*(9), 18; Caballero, R., & Yerema, R. (2009, February 19). Employer Review: Boeing Canada Operations Limited: Chosen as one of Canada's best diversity employers for 2009. www.eluta.ca/diversity-at-boeing-canada.

59. Caballero, R., & Yerema, R. (2009, March 21). Employer Review: Corus Entertainment Inc.: Chosen as one of Canada's best diversity employers for 2009. www.eluta.ca/diversity-at-corus-entertainment.

60. Caudron, S. (1993, April). Training can damage diversity efforts. *Personnel Journal,* 51–62.

61. Jayne, M.E.A., & Dipboye, R.L. (2004). Leveraging diversity to improve business performance: Research findings and recommendations for organizations. *Human Resource Management, 43,* 409–424.

62. Mayer, R.C., & Davis, J.H. (1999). The effect of the performance appraisal system on trust for management: A field quasi-experiment. *Journal of Applied Psychology, 84,* 123–136.

63. Lee, C. (1997, January). Trust. *Training, 34*(1), 28–37.

64. Mayer & Davis, 1999; Davis, J.H., Mayer, R.C., & Schoorman, F.D. (1995, October). The trusted general manager and firm performance: Empirical evidence of a strategic advantage. Paper presented at the 15th annual meeting of the Strategic Management Society, Mexico City, Mexico. Cited in Mayer & Davis, 1999.

65. Davis, Mayer, & Schoorman, 1995; Mayer, R.C., Davis, J.H., & Schoorman, F.D. (1995). An integrative model of organizational trust. *Academy of Management Review, 20,* 709–734; Rousseau, D.M., Sitkin, S.B., Burt, R.S., & Camerer, C. (1998). Not so different after all: A cross-discipline view of trust. *Academy of Management Review, 23,* 393–404.

66. Mayer, Davis, & Schoorman, 1995.

67. Mayer & Davis, 1999; Mayer, Davis, & Schoorman, 1995.

68. Dirks, K.T., & Ferrin, D.L. (2002). Trust in leadership: Meta-analytic findings and implications for research and practice. *Journal of Applied Psychology, 87,* 611–628.

69. Neto, J.T. (2009, April 6). About this survey. *A special national report for the Great Place to Work Institute Canada. Globe and Mail,* GPTW2.

70. Rhoades, L., & Eisenberger, R. (2002). Perceived organizational support: A review of the literature. *Journal of Applied Psychology, 87,* 698–714.

71. Rhoades & Eisenberger, 2002.

72. Shanock, L.R., & Eisenberger, R. (2006). When supervisors feel supported: Relationships with subordinates' perceived supervisor support, perceived organizational support, and performance. *Journal of Applied Psychology, 91,* 689–695.

73. Allen, D.G., Shore, L.M., & Griffeth, R.W. (2003). The role of perceived

organizational support and supportive human resource practices in the turnover process. *Journal of Management, 29*(1), 99–118.

74. Campion, M.A., Palmer, D.K., and Campion, J.E. (1997). A review of structure in the selection interview. *Personnel Psychology, 50*, 655–702; McDaniel, M.A., Whetzel, D.L., Schmidt, F.L., & Maurer, S.D. (1994). The validity of employment interviews: A comprehensive review and meta-analysis. *Journal of Applied Psychology, 79*, 599–616; Wiesner, W.H., & Cronshaw, S.F. (1988). A meta-analytic investigation of the impact of interview format and degree of structure on the validity of the employment interview. *Journal of Occupational Psychology, 61*, 275–290.

75. Hakel, M.D. (1982). Employment interviewing. In K.M. Rowland & G.R. Ferris (Eds.), *Personnel management*. Boston: Allyn and Bacon.

76. Hakel, 1982; Dipboye, R.L. (1989). Threats to the incremental validity of interviewer judgments. In R.W. Eder & G.R. Ferris (Eds.), *The employment interview: Theory, research, and practice*. Newbury Park, CA: Sage.

77. Hollmann, T.D. (1972). Employment interviewers' errors in processing positive and negative information. *Journal of Applied Psychology, 56*, 130–134.

78. Rowe, P.M. (1989). Unfavorable information in interview decisions. In R.W. Eder & G.R. Ferris (Eds.), *The employment interview: Theory, research, and practice*. Newbury Park, CA: Sage.

79. Maurer, T.J., & Alexander, R.A. (1991). Contrast effects in behavioral measurement: An investigation of alternative process explanations. *Journal of Applied Psychology, 76*, 3–10; Maurer, T.J., Palmer, J.K., & Ashe, D.K. (1993). Diaries, checklists, evaluations, and contrast effects in measurement of behavior. *Journal of Applied Psychology, 78*, 226–231; Schmitt, N. (1976). Social and situational determinants of interview decisions: Implications for the employment interview. *Personnel Psychology, 29*, 70–101.

80. Chapman, D.S., & Zweig, D.I. (2005). Developing a nomological network for interview structure: Antecedents and consequences of the structured selection interview. *Personnel Psychology, 58*, 673–702.

81. For other reasons and a review of the interview literature, see Harris, M.M. (1989). Reconsidering the employment interview: A review of recent literature and suggestions for future research. *Personnel Psychology, 42*, 691–726.

82. Rynes, S.L., Bretz, R., & Gerhart, B. (1991). The importance of recruitment in job choice: A different way of looking. *Personnel Psychology, 44*, 487–521.

83. Hausknecht, J.P., Day, D.V., & Thomas, S.C. (2004). Applicant reactions to selection procedures: An updated model and meta-analysis. *Personnel Psychology, 57*, 639–683.

84. Balzer, W.K., & Sulsky, L.M. (1992). Halo and performance appraisal research: A critical examination. *Journal of Applied Psychology, 77*, 975–985; Cooper, W.H. (1981). Ubiquitous halo. *Psychological Bulletin, 90*, 218–244; Murphy, K.R., Jako, R.A., & Anhalt, R.L. (1993). Nature and consequences of halo error: A critical analysis. *Journal of Applied Psychology, 78*, 218–225.

85. Kingstrom, P.D., & Bass, A.R. (1981). A critical analysis of studies comparing behaviorally anchored rating scales (BARS) and other rating formats. *Personnel Psychology, 34*, 263–289; Landy, F.J., & Farr, J.L. (1983). *The measurement of work performance*. New York: Academic Press.

86. Mayer & Davis, 1999.

Chapter 4

1. Excerpted from Nebenzahl, D. (2009, February 28). Managing the generation gap. *The Gazette* (Montreal), G1–G2. Reprinted by the express permission of Montreal Gazette Group Inc., a CanWest Partnership.

2. Hofstede, G. (1980). *Culture's Consequences: International differences in work-related values*. Beverly Hills, CA: Sage, 19; see also Rokeach, M. (1973). *The nature of human values*. New York: Free Press.

3. Meglino, B.M., & Ravlin, E.C. (1998). Individual values in organizations: Concepts, controversies, and research. *Journal of Management, 24*, 351–389.

4. Schwartz, S.H. (1992). Universals in the content and structure of values: Theoretical advances and empirical tests in 20 countries. *Advances in Experimental Social Psychology, 25*, 1–65.

5. See for example Hammill, G. (2005, Winter/Spring). Mixing and managing four generations of employees. *FDU Magazine*(online), http://view.fdu.edu/default.aspx?id=1144.

6. Cennamo, L., & Gardner, D. (2008). Generational differences in work values, outcomes and person–organisation fit. *Journal of Managerial Psychology, 23*, 891–906; Hess, N., & Jepsen, D.M. (2009). Career stage and generational differences in psychological contracts. *Career Development International, 14*, 261–283; Wong, M., Gardiner, E., Lang, W., & Coulon, L. (2008). General differences in personality and motivation: Do they exist and what are the implications for the workplace? *Journal of Managerial Psychology, 23*, 878–890; Deal, J.J. (2007). *Retiring the generation gap: How employees young and old can find common ground*. San Francisco: Jossey-Bass.

7. Westerman, J.W., & Yamamura, J.H. (2007). Generational preferences for work environment fit: Effects on employee outcomes. *Career Development International, 12*, 150–161; Cennamo & Gardner, 2008; Wong et al., 2008.

8. Twenge, J.M., & Campbell, S.M. (2008). Generational differences in psychological traits and their impact on the workplace. *Journal of Managerial Psychology,23*, 862–877.

9. Cennamo & Gardner, 2008; Westerman & Yamamura, 2007; Smola, K.W., & Sutton, C.D. (2002). Generational differences: Revisiting generational work values for the new millennium. *Journal of Organizational Behavior, 23*, 363–382.

10. Deal, 2007.

11. Meglino & Ravlin, 1998; Kristof, A.L. (1996). Person-organization fit: An integrative review of its conceptualizations, measurement, and implications. *Personnel Psychology, 49*, 1–49.

12. Black, J.S., & Mendenhall, M. (1990). Cross-cultural training effectiveness: A review and theoretical framework for future research. *Academy of Management Review, 15*, 113–136.

13. MOW International Research Team. (1987). *The meaning of working*. London: Academic Press.

14. Hofstede, 1980. For a critique of this work, see Dorfman, P.W., & Howell, J.P. (1989). Dimensions of national culture and effective leadership patterns: Hofstede revisited. *Advances in International Comparative Management, 3*, 127–150.

15. Hofstede, G. (1991). *Cultures and organizations: Software of the mind*. London: McGraw-Hill; Hofstede, G., & Bond, M.H. (1988). The Confucius connection: From cultural roots to economic growth. *Organizational Dynamics, 16*(4), 4–21.

16. House, R.J., Hanges, P.J., Javidan, M., Dorfman, P.W., & Gupta, V. (Eds.) (2004). *Culture, leadership, and organizations: The GLOBE study of 62 societies*. Thousand Oaks, CA: Sage.

17. Hofstede, G. (1984). The cultural relativity of the quality of life concept. *Academy of Management Review, 9,* 389–398; Hofstede, G. (1993, February). Cultural constraints in management theories. *Academy of Management Executive,* 81–94.

18. Young, S.M. (1992). A framework for successful adoption and performance of Japanese manufacturing practices in the United States. *Academy of Management Review, 17,* 677–700; Basadur, M. (1992, May). Managing creativity: A Japanese model. *Academy of Management Executive,* 29–42.

19. Glasman, L.R., & Albarracín, D. (2006). Forming attitudes that predict future behavior: A meta-analysis of the attitude-behavior relation. *Psychological Bulletin, 132,* 778–821.

20. The following syllogistic construction of attitudes can be found in Jones, E.E., & Gerard, H.B. (1967). *Foundations of social psychology.* New York: Wiley.

21. Wood, W. (2000). Attitude change: Persuasion and social influence. *Annual Review of Psychology, 51,* 539–570.

22. Harrison, D.A., Newman, D.A., & Roth, P.L. (2006). How important are job attitudes? Meta-analytic comparisons of integrative behavioral outcomes and time sequences. *Academy of Management Journal, 49,* 305–325.

23. Locke, E.A. (1976). The nature and causes of job satisfaction. In M.D. Dunnette (Ed.), *Handbook of industrial and organizational psychology.* Chicago: Rand McNally. See also Rice, R.W., Gentile, D.A., & McFarlin, D.B. (1991). Facet importance and job satisfaction. *Journal of Applied Psychology, 76,* 31–39.

24. Smith, P.C. (1992). In pursuit of happiness: Why study general job satisfaction? In C.J. Cranny, P.C. Smith, & E.F. Stone (Eds.), *Job satisfaction.* New York: Lexington.

25. Smith, P.C., Kendall, L.M., & Hulin, C.L. (1969). *The measurement of satisfaction in work and retirement.* Chicago: Rand McNally; Smith, P.C., Kendall, L.M., & Hulin, C.L. (1985). *The job descriptive index* (Rev. ed.). Bowling Green, OH: Department of Psychology, Bowling Green State University.

26. Weiss, D.J., Dawis, R.V., England, G.W., & Lofquist, L.H. (1967). *Manual for the Minnesota satisfaction questionnaire: Minnesota studies in vocational rehabilitation.* Minneapolis: Vocational Psychology Research, University of Minnesota.

27. Locke, E.A. (1969). What is job satisfaction? *Organizational Behavior and Human Performance, 4,* 309–336; Rice, R.W., McFarlin, D.B., & Bennett, D.E. (1989). Standards of comparison and job satisfaction. *Journal of Applied Psychology, 74,* 591–598.

28. Williams, M.L., McDaniel, M.A., & Nguyen, N.T. (2006). A meta-analysis of the antecedents and consequences of pay level satisfaction. *Journal of Applied Psychology, 91,* 392–413.

29. For a good overview of fairness research, see Greenberg, J., & Colquitt, J.A. (2005). *Handbook of organizational justice.* Mahwah, NJ: Lawrence Erlbaum Associates. For empirical reviews of the literature, see Colquitt, J.A., Conlon, D.E., Wesson, M.J., Porter, C.O.L.H., & Ng, K.Y. (2001). Justice at the millennium: A meta-analytic review of 25 years of organizational justice research. *Journal of Applied Psychology, 86,* 425–445; Cohen-Charash, Y., & Spector, P.E. (2001). The role of justice in organizations: A meta-analysis. *Organizational Behavior and Human Decision Processes, 86,* 278–321.

30. Adams, J.S. (1963). Toward an understanding of inequity. *Journal of Abnormal and Social Psychology, 67,* 422–436.

31. See Kulik, C.T., & Ambrose, M.L. (1992). Personal and situational determinants of referent choice. *Academy of Management Review, 17,* 212–237.

32. Sharp, I. (2009, April 15). A few bumps in the road. *Globe and Mail,* B3.

33. Greenberg, J. (1987). A taxonomy of organizational justice theories. *Academy of Management Review, 12,* 9–22.

34. Brockner, J., & Wisenfeld, B.M. (1996). An integrative framework for explaining reactions to decisions: Interactive effects of outcomes and procedures. *Psychological Bulletin, 120,* 189–208; Brockner, J., & Wiesenfeld, B. (2005). How, when, and why does outcome favorability interact with procedural fairness? In Greenberg & Colquitt, 2005.

35. Cropanzano, R., & Folger, R. (1989). Referent cognitions and task decision autonomy: Beyond equity theory. *Journal of Applied Psychology, 74,* 293. See also Folger, R. (1987). Reformulating the preconditions of resentment: A referent cognitions model. In J.C. Masters & W.P. Smith (Eds.), *Social comparison, justice, and relative deprivation: Theoretical, empirical, and policy perspectives.* Hillsdale, NJ: Erlbaum.

36. Colquitt, J.A., Greenberg, J., & Zapata-Phelan, C.P. (2005). What is organizational justice? A historical overview. In Greenberg & Colquitt, 2005; Bies, R.J. (2005). Are procedural justice and interactional justice conceptually distinct? In Greenberg & Colquitt, 2005.

37. Greenberg, J. (2006). Losing sleep over organizational injustice: Attenuating insomniac reactions to underpayment inequity with supervisory training in interactional justice. *Journal of Applied Psychology, 91,* 58–69.

38. Judge, T.A. (1992). The dispositional perspective in human resources research. *Research in Personnel and Human Resources Management, 10,* 31–72. See also Staw, B.M., & Cohen-Charash, Y. (2005). The dispositional approach to job satisfaction: More than a mirage, but not yet an oasis. *Journal of Organizational Behavior, 26,* 59–78.

39. Judge, T.A., Heller, D., & Mount, M.K. (2002). Five-factor model of personality and job satisfaction: A meta-analysis. *Journal of Applied Psychology, 87,* 530–541.

40. Judge, T.A., Bono, J.E., & Locke, E.A. (2000). Personality and job satisfaction: The mediating role of job characteristics. *Journal of Applied Psychology, 85,* 237–249.

41. Weiss, H.M., & Cropanzano, R. (1996). Affective events theory: A theoretical discussion of the structure, causes and consequences of affective experiences at work. *Research in Organizational Behavior, 18,* 1–74.

42. Barsade, S.G. (2002). The ripple effect: Emotional contagion and its influence on group behavior. *Administrative Science Quarterly, 47,* 644–675.

43. Grandey, A.A., Dickter, D.N., & Sin, H.P. (2004). The customer is *not* always right: Customer aggression and emotion regulation of service employees. *Journal of Organizational Behavior, 25,* 397–418.

44. Côté, S., & Morgan, L.M. (2002). A longitudinal analysis of the association between emotion regulation, job satisfaction, and intentions to quit. *Journal of Organizational Behavior, 23,* 947–962; Diefendorff, J.M., & Richard, E.M. (2003). Antecedents and consequences of emotional display rule perceptions. *Journal of Applied Psychology, 88,* 284–294; Schaubroeck, J., & Jones, J.R. (2000). Antecedents of workplace emotional labor dimensions and moderators of their effects on physical symptoms. *Journal of Organizational Behavior, 21,* 163–183.

45. Côté & Morgan, 2002.

46. Glomb, T.M., Kammeyer-Mueller, J.D., & Rotundo, M. (2004). Emotional labor demands and compensating wage differentials. *Journal of Applied Psychology, 89*, 700–714.

47. This material draws upon Locke, 1976.

48. Hackett, R.D. (1989). Work attitudes and employee absenteeism: A synthesis of the literature. *Journal of Occupational Psychology, 62*, 235–248; Hackett, R.D., & Guion, R.M. (1985). A reevaluation of the absenteeism-job satisfaction relationship. *Organizational Behavior and Human Decision Processes, 35*, 340–381.

49. Johns, G. (2008). Absenteeism and presenteeism: Not at work or not working well. In C.L. Cooper & J. Barling (Eds.), *The Sage handbook of organizational behavior*(Vol. 1). London: Sage; Nicholson, N., & Johns, G. (1985). The absence culture and the psychological contract—Who's in control of absence? *Academy of Management Review,10*, 397–407.

50. Warr, P.B. (1987). *Work, unemployment, and mental health*. Oxford: Oxford University Press; Jamal, M., & Mitchell, V.F. (1980). Work, nonwork, and mental health: A model and a test. *Industrial Relations, 19*, 88–93; Judge, T.A., & Watanabe, S. (1993). Another look at the job satisfaction-life satisfaction relationship. *Journal of Applied Psychology, 78*,939–948.

51. Farris, G.F. (1971). A predictive study of turnover. *Personnel Psychology, 24*, 311–328. However, the more general relationship between performance and voluntary turnover is negative, as shown by Bycio, P., Hackett, R.D., & Alvares, K.M. (1990). Job performance and turnover: A review and meta-analysis. *Applied Psychology: An International Review, 39*, 47–76; Williams, C.R., & Livingstone, L.P. (1994). Another look at the relationship between performance and voluntary turnover. *Academy of Management Journal, 37*, 269–298.

52. Hom, P.W., & Griffeth, R.W. (1995). *Employee turnover*. Cincinnati, OH: South-Western.

53. This model is based on Hom & Griffeth, 1995; Lee, T.W., & Mitchell, T.R. (1994). An alternative approach: The unfolding model of voluntary employee turnover. *Academy of Management Review, 19*, 51–89; Mitchell, T.R., Holtom, B.C., Lee, T.W., Sablynski, C.J., & Erez, M. (2001). Why people stay: Using job embeddedness to predict voluntary turnover. *Academy of Management Journal, 44*, 1102–1121.

54. Hom & Griffeth, 1995.

55. Carsten, J.M., & Spector, P.E. (1987). Unemployment, job satisfaction, and employee turnover: A meta-analytic test of the Muchinsky model. *Journal of Applied Psychology, 72*, 374–381.

56. Boswell, W.R., Boudreau, J.W., & Tichy, J. (2005). The relationship between employee job change and job satisfaction: The honeymoon-hangover effect. *Journal of Applied Psychology, 90*, 882–892.

57. Judge, T.A., Thoresen, C.J., Bono, J.E., & Patton, G.K. (2001). The job satisfaction-job performance relationship: A qualitative and quantitative review. *Psychological Bulletin, 127*, 376–407.

58. Iaffaldano, M.T., & Muchinsky, P.M. (1985). Job satisfaction and job performance: A meta-analysis. *Psychological Bulletin, 97*, 251–273.

59. Lawler, E.E., III (1973). *Motivation in organizations*. Monterey, CA: Brooks/Cole.

60. Riketta, M. (2008). The causal relationship between job attitudes and performance: A meta-analysis of panel studies. *Journal of Applied Psychology, 93*, 472–481.

61. Organ, D.W. (1988). *Organizational citizenship behavior: The good soldier syndrome*. Lexington, MA: Lexington; Podsakoff, P.M., MacKenzie, S.B., Paine, J.B., & Bachrach, D.G. (2000). Organizational citizenship behaviors: A critical review of the theoretical and empirical literature and suggestions for future research. *Journal of Management, 26*, 513–563.

62. Lepine, J.A., Erez, A., & Johnson, D.E. (2002). The nature and dimensionality of organizational citizenship behavior: A critical review and meta-analysis. *Journal of Applied Psychology, 87*, 52–65; Organ, D.W., & Ryan, K. (1995). A meta-analytic review of attitudinal and dispositional predictors of organizational citizenship behavior. *Personnel Psychology, 48*, 775–802; Hoffman, B.J., Blair, C.A., Meriac, J.P., & Woehr, D.J. (2007). Expanding the criterion domain? A quantitative review of the OCB literature. *Journal of Applied Psychology, 92*, 555–566.

63. Organ, 1988.

64. Lepine et al., 2002; Fassina, N.E., Jones, D.A., & Uggerslev, K.L. (2008). Meta-analytic tests of relationships between organizational justice and citizenship behavior: Testing agent-system and shared-variance models. *Journal of Organizational Behavior, 29*, 805–828.

65. George, J.M. (1991). State or trait: Effects of positive mood on prosocial behaviors at work. *Journal of Applied Psychology, 76*, 299–307;

66. Podsakoff, N.P., Whiting, S.W., Podsakoff, P.M., & Blume, B.D. (2009). Individual- and organizational-level consequences of organizational citizenship behaviors: A meta-analysis. *Journal of Applied Psychology, 94*, 122–141.

67. Leavy, B. (2005). Innovation at Xilinx: A senior operating manager's view. *Strategy & Leadership,33*(4), 33–37.

68. Harter, J.K, Schmidt, F.L., & Hayes, T.L. (2002). Business-unit level relationship between employee satisfaction, employee engagement, and business outcomes: A meta-analysis. *Journal of Applied Psychology, 87*, 268–279.

69. Laabs, J. (1999, March). The HR side of Sears' comeback. *Workforce*, 24–29.

70. Meyer, J.P., & Allen, N.J. (1997). *Commitment in the workplace*. Thousand Oaks, CA: Sage.

71. Meyer, J.P., Allen, N.J., & Topolnytsky, L. (1998). Commitment in a changing world of work. *Canadian Psychology, 39*, 83–93; see also Meyer, J.P., Jackson, T.A., & Maltin, E.R. (2008). Commitment in the workplace: Past, present, and future. In J. Barling & C.L. Cooper (Eds.), *The Sage handbook of organizational behavior* (Vol. 1). London: Sage.

72. Meyer, J.P, Stanley, D.J., Herscovitch, L., & Topolnytsky, L. (2002). Affective, continuance, and normative commitment to the organization: A meta-analysis of antecedents, correlates, and consequences. *Journal of Vocational Behavior, 61*, 20–52.

73. Meyer et al., 2002.

74. Meyer et al., 2002; for a careful study, see Jaros, S.J., Jermier, J.M., Koehler, J.W., & Sincich, T. (1993). Effects of continuance, affective, and moral commitment on the withdrawal process: An evaluation of eight structural equation models. *Academy of Management Journal, 36*, 951–995.

75. Meyer, J.P., Becker, T.E., & Vandenberghe, C. (2004). Employee commitment and motivation: A conceptual analysis and integrative model. *Journal of Applied Psychology, 89*, 991–1007.

76. Meyer, J.P., Paunonen, S.V., Gellatly, I.R., Goffin, R.D., & Jackson, D.N. (1989). Organizational commitment and job performance: It's the nature of the commitment that counts. *Journal of Applied Psychology, 74*, 152–156.

77. Randall, D.M. (1987). Commitment and the organization: The organization man revisited. *Academy of Management Review, 12*, 460–471.

78. Meyer, Allen, & Topolnytsky, 1998.
79. Cascio, W.F. (1993, February). Downsizing: What do we know? What have we learned? *Academy of Management Executive*, 95–104.
80. Meyer et al., 1998; see also Meyer et al., 2008.

Chapter 5

1. Brooks, Y. (2006, December). Handle with care. *BC Business*(online),bcbusinessonline.ca; Colman, R. (2007, March). Packing the perfect HR punch: Great Little Box Company president and CEO Robert Meggy, CMA, FCMA, knows that people make a business. His unique approach to employee engagement proves it. *Entrepreneur*(online),-www.entrepreneur.com; Great Little Box Company: A team approach to success. *Managing for Business Success.*Industry Canada, www.ic.gc.ca; Atkinson, C. (2008, July 2). The total package: Anatomy of a great place to work, *Globe and Mail,*B6; Brent, P. (2005, October). Packaging loyalty: A Vancouver maker thrives by finding employees who fit. *National Post,*WK2; Yerema, R. (2009, January 12). Employer Review: The Great Little Box Company Ltd.: Chosen as one of Canada's Top 100 employers and BC's top employers for 2009. www.eluta.ca; Great Little Box Company, www.greatlittlebox.com/about/history.
2. Great Little Box Company: A team approach to success. *Managing for Business Success.*Industry Canada, www.ic.gc.ca.
3. Campbell, J.P., Dunnette, M.D., Lawler, E.E., Iii, & Weick, K.E., Jr. (1970). *Managerial behavior, performance, and effectiveness.* New York: McGraw-Hill. Also see Blau, G. (1993). Operationalizing direction and level of effort and testing their relationship to job performance. *Organizational Behavior and Human Decision Processes, 55,* 152–170.
4. Dyer, L., & Parker, D.F. (1975). Classifying outcomes in work motivation research: An examination of the intrinsic-extrinsic dichotomy. *Journal of Applied Psychology, 60,* 455–458; Kanungo, R.N., & Hartwick, J. (1987). An alternative to the intrinsic-extrinsic dichotomy of work rewards. *Journal of Management, 13,* 751–766. Also see Brief, A.P., & Aldag, R.J. (1977). The intrinsic-extrinsic dichotomy: Toward conceptual clarity. *Academy of Management Review, 2,* 496–500.

5. Gagné, M., & Deci, E.L. (2005). Self-determination theory and work motivation. *Journal of Organizational Behavior, 26,*331–362.
6. Vallerand, R.J. (1997). Toward a hierarchical model of intrinsic and extrinsic motivation. *Advances in Experimental Social Psychology, 29,* 271–360.
7. Deci, E.L., & Ryan, R.M. (1985). *Intrinsic motivation and self-determination in human behavior.* New York: Plenum.
8. Deci & Ryan, 1985.
9. Eisenberger, R., & Cameron, J. (1996). Detrimental effects of reward: Reality or myth? *American Psychologist, 51,* 1153–1166.
10. Guzzo, R.A. (1979). Types of rewards, cognitions, and work motivation. *Academy of Management Review, 4,* 75–86; Wiersma, U.J. (1992). The effects of extrinsic rewards in intrinsic motivation: A meta-analysis. *Journal of Occupational and Organizational Psychology, 65,* 101–114.
11. Based on Campbell, J.P., & Pritchard, R.D. (1976). Motivation theory in industrial and organizational psychology. In M.D. Dunnette (Ed.), *Handbook of industrial and organizational psychology.* Chicago: Rand McNally.
12. O'Reilly, C.A. Iii, & Chatman, J.A. (1994). Working smarter and harder: A longitudinal study of managerial success. *Administrative Science Quarterly, 39,* 603–627.
13. Hunter, J.E. (1986). Cognitive ability, cognitive aptitudes, job knowledge, and job performance. *Journal of Vocational Behavior, 29,* 340–362; Schmidt, F.L., & Hunter, J.E. (1998). The validity and utility of selection methods in personnel psychology: Practical and theoretical implications of 85 years of research findings. *Psychological Bulletin, 124,* 262–274.
14. Mayer, J.D., Caruso, D.R., & Salovey, P. (2000). Emotional intelligence meets traditional standards for an intelligence. *Intelligence, 27,* 267–298; Salovey, P., & Mayer, J.D. (1990). Emotional intelligence. *Imagination, Cognition and Personality, 9,*185–211.
15. Mayer, Caruso, & Salovey, 2000.
16. George, J.M. (2000). Emotions and leadership: The role of emotional intelligence. *Human Relations, 53,*1027–1055.
17. George, 2000.
18. George, 2000.
19. Van Rooy, D.L., & Viswesvaran, C. (2004). Emotional intelligence: A meta-analytic investigation of predictive validity and nomological net.

*Journal of Vocational Behavior, 65,*71–95.
20. Schutte, N.S., Malouff, J.M., Hall, L.E., Haggerty, D.J., Cooper, J.T., Golden, C.J., & Dornheim, L. (1998). Development and validation of a measure of emotional intelligence. *Personality and Individual Differences, 25,* 167–177; Wong, C., & Law, K.S. (2002). The effects of leader and follower emotional intelligence on performance and attitude: An exploratory study. *The Leadership Quarterly, 13,* 243–274; Daus, C.S., & Ashkanasy, N.M. (2005). The case for the ability-based model of emotional intelligence in organizational behaviour. *Journal of Organizational Behavior, 26,*453–466.
21. Côté, S., & Miners, C.T.H. (2006). Emotional intelligence, cognitive intelligence, and job performance. *Administrative Science Quarterly, 51,* 1–28.
22. See Henkoff, R. (1993, March 22). Companies that train best. *Fortune,* 62–75.
23. The distinction between need (content) and process theories was first made by Campbell et al., 1970.
24. Maslow, A.H. (1970). *Motivation and personality* (2nd ed.). New York: Harper & Row.
25. Alderfer, C.P. (1969). An empirical test of a new theory of human needs. Organizational Behavior and Human Performance, 4, 142–175. Also see Alderfer, C.P. (1972). *Existence, relatedness, and growth: Human needs in organizational settings.* New York: The Free Press.
26. McClelland, D.C. (1985). *Human motivation.* Glenview, IL: Scott, Foresman.
27. McClelland, D.C., & Winter, D.G. (1969). *Motivating economic achievement.* New York: The Free Press, 50–52.
28. McClelland, D.C., & Boyatzis, R.E. (1982). Leadership motive pattern and long-term success in management. *Journal of Applied Psychology, 67,* 737–743; McClelland, D.C., & Burnham, D. (1976, March–April). Power is the great motivator. *Harvard Business Review,* 159–166. However, need for power might not be the best motive pattern for managers of technical and professional people. See Cornelius, E.T., Iii, & Lane, F.B. (1984). The power motive and managerial success in a professionally oriented service industry organization. *Journal of Applied Psychology, 69,* 32–39.
29. Wahba, M.A., & Bridwell, L.G. (1976). Maslow reconsidered: A review of research on the need hierarchy theory. *Organizational Behavior*

and Human Performance, 15, 212–240.

30. Schneider, B., & Alderfer, C.P. (1973). Three studies of measures of need satisfaction in organizations. *Administrative Science Quarterly, 18,* 498–505. Also see Alderfer, C.P., Kaplan, R.E., & Smith, K.K. (1974). The effect of relatedness need satisfaction on relatedness desires. *Administrative Science Quarterly, 19,* 507–532. For a disconfirming test, see Rauschenberger, J., Schmitt, N., & Hunter, J.E. (1980). A test of the need hierarchy concept by a Markov model of change in need strength. *Administrative Science Quarterly, 25,* 654–670.

31. McClelland, 1985; Spangler, W.D. (1992). Validity of questionnaire and TAT measures of need for achievement: Two meta-analyses. *Psychological Bulletin, 112,* 140–154.

32. Great Little Box Company: A team approach to success. *Managing for Business Success.*Industry Canada, www.ic.gc.ca.

33. Herzberg, F. (1966). *Work and the nature of man.* Cleveland: World Publishing.

34. Lawler, E.E., III. (1973). *Motivation in work organizations.* Monterey, CA: Brooks/Cole.

35. Vroom, V.H. (1964). *Work and motivation.* New York: Wiley.

36. Mitchell, T.R. (1974). Expectancy models of job satisfaction, occupational preference, and effort: A theoretical, methodological, and empirical appraisal. *Psychological Bulletin, 81,* 1053–1077. Also see Pinder, C.C. (1984). *Work motivation: Theory, issues, and applications.* Glenview, IL: Scott, Foresman; Kanfer, R. (1990). Motivation theory in industrial and organizational psychology. In M.D. Dunnette & L.M. Hough (Eds.), *Handbook of industrial and organizational psychology* (2nd ed., Vol. 1). Palo Alto, CA: Consulting Psychologists Press.

37. A good discussion of how managers can strengthen expectancy and instrumentality relationships is presented by Strauss, G. (1977). Managerial practices. In J.R. Hackman & J.L. Suttle (Eds.), *Improving life at work: Behavioral science approaches to organizational change.* Glenview, IL: Scott, Foresman.

38. Adams, J.S. (1965). Injustice in social exchange. *Advances in Experimental Social Psychology, 2,* 267–299.

39. Kulik, C.T., & Ambrose, M.L. (1992). Personal and situational determinants of referent choice. *Academy of Management Review, 17,* 212–237.

40. Carrell, M.R., & Dittrich, J.E. (1978). Equity theory: The recent literature, methodological considerations, and new directions. *Academy of Management Review, 3,* 202–210; Mowday, R.T. (1991). Equity theory predictions of behavior in organizations. In R.M. Steers & L.W. Porter (Eds.), *Motivation and work behavior,* 111–131. New York: McGraw-Hill.

41. Mowday, 1991; Carrell & Dittrich, 1978.

42. See Kulik & Ambrose, 1992.

43. Colman, R. (2007, March).

44. Locke, E.A., & Latham, G.P. (2002). Building a practically useful theory of goal setting and task motivation. *American Psychologist, 57,* 705–717.

45. The best-developed theoretical position is that of Locke, E.A., & Latham, G.P. (1990). *A theory of goal setting and task performance.* Englewood Cliffs, NJ: Prentice-Hall.

46. Locke & Latham, 2002.

47. Locke & Latham, 2002.

48. Locke, E.A., Latham, G.P., & Erez, M. (1988). The determinants of goal commitment. *Academy of Management Review, 13,* 23–39.

49. See Erez, M., Earley, P.C., & Hulin, C.L. (1985). The impact of participation on goal acceptance and performance: A two-step model. *Academy of Management Journal, 28,* 50–66.

50. Latham, G.P., Erez, M., & Locke, E.A. (1988). Resolving scientific disputes by the joint design of crucial experiments by the antagonists: Application to the Erez-Latham dispute regarding participation in goal setting. *Journal of Applied Psychology, 73,* 753–772.

51. Latham, G.P., Mitchell, T.R., & Dosset, D.L. (1978). The importance of participative goal setting and anticipated rewards on goal difficulty and job performance. *Journal of Applied Psychology, 63,* 163–171; Saari, L.M., & Latham, G.P. (1979). The effects of holding goal difficulty constant on assigned and participatively set goals. *Academy of Management Journal, 22,* 163–168.

52. For a discussion of this issue, see Saari & Latham, 1979.

53. Payne, S.C., Youngcourt, S.S., & Beaubien, J.M. (2007). A meta-analytic examination of the goal orientation nomological net. *Journal of Applied Psychology, 92,*128–150; Zweig, D., & Webster, J. (2004). Validation of a multidimensional measure of goal orientation. *Canadian Journal of Behavioural Science, 36:3,* 232–243.

54. VandeWalle, Brown, Cron, & Slocum, 1999; Seijts, G.H., Latham, G.P., Tasa, K., & Latham, B.W. (2004). Goal setting and goal orientation: An integration of two different yet related literatures. *Academy of Management Journal, 47,* 227–239; Button, S.B., Mathieu, J.E., & Zajac, D.M. (1996). Goal orientation in organizational research: A conceptual and empirical foundation. *Organizational Behavior and Human Decision Processes, 67,* 26–48; VandeWalle, D., Brown, S.P., Cron, W.L., & Slocum, J.W., Jr. (1999). The influence of goal orientation and self-regulation tactics on sales performance: A longitudinal field test. *Journal of Applied Psychology, 84,* 249–259; VandeWalle, D., Cron, W.L., & Slocum, J.W., Jr. (2001). The role of goal orientation following performance feedback. *Journal of Applied Psychology, 86,* 629–640; Kozlowski, S.W.J., Gully, S.M., Brown, K.G., Salas, E., Smith, E.M., & Nason, E.R. (2001). Effects of training goals and goal orientation traits on multidimensional training outcomes and performance adaptability. *Organizational Behavior and Human Decision Processes, 85,* 1–31; VandeWalle, Brown, Cron, & Slocum, 1999.

55. Latham, G.P., & Seijts, G.H. (1999). The effects of proximal and distal goals on performance on a moderately complex task. *Journal of Organizational Behavior, 20,*421–429; Seijts, G.H., & Latham, G.P. (2001). The effect of distal learning, outcome, and proximal goals on a moderately complex task. *Journal of Organizational Behavior, 22,*291–307.

56. Locke, E.A., & Latham, G.P. (1984). *Goal setting—A motivational technique that works.* Englewood Cliffs, NJ: Prentice-Hall.

57. Latham, G.P., & Baldes, J.J. (1975). The "practical significance" of Locke's theory of goal setting. *Journal of Applied Psychology, 60,* 122–124; Latham, G.P., & Locke, E. (1979, Autumn). Goal setting—a motivational technique that works. *Organizational Dynamics, 8(2),* 68–80.

58. Payne et al., 2007; Seijts, Latham, Tasa, & Latham, 2004; Seijts, G., & Latham, G.P. (2005). Learning versus performance goals: When should each be used? *Academy of Management Executive, 19,*124–131.

59. Latham & Seijts, 1999; Seijts & Latham, 2001.

60. O'Leary-Kelly, A.M., Martocchio, J.J., & Frink, D.D. (1994). A review of the influence of group goals on group performance. *Academy of Management Journal, 37,* 1285–1301.

61. Seijts, Latham, Tasa, & Latham, 2004; Seijts & Latham, 2005; Latham & Seijts, 1999; Seijts & Latham, 2001.

62. Kagitcibasi, C., & Berry, J.W. (1989). Cross-cultural psychology: Current research and trends. *Annual Review of Psychology, 40*, 493–531.

63. Hofstede, G. (1980). *Culture's consequences: International differences in work-related values.* Beverly Hills, CA: Sage.

64. For a review, see Kagitcibasi & Berry, 1989.

65. Adler, N.J. (1992). *International dimensions of organizational behavior* (2nd ed.). Belmont, CA: Wadsworth.

66. Locke & Latham, 2002.

67. Kirkman, B.L., & Shapiro, D.L. (1997). The impact of cultural values on employee resistance to teams: Toward a model of globalized self-managing work team effectiveness. *Academy of Management Review, 22*, 730–757.

68. Adler, 1992, 159.

Chapter 6

1. (2009). Employer Review: WestJet Airlines Ltd.: Chosen as one of Alberta's ttop employers for 2009. eluta.ca/top-employer-westjet-airlines; Jang, B. (2009, February 16). WestJet sets steady course for supremacy. *Globe and Mail*,B1, B8; Quinn, P. (2008, January 30). WestJet locks in top spot on corporate culture honour poll. *Financial Post*(online),-www.financialpost.com; (2009). *Canada's 10 Most Admired Corporate Cultures 2008.*Toronto: Waterstone Human Capital; (2008). *Canada's 10 Most Admired Corporate* Cultures 2007.Toronto: Waterstone Human Capital. Alphonso, C. (2002, March 15). Street expects soaring WestJet to fly higher. *Globe and Mail*, B9; Heath-Rawlings, J. (2003, June 6). WestJet seen gliding through turbulence. *Globe and Mail*, B12; Menzies, P. (1999, July 2). Upstart WestJet proves free market can fly. *National Post*, C7; Verburg, P. (2000, December 25). Prepare for takeoff. *Canadian Business, 73(24)*, 94–99; Davis, A.A. (2006). Missing the turbulence. *WestJet's* 10th Anniversary Magazine.Calgary, Alberta: Red Point Media Group; Davis, A.A. (2006). Looking back to the future. *WestJet's 10th Anniversary Magazine.* Calgary, Alberta: Red Point Media Group; Magnan, M. (2005, October 10–23). People power. *Canadian Business, 78(20)*, 125; Wahl, A. (2005, October 10–23). Culture shock. *Canadian Business, 78(20),*

115; Jang, B. (2006, April 28). WestJet soars to record profit. *Globe and Mail*,B5; Anonymous (2006, August 3). WestJet earnings soar to record. *Toronto Star*, C3.

2. Rynes, S.L., Gerhart, B., & Minette, K.A. (2004). The importance of pay in employee motivation: Discrepancies between what people say and what they do. *Human Resource Management, 43*, 381–394.

3. Jenkins, G.D., Jr., Mitra, A., Gupta, N., & Shaw, J.D. (1998). Are financial incentives related to performance? A meta-analytic review of empirical research. *Journal of Applied Psychology, 83*, 777–787; Sturman, M.C., Trevor, C.O., Boudreau, J.W., & Gerhart, B. (2003). Is it worth it to win the talent war? Evaluating the utility of performance-based pay. *Personnel Psychology, 56*, 997–1035; Rynes, Gerhart, & Minette, 2004.

4. For reviews, see Chung, K.H. (1977). *Motivational theories and practices.* Columbus, OH: Grid; Lawler, E.E., III. (1971). *Pay and organizational effectiveness: A psychological view.* New York: McGraw-Hill. For a careful study, see Wagner, J.A., Iii, Rubin, P.A., & Callahan, T.J. (1988). Incentive payment and nonmanagerial productivity: An interrupted time series analysis of magnitude and trend. *Organizational Behavior and Human Decision Processes, 42*, 47–74.

5. Locke, E.A., Feren, D.B., McCaleb, V.M., Shaw, K.N., & Denny, A.T. (1980). The relative effectiveness of four methods of motivating employee performance. In K.D. Duncan, M.M. Gruneberg, & D. Wallis (Eds.), *Changes in working life.* London: Wiley.

6. Fein, M. (1973, September). Work measurement and wage incentives. Industrial Engineering, 49–51.

7. Inspire your team. *Success*, 12; Perry, N.J. (1988, December 19). Here come richer, riskier pay plans. *Fortune*, 50–58; Sharplin, A.D. (1990). Lincoln Electric Company, 1989. In A.A. Thompson, Jr., & A.J. Strickland, III. *Strategic management: Concepts and cases.* Homewood, IL: BPI/Irwin.

8. For a general treatment of why firms fail to adopt state-of-the-art personnel practices, see Johns, G. (1993). Constraints on the adoption of psychology-based personnel practices: Lessons from organizational innovation. *Personnel Psychology, 46*, 569–592.

9. Posner, B.G. (1989, May). If at first you don't succeed. *Inc.*, 132–134, 132.

10. Lawler, 1971.

11. Lawler, 1971; Nash, A., & Carrol, S. (1975). *The management of compensation.* Monterey, CA: Brooks/Cole.

12. Bertin, O. (2003, January 31). Is there any merit in giving merit pay? *Globe and Mail*, C1, C7.

13. Sethi, C. (2006, September 5). Calgary wages rising at record pace. *Globe and Mail*, B1, B2.

14. Chu, K. (2004, June 15). Firms report lacklustre results from pay-for-performance plans. Wall Street Journal, D2.

15. Heneman, R.L. (1990). Merit pay research. *Research in Personnel and Human Resources Management, 8*, 203–263; Tosi, H.L., & Gomez-Mejia, L.R. (1989). The decoupling of CEO pay and performance: An agency theory perspective. *Administrative Science Quarterly, 34*, 169–189; Ungson, G.R., & Steers, R.M. (1984). Motivation and politics in executive compensation. *Academy of Management Review, 9*, 313–323.

16. Haire, M., Ghiselli, E.E., & Gordon, M.E. (1967). A psychological study of pay. *Journal of Applied Psychology Monograph, 51*, (Whole No. 636).

17. Lublin, J.S. (1997, January 8). Why more people are battling over bonuses. *Wall Street Journal*, B1, B7.

18. Meyer, H.H. (1991, February). A solution to the performance appraisal feedback enigma. *Academy of Management Executive*, 68–76.

19. See Zenga, T.R. (1992). Why do employers only reward extreme performance? Examining the relationships among pay, performance, and turnover. *Administrative Science Quarterly, 37*, 198–219.

20. Lawler, E.E., Iii, (1972). Secrecy and the need to know. In H.L. Tosi, R.J. House, & M.D. Dunnette (Eds.), *Managerial motivation and compensation.* East Lansing, MI: Michigan State University Press.

21. Futrell, C.M., & Jenkins, O.C. (1978). Pay secrecy versus pay disclosure for salesmen: A longitudinal study. *Journal of Marketing Research, 15*, 214–219, 215.

22. For a study of the prevalence of these plans, see Lawler, E.E. Iii, Mohrman, S.A., & Ledford, G.E. (1992). *Employee involvement and total quality management: Practices and results in Fortune 1000 companies.* San Francisco: Jossey-Bass.

23. Vermond, K. (2008, October 11). Bonus planning in a bear market. *Globe and Mail*,B16; Gooderham, M. (2007, November 20). A piece of the pie as motivational tool. *Globe and Mail*, B8.

24. (2003, October). The goals of stock option programs. www.workforce.com.

25. Gordon, A. (February 2000). 35 best companies to work for. *Report on Business Magazine*, 24–32.

26. Brearton, S., & Daly, J. (2003, January). The 50 Best Companies to Work for in Canada. *Report on Business*, 53–65.

27. Hays, S. (February 1990). "Ownership cultures" create unity. *Workforce*, 78(2), 60–64.

28. Vermond, K. (2008, March 29). Worker as shareholder: Is it worth it? *Globe and Mail*, B21.

29. Graham-Moore, B., & Ross, T.L. (1990). *Gainsharing: Plans for improving performance*. Washington, DC: Bureau of National Affairs; Markham, S.E., Scott, K.D., & Little, B.L. (1992, January–February). National gainsharing study: The importance of industry differences. *Compensation & Benefits Review*, 34–45; Miller, C.S., & Shuster, M.H. (1987, Summer). Gainsharing plans: A comparative analysis. *Organizational Dynamics*, 44–67.

30. Davis, V. (1989, April). Eyes on the prize. *Canadian Business*, 93–106.

31. Graham-Moore & Ross, 1990; Moore, B.e, & Ross, T.L. (1978). *The Scanlon way to improved productivity: A practical guide*. New York: Wiley.

32. Perry, N.J. (1988, December 19). Here come richer, riskier pay plans. *Fortune*, 50–58; Lawler, E.E. (1984). Whatever happened to incentive pay? *New Management*, 1(4), 37–41.

33. Arthur, J.B., & Huntley, C.L. (2005). Ramping up the organizational learning curve: Assessing the impact of deliberate learning on organizational performance under gainsharing. *Academy of Management Journal, 48*, 1159–1170.

34. Hammer, T.H. (1988). New developments in profit sharing, gainsharing, and employee ownership. In J.P. Campbell & R.J. Campbell (Eds.), *Productivity in organizations*. San Francisco: Jossey-Bass.

35. Cooper, C.L., Dyck, B., & Frohlich, N. (1992). Improving the effectiveness of gainsharing: The role of fairness and participation. *Administrative Science Quarterly, 37*, 471–490.

36. Lawler, E.E., Iii, & Jenkins, G.D., Jr. (1992). Strategic reward systems. In M.D. Dunette & L.M. Hough (Eds.), *Handbook of industrial and organizational psychology* (2nd ed., Vol. 3). Palo Alto, CA: Consulting Psychologists Press.

37. Murray, B., & Gerhart, B. (1998). An empirical analysis of a skill–based pay program and plant performance outcomes. *Academy of Management Journal, 41*, 68–78.

38. Peterson, S., & Luthans, F. (2006). The impact of financial and nonfinancial incentives on business-unit outcomes over time. *Journal of Applied Psychology, 91*, 156–165.

39. Immen, W. (2009, February 27). Meaning means more than money at work: Poll. *Globe and Mail*, B14; Immen, W. (2008, January 23). Forget pay: Challenging work counts for top talent. *Globe and Mail*, C2.

40. Taylor, F.W. (1967). *The principles of scientific management*. New York: Norton.

41. This discussion draws upon Gibson, J.L., Ivancevich, J.M., & Donnelly, J.H., Jr. (1991). *Organizations*, 7th edition. Homewood, IL: Irwin.

42. Ray, R. (2006, April 19). New assignments a stretch but not a yawn. *Globe and Mail*, C1, C6.

43. Immen, W. (2007, October 17). Starting rotation adds bench strength. *Globe and Mail*, C1, C2.

44. Hackman, J.R., & Oldham, G.R. (1980). *Work redesign*. Reading, MA: Addison-Wesley.

45. Oldham, G.R., Hackman, J.R., & Stepina, L.P. (1979). Norms for the job diagnostic survey. *JSAS Catalog of Selected Documents in Psychology, 9*, 14. (Ms. No. 1819).

46. See, for example, Johns, G., Xie, J.L., & Fang, Y. (1992). Mediating and moderating effects in job design. *Journal of Management, 18*, 657–676.

47. Humphrey, S.E., Nanhrgang, J.D., & Morgeson, F.P. (2007). Integrating motivational, social, and contextual work design features: A meta-analytic summary and theoretical extension of the work design literature. *Journal of Applied Psychology, 92*, 1332–1356.

48. Johns et al., 1992; Tiegs, R.B., Tetrick, L.E., & Fried, Y. (1992). Growth need strength and context satisfactions as moderators of the relations of the Job Characteristics Model. *Journal of Management, 18*, 575–593.

49. Brown, S.P. (1996). A meta-analysis and review of organizational research on job involvement. *Psychological Bulletin, 120*, 235–255.

50. This section draws in part on Hackman & Oldham, 1980.

51. Dumaine, B. (1989, November 6). P&G rewrites the marketing rules. *Fortune*, 34–48, 46.

52. Campion, M.A., Mumford, T.V., Morgeson, F.P., & Nahrgang, J.D. (2005). Work redesign: Eight obstacles and opportunities. *Human Resource Management, 44*, 367–390.

53. Stonewalling plant democracy (1977, March 28). *Business Week*.

54. Morgeson, F.P., & Humphrey, S.E. (2006). The work design questionnaire (WDQ): Developing and validating a comprehensive measure for assessing job design and the nature of work. *Journal of Applied Psychology, 91*, 1321–1339; Humphrey et al., 2007.

55. Good descriptions of MBO programs can be found in Mali, P. (1986). *MBO updated: A handbook of practices and techniques for managing by objectives*. New York: Wiley; Odiorne, G.S. (1965). *Management by objectives*. New York: Pitman; Raia, A.P. (1974). *Managing by objectives*. Glenview, IL: Scott, Foresman.

56. Beer, M., & Cannon, D. (2004). Promise and peril in implementing pay-for-performance. *Human Resource Management, 43*, 3–48.

57. Brearton, S., & Daly, J. (2003, January). The 50 best companies to work for in Canada. *Report on Business*, 53–66.

58. Brearton & Daly, 2003; Rodgers, R., & Hunter, J.E. (1991). Impact of management by objectives on organization productivity. *Journal of Applied Psychology, 76*, 322–336.

59. Rodgers & Hunter, 1991.

60. See Rodgers, R., Hunter, J.E., & Rogers, D.L. (1993). Influence of top management commitment on management program success. *Journal of Applied Psychology, 78*, 151–155.

61. For discussions of these and other problems with MBo, see Levinson, H. (1979, July–August). Management by whose objectives. *Harvard Business Review*, 125–134; McConkey, D.D. (1972, October). 20 ways to kill management by objectives. *Management Review*, 4–13; Pringle, C.D., & Longenecker, J.G. (1982). The ethics of MBO. *Academy of Management Review, 7*, 305–312.

62. Chisholm, P. (2000, May 29). What the boss needs to know. *Maclean's, 113*(22), 18–22; Chisholm, P. (2001, March 5). Redesigning work. *Maclean's, 114*(10), 34–38.

63. See Nollen, S.D. (1982). *New work schedules in practice: Managing time in a changing society*. New York: Van Nostrand Reinhold; Ronen, S. (1981). *Flexible working hours: An innovation in the quality of work life*. New York: McGraw-Hill; Ronen, S. (1984). *Alternative work schedules: Selecting, implementing, and evaluating*. Homewood, IL: Dow Jones-Irwin.

64. For a good study showing absence reduction, see Dalton, D.R., & Mesch, D.J. (1990). The impact of flexible scheduling on employee attendance and turnover. *Administrative Science Quarterly, 35,* 370–387.

65. Baltes, B., Briggs, T.E., Huff, J.W., Wright, J.A., & Neuman, G.A. (1999). Flexible and compressed workweek schedules: A meta-analysis of their effects on work-related criteria. *Journal of Applied Psychology, 84,* 496–513.

66. Golembiewski, R.T., & Proehl, C.W. (1978). A survey of the empirical literature on flexible workhours: Character and consequences of a major innovation. *Academy of Management Review, 3,* 837–853; Pierce, J.L., Newstrom, J.W., Dunham, R.B., & Barber, A.E. (1989). *Alternative work schedules.* Boston: Allyn and Bacon; Ronen, 1981 and 1984.

67. Baltes et al., 1999.

68. Ronen, 1984; Nollen, 1982.

69. Pierce et al., 1989; Ronen, 1984; Ronen, S., & Primps, S.B. (1981). The compressed workweek as organizational change: Behavioral and attitudinal outcomes. *Academy of Management Review, 6,* 61–74.

70. Pierce et al., 1989; Ivancevich, J.M., & Lyon, H.L. (1977). The shortened workweek: A field experiment. *Journal of Applied Psychology, 62,* 34–37.

71. Johns, G. (1987). Understanding and managing absence from work. In S.L. Dolan & R.S. Schuler (Eds.), *Canadian readings in personnel and human resource management.* St. Paul, MN: West.

72. Ivancevich & Lyon, 1977; Calvasina, E.J., & Boxx, W.R. (1975). Efficiency of workers on the four-day workweek. Academy of Management Journal, 18, 604–610; Goodale, J.G., & Aagaard, A.K. (1975). Factors relating to varying reactions to the 4-day workweek. *Journal of Applied Psychology, 60,* 33–38.

73. Baltes et al., 1999.

74. This section relies on Pierce et al., 1989.

75. Popplewell, B. (2009, March 10). Staying at home so others don't have to. *Toronto Star,*B1, B4; Grant, T. (2009, June 23). "Buying jobs and buying time." *Globe and Mail,*B4.

76. DeFrank, R.S., & Ivancevich, J. M. (1998). Stress on the job: An executive update. *Academy of Management Executive, 12,* 55–66.

77. Grensing-Pophal, L. (1997, March). Employing the best people—from afar. *Workforce, 76(3),* 30–38; Piskurich, G.M. (1998). *An organizational guide to telecommuting: Setting up and running a successful telecommuter program.* Alexandria, VA: American Society for Training and Development.

78. Grensing-Pophal, 1997.

79. DeFrank & Ivancevich, 1998; Goldsborough, R. (1999, May 14). Make telecommuting work for you. *Computer Dealer News,* 19–20; Fortier, B. (2005, June 6). Ergonomics for teleworkers often overlooked. *Canadian HR Reporter, 18*(11),18, 21.

80. Galt, V. (2003, September 24). Drive is on for telework. *Globe and Mail,*C7; Vu, U. (2006, August 14). A variety of options gives boost to remote work. *Canadian HR Reporter, 19*(14),15, 21; Myers, R.C. (2008, March 8). The back and forth of working from home.*Globe and Mail,* B16.

81. DeFrank & Ivancevich, 1998; Grensing-Pophal, 1997.

82. Gajendran, R.S., & Harrison, D.A. (2007). The good, the bad, and the unknown about telecommuting: Meta-analysis of psychological mediators and individual consequences. *Journal of Applied Psychology, 92,* 1524–1541.

83. Bailey, D.S., & Foley, J. (1990, August). Pacific Bell works long distance. *HRMagazine,* 50–52.

84. Myers, 2008.

85. Klie, S. (2008, June 2). Mistrust "number one barrier" to telework. *Canadian HR Reporter, 21*(11),13, 19; Grensing-Pophal, 1997.

86. Rynes et al., 2004.

Chapter 7

1. Excerpted with minor edits from Kibbe, D.R., & Casner-Lotto, J. (2002, Summer). Ralston Foods: From Greenfield to maturity in a team-based plant. *Global Business and Organizational Excellence,* 21, 57–67. Copyright © 2002 John Wiley & Sons, Inc. Reprinted with permission of John Wiley & Sons, Inc.

2. Tuckman, B.W. (1965). Developmental sequence in small groups. *Psychological Bulletin,* 63, 384–399; Tuckman, B.W., & Jensen, M.A.C. (1977). Stages of small-group development revisited. *Group & Organization Studies, 2,* 419–427.

3. Harris, S.G., & Sutton, R.I. (1986). Functions of parting ceremonies in dying organizations. *Academy of Management Journal,* 29, 5–30.

4. Seger, J.A. (1983). No innate phases in group problem solving. *Academy of Management Review,* 8, 683–689. For a study comparing phases with punctuated equilibrium, see Chang, A., Bordia, P., & Duck, J. (2003). Punctuated equilibrium and linear progression: Toward a new understanding of group development. *Academy of Management Journal,* 46, 106–117.

5. Ginnett, R.C. (1990). Airline cockpit crew. In J.R. Hackman (Ed.), *Groups that work (and those that don't).* San Francisco: Jossey-Bass.

6. Gersick, C.J.G. (1989). Marking time: Predictable transitions in task groups. *Academy of Management Journal, 32,* 274–309; Gersick, C.J.G. (1988). Time and transition in work teams: Toward a new model of group development. *Academy of Management Journal, 31,* 9–41.

7. Gersick, 1989, 1988; Hackman, J.R., & Wageman, R. (2005). A theory of team coaching. *Academy of Management Review, 30,* 269–287.

8. Hare, A.P. (1976). *A handbook of small group research.* New York: The Free Press; Shaw, M.E. (1981). *Group dynamics: The psychology of small group behavior* (3rd ed.). New York: McGraw-Hill; Jones, E.E., & Gerard, H.B. (1967). *Foundations of social psychology.* New York: Wiley.

9. Hare, 1976; Shaw, 1981.

10. The following discussion relies upon Steiner, I.D. (1972). *Group process and productivity.* New York: Academic Press.

11. Steiner, 1972; Hill, G.W. (1982). Group versus individual performance: Are n+1 heads better than one? Psychological Bulletin, 91, 517–539.

12. Williams, K.Y., & O'Reilly, C.A. III. (1998). Demography and diversity in organizations: A review of 40 years of research. *Research in Organizational Behavior, 20,* 77–140; Jackson, S.E., Stone, V.K., & Alvarez, E.B. (1993). Socialization amidst diversity: The impact of demographics on work team oldtimers and newcomers. *Research in Organizational Behavior, 15,* 45–109.

13. Watson, W.E., Kumar, K., & Michaelson, L.K. (1993). Cultural diversity's impact on interaction process and performance: Comparing homogeneous and diverse task groups. *Academy of Management Journal,* 36, 590–602.

14. Webber, S.S., & Donahue, L.M. (2001). Impact of highly and less job-related diversity on work group cohesion and performance: A meta-analysis. *Journal of Management, 27,* 141–162.

15. Guzzo, R.A., & Dickson, M.W. (1996). Teams in organizations: Recent research on performance and effectiveness. *Annual Review of Psychology, 47,* 307–338.

16. Harrison, D.A., Price, K.H., & Bell, M.P. (1998). Beyond relational demography: Time and effects of surface- and

deep-level diversity on work group cohesion. *Academy of Management Journal, 41,* 96–107; see also Bell, S.T. (2007). Deep-level composition variables as predictors of team performance: A meta-analysis. *Journal of Applied Psychology, 92,* 595–615.

17. For an example of the social process by which this sharing may be negotiated in a new group, see Bettenhausen, K., & Murnighan, J.K. (1991). The development of an intragroup norm and the effects of interpersonal and structural challenges. *Administrative Science Quarterly, 36,* 20–35.

18. Kanter, R.M. (1977). *Men and women of the corporation.* New York: Basic Books, 37.

19. Leventhal, G.S. (1976). The distribution of rewards and resources in groups and organizations. In L. Berkowitz & E. Walster (Eds.), *Advances in experimental social psychology* (Vol. 9). New York: Academic Press.

20. See Mitchell, T.R., Rothman, M., & Liden, R.C. (1985). Effects of normative information on task performance. *Journal of Applied Psychology, 70,* 48–55.

21. Jackson, S.E., & Schuler, R.S. (1985). A meta-analysis and conceptual critique of research on role ambiguity and role conflict in work settings. *Organizational Behavior and Human Decision Processes, 36,* 16–78. For a methodological critique of this domain, see King, L.A., & King, D.W. (1990). Role conflict and role ambiguity: A critical assessment of construct validity. *Psychological Bulletin, 107,* 48–64.

22. Jackson & Schuler, 1985; Tubre, T.C., & Collins, J.M. (2000). Jackson and Shuler (1985) revisited: A meta-analysis of the relationship between role ambiguity, role conflict, and job performance. *Journal of Management, 26,* 155–169.

23. O'Driscoll, M.P., Ilgen, D.R., & Hildreth, K. (1992). Time devoted to job and off-job activities, interrole conflict, and affective experiences. *Journal of Applied Psychology, 77,* 272–279.

24. See Latack, J.C. (1981). Person/role conflict: Holland's model extended to role-stress research, stress management, and career development. *Academy of Management Review, 6,* 89–103.

25. Jackson & Schuler, 1985.

26. Shaw, 1981.

27. Kiesler, S., & Sproull, L. (1992). Group decision making and communication technology. *Organizational Behavior and Human Decision Processes, 52,* 96–123.

28. Strodbeck, F.L., James, R.M., & Hawkins, C. (1957). Social status in jury deliberations. *American Sociological Review, 22,* 713–719.

29. Kiesler & Sproull, 1992.

30. For other definitions and a discussion of their differences, see Mudrack, P.E. (1989). Defining group cohesiveness: A legacy of confusion? *Small Group Behavior, 20,* 37–49.

31. Stein, A. (1976). Conflict and cohesion: A review of the literature. *Journal of Conflict Resolution, 20,* 143–172. For an interesting example, see Haslam, S.A.., & Reicher, S. (2006). Stressing the group: Social identity and the unfolding dynamics of responses to stress. *Journal of Applied Psychology, 91,* 1037–1052.

32. Cartwright, D. (1968). The nature of group cohesiveness. In D. Cartwright & A. Zander (Eds.), *Group dynamics* (3rd ed.). New York: Harper & Row.

33. Lott, A., & Lott, B. (1965). Group cohesiveness as interpersonal attraction: A review of relationships with antecedent and consequent variables. *Psychological Bulletin, 64,* 259–309.

34. Anderson, A.B. (1975). Combined effects of interpersonal attraction and goal-path clarity on the cohesiveness of task-oriented groups. *Journal of Personality and Social Psychology, 31,* 68–75; see also Cartwright, 1968.

35. Aronson, E., & Mills, J. (1959). The effects of severity of initiation on liking for a group. *Journal of Abnormal and Social Psychology, 59,* 177–181.

36. Cartwright, 1968; Shaw, 1981.

37. Schacter, S. (1951). Deviation, rejection, and communication. *Journal of Abnormal and Social Psychology, 46,* 190–207; see also Barker, J.R. (1993). Tightening the iron cage: Concertive control in self-managing teams. *Administrative Science Quarterly, 38,* 408–437.

38. Beal, D.J., Cohen, R.R., Burke, M.J., & McLendon, C.L. (2003). Cohesion and performance in groups: A meta-analytic clarification of construct relations. *Journal of Applied Psychology, 88,* 989–1004; Mullen, B., & Copper, C. (1994). The relation between group cohesiveness and performance: An integration. *Psychological Bulletin, 115,* 210–227.

39. Podsakoff, P.M., MacKenzie, S.B., & Ahearne, M. (1997). Moderating effects of goal acceptance on the relationship between group cohesiveness and productivity. *Journal of Applied Psychology, 82,* 974–983.

40. Seashore, S. (1954). Group cohesiveness in the industrial workgroup. Ann Arbor, MI: Institute for Social Research; see also Stogdill, R.M. (1972). Group productivity, drive, and cohesiveness. *Organizational Behavior and Human Performance, 8,* 26–43. For a critique, see Mudrack, P.E. (1989). Group cohesiveness and productivity: A closer look. *Human Relations, 42,* 771–785.

41. Gulley, S.M., Devine, D.J., & Whitney, D.J. (1995). A meta-analysis of cohesion and performance: Effects of level of analysis and task interdependence. *Small Group Research, 26,*497–520.

42. Shepperd, J.A. (1993). Productivity loss in small groups: A motivation analysis. *Psychological Bulletin, 113,* 67–81; Kidwell, R.E., III, & Bennett, N. (1993). Employee propensity to withhold effort: A conceptual model to intersect three avenues of research. *Academy of Management Review, 18,* 429–456.

43. Shepperd, 1993; Kidwell & Bennett, 1993; George, J.M. (1992). Extrinsic and intrinsic origins of perceived social loafing in organizations. *Academy of Management Journal, 35,* 191–202.

44. Guzzo & Dickinson, 1996.

45. Kirkman, B.L., & Shapiro, D.L. (1997). The impact of cultural values on employee resistance to teams: Toward a model of globalized self-managing work team effectiveness. *Academy of Management Review, 22,* 730–757.

46. Guzzo & Dickinson, 1996; Kirkman & Shapiro, 1997; Banker, R.D., Field, J.M., Schroeder, R.G., & Sinha, K.K. (1996). Impact of work teams on manufacturing performance: A longitudinal field study. *Academy of Management Journal, 39,* 867–890.

47. Tasa, K., Taggar, S., & Seijts, G.H. (2007). The development of collective efficacy in teams: A multi-level and longitudinal perspective. *Journal of Applied Psychology, 92,* 17–27; Gibson, C.B., & Earley, P.C. (2007). Collective cognition in action: Accumulation, interaction, examination, and accommodation in the development and operation of efficacy beliefs in the workplace. *Academy of Management Review, 32,* 438–458.

48. Hackman, J.R. (1987). The design of work teams. In J.W. Lorsch (Ed.), *Handbook of organizational behavior.* Englewood Cliffs, NJ: Prentice-Hall; see also Hackman, J.R. (2002). *Leading teams: Setting the stage for great performances.* Boston: Harvard Business School Press.

49. Campion, M.A., Medsker, G.J., & Higgs, A.C. (1993). Relations between work group characteristics and effectiveness: Implications for designing effective work groups. *Personnel Psychology, 46,* 823–850.

50. Wall, T.D., Kemp, N.J., Jackson, P.R., & Clegg, C.W. (1986). Outcomes of autonomous workgroups: A field experiment. *Academy of Management Journal, 29,* 280–304, 283.

51. Parts of this section rely on Hackman, 1987.

52. See Ashforth, B.E., & Mael, F. (1989). Social identity theory and the organization. *Academy of Management Review, 14,* 20–39.

53. Wall et al., 1986; Cordery, J.L., Mueller, W.S., & Smith, L.M. (1991). Attitudinal and behavioral effects of autonomous group working: A longitudinal field study. *Academy of Management Journal, 34,* 264–276.

54. Bainbridge, J. (2009). Inspire and innovate: Personal services. www.guardian.co.uk.

55. Hayward, D. (2003, May 20). Management through measurement. *Financial Post,* BE5.

56. Manz, C.C., & Sims, H.P., Jr. (1987). Leading workers to lead themselves: The external leadership of self-managing work teams. *Administrative Science Quarterly, 32,* 106–128.

57. For reviews of research on self-managed teams, see Chapter 3 of Cummings, T.G., & Molloy, E.S. (1977). *Improving productivity and the quality of working life.* New York: Praeger; Goodman, P.S., Devadas, R., & Hughes, T.L.G. (1988). Groups and productivity: Analyzing the effectiveness of self-managing teams. In J.P. Campbell & R.J. Campbell (Eds.), *Productivity in organizations.* San Francisco: Jossey-Bass; Pearce, J.A., III, & Ravlin, E.C. (1987). The design and activation of self-regulating work groups. *Human Relations, 40,* 751–782.

58. Campion, M.A., Papper, E.M., & Medsker, G.J. (1996). Relations between work team characteristics and effectiveness: A replication and extension. *Personnel Psychology, 49,* 429–452; Campion, Medsker, & Higgs, 1993.

59. Hyatt, D.E., & Ruddy, T.M. (1997). An examination of the relationship between work group characteristics and performance: Once more into the breech. *Personnel Psychology, 50,* 553–585.

60. Kirkman & Shapiro, 1997; Banker et al., 1996.

61. Farnham, A. (1994, February 7). America's most admired company. *Fortune,* 50–54; Dumaine, B. (1993, December 13). Payoff from the new management. *Fortune,* 103–110.

62. Waterman, R.H., Jr. (1987). *The renewal factor.* New York: Bantam Books; McElroy, J. (1985, April). Ford's new way to build cars. *Road & Track,* 156–158.

63. Pinto, M.B., Pinto, J.K., & Prescott, J.E. (1993). Antecedents and consequences of project team cross-functional cooperation. *Management Science, 39,* 1281–1297; Henke, J.W., Krachenberg, A.R., & Lyons, T.F. (1993). Cross-functional teams: Good concept, poor implementation! *Journal of Product Innovation Management, 10,* 216–229. Mustang examples from White, J.B., & Suris, O. (1993, September 21). How a "skunk works" kept the Mustang alive—on a tight budget. *Wall Street Journal,* A1, A12.

64. Mathieu, J., Maynard, M.T., Rapp, T., & Gilson, L. (2008). Team effectiveness 1997–2007: A review of recent advancements and a glimpse into the future. *Journal of Management, 34,* 410–476; Mesmer-Magnus, J.R., & DeChurch, L.A. (2009). Information sharing and team performance. *Journal of Applied Psychology, 94,* 535–546.

65. Cronin, M.A., & Weingart, L.R. (2007). Representational gaps, information processing, and conflict in functionally diverse teams. *Academy of Management Review, 32,* 761–773, p. 761.

66. Lipnack, J., & Stamps, J. (2000). Virtual teams: People working across boundaries with technology. (2nd ed.). New York: Wiley; Axtell, C.M., Fleck, S.J., & Turner, N. (2004). Virtual Teams: Collaborating across distance. *International Review of Industrial and Organizational Psychology, 19,* 205–248.

67. Willmore, J. (2000, February). Managing virtual teams. *Training Journal,* 18–21.

68. Joinson, C. (2002, June). Managing virtual teams. *HR Magazine,* 68–73.

69. Cascio, W.F. (2000, August). Managing a virtual workplace. *Academy of Management Executive,* 81–90; see also Malhotra, A., Majchrzak, A., & Rosen, B. (2007). Leading virtual teams. *Academy of Management Perspectives,* 60–70, and Gibson, C.B., & Gibbs, J.L. (2006). Unpacking the concept of virtuality: The effects of geographic dispersion, electronic dependence, dynamic structure, and national diversity on team innovation.

Administrative Science Quarterly, 51, 451–495.

70. Willmore, 2000.

71. Kirkman, B.L., Rosen, B., Gibson, C.B., Telusk, P.E., & McPherson, S.O. (2002, August). Five challenges to virtual team success: Lessons from Sabre, Inc. *Academy of Management Executive, 67*–79.

72. Cascio, 2000; Joinson, 2002; Kirkman et al., 2002.

73. Allen, N.J., & Hecht, T.D. (2004). The "romance of teams": Toward an understanding of its psychological underpinnings and implications. *Journal of Occupational and Organizational Psychology, 77,* 439–461.

74. Vallas, S.P. (2003). Why teamwork fails: Obstacles to workplace change in four manufacturing plants. *American Sociological Review, 68,* 223–250; Tudor, T.R., Trumble, R.R., & Diaz, J.J. (1996, Autumn). Work-teams: Why do they often fail? *S.A.M. Advanced Management Journal,* 31–39.

Chapter 8

1. Anonymous (2009, April 6). Canada's best workplaces: Google Canada, World's top search engine also ranked Canada's best place to work. *A Special National Report for the Great Place to Work Institute, Globe and Mail,*GPTW1, GPTW3; Abel, K. (2008, November 24). Google Canada's new eco-friendly home enjoys playful work philosophy: Part One and Part Two [Web log message]. www.krisable.ctv.ca/blog; Mills, E. (2007, April 27). Newsmaker: Meet Google's culture czar. CNET News, www.news.cnet.com; Google Corporate Information, The Google Culture, www.google.ca.

2. See Morrison, E.W. (1993). Newcomer information seeking: Exploring types, modes, sources, and outcomes. *Academy of Management Journal, 36,* 557–589.

3. The terms information dependence and effect dependence are used by Jones, E.E., & Gerard, H.B. (1967). *Foundations of social psychology.* New York: Wiley.

4. Festinger, L. (1954). A theory of social comparison processes. *Human Relations, 7,* 117–140; Thomas, J., & Griffin, R. (1983). The social information processing model of task design: A review of the literature. *Academy of Management Review, 8,* 672–682.

5. Kelman, H.C. (1961). Processes of opinion change. *Public Opinion Quarterly, 25,* 57–78.

6. Bauer, T.N., Morrison, E.W., & Callister, R.R. (1998). Organizational socialization: A review and directions for future research. In G.R. Ferris & K.M. Rowland (Eds.), *Research in Personnel and Human Resources Management*, Volume 16. (pp. 149–214). Greenwich, CT: JAI Press; Saks, A.M., & Ashforth, B.E. (1997a). Organizational socialization: Making sense of the past and present as a prologue for the future. *Journal of Vocational Behavior, 51*, 234–279.

7. Saks, A.M., & Ashforth, B.E. (1997). A longitudinal investigation of the relationships between job information sources, applicant perceptions of fit, and work outcomes. *Personnel Psychology, 50*, 395–426.

8. Kristof-Brown, A.L., Zimmerman, R.D., & Johnson, E.C. (2005). Consequences of individuals' fit at work: A meta-analysis of person-job, person-organization, person-group, and person-supervisor fit. *Personnel Psychology, 58*, 281–342; Kristof, A.L. (1996). Person-organization fit: An integrative review of its conceptualizations, measurement, and implications. *Personnel Psychology, 49*, 1–49; Saks & Ashforth, 1997; Saks, A.M., & Ashforth, B.E. (2002). Is job search related to employment quality? It all depends on the fit. *Journal of Applied Psychology, 87*, 646–654.

9. Ashforth & Saks, 1996; Riketta, M. (2005). Organizational identification: A meta-analysis. *Journal of Vocational Behavior, 66*, 358–384.

10. Van Maanen, J., & Schein, E.H. (1979). Toward a theory of organizational socialization. *Research in Organizational Behavior, 1*, 209–264.

11. Feldman, D.C. (1976). A contingency theory of socialization. *Administrative Science Quarterly, 21*, 433–452.

12. Wanous, J.P. (1992). *Organizational entry: Recruitment, selection, orientation, and socialization of newcomers.* (2nd ed.). Reading, MA: Addison-Wesley.

13. Wanous, J.P. (1976). Organizational entry: From naive expectations to realistic beliefs. *Journal of Applied Psychology, 61*, 22–29; Wanous, J.P., Poland, T.D., Premack, S.L., & Davis, K.S. (1992). The effects of met expectations on newcomer attitudes and behaviors: A review and meta-analysis. *Journal of Applied Psychology, 77*, 288–297.

14. See Breaugh, J.A. (1992). *Recruitment: Science and practice.* Boston: PWS-Kent.

15. Morrison, E.W., & Robinson, S.L. (1997). When employees feel betrayed: A model of how psychological contract violation develops. *Academy of Management Review, 22*, 226–256.

16. Robinson, S.L., & Rousseau, D.M. (1994). Violating the psychological contract: Not the exception but the norm. *Journal of Organizational Behavior, 15*, 245–259.

17. Zhao, H., Wayne, S.J., Glibkowski, B.C., & Bravo, J. (2007). The impact of psychological contract breach on work-related outcomes: A meta-analysis. *Personnel Psychology, 60*, 647–680.

18. Morrison & Robinson, 1997.

19. Morrison & Robinson, 1997.

20. Wanous, 1992; Breaugh, 1992.

21. Wanous, 1992; Breaugh, 1992.

22. Galt, V. (2005, March 9). Kid-glove approach woes new grads. *Globe and Mail*, C1, C3.

23. Harding, K. (2003, July 16). Police aim to hire officers. *Globe and Mail*, C1.

24. Phillips, J.M. (1998). Effects of realistic job previews on multiple organizational outcomes: A meta-analysis. *Academy of Management Journal, 41*, 673–690.

25. Premack, S.L., & Wanous, J.P. (1985). A meta-analysis of realistic job preview experiments. *Journal of Applied Psychology, 70*, 706–719. See also Wanous, J.P., Poland, T.D., Premack, S.L., & Davis, K.S. (1992). The effects of met expectations on newcomer attitudes and behaviors: A review and meta-analysis. *Journal of Applied Psychology, 77*, 288–297.

26. Premack & Wanous, 1985; McEvoy, G.M., & Cascio, W.F. (1985). Strategies for reducing employee turnover: A meta-analysis. *Journal of Applied Psychology, 70*, 342–353.

27. Morrison & Robinson, 1997.

28. Wanous, J.P., & Reichers, A.E. (2000). New employee orientation programs. *Human Resource Management Review, 10*, 435–451.

29. Gruner, S. (1998, July). Lasting impressions. *Inc., 20*(10), 126.

30. Klein, H.J., & Weaver, N.A. (2000). The effectiveness of an organizational-level orientation training program in the socialization of new hires. *Personnel Psychology, 53*, 47–66.

31. Schettler, J. (2002, August). Welcome to ACME Inc. *Training, 39*(8), 36–43.

32. Van Maanen, J., & Schein, E.H. (1979). Toward a theory of organizational socialization. In B.M. Staw (Ed.), *Research in organizational behavior,* Vol. 1. Greenwich, CT: JAI Press, 209–264.

33. Ashforth, B.E., & Saks, A.M. (1996). Socialization tactics: Longitudinal effects on newcomer adjustment. *Academy of Management Journal, 39*, 149–178; Jones, G.R. (1986). Socialization tactics, self-efficacy, and newcomers' adjustments to organizations. *Academy of Management Journal, 29*, 262–279.

34. Ashforth & Saks, 1996; Jones, 1986; Cable, D.M., & Parsons, C.K. (2001). Socialization tactics and person-organization fit. *Personnel Psychology, 54*, 1–23; Rollag, K., Parise, S., & Cross, R. (2005). Getting new hires up to speed quickly. *MIT Sloan Management Review*, 35–41.

35. Kram, K. (1985). *Mentoring.* Glenview, IL: Scott, Foresman.

36. Allen, T.D., Eby, L.T., & Lentz, E. (2006a). Mentorship behaviours and mentorship quality associated with formal mentoring programs: Closing the gap between research and practice. *Journal of Applied Psychology, 91*, 567–578; Murray, M. (1991). *Beyond the myths and magic of mentoring: How to facilitate an effective mentoring program.* San Francisco, CA: Jossey-Bass; Lawrie, J. (1987). How to establish a mentoring program. *Training & Development Journal, 41*(3), 25–27.

37. Harding, K. (2003, March 12). Your new best friend. *Globe and Mail*, C1, C10.

38. Cox, T., Jr. (1993). *Cultural diversity in organizations: Theory, research, & practice.* San Francisco: Berrett-Koehler; Noe, R.A. (1988). Women and mentoring: A review and research agenda. *Academy of Management Review, 13*, 65–78; Ragins, B.R. (1989). Barriers to mentoring: The female manager's dilemma. *Human Relations, 42*, 1–22.

39. Dreyfus, J., Lee, M.J., & Totta, J.M. (1995, December). Mentoring at the Bank of Montreal: A case study of an intervention that exceeded expectations. *Human Resource Planning, 18*(4), 45–49.

40. Ragins, B., & McFarlin, D. (1990). Perceptions of mentor roles in cross-gender mentoring relationships. *Journal of Vocational Behavior, 37*, 321–339.

41. Burke, R., & McKeen, C. (1990). Mentoring in organizations: Implications for women. *Journal of Business Ethics, 9*, 317–322; Dennett, D. (1985, November). Risks, mentoring helps women to the top. *APA Monitor, 26*; Morrison, A., White, R., & Van Velsor, E. (1987). *Breaking the glass ceiling: Can women reach the top of America's largest corporations?* Reading, MA: Addison-Wesley.

42. Purden, C. (2001, June). Rising to the challenge. *Report on Business Magazine, 17*(12), 31.

43. Purden, 2001.

44. Church, E. (2001, March 8). Mentors guide women through career roadblocks. *Globe and Mail*, B12.

45. Cox, 1993; Ibarra, H. (1993). Personal networks of women and minorities in management. *Academy of Management Review, 18*, 56–87.

46. Nkomo, S., & Cox, T. (1989). Gender differences in the upward mobility of black managers: Double whammy or double advantage? *Sex Roles, 21*, 825–839.

47. Thomas, D. (1989). Mentoring and irrationality: The role of racial taboos. *Human Resource Management, 28*, 279–290; Thomas, D. (1990). The impact of race on managers' experiences of developmental relationships: An intraorganizational study. *Journal of Organizational Behavior, 11*, 479–492.

48. Papmehl, A. (2002, October 7). Diversity in workforce paying off, IBM finds. *Toronto Star*. Retrieved November 30, 2003, from www.thestar.com.

49. Dalton, G.W., Thompson, P.H., & Price, R. (1977, Summer). The four stages of professional careers—A new look at performance by professionals. *Organizational Dynamics*, 19–42; Fagenson, E. (1988). The power of a mentor: Protégés and nonprotégés' perceptions of their own power in organizations. *Group and Organization Studies, 13*, 182–192; Fagenson, E. (1989). The mentor advantage: Perceived career/job experiences of protégés versus non-protégés. *Journal of Organizational Behavior, 10*, 309–320; Scandura, T. (1992). Mentorship and career mobility: An empirical investigation. *Journal of Organizational Behavior, 13*, 169–174; Dreher, G., & Ash, R. (1990). A comparative study of mentoring among men and women in managerial, professional and technical positions. *Journal of Applied Psychology, 75*, 539–546; Whitely, W., Dougherty, T., & Dreher, G. (1991). Relationship of career mentoring and socioeconomic origin to managers' and professionals' early career progress. *Academy of Management Journal, 34*, 331–351.

50. Allen, T.D., Eby, L.T., Poteet, M.L., Lentz, E., & Lima, L. (2004). Career benefits associated with mentoring for protégés: A meta-analysis. *Journal of Applied Psychology, 89*, 127–136.

51. Chao, G., Walz, P., & Gardner, P. (1992). Formal and informal mentorships: A comparison on mentoring functions and contrast with nonmentored counterparts. *Personnel Psychology, 45*, 619–636; Noe, R. (1988). An investigation of the determinants of successful assigned mentoring relationships. *Personnel Psychology, 41*, 457–479; Allen, Eby, & Lentz, 2006a; Allen, T.D., Eby, L.T., & Lentz, E. (2006b). The relationship between formal mentoring program characteristics and perceived program effectiveness. *Personnel Psychology, 59*, 125–153.

52. Ostroff, C., & Kozlowski, S.W.J. (1992). Organizational socialization as a learning process: The role of information acquisition. *Personnel Psychology, 45*, 849–874; Saks, A.M., & Ashforth, B.E. (1996). Proactive socialization and behavioral self-management. Journal of Vocational Behavior, 48, 301–323.

53. Morrison, E.W. (1993). Newcomer information seeking: Exploring types, modes, sources, and outcomes. *Academy of Management Journal, 36*, 557–589; Morrison, E.W. (1993). Longitudinal study of the effects of information seeking on newcomer socialization. *Journal of Applied Psychology, 78*, 173–183.

54. Ashford, S.J., & Black, J.S. (1996). Proactivity during organizational entry: The role of desire for control. *Journal of Applied Psychology, 81*, 199–214; Griffin, A.E.C., Colella, A., & Goparaju, S. (2000). Newcomer and organizational socialization tactics: An interactionist perspective. *Human Resource Management Review, 10*, 453–474; Wanberg, C.R., & Kammeyer-Mueller, J.D. (2000). Predictors and outcomes of proactivity in the socialization process. *Journal of Applied Psychology, 85*, 373–385; Whitely, W.T., Peiró, J.M., Feij, J.A., & Taris, T.W. (1995). Conceptual, epistemological, methodological, and outcome issues in work-role development: A reply. *Journal of Vocational Behavior, 46*, 283–291.

55. Ostroff & Kozlowski, 1992; Ashforth, B.E., Sluss, D.M., & Saks, A.M. (2007). Socialization tactics, proactive behavior, and newcomer learning: Integrating socialization models. *Journal of Vocational Behavior, 70*, 447–462.

56. For a more complete discussion of various definitions, theories, and concepts of culture, see Allaire, Y., & Firsirotu, M.E. (1984). Theories of organizational culture. *Organization Studies, 5*, 193–226; Hatch, M.J. (1993). The dynamics of organizational culture. *Academy of Management Review, 18*, 657–693; Schein, E.H. (1992). *Organizational culture and leadership*, 2nd edition. San Francisco: Jossey-Bass; Smircich, L. (1983). Concepts of culture and organizational analysis. *Administrative Science Quarterly, 28*, 339–358.

57. Sackmann, S.A. (1992). Culture and subculture: An analysis of organizational knowledge. *Administrative Science Quarterly, 37*, 140–161.

58. Gregory, K.L. (1983). Native-view paradigms: Multiple cultures and culture conflicts in organizations. *Administrative Science Quarterly, 28*, 359–376.

59. Deal, T.E., & Kennedy, A.A. (1982). *Corporate cultures: The rites and rituals of corporate life*. Reading, MA: Addison-Wesley; Kilmann, R., Saxton, M.J., & Serpa, R. (1986, Winter). Issues in understanding and changing culture. *California Management Review*, 87–94. For a critique, see Saffold, G.S., III. (1988). Culture traits, strength, and organizational performance: Moving beyond "strong" culture. *Academy of Management Review, 13*, 546–558.

60. Holloway, A. (2006, April 10–23). Hilti (Canada) Corp. *Canadian Business, 79*(8), 78.

61. Quinn, P. (2008, January 30). WestJet locks in top spot on corporate culture honour poll. *Financial Post*(online),-www.financialpost.com; (2009). *Canada's 10 Most Admired Corporate Cultures 2008*. Toronto: Waterstone Human Capital; (2008). *Canada's 10 Most Admired Corporate Cultures 2007.*Toronto: Waterstone Human Capital.

62. Verburg, P. (2000, December 25). Prepare for takeoff. *Canadian Business, 73*(24), 94–99; (2008). *Canada's 10 Most Admired Corporate Cultures 2007.* Toronto: Waterstone Human Capital.

63. Gordon, G.G., & Di Tomaso, N. (1992). Predicting corporate performance from organizational culture. *Journal of Management Studies, 29*, 783–798. For a critique of such work, see Siehl, C., & Martin, J. (1990). Organizational culture: A key to financial performance. In B. Schneider (Ed.), *Organizational climate and culture*. San Francisco: Jossey-Bass.

64. Sheridan, J.E. (1992). Organizational culture and employee retention. *Academy of Management Journal, 35*, 1036–1056.

65. Lorsch, J.W. (1986, Winter). Managing culture: The invisible barrier to strategic change. *California Management Review*, 95–109.

66. Verburg, P. (2000, December 25).

67. (2009). *Canada's 10 Most Admired Corporate Cultures 2008*. Toronto: Waterstone Human Capital.

68. Mount, I. (2002, August). Out of control. *Business 2.0, 3(8)*, 38–44.

69. Cartwright, S., & Cooper, C.L. (1993, May). The role of culture compatibility in successful organizational marriage. *Academy of Management Executive*, 57–70.

70. Fordahl, M. (2002, March 28). Hp, Compaq face ghosts of mega-mergers past. *Globe and Mail*, B17.

71. Kets de Vries, M.F.R., & Miller, D. (1984). *The neurotic organization: Diagnosing and changing counterproductive styles of management*. San Francisco: Jossey-Bass.

72. Lardner, J. (2002, March). Why should anyone believe you? *Business 2.0, 3(3)*, 40–48; Waldie, P., & Howlett, K. (2003, June 11). Reports reveal tight grip of Ebbers on WorldCom. *Globe and Mail*, B1, B7; Wells, J. (2009, August 6). Now playing: Garth Drabinsky stars in the 7-year stretch. *Toronto Star*, A1, A12; Blackwell, R., & MacMillan, J. (2009, August 6). They built a theatre empire that crumbled, bilking investors and cleaning out creditors. Now Garth Drabinsky and his partner are going to jail for their "deception" and "dishonest dealing." *Globe and Mail*, A1, A7.

73. McKenna, B. (2003, August 27). Shuttle probe blasts NASA's dysfunctional atmosphere. *Globe and Mail*, A9; Schwartz, J., & Wald, M.L. (2003, August 27). Shuttle probe faults NASA. *Toronto Star* (online), www.thestar.ca (orig. pub. *New York Times*).

74. See Schein, 1992.

75. Papmehl, 2002.

76. Uttal, B. (1985, August 5). Behind the fall of Steve Jobs. *Fortune*, 20–24.

77. Pascale, R. (1985, Winter). The paradox of "corporate culture": Reconciling ourselves to socialization. *California Management Review*, 26–41. For some research support, see Caldwell, D.F., Chatman, J.A., & O'Reilly, C.A. (1990). Building organizational commitment: A multifirm study. *Journal of Occupational Psychology, 63*, 245–261.

78. Gordon, A. (2000, February). 35 best companies to work for. *Report on Business Magazine*, 24–32.

79. Hatch, 1993; Ornstein, S. (1986). Organizational symbols: A study of their meanings and influences on perceived organizational climate. *Organizational Behavior and Human Decision Processes, 38*, 207–229.

80. Nulty, P. (1989, February 27). America's toughest bosses. *Fortune*, 40–54.

81. Trice, H.M., and Beyer, J.M. (1984). Studying organizational cultures through rites and ceremonials. *Academy of Management Review, 9*, 653–669.

82. Martin, J., Feldman, M.S., Hatch, M.J., & Sitkin, S.B. (1983). The uniqueness paradox in organizational stories. *Administrative Science Quarterly, 28*, 438–453.

83. Peters, T., & Austin, N. (1985). *A passion for excellence: The leadership difference*. New York: Random House.

Chapter 9

1. Pitts, G. (2008, December). The testing of Michael McCain. *Report on Business*, 60–66; Pitts, G. (2008, August 30). Man under fire. *Globe and Mail*, B1, B6; Greenwood, J. (2009, February 3). Listeria costs Maple Leaf $27M. *National Post*, FP7; Anonymous (2009, February 2). Corporate honesty. *Winnipeg Free Press*, A11; Charlebois, S., & Levene, K. (2009, January 13). Good leadership in trying times: PR strategy: Maple Leaf CEO steers his firm through crisis. *National Post*, FP7; Maple Leaf Foods Inc. Biography Michael H. McCain, www.mapleleaf.com/en/corporate/company-info/management-team/michael-h-mccain.

2. Daly, J. (2003, February). The toughest SOBs in business. *Report on Business Magazine, 19*(8), 34–42; Various contributors (2005, November). The power 25. *Report on Business Magazine, 22*(4), 49–82.

3. Ireland, R.D., & Hitt, M.A. (1999). Achieving and maintaining strategic competitiveness in the 21st century: The role of strategic leadership. *Academy of Management Executive, 13*, 43–57.

4. Bass, B.M. (1990). *Bass & Stogdill's handbook of leadership: A survey of research* (3rd ed.). New York: Free Press.

5. This list is derived from Bass, 1990; House, R.J., & Baetz, M.L. (1979). Leadership: Some empirical generalizations and new research directions. *Research in Organizational Behavior, 1*, 341–423; Locke, E.A. & Associates (1992). *The essence of leadership: The four keys to leading effectively*. New York: Free Press; Lord, R.G., DeVader, C.L., & Alliger, G.M. (1986). A meta-analysis of the relationship between personality traits and leadership perceptions: An application of validity generalization procedures. *Journal of Applied Psychology, 71*, 402–410.

6. Judge, T.A., & Bono, J.E. (2000). Five-factor model of personality and transformational leadership. *Journal of Applied Psychology, 85*, 751–765; Judge, T.A., Colbert, A.E., & Ilies, R. (2004). Intelligence and leadership: A quantitative review and test of theoretical propositions. *Journal of Applied Psychology, 89*, 542–552.

7. Kirkpatrick, S.A., & Locke, E.A. (1991). Leadership: Do traits matter? *Academy of Management Executive, 5*, 48–60.

8. Hannon, G. (2004, January). The great transformation. *Report on Business Magazine, 20*(7), 43–46.

9. Judge, T.A., Piccolo, R.F., & Ilies, R. (2004). The forgotten ones? The validity of consideration and initiating structure in leadership research. *Journal of Applied Psychology, 89*, 36–51.

10. Kerr, S., Schriesheim, C.A., Murphy, C.J., & Stogdill, R.M. (1974). Toward a contingency theory of leadership based upon the consideration and initiating structure literature. *Organizational Behavior and Human Performance, 12*, 62–82.

11. Podsakoff, P.M., Bommer, W.H., Podsakoff, N.P., & MacKenzie, S.B. (2006). Relationships between leader reward and punishment behaviour and subordinate attitudes, perceptions, and behaviors: A meta-analytic review of existing and new research. *Organizational Behavior and Human Decision Processes, 99*, 113–142.

12. Verburg, P. (2000, December 25). Prepare for takeoff. *Canadian Business, 73*(24), 94–99.

13. Fiedler, F.E. (1967). *A theory of leadership effectiveness*. New York: McGraw-Hill; Fiedler, F.E. (1978). The contingency model and the dynamics of the leadership process. In L. Berkowitz (Ed.), *Advances in experimental social psychology* (Vol. 11). New York: Academic Press; Fiedler, F.E., & Chemers, M.M. (1974). *Leadership and effective management*. Glenview, IL: Scott, Foresman.

14. For a summary, see Fiedler, 1978.

15. See Ashour, A.S. (1973). The contingency model of leader effectiveness: An evaluation. *Organizational Behavior and Human Performance, 9*, 339–355; Graen, G.B., Alvares, D., Orris, J.B., & Martella, J.A. (1970). The contingency model of leadership effectiveness: Antecedent and evidential results. *Psychological Bulletin, 74*, 285–296.

16. Peters, L.H., Hartke, D.D., & Pohlmann, J.T. (1985). Fiedler's contingency theory of leadership: An application of the meta-analysis

procedures of Schmidt and Hunter. *Psychological Bulletin, 97,* 274–285; Schriesheim, C.A., Tepper, B.J., & Tetreault, L.A. (1994). Least preferred co-worker score, situational control, and leadership effectiveness: A meta-analysis of contingency and performance predictions. *Journal of Applied Psychology, 79,* 561–573; Strube, M.J., & Garcia, J.E. (1981). A meta-analytic investigation of Fiedler's contingency model of leadership effectiveness. *Psychological Bulletin, 90,* 307–321.

17. Fiedler, F.E. (1989). The effective utilization of intellectual abilities and job-relevant knowledge in group performance: Cognitive resource theory and an agenda for the future. *Applied Psychology: An International Review, 38,*289–304. Fiedler, F.E. (1995). Cognitive resources and leadership performance. *Applied Psychology: An International Review, 44,*5–28.

18. Fiedler, 1995; Fiedler, F.E., Murphy, S.E., & Gibson, F.W. (1992). Inaccurate reporting and inappropriate variables: A reply to Vecchio's (1990) examination of cognitive resource theory. *Journal of Applied Psychology, 77,*372–374.

19. Fiedler, Murphy, & Gibson, 1992; Vecchio, R.P. (1990). Theoretical and empirical examination of cognitive resource theory. *Journal of Applied Psychology, 75,*141–147.

20. House, R.J., & Dessler, G. (1974). The path-goal theory of leadership: Some post hoc and a priori tests. In J.G. Hunt & L.L. Larson (Eds.), *Contingency approaches to leadership.* Carbondale, IL: Southern Illinois University Press; House, R.J., & Mitchell, T.R. (1974, Autumn). Path-goal theory of leadership. *Journal of Contemporary Business,* 81–97. See also Evans, M.G. (1970). The effects of supervisory behavior on the path-goal relationship. *Organizational Behavior and Human Performance, 5,* 277–298.

21. Filley, A.C., House, R.J., & Kerr, S. (1976). *Managerial process and organizational behavior* (2nd ed.). Glenview, IL: Scott, Foresman; House & Dessler, 1974; House & Mitchell, 1974; Wofford, J.C., & Liska, L.Z. (1993). Path-goal theories of leadership: A meta-analysis. *Journal of Management, 19,* 857–876.

22. See, for example, Greene, C.N. (1979). Questions of causation in the path-goal theory of leadership. *Academy of Management Journal, 22,* 22–41; Griffin, R.W. (1980). Relationships among individual, task design, and leader behavior variables. *Academy of Management Journal, 23,* 665–683.

23. Mitchell, T.R. (1973). Motivation and participation: An integration. *Academy of Management Journal, 16,* 160–179.

24. Maier, N.R.F. (1970). *Problem solving and creativity in individuals and groups.* Belmont, CA: Brooks/Cole; Maier, N.R.F. (1973). *Psychology in industrial organizations* (4th ed.). Boston: Houghton Mifflin.

25. Maier, 1970, 1973.

26. Vroom, V.H., & Jago, A.G. (1988). *The new leadership: Managing participation in organizations.* Englewood Cliffs, NJ: Prentice-Hall; Vroom, V.H., & Yetton, P.W. (1973). *Leadership and decision-making.* Pittsburgh: University of Pittsburgh Press.

27. Vroom & Yetton, 1973, 13.

28. See Vroom & Jago, 1988, for a review. See also Field, R.H.G., Wedley, W.C., & Hayward, M.W.J. (1989). Criteria used in selecting Vroom-Yetton decision styles. *Canadian Journal of Administrative Sciences, 6*(2), 18–24.

29. Reviews on participation reveal a complicated pattern of results. See Miller, K.I., & Monge, P.R. (1986). Participation, satisfaction, and productivity: A meta-analytic review. *Academy of Management Journal, 29,* 727–753; Wagner, J.A., Iii, & Gooding, R.Z. (1987a). Shared influence and organizational behavior: A meta-analysis of situational variables expected to moderate participation–outcome relationships. *Academy of Management Journal, 30,* 524–541; Wagner, J.A., Iii, & Gooding, R.Z. (1987b). Effects of societal trends on participation research. *Administrative Science Quarterly, 32,* 241–262.

30. Graen, G.B., & Uhl-Bien, M. (1995). Relationship-based approach to leadership: Development of leader–member exchange (LMX) theory of leadership over 25 years: Applying a multi-level, multi-domain perspective. *Leadership Quarterly, 6*(2), 219–247.

31. Gerstner, C.R., & Day, D.V. (1997). Meta-analytic review of leader-member exchange theory: Correlates and construct issues. *Journal of Applied Psychology, 82,* 827–844; Graen, & Uhl-Bien, 1995; Schriesheim, C.A., Castro, S.L., & Cogliser, C.C. (1999). Leader–member exchange (LMX) research: A comprehensive review of theory, measurement, and data-analytic practices. *Leadership Quarterly, 10*(1), 63–113; House, R.J., & Aditya, R.N. (1997). The social scientific study of leadership: Quo vadis? *Journal of Management, 23,* 409–473;

Tierney, P., Farmer, S.M., & Graen, G.B. (1999). An examination of leadership and employee creativity: The relevance of traits and relationships. *Personnel Psychology, 52,* 591–620.

32. Gerstner, & Day, 1997; Graen, & Uhl-Bien, 1995; Ilies, R., Nahrgang, J.D., & Morgeson, F.P. (2007). Leader-member exchange and citizenship behaviors: A meta-analysis. *Journal of Applied Psychology, 92,*269–277.

33. Judge, T.A., & Piccolo, R.F. (2004). Transformational and transactional leadership: A meta-analytic test of their relative validity. *Journal of Applied Psychology, 89,*755–768.

34. The transformational/transactional distinction is credited to Burns, J.M. (1978). *Leadership.* New York: Harper & Row.

35. Bass, B.M. (1985). *Leadership and performance beyond expectations.* New York: Free Press; Bass, B.M. (1990, Winter). From transactional to transformational leadership: Learning to share the vision. *Organizational Dynamics,* 19–31.

36. Judge & Piccolo, 2004.

37. Judge & Piccolo, 2004; Bono, J.E., & Judge, T.A. (2004). Personality and transformational and transactional leadership: A meta-analysis. *Journal of Applied Psychology, 89,*901–910.

38. House, R.J. (1977). A 1976 theory of charismatic leadership. In J.G. Hunt & L.L. Larson (Eds.), *Leadership: The cutting edge.* Carbondale, IL: Southern Illinois University Press.

39. House, R.J., Woycke, J., & Fodor, E.M. (1988). Charismatic and non-charismatic leaders: Differences in behavior and effectiveness. In J.A. Conger & R.N. Kanungo (Eds.), *Charismatic leadership: The elusive factor in organizational effectiveness.* San Francisco: Jossey-Bass.

40. DeGroot, T., Kilker, D.S., & Cross, T.C. (2000). A meta-analysis to review organizational outcomes related to charismatic leadership. Canadian Journal of Administrative Sciences, 17, 356–371; Fuller, J.B., Patterson, C.E.P., Hester, K., & Stringer, D.Y. (1996). A quantitative review of research on charismatic leadership. *Psychological Reports, 78,* 271–287.

41. Agle, B.R., Nagarajan, N.J., Sonnenfeld, J.A., & Srinivasan, D. (2006). Does CEO charisma matter? An empirical analysis of the relationships among organizational performance, environmental uncertainty, and top management team perceptions of CEO charisma. *Academy of Management Journal, 49,*161–174; Waldman, D.A., Ramirez, G.G., House, R.J., &

Puranam, P. (2001). Does leadership matter? CEO leadership attributes and profitability under conditions of perceived environmental uncertainty. *Academy of* Management Journal, 44, 134–143; Colbert, A.E., Kristof-Brown, A.L., Bradley, B.H., & Barrick, M.R. (2008). CEO transformational leadership: The role of goal importance congruence in top management teams. *Academy of Management Journal, 51*,81–96; Ling, Y., Simsek, Z., Lubatkin, M.H., & Veiga, J.F. (2008). The impact of transformational CEOs on the performance of small- to medium-sized firms: Does organizational context matter? *Journal of Applied Psychology, 93*,923–934.

42. Howell, J.M. (1988). Two faces of charisma: Socialized and personalized leadership in organizations. In J.A. Conger & R.N. Kanungo (Eds.), *Charismatic leadership: The elusive factor in organizational effectiveness*. San Francisco: Jossey-Bass; Howell, J.M., & Avolio, B.J. (1992, May). The ethics of charismatic leadership. Submission or liberation? *Academy of Management Executive*, 43–54.

43. Judge & Piccolo, 2004; Herold, D.M., Fedor, D.B., Caldwell, S., & Liu, Y. (2008). The effects of transformational and change leadership on employees' commitment to a change: A multilevel study. *Journal of Applied Psychology, 93*, 346–357.

44. Wang, H., Law, K.S., Hackett, R.D., Wang, D., & Chen, Z.X. (2005). Leader-member exchange as a mediator of the relationship between transformational leadership and followers' performance and organizational citizenship behaviour. *Academy of Management Journal, 48*,420–432; Piccolo, R.F., & Colquitt, J.A. (2006). Transformational leadership and job behaviours: The mediating role of core job characteristics. *Academy of Management Journal, 49*,327–340; Walumbwa, F.O., Avolio, B.J., & Zhu, W. (2008). How transformational leadership weaves its influence on individual job performance: The role of identification and efficacy beliefs. *Personnel Psychology, 61*, 793–825.

45. Brown, M.E., Trevino, L.K., & Harrison, D.A. (2005). Ethical leadership: A social learning perspective for construct development and testing. *Organizational Behavior and Human Decision Processes, 97*,117–134.

46. Olive, D. (2006, June 25). Nothing like a crisis to test corporate mettle. *Globe and Mail*,A19; Various contributors (2005, November). The power

25: Rick George. *Report on Business Magazine, 22(4)*, 49–82.

47. Thomas, Schermerhorn, & Dienhart, 2004.

48. Carpenter, D. (2006, July 3). Boeing CEO sitting pretty one year in. *Globe and Mail*, B5.

49. Brown, Trevino, & Harrison, 2005; Schminke, Ambrose, & Neubaum, 2005; Mayer, D.M., Kuenzi, M., Greenbaum, R., Bardes, M., & Salvador, R. (2009). How low does ethical leadership flow? Test of a trickle-down model. *Organizational Behavior and Human Decision Processes, 108*, 1–13.

50 Pitts, 2008.

51. Walumbwa, F.O., Avolio, B.J., Gardner, W.L., Wernsing, T.S., & Peterson, S.J. (2008). Authentic leadership: Development and validation of a theory-based measure. *Journal of Management, 34*,89–126.

52. Walumbwa et al., 2008.

53. Javidan, M., Dorfman, P.W., de Luque, M.S., & House, R.J. (2006). In the eye of the beholder: Cross-cultural lessons in leadership from Project GLOBE. *Academy of Management Perspectives, 20*, 67–90.

54. Javidan et al., 2006.

55. Javidan et al., 2006.

56. Gregersen, H.B., Morrison, A.J., & Black, J.S. (1998, Fall). Developing leaders for the global frontier. *Sloan Management Review*, 21–32.

57. Javidan et al., 2006.

58. Kingston, A. (2009, March 16). Bonnie of the Bay. *Maclean's, 122(9)*,34–36.

59. Gregersen, Morrison, & Black, 1998.

60. Gregersen, Morrison, & Black, 1998; Javidan et al., 2006.

61. Javidan et al., 2006.

62. Gregersen, Morrison, & Black, 1998; Church, E. (1999, January 7). Born to be a global business leader. *Globe and Mail*, B8.

63. Moore, K. (2002, August 21). Multicultural Canada breeds managers with global outlook. *Globe and Mail*, B9.

64. Eagley, A.H., & Johnson, B.T. (1990). Gender and leadership style: A meta-analysis. *Psychological Bulletin, 108*, 233–256.

65. Kass, S. (September 1999). Employees perceive women as better managers than men, finds five-year study. *ADA Monitor, 30(8)*, 6.

66. Eagly, A.H., Johannesen-Schmidt, M.C., & van Engen, M.L. (2003). Transformational, transactional, and laissez-faire leadership styles: A meta-analysis comparing women and men. *Psychological Bulletin, 120*, 569–591.

67. Nuttall-Smith, C., & York, G. (2007, March). Orange China. *Report on Business*,24–38; Salewicz, G. (2007, March). Editor's Desk. *Report on Business*,4.

68. Klie, S. (2009, April 6). Women make small gains. *Canadian HR Reporter, 22(7)*,1, 2; Morra, M. (2008, June–July). The broad perspective. *HR Professional*, 22–28.

69. Eagly, A.H., & Carli, L.L. (2007, September). Women and the labyrinth of leadership. *Harvard Business Review, 85*,63–71.

70. Eagly & Carli, 2007.

Chapter 10

1. Davies, M., & Siew, W. (2009, March 10). 45 percent of world's wealth destroyed: Blackstone CEO. *Reuters.*-www.reuters.com; Faiola, A., Nakashima, E., & Drew, J. (2008, October 15). What Went Wrong? *Washington Post*, A01; Guenther, K.A. (2003).Promoting homeownership. *Independent Banker, 53(6), 46–50*; Dow Jones Industrial averages from www.djaverages.com; Bank of Canada rates from www.bankofcanada.ca; Energy Information Administration oil prices from www.eia.doe.gov.

2. Mintzberg, H. (1979). *The structuring of organizations*. Englewood Cliffs, NJ: Prentice-Hall.

3. MacCrimmon, K.R., & Taylor, R.N. (1976). Decision making and problem solving. In M.D. Dunnette (Ed.), *Handbook of industrial and organizational psychology*. Chicago: Rand McNally.

4. Anonymous. (2008, November). No left turn. *Road & Track*, 40.

5. Anonymous. (2008, November 20, 21). www.cnn.com.

6. Simon, H.A. (1957). *Administrative behavior* (2nd ed.). New York: Free Press. See also: Kahneman, D. (2003). A perspective in judgment and choice: Mapping bounded rationality. *American Psychologist, 56*, 697–720.

7. Bazerman, M. (2006). *Judgment in managerial decision making* (6th ed.). Hoboken, NJ: Wiley; Kahneman, 2003.

8. Russo, J.E., & Schoemaker, P.J.H. (1989). *Decision traps*. New York: Doubleday; Whyte, G. (1991, August). Decision failures: Why they occur and how to prevent them. *Academy of Management Executive*, 23–31.

9. The latter two difficulties are discussed by Huber, G.P. (1980). *Managerial decision making*. Glenview, IL: Scott, Foresman. For further discussion of problem identification, see Cowan, D.A. (1986).

Developing a process model of problem recognition. *Academy of Management Review, 11,* 763–776; Kiesler, S., & Sproull, L. (1982). Managerial response to changing environments: Perspectives on problem sensing from social cognition. *Administrative Science Quarterly, 27,* 548–570.

10. Whyte, 1991; Russo & Schoemaker, 1989.

11. Tversky, A., & Kahneman, D. (1973). Availability: A heuristic for judging frequency and probability. *Cognitive Psychology, 5,* 207–232. Also see Taylor, S.E., & Fiske, S.T. (1978). Salience, attention, and attribution: Top of the head phenomena. In L. Berkowitz (Ed.), *Advances in experimental social psychology* (Vol. 11). New York: Academic Press.

12. Lichtenstein, S., Fischhoff, B., & Phillips, L.D. (1982). Calibration of probabilities: The state of the art in 1980. In D. Kahneman, P. Slovic, & A. Tversky (Eds.), *Judgment under uncertainty: Heuristics and biases.* Cambridge: Cambridge University Press.

13. Tingling, P. (2009, April 21). Fact or fantasy. *National Post,* FP12.

14. Miller, J.G. (1960). Information input, overload, and psychopathology. *American Journal of Psychiatry, 116,* 695–704.

15. Manis, M., Fichman, M., & Platt, M. (1978). Cognitive integration and referential communication: Effects of information quality and quantity in message decoding. *Organizational Behavior and Human Performance, 22,* 417–430; Troutman, C.M., & Shanteau, J. (1977). Inferences based on nondiagnostic information. *Organizational Behavior and Human Performance, 19,* 43–55.

16. Tsai, C.I., Klayman, J., & Hastie, R. (2008). Effects of amount of information on judgment accuracy and confidence. *Organizational Behavior and Human Decision Processes, 107,* 97–105.

17. Feldman, M.S., & March, J.G. (1981). Information in organizations as signal and symbol. *Administrative Science Quarterly, 26,* 171–186.

18. Gino, F. (2008). Do we listen to advice just because we paid for it? The impact of advice cost on its use. *Organizational Behavior and Human Decision Processes,107,* 234–245. For a review of advice taking, see Bonaccio, S., & Dalal, R.S. (2006). Advice taking and decision-making: An integrative literature review and implications for the organizational sciences. *Organizational Behavior and Human Decision Processes,101,* 127–151.

19. Kahneman et al., 1982; Tversky, A., & Kahneman, D. (1976). Judgment under uncertainty: Heuristics and biases. *Science, 185,* 1124–1131.

20. Northcraft, G.B., & Neale, M.A. (1987). Experts, amateurs, and real estate: An anchoring-and-adjustment perspective on property pricing decisions. *Organizational Behavior and Human Decision Processes, 39,* 84–97.

21. Johns, G. (1999). A multi-level theory of self-serving behavior in and by organizations. *Research in Organizational Behavior, 21,* 1–38; Tetlock, P.E. (1999). Accountability theory: Mixing properties of human agents with properties of social systems. In L.L. Thompson, J.M. Levine, & D.M. Messick (Eds.), *Shared cognition in organizations: The management of knowledge.* Mahwah, N.J.: Lawrence Erlbaum.

22. Nutt, P.C. (2004, November). Expanding the search for alternatives during strategic decision-making. *Academy of Management Executive,*13–28.

23. Simon, H.A. (1957). *Models of man.* New York: Wiley; Cyert, R.M., & March, J.G. (1963). *A behavioral theory of the firm.* Englewood Cliffs, NJ: Prentice-Hall. For an example, see Bower, J., & Zi-Lei, Q. (1992). Satisficing when buying information. *Organizational Behavior and Human Decision Processes, 51,* 471–481.

24. Bazerman, M. (1990). *Judgment in managerial decision making* (2nd ed.). New York: Wiley.

25. Kahneman, D., & Tversky, A. (1979). Prospect theory: An analysis of decision under risk. *Econometrica, 47,* 263–291.

26. Sitkin, S.B., & Pablo, A.L. (1992). Conceptualizing the determinants of risk behavior. *Academy of Management Review, 17,* 9–38.

27. For a detailed treatment and other perspectives, see Northcraft, G.B., & Wolf, G. (1984). Dollars, sense, and sunk costs: A life cycle model of resource allocation decisions. *Academy of Management Review, 9,* 225–234.

28. Brockner, J. (1992). The escalation of commitment to a failing course of action: Toward theoretical progress. *Academy of Management Review, 17,* 39–61; Staw, B.M. (1997). Escalation of commitment: An update and appraisal. In Z. Shapira (Ed.), *Organizational decision making.* Cambridge: Cambridge University Press.

29. Staw, B.M. (1981). The escalation of commitment to a course of action. *Academy of Management Review, 6,*

577–587. For the limitations on this view, see Knight, P.A. (1984). Heroism versus competence: Competing explanations for the effects of experimenting and consistent management. *Organizational Behavior and Human Performance, 33,* 307–322.

30. Arkes, H.R., & Blumer, C. (1985). The psychology of sunk cost. *Organizational Behavior and Human Decision Processes, 35,* 124–140.

31. Whyte, G. (1986). Escalating commitment to a course of action: A reinterpretation. *Academy of Management Review, 11,* 311–321.

32. Wong, K.F.E., Yik, M., & Kwong, J.Y.Y. (2006). Understanding the emotional aspects of escalation of commitment: The role of negative affect. *Journal of Applied Psychology, 91,* 282–297.

33. Ku, G., Malhorta, D., & Murnighan, J.K. (2005). Towards a competitive arousal model of decision-making: A study of auction fever in live and internet auctions. *Organizational Behavior and Human Decision Processes, 96,* 89–103.

34. Simonson, I., & Nye, P. (1992). The effect of accountability on susceptibility to decision errors. *Organizational Behavior and Human Decision Processes, 51,* 416–446; Simonson, I., & Staw, B.M. (1992). Deescalation strategies: A comparison of techniques for reducing commitment to losing courses of action. *Journal of Applied Psychology, 77,* 419–426; Whyte, 1991.

35. Whyte, G. (1993). Escalating commitment in individual and group decision making: A prospect theory approach. *Organizational Behavior and Human Decision Processes, 54,* 430–455.

36. Hawkins, S.A., & Hastie, R. (1990). Hindsight: Biased judgments of past events after outcomes are known. *Psychological Bulletin, 107,* 311–327.

37. Greenwald, A.G. (1980). The totalitarian ego: Fabrication and revision of personal history. *American Psychologist, 35,* 603–618.

38. Forgas, J.P., & George, J.M. (2001). Affective influences on judgments and behavior in organizations: An information processing perspective. *Organizational Behavior and Human Decision Processes, 86,* 3–34.

39. Hayward, M.L.A., & Hambrick, D.C. (1997). Explaining the premiums paid for large acquisitions: Evidence of CEO hubris. *Administrative Science Quarterly, 42,* 103–127.

40. Forgas & George, 2001; Weiss, H.M. (2002). Conceptual and empirical foundations for the study of affect at

work. In R.G. Lord, R.J. Klimoski, & R. Kanfer (Eds), *Emotions in the workplace: Understanding the structure and role of emotions in organizational behavior*. San Francisco: Jossey-Bass; Davis, M.A. (2009). Understanding the relationship between mood and creativity: A meta-analysis. *Organizational Behavior and Human Decision Processes, 108*, 25–38; Baas, M., De Dreu, C.K.W., & Nijstad, B.A. (2008). A meta-analysis of 25 years of mood-creativity research: Hedonic tone, activation, or regulatory focus? *Psychological Bulletin, 134*, 779–806.

41. Au, K., Chan, F., Wang, D., & Vertinsky, I. (2003). Mood in foreign exchange trading: Cognitive processes and performance. *Organizational Behavior and Human Decision Processes, 91*, 322–338.

42. Mitchell, T.R., & Beach, L.R. (1977). Expectancy theory, decision theory, and occupational preference and choice. In M.F. Kaplan & S. Schwartz (Eds.), *Human judgment and decision processes in applied settings*. New York: Academic Press.

43. Pinfield, L.T. (1986). A field evaluation of perspectives on organizational decision making. *Administrative Science Quarterly, 31*, 365–388.

44. Nutt, P.C. (1989). *Making tough decisions*. San Francisco: Jossey-Bass.

45. Nutt, P.C. (1999, November). Surprising but true: Half the decisions in organizations fail. *Academy of Management Executive*, 75–90.

46. Lord, R.G., & Maher, K.J. (1990). Alternative information-processing models and their implications for theory, research, and practice. *Academy of Management Review, 15*, 9–28.

47. Shaw, M.E. (1981). *Group dynamics* (3rd ed.). New York: McGraw-Hill, 78.

48. Hill, G.W. (1982). Group versus individual performance: Are n+1 heads better than one? *Psychological Bulletin, 91*, 517–539.

49. Shaw, 1981; Davis, J.H. (1969). *Group performance*. Reading, MA: Addison-Wesley; Libby, R., Trotman, K.T., & Zimmer, I. (1987). Member variation, recognition of expertise, and group performance. *Journal of Applied Psychology, 72*, 81–87.

50. Van Ginkel, W.P., & van Knippenberg, D. (2009). Knowledge about the distribution of information and group decision making: When and why does it work? *Organizational Behavior and Human Decision Processes, 108*, 218–229; Brodbeck, F.C., Kerschreiter, R., Mojzisch, A., & Schulz-Hardt, S.

(2007). Group decision making under conditions of distributed knowledge: The information asymmetries model. *Academy of Management Review, 32*, 459–479.

51. Janis, I.L. (1972). *Victims of groupthink*. Boston: Houghton Mifflin.

52. Esser, J.K. (1998). Alive and well after 25 years: A review of groupthink research. *Organizational Behavior and Human Decision Processes, 73*, 116–141.

53. Aldag, R.J., & Fuller, S.R. (1993) Beyond fiasco: A reappraisal of the groupthink phenomenon and a new model of group decision processes. *Psychological Bulletin, 113*, 533–552; McCauley, C. (1989). The nature of social influence in groupthink: Compliance and internalization. *Journal of Personality and Social Psychology, 57*, 250–260; Baron, R.S. (2005). So right it's wrong: Groupthink and the ubiquitous nature of polarized group decision making. *Advances in Experimental Social Psychology, 37*, 219–253.

54. Janis, 1972.

55. This is our analysis. The data cited is from Capers, R.S., & Lipton, E. (1993, November). Hubble error: Time, money, and millionths of an inch. *Academy of Management Executive*, 41–57 (originally published in *Hartford Courant*).

56. Hart, P. (1998). Preventing groupthink revisited: Evaluating and reforming groups in government. *Organizational Behavior and Human Decision Processes, 73*, 306–326.

57. Stoner, J.A.F. (1961). *A comparison of individual and group decisions involving risk*. Unpublished Master's thesis. School of Industrial Management, Massachusetts Institute of Technology.

58. Lamm, H., & Myers, D.G. (1978). Group-induced polarization of attitudes and behavior. In L. Berkowitz (Ed.), *Advances in experimental social psychology* (Vol. 11). New York: Academic Press.

59. Isenberg, D.J. (1986). Group polarization: A critical review and meta-analysis. *Journal of Personality and Social Psychology, 50*, 1141–1151.

60. Kiesler, S., & Sproull, L. (1992). Group decision making and communication technology. *Organizational Behavior and Human Decision Processes, 52*, 96–123; Sia, C.L., Tan, B.C.Y., & Wei, K.K. (1999). Can a GSS stimulate group polarization? An empirical study. *IEEE Transactions on Systems, Man, and Cybernetics Part C—Applications and Reviews, 29*, 227–237.

61. Nutt, 1999.

62. Maier, N.R.F. (1973). *Psychology in industrial organizations* (4th ed.). Boston: Houghton Mifflin; Maier, N.R.F. (1970). *Problem solving and creativity in individuals and groups*. Belmont, CA: Brooks/Cole.

63. Tjosvold, D. (2000). *Learning to manage conflict: Getting people to work together productively*. Lanhan, MD: Lexington; Tjosvold, D. (1985). Implications of controversy research for management. *Journal of Management, 11*(3), 21–37.

64. Schwenk, C.R. (1984). Devil's advocacy in managerial decision-making. *Journal of Management Studies, 21*, 153–168. For a study, see Schwenk, C., & Valacich, J.S. (1994). Effects of devil's advocacy and dialectical inquiry on individuals versus groups. *Organizational Behavior and Human Decision Processes, 59*, 210–222.

65. Osborn, A.F. (1957). *Applied imagination*. New York: Scribners.

66. See for example Madsen, D.B., & Finger, J.R., Jr. (1978). Comparison of a written feedback procedure, group brainstorming, and individual brainstorming. *Journal of Applied Psychology, 63*, 120–123.

67. Sutton, R.I., & Hargadon, A. (1996). Brainstorming groups in context: Effectiveness in a product design firm. *Administrative Science Quarterly, 41*, 685–718.

68. Gallupe, R.B., Dennis, A.R., Cooper, W.H., Valacich, J.S., Bastianutti, L.M., & Nunamaker, J.F., Jr. (1992). Electronic brainstorming and group size. *Academy of Management Journal, 35*, 350–369. See also Dennis, A.R., & Valacich, J.S. (1993). Computer brainstorms: More heads are better than one. *Journal of Applied Psychology, 78*, 531–537.

69. Delbecq, A.L., Van de Ven, A.H., & Gustafson, D.H. (1975). *Group techniques for program planning*. Glenview, IL: Scott, Foresman, 8.

70. Delbecq et al., 1975.

Chapter 11

1. Sources include Broughton, P.D. (2002, January 29). Enron lived "on edge—sex, money, all of it." *National Post*, A1; Dube, R. (2006, July 6). Will Lay's legacy be greed or innovation? *Globe and Mail*, B1; Farrell, G. (2003, March 3). Former Andersen exec tells of stressful internal culture. *USA Today*, 3B; Farrell, G., & Jones, D. (2002, January 14). How did Enron come unplugged? *USA Today*, 1B; Feder, B.J. (2003, June 10). Manage-

ment practices enabled huge fraud, 2 investigations find. *New York Times*, C1; Roberts, J.L., & Thomas, E. (2002, March 11). Enron's dirty laundry. *Newsweek*, 22–28; Sloan, A., & Isikoff, M. (2002, January 28). The Enron effect. *Newsweek*, 34–36; Sloan, A. (2006, June 5). Laying Enron to rest: Convicted felons Ken Lay and Jeff Skilling may be trading pinstripes for prison stripes. These were "the smartest guys in the room"? *Newsweek*, 24–30; Zellner, W., Forest, S.A., Thornton, E., Coy, P., Timmons, H., Lavelle, L., & Henry, D. (2001, December 17). The fall of Enron. *Business Week*, 30–36; Zellner, W., Palmeri, C., France, M., Weber, J., & Carney, D. (2002, February 11). Jeff Skilling: Enron's missing man. *Business Week*, 38–40; Clark, A. (2009, January 6). US court orders Enron fraudster Jeffery Skilling to be resentenced. www.guardian.co.uk.

2. Brass, D.J., & Burkhardt, M.E. (1993). Potential power and power use: An investigation of structure and behavior. *Academy of Management Journal*, 36, 441–470; see also Kim, P.H., Pinkley, R.L., & Fragale, A.R. (2005). Power dynamics in negotiation. *Academy of Management Review*, 30, 799–822.

3. These descriptions of bases of power were developed by French, J.R.P., Jr., & Raven, B. (1959). In D. Cartwright (Ed.), *Studies in social power*. Ann Arbor, MI: Institute for Social Research.

4. Rahim, M.A. (1989). Relationships of leader power to compliance and satisfaction with supervision: Evidence from a national sample of managers. *Journal of Management*, 15, 545–556; Tannenbaum, A.S. (1974). *Hierarchy in organizations*. San Francisco: Jossey-Bass.

5. Podsakoff, P.M., & Schriesheim, C.A. (1985). Field studies of French and Raven's bases of power: Critique, reanalysis, and suggestions for future research. Psychological Bulletin, 97, 387–411.

6. Heider, F. (1958). *The psychology of interpersonal relations*. New York: Wiley.

7. Podsakoff & Schriesheim, 1985.

8. Ragins, B.R., & Sundstrom, E. (1990). Gender and perceived power in manager-subordinate dyads. *Journal of Occupational Psychology*, 63, 273–287.

9. The following is based upon Kanter, R.M. (1977). *Men and women of the corporation*. New York: Basic Books. For additional treatment see Pfeffer, J. (1992). *Managing with power: Politics and influence in organizations*. Boston: Harvard Business School Press.

10. See Thomas, K.W., & Velthouse, B.A. (1990). Cognitive elements of empowerment: An "interpretative" model of intrinsic task motivation. *Academy of Management Review*, 15, 668–681; Conger, J.A., & Kanungo, R.N. (1988). The empowerment process: Integrating theory and practice. *Academy of Management Review*, 13, 471–482. For a good review of this area, see Spreitzer, G. (2008). Taking stock: A review of more than twenty years of research on empowerment at work. In J. Barling and C.L. Cooper (Eds.), *The Sage handbook of organizational behavior* (Vol.1). London: Sage.

11. Chen, G., Kirkman, B.L., Kanter, R., Allen, D., & Rosen, B. (2007). A multilevel study of leadership, empowerment, and performance in teams. *Journal of Applied Psychology*, 92, 331–346; Srivastava, A., Bartol, K.M., & Locke, E.A. (2006). Empowering leadership in management teams: Effects on knowledge sharing, efficacy, and performance. *Academy of Management Journal*, 49, 1239–1251.

12. Tichy, N.M., & Sherman, S. (1993, June). Walking the talk at GE. *Training and Development*, 26–35.

13. Lowe, E. (2005, October). Responseability and the Power to Please: Delta Hotels. *Social Innovations*, 7–8, Vanier Institute of the Family. www.vifamily.ca/library/social/delta.html.

14. Seibert, S.E., Silver, S.R., & Randolph, W.A. (2004). Taking empowerment to the next level: A multiple-level model of empowerment, performance, and satisfaction. *Academy of Management Journal*, 47, 332–349; Laschinger, H.K.S., Finegan, J.E., Shamian, J., & Wilk, P. (2004). A longitudinal analysis of the impact of workplace empowerment on work satisfaction. *Journal of Organizational Behavior*, 25, 527–545; Patterson, M.G., West, M.A., & Wall, T.D. (2004). Integrated manufacturing, empowerment, and company performance. *Journal of Organizational Behavior*, 25, 641–665; Wall, T.D., Wood, S.J., & Leach, D.J. (2004). Empowerment and performance. *International Review of Industrial and Organizational Psychology*, 19, 1–46.

15. Bowen, D.E., & Lawler, E.E., III. (1992, Spring). The empowerment of service workers: What, why, how, and when. *Sloan Management Review*, 31–39.

16. Kipnis, D., Schmidt, S.M., & Wilkinson, I. (1980). Intraorganizational influence tactics: Explorations in getting one's way. *Journal of Applied Psychology*, 65, 440–452; Kipnis, D., & Schmidt, S.M. (1988). Upward-influence styles: Relationship with performance evaluation, salary, and stress. *Administrative Science Quarterly*, 33, 528–542.

17. See Brass & Burkhardt, 1993.

18. Kipnis et al., 1980. See also Keys, B., & Case, T. (1990, November). How to become an influential manager. *Academy of Management Executive*, 38–51.

19. Kipnis & Schmidt, 1988

20. Westphal, J.D., & Stern, I. (2006). The other pathway to the boardroom: Interpersonal influencing behavior as a substitute for elite credentials and majority status in obtaining board appointments. *Administrative Science Quarterly*, 51, 169–204.

21. Kipnis, D. (1976). *The powerholders*. Chicago: University of Chicago Press.

22. McClelland, D.C. (1975). *Power: The inner experience*. New York: Irvington.

23. Winter, D.G. (1988). The power motive in women—and men. *Journal of Personality and Social Psychology*, 54, 510–519.

24. McClelland, D.C., & Burnham, D.H. (1976, March–April). Power is the great motivator. *Harvard Business Review*, 100–110.

25. Ashforth, B.E. (1989). The experience of powerlessness in organizations. *Organizational Behavior and Human Decision Processes*, 43, 207–242.

26. Salancik, G.R., & Pfeffer, J. (1977, Winter). Who gets power—and how they hold on to it: A strategic contingency model of power. *Organizational Dynamics*, 3–21.

27. Salancik, G.R., & Pfeffer, J. (1974). The bases and use of power in organizational decision making: The case of a university. *Administrative Science Quarterly*, 19, 453–473. Also see Pfeffer, J., & Moore, W.L. (1980). Power in university budgeting: A replication and extension. *Administrative Science Quarterly*, 25, 637–653. For conditions under which the power thesis breaks down, see Schick, A.G., Birch, J.B., & Tripp, R.E. (1986). Authority and power in university decision making: The case of a university personnel budget. *Canadian Journal of Administrative Sciences*, 3, 41–64.

28. Hickson, D.J., Hinings, C.R., Lee, C.A., Schneck, R.E., & Pennings, J.M.

(1971). A strategic contingency theory of intraorganizational power. *Administrative Science Quarterly, 16,* 216–229; for support of this theory, see Hinings, C.R., Hickson, D.J., Pennings, J.M., & Schneck, R.E. (1974). Structural conditions of intra-organizational power. *Administrative Science Quarterly, 19,* 22–44; Saunders, C.S., & Scamell, R. (1982). Intraorganizational distributions of power: Replication research. *Academy of Management Journal, 25,* 192–200; Hambrick, D.C. (1981). Environment, strategy, and power within top management teams. *Administrative Science Quarterly, 26,* 253–276.

29. Kanter, 1977, 170–171.

30. Hickson et al., 1971; Hinings et al., 1974.

31. Hickson et al., 1971; Hinings et al., 1974; Saunders & Scamell, 1982.

32. Nulty, P. (1989, July 31). The hot demand for new scientists. *Fortune,* 155–163.

33. Nord, W.R., & Tucker, S. (1987). *Implementing routine and radical innovations.* Lexington, MA: Lexington Books.

34. Mayes, B.T., & Allen, R.W. (1977). Toward a definition of organizational politics. *Academy of Management Review, 2,* 672–678.

35. Porter, L.W., Allen, R.W., & Angle, H.L. (1981). The politics of upward influence in organizations. *Research in Organizational Behavior, 3,* 109–149.

36. Porter et al., 1981; Madison, D.L., Allen, R.W., Porter, L.W., Renwick, P.A., & Mayes, B.T. (1980). Organizational politics: An exploration of managers' perceptions. *Human Relations, 33,* 79–100.

37. Kacmar, K.M., & Baron, R.A. (1999). Organizational politics: The state of the field, links to related processes, and an agenda for future research. *Research in Personnel and Human Resources Management, 17,* 1–39.

38. Treadway, D.C., Ferris, G.R., Hochwarter, W., Perrewé, P., Witt, L.A., & Goodman, J.M. (2005). The role of age in the perceptions of politics-job performance relationship: A three-study constructive replication. *Journal of Applied Psychology, 90,* 872–881.

39. Ferris, G.D., Davidson, S.L., & Perrewé, P.L. (2005). *Political skill at work: Impact on effectiveness.* Mountain View, CA: Davies-Black, 7; see also Ferris, G.R., Treadway, D.C., Kolodinsky, R.W., Hochwarter, W.A., Kacmar, C.J., Douglas, C., & Frink, D.D. (2005). Development and validation of the Political Skill Inventory. *Journal of Management, 31,* 126–152.

40. Perrewé, P.L., Zellars, K.L., Ferris, G.R., Rossi, A.M., Kacmar, C.J., & Ralston, D.A. (2004). Neutralizing job stressors: Political skill as an antidote to the dysfunctional consequences of role conflict. *Academy of Management Journal, 47,* 141–152; Harvey, P., Harris, R.B., Harris, K.J., & Wheeler, A.R. (2007). Attenuating the effects of social stress: The impact of political skill. *Journal of Occupational Health Psychology, 12,* 105–115.

41. Kotter, J.P. (1982). *The general managers.* New York: Free Press.

42. Forret, M.L., & Dougherty, T.W. (2004). Networking behaviors and career outcomes: Differences for men and women. *Journal of Organizational Behavior, 25,* 419–437; Forret, M.L., & Dougherty, T.W. (2001). Correlates of networking behavior for managerial and professional employees. *Group & Organization Management, 26,* 283–311.

43. See also Wolff, H-G., & Maser, K. (2009). Effects of networking on career success: A longitudinal study. *Journal of Applied Psychology, 94,* 196–206.

44. Brass, D.J., Galaskiewicz, J., Greve, H.R., & Tsai, W. (2004). Taking stock of networks and organizations: A multilevel perspective. *Academy of Management Journal, 47,* 795–817.

45. Cross, R., Cowen, A., Vertucci, L., & Thomas, R.J. (2009). How effective leaders drive results through networks. *Organizational Dynamics, 38,* 93–105.

46. Geis, F., & Christie, R. (1970). Overview of experimental research. In R. Christie & F. Geis (Eds.), *Studies in Machiavellianism.* New York: Academic Press; Wilson, D.S., Near, D., & Miller, R.W. (1996). Machiavellianism: A synthesis of the evolutionary and psychological literatures. *Psychological Bulletin, 119,* 285–299.

47. Geis & Christie, 1970; Wilson et al., 1996.

48. What follows relies on Ashforth, B.E., & Lee, R.T. (1990). Defensive behavior in organizations: A preliminary model. *Human Relations, 43,* 621–648.

49. Boeker, W. (1992). Power and managerial dismissal: Scapegoating at the top. *Administrative Science Quarterly, 37,* 400–421.

50. Galloway, G. (2009, May 21). Watchdog predicted reactor's demise. *Globe and Mail,* A5; (2008, January 16). Nuclear safety watchdog head fired for "lack of leadership": Minister. www.cbc.ca/news.

51. This draws loosely on Glenn, J.R., Jr. (1986). *Ethics in decision making.* New York: Wiley.

52. For reviews, see Treviño, L.K. (1986). Ethical decision making in organizations: A person-situation interactionist model. *Academy of Management Review, 11,* 601–617; Tsalikis, J., & Fritzsche, D.J. (1989). Business ethics: A literature review with a focus on marketing ethics. *Journal of Business Ethics, 8,* 695–743.

53. Tyson, T. (1992). Does believing that everyone else is less ethical have an impact on work behavior? *Journal of Business Ethics, 11,* 707–717.

54. Treviño, L.K., Weaver, G.R., & Brown, M.E. (2008). It's lovely at the top: Hierarchical levels, identities, and perceptions of organizational ethics. *Business Ethics Quarterly, 18,* 233–252.

55. Tsalikis & Fritzsche, 1989.

56. Kaynama, S.A., King, A., & Smith, L.W. (1996). The impact of a shift in organizational role on ethical perceptions: A comparative study. *Journal of Business Ethics, 15,* 581–590.

57. McCabe, D.L., Butterfield, K.D., & Treviño, L.K. (2006). Academic dishonesty in graduate business programs: Prevalence, causes, and proposed action. *Academy of Management Learning & Education, 5,* 294–305.

58. Tenbrunsel, A.E., & Smith-Crowe, K. (2008). Ethical decision making: Where we've been and where we're going. *Academy of Management Annals, 2,* 545–607.

59. Tsalikis & Fritzsche, 1989.

60. Bird, F., & Waters, J.A. (1987). The nature of managerial moral standards. *Journal of Business Ethics, 6,* 1–13.

61. Hegarty, W.H., & Sims, H.P., Jr. (1978). Some determinants of unethical behavior: An experiment. *Journal of Applied Psychology, 63,* 451–457; Treviño, L.K., Sutton, C.D., & Woodman, R.W. (1985). *Effects of reinforcement contingencies and cognitive moral development on ethical decision-making behavior: An experiment.* Paper presented at the annual meeting of the Academy of Management, San Diego.

62. Levine, D.B. (1990, May 21). The inside story of an inside trader. *Fortune,* 80–89, 82.

63. Grover, S.L. (1993). Why professionals lie: The impact of professional role conflict on reporting accuracy.

Organizational Behavior and Human Decision Processes, 55, 251–272.

64. Staw, B.M., & Szwajkowski, E.W. (1975). The scarcity-munificence component of organizational environments and the commission of illegal acts. *Administrative Science Quarterly, 20,* 345–354.

65. Sonnenfeld, J., & Lawrence, P.R. (1989). Why do companies succumb to price fixing? In K.R. Andrew (Ed.), *Ethics in practice: Managing the moral corporation.* Boston: Harvard Business School Press.

66. Detert, J.R., Treviño, L.K., & Sweitzer, V.L. (2008). Moral disengagement in ethical decision making: A study of antecedents and outcomes. *Journal of Applied Psychology, 93,* 374–391.

67. Hegarty & Sims, 1978; Hegarty, W.H., & Sims, H.P., Jr. (1979). Organizational philosophy, policies, and objectives related to unethical decision behavior: A laboratory experiment. *Journal of Applied Psychology, 64,* 331–338.

68. Colby, A., & Kohlberg, L. (1987). *The measurement of moral judgment. Volume 1: Theoretical foundations and research validation.* Cambridge: Cambridge University Press; see also Treviño, 1986; Grover, 1993.

69. Detert et al., 2008.

70. Reynolds, S.J., (2008). Moral attentiveness: Who pays attention to the moral aspects of life? *Journal of Applied Psychology, 93,* 1027–1041.

71. Victor, B., & Cullen, J.B. (1988). The organizational bases of ethical work climates. *Administrative Science Quarterly, 33,* 101–125.

72. Tenbrunsel & Smith-Crowe, 2008.

73. Baucus, M.S., & Near, J.P. (1991). Can illegal corporate behavior be predicted? An event history analysis. *Academy of Management Journal, 34,* 9–16.

74. Anand, V., Ashforth, B.E., & Joshi, M. (2004, May). Business as usual: The acceptance and perpetuation of corruption in organizations. *Academy of Management Executive,* 39–53.

75. Sonnenfeld & Lawrence, 1989; see also Hosmer, L.T. (1987). The institutionalization of unethical behavior. *Journal of Business Ethics, 6,* 439–447.

76. Morgan, R.B. (1993). Self- and co-worker perceptions of ethics and their relationships to leadership and salary. *Academy of Management Journal, 36,* 200–214.

77. This definition and other material in this paragraph are from Miceli, M.P., & Near, J.P. (2005). Standing up or standing by: What predicts blowing the whistle on organizational wrongdoing? *Research in Personnel and Human Resources Management, 24,* 95–136.

78. Moore, D.A, Tetlock, P.H., Tanlu, L., & Bazerman, M.H. (2006). Conflicts of interest and the case of auditor independence: Moral seduction and strategic issue cycling. *Academy of Management Review, 31,* 10–29.

79. Ripley, A. (2002, December 30/2003, January 6). The night detective. *Time,* 45; Morse, J., & Bower, A. (2002, December 30/2003, January 6). The party crasher. *Time,* 53.

80. Peirce, E., Smolinski, C.A., & Rosen, B. (1998, August). Why sexual harassment complaints fall on deaf ears. *Academy of Management Executive,* 41–54.

81. O'Leary–Kelly, A.M., Bowes-Sperry, L., Bates, C.A., & Lean, E.R. (2009). Sexual harassment at work: A decade (plus) of progress. *Journal of Management, 35,* 503–536; Willness, C.R., Steel, P., & Lee, K. (2007). A meta-analysis of the antecedents and consequences of workplace sexual harassment. *Personnel Psychology, 60,* 127–162.

82. Schneider, K.T., Swan, S., & Fitzgerald, L.F. (1997). Job-related and psychological effects of sexual harassment in the workplace: Empirical evidence from two organizations. *Journal of Applied Psychology, 82,* 401–415.

83. O'Leary-Kelly et al., 2008.

84. Seppa, N. (1997, May). Sexual harassment in the military lingers on. *APA Monitor,* 40–41.

85. Seppa, 1997.

86. Peirce et al., 1998; Seppa, 1997.

87. Peirce et al., 1998.

88. Peirce et al., 1998.

89. Peirce et al., 1998.

90. Flynn, G. (1997, February). Respect is key to stopping harassment. *Workforce,* 56.

91. Peirce et al., 1998.

92. This draws on Waters, J.A., & Bird, F. (1988). *A note on what a well-educated manager should be able to do with respect to moral issues in management.* Unpublished manuscript.

93. See Jones, T.M. (1991). Ethical decision making by individuals in organizations: An issue-contingent model. *Academy of Management Journal, 16,* 366–395.

94. Weber, J. (1990). Measuring the impact of teaching ethics to future managers: A review, assessment, and recommendations. *Journal of Business Ethics, 9,* 183–190.

Chapter 12

1. Excerpted from Kelly, C. (2009, June 17). Rival Yorkville hair salons in ugly battle. www.thestar.com. Reprinted with permission of TorStar Syndication Services.

2. Kolb, D.M., & Bartunek, J.M. (Eds.) (1992). *Hidden conflict in organizations: Uncovering behind-the-scenes disputes.* Newbury Park, CA: Sage.

3. This section relies partly on Walton, R.E., & Dutton, J.M. (1969). The management of interdepartmental conflict: A model and review. *Administrative Science Quarterly, 14,* 73–84; see also De Dreu, C.K.W., & Gelfand, M.J. (2008). Conflict in the workplace: Sources, functions, and dynamics across multiple levels of analysis. In C.K.W. De Dreu & M.J. Gelfand (Eds.), *The psychology of conflict and conflict management in organizations.* New York: Lawrence Erlbaum.

4. Ashforth, B.E., & Mael, F. (1989). Social identity theory and the organization. *Academy of Management Review, 14,* 20–39; Kramer, R.M. (1991). Intergroup relations and organizational dilemmas: The role of categorization processes. *Research in Organizational Behavior, 13,* 191–228; Messick, D.M., & Mackie, D.M. (1989). Intergroup relations. *Annual Review of Psychology, 40,* 45–81.

5. Johns, G. (1994). Absenteeism estimates by employees and managers: Divergent perspectives and self-serving perceptions. *Journal of Applied Psychology, 79,* 229–239.

6. See Whyte, W.F. (1948). *Human relations in the restaurant industry.* New York: McGraw-Hill.

7. Moritz, M. (1984). *The little kingdom: The private story of Apple Computer.* New York: Morrow, 246–247.

8. Jehn, K.A., & Mannix, E.A. (2001). The dynamic nature of conflict: A longitudinal study of intragroup conflict and group performance. *Academy of Management Journal, 44,* 238–251.

9. For evidence of the pervasively negative impact of conflict, see De Dreu, C.K.W., & Weingart, L.R. (2003). Task versus relationship conflict, team performance, and team member satisfaction: A meta-analysis. *Journal of Applied Psychology, 88,* 741–749. For exceptions for task conflict, see Jehn & Mannix, 2001; Jehn, K.A. (1997). A qualitative analysis of conflict types and dimensions in organizational groups. *Administrative Science Quarterly, 42,* 530–557.

10. See Blake, R.R., Shepard, M.A., & Mouton, J.S. (1964). *Managing inter-*

group conflict in industry. Houston: Gulf; Sherif, M. (1966). *In common predicament: Social psychology of intergroup conflict and cooperation*. Boston: Houghton Mifflin; Wilder, D.A. (1986). Social categorization: Implications for creation and reduction of intergroup bias. *Advances in Experimental Social Psychology, 19*, 291–349; Pruitt, D.G. (2008). Conflict escalation in organizations. In De Dreu & Gelfand, 2008.

11. Thomas, K.W. (1992). Conflict and negotiation in organizations. In M.D. Dunnette & L.M. Hough (Eds.), *Handbook of industrial and organizational psychology* (2nd ed., Vol. 3). Palo Alto, CA: Consulting Psychologists Press.

12. Seabrook, J. (1994, January 10). E-mail from Bill. *The New Yorker*, 48–61, 52.

13. Johnson, D.W., Maruyama, G., Johnson, R., Nelson, D., & Skon, L. (1981). Effects of cooperative and individualistic goal structures on achievement: A meta-analysis. *Psychological Bulletin, 89*, 47–62; see also Tjosvold, D. (1991). *The conflict-positive organization*. Reading, MA: Addison-Wesley.

14. Tjosvold, D., Dann, V., & Wong, C. (1992). Managing conflict between departments to serve customers. *Human Relations, 45*, 1035–1054.

15. Neale, M.A., & Bazerman, M.H. (1992, August). Negotiating rationally: The power and impact of the negotiator's frame. *Academy of Management Executive*, 42–51, p. 42.

16. Wall, J.A., Jr. (1985). *Negotiation: Theory and practice*. Glenview, IL: Scott, Foresman.

17. Walton, R.E., & McKerzie, R.B. (1991). *A behavioral theory of labor negotiations* (2nd ed.). Ithaca, NY: ILR Press.

18. What follows draws on Pruitt, D.G. (1981). Negotiation behavior. New York: Academic Press.

19. Wall, J.A., Jr., & Blum, M. (1991). Negotiations. *Journal of Management, 17*, 273–303.

20. Wall & Blum, 1991.

21. Stuhlmacher, A.F., and Walters, A.E. (1999). Gender differences in negotiation outcome: A meta-analysis. *Personnel Psychology, 52*, 653–677.

22. Bazerman, M.H. (1990). *Judgment in managerial decision making* (2nd ed.). New York: Wiley.

23. The following draws on Bazerman, M.H., & Neale, M.A. (1992). *Negotiating rationally*. New York: The Free Press; see also Bazerman, M.H. (2006). *Judgment in managerial*

decision making (6th ed.). Hoboken, NJ: Wiley.

24. Sherif, 1966; Hunger, J.D., & Stern, L.W. (1976). An assessment of the functionality of the superordinate goal in reducing conflict. *Academy of Management Journal, 19*, 591–605.

25. Goldman, B.M., Cropanzano, R., Stein, J., & Benson, L. III. (2008). The role of third parties / mediation in managing conflict in organizations. In De Dreu & Gelfand, 2008.

26. Pruitt, 1981; Kressel, K., & Pruitt, D.G. (1989). *Mediation research*. San Francisco: Jossey-Bass.

27. Kressel & Pruitt, 1989.

28. Pruitt, 1981; Wall & Blum, 1991.

29. Moore, M.L., Nichol, V.W., & McHugh, P.P. (1992). Review of no-fault absenteeism cases taken to arbitration, 1980–1989: A rights and responsibilities analysis. *Employee Rights and Responsibilities Journal, 5*, 29–48; Scott, K.D., & Taylor, G.S. (1983, September). An analysis of absenteeism cases taken to arbitration: 1975–1981. *The Arbitration Journal*, 61–70.

30. For a spirited debate on this, see De Dreu, C.K.W. (2008). The virtue and vice of workplace conflict: Food for (pessimistic) thought. *Journal of Organizational Behavior, 29*, 5–18, and Tjosvold, D. (2008). The conflict-positive organization: It depends on us. *Journal of Organizational Behavior, 29*, 19–28.

31. Robbins, S.P. (1974). *Managing organizational conflict: A nontraditional approach*. Englewood, Cliffs, NJ: Prentice-Hall, 20.

32. Brown, L.D. (1983). *Managing conflict at organizational interfaces*. Reading, MA: Addison-Wesley.

33. Robbins, 1974; see also Brown, 1983.

34. Raynal, W., & Wilson, K.A. (2001, October 15). What about Bob? *Autoweek*, 5.

35. Ramsay, L. (1999, March 15). Stress, the plague of the 1990s. *National Post*, D10. Best, P. (1999, February). All work (Stressed to the max? Join the club). *Report on Business Magazine*, 3.

36. Keita, G.P. (2006, June). The national push for workplace health. *Monitor on Psychology*, 32.

37. Price, M. (2009, July–August). The recession is stressing men more than women. *Monitor on Psychology*, 10.

38. Tangri, R. (2007, September). Putting a price on stress. *Canadian Healthcare Manager, 14*, 24–25.

39. This model has much in common with many contemporary models of work stress. For a comprehensive summary,

see Kahn, R.L., & Byosiere, P. (1992). Stress in organizations. In M.D. Dunnette & L.M. Hough (Eds.), *Handbook of industrial and organizational psychology* (2nd ed., Vol. 3). Palo Alto, CA: Consulting Psychologists Press.

40. McGrath, J.E. (1970). A conceptual formulation for research on stress. In J.E. McGrath (Ed.), *Social and psychological factors in stress*. New York: Holt, Rinehart, Winston.

41. Roth, S., & Cohen, L.J. (1986). Approach, avoidance, and coping with stress. *American Psychologist, 41*, 813–819.

42. Glazer, S., & Beehr, T.A. (2005). Consistency of implications of three role stressors across four countries. *Journal of Organizational Behavior, 26*, 467–487.

43. Ng, T.W.H., Sorensen, K.L., & Eby, L.T. (2006). Locus of control at work: A meta-analysis. *Journal of Organizational Behavior, 27*, 1057–1087.

44. Friedman, M., & Rosenman, R. (1974). *Type A Behavior and your heart*. New York: Knopf.

45. Chesney, M.A., & Rosenman, R. (1980). Type A behavior in the work setting. In C.L. Cooper and R. Payne (Eds.), *Current concerns in occupational stress*. Chichester, England: Wiley. For a typical study, see Jamal, M., & Baba, V.V. (1991). Type A behavior, its prevalence and consequences among women nurses: An empirical examination. *Human Relations, 44*, 1213–1228.

46. Fine, S., & Stinson, M. (2000, February 3). Stress is overwhelming people, study shows. *Globe and Mail*, A1, A7; Matthews, K.A. (1982). Psychological perspectives on the Type A behavior pattern. *Psychological Bulletin, 91*, 293–323.

47. Booth-Kewley, S., & Friedman, H.S. (1987). Psychological predictors of heart disease: A quantitative review. *Psychological Bulletin, 101*, 343–362; Smith, D. (2003, March). Angry thoughts, at-risk hearts. *Monitor on Psychology*, 46–48; Ganster, D.C., Schaubroeck, J., Sime, W.E., & Mayes, B.T. (1991). The nomological validity of the Type A personality among employed adults. *Journal of Applied Psychology, 76*, 143–168.

48. Houkes, I., Janssen, P.P.M., de Jonge, J., & Bakker, A.B. (2003). Personality, work characteristics, and employee well-being: A longitudinal analysis of additive and moderating effects. *Journal of Occupational Health Psychology, 8*, 20–38; Grant, S., & Langan-Fox, J. (2007). Personality

and the stressor-strain relationship: The role of the Big Five. *Journal of Occupational Health Psychology, 12,* 20–33; Kammeyer-Mueller, J.D., Judge, T.A., & Scott, B.A. (2009). The role of core self-evaluations in the coping process. *Journal of Applied Psychology, 94,* 177–195.

49. Spector, P.E., Zapf, D., Chen, P.Y., & Frese, M. (2000). Why negative affectivity should not be controlled in stress research: Don't throw out the baby with the bath water. *Journal of Organizational Behavior, 21,* 79–95. For a relevant study, see Barsky, A., Thoresen, C.J., Warren, C.R., & Kaplan, S.A. (2004). Modeling negative affectivity and job stress: A contingency-based approach. *Journal of Organizational Behavior, 25,* 915–936.

50. Fine, S., & Stinson, M. (2000, February 3). Stress is overwhelming people, study shows. Globe and Mail, A1, A7.

51. Parasuraman, S., & Alutto, J.A. (1981). An examination of the organizational antecedents of stressors at work. *Academy of Management Journal, 24,* 48–67.

52. Mintzberg, H. (1973). *The nature of managerial work.* New York: Harper & Row.

53. An excellent review of managerial stressors can be found in Marshall, J., & Cooper, C.L. (1979). *Executives under pressure.* New York: Praeger.

54. Xie, J.L., & Johns, G. (1995). Job scope and stress: Can job scope be too high? *Academy of Management Journal, 38,* 1288–1309.

55. Maslach, C., Leiter, M.P., & Schaufeli, W. (2009). Measuring burnout. In S. Cartwright & C.L. Cooper (Eds.), *The Oxford handbook of organizational well-being.* Oxford: Oxford University Press; Maslach, C., & Leiter, M.P. (2008). Early predictors of burnout and engagement. *Journal of Applied Psychology, 93,* 498–512; Maslach, C., & Jackson, S.E. (1984). Burnout in organizational settings. In S. Oskamp (Ed.), *Applied social psychology annual* (Vol. 5). Beverly Hills, CA: Sage.

56. Maslach, C., Schaufeli, W.B., & Leiter, M.P. (2001). Job burnout. *Annual Review of Psychology, 52,* 397–422; Cordes, C.L., & Dougherty, T.W. (1993). A review and integration of research on job burnout. *Academy of Management Review, 18,* 621–656. For a comprehensive study, see Lee, R.T., & Ashforth, B.E. (1993). A longitudinal study of burnout among supervisors and managers: Comparisons of the Leiter and Maslach (1988) and Golembiewski et al. (1986) models. *Organizational Behavior and Human Decision Processes, 54,* 369–398.

57. See Pines, A.M., & Aronson, E. (1981). *Burnout: From tedium to personal growth.* New York: The Free Press.

58. Galt, V. (2005, November 15). Fewer workers willing to put in 110%. *Globe and Mail,* B8; Carniol, N. (2005, November 15). Fewer workers willing to give 100 percent. *Toronto Star,* D1, D11; Galt, V. (2005, January 26). This just in: Half your employees ready to jump ship. *Globe and Mail,* B1, B9.

59. Schaufeli, W.B., Bakker, A.B., & Van Rhenen, W. (in press). How changes in job demands and resources predict burnout, work engagement, and sickness absenteeism. *Journal of Organizational Behavior;* see also Bakker, A.B., & Demerouti, E. (2008). Towards a model of work engagement. *Career Development International, 13,* 209–223.

60. Bakker, A.B., & Demerouti, E. (2007). The job-demands-resources model: State of the art. *Journal of Managerial Psychology, 22,* 309–328.

61. Bakker & Demerouti, 2007; Schaufeli et al., in press.

62. Salin, D. (2003). Ways of explaining workplace bullying: A review of enabling, motivating and precipitating structures in the work environment. *Human Relations, 56,* 1213–1232.

63. Bowling, N.A., & Beehr, T.A. (2006). Workplace harassment from the victim's perspective: A theoretical model and meta-analysis. *Journal of Applied Psychology, 91,* 998–1012.

64. Salin, 2003; Rayner, C., & Keashly, L. (2005). Bullying at work: A perspective from Britain and North America. In S. Fox & P.E. Spector (Eds.), *Counterproductive work behavior: Investigations of actors and targets.* Washington, DC: American Psychological Association.

65. This is one interpretation of the distinction between bullying and mobbing. See Zapf, D., & Einarsen, S. (2005). Mobbing at work: Escalated conflicts in organizations. In Fox & Spector, 2005.

66. Meyers, L. (2006, July–August). Still wearing the "kick me" sign. *Monitor on Psychology,* 68–70.

67. Dingfelder, S.F. (2006, July–August). Banishing bullying. *Monitor on Psychology,* 76–78.

68. See Ford, M.T., Heinen, B.A., & Langkamer, K.L. (2008). Work and family satisfaction and conflict: A meta-analysis of cross-domain relations. *Journal of Applied Psychology, 92,* 57–80.

69. Duxbury, L., & Higgins, C. (2003). *Work–life conflict in Canada in the new millennium: A status report.* Ottawa: Health Canada.

70. Bellavia, G.M., & Frone, M.R. (2005). Work-family conflict. In J. Barling, E.K. Kelloway, & M.R. Frone (Eds.), *Handbook of work stress.* Thousand Oaks, CA: Sage.

71. Dierdorff, E.C., & Ellington, J.K. (2008). It's the nature of the work: Examining behavior-based sources of work-family conflict across occupations. *Journal of Applied Psychology, 93,* 883–892.

72. For job loss in particular, see McKee-Ryan, F.M., Song, Z., Wanberg, C.R., & Kinicki, A.J. (2005). Psychological and physical well-being during unemployment: A meta-analytic study. *Journal of Applied Psychology, 90,* 53–76; for mergers and acquisitions, see Cartwright, S. (2005). Mergers and acquisitions: An update and appraisal. *International Review of Industrial and Organizational Psychology, 20,* 1–38.

73. DeFrank, R.S., & Ivancevich, J.M. (1998, August). Stress on the job: An executive update. *Academy of Management Executive,* 55–66.

74. Jackson, S.E., & Schuler, R.S. (1985). Meta-analysis and conceptual critique of research on role ambiguity and conflict in work settings. *Organizational Behavior and Human Decision Processes, 36,* 16–78. For a critique of some of this research, see Fineman, S., & Payne, R. (1981). Role stress—A methodological trap? *Journal of Occupational Behaviour, 2,* 51–64.

75. Fitzgerald, L.F., Drasgow, F., Hulin, C.L., Gelfand, M.J., & Magley, V.J. (1997). Antecedents and consequences of sexual harassment in organizations: A test of an integrated model. *Journal of Applied Psychology, 82,* 578–589; Schneider, K.T., Swan, S., & Fitzgerald, L.F. (1997). Job-related and psychological effects of sexual harassment in the workplace: Empirical evidence from two organizations. *Journal of Applied Psychology, 82,* 401–415.

76. Fitzgerald et al., 1997; Schneider et al., 1997.

77. O'Leary-Kelly, A.M., Bowes-Sperry, L., Bates, C.A., & Lean, E.R. (2009). Sexual harassment at work: A decade (plus) of progress. *Journal of Management, 35,* 503–536; Willness, C.R., Steel, P., & Lee, K. (2007). A meta-analysis of the antecedents and consequences of

workplace sexual harassment. *Personnel Psychology, 60*, 127–162.

78. Peirce, E., Smolinski, C.A., & Rosen, B. (1998, August). Why sexual harassment complaints fall on deaf ears. *Academy of Management Executive*, 41–54; Schneider et al., 1997.

79. Fitzgerald et al., 1997; Glomb, T.M., Munson, L.J., Hulin, C.L., Bergman, M.E., & Drasgow, F. (1999). Structural equation models of sexual harassment: Longitudinal explorations and cross-sectional generalizations. *Journal of Applied Psychology, 84*, 14–28.

80. Cohen, S., & Wills, T.A. (1985). Stress, social support, and the buffering hypothesis. *Psychological Bulletin, 98*, 310–357; Kahn & Byosiere, 1992. For a recent treatment of social support and relational views of work, see Grant, A.M., & Parker, S.K. (2009). Redesigning work design theories: The rise of relational and proactive perspectives. *Academy of Management Annals, 3*, 317–375.

81. Gilboa, S., Shirom, A., Fried, Y., & Cooper, C. (2008). A meta-analysis of work demand stressors and job performance: Examining main and moderating effects. *Personnel Psychology, 61*, 227–271. For a classic study, see Jamal, M. (1984). Job stress and job performance controversy: An empirical assessment. *Organizational Behavior and Human Performance, 33*, 1–21.

82. LePine, J.A., Podsakoff, N.P., & LePine, M.A. (2005). A meta-analytic test of the challenge stressor-hindrance stressor framework: An explanation for inconsistent relationships among stressors and performance. *Academy of Management Journal, 48*, 764–775.

83. Johns, G. (1997). Contemporary research on absence from work: Correlates, causes and consequences. *International Review of Industrial and Organizational Psychology, 12*, 115–173; Darr, W., & Johns, G. (2008). Work strain, health, and absenteeism from work: A meta-analysis. *Journal of Occupational Health Psychology, 13*, 293–318; Podsakoff, N.P., LePine, J.A., & LePine, M.A. (2007). Differential challenge stressor-hindrance stressor relationships with job attitudes, turnover intentions, turnover, and withdrawal behavior: A meta-analysis. *Journal of Applied Psychology, 92*, 438–454.

84. Beehr, T.A., & Newman, J.E. (1978). Job stress, employee health, and organizational effectiveness: A facet analysis, model, and literature review. *Personnel Psychology, 32*, 665–699;

Kahn & Byosiere, 1992; Frone, M.R. (2008). Employee alcohol and illicit drug use: Scope, causes, and organizational consequences. In J. Barling & C.L. Cooper (Eds.), *Sage handbook of organizational behavior* (Vol 1). London: Sage.

85. For reviews, see Cramer, P. (2000). Defense mechanisms in psychology today: Further processes for adaptation. *American Psychologist, 55*, 637–646; Baumeister, R.F., Dale, K., & Sommer, K.L. (1998). Freudian defense mechanisms and empirical findings in modern social psychology: Reaction formation, projection, displacement, undoing, isolation, sublimation, and denial. *Journal of Personality, 66*, 1081–1124.

86. Beehr & Newman, 1978. For a later review and a strong critique of this work, see Fried, Y., Rowland, K.M., & Ferris, G.R. (1984). The physiological measurement of work stress: A critique. *Personnel Psychology, 37*, 583–615. See also Fried, Y. (1989). The future of physiological assessments in work situations. In C.L. Cooper & R. Payne (Eds.), *Causes, coping, and consequences of stress at work*. Chichester, England: Wiley & Sons.

87. Cohen, S., & Herbert, T.B. (1996). Health psychology: Psychological and physical disease from the perspective of human psychoneuroimmunology. *Annual Review of Psychology, 47*, 113–142; Cohen, S., & Williamson, G.M. (1991). Stress and infectious disease in humans. *Psychological Bulletin, 109*, 5–24.

88. Melamed, S., Shirom, A., Toker, S., Berliner, S., & Shapira, I. (2006). Burnout and risk of cardiovascular disease: Evidence, possible causal paths, and promising research directions. *Psychological Bulletin, 132*, 327–353; Kivimaki, M., Virtanen, M., Elovainio, M., Kouvonen, A., Vaananen, A., & Vahtera, J. (2006). Work stress in the etiology of coronary heart disease: A meta-analysis. *Scandinavian Journal of Work, Environment and Health, 32*, 431–442; see also the special issue Stress and the Heart, *Stress and Health*, August 2008.

89. Grandey, A.A., Fisk, G.M., & Steiner, D.D. (2005). Must "service with a smile" be stressful? The moderating role of personal control for American and French employees. *Journal of Applied Psychology, 90*, 893–904; Grandey, A.A., Dickter, D.N., & Sin, H.P. (2004). The customer is not always right: Customer aggression and emotion regulation of service

employees. *Journal of Organizational Behavior, 25*, 397–418.

90. See Spriggs, C.A., & Jackson, P.R. (2006). Call centers as lean service environments: Job related strain and the mediating role of work design. *Journal of Occupational Health Psychology, 11*, 197–212.

91. This section relies on a *Wall Street Journal* special section on Work & Family (1993, June 21) and Shellenbarger, S. (1993, June 29). Work & family. *Wall Street Journal*, B1.

92. Kelly, E.L., Kossek, E.E., Hammer, L.B., Durhman, M., Bray, J., Chermack, K., Murphy, L.A., & Kaskubar, D. (2008). Getting there from here: Research on the effects of work-family initiatives on work-family conflict and business outcomes. *Academy of Management Annals, 2*, 305–309.

93. Richardson, K.M., & Rothstein, H.R. (2008). Effects of occupational stress management intervention programs: A meta-analysis. *Journal of Occupational Health Psychology, 13*, 69–93; Ivancevich, J.M., Matteson, M.T., Freedman, S.M., & Phillips, J.S. (1990). Worksite stress management interventions. *American Psychologist, 45*, 252–261; Cartwright, S., & Cooper, C. (2005). Individually targeted interventions. In Barling et al., 2005.

94. Richardson & Rothstein, 2008; Ivancevich et al., 1990.

95. Lush, T. (1998, October 3). Company with a conscience. *The Gazette (Montreal)*, C3.

96. Immen, W., & Brown-Bowers, A. (2008, April 16). Employers get the fitness bug. *Globe and Mail*, C1, C2.

97. Parks, K.M., & Steelman, L.A. (2008). Organizational wellness programs: A meta-analysis. *Journal of Occupational Health Psychology, 13*, 58–63; DeGroot, T., & Kiker, D.S. (2003). A meta-analysis of the non-monetary effects of employee health management programs. *Human Resource Management, 42*, 53–69; Jex, S.M. (1991). The psychological benefits of exercise in work settings: A review, critique, and dispositional model. *Work & Stress, 5*, 133–147.

Appendix

1. Rousseau, D.M. (2006). Is there such a thing as "evidence-based management"? *Academy of Management Review, 31*, 256–269; Pfeffer, J., & Sutton, R.I. (2006). Evidence-based management. *Harvard Business Review*, 62–74.

2. Sutton, R.I. (1991). Maintaining norms about expressed emotions: The case of bill collectors. *Administrative Science Quarterly, 36,* 245–268.

3. Lupton, T. (1963). *On the shop floor.* Oxford: Pergamon.

4. Bensman, J., & Gerver, I. (1963). Crime and punishment in the factory: The function of deviancy in maintaining the social system. *American Sociological Review, 28,* 588–598.

5. Mintzberg, H. (1973). *The nature of managerial work.* New York: Harper & Row.

6. Ragins, B.R., & Cotton, J.L. (1993). Gender and willingness to mentor in organizations. *Journal of Management, 19,* 97–111.

7. Ivancevich, J.M., & Lyon, H.L. (1977). The shortened workweek: A field experiment. *Journal of Applied Psychology, 62,* 34–37.

8. Sutton, R.I., & Rafaeli, A. (1988). Untangling the relationship between displayed emotions and organizational sales: The case of convenience stores. *Academy of Management Journal, 31,* 461–487.

9. Greenwood, R.G., & Wrege, C.D. (1986). The Hawthorne studies. In D.A. Wren & J.A. Pearce II (Eds.), *Papers dedicated to the development of modern management.* The Academy of Management; Roethlisberger, F.J., & Dickson, W.J. (1939). *Management and the worker.* Cambridge, MA: Harvard University Press.

10. Adair, J.G. (1984). The Hawthorne effect: A reconsideration of the methodological artifact. Journal of Applied Psychology, 69, 334–345.

11. See Academy of Management (2008). Academy of Management code of ethics. *Academy of Management Journal, 51,* 1246–1253; Lowman, R.L. (Ed.). (1998). *The ethical practice of psychology in organizations.* Washington, DC: American Psychological Association.

Chapter 1

Page 3: © 2008 Richard Johnson Photography Inc.; page 4: © Tim Wright/CORBIS; page 9: Chris So/GetStock.com; page 17: CP/AP Photo/Jacquelyn Martin; page 18: Michael Newman/PhotoEdit.

Chapter 2

Page 39: © DundeeWealth Inc.; page 60: David Anderson; page 61: Courtesy of Keller Williams Ottawa Realty.

Chapter 3

Page 72: Courtesy of Canada Post; page 73: P.C. Vey; page 89: © Queen's Printer for Ontario, 2003. Reproduced with permission; page 91: Shy Ing, Ottawa Police Service; page 97: © Masterfile.

Chapter 4

Page 111: Phil Carpenter, © Gazette 2009; page 114: Kyodo /Landov; page 130: AP Photo/Mark Lennihan; page 134: A.G.E. Foto Stock/Firstlight.ca.

Chapter 5

Page 145: Courtesy of Great Little Box Company; page 167: Weyerhauser Co.; page 168: Dick Hemingway; page 169: Bebeto Matthews/CP.

Chapter 6

Page 179: CP/Adrian Wyld; page 181: Matt Hall Adjunct Advocate; page 182: Mikhallshin Iqor/ITAR-TASS/Landov; page 185: David Cooper/GetStock.com; page 190: Jean B. Heguy Photo/Firstlight.ca; page 193: PHOTOFEST; page 203: David W. Harbaugh; page 205: David Anderson.

Chapter 7

Page 217: Mark Richards/PhotoEdit Inc.; page 229: © Ashley Cooper/CORBIS; page 238: Norman Mayersohn/The New York Times/Redux; page 241: Eyecandy Images/GetStock.com.

Chapter 8

Page 251: Courtesy of Kris Abel; page 262: © Leif Skoogfors/Corbis; page 265: © Dennis MacDonald/Alamy; page 273: Adrian Wyld/CP Picture Archive; page 274: Gordon Beck/CP Picture Archive; page 276: Daniel Alan/Stone/Getty.

Chapter 9

Page 286: THE CANADIAN PRESS/Ryan Remiorz; page 288: Photo courtesy of Business Development Bank of Canada; page 289: Roy Delgado; page 291: Philip Lengden; page 293: Kevin Frayer/CP Photo Archive; page 304: Aaron Harris/CP Photo Archive; page 305: Jeff McIntosh/CP Picture Archive; page 310: Richard Lautens/GetStock.com; page 312: Dick Loek/GetStock.com.

Chapter 10

Page 358: Ken Howard/GetStock.com; page 362: ScienceCartoonsPlus.com; page 364: © allOver photography/Alamy; page 370: © Ariel Skelley/Corbis; page 373: Brasiliao/Shutterstock.

Chapter 11

Page 391: © Greg Smith/Corbis; page 398: Steve White/CP Picture Archive; page 399: Philip Bird/GetStock.com; page 406: © Mark Leibowitz/Masterfile; page 411: SCOTT AUDETTE/Reuters/Landov.

Chapter 12

Page 425: CARLOS OSORIO/TORONTO STAR; page 432: Michael Stuparyk/GetStock.com; page 440: Randy Glasbergen; page 446: Chip Somodevilla/Getty Images; page 451: CP/Fred Chartrand; page 452: Dick Hemingway.